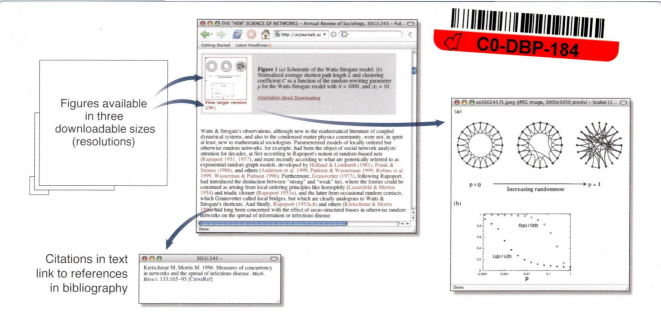

Figures available in three downloadable sizes (resolutions)

Citations in text link to references in bibliography

References in Annual Reviews article bibliography link out to sources of cited articles online

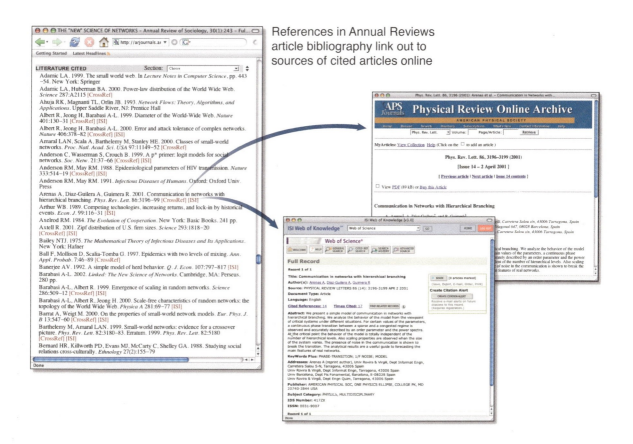

Annual Review of
Resource Economics

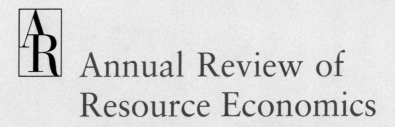

Annual Review of Resource Economics

Volume 1, 2009

Gordon Rausser, *Editor*
University of California, Berkeley

Kerry Smith, *Associate Editor*
Arizona State University, Tempe

David Zilberman, *Associate Editor*
University of California, Berkeley

www.annualreviews.org • science@annualreviews.org • 650-493-4400

Annual Reviews
4139 El Camino Way • P.O. Box 10139 • Palo Alto, California 94303-0139

Annual Reviews
Palo Alto, California, USA

International Standard Serial Number: 1941-1340
International Standard Book Number: 978-0-8243-4701-7

TYPESET BY DARTMOUTH JOURNAL SERVICES
PRINTED AND BOUND BY MALLOY INCORPORATED, ANN ARBOR, MICHIGAN

Preface

The *Annual Review of Resource Economics* is being launched simultaneously with the new *Annual Review of Economics* and the *Annual Review of Financial Economics*. The purpose of all of these Reviews is to provide authoritative critical reviews evaluating the most significant research developments in each field. The groundbreaking *Annual Review of Resource Economics* will provide a forum in which emerging and leading scholars will evaluate the most important contemporary advances in the broad field of resource economics, focusing on agricultural economics, environmental economics, renewable resources, exhaustible resources, and economic development. Scholars authoring articles in each volume will lay out the most important recent developments based on the *significant* findings contributing to the total literature in the field, writing with technical precision for a broad audience of scholars across the economics and related disciplines. Our strategy in commissioning these articles is different from other reviews. We deliberately target research frontier questions—where different methodologies are available to address closely related problems or where different results have coexisted without efforts to reconcile them.

Each volume is designed for audiences with a general background in economics as well as a broad range of scientists interested in the core of analytical economics, the natural sciences, and public policy. In the final analysis, it is the intention of the editorial committee of the *Annual Review of Resource Economics* to present in each volume a rolling textbook or desk reference for all those professionals seeking authoritative, peer-reviewed, and up-to-date analysis on the nexus between resource economics, natural science, and public policy.

In this first volume of the *Annual Review of Resource Economics*, we have organized the contributions around four broad themes: policy analysis and design (nine articles), resource dynamics (seven articles), ecology and space (six articles), and technology and innovation (six articles). Within each of these categories, the articles are sequenced to move from the more general to the more specific. In the policy analysis and design category, the articles begin with the broad picture of the role of agriculture in economic development. They then continue with the economics of transition in developing economies; global distortions in economic sectors resulting from governmental intervention; financial contracts between the public and private sectors; environmental regulations and their influence on market structure; the development of new risk markers; policy reactions to the so-called curse of natural resources; experimental economics analysis of the intersection of the environment and development; and finally, the evaluation of designed experiments on choice behavior, the environment, and health in developing countries.

The resource dynamics category begins with analyses of irreversibility, a current assessment of the seminal work of Hotelling and the intertemporal modeling of risk and uncertainty. It continues with an overview of rent taxation for exhaustible resources, assessments of the interaction between climate change and both land use and urban growth, and ends with a comparison of reduced-form and structural modeling in environmental and resource economics. In the third category (ecology and space), issues of land use, water allocation, and biodiversity are assessed, beginning with the integration of ecological and economic models, our progress on land use, endangered species, and water allocation and pricing. The final category on technology and innovation is initiated with an authoritative assessment of the economics of R&D, particularly in agriculture and food systems, followed by electricity markets in the developing world; energy efficiency economics; and recent developments in renewable technologies, biofuels, and biotechnology.

We adopt the tradition of Annual Reviews volumes of honoring one of our field's most distinguished scholars with an invited prefatory essay. Robert M. Solow, a Nobel Prize winner in Economics, inaugurates this tradition with his customary charm and grace, providing a rich overview of resource economics focusing on the thorny issue of sustainability, its conceptualization, and its empirical formulations. After articulating what had been accomplished, he sets an agenda that focuses largely on future research at the core of production economics.

For all of our future volumes of the *Annual Review of Resource Economics*, we anticipate and welcome the advice and counsel of our colleagues as well as readers of this first volume. For the time being, we extend our gratitude to all those who have contributed to the launch of this series and thank those who have worked behind the scenes to contribute to what promises to be an exciting new intellectual venture. Our ultimate objective is to establish a forum in which emerging and leading scholars advance and explain the most important contemporary developments in our field.

Gordon Rausser,
Editor, Robert Gordon Sproul Distinguished Professor,
University of California, Berkeley

Kerry Smith,
Associate Editor, W.P. Carey Professor of Economics,
Arizona State University, Tempe

David Zilberman,
Associate Editor, Robinson Chair in Agricultural Economics,
University of California, Berkeley

Annual Review of
Resource Economics

Volume 1, 2009

Contents

Resource Dynamics

Ecology and Space

Technology and Innovation

Errata

An online log of corrections to *Annual Review of Resource Economics* articles
may be found at http://resource.AnnualReviews.org

Related Articles

Robert M Solow

An Amateur Among Professionals

Robert M. Solow

Department of Economics, Massachusetts Institute of Technology,
Cambridge, Massachusetts 02139; email: jamu@mit.edu

Annu. Rev. Resour. Econ. 2009. 1:1–14

First published online as a Review in Advance on
June 22, 2009

The *Annual Review of Resource Economics* is
online at resource.annualreviews.org

This article's doi:
10.1146/annurev.resource.050708.144305

1941-1340/09/1010-0001$20.00

Key Words

resource economics, Hotelling condition, sustainability, backstop
technology

Abstract

This brief retrospective note describes the author's occasional contributions to the economics of natural resources. It emphasizes the
role and interpretation of the Hotelling condition and discusses
the reasons why that result plays so small a role empirically. The
concept of sustainability is introduced in the simplest possible
content, that of directly consuming a finite stock over infinite time.
When the resources flow is an input into production along with
capital that can be accumulated, the nature of sustainability
changes and becomes more interesting. It is suggested, however,
that to consider instead the eventual availability of a resource-free
backstop technology may be just as interesting and more relevant.
That concept is illustrated in the direct-consumption context but
awaits further development in production economies.

For good reason, this is a very short example of the genre "retrospective essay." Although I have had a long career as an economist, I have only a very brief and episodic record as a resource (and environmental) economist. There is not a lot to retrospect about. But my timing has been pretty good, and maybe not accidentally.

The theory of economic growth, and the role of capital accumulation in it, has been a long-time preoccupation, however. I think I was always sort of subliminally aware (and often superliminally aware) that natural-resource limitations (including those imposed or mediated by the environment) were absent from theoretical and empirical model-building. Most of the time that seemed to be more an intellectual gap than a practical error. I was well acquainted with the book by Barnett & Morse (1963). (Harold Barnett was a friend from my graduate-student days.) So resource scarcity did not seem to be a pressing practical problem. And I remembered having been told by a distinguished chemist friend that untold quantities of nitrogen could be fixed from the air (given only a large supply of cheap energy), that the energy would eventually be available from the Sun in one form or another, and that nitrogen could provide the basis of a whole materials economy. For a macroeconomist like me, there were other things to think about.

Then came the splash over the Club of Rome's *Limits to Growth* (Meadows et al. 1971). I tend to react badly when opprobrium, especially ignorant opprobrium, is heaped upon "economists." When I read the book, it seemed to me to draw sweeping conclusions from unverified assumptions and thin-air-invented dynamics, meanwhile ignoring some normal market mechanisms. I commented on the book twice (Solow 1972, 1973), but in rather inaccessible places. Probably not coincidentally, in 1974, came two opportunities: to contribute an article to a special issue of the *Review of Economic Studies* (Solow 1974a) devoted to the economics of natural resources and to give the Ely Lecture (Solow 1974b) at the annual convention of the American Economic Association. So I could do some academic research that fit into my normal scheme of things and also help to open up the analytical issue of resource limitations to a wider group of economists who would actually understand the substance. And so began my mini career as a resource economist.

A second active current of thought also helped to lead me—as if by an Invisible Hand?—to the topic of the technical paper "Intergenerational Equity and Exhaustible Resources" (Solow 1974a), introducing the theory of optimal economic growth stemming from Frank Ramsey's (1928) famous article. The connection is easy to see in terms of the simplest "cake-eating" problem. Consider a cake of finite size to be consumed over the infinite future: At what rate should it be consumed? Diminishing marginal utility of cake suggests equal consumption in every interval, but no constant consumption level other than zero is feasible forever. So perhaps future utility should be discounted according to subjective time preference. (Ramsey opposed this practice on ethical grounds.) That would suggest equalizing discounted marginal utility over time. With a constant discount rate—the only time-consistent possibility—the marginal utility of cake would have to grow exponentially and indefinitely with time, so the rate of consumption would have to converge to zero. That is feasible, but it does not seem fair to the future. (I hardly need to mention that these same puzzles about discounting—it matters so much and rests on so little—are again at the center of controversies about the proper response to global warming.)

The finite-cake story seems relevant to the problem of exhaustible or nonrenewable resources, but it misses too much. (It is understood that the notion of "running out" can be replaced by the notion of prohibitively rising extraction costs.) The natural resources we are concerned about are not consumed directly; they are used in varying amounts, along with other inputs, to produce the goods we consume. The finite-resource problem needs to be embedded in a model of production and consumption. Then the urgency of the resource-scarcity problem will, in a commonsense way, depend on the importance of resource inputs, on the ease or difficulty with which other inputs can be substituted for nonrenewable resources, and on technological progress that allows more consumable output to be extracted from any combination of natural-resource and other inputs.

The notion that technological progress could make the resource-scarcity problem go away seemed too simple and obvious, even if possibly true, so I started from a fairly traditional growth model without technological change. The problem was then to find and characterize the largest constant level of consumption that could be permanently sustained, starting with a finite stock of a nonrenewable resource that was essential to production (in the sense that zero resource input implied zero output). The other productive inputs were capital and labor. With the supply of labor constant for the very long run, the game was all about the accumulation of capital played against the depletion of the resource. In this setting, constant positive consumption forever cannot simply be ruled out, as it can in the cake-eating case. Indeed, intuition was confirmed and made precise: Enough substitutability would do the trick, and in the borderline case, the outcome depended on the relative importance of capital and resources as inputs (as measured by the elasticity of output with respect to each of those inputs).

That sort of logic was clearly a way of getting at the general issue of sustainability. A large, ingenious, and useful literature has evolved on these important questions, some of which is summarized in a recent note by John Hartwick (2009). One especially interesting result was what I called Hartwick's Rule: The investment of all (competitive) resource rents along an efficient path leads to just enough capital accumulation to maintain a constant level of consumption. This thought, too, has been further elaborated in the literature.

My only further contribution was expository. In one invited lecture (Solow 1992b), I tried to explain to a scientifically literate audience that "sustainability" did not and should not mean the preservation of every individual resource and environmental amenity, but rather the preservation of a general capacity to produce well-being. The common injunction to leave Nature as we found it is neither feasible nor sensible. In another lecture (Solow 1992a), I used Hartwick's Rule to argue for comprehensive "green" national accounts that would, among other benefits, allow some approximation to the volume of net investment in reproducible capital required for sustainability of national consumption.

The Ely Lecture "The Economics of Resources and the Resources of Economics" (Solow 1974) was intended not only to introduce a broad audience of economists to the economic theory of nonrenewable resources, but also to defend our fair discipline against ignorant statements about its incapacity to deal with the role of nature in economic life. The particular device that came naturally was to treat Hotelling's original analysis as an application of capital theory to a nonreproducible resource. There is no need to rehearse those ideas here, but see Hartwick (2009) and other articles in the symposium in the first issue of the *Journal of Natural Resources Policy Research*.

I would like to comment, however, on one aspect of the Hotelling-based theory. It leads, as is well known, to the proposition that the scarcity rent on a nonrenewable resource, the excess of price over marginal extraction cost, should be rising through time at a proportional rate equal to the (real) rate of interest. But empirical work aimed at testing this proposition against facts has yielded, at best, mixed results, and probably less. It is safe to say that it is very difficult to detect this sort of price behavior in actual time series, for several reasons.

For one thing, it is possible that, in many cases, the scarcity rent has been relatively small during the period of observation, if the ultimate exhaustibility of the resource is seen as a very distant or even unlikely event. Then its movement through time could be lost in the noise. More important, for many natural-resource products, short-run supply and demand curves may be rather inelastic with respect to price. Then the inevitable shifts in supply and demand curves—related to weather, politics, the business cycle, downstream shifts in demand, occasional innovations, and so forth—will generate large and erratic changes in price, perhaps further exaggerated by speculation. Modest scarcity rents will be even harder to detect and isolate.

A recent and as yet unpublished paper by James D. Hamilton (2008) makes this point well and concludes, "The $140/barrel price in the summer of 2008 and the $60/barrel in November of 2008 could not both be consistent with the same calculation of a scarcity rent warranted by long-term fundamentals. Notwithstanding, the algebra of compound growth suggests that if demand growth resumes in China and other countries at its previous rate, the date at which the scarcity rent will start to make an important contribution to the price, if not here already, can not be far away." That sounds reasonable.

Considerations like this may help to account for the apparent empirical irrelevance of the Hotelling (1931) model. But they also remind us of the proper function of an abstract theory of that kind. It is both a guide to the intuition and a very general framework, not a precise template, for empirical investigation. Hotelling reminds us that the existing stock of a natural resource, renewable or nonrenewable, is a capital asset, even if it has some special characteristics not shared with other types of capital assets such as printing presses or inventories of canned goods. So we have a notion of how to start thinking about them and observing what happens in their markets. Even apart from the particular difficulties mentioned above, you would not expect to see the price of oil or copper behaving exactly like a well-defined marginal extraction cost plus an exponentially rising scarcity rent, any more than you would expect to see the price of spinach looking exactly like the ratio of the marginal utility of spinach to the marginal utility of income for the well-defined marginal buyer of spinach.

Nowadays the main practical focus of attention in the economics of natural resources is the future supply of energy. The rapid growth of the large Chinese and Indian economies; the possibility that the peak of world oil production is just ahead or already behind us; and the special difficulties, political and environmental, associated with coal and nuclear energy have all conspired to create a lively interest in alternative, nonfossil-fuel-based sources of usable energy. With this in mind, I mention a line of thought and research that brings together the insights of the Hotelling model and the issue of sustainability, the two topics I have been discussing so parochially in terms of my own writing.

In 1973, needing it to establish reasonable terminal conditions for an intertemporal model of oil production, William Nordhaus (1973) introduced the concept of a "backstop technology." In context he meant a technology for producing useful energy that was not dependent on a nonrenewable resource base and, thus, could provide an indefinitely sustainable tail to an episode of oil-based economic life. The idea was that the backstop technology might not be available at all until some time in the future or that it might be available now but at an uneconomically high cost, although this cost could be expected to fall over time. Eventually the Oil Age links up with the Backstop Age, with or without an interval of overlap, until the Oil Age ends and the (in principle, infinite) Backstop Age begins.

This struck me at the time—I was teaching a course on the economics of natural resources—as a more sensible, more realistic, way to think about the very long run than the kind of maximum-feasible-constant-consumption-path exercise I described above. This backstop-technology concept is probably what will eventually play out in history. So far as I know, there has not been much literature, either purely theoretical or empirically calibrated, following up Nordhaus's idea. There should be more, and the widespread interest in energy from direct solar, wind, biofuels, and the like should stimulate this research.

At a summer school in 2003 (see Appendix below), I gave a lecture whose broad topic was the relation between ecology and economics. There I tried to offer an expository but fairly complete treatment of the backstop-technology idea applied to the simplest cake-eating problem. It does manage to synthesize the Hotelling model with intuitions about sustainability, without any need for time discounting. I never published that lecture, but I include it here as an Appendix (see section below), in the hope of stirring up some more sophisticated work on what seems to me to be the right way in practice—in theoretical practice, that is—to deal with the sustainability issue. Once again, the backstop idea needs to be embedded in a model with production. There will be some difficult modeling decisions: For example, is the capital employed in the resource-using technology shiftable to the backstop technology when the transition occurs? It is hard to guess in advance whether anything very different will happen, but the presence of more margins to play with should lead to some interesting economics.

An explicitly retrospective essay like this may tend to encourage an unhealthy concern with oneself. I want to mention—for a reason, I hasten to say—that I can remember writing only two papers on renewable resources, although I always included them in my teaching. The first (Solow 1976) was on an optimal fishing strategy when a natural predator on the valued species is present; I did the best I could, but I was unhappy that I could provide only a dual characterization of the optimal strategy, not a straightforward primal description. The second (Solow 2002) was a modification of the standard when-to-cut-a-tree formula if the standing stock of trees also conveyed a benefit.

I mention this to point out that both papers were composed for *Festschriften*: the first in honor of William Vickrey, who was interested in everything, the second in honor of Karl-Göran Mäler, a mainstay of the field. It has struck me that essentially everything I have written on resource economics, with maybe a fractional exception for the first paper on constant-consumption paths, has been a response to an invitation: a lecture, a *Festschrift*, a conference. That is what happens to a (curious) amateur among professionals.

APPENDIX: BACK TO BACKSTOP TECHNOLOGY

The following is extracted, with minor revision, from a previously unpublished talk given at the Summer School on Economics and Ecology held in Trieste, Italy, in June 2003.

This is not a talk on sustainability. The notion of sustainability has become a buzzword in current discourse about economic policy. The path traced by the concept is a rather familiar one in economics. It starts as a fairly vague, but not meaningless, characteristic of possible paths for an economy or part of an economy, and generally a desirable characteristic at that. The next step was to give the notion some precision. In the intellectual style of modern economics, this meant embedding it in a well-conceived model, so that we could discuss things like measurement, implications, trade-offs, equilibrium conditions, optimality properties, and the rest of the routine apparatus.

Then, in the spirit of the man who said "I know how to spell 'banana' but I don't know when to stop," we continued to refine the concept well past our capacity to actually use it. This is not necessarily bad; the marginal value of refinement may be pretty low, but very likely the marginal cost is even lower. [By the way, Y. Hossein Farzin (2002a,b) provides a very useful recent attempt to put some order and simplicity into the literature on sustainability.]

Nevertheless, the point I want to make in this talk is that, for practical purposes, there is a more useful set of theoretical and empirical investigations we could be pursuing with roughly the same applied-analytical goal in mind, namely understanding the constraints imposed on economic evolution by the natural environment (more realistically, by some aspects of the natural environment).

Some 30 years ago, set in motion by the first OPEC oil shock, Professor William Nordhaus of Yale University sketched a programming model of the world oil economy. His immediate goal was to estimate the shadow price, i.e., the true scarcity value, of a barrel of crude oil in the ground. You can easily understand how interesting and significant it would have been to compare this shadow price with the world market price of crude oil in 1974. (One of my favorite professorial reminiscences is connected with that paper. I was explaining Nordhaus's work in a graduate course I was then teaching on the economic theory of natural resources. As a strong believer in economics as a handicraft industry, I mentioned, teasingly, to the class that this remarkable piece of work had been done by an extraordinarily powerful research apparatus, not to be undervalued by advocates of Big Economics: one professor and one undergraduate research assistant. When the class was over, one of the students came shyly up to me and said, "I was the undergraduate research assistant." It turned out to be Paul Krugman. Teaching can be an unexpected pleasure.)

Today's shadow value of an oil deposit is a forward-looking concept, like any other asset price. To take an obvious example, it must depend on expected future discoveries of oil, on future availability of alternative sources of energy, as well as on future demand. There is an obvious connection with sustainability: Along an unsustainable path, one would expect the shadow price to be rising, and this must have an effect on the current price.

Nordhaus chose a way of dealing with this problem that still strikes me as sensible. Instead of worrying about the infinite-time possibilities for an economy with a finite stock of oil, he took it for granted that the world would sooner or later revert to a technology for mobilizing energy that was not based on an exhaustible resource. He called this the "backstop technology." Such technologies already exist, and they existed then; they have not yet taken over from fossil-fuel technologies because they are more costly. But they will eventually become cheaper than fossil-fuel-based technologies both because the backstop technology will improve over time and because the shadow price of oil will increase (for reasons already discerned by Harold Hotelling in 1931).

So Nordhaus made what seemed like plausible assumptions about the evolution of energy costs associated with the most likely backstop technologies; he used these assumptions to anchor the future shadow price of oil, from which he could work backward toward the current shadow price. This was an application of Herbert Stein's deep philosophical remark to the effect that, "Anything that can not possibly go on will stop." Since I was teaching a graduate course in the economic theory of natural resources, I went on to work out for my class the timing and details of the transition from an exhaustible-resource-based technology to a resource-free (or renewable-resource-based) technology.

I really like those refinements, and I think that learning about them is an important part of the education of an economist. I also think that it is probably more useful to investigate the emergence of backstop technologies and their implications than to focus on the version of sustainability that motivates the literature today. I want to say clearly that this is not an aesthetic or theoretical judgment, but an empirical one. The backstop scenario is a more likely one to play out in the future, so the value of a marginal refinement in that arena is likely to exceed the value of further refinements in modeling sustainability.

I propose to illustrate the nature of the backstop story by dealing informally with the oldest and simplest problem of allocating a finite resource over infinite time, indeed a case in which there is obviously no indefinitely sustainable path in the usual sense. You will guess that I have in mind the so-called cake-eating problem. It has the advantage that I can make the important general points without technical detail.

Let me remind you of the story. An economy—possibly a single shipwrecked sailor, possibly something more complex—has at its disposal a given stock S of an essential resource. A flow use of the resource can serve as a productive input, and that can lead to some interesting economics, now well explored, but it is simpler if we imagine the resource to be directly consumed. The instantaneous social utility function is $u(c)$, with all the usual properties and, to make things easy but still interesting, $u(0) = 0$ and $u'(0) = \infty$, so that zero consumption is truly painful. [The alternative assumption that $u(0) = -\infty$ may be more interesting, but it requires more detail than is useful here.] The question is, What is the best time pattern of use of the stock S? A strong assumption, almost always adopted in this part of economics, is that utility is time additive: The criterion of goodness is $\int_0^\infty u(c(t))dt$. Notice that I have not allowed for a utility discount rate. I will have to say more about that soon; I would be very happy to be able to do without it, because it was never struck me as a convincing assumption, neither for a shipwrecked sailor nor for a society.

If the stock S had to last only for a finite time T, then the obvious solution is steady use: $c(t) = S/T$ for $0 < t < T$. Mere diminishing marginal utility tells us that any nonconstant flow can be improved by transferring some consumption from an instant with higher flow (and therefore lower marginal utility) to an instant with lower flow (and therefore higher marginal utility). The value for that path is $Tu(S/T)$. Once S is used up, however, the society or the sailor is condemned to utter misery for the rest of time; so that is not really a good solution. If we ignore this crucial fact for a moment, it is easy to calculate that $d/dT[Tu(S/T)] = u(S/T) - (S/T)u'(S/T) > 0$. (This is where the assumption that $u(0) = 0$ helps.) In that sense, a longer period of lower use is always better than a shorter period of higher use. In contrast, $T = \infty$ is not a solution because then $c = 0$; that is a way of saying that there is no sustainable pay for this economy. We have reached a well-known impasse.

The standard way out of this box, as I assume everyone knows, is to introduce a positive utility-discount rate, so that the society or the sailor maximizes $\int e^{-rt} u(c(t))dt$. This leads to the equalization of discounted marginal utility at every instant, or $u'(c(t)) = ke^{rt}$, with the constant k chosen so as exactly to use up the initial stock S. But then consumption decreases steadily toward zero, and instantaneous social utility decreases with increasing painfulness to zero. Exponential discounting cleans up the mathematical mess and leaves everything finite. The trouble with this "solution" is that discounting is so arbitrary and therefore ultimately unconvincing. There is an intelligent but inconclusive literature that tries to evade this arbitrariness. (The most up-to-date source is probably Portney & Weyant 1999.) This is not what I want to discuss. One of my goals is precisely to be able to do without an arbitrary discount rate.

Instead I introduce a backstop technology. Suppose there is now, or will be in the future, a way of producing a perfect (meaning very close) substitute for the nonrenewable resource. That is to say, it is possible even now, or will be possible in the future, to get along without the resource, but perhaps—though not necessarily—at a very low level of utility. It should be understood that this is not intended as some kind of analytical device; it is an assumption about the physical world (and not about preferences). I think it is worth exploring because I think it is usually empirically true. If it is not empirically valid, it is pointless.

The historically interesting situation is that a primitive backstop technology is known, but it is expected to become more productive in the future. Obviously the future productivity of any backstop technology is uncertain; I will argue deterministically, but a probabilistic theory is needed if the basic idea is useful. My basic belief is that the theoretical and empirical investigation of backstop technologies is a better use of intellectual effort than the refinement of arguments about discounting and sustainability.

The simplest case for elementary exposition is that the backstop technology already exists and is not expected to improve. We can cut out some intermediate steps (like calculating the maximum level of utility achievable using only the backstop technology) by simply assuming that the best such utility level is u_b. In addition I will assume that the resource-based and backstop technologies cannot be used simultaneously; it is a case of one or the other at any time. This simplification is inessential, but it economizes on routine calculation.

The problem can now be formulated in this way: Over how long an interval T should the nonrenewable resource be used? While it is being used, it should be used at a constant rate, for the diminishing-marginal-utility reasons already mentioned, so the utility level achieved will be $u(S/T)$. In the absence of discounting, it does not matter when that interval occurs, or even whether it consists of one interval or several with lengths adding up to T. I put resource use at the very beginning, for definiteness. This is obviously the right thing to do if the backstop technology is expected to improve over time; this is the realistic presumption, and I take it up in a moment.

Suppose the Oil Age extends from 0 to T and the Solar Age extends from T to Z, where Z is some arbitrary date that will turn out to play no role at all. I stay with the conventional assumption of time additivity. Then total undiscounted utility is $Tu(S/T) + (Z - T)u_b$. The best value of T satisfies $u(S/T) - (S/T)u'(S/T) - u_b = 0$. Obviously, then, T^* is independent of Z. So this solution (steady flow of resource use for the first T^* units of time, best use of backstop technology thereafter) is valid for all time, with zero discounting. There is a simple graphical solution for T^*. **Figure 1** plots the utility function $u(c)$. Rotate a ray starting at $(0,u_b)$ until it is tangent to the utility function at c^*. Then $T^* = S/c^*$.

The utility path for the economy is shown in **Figure 2**. It may be worth mentioning explicitly that if $u_b > u(c)^*$, then the economy never consumes its nonrenewable resource; the backstop technology is superior. But that is uninteresting: The "deposit" would not even be seen as a "resource."

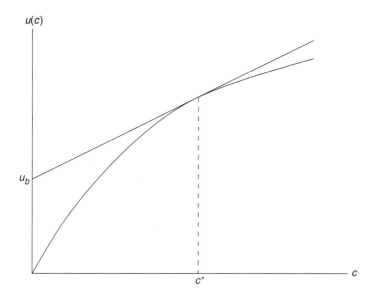

Figure 1

Optimal current consumption c^* is determined by the tangecy of the line from u^b with $u(c)$. Then $T^* = S/c^*$. Variables: c^*, the optimal level of consumption; S, the original stock; T^*, the optimal time over which to exhaust the original stock; u_b, the level of utility achievable with the backstop technology; $u(c)$, the level of utility associated with consumption level c.

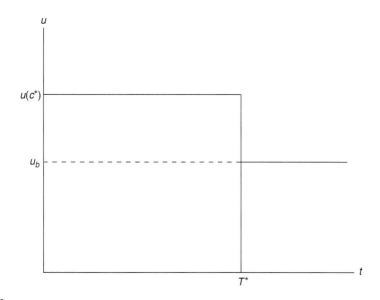

Figure 2

The corresponding path for $u(c)$, from which the path for c follows. Variables: c^*, the optimal level of consumption; t, time; T^*, the optimal time over which to exhaust the original stock; u_b, the level of utility achievable with the backstop technology.

A more interesting and more "realistic" scenario occurs when the net social value associated with the backstop technology is an increasing function of calendar time $u_b(t)$. The backstop technology may not even be available now or in the near future, but it is expected to appear at a fixed date in the future, say t_1, and to improve in productivity from then on. [There is room for elaboration here: $u_b(t)$ should be probabilistic rather than known with certainty, and a more inclusive model could allow for learning by doing or some other endogenous influences on $u_b(t)$.] So the situation is as described in **Figure 3**, and the problem is once again to choose the best pattern of use of the stock S of the natural resource in these circumstances.

As always, when the resource-based technology is in use, the flow should be constant; peaks and valleys are wasteful. Now, however, the interval of use of the resource should definitely come at the beginning, even without discounting. It is better to use the backstop technology when it is more productive rather than less (unless possibly if there is a learn-by-doing component). A time interval $(0,T^*)$ is to be chosen, with the resource being used up at the rate $c^* = S/T^*$; thereafter the backstop technology is employed, yielding social utility $u_b(t)$.

More can be said, without much fuss. For instance, the path shown in **Figure 4** is not efficient. When the resource is exhausted at T^*, there should not be a discrete upward jump in social utility as the economy switches to the backstop technology. The reason is that a slightly smaller value of T^* (larger value of c^*) would improve social welfare during the (slightly shorter) resource-use period, and the first stages of use of the backstop technology would still improve on the last stages of resource use under the initial trail program. So $u(c^*) \geq u_b(T^*)$.

Can social welfare take a discrete drop at T^*? Yes, it can. Start with the path in **Figure 5**.

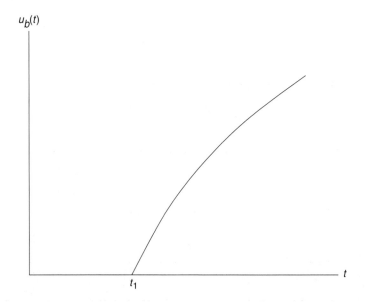

Figure 3

A backstop technology that is first available at t_1 and then becomes more productive over time. Variables: t, time; u_b, the level of utility achievable with the backstop technology.

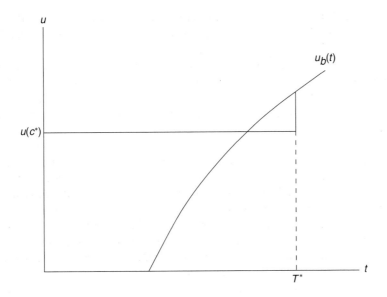

Figure 4

A nonoptimal value of T^*: A slightly smaller value would increase utility as an interval with no decrease elsewhere. Variables: t, time; T^*, the optimal time over which to exhaust the original stock; $u(c)$, the level of utility associated with consumption level c; u_b, the level of utility achievable with the backstop technology.

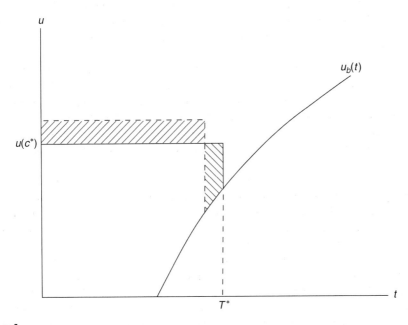

Figure 5

A discrete decrease in c and u at T^* is optimal. Variables: t, time; T^*, the optimal time over which to exhaust the original stock; u_b, the level of utility achievable with the backstop technology; $u(c)$, the level of utility associated with consumption level c.

Would it be better to choose a slightly smaller T^*? That would increase the flow of social utility during the new resource-use phase. But that phase would end sooner. The net gain in undiscounted social welfare would be the area of the horizontal shaded sliver, offset by a loss equal to the area of the shaded vertical sliver at the end shown in **Figure 5**. The comparison could go either way, depending on the exact shape of $u_b(t)$ and the utility function $u(c)$. Actually, assuming only that $u_b(t)$ is smoothly increasing, it is easy to see that there must be a discrete reduction in instantaneous social utility at the instant at which the economy switches from the resource-based to the backstop technology. [Social welfare for any choice to T is $W = Tu(S/T) + \int_T^Z u_b(t)dt$, where the irrelevant Z is introduced. So $dW/dT = u(S/T) - (S/T)u'(S/T) - u_b(T)$. If $u(S/T) \leqq u_b(T)$, it follows that $dW/dT < 0$ at T. It would be an improvement to reduce T a little, which would create a positive gap between $u(S/T)$ and $u_b(T)$. It is amusing that I can see this in **Figure 5**, but I have a hard time putting it into words.]

It should be understood that this kind of model can be elaborated in several directions. The resource-based and backstop technologies could be specified in more detail, with labor and other costs made explicit. Then there would be a normal allocation problem within the economy, to be studied in the usual way. A demand side could be added, with consumption and investment endogenized. It would be possible to relax the assumption that only one of the resource-based and backstop technologies can be used at any time, so that there could be an interval when oil and solar share the energy market. In brief, a whole general equilibrium apparatus can be built and wrapped around the basic technological choice.

I repeat, this technical maneuver is precisely not the prospect that interests me now. It seems to me that the organization and development of backstop technologies is in fact the way a growing economy typically evades the sustainability problem. Societies typically do not conserve scarce nonrenewable resources; instead, societies typically work around them, either by shifting to technologies based on more abundant resources or, in the limit, by reducing use of scarce resources to a minimum. Two or three decades ago, when I first got interested in this part of economics, I asked an eminent chemist friend (Professor Paul Doty of Harvard University) how far he thought it would ultimately be possible to economize on scarce nonrenewable resources. He answered that, with cheap enough energy and more or less unlimited access to nitrogen (a very abundant element in the atmosphere), it would be possible to create new materials and, with them, manufacture just about everything.

I do not know if that forecast looks valid today. But that way of thinking certainly suggests that the algebra of backstop technologies is more relevant to sustainability in our society than the refined algebra of conservation of exhaustible resources and the fairly unproductive discussion of the logic and morality of discounting that seems to accompany it. At least there are some rough empirical calculations to be made.

In taking the first steps in this direction, it is convenient to assume that the backstop technology produces a perfect substitute for the resource-based output. This is certainly the case with electric energy, usually the first context one thinks of. Obviously "very good substitute" is a very good substitute for "perfect substitute." There are also contexts in which the backstop perspective may be inappropriate. Think of scenic wonders—natural or man-made—for instance. Could we provide a near-perfect substitute for the Giant Sequoia or the Parthenon? What makes me suspicious is that people might have to be "taught" that some other species of tree—or fish or landscape—is "just as good as" the giant redwoods. This puts one in mind of the sort of brainwashing described by Aldous Huxley (1932) in his anti-utopia *Brave New World*. Once that analogy occurs to you, it looks more attractive to leave the Giant Sequoia alone. (A rule of reason should apply: The lack of perfect substitute for an enormous old redwood does not imply that none exists for a not-very-distinguished species of fish.)

Recent public discussions of possible backstop technologies for energy have not been exactly confidence inspiring. Many alternatives to oil and gas have been mentioned: direct solar, wind, biomass, hydrogen, fuel cells, tar sands. But the accompanying analysis often has the faint odor of hype. Too often we are told that backstop technology X will become viable when the real price of oil rises $Y a barrel; if the real price of oil does just that, we are told that the next increment of $Y will be the key. Obviously that kind of research would be better taken out of the hands of interested parties, including governments.

I am only too conscious that the trail I have been following is resource economic rather than ecologic economic in substance. When I began working in this field, the resource-economic research area was the economics of fisheries. Ecological economics began to take shape only when I was working on other things altogether, so I am not up to date. I tend to doubt that it has taken shape yet; maybe this conference will mark an inflection. In any case, as an old dog, I could not hope to contribute new tricks to ecological economics.

There is a generic difference between resource economics and ecological economics. In the first, the resource stock does not react to its exploitation (except, of course, by becoming depleted). In the second, it does. In ecological economics, the resource stock has an interesting and important dynamic of its own. The case of the fishery, in its early development, was sort of intermediary. The fish population does have a dynamic, but in the old days, it was modeled as pretty simple, usually logistic. Maybe modern fishery economics pays more attention to the interrelated ecology of the ocean. (I did once, about 30 years ago, write a paper introducing a natural predator into an otherwise standard fishery model but did not get very far, probably because computer simulation was not then as available as it is now.)

The function of economic theory is to help train the intuition of economists and, as part of that process, to help guide empirical work. I have kept emphasizing, perhaps to the point of boredom, that models combining an exhaustible resource with a backstop technology are interesting only if access to backstop technologies is, in fact, an important part of the history of societies casting about for sustainability. In that case, it is a good idea for economists to polish their intuition on problems associated with the transition to backstop technologies, and perhaps to the endogenous evolution of such technologies.

I am not sure that I can provide a lesson for ecological economics, nor am I sure that it is my duty to provide one. If my earlier suggestion is correct, that the significant difference between ecological economics and resource economics is that the reciprocal dynamics of an ecological system subject to human exploitation is radically more complicated than that of a simple resource, then one natural object of research is to classify and categorize those dynamic responses. I am a great believer in simple models and "representative" special cases. That may be the proper approach in this bilaterally complicated field. The problem may be to locate the key simplifications, whether they are on the ecological or the economic side. Probably, they will have to be on both sides.

If one were setting out to model the interaction of economists and ecologists in creating and extending a subdiscipline of ecological economics, it would be interesting to observe conferences like this and to think whether a predator-prey model is appropriate—and who is the predator and who is the prey—or else a situation where complementarities are exploited and cooperation rules. I am hoping for the best.

DISCLOSURE STATEMENT

The author is not aware of any affiliations, memberships, funding, or financial holdings that might be perceived as affecting the objectivity of this review.

LITERATURE CITED

Barnett HJ, Morse C. 1963. *Scarcity of Growth: The Economics of Mineral Extraction*. Baltimore, MD: Johns Hopkins Univ. Press

Farzin YH. 2002a. *Can an exhaustible resource economy be sustainable?* Work Pap. 47.2002, FEEM. doi: 10.2139/ssrn.317933

Farzin YH. 2002b. *Sustainability and Hamiltonian value*. Work. Pap. 48.2002, FEEM. doi: 10.2139/ssrn.317959

Hamilton JD. 2008. *Understanding crude oil prices*. Work. Pap., Dep. Econ, Univ. Calif., San Diego

Hartwick J. 2009. What would Solow say? *J. Nat. Resour. Policy Res.* 1(1):1–6

Hotelling H. 1931. The economics of exhaustible resources. *J. Polit. Econ.* 39(2):137–75

Huxley A. 1932. *Brave New World*. New York: Harper & Brothers Publ.

Meadows DH, Meadows DL, Randers J, Behrens WW. 1971. *The Limits to Growth*. New York: Universe Books

Nordhaus W. 1973. The allocation of energy resources. *Brook. Pap. Econ. Act.* 3:529–70

Portney P, Weyant JP, eds. 1999. *Discounting and Intergenerational Equity*. Washington, DC: Resour. Future

Ramsey F. 1928. A mathematical theory of saving. *Econ. J.* 38(Dec.):543–59

Solow R. 1972. Notes on 'Doomsday Models.' *Proc. Natl. Acad. Sci. USA* 69(2):3832–33

Solow R. 1973. Is the end of the world at hand? *Challenge* 16(1):39–50

Solow R. 1974a. Intergenerational equity and exhaustible resources. *Rev. Econ. Stud.* 41:29–45 [1973. Work. Pap. 103, Dep. Econ., MIT]

Solow R. 1974b. The economics of resources or the resources of economics? *Am. Econ. Rev. Pap. Proc.* 64(2):1–14

Solow R. 1976. Optimal fishing with a natural predator. In *Public and Urban Economics: Essays in Honor of William S. Vickrey*, ed. R Grieson. Lexington, MA: Lexington Books

Solow R. 1992a. An almost practical step toward sustainability. Invited lecture on the occasion of the 40th Anniversary of Resources for the Future, Washington, DC, October 8, 1992. *Resour. Policy* 19(3):162–72

Solow R. 1992b. Sustainability: an economist's perspective. *Res. Explor.* 8(1):3–6 [Condensed from the 18th J. Seward Johnson Lecture, 14 June 1991, Marine Policy Cent., Woods Hole Oceanogr. Inst., Woods Hole, MA]

Solow R. 2002. What if Jevons had actually liked trees? In *Economic Theory for the Environment, Essays in Honour of Karl-Göran Mäler*, ed. B Kriström, P Dasgupta, K-G Löfgren. Cheltenham, UK/Northampton, MA: Edward Elgar

Agriculture for Development: Toward a New Paradigm

Derek Byerlee,[1] Alain de Janvry,[2] and Elisabeth Sadoulet[2]

[1]The World Bank, Washington, D.C. 20433; email: dbyerlee@gmail.com

[2]Department of Agricultural and Resource Economics, University of California, Berkeley, California 94720; email: alain@are.berkeley.edu, sadoulet@are.berkeley.edu

Annu. Rev. Resour. Econ. 2009. 1:15–31

First published online as a Review in Advance on May 21, 2009

The *Annual Review of Resource Economics* is online at resource.annualreviews.org

This article's doi: 10.1146/annurev.resource.050708.144239

Key Words

agriculture, development, strategies, policies, poverty reduction

Abstract

The fundamental role that agriculture plays in development has long been recognized. In the seminal work on the subject, agriculture was seen as a source of contributions that helped induce industrial growth and a structural transformation of the economy. However, globalization, integrated value chains, rapid technological and institutional innovations, and environmental constraints have deeply changed the context for agriculture's role. We argue that a new paradigm is needed that recognizes agriculture's multiple functions for development in that emerging context: triggering economic growth, reducing poverty, narrowing income disparities, providing food security, and delivering environmental services. Yet, governments and donors have neglected these functions of agriculture with the result that agriculture growth has been reduced, 75% of world poverty is rural, sectoral income disparities have exploded, food insecurity has returned, and environmental degradation is widespread, compromising sustainability. Mobilizing these functions requires shifting the political economy to overcome antiagriculture policy biases, strengthening governance for agriculture, and tailoring priorities to country conditions.

INTRODUCTION

A rich literature, both theoretical and empirical, has examined the process of structural transformation of economies, from the least developed in which economic activity is based largely on agriculture, to the high income in which agriculture typically accounts for less than 5% of GDP. This literature has articulated agriculture's role as the precursor to the acceleration of industrial growth from England in the mid-eighteenth century to Japan in the late-nineteenth century as well as much of Asia in the late-twentieth century (Bairoch 1973, Timmer 1988, Diao et al. 2005). As shown in **Figure 1** (see color insert), the structural transformation where the shares of agriculture in employment and GDP decline as per capita income rises is a striking cross-country empirical regularity.

The thinking on the role of agriculture in this structural transformation has evolved over time. Classical theorists, led by Lewis (1954), viewed economic development as a growth process of relocating labor from an agricultural sector characterized by low productivity and the use of traditional technology to a modern urban-industrial sector with higher labor productivity. Lewis's theory was employed to support the industrialization-led strategies adopted by many developing countries during the 1950s and 1960s, which resulted in a pronounced "urban bias" in policy and investment decisions throughout this period (Staatz & Eicher 1998).

Beginning in the 1960s, a major revision in development thinking argued for a central role for agriculture as a driver of growth, especially in the early stages of industrialization (Johnston & Mellor 1961). This view of agriculture's lead role, stimulated in large part by the emerging experience in Asia, was founded on two core contributions. First, leading scholars such as Schultz (1964) and Hayami & Ruttan (1971) recognized that traditional agriculture could be transformed rapidly into a modern sector through the adoption of science-based technology, thereby making a large contribution to overall growth. Second, economists now explicitly identified the strong growth linkages and multiplier effects of agricultural growth to the nonagricultural sectors (Mellor 1998). A large share of manufacturing in the early stages of development is agriculturally related. More importantly, rising incomes of rural households were seen as vital to providing a market for domestically produced manufactures and services (Adelman 1984). Even when labor was believed to be in surplus in the rural sector, technological change and productivity growth were considered essential for industrialization to prevent rising food prices and nominal wage costs from undermining industrial development (Lele & Mellor 1981). The successful transfer of labor to the urban-industrial sector required important investment in rural human capital (Lucas 2004).

Following the Green Revolution experience in Asia, it was argued that these growth and employment linkages are most powerful when agricultural growth is driven by broad-based productivity increases in a rural economy dominated by small farms, as in much of Asia (Mellor 1976). Small- to medium-sized farm households typically have more favorable expenditure patterns for promoting growth of the local nonfarm economy, including rural towns, since they spend higher shares of income on rural nontraded goods and services, which are also generally more labor intensive (King & Byerlee 1978, Haggblade et al. 2008). This development of the rural nonfarm economy has been key to rural poverty reduction, particularly in China (Gulati & Fan 2007).

Despite broad acceptance of the structural transformation paradigm, this paper argues that it is time to rethink agriculture's roles in development for two reasons. First, the structural transformation models even with their more nuanced view of the role of agriculture still see agriculture as the handmaiden of industrialization. Yet, given the sheer size of the agricultural sector with an estimated 2.5 billion persons dependent on this activity, with three quarters of all poor people living in rural areas, and with agriculture as the largest user of natural resources, it is increasingly recognized that realization of the global development agenda will not be possible without explicitly focusing on the role of agriculture for development rather than agriculture in industrialization.

This recognition of agriculture's broader roles for development started in the 1970s with the focus on equity and employment, and the growing evidence that productivity growth across millions of smallholders was strongly pro-poor. During the 1990s, the development community explicitly recognized poverty reduction as the major objective of development programs and a burgeoning literature started to demonstrate the links between agriculture and poverty reduction (Timmer 2002, Thirtle et al. 2003, Christiaensen & Demery 2007).

Meanwhile, since the 1992 Earth Summit in Rio de Janeiro, the central role of agriculture for meeting the environmental agenda has been widely recognized, given that agriculture is the major user and often abuser of natural resources. This broader agenda was enshrined in the eight Millennium Development Goals agreed to in 2000 by all 191 United Nations member states. Agriculture relates to nearly all these goals and is central to at least three of them—reducing poverty and hunger, fostering gender equality, and sustainable management of the environment. In addition, agriculture's role in economic growth remains critical to achieving all these goals.

Second, even within a broader paradigm of agriculture for development, the world in which agriculture operates has changed drastically as a result of globalization, new technologies and institutions, and new more demanding markets. Globalization has spurred rapid growth in demand for agricultural exports especially for higher value products, while opening the potential for developing countries to import food. At the same time, tightly coordinated supply chains have emerged that now operate on a far larger scale, which have unleashed a massive transformation in the organization of agricultural markets. Similarly, new biotechnologies, as well as emerging new markets for agriculture such as the production of biofuels and the provision of environmental services for the mitigation of climate change, offer scope for faster growth of the sector. Finally, major institutional innovations in governance; civil society organizations; and services such as finance, insurance, and information imply a greatly increased role of the private sector and civil society as well as a more decentralized but smaller presence of the state.

Some of these changes are favorable to an agriculture-for-development agenda. Expanded markets for labor-intensive nontraditional exports create new opportunities for farmers in developing countries. But other changes challenge the implementation of this development agenda. The competitiveness of agriculture in the poorest countries and the viability of the family farm are called into question by restricted access to proprietary technological innovations, economies of scale in provisioning more demanding supply chains, and a declining role and capacity of the state in servicing the small-farm sector.

This paper reviews these wider roles of agriculture for development and argues that, even in the dramatically changed context of the twenty-first century, agriculture remains critical to the development agenda. Departing from the standard structural transformation paradigm, the paper outlines agriculture's multiple roles in five central pillars of the development agenda—economic growth, poverty reduction, equity including by gender, food security, and environmental sustainability—identifying important synergies and trade-offs between them.

Yet, despite the powerful arguments for raising the profile of agriculture for development, the political economy of national development strategies and international development assistance has widely shortchanged the sector. The final section addresses this political economy and suggests ways to maintain the momentum in the wake of renewed interest in agriculture for development, following the 2008 global food crisis.

AGRICULTURE AS A TRIGGER OF ECONOMIC GROWTH

Agriculture's central role in growth is the major contribution of the more recent literature on structural transformation discussed above. A key question is whether agriculture continues to be an effective engine for growth especially in late-developing countries, mostly in Africa, in light of the rapidly changing context and the potential to import food. We argue that the answer is yes in terms of the importance of domestic food production as well as the comparative advantage of agriculture in export-led growth in the early stages of development.

Many staples in Africa are nontradable, either because of local preferences (e.g., banana plantain in Central Africa) or because of high transactions costs (e.g., cassava). In addition, in many countries, because of frequent shortages of foreign exchange for importing substitute cereals, food production has to keep up with domestic demand in order to maintain affordable food prices, which are critical to overall growth. Even in the Asian countries that have experienced a Green Revolution, increasing yields for staple crops remains critical for growth. Staple crops are still the largest agricultural subsector (slightly more than one third of agricultural output in China and India, and slightly more than half in Vietnam). Many of these countries have rice as the major staple, and given their size relative to world markets, they need to continue to produce most of their food domestically to secure low-cost food essential for growth.

In addition, agriculture is often the lead export sector and foreign exchange earner because it is the sector with strong comparative advantage in the early stages of development. Most African countries are relatively rich in natural resources, but poor in skilled labor, suggesting comparative advantage for unprocessed primary products. This is re-enforced by a weak business investment climate in terms of infrastructure (roads, electricity, communications) and institutions (legal, financial, regulatory) that constrain private investment in the formal manufacturing and service industries. In some countries, a combination of natural resources, human capital endowments, and an improving business environment point to comparative advantage in processed primary commodities as a potential entry point for building a competitive manufacturing sector.

Although globalization and new dynamic producers have increased competition in traditional agricultural exports, recent successes such as coffee in Vietnam and cocoa in Ghana suggest that agricultural exports can be a major sources of growth. In Ghana, increased productivity in cocoa has been a major driver of its successful agricultural growth and poverty reduction since 1995. African countries, such as Senegal, Kenya, and Ethiopia, are also increasingly successful in rapidly growing exports markets for horticultural products and flowers.

Even if there is general agreement on the importance of agriculture in economic growth in the early stages, it is sometimes argued that rapid agricultural growth will be difficult in

Share of Labor in Agriculture and Share of Agriculture in GDP

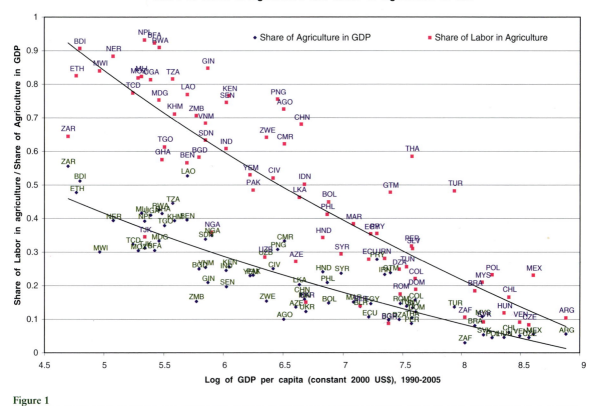

Figure 1

The structural transformation as income per capita rises.

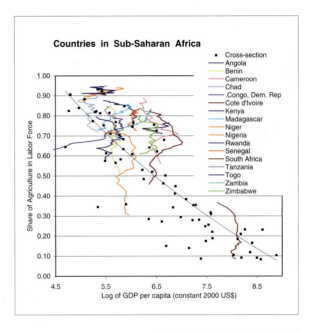

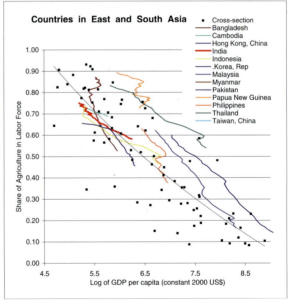

Figure 2

Contrasted structural transformations of countries in (*top*) Sub-Saharan Africa and (*bottom*) East and South Asia.

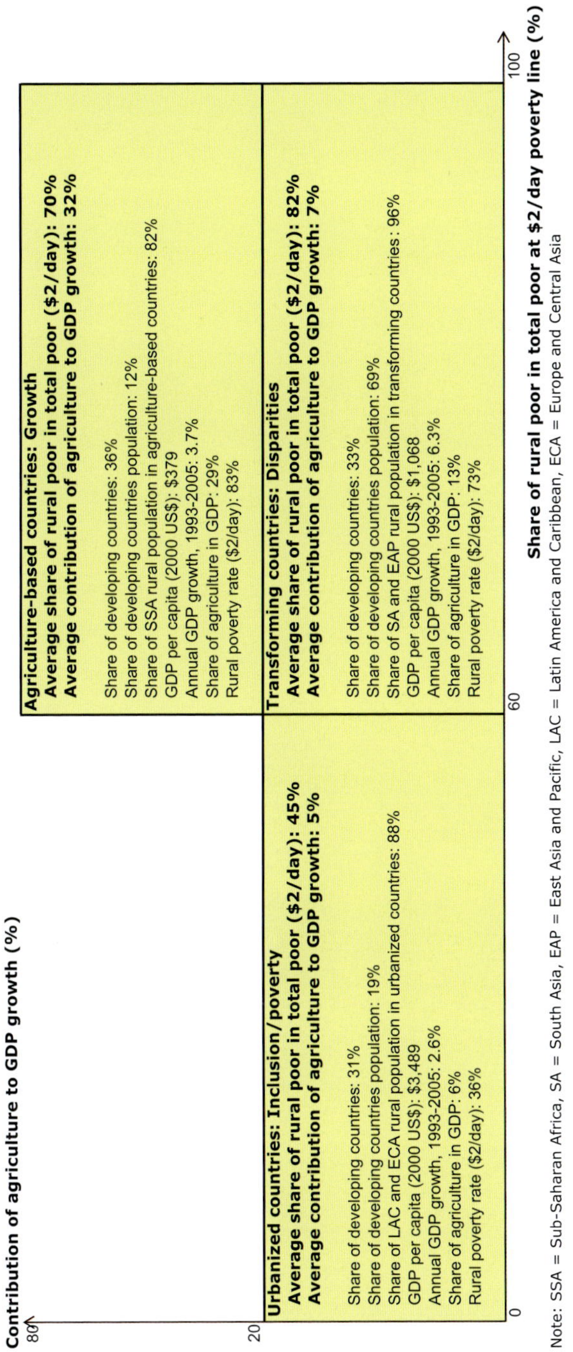

Contribution of agriculture to GDP growth (%)

Agriculture-based countries: Growth
Average share of rural poor in total poor ($2/day): 70%
Average contribution of agriculture to GDP growth: 32%

Share of developing countries: 36%
Share of developing countries population: 12%
Share of SSA rural population in agriculture-based countries: 82%
GDP per capita (2000 US$): $379
Annual GDP growth, 1993–2005: 3.7%
Share of agriculture in GDP: 29%
Rural poverty rate ($2/day): 83%

Transforming countries: Disparities
Average share of rural poor in total poor ($2/day): 82%
Average contribution of agriculture to GDP growth: 7%

Share of developing countries: 33%
Share of developing countries population: 69%
Share of SA and EAP rural population in transforming countries: 96%
GDP per capita (2000 US$): $1,068
Annual GDP growth, 1993–2005: 6.3%
Share of agriculture in GDP: 13%
Rural poverty rate ($2/day): 73%

Urbanized countries: Inclusion/poverty
Average share of rural poor in total poor ($2/day): 45%
Average contribution of agriculture to GDP growth: 5%

Share of developing countries: 31%
Share of developing countries population: 19%
Share of LAC and ECA rural population in urbanized countries: 88%
GDP per capita (2000 US$): $3,489
Annual GDP growth, 1993–2005: 2.6%
Share of agriculture in GDP: 6%
Rural poverty rate ($2/day): 36%

Share of rural poor in total poor at $2/day poverty line (%)

Note: SSA = Sub-Saharan Africa, SA = South Asia, EAP = East Asia and Pacific, LAC = Latin America and Caribbean, ECA = Europe and Central Asia

Figure 3

Typology of functions of agriculture for development. Abbreviations: ECA, Europe and Central Asia; EAP, East Asia and Pacific; LAC, Latin America and Caribbean; SA, South Asia; SAA, Sub-Saharan Africa.

Africa because of an inherently unfavorable agro-ecological base, degraded soils, low population density, poorly functioning markets, and competition from the rest of the world (Maxwell et al. 2001). Yet, agriculture has been the most dynamic sector in Africa with growth rates of 3.7% annually exceeding the growth in the nonagricultural sector over the 1993–2005 period. Growth above 4% over this period was observed in Malawi, Rwanda, Cameroon, Benin, and Guinea. Over the long term in most countries, agriculture is likely to grow more slowly than nonagricultural sectors, given Engel's Law according to which, as incomes rise, the proportion spent on food falls. However, globalization can also help relax this constraint by providing access to deeper markets with highly elastic demands for products such as fresh horticultural and organic produce and animal and fish products.

AGRICULTURE'S POWER FOR POVERTY REDUCTION

Three out of four poor people in developing countries—890 million people—lived in rural areas in 2002. Even with rapid urbanization, the developing world is expected to remain predominantly rural in most regions until around 2020, and the majority of the poor are projected to continue to live in rural areas until 2040 (Ravallion et al. 2007). This reflects a large and persistent gap between the share of agriculture in GDP and the share of agriculture in the labor force due to the slow movement of labor out of agriculture, as shown in **Figure 1**.

The persistent concentration of absolute and relative poverty in rural areas, even with rapid economic growth, illustrates the difficulty of redistributing income generated outside of agriculture and the deep inertia in people's occupational transformation as economies restructure. Migrating out of agriculture to urban areas is often hampered by lack of information, cost, skill gaps, aging, and family and social ties.

There is now overwhelming evidence that growth in the rural economy is essential for reducing poverty in most developing countries. From a simple decomposition analysis, 81% of the worldwide reduction in rural poverty during the 1993–2002 period can be ascribed to improved conditions in rural areas; migration accounted for only 19% of the reduction (World Bank 2007).[1]

Cross-country econometric evidence indicates that GDP growth generated in agriculture is particularly effective in benefiting the poor. Among 42 developing countries over 1981–2003, 1% GDP growth originating in agriculture increased the expenditures of the five poorest deciles on average by 3.7%, far more than the 0.9% induced by 1% GDP growth originating in the rest of the economy (Ligon & Sadoulet 2007). Similarly, Bravo-Ortega & Lederman (2005) found that an increase in overall GDP coming from agricultural labor productivity is on average 2.9 times more effective in raising the incomes of the poorest quintile in developing countries than an equivalent increase in GDP coming from nonagricultural labor productivity.

Similar results hold for the agricultural growth-poverty linkages at the country level. In China, where land is relatively equally distributed, the reduction in poverty was almost four times higher from GDP growth originating in agriculture than from GDP growth originating in industry or services (Ravallion & Chen 2007). Rapid agricultural develop-

---

[1]This decomposition abstracts from indirect effects of urbanization on rural poverty through remittances and rural wage changes through tighter rural labor markets. Yet, it also conservatively assumes that all rural-urban migrants are poor, which is unlikely because migrants are often the more educated and entrepreneurial.

ment also contributed substantially to the dramatic poverty reduction in Vietnam over the past 15 years and is likely to remain an important pathway out of poverty for many of Vietnam's poor (van de Walle & Cratty 2004). But in some countries, rural poverty did not decline, despite rapid agricultural growth—for example, in Bolivia, Peru, and Brazil, where growth was concentrated in an export-oriented sector of large capital-intensive farms.

Some of the impact of agricultural productivity growth on poverty reduction is obtained directly through raising farm incomes, but much of it is indirect through employment and food prices. Econometric studies of India for 1958–1994, where many of the rural poor are landless, report price and wage effects of food crop productivity to be more important in reducing rural poverty in the long run than direct effects of farm profits, which dominated in the short run (Datt & Ravallion 1998). Although lower food prices reduce farm incomes, the experience from the Green Revolution in Asia was that total factor productivity rose faster than food prices declined, leading to a win-win for poor producers and consumers (Lipton 2005). In addition to the urban poor and the rural landless, more than half of poor farm households are typically net food buyers who benefit from lower food prices. When a food crisis hits, a majority of poor smallholders are, in fact, hurt by rising prices, a somewhat counterintuitive outcome.

With rising incomes, growth is increasingly driven by the rapidly expanding demand for livestock products and high-value crops, which are also more labor intensive. The poverty impact of growth in the agricultural sector will thus depend increasingly on the poor connecting to these new growth processes, either as smallholders or as laborers in large farms. Vertically integrated supply chains and supermarkets pose particular challenges for them, although recent evidence from China suggests that small and poor farmers can take an active part in the rapidly expanding horticulture economy (Wang et al. 2006). A similar pro-poor pattern holds for India's dynamic dairy industry. Success stories in smallholder competitiveness in high-value activities typically depend on membership in effective producer organizations that can address the challenges of economies of scale in marketing and processing.

Agricultural productivity growth also contributes to poverty reduction by stimulating rural nonfarm growth, especially where infrastructure and the investment climate are already in place (Barnes & Binswanger 1986, Hazell & Haggblade 1991). In India and Indonesia, growth in rural services was estimated to contribute at least as much as growth in agriculture toward reducing poverty.

ADDRESSING WIDENING DISPARITIES

Rural-Urban Disparity

Even in countries that have experienced rapid reduction in rural poverty, mostly in Asia, disparities between rural and urban incomes have tended to widen. In a sample of almost 70 countries, the median urban income (consumption) is at least 80% higher than rural income in half the countries. These differences have been increasing in many countries. In India, rural and urban incomes were fairly similar in 1951, but the gap has since widened substantially. In China, the gap between urban and rural incomes narrowed in the early reform years, when rapid agricultural growth drove overall economic growth, but it has since opened again from a ratio of 2.1 in 1993 to 3.5 in 2002 (Yang 1999, Ravallion & Chen 2007). In China, the incidence of urban poverty declined twice as fast as that of rural poverty between 1980 and 2001; in Indonesia, 2.5 times as fast over the same period; and in Thailand, 3.7 times as fast between 1970 and 1999.

These growing rural-urban gaps have often been accompanied by widening regional imbalances among rural areas in many countries. Examples abound of lagging regions within countries of above-average agricultural performance—northeast Brazil, Bihar in India, the Peruvian highlands, and western China.

In the short to medium term, rising inequality is causing social and political tensions. This is being reflected in recent efforts in countries with diverse political systems, from India to China, to focus policies on raising rural incomes. Over the long term, growing inequality is likely to reduce overall growth as well (World Bank 2005).

Policies that alter the terms of trade toward agriculture through subsidies and protection may be a quick fix to rising disparities. But weak fiscal capacity to sustain transfers large enough to reduce the income gaps, as well as competition from extensive unmet demands for public goods and continuing urban demands for low food prices, create a policy dilemma (Hayami 2005). Raising autonomous incomes in agriculture and the rural non-farm economy via competitive investments must therefore be the essence of the solution.

Gender Disparities

Another major source of inequality, too often unrecognized, is gender differences in access to resources and markets that result in forgone agricultural output, higher levels of poverty, and food and nutrition insecurity. Given that agriculture is the largest source of women's employment, mainstreaming gender in agricultural policies and programs is essential for the success of development.

Gender inequality starts with unequal access to resources. Women are less likely than men to own land, and even when they do own land, their landholdings are smaller (Deere & León 2003). Likewise, inequality is often embedded in the distribution of water rights, with the rights of women controlled by their husbands. This inequality is driven by weak positioning in intrahousehold bargaining that originates in unfavorable marital and inheritance laws, family and community norms, and unequal access to labor markets.

Because of differential access to assets, markets, and technical assistance, household welfare can often be improved by within-household reallocation of assets to women. Evidence from Burkina Faso suggests that overall output of crops grown by the household could increase by 6% if some labor and fertilizer were reallocated within the household from men's to women's plots (Udry et al. 1995).

Because of poor access to markets, finance, and technical advice, the role of women is often restricted to subsistence food crops with low potential to generate higher incomes. Enabling women to move beyond subsistence production and into high-value farming is a key pathway out of poverty for them, facilitated by better access to resources. Women, more than men, spend their income on food, thus improving household food and nutrition security and particularly the development of children (Katz 1995).

A CONTINUING ROLE IN FOOD SECURITY

Agriculture's role in food security has shifted over time. With rapid population growth and growing food aid in Asia in the 1950s and 1960s and the global food crisis of the mid-1970s, attention was focused on food availability at the global and national levels. From the mid-1970s to the 2008 food crisis, the world was generally food secure, producing enough food to meet the dietary needs of today's global population. However, the 2008 crisis was a sharp reminder that global food security should not be taken for granted because of uncertainties from growing resource scarcity, rising energy prices, new demands such as biofuels, and climate change.

At the country level, trade can stabilize food availability and prices in countries with rising and diversified foreign exchange earnings—the case for most countries in Asia and Latin America. However, domestic food availability is still a challenge for many countries in Africa that experience some combination of negative per capita annual growth rates in staple food, large production fluctuations caused by climatic variability, low foreign exchange earnings, and landlocked status or poor infrastructure to import food staples. World price fluctuations place additional strain on import capacity; therefore, increasing domestic food availability and stability remains essential for development in these countries.

Because of the low price elasticity of demand for food staples and the thinness of international markets, small changes in food availability translate into large spikes in domestic prices and reductions in real incomes of poor consumers, many of whom are farmers. The 2008 food price spike is estimated to have moved an additional 130–155 million people into poverty (World Bank 2008).

However, even with adequate global supplies, more than 800 million people remain undernourished and more than 5 million children die each year from causes linked to undernutrition (Gross & Webb 2006). Accordingly, the concept of food security evolved in the 1980s to include access—the means to acquire food and, most recently, the human right to adequate food. Food access puts emphasis on food security at the level of households and individuals within households (especially women and children).

Within this broader perspective, the channels between agricultural production and food security are complex and multiple. Rising productivity increases rural incomes and lowers food prices, making food more accessible to the poor. Other investments—such as improved irrigation and drought-tolerant crops—reduce price and income variability by mitigating the impact of climatic shocks. Productivity gains are key to food security in countries with foreign exchange shortage or limited infrastructure to import food. The same applies to households in remote areas with poor access to food markets.

For most of the malnourished, the lack of access to food is a greater problem than food availability. Today, agriculture's ability to generate income for the poor is often more important for food security than its ability to increase local food supplies. Women, more than men, spend their income on food, so efforts to redress gender biases can provide payoffs to food security as well.

Beyond food supply and access, lack of dietary diversity can lead to micronutrient malnutrition, even when energy intakes are sufficient. This "hidden hunger" can cause illness, blindness, and premature death as well as impair the cognitive development of survivors. Recent experience indicates that it is possible to develop crop varieties with higher levels of vitamins and minerals, providing yet another example of the link between agriculture and food security.

HARNESSING AGRICULTURE AS A STEWARD OF THE ENVIRONMENT

Agriculture is the major user of scarce natural resources (85% of the developing world's fresh water withdrawal and 42% of its land). It is also a leading cause of underground water depletion, agrochemical pollution, soil exhaustion, loss of biodiversity through deforestation, and an important contributor to global climate change, accounting for up to 30% of greenhouse gas emissions. At the same time, degradation of these natural resources undermines the basis for future agricultural production and increases vulnerability to risk (Millennium Ecosystem Assessment 2005).

The environmental costs of agriculture relate to both intensification and extensification strategies pursued to varying degrees in different regions. In Green Revolution areas, agricultural intensification has generated environmental problems from reduced biodiversity, mismanaged irrigation water, agrochemical pollution, and health costs and deaths from pesticide poisoning. The rapid rise of intensive livestock production in middle-income countries has its own environmental costs through animal waste and the spread of animal diseases such as avian influenza.

Yet, areas that have not experienced intensification, especially in Sub-Saharan Africa, suffer from deforestation, soil erosion, desertification, and degradation of pastures and watersheds from unsustainable expansion of the agricultural frontier with growing rural populations pushed into more marginal and fragile zones. For these areas, agricultural intensification—based on a "doubly Green Revolution" (Conway 1999)—must be part of the solution. The challenge is to manage the trade-offs from agricultural intensification by seeking more sustainable production systems and to enhance agriculture's environmental services. Many promising technological and institutional innovations can make agriculture more sustainable with minimum trade-offs on growth and poverty reduction. For example, one of agriculture's global success stories in the past two decades is conservation tillage. This win-win approach has worked in commercial agriculture in Latin America and among smallholders in South Asia's rice-wheat systems. In less-favored regions, community-based approaches have succeeded in many areas to better manage watersheds and forests.

But widespread adoption of more sustainable approaches has often been hindered by inappropriate incentive policies that encourage mining of resources, such as electricity subsidies that encourage underground water extraction in India. Strengthening property rights and providing long-term incentives for natural resource management with off-farm benefits are necessary in both intensive and extensive farming areas to manage externalities. However, these reforms are often politically difficult to implement.

Agriculture can also provide positive environmental services such as clean drinking water, stable water flows to irrigation systems, carbon sequestration, and protection of biodiversity. There is growing interest in payments for these services to help overcome market failures in managing environmental externalities, especially in Latin America (Food and Agricultural Organization 2007). Environmental certification of products also allows consumers to pay for sustainable environmental management, as practiced under fair trade or shade-grown coffee. In the future, carbon-trading schemes—especially if their coverage is extended to provide financing for avoided deforestation and soil carbon sequestration—offer significant potential to reduce emissions from land-use change in agriculture.

Managing the connections among agriculture, natural resource conservation, and the environment must be an integral part of using agriculture for development. This will not be easy—with rising competition for natural resources from nonfarm sectors and new agricultural markets, such as biofuels, the tensions and trade-offs are likely to grow. Weak governance for agriculture also limits the scope for regulatory interventions to internalize externalities, putting a premium on simple and effective incentive schemes.

THE UNDERUTILIZATION OF AGRICULTURE'S POTENTIAL FOR DEVELOPMENT

Too often, the agriculture-for-development connections revealed by the evidence reviewed here have been insufficiently exploited. Agriculture has yet to perform as an engine of growth in most Sub-Saharan countries, where the labor force is rapidly urbanizing without per capita income growth, resulting in failed structural transformations compared with what happened in Asia. In Sub-Saharan countries (**Figure 2a**, see color insert), the share of agriculture in the labor force declined over the long 1961–2003 period without gains in GDP per capita; by contrast, in the East and South Asian countries (**Figure 2b**, see color insert), a declining share of agriculture in the labor force was accompanied by rising GDP per capita. Even in the transforming countries (defined as countries with a high share of total poverty located in the rural sector, but with most of their GDP growth originating outside agriculture, see below), the rural poverty and income disparity challenges remain huge, despite spectacular progress in some countries in overall economic growth. Premature and unduly high extraction of the agricultural surplus to finance industrialization, and a lack of public investment in agriculture despite good growth potential, are key reasons for sluggish agricultural performance in many agriculture-based countries (defined as countries with a high share of total poverty located in the rural sector and with most of their GDP growth originating in agriculture, see below).

The landmark study by Krueger et al. (1991) on the political economy of agricultural pricing policy documented how 16 of the 18 developing countries analyzed taxed agriculture relative to other sectors. Interventions induced a 30% decline in the relative price of agricultural products with respect to a nonagricultural price index. This policy bias was largest in Sub-Saharan Africa, with overvalued exchange rates, high tariff protection in industry, and taxes on agricultural exports all contributing to the bias. In addition, the bias was costly in foregone growth. It was estimated that a 10 percentage points reduction in total taxation to the sector would increase overall annual growth by 0.43 percentage points.

Since then, most developing countries have substantially improved their macroeconomic policy and reduced their biases against agriculture. Between 1980–1984 and 2000–2004, net agricultural taxation declined on average from 28% to 10% in agriculture-based countries, most of which were in Africa (Anderson 2008). A large part of the gain has been through better macroeconomic policies. A composite score comprising three key elements of sound macroeconomic policy (fiscal, monetary, and exchange rate) shows a clear improvement since the mid-1990s in almost all African countries (World Bank 2007). A positive association is also observed between improvements in that score and the performance of agriculture.[2]

The structural transformation paradigm has highlighted the art of successful countries in balancing investment in agriculture and taxing it (directly and indirectly) to finance industrial development (Teranishi 1997, Thorbecke & Wan 2004). It was the heavy exploitation of agriculture before meaningful (public) investment in agricultural development that proved lethal in Africa. Even today, the share of public spending on agriculture in agriculture-based countries (mostly in Africa) is significantly less (4% in

---

[2]However, trade policies, especially of industrialized countries, continue to depress world prices and create a loss of 0.3 percentage points of annual agricultural output growth for developing countries (World Bank 2007).

2004) than in the transforming countries of Asia during their agricultural growth spurt (10% in 1980). At the same time, the share of agriculture in official development assistance declined sharply over the past two decades, from a high of 18.1% in 1979 to 3.5% in 2004.

Well-targeted public investments have high payoffs to growth and poverty reduction. In particular, high returns to agricultural research and extension have been well documented (Alston et al. 2002). Yet, agricultural spending has often been biased toward subsidizing private goods (fertilizer, credit) and making socially regressive transfers. These are overall substantially less productive than investments in core public goods (López & Galinato 2006). The bias toward private goods often worsens as countries' fiscal capacity rises, as in India, where agricultural subsidies rose from 40% of agricultural public expenditures in 1975 to 75% in 2002. Underinvestment in agriculture is thus further compounded by extensive misinvestment.

Failed agricultural development efforts such as integrated rural development in the 1970s and training-and-visit extension in the 1980s also negatively influenced spending. Poor understanding of agrarian dynamics, weak governance, and the tendency for donors to seek one-size-fits-all approaches contributed to these failures. Implementation difficulties are especially challenging in agriculture, with the cross-sectoral nature of many investments, extensive market failures requiring effective state intervention, and the need for technical skills on both the government and donor sides. This experience underlines the needs to strengthen donor and country capacity for policy analysis and project design and to invest in governance and institutions for effective implementation.

SECOND CHANCE: RENEWED INTEREST IN AGRICULTURE FOR DEVELOPMENT

The agriculture-for-development agenda presents two challenges for implementation. One is managing the political economy of agricultural policies to overcome policy biases, underinvestment, and misinvestment. The other is strengthening governance for the implementation of agricultural policies, particularly in the many developing countries where governance gets low scores.

There is evidence that the political economy has been changing in favor of agriculture and rural development. Since 2001, government and donor interest in agriculture has increased, with a sharp jump in commitments during the food crisis. In particular, the New Partnership for Africa's Development set in 2002 the target for African countries of spending 10% of public expenditures on agriculture, up from an average of 4% (Food and Agriculture Organization 2002). In 2008, the World Bank committed to double assistance to agriculture in Africa by 2010. This is happening because of higher and more volatile commodity prices; growing recognition among developing-country governments and donors of the multiple roles of agriculture for development; and new approaches to agricultural development based on decentralization, participation, and public-private partnerships, with greater likelihood of success.

Rural civil society organizations are also playing a much larger role that rivals that of many government and donor organizations. The private agribusiness sector has become more prevalent and foreign private investment is now flowing into the sector, including in Africa. And large philanthropic organizations such as the Bill and Melinda Gates Foundation have become major players in assistance to agriculture. These new actors can play important roles in enhancing the political economy of agriculture for development.

In this new context, strong public policy and state capacity is needed to secure desirable social outcomes, especially inclusive and sustainable agricultural growth. Yet, the renewed interest in agriculture for development is fragile as a result of weak and widely eroded state capacity following structural adjustment policies as well as the complexity of the agenda. Strengthening the capacity of the state in its new roles of coordinating across sectors and of partnering with the private sector and civil society is urgently needed. In most countries, ministries of agriculture are in need of far-reaching reforms. Other ministries play even greater roles in many aspects of the agenda such as the environment, nutrition, and regional development, but coordination remains weak.

By bringing government closer to rural people, decentralization holds the potential to deal with the localized and heterogeneous aspects of agriculture, especially for extension. Community-driven development can harness the potential of rural communities—their local knowledge, creativity, and social capital. Territorial development can help manage economic projects with a broader scale than the community-driven development approaches.

A stronger state will not be enough. The "third sector"—communities, producer and other stakeholder organizations, and nongovernmental organizations—can improve representation of the rural poor and, in so doing, also improve governance (World Bank 2007). Producer organizations can give political voice to smallholders and hold policy makers and implementing agencies accountable. Freedom of association, a free press, and investment in the social capital of rural organizations, including women's organizations, are important for such demand-side strategies of improving governance.

Donors must also improve their effectiveness as they scale up their investments once again. Country-led agricultural strategies and the broader poverty reduction strategy papers provide a framework for donors to align their support to the agricultural sector and with each other, using the government's public expenditure and procurement systems as mechanisms for program implementation. However, donor organizations' technical skills in agriculture have been severely depleted and must be adjusted to the new conditions if agriculture is to be used effectively for development.

Finally, the agriculture-for-development agenda cannot be realized without more and better international commitments. The global agricultural agenda has a multiplicity of dimensions: establishing fair rules for international trade, agreeing on product standards and intellectual property rights, facilitating R&D spillovers for the benefit of the poor, avoiding such negative spillovers as animal diseases, conserving the world's biodiversity, and mitigating and adapting to climate change. Current international organizations—that were largely defined in the 1950s in a vastly different world for development—are poorly prepared for this new agenda, and institutional reforms and innovations are needed to rebuild capacity in agriculture and facilitate greater coordination across international agencies and with the new actors in the global arena, including civil society, the business sector, and philanthropy.

SETTING PRIORITIES IN AGRICULTURE FOR DEVELOPMENT: TYPOLOGY OF FUNCTIONS

In the paradigm of agriculture fulfilling multiple functions for development, priorities in using these functions must be clearly established. This is important as trade-offs usually arise in achieving these functions. For instance, how growth is achieved has strong implications for poverty reduction, income disparities, and environmental impacts. However, the main functions that agriculture provides for development vary across countries depending on the structure of poverty and the importance of agriculture as a source of growth. The *World Development Report 2008* (World Bank 2007) summarized these contributions by categorizing countries according to the contribution of agriculture to GDP growth over the period 1991–2005 and the most recent estimate of the share of the rural poor in the total number of poor, using the $2-a-day poverty line (**Figure 3**, see color insert).

Three clusters of structurally different economies emerge, each with distinct priority functions in using agriculture for development. In the agriculture-based countries (most of them in Sub-Saharan Africa), agriculture contributed approximately one third of overall growth, and 70% of the poor are concentrated in rural areas. By its mere size, the agricultural sector is critical for growth, at least in the medium term. The staple crop sector is typically the largest subsector and must be a focus of development strategies aimed at accelerating growth, food security, and poverty reduction.

In the transforming economies (mostly in East Asia and the Pacific, South Asia, and North Africa and the Middle East), agriculture contributed only 7% to growth during 1993–2005 and 13% of the economy, but it employs 57% of the labor force. Despite rapid growth and declining poverty rates in most of these countries, poverty remains widespread and overwhelmingly rural—82% of the poor live in rural areas and the disparity between rural and urban incomes is widening even as rural poverty falls.

In these countries, the transition of people out of agriculture and rural areas is not keeping pace with the restructuring of economies away from agriculture due to limited labor mobility and skills. One policy response is facilitating faster absorption of the agricultural labor force in the urban economy through investments in human capital. But the time lags in educating people for nonagricultural employment are substantial. For the medium term, the main function of agriculture is to reduce sectoral disparities through, for example, tapping rapidly growing markets for labor-intensive, high-value products and related rural nonfarm industries and services.

In the urbanized countries (mostly in Latin America and the Caribbean as well as Eastern Europe and Central Asia), agriculture makes up only 6% of GDP and contributed 5% to growth. Although almost three quarters of the population of urbanized countries live in urban areas, 45% of the poor are still in rural areas, and 18% of the labor force works in agriculture.

In these countries, agriculture acts like other tradable sectors, often economically important in subregions that maintain agriculture-based features. It provides growth opportunities in subsectors with a comparative advantage and dynamic markets. The main divide is now between the traditional rural sector and the modern rural and urban sectors. The function of agriculture for development in the these countries is social inclusion for poverty reduction: to create opportunities for smallholders by supplying the modern food markets and good jobs in agriculture and the rural nonfarm economy.

Given its multiplicity of functions for development, and the trade-offs that generally prevail among such functions, setting priorities in using agriculture for development in specific countries and regions is an essential exercise. This requires putting into place informed and participatory consultative processes whereby priorities are set and strategies are established as to how resources will be allocated and coordination achieved to attain the set priorities.

CONCLUSION

With risk of failure in meeting the Millennium Development Goals as the 2015 deadline approaches, the high social costs of the recent food crisis, and the increasingly ominous symptoms of the impacts of climate change on agriculture and the rural poor, there is growing recognition among governments and donors that, contrary to neglect over the past 25 years, agriculture must be given a more prominent place on the development agenda. But returning to agriculture does not imply business as usual. As greater attention is given to agriculture, there is also recognition that a new paradigm has emerged regarding the functions of agriculture for development, beyond serving as an instrument for industrialization through successful structural transformations. The functions of agriculture for development include growth, poverty reduction, reduced sectoral disparities, food security, and providing environmental services. Priorities vary by country type: Accelerating growth is dominant in the agriculture-based countries, reducing disparities is primary in the transforming countries, and enhancing smallholder inclusion is most important in the urbanized countries. Today's greater willingness to invest in agriculture requires careful prioritization of the functions of agriculture and selection of the corresponding instruments to achieve these functions. The current attention given to agriculture and the new paradigm in using agriculture for development offer unique opportunities to address the extensive remaining development issues.

SUMMARY POINTS

1. The accepted wisdom in development economics is that agriculture is a source of product, factor, foreign exchange, and market contributions that all helped trigger industrial growth and a decline in the share of agriculture in the economy.
2. Today, however, the context in which this role is being played is quite different, characterized by globalization, integrated value chains, rapid technological and institutional innovations, and environmental constraints.
3. In this context, a new paradigm is needed that recognizes the multiple functions of agriculture for development: triggering GDP growth in early stages, reducing poverty, narrowing income disparities, providing food security, and delivering environmental services.
4. Governments and donors have neglected these functions of agriculture over the past 25 years, with negative impacts on development. However, this is changing as agriculture's multiple functions are increasingly recognized, in part in response to the food, poverty (in relation to the Millennium Development Goals), and climate change crises.
5. Mobilizing these functions requires shifting the political economy to overcome antiagriculture policy biases, strengthening governance for agriculture, and prioritizing agriculture's functions in relation to country types.

FUTURE ISSUES

1. What are the important trade-offs between the various functions of agriculture for development, and how may these be minimized?
2. What factors determine the political economy of policy and investment biases against agriculture in developing countries?
3. How can governance for agriculture be better characterized, and what factors determine its quality?

DISCLOSURE STATEMENT

The authors are not aware of any affiliations, memberships, funding, or financial holdings that might be perceived as affecting the objectivity of this review.

ACKNOWLEDGMENTS

This paper is based largely on the *World Development Report 2008, Agriculture for Development*. We are grateful to many other members of the team for their intellectual contributions.

LITERATURE CITED

Adelman I. 1984. Beyond export-led growth. *World Dev.* 12(9):937–49

Alston J, Chan-Kang C, Marra C, Pardey P, Wyatt TJ. 2002. *A Meta-Analysis of the Rates of Return to Agricultural R&D: ex pede herculem?* Washington, DC: IFPRI

Anderson K. 2008. *Distortions in Agricultural Incentives: A Global Perspective.* London: Palgrave Macmillan

Bairoch P. 1973. Agriculture and the Industrial Revolution, 1700–1914. In *The Fontana Economic History of Europe: The Industrial Revolution*, Vol. 3, ed. CM Cipolla. London: Collinis/Fontana

Barnes DF, Binswanger H. 1986. Impact of rural electrification and infrastructure on agricultural changes. *Econ. Polit. Wkly.* 21:26–34

Bravo-Ortega C, Lederman D. 2005. *Agriculture and national welfare around the world: causality and international heterogeneity since 1960.* Policy Res. Work. Pap. 3499, World Bank

Christiaensen L, Demery L. 2007 *Down to earth: agriculture and poverty reduction in Africa, directions in development.* Washington, DC: World Bank

Conway G. 1999. *The Doubly Green Revolution: Food for All in the Twenty-First Century.* Ithaca, NY: Cornell Univ. Press

Datt G, Ravallion M. 1998. Farm productivity and rural poverty in India. *J. Dev. Stud.* 34(4):62–85

Deere CD, León M. 2003. The gender asset gap: land in Latin America. *World Dev.* 31(6):925–47

Diao X, Hazell P, Resnick D, Thurlow J. 2005. *The Role of Agriculture in Pro-Poor Growth in Sub-Saharan Africa.* Washington, DC: IFPRI

Food Agric. Organ. 2002. *Comprehensive Africa Agriculture Development Program.* Rome: New Partnersh. Africa's Dev.

Food Agric. Organ. 2007. *The State of Food and Agriculture 2007. Paying Farmers for Environment Services.* Rome: FAO

Gross R, Webb P. 2006. Wasting time for wasted children: severe child undernutrition must be resolved in non-emergency settings. *Lancet* 367:1209–11

Gulati A, Fan S. 2007. *The Dragon and the Elephant: Agricultural and Rural Reforms in China and India*. Baltimore, MD: Johns Hopkins Univ. Press

Haggblade S, Hazell P, Reardon T. 2008. *Transforming the Rural Non-Farm Economy: Opportunities and Threats in the Developing World*. Baltimore, MD: Johns Hopkins Univ. Press

Hayami Y. 2005. *An emerging agriculture problem in high-performing Asian economies*. Presented at Conf. Asian Soc. Agric. Econ., 5th, Zahedan, Iran

Hayami Y, Ruttan V. 1971. *Agricultural Development: An International Perspective*. Baltimore, MD: Johns Hopkins Univ. Press

Hazell P, Haggblade S. 1991. Rural-urban growth linkages in India. *Indian J. Agric. Econ.* 46(4):515–29

Johnston BG, Mellor JW. 1961. The role of agriculture in economic development. *Am. Econ. Rev.* 87(2):566–93

Katz E. 1995. Gender and trade within the household: observations from rural Guatemala. *World Dev.* 23(2):327–42

King RP, Byerlee D. 1978. Factor intensity and locational impacts of rural consumption patterns in Sierra Leone. *Am. J. Agric. Econ.* (60):197–206

Krueger A, Schiff M, Valdés A. 1991. *The Political Economy of Agricultural Pricing Policy*. Baltimore, MD: Johns Hopkins Univ. Press

Lele U, Mellor J. 1981. Technological change, distributive bias, and labor transfers in a two-sector economy. *Oxf. Econ. Pap.* 33(3):426–41

Lewis WA. 1954. Economic development with unlimited supplies of labor. *Manchester Sch. Econ. Soc. Stud.* 22(2):139–91

Ligon E, Sadoulet E. 2007. Estimating the effects of aggregate agricultural growth on the distribution of expenditures. In *Background Note for the World Development Report 2008*. Washington, DC: World Bank

Lipton M. 2005. *The family farm in a globalizing world: the role of crop science in alleviating poverty*. 2020 Vision Discuss. Pap. 20, Int. Food Policy Res. Inst.

López R, Galinato GI. 2006. Should governments stop subsidies to private goods? Evidence from rural Latin America. *J. Public Econ.* 91(5-6):1071–94

Lucas R. 2004. Life earnings and rural-urban migration. *J. Polit. Econ.* 112(S1):S29–59

Maxwell S, Urey I, Ashley C. 2001. Emerging issues in rural development: an issues paper. *Dev. Policy Rev.* 19(4):395–426

Mellor JW. 1976. *The New Economics of Growth*. Ithaca, NY: Cornell Univ. Press

Mellor J. 1998. Agriculture on the road to industrialization. In *International Agricultural Development*, ed. C Eicher, J Staatz. Baltimore, MD: Johns Hopkins Univ. Press

Millenn. Ecosyst. Assess. 2005. *Current State and Trends Assessment*. Washington, DC: Island Press

Ravallion M, Chen S. 2007. China's (uneven) progress against poverty. *J. Dev. Econ.* 82(1):1–42

Ravallion M, Chen S, Sangraula P. 2007. New evidence on the urbanization of global poverty. In *Background Note for the World Development Report 2008*. Washington, DC: World Bank

Schultz TW. 1964. *Transforming Traditional Agriculture*. New Haven, CT: Yale Univ. Press

Staatz JM, Eicher CK. 1998. Agricultural development ideas in historical perspective. In *International Agricultural Development*, ed. CK Eicher, JM Staatz. Baltimore, MD: Johns Hopkins Univ. Press

Teranishi J. 1997. Sectoral resource transfer, conflict, and macrostability in economic development: a comparative analysis. In *The Role of Government in East Asian Economic Development: Comparative Institutional Analysis*, ed. M Aoki, HK Kim, M Okuno-Fujiwara. Oxford, UK: Clarendon

Thirtle C, Lin L, Piesse J. 2003. The impact of research-led agriculture productivity growth on poverty reduction in Africa, Asia, and Latin America. *World Dev.* 31(12):1959–75

Thorbecke E, Wan H Jr. 2004. *Revisiting East (and South) Asia's development model*. Presented at 75 Years Dev. Conf., Ithaca, NY

Timmer CP. 1988. The agricultural transformation. In *Handbook of Development Economics*, Vol. 1, ed. H Chenery, TN Srinivasan. Amsterdam: North-Holland

Timmer CP. 2002. Agriculture and economic development. In *Handbook of Agricultural Economics*, Vol. 2, ed. B Gardner, G Rausser, pp. 1487–546. Amsterdam: Elsevier Sci.

Udry C, Hoddinott J, Alderman H, Haddad L. 1995. Gender differentials in farm productivity: implications for household efficiency and agricultural policy. *Food Policy* 20(5):407–23

van de Walle D, Cratty D. 2004. Is the emerging on-farm market economy the route out of poverty in Vietnam? *Econ. Transit.* 12(2):237–74

Wang H, Dong X, Rozelle S, Huang J, Reardon T. 2006. *Producing and procuring horticultural crops with Chinese characteristics: a case study in the greater Beijing area.*, Staff Pap., Agric. Econ. Dep., Mich. State Univ.

World Bank. 2005. *World Development Report 2006: Equity and Development*. Washington, DC: World Bank

World Bank. 2007. *World Development Report 2008: Agriculture for Development*. Washington, DC: World Bank

World Bank. 2008. *Global Economic Prospects 2009: Commodities at the Crossroad*. Washington, DC: World Bank

Yang DT. 1999. Urban-biased policies and rising income inequality in China. *Am. Econ. Rev.* 89(2):306–10

Governance Structures and Resource Policy Reform: Insights from Agricultural Transition

Johan F.M. Swinnen[1] and Scott Rozelle[2]

[1]Department of Economics and LICOS Centre for Institutions and Economic Performance, University of Leuven, B-3000 Leuven, Belgium; email: jo.swinnen@econ.kuleuven.be

[2]Freeman Spogli Institute, Stanford University, Stanford, California 94305; email: rozelle@stanford.edu

Annu. Rev. Resour. Econ. 2009. 1:33–54

First published online as a Review in Advance on June 26, 2009

The *Annual Review of Resource Economics* is online at resource.annualreviews.org

This article's doi: doi: 10.1146/annurev.resource.050708.144122

Key Words

political economy, liberalization, China, Soviet Union, Eastern Europe

Abstract

New research on the political economy of policy-induced distortions to incentives for optimal resource use in agriculture and insights from the study of the dramatic reforms in former state-controlled economy has led to enhanced insights on the role of governance structures on policy making in agricultural and natural resources. This paper reviews these research developments and key new insights.

INTRODUCTION

Policy-induced distortions to incentives for optimal resource use come in many forms. In this review we focus on two widely observed forms of policy distortions with important implications for economic development, agricultural production, and food consumption. The first policy (distortion) we focus on is how governments have affected the nature of property rights in resource use, as well as in the production and processing of food and other agricultural-derived commodities. As is well known, the nature of these rights has major effects on both equity and efficiency (de Janvry et al. 2001, Deininger & Feder 2002). The second policy we focus on is how governments have affected the incentives to produce and consume food and agricultural-derived commodities by their interventions that have influenced consumer and producer prices. Such policy initiatives have taken many forms, such as outright bans of markets, impositions of government-controlled supply and exchange, price-setting, the use of trade restrictions (such as import bans and export embargoes, taxes, and quotas), and the manipulation of exchange rates (Anderson 2009a, Krueger et al. 1988).

In the 1960s and 1970s many poor and middle-income countries, representing a large share of the world's rural population, were heavily affected by state interventions. This was most extreme in the Communist world, spreading from Central Europe to East Asia, where the entire economic system was under direct control of the state. However, also outside the Socialist Bloc, in many African, Latin-American, and South Asian countries the state played an important role in the economy.

In the past decades there have been tremendous changes in the nature of these distortions as a result of a series of reforms. The first major liberalization pushes began in the late 1960s in Indonesia and Sri Lanka. The most dramatic set of reforms began toward the end of the 1970s and beginning of the 1980s when China embarked on its reform path by property rights reforms, market liberalization, and a reduction of price distortions in the economy. Vietnam followed in the mid-1980s. The reforms in China and Vietnam have been heralded as lifting hundreds of millions of people out of dire poverty (World Bank 2000), as "the biggest antipoverty program the world has ever seen" (McMillan 2002, p. 94), and as having led to "the greatest increase in economic well-being within a 15-year period in all of history" (Fischer 1994, p. 131).

Countries in Sub-Saharan Africa, in Central and Eastern Europe (CEE), and in the former Soviet Union (FSU) introduced a series of reforms in the 1980s and 1990s that were targeted at removing state intervention and distortions to producer incentives, because such policy distortions were thought to pose major constraints on productivity, income growth, and poverty reduction (e.g., Krueger et al. 1988, Lipton 1977, Timmer 1986). Better incentives were expected to yield growth, thereby raising incomes and reducing poverty. However, in contrast to the East Asian reforms, the effects were quite different, causing a rigorous debate on the optimal reform choices (Clague & Rausser 1992, Dewatripont & Roland 1992, Sachs & Woo 1994).

Although there is a large literature on the effects of these reforms (Macours & Swinnen 2002, Roland 2000, Rozelle & Swinnen 2004), in this review we focus on the determinants. Specifically, we are interested in explaining the political economy of these reforms. In addition, within the broader set of the political economy issues, we explore how changes or differences in political governance have affected these reforms. Overall, we show how the study of these reforms has contributed to important new insights on how (changes in) governance structures, including domestic political regimes, have caused policy (reforms), or not.

Because of the broad nature of these questions, we necessarily need to restrict our analysis to, arguably, the most dramatic reforms in the past decades and on the lessons that can be drawn from them. We present these insights within the framework of the new theoretical developments on the political economy of reforms. The recent decade has yielded a rich new literature on this set of questions. The reforms in the 1980s and 1990s triggered many studies trying to understand the effects and reasons for the reforms. They have also triggered an important growth in the literature on the more general questions of the effects and the determinants of reforms as well as a reinvestigation of older institutional and policy reforms in these areas. Our review also draws upon the new studies covering general issues and older questions to the extent that they contribute relevant new insights for the focus of this paper.

EXPLAINING POLICY DISTORTIONS: FROM STRUCTURAL CAUSES TO GOVERNANCE

Research in the field of political economy of agricultural policy and distortions was triggered by the puzzling question: Why is agriculture supported in rich countries and taxed in poor countries? Empirical evidence on agricultural protection/taxation that emerged from numerous studies in the 1980s and the 1990s can be summarized by referring to three sets of policies or patterns: the development pattern, the antitrade pattern, and the anticomparative advantage pattern (or relative income pattern). These are documented by Anderson & Hayami (1986), Gardner (1987), Honma & Hayami (1986), and Lindert (1991) for countries of North America and East Asia; Bates (1989) and Krueger et al. (1991) for developing countries; Tracy (1989) for Western Europe; and see Anderson (2009a) for recent global evidence.

The development pattern refers to two observations. First, empirical evidence from countries across the world shows a positive correlation between agricultural protection and average country incomes. Second, historically (over time) most nations shift from taxation of agricultural producers to protection as they develop economically. The antitrade pattern refers to the observation that import-competing sectors (products) tend to be more assisted (or taxed less) than sectors producing exportable products. The anticomparative advantage pattern refers to the observation that protection is lower (or taxation higher) for products with a comparative advantage and that protection increases when the share of farm income in GDP falls relative to the rest of the economy.

The starting point of the literature is the observations that these global patterns of agricultural distortions could not be explained by traditional economic arguments. Drawing on the general theories of "new political economy," coming out of the University of Chicago—with the important contributions of Stigler (1971), Peltzman (1976), and Becker (1983), the public choice school from Buchanan & Tullock (1962), and the influential work by Downs (1957) and Olson (1965)—the political economy explanations put forward in the 1980s and the 1990s focused importantly on (economic) structural factors. Changes in structural conditions in an economy—for example, those coinciding with economic development or those associated with different commodities for a given level of development—have an impact on (*a*) the costs and distribution of the distortions associated with protection,[1] (*b*) the intensity of political activities,[2] and (*c*) the ability to organize politically and influence the government[3] (for a review, see de Gorter & Swinnen 2002).

Although the importance of political systems for policy has long been emphasized, for example in the seminal work by Buchanan and Tullock (1962), these arguments received relatively little attention in the early studies. The past decade and a half, however, have witnessed a growing set of studies analyzing the role of political regimes and ideology on policy making. Surveys of recent developments are provided by Dewan & Shepsle (2008a,b), Gawande & Krishna (2003), Grossman & Helpman (2002), Persson & Tabellini (2000, 2003), Rausser et al. (2008), Roland (2000), Swinnen (2009b), and Weingast & Wittman (2006). To relate some of these insights to agricultural and resource policy, it is useful to look at the part of the literature that considers the political regime (or the "constitutional choice" in the framework of, e.g., Aghion et al. 2004) as providing a degree of insulation for policy makers. As such, the political regime determines to what extent the government, once appointed, can rule with ex post control, or not; what type of majorities it needs to ensure its ability to pass legislation; and whether groups have veto power. Different mechanisms can translate the preferences of citizens into controls on the government, majority formations, and, hence, policies (Rausser & Roland 2009). These issues relate to the differential effects of democracy and autocratic regimes (Acemoglu & Robinson 2006, North et al. 2006); to the effect of different electoral systems (Persson & Tabellini 2003), including systems set up on the basis of proportional representation versus majoritarian systems (Roelfsema 2004, Rogowski & Kayser 2002); and to the effect of autonomy given to bureaucrats and implementing institutions (Prendergast 2007).[4]

In terms of empirical predictions, the greater insulation of decision makers implies that they can follow their private preferences to a greater extent. However, this in itself has little predictive power, since there is no direct relationship to be expected between the preferences of rulers and the nature of political regimes on issues such as protectionism or property rights (O'Rourke & Taylor 2002). One implication, however, is that there should be more variation in policy choices under dictatorial regimes than under

---

[1]See Anderson (1995) and Swinnen (1994) for theoretical analyses of how changes in the structure of the economy affect the political costs and benefits of agricultural protection and thus the government's political incentives in decision making: for example, the share of food in consumer expenditures as a share in total expenditures, which reduces the opposition of consumers to agricultural protection, as well as the opposition of capital owners in other sectors who oppose the (wage) inflation pressures that come from increased food costs with agricultural protection.

[2]With economic development, incomes in the rest of the economy grow faster than in agriculture. This creates political incentives (both on the demand—or farmers—side and the supply—or politician—side to exchange government transfer in exchange for political support. Farms look for government support either because returns to their investment are larger in lobby activities than in market activities or because the willingness to vote for/support politicians is stronger as the impact on utility is relatively stronger. For similar reasons, governments are more likely to support sectors with a comparative disadvantage than sectors with a comparative advantage (e.g., de Gorter & Tsur 1991, Swinnen & de Gorter 1993, Hillman 1982, Krueger 1990).

[3]With a declining share of agriculture in employment, studies drawing on Olson's (1965) logic of collection action argument have reasoned that this makes political organization of farmers less costly and is therefore likely to increase the effective lobbying of farmers.

[4]In an application of these issues to decision making on agricultural policy in the European Union, Pokrivcak et al. (2007) showed how E.U. agricultural policy reforms are determined by a complex interaction of majority voting rules, changes in the external environment, and the preferences of the European Commission (the agenda-setting bureaucracy in Brussels).

democracy, *ceteris paribus*, if dictatorial leaders are less constrained in setting policies. This hypothesis, in fact, is consistent with the regression model of Olper (2007), which performs better in democracies than in dictatorships, presumably because governmental response to pressure from interest groups is stronger in democracies. This may also be the reason why early studies that focused only on the simple relations between agricultural policy and political regimes in cross-section studies find limited impact (Beghin & Kherallah 1994).

Taking a different tack, Dutt & Mitra (2005) emphasized the role of ideology. In their work they found that left-wing governments (that attach higher weights to the welfare of workers/laborers) are more protectionist when they are in capital-abundant countries, but less protectionist when they are in capital-scarce countries. An application of this argument to agricultural policy, however, is not straightforward because increasing food costs through agricultural protection hurts both workers and those who invest industrial capital. Hence, rulers who support "labor" and "capital" should also oppose agricultural protection—as they did historically in Europe (Findlay & O'Rourke 2007, Kindleberger 1975, Schonhardt-Bailey 1998). Olper (2001) found that, on average, right-wing governments are more protectionist in terms of agriculture than are left-wing ones. This is consistent with studies such as those by Bates (1983), who argues that socialist rulers in Africa imposed lower commodity prices on farmers (or taxed farmers), and by Tracy (1989), who found that right-wing governments in Europe (such as those dominated by Catholic parties and conservative parties, including the Nazi party in Germany) tended to support farm interests and increase protection.

However, a closer reading of the literature suggests that these conclusions require refinement. First, cross-section studies are quite limited in what they are able to illuminate. Longer-run studies, in contrast, allow the researcher to more carefully measure the impact of shifts from one system (or set of political institutions) to another. For example, Swinnen et al. (2001) demonstrated how some changes in voting rules in Belgium had an effect on agricultural protection, whereas other changes had no effect. In particular, those changes in electoral rules that disproportionately benefited people involved in agriculture (e.g., by extending voting rights to small farmers and tenants in the early twentieth century) induced an increase in agricultural protection. However, electoral changes (such as extending voting rights to women) did not affect agricultural protection as they increased voting rights both of those in favor and of those against protection.

Empirical observations also suggest an interaction between the effects of ideology and economic development. Consider, for example, the agricultural policies of extreme left-wing regimes. Communist dictators, such as Stalin in Russia, Mao in China, and Hoxha in Albania, heavily taxed agriculture. However, farmers were subsidized under Brezhnev in the Soviet Union and in most East European Communist countries in the 1970s and 1980s (Rozelle & Swinnen 2009b).

The ideology effect is also conditional on inequality. Despite supporting agriculture less on average, left-wing governments tend to support farmers more in unequal societies (Olper 2007).[5] Interestingly, this is counter to the traditional, Olson-type arguments that large farmers are better in overcoming collective action problems. La Ferrara (2002) argued that inequality may cause collective action problems, which could explain why

---

[5]Dutt & Mitra (2002) also found that a labor-abundant economy will be affected differently by a rise in asset inequality than a capital-abundant economy will be.

protection is negatively correlated with inequality. Historical evidence on this is also found in Europe (Schonhardt-Bailey 2006, Swinnen 2009a). Strong inequality in England, Germany, and France at the end of the nineteenth century weakened the protariff demands of large grain farmers as they were opposed by small farmers, many of whom were livestock producers. Further highlighting this inequality, in France large and small farms were organized in different unions and associated with different political parties.

The part of the empirical literature that has attempted to quantify some of the assertions has focused on explaining price distortions. The distortions of property rights have been addressed mostly in a separate literature: See, for example, Binswanger et al. (1995b), Hayami et al. (1990), Swinnen (1997), and various chapters in de Janvry et al. (2001). Despite the absence of attention to these issues in the quantitative literature, political fights over policy reforms have focused on property rights as much as they have on price incentives. For example, with highly unequal land distribution, small peasants and landless rural workers are less likely to align with landlords to demand agricultural tariffs and are more likely to fight them to demand a redistribution of rights. Studies on the political economy of property rights reforms generally put a strong emphasis on the interaction with governance issues because land rights reforms were often associated with changes in the political regime (Binswanger et al. 1995a, de Janvry 1981, Rausser et al. 2009).

There is also an interesting hypothesis that important policy reforms require the combination of both a change in political regimes and a "crisis" (Acemoglu & Robinson 2001, 2006). Crises may be needed to overcome the inherent status quo in the political-institutional equilibrium that exists in a society and to break the power of interest groups that are entrenched in the institutions as they exist in a society (Rausser et al. 2008). Examples include reforms in Western Europe in the early twentieth century when the combination of enhanced political rights for farmers and a dramatic rural crisis caused major changes in agricultural policies, including land reforms (Swinnen 2001) and reforms in China in the 1970s when the combination of widespread hunger in the countryside and the death of Mao allowed major reforms to occur (see below).

For these reasons, it is important to complement statistical studies with the analysis of specific reforms into greater detail to understand the complexities of the causal mechanisms. In the rest of this paper we review insights on governance and policy reforms from the most dramatic reforms in the past decades, i.e., those implemented in the transition countries of Europe and Asia.

POLITICAL CHANGE AND POLICY REFORMS IN TRANSITION AGRICULTURE

The importance of the following nations as well as their political systems is undeniable. Until the late 1970s, a large share of the globe—from the center of Europe to the southeast regions of Asia—was under Communist rule. The lives of more than 1.5 billion people were directly controlled by Communist leaders, and incentives in these states were massively distorted. The leaders of the Soviet Bloc and China were committed to Socialist ideology and designed their economies to be insulated from the world and the global economic market. Even though the reforms implemented since the end of the Cold War have differed among countries, changes in political regimes played an important role in triggering reforms in all countries.

From Mao to Deng in China

The economic transition in China followed the political transition from Mao Zedong to Deng Xiaoping. Before 1980, the influence of Mao was inescapable. Mao's fear of the outside world, his commitment to Socialism, and his skepticism of markets helped produce the prereform economic system. It was a system fundamentally closed to trade, run without markets, and administered by a controlled pricing system that discriminated against agriculture. It was a system that also failed to raise per capita income and to produce rises in total factor productivity.

There was no dramatic overthrow of the Communist Party after Mao's death. Deng assumed power from within the system. The Communist Party was in control both before and after Deng's accession to the position of supreme leader. Moreover, although Deng had a number of bold ideas, he also was essentially committed to the same system that had been built during the previous three decades (Yang 1996).

Nonetheless, the beginning of the Reform Era is clearly marked by the political rise of Deng in the wake of Mao's death. Committed to a self-taught belief in incentives and pragmatism while also being attracted by the rapid growth that was transforming most of the rest of East Asia, Deng's policy approach could not have been more different from Mao's had there been a revolution. Deng believed in technology whatever its source—from foreign direct investment or an investment into domestic science and engineering. Deng wanted to incentivize the economy.

Although Deng's first reform move was bold—the Household Responsibility System (HRS) reforms decollectivized agricultural production and replaced it with a system of household-based farming (Lin 1992)—the initial years afterward showed no move to continue with radical changes to the economy (Sicular 1995). Prices were administratively raised by officials in the planning bureau who retained control over the economy. It was not until property rights had been fully reformed in the mid-1980s that the leadership decided to move toward marketing and other reforms.[6] McMillan & Naughton (1992) described this process as one that is gradual and deliberate but unplanned.

From Stalin to Brezhnev in the Soviet Union

Interestingly, the distortions under Mao in China resemble the distortions under Stalin in the Soviet Union of the 1930s much more than the distortions in the Soviet Union in the 1970s (Wädekin 1990). Stalin's desire to modernize quickly and his commitment to heavy industry—and his distrust of the farming population—led to his policy of using his centrally controlled economic system to tax the countryside to finance industrial development. This system, as in Mao's China, reduced incentives for farms to invest and produce and left agriculture stagnant.

Soviet agricultural policy, however, changed after World War II. When Kruzhnev took over as Soviet leader following Stalin's death, he initially continued Stalin's agricultural policies. However, he gradually introduced important changes. He reduced taxes on agri-

---

[6]The subsequent reforms increasingly allowed farmers to sell their output to private traders (Park et al. 2002). Entry by nonstate entities and individuals was gradually allowed. Ultimately, competition forced the entire state-owned marketing system to be disbanded. It took 20 years to replace China's planned agricultural marketing system of the early 1980s with a system of competitive markets (Huang et al. 2004). Tariff reductions and trade liberalization finished the process (Huang et al. 2008). Pingali & Xuan (1992) described largely the same strategy in Vietnam.

culture and started to provide substantial assistance from the state, both in terms of investment support and in terms of higher prices. This proagricultural policy was continued and reinforced under Brezhnev's Soviet leadership in the 1960s and 1970s (Wegren 1998). During the period between 1975 and 1985 almost 30% of total Soviet investment went into agriculture (Gray 1990). A similar situation occurred in Central and Eastern European countries where farm workers lived relatively well as a result of large subsidies to overstaffed and inefficient farms (Liefert & Swinnen 2002).

Failed Reform Attempts Under Gorbachev

Only a series of timid rights reforms was tried out in the FSU. Although the Soviet Union reduced taxation of agriculture through its pricing policy after World War II, the Soviet leadership never let go of its centrally imposed collective and state farm system. In 1978 shortly after the time that the HRS reforms started in China, there was a state-led effort in the Soviet Union when Mikhail Gorbachev became the head of the agricultural department of the Central Committee of the Soviet Communist Party. Gray (1990, p. 4) argues that, in March 1985, when Gorbachev became the General Secretary of the Communist Party, "the top Soviet leader [was] the main proponent of economic reform" and that "perhaps at few times in history has high authority been so responsive to new ideas from intellectuals, most of whom are acutely aware of foreign examples."

During the Gorbachev years several agricultural reforms were designed and promoted in an attempt to impose financial discipline on farm workers and to reward them by basing remuneration more directly on their performance (Brooks 1990, Wegren 1998). Although the reforms were tried across a widespread region, they largely failed (Lerman & Brooks 2001, van Atta 1993). Similarly, some of the CEE experimented with reforms in the 1970s and 1980s, but these reforms had modest impacts at best (Wädekin 1990) or made things worse (Wyzan 1990).

Initially, the reform experiments were based on collective farming. Later, they moved beyond their initial proposals and made an assault on the basic principles of collective agriculture. Similar to Deng, Gorbachev proposed to allow households to lease land, gain access to factors of production, and claim rights to the residual income after certain payments were made. However, these reforms were met with little success.

What is remarkable is that the Soviet leadership under Gorbachev in the second half of the 1980s introduced reform proposals similar to those of China's leadership almost a decade earlier (van Atta 1993). It is also interesting to note that the early reform path by Gorbachev was preferred by the conservative faction of China's leadership as it was considered to be ideologically less radical than that of the HRS.

The main difference in the reform process appears to be less in the nature of the policies than in the dynamics of the relationships among the actors involved in the reforms. In the Soviet Union, reform was driven primarily by a Communist leadership that was unsatisfied with previous reform attempts. The central leadership in the Soviet Union, however, had little support from farmers or local officials. In contrast, China's leadership, albeit supportive of reform efforts, at times seemed to be driven by the force of the farmers.

The Fall of the Berlin Wall and the Collapse of Communism in Europe

So why did reform finally happen? In fact, it took a dramatic political reform (the fall of the Communist regimes) to trigger fundamental policy reforms in Europe. The fall of the

Berlin Wall in 1989 signaled the beginning of the collapse of the Communist regimes throughout Eastern Europe and the (former) Soviet Union. It was at this time (of crisis) that many nations implemented a bold series of reform policies—a "big bang"—that often went far beyond the reforms that had been implemented in China and Vietnam. Within a short period of time, prices and trade were liberalized, subsidies cut, property rights privatized, and production and trade organizations restructured. The entire agri-food system was privatized and support for agriculture fell to very low levels (Anderson & Swinnen 2008).

A strong positive relationship has been shown among political reform, market liberalization, and land reforms (Swinnen & Heinegg 2002). However, political changes did not occur everywhere in the FSU. Even now, 20 years after the changes, some of the leaders have not changed. This is the case, for example, in countries such as Belarus, Turkmenistan, and Uzbekistan. In other countries, such as Russia, political freedoms have been reduced again.

Why Was Reform Possible with the Communist Party in China But Not in the Former Soviet Union?

The above discussion raises an interesting question: Why were radical reforms of the property rights system and further gradual market liberalization possible in China but not in the Soviet Union under the Communist regime? Swinnen & Rozelle (2006) argue that radical property rights reforms under the Communist regimes could occur only when the reforms received support simultaneously from the grass roots and from the top of the Communist Party. Reform failed in China in the 1960s because there was no support from the top leadership (Mao) for radical decollectivization demanded by households at the grassroots level (Lardy 1983). Reform failed in Russia in the 1970s because there was neither grassroots nor leadership support for radical changes (Brada & Wädekin 1988). Agricultural reform failed in the 1980s in Russia because the reform proposals from the top of the Communist leadership under Gorbachev were not supported at the grassroots level (Gray 1990). Only in China at the end of the 1970s and the early 1980s was there a confluence of interests in favor of radical reforms at the top and at the grass roots, from both farm households and local officials.

From this perspective it is important to clarify further the interaction between rural initiatives in HRS and political debate among Chinese leaders. The reforms are the result of a delicate balance between pressure from the grass roots and preference to reform from an important part of the top leadership. In the temporary leadership vacuum that existed after Mao's death, both factors reinforced each other in China (McMillan 2002). The success of the HRS reforms in increasing output, reducing poverty, and maintaining social stability in China's countryside reinforced the positions of the proreform groups in Beijing. Inversely, the enhanced position of the proreform groups created the policy space that was necessary for the grassroots initiatives to spread across rural China.

The HRS reforms started in some of the more drought-prone rural areas of China several years before they began to be openly allowed (or encouraged) by even the more reform-minded leaders in Beijing in the late 1970s. When decollectivization started in China's countryside in 1978, those who favored reform at the top of the Communist Party were still in the midst of a power battle with conservative forces and not yet in charge. The power struggle among different factions continued throughout the 1978–1982 period

(Yang 1996), during which the official party policy did not openly encourage the HRS reforms. It was not until the summer of 1982 that a central policy document was drafted formally praising the HRS. By this time 68% of all households had adopted the HRS in agriculture, and by the time the document made decollectivization official dogma in 1983, more than 90% of China's villages had decollectivized.

The attitudes of Chinese and Soviet farm workers and local officials toward decollectivization were distinct because of differences in technology and price distortions in prereform collective agriculture. In rural China more than 30% of households lived in utmost poverty in the mid-1970s (Lardy 1983, World Bank 1992). Reforms started clandestinely in several regions in China, especially those regions that suffered heavily during the famine that followed the Great Leap Forward (Zhou 1996).

In contrast, farm workers in CEE and the Soviet Union benefited from large government subsidies and high wages, and they were covered by social welfare benefits (OECD 1996). Despite low farm productivity, workers in the Soviet Union's state farms and collectives enjoyed standards of living far higher than those in China's rural sector. In several CEE countries, rural incomes were actually higher than urban incomes (Ellman 1988). With a reduction of distortions, farm incomes would have fallen, effort by farm laborers would have needed to increase, and risk would have been higher. Moreover, with overemployment and soft-budget constraints, agricultural reform would trigger layoffs. Not surprisingly, many farm workers in the Soviet Union and CEE resisted agricultural reforms.

Differences in technology reinforced these differences in attitudes that were being shaped by the preexisting conditions. Farmers in China purchased few of their inputs and sold relatively little of their output to the market. Almost no farmers interfaced with processors. Most importantly, given the high labor factor share, the potential for effort efficiency-enhanced output would mean significantly higher incomes for farmers. In contrast, farms in the Soviet Union and Eastern Europe were more integrated into an industrialized production system and a complex network of relations with input suppliers and processors (Johnson & Brooks 1983). Moreover, they were more capital and land intensive. Under these conditions, farms were less likely to get a large boost from incentive improvements and more likely to face serious disruptions (Macours & Swinnen 2002).

INTERNAL GOVERNANCE: THE ROLE OF THE BUREAUCRACY AND ADMINISTRATIVE ORGANIZATION

The support by officials for reforms in China was sustained by their personal interests as farm village leaders (Oi 1989). Subsequent bureaucratic reforms as well as rural industrialization and fiscal reforms sustained the initial reforms (Qian & Weingast 1997).[7] These changes stimulated interest by bureaucrats in local economic growth. In the Soviet Union, little change took place in the bureaucracy (Shleifer 1997), and because the interests of local officials were aligned with those of the farm managers, the rational response of both was to resist, not support, reform. Frye & Shleifer (1997) refer to the different

---

[7]Deng Xiaoping imposed a mandatory retirement program in 1980, effectively removing the old guard and replacing them with younger and more proreform people (Lee 1991). In the mid-1980s, he allowed bureaucrats to quit government positions and join business, which stimulated bureaucrat interest in economic growth and enterprise development (Li 1998).

bureaucratic attitudes in implementing the reforms as the "grabbing hand" in Russia and the "helping hand" in China.

Several authors have argued that the decentralized nature of China's economy may have given China an advantage over Russia, enabling China to make the agricultural reforms more successful. The differing organizational and hierarchical structures of the central planning systems of China and Russia allowed for more reform experimentation by Communist leaders in China and therefore aided their reform process because China could take a trial-and-error approach (Qian & Xu 1993).[8]

We find little support for these arguments in the case of China's initial reforms. Although the introduction of China's HRS reforms was regionally concentrated, this had little to do with the design of planners, but more with grassroots initiatives. In fact, the location of the start of the reforms—often in remote outlying regions—was often determined by the relative absence of control by the planners (Yang 1996), contrary to what would be expected from a government-designed experiment. The spread of the HRS system—across nearly one million brigades and more than ten million teams in less than five years—did not reflect careful planning, but instead, as one village official in China is quoted by McMillan (2002), "HRS spread like the flu."

If there was any tendency for experimenting with reform, it happened mostly in the Soviet Union. In fact, significant experimentation occurred in the former Soviet agricultural system in the late 1970s and early 1980s (van Atta 1993). Experiments with new forms of agricultural management were attempted on a regional basis (Radvanyi 1988). Not until the 1990s would the decentralized nature of China play a more important role, for example in market liberalization, in the implementation of fiscal reforms, and in the emergence of Town and Village Enterprises and similar policies (Wong 1997, Nyberg & Rozelle 1999, Zhang 2006).

LEGITIMACY AND SEQUENCING OF THE REFORMS: BIG BANG VERSUS GRADUALISM

Unlike the situation in Soviet Union, where the lack of significant reforms ultimately contributed to the fall of the Communist leadership, the radical, though partial, economic reforms in the Chinese countryside did much to reinforce the Communist Party's power (Oi 1989). The radical reforms on the land rights and production structure in China, which looked like moves away from Socialism, may have done more to consolidate the rule of the Communist Party than any other measures taken during this period. The changes directly affected more than 70% of the population living in the rural areas. The rise in food production also increased food supplies to cities and took a lot of pressure off the government.[9] These conclusions are important to understand the difference in reform sequencing. Once China had successfully implemented property rights reform and restructured its farms (as well as adjusted prices to reduce the implicit tax on farmers),

---

[8]Qian & Xu (1993) refer to these differences as a U-form (Soviet-Union) versus an M-form (China) hierarchy, based on typologies used by Williamson (1975). Roland (2000) argues that while China's planning system was based on the regional duplication of industries, the Soviet system was organized to exploit economies of scale and division of labor on a much wider scale. Qian et al. (1999) argue that the benefits from learning relative to the possible costs of reversal of a reform experiment were significantly higher in China's regionally organized system compared with the Soviet functional organization of central planning.

[9]Many of the same dynamics occurred in Vietnam (Pingali & Xuan 1992, Wurfel 1993).

liberalizing markets became less imperative (Rozelle 1996). The early pricing changes (which were not implemented through markets, but by the planning bureaucracy) and HRS helped the reformers to meet their initial objectives of increasing agricultural productivity, farm incomes, and food output (Sicular 1988, Lin 1992). The reforms fueled economic growth and reduced concerns about food security. The legitimacy of leaders able to run a government that could raise people's standard of living was at least temporarily satisfied. A new set of radical reforms might have exposed the leaders to new risks (Putterman 1993). With the urgency for additional reforms dampened for top leaders (because their goals were met) as well as farmers (because their incomes and control over the means of production both had improved), there was less policy pressure from both the top and the grass roots.

The situation was very different in the Soviet Union and CEE states in the late 1980s. Communist leaders in these regions had failed to reform substantially for decades [see Acemoglu & Robinson (2006, 2008) for an analysis of conditions in which the (in)ability of existing governments to introduce sufficient redistribution through fiscal means will lead to or prevent revolutions that indicate a redistribution of economic and political rights]. Once the Soviet and CEE leaders lost power, the anticommunist political forces that took over were determined to eliminate the Communist system and introduce political changes (e.g., democracy) and economic changes (such as a market economy), each of which reinforced the other (Balcerowicz 1994).[10] Reforms were launched despite resistance by farm managers, workers, and local officials. Reformers chose to push through as much of the reform agenda as possible at the time that they were (still) in charge. Hence, for both political and economic reasons, a comprehensive set of radical reforms was pursued. Because the previous reforms had failed to result in efficiency improvements, yielding only marginal and slow policy shifts, in the view of the reformers a more radical and broad-based reform approach was necessary.

A broad and encompassing reform strategy was also required for technical and administrative reasons. First, the more industrialized nature of the Soviet agricultural production system and the inefficiencies imbedded in the agro-food supply chain required an approach beyond the confines of the farming sector (Johnson & Brooks 1983). Second, the more complicated technologies in Soviet and CEE agriculture meant a more complex set of exchanges between a larger number and greater variety of firms, which required massive information to design an optimal sequence of policies (Goodhue et al 1998, McMillan 2002). Third, unlike in China, agriculture in the Soviet Union and the CEE was less important to the economy, requiring a much broader reform agenda.

ENDOGENOUS GOVERNANCE AND RIGHTS REFORMS

The mixture of political and economic objectives was especially paramount in property rights reform. The reform of land rights was one of the most hotly disputed issues, as such reform aimed to influence the political constellation, i.e., the distribution of power and

---

[10]The ultimate political reform objective may still be economic efficiency, which is achieved not only by influencing the economy's production function, but also by how the posttransition governments can distort the economy (Lyons et al. 1994, Rausser & Simon 1992). There are many examples of such mixed political and economic objectives, including Thatcher's privatization policies in the 1980s in the United Kingdom (Studlar et al. 1990) and nineteenth-century rural reforms in Western Europe to stop the growth of socialist influence (Craeybeckx 1973).

wealth in the posttransition period (Swinnen, 1999). Interestingly, the choice of policies differs sharply among countries (Lerman et al. 2004).

The radical approach to restitute land rights to former land owners in many Eastern European countries can be interpreted within a political framework. In several countries the objectives of anti-Communist (or anti-Soviet) political parties were made explicit by their use of land restitution policy to break the rural power and organizational structure of (former) communist groups. Two examples are Bulgaria, where the communist party continued to control the countryside (Lyons et al. 1994, Swinnen 1997), and Latvia, where restitution concentrated the land in the hands of the native Latvian population and wrested control away from Russian migrants (Rabinowicz 1997).

In addition to the political factors mentioned above, historical legacies also affected policy reform. In CEE the history of private land rights and the tradition of private farming in the countries provided strong incentives for CEE reformers to privatize land (Rizov et al. 2001). Proximity to the European Union reinforced this approach. In contrast, in Russia and Central Asia where no such tradition existed, there was a popular preference that land should not be privately owned (Swinnen & Heinegg 2002). For different reasons, a similar approach was found in China and Vietnam, where the continuation of the Communist regime and its ideology played an important role (Jacoby et al. 2002). With land as the most basic factor of production in agriculture in a Communist country, leaders believe that the state, or its representative, the collective, should control it. In both nations, reformers also provided (increasingly) well-defined control and income rights, and the de facto difference regarding land ownership decreased.

DEVELOPMENT AND ANTITRADE PATTERNS IN PRICE DISTORTIONS AND REFORMS

The positive relation between economic development and agricultural support, which is widely observed in market economies (see above), is also found in posttransition countries. On average, current farmer assistance tends to be higher in higher-income countries and for import-competing enterprises than it is for export-oriented ones (Anderson & Swinnen 2008). Heavy negative government intervention in the form of depressed incentives also tends to be concentrated on commodities that have the potential to provide export tax revenue for the government. This is especially the case in the cotton sectors of Uzbekistan, Turkmenistan, and Tajikistan (Pomfret 2008), where the government controls the cotton chain as a means of extracting rents, thereby depressing farm prices and production incentives. In addition, traditional grain-exporting countries such as Ukraine and Bulgaria as well as (surplus regions of) Russia are characterized by regular strong government interventions. For example, in the mid-1990s in Bulgaria, ministers of agriculture had to resign regularly following reports of grain shortfalls or unregulated exports threatening the local grain supply (Swinnen 1996). In Ukraine, ad hoc grain market interventions have continued in recent years (von Cramon-Taudabel et al. 2008).

In the case of China, although farmers were taxed heavily in the past, in recent years they have begun to receive greater assistance from the state (Huang et al. 2008). In 2007, for example, farmers received up to US$20 per acre (in RMB equivalents) in production subsidies (Rozelle et al. 2008). Although it is unclear if the new subsidies are distorting, the tendency in China is to support agriculture as the nation's economy grows.

An interesting issue arises whether this development pressure is also behind the remarkable switch from agricultural taxation to agricultural subsidization in the Soviet Union over the 1930–1970 period.[11] Rozelle & Swinnen (2009a) analyzed the relationship between income and the shift from taxation to subsidization in the Soviet Union and the current policy developments in China. The data suggest that the change in the Soviet Union occurred when GDP per capita was approximately US$3500, which is roughly the current level of income in China. Hence, these observations are consistent with the interpretation that the pressure to start subsidizing agriculture is real in China and will lead to a net subsidization of agriculture in the future—in the absence of strict constraints, such as those the World Trade Organization (WTO) may provide.

In addition, improvements in the government's budgetary situation, which allowed more subsidies to be given to farmers than were possible in the early years of transition, also play a role. This situation is particularly important in Russia and some of its neighbors, such as Kazakhstan, where recovery from the post-1998 fiscal crisis has been aided by windfall gains from the dramatic rise in the prices of their oil and gas exports between 1998 and 2008. China's nascent use of subsidies coincides with the rebound of fiscal revenues under the control of the central government.

INTERNATIONAL GOVERNANCE STRUCTURES

So far the discussion has focused on the impact of domestic governance structures. However, an interesting issue is the impact of international governance structures on policy reform (Anania et al. 2004, Bagwell & Staiger 2002, Dutt & Mitra 2009, Josling et al. 1996, Rausser 1995). Examples of these structures include agreements by the WTO, NAFTA, as well as E.U. enlargement.

According to the literature, the impact of the WTO is mixed.[12] Some of the transition countries, such as the Czech Republic, Slovakia, Hungary, Poland, Romania, and Slovenia, were members of the GATT and have been members of the WTO since its creation in 1995. China, Bulgaria, Estonia, Lithuania, Latvia, Kyrgyz, Armenia, Georgia, and Albania joined the WTO later. Ukraine, Russia, and Kazakhstan are in various stages of discussion regarding WTO accession. Countries that were founding members in 1995 have not been strongly disciplined by WTO accession. Their commitments were based on high support levels of the 1980s and therefore produced little constraints on their policies in the 1990s (Bacchetta & Drabek 2002).

However, for those that had to negotiate their entry in the latter 1990s, the constraints on introducing or maintaining distortions are more serious. In China, perhaps more than any other acceding country, the accession process has led to a significant fall in distortions (Huang et al. 2008). China's desire to enter the WTO led to two phases of adjustments in

---

[11]These processes are consistent with broad patterns of agricultural policy identified by studies that ignored ideology (see Explaining Policy Distortions: From Structural Causes to Governance, section above). Dutt & Mitra (2009), Olper (2007), and Olper & Raimundi (2009), using cross-country evidence, found that there are interactions between ideological preferences of rulers and development in determining support for agriculture, but they came to different conclusions on the source of the effects.

[12]In general, most experts agree that the Uruguay Round Agreement on Agriculture may have constrained the growth of agricultural protection but has done little to reduce it, at least in the countries that were GATT members during the negotiations (Anania et al. 2004). The GATT/WTO impact may have been more important for the instruments than for the level of support. For example, GATT/WTO accession triggered an important change in the instrument choice in the European Union over the past decades, but much less on the level of protection.

protection. Huang & Chen (1999) demonstrated that, even before China's accession, leaders aggressively reduced protection on a number of commodities (including many importables such as soybeans and cotton) in anticipation of the negotiations. Upon accession, protection fell even further (Huang et al. 2004). The constraints imposed on China as a newly acceding country by international agreements have been real and have led to falling rates of the positive protection—especially for a significant number of importable commodities.

For the CEE countries, the most important WTO impact has been indirect: In anticipation of eastward enlargement, the European Union was forced to introduce major changes to its Common Agricultural Policy, which in turn has affected postaccession agricultural distortions. E.U. accession, both prospective and actual, has had obvious and profound influences on policy choices (Swinnen 2002). The CEE countries that joined in 2004 have raised domestic agricultural and food prices toward E.U. levels. These countries had to undertake major regulatory improvements to stimulate their markets, including private investments in the food chain and public rural infrastructure investments. Their trade policies have likewise changed so as to allow free access for all products from other E.U. countries and, in most cases, also freer access for nonagricultural products from non-E.U. countries (Ciaian & Swinnen 2008).

Finally, the role of other international institutions, such as the World Bank and International Monetary Fund, was important at the start of transition, as it provided policy guidance in all these countries. However, in more recent years this guidance has been less effective. In contrast, policy advice from the European Union was perceived as more relevant for those countries joining this collective, especially E.U. accession countries. Countries aspiring to join the European Union (such as most of the Balkan countries and as far east as Ukraine), or those seeing the accession countries as models for their own development strategies, also take seriously any policy advice from the European Union. Another reason for the declining influence of some international financial institutions is that the improved fiscal and macroeconomic situations of many countries have made them less beholden to those institutions requiring reforms as a condition to providing loans or financial assistance.

CONCLUSION

In this paper we review the literature on governance structures and policy reform related to agricultural price distortions and land rights reform. We draw insights from the theoretical and quantitative literature and from studies on the dramatic reforms in transition countries. Evidence exists supporting the general conclusion that regime changes contribute to policy reforms: Whenever a major policy reform occurred, a regime change (of some sort) preceded it or coincided with it. In some cases, particularly in China, this regime change was within the Communist party. In many other countries economic changes occurred only when the Communist regime collapsed. There is also evidence that a combination of regime change and events that cause strong demand at the grassroots level for policy reform (such as an income crisis) is needed to trigger important policy reforms in an authoritarian political system. In our review of the history of the Communist regimes we find that only in China in the late 1970s was such combination present.

In general, the specific nature of the relationship between (changes in) governance structures and policy reform is complicated and nuanced. This relationship is conditional on several factors including ideology, inequality, and level of development. The impact of changes in political regimes on policy reform depends on the preference of the rulers (ideology) under the various regimes and the extent to which they can enforce their private preferences. Inequality matters in several ways. For example, whether farming is dominated by large landlords or by small-scale resource poor farmers is likely to affect the policies, either because of their ability to influence the government through lobbying or because of the government's ideological preferences. In addition, the ability of landlords, peasants, and landless workers to form a coalition to demand proagriculture fiscal policies, or the possibility of them spending their political activities on fighting each other over the distribution of property rights, depends on the initial distribution of these rights.

Although it is well known that the structural characteristics of the economy affect trade and fiscal policies toward agriculture, until recently there was much less information on how this process interacts with the nature of the political regimes. Our survey suggests that, even in autocratic regimes, important structural changes in the economy appear to be correlated with commonly observed changes in policy, e.g., subsidies to agriculture are positively correlated with economic development. Changes in agricultural subsidization and taxation under Communist regimes, i.e., over the 1930–1980 period in the Soviet Union and over the past 40 years in China, are consistent with these observations.

In many cases governance and policy reform affect one another in a dynamic and bidirectional fashion, with economic reforms also affecting the governance structure. In China the dramatic success of the early economic reforms contributed to the legitimacy and the survival of the Communist Party and mitigated the pressures for further economic reforms. In the Soviet Union the opposite occurred: The failure of timid reforms contributed to the decline in the legitimacy of the Communist Party, and once changes were possible, opponents tried to implement reforms that were intended both to reform the economic system and to change the future political regime.

An important final issue for future research is the interaction of different reforms within a political economy framework and the normative implications. Most normative studies focus on a single policy and its effects. However, if some specific reform policies are elements of broader reform packages, as our review indicates to be important, such single-policy evaluation may not be the right framework for drawing normative conclusions. In a broader reform strategy, specific policies may play a (political) role to reinforce the overall reform strategy, or they may play a role as compensation instruments. On the one hand, agricultural protection can be part of a "social contract" in which more general reforms are promoted to stimulate productivity growth and restructuring and where agricultural protection is used to cushion the blows for the least mobile—as has been suggested more generally by Rausser (1982) and de Gorter et al. (1992) and for which there is empirical evidence (e.g., Swinnen et al. 2000). On the other hand, policy reform can be one element of a much broader paradigm shift such as in CEE, the FSU, and China. Within this set of policy reforms, specific reforms (such as the restitution of land rights to former owners in CEE) can be an element of a broader reform package to create an irreversible set of direct and indirect changes: The former would affect economic incentives; the latter would stimulate, through an induced change in political preferences, a reduction of distortions in the long run. The welfare effects of these policies should thus be interpreted in this broader perspective. There is an important need for further research to incorporate such interactions for normative interpretations of reform effects.

DISCLOSURE STATEMENT

The authors are not aware of any affiliations, memberships, funding, or financial holdings that might be perceived as affecting the objectivity of this review.

ACKNOWLEDGMENTS

We thank Gordon Rausser for guidance.

LITERATURE CITED

Acemoglu D, Robinson JA. 2001. A theory of political transitions. *Am. Econ. Rev.* 91:938–63

Acemoglu D, Robinson JA. 2006. *Economic Origins of Dictatorship and Democracy.* Cambridge, UK: Cambridge Univ. Press

Acemoglu D, Robinson JA. 2008. Persistence of power, elites and institutions. *Am. Econ. Rev.* 98 (1):267–93

Aghion P, Alesina A, Trebbi F. 2004. Endogenous political institutions. *Q. J. Econ.* 119(2):565–612

Anania G, Bohman ME, Carter CA, McCalla AF, eds. 2004. *Agricultural Policy Reform and the WTO: Where Are We Heading?* London: Edward Elgar

Anderson K. 1995. Lobbying incentives and the pattern of protection in rich and poor countries. *Econ. Dev. Cult. Change* 43(2):401–23

Anderson K, ed. 2009a. *Distortions to Agricultural Incentives: A Global Perspective.* Washington, DC: World Bank. In press

Anderson K, ed. 2009b. *The Political Economy of Distortions to Agriculture.* Washington, DC: World Bank. In press

Anderson K, Hayami Y. 1986. *The Political Economy of Agricultural Protection: East Asia in International Perspective.* London: Allen Unwin

Anderson K, Swinnen JFM, eds. 2008. *Distortions to Agricultural Incentives in Europe's Transition Economies.* Washington, DC: World Bank

Bacchetta M, Drabek Z. 2002. *Effects of WTO accession on policy-making in sovereign states: preliminary lessons from the recent experience of transition countries.* Work. Pap. DERD-2002-02, WTO

Becker GS. 1983. A theory of competition among pressure groups for political influence. *Q. J. Econ.* 98(3):371–400

Bagwell K, Staiger RW. 2002. *The Economics of the World Trading System.* Cambridge, MA: MIT Press

Balcerowicz L. 1994. Common fallacies in the debate on the transition to a market economy. *Econ. Polit.* 9(19):17–50

Bates RH. 1983. Patterns of market intervention in agrarian Africa. *Food Policy* 8(4):297–304

Bates RH. 1989. *Beyond the Miracle of the Market: The Political Economy of Agrarian Development in Rural Kenya.* Cambridge, U.K.: Cambridge Univ. Press

Beghin JC, Kherallah M. 1994. Political institutions and international patterns of agricultural protection. *Rev. Econ. Stat.* 76(3):482–9

Binswanger H, Deininger K, Feder G. 1995a. Agricultural land relations in the developing world. *Am. J. Agric. Econ.* 75:1242–8

Binswanger H, Deininger K, Feder G. 1995b. Power, distortions, revolt and reform in agricultural land relations. In *Handbook of Development Economics*, Vol. 3, ed. C Hollis, TN Srinivasan, pp. 2659–72. Amsterdam: North-Holland

Brada JC, Wädekin K, eds. 1988. *Socialist Agriculture in Transition: Organizational Response to Failing Performance.* Boulder, CO: Westview

Brooks KM. 1990. Soviet agricultural policy and pricing under Gorbachev. In *Soviet Agriculture: Comparative Perspectives*, ed. RG Kenneth, pp. 116–29. Ames, IA: Iowa State Univ. Press

Buchanan JM, Tullock G. 1962. *The Calculus of Consent: Logical Foundations of Constitutional Democracy*. Ann Arbor, MI: Univ. Mich. Press

Ciaian P, Swinnen JFM. 2008. Distortions to agricultural incentives in Central and Eastern Europe. See Anderson & Swinnen 2008, pp. 58–87

Clague C, Rausser GC. 1992. *The Emergence of Market Economies in Eastern Europe*. Cambridge, MA: Blackwell

Craeybeckx J. 1973. De agrarische depressie van het einde der XIXe eeuw en de politieke strijd om de boeren I. *Belg. Tijdschr. Nieuwste Geschied.* 4:190–230

de Gorter H, Nielson DJ, Rausser GC. 1992. Productive and predatory public policies: research expenditures and producer subsidies in agriculture. *Am. J. Agric. Econ.* 74(1):27–37

de Gorter H, Swinnen JFM. 2002. Political economy of agricultural policies. In *Handbook of Agricultural Economics Volume 2B: Agricultural and Food Policy*, ed. BL Gardner, GC Rausser, pp. 2073–123. Amsterdam: Elsevier Sci. Ltd.

de Gorter H, Tsur Y. 1991. Explaining price policy bias in agriculture: the calculus of support-maximizing politicians. *Am. J. Agric. Econ.* 73(4):1244–54

de Janvry A. 1981. *The Agrarian Question and Reformism in Latin America*. Baltimore, MD: Johns Hopkins Univ. Press

de Janvry A, Gordillo G, Platteau JP, Sadoulet E, eds. 2001. *Access to Land, Rural Poverty, and Public Action*. Oxford, UK: Oxford Univ. Press

Deininger K, Feder G. 2002. Land institutions and land markets. In *Handbook of Agricultural Economics*, ed. B Gardner, G Rausser. Amsterdam: Elsevier Sci.

Dewan T, Shepsle KA. 2008a. Recent economic perspectives on political economy. Part I. *Br. J. Polit. Sci.* 38(2):363–82

Dewan T, Shepsle KA. 2008b. Recent economic perspectives on political economy. Part II. *Br. J. Polit. Sci.* 38(3):543–64

Dewatripont M, Roland G. 1992. The virtues of gradualism and legitimacy in the transition to a market economy. *Econ. J.* 102(411):291–300

Downs A. 1957. *An Economic Theory of Democracy*. New York: Harper Row

Dutt P, Mitra D. 2002. Endogenous trade policy through majority voting: an empirical investigation. *J. Int. Econ.* 58(1):107–33

Dutt P, Mitra D. 2005. Political ideology and endogenous trade policy: an empirical investigation. *Rev. Econ. Stat.* 87(1):59–72

Dutt P, Mitra D. 2009. Political economy of agricultural distortion patterns: the roles of ideology, inequality, lobbying and public finance. See Anderson 2009b, In press

Ellman M. 1988. Contract brigades and normless teams in Soviet agriculture. See Brada & Wädekin 1988, pp. 23–33

Findlay R, O'Rourke KH. 2007. *Power and Plenty. Trade, War, and the World Economy in the Second Millennium*. Princeton NJ: Princeton Univ. Press

Fischer S. 1994. Structural factors in the economic reforms of China, Eastern Europe, and the former Soviet Union. Discussion. *Econ. Polit.* 9(1):131–35

Frye T, Shleifer A. 1997. The invisible hand and the grabbing hand. *Am. Econ. Rev.* 87(2):354–58

Gardner BL. 1987. Causes of U.S. farm commodity programs. *J. Polit. Econ.* 95(2):290–310

Gawande K, Krishna P. 2003. The political economy of trade policy: empirical approaches. In *Handbook of International Trade*, ed. E Kwan Choi, J Harrigan, pp. 213–50. Oxford: Blackwell

Goodhue R, Rausser GC, Simon LK. 1998. Privatization, market liberalization and learning in transition economies. *Am. J. Agric. Econ.* 80(4):724–37

Gray KR, ed. 1990. *Soviet Agriculture: Comparative Perspectives*. Ames, IA: Iowa State Univ. Press

Grossman GM, Helpman E. 2002. *Interest Groups and Trade Policy*. Trenton, NJ: Princeton Univ. Press

Hayami Y, Quisumbing MA, Adriano L. 1990. *Toward an Alternative Land Reform Paradigm: A Philippine Perspective*. Quezon City: Ateneo de Manila Univ. Press

Hillman AL. 1982. Declining industries and political-support protectionist motives. *Am. Econ. Rev.* 72(5):1180–87

Honma M, Hayami Y. 1986. The determinants of agricultural protection levels: an econometric analysis. In *The Political Economy of Agricultural Protection*, ed. K Anderson, Y Hayami. London: Allen Unwin

Huang J, Chen C. 1999. *Effect of trade liberalization on agriculture in China: institutional and structural aspects.* Work. Pap. Series N 42, United Nations, ESCAP Cent. Res. Dev. Coarse Grains Pulses Roots Tuber Crops

Huang J, Liu Y, Martin W, Rozelle S. 2008. Distortions to agricultural incentives in China. In *Distortions to Agricultural Incentives in Asia*, ed. K Anderson, W Masters. Washington, DC: World Bank

Huang J, Rozelle S, Chang M. 2004. The nature of distortions to agricultural incentives in China and implications of WTO accession. *World Bank Econ. Rev.* 18(1):59–84

Jacoby H, Li G, Rozelle S. 2002. Hazards of expropriation: tenure insecurity and investment in rural China. *Am. Econ. Rev.* 92(5):1420–47

Johnson DG, Brooks KM, eds. 1983. *Prospects for Soviet Agriculture in the 1980s.* Bloomington, IN: Indiana Univ. Press

Josling TE, Tangermann S, Warley TK. 1996. *Agriculture in the GATT.* Basingstoke, UK: McMillan

Kindleberger CP. 1975. The rise of free trade in Western Europe, 1820–1875. *J. Econ. Hist.* 35(1):20–55

Krueger AO. 1990. *Government failures in development.* Work. Pap. 3340, NBER

Krueger AO, Schiff M, Valdes A. 1988. Agricultural incentives in developing countries: measuring the effects of sectoral and economy wide policies. *World Bank Econ. Rev.* 3(2):225–71

Krueger AO, Schiff M, Valdés A. 1991. *The Political Economy of Agricultural Pricing Policy.* London: Johns Hopkins Univ. Press

La Ferrara E. 2002. Inequality and group participation: theory and evidence from rural Tanzania. *J. Public Econ.* 85(2):235–73

Lardy N. 1983. *Agriculture in China's Modern Economic Development.* Cambridge, UK: Cambridge Univ. Press

Lee HY. 1991. *From Revolutionary Cadres to Party Technocrats in Socialist China.* Berkeley, CA: Univ. Calif. Press

Lerman Z, Brooks K. 2001. *Turkmenistan: An Assessment of Leasehold-based Farm Restructuring.* Tech. Pap. 500, World Bank

Lerman Z, Csaki C, Feder G. 2004. *Agriculture in Transition: Land Policies and Evolving Farm Structures in Post-Soviet Countries.* Landham, MD: Lexington Books

Li DD. 1998. Changing incentives of the Chinese bureaucracy. *Am. Econ. Rev.* 88(2):393–97

Liefert WM, Swinnen JFM. 2002. *Changes in agricultural markets in transition economics.* Agric. Econ. Rep. 806, ERS, USDA

Lin JY. 1992. Rural reforms and agricultural growth in China. *Am. Econ. Rev.* 82(1):34–51

Lindert PH. 1991. Historical patterns of agricultural policy. In *Agriculture and the State: Growth, Employment, and Poverty*, ed. C Timmer, ch. 2. Ithaca, NY: Cornell Univ. Press

Lipton M. 1977. *Why Poor People Stay Poor: A Study of Urban Bias in World Development.* Cambridge, MA: Harvard Univ. Press

Lyons R, Rausser G, Simon L. 1994. Disruption and continuity in Bulgaria's agrarian reform. In *Privatization of Agriculture in New Market Economies: Lessons from Bulgaria*, ed. A Schmitz, K Moulton, A Buckwell, S Davidova, pp. 87–117. Norwell, MA: Kluwer Acad.

Macours K, Swinnen JFM. 2002. Patterns of agrarian transition. *Econ. Dev. Cult. Change* 50(2):365–94

McMillan J. 2002. *Reinventing the Bazaar. The Natural History of Markets.* New York: WW Norton

McMillan J, Naughton B. 1992. How to reform a planned economy: lessons from China. *Oxf. Rev. Econ. Policy* 8:130–43

Nyberg A, Rozelle S. 1999. *Accelerating Development in Rural China. World Bank Monograph Series, Rural Development Division*. Washington, DC: World Bank

North DC, Wallis JJ, Weingast BR. 2006. *A conceptual framework for interpreting recorded human history*. Work. Pap. 12795, NBER

OECD. 1996. *Agricultural Policies in Non-Member Countries*. Paris: OECD

Oi J. 1989. Market reforms and corruption in rural China. *Stud. Comp. Communism* 22(2/3):221–33

Olper A. 2001. Determinants of agricultural protection: the role of democracy and institutional setting. *J. Agric. Econ.* 52(2):75–92

Olper A. 2007. Land inequality, government ideology and agricultural protection. *Food Policy* 32 (1):67–83

Olper A, Raimundi V. 2009. Constitutional rules and agricultural protection. See Anderson 2009b, In press

Olson M. 1965. *The Logic of Collective Action*. New Haven: Yale Univ. Press

O'Rourke K, Taylor AM. 2002. *Democracy and protection*. Work. Pap. 12250, NBER

Park A, Jin H, Rozelle S, Huang J. 2002. Market emergence and transition: transition costs, arbitrage, and autarky in China's grain market. *Am. J. Agric. Econ.* 84(1):67–82

Peltzman S. 1976. Towards a more general theory of regulation. *J. Law Econ.* 19(2):211–40

Persson T, Tabellini GE. 2000. *Political Economics—Explaining Economic Policy*. Cambridge, MA: MIT Press

Persson T, Tabellini GE. 2003. *The Economic Effects of Constitutions: What Do the Data Say?* Cambridge, MA: MIT Press

Pingali PL, Xuan V. 1992. Vietnam: decollectivization and rice productivity growth. *Econ. Dev. Cult. Change* 40(4):697–718

Pokrivcak J, Crombez C, Swinnen JFM. 2007. The status quo bias and reform of the common agricultural policy: impact of voting rules, the European Commission, and external changes. *Eur. Rev. Agric. Econ.* 33(4):562–90

Prendergast C. 2007. The motivation and bias of bureaucrats. *Am. Econ. Rev.* 97(1):180–96

Qian Y, Roland G, Xu C. 1999. Why is China different from Eastern Europe? Perspectives from organization theory. *Eur. Econ. Rev.* 43(4):1085–94

Qian Y, Weingast BR. 1997. Federalism as a commitment to preserving market incentives. *J. Econ. Perspect.* 11(4):83–92

Qian Y, Xu C. 1993. Why China's economic reforms differ: the M-form hierarchy and entry/expansion of the non-state sector. *Econ. Transit.* 1(2):135–70

Pomfret R. 2008. Distortions to agricultural incentives in Kazakhstan. See Anderson & Swinnen 2008, pp. 219–64

Putterman L. 1993. *Continuity and Change in China's Rural Development*. New York: Oxford Univ. Press

Rabinowicz E. 1997. The political economy of land reform in the Baltics. In *The Political Economy of Agrarian Reform in Central and Eastern Europe*, ed. JFM Swinnen. Aldershot: Ashgate

Radvanyi J. 1988. The experiments in Georgia, 1974-1984: quest for a new organization in the Soviet agricultural system. See Brada & Wädekin 1988, pp. 110–24

Rausser GC. 1982. Political economic markets: PERTs and PESTs in food and agriculture. *Am. J. Agric. Econ.* 64(5):821–33

Rausser GC. 1995. *GATT Negotiations and the Political Economy of Policy Reform*. Berlin/Heidelberg/New York: Springer-Verlag

Rausser GC, Roland G. 2009. Special interests versus the public interest: the determination of policy instruments. See Anderson 2009b, In press

Rausser GC, Simon LK. 1992. The political economy of transition in Eastern Europe: packaging enterprises for privatization. In *The Emergence of Market Economies in Eastern Europe*, ed. C Clague, G Rausser, ch. 14, pp. 245–70. Cambridge, MA: Blackwell

Rausser GC, Swinnen JFM, Zusman P. 2008. *Political power and endogenous policy formation. Mimeogr.*, Univ. Calif. Berkeley

Rizov M, Gavrilescu D, Gow HR, Mathijs E, Swinnen JFM. 2001. Transition and enterprise restructuring: the development of individual farming in Romania. *World Dev.* 29(7):1257–74

Roelfsema H. 2004. *Political institutions and trade protection.* Work. Pap. 04-06, Tjalling C Koopmans Res. Inst., Univ. Utrecht

Rogowski R. 1989. *Commerce and Coalitions. How Trade Affects Domestic Political Alignments.* Princeton NJ: Princeton Univ. Press

Rogowski R, Kayser MA. 2002. Majoritarian electoral systems and consumer power: price-level evidence from the OECD countries. *Am. J. Polit. Sci.* 46(3):526–39

Roland G. 2000. *Transition and Economics: Politics, Markets and Firms.* Cambridge, MA: MIT Press

Rozelle S. 1996. Gradual reform and institutional development: the keys to success of China's rural reforms. In *Reforming Asian Socialism: The Growth of Market Institutions*, ed. J McMillan, B Naughton, pp. 197–220. Ann Arbor, MI: Univ. Mich. Press

Rozelle S, Huang J, Otsuka K. 2008. Agriculture in China's development. In *China's Great Economic Transformation*, ed. L Brandt, T Rawski, pp. 467–505. New York: Cambridge Univ. Press

Rozelle S, Swinnen JFM. 2004. Success and failure of reform: insights from the transition of agriculture. *J. Econ. Lit.* 42(2):404–56

Rozelle S, Swinnen JFM. 2009a. The political economy of agricultural distortions in the transition countries of Europe and Asia. See Anderson 2009b, In press

Rozelle S, Swinnen JFM. 2009b. Why did the communist party reform in China and not in the Soviet Union? *China Econ. Rev.* In press

Sachs JD, Woo W-T. 1994. Structural factors in the economic reforms of China, Eastern Europe and the former Soviet Union. *Econ. Polit.* 9(1):101–45

Schonhardt-Bailey C. 1998. Parties and interests in the 'marriage of iron and rye.' *Br. J. Polit. Sci.* 28:291–330

Schonhardt-Bailey C. 2006. *From the Corn Laws to Free Trade. Interests, Ideas and Institutions in Historical Perspective.* Cambridge MA: MIT Press

Shleifer A. 1997. Government in transition. *Eur. Econ. Rev.* 41(3-5):385–410

Sicular T. 1988. Plan and market in China's agricultural commerce. *J. Polit. Econ.* 96(2):283–307

Sicular T. 1995. Redefining state, plan, and market: China's reforms in agricultural commerce. *China Q.* 144:1020–46

Stigler GJ. 1971. The economic theory of regulation. *Bell J. Econ. Manag. Sci.* 2:3–21

Studlar DT, McAllister I, Ascui A. 1990. Privatization and the British electorate: microeconomic policies, macroeconomic evaluations, and party support. *Am. J. Pol. Sci.* 34(4):1077–101

Swinnen JFM. 1994. A positive theory of agricultural protection. *Am. J. Agric. Econ.* 76(1):1–14

Swinnen JFM. 1996. Endogenous price and trade policy developments in Central European agriculture. *Eur. Rev. Agric. Econ.* 23(2):133–60

Swinnen JFM, ed. 1997. *The Political Economy of Agrarian Reform in Central and Eastern Europe.* Aldershot: Ashgate

Swinnen JFM. 1999. The political economy of land reform choices in Central and Eastern Europe. *Econ. Transit.* 7(3):637–64

Swinnen JFM. 2001. Political reforms, rural crises, and land tenure in Western Europe. *Food Policy* 27(4):371–94

Swinnen JFM. 2002. Transition and integration in Europe: implications for agricultural and food markets, policy and trade agreements. *World Econ.* 25(4):481–501

Swinnen JFM. 2009a. Agricultural protection growth in Europe 1870–1969. See Anderson 2009b, In press

Swinnen JFM. 2009b. The political economy of agricultural policies: the literature to date. See Anderson 2009b, In press

Swinnen JFM, Banerjee AN, de Gorter H. 2001. Economic development, institutional change, and the political economy of agricultural protection: an econometric study of Belgium since the 19th century. *Agric. Econ.* 26(1):25–43

Swinnen JFM, de Gorter H. 1993. Why small groups and low income sectors obtain subsidies: the 'altruistic' side of a 'self-interested' government. *Econ. Polit.* 5(3):285–96

Swinnen JFM, de Gorter H, Rausser GC, Banerjee AN. 2000. The political economy of public research investment and commodity policies in agriculture: an empirical study. *Agric. Econ.* 22 (2):111–22

Swinnen JFM, Heinegg A. 2002. On the political economy of land reforms in the former Soviet Union. *J. Int. Dev.* 14(7):1019–31

Swinnen JFM, Rozelle S. 2006. *From Marx and Mao to the Market: The Economics and Politics of Agricultural Transition.* New York: Oxford Univ. Press

Timmer CP. 1986. *Getting Prices Right: The Scope and Limits of Agricultural Price Policy.* New York: Cornell Univ. Press

Tracy M. 1989. *Government and Agriculture in Western Europe 1880-1988.* New York: Harvester Wheatsheaf, 3rd ed.

van Atta D. 1993. *The 'Farmer Threat': The Political Economy of Agrarian Reform in Post-Soviet Russia.* Boulder, CO: Westview

von Cramon–Taubadel S, Nivyevskiy O, von der Malsburg EE, Movchan V. 2008. Distortions to agricultural incentives in Ukraine. See Anderson & Swinnen 2008, pp. 175–217

Wädekin K-E. 1990. Determinants and trends of reform in communist agriculture: a concluding essay. In *Communist Agriculture: Farming in the Soviet Union and Eastern Europe*, ed. K-E Wädekin, pp. 321–39. London/New York: Routledge

Wegren SK, ed. 1998. *Land Reform in the Former Soviet Union and Eastern Europe.* London: Routledge

Weingast BR, Wittman D, eds. 2006. *The Oxford Handbook of Political Economy.* New York: Oxford Univ. Press

Williamson OE. 1975. *Markets and Hierarchies.* New York: Free Press

Wong CPW, ed. 1997. *Financing Local Government in the People's Republic of China.* Hong Kong: Oxford Univ. Press

World Bank. 1992. *China: Strategies for Reducing Poverty in the 1990s.* Washington, DC: World Bank

World Bank. 2000. *World Development Report 2000/2001: Attacking Poverty.* Washington, DC: World Bank

Wurfel D. 1993. Doi Moi in comparative perspective. In *Reinventing Vietnamese Socialism: Doi Moi in Comparative Perspective*, ed. W Turley, M Selden, pp. 165–207. Boulder, CO: Westview

Wyzan ML. 1990. The Bulgarian experience with centrally planned agriculture: lessons for Soviet reformers? In *Soviet Agriculture: Comparative Perspectives*, ed. KG Gray, pp. 220–42. Ames, IA: Iowa State Univ. Press

Yang D. 1996. *Calamity and Reform in China: State, Rural Society, and Institutional Change Since the Great Leap Famine.* Stanford, CA: Stanford Univ. Press

Zhang X. 2006. Fiscal decentralization and political centralization in China: implications for growth and inequality. *J. Comp. Econ.* 34:713–26

Zhou KX. 1996. *How the Farmers Changed China: Power of the People.* Boulder, CO: Westview

Distortions to Agricultural Versus Nonagricultural Producer Incentives

Kym Anderson

World Bank; CEPR; and School of Ecnomics, University of Adelaide, Adelaide SA 5005 Australia; email: kym.anderson@adelaide.edu.au

Annu. Rev. Resour. Econ. 2009. 1:55–74

The *Annual Review of Resource Economics* is online at resource.annualreviews.org

This article's doi: 10.1146/annurev.resource.050708.144236

Key Words

distorted farm prices, trade policy reforms, inefficient resource use

Abstract

For more than a century, government policies have grossly distorted resource use in agriculture, both within and between countries. Earnings from farming in many developing countries have been depressed by a prourban bias in own-country policies as well as by governments of richer countries favoring their farmers with import barriers and subsidies. Both sets of policies reduce national and global economic welfare and inhibit economic growth; they also add to inequality and poverty in developing countries. Since the 1980s, however, numerous developing and some high-income country governments have reduced their sectoral and trade policy distortions. This paper draws on new empirical studies to show the changing extent of policy distortions to prices faced by the world's farmers since the 1950s. Modeling results provide an indication of how far those reforms proceeded between the early 1980s and 2004 and of how much scope remains for removing continuing inefficiencies in global agricultural resource use.

THE ISSUE AND ITS IMPORTANCE

Resource use in agriculture, both within and between countries, has been grossly distorted for more than a century by government price and trade policies in both rich and poor countries. Earnings from farming in many developing countries have been depressed by a prourban bias in own-country policies as well as by governments of richer countries favoring their farmers with import barriers and subsidies. Both sets of policies reduce national and global economic welfare and inhibit economic growth. They also add to inequality and poverty in developing countries and slow structural adjustment in growing economies. Since the 1980s, however, numerous developing and some high-income country governments have been reducing their sectoral and trade policy distortions and are relying on more-direct forms of taxation and support that are less wasteful of resources.

For growing economies, the most common reason for restrictions on imports of farm products has been to protect the value of assets of domestic farmers and associated agribusinesses producers from import competition as they come under competitive pressure to shed labor in the course of economic development. But, in the process, those protective measures hurt not only domestic consumers and exporters but also foreign producers and traders of farm products. Their distorting effects on resource use and consumer purchases reduce national and global economic welfare, the latter through depressing international prices of farm products, which in turn lowers the earnings of farmers and associated rural businesses in other countries.

This external policy influence on other countries is not the only thing affecting their farmers though. The governments of many (especially newly independent) developing countries have a history of taxing their farmers heavily. A well-known example is the taxing of exports of plantation crops in postcolonial Africa (Bates 1981). The use of multiple exchange rates also introduced an antitrade bias in many developing countries. In addition, most developing countries chose to pursue an import-substituting industrialization strategy, predominantly by restricting imports of manufactures. This indirectly taxed other tradable sectors, including agriculture, in those developing economies.

This disarray in world agriculture, as described by Johnson (1991) in the title of his seminal book, means there has been overproduction of farm products in high-income countries and underproduction in developing countries. It also means there has been less international trade in farm products than would be the case under free trade, thereby thinning markets for these weather-dependent products and thus making them more volatile. Using a stochastic model of world food markets, Tyers & Anderson (1992, table 6.14) found that instability of international food prices in the early 1980s was three times greater than it would have been under free trade in those products.

During the past quarter century, however, numerous countries have begun to reform their agricultural price, trade, and exchange rate policies. Such reform raises the question as to how far the world has come in reducing market distortions relative to how far it still has to go before agricultural and other resources are free to be attracted to their most productive uses.[1]

---

[1] Of course, laissez faire may not be optimal in the presence of externalities, nor should it be forgotton that raising tax revenue to provide public goods is a legitimate goal of government. But agricultural price and trade policies are almost never first-best ways to overcome externalities or raise taxes (Corden 1997, chs. 4 and 13). Throughout this article, it is assumed that reducing government distortions to product prices is a step in the direction of improving resource allocation, in the sense that this then allows governments to find more-efficient domestic policy measures for dealing with externalities and raising taxes. Such reforms may incidentally also contribute to those goals (e.g., by lowering pollutive farm production or expanding the volume of imports enough to more than compensate for the reduction in the rate of import taxation).

This article begins with a survey of the methodology required to measure the extent of own-country distortions to incentives faced by farmers relative to producers of other tradable goods. It then surveys analyses of the effects of price and trade policies on producer and consumer incentives over time, focusing on the worsening of that situation between the 1950s and mid-1980s and the progress that has been made over the subsequent 25 years. Economy-wide computable general equilibrium (CGE) modeling results then provide a further indication of how far those reforms have proceeded between the early 1980s and 2004 and of how much scope remains for removing continuing inefficiencies in global agricultural resource use. This paper concludes by assessing the prospects for reducing remaining distortions.

CGE: Computable general equilibrium

NATIONAL DISTORTIONS TO INCENTIVES: BASIC THEORY

Bhagwati (1971) and Corden (1997) define the concept of a policy distortion to a product market as something imposed by governments and that creates a gap between the marginal social return to a seller and the marginal social cost to a buyer in a transaction. [Also see Anderson et al. (2008), from which this section draws heavily.] Such a distortion imposes an economic cost on society that can be estimated using welfare techniques such as those pioneered by Harberger (1971). As Harberger notes, this focus allows a great simplification in evaluating the marginal costs of a set of distortions: Changes in economic costs can be evaluated taking into account the changes in volumes directly affected by such distortions, ignoring all other changes in prices. In the absence of divergences such as externalities, the measure of a distortion is the gap between the price paid and the price received, irrespective of whether the level of these prices is affected by the distortion. Once the extent of that price wedge is measured for a product, it can be used as an input into a model of the market for that good to estimate what the market price effect is of that distortion, if any (Just et al. 2004).

Other developments that change incentives facing producers and consumers can include flow-on consequences of the distortion, but these should not be confused with the direct price distortion that needs to be estimated. If, for instance, a country is large in world trade for a given commodity, imposition of an export tax may raise the price in international markets, reducing the adverse impact of the distortion on producers in the taxing country. Other flow-on consequences include the effect of trade distortions on the real exchange rate, which is the price of traded goods relative to nontraded goods, or on the market for substitutes or complements in production or consumption. None of these flow-on effects are of immediate concern, however, because if the product market's direct distortions are accurately estimated, they can be incorporated as price wedges into an appropriate national or global economy-wide CGE model, which in turn will be able to capture the full general equilibrium impacts (inclusive of terms of trade, real exchange rate, and substitution effects) of the various direct distortions to the producer and consumer prices of the product.

The total effect of distortions on the agricultural sector will depend not just on the size of the direct agricultural policy measures, but also on the magnitude of distortions generated by direct policy measures altering incentives in nonagricultural sectors. Relative prices and hence relative rates of government assistance affect producers' incentives. In a two-sector model of an economy, an import tax has the same effect on the export sector as an export tax: the Lerner (1936) Symmetry Theorem. This carries over to a model that has

CTE: Consumer tax
equivalent
NRA: Nominal rate of
assistance

many sectors and is unaffected given imperfect competition domestically or internationally or if some of those sectors produce only nontradables (Vousden 1990, pp. 46–47). The symmetry theorem is therefore also relevant for considering distortions within the agricultural sector. In particular, the protection of import-competing farm industries, for example, via import tariffs, has similar adverse effects on incentives to produce exportables as does an explicit tax on agricultural exports; and if both measures are in place, this is a double imposition on farm exporters.

In what follows, we begin by focusing first on direct distortions to agricultural incentives, before turning to those affecting the sector indirectly via policies directed at nonagricultural sectors.

Direct Agricultural Distortions

Consider a small, open, perfectly competitive national economy with many firms producing a homogeneous farm product with just primary factors. In the absence of externalities, processing, producer-to-consumer wholesale plus retail marketing margins, exchange rate distortions, and domestic and international trading costs, that country would maximize national economic welfare by allowing both the domestic farm product price and the consumer price of that product to equal E times P, where E is the domestic currency price of foreign exchange and P is the foreign currency price of this identical product in the international market. That is, any government-imposed diversion from that equality, in the absence of any market failures or externalities, would be welfare reducing for that small economy.

Price-Distorting Trade Measures at the National Border

The most common distortion is an *ad valorem* tax on competing imports (usually called a tariff), t_m. Such a tariff on an imported product that is a perfect substitute for the domestically produced good is the equivalent of a production subsidy and a consumption tax both at rate t_m. If that tariff on the imported primary agricultural product is the only distortion, its effect on producer incentives can be measured as the nominal rate of assistance (NRA) to farm output conferred by border support (NRA_{BS}), which is the unit value of production at the distorted price less its value at the undistorted free market price expressed as a fraction of the undistorted price:[2]

$$NRA_{BS} = \frac{E \times P(1 + t_m) - E \times P}{E \times P} = t_m. \tag{1}$$

The effect of that import tariff on consumer incentives in this simple economy is to generate a consumer tax equivalent (CTE) on the agricultural product for final consumers:

$$CTE = T_m. \tag{2}$$

The effects of an import subsidy are identical to those in Equations 1 and 2 for an import tax, but t_m in that case would have a negative value.

---

[2]The NRA_{BS} thus differs from the producer support estimate (PSE) as calculated by the OECD, in that the PSE is expressed as a fraction of the distorted value. It is thus $t_m/(1 + t_m)$, and for a positive t_m, the PSE is smaller than the NRA_{BS} and is necessarily less than 100%.

Governments sometimes also intervene with an export subsidy s_x (or an export tax in which case s_x would be negative). If that were the only intervention, then

$$NRA_{BS} = CTE = s_x. \qquad (3)$$

If any of these trade taxes or subsidies were specific rather than *ad valorem* (e.g., $y/kg rather than z percent), its *ad valorem* equivalent can be calculated using slight modifications of Equations 1, 2, and 3.

Domestic Producer and Consumer Price-Distorting Measures

Governments sometimes intervene with a direct production subsidy for farmers, s_f (or production tax, in which case s_f is negative, including via informal taxes in kind by local and provincial governments). In that case, if only this distortion is present, the effect on producer incentives can be measured as the NRA to farm output conferred by domestic price support (NRA_{DS}), which is as above except s_f replaces t_m or s_x, but the CTE in that case is zero. Similarly, if the government imposes only a consumption tax c_c on this product (or consumption subsidy, in which case c_c is negative), the CTE is as above except c_c replaces t_m or s_x, but the NRA_{DS} in that case is zero.

The combination of domestic and border support provides the total rate of assistance to output, NRA_o, where

$$NRA_o = NRA_{BS} + NRA_{DS}. \qquad (4)$$

If there are distortions to input costs, their *ad valorem* equivalent can be accounted for by summing each input's NRA times its input-output coefficient to obtain the combined NRA_i, and adding that to the farm industry's nominal rate of direct assistance to farm output, NRA_o, to get the total NRA to farm production.

What If the Exchange Rate System Also Distorts Prices?

Should a multitier foreign exchange rate regime be in place, then another policy-induced price wedge exists. A simple two-tier exchange rate system creates a gap between the price received by all exporters and the price paid by all importers for foreign currency, changing both the exchange rate received by exporters and that paid by importers from the equilibrium rate E that would prevail without this distortion in the domestic market for foreign currency (Bhagwati 1978).

Exchange rate overvaluation of the type considered here requires controls by the government on current account transfers. A common requirement is that exporters surrender their foreign currency earnings to the central bank to change to local currency at a low official rate. This is equivalent to a tax on exports to the extent that the official rate is below what the exchange rate would be in a market without government intervention. That implicit tax on exporters reduces their incentive to export and hence the supply of foreign currency flowing into the country. With less foreign currency, demanders are willing to bid up its purchase price, thereby providing a potential rent for the government, which can be realized by auctioning off the limited supply of foreign currency extracted from exporters or creating a legal secondary market. Either mechanism will create a gap between the official and parallel rates (de Melo & Robinson 1989, Dervis et al. 1981). Should the government allow the exporters to exchange part of their foreign exchange earnings in the secondary market (or not be able to prevent them from creating an unofficial secondary market), this would reduce the gap between the official and secondary market prices.

What matters for present purposes is that, when a country has distortions in its domestic market for foreign currency, the exchange rate relevant for calculating the NRA_o or the CTE for a particular tradable product depends, in the case of a dual exchange rate system, on whether the product is an importable or an exportable. By contrast, in the case of multiple exchange rates, it depends on the specific rate applying to a given product each year.

What About Post-Farm-Gate Costs?

If a state trading corporation is charging excessively for its marketing services and thereby lowering the farm-gate price of a product, for example as a way of raising government revenue in place of an explicit tax, the extent of that excess should be treated as if it is an explicit tax. Some farm products, including some that are not internationally traded, are inputs into a processing industry that may also be subject to government interventions. In that case, the effect of those interventions on the price received by farmers for the primary product also needs to be taken into account.

The Mean of Agricultural NRAs

When it comes to averaging across countries, each polity is an observation of interest, so a simple average is meaningful for the purpose of political economy analysis. But if one wants a sense of how distorted agriculture is in a whole region, a weighted average is needed. The weighted average, NRA, for covered primary agriculture can be generated by multiplying each primary industry's value share of production (valued at the farm-gate equivalent undistorted prices) by its corresponding NRA and adding these across industries.[3] The overall sectoral rate, $NRAag$, could also include actual or assumed information for the noncovered commodities and, where it exists, the aggregate value of non-product-specific assistance to agriculture. A weighted average can be similarly generated for the tradables part of agriculture—including those industries producing products such as milk and sugar that require only light processing before they can be traded—by assuming that its share of non-product-specific assistance equals its weight in the total. Call that $NRAag^t$.

The Dispersion of Agricultural NRAs

In addition to the mean, it is important to provide a measure of the dispersion or variability of the NRA estimates across the covered products. The cost of government policy distortions to incentives in terms of resource misallocation tends to increase with the degree of substitution in production (Lloyd 1974). In the case of agriculture that involves the use of farm land that is sector specific but transferable among farm activities, the greater the variation of NRAs across industries within the sector, the higher will be the

---

[3]Corden (1971) proposed that free-trade volume be used as weights, but because they are not observable (and an economy-wide model is needed to estimate them), the common practice is to compromise by using actual distorted volumes but undistorted unit values or, equivalently, distorted values divided by (1+ NRA). If estimates of own- and cross-price elasticities of demand and supply are available, a partial equilibrium estimate of the quantity at undistorted prices could be generated, but if those estimated elasticities are unreliable, this may introduce more error than it seeks to correct.

welfare cost of those market interventions. A simple indicator of dispersion is the standard deviation of industry NRAs within agriculture.

TBI: Trade bias index
WRI: Welfare reduction index

Anderson & Neary (2005) showed the possibility of developing a single index that captures the extent to which the mean and standard deviation of protection together contribute to the welfare cost of distortionary policies. This index recognizes the relation of welfare cost of a government-imposed price distortion to the square of the price wedge, and so it is larger than the mean and is positive regardless of whether the government's agricultural policy is favoring or hurting farmers. When only import restrictions are distorting agricultural prices, the index provides a percentage tariff equivalent that, if applied uniformly to all imports, would generate the same welfare cost as the actual intrasectoral structure of protection from import competition. Lloyd et al. (2009) showed that, once NRAs and CTEs have been calculated, these values can be used to generate such an index even in the more complex situation where domestic producer or consumer taxes or subsidies may be present in addition to not only import tariffs but also any other trade taxes or subsidies or quantitative restrictions. This measure, termed a welfare reduction index (WRI), is the percentage agricultural trade tax (or uniform NRA and CTE), which, if applied uniformly to all agricultural tradables, would generate the same reduction in national economic welfare as the actual intrasectoral structure of distortions to domestic prices of tradable farm goods. Lloyd et al. also showed that, if one is willing to assume that domestic price elasticities of supply (demand) are equal across farm commodities, then the only information needed to estimate the WRI, in addition to the NRAs and CTEs, is the share of each commodity in the domestic value of farm production (consumption) at undistorted prices.

Trade Bias in Agricultural Assistance

A trade bias index (TBI) is also needed to indicate the changing extent to which a country's policy regime has an antitrade bias within the agricultural sector. This is important because, as indicated by Lerner (1936), a tariff assisting import-competing farm industries has a similar effect on farmers' incentives as a tax on agricultural exports, and the presence of both measures represents a double imposition on farm exports. A dual exchange rate system would add further to the antitrade bias. The higher is the NRA to import-competing agricultural production ($NRAag_m$) relative to that for exportable farm activities ($NRAag_x$), the more incentive producers in that subsector will have to bid for mobile resources that would otherwise have been employed in export agriculture, other things equal.

Once each farm industry is classified as import competing, a producer of exportables, or as producing a nontradable (its status could change over time), it is possible to generate for each year the weighted average NRAs for the two different groups of tradable farm industries. They can then be used to generate an agricultural TBI defined as

$$TBI = \left[\frac{1 + NRAag_x}{1 + NRAag_m} - 1 \right], \tag{5}$$

where $NRAag_m$ and $NRAag_x$ are the average NRAs for the import-competing and exportable parts of the agricultural sector, respectively (their weighted average is $NRAag^t$). This index has a value of zero when the import-competing and export subsectors are equally assisted, and its lower bound approaches -1 in the most extreme case of an antitrade policy bias.

RRA: Relative rate of assistance
TRI: Trade reduction index

Anderson & Neary (2005) showed that it is possible to develop a single index that captures the extent to which import protection reduces the volume of trade. Once NRAs and CTEs have been calculated, Lloyd et al. (2009) showed how they can be used to generate a more-general trade reduction index (TRI), which also allows for the trade effects of domestic price-distorting policies, regardless of whether they (or the trade measures) are positive or negative. Such a measure is the percentage agricultural trade tax (or uniform NRA and CTE), which, if applied uniformly to all agricultural tradables, would generate the same reduction in trade volume as the actual intrasectoral structure of distortions to domestic prices of tradable farm goods. Lloyd et al. further showed that, if the domestic price elasticities of supply (demand) are equal across farm commodities, then the only information needed to estimate the TRI, in addition to the NRAs and CTEs, is the share of each commodity in the domestic value of farm production (consumption) at undistorted prices.

Indirect Agricultural Assistance/Taxation via Nonagricultural Distortions

In addition to direct assistance to or taxation of farmers, the Lerner (1936) Symmetry Theorem demonstrates that farmers' incentives are also affected indirectly by government assistance to nonagricultural production in the national economy. All things being equal, the higher the NRA is to nonagricultural tradables production ($NRAnonag^t$), the more incentive producers in other tradable sectors will have to bid up the value of mobile resources that would otherwise have been employed in agriculture. If $NRAag^t$ is below $NRAnonag^t$, one might expect fewer resources in agriculture than there would be under free market conditions in the country, notwithstanding any positive direct assistance to farmers. Given converse conditions, the opposite would be expected.

One way to capture this is to calculate a relative rate of assistance (RRA), defined as

$$RRA = \left[\frac{1 + NRAag^t}{1 + NRAnonag^t} - 1 \right]. \quad (6)$$

Because an NRA cannot be less than −1 if producers are to earn anything, neither can RRA. This measure is a useful indicator for providing international comparisons over time of the extent to which a country's policy regime has an anti- or proagricultural bias.

NATIONAL DISTORTIONS TO AGRICULTURAL INCENTIVES: EMPIRICAL ESTIMATES

The history of agricultural protection growth in high-income countries is well known and well documented, so it need not be rehearsed here. The evolution of price distortions in developing countries from the 1950s, as many of them became independent from their colonial masters, is somewhat more heterogeneous, and so it is worth briefly summarizing before turning to empirical estimates of the magnitude of price distortions. We begin with the first of the newly industrializing regions, namely Northeast Asia.

The Evolution of Policies in Developing Countries

In South Korea and Taiwan in the 1950s, as in many newly independent developing countries, an import-substituting industrialization strategy, which harmed agriculture, was initially adopted. Unlike most other developing countries, South Korea and Taiwan replaced that policy in the early 1960s with a more-neutral trade policy that resulted in their very rapid export-oriented industrialization. This development strategy in those densely populated economies imposed competitive pressure on the farm sector, which, just as in Japan in earlier decades, prompted farmers to lobby (successfully, as it happened) for ever-higher levels of protection from import protection (Anderson & Hayami 1986, ch. 2).

Many less-advanced and less-rapidly growing developing countries not only adopted import-substituting industrialization strategies in the late 1950s and early 1960s (Little et al. 1970, Balassa & Associates 1971), but also imposed direct taxes on their exports of farm products (Bates 1981). It was common in the 1950s and 1960s, and in some cases through to the 1980s also, to use dual or multiple exchange rates so as to indirectly tax both exporters and importers (Bhagwati 1978, Krueger 1978). This added to the antitrade bias of developing countries' trade policies. Certainly within the agricultural sector of each country, import-competing industries tended to enjoy more government support than those that were more competitive internationally (Krueger et al. 1988, 1991; Herrmann et al. 1992). The study by Krueger et al. also reveals, at least up to the mid-1980s, that direct disincentives for farmers such as agricultural export taxes were less important than indirect disincentives in the form of import protection for the manufacturing sector or overvalued exchange rates, both of which attracted resources away from agricultural industries producing tradable products.

In short, historically agrarian developing countries have tended to tax agriculture relative to manufacturing. However, those countries that manage to have an industrial takeoff gradually change from taxing to subsidizing agriculture relative to other sectors in the course of their economic development. This transition is less sudden, and occurs at a later stage of development, the stronger a country's comparative advantage in agriculture (Anderson & Hayami 1986, Lindert 1991). Hence, at any point in time, farmers in poor countries tended to face depressed terms of trade relative to product prices in international markets, while the opposite was true for farmers in rich countries (Anderson 1995). The exceptions were not only poor countries with an extreme comparative disadvantage in agriculture (such as South Korea), but also rich countries with an extreme comparative advantage in agriculture (Australia, New Zealand).

Whereas the earlier policy history of developing countries has been described in previous surveys (e.g., Krueger 1984), less well-known is the actual extent to which many emerging economies have belatedly followed the example of South Korea and Taiwan in abandoning import substitution and opening their economies. Some (e.g., Chile) started in the 1970s, whereas others (e.g., India) did not do so in a sustained way until the 1990s. Some countries have adopted a very gradual pace of reform, with occasional reversals, whereas others have moved rapidly to open markets. Finally, some countries have adopted the rhetoric of reform but in practice have done little to free up their economies. To get a clear sense of the overall impact of these reform attempts, as well as those of high-income countries, there is no substitute for empirical analysis that quantifies over time the types of indicators raised in the theory section above.

Estimates of Distortions Since the 1950s

After postwar reconstruction, Japan raised its agricultural protection, just as had been happening in Western Europe, but to even higher levels. Domestic prices exceeded international market prices for grains and livestock products by less than 40% in both Japan and the European community in the 1950s (Gulbrandsen & Lindbeck 1973). By the early 1980s, the difference was more than 80% for Japan but was still approximately 40% for the European Community—and was still close to zero for the agricultural-exporting rich countries of Australasia and North America (Anderson & Hayami 1986, table 2.5). Virtually all assistance to Japanese and European farmers in that period was due to restrictions on imports of farm products.

OECD: Organization for Economic Cooperation and Development

Since 1986, the OECD Secretariat has been computing annual producer and consumer support estimates by member countries (OECD 2008a). For the OECD member countries as a group, the producer support estimate rose between 1986–1988 and 2005–2007 in U.S. dollars from $239 to $263 billion, but it has come down when expressed as a share of support-inclusive returns to farmers (from 37% to 26%, or from 59% to 35% when expressed as a percentage of undistorted prices). Because of some switching of support instruments, including to measures that are based on noncurrent production or on long-term resource retirement, the share of assistance provided via market price support measures has fallen from three quarters to one half. This suggests OECD policies have become considerably less trade distorting at least in proportional terms, even though farmer support in high-income countries has continued to grow in dollar terms because of growth in the value of their farm output.

For developing countries outside Northeast Asia, the main comprehensive set of pertinent estimates over time covers the period just prior to when reforms became widespread. They were generated as part of a major study of 18 developing countries conducted from the 1960s to the mid-1980s by Krueger et al. (1988, 1991). That study sponsored by the World Bank, whose estimates are summarized in Schiff & Valdés (1992), shows that the depression of incentives facing farmers has been due only partly to various forms of agricultural price and trade policies, including subsidies to food imports. In many cases, the nonagricultural policies of those developing countries have been even more important in hurting their farmers, albeit indirectly. The two key nonagricultural policies have been manufacturing protectionism (which attracts resources from agriculture to the industrial sector) and overvalued exchange rates (which attract resources to sectors producing nontradables, such as services). The study by Krueger et al. (1988, 1991) revealed that disincentives for farmers and for producers of exportables (as compared with import-competing farm producers) were greater the poorer the country was, suggesting a strong antitrade bias for the sector as a whole.

Because there were no comprehensive multicountry, multiregion studies of the Krueger-Schiff-Valdés type for developing countries that monitored progress over the reform period [but see Valdés (1996, 2000) for a sample of Latin American and European transition economies and a recent study of four Asian countries by Orden et al. (2007)], a new study was launched by the World Bank in 2006 aimed at filling this lacuna. The new study covers not only 41 developing countries, but also 14 European transition economies as well as 20 high-income countries. Anderson (2009) provides a global overview of the results, and the detailed country case studies are reported in four regional volumes covering Africa, Asia, Latin America, and Europe's transition economies. Anderson & Valenzuela (2008) provide the global database that brings together the 50 years of distortion estimates. The results from this study reveal a substantial reduction in distortions to agricultural incentives in developing countries over the past two to three decades. They also reveal that progress has not been uniform across countries and regions, and that—contrary to some earlier claims (e.g., Jensen et al. 2002)—the reform process is far from complete. In particular, many countries still have a strong antitrade bias in the structure of assistance within their agricultural sector, and some countries have "overshot" in the sense that they have moved from having an average rate of assistance to farmers that was negative to one that is positive, rather than stopping at the welfare-maximizing rate of zero. Moreover, the variance in rates of assistance across commodities within each country, and in aggregate rates across countries, remains substantial, and the begger-thy-neighbor practice of insulating domestic markets from international food price fluctuations continues, thereby exacerbating this volatility.

A global summary of these new results is provided in **Figure 1**. It reveals that the NRA to farmers in high-income countries rose steadily over the post–World War II period

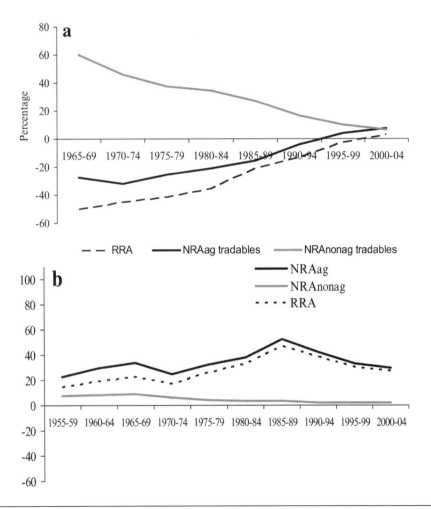

Figure 1

Nominal rates of assistance (NRAs) to agricultural and nonagricultural sectors and relative rate of assistance (RRA) for (*a*) developing and (*b*) high-income countries, 1955–2004 (percentages are production-weighted averages across countries). The RRA is defined as $100*[(100 + \text{NRAag}^t)/(100 + \text{NRAnonag}^t) - 1]$, where NRAag^t and NRAnonag^t are the percentage NRAs for the tradable parts of the agricultural and nonagricultural sectors, respectively. Source: Anderson (2009, ch. 1), based on estimates in Anderson & Valenzuela (2008).

through to the end of the 1980s, apart from a small dip when international food prices spiked around 1973–1974. After peaking at more than 50% in the mid-1980s, the average NRA for high-income countries has fallen slightly, although the extent of the dip shown assumes that the farm programs claimed to be decoupled from production do not have influence on production decisions. For developing countries, the average NRA for agriculture has been rising, but from a level of around -25% during the period from the mid-1950s to the early 1980s to a level of nearly 10% in the first half of the present decade.

GSE: Gross subsidy equivalent

When rates of assistance are expressed in terms of the gross subsidy equivalent (GSE), the rise in high-income assistance effectively offset the rise in negative assistance to developing-country farmers prior to the 1980s, but then the rise in developing-country NRAs has more than offset the fall in NRAs for high-income country farmers since the 1980s. As a result, the estimated GSE of government assistance to farmers globally has risen very substantially in constant (2000) U.S. dollar terms, from close to zero up to the mid-1970s to more than $200 billion per year at the farm gate since the mid-1990s. When expressed on a per farmer basis, it varies enormously between high-income and developing countries. In 1980–1984, the GSE in high-income countries was already approximately $8000, and by 2000–2004, it had risen to $10,000 on average (and up to $25,000 in Norway, Switzerland, and Japan) or to $13,500 when decoupled payments are included. By contrast, the GSE in developing economies was -$140 per farmer in the first half of the 1980s, which is a nontrivial tax when one recalls that the majority of these households were surviving on less than $1 a day per capita. By 2000–2004, farmers received on average $50 each (Anderson 2009, ch. 1). Although a major improvement, this support is only 0.5% of that received by the average farmer in high-income countries.

The improvement in farmers' incentives in developing countries is understated by the above NRAag estimates, because those countries have also reduced their assistance to producers of nonagricultural tradable goods, most notably manufacturers. The decline in the weighted average NRA for the latter, depicted in **Figure 1a**, was clearly much greater than the increase in the average NRA for tradable agricultural sectors up to the mid-1980s, consistent with the finding of Krueger et al. (1988, 1991). Since the mid-1980s, changes in both sectors' NRAs have contributed almost equally to the improvement in farmer incentives. The RRA, captured in Equation 6 above, provides a useful indicator of relative price change: The RRA for developing countries as a group went from -46% in the second half of the 1970s to 1% in the first half of the present decade. This increase (from a coefficient of 0.54–1.01) is equivalent to an almost doubling in the relative price of farm products, which is a huge change in the fortunes of developing-country farmers in only one generation. This increase is due largely to the changes in Asia, but even for Latin America that relative price hike is one half. For Africa, that indicator improves by only one eighth. For high-income countries, assistance to manufacturing was on average much smaller than assistance to farmers even in the 1950s, and its decline since then has had only a minor impact on that group's average RRA (**Figure 1b**).[4]

Whereas the RRA captures the extent of anti- or proagricultural bias in policies across sectors, the TBI defined in Equation 5, above, captures the extent to which the exporting and import-competing subsectors of agriculture have very different NRAs. **Figure 2** shows agriculture's TBI on the horizontal axis and the RRA on the vertical axis. An economy

---

[4]Clear exceptions are Australia and New Zealand, where manufacturing protection had been very high and its decline occurred several decades later than in other high-income countries (Anderson et al. 2007).

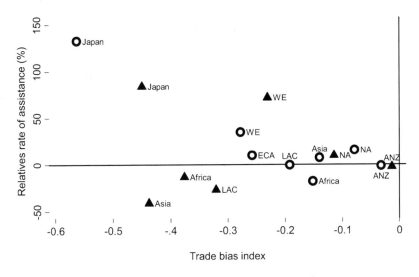

Figure 2

Relationship between relative rate of assistance (RRA) and the trade bias index for agriculture in various regions, 1980–1984 and 2000–2004. Abbreviations: ANZ, Australia and New Zealand; ECA, Eastern Europe and Central Asia; LAC, Latin America and Caribbean; NA, North America; WE, Western Europe. Source: Anderson (2009, ch. 1), using the formulae in Equations 5 and 6, and nominal rate of assistance and RRA estimates in Anderson & Valenzuela (2008).

with no anti- or proagricultural bias (RRA = 0) and no anti- or protrade bias within the farm sector (TBI = 0) would be located at the intersection of these two axes. As of 1980–1984, Africa, Asia, and Latin America were all well to the southwest of that neutral point, but by 2000–2004, all had moved to become much closer to the vertical axis (meaning they had reduced their antitrade bias in agriculture), and all but Africa had become closer to the horizontal axis. Asia is now above, rather than below, that axis, which means those developing countries are assisting farmers relative to producers of other tradable products. Although such assistance can lead to as much waste of resources as the earlier antiagricultural policy bias, only in Korea and Taiwan is the 2000–2004 RRA well above zero (RRA is only 1% for China and 4% for Southeast Asia).

To provide single indicators of distortions imposed by each country's border and domestic policies on its economic welfare and its trade volume, Lloyd et al. (2009) defined a WRI and a TRI and estimated them for the 75 countries in the above-mentioned World Bank study, taking into account that the NRA differs from the CTE for some products (while ignoring indirect effects of sectoral and trade policy measures directed at nonagricultural sectors). The WRI measure reflects the true welfare cost of agricultural price-distorting policies better than the NRA because it captures the disproportionately higher welfare costs of peak levels of assistance or taxation. Thus, WRI measures better approximate what a CGE model can provide in the way of estimates of the trade and welfare (and other) effects of the price distortions captured by the product NRA and CTE estimates, and they have the advantage over CGE models of being able to provide an annual time series. Global five-year averages of those two indexes, along with the global average NRA, are provided in **Figure 3**.

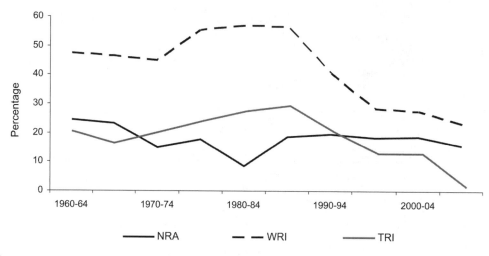

Figure 3

Nominal rate of assistance (NRA), welfare reduction index (WRI), and trade reduction index (TRI) for the world's tradable farm products, 1960–2004 (shown as percentages of total production). Estimates of these indicators are taken from a sample of 75 countries (see Anderson & Valenzuela 2008) that in 2000–2004 accounted for 92% of global agricultural GDP. Source: Lloyd et al. (2009).

On the one hand, the WRI results in **Figure 3** indicate a fairly constant tendency for agricultural policies to reduce welfare from the 1960s to the 1980s, despite some decline in the 1990s. This reflects the fact that NRAs for high-income and developing countries diverged (in opposite ways) away from zero in the first half of the period under study and then converged toward zero in the most recent quarter century. Thus, their weighted average NRA traces out a fairly flat trend, whereas the WRI traces out a hill-shaped path and provides a less misleading indicator of resource misallocation in world agricultural markets.

On the other hand, TRI indicates that the trade restrictiveness of agricultural policy for developing countries as a group was roughly constant until the early 1990s and thereafter it declined, especially for Asia and Latin America, whereas for high-income countries, the TRI decline began a few years later. The TRI for developing countries is driven by the exportables subsector, which was being taxed until recently, and the import-competing subsector, which was and is increasingly being protected (albeit by less than in high-income countries). For high-income countries, policies have supported both exporting and import-competing agricultural products, and even though the policies favor the latter much more heavily, the assistance to exporters has offset somewhat the antitrade bias from the protection of import-competing producers. The net result, shown in **Figure 3**, is that the global TRI rises from approximately 20% in the 1960s to approximately 30% in the latter 1980s before falling to a little above 10% by the late 1990s.

ECONOMY-WIDE EFFECTS OF PAST REFORMS AND REMAINING POLICIES

As discussed above, a great deal of reform has occurred over the past quarter century in policy distortions to agricultural incentives throughout the world: The antiagricultural and antitrade biases of policies of many developing countries have been reduced, export subsidies of high-income countries have been cut, and some reinstrumentation toward less inefficient and less trade-distorting forms of support, particularly in Western Europe, has begun. [A thorough discussion of farm policy re-instrumentation is available in Rausser (1995).] However, protection from agricultural import competition has continued to be on an upward trend in both rich and poor countries, notwithstanding the Uruguay Round Agreement on Agriculture, which aimed to bind and reduce farm tariffs. What, then, have been the net economic effects of agricultural price and trade policy changes around the world since the early 1980s? And how do those effects on global markets, farm incomes, and economic welfare compare with the effects of policy distortions still in place as of 2004? Valenzuela et al. (2009) used a global economy-wide model known as LINKAGE (van der Mensbrugghe 2005) to provide a combined retrospective and prospective analysis that seeks to assess how far the world has come, and how far it still has to go, in removing the disarray in world agriculture. It quantifies the impacts both of past reforms and of current policies by comparing the effects of the distortion estimates from the recent World Bank project for the period 1980–1984 with those of 2004.

Several key findings from that economy-wide modeling study are worth emphasizing. First, the policy reforms from the early 1980s to the mid-2000s improved global economic welfare by $233 billion per year, and removing the distortions remaining as of 2004 would add another $168 billion per year (in 2004 U.S. dollars). This suggests that in a global welfare sense the world had moved three fifths of the way toward global free trade in goods over that quarter century.

Second, developing economies benefited proportionately more than high-income economies (1.0% compared with 0.7% of national income) from those past policy reforms and would gain nearly twice as much as high-income countries if all countries were to complete that reform process (an average increase of 0.9% compared with 0.5% for high-income countries). Of those prospective welfare gains from global liberalization, 60% would come from agriculture and food policy reform. This is a striking result given that the shares of agriculture and food in global GDP and global merchandise trade are only 3% and 6%, respectively. The contribution of farm and food policy reform to the prospective welfare gain for developing countries alone is even greater, at 83%.

Third, the share of global farm production exported (excluding intra-E.U. trade) in 2004 was slightly smaller as a result of those reforms since 1980–1984 because of fewer farm export subsidies. Agriculture's 8% share in 2004 contrasts with the 31% share for other primary products and the 25% for all other goods—a "thinness" that is an important contributor to the volatility of international prices for weather-dependent farm products. If the policies distorting goods trade in 2004 were removed, the share of global production of farm products that is exported would rise from 8% to 13%, thereby reducing instability of prices and quantities of those products traded.

Fourth, the developing countries' share of the world's primary agricultural exports rose from 43% to 55%, and their farm output share increased from 58% to 62%, because of the reforms since the early 1980s. Rises were seen in nearly all agricultural industries except rice and sugar. Removing remaining goods market distortions would boost their export and output shares even further to 64% and 65%, respectively.

Fifth, the average real price in international markets for agricultural and food products would have been 13% lower had policies not changed over the past quarter century. Evidently, the impact of the RRA fall in high-income countries (including the cuts in farm export subsidies) in raising international food prices more than offset the opposite impact of the RRA rise (including the cuts in agricultural export taxes) in developing countries over that period. By contrast, removing remaining distortions as of 2004 is projected to raise the international price of agricultural and food products by less than 1% on average. This is contrary to earlier modeling results based on the GTAP protection database. For example, Anderson et al. (2006) estimated international prices would rise by 3.1% or, for primary agriculture, by 5.5%. The lesser impact in these new results is because export taxes in developing countries based on the above NRA estimates for 2004 are included in the new database (most notably for Argentina) and their removal would offset the international price-raising effect of eliminating import protection and farm subsidies elsewhere.

Sixth, for developing countries as a group, net farm income (value added in agriculture) is estimated to be 4.9% higher than it would have been without the reforms of the past quarter century, which is more than ten times the proportional gain for nonagriculture. If policies remaining in 2004 were removed, net farm incomes in developing countries would rise a further 5.6%, compared with just 1.9% for nonagricultural value added. In addition, returns to unskilled workers in developing countries—the majority of whom work on farms—would rise more than returns to other productive factors from that liberalization. Together, these findings suggest both inequality and poverty could be alleviated by such reform, given that three quarters of the world's poor are farmers in developing countries (Chen & Ravallion 2008).

Finally, removal of agricultural price-supporting policies in high-income countries would undoubtedly lead to painful reductions in income and wealth for farmers if they were not compensated—although the majority of farm household income in high-income countries comes from off-farm sources (OECD 2008b). The gainers in the rest of high-income countries could readily afford to compensate their farmers fiscally from the benefits of freeing trade, bearing in mind that farmers constitute less than 3% of the workforce in high-income countries.

PROSPECTS FOR FURTHER REDUCTIONS IN DISTORTIONS

The RRAs summarized above could lead one to view developments from the early 1960s to the mid-1980s as an aberrant period of welfare-reducing policy divergence (negative and declining RRAs in low-income countries, positive and rising RRAs in most high-income countries) that has given way to welfare-improving and poverty-reducing reforms during which the two country groups' RRAs are converging. However, the convergence of RRAs to near zero hides the continuing difference in NRAs between exporting and import-competing subsectors of agriculture: The former trended toward zero, which was almost certainly welfare improving, while the latter was above zero from the 1950s and is trending upward over time at the same rate as in high-income countries (notwithstanding the Uruguay Round Agreement on Agriculture, which was aimed at tariffying and reducing import protection).

Why have some countries reformed their price-distorting agricultural and trade policies more than others in recent decades? Some have reformed unilaterally, having become convinced that it is in their own national interest to do so. Dramatic and significant examples of the past three decades are China, among developing countries, and Australia and New Zealand, among the high-income countries (Huang et al. 2009, Anderson et al. 2007). Other countries may have reformed their policies to secure bigger and better loans from international financial institutions, and having taken that first step, they have continued the process, even if somewhat intermittently. India is one example, but numerous examples can also be found in Africa and Latin America. Few have gone backward in terms of increasing their antiagricultural bias, although Zimbabwe and perhaps Argentina present exceptions during the current decade, and numerous countries joined them in 2008, at least temporarily, in response to the sudden upward spike in international food prices. Some countries have reduced their agricultural subsidies and import barriers at least partly in response to the GATT's multilateral Uruguay Round Agreement on Agriculture; the European Union is the most important example (helped by its desire for otherwise-costly preferential trade agreements, including its expansions eastward in 2004 and 2007).

The European Union reforms suggest agricultural protection growth can be slowed and even reversed if accompanied by reinstrumentation away from price supports to decoupled measures or more direct forms of farm income support (Rausser 1995, Josling 2009). The starker examples of Australia and New Zealand show that one-off buyouts can bring faster and even complete reform (Anderson et al. 2007). For a detailed analysis of the buyout option versus the slower and less complete cashout option (moving to direct payments), as well as the uncompensated gradual squeeze-out or sudden cutout options, see Orden and Diaz-Bonilla (2006). However, in the developing countries where rates of agricultural protection are generally below those for high-income countries, there are fewer signs of a slowdown of the upward trend in agricultural protection from import competition over the past half century. Indeed, numerous signs indicate that developing-country governments want to keep open their options to raise agricultural NRAs in the future, particularly via import restrictions. One is the high tariff bindings that developing countries committed themselves to by signing the Uruguay Round Agreement on Agriculture: As of 2001, actual applied tariffs on agricultural products (averaging 21%) were less than half the corresponding bound tariffs for developing countries (at 48%) and less than one sixth in the case of least-developed countries (Anderson & Martin 2006, table 1.2). Another is the unwillingness of many developing countries to agree to major cuts in bound agricultural tariffs in the on-going Doha round of multilateral trade negotiations by the World Trade Organization (WTO). The demands of developing countries in the multilateral trading system's agricultural negotiations for exemptions for "special products" and for a "special safeguard mechanism" represent two other signs.

Developing countries that continue to free up domestic markets and practice good macroeconomic governance will keep growing, and typically the growth will be more rapid in manufacturing and service activities than in agriculture, especially in the more densely populated countries where agricultural comparative advantage is likely to decline. Whether such economies become more dependent on imports of farm products depends, however, on what happens to their relative RRAs. The first wave of Asian industrializers (Japan, and then Korea and Taiwan) chose to slow the growth of food import dependence by raising their NRA for agriculture even as they were reducing their NRA for nonfarm tradables, such that their RRA rose increasingly above the neutral zero level. A key question is, Will later industrializers follow suit, given the past close association of RRAs with rising per capita income and falling agricultural comparative advantage?

One new force is disciplines on farm subsidies and protection policies of WTO member countries following the Uruguay Round Agreement on Agriculture. Earlier industrializers were not bound under GATT to keep down their agricultural protection. Had there been strict disciplines on farm trade measures at the time Japan and Korea joined GATT in 1955 and 1967, respectively, their NRAs may have been halted at less than 20% (Anderson 2009, figure 1.12). At the time of China's accession to WTO in December 2001, its NRA was less than 5% according to Huang et al. (2009) or 7.3% for import-competing agriculture. Its average bound import tariff commitment was approximately twice that rate (16% in 2005), but what matters most is China's out-of-quota bindings on the items whose imports are restricted by tariff rate quotas. The latter tariff bindings as of 2005 were 65% for grains, 50% for sugar, and 40% for cotton (Anderson et al. 2009). As such, the legal commitments, including those made by China, on acceding to WTO are far from current levels of support for its farmers and are unlikely to constrain the government much in the next decade or so. The legal constraints on developing countries that joined the WTO earlier are even less constraining. For India, Pakistan, and Bangladesh, for example, their estimated NRAs for agricultural importables in 2000–2004 are 34%, 4%, and 6%, respectively, whereas the average bound tariffs on their agricultural imports are 114%, 96%, and 189%, respectively (WTO, ITC, UNCTAD 2007).

It is hoped that developing countries will choose not to make use of the legal wiggle room they have allowed themselves in their WTO bindings to follow Japan, Korea, and Taiwan into high agricultural protection. A much more efficient and equitable strategy would be to treat agriculture in the same way they have been treating nonfarm tradable sectors. Such a strategy would involve opening the sector to international competition and relying on more-efficient domestic policy measures for raising government revenue (e.g., income and consumption or value-added taxes) and for assisting farm families [e.g., public investment in rural education and health, rural infrastructure, and agricultural research and development (see Fan 2008)].

As for high-income countries, they have all lowered the price supports for their farmers since the 1980s. In some countries, the decline in price support has been partly replaced by assistance that is at least somewhat decoupled from production. If that trend continues at the pace of the past quarter century, and if there is no growth of agricultural protection in developing countries, then before the middle of this century most of the disarray in world food markets will have been removed. However, if the WTO's Doha Development Agenda is not brought to a successful conclusion, and governments thereby find it more difficult to ward off agricultural protection lobbies, it is all the more likely that developing countries will follow the same agricultural protection path in this century as that which was taken by high-income countries in the past century.

DISCLOSURE STATEMENT

The author is not aware of any affiliations, memberships, funding, or financial holdings that might be perceived as affecting the objectivity of this review.

ACKNOWLEDGMENTS

This paper draws heavily on a World Bank research project, Distortions to Agricultural Incentives, which I directed from 2006 to 2009 (**http://www.worldbank.org/agdistortions**). I am grateful for helpful comments on earlier project outputs from various workshop and conference participants, for the efforts of nearly 100 authors who provided the country case studies for the Agricultural Distortions project, for computational assistance from a team of assistants led by Ernesto Valenzuela that brought together the global Agricultural Distortions database, and for funding from various World Bank Trust Funds, particularly those provided by the governments of the Netherlands (BNPP) and the United Kingdom

(DfID). Views expressed are mine alone and not necessarily those of the World Bank or its Executive Directors.

LITERATURE CITED

Anderson J, Neary P. 2005. *Measuring the Restrictiveness of International Trade Policy*. Cambridge, MA: MIT Press

Anderson K. 1995. Lobbying incentives and the pattern of protection in rich and poor countries. *Econ. Dev. Cult. Change* 43(2):401–23

Anderson K, ed. 2009. *Distortions to Agricultural Incentives: A Global Perspective, 1955 to 2007*. London: Palgrave Macmillan; Washington, DC: World Bank. In press

Anderson K, Hayami Y. 1986. *The Political Economy of Agricultural Protection*. Boston/London/ Sydney: Allen Unwin

Anderson K, Kurzweil M, Martin W, Sandri D, Valenzuela E. 2008. Measuring distortions to agricultural incentives, revisited. *World Trade Rev.* 7(4):675–704

Anderson K, Lloyd P, MacLaren D. 2007. Distortions to agricultural incentives in Australia since World War II. *Econ. Rec.* 83(263):461–82

Anderson K, Martin W, eds. 2006. *Agricultural Trade Reform and the Doha Development Agenda*. London: Palgrave Macmillan; Washington, DC: World Bank

Anderson K, Martin W, Valenzuela E. 2009. Long run implications of WTO accession for agriculture in China. In *China's Agricultural Trade: Issues and Prospects*, ed. C Carter, I Sheldon. London: CABI. In press

Anderson K, Martin W, van der Mensbrugghe D. 2006. Distortions to world trade: impacts on agricultural markets and farm incomes. *Rev. Agric. Econ.* 28(2):168–94

Anderson K, Valenzuela E. 2008. *Estimates of Distortions to Agricultural Incentives, 1955 to 2007*. Washington, DC: World Bank. http://www.worldbank.org/agdistortions

Balassa B and Associates. 1971. *The Structure of Protection in Developing Countries*. Baltimore, MD: Johns Hopkins Univ. Press

Bates R. 1981. *Market and States in Tropical Africa: The Political Basis of Agricultural Policies*. Berkeley, CA: Univ. Calif. Press

Bhagwati J. 1971. The generalized theory of distortions and welfare. In *Trade, Balance of Payments and Growth*, ed. JN Bhagwati, RW Jones, RA Mundell, J Vanek. Amsterdam: North-Holland

Bhagwati J. 1978. *Foreign Trade Regimes and Economic Development: Anatomy and Consequences of Exchange Control Regimes*. Cambridge, MA: Ballinger

Chen S, Ravallion M. 2008. *The developing world is poorer than we thought, but no less successful in the fight against poverty*. Policy Res. Work. Pap. 4703, World Bank

Corden W. 1971. *The Theory of Protection*. Oxford, UK: Clarendon

Corden W. 1997. *Trade Policy and Economic Welfare*. Oxford, UK: Clarendon. 2nd ed.

de Melo J, Robinson S. 1989. Product differentiation and the treatment of foreign trade in computable general equilibrium models of small economies. *J. Int. Econ.* 27:47–67

Dervis K, de Melo J, Robinson S. 1981. A general equilibrium analysis of foreign exchange shortages in a developing country. *Econ. J.* 91:891–906

Fan S. 2008. *Public Expenditures, Growth and Poverty in Developing Countries: Issues, Methods and Findings*. Baltimore, MD: Johns Hopkins Univ. Press

Gulbrandsen O, Lindbeck A. 1973. *The Economics of the Agricultural Sector*. Uppsala: Almquist Wicksell

Harberger A. 1971. Three basic postulates for applied welfare economics: an interpretative essay. *J. Econ. Lit.* 9(3):785–97

Herrmann R, Schenck P, Thiele R, Wiebelt M. 1992. *Discrimination Against Agriculture in Developing Countries?* Tubingen: JCB Mohr

Huang J, Rozelle S, Martin W, Liu Y. 2009. China. In *Distortions to Agricultural Incentives in Asia*, ed. K Anderson, W Martin, ch. 3. Washington, DC: World Bank

Jensen H, Robinson S, Tarp F. 2002. General equilibrium measures of agricultural policy bias in fifteen developing countries. TMD Discuss. Pap. 105, IFPRI

Johnson D. 1991. *World Agriculture in Disarray*. London: St Martin's. Rev. ed.

Josling T. 2009. Western Europe. See Anderson 2009, ch. 3

Just R, Hueth D, Schmitz A. 2004. *The Welfare Economics of Public Policy: A Practical Approach to Project and Policy Evaluation*. London: Edward Elgar

Krueger A. 1978. *Foreign Trade Regimes and Economic Development: Liberalization Attempts and Consequences*. Cambridge, MA: Ballinger

Krueger A. 1984. Trade policies in developing countries. In *Handbook of International Economics, Vol. 1: International Trade*, ed. RW Jones, PB Kenen, ch. 11. Amsterdam: North-Holland

Krueger A, Schiff M, Valdés A. 1988. Agricultural incentives in developing countries: measuring the effect of sectoral and economy-wide policies. *World Bank Econ. Rev.* 2(3):255–72

Krueger A, Schiff M, Valdés A. 1991. *The Political Economy of Agricultural Pricing Policy, Volume 1: Latin America, Volume 2: Asia, and Volume 3: Africa and the Mediterranean*. Baltimore, MD: Johns Hopkins Univ. Press

Lerner A. 1936. The symmetry between import and export taxes. *Economica* 3(11):306–13

Lindert P. 1991. Historical patterns of agricultural protection. In *Agriculture and the State*, ed. P Timmer. Ithaca: Cornell Univ. Press

Little I, Scitovsky T, Scott M. 1970. *Industry and Trade in Some Developing Countries: A Comparative Study*. London: Oxford Univ. Press

Lloyd P. 1974. A more general theory of price distortions in an open economy. *J. Int. Econ.* 4(4):365–86

Lloyd P, Croser J, Anderson K. 2009. Welfare- and trade-reducing indexes of distortions to agricultural incentives. See Anderson 2009, ch. 11

OECD. 2008a. *Producer and consumer support estimates*. http://www.oecd.org

OECD. 2008b. *The role of farm households and the agro-food sector in the economy of rural areas: evidence and policy implications*. Mimeogr., TAD/CA/APM/WP(2008)25, OECD

Orden D, Cheng F, Nguyen H, Grote U, Thomas M, et al. 2007. *Agricultural Producer Support Estimates for Developing Countries: Measurement Issues and Evidence from India, Indonesia, China and Vietnam, IFPRI Research Report 152*. Washington, DC: Int. Food Policy Res. Inst.

Orden D, Diaz-Bonilla E. 2006. Holograms and ghosts: new and old ideas for reforming agricultural policies. In *Agricultural Trade Reform and the Doha Development Agenda*, ed. K Anderson, W Martin, ch. 11. London: Palgrave Macmillan; Washington, DC: World Bank

Rausser G. 1995. *GATT Negotiations and the Political Economy of Policy Reform*. Berlin/Heidelberg/New York: Springer-Verlag

Schiff M, Valdés A. 1992. *A Synthesis of the Economics in Developing Countries. The Political Economy of Agricultural Pricing Policy*, Vol. 4. Baltimore, MD: Johns Hopkins Univ. Press

Tyers R, Anderson K. 1992. *Disarray in World Food Markets: A Quantitative Assessment*. Cambridge, UK/New York: Cambridge Univ. Press

Valdés A. 1996. Surveillance of agricultural price and trade policy in Latin America during major policy reforms. Discuss. Pap. 349, World Bank

Valdés A, ed. 2000. *Agricultural support policies in transition economies*. Tech. Pap. 470, World Bank

Valenzuela E, van der Mensbrugghe D, Anderson K. 2009. General equilibrium effects of price distortions on global markets, farm incomes and welfare. See Anderson 2009, ch. 13

van der Mensbrugghe D. 2005. LINKAGE *technical reference document: version 6.0*. Mimeogr., World Bank. http://www.worldbank.org/prospects/linkagemodel

Vousden N. 1990. *The Economics of Trade Protection*. Cambridge, UK: Cambridge Univ. Press

WTO, ITC, UNCTAD. 2007. *Tariff Profiles 2006*. Geneva: WTO

Public-Private Partnerships: Goods and the Structure of Contracts

Gordon Rausser[1] and Reid Stevens[2]

[1]Robert Gordon Sproul Distinguished Professor, University of California, Berkeley, California 94720; email: grausser@are.berkeley.edu

[2]Department of Agricultural and Resource Economics, University of California, Berkeley, California 94720

Annu. Rev. Resour. Econ. 2009. 1:75–97

First published online as a Review in Advance on May 21, 2009

The *Annual Review of Resource Economics* is online at resource.annualreviews.org

This article's doi:
10.1146/annurev.resource.050708.144233

Key Words

incomplete contracting, control rights, impure goods, environmental remediation, infrastructure development, water sanitation, public goods research

Abstract

This paper presents a framework for analyzing the structure of contracts for public-private partnerships (PPP) that produce products and services that generally include mixtures of both public and private goods. A three-stage framework, sourced with the incomplete contracting and control rights literature, is advanced to evaluate the successes and failures of a variety of PPP in the natural resources. These case studies provide unique insights into the contract structures that are typically designed for the management and provision of impure public goods. We demonstrate the desired contract structure of a PPP depends on the type of good or service produced, and it is this pivotal point that generally results in shared authority in the extraction or production and consumptive distribution of natural resources.

1. INTRODUCTION

Public-private partnerships (PPPs) are pervasive. Governments have partnered with the private sector to solve problems ranging from social security to nuclear waste management. In the United Kingdom, between 1992–2003, the government invested more than £36 billion in nearly 600 PPPs and is expected to spend another £110 billion between 2004 and 2029 (Allen 2003; Hodges & Mellett 2003, 2004). These partnerships are estimated to have reduced costs more than 17% over the previous forms of public provision (Pina & Torres 2001). In the European Union, 7% of all services provided by local governments are provided by PPPs, and in small cities, PPPs account for 33% of service provision.

Developing countries have also reduced costs and improved quality by using PPPs to provide services and infrastructure (Boubakri & Cosset 1998; World Bank 2002, 2004). In the 1990s, more than 15% of investments in water and sanitation in developing countries came through private firms working with local governments. Overall, private firms contributed more than $580 billion to infrastructure in developing countries, accounting for nearly 20% of total annual investments. Recently, governments around the world have announced their intention to form PPPs in the financial sector to control systemic risks. Though there has been much discussion in both the popular press and academic community, no consensus has been reached on the optimal contract structure for these partnerships (Savas 1982, Donahue 1989, Shapiro & Willig 1990, Shaoul 2005).

PPPs have been especially prevalent in countries attempting to improve management and service provisions of natural resources. In this paper, we focus on PPPs that have been designed and implemented in natural resources. We define natural resources to include both market and nonmarket goods and services that arise from, inter alia, water, land use, mining, environmental remediation, forestry, fisheries, or public/private goods research. Partnerships in natural resources provide unique insights into the optimal PPP structure because they must address the management and provision of impure public goods.[1] The optimal structure of a PPP depends on the type of good or service produced, and it is this pivotal point that generally results in shared authority in the extraction or production and consumptive distribution of natural resources.

Contracts for PPPs in the natural resources, and their associated control and property rights, come in many forms, ranging from large, multiproject, multiyear alliances to small-scale projects. We present a three-stage operational framework to analyze these contracts. This structure is based on control rights that stem from contingencies in the partnership's production process and are embedded in the contract. In Stage 1, the public and private partners negotiate to determine the allocation of the front-end control rights and the back-end property rights.[2] The front-end control rights determine the nature and scope of the activities that the partnership will undertake as well as decision-making authority over those activities, whereas back-end property rights determine ownership and how any benefits generated by the partnership will be distributed. The partners also make relationship-specific investments according to the contract in Stage 1. In Stage 2, the partners bargain over management decisions with bargaining power determined by the contract

---

[1]Impure public goods are goods that are either nonrival or nonexcludable but not both (if both, then the good is a pure public good).

[2]There is no consistent definition of control rights and property rights in the literature. In this paper, we use control rights to refer to the authority to make decisions during the production process (the front end) and property rights to refer to ownership of either the partnership's assets or the goods produced by the partnership (the back end).

and investments made in Stage 1. The equilibrium outcome of this bargaining process is either a noncooperative decision (commonly referred to as a default outcome or a disagreement payoff) or a cooperative solution that maximizes the joint benefit. In Stage 3, there is an unanticipated shock that causes the partners or stakeholders to revisit their control and property rights. Depending on the nature of the shock, the partners may engage in renegotiation that reassigns control and property rights (and return to Stage 1) or they may conclude the partnership.

Our analysis and evaluation are organized as follows: In Section 2, we provide a survey of the relevant theory; in Section 3, we present the three-stage framework for evaluating PPP contracts; in Section 4, we apply this framework to a variety of PPPs in the natural resources; and in Section 5, we offer concluding remarks.

2. REVIEW OF PUBLIC-PRIVATE PARTNERSHIP THEORY

The core of any framework for evaluating PPPs is sourced with incomplete contracting literature (Hart & Moore 1988, Aghion & Bolton 1992, Aghion et al. 1994, Dewatripont & Maskin 1995, Hart 1995, Aghion & Tirole 1997, Hart et al. 1997, Hart & Moore, 1999, Tirole 1999).[3] Of particular relevance to PPP contracts is the determination of control rights. In this literature, a control right is the authority to make a decision with respect to both anticipated events and events that are not foreseen in the contract. The allocation of control rights can determine whether a partnership will operate efficiently (Schmidt 1996a,b; Helmut 2005).

In the case of a partnership that produces a pure private good, the partners have an incentive to underinvest because the benefits from their investment can be lost in ex-post renegotiation (Grossman & Hart 1986, Hart & Moore 1990). Grossman & Hart (1986) used a two-period model with two firms. In the first period, the firms create a contract that allocates control rights and each firm makes relationship-specific investments, (a_1, a_2). In the second period, each partner makes production decisions, (c_1, c_2), based on the control rights assigned in the contract, which determine the partnership value for partners 1 and 2, $B_1[a_1, c_1, c_2]$ and $B_2[a_2, c_1, c_2]$. Both the investments and the decisions are uncontractible in period 1, but once the decisions are made, each partner is presumed to have equivalent information about their values.

In the first period, the firms make the relationship-specific investments noncooperatively. After these investments are observed, the second period begins and the control rights, which were allocated by the first-period contract, are exercised. These decisions can be made noncooperatively or cooperatively, through costless renegotiation, because the choice of c becomes contractible in period 2. It is unlikely that the noncooperative equilibrium decisions, $(\hat{c}_1, \hat{c}_2)$, will maximize the partnership's value, so the firms can benefit from renegotiation in period 2, after observing the investment decisions from period 1, which are chosen in anticipation of the renegotiation, and create a contract specifying the optimal c_1 and c_2. Grossman & Hart (1986) and Hart & Moore (1990) assumed the firms divide the surplus from the joint venture symmetrically. This outcome will generally be inefficient as both firms underinvest and do not maximize ex-ante value of the partnership.

---

[3]A contract is incomplete in the sense that there is a set of events, that can influence the partnership, that have not been enumerated in the contract.

If one firm's first-period investment has a larger effect on the partnership's value than the other firm's, the contract should assign the firm with the more valuable investment full control over decision making in the second period. Under this circumstance, the allocation of control in the first period provides the firm with the most valuable investment an incentive to invest optimally. When the firm whose investment has a larger impact on the partnership's value invests optimally, the partnership's value is maximized. Thus, under-investment can be mitigated, in a joint venture that produces a private good, if the contract assigns agents control rights to assets on which their production is dependent.

Hart (2003) used the incomplete contract theory to evaluate a PPP that creates infrastructure that must be constructed and operated. The government can "bundle" the construction and operation by forming a partnership with a private firm or "unbundle" the project using different firms, one to construct and another firm to operate the infrastructure. The advantage of bundling is the private firm internalizes the benefits of investments made during construction. A firm that manages a bundled project will be more willing to make investments in construction that lead to more efficient operation than a firm that is responsible for construction only. If the quality of the infrastructure cannot be specified in the contract, but the quality of the service can be specified, a PPP could provide the best incentives for the private firm to invest optimally in construction.

Besley & Ghatak (2001) extended the incomplete contracting framework to a partnership that produces a public good. In their model, two agents, n and g, make relationship-specific investments, a_n, a_g, that increase the nonrival and nonexcludable benefits generated by a project, $B(a_n, a_g)$. Each agent's valuation parameter, θ_i, determines his or her respective payoffs: g's payoff is $\theta_g B(a_n, a_g) - a_g$ and n's payoff is $\theta_n B(a_n, a_g) - a_n$. The first-best levels of investment, which maximize the joint payoff $(\theta_g + \theta_n)B(a_n, a_g) - a_g - a_n$, are generally not reached because the investments are not contractible and each agent will possess bargaining power once the investments are sunk. If the parties engage in ex-post Nash bargaining, with a symmetric split of the surplus, the ex-ante investment decisions will not be optimal because the partners will receive only a fraction of the social benefit generated by their investment.

Besley & Ghatak (2001) demonstrated that the project's joint surplus will be maximized by allocating all control rights to the partner that assigns the highest monetary value to the project. The partner with the highest valuation has the incentive to invest optimally and this assignment of authority allows that partner to do so. Thus, when a public good is produced by a partnership, the agent's valuation of the output generated, and not the relative value of their investment, should determine the allocation of control rights.

Most of the control rights literature has focused on the optimal allocation of control rights when producing either a private good or a public good, and though we can glean useful lessons, it does not provide a complete framework to evaluate PPPs in the natural resources that produce impure goods such as environmental remediation, water sanitation, or infrastructure. For such goods, Francesconi & Muthoo (2006) developed a framework for allocating control rights in PPPs. Initially, two agents, g and n, divide the control rights between themselves. The partner g holds a share $c \varepsilon [0, 1]$ of the control rights, and the remaining $(1 - c)$ of the control rights are held by the partner n. After the control rights are allocated, g and n invest $a_g, a_n \geq 0$, respectively, in the project. Once the investments are made, the partners can make decisions either unilaterally or jointly through cooperative bargaining. If the partners do not cooperate, the project's value will be $B(c, a_g, a_n)$; if they cooperate, the value will be $b(a_g, a_n)$, where $b(a_g, a_n) > B(c, a_g, a_n)$.

Table 1 Optimal assignment of control rights in a public-private partnership by type of good

	Control rights assigned to the firm(s) with the highest valuation of the project	Control rights assigned to the firm(s) with the most valuable investments
Private good (Grossman & Hart 1986, Hart & Moore 1990)		X
Public good (Besley & Ghatak 2001)	X	
Impure good (Francesconi & Muthoo 2006)	X[a]	X[a]

[a]Depending on the impunity of the good produced by the partnership

The noncooperative project value, $B(c, a_g, a_n)$, is assumed to be a linear function of control rights: $B(c, a_g, a_n) = cB^g(a_g, a_n) + (1 - c)B^n(a_g, a_n)$, where $B^i(a_g, a_n)$ is the project's value for partner i when i has sole decision-making authority.

The players bargain over whether the decisions are to be made cooperatively or noncooperatively and what, if any, transfers there will be from g to n or n to g. If g and n cooperate, their payoffs are $\theta_g b(a_g, a_n) + t$ and $\theta_n b(a_g, a_n) - t$, respectively, where the valuation parameters, θ_n and θ_g, determine each partner's valuation of the project, and t is a monetary transfer from n to g, which can be positive or negative. But if the partners choose to make decisions noncooperatively, the payoffs are $\theta_g[cB^g(a_g, a_n) + (1 - \alpha)(1 - c)B^n(a_g, a_n)]$ and $\theta_n[(1 - \alpha)cB^g(a_g, a_n) + (1 - c)B^n(a_g, a_n)]$, respectively, where the impurity of the good produced by the project is measured by the parameter $\alpha \varepsilon [0, 1]$. The α parameter allows this framework to be extended to PPPs that produce any good on the spectrum between pure private goods and pure public goods.

If the partnership produces a pure private good ($\alpha = 1$) or a pure public good ($\alpha = 0$), the model yields the results from Grossman & Hart (1986), Hart & Moore (1990), or Besley & Ghatak (2001). However, if the PPP produces an impure good, $\alpha \varepsilon (0, 1)$, and each partner's investment is equally important, the low-valuation partner should have sole authority. Intuitively, high-valuation partners already have an incentive to invest because they will enjoy some of the benefits of the impure good even without decision-making authority, and low-valuation partners will be more willing to invest if they gain a greater share of the control rights. For a summary of the model results for the three types of goods, see **Table 1**.

The broad themes developed in these papers yield useful results when applied to PPPs in specific industries. Bundling the construction and operation of a project reduces under-investment when the quality of investment cannot be observed (Hart 2003) as well as when the quality of the investment can be observed (Bennett & Iossa 2006).[4] When there is an externality between the construction and management or operation of infrastructure, the two should be bundled only when the externality is positive, that is, when the externality resulting from increases in the quality of design in turn decreases operating costs (Martimort & Pouyet 2006).

---

[4]Investments with unobservable quality, like managerial effort, cannot be verified by other parties, whereas investments with observable quality, like construction equipment, can be verified (Kessler & Lülfesmann, 2000).

PPPs that conduct research related to natural resources can be structured so that private firms sponsor research that benefits public goods research (Spielman et al. 2007, Rausser et al. 2008). Public investment in research can stimulate private investment by creating new technologies that can be profitably exploited by the private sector (Wang 2007). In forming these relationships, PPPs cannot be justified solely as a fundraising device where public funds are replaced with private funds, because the payout to the private firm can cause greater distortions than a tax levied by the public sector (Sadka 2006, Engel et al. 2007).[5]

3. OPERATIONAL FRAMEWORK

The theoretical papers on incomplete PPP contracts have been developed in terms of primitives and, as the authors acknowledge, ignore important details found in PPP contracts. For example, the papers typically assume symmetric bargaining power, though this is rarely the case. Using these frameworks as a guide, we develop a three-stage framework to evaluate PPP contracts. In Stage 1, the public and private partners negotiate an incomplete contract that assigns front-end control rights over decision making and back-end property rights over the partnership's assets and the goods produced by the PPP. Once these rights are assigned, the partners make investments. In the following stage, the partners make management decisions through bargaining. This bargaining will lead either to the noncooperative bargaining solution or to the cooperative bargaining solution that maximizes the joint benefit to both partners. In Stage 3, the partners respond to an unanticipated shock by either concluding their partnership or beginning this process again at Stage 1 by renegotiating the allocation of control rights and property rights. If the partners choose to renegotiate, the control rights will generally be distributed differently.

An operational conceptual lens is necessary to analyze PPP contracts in natural resources that includes the terms and conditions used to assign front-end control rights and back-end property rights. The following three-stage framework provides a lens that allows us to evaluate PPP contracts.

3.1. Stage 1: Setting the Bargaining Space and Negotiating the Contract

In Stage 1, the partners negotiate a contract and make investments. The PPP is based on a contractual commitment that involves more than public sector regulations being imposed on a private party. The public institution should begin this process with a self-assessment to identify their primary objectives in seeking out private partners, their strengths and assets, and the desired complementarities. This assessment is essential to form an efficient partnership.

Though the order in which partnership negotiations proceed is of little material consequence, it is vital for the public institution to be deliberate early in the process, when seemingly innocuous decisions ex-ante may severely limit its control or flexibility at crucial junctures ex-post. At each point in a relationship, it is important for the public

---

[5]Engel et al. (2007) make the standard assumption that raising $1 in taxes costs society $\lambda > 1$ dollars. An additional dollar invested by a private firm saves society $\lambda - 1 > 0$ dollars in taxes. However, the firm must be compensated for its investment with at least an additional $1 in present value. Because this future revenue could have been used by the government to reduce distortions created by taxes, the opportunity cost of losing the future $1 in user fees is the shadow cost of public funds, λ.

institution to consider the long-term consequences of all relationship-related decisions. In finding and selecting a partner, firms often seek government contracts and make specific offers, leaving public institutions in a passive role of waiting to be approached. Alternatively, the public institution can take a proactive role. Given the results of the self-assessment, the public institution can seek out well-matched partners that complement their strengths. Although deliberately seeking out partners, rather than waiting to be approach with a proposal, requires more effort initially, it provides the public institution the greatest degree of control over the selection of partners, which implicitly defines the control the public institution has over the remainder of the structuring process. In addition, by actively approaching potential partners in the private sector, a public institution can form a consortium with a group of specialized partners if that better suits the public institution's objective. This active approach can substantially broaden the public institutions choice set. Likewise, a proactive approach on the part of a private firm can increase its control in the bargaining process.

Once a partner is selected, the public and private institutions engage in negotiations that result in a contract that allocates to each of the i partners, $i = 1, 2$, a share of the front-end control rights, c_i, and back-end property rights, r_i, where $0 \leq c_i \leq 1$, $0 \leq r_i \leq 1$ for all i and $\sum_{i=1}^{2} c_i = 1$, $\sum_{i=1}^{2} r_i = 1$. The front-end control rights enumerate the resources committed by both partners and give the partners decision-making power over the partnership's investment and production processes. The back-end property rights assign ownership of assets and specify the manner in which the partnership's assets will be distributed. The project's risks are implicitly assigned through this allocation of property and control rights. The contract also specifies each partner's investments, which are made during the first stage.

In the first stage, each partner works to minimize its share of input while making sure the combined resources will be sufficient for a successful joint effort. The commitment of resources in the front-end is fairly transparent; however, the implications of choosing particular governing structures for the partnership are less transparent. Given the diversity of assets, it is difficult for potential partners to balance their respective asset contributions. These assets can be tangible, as with financial assets or equipment, or intangible "knowledge" assets (Rausser et al. 2000). Unlike tangible assets, the value of intangible assets is not easily defined as it relies on many factors such as the nature of the assets and the degree of complementarity.

Identifying these aspects of the partner's assets is important to create complementarities among the different assets held by the public and private partners and when negotiating over the contributions each partner will make to the relationship. Private institutions are likely to have more access to funding, state-of-the-art scientific tools, commercialization expertise, and marketing resources. In return, public institutions can give the private partner rights in a natural monopoly, preferential access to natural resources, and assistance in navigating bureaucracies. The objective of the contract is to utilize each partner's assets in the most productive combinations (Leavitt & Morris 2004).

The governance structure of the partnership must be determined in the first stage. Fundamentally, it defines each partner's front-end control rights and back-end property rights. This assignment of control and ownership will determine how the partners will interact, make decisions, resolve conflicts, and terminate the agreement if necessary. An important consequence of the governance structure is that it determines how the project will be evaluated and under what conditions the scope will be changed (i.e., the agreement extended or terminated). At the conclusion of the partnership, the options in the agreement determine how benefits are disseminated and the process for establishing ownership through property rights. Each of these issues is crucial in determining how both the pecuniary and nonpecuniary benefits of the project are shared by the partners and by the public.

3.2. Stage 2: Decision Making Through Bargaining

In Stage 2, the partners jointly manage the partnership by making decisions based on a two-person, two-phase bargaining game [see Rausser et al. (2009) for an extension of this analysis to an n-person bargaining game]. In the first phase, the public partner and the private partner decide what threats to invoke if no agreement is reached, where the threat strategies are chosen to maximize their payoff while minimizing effort and are based on the control rights and property rights assigned in Stage 1. These threat strategies, $(\tilde{c}_i, \tilde{r}_i)$, determine the disagreement payoffs, $[B_1(\tilde{c}_1, \tilde{r}_1), B_2(\tilde{c}_2, \tilde{r}_2)]$, where B_i is the ith partner's objective function, and these strategies are taken as given in the second phase. These strategies need not actually be carried out and may not even be explicit; all that is required is the potential of threat.

From the endogenous determination of the noncooperative equilibrium, a Pareto move to a cooperative outcome can be easily determined. The latter outcome is found by choosing (c_1, r_1) and (c_2, r_2) to maximize the product, $[B_1(c_1, r_1) - B_1(\tilde{c}_1, \tilde{r}_1)][B_2(c_2, r_2) - B_2(\tilde{c}_2, \tilde{r}_2)]$, such that $B_i(c_i, r_i) - B_i(\tilde{c}_i, \tilde{r}_i) \geq 0$, $i = 1, 2$. In this stage, the partners will achieve an efficient outcome, in which the partners exercise their rights and share the payoff. The partner holding the relevant right is aware of the noncontrolling partner's influence and unilaterally selects an action that maximizes the controlling partner's objective function given the noncontrolling partner's active threats (penalties or rewards or its reactive pattern) (Rausser et al. 2008).

Beyond their choice of influence strategy, each partner may exercise control over the resources dedicated to the relationship depending on the results of Stage 1. For example, if a public institution is approached by a single firm and considers only their offer, it has a very limited choice set and is likely to have little leverage over that firm's resources. However, if a public institution considers multiple offers from partners with varied assets, its choice set is broader.

3.3. Stage 3: Is There a Shock?

In the final stage of the agreement (Stage 3), the partners respond to unanticipated shocks. For our purposes, a shock is an event that affects the partnership over which there is no explicit contingency. When there is a shock, the partners have two options: (a) They can conclude the partnership and exercise their back-end property rights over the assets and goods produced by the partnership, or (b) they can renegotiate the control rights and property rights assigned and begin again at Stage 1. If the partners choose to renegotiate, the allocation of bargaining power in renegotiation may be different from the allocation in the previous stages. By this stage, a partner may find itself in a more vulnerable position as a result of the nature of the shock or relationship-specific investments. This potential for changes in relative bargaining power could lead to a reassignment of control rights.

After Stage 3, the partners assess the outcome of their partnership and consider whether to renew the agreement. Public institutions, lacking until now a formal method for review of partnerships with private institutions, have developed a variety of evaluation policies. See the United Kingdom's *Value for Money Assessment Guidelines* (Treasury 2006) for one such leading example. These policies rely mainly on anecdotal feedback from involved personnel to measure the merits of specified projects and monitor unintended consequences. The informal reviews and vague impression of both partners are coupled with more tangible outcomes, such as the PPP's output value, in assessing the success of a partnership.

A key policy issue is developing concrete measures of PPP productivity. Much of the literature on PPPs focuses on developing proper incentives within the scope of an individual agreement, but little consideration is given to incentives that fall outside a specific agreement. Because many of these agreements are up for renewal once completed, there are incentives for the public institution to ensure that the private partner is satisfied with the outcome of the agreement, and under increasing financial pressure, this may affect behavior within a current agreement. In other words, these agreements are not necessarily one-shot games; instead, they may be a single round of a repeated game. As such, there are incentives for the public institution to develop a certain reputation so that the private partner will support a renewed relationship. This speaks to one of the primary concerns with PPP agreements—that public institutions will fail to look for funding from other sources and thus become dependent on renewing these agreements. As a result, the public institution may lose its ability to walk away from negotiations and, therefore, much of its bargaining power. If recognized, these issues may be addressed by choosing a partner with which there is strong incentive alignment as well as safeguards in the agreement.

4. CASE STUDIES

In this section, we apply our operational framework to PPPs in natural resources. These case studies allow us to examine the outcome of a variety of PPP contracts in environmental remediation, infrastructure, water and wastewater management, and public goods research. PPPs in the natural resources typically have long-term project horizons (10–20 years). Because our concern is with PPPs that have completed all three stages of our framework, recently established PPPs are omitted.

4.1. PPPs and Environmental Remediation

The public sector often lacks sufficient funding and clear definitions of roles and procedures to manage efficiently with environmental protection and remediation. Because environmental remediation is an impure public good, the private sector does not have incentives to invest the socially optimal amount on its own. By forming PPPs, the public sector, especially in developing countries, draws on the experience and technical expertise of the private sector to manage environmental investments. PPPs can be formed to work exclusively on environmental remediation, or environmental remediation can be included in the contract of a larger project involving the PPP. These PPPs can often construct facilities and provide ongoing services at a lower cost than can the public sector, resulting primarily from superior private sector scale efficiencies and technical expertise.

A leading example of PPPs in environmental remediation are those the U.S. Department of Energy (DOE) initiated in 1994 to reform management of the Department's legacy nuclear waste. The DOE's management of nuclear waste was notoriously unreliable and inefficient, so the Department formed partnerships with the private sector to strengthen oversight capabilities and lower costs. Prior to 1994, the DOE hired private sector contractors to dispose of nuclear waste under cost-plus-fixed-fee contracts. In these contracts, contractors were repaid all of their expenses, plus some negotiated profit margin in the form of either a fixed percentage of total costs or a fixed dollar amount. In addition to these predetermined earnings, an incentive award was usually granted in recognition of the contractor's ability to meet general performance expectations. Though cost-plus contracts are thought to be effective where uncertainty is high or when the project has not been completely specified, these contracts were plagued by unanticipated cost increases and time extensions. These contracts were also inefficient because they dealt with the provision of an impure public good, and without joint decision making in Stage 2, the contractors would not provide the socially optimal level of investment. Under pressure to improve performance from the General Accountability Office and Congress, the DOE began forming PPPs to manage environmental remediation.

The DOE initiated performance-based incentive contracts in these new partnerships with the private sector. Though the structure of the contract varied by project, each contract comprised a system of rewards and penalties (working on the premise that contractors will tailor their work so as to earn the former while avoiding the latter) that were selected to dictate the level of financial risk sharing between parties. In 1995, the DOE formed a PPP to construct and operate a nuclear waste disposal facility at the nuclear production complex in Hanford, Washington. This partnership would replace the efforts of contractors, hired with cost-reimbursable contracts, that had unsuccessfully managed the site. In addition to lowering costs and speeding up production, the DOE planned on transferring some of the risks associated with nuclear waste disposal to the private partners.

The DOE began Stage 1 by actively seeking out partners in the private sector that would be willing to form a consortium capable of handling the complex disposal process to increase the set of potential partners. The Department, in an effort to determine whether interested firms had resources at their disposal to complete the project, used a two-phase process to form the partnership. During the first phase, the DOE established the requirements, both technical and financial, potential partners would be expected to meet. To foster competition, the Department selected two groups of firms for the first phase of the project and entered into short-term contracts with both groups. At the end of this phase, the firms presented a financing and development proposal based on their on-site waste tests and negotiations with financial institutions. The DOE created a final contract, expected to last 10–14 years, which included a plan for design, construction, operation, and financing, with a group of firms that included Betchel National, Inc., and British Nuclear Fuels. At the end of this contract, the second phase would begin, during which the DOE would create a new contract, based on lessons learned during phase 1, with any qualified firm to manage the disposal of the remaining waste.

The Department attempted to implement a performance-based contract in Stage 1 that allocated the control rights over the production process to the private partners to avoid cost overruns and construction delays, which could lead to further contamination of the area (Diprinzio 2000). Rather than share decision-making authority in Stage 2, as is optimal when producing an impure public good, the private firms would make all decisions regarding the nuclear waste processing process and receive payments from the DOE at the agreed on fixed rate. The DOE included construction and processing benchmarks in the contract that specified the time the facility would be completed and the level of waste it would be expected to process. Though the DOE did not retain any decision-making authority over the production process, the Department did provide incentives for the private firms to use their control rights to meet the processing benchmarks through a three-tier payment system. The firms would receive a base payment to cover their operational costs and debt obligations for meeting specified output levels before the facility reached full capacity. Once output reached full capacity, the firms would receive a contract capacity payment for output that reached the DOE's minimum order threshold. If the firm's output exceeded the minimum output stipulated in the contract, a premium capacity payment would be made. The pricing structure was designed to provide incentives for the firms to exceed the production level. The DOE was responsible for providing an adequate level of waste for the firms to meet their benchmarks.

The incentive system, which used benchmarks and payments rather than joint decision making to reach production goals, proved ineffective as the partnership experienced an unexpected shock in Stage 3 that increased construction costs (Akintoye et al. 2003). The contract originally called for a small-scale waste disposal facility that would be used only in the short-term and that would be replaced by a permanent facility in the second phase. As the private firms began to design and construct the facility, it became clear that a temporary facility would cost as much as a permanent facility, because of strict federal regulations regarding nuclear waste disposal, which drastically increased the cost and complexity of the project. Rather than renegotiate the control rights and property rights to provide appropriate incentives for the firms to construct a permanent facility, the DOE made only minor changes that did not adequately adjust the contract in response to the shock. Because the DOE did not return to Stage 1 to carefully align incentives during the renegotiations that followed unanticipated shocks in Stage 3, the Department unintentionally decreased the partnership's probability of success.

In Stage 2, bargaining over the project's financing led to a shock that also required renegotiation and changes to the initial contract. The contract initially gave the private firms sole decision-making authority to arrange for the project's funding through debt and equity financing. Though this assignment of control rights limited the Department's financial risk and gave the firms an incentive to secure a loan with favorable terms, the government made postcontract efforts to be granted termination-for-convenience rights that would allow the Department to terminate the contract at any time and be responsible only for paying the private partner's termination costs. These rights are usually found in government contracts but are not typically part of industry contracts.

As termination-for-convenience rights were bargained over in Stage 2, it became clear that the Department's payment to its partners would not cover the outstanding principal and interest, which substantially increased the firm's financial exposure. The firms, anticipating nearly $4 billion in debt financing, in addition to their own equity, were unable to bear the risk associated with this clause. The government had little leverage in the bargaining and subsequent renegotiation because the contract allocated sole financial decision-making authority to the firms.

During renegotiation in Stage 3, the government agreed to accept most of the project's financial risk in exchange for right-to-termination rights, which skewed the private firm's incentives for securing efficient financing. Similar concessions that changed the private firm's incentives were made during renegotiation in response to bargaining over the

Department's effort to include other provisions typically used in government contracts, including adherence to Federal Cost Accounting Standards and submission to audits by the Defense Contractor Auditing Agency (Diprinzio 2000). Because the DOE did not address these unanticipated shocks by returning to Stage 1 to reassign decision-making authority and ownership optimally, the private partner's incentives to complete the project efficiently were gradually eroded. By May 2000, the project's expected costs increased to 120% of the original projection, and with the project over budget and unable to meet construction benchmarks, the project was terminated (U.S. Government Accountability Office 2004).

4.2. PPPs and Infrastructure Investment

Infrastructure development projects carry significant risk as they require large capital investments over a long time period to construct, operate, and maintain assets. Traditionally, infrastructure development was pursued only by the public sector because many of the projects (bridges, roads, telecommunications, railroads, energy, etc.) dealt with natural resources and produced impure public goods. But as infrastructure development has grown increasingly complex and expensive, governments have looked to improve efficiency by using private sector expertise and financing through PPPs (Engel et al. 1997; Ramamurti 1997; Estache et al. 2000, 2007). PPPs also allow the government to avoid levying distortionary taxes by tapping private sector funding, which can be repaid by user fees generated by the partnership. PPPs can also reduce the public sector's financial risk in both the cost of the project and the future revenue streams, and some public agencies argue that this risk transfer is the primary benefit flowing from the use of financing by PPPs.

When an infrastructure PPP is formed, the private firms usually manage the finance, planning, and construction of the asset base for the services to be generated. Upon completion of the project, the firm is allowed to manage and collect rents from the asset for a length of time, after which the asset reverts to the government. In developing countries, infrastructure financing by PPPs is particularly promising as it allows governments without sufficient funding, risk-bearing capability, or intellectual capital to build their country's infrastructure (Irwin et al. 1997, Alonso-Conde et al. 2007).

Infrastructure development projects are typically long lived, illiquid, capital intensive, and difficult to value, carrying with them significant risks (construction risk, operating risk, revenue risk due to volume shortfall, financial risk, force majeure risk, regulatory risk, and environmental risk). A major challenge in securing private sector involvement in the provision of public infrastructure has been to design contracts that result in appropriate risk sharing. Contracts for infrastructure PPPs can reduce these risks by carefully structuring the renegotiation process so as not to distort each partner's incentives (Gausch 2004).

A leading example occurred in Australia where the government has been successful in using PPPs to increase the provision of an impure public good (roads) by forming contracts that directly address the private sector's concerns about risk sharing (Brown 2005). The government has repeatedly created successful partnerships that have led private firms to invest over $9 billion in the country's roads. In Stage 1, the government learned that the private partners would enter into a contract only if it included price-setting mechanisms that correctly reflected the risks they assumed by financing and operating these projects. The Australian government addressed this concern by sharing price-setting control rights with the firms in the Stage 1 contract. The partners would jointly set prices in Stage 2 to reflect the private firm's risks and allow for price flexibility in response to unanticipated shocks. By assigning the firms some control rights for setting prices in the face of unanticipated events and setting prices according to the firm's risks, these contracts aligned the partner's expectations for pricing, which reduced the private firm's risk and the need for renegotiation. This assignment of control rights has decreased unanticipated shocks (Stage 3) and allowed the Australian government to form successful contracts with the private sector to finance infrastructure.

Another leading example are the build-operate-transfer (BOT) partnerships the Mexican Government formed with private contractors during their National Highway Program (1989–1994). In a typical BOT partnership, the contractors construct, operate, and capture revenues in Stage 2 and, after a fixed period of time, transfer ownership to the government in Stage 3 (Ruster 1997, Rogozinski 1998). In Stage 1, the Mexican government created contracts for the partnerships that used the firm's construction cost and revenue projections to estimate the operation time. Since the government chose private partners based solely on their projected costs, the firms had an incentive to underbid the competition with unrealistic estimates. As a result, in Stage 3, when construction and management costs were much higher than anticipated (a shock the government did not anticipate), the partners would renegotiate with the government to extend the operation period, and the associated control rights, to recover their costs. Rather than terminate these contracts in Stage 3, the government renegotiated, but it did not share decision-making authority or provide incentives and benchmarks to encourage efficient use of control rights.

As the government's willingness to renegotiate became clear, contractors would also overcapitalize costs, because larger investments by the private partners invariably led to the government granting longer operation times. The government was unable to prevent overcapitalization because there was no shared decision-making authority in the Stage 1 contract over the construction and management process that took place in Stage 2. The Mexican BOT partnerships were not successful because the lack of shared decision-making authority led to Stage 3 renegotiations that distorted the private partner's incentives.

With the Mexican experience in mind, the Chilean government embarked on a similar BOT partnership to improve the country's roads (Lobo & Hinojosa 1999). To avoid renegotiations, the partners shared decision-making authority, which led to efficient outcomes because these infrastructure partnerships produced impure public goods. In Stage 1, the contracts allocated some price-setting control rights to the government in anticipation of attempts to renegotiate in response to low revenue. To establish a floor for the firm's expected earnings, all contracts fixed the duration of the operation period and gave the government decision-making authority over minimum toll levels. The contracts also set a ceiling on revenue during the operation period and required the private partner to give the government any revenue in excess of that ceiling. Finally, the government agreed to pay fixed subsidies if the revenue from operating a toll road did not cover costs. By using shared authority to establish a clear range for expected earnings and establish a framework for earnings outside of that range in the contract, the Chilean government avoided losing bargaining power in renegotiation due to unanticipated shocks in Stage 3.

4.3. PPPs in Water and Wastewater Management

PPPs are often the most efficient choice for governments looking to trim budgets and improve quality by transferring control of public utilities to the private sector (Seppala et al. 2001, Lorena et al. 2002, Foster 2005, Chong et al. 2007, Auriol & Blanc 2007). Public utilities that use natural resources (water, power, etc.) provide impure public goods. If these public utilities are sold to and operated by the private sector, we would expect the firms to exercise market power by setting prices above the optimal level and producing quantity below the optimal level. By forming a PPP, the government retains some control over production and pricing decisions and can limit the private firm's use of market power (Limi 2008). Beyond limiting the use of market power, forming partnerships between public utilities and the private sector can improve quality and decrease operating costs.

Drinking water in the United States is an impure public good provided by regional governments. Local provision prevents local public sectors from realizing returns to scale in water purification technology and customer service. These smaller public providers can improve operation by finding partners in the private sector that complement the public sector's capabilities. Local governments have created successful partnerships by identifying partners in the private sector with complementary assets and by creating contracts that provide incentives for the private partner to efficiently use those resources.

A leading example of PPPs in this field was the five-year partnership formed in 1997 by the Buffalo Water Authority which delivers water to more than 77,000 people in Buffalo, New York, with American Water to repair and operate the city's water system. The size of the city's water services did not justify in-house development of the technology necessary to manage its services more efficiently. In Stage 1, the Buffalo Water Authority actively approached private sector firms and chose its partner on the basis of its experience and technological capacity in managing water services for more than 13 million people. Because water is an impure public good, the Stage 1 contract established shared authority by assigning the city and the private partner partial control rights to ensure socially optimal provision. During Stage 2, the partners decided to use American Water's collection management system to collect bills, the partnership's primary source of revenue, which led to an increase in payment rates from 80% to 97%. The partners also jointly managed water provision technology and customer service. Cost and services benchmarks were set by the partners, with compensation for meeting those benchmarks, to provide incentives for the firm to use their control rights efficiently. The firm exceeded the benchmarks, and net of compensation payments, Buffalo saved $21 million over the course of the partnership in operational costs and eliminated redundancies.

Following Buffalo's example, Indianapolis Water formed a partnership in 2002 to improve the quality of drinking water and decrease costs. Like the Buffalo Water Authority, Indianapolis Water began Stage 1 by actively seeking private partners that had the resources to improve the city's water provision. Indianapolis chose to partner with the multinational corporation Veolia Water, which gave the city access to water-purifying technology and expertise that would have otherwise been prohibitively expensive. The city created a shared authority contract that provided incentives for Veolia to invest the socially optimal amount in technology it otherwise would not, because water is an impure public good, by retaining the control rights over price setting.

Indianapolis used this decision-making authority to stipulate that the rates charged for water would be fixed for five years, which meant that any reductions in cost would increase the revenue Veolia shared with the city. This incentive structure led Veolia, which held control rights over the production processes, to lower costs consistently over the five-year period. The Stage 1 contract also provided incentives for the private partner to improve quality by including measurable quality standards and rewards, in addition to the base fee, if those standards were met. Veolia exceeded these benchmarks and significantly improved the city's water quality. By choosing partners that could compensate for the public sector's deficiencies and providing proper incentives in Stage 1 through a contract with shared authority, these partnerships have been more successful than provision by either a public or private entity.

Wastewater management in the United States faces a similar challenge: Wastewater is an impure public good that is managed at the local level and systems implemented by smaller cities are not as efficient as those in larger cities because of the economies of scale. Some local governments have realized significant cost reductions by forming PPPs instead of hiring contractors to manage wastewater. The first long-term PPP in wastewater management in the United States was formed in 1992 by the city of Glen Cove, New York, and the British water company Severn Trent, a water supplier and wastewater treatment firm.

Glen Cove began looking for a private partner (Stage 1) in response to a requirement from the State of New York Department of Environmental Conservation to reduce the city's Water Pollution Control Plant effluent by 58.5% within 15 years. The city was awarded a $3.4-million-dollar grant to make the necessary improvements to the facility that served the city's 30,000 residents. The city, looking to decrease costs and limit liability, formed a 20-year partnership with Severn Trent.

Meeting New York's effluent-reduction benchmark would require large investments in the wastewater management facility that were not feasible for Glen Cove. In Stage 1, the city used the contract to provide incentives for its private partner to make the needed investments in this impure good by assigning the firm all liability for environmental damage. Because Severn Trent indemnified the city against any and all liability for damages, joint bargaining in Stage 2 led the firm to invest over $3 million in cost-lowering safety technology within the first two years of the partnership to decrease the likelihood of a wastewater accident, even though the firm was contractually obligated to invest only $900,000. These investments increased the plant's environmental compliance and saved Glen Cove $200,000 in operating costs per year.

During Stage 2, cooperative decision making also led the partners to improve the efficiency of the plant's workers. The private partner's investments gave the partnership an opportunity to lower costs by decreasing the plant's hours of manned operation from 24 to 16. Working with the city, Severn Trent restructured the facility's workforce and provided health and safety training, which led to a 100% reduction in lost-time accidents.

4.4. PPPs and Public Goods Research

As public funding of scientific research has declined, and knowledge inputs have played an increasingly important role in industrial processes, universities and other public research institutions have looked to private sources to increase their research budgets. Many lessons have been learned as public criticism and scrutiny of these research partnerships have evolved (Press & Washburn 2000). Issues such as conflict of academic and industry interests; ownership of, and access to, intellectual property (e.g., issues of hold-up and blocking patents); and publication delays have fueled the current debate and often present insurmountable obstacles to forming research partnerships (Lach & Schankerman 2004).

A host of external forces have shaped the current environment in which public researchers are seeking to engage actively with private researchers. Among these are diminishing federal and state funds for public goods research and increased state funding for private-public research. In addition, legislation (e.g., the Bayh-Dole Act), the restructuring of many large life sciences firms, and an alignment of private and public research incentives have contributed to this trend (Rausser 1999). Moreover, the traditional research paradigm that presumes there is a one-way flow from basic science conducted in public institutions to applied research and commercialization undertaken by private industry has begun to be replaced by a chaotic research and development feedback-loop paradigm (Rausser 1999, Rausser et al. 2008). Increasingly, public universities and private companies are engaging in joint research, establishing relationships with exchange and collaboration in all stages of research (Henderson et al. 1998, Jensen & Thursby 2001).

The potential benefits from university-industry partnerships have been well articulated. Complementarities between scientific and practical knowledge have the capacity to generate rapid and far-reaching innovation. It follows that each partner is seeking attributes and assets in prospective partners that complement their own abilities and resources. Industry is interested in combining its knowledge of markets with information on new research and innovation to identify those developments that are likely to lead to commercial applications (Aghion & Tirole 1994, Aghion et al. 2005). This motivation may be obvious, but industry is also interested in more subtle assets such as access to academic expertise, networks, and first-hand information about up-and-coming scientists (current graduate students). Although universities are clearly interested in financial capital, they also seek intellectual capital, cutting-edge research technologies, proprietary research tools (e.g., databases), and, in many instances, enabling intellectual property (Heller & Eisenberg 1998, Blumenstyk 2001). Access to these research assets enhances a university's ability to provide a first-rate education to its graduate students.

Although the potential benefits of research partnerships are reasonably transparent, the potential risks to both parties are opaque. These risks pose serious obstacles to the successful formation of public-private research partnerships. In addition to the uncertainty inherent in any research process, the differences between university educational objectives and corporate goals are an important source of risk in these relationships (Slaughter & Leslie 1997, Graff et al. 2002). Recent data show that almost 70% of research in universities has been categorized by the National Science Foundation as basic, whereas the proportion is reversed in industry. In 2000, although universities accounted for only 14% of total research and development funding in the United States, they performed approximately 50% of the total basic research (Scotchmer 2004). With private financing comes concerns arise that the traditional orientation of the academic research agenda toward basic, public goods research will be directed toward more applied, appropriable research that serves the objectives of the private partner and that this, in turn, will result in a loss of academic integrity.

Not only research direction but research results from sponsored studies may be biased toward sponsors' interests. Bekelman et al. (2003), for instance, showed that in biomedical research there is a statistically significant association between industry sponsorship and proindustry conclusions. Industrial sponsors may also impose constraints on communication between grantees and other colleagues that, in turn, may hinder research progress and increase research costs (Scotchmer 2004). Planning horizons tend to differ; university researchers focus on long-term research, while companies often seek quick payoff projects. In addition, the cultures and values of research partners may simply clash, creating insurmountable blocks to a continuing relationship. Furthermore, the incentives to secure a renewal or extension of an existing contractual agreement may adversely influence university scientists' behavior under a current collaboration.

Rights to intellectual property are especially contentious (Kenney 1986, Slaughter 1988, Brooks 1993). Hold-up and background rights are of primary concern to an industry partner interested in commercializing the products of a research partnership. Researchers at universities and other public institutions often use proprietary or enabling intellectual property research tools in their research without obtaining rights. They are sometimes blocked, however, from using these tools for commercial purposes. Generally, one researcher in a university institution may freely access another researcher's patented research tool for academic study. This opportunity does not typically extend to private researchers unless a formal agreement is forged. Thus a private company looking to partner with a particular researcher, for example, may experience hold-up at the commercialization stage because the public research partner did not obtain formal rights to all research inputs (i.e., background rights) from some other private company. Note also that if numerous university researchers and graduate students are involved in a research project, industry risks loss of privacy and protection for proprietary information.

The interests of parties outside a research agreement (i.e., third parties) are also at risk under public-private research agreements. If an agreement is not effectively structured with regard to patenting and licensing rights, a third-party interest in having reasonable access to research discoveries and innovations may not be adequately represented. In fact, blocking patents can and do arise (Heller & Eisenberg 1998).

In summary, the cooperation between universities and industry prompts a series of questions: Does the profit-driven sponsor shift the university's mission away from basic research? Does industry's desire to exploit intellectual property rights interfere with communication within and between universities to an extent harmful to open science (Scotchmer 2004)? These conflicts are an inevitable consequence of a fundamental clash between a public system that encourages openness in science and an industrial system that gives financial rewards based on secrecy. In the end, this all boils down to one question: Can a university-industry partnership be socially beneficial or, more precisely, Pareto improving?

Scotchmer (2004) argued that a public-private venture is justifiable for big science projects. On the one hand, for certain large projects, the public sector may face the problem of choosing the right investments (those with high probability of success) and making sure the funds are used as intended; on the other hand, the private sector has the expertise needed to screen likely successful projects but sometimes cannot reap unappropriable social benefits, thus is unable to recover the cost of research (Sheridan 2007). In this situation, a PPP can help solve the duality problem. If this asymmetric information problem does exist, however, then industry can strategically engage the public sector into subsidizing its privately profitable projects.

A leading example of university-private research partnerships was formed by the University of California (UC), Berkeley, and Novartis Agricultural Discovery Institute, Inc. (NADI), in 1998. The partnership's Stage 1 contract allowed UC Berkeley to retain control of an open research agenda. The research agenda is determined in Stage 2 when an open call is put out to participating faculty for research proposals—neither UC Berkeley nor NADI defines the type of project proposals to be considered. Furthermore, the committee that allocates funding to each project in Stage 2 (all proposed projects receive some amount of funding) is made up of three UC Berkeley faculty members and two members representing NADI. The criteria used for ranking projects include the quality and intellectual merit of the proposed research, potential advancement of discovery, and the past and present productivity of the research—the interest of the project to NADI is not considered.

An alternative structure governs a biological research agreement in another leading example: the partnership between Washington University (WU), St. Louis, and the plant biotechnology company Monsanto. This partnership's Stage 1 contract assigned both partners control over the research agenda, which gave Monsanto control over research funding decisions that NADI did not have. In Stage 2, the agreement specifically directs an advisory committee to solicit proposals and identify and fund those projects that not only have exceptional academic merit, but also serve the research interests of Monsanto. In this case, the advisory committee is equally split with three WU members and three representatives from Monsanto. This joint assignment of control rights over the research agenda gives the interests of Monsanto more weight, both in defining the choice set of research proposals that will be considered by the committee and in selecting which of those proposals are funded, than NADI has in its agreement with UC Berkeley.

Depending on the mission of the university and its role in the community, both of these alternative contract structures, with the associated control rights, have merits. Because the research interests of the private partner carry more weight, the WU/Monsanto agreement may be more likely to generate innovations that result in commercial applications, meeting the objective of serving the community with successful technology transfers. On the other hand, the UC Berkeley/NADI agreement more adequately protects the academic freedom of participating faculty. What is important is that the public institutions make conscience decisions about where they are comfortable on this spectrum of control over the research agenda and that they are fully aware of the implicit tradeoffs contained in the related contract language.

The primary interest of universities is to share their research results with colleagues as rapidly as possible, through publications and presentations at conferences, with the hope that scientific knowledge and research will be advanced. This academic mission conflicts with the private partner's interest in appropriating innovation and technological advancements, which requires, for a certain amount of time, that research results be kept from competing interests until the private partner establishes rights to the innovation.

Including publication-delay provisions in Stage 1 research agreements usually comes under considerable scrutiny. In fact, guidelines issued by the National Institutes of Health (1994) recommend a delay of no more than 30–60 days. A more relevant question concerns control of the option for terminating the delay period rather than the specified maximum length of this period. In Stage 1, the UC Berkeley/NADI contract assigns both partners authority over publication delay. NADI was assigned the right to decide whether an innovation has the potential to be patented during an initial 30-day delay. If they decide that the parties should proceed with a patent application, publications can be delayed only up until the time the patent application is filed or 90 days—whichever is shorter. UC Berkeley was assigned the right to file the patent application at any time. The filing process can be expedited, with an initial application filed in a day or so. Therefore, under this agreement, although the maximum publication delay is 120 days, UC Berkeley has complete control to end the delay (past the initial 30-day period). In contrast, in the WU/Monsanto agreement, WU does not have control over the end of the delay. Monsanto has the right to review all research prior to publication and request a short delay to begin the process of filing for a patent. In both agreements, the private partner is responsible for managing and paying for any patents they choose to file. WU can license the patent to others only if Monsanto does not elect to file for a patent.

A more subtle issue is whether a university is obligated to file for a patent if requested to do so by the industry partner, or whether it has some discretion. A university partner may wish to avoid expending the effort required to patent innovations if it does not foresee that the patent will be applied commercially. For example, under the UC Berkeley/NADI agreement, the partners share authority over the patent decision process, so UC Berkeley can elect not to file for a patent that NADI does not intend to commercialize. In other words, UC Berkeley can make sure that innovation, or know-how, that would not otherwise be commercialized remains freely available to the public and that limited administrative resources are not diverted to pursue meaningless patents.

Of vital importance for industry-university research agreements is the nature of the licensing options. Currently, it is common for the industry partner to be given a first-to-negotiate licensing option for some subset of the innovations generated under the research agreement. Generally, these options must be exercised within a specified time period, or else the option is extended to third parties. In response to public outcry concerning previous, poorly structured agreements, such as the Sandoz/Scripps agreement,[6] and concern about blocking patents, right-of-first-refusal options evolved into right-to-negotiate options. In theory, if the industry partner is granted the more limited option of right-to-negotiate, a university has greater control over licensing rights and can prevent blocking patents from being awarded.

Other aspects of licensing agreements receive less attention but are also critical. One such aspect is the percentage of the total innovation for which the industry partner holds an option to negotiate an exclusive license (i.e., access option). Under the UC Berkeley/NADI agreement, NADI can exercise this option for an "allowable percentage" of patents, equal to the percentage of the research funding that came from NADI. As a result, NADI had limited access options. Under other agreements, the industry partner holds this option for all patented discoveries generated by the agreement.

Third-party options are also a critical aspect of licensing options. These options are the rights that parties outside the agreement have to innovation generated by the agreement. In the UC Berkeley/NADI agreement, these options are managed jointly in Stage 2. UC Berkeley can give third parties open options on patents not included in the allowable percentage and on patented innovations either covered by nonexclusive license or for which the first-to-negotiate option has expired for NADI. NADI has no recourse once their licensing option has expired, and UC Berkeley is free to enter into licensing negotiations with third parties. In contrast, under the WU/Monsanto agreement, the contract grants Monsanto much more control in Stage 2, and third parties hold only a conditional option. Monsanto has right-of-first-refusal on any licensing arrangement between WU and third parties, even if Monsanto's original licensing option has expired. Thus, Monsanto is guaranteed an option of first refusal on any third party offers made to WU. This severely limits the options available to third parties.

---

[6]In 1993, the publicly funded Scripps Research Institute agreed to form a research partnership with Sandoz Pharmaceuticals. Sandoz would provide $300 million in funding for research over 10 years in return for a world-wide license of all discoveries made by researchers at Scripps. This controversial agreement, which would have given Sandoz licensing rights to nearly $1 billion worth of research funded by the federal government, was restructured after the government threatened to cut off funding to the institute.

5. CONCLUSION

As PPPs in the natural resources become more common, it is important to use a conceptual framework that takes into account the type of good the partnership produces to guide contract structure and evaluate performance. We turn to the incomplete contracts literature to create a three-stage framework that focuses on the allocation of front-end control rights and back-end property rights. In Stage 1, the partners form a contract that assigns control and property rights. Once these rights are assigned, the partners bargain in Stage 2 over whether management decisions will be made cooperatively or noncooperatively. In Stage 3, the partnership may experience an unanticipated shock. In response to this shock, the partners may return to Stage 1 by renegotiating the assignment of control and property rights or they may conclude the partnership.

We use this framework to evaluate various PPPs in the natural resources and find that the assignment of control and property rights can determine a PPP's success. Whether in environmental remediation, infrastructure development, water provision, or public/private research, either the assignment of these rights will provide the partners incentives to manage the partnership efficiently (e.g., the UC Berkeley/NADI partnership, the Buffalo/American Water partnership) or it will not (e.g., the DOE's Hanford partnership, the Mexican BOT highway partnerships).

Though partnerships have been efficiently applied in Europe and some developing countries, PPPs in the United States and Canada have not been as successful. For example, surveys of infrastructure PPPs have found governments were unable to reduce their budgets while the private partners have had trouble generating a profit (Swimmer 2001, Boardman et al. 2006). In these projects, as in our case studies, the partners generally failed because their incentives were misaligned as a result of the assignment of control and property rights. Using our operational framework to assign control and property rights that align incentives, PPPs in North America could become more successful.

DISCLOSURE STATEMENT

The authors are not aware of any affiliations, memberships, funding, or financial holdings that might be perceived as affecting the objectivity of this review.

ACKNOWLEDGMENTS

We are grateful to David Zilberman and George Wolf for their valuable suggestions and comments on an earlier draft of this paper.

LITERATURE CITED

Aghion P, Bolton P. 1992. An incomplete contracts approach to financial contracting. *Rev. Econ. Stud.* 59(3):473–94

Aghion P, Dewatripont M, Rey P. 1994. Renegotiation design with unverifiable information. *Econometrica* 62(2):257–82

Aghion P, Dewatripont M, Stein J. 2005. *Academic freedom, private-sector focus, and the process of innovation.* Discuss. Pap. 2089, Inst. Econ. Res., Harvard Univ.

Aghion P, Tirole J. 1994. The management of innovation. *Q. J. Econ.* 109(4):1185–209

Aghion P, Tirole J. 1997. Formal and real authority in organizations. *J. Polit. Econ.* 105(1):1–29

Akintoye A, Beck M, Hardcastle C, eds. 2003. *Public-Private Partnerships: Managing Risks and Opportunities*. Oxford, UK: Blackwell Sci.

Allen G. 2003. *The private finance initiative*. Res. Pap. 01/117, House Commons Libr.

Alonso-Conde A, Brown C, Javier RS. 2007. Public private partnerships: incentives, risk transfer and real options. *Rev. Financ. Econ.* 16(4):335–49

Auriol E, Blanc A. 2007. *Public private partnerships in water and electricity in Africa*. Work. Pap. 38, Agence Fr. Dev.

Bekelman J, Gross C, Li Y. 2003. Scope and impact of financial conflicts of interest in biomedical research. *JAMA* 289(4):454–65

Bennett C, Iossa E. 2006. Delegation of contracting in the private provision of public services. *Rev. Ind. Organ.* 29(1):75–92

Besley T, Ghatak M. 2001. Government versus private ownership of public goods. *Q. J. Econ.* 116(4):1343–72

Blumenstyk G. 2001. Temple University shuts down for-profit distance-education company. *Chron. High. Educ.* 47(45):29–30

Boardman A, Poschmann F, Vining A. 2006. Public-Private Partnerships in the U.S. and Canada: there are no free lunches. *J. Comp. Policy Anal.* 7(3):1–22

Boubakri N, Cosset J. 1998. The financial and operating performance of newly privatized firms: evidence from developing countries. *J. Financ.* 53(3):1081–110

Brooks H. 1993. Research universities and the social contract for science. In *Empowering Technology: Implementing a US Policy*, ed. L Brascome. Cambridge, MA: MIT Press

Brown C. 2005. Financing transport infrastructure: for whom the road tolls. *Aust. Econ. Rev.* 38(4):431–8

Chong E, Huet F, Saussier S, Steiner F. 2007. Public-private partnerships and prices: evidence from water distribution in France. *Rev. Ind. Organ.* 29(1):149–69

Dewatripont M, Maskin E. 1995. Contractual contingencies and renegotiation. *Rand J. Econ.* 26(4):704–19

Diprinzio R. 2000. The US Department of Energy and the privatization of the Hanford Tank Waste Remediation System. *J. Proj. Financ.* 6(3):54–60

Donahue J. 1989. *The Privatization Decision: Public Ends, Private Means*. New York: Basic Books

Engel E, Fisher R, Galetovic A. 1997. Highway franchising: pitfalls and opportunities. *Ar. Econ. Rev. Pages Proc.* 87(2):68–72

Engel E, Fischer R, Galetovic A. 2007. *The basic public finance of public-private partnerships*. Work. Pap. 13284, NBER

Estache A, Juan E, Trujillo L. 2007. *Public-private partnerships in transport*. Work. Pap. 4436, World Bank

Estache A, Romero M, Strong J. 2000. *The long and winding path to private financing and regulation of toll roads*. Work. Pap. 2387, World Bank

Foster V. 2005. *Ten years of water service reforms in Latin America: toward an Anglo-French model*. Discuss. Pap. 3, Water Supply Sanit. Sect., World Bank

Francesconi M, Muthoo A. 2006. *Control rights in public-private partnerships*. Discuss. Pap. 2143, IZA

Gausch J. 2004. Granting and renegotiating infrastructure concessions: doing it right. In *WBI Development Studies*. Washington, DC: World Bank

Graff G, Heiman A, Zilberman D. 2002. University research and offices of technology transfer. *Calif. Manag. Rev.* 45(1):89–115

Grossman S, Hart O. 1986. The costs and benefits of ownership: a theory of vertical and lateral integration. *J. Polit. Econ.* 94(4):691–719

Hart O. 1995. *Firms, Contracts, and Financial Structure*. Oxford, UK: Oxford Univ. Press

Hart O. 2003. Incomplete contracts and public ownership: remarks, and an application to public-private partnerships. *Econ. J.* 113(486):C69–76

Hart O, Moore J. 1988. Incomplete contracts and renegotiation. *Econometrica* 56(4):755–85

Hart O, Moore J. 1990. Property rights and the nature of the firm. *J. Polit. Econ.* 98(6):1119–58

Hart O, Moore J. 1999. Foundations of incomplete contracts. *Rev. Econ. Stud.* 66(1):115–38

Hart O, Shleifer A, Vishny R. 1997. The proper scope of government: theory and an application to prisons. *Q. J. Econ.* 112(4):1126–61

Heller M, Eisenberg R. 1998. Can patents deter innovation? The anticommons in biomedical research. *Science* 280(5634):698–701

Helmut B. 2005. *Externalities, communication and the allocation of decision rights*. Discuss. Pap. 5391, CEPR

Henderson R, Jaffe A, Trajenberg M. 1998. Universities as a source of commercial technology: a detailed analysis of university patenting, 1965–1988. *Rev. Econ. Stat.* 80(1):119–27

Hodges R, Mellett H. 2003. Reporting public sector financial results. *Public Manag. Rev.* 5(1): 99–114

Hodges R, Mellett H. 2004. Reporting PFI in annual accounts: a user's perspective. *Public Money Manag.* 24(3):153–8

Irwin T, Klein M, Perry G, Thobani M. 1997. *Dealing with Public Risk in Private Infrastructure.* Washington, DC: World Bank

Jensen R, Thursby M. 2001. Proofs and prototypes for sale: the licensing of university inventions. *Am. Econ. Rev.* 91(1):240–59

Kenney M. 1986. *Biotechnology: The University-Industrial Complex.* New Haven, CT: Yale Univ. Press

Kessler A, Lülfesmann C. 2000. *Monitoring and productive efficiency: a comparison of public and private ownership.* Discuss. Pap. 608, Ser. A, Univ. Bonn

Lach S, Schankerman M. 2004. Royalty sharing and technology licensing in universities. *J. Eur. Econ. Assoc.* 2(2–3):252–64

Leavitt W, Morris J. 2004. In search of middle ground: the public authority as an alternative to privatization. *Public Works Manag. Policy* 9(2):154–63

Limi A. 2008. *(Un)bundling public-private partnership contracts in the water sector: competition in auctions and economies of scale in operation.* Work. Pap. 4459, World Bank

Lobo A, Hinojosa S. 1999. *Broad roads in a thin country: infrastructure concessions in Chile.* Work. Pap. 2279, World Bank

Lorena A, Abdala M, Shirley M. 2002. The Buenos Aires water concession. In *Thirsting for Efficiency: The Economics and Politics of Urban Water System Reform*, ed. M Shirley. Oxford, UK: Elsevier Sci.

Martimort D, Pouyet J. 2006. *"Build it or not": normative and positive theories of public-private partnerships.* Discuss. Pap. 5610, CEPR

National Institutes of Health. 1994. *NIH Guidelines for Research Involving Recombinant DNA Molecules.* Washington, DC: Dep. Health Human Serv.

Pina V, Torres L. 2001. Analysis of the efficiency of local governments services delivery: an application to urban public transport. *Transp. Res.* 35(10):929–44

Press E, Washburn J. 2000. The kept university. *Atl. Mon.* 285(3):39–54

Ramamurti R. 1997. Testing the limits of privatization: Argentine railroads. *World Dev.* 25(12): 1973–93

Rausser G. 1999. Private/public research: knowledge assets and future scenarios. *Am. J. Agric. Econ.* 81(5):1011–27

Rausser G, Ameden H, Simon L. 2000. Public-private alliances in biotechnology: Can they narrow the knowledge gaps between rich and poor? *Food Policy* 25(4):499–513

Rausser G, Simon L, Stevens R. 2008. Public vs. private good research at land-grant universities. *J. Agric. Food Ind. Organ.* 6(2): artic. 4

Rausser G, Swinnen J, Zusman P. 2009. *Political Power and Endogenous Policy Formation.* Cambridge, UK: Cambridge Univ. Press. In press

Rogozinski J. 1998. *High Price for Change: Privatization in Mexico*. Washington, DC: Inter-Am. Dev. Bank

Ruster J. 1997. *A Retrospective on the Mexican Toll Road Program (1989–1994). The Private Sector in Infrastructure: Strategy, Regulation, and Risk*. Washington, DC: World Bank

Sadka E. 2006. *Public-private partnerships: a public economics perspective*. Work. Pap. 06/77, IMF

Savas E. 1982. *Privatizing the Public Sector: How to Shrink Government*. Chatham, NJ: Chatham House

Schmidt K. 1996a. The costs and benefits of privatization: an incomplete contracts approach. *J. Law Econ. Organ.* 12(1):1–24

Schmidt K. 1996b. Incomplete contracts and privatization. *Eur. Econ. Rev.* 40(3–5):569–79

Scotchmer S. 2004. *Innovation and Incentives*. Cambridge, MA: MIT Press

Seppala O, Hukka J, Katko T. 2001. Public-private partnerships in water and sewerage services. *Public Works Manag. Policy* 6(1):42–58

Shaoul J. 2005. The private finance initiative or the public funding of private profit? In *The Challenge of Public-Private Partnerships: Learning from International Experience*, ed. G Hodge, C Creve. Cheltenham, UK: Edward Elgar

Shapiro C, Willig R. 1990. Economic rationales for the scope of privatization. In *The Political Economy of Private Sector Reform and Privatization*, ed. E Suleiman, J Waterbury. Boulder, CO: Westview

Sheridan C. 2007. Big oil's biomass play. *Nat. Biotechnol.* 25(11):1201–3

Slaughter S. 1988. Federal policy and supply-side institutional resource allocation at public research universities. *Rev. High. Educ.* 8:295–318

Slaughter S, Leslie L. 1997. *Academic Capitalism: Politics, Policies, and the Entrepreneurial University*. Baltimore, MD: Johns Hopkins Press

Spielman D, Hartwich F, Grebmer K. 2007. *Sharing science, building bridges, and enhancing impact: public–private partnerships in the CGIAR*. Discuss. Pap. 00708, IFPRI

Swimmer D. 2001. The current state of Canadian infrastructure. In *Building the Future: Issues in Public Infrastructure in Canada*, ed. A Vining, J Richards. Toronto: CD Howe Institute

Tirole J. 1999. Incomplete contracts: where do we stand? *Econometrica* 67(4):741–81

Treasury HM. 2006. *Value for Money Assessment Guidance*. London: Scottish Futures Trust

US Gov. Account. Off. 2004. Nuclear waste: absence of key management reforms on Hanford's Cleanup Project adds to challenges of achieving cost and schedule goals. *Rep. GAO-04-611, Comm. Gov. Reform, House Represent.*

Vonortas N. 1991. *Cooperative Research in R&D-Intensive Industries*. Aldershot, UK: Avebury Acad.

Wang C. 2007. *Public investment policy and industry incentives in life science research*. PhD thesis, Oregon State Univ.

World Bank. 2002. *World Development Report 2002: Building Institutions for Markets*. New York: Oxford Univ. Press

World Bank. 2004. *World Development Report 2004: Making Services Work For Poor People*. New York: Oxford Univ. Press

Environmental Regulations and Economic Activity: Influence on Market Structure

Daniel L. Millimet,* Santanu Roy, and
Aditi Sengupta

Department of Economics, Southern Methodist University, Dallas,
Texas 75275-0496; email: millimet@smu.edu, sroy@smu.edu,
asengupt@smu.edu

Annu. Rev. Resour. Econ. 2009. 1:99–117

First published online as a Review in Advance on
June 22, 2009

The *Annual Review of Resource Economics* is
online at resource.annualreviews.org

This article's doi:
10.1146/annurev.resource.050708.144100

1941-1340/09/1010-0099$20.00

*Corresponding author

Key Words

environmental regulation, economic activity, industry dynamics

Abstract

We survey recent developments in the theoretical and empirical
literature on the economic effects of environmental regulation on
various aspects of market structure including entry, exit, and size
distribution of firms and market concentration.

1. INTRODUCTION

The environment and the economy are inextricably linked; policy makers cannot discuss the former without the conversation turning immediately to the latter. In light of the recent economic crisis in the United States, combined with the growing concern over climate change, circumventing the rhetoric and understanding the impact of environmental regulation on economic activity are crucial. Here, we provide a (necessarily incomplete) survey of one aspect of this literature. Specifically, we focus on the effect of environmental regulation on market structure.

Although significantly smaller than the literature assessing the impact of environmental regulation on trade and investment flows and plant location, the literature analyzing the potential effect of environmental regulation on market structure of regulated industries is growing. The market structure of an industry mainly refers to the degree of market concentration that depends on the number of firms in the industry and the distribution of market shares (and the related size distribution of firms). Environmental regulation may affect market structure by modifying, among other things, the possibility of entry of new firms, exit of incumbent firms, and the relative competitive advantage of active firms. Much of the existing literature assessing the impact of environmental regulation on market structure tends to focus on entry, exit, and the number of active firms. A somewhat smaller literature examines the impact on size distribution of firms; their degree of asymmetry; and the market share, entry, and exit of large versus small firms. Also, much of the literature tends to treat regulation as exogenous (with the exception of the rent-seeking literature that tends to view the level of regulation as endogenous).

The literature we survey is not homogeneous; one of the important sources of difference across various strands of the literature arises from variances in the underlying mechanism by which environmental regulation is presumed to influence market structure. We divide the literature into categories based on the underlying mechanism. In particular, we divide the literature into strands where environmental regulation impacts market structure through (*a*) simply raising production costs, (*b*) modifying the firm-level economies of scale (from the use of pollution abatement technologies), (*c*) technological innovation and investment to reduce future compliance and abatement costs, and (*d*) rent-seeking behavior by firms that strategically influence the level of regulation. In each category, we first discuss some key theoretical contributions and then provide a brief overview of the relevant empirical evidence.

Our decision to focus on market structure is based on two pillars. First, the ability of environmental regulation to alter market structure unintentionally has been, in our opinion, relatively neglected to date. In particular, this literature has taken a backseat to studies concerned with the impact of environmental regulation on competitiveness and productivity. Second, changes in market structure affect the degree of competition in the market, the extent of market power, and consumer and producer welfare. Furthermore, it may affect the government's ability to enforce environmental regulation and thus protect the environment. Understanding the impact of environmental regulation on market structure is crucial for assessing the effectiveness and welfare effects of such policies.

Perhaps the most well-known survey on environmental regulation within economics is provided by Jaffe et al. (1995). The authors discuss the literature concerning the effect of environmental regulation on competitiveness. In practice, this corresponds to studies addressing the impact of environmental regulation on international trade patterns, foreign versus domestic investment decisions, firm location, and total factor productivity. The authors conclude (Jaffe et al. 1995, p. 157), "Overall, there is relatively little evidence to support the hypothesis that environmental regulations have had a large adverse effect on competitiveness, however that elusive term is defined."

More recent surveys are provided by Jeppesen et al. (2002), Batabyal & Nijkamp (2004), and Press (2007). Jeppesen et al. (2002) and Press (2007) discuss the prior literature on the ability of environmental regulation to influence firm location, emphasizing the mixed empirical evidence to date. In addition, Press (2007) reviews the literature on the role of environmental regulation in technological innovation. Finally, Batabyal & Nijkamp (2004) provide a nice survey of a larger set of environmental issues within the regional science literature. Concerning the general topics of environmental regulation and economic activity, the authors discuss several empirical studies relating environmental regulation to regional economic development. Consonant with the conclusions drawn in Jaffe et al. (1995), the authors summarize that most empirical work fails to find an adverse impact of environmental regulation. However, the authors are quick to note that methodological issues may plague much of this literature. Lastly, additional surveys by Fullerton (2001, 2008), Jaffe et al. (2003), and Requate (2005) address issues related to the choice of regulatory instrument (e.g., taxes, subsidies, command and control, permits, etc.), incentives for technology adoption and diffusion, and the larger distributional implications of environmental policy.

Before turning to our review of the literature on the impact of environmental regulation on market structure, it is worth updating and extending some of the statistics provided in Jaffe et al. (1995). These statistics provide a vital backdrop for understanding the concern over the potentially deleterious economic effects of environmental regulation. As noted in Jaffe et al. (1995), between 1970 and 1990, aggregate annual (air) emissions of sulfur dioxide declined by 26%, volatile organic compounds by 36%, carbon monoxide by 45%, and lead by 97%. **Table 1** reveals that these declines, as well as for particulate matter, ammonia, and nitrogen oxides, continued over the period 1990–2007. Moreover, declining emissions between 1990 and 2007 occurred despite gross domestic product (GDP) rising 63%, vehicle miles traveled increasing 45%, U.S. population growing 21%, and energy consumption rising 20% (U.S. EPA 2008).

Achieving such reductions is not without cost. Pollution-abatement capital expenditures by manufacturing establishments with 20 or more employees were $7.88 billion in 1994 (U.S. Census Bureau 1996). Moreover, these expenditures are not distributed uniformly throughout the United States, either by industry or geography: Seventy-three percent occurred in four industries (chemicals and allied products, petroleum and coal products, paper and allied products, and primary metal industries), and 35% occurred within three states (Texas, California, and Louisiana). Aggregate operating costs related to pollution-abatement activities were $20.67 billion in 1994. Air pollution was responsible for $10.45 billion of the total pollution abatement capital expenditures and operating costs ($28.55 billion).

In 2005, the most recent year such data were collected, pollution-abatement capital expenditures by manufacturing establishments with 20 or more employees declined to $5.91 billion (U.S. Census Bureau 2008). Again, though, the expenditures were not distributed uniformly; the same four industries discussed above accounted for 63%, and Texas, California, and Louisiana continued to account for over 30%. Aggregate operating

Table 1 Change in annual national emissions by source category from 1990–2007[a]

Pollutant	Source category				Total change	Percent change
	Stationary fuel combustion	Industrial and other processes	Highway vehicles	Nonroad mobile		
$PM_{2.5}$	−693	−224	−223	−49	−1189	−51%
PM_{10}	−722	−43	−235	−62	−1062	−33%
NH_3	40	−353	152	−28	−189	−4%
SO_2	−9036	−844	−412	−25	−10,267	−45%
NO_x	−4894	229	−4029	383	−8311	−33%
VOC	621	−2809	−5786	−12	−7986	−35%
CO	−207	8442	−68,645	−2685	−63,095	−44%
Pb^b	−0.410	−2.621	−0.421	−0.153	−3.604	−72%

[a]Amounts are measured in thousands of tons. Abbreviations: NH_3, ammonia; CO, carbon monoxide; NO, nitrogen oxide; Pb, lead; PM, particulate matter; SO_2, sulfur dioxide; VOC, volatile organic compound. Source: http://www.epa.gov/air/airtrends/2008/report/AirPollution.pdf.
[b]Emission changes are from 1990 to 2002 only.

costs related to pollution-abatement activities were $20.68 billion in 2005. Between 1994 and 2005, combined pollution-abatement capital expenditures and operating costs attributable to air pollution were $12.51 billion; thus, the fraction devoted to air pollution rose from roughly 37% to 47% over this period.

The Enforcement and Compliance Program of the Environmental Protection Agency (EPA) provides further confirmation that environmental regulations have economic consequences in the United States. The EPA conducted between 20,000 and 23,000 inspections/evaluations annually in fiscal years 2004–2008. The criminal enforcement program initiated at least 300 environmental crime cases per annum over this time period as well (see http://www.epa.gov/compliance/resources/reports/endofyear/eoy2008/fy2008results.pdf). Civil and criminal enforcement actions concluded in fiscal year 2008 alone required polluters to invest roughly $11.8 billion in pollution reduction, clean up of contaminated land and water, achievement of compliance, and implementation of environmentally beneficial projects (see http://www.epa.gov/compliance/resources/reports/endofyear/eoy2008/fy2008.html). This is up from approximately $5.5 billion in fiscal year 2004. In total, the EPA touts that, "EPA enforcement actions have required companies to invest an estimated inflation adjusted total of $45 billion in pollution control equipment and clean up plus environmentally beneficial projects over the last 5 years. This is equal to $36 million/work day" (see http://www.epa.gov/compliance/resources/reports/endofyear/eoy2008/fy2008 results.pdf).

Finally, although comparative data on international environmental regulatory stringency are still relatively difficult to obtain, information is becoming increasingly available. One recent assessment, provided in Esty et al. (2008), sheds some light on the severity (or lack thereof) of environmental regulation in the United States. The authors compute an Environmental Performance Index (EPI) for 2008 for 149 countries. The EPI focuses on two main objectives: environmental health and ecosystem vitality. These objectives are then mapped into six main policy categories: environmental health, air pollution, water, biodiversity and habitat, productive natural resources, and climate change. Finally, the six policy categories are measured using a total of 25 environmental indicators including sanitation, air pollution, water quality, habitat protection, pesticide regulation, and industrial carbon intensity. According to the EPI, the United States ranks 39th out of 149, placing it ahead of seven E.U. countries and prominent Asian economics such as China, India, South Korea, and Taiwan.

In sum, although many may not consider the United States to be a global, environmental leader, the potential for current environmental regulation to have an adverse effect on economic activity is one that cannot be neglected. Moreover, growing concern over climate change is likely to lead to more stringent regulation in the future. However, sound policy-making requires accurate information on just what those adverse effects may be.

In Section 2, we discuss the literature emphasizing rising production costs under environmental regulation. Section 3 reviews the literature stressing economies of scale in the compliance with environmental regulation. Section 4 assesses the literature on the interplay between environmental regulation and technological innovation. Section 5 discusses a small literature on rent-seeking behavior arising from opportunities created by environmental regulation. Finally, Section 6 concludes by offering some directions for future research.

2. PRODUCTION COSTS

The primary mechanism by which environmental regulation may affect market structure is through the cost of production of firms. The theoretical literature emphasizing the production-cost aspect of environment has studied the effect of regulation on the equilibrium number of firms in a static framework. Although this literature allows for endogenous entry and exit of firms, it has abstracted from issues related to economies of scale (say, in the abatement technology); furthermore, the static framework precludes the introduction of technological innovation. Consequently, greater production costs adversely affect the profitability of firms, thereby altering incentives for the entry and exit of firms into the market.

In particular, a significant strand of literature has focused on the theoretical analysis of symmetric (identical firms) oligopolistic markets with endogenous entry and exit. The goal of such analysis is to characterize the comparative statics of regulation on the equilibrium number of active firms. Much of the analysis is carried out under the assumption that firms compete in quantity (Cournot competition). While allowing for fixed cost of entry, the production technology of firms that enter is generally assumed to be characterized by nonincreasing returns to scale (convex net cost functions). A negative relationship between the number of firms and regulatory stringency indicates that more stringent regulation has a negative effect on the entry of new firms and a positive effect on the exit of existing firms.

Katsoulacos & Xepapadeas (1996) consider the special case of a linear demand function and a cost function that is additively separable in outputs and emissions. Under this setup, the authors find that the equilibrium number of firms in the market is decreasing in the unit emission tax. Building on this result, Katsoulacos & Xepapadeas (1995) show that the second-best socially optimal outcome can be achieved by a regulatory scheme that combines an entry license fee and an emission tax because the second-best optimal emission tax does not restrict the number of firms to the second-best social optimum. Shaffer (1995) and Lee (1999) extended this analysis to more general demand and production-cost functions, while assuming that emissions are proportional to output. Here, the effect of an increase in the emission tax on firm output is ambiguous, but the impact on the equilibrium number of firms in the market is always negative.

More recently, Lahiri & Ono (2007) analyze the effect of an increase in an emission tax on a symmetric oligopoly when firms can reduce emissions using abatement technologies (in addition to modifying output). The authors find that an increase in the emission tax unambiguously decreases aggregate output, but it has an ambiguous effect on output per firm, with the direction depending on the curvature of the inverse demand function. If the inverse demand function is concave (a relatively standard assumption in the Cournot model), output per firm is unambiguously higher as a result of an increase in the emission tax, implying a decline in the equilibrium number of firms in the market. However, the converse may be true if the inverse demand function is convex.

The analysis in Lahiri & Ono (2007) is similar to that contained in Requate (1997), who also discusses the effect of absolute versus relative emission standards on the equilibrium number of firms. An absolute standard is one that taxes firms per unit of emission; a relative standard restricts emissions per unit of output by firms. Requate (1997) finds that a more stringent absolute emission standard always reduces the equilibrium number of firms. However, the effect of a more stringent relative emission standard on market structure is ambiguous. The latter result is also noted in Lahiri & Ono (2007). In their model, an increase in the relative emission standard reduces aggregate output at the industry level, but it also reduces output per firm if the inverse demand function is convex. As such, the effect on the number of firms in the market is ambiguous. If the inverse demand function is concave, the effect on output per firm is ambiguous, continuing to yield no clear prediction on the change in the number of firms in equilibrium.

Abandoning the oligopoly setup, Lange & Requate (1999) and Requate (2005) analyze the effect of an increase in an emission tax on the equilibrium number of firms in theoretical models of symmetric monopolistic competition. Here, the authors find an inverse relationship between the severity of the tax and the equilibrium number of firms under reasonable parametric restrictions.

Finally, in a symmetric Cournot oligopoly with endogenous entry, Farzin (2003) treats environmental quality as complementary to the consumption of the industry product. The author derives conditions under which this assumption generates a positive relationship between the stringency of the emission standard and the equilibrium number of firms. In particular, the author finds that the rate of entry increases with the price elasticity of the industry demand function.

In sum, theoretical analysis of static markets with endogenous entry and symmetric firms indicates that an increase in absolute standards discourages entry, induces exit, and increases market concentration unless the improvement in environmental quality resulting from the change in standard has a significant positive effect on demand for industry output. An increase in emission tax leads to similar qualitative effects under (at least) three conditions: (*a*) There is no viable abatement technology available to firms (and therefore firms can reduce emissions only by reducing output), (*b*) the demand function for the final good produced by the industry satisfies restrictions on curvature (such as concavity), or (c) firms do not have sufficient strategic interaction in the market (as in the case of monopolistic competition). In contrast, the effect of an increase in a relative emission standard on the equilibrium number of firms is quite ambiguous; no easily interpretable conditions exist under which the net effect on the number of firms can be signed in either direction.

There exists a relatively sizeable empirical literature assessing the impact of environmental regulation on various aspects of market structure: location decisions by plants, entry and exit propensities, employment. Interpretation of the results is, however, not necessarily straightforward; one must pay attention to the source of the variation that is used to identify the effect of environmental regulation. If the variation arises spatially—across counties or states—then negative effects of more stringent environmental regulation may not affect the level and structure of the market at the industry level, but instead only the spatial distribution of economic activity is affected. Unfortunately, most existing empirical studies rely on this type of variation.

Early empirical studies of the effect of environmental regulation on firm location are provided in Bartik (1988), McConnell & Schwab (1990), and Levinson (1996). Bartik (1988) and Levinson (1996) rely on variation in compliance costs across states, whereas McConnell & Schwab (1990) rely predominantly on intercounty variation arising from differences in attainment status under the Clean Air Act. All three studies obtain relatively small or insignificant effects of environmental regulation on new plant location decisions.

More recent studies, however, have built on McConnell & Schwab (1990) by identifying the impact of environmental stringency through spatial and temporal variation arising from differences in county-level attainment status. These studies find statistically and economically meaningful impacts of environmental regulation. Once again, it is not clear whether these results reflect only a shift in production from nonattainment to attainment counties, a shift in production overseas, a decrease in aggregate output, or some combination thereof.

Henderson (1996) finds that three consecutive years of nonattainment status by a county reduce the stock of establishments located therein. In addition, the effect is larger for plants in more pollution-intensive sectors. Becker & Henderson (2000) estimate large reductions in the number of new plants in pollution-intensive industries opening in counties when in nonattainment (relative to when in attainment) using data over the period 1967–1992. The authors find that sectors with larger plants are differentially affected, thereby shifting the structure of the market to new, single-plant firms in less regulated areas. In addition, the authors provide some evidence that survival rates of new plants are higher in nonattainment counties during some periods, perhaps owing to grandfathering provisions contained in environmental regulation or owing to greater sunk costs acting as a barrier to exit (Rivoli & Salorio 1996).

Similarly, Greenstone (2002) finds significant reductions in economic activity of pollution-intensive plants (relative to nonpolluters) in nonattainment counties (relative to counties in attainment). Using data spanning the period 1972–1987, counties in nonattainment under the Clean Air Act suffered a loss of approximately 600,000 jobs and $75 billion (in 1987 dollars) in output in pollution-intensive industries relative to counties in attainment. Using panel data on counties in the state of New York over the period 1980–1990, List et al. (2003b) find that counties in nonattainment obtain significantly fewer new manufacturing plants in pollution-intensive (relative to nonpolluting) manufacturing sectors. List et al. (2003a), relying on the same data, find that nonattainment counties are significantly less likely to be the location choice of relocating, pollution-intensive plants.

Two other studies that do not rely on variation in county-level attainment status for identification are of note. Gray (1997) uses state-level, panel data on new plant "births" from 1963 to 1987 along with several measures of state-level environmental stringency. The author finds that states with more stringent environmental regulation have a lower birth rate of new manufacturing plants, although, surprisingly, the magnitudes of the effects are no greater for industries deemed to be high-pollution industries. Building on this work, Gray & Shadbegian (2002) use panel data on the pulp and paper industry from 1967 to 2002. The authors find that firms shift production across state lines, reallocating production shares to states with less stringent regulation. However, two-thirds of this reallocation occurs within existing plants; the remaining one-third is equally attributable to plant openings and closings.

The fact that such interstate shifting occurs is significant, and it reinforces the above claim that the results of the studies discussed to this point do not necessarily indicate a reduction in industry-level output from more stringent environmental regulation. Greenstone (2002, pp. 1211–12) summarized this succinctly:

It would be informative if the estimated regulation effects could be used to determine how much production (and employment) was shifted abroad as a result of the non-attainment designations. This would provide one measure of the national costs of these regulations. Unfortunately, such a calculation is not possible because it cannot be determined whether the lost activity in non-attainment counties moved to foreign countries or attainment counties. Since it is likely that the regulation effects partially reflect some shifting of manufacturing activity within the United States, they probably overstate the national loss of activity due to the non-attainment designations. Moreover, the possibility of intra-country shifting means that the regulation effects are also likely to overstate losses in non-attainment counties. The reason is that the identification strategy relies on comparisons between non-attainment and attainment counties, which leads to 'double counting' when production is moved from a non-attainment county to an attainment one.

Studies at the industry level address this shortcoming at least to some extent, although then the issue of whether the resulting estimates reflect a causal effect of environmental regulation becomes more prominent.

In this vein, Ollinger & Fernandez-Cornejo (1998) analyze the role of sunk environmental regulatory costs on the number of innovative pesticide firms over the period 1972–1989. The authors find a sizeable negative effect of sunk costs related to environmental and health regulation. The negative impact is markedly stronger on the number of smaller firms. In sum, the authors conclude that greater regulatory costs force firms to expand, and firms unable to do so suffer a loss in profits and ultimately exit the industry.

Two more recent studies in a similar spirit are provided by Blair & Hite (2005) and Ryan (2006). Blair & Hite (2005) analyze the effect of environmental regulation on the structure of the public landfill market in Ohio over the period 1989–1997. More stringent federal regulation emanating from concern over groundwater contamination and other negative externalities was implemented during the sample period. The authors estimate that the more stringent regulation led to a 16.6% reduction in the probability of a county containing a public landfill, resulting in a more concentrated market. Ryan (2006) analyzes the dynamic effects of environmental regulation under the Clean Air Act on the cement industry in Portland, Ohio. The primary finding is that regulation leads to a sizable increase in the sunk cost of entry. This entry barrier leads to greater concentration in the industry.

A smaller literature has focused explicitly on the exit decision of firms. Deily & Gray (1991) analyze data from 1977 to 1986 on EPA enforcement activity, finding that steel mills facing the likelihood of stringent regulatory enforcement (i.e., those with higher predicted probabilities of future inspections) were more likely to close. However, the authors also find that inspectors are more likely to bypass mills with a higher likelihood of closing if inspected. Similarly, Helland (1998) analyzes EPA inspections of pulp and paper mills in one EPA region over the period 1990–1993. The author finds that less profitable mills are less likely to be inspected, mitigating at least some of the potential impact of environmental regulation on closures. Snyder et al. (2003) estimate the impact of regulation on the exit decisions of chlorine-manufacturing plants using data from 1976 to 2001. The authors find some evidence that exits were induced by more stringent regulation, leading to a greater market share by cleaner firms. List et al. (2004) find moderate evidence of an effect on closure rates of pollution-intensive (relative to nonpolluting) plants from nonattainment status. Interestingly, the only statistically significant effect the authors find is for closures accompanied by a partial or complete move to a different state. This result is consonant with spatial variation in environmental regulation affecting the distribution of economic activity—and not necessarily the aggregate level of activity.

Of note, there is some empirical support for regulation actually discouraging exit in Europe. Analyzing Norwegian data for three manufacturing sectors, Golombek & Raknerud (1997) find that regulated establishments had significantly lower probability of exit than the nonregulated units in two of three sectors; results for the third sector are statistically insignificant. Using the same Norwegian data, Biorn et al. (1998) estimate the exit probability of a regulated establishment to be approximately one-third that of a nonregulated one.

3. ECONOMIES OF SCALE

Environmental regulation may alter the economies of scale for individual firms. In particular, the economies and diseconomies of scale associated with the cost of regulatory compliance and the pollution abatement technology available to firms (to bring down their compliance costs) may affect the level and shape of the net average and marginal cost curves of firms, thus impacting their minimum efficient scale. This, in turn, affects the number and size of firms in the market in equilibrium. The precise effect of regulation on scale economies is likely to be sensitive to the particular instruments used for regulation, as well as the political environment surrounding the enforcement of regulation and the legal environment in which the firm operates. As in the theoretical literature emphasizing production costs, the theoretical literature on economies of scale is carried out in a static framework, with entering and exiting firms typically being "small" (i.e., price takers).

In such a setup, Conrad & Wang (1993) analyze the impact of an increase in emissions tax in a market with endogenous entry of price-taking firms. The assumptions in the papers on production and abatement technology imply decreasing returns to scale; they show that the optimal scale of firms declines with increase in regulation. As the effective marginal cost curve increases with regulation, equilibrium price increases and the total output sold in equilibrium declines. The net effect of an increase in regulation on the equilibrium number of firms is therefore ambiguous. Conrad & Wang (1993) also show that the equilibrium number of firms declines with an increase in the emission tax if the demand function for the final product is sufficiently elastic. If the demand function is sufficiently inelastic, however, the equilibrium number of firms may rise. For the case of a dominant firm with a competitive fringe, the authors show that an increase in the emission tax reduces the number of firms if the elasticity of the residual demand curve is high and/or the marginal cost curve of the competitive firms is steep. In a comment on Conrad & Wang (1993), Kohn (1997) argues that if there are sufficient economies of scale in the abatement technology, then the optimal scale and output of polluting firms may increase with emission tax and, in such situations, the imposition of a (Pigouvian) emission tax is more likely to reduce the number of firms (even if the demand curve for the final product is sufficiently inelastic).

Taking a different approach, Spulber (1985) compares various regulatory instruments assuming free entry and exit. The author finds that if an optimal per-firm environmental standard is employed, excessive entry of small firms will occur. Moreover, aggregate pollution will exceed the social optimum, and production level of each firm will be below the socially efficient scale.

A significant number of empirical findings have indicated the presence of positive economies of scale with respect to environmental regulation that, in turn, leads to reduced entry and greater exit of firms. Dean & Brown (1995) provide evidence that environmental regulation is a net deterrent on the entry of new manufacturing firms. Although the authors do not assess empirically the underlying mechanisms behind this finding, they do provide an extensive review of the arguments, suggesting an increase in the minimum efficient scale of production from greater regulatory stringency. Pashigan (1984) provides evidence for the manufacturing industry as a whole indicating that the minimum efficient scale increases with the stringency of environmental regulation. Pittman (1981) provides similar evidence for pulp and paper mills. Examining new business formations across 170 manufacturing industries over a ten-year span, Dean et al. (2000) find that more stringent environmental regulation is associated with fewer small business formations; no impact is found on the creation of new, large establishments. Becker & Henderson (2000) find that new plants in nonattainment areas are significantly larger than those originating in attainment counties, reflecting greater initial capital investment. However, plant sizes converge across in attainment and nonattainment counties over time. Finally, Berman & Bui (2001) analyze the effect of environmental regulations adopted in Los Angeles Basin (California) over the period 1979–1992 on labor demand at manufacturing plants. The results indicate little adverse effect on labor demand and even some positive effects attributable to the complementarity between labor and abatement activity. Together, these findings suggest a unit cost advantage to larger firms resulting from environmental regulation and a resulting greater market share for larger establishments. Similar evidence is available from Norway; Golombek & Raknerud (1997) find that regulated establishments increase employment levels.

More recently, Yin et al. (2007) directly address the issue of exit of firms/facilities upon imposition of one specific environmental regulation, namely underground storage tanks, on the petroleum retail market. The authors identify economies of scale and liquidity constraints as the fundamental reasons behind the exit of small outlets/firms from the industry. Large outlets enjoy a competitive advantage in the market, as it is difficult for the smaller outlets to pass on the compliance costs to the customers in the presence of economies of scale. Similarly, liquidity-constrained, smaller firms are forced to exit the industry because they are unable to replace or upgrade equipment as required by standards for underground storage tanks.

The discussion on economies of scale to this point has implicitly assumed that firms are homogeneous. Thus, stricter regulation has identical effects on all firms, and any intra-industry variation in firm size is attributable to spatial variation in environmental regulation. However, this may be unrealistic. Environmental regulation may be associated with differences in abatement costs (and related scale economies) across firms, thereby creating different incentives for firms to adopt or develop new abatement technology.

Brock & Evans (1985) provide a theoretical model addressing the question of whether the government should practice regulatory tiering (i.e., regulate smaller firms less stringently than larger firms). Although not directly relevant to the question here, the model posits that firm size is increasing in access to a scarce factor—interpreted as managerial ability—and that this factor also reduces the administrative costs associated with regulatory compliance. Thus, absent regulatory tiering, the cost of compliance with environmental regulation varies across firms and is decreasing in firm size. Empirical evidence concerning compliance costs with nonenvironmental regulation affirms the negative relationship between firm size and compliance costs (for citations, see Brock & Evans 1985).

Of more direct relevance is the theoretical model provided in Carraro & Soubeyran (1996). Analyzing an asymmetric oligopoly, the authors show that a uniform emission tax imposed on all firms can increase the market share of a firm if the firm is already relatively large (i.e., enjoys an initial cost advantage). As a result, the dispersion in market share increases as a result of environmental regulation.

The empirical literature provides some validation; there is evidence of heterogeneous responses to environmental regulation within an industry. Gray & Shadbegian (2002), discussed above, find differential reallocation of production across states in response to variation in state-level environmental regulatory stringency. Specifically, firms with high compliance rates with environmental regulation appear to slightly favor states with more stringent regulation. The authors attribute such heterogeneity to differences in the cost of regulatory compliance across firms: Firms facing high costs of compliance prefer to reallocate production to more environmentally lax states, whereas firms with low costs of compliance have a slight preference for environmentally stringent states.

Millimet (2003) finds that the number of establishments of a certain size located within a county depends on environmental regulation measured at both the state and industry level. Only if both are strict (i.e., establishments belong to a heavily regulated industry measured at the national level and are located in a state with strict regulations) does the stock of large establishments increase and the stock of small establishments decline. In other words, if state-level environmental regulation becomes more strict, then the stock of large (small) establishments in industries that face relatively stringent environmental regulation nationally becomes larger (smaller). However, the stock of large (small) establishments in industries that face relatively lax environmental regulation nationally becomes smaller (larger). This result is consonant with firms finding it optimal to comply with stricter state-level regulation and, as a result, becoming larger only when competitors located elsewhere also face strict regulation. In the absence of stringent regulation on competitors, establishments either downsize or are replaced with new, smaller establishments perhaps to avoid detection of noncompliance.

4. TECHNOLOGICAL INNOVATION

The discussion to this point, particularly within the theoretical literature, has been static in nature. Understanding the impact of environmental regulation on market structure, however, is incomplete without accounting for dynamic considerations. In a dynamic setting, environmental regulation affects the incentive of firms to invest in technology adoption, innovation, and research and development (R&D) in pollution abatement to bring down future compliance and abatement costs. Such investment, in turn, affects current and future economies of scale (i.e., changes future average and marginal cost curves of firms) and potentially contributes to heterogeneity in firm size. It also creates the need to generate surplus to compensate firms for past investment. These, in turn, affect the dynamic incentives for entry and exit of firms.

The existing literature on environmental regulation and investment has predominantly focused on the so-called Porter hypothesis (Porter 1991, Porter & van der Linde 1995). According to the hypothesis, stringent environmental regulation encourages firms to innovate and develop more cost-effective methods of achieving regulatory compliance. However, in the process, firms may also discover new technologies that reduce emissions and production costs. As stated in Section 1, surveys on the productivity effects of environmental regulation, as well as the impact of regulatory instruments on technology investments, are provided elsewhere. However, very little is known about the interrelationship between environmental regulation, technological investments, and the entry and exit of firms and their intertemporal size distribution.

Parry (1995) considers an upstream market that carries out R&D to develop new abatement technology for a downstream polluting sector. Both markets are characterized by free entry and success in R&D is stochastic. The upstream firm that succeeds in developing a new abatement technology becomes a monopolist and sets a license fee that must be paid by any downstream firm wishing to adopt it. The author shows that an increase in an emissions tax raises the license fee and reduces the number of firms in the downstream market.

Mason & Swanson (2002) consider the ability of a patent-holding incumbent firm to utilize environmental regulation to gain a competitive advantage or act as a barrier to entry. Specifically, the authors consider the case where regulation is used to ban further consumption of a natural resource as an input in the production process once the usage reaches a certain limit. Thus, the combination of regulation and technological innovation result in a less competitive industry.

Recently, Sengupta (2008) shows in a two-period model that an exogenous environmental regulation imposed on a competitive industry induces *ex ante* identical firms to undertake investment to reduce their future cost of regulatory compliance. This, in turn, generates interfirm heterogeneity and shake-out of firms over an equilibrium dynamic path. Policy-induced investment by firms enables the firms that choose to be cleaner and larger to survive, whereas firms that choose to be dirtier and smaller may eventually exit as the industry matures. Under certain conditions, the equilibrium dynamic path of the competitive industry entails greater heterogeneity among firms and shake-out of firms with relatively stringent regulation. However, conditions exist under which exit may not occur.

There is no empirical evidence, to our knowledge, on the role of regulatory-induced technological innovation affecting market structure. There is, however, evidence related to the ability of environmental regulation to induce technological change. Gray & Shadbegian (1998) find that more stringent environmental regulation alters the technology choices of paper mills: Mills in states with more strict regulation choose cleaner production technologies. In addition, investment in abatement technology crowds out investment in productive technology at the plant level. At the firm level, productive investments are reallocated to plants located in states with more lax environmental regulation. Using data on offshore oil and gas production in the Gulf of Mexico from 1968 to 1998, Managi et al. (2005) find that environmental regulation induces technological change (measured by a shifting out of the production frontier). Jaffe & Palmer (1997) analyze panel data at the industry-level from 1974 to 1991. The authors find that lagged abatement expenditures are positively related to current R&D. However, they fail to find any link between lagged abatement expenditures and innovative output, measured by patent activity. Similarly, Snyder et al. (2003) fail to find any regulatory-induced effect on the decision by chlorine-manufacturing plants to adopt cleaner, membrane cell technology. Conversely, Brunnermeier & Cohen (2005) analyze panel data on manufacturing industries from 1983 to 1992 and find abatement expenditures to be positively associated with successful environmental patent applications. However, greater enforcement of environmental regulation did not provide any additional incentive to innovate.

In a somewhat different vein, List et al. (2004) study the impact of the New Source Review (NSR) provision of the Clean Air Act. Under the NSR, existing plants that wish to undertake modifications that are expected to yield a net increase in emissions must comply with pollution-control standards for new sources. As such, modifications relieve the plant of any grandfathering privileges it may possess. Because the NSR requirements are more strict for plants located in nonattainment counties, List et al. (2004) analyze the impact of nonattainment status on plant-level modification decisions in pollution-intensive (relative to nonpolluting) sectors. The authors find a statistically and meaningful deterrent effect of the NSR on modifications. Consequently, grandfathering provisions of environmental regulation encourage the continued use of inefficient technologies as well as potentially higher pollution levels.

5. RENT-SEEKING BEHAVIOR

The final mechanism by which environmental regulation may alter market structure is through strategic behavior on the part of incumbent firms. Incumbent firms may strategically invest in new abatement technology to reduce their abatement cost so as to create incentives for the regulator to increase future regulation that can, in turn, place other firms at a competitive disadvantage. This is particularly relevant when some firms have exclusive access to a technology or other cost advantage over rival firms. In such cases, firms may even lobby for novel and stricter regulations to exploit their first-movers' advantage. By increasing rivals' costs through induced regulation, innovating firms may cause rivals to exit, limit entry by potential competitors, or increase heterogeneity in market shares among existing firms in the industry.

The potential for environmental regulation to raise rivals' costs and act as a barrier to entry creates demand for more stringent regulation by those possessing some initial advantage (Salop & Scheffman 1983; Barrett 1991, 1992; Fri 1992). Firms that have adopted investments with little to no reversibility wish for the government to impose a regulatory standard that is at par with their environmental performance, and this creates additional impediments for potential entrants in the industry.

Buchanan & Tullock (1975) were the first to point out that regulation that relied on a nontransferable permit to limit a firm's pollution-producing output creates a barrier to entry and, consequently, generates rents for incumbents. This rent-creating potential for incumbent firms through entry barriers continues to exist when such permits are coupled with environmental standards (such as technology forcing) that reduce the scale economies for individual firms (Maloney & McCormick 1982).

More recently, Denicolò (2008) shows that when firms choose abatement technology and have private information about their own production costs (resulting from any choice of abatement technology), an incumbent firm may voluntarily choose a cleaner technology (than the one mandated by existing regulation) in order to signal low production cost (when it adopts this cleaner technology) so as to induce the government to impose more stringent regulation. This, in turn, can deter potential entry (in the presence of a fixed entry cost) or reduce the scale of the entrant (if the entrant has a higher compliance cost). Thus, voluntary overcompliance can be used by firms in a strategic attempt to signal that the existing regulation is not overly burdensome. If the government then acts on this signal by effecting stricter regulation in the future, the overcompliant firm can retain or increase market dominance. See Lyon & Maxwell (2004) for a more comprehensive review of environmental overcompliance by firms. Similarly, Schoonbeek & de Vries (2008) discuss a model where a monopolist faces a potential entrant. They show that the socially optimal level of regulation may preserve the monopoly and, as such, that the preferences of the welfare-maximizing government and the incumbent firm may coincide.

Some empirical support for this line of thought is contained in Helland & Matsuno (2003), who find that an increase in compliance cost due to environmental regulation increases the rent (Tobin's q) for larger firms. Additional support comes from two case studies. First, DuPont broke from the industry norm in the mid-1980s and lobbied in favor of stricter regulation concerning the use of chlorofluorocarbon because they held the patent rights on chlorofluorocarbon substitutes. Resulting tighter regulation did increase DuPont's market position (Lyon & Maxwell 2004, Denicolò 2008). Consonant with Rivoli & Salorio (1996), once an irreversible investment is made by a firm, the cost is sunk; thus, *ex post*, it acts as an exit barrier. Second, in the early 1990s, California implemented a new phase of regulation on reformulated gasoline. Whereas most of the industry opposed the move, the state's largest gasoline retailer, Arco, supported the regulation. Brown (2008) finds that the regulation resulted in greater industry concentration and higher profits for surviving firms as the resulting price increase for wholesale gasoline exceeded the increase in average variable compliance costs.

Strategic positioning by incumbent firms in markets for tradable emission permits can also act as entry barriers (e.g., Sartzetakis 1997, Koutstaal 2002). Focusing on the tradable permit market, Misiolek & Elder (1984) examine if firms with market power use exclusionary manipulation to reduce competition in the product market from rivals or potential entrants. Bohm (1994) argues that, under imperfect capital markets, grandfathering of permits can act as a barrier to entry. Koutstaal (1997) finds empirical support for this hypothesis in the context of carbon dioxide emission trading in the Netherlands. In a study of the E.U. electrical utility sector, Svendsen & Vesterdal (2002) find evidence that the grandfathering of emission permits acts as barrier to entry.

6. SOME DIRECTIONS FOR FUTURE RESEARCH

The most important development in the field of industrial organization over the past 20 years is the systematic empirical investigation and establishment of observed regularities related to the dynamics of industries and the product life cycle (including entry, exit, turnover, growth, and survival of firms as well as changes in their size distribution, age distribution, scale, and capital structure over time). A large theoretical literature on industry dynamics has followed in which evolutionary and competitive (both perfectly competitive as well as strategic) models of dynamic industries with endogenous entry, exit, and technological change (through investment or learning) are analyzed to explain the various empirical regularities.

Perhaps the most striking gap in the literature on environmental regulation is its inability to connect to this rich literature on dynamic industry models in order to understand the long-term impacts of environmental regulation on industries and firms. The response of firms to any level of environmental regulation is spread over time as firms gradually adjust their investment in the development and adoption of abatement technology, their production capacity, their cost of compliance, and their entry and exit decisions. Learning about more efficient means of complying with regulation will also affect firms' responses to environmental regulation. These, in turn, have spillover effects and affect other firms (both incumbents and potential entrants). Furthermore, the outcomes of endogenous learning and investment, as well as the propagation of externalities, are subject to uncertainty.

The resulting industry dynamics are interesting from the standpoint of both positive and normative economics. From a positive point of view, they enable us to understand the lagged effects of regulation on market structure, size and age distribution, and turnover of firms. From a normative point of view, they determine the true intertemporal cost and benefit of regulation (including the dynamic environmental impact of any regulation), which, in turn, are useful for determining the appropriate levels of environmental regulation. Static analysis of the impact of regulation on industries misses out on these important positive and normative aspects. In addition, important insights can be derived from empirical studies of specific industries along the lines of the literature concerning product life cycle and by accounting for historical changes in levels of environmental regulation on such industries.

Differences in the enforcement of regulation also affect the impact of such regulation on size distribution of firms as well as entry and exit. Certain regulations may favor smaller firms through regulatory tiering, and, in many circumstances, smaller firms can evade or escape compliance with little probability of being penalized (by the government as well as from lawsuits or negative publicity brought by individuals or groups). This, in turn, may create incentives for firms to limit their scale of production and forego the economies of scale in order to save on compliance costs, which, in turn, can lead to the coexistence of larger, more efficient, compliant firms with noncompliant, smaller firms. This endogenous difference between firms created through regulation, along with the relative market shares and technologies of the different types of firms in the market, determines the eventual net benefit to society from regulation (including the impact on the environment). A proper economic analysis of the strategic endogenous compliance and investment/capacity decisions of firms under weak, and possibly politically motivated, regulatory enforcement is clearly needed.

Finally, the existing literature focuses predominantly on the private costs of environmental regulation incurred by firms and the benefits of environmental quality enjoyed by society. Relatively neglected is the potential for firms to benefit from environmental regulation, not for reasons put forth in the Porter hypothesis, but from an increase in product demand by "green" consumers. If such green consumerism is of sufficient magnitude, stricter environmental regulation may encourage the entry of new firms in the industry. However, it is unclear whether mandatory regulation is sufficient to generate increases in consumer demand or if positive demand effects are realized only when the regulation is self-imposed (through voluntary regulation where none exists or through overcompliance).

DISCLOSURE STATEMENT

The authors are not aware of any affiliations, memberships, funding, or financial holdings that might be perceived as affecting the objectivity of this review.

LITERATURE CITED

Barrett S. 1991. Environmental regulations for competitive advantage. *Bus. Strateg. Rev.* 2:1–15

Barrett S. 1992. Strategy and the environment. *Columbia J. World Bus.* 27:202–8

Bartik TJ. 1988. The effects of environmental regulation on business location in the United States. *Growth Change* 19:22–44

Batabyal AA, Nijkamp P. 2004. The environment in regional science: an eclectic review. *J. Reg. Sci.* 83:291–316

Becker R, Henderson V. 2000. Effects of air quality regulations on polluting industries. *J. Polit. Econ.* 108:379–421

Berman E, Bui LTM. 2001. Environmental regulation and labor demand: evidence from the South Coast Air Basin. *J. Public Econ.* 79:265–95

Biorn E, Golombek R, Raknerud A. 1998. Environmental regulations and plant exit: a logit analysis based on establishment panel data. *Environ. Resour. Econ.* 11:35–59

Blair B, Hite D. 2005. The impact of environmental regulations on the industry structure of landfills. *Growth Change* 36:529–50

Bohm P. 1994. *Government revenue implications of carbon taxes and tradable carbon permits: efficiency aspects.* Presented at the 50th Congr. Int. Inst. Public Financ., Harvard Univ., Cambridge, MA

Brock W, Evans D. 1985. The economics of regulatory tiering. *Rand J. Econ.* 16:398–409

Brown J. 2008. *Raising rivals' costs via California's environmental regulations: an empirical test.* Work. Pap., East. Conn. State Univ.

Brunnermeier S, Cohen M. 2005. Determinants of environmental innovation in US manufacturing industries. *J. Environ. Econ. Manag.* 45:278–93

Buchanan JM, Tullock G. 1975. Polluters' profits and political response: direct controls versus taxes. *Am. Econ. Rev.* 65:139–47

Carraro C, Katsoulacos Y, Xepapadeas A, eds. 1996. *Environmental Policy and Market Structure.* Dordrecht: Kluwer Acad.

Carraro C, Soubeyran A. 1996. Environmental taxation, market share, and profits in oligopoly. See Carraro et al. 1996, pp. 23–44

Conrad K, Wang J. 1993. The effect of emission taxes and abatement subsidies on market structure. *Int. J. Ind. Organ.* 11:499–518

Dean T, Brown R. 1995. Pollution regulation as a barrier to new firm entry: initial evidence and implications for future research. *Acad. Manag. J.* 38:288–303

Dean T, Brown R, Stango V. 2000. Environmental regulation as a barrier to the formation of small manufacturing establishments: a longitudinal examination. *J. Environ. Econ. Manag.* 40:56–75

Deily ME, Gray WB. 1991. Enforcement of pollution regulations in a declining industry. *J. Environ. Econ. Manag.* 21:260–74

Denicolò V. 2008. A signaling model of environmental overcompliance. *J. Econ. Behav. Organ.* 68:293–303

Esty DC, Levy MA, Kim CH, de Sherbinin A, Srebotnjak T, Mara V. 2008. *2008 Environmental Performance Index*. New Haven, CT: Yale Cent. Environ. Law Policy

Farzin Y. 2003. The effects of emissions standards on industry. *J. Regul. Econ.* 24:315–27

Fri R. 1992. The corporation as a nongovernmental organization. *Columbia J. World Bus.* 27:91–5

Fullerton D. 2001. A framework to compare environmental policies. *South. Econ. J.* 68:224–48

Fullerton D. 2008. *Distributional effects of environmental and energy policy: an introduction*. Work. Pap. 14241, NBER

Golombek R, Raknerud A. 1997. Do environmental standards harm manufacturing employment? *Scand. J. Econ.* 91:29–44

Gray W. 1997. *Manufacturing plant location: Does state pollution regulation matter?* Work. Pap. 5880, NBER

Gray W, Shadbegian R. 1998. Environmental regulation, investment timing, and technology choice. *J. Ind. Econ.* 46:235–56

Gray W, Shadbegian R. 2002. *When do firms shift production across states to avoid environmental regulation?* Work. Pap. 8705, NBER

Greenstone M. 2002. The impacts of environmental regulations on industrial activity: evidence from the 1970 and 1977 Clean Air Act Amendments and the Census of Manufactures. *J. Polit. Econ.* 110:1175–219

Helland E. 1998. The enforcement of pollution control laws: inspections, violations, and self-reporting. *Rev. Econ. Stat.* 80:141–53

Helland E, Matsuno M. 2003. Pollution abatement as a barrier to entry. *J. Regul. Econ.* 24:243–59

Henderson JV. 1996. Effects of air quality regulation. *Am. Econ. Rev.* 86:789–813

Jaffe A, Newell RG, Stavins RN. 2003. Technological change and the environment. In *Handbook of Environmental Economics*, ed. K Mäler, J Vincent, 1:461–516. Amsterdam: Elsevier

Jaffe AB, Palmer K. 1997. Environmental regulation and innovation: a panel data study. *Rev. Econ. Stat.* 79:610–19

Jaffe AB, Peterson SR, Portney PR, Stavins RN. 1995. Environmental regulation and the competitiveness of U.S. manufacturing: What does the evidence tell us? *J. Econ. Lit.* 33:132–63

Jeppesen T, List JA, Folmer H. 2002. Environmental regulations and new plant location decisions: evidence from a meta-analysis. *J. Reg. Sci.* 42:19–49

Katsoulacos Y, Xepapadeas A. 1995. Environmental policy under oligopoly with endogenous market structure. *Scand. J. Econ.* 97:411–20

Katsoulacos Y, Xepapadeas A. 1996. Emission taxes and market structure. See Carraro et al. 1996, pp. 3–22

Kohn RE. 1997. The effect of emission taxes and abatement subsidies on market structure. Comment. *Int. J. Ind. Organ.* 15:617–28

Koutstaal P. 1997. *Economic Policy and Climate Change: Tradable Permits for Reducing Carbon Emissions*. Cheltenham, UK: Edward Elgar

Koutstaal P. 2002. Tradable permits in economic theory. In *Handbook of Environmental Resource Economics*, ed. J Bergh, pp. 265–74. Cheltenham, UK: Edward Elgar

Lange A, Requate T. 1999. Emission taxes for price-setting firms: differentiated commodities and monopolistic competition. In *Environmental Regulation and Market Power, Competition, Time Consistency and International Trade*, ed. E Petrakis, E Sartzetakis, A Xepapadeas. Cheltenham, UK: Edward Elgar

Lahiri S, Ono Y. 2007. Relative emission standard versus tax under oligopoly: the role of free entry. *J. Econ.* 91:107–28

Lee S-H. 1999. Optimal taxation for polluting oligopolists with endogenous market structure. *J. Regul. Econ.* 15:293–308

Levinson A. 1996. Environmental regulations and manufacturer's location choices: evidence from the Census of Manufactures. *J. Public Econ.* 62:5–30

List JA, McHone WW, Millimet DL. 2003a. Effects of air quality regulation on the destination choice of relocating plants. *Oxf. Econ. Pap.* 55:657–78

List JA, Millimet DL, Fredriksson PG, McHone WW. 2003b. Effects of environmental regulations on manufacturing plant births: evidence from a propensity score matching estimator. *Rev. Econ. Stat.* 85:944–52

List JA, Millimet DL, McHone WW. 2004. The unintended disincentive in the clean air act. *B.E. J. Econ. Anal. Policy* 4(2): artic. 2

Lyon TP, Maxwell JW. 2004. *Corporate Environmentalism and Public Policy*. Cambridge, UK: Cambridge Univ. Press

Maloney M, McCormick R. 1982. A positive theory of environmental quality regulation. *J. Law Econ.* 25:99–123

Managi S, Opaluch J, Jin D, Grigalunas T. 2005. Environmental regulations and technological change in the offshore oil and gas industry. *Land Econ.* 81:303–19

Mason R, Swanson T. 2002. The costs of uncoordinated regulation. *Eur. Econ. Rev.* 46:143–67

McConnell VD, Schwab RM. 1990. The impact of environmental regulation on industry location decisions: the motor vehicle industry. *Land Econ.* 66:67–81

Millimet DL. 2003. Environmental abatement costs and establishment size. *Contemp. Econ. Policy* 21:281–96

Misiolek W, Elder H. 1984. Exclusionary manipulation of markets for pollution rights. *J. Environ. Econ. Manag.* 11:244–63

Ollinger M, Fernandez-Cornejo J. 1998. Sunk costs and regulation in the U.S. pesticide industry. *Int. J. Ind. Organ.* 16:139–68

Parry I. 1995. Optimal pollution taxes and endogenous technological progress. *Resour. Energy Econ.* 17:69–85

Pashigian BP. 1984. The effect of environmental regulation on optimal plant size and factor shares. *J. Law Econ.* 26:1–28

Pittman RW. 1981. Issue in pollution control: interplant cost differences and economies of scale. *Land Econ.* 57:1–17

Porter M. 1991. America's green strategy. *Sci. Am.* 264:168

Porter M, van der Linde C. 1995. Green and competitive: ending the stalemate. *Harv. Bus. Rev.* Sept-Oct:120–34

Press D. 2007. Industry, environmental policy, and environmental outcomes. *Annu. Rev. Environ. Resour.* 32:317–44

Requate T. 1997. Green taxes in oligopoly if the number of firms is endogenous. *Finanzarchiv* 54:261–80

Requate T. 2005. Dynamic incentives by environmental policy instruments—a survey. *Ecol. Econ.* 54:175–95

Rivoli P, Salorio E. 1996. Foreign direct investment and investment under uncertainty. *J. Int. Bus. Stud.* 27:335–57

Ryan SP. 2006. *The costs of environmental regulation in a concentrated industry*. Work. Pap., MIT

Salop S, Scheffman D. 1983. Raising rival's cost. *Am. Econ. Rev.* 73:38–39

Sartzetakis E. 1997. Raising rivals' costs via emission permits markets. *Rev. Ind. Organ.* 21:751–65

Schoonbeek L, de Vries F. 2008. *Environmental taxes and industry monopolization.* Discuss. Pap. 19, Stirling Econ.

Sengupta A. 2008. *Environmental regulations and industry dynamics.* Work. Pap., Dep. Econ., South. Methodist Univ.

Shaffer S. 1995. Optimal linear taxation of polluting oligopolists. *J. Regul. Econ.* 7:85–100

Snyder L, Miller N, Stavins R. 2003. The effects of environmental regulation on technology diffusion: the case of chlorine manufacturing. *Am. Econ. Rev.* 93:431–35

Spulber D. 1985. Effluent regulation and long run optimality. *J. Environ. Econ. Manag.* 12:103–16

Svendsen G, Vesterdal M. 2002. *CO_2 trade and market power in the EU electricity sector.* Work. Pap., Aarhus Sch. Bus.

U.S. Census Bureau. 1996. *Pollution Abatement Cost and Expenditures: 1992.* Washington, DC: US Gov. Print. Off.

U.S. Census Bureau. 2008. *Pollution Abatement Costs and Expenditures: 2005.* Washington, DC: US Gov. Print. Off.

U.S. EPA. 2008. *National Air Quality—Status and Trends through 2007.* Washington, DC: US Gov. Print. Off.

Yin H, Kunreuther H, White MW. 2007. *Do environmental regulations cause firms to exit the market? Evidence from Underground Storage Tank (UST) regulations.* Work. Pap., Erb Inst. Glob. Sustain. Enterp., Univ. Mich.

The Development of New Catastrophe Risk Markets

Howard C. Kunreuther[*] and
Erwann O. Michel-Kerjan

Center for Risk Management and Decision Processes, Wharton School
of the University of Pennsylvania, Philadelphia, Pennsylvania 19104;
email: kunreuther@wharton.upenn.edu, erwannmk@wharton.upenn.edu

Annu. Rev. Resour. Econ. 2009. 1:119–37

The *Annual Review of Resource Economics* is
online at resource.annualreviews.org

This article's doi:
10.1146/annurev.resource.050708.144302

1941-1340/09/1010-0119$20.00

*Corresponding author

Key Words

extreme events, mitigation, alternative risk transfer instruments,
long-term insurance

Abstract

The large-scale disasters that have occurred since 2001 suggest that
we have entered a new era of catastrophes. We are more vulnerable
to extreme events as a result of the increasing concentration of
population and activities in exposed areas of the country. The
question is not whether large-scale catastrophe will occur, but
when and how frequently they will strike. One key question is,
Who will pay for the economic losses future disasters will inflict?
This paper discusses how new catastrophe risk markets can be
developed to provide the necessary financial coverage to make our
country more resilient. We look specifically at insurance-linked
financial instruments to complement traditional insurance and reinsurance. We also propose the development of long-term insurance and long-term loans to overcome behavioral biases such as
myopia and misperception of risks. The paper concludes by pro-
posing risk management strategies that apply to other extreme
events such as the financial crisis of 2008–2009.

1. A CAUSE FOR CONCERN

Over the past few decades, natural disasters have caused significant fatalities, injuries, and property damage. **Table 1** illustrates the new era of costly catastrophes we have entered: Of the 25 most costly insured catastrophes in the world between 1970 and 2008, all of

Table 1   The 25 most costly insured catastrophes in the world 1970–2008 (2008 prices)[a]

$ billion	Event	Victims (dead or missing)	Year	Area of primary damage
48.1	Hurricane Katrina	1836	2005	USA, Gulf of Mexico
36.8	9/11 attacks	3025	2001	USA
24.6	Hurricane Andrew	43	1992	USA, Bahamas
20.3	Northridge Earthquake	61	1994	USA
16.0	Hurricane Ike	348	2008	USA, Caribbean
14.6	Hurricane Ivan	124	2004	USA, Caribbean
13.8	Hurricane Wilma	35	2005	USA, Gulf of Mexico
11.1	Hurricane Rita	34	2005	USA, Gulf of Mexico
9.1	Hurricane Charley	24	2004	USA, Caribbean
8.9	Typhoon Mireille	51	1991	Japan
7.9	Hurricane Hugo	71	1989	Puerto Rico, USA
7.7	Winterstorm Daria	95	1990	France, UK
7.5	Winterstorm Lothar	110	1999	France, Switzerland
6.3	Winterstorm Kyrill	54	2007	Germany, UK, Netherlands, France
5.9	Storms and Floods	22	1987	France, UK
5.8	Hurricane Frances	38	2004	USA, Bahamas
5.2	Winterstorm Vivian	64	1990	Western/Central Europe
5.2	Typhoon Bart	26	1999	Japan
5.0	Hurricane Gustav	153	2008	USA, Caribbean
4.7	Hurricane Georges	600	1998	USA, Caribbean
4.4	Tropical Storm Alison	41	2001	USA
4.4	Hurricane Jeanne	3034	2004	USA, Caribbean
4.0	Typhoon Songda	45	2004	Japan, South Korea
3.7	Storms	45	2003	USA
3.6	Hurricane Floyd	70	1999	USA, Bahamas, Colombia

[a]Payments for floods by the National Flood Insurance Program in the United States are excluded.
Abbreviations: USA, United States; UK, United Kingdom.
Sources: Wharton Risk Center with data from Swiss Re and Insurance Information Institute.

them occurred after 1987, 17 of them since 2001. Furthermore, except for the terrorist attacks on September 11, 2001, all of these events were natural disasters.

To deal with the increase in losses from these events, more attention has been devoted to ways to reduce future losses in hazard-prone areas, and there has been increased interest in the role that insurance-linked securities can play in providing financial protection against catastrophic losses with the volume of these instruments. We explore both of these developments in this article.

Section 1 details the evolution of the economic and insured losses from natural disasters over the past four decades. We then explore the key drivers of this recent change (Section 2) and discuss the challenges faced by insurers today in continuing to provide coverage against such catastrophes (Section 3). The market for catastrophe financial protection is then analyzed in Section 4. Given the behavioral biases of decision makers described in Section 5, we argue for the importance of long-term contracts as a way of providing stability and incentivizing individuals to invest in risk-reduction measures (Section 6). The article concludes by showing how the lessons from natural disasters can help us to better manage other extreme events.

Between 1970 and the mid-1980s, insured losses due to natural disasters in the world were in the range of $3 to $4 billion a year (unless noted, all figures presented in this section are in 2008 U.S. dollars). In fact, until Hurricane Hugo [which cost insurers more than $4 billion in 1989 prices (or $7.9 billion in 2008 prices)] hit the Charleston, South Carolina, area in 1989, there was not a single disaster that cost insurers more than $1 billion. In the early 1990s, the scale of insured losses from major natural disasters changed radically, for reasons we explain in the next section. The occurrence of Hurricane Andrew in 1992 cost the insurance industry $15.5 billion ($24.6 billion in 2008 prices) and caused nine small insurance companies to become insolvent. Several large insurers were also severely impacted by the disaster. For example, the Florida branch of State Farm Fire and Casualty (the largest homeowner insurer in the United States) suffered a $4 billion loss and survived only because it was rescued by its parent company in Illinois. The Florida branch of Allstate, the other major player in the state at the time, paid approximately $1.9 billion in claims. This loss exceeded by $500 million the total profits that Allstate earned from all types of insurance they marketed in Florida during the 53 years the firm had been in business in the state.

Hurricane Andrew was a wake-up call for the insurance industry. Companies recognized that they were not well equipped to estimate the potential loss distribution from disasters and began to utilize catastrophic models to estimate the likelihood and consequences from specific hazards that might cause damage in specific locations (Grossi & Kunreuther 2005). Since that time, insurers have improved their underwriting processes against catastrophe risks. No insurance company declared insolvency as a result of the September 11, 2001, terrorist attacks, and only one insurer became insolvent after the series of hurricanes that devastated Florida in 2004 (U.S. Government Accountability Office 2005).

Extreme events have continued to inflict major losses on insurers. A new record was reached in 2004 with global insured losses of $49 billion (Swiss Re 2005). This upward trend continued in 2005 with total insured losses from natural catastrophes of $87 billion (which excludes $17 billion in flood insurance claims paid by the U.S. National Flood Insurance Program). Hurricane Katrina alone cost insurers and reinsurers $48.1 billion. Losses due to natural catastrophes and man-made disasters were far below the long-term trend in 2006. Of the $48 billion in catastrophe-related economic losses worldwide, $16 billion was covered by insurance ($11 and $5 billion for natural and man-made

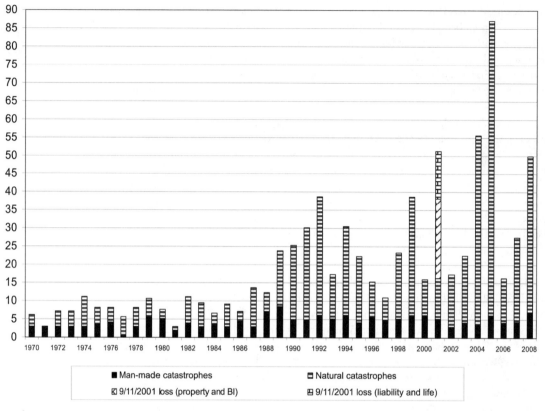

Figure 1

Worldwide evolution of catastrophe insured losses 1970–2008.

Note: Losses in dollars are indexed to 2008, which is in current dollars. Vertical axis measures US$ billion, by which losses are measured.

Source: Wharton Risk Center with data from Swiss Re and Insurance Information Institute.

disasters, respectively). Insured losses were lower than in 2006 in only two years (1988 and 1997) during the period 1987–2006.

According to Munich Re, there were 950 natural catastrophes in 2007, the most since 1974, which inflicted nearly $27 billion in insured losses. With Tropical Storms Fay and Hanna and Hurricanes Gustav and Ike[1] occurring in the North Atlantic in 2008 coupled with earthquakes in China, Japan, and Indonesia, and typhoons and floods in other parts of the world, total economic losses in 2008 were estimated to be $200 billion, the third most expensive year on record after 1995 and 2005 (Munich Re 2008).

Figure 1 depicts the evolution of worldwide insured losses due to catastrophes between 1970 and 2008 (in 2008 indexed prices). The increased losses during the past 20 years (1989–2008) compared with the previous 19 years (1970–1988) are clearly displayed.

---

[1]If preliminary estimates of damage from Hurricane Ike at $25 billion are borne out, it would be the third-costliest hurricane in U.S. history.

2. REASONS FOR INCREASED LOSSES IN RECENT YEARS

What are the key drivers of the increase in these losses? More specifically, what role have socioeconomic factors played? How is a change in climate likely to affect the number and severity of catastrophes in the future? To answer these questions, we draw on material in Kunreuther & Michel-Kerjan (2009, ch. 1).

2.1. Increasing Urbanization and Value at Risk

The two socioeconomic factors that directly influence the level of economic losses from natural disasters are degree of urbanization and value at risk. In 2000, approximately 50% of the world's population (6 billion people) lived in cities, compared with only 30% (2.5 billion people) 50 years earlier. Projections by the United Nations show that by 2025 this figure will have increased up to 60% (i.e., 8.3 billion people). A direct consequence of this trend is the increasing number of so-called mega-cities with populations above 10 million. In 1950, New York City was the only mega-city. Forty years later, there were 12 such cities. By 2015, there are estimated to be 26, including Tokyo (29 million inhabitants), Shanghai (18 million), New York City (17.6 million), and Los Angeles (14.2 million inhabitants) (Crossett et al. 2004). **Figure 2** (see color insert) depicts the increase in population by county in the United States between 1990 and 2000. Coupled with the growth of urban areas has been a large movement of individuals to coastal areas that are subject to losses from hurricanes and flooding.

In 2003, 53% of the nation's population (153 million people) resided in the 673 U.S. coastal counties (including near lakes), an increase of 33 million people since 1980, according to the National Oceanic Atmospheric Administration. And the nation's coastal population is expected to increase by more than 12 million by 2015 (Crossett et al. 2004).

The development of Florida as a home for retirees illustrates this trend. According to the U.S. Bureau of the Census, the population of Florida has increased significantly over the past 50 years: 2.8 million inhabitants in 1950, 6.8 million in 1970, 13.0 million in 1990, and a projected 19.3 million population in 2010 (an increase of almost 600% since 1950), increasing the likelihood of severe economic and insured losses unless cost-effective mitigation measures are implemented.

To understand more fully the implications of growing urbanization, one can calculate the total direct economic cost of specific disasters that occurred decades ago and see how much a similar catastrophe would cost today. A recent study by Pielke et al. (2008) normalizes to the year 2005 mainland U.S. hurricane damage during the period 1900–2005 by adjusting for inflation, population, and wealth. The data reveal that the 1926 hurricane that hit Miami, Florida, would have been almost twice as costly as Hurricane Katrina had it occurred in 2005 given the growth of the area. The Galveston, Texas, hurricane of 1900 would have had total direct economic costs similar to Hurricane Katrina if it had occurred in 2005. These findings suggest that, independent of changes in weather patterns, we are likely to see increasingly devastating disasters in the coming years because of the ongoing growth in population and property values in hazard-prone areas.

In summary, increased urbanization and an increase in real property values in hazard-prone areas will have a major impact on the level of economic and insured losses from future natural catastrophes. In low- and middle-income countries, many large cities have very high population densities compared to most North American and European cities.

This concentration poses a challenge with respect to timely evacuation and rescue operations for reducing the number of injuries and fatalities from a major disaster.

2.2. Impact of Climate Change

Is a change in climate likely to affect the number and severity of future weather-related catastrophes? Landsea et al. (2006) pointed out that subjective measurements and variable procedures make existing tropical cyclone databases insufficiently reliable to detect trends in the frequency of extreme cyclones. This conclusion is reinforced in a recent summary of articles on global climate change by Patrick Michaels, past president of the American Association of State Climatologists, who notes that all studies of hurricane activity that claim a link between human causation and the recent spate of hurricanes must also account for the equally active period around mid-twentieth century. Studies using data from 1970 onward begin at a cool point in the hemisphere's temperature history and, hence, may draw erroneous conclusions regarding global climate change and hurricane activity (Michaels 2006).

The current debate in the scientific community regarding changes in the frequency and intensity of hurricanes and their relationship to global climate change is likely to be with us for a long time to come. The results to date raise issues for the insurance industry to the extent that an increase in the number of major hurricanes over a shorter period of time is likely to translate into a greater number hitting the coasts, with a greater likelihood of damage to a much larger number of residences and commercial buildings today than in the 1950s. For more discussion on this issue, see Mills (2005) and Höppe & Pielke (2006).

Moreover, recent work by the Intergovernmental Panel on Climate Change (2007) indicates that one of the impacts of a change in climate will be an increase in weather extremes. We are likely to witness not only more intense storms, but also more intense heat waves, droughts, and flooding episodes. This will also translate into a much higher level of volatility from one year to the next and increased uncertainty by insurers. We turn to this aspect now.

3. CHALLENGES FACING INSURERS IN PROVIDING PROTECTION AGAINST CATASTROPHIC RISKS

Given the recent history of catastrophes, insurers and reinsurers are reexamining their ability to provide protection against catastrophic risks and are asking whether these events are still insurable and, if so, at what price (for details on which this discussion draws, see Kunreuther & Michel-Kerjan 2009, ch. 6). To understand the concept of insurability, consider a standard policy whereby premiums are paid at the start of a given time period to cover losses during this interval (usually a year). Two conditions must be met before insurance providers are willing to offer coverage against an uncertain event. The first is the ability to identify and quantify, or estimate, the chances of the event occurring and the extent of losses likely to be incurred. The second is the ability to set premiums for each potential customer or class of customers at prices that provide a competitive return at the assumed level of risk.

If both conditions are satisfied, a risk is considered to be insurable. But it still may not be profitable. In other words, it may be impossible to specify a premium for which there is sufficient demand and incoming revenue to cover the development, marketing, operating, cost of holding capital, and claims processing costs of the insurer and yield a net positive profit over a prespecified time horizon. In such cases, the insurer will not want to offer coverage against this risk. In his study on insurers' decision making as to when they would market coverage for a specific risk, Stone (1973) developed a model whereby firms maximize expected profits subject to satisfying a constraint related to the survival of the firm. Insurers satisfy their survival constraint by choosing a portfolio of risks that has a likelihood of experiencing total claim payments greater than some predetermined amount (L^*) that is less than some threshold probability p_1.

In determining what premiums to charge for catastrophic risks, insurers must consider problems associated with the ambiguity of the risk and degree of correlation of the risk. We briefly examine each of these factors below.

3.1. Ambiguity of the Risk

Figure 3 illustrates the total number of loss events from 1950 to 2000 in the United States for three types of natural disasters: earthquakes, floods, and hurricanes. Events were selected that had at least $1 billion of economic damage and/or more than 50 deaths. Looking across all the disasters of a particular type (earthquake, hurricane, or flood), for this 50-year period, the median loss is low while the maximum loss is very high. The 2004 and 2005 seasons have already dramatically changed the upper limits in **Figure 3**. Hurricane Katrina is estimated to have caused between $150 billion and $170 billion in economic losses, more than four times the most costly hurricane between 1950 and 2000. Given this wide variation in loss distribution, it is not surprising that insurers are concerned about the uncertainty of the loss in estimating premiums or about providing any coverage in certain hazard-prone areas.

The infrequency of major catastrophes in a single location implies that the loss distribution is not well specified. The ambiguities associated with both the probability of an extreme event occurring and with the outcomes of such an event raise a number of

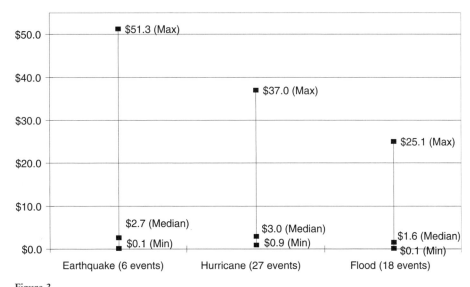

Figure 3

Historical economic losses in billions of dollars versus type of significant U.S. natural disasters for the 50-year period from 1950 to 2000.

challenges for insurers with respect to pricing their policies. As shown by a series of empirical studies, actuaries and underwriters are averse to ambiguity and want to charge much higher premiums when the likelihood and/or consequences of a risk are highly uncertain than if these components of risk are well specified (Kunreuther et al. 1995).

In a survey of 78 actuaries in France, Cabantous (2007) showed that the annual mean premium was 32% higher when the ambiguity came from an imprecise forecast than when the risk was well understood. A Web-based survey of U.S. actuaries and underwriters' decision making under risk in 2007 utilized nine different scenarios by crossing three different types of natural hazards (fire, flood, and hurricane) with three types of information about the probability of a disaster (precise probability, imprecise probability, and conflicting probability). For a one-year contract, mean annual premiums when the probability is ambiguous are 25% higher than when it is given precisely (Cabantous et al. 2009).

3.2. Correlated Risks

For extreme events, the potential for high correlation between risks will have an impact on the tail of the loss distribution. This requires additional capital for insurers to protect themselves against large losses. Insurers normally face spatially correlated losses from large-scale natural disasters. State Farm and Allstate paid $3.6 billion and $2.3 billion in claims, respectively, in the wake of Hurricane Andrew in 1992 owing to their high concentration of homeowners' policies in the Miami-Dade County area of Florida. Given this unexpectedly high loss, both companies began to reassess their strategies of providing coverage against wind damage in hurricane-prone areas (Lecomte & Gahagan 1998).

Hurricanes Katrina and Rita, which devastated the U.S. Gulf Coast in August and September 2005, had dramatic impacts on several lines of insurance, notably property damage and business interruption. Edward Liddy, chairman of Allstate, which provided insurance coverage to 350,000 homeowners in Louisiana, Mississippi, and Alabama, shortly after Katrina was quoted in the *Wall Street Journal* saying, "Extensive flooding has complicated disaster planning and the higher water has essentially altered efforts to assess damage. We now have 1,100 adjusters on the ground. We have another 500 who are ready to go as soon as we can get into some of the most-devastated areas. It will be many weeks, probably months, before there is anything approaching reliable estimates" (Francis 2005).

4. DEALING WITH THE CHALLENGES OF CATASTROPHIC LOSSES

To protect themselves against the possibility of catastrophic losses, insurers have traditionally relied on reinsurance (this section draws on Michel-Kerjan & Morlaye 2008). Reinsurance provides protection to private insurers in much the same way that insurance provides coverage to policyholders. Reinsurers offer coverage against the catastrophic portion of a loss for which insurers do not want to be financially responsible. In this type of arrangement, the reinsurer charges a premium to indemnify an insurance company against a layer of the catastrophic losses that the insurer would otherwise be responsible for covering.

One of the key features of the reinsurance market is the lack of price regulation, which exists for insurance. Thus, there was a significant increase in reinsurance prices for catastrophic risks in the United States in the aftermath of the 2005 hurricane season (from +50% to +100% depending on the risk and insurer's characteristics). This provided an impetus for the expansion of alternative risk transfer instruments, such as insurance-linked securities, that transfer part of the exposure to catastrophic losses directly to investors in the financial markets.

Since their inception more than a decade ago, insurance-linked securities have often been presented as a promising solution to address the capital needs of companies exposed to potential catastrophic risk. In a relative sense, the 2005–2007 period has been a clarion call for new investment opportunities, and we have witnessed historic records in catastrophe bond (cat bond) issuance and the development of a multibillion-dollar market for other innovative instruments. For a comprehensive discussion of alternative risk transfers markets at the beginning of the 2000s, see Lane (2002) and Dischel (2002). In the following sections, we discuss two types of insurance-linked securities instruments provided by the capital markets: industry loss warranties (ILWs) and cat bonds.

4.1. Industry Loss Warranties

The first ILWs were issued in the 1980s to cover airline industry losses. They were then developed in the property and casualty insurance industry in the aftermath of major natural disasters that occurred in the past 15 years. As the name indicates, an ILW (also known as original loss warranty, OLW) is a financial instrument designed to protect insurers and reinsurers from severe losses due to extreme events such as natural disasters. The ILW market today focuses almost exclusively on catastrophic risks, and it has increased significantly after Hurricanes Katrina, Rita, and Wilma.

ILWs operate as follows: The buyer who wants to hedge his risk pays the seller a premium at the inception of the contract. In return, the buyer can make a claim in the event of a major industry loss. The payout of an ILW can be structured in a simplified way such that the buyer can make a claim equal to the limit (L) of the ILW if a predefined industry loss index (IL) exceeds a threshold known as the trigger (T) for a particular state/ region, regardless of the buyer's actual amount of incurred loss.[2]

$$Claims = L \text{ if } IL \geq T$$
$$Claims = 0 \text{ if } IL \geq T$$

For example, the buyer of a $200 million limit U.S. wind ILW in New York in 2010 attached at $20 billion will pay a premium to a protection writer (e.g., a hedge fund acting as a reinsurer) and in return will receive $200 million if total losses to the insurance industry from a single U.S. hurricane in New York in 2010 exceed $20 billion.

One of the main advantages of ILWs is that they involve relatively low transaction costs both for the buyers (insurers or reinsurers) and sellers (e.g., hedge funds). The sellers do not have to evaluate the expected loss to the (re)insured portfolio of a specific company from the trigger event; instead, they need to evaluate only the exceedance probability curve of the entire industry, which typically reduces the uncertainty and hence the cost associated with a higher level of volatility.

The ILW market has grown significantly in the aftermath of Hurricane Katrina, which indicates a strong appetite from insurers and reinsurers for access to sources of capital other than traditional reinsurance or retrocession. It is estimated that nearly $4

---

[2]We give here the example of a derivative swap, which is the most commonly used ILW contract. But it does not have to be. There could be a first indemnity trigger (loss encounter by the buyers), then a second trigger based on industry loss. Several thresholds associated with different payments (L) could also exist.

billion in ILWs were issued between September 2005 and September 2006 (State Board of Administration of Florida 2006). However, because most of these transactions transpired directly between companies, and details of the deals are not necessarily made public, knowing the precise aggregate volume and prices is difficult.

4.2. Catastrophe Bonds

Cat bonds enable an insurer or reinsurer to access funds if a severe disaster produces large-scale damage, in a manner similar to ILWs. To illustrate how cat bonds work, consider an insurer or reinsurer, "SafeCompany," who would like to cover part of its exposure against catastrophic losses. Suppose the losses from a disaster covered by the cat bond exceed a prespecified trigger. Then the interest on the bond, the principal, or both, are forgiven, depending on the specifications of the issued cat bond. These funds are then provided to SafeCompany to help cover its claims from the event.

In 2007, State Farm issued a jumbo cat bond: a $1.2 billion risk capital bond, which as of June 2009 is the largest cat bond ever issued. (The original attempt had been to issue a $4 billion bond, but it was scaled down to the $1.2 billion note and term loan.) The bond is innovative in that it is cumulative: The company covers its portfolio in the case of cumulative losses due to a series of predefined events (e.g., hurricanes in the United States, earthquakes in Japan) over the three-year maturity of the bond.

One advantage of cat bonds over traditional one-year reinsurance contracts is that they can typically offer longer term coverage—one to five years. Over time, the proportion of cat bonds with longer maturity has increased, an indication that these instruments are gaining trust within the reinsurance/finance community. **Table 2** specifies the maturity of cat bonds that were issued between 1997 and 2007. The average maturity is approximately three years: Some cat bonds have only a one-year maturity, whereas others have five or more years. In the context of highly volatile reinsurance prices that often occur after large catastrophes, cat bonds offer an important element of stability for insurers by guaranteeing a predefined price over several years, assuming that the entire capital of the bond is not triggered (in which case a new bond has to be issued under price conditions that are likely to differ). We believe that this stability has been largely undervalued so far.

Bonds do not have to cover only natural disasters, nor are they issued only to protect a commercial enterprise. For example, the first bond that insured against terrorism was issued in Europe in August 2003. The world-governing organization of football (soccer), the International Federation of Association Football (FIFA), which organized the 2006 World Cup in Germany, developed a $262 million bond to protect its investment. Under very specific conditions, the cat bond covered losses resulting from both natural and terrorist extreme events that would have resulted in the cancellation of the World Cup final game without the possibility of it being rescheduled to 2007 (Kunreuther & Michel-Kerjan 2004). Moreover, through its FONDEN facility, the government of Mexico sponsored the $160 million CAT-Mex transaction in May 2006, making it the first government to issue a cat bond.[3]

---

[3]The cat bonds were part of a $450 million reinsurance transaction with European Finance Reinsurance, a wholly owned subsidiary of the reinsurance company, Swiss Re. Swiss Re retained $290 million of the contract exposure and issued $160 million in cat bonds with a three-year maturity through a special purpose vehicle, CAT-Mex.

Table 2   Maturity of cat bonds issued between 1997 and 2007[a]

Maturity	1 year	2 year	3 year	4 year	5 year	10 year
1997	2	1	1	0	0	1
1998	7	0	0	0	1	0
1999	5	0	3	0	2	0
2000	3	1	4	0	1	0
2001	2	1	3	1	0	0
2002	0	1	4	2	0	0
2003	0	1	3	1	2	0
2004	1	2	1	1	2	0
2005	1	2	7	0	1	0
2006	2	4	12	1	1	0
2007	4	5	12	3	5	0
Total (91)	27	18	50	9	15	1

[a]Source: Michel-Kerjan & Morlaye (2008).

An increasing number of cat bonds cover multiple events. In 2005, 2006, and 2007, over half of the capital at risk through cat bonds was for multievent bonds rather than single-event bonds. In terms of outstanding capital, U.S. earthquakes and hurricanes represented the largest volume in both 2006 and 2007, followed by storm exposure in Europe, then typhoons and earthquakes in Japan. Whether more companies, trade associations, and state and federal governments working in collaboration with experts in the field will diversify their coverage through insurance-linked securities shall be a key factor in developing these instruments.

Cat bonds have been on the market for approximately 10 years now, which enables one to make some comparisons about the evolution of issuances and outstanding capital. **Figure 4** (see color insert) illustrates the evolution of risk capital issued and outstanding, indicated by the number of bonds issued between 1997 and December 2007. At the end of 2004, nearly $4 billion in cat bond principal was outstanding (including $1.14 billion of new issuances that year). In 2007, 27 new cat bonds were issued for a total of $7 billion in capital and an additional $14 billion was outstanding.

The recent evolution of insurance-linked securities is promising. With more than $25 billion of outstanding capital in 2007 for property/casualty coverage coupled with the annual rate of growth witnessed in recent years, we could continue to see an increasing volume of capital issued to cover catastrophes. As we write this paper, however, how the 2008–2009 financial crisis will impact this market remains unclear. On the one hand, investors might be more cautious by not investing in assets they can lose overnight. On the other hand, as investors look at a new class of assets that is not correlated with traditional financial markets, catastrophe insurance-linked securities may present some advantage (Cummins & Weiss 2008).

5. BEHAVIORAL CHALLENGES: THE DEMAND FOR INSURANCE AND MITIGATION

Although insurance, reinsurance, and financial instruments transfer the risk of catastrophes to other parties, they do not reduce the risk itself. In the case of natural disasters, one needs to focus on investments in measures that decrease the level of risk associated with the hazard.

How effective can mitigation be in reducing exposure to future disaster? To shed some light on this question, we undertook an analysis of the impact that mitigation would have on reducing losses from hurricanes that occurred in four states: Florida, New York, South Carolina, and Texas (Kunreuther & Michel-Kerjan 2009). In our analysis of the impact of mitigation, we considered two extreme cases: one in which no homeowners have invested in mitigation, the other in which all homeowners have invested in predefined mitigation measures for residential structures based on the latest building codes in these four states. In Florida, we used the requirements as defined by the Institute for Business and Home Safety (2009) to incorporate mitigation. From the U.S. Hurricane Model developed by the catastrophe modeling firm Risk Management Solutions, losses were calculated on a ground-up and gross basis, assuming an appropriate mitigation measure across the insured portfolio.

The analysis reveals that mitigation has the potential to provide significant cost savings in all four states, ranging from 61% in Florida for a 100-year return period loss to 31% in New York for a 500-year return period loss. In Florida alone, the use of mitigation leads to a $51 billion savings for a 100-year event and $83 billion for a 500-year event. These findings are important given the costly capital needed to cover the tail of the distribution of extreme events. Enforcing mitigation significantly reduces, if not eliminates, this tail.

The challenge, however, lies in making sure residents in hazard-prone areas adopt this mitigation measure. Indeed, many people tend not to invest in such protection until after a disaster has occurred, in what has been termed the natural disaster syndrome (Kunreuther 1996). There are a range of informal mechanisms that explain this syndrome. One relates to framing the problem imperfectly: Experts focus on likelihood and consequences as two key elements of the risk. Several studies show, however, that individuals rarely seek out probability estimates when making their decisions. When these data are given to them, decision makers often do not use the information. In one study, researchers found that only 22% of subjects sought out probability information when evaluating several risky managerial decisions (Huber et al. 1997). People have a particular difficulty dealing with probabilistic information for small-likelihood events. In one study, individuals could not distinguish the relative safety of a chemical plant that had an annual chance of experiencing a catastrophic accident that varied from 1 in 10,000 to 1 in 1 million (Kunreuther et al. 2001).

There is also evidence that firms and residents tend to ignore risks whose subjective odds are seen as falling below some threshold. Prior to a disaster, many individuals perceive its likelihood as sufficiently low that they argue, "It will not happen to me." As a result, they do not feel the need to invest voluntarily in mitigation measures such as strengthening their house or protecting themselves financially by purchasing insurance. It is only after the disaster occurs that these same individuals express remorse that they did not undertake protective measures.

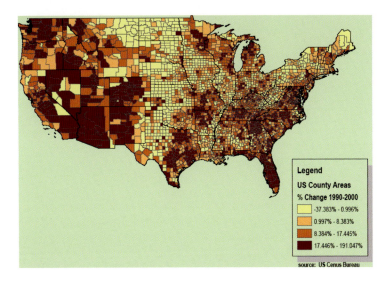

Figure 2

Evolution of the U.S. population between 1990 and 2000.

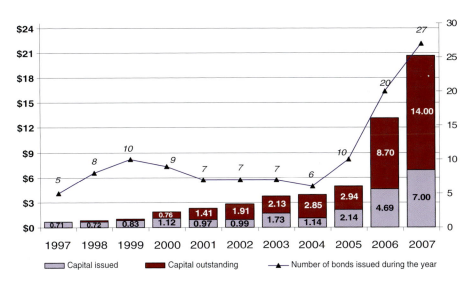

Figure 4

Natural catastrophe bonds: capital risk issued and outstanding 1997–2007 (in billions of dollars, *left vertical axis*). Years are noted in the right vertical axis. Bonds for natural disasters in the United States and abroad are combined; also included is the first liability cat bond (Avalon Re) issued by Oil Casualty Company in 2005 for $405 million. Sources: Data from Swiss Re Capital Markets, Goldman Sachs, and Guy Carpenter.

Another reason that individuals do not invest in protective measures is that they are highly myopic and tend to focus on the returns over only the next couple of years. In addition, there is extensive experimental evidence showing that human temporal discounting tends to be hyperbolic, where temporally distant events are disproportionately discounted relative to immediate ones. As an example, people are willing to pay more to have the timing of the receipt of a cash prize accelerated from tomorrow to today, than they are to have it accelerated from the day after tomorrow to tomorrow (Loewenstein & Prelec 1991).

There is extensive evidence that residents in hazard-prone areas do not undertake loss-prevention measures voluntarily. A 1974 survey of more than 1000 California homeowners in earthquake-prone areas revealed that only 12% of the respondents had adopted any protective measures (Kunreuther et al. 1978). Fifteen years later, there was little change despite the increased public awareness of the earthquake hazard. In a 1989 survey of 3500 homeowners in four California counties at risk from earthquakes, only 5–9% of the respondents in these areas reported adopting any loss-reduction measures (Palm et al. 1990). Burby et al. (1988), and Laska (1991) found a similar reluctance by residents in flood-prone areas to invest in mitigation measures.

Even after the devastating 2004 and 2005 hurricane seasons, a large number of residents had still not invested in relatively inexpensive loss-reduction measures with respect to their property, nor had they undertaken emergency-preparedness measures. In May 2006, a survey of 1100 adults living along the Atlantic and Gulf coasts revealed that 83% of the respondents had taken no steps to fortify their home, 68% had no hurricane survival kit, and 60% had no family disaster plan (Goodnough 2006).

Homeowners who do not invest in cost-effective mitigation measures if they are not required to do so should not simply be considered irrational. There are a number of reasons that people have for not taking these actions until after the next disaster occurs. We thus turn to the need for long-term contracts to address these issues.

6. AN INNOVATIVE MARKET-BASED SOLUTION: LONG-TERM RISK FINANCING CONTRACTS

To address the problem of the volatility of homeowners' failure to protect their property against disaster, we propose a new approach to providing homeowners' coverage: long-term insurance (LTI) contracts rather than the usual annual policies on residential property (information in this section is based in part on Jaffee et al. 2008). For an LTI policy to be feasible, insurers would have to be able to charge a premium that reflects their best estimate of the risk over a given time period (say, 10 or 25 years). The uncertainty surrounding these estimates could be reflected in the premium as a function of the length of the insurance contract in much the same way that the interest rate on fixed-rate mortgages varies among 15-, 25-, and 35-year loans.

The obvious advantage of an LTI contract from the point of view of policyholders is that it provides them with stability and an assurance that their property is protected for as long as they own it. This has been a major concern in hazard-prone areas where insurers have canceled policies following severe disasters such as those that occurred during the 2005 hurricane season. With an LTI policy in place, homeowners in hazard-prone areas would be protected from one disaster to the next, providing them with financial resources for recovery and reducing the need for liberal disaster assistance.

6.1. Benchmark from the Mortgage Industry

The mortgage market in the United States provides a useful benchmark for developing LTI. Although home loans today typically have maturities of 20 or 30 years, until the Great Depression, such long-term mortgages were rare. For instance, U.S. bank mortgages were commonly short term (maturities 1 to 4 years) with the full principal due at maturity. As house prices fell under dire Depression conditions, the loan balances of most homes began to exceed the house value, giving the borrower further incentive to default. A vicious circle then ensued, as falling house prices begot more mortgage defaults and mortgage defaults begot greater declines in house prices. To curtail this process, the Federal Home Owners Loan Corporation (HOLC) was created in 1933 to recycle the failing home mortgages (reminiscent of government programs now being proposed to deal with subprime mortgages). The HOLC also expanded the use of long-term, fixed-payment, and fully amortizing mortgages in the United States. Having concluded its objectives, the HOLC was closed by 1935, a notable achievement. It was replaced by the Federal Housing Administration, established under the National Housing Act of 1934, to oversee a program of home mortgage insurance against default and which continued to promote the use of long-term mortgages (Aaron 1972).

6.2. Encouraging Adoption of Mitigation Measures

LTI provides economic incentives for homeowners to invest in mitigation, whereas current annual insurance policies (even if they are risk based) are unlikely to do so. To illustrate this point, consider the following simple example where insurance premiums reflect the actuarial risk. Suppose that the "Lowland" family could invest $1500 to strengthen the roof of its house so as to reduce the damage by $30,000 from a future hurricane with an annual probability of 1 in 100. An insurer charging a risk-based premium would be willing to reduce the annual charge by $300 (1/100 × $30,000) to reflect the lower expected losses that would occur if a hurricane hit the area in which the policyholder was residing. If the house was expected to last for 10 or more years, the net present value of the expected benefit of investing in this measure would exceed the up-front cost at an annual discount rate as high as 15%.

Under current annual insurance contracts, many property owners would be reluctant to incur the $1500 expenditure, because they would get only $300 back next year and are likely to consider only the benefits over the next few years when making their decisions. If they underweigh the future, the expected discounted benefits would likely be less than the $1500 up-front costs. In addition, budget constraints could discourage them from investing in the mitigation measure. Other considerations could also play a role in a family's decision not to invest in these measures. For example, the family may know how long they will reside in the house, or their insurer might not reward them again when their policy is renewed.

Suppose a 20-year required insurance policy were tied to the property rather than to the individual. The homeowner could then take out a $1500 home-improvement loan at an annual interest rate of 10%, resulting in payments of $145 per year. If the insurance premium was reduced by $300, the savings to the homeowner each year would be $155. Alternatively, this loan could be incorporated as part of the mortgage at an interest rate below 10%.

These mitigation loans would constitute a new financial product. A bank would have a financial incentive to provide this type of loan, because it is now better protected against a catastrophic loss to the property. In addition, the insurer knows that its potential loss from a major disaster is reduced. Moreover, the general public will now be less likely to have large amounts of their tax dollars going toward disaster relief (Kunreuther 2006)—a win-win-win situation for all!

There is an additional benefit to insurers in having banks encourage individuals to invest in cost-effective mitigation measures. The cost of reinsurance, which protects insurers against catastrophic losses, should now decrease. If reinsurers know that they are less likely to make large payments to insurers because each piece of property in a region now has a lower chance of experiencing a large loss, then they will reduce their premiums to the insurer for the same reason that the insurer is reducing its premium to the property owner.

Suppose that an insurer had 1000 identical insurance policies in a particular area and that each would expect to make claims payments of $40,000 following a hurricane if home-owners had not strengthened their roofs. The insurer's loss from such a disaster would be $40 million. Suppose also that the insurer would want to have $25 million in coverage from a reinsurer to protect its surplus. If the hypothetical hurricane has a 1-in-100 chance of hitting the region where these families reside, the expected loss to a reinsurer would be $250,000 and the premium charged to the insurer would reflect this. If the bank required that all 1000 homes had their roofs mitigated to meet the local building code and each homeowner's loss were reduced to $10,000, then the insurer's total loss would be $10 million should all 1000 homes be affected, and it would not require reinsurance. These savings would be passed on by the insurer to the homeowner in the form of a lower premium.

In addition to all these benefits, LTI would also reduce transaction costs from the consumer's and insurer's point of view. More specifically, an insurer who offers an LTI policy has reduced marketing costs because this is incurred only at the time the contract is offered rather than every year. Similarly, consumers with one-year policies whose contracts are canceled at the end of the year are able to avoid the search costs of looking for another policy by buying an LTI policy. The expected social welfare benefits to the consumer based on a long-term policy can be quite substantial.

6.3. Why Does a Market for Long-Term Insurance Not Exist Today?

To move forward in developing a market for LTI, it is important to consider some of the reasons why this market does not exist today. In his seminal work on uncertainty and welfare economics, Kenneth Arrow defined "the absence of marketability for an action which is identifiable, technologically possible and capable of influencing some individuals' welfare…as a failure of the existing market to provide a means whereby the services can be both offered and demanded upon the payment of a price" (Arrow 1963). Here we discuss several factors that have contributed to the nonmarketability of LTI for protecting homeowners' property against losses from fire, theft, and large-scale natural disasters. We discuss elements that affect both the supply and demand sides.

6.3.1. Supply side. Insurance rates in the United States are frequently restricted to be artificially low in hazard-prone areas. The result is that the risks most subject to catastrophic losses also become the most unattractive for insurers to market. A second stumbling block, derived from premium regulation, is that insurers are unclear as to how much they will be allowed to charge in the future.

Uncertainty regarding costs of capital and changes in risk over time may also deter insurers from providing LTI. In principle, insurers could add a component in their premium quotes to account for the costs created by these factors. The problem is that the insurance regulator presumed to be representing consumer interests may not allow these costs to be embedded in the approved premiums. Furthermore, it is unclear what the voluntary demand for coverage will be, given the resulting premium. In a real sense, a new and less intrusive format for government regulation of insurance markets may be required if the private markets are to be successful in dealing with time-varying risks and capital. Impediments to risk spreading across insurance firms is another source of market failure.

6.3.2. Demand side. Some homeowners may worry about the financial solvency of their insurer over a long period, particularly if they have the feeling they would be locked-in if they sign an LTI contract. Consumers might also fear being overcharged if insurers set premiums that reflect the uncertainty associated with long-term risks. Furthermore, those who have not suffered a loss for 10 years but have a 25-year LTI may feel that the premiums are unfairly priced. It is thus essential that the design of an LTI contract anticipates these concerns. The policy may also include specific features that allow contract terms to change over time.

6.3.3. Open issues. There are many issues that have to be addressed in the development of long-term property insurance contracts:

- Could insurers offer adjustable rate policies similar to these types of mortgage contracts?
- Could property owners change their insurance policy over time in a manner similar to refinancing a mortgage?
- What role would the modeling companies and the scientific community studying climate science play in providing estimates for developing risk-based premiums and for suggesting a rationale for changes over time as new information becomes available from the scientific community?
- What types of risk-transfer instruments would emerge from the reinsurance market as well as from the capital markets to protect insurers against catastrophic losses?
- What role would the federal government play in providing such protection?
- Should property owners be required to purchase insurance or would this be at the discretion of the banks issuing a mortgage?

Although these issues will have to be resolved before such policies are marketed, we feel that the idea should be introduced as a way of dealing with the issue of myopia that often discourages individuals and firms from investing in cost-effective mitigation measures.

7. CONCLUSION: LESSONS FROM NATURAL DISASTERS TO OTHER EXTREME EVENTS

Our analysis in this article deals with one type of catastrophe (natural hazard) and one country (the United States), but we believe the findings apply to a broader set of extreme events and extend to other countries (see also Kunreuther & Michel-Kerjan 2009, ch. 15). We expand on this point below by focusing on the myth of low-probability events and suggesting ways of linking risk assessment and risk perception with risk management for catastrophic events as part of a more coherent strategy for dealing with extreme events.

7.1. The Myth of Low-Probability Events

Conventional wisdom holds that major accidents and disasters are low-probability events. From the viewpoint of any individual or any community these events may indeed have a small chance of occurring. However, when one expands the lens to a state, country, or the global community, the likelihood of a catastrophic event increases.

It is somewhat sobering, for instance, to learn that the probability that at least $10 billion of insured properties will be destroyed by hurricanes in Florida next year is one in six. This is equivalent to the chance of getting the number three when one tosses a die—hardly a low probability. If we extend the time horizon from 1 year to 10 years while keeping the population of Florida constant, the likelihood of damage exceeding this amount is greater than five in six.

With more economic development in coastal areas and the possible increased intensity of hurricanes due to global warming, we are almost certain to experience a disaster of $10 billion or greater in Florida in the next decade. If one extends the event space to include all natural disasters and the sample space to encompass the globe, then it should be clear that we have to modify our definition of a low-probability event. In other words, we expect large-scale catastrophes to unfold at an accelerating rhythm in the coming years. What should be done to meet this new challenge?

7.2. Risk Management Strategies for Extreme Events

Catastrophic risk management strategies should be based on assessments of the risk, recognize interdependencies, and address behavioral biases and heuristics used by decision makers who can influence the risk. The capabilities of the private sector should be utilized to develop risk management strategies in combination with public sector initiatives that address the aforementioned pitfalls.

In the context of natural disasters, we propose the development of long-term contracts such as multiyear insurance policies with premiums reflecting risk and multiyear financial loans to encourage homeowners to invest in cost-effective loss-reduction measures. Given the vulnerability associated with poorly designed structures, there is a need for well-enforced building codes for new structures in hazard-prone areas.

Turning to other extreme events, we believe that similar risk management strategies may be appropriate for reducing future losses. Rather than assuming that an event will not happen, one should develop worst-case scenarios to determine whether there are steps that can be taken to reduce the impact. For example, with respect to the recent financial crisis, there has been extensive documentation as to how the subprime mortgage crisis could have easily been predicted had the industry developed scenarios where housing prices fell nationally by a large amount. Similarly the *New Orleans Times Picayune*(2002) had a series of articles predicting Hurricane Katrina and the *National Geographic* published an article (Bourne 2004) characterizing the devastation that a disaster such as Katrina could do to the city. The disaster occurred 10 months later. The challenge is to develop economic incentives to reward individuals and organizations for taking these scenarios seriously, as there are often competing interests to be satisfied immediately.

There are also opportunities for developing long-term contracts that take the behavioral biases and heuristics utilized by decision makers into account. For example, presenting probabilities of extreme events in the context of a multiyear horizon may also lead individuals to pay attention to the resulting outcomes. To illustrate, rather than providing information in terms of a 1-in-100 chance of an event occurring next year, one could indicate that the chance of at least one of these events occurring in the next 25 years is greater than one in five.

At the end of the day, the paradox in waging a war against the weather and other extreme events is that we are our own worst enemy. As individuals, we may decide to build in risky areas. As decisions makers in the public sector, we may permit millions of people to live in these high-hazard areas without requiring them to adopt appropriate risk-reduction measures. In refusing to take steps in a proactive manner to reduce our vulnerabilities, we plant seeds for future disasters that will affect our future well-being and social welfare.

DISCLOSURE STATEMENT

The authors are not aware of any affiliations, memberships, funding, or financial holdings that might be perceived as affecting the objectivity of this review.

LITERATURE CITED

Aaron H. 1972. *Shelter and Subsidies: Who Benefits from Federal Housing Policies*. Washington, DC: Brook. Inst.

Arrow K. 1963. Uncertainty and the welfare economics of medical care. *Am. Econ. Rev.* 53(5):941–73

Bourne JK Jr. 2004. Gone with the water. *Natl. Geogr. Mag.* 206:88–105

Burby R, Bollens S, Kaiser E, Mullan D, Sheaffer J. 1988. *Cities Under Water: A Comparative Evaluation of Ten Cities' Efforts to Manage Floodplain Land Use*. Boulder, CO: Inst. Behav. Sci. Univ. Colo.

Cabantous L. 2007. Ambiguity aversion in the field of insurance: insurers' attitude to imprecise and conflicting probability estimates. *Theory Decis.* 62:219–35

Cabantous L, Hilton D, Kunreuther H, Michel-Kerjan E. 2009. *Is imprecise knowledge better than conflicting expertise? The impacts of imprecise and of conflicting probabilities on insurance pricing*. Work. Pap., Wharton Risk Manag. Decis. Process. Cent., Wharton Sch., Univ. Pa.

Crossett KM, Culliton TJ, Wiley PC, Goodspeed TR. 2004. *Population Trends Along the Coastal. United States: 1980–2008*. Silver Spring, MD: Natl. Ocean. Atmos. Admin.

Cummins JD, Weiss MA. 2008. *Convergence of insurance and financial markets: hybrid and securitized risk transfer solutions*. Work. Pap., Temple Univ.

Dischel RS. 2002. *Climate Risk and the Weather Market, Financial Risk Management with Weather Hedges*. United Kingdom: Risk Books

Francis T. 2005. After Katrina, insurance costs to rise. *Wall Street Journal*, Sept. 5: C1

Goodnough A. 2006. As hurricane season looms, states aim to scare. *New York Times*, May 31: A16

Grossi P, Kunreuther H, eds. 2005. *Catastrophe Modeling: A New Approach to Managing Risk*. New York: Springer

Höppe P, Pielke R, eds. 2006. *Workshop on climate change and disaster losses: understanding and attributing trends and projections*. SPARC Workshop Rep., Univ. Colo., May 25-26, Hohenkammer, Germany

Huber O, Wider R, Huber O. 1997. Active information search and complete information presentation in naturalistic risky decision tasks. *Acta Psychol. (Amst.)*. 95:15–29

Institute for Business and Home Safety. 2009. *Fortified... for safer living.* http://www.ibhs.org/pro perty_protection/default.asp?id=8

Intergovernmental Panel on Climate Change. 2007. *Climate Change 2007: The Physical Science Basis. Contribution of Working Group I to the Fourth Assessment Report of the Intergovernmental Panel on Climate Change*, ed. S Solomon, D Qin, M Manning. Cambridge, UK: Cambridge Univ. Press

Jaffee D, Kunreuther H, Michel-Kerjan E. 2008. *Long term insurance (LTI) for addressing catastrophic market failure.* Work. Pap. 14210, NBER

Kunreuther H. 1996. Mitigating disaster losses through insurance. *J. Risk Uncertain.* 12:171–87

Kunreuther H. 2006. Disaster mitigation and insurance: learning from Katrina. *Ann. Am. Acad. Polit. Soc. Sci.* 604:208–27

Kunreuther H, Ginsberg R, Miller L, Sagi P, Slovic P, et al. 1978. *Disaster Insurance Protection: Public Policy Lessons.* New York: Wiley & Sons

Kunreuther H, Meszaros J, Hogarth R, Spranca M. 1995. Ambiguity and underwriter decision processes. *J. Econ. Behav. Organ.* 26:337–52

Kunreuther H, Michel-Kerjan E. 2004. Policy-watch: challenges for terrorism insurance in the United States. *J. Econ. Perspect.* 18(4):201–14

Kunreuther H, Michel-Kerjan E. 2009. *At War with the Weather: Managing Large-Scale Risks in a New Era of Catastrophes.* New York: MIT Press

Kunreuther H, Novemsky N, Kahneman D. 2001. Making low probabilities useful. *J. Risk Uncertain.* 23:103–20

Landsea CW, Harper BA, Hoarau K, Knaff JA. 2006. Can we detect trends in extreme tropical cyclones? *Science* 313:452–54

Lane M, ed. 2002. *Alternative Risk Strategies.* London: Risk Waters Grp.

Laska SB. 1991. *Floodproof Retrofitting: Homeowner Self-Protective Behavior.* Boulder, CO: Inst. Behav. Sci. Univ. Colo.

Lecomte E, Gahagan K. 1998. Hurricane insurance protection in Florida. In *Paying the Price: The Status and Role of Insurance Against Natural Disasters in the United States*, ed. H Kunreuther, R Roth. Washington, D.C: Joseph Henry Press

Loewenstein G, Prelec D. 1991. Negative time preference. *Am. Econ. Rev.* 81(2):347–52

Michaels P. 2006. *Is the sky really falling? A review of recent global warming scare stories.* Policy Anal. 576, Cato Inst.

Michel-Kerjan E, Morlaye F. 2008. Extreme events, global warming, and insurance-linked securities: how to trigger the "tipping point." *Geneva Pap. Risk Insur. Issues Pract.* 33:153–76

Mills E. 2005. Insurance in a climate of change. *Science* 308:1040–44

Munich Re. 2008. *Catastrophe figures for 2008 confirm that climate agreement is urgently needed.* Munich Re Press Release, Dec. 29

New Orleans Times Picayune. 2002. *Special report: washing away.* Five-part series June 23–27. http://chss.montclair.edu/english/furr/essays/tpnoseries02.pdf

Palm R, Hodgson M, Blanchard RD, Lyons D. 1990. *Earthquake Insurance in California: Environmental Policy and Individual Decision Making.* Boulder, CO: Westview

Pielke R Jr, Gratz J, Landsea C, Collins D, Saunders M, Musulin R. 2008. Normalized hurricane damage in the United States: 1900–2005. *Nat. Hazard Rev.* 9:29–42

State Board of Administration of Florida. 2006. *A Study of Private Capital Investment Options and Capital Formation Impacting Florida's Residential Insurance Market.* Tallahassee, FL: SBA Florida

Stone J. 1973. A theory of capacity and the insurance of catastrophe risks: part I and part II. *J. Risk Insur.* 40:231–43, 339–55

Swiss Re. 2005. *Natural catastrophes and man-made disaster in 2004: more than 300,000 fatalities, record insured losses.* Sigma Study 1, Swiss Re

U.S. Government Accountability Office. 2005. Catastrophe risk: U.S. and European approaches to insure natural catastrophe and terrorism risks. Appendix III. *GAO Rep. GAO-05-199*, Washington, DC

The Curse of Natural Resources

Katharina Wick[1] and Erwin Bulte[2]

[1]Department of Economics, Tilburg University, 5000 LE Tilburg, The Netherlands

[2]Development Economics Group, Wageningen University, 6700 EW Wageningen, Netherlands; Oxford Center for the Analysis of Resource-Rich Economies (OxCarre), Oxford, OX1 3UQ, United Kingdom; email: erwin.bulte@wur.nl

Annu. Rev. Resour. Econ. 2009. 1:139–55

First published online as a Review in Advance on May 12, 2009

The *Annual Review of Resource Economics* is online at resource.annualreviews.org

This article's doi: 10.1146/annurev.resource.050708.144219

Key Words

institutions, resources and conflict, resources and economic performance

Abstract

A large literature has developed that documents a negative association between the presence of natural resources and economic development. In this paper we explore the empirics and theories of the so-called resource curse and try to assess its robustness. We conclude that there are many open questions and that the case of the curse needs revision and nuance.

1. INTRODUCTION

One of the controversial topics in the field of resource economics during the past decade is the so-called resource curse hypothesis. The resource curse refers to the apparently paradoxical result that to have more of a good thing can be bad. In terms of the curse, economists and political scientists have amassed a body of evidence that suggests an abundance of resources is associated with (*a*) slow growth, (*b*) an enhanced risk of civil war, and (*c*) autocratic political regimes. Arguably these three dimensions are interdependent.

In this article we review the emerging literature on the resource curse, focusing on the linkage between resources and slow growth, as this is the domain where economists have contributed most. We present the evidence and set out to discuss the most prominent explanations for the curse. We pay special attention to the pivotal role of institutional quality as a conditional factor. After this, we discuss some of the policy responses to the curse. Finally, we review some of the most recent evidence that challenges the robustness or even existence of the curse. Turning the curse paradigm on its head, these new findings suggest that resources may be a blessing. We conclude that resources do not necessarily spell doom for development and argue that more care must be taken to identify conditions under which the resource curse materializes. As in other fields, simple blanket recommendations are counterproductive.

2. THE PARADOX IS BORN

Concerns about the potential adverse consequences of resource-based development may be traced back to the 1950s. Since then, Gelb (1988) and Auty (1990) have been credited as early analysts of the curse. However, the most influential contribution, and the one that firmly placed the resource curse concept on the academic map, is a paper by Sachs & Warner (1997). They collected data for a large number of countries and estimated a multivariate regression equation to explain average economic growth over the period 1970–1990. One of their reduced-form growth regression equations is as follows:

$$Ln(Y_t/Y_0)/T = \alpha_0 + \alpha_1 LnY_0 + \alpha_2 SXP + \alpha_3 Z + \varepsilon,$$

where Y_t is income at time t (thus, Y_0 is initial income), SXP is the resource measure advanced by Sachs and Warner (the ratio of primary exports to GDP in 1970), and Z is a vector of the usual control variables in cross country growth regressions (e.g., openness of the economy, investment proxies, bureaucratic quality) [in a follow-up paper, Z also included a series of geographical variables (see Sachs & Warner 2001)]. When estimating the above equation, or variants thereof, the coefficient for the resource measure entered significantly and with a negative sign. Specifically, Sachs & Warner (1997) found that a one standard deviation increase in their resource measure is associated with a reduction in the annual per capita growth rate of approximately 1%. Similar results are found when trying alternative specifications, including ones where outliers are removed or when correcting for scale effects. It is easy to imagine why such a paradoxical result appealed to both empiricists and theoretical model builders—they were invited to consider the curse's robustness and explore potential mechanisms to explain its existence.

In the years that followed, a flurry of research results became available—mostly confirming the earlier negative association between resources and growth. Among the key insights obtained was the result that curse-like outcomes are more likely to emerge for so-called point resources than for diffuse resources. Point resources are natural resources that are clustered in space and can be controlled or defended by one party (perhaps promoting inequality due to highly skewed access to enduing resource rents). Examples include oil fields and diamond mines. In contrast, diffuse resources are spread out thinly—think of fertile land.

In addition to the cross-country growth regressions, there have been several careful case studies of individual countries that support the view that resources may be a hindrance to development. For example, using case studies from Southeast Asia, Ross (2001b) analyzed the destructive effect of timber booms on the quality of the institutions that are supposed to manage timber harvesting. Karl (1997) observed that a large flow of "petrodollars" may weaken the state and undermine the government's ability to manage the economy, resulting in poor economic performance.

Does the curse spill over to domains other than economic growth? Some of the early evidence suggests that it does—the curse has different faces. For example, Bulte et al. (2005) estimated a basic development equation, where several development indicators are explained rather than income growth—think of the share of the population that is undernourished or lacks access to safe water, life expectancy, and the overall human development indicator. Distinguishing between point and diffuse resources, the results are generally consistent with the findings of the growth literature: Negative associations exist between point resources and the various proxies of development, but there are no significant results for diffuse resources.

Another dimension of the resource curse concerns the connection between certain natural resources and regime type. Ross (2001a) and Jensen & Wantchekon (2004) provide empirical evidence that links oil to autocratic regimes. Other evidence also implicates nonoil minerals as impeding the emergence of democratic structures. Resource proceeds give an authoritarian leader an incumbency advantage and may hinder transition to democracy. Resource wealth often induces a rentier effect (an issue we return to in more depth below), associated with buying political power through "white elephant" projects (Robinson & Torvik 2005), clientism (Robinson et al. 2006), and military repression (Azam 2001). Recently, Ross (2008b) suggested that the effect of oil wealth stretches even further and can also partially explain the underrepresentation of women in public service as well as the slow progress toward gender equality in the Middle East.

In parallel with the literature on resources and economic outcomes, Collier & Hoeffler (1998, 2004) pioneered the literature examining the impact of resources on the onset of conflict. Using the same resource measure as used by Sachs and Warner, i.e., the ratio of resource exports over GDP, they presented evidence suggesting resources fuel civil war. The Collier-Hoeffler results provide support for the view that, in addition to grievance-based reasons for engaging in a rebellion, greed may also play a role. According to this perspective, civil war is a special form of noncooperative behavior, reflecting opportunities for rebels (or rebel leaders) to enrich themselves, for example by seizing resource rents. Rebels are viewed as rational predators or, using terms with a less negative connotation, as entrepreneurs following up on a profitable opportunity. Grievance, in contrast, is rooted in a behavioral paradigm and emphasizes relative deprivation, social exclusion, and inequality (e.g., that due to ethnic or religious divides). In the context of resource-rich societies, grievance may be exacerbated by insufficiently compensated land expropri-ation, environmental degradation, inadequate job opportunities, and labor migration (e.g., Rosser 2006). Relevant for both the greed and grievance motive is that resource rents provide a potential source of funding for the start-up costs associated with initiating a rebel organization.

A government wishing to avoid conflict can choose between two distinct strategies: suppressing the people by force or bribing them into production by providing productivity-enhancing public goods (e.g., Wick 2008). Such choices have implications for economic outcomes, cementing a link between different dimensions of the curse. Moreover, in line with observations in the literature dealing with resources and slow growth, point resources are more likely to invite conflict than are diffuse resources [e.g., see Wick & Bulte (2006) for a theoretical analysis and Ross (2008a) for recent evidence on the relation between oil and conflict].

3. LINKING RESOURCES TO SLOW GROWTH

Why are natural resources associated with slow economic growth? A number of possible explanations have been advanced. Long before the curse concept became "en vogue," a group of economists pointed to the dangers of resource-based development strategies. Taken together, the theories developed in the 1950s may be classified as structuralist explanations. They focus on long-run declining terms of trade for primary commodities (Prebisch 1950, Deaton 1999), fluctuations in the prices of such commodities, or the lack of linkages between resource extraction enclaves and the rest of the economy (Hirschman 1958). However, none of these early explanations have stood the test of closer empirical scrutiny (Ross 1999). There are many exceptions to the structuralist's dismal predictions, despite their relevance for certain resources during specific episodes (e.g., Tan 1983, Moran 1983, Behrman 1987, Cuddington 1992, Lutz 1994, Dawe 1996, Fosu 1996).

So the hunt for alternative explanations has been on. The list of candidate stories includes work by Manzano & Rigobon (2001), who focus on the pivotal role of debt overhang. They argued that resource-abundant countries, using their stocks as collateral, incurred large debts in the 1970s (when resource prices were high) that adversely affected their growth potential in the 1980s (after resource prices fell). This is consistent with an earlier observation by Davis (1983), who demonstrated that windfall gains triggered large-scale imports in a number of coffee-exporting countries. Imports rose as much as exports when coffee prices increased because countries wanted to use their sudden wealth to promote development. As a result, spending exceeded levels that could sustainably be afforded, and after the boom, contractionary measures, with detrimental effects on growth, were necessary to balance the current account.

Manzano & Rigobon (2001) also demonstrated that introducing credit constraints (the value of a country's debt over its GDP) into a growth regression renders the coefficient on the resource measure insignificant. This suggests that curse-type outcomes were caused by credit constraints faced by resource-rich countries after the commodity booms of the 1970s. However, two interesting questions arise: Why did resource-abundant countries accumulate larger debts than they could reasonably service, and why did they fail to invest their loans in sufficiently productive projects? Consistent with earlier suggestions by Auty (1990), these questions point to some form of policy failure—perhaps akin to institutional failure—to which we return below.

Another class of explanations comprises so-called Dutch disease theories. Traditionally, Dutch disease refers to outcomes in which the manufacturing sector in resource exporting countries shrinks during a boom as domestic prices increase (making investment goods more expensive) and the domestic currency is appreciated (undermining the international competitiveness of the sector) (see van Wijnbergen 1984, Krugman 1987). The term Dutch disease was coined by *The Economist* (1977) to describe the fate of the Netherlands following the discovery of sizable natural gas reserves. Capital and labor were drawn away from the manufacturing sector, which became less competitive. If one believes that the manufacturing (tradables) sector is the long-term engine of growth for economies—for example because of external effects, technology spillovers, or learning by doing effects, which result in increasing returns to scale at the sector level—then it is possible to explain curse-like outcomes (see Matsuyama 1992).

In its simplest form, Dutch disease models have a rather blunt prediction: Resource-rich countries should suffer from the curse. The evidence suggests a more mixed picture, with some countries benefiting from their resource endowments. Think of the diverging experiences of Botswana and Malaysia versus those of Nigeria and Venezuela. In light of this observation, it may come as no surprise that existing empirical work suggests that Dutch disease plays, at best, a minor role in explaining the curse (e.g., Leite & Weidmann 2002, Sala-i-Martin & Subramanian 2003). According to Matsen & Torvik (2005), traditional Dutch disease models fail to account for public savings and incorrectly assume that resource revenues must be spent immediately. In reality, (public) savings decisions may play an important role in some resource-rich states—think of the Norwegian pension fund, which is projected to grow until a size more than double the Norwegian GDP. Allowing for optimal savings implies trading off consumption today with tomorrow (the usual user cost) as well as decreased future productivity growth (due to Dutch disease effects). As a result, optimal consumption growth is higher in resource-rich countries than it is in resource-poor ones, and a greater share of income should be saved today. One explanation for diverging economic fates of resource-rich countries may lie in the inability of some countries to save optimally.

But there are other candidate explanations. In resource-rich countries the primary sector tends to be large. This has several counteracting effects on the (incentives for) human capital accumulation in the economy, which in turn impact long-term growth if there are positive externalities associated with schooling. Indeed, a negative correlation appears between resources and various proxies of educational attainment in countries (e.g., Gylfason 2001, Papyrakis & Gerlagh 2004). Schooling may be hampered by Dutch disease effects—a real exchange-rate appreciation impairs the development of human capital intensive sectors (Gylfason et al. 1999). Moreover, if the primary sector requires low-skill levels, then incentives to invest in human capital are reduced further—both for individual workers and for the government. Resource wealth may also act as a "sugar daddy" by inviting sloth and reducing incentives to work or study. To the extent that such responses are "irrational," that is, not explained by enhanced demand for leisure due to an income effect, these extraeconomic explanations are usually frowned upon by economists.

Papyrakis & Gerlagh (2004) explored several potential channels via which the curse may work, including reduced investment, schooling, or openness to trade as well as worsening terms of trade or corruption levels. When controlling for all these mechanisms, the curse disappears, suggesting that the curse works indirectly—via one of these channels. Their results implicate the investment channel as the most significant one. Thus, a steady stream of resource revenues may attenuate incentives to put aside capital now and undertake productive investments.

Debts, Dutch disease effects, and reduced schooling or investment may be viewed as proximate causes. One may probe deeper and consider ultimate causes: Why do some countries fail to respond optimally to windfall gains? This suggests a pivotal role for policy making or institutions. Indeed, it appears as if a consensus is now growing that points to institutional quality—or the lack thereof—as a driver or the curse. Including the institutional dimension allows analysts to account for the mixed experiences of resource-rich countries whereby some, but not others, escape the curse.

4. A FOCUS ON INSTITUTIONS

Institutional quality is now recognized as a key driver of development. Indeed, the emphasis on institutions in current development thinking has reached such levels that Rodrik argued we are now in the midst of a phase of "institutions fundamentalism" (which follows the "market fundamentalism" of getting prices right associated with the Washington Consensus of the 1980s and early 1990s). The popularity of institutions has been triggered in part by the seminal work of Sokoloff & Engerman (2000) and Acemoglu et al. (2001).

Sokoloff & Engerman (2000) found that extractive colonies based on plantation crops (sugar and coffee) were established in places where physical conditions were suitable for plantation agriculture (benefiting from returns to scale) and where cheap labor was locally available or could be imported. Once in place, institutions based on unequal distribution of power and income are beneficial for (domestic) elites and are therefore perpetuated and reproduced over time. In contrast, development in North America was based on different factor endowments, favoring household farms and triggering a relatively equal distribution of wealth and power. These egalitarian beginnings affected the way American society is currently organized. One hypothesis, therefore, is that colonies with diffuse resources (arable land) developed favorable institutions, conducive to long-term growth, whereas colonies endowed with pointy resources or conditions enabling plantation agriculture moved in other directions. Inspired by this approach, Acemoglu and coworkers (2001) used settler mortality as an instrumental variable for institutional quality and addressed the endogeneity concerns that hampered earlier work on the role of institutions in explaining income differentials. Follow up work by Rodrik et al. (2004) and Easterly & Levine (2003) confirmed the pivotal role of institutions, firmly placing this issue at the heart of modern development economics. The resource-curse literature has naturally absorbed some of this mainstream thinking.

Why would institutions matter for growth? Governance proxies such as property rights security (one key component of the institutional framework) matter because they determine to what extent potential investors expect to be able to reap the benefits from their investments. However, additional—perhaps more indirect—avenues via which institutions matter may also exist. For example, institutional quality codetermines a country's ability to react to external shocks. As Rodrik (1998) noted, "When social divisions run deep and the institutions of conflict management are weak, the economic costs of exogenous shocks—such as deteriorations in the terms of trade—are magnified by the distributional conflicts triggered." Dealing with shocks may require unpopular and painful measures to be borne by (parts of) the population, and if civil peace is unstable as a result of smoldering conflicts between factions in the country, implementing appropriate policies may be quite a challenge.

Broadly speaking, two streams of literature can be distinguished. The first analyzes the growth (or conflict) effects of resources, conditional on the quality of institutions. The second endogenizes institutional quality and explicitly considers the impact of natural resources on the institutional framework. Within the latter stream, papers focus on the adverse effect of natural resources on the nature of political regimes (e.g. less democracy) and governance quality (e.g. more corruption).

First consider the case where the institutional context is taken as given. Mehlum et al. (2006) provide a successful attempt to analyze why the curse occurs in some economies and not in others. They developed a model where some entrepreneurs have to divide themselves across two sectors: the rent-seeking sector and a modern manufacturing sector. When rent seeking, entrepreneurs are unproductive and live off resource rents. In contrast, the modern manufacturing sector is productive and even subject to increasing returns to scale at the sector level (such that entry of one new modern manufacturer raises the income of all others in that sector). Entrepreneurs in manufacturing may also, to some extent, share in the available resource rents, depending on the quality of institutions. Movement of talent occurs to equate the return to entrepreneurial skills—in equilibrium, income differentials between the sectors have been arbitraged away.

When institutions are bad ("grabber-friendly economies"), the rent seekers are able to grab a large share of the national resource pie for their private benefit. Instead, when institutions are good ("producer-friendly economies"), rents are shared more equally, and the returns to rent seeking are low. Mehlum and coworkers solved for the equilibrium allocation of talent across sectors as well as the ensuing income levels. Next, they considered what happens during resource booms—when the resource pie suddenly increases in size. The model predicts that resource booms tend to reduce total income in grabber-friendly economies and raise income in producer-friendly economies. The latter effect follows because extra income is poured into the economy. The former effect is more counterintuitive and follows from the reallocation of talent from the manufacturing to the rent-seeking sector after a boom. The structure of the economy, with increasing returns to scale in manufacturing, implies that everybody's income will fall as a result of such a reallocation. These theoretical predictions are confirmed in an empirical analysis, where the resource measure is interacted with a measure of institutional quality.

Additional papers have taken rent seeking as a starting point. Resource rents accrue to resource owners, so in practice they often fall in the hands of the government who can then allocate them to certain uses. It has been argued that such rents are easily appropriable by elites, leading to bribes and distortions in public policies (Karl 1997, Tornell & Lane 1999, Torvik 2002). Rent seeking may also affect economic production in the formal economy through crowding out of talent, and it may shift entrepreneurial activity from manufacturing to the resource sector. Atkinson & Hamilton (2003) captured the adverse effects of rent seeking on an economy using the concept of the genuine savings rate. The term refers to the net national savings adjusted for natural resource depletion (i.e., extracting a resource is equivalent to de-saving). In an empirical analysis they found that resource-rich countries with low or negative genuine saving rates (i.e., that use resource money for government consumption rather than investment) fall prey to the resource curse.

Several papers have analyzed the potentially adverse effects of resources, conditional on the institutional setting. For example, Robinson et al. (2006) focused on the political foundations of the curse and highlighted perverse incentives for incumbent policy makers.

Because resource booms raise the value of staying in power, unaccountable policy makers are tempted to create unproductive public sector employment (e.g., nepotism, clientelism). If incumbents want to prolong their reign by appointing friends to positions of power, thereby redistributing income to influence elections, resource curse–type outcomes may eventuate. However, it is important to note that the degree to which this is feasible depends on the institutional setting within which policy makers operate.

The "policies for sale" approach, pioneered by Bernheim & Whinston (1986) and Grossman & Helpman (1994), provides another avenue to link resource abundance to policy making. According to this model, politicians trade with interest groups (industries), exchanging policies for support (bribes). In equilibrium, bribing is truthful—firms pay more money in return for greater benefits from the policies. Bulte & Damania (2008) developed a simple general equilibrium model in which the manufacturing sector (characterized by increasing returns to scale at the sector level) and the resource sector purchase "supporting policies" from a selfish government (such as investments in education for the manufacturing sector, and physical infrastructure for the resource sector). In this model, resource booms and discoveries tilt the balance in favor of the resource sector, yielding a reorientation of support to this sector. As policy support for manufacturing falls, entrepreneurs exit from that sector. In spite of the windfall gain, aggregate income in the economy falls. There exist, however, conditions under which the dismal outcome described above need not materialize—again an example where the institutional structure matters and determines whether the curse materializes. When there is a political challenger waiting in the wings to oust the incumbent government, the story changes. In particular, the threat of a political transition "disciplines" incumbents, so that they are forced to care about aggregate income as well as the bribes they can pocket for themselves. A Sachs-Warner-style growth regression, but including an interaction term for political competition multiplied by resource abundance, supports the central idea that abundant point resources can lead to bad policies and bad economic performance, but only in the absence of political competition.

As a final example of how the resource curse can materialize in some settings, and not in others, consider the work of Andersen & Aslaksen (2006), which hones in on constitutional design. Their work is based on insights by Persson & Tabellini (2004), who pioneered the notion that constitutional design has consequences for economic policies. Key concepts in their analysis are accountability and representativeness of a country's executive body. Andersen & Aslaksen (2006) found that both presidential regimes and majoritarian electoral rules (as opposed to parliamentarian systems and proportional representation) tend to be associated with more spending for special interests, at the expense of public goods that benefit a wider swathe of voters (and that could enhance economic growth). The reason is that presidential regimes and majoritarian rules imply that the incumbent decision maker is not dependent on a stable majority among the legislators and is therefore more likely to cater to the interests of powerful minorities. In this light, it is no surprise that sectoral lobbying for preferential treatment is more successful in presidential than in parliamentary systems.

As mentioned above, a growing literature goes one step further and attempts to endogenize institutional quality in the analysis. A prominent and motivating contribution in this vein is provided by Ross (2001a), who demonstrated a negative correlation between resource measures—especially the presence of oil—and the level of democracy in a large sample of countries. This analysis has developed into one of the dimensions of the resource curse described in the Introduction—a negative association between resources and political regimes [see also Aslaksen & Torvik (2006), who analytically showed how resource wealth may decrease the probability of sustained democracy].

Leite & Weidmann (2002) provide another early attempt to capture this phenomenon and deal with a different "level" of institutional quality. They distinguished between point and diffuse resources and argued that abundant point resources tend to stimulate corruption and that corruption, in turn, retards economic growth. After controlling for the level of corruption, resource abundance is no longer significant in growth regressions. Corruption lowers the incentive to invest and innovate, as it tends to raise uncertainty and decreases returns (by effectively imposing an investment tax). This evidence suggests that the main effect of resources on economic performance is indirect—through the level of corruption. Researchers often use the level of corruption in countries as a governance measure, providing one specific type of institutional quality (see Williamson 2000).

Isham et al. (2005) confirmed the findings by Leite and Weidmann and placed them in a more general context. In addition to corruption, they considered the governance proxies Voice and Accountability and Government Effectiveness made available by the World Bank. They analyzed the association between (point) resources and economic growth, examining direct and indirect links. Given a certain level of institutional quality, natural resources have no separate effect on growth. However, point resources tend to result in worse institutions (whereas diffuse resources do not).

How may resources affect institutional quality? It is easy to imagine that resource rents have a direct income effect. To the extent that rents translate into government income, one may expect they could be used to improve the provision of public goods (including the quality of the institutional system). Various indirect mechanisms could also play a role—some of which have negative consequences that could easily dominate any positive income effect. For example, Hodler (2006) presented a model in which a certain dimension of institutional quality, namely property rights, is endogenously determined. According to his model a resource boom triggers an increase in fighting activities in an economy. The increase in appropriating activities leads to a general worsening of the property rights in the economy. This contribution thus ties together the slow growth and conflict dimension of the resource curse.

Yet other mechanisms, perhaps more subtle ones, may also be at play. In political science the concept of rentier states is well known and often used to explain why resource-rich countries may suffer from bad institutions and policies (e.g., Karl 1997, Ross 1999). This concept identifies a "disconnection" between the state and its citizens as one of the main causes for weak institutional capacity. As Moore (2001) pointed out, when the state can control resource rents associated with extraction, then it does not rely on taxation of citizens for revenues. Several things happen when the state does not have to "earn its income" but lives off rents. First, citizens may care less about how the government spends its income (as they do not have to pay for it directly) and are less inclined to scrutinize public expenditures and hold the government accountable—possibly giving rise to exorbitant private consumption of the government or hopelessly inefficient bureaucracies. Second, because the government does not need to generate its income from the people, the interests of the state and the people do not necessarily run parallel. The state has a weaker incentive to provide the public goods needed by the people to enhance production (such as the rule of law). Furthermore, the state may have less knowledge about what the people desire. Third, the state has ample means to quell potential opposition—either by wasteful public spending programs and patronage or by investments in repression. The latter may also be induced by the fact that resource wealth could trigger ethnic or regional conflict. One response would be to invest in a larger military apparatus, so as to "keep the peace" in the region. As mentioned above, this means that income from resource rents may support authoritarian, rather than democratic, regimes.

Another difference between rentier states and states relying on taxing citizens is that the former are more attractive to take over by force. Whereas tax revenues flow only if the whole complex revenue mechanism is kept going, the immediate rewards for obtaining access to point resources are far greater. In rentier states, therefore, the danger of violent strife is greater—a prediction consistent with stylized facts.

5. EXORCISING THE CURSE?

Some of the poorest countries in the world, for example in Sub-Saharan Africa, appear to be suffering from the natural resource curse. A better understanding of the phenomenon and its driving mechanisms—whether or not the result of institutional erosion—enables formulation of appropriate policy recommendations. Not surprisingly, this has become a priority for both the academic and policy-making world in recent years.

Sala-i-Martin & Subramanian (2003) provide an innovative perspective. They suggested distributing rents to the people as a means around the rentier state problem. Distributing resource rents to the population in a lump-sum fashion and subsequently requiring the government to tax part of it back to finance any state activity would reintroduce a stronger linkage between the state and its people. If so, perhaps the government would be held more accountable for the way the money is spent. Sandbu (2006) argued that such a strategy would trigger two effects, each one helping to alleviate resource curse–type problems. First, an "endowment effect" would be created—people care more about the usage of money, which they have formerly possessed and had to give up through taxation, than about the spending of resource rents they never owned in the first place. Second, owing to an "information effect," citizens of countries where the government relies on taxation are more aware about the amount of money the government has at its disposal.

Another avenue to exorcize the curse is provided by proponents of Dutch disease explanations who point to the Norwegian pension fund fueled by petro-rents. When only the interest of this fund is spent, oil wealth is converted into a key asset for future as well as current generations. By investing rents abroad, appreciation of the currency and associated adverse Dutch disease effects for local manufacturers are avoided. Many resource-rich countries have expressed an interest in following the Norwegian example, but this approach requires high-quality (political) institutions as well as strong political commitment. It is not evident that this approach can be easily mimicked by a large set of developing countries.

Yet another avenue to mitigate the curse may be through regulation of trade in resources. The issue of so-called blood diamonds (the sales of which allegedly finance rebel movements, prolonging civil wars in several African countries) was tackled by the establishment of the Kimberley Process Certification Scheme in 2003. The 48 participants (representing 74 countries) commit to trading only rough diamonds among each other. Each exporting country has to certify its traded diamonds, ensuring buying companies and customers that their money is not fueling conflicts (Bannon & Collier 2003, Kimberley

Process Certification Scheme Working Group 2006). So far, this approach seems promising. A large part of traded diamonds are considered conflict free (United Nations General Assembly 2006, Kimberley Process Certification Scheme Working Group 2006). However, the scheme has been criticized for being based on the voluntary cooperation of participants. Peer review by participating countries is one way to ensure compliance, but some argue that the scheme does not go far enough in its requirements (see, for example, Amnesty International 2006).

Finally, to address the concern that resource spoils trigger institutional deterioration via rent seeking and corruption the Extractive Industries Transparency Initiative (EITI) was launched. The EITI is supported by many institutions, including the World Bank, the International Monetary Fund, the African Development Bank, and the European Bank for Reconstruction and Development as well as many nongovernmental organizations. The aim of the initiative is to strengthen and improve governance in resource-rich countries so that many of the problems discussed above (resulting from bad institutional quality) can be avoided. This goal will be achieved by improving transparency and accountability in relation to natural resources. As discussed, one of the major problems identified is that the population lacks detailed information about the magnitude of resource rents and thus cannot hold the government accountable. The EITI aims to publicize company payments in exchange for usage of natural resources and to provide full accounts of government revenue. So far, 21 countries have joined the initiative, among them Congo, Nigeria, and Peru. However, the EITI is still in the preparation phase, and currently the success of the project is unclear. Yet, several problems have been encountered, including a large discrepancy between rhetoric and concrete actions of government leaders. There is also evidence that some governments fail to recognize the important role of civil society organizations in the process, resulting in marginalization and intimidation of civil society activists (see, for example, Revenue Watch Institute 2006).

6. CHALLENGING THE RESOURCE CURSE EVIDENCE

Slowly but steadily, a consensus perspective on the curse is emerging: (*a*) An abundance of resources is bad for development, peace, and political freedoms; (*b*) the ultimate and proximate causes of the curse are debatable, but likely involve institutional quality as a pivotal variable; and (*c*) through careful policy response, it is possible to exorcize the curse or at least attenuate its implications. This consensus caught root beyond the realm of academia and was shared by nongovernmental organizations, multilateral organizations (the International Monetary Fund and World Bank), as well as some corporations. Trade measures have been implemented, transparency initiatives have been started, and British Petroleum funded a research unit at Oxford University aimed at analyzing resource-rich economies.

At the same time, new evidence has started to trickle down casting doubts on the foundations of the curse. Several questions arise: Does the phenomenon exist at all? If so, how widespread is it? The resource curse literature is, to a very large extent, driven by empirical results—with theoretical analyses added later. It now appears as if the empirical roots of the curse may not stand to close scrutiny.

First, and at a conceptual level, one may argue that empirical work on the curse has been mis-specified. Indeed, the evidence presented may not allow the inference that resources are somehow bad, even if there exists a negative correlation between resources and economic growth. Referring back to traditional Hotelling-style extraction models, Boyce & Emery (2008) make clear that one should not expect that resource discoveries raise economic growth rates. Instead, such a discovery should instantaneously raise income levels, but theory predicts that resource rents will fall during the extraction phase as the stock gets exhausted. Hence, economic growth is lower (or even negative), but during the extraction phase, income will be higher than in the counterfactual case without resources (and if resource rents are invested wisely income levels will remain higher). As a result, the standard economic model is hard to reconcile with the resource curse perspective—why would countries be "cursed" if their income levels are (temporarily) raised? Evidence provided by Boyce & Emery (2008) and by Bravo-Ortega & de Gregorio (2005) supports the idea that a positive correlation exists between income levels and resource measures.

Second, doubts are rising about the robustness of the claimed results. Manzano & Rigobon (2001) not only used cross-section analysis to analyze the relation between resources and economic growth (as is commonly done in the literature inspired by Sachs and Warner), but also estimated the growth model using panel data. When controlling for fixed effects, the negative effect of resource abundance disappears. The authors thus inferred that the conventional resource curse result is due to an omitted variable bias. They suggested that the omitted variable is "credit constraints." Once one introduces a measure for credit constraints into the (cross-country) regression, the negative effect of resources disappears. Mackay (2008) went one step further. His panel analyses, which allows for the impact of resources on growth to vary over time, suggested that the curse has been transformed into a blessing in the most recent decades.

Similar findings have been obtained in the literature that focuses on resources and political regimes. Focusing on the most contentious resource of all (oil!), a recent study by Horiuchi & Waglé (2008) found that the negative correlation between resource rents and autocracy measures disappears when a panel model with fixed effects is used. They concluded that current undemocratic and oil-abundant countries were not democratic states before oil began to be discovered and exploited commercially. There is no evidence that the already democratic countries became less democratic under the influence of oil wealth. This study thus points to another omitted variable in most regressions—the overhang of history.

A third concern has arisen about the way resources are measured in the typical growth, conflict, or democracy regression. Sachs & Warner (1997, 2001) and most others used the ratio of primary exports to GDP. However, scaling resource output by the size of the economy implies that this measure captures dependence, rather than resource wealth or abundance. These concepts may be correlated—countries with large resource stocks may derive high incomes from extraction and, because of Dutch disease arguments, may specialize in primary exports and become dependent on resources. Yet, some resource-abundant countries are not dependent on resources, and some relatively resource-scarce countries are.

Moreover, the traditional Sachs and Warner "flow" variable may be subject to serious endogeneity concerns. The typical curse story, as discussed above, views a negative correlation between resource dependence and institutional quality as evidence that resources undermine institutions. However, and alternatively, such a correlation may capture that the resource sector is the default sector in the absence of decent institutions, as nobody is willing to invest in alternative forms of capital. If so, GDP will be low, and the conventional curse variable takes on high values. Similarly, a positive correlation between resource dependence and the onset of conflict may mean that resources trigger conflict. However, it may also mean that conflict makes countries dependent on resource extraction—the default activity that still takes place after other economic sectors (which may be more mobile or perhaps better linked to the rest of the economy) have ceased. So, which story is true? Do resources undermine institutions, cause slow growth, and trigger conflict, or is the causality running in the opposite direction? Are resources a curse to development and peace, or do they provide a safety net so that people, communities, and economies are able to eke out an existence even under the most adverse circumstances?

Evidence is mounting suggesting that the resource curse claim is not very robust to alternative (arguably more exogenous) resource measures. For example, Stijns (2002) used a physical measure of energy and mining reserves and found that the curse does not spill over to this measure. Ding & Field (2005) distinguished between measures of resource dependence and abundance. After including a physical measure of resource abundance in the traditional model, they found a positive effect of resource abundance on economic growth. Brunnschweiler & Bulte (2008c) confirmed this finding. They instrumented for resource dependence (to identify exogenous variation of this variable) and found that the Sachs and Warner resource measure no longer enters significantly in growth regressions. In contrast, a resource-abundance measure (based on the discounted value of resource rents) is positively correlated with growth and income levels. In a follow-up paper they demonstrated that similar results are obtained in the resource-conflict model (Brunnschweiler & Bulte 2008b). Conflict makes countries dependent on resource extraction, not vice versa, and resource abundance attenuates the risk of civil war via a positive effect on income (which in turn is negatively correlated with the risk of war). Brunnschweiler & Bulte (2008a) summarized these results.

7. DISCUSSION AND CONCLUSIONS

A long-standing tradition in economics and political science argues against development strategies based on exports of primary products. These so-called structuralist theories point to declining long-term price trends, deteriorating terms of trade, volatile prices, enclave production, and the absence of economies of scale. Nevertheless, standard comparative advantage arguments imply a strong case for exports of primary commodities, and in light of the favorable experiences in countries like Australia, the United States, and Canada, the dominant view until the mid-1990s was that an abundance of natural resources is a blessing for development. This perspective changed in the 1990s after seminal work by Sachs & Warner (1997, 2001) (in the growth domain) and Collier & Hoeffler (1998, 2004) (in the conflict domain). In the words of Rosser (2006), "the conventional wisdom is now arguably the exact opposite of what it was prior to the late 1980s." The resource curse was born and widely embraced by the scientific community.

After a decade of empirical and analytical research, the resource curse literature now appears to be at a crossroad. Whereas some analysts have tried to carefully build a structure that accommodates the stylized facts, sorting out proximate and ultimate effects and identifying causal mechanisms via which the curse may work, others have undermined the foundations of such a structure by casting doubts on the empirical validity of the curse results. The evidence presented in the previous section of this article seems to seal the fate of the resource curse. After the intellectual "buzz" that surrounded the curse, it now appears as though the profession has been beating a dead horse. However, such a conclusion is premature—the empirical picture remains mixed, and it is too early to dismiss the curse concept altogether.

For example, Norman (2005) found evidence of a resource curse when physical reserves as opposed to export intensity are used as the key explanatory variable. Atkinson & Hamilton (2003) employed a proxy for resource abundance different from the one used by Sachs & Warner (1997, 2001) and found that the curse emerges for a subset of countries. In addition, Bravo-Ortega & de Gregorio (2005) reported specifications where the resource curse "survives" fixed effects panel estimates.

Most interesting, perhaps, are recent attempts to move beyond aggregate models that yield blanked recommendations and more carefully embrace the diversity of both the resources as well as the economies that are trading them. As discussed above, resources may generate both level and growth effects, and economies vary in their level of institutional quality. Moreover, resources differ in terms of their value, the ease with which they can be grabbed and smuggled, and the capital intensity of production. For example, Lujala et al. (2005) demonstrated that, although no relation exists between an aggregate measure of diamonds and conflict onset, lootable (alluvial) and nonlootable (i.e., underground) diamonds have opposite effects on the incidence of conflict.

The temporal dimension may also matter. Collier & Goderis (2007) distinguished between short-term and long-term effects of resource extraction and found that long-term effects on development are generally worse. It is also overly simplistic to lump all domestic conflict together under the single header of civil war—the magnitude of the conflict varies, the intentions and motives may be different (e.g., secessionist wars versus nonsecessionist wars), and the international context is also too easily overlooked. To embrace the diversity of resources and economies, more careful econometric evidence is needed. This should involve "new" approaches like Bayesian model averaging, which allow greater flexibility.

In sum, the resource curse hypothesis remains controversial. Although great progress has been made, it is fair to conclude that crucial elements are still unknown or ill understood. It is also fair to say that the curse offers ample scope for future research and will remain a lively research field in the years to come.

DISCLOSURE STATEMENT

The authors are not aware of any affiliations, memberships, funding, or financial holdings that might be perceived as affecting the objectivity of this review.

LITERATURE CITED

Acemoglu D, Johnson A, Robinson JA. 2001. The colonial origins of comparative development: an empirical investigation. *Am. Econ. Rev.* 91:1369–401

Amnesty International. 2006. External document POL 30/024/2006. *News Serv. No. 158, Amnesty Int.*

Andersen JJ, Aslaksen S. 2006. *Constitutions and the resource curse.* Work. Pap. Ser. 7506, Dep. Econ., Norwegian Univ. Sci. Tech.

Aslaksen S, Torvik R. 2006. A theory of civil conflict and democracy in rentier states. *Scand. J. Econ.* 108(4):571–85

Atkinson G, Hamilton K. 2003. Savings, growth and the resource curse hypothesis. *World Dev.* 31:1793–807

Auty RM. 1990. *Resource Based Industrialization: Sowing the Oil in Eight Less Developed Countries.* Oxford, UK: Clarendon

Azam JP. 2001. The redistributive state and conflicts in Africa. *J. Peace Res.* 38:429–44

Bannon I, Collier P. 2003. *Natural Resources and Violent Conflict: Options and Actions.* Washington, DC: World Bank

Behrman J. 1987. Commodity price instability and economic goal attainment in developing countries. *World Dev.* 15:559–73

Bernheim BD, Whinston M. 1986. Menu actions, resource allocation and economic influence. *Q. J. Econ.* 101:1–31

Boyce J, Emery H. 2008. *What can exhaustible resource theory tell us about per capita income levels and growth in resource abundant economies?* Mimeogr., Dep. Econ., Univ. Calgary

Bravo-Ortega C, de Gregorio J. 2005. *The relative richness of the poor? Natural resources, human capital, and economic growth.* Work. Pap. 3484, World Bank Policy Res.

Bulte EH, Damania R, Deacon RT. 2005. Resource intensity, institutions and development. *World Dev.* 33:1029–44

Bulte EH, Damania R. 2008. Resources for sale: corruption, democracy and the natural resource curse. *B.E. J. Econ. Anal. Policy* 8(1): artic. 5

Brunnschweiler CN, Bulte EH. 2008a. Linking natural resources to slow growth and more conflict. *Science* 320(5876):616–17

Brunnschweiler CN, Bulte EH. 2008b. *Natural resources and violent conflict: resource abundance, dependence and the onset of civil wars.* Econ. Work. Pap. Ser. 08/78, ETH Zurich

Brunnschweiler CN, Bulte EH. 2008c. The resource curse revisited and revised: a tale of paradoxes and red herrings. *J. Environ. Econ. Manag.* 55:246–64

Collier P, Goderis B. 2007. *Commodity priced, growth, and the natural resource curse: reconciling a conundrum.* Work. Pap. 2007-15, CSAE, Oxford Univ.

Collier P, Hoeffler A. 1998. On economic causes of civil war. *Oxf. Econ. Pap.* 50:563–73

Collier P, Hoeffler A. 2004. Greed and grievance in civil war. *Oxf. Econ. Pap.* 56(4):563–95

Cuddington JT. 1992. Long-run trends in 26 primary commodity prices. *J. Dev. Econ.* 39:207–27

Davis JM. 1983. The economic effects of windfall gains in export earnings. *World Dev.* 2:119–39

Dawe D. 1996. A new look at the growth in developing countries. *World Dev.* 24:1905–14

Deaton A. 1999. Commodity prices and growth in Africa. *J. Econ. Perspect.* 13:23–40

Ding N, Field BC. 2005. Natural resource abundance and economic growth. *Land Econ.* 81(4): 496–502

Easterly W, Levine R. 2003. Tropics, germs, and crops: the role of endowments in economic development. *J. Monet. Econ.* 50(1):3–39

The Economist. 1977. The Dutch disease. *Economist*, Nov. 26:82–83

Fosu A. 1996. Primary exports and economic growth in developing countries. *World Econ.* 19:465–75

Gelb A. 1988. *Windfall Gains: Blessing or Curse?* Oxford, UK: Oxford Univ. Press

Grossman G, Helpman E. 1994. Protection for sale. *Am. Econ. Rev.* 84:833–50

Gylfason T. 2001. Natural resources, education, and economic development. *Eur. Econ. Rev.* 45:847–59

Gylfason T, Herbertsson TT, Zoega G. 1999. A mixed blessing: natural resources and economic growth. *Macroecon. Dyn.* 3:204–25

Hirschman AO. 1958. *The Strategy of Economic Development.* New Haven, CT: Yale Univ. Press

Hodler R. 2006. The curse of natural resources in fractionalized countries. *Eur. Econ. Rev.* 50(6): 1367–86

Horiuchi Y, Waglé S. 2008. *100 years of oil: Did it depress democracy and sustain autocracy?* Work. Pap., Crawford Sch. Econ. Gov., ANU Coll. Asia Pac., Aust. Natl. Univ.

Isham J, Woodcock M, Pritchett L, Busby G. 2005. The varieties of resource experience: natural resource export structures and the political economy of economic growth. *World Bank Econ. Rev.* 19(2):141–74

Jensen N, Wantchekon L. 2004. Resource wealth and political regimes in Africa. *Comp. Polit. Stud.* 37:816–41

Karl T. 1997. *The Paradox of Plenty: Oil Booms and Petro-States.* Berkeley, CA: Univ. Calif. Press

The Kimberley Process Certification Scheme Working Group. 2006. *Third Year Review.* Windhoek, Namib.: KPCS

Krugman P. 1987. The narrow moving band, the Dutch disease, and the competitive consequences of Mrs. Thatcher: notes on trade in the presence of dynamic scale economies. *J. Dev. Econ.* 37:41–55

Leite C, Weidmann J. (2002). Does Mother Nature corrupt? Natural resources, corruption and economic growth. In *Governance, Corruption, and Economic Performance*, ed. G Abed, S Gupta, pp. 159–96. Washington, DC: IMF

Lujala P, Gleditsch NP, Gilmore E. 2005. A diamond curse? Civil war and a lootable resource. *J. Confl. Resolut.* 49:538–62

Lutz M. 1994. The effects of volatility in the terms of trade on output growth: new evidence. *World Dev.* 22:1959–75

Mackay SH. 2008. *Natural resources: from curse to blessing?* Work. Pap., Dep. Econ., Univ. Manch.

Manzano O, Rigobon R. 2001. *Resource curse or debt overhang?* Work. Pap. W8390, NBER

Matsen E, Torvik R. 2005. Optimal Dutch disease. *J. Dev. Econ.* 78(2):494–515

Matsuyama K. 1992. Agricultural productivity, comparative advantage and economic growth. *J. Econ. Theory* 58:317–34

Mehlum H, Moene K, Torvik R. 2006. Institutions and the resource curse. *Econ. J.* 116(508):1–20

Moore M. 2001. Political underdevelopment: what causes bad governance? *Public Manag. Rev.* 3:1–34

Moran C. 1983. Export fluctuations and economic growth. *J. Dev. Econ.* 12:195–218

Norman CS. 2005. *Rule of law and the resource curse: abundance versus intensity.* Discuss. Pap., Dep. Econ., Univ. Calif. Santa Barbara

Papyrakis E, Gerlagh R. 2004. The resource curse hypothesis and its transmission channels. *J. Comp. Econ.* 32(1):1–196

Persson T, Tabellini G. 2004. Constitutional rules and fiscal policy outcomes. *Am. Econ. Rev.* 94:25–46

Prebisch R. 1950. *The economic development of Latin America and its principal problems.* New York: United Nations

Revenue Watch Institute. 2006. *Eye on EITI: Civil Society Perspectives and Recommendations on the Extractive Industries Transparency Initiative.* New York: Revenue Watch Inst.

Robinson JA, Torvik R. 2005. White elephants. *J. Public Econ.* 89:197–210

Robinson JA, Torvik R, Verdier T. 2006. Political foundations of the resource curse. *J. Dev. Econ.* 79(2):447–68

Rodrik D. 1998. Where did all the growth go? External shocks, social conflict, and growth collapses. *J. Econ. Growth* 4(4):358–412

Rodrik D, Subramanian A, Trebbi F. 2004. Institutions rule: the primacy of institutions over geography and integration in economic development. *J. Econ. Growth.* 9(2):131–65

Ross ML. 1999. The political economy of the resource curse. *World Polit.* 51:297–322

Ross ML. 2001a. Does oil hinder democracy? *World Polit.* 53:325–61

Ross ML. 2001b. *Timber Booms and Institutional Breakdown in Southeast Asia.* Cambridge, UK: Cambridge Univ. Press

Ross ML. 2008a. Blood Barrels. *Foreign Aff.* 87:2–9

Ross ML. 2008b. Oil, Islam and women. *Am. Polit. Sci. Rev.* 102(1):107–23

Rosser ML. 2006. *The political economy of the resource curse: a literature survey.* Work. Pap. 268, IDS

Sachs JD, Warner AM. 1997. *Natural resource abundance and economic growth*. Work. Pap. 5398, NBER

Sachs JD, Warner AM. 2001. The curse of natural resources. *Eur. Econ. Rev.* 45:827–38

Sala-i-Martin X, Subramanian A. 2003. *Addressing the natural resource curse: an illustration from Nigeria*. Work. Pap. 9804, NBER

Sandbu M. 2006. Natural wealth accounts: a proposal for alleviating the natural resource curse. *World Dev.* 34(7):1153–70

Sokoloff KL, Engerman SL. 2000. Institutions, factor endowments and paths of development in the New World. *J. Econ. Perspect.* 14:217–32

Stijns J. 2002. *Natural resource abundance and economic growth revisited*. Mimeogr., Dep. Econ., Univ. Calif. Berkeley

Tan G. 1983. Export instability, export growth and GDP growth. *J. Dev. Econ.* 12:219–27

Tornell A, Lane P. 1999. The voracity effect. *Am. Econ. Rev.* 89:22–46

Torvik R. 2002. Natural resources, rent seeking and welfare. *J. Dev. Econ.* 67:455–70

United Nations General Assembly. 2006. *The role of diamonds in fuelling conflict: breaking the link between the illicit transaction of rough diamonds and armed conflict as a contribution to prevention and settlement of conflicts*. Work. Pap., United Nations

van Wijnbergen S. 1984. The "Dutch disease": a disease after all? *Econ. J.* 94:41–55

Wick K. 2008. Conflict and production: an application to natural resources. *B.E. J. Econ. Anal. Policy* 8(1): artic. 2

Wick K, Bulte EH. 2006. Contesting resources—rent seeking, conflict and the natural resource curse. *Public Choice* 128(3):457–76

Williamson OE. 2000. The new institutional economics: taking stock, looking ahead. *J. Econ. Lit.* 38(3):595–613

Experiments in Environment and Development

Juan Camilo Cárdenas

Facultad de Economía, CEDE, Universidad de los Andes, Bogota, Colombia;
email: jccarden@uniandes.edu.co

Annu. Rev. Resour. Econ. 2009. 1:157–82

First published online as a Review in Advance on July 9, 2009

The *Annual Review of Resource Economics* is online at resource.annualreviews.org

This article's doi:
10.1146/annurev.resource.050708.144056

Key Terms

field experiments, development economics, environmental economics, resource economics

Abstract

Many of the main scientific challenges in the fields of development, environment, and resource economics have a microeconomic foundation wherein behavioral elements play a significant role. Preferences with respect to risk, time, societal others, and the environment shape the decision-making processes of individuals. Economic experiments have been extensively carried out in the lab and in the field to test the predictions of behavioral theories; some have had a particular focus on development and environmental issues. Random interventions have also proven to be an important source of information with respect to experimentation in development and policy design. This article identifies the contributions of experiments and random interventions and reflects on the value of having a productive dialogue—in connection with said experiments—with the main stakeholders regarding the problems being studied.

Wherever experimental science is done, young men and women are learning to build instruments, using the new materials and new concepts that science has made available. And then, the crafts that were nurtured in the laboratory find uses in the world outside. We remain tool-making animals, and science will continue to exercise the creativity programmed into our genes.

Freeman J. Dyson, *Science*, 15 May 1998, 280(5366):1014–15

1. MOTIVATIONS

The decision-making processes aimed at optimizing one's well-being will most likely affect and be affected by the environment, place of residency (whether a town or village), or both. Such decisions will be not only constrained by budget considerations, but also determined by the information available, similar to the way behavioral biases in humans have evolved over generations. These biases may include particular nonmonetary motivations with respect to other people, future generations, or the environment. Individuals' decisions may also be mediated by a myopic view of the long-run consequences of their actions or by certain biases against risk, loss, or ambiguity. At the same time, the examples set by others or the beliefs individuals have about others will also likely guide individuals' decisions. Over the long run, the level of development attained as well as the state of the environment will be the result of the aggregation of all these behavioral traits and choices. The manner in which individuals value choices and decide among them has been a focus of research in the social and behavioral sciences for decades. The use of experimental methods for exploring the behavioral components of human interaction, the well-being of humans, as well as their environment has greatly enabled addressing these questions.

Some major issues, including those relating to the promotion of growth and well-being as well as the preservation of ecosystems in order to achieve a more sustainable pattern of development, remain and have generated serious academic debate in the field of economics. These issues are concerned primarily with the search for an adequate balance between sustaining consumption and preserving natural capital (Arrow et al. 2004). Average growth coincides with persistent or increasing levels and types of global inequalities. The lack of stable access to basic nutrition, health, education, housing, water, land, and credit continues to affect a large proportion of the 5 billion people who make up the so-called developing world. Meanwhile, global and local environmental problems continue to pose both current and future threats to the rich and poor alike, whether from global warming, the polluting of village water springs, the depletion of global fisheries, or the exhaustion of the main income and nutrition sources of small communities situated in and dependent on mangrove forests. Biodiversity remains a puzzling challenge as, over the short run, it correlates quite strongly with the supply of goods and services for the poor. With respect to many societies, biological diversity is also strongly linked with cultural diversity and, consequently, faces potential losses; the most significant threat may be the extinction of a great number of species owing to human activity.

The challenges are immense: The focus of recent *World Development Reports* (World Bank 2001, 2003, 2006, 2008, 2010) are indicative of the challenges that may guide those interested in where biological and cultural diversity intersect. The current trends that motivated the eight Millennium Development Goals (**http://www.un.org/millennium goals/**) and their 18 targets are also indicative of the challenges ahead with respect to development and the sustainable use of ecosystems. Fortunately, the fields of natural resource, environmental, and development economics are up to the task. All three disciplines have not been indifferent to these issues. Furthermore, they have embraced the experimental approach of science and, over the past several decades, have contributed greatly to the enrichment of relevant tools, theories, models, and policy recommendations. Many of the problems mentioned above have a microeconomic and behavioral foundation; therefore, they suggest challenges suitable to the behavioral and experimental tools used in the profession. The recent laboratory approach to economics has allowed researchers to focus on testing different theories—whereby some are rejected and others are polished—so as to create the necessary conditions for inventing new models of economic behavior, designing markets and regulatory institutions, and achieving a better understanding of self-governance.

An overview of several works collected for this article suggests that today we know much more about the patterns of behavior, the micromotives of key actors with respect to the environment, and some of the main issues related to development. This paper does not aim to survey the above-noted fields, as others have already done this: See recent works by Sturm & Weimann (2006), Ehmke & Shogren (2009), and Cárdenas & Carpenter (2008) for reviews of the recent academic work by experimentalists addressing research questions related to environmental and development economics.[1] In addition, Harrison (2006) reviewed the literature on laboratory experiments aimed at addressing criticisms related to hypothetical bias in the stated and revealed preferences of approaches that emphasize environmental valuation [also see his work with Neill et al. (1994) concerning the early debates]. Murphy & Stevens (2004) likewise evaluated the use of experiments to correct for problems of hypothetical bias in contingent valuation studies, and they called for the study of the reasons underlying such bias. Readers should also look at a meta-analysis conducted by List & Gallet (2001), which addresses the issue of hypothetical versus experimental valuations of environmental goods and shows an increase in the use of experimental methods for studying environmental and resource economics questions. In fact, the literature on the use of experiments to address problems of hypothetical bias goes back at least two decades, to when direct and indirect valuation techniques were experiencing a boom. The handbook chapter by Shogren (2005), dealing with how experiments have addressed the challenges of environmental valuation, considers the test of rationality in environmental choices, the particular problem of estimating the value of environmental goods, and the challenge of designing incentives dependent on the elicitation method. As noted by Shogren (2005), since the 1980s several authors began calling attention to experimentation as something complementary to nonmarket valuation exercises, which were fashionable at the time. Turning to natural resource management, Ostrom (2006) surveyed the value of conducting laboratory and field experiments vis à vis the study of common-pool resources and the so-called tragedy of the commons. Experimentation has confirmed what ethnographic studies had already discovered—that through cooperation, humans may be able to escape the tragedy trap.

Several works provide a compilation of the research (which continues to thrive) using field experimentation in economics (e.g., Harrison & List 2004, Levitt & List 2007) and examining the role of experiments and randomization in development economics

---

[1]Oosterbeek et al. (2004) also conducted a meta-analysis of ultimatum game results from around the world, although their focus is not on developmental or environmental questions. For our purposes, the value of their analysis is derived from the sample that includes several developing nations.

(e.g., Banerjee & Duflo 2009) as well as the application of field experiments with respect to environmental (e.g., Sturm & Weimann 2006) and developmental (e.g., Cárdenas & Carpenter 2008) issues.

Replications of experiments on social preferences in both the industrialized and developing worlds suggest that humans manifest robust patterns of prosociality with respect to altruism, fairness, reciprocity, and a willingness to cooperate with others as well as a propensity for social punishment even at a personal cost. Such findings are not new in the development economics literature or in the overall economics discipline. The notion of sympathy has its earliest and clearest defender in Adam Smith. Further augmenting the field of development economics is the work on altruism by Stark (1999), which focuses on how altruism affects intergenerational transfers within families or groups in terms of the willingness of families to make sacrifices in order to raise and educate their children as well as on decisions related to migration and the sending of remittances. Also important is Stark's (1996) work on modeling the manner in which altruistic behavior might evolve.

In addition, cross-country comparisons and meta-analysis suggest that some cultural factors shift entire groups around observed means, indicating that context does matter. See Hermann et al. (2008) for a recent study on urban dwellers in 16 cities across several continents, and Marlowe et al. (2008) and Henrich et al. (2006) for new evidence regarding small-scale societies around the world. Variations in the lab and in controlled experiments in the field have also shown that humans respond to framing, context, the attributes of others, the experimenter's effects, and several additional factors that may shift prosocial behavior.

Besides including social preferences within analysis, other patterns of observed behavior in experiments also need to be mentioned. With regard to time and risk, a convergence of findings seems to suggest that, on average, individuals are moderately risk averse, although sufficiently high variation exists such that, with respect to any given individual, psychological traits need to be taken into account. Based on both lab and field experiments, the simplest case, which is well documented, indicates that women are less risk tolerant than men. This finding has implications for the design of microfinance institutions and products.

After identifying the modest but steady rise of experimental studies in agricultural and resource journals, Fisher et al. (1993) introduced the question of whether policy makers should pay attention to experiments. A decade and a half later, Venkatachalam (2008) suggested that mainstream policy analysis and design are still based on a behavioral model that ignores much of the knowledge accumulated by behavioralists and experimentalists. Gintis (2000a) reviewed a few decision-making scenarios in which the interaction between humans and the environment would be better understood if examined through a behavioral lens. These include scenarios of "games against nature," where time inconsistencies and time discounting, risk and uncertainty, loss aversion, and status-quo biases are all of obvious relevance to environmental outcomes. With regard to strategic interactions, Gintis (2000a) also highlighted well-known bargaining games used to measure fairness (e.g., ultimatum games) as well as games reflective of social dilemmas (such as public goods and common-pool resource games) and games confirming the argument that individuals do, in fact, incorporate other-regarding preferences into their decision making. These strategic games have found several applications to the problems of development and the environment, and they have inspired framed and artifactual experiments.

These authors' concerns do not, however, imply that researchers have ignored behavioral approaches to the problems of rationality in development and environmental models. With Adam Smith as the first behavioral economist (Ashraf et al. 2005), we have a long history of incorporating phenomena such as sympathy into the scientific study of economic behavior and without the indifference associated with the fields of development or environmental economics. The issue of omission is valid, however, in terms of the construction of public policies, incentives, and programs for which much less consideration has been taken toward design, implementation, or evaluation. In the developing world, many incentives such as those for payments for environmental services, taxes, and subsidies continue to assume a rational agent with self-oriented preferences and an essentially perfect capacity for the calculations of probability over uncertain outcomes and discounting of costs and benefits over time.

Nonetheless, the use of experimentation is not free of criticism. Responding to the problem of external validity (Loewenstein 1999; Loomes, 1999a, 1999b), more experimental economists have left the campus lab to recruit people from nonstudent subject pools (see, for instance, Carpenter et al. 2005, Harrison & List 2004). Early pioneers include Peter Bohm (see Dufwenberg & Harrison 2008) and Hans Binswanger (1980, 1981), who carried out their experiments several decades ago. Then, in the mid-1990s, there was a surge in experimentation on small-scale societies that specifically targeted either development or natural resource issues. This included a series of doctoral dissertations (including those by Abigail Barr in Zimbabwe, Joe Henrich in South America, and myself in Colombia) that involved traveling to rural areas and conducting canonical games of fairness, altruism, and cooperation with local villagers.

In this article, I focus on certain particularities evident in development and environmental problems and discuss how they pose challenges yet also present opportunities for the innovative use of experimental tools to understand better the interaction among behavior, institutions, and ecosystems. Furthermore, although certain crucial components of these interactions have been the focus of experimental research over the past several decades, there remain areas of promising and urgent research that have not been fully explored.

Given the rich literature mentioned above, this article proposes a set of questions and discussions, both of which have emerged from observations made in connection with field experiments conducted with villagers during the past several decades. These villagers are confronting the very problems being targeted in the above-noted economics fields. As such, their experience is relevant to scholars interested in bringing about social change through experimentation and institutional design.

This article also aims to establish a productive dialogue between lab and field experimentation, in particular between random interventions and field experiments.[2] The strategy of randomization in development economics has a long tradition and has recently seen a rise in popularity (Duflo 2005), a development likely influenced by the revival of the microeconomic approach in development economics. Banerjee & Duflo (2009) reported that there are 67 ongoing randomized evaluations in Africa alone.

---

[2]The issue of terminology will also have to be addressed eventually, as some leading authors (see Banerjee & Duflo 2009) use random interventions to mean field experiments. Thus, under the typology used by Harrison & List (2004) and Levitt & List (2007), these random interventions would be considered as either framed field, natural field, or natural experiments.

The importance of these behavioral foundations is clearly stated by Bardhan & Udry (1999, p. 5): "Development economics is full of examples of apparently irrational behavior that may be successfully explained as an outcome of more complex exercises in rationality, particularly with deeper probes into the nature of the feasibility constraints or the preference patterns." The invitation to consider carefully the conditions under which institutions and behavior interact within contemporary developing contexts is also stressed by Stiglitz (1991, p. 27): "[M]odels focusing on fully informed rational peasants working within 'rational' and efficient institutions are likely to be not only inadequate, but seriously misleading, just as models that simply hypothesize that peasants are rule (tradition)-bound, irrational, and non-economic are almost certainly misleading. Peasants are rational, but they are not fully informed. And imperfect information (as well as a variety of other transaction costs), besides limiting the effective degree of competition, creates institutional rigidities, allowing the persistence of seemingly inefficient institutions."

Progress has also been made within the area of behavioral game theory (Gintis 2000b, Camerer 2003, Bowles 2004), with the development of models that incorporate particular elements of preference and choice with respect to time, risk, uncertainty, society, fairness, social norms, and the environment, to name just a few. The experimental lab has provided a rich setting to test the hypotheses of most of these theoretical developments; this has allowed new models of behavior with refutable hypotheses to be proposed.

With a solid array of experiments, a more robust experience enabling the replication of lab experiments in the field, and improved behavioral models, there are greater possibilities for a productive exchange between lab and field researchers of findings that address developmental and environmental issues. The realization of this potentiality is not entirely new. Banerjee & Duflo (2009) mentioned the value of establishing a rich exchange between economists and the nongovernmental organizations (NGOs) and state agencies with which they work, and they evaluated the risks associated with the selection of partners in random interventions, particularly when scaling-up programs. Levitt & List (2007), likewise, proposed a new generation of field experiments with private partners interested in focusing on untapped areas of industrial organization, areas where experimentation could answer some of the key questions confronting academia as well as respective industries.

It is interesting to note that both Banerjee & Duflo (2009) and Levitt & List (2007) found agreement on a number of points. Both noted that those conducting experiments would benefit greatly from teaming up with key partners in the field, including private, state, and NGO stakeholders. Both also agreed that, by maintaining a close link with theory, experimentation will continue to make a productive contribution to science, so long as randomization remains one of its fundamentals. Finally, both noted the importance of ethical issues in experimentation, although Levitt & List (2007) stressed this more explicitly.

2. QUESTIONS TO GUIDE EXPERIMENTAL RESEARCH

The questions driving the scientific community in the development and environmental fields of economics are constantly evolving; at the same time, they continue to encompass many of the same essential components that have informed the discipline from the start. Creating growth, augmenting quality of life of households, reducing inequality and the social losses caused by the negative externalities of public goods, and resolving the tragedies of the commons have all been central to these fields and the

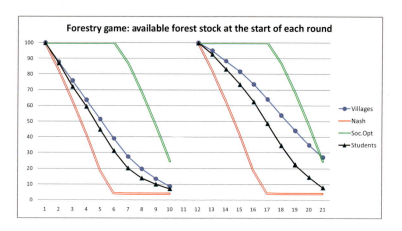

Figure 1

Depiction of forestry game in which five players exploit a forest with an initial stock of 100 trees: Results are shown for first 10 rounds (*left panel*) and second 10 rounds (*right panel*), i.e., under the new set of rules. The panels also provide the Nash and social optimal benchmarks for comparison.

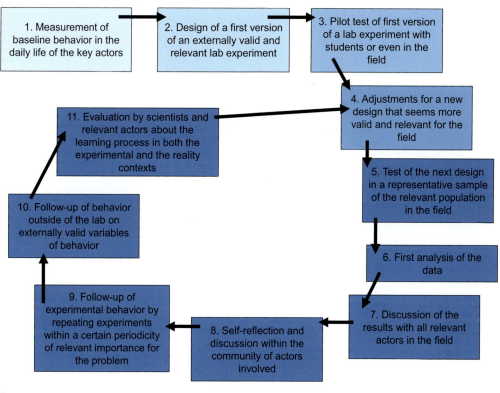

Figure 3

Sequence of steps possible to carry an iterative experiment between the lab and the field.

discipline as a whole for much of its existence. What fraction of proposed solutions is market based, state based, or derived from self-governed institutions has also been an essential concern. I focus on some of the challenges evident in these fields today and discuss where the behavioral sciences and experimentation may provide some answers. A list of suggested issues is presented in **Table 1**, with the purpose of connecting questions to possible experimental designs in the areas of development and environmental economics.

The items noted in **Table 1** are by no means exhaustive. However, they represent cases that have high potential in terms of formulating relevant questions that have important behavioral aspects and that are potentially interesting and feasible with respect to possible experimental designs. Furthermore, some of these issues correspond to areas of common interest with respect to both development and environmental economics, areas where behavioral models and experimental techniques seem to coincide in a useful way. These include the determinants of extreme poverty, the provision of public goods, the sustainability of common-pool resources at the local level, and the behavioral aspects of ecosystems conservation. A vast fraction of the developing world currently faces these problems on a regular (even daily) basis, particularly at a micro level (in households, neighborhoods, and villages). Associated with these problems are several behavioral components of economic decision making, including preferences with regard to time, risk, and the environment (see column 2 in **Table 1**). As indicated by the references noted in **Table 1**, several experimental designs have been widely used for measuring behavior as well as responses to changes in the experimental conditions or context.

Some of these issues occasionally overlap and become combined in experimental studies. One example is the problem of technological change and the adoption of sustainable practices, which usually involves risk, but is also reflective of preferences toward others and the environment (see Engle-Warnick et al. 2007). In addition, **Table 1** and the corresponding footnotes identify a series of experimental studies with such a question and design in mind. These works are by no means exhaustive, but they provide a reference to a reader interested in looking at more specific experiments and results, many of them in the contexts of development, natural resources, or the environment.

A valuable exercise is to identify the current context and conditions for the poor, i.e., the focus of this article. Banerjee & Duflo (2007, 2009) compiled a set of findings describing the context in which the poor live; if we wish to understand the behavioral aspects of being poor—in terms of trying to get out of poverty and the constraints related to it—such a description must inform our experimental designs, in both the lab and the field. According to these authors, the poor live in households consisting of large numbers of family members, usually including several children. These households spend a substantial portion (though not all) of their income on food, and thus they suffer in a significant way the consequences of rising food prices in the market place. They also spend a portion of their income on goods and services in ways reflective of cultural values and social norms (e.g., on alcohol, tobacco, festivities, funerals, weddings, etc.).

Given these findings, the reader can begin to see how prosocial behavior among the poor is related to kin versus nonkin transfers with respect to food sharing and safety nets and how research may include variations on experiments about sharing and

Table 1 Questions, behavioral aspects, and experimental strategies[a]

Issues in development and the environment	Preferences involved	Trade-offs and interesting questions	Experimental designs from the field and the lab
• Risk exposure, risk aversion, and poverty	• Risk aversion, ambiguity aversion, loss aversion	• Risk versus higher returns • Technology adoption	• Lotteries, varying variance, and expected returns[b]
• Time discounting, saving rates, pensions	• Time preferences • Life-cycle decisions	• Consumption today versus consumption tomorrow	• Payments spaced in time[c]
• Prosociality toward others today (fairness, inequality) • Prosociality toward kin in the future • Prosociality toward nonkin in the future	• Other-regarding preferences (altruism, fairness, inequality aversion) • Time preferences	• My consumption today versus sharing with kin today • My consumption today versus sharing with others today • My consumption today versus saving for kin tomorrow	Social preferences: • Altruism (DG, UG)[d] • Reciprocity and trust (UG, TG, gift exchange)[e] • Cooperation (PD, CPR, VCM)[f] • Third-party punishment[g]
• Protection of the environment	• Ecological preferences • Time preferences • Other-regarding preferences	• Consumption today versus resource exhaustion tomorrow • Consumption today versus extinction tomorrow • Protecting today versus consumption of others (next generations) tomorrow	• WTA/WTP (hypothetical, experimental) offers[h] • Donations to environmental protection programs and charities • Ecological or environmental intrinsic values[i] • Common-pool resource and public-goods games[f]
• Environmental institutions and mechanisms	.	• Market- versus state- versus community-based management of the local and global commons	• Market-based institutions (ITQs, fees, quotas, command and control)[j] • CPR games, VCM games[f]
• Market-based growth through competition, specialization and access to credit and microfinance	• Entrepreneurship • Other-regarding preferences • Risk aversion	• Cooperation versus competition (complementary? conflicting?) • Innovation versus risk for the uninsured • Adaptive (resilient) multitasking versus specialization	• Market behavior (double auction, posted offers, etc.)[k]
• Provision of public goods, regulation, and corruption (education, health, security, recreation, etc.)	• Other-regarding preferences	• Market- versus state- versus community-based provision of local public goods • Rule of law, compliance, rent-seeking	• CPR games, VCM games[f] • Endogenous versus external regulations[l] • Corruption[m]

(Continued)

Table 1 (*Continued*)

Issues in development and the environment	Preferences involved	Trade-offs and interesting questions	Experimental designs from the field and the lab
• Self-government and social networks	• Other-regarding preferences • Risk preferences	• Private versus state versus communal insurance over risks	• (Lotteries) risk and risk-pooling games[b] • Existing and controlled social networks experiments in combination with social preferences experiments[n]

[a]Abbreviations: CPR, common-pool resources; DG, dictator game; ITQ, individual transferable quota; PD, prisoner's dilemma; TG, trust game; UG, utility game; VCM, voluntary contributions mechanism; WTA, willingness to accept; WTP, willingness to pay.

[b]Binswanger (1980, 1981), Barr (2003b), Engle-Warnick & Laszlo (2006), Engle-Warnick et al. (2007), Harrison et al. (2005).

[c]Harrison et al. (2002), Kirby et al. (2002).

[d]Ashraf et al. (2005), Barr et al. (2009), Bettinger & Slonim (2006), Carpenter et al. (2005), Gowdy et al. (2003), Henrich et al. (2006), Holm & Danielson (2005), Marlowe et al. (2008).

[e]Ashraf et al. (2005, 2006a, 2006b), Berg et al. (1995), Bohnet & Zeckhauser (2004), Bouma et al. (2008), Buchan et al. (2003), Burks et al. (2003), Cassar et al. (2007), Chong et al. (2008), Danielson & Holm (2007), Fong (2007), Fong & Luttmer (2009), Gurven (2004), Johanson-Stenman et al. (2004), Holm & Danielson (2005), Ñopo et al. (2008), Lazzarini et al. (2004), Rodriguez et al. (2008).

[f]Alpizar et al. (2008a, 2008b), Barr (2003), Cárdenas (2003), Cárdenas et al. (2000, 2002), Cárdenas & Carpenter (2005), Cárdenas & Ostrom (2004), Carpenter & Seki (2006), Carpenter et al. (2004), Chong et al. (2008), Cooper et al. (1996), Gaechter et al. (2004), Herrmann et al. (2008), Ibañez & Carlsson (2009), Karlan (2005), Lopez et al. (2009), Ñopo et al. (2008), Osés-Erasoa & Viladrich-Grau (2007), Rodriguez et al. (2006), Rondeau et al. (2005), Tyson et al. (1998), Velez et al. (2006), Vyrastekova & van Soest (2003).

[g]Marlowe et al. (2008).

[h]List & Gallet (2001), Knetsch & Sinden (1984), Knetsch (1989), Harrison (2006), Shogren (2005), Sturm & Weimann (2006).

[i]Boyce et al. (1992), Casey et al. (2008), Jack (2008), Jack et al. (2009), Marette et al. (2008), Sandhua et al. (2008), Vollan (2008).

[j]Murphy & Stranlund (2007).

[k]Capra et al. (2009), Jack (2008).

[l]Fiore et al. (2009).

[m]Alatas et al. (2006), Barr et al. (2004).

[n]Leider et al. (2009), Cárdenas & Jaramillo (2007).

altruism where transfers among kin may be substantially higher than in other nonpoor groups.[3] The intrahousehold dynamics of bargaining and sharing, and the gender biases that may mediate between such processes and social exchanges outside the household, create an increasingly complicated setting with respect to consumption optimization among the poor than has been fully explored till now in the laboratory. Sharing among nonkin remains an important source of income among the rural and urban poor, not only in developing countries but also in industrialized countries such as the United States. Haider & McGarry (2006) studied resource sharing among the poor in the Untied States, and on the basis of their results, they concluded that "while transfers respond significantly to macroeconomic conditions, there has also been a steady increase in shared living arrangements that is unexplained by macroeconomic and demographic changes. We

---

[3]The data reported by Banerjee & Duflo (2009) do not include nonmonetary transfers to neighbors and members of extended families. This is an important component of calories entering and exiting the household among many poor rural and urban groups. Its measurement is much more difficult, but it is of utmost importance to the understanding of survival strategies.

hypothesize that these changes may be due to changes in attitudes and social norms." They found that a substantial part of these private transfers occur within shared residency settings and among less-educated women. In other studies, anthropologists have looked at sharing among indigenous groups and in some cases compared their findings with the results from experimental tests about prosocial behavior in these societies (Gurven et al. 2000, Gurven 2004).

Land ownership among the poor continues to be very common, although much variation exists across and within countries explaining inequality as well as constraints to access to other markets such as credit. Apart from land, the poor own few durable assets, and in both rural and urban areas, they lack formal property rights that could facilitate entering formal markets of credit. Their low levels of food consumption, although not necessarily constrained by income (see Banerjee & Duflo 2009), affect health and health expenditure in various ways. The expenditure on education is small, but this is mostly explained by the access the poor have in developing nations to publicly provided and/or free education. Many among the poor are also small-scale entrepreneurs, engaging in a variety of activities. In fact, agriculture is no longer the main occupation for many of the poor around the world, although land cultivation remains important.

The formal and informal participation of the poor in the financial sector has been the focus of a more active research agenda using behavioral and experimental approaches and is not described here in detail (see, for instance, Siwan & Baland 2002, Karlan 2005, Ashraf et al. 2006b).

Many of the more vulnerable groups in the developing world use local commons directly or indirectly, and there exists frequent interactions related to the extraction and use of resources and other environmental services derived from local ecosystems. Ostrom et al. (2007) reported that approximately 100,000 areas around the globe are under some kind of authority or environmental protection institution. Some areas are designated as state property and are thus under state management, others are probably part of private or NGO initiatives, and yet others are most likely communally owned. Each of these local ecosystems is subject to the essential problems motivating this article—they are most likely subject to rural poverty, with weak or only partially effective formal regulatory institutions. Moreover, respective inhabitants (those living within and/or around these areas) are generally highly dependent on the ecosystems' resources. Long-run and short-run needs face serious trade-offs, and collective action is probably a major issue within those communities. Social networks—the reciprocity and sharing of norms—are likely an important part of the daily life of these communities. Risk and uncertainty pose significant challenges for those who are uninsured and engage in agricultural or nonagricultural activities to complement their regular income. However, it is very likely that these same households interact with market and state institutions in several ways. These issues are the components of behavioral questions that have motivated the work of experimentalists from the very beginning.

3. A FORESTRY FIELD EXPERIMENT IN THAILAND AND COLOMBIA: AN EXAMPLE WITH UNEXPECTED RESULTS

To illustrate the above points, I now discuss a specific example of a simple experimental design together with a field and lab test featuring participants in Thailand and Colombia (Cárdenas et al. 2009). In this forestry game, five players exploit a forest with an initial stock of 100 trees. During each round, the forest can grow at a rate of 10%, that is, for each 10 standing trees, one more tree might grow; altogether, the forest can grow up to 100 trees. During each round of the first stage, a player can cut up to 5 trees. If the stock falls below 25 trees, the maximum trees allowed to each player decreases monotonically such that the group maximum does not exceed the total number of trees available. Decisions are made in private and are kept confidential, and during each round, only the total group extraction is announced. The first stage consists of a maximum of 10 rounds with no communication allowed among the five players. A second stage of 10 rounds follows, with a renewed forest of 100 trees. Participants face a set of new rules on which they may vote; all possibilities are aimed at maximizing group earnings. At the end of the two stages (20 rounds in total), the number of trees cut by each player is calculated, and the related amount in cash is paid out in private. The trees that remain standing in the forest at the end of either stage have no monetary value for the players.

During the first stage, each player should extract the maximum number of trees allowed for each round. Assuming that in every round 25 trees will be cut, the forest should be wiped out by the sixth round. Under this Nash strategy, the group would amass a total of 119 trees. A socially efficient sustainable path of extraction should postpone exhaustion of the forest until the tenth round of that stage, thus maximizing the group's earnings over 10 rounds, at 166 trees. In either case, the final forest stock will be zero trees, given that at the end of the tenth round any remaining trees have no value to the players.

Figure 1 (see color insert) presents the data for the 24 sessions of the game played out in six villages, and the 8 sessions run with students in the two countries for a total of 160 participants. As we expected on the basis of the previous field and lab literature, the players approach neither the pure Nash equilibrium of self-interested maximizers, nor the socially optimal solution. Additionally, we observe a significant difference in the forest stocks between students and villagers (Wilcoxon rank-sum p-value = 0.0083); the difference is even greater during the second stage.

What we did not expect was that the players, particularly the villagers, would leave trees standing as of the end of the game, given that the trees had no monetary value after the completion of the tenth round. We need to consider only the data for those cases where trees remained standing at the end of a stage (that is, after round 10 or round 20) and where the maximum allowed was a positive number. This happened at the end of the first stage in 50% of the village sessions and in 25% of the student ones. In the rest of the sessions, the forest was exhausted prior to the tenth round. Meanwhile, the number of sessions with an available stock of trees at the beginning of the tenth round during the second stage was 80% for the villages and only 37.5% for the students. Recall that for both stages, any trees left standing in the forest during the final round yielded no income to the players unless they were extracted. On average, these villager subsamples had an available stock of 14.75 trees by round 10 and 33.6 available trees by round 20; in the first case, they extracted 6 trees, and in the second, 10 trees, thus leaving on average 8.8 and 23.5 trees standing, respectively (p-value = 0.005 and 0.0003, respectively). In the students case, the difference between the initial stock and the number of trees extracted is not statistically significant for the tenth round (p-value = 0.1974) and only significant at the 10% level for round 20 (p-value = 0.0617). Clearly, the participants—particularly the villagers—were leaving money on the table. Furthermore, under the new set of rules imposed during the second stage, the number of trees remaining following final round extraction was greater than during the first stage! The question is, Why were the participants not getting those earnings? Altruistic motivations cannot be argued as the earnings do not go to anyone.

A series of interviews and a follow-up workshop in each of the six villages in the two countries allowed us to interpret this behavior. Our first concern was that the design may not have been properly understood and that the trees were not extracted owing to error. Our field participants explained this behavior by linking it to the symbolic value of the standing trees and the forest as a whole. Phrases like "one should not extract the last trees, there will be children and grandchildren who could use them" and "one should always leave part of the forest for others" were very frequent, and they reflected common practice in the field, even under open or joint access to forests. One could argue that, in actual forests, the marginal cost of cutting the remaining trees would not be compensated by the income from its extraction and sale. Yet in our experimental design, we included no marginal cost for cutting units.

This opens a series of questions that deserve further inquiry. It seems that the intrinsic value of leaving behind those last trees was greater than the opportunity cost of not cutting them—i.e., the foregone income—even though these were not actual trees, but rather just magnets on a board. Nevertheless, this valuation of standing trees does not necessarily carry backward to previous rounds, where we observed players extracting the maximum quota allowed more frequently. This finding teaches us some lessons. First, the comparison of students against villagers using the same design and incentives allowed us to detect a possible nonextraction value that was not as salient in the lab data featuring only students. Second, the interviews and the workshop later conducted in the villages allowed us to confirm that such valuation of trees left standing had a symbolic meaning, one associated with the nonuse values of forests. Most likely, this was driven by the loose frame of our design; nonetheless, it tells us something about the villagers' broader perception of forests.

In a next design, we should test the effects of incorporating payoffs from trees left standing (e.g., conservation values) and of increasing marginal costs of extraction on the level of degradation. We should also test framing effects by trying the same design with no reference to trees and a forest, but rather as an abstract pool of tokens that can be taken or left behind. These experiments suggest that people in the field are resistant to the simplification of the logging value of forests and thus instinctively incorporate other values that are inseparable from them.

Such an understanding is evident in the study of biodiversity conservation and its attendant challenges. In a recent exercise (Sutherland et al. 2009), a group of 12 academics, 21 international organizations, and more than 700 individuals selected 100 key questions representative of the challenges involved in the conservation of the world's biodiversity. Among the academics, only one economist was invited to join the team for the final selection. Nevertheless, many of the questions had a direct link to the understanding of behavior and the functioning of economic systems. Assuming that these questions are welcomed as relevant, at least eight of them could inspire the design of experiments that adapt currently available designs to help us find answers. The questions are as follows:

- What factors affect the extent to which practitioners integrate consideration of human needs and preferences into policy and practice?
- What are the biodiversity impacts of changes in energy prices?

- How do tenure systems shape conservation outcomes in different social and ecological contexts?
- How do economic subsidies affect biodiversity within the recipient country and elsewhere?
- How do different values (e.g., use versus preservation) and the framing of these values (e.g., ecosystem services versus species) motivate policy makers to assign public resources to conservation programs and policies?
- What factors shape individual and state compliance with local, national, and international conservation regimes?
- What are the impacts of different conservation incentive programs on biodiversity and human well-being?
- How does providing information to resource users affect individual behavior and support for collective restrictions, and how does the effect vary with different means of providing the information?

Combining a few of these questions, one could envision a large longitudinal study incorporating lab and field experiments and random interventions within several control and treatment communities featuring different types of cultural background and histories of traditional to modern management of forests. Respective villages could be subjected to variations of treatment variables (monetary and nonmonetary incentives) and degrees of information and framing regarding the importance of conservation and trade-offs between preservation and forest resource use. The study should include a longitudinal survey, inclusive of incentivized experiments, in order to capture behavior regarding risk, time, other-regarding, and ecological preferences as well as behavior related to parcels and forests. Changes in attitudes due to the different treatments should also be included. A close collaboration with NGOs and local, regional, or national governments as part of the experimental design would allow the study to capture the role these external actors play in shaping preferences and behavior through the different mechanisms they use (e.g., payment for environmental services, taxes, campaigns, tenure changes, etc.).

4. THE CHALLENGES AHEAD AND A PROPOSAL: WORKSHOP EXPERIMENTS

To realistically define areas of promising research, one needs to establish a research strategy that is compatible with the problems under study, in this case the relationship between development and the environment. In building such a strategy, we cannot ignore the possibility of a permanent tension between generalization and specificity. Likewise, the debate over the utility of using panaceas for addressing environmental problems must be addressed.[4]

As Ostrom et al. (2007) put it:

> Advocates of panaceas make two false assumptions: (i) all problems, whether they are different challenges within a single resource system or across a diverse set of resources, are similar enough to be represented by a small class of formal models; and (ii) the set of preferences, the possible roles of

---

[4]Currently, the scientific community dealing with fisheries is engaged in a heated debate over the worldwide potential of using individual tradable quota mechanisms to regulate stocks in a sustainable manner.

information, and individual perceptions and reactions are assumed to be the same as those found in developed Western market economies ... Large studies of land-use and land-cover change have not found evidence for any single, ever-present driver of change. Experimental and field research has consistently found that individuals overtly facing the same situation vary substantially in their behavior. As Ackoff ... has reflected, "panacea proneness is a diluted form of fundamentalism rather than a method of serious diagnosis."

4.1. The Need for Iterations Among Models, Experiments, and Reality

A natural way for experimentalists to think about experiments is to test theory and models against reality or to enrich, even debunk and recreate, theory so that it fits and serves reality better. Theory may also inspire experimental testing to verify its internal validity, but once again, it must ultimately pass the external validity test. In **Figure 2**, I put these iterations and several more in a simple graphical model to set the framework for the following discussion. The same argument holds for policy design and testing. Ostrom (2007) warned against applying the unique prescription policy solution to the problems of complex socioecological systems. Instead, iterations between policy makers, analysis, and the stakeholders on the ground may provide an environment for tailoring solutions to the specifics of the socioecological system.

Well-known iterations in experimental economics include the design and study of the double-auction mechanism in competitive markets by Vernon Smith (2003) and the work of Alvin Roth (2002) in matching markets. Such productive dialogue (iterations A-D) between theory and experiments has enriched the sophistication of the competitive market and the matching models, the test of their robustness, and the need or lack thereof for certain assumptions to hold. Furthermore, such iterations have led to rich exchange with reality (iterations F-C and B-E) in areas of auction design; government auctions of spectra; design of electricity, gas, and water markets; and matching markets for public education, judges, doctors, or exchange of kidneys. Smith (2003) and Roth (2002) have made the model-experiment interactions in our framework contribute to reality. They also have been acute observers of reality to enrich their research and theories. In that manner, they both epitomize the role of the economics designer/engineer.

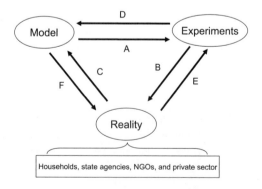

Figure 2

Schematic demonstrating the relationship between theoretical models, experiments, and reality.

Such iterations are of prime interest to those of us concerned with the issues of development and the environment. The rest of this article reflects on such potentials by identifying untapped areas of research and discussing some promising iterations already happening. In the following, the iterations (B-E) between reality and experimentation are emphasized.

There is a great deal of work to be exploited by getting key actors on the ground to participate actively not only as subjects in experiments but also as learners and sources of input to better designs. As more experimenters open dialogues with citizens, communities, NGOs, state agencies, and the private sector, more input about the external validity and applicability of experiments influences the daily action of these actors. Meanwhile, the participation of these actors in the experimental process as subjects, monitors, implementers, or users of the experimental data may open a door for self-reflection and learning that could be harnessed for the development and environmental goals motivating our work.

The involvement of the experimental participants in the research poses an immense puzzle for those interested in experimentation. The dialogue between theory and experimentation (iterations A-D) is heavily justified on the grounds of replication and generalization and given the possibility of building refutable hypotheses from tractable models. In addition, those who have conducted field experiments know the great value of having experimental tools that are adaptable with respect to local context and the particular participants involved. Shogren (2005, p. 976) eloquently described the dilemma:

> [O]ne researcher's gain of control can be another's loss of context ... These researchers argue that it is these confounding factors (e.g., uncontrolled body language sent in face-to-face bargaining) that provide the rich economic context that motivates real-world behavior. They point out that striving for complete control is self-defeating because it creates an economic environment that is too sterile, too abstract, too unreal, with no parallel in the real-world, and therefore generates subjects who are motivated by salient payoffs, but unmotivated by the context in which these payoffs are earned.

The tension between replicability and adaptability in experimental research can be dealt with by moving in the direction of what I refer to here as "workshop" experiments. Such workshop experiments are meant to create an environment where experimenters and ground actors collaborate in order to design, test, redesign, and learn from experiments: This would be accomplished through the adaptive use of research tools to solve each particular problem encountered (e.g., iterations B-E in the original framework presented in **Figure 2**). Throughout the process, analysts should be careful to secure/uphold their scientific foundations by continually referencing theory (iterations A-D), even while being inspired by iterations B-E.

The concept of workshop experimentation proposed here emerges following a decade of conducting field experiments in different rural and urban contexts.[5] Also inspiring this approach is the legacy of the work carried out by key contributors to the development, environmental, and experimental literature—individuals such as Elinor Ostrom, Alvin Roth, and Vernon Smith, who have always maintained a reference point when conducting

---

[5]One particular collaboration with Marco Janssen and Francois Bousquet on a project funded by the National Science Foundation, "The Dynamics of Rules and Commons Dilemmas," also inspired many of the ideas here presented. For more information, see **http://www.public.asu.edu/~majansse/dor/nsfhsd.htm**.

their work using experiments and behavioral models. Vernon Smith and Alvin Roth have also worked with key actors on the ground, including, for instance, regulators or the final users of matching or network markets. As demonstrated by them, moving between the lab and actors on the ground is fruitful for designing better auctions and matching algorithms. Several of these designs are currently being tested in a more "natural" manner in different public domains, albeit in ways not directly related to development and environmental issues.

In addition, a series of new efforts, best exemplified by the Poverty Action Lab at the Massachusetts Institute of Technology and the Innovations for Poverty Action at Yale University, relies on random interventions[6] to address the challenge of poverty reduction. Banerjee & Duflo (2009) documented a part of the experience gained from several of their projects, which allowed for multiple iterations, albeit in various forms. They reported on the different trials used and the incentives piloted in the random interventions. They also reported on how the input from NGOs shaped the project that was finally implemented. Similarly, Levitt & List (2007) drew attention to the value of establishing productive partnerships with those on the ground when designing and testing field experiments. Note, however, that the examples highlighted by them come from the private sector, where the focus was on economic issues related to industrial organization.

The concept of viewing experimental settings as workshops, where artisans deal with each specific problem as a craft science and use existing tools while making or adapting other tools in order to carry out the analysis, is not only based on my own experience in the field; it is also a product of the legacy of Elinor and Vincent Ostrom, who developed their workshop in political theory and policy analysis at Indiana University utilizing a similar analogy (J.C. Cárdenas, personal communication). For years, both worked on a weekly basis in a furniture-making workshop, where they learned the productive value of collaboration, artisanship, and tool making. In the workshop, the carpenter needs to tailor each table and chair to the specific needs of the customer as well as to the availability of materials and tools, while maintaining a generic set of common components and rules of design. Furthermore, in carpentry, just as in the workshop experiments, one needs to be tool maker and adapt the available tools to each new problem. Ostrom (1980) discussed these ideas in the context of science, emphasizing the artisanship necessary to study organizations as artifacts. Humans are both the artisans and the main component of the artifact, namely the organization. As observers and learners, Ostrom (1980) argued, humans have the capacity to transform their own object of study. Recognizing the experimenter's role as artisan and tool maker—while establishing within the workshop a dialogue with other individuals involved in the problem being studied—can lead to a richer environment of reflection, one wherein a better understanding and crafting of superior organizations and institutions may be achieved.

The proposed workshop experiments include a dynamic exchange between scientists and the key actors on the ground. The exchange, represented by iterations B-E in **Figure 2**, could transpire as a cycle of iterations, one that starts with the first lab experiment and is then taken into the field, where it is transformed into a dialogue with the key actors relevant to

---

[6]Levitt & List (2007) identified these as framed field experiments, although their category of natural field experiments also includes certain random interventions, for instance, those where the subjects involved in the intervention do not know that they are part of a random trial.

the question being considered. **Figure 3** (see color insert) shows a suggested sequence of steps, one that would then continue through as many cycles as proves necessary.

4.2. Field Experiments as Pedagogical Tools

The possibility that controlled experiments should become pedagogical tools has been mentioned frequently in the field by actors including NGOs outside of academia. Indeed, the International Potato Center recently published a field practitioners handbook with such a purpose: See **http://www.cipotato.org/publications/publication.asp?cod=003620**.

Business schools worldwide have relied for many years now on simulation games and incentivized experiments to teach students the skills needed to excel in the competitive private sector. Trial and error, careful observation over long periods of time, and iterations over semesters or even years have all provided rich data and valuable experience for the real world of business. With respect to teaching economics, the use of experimentation in the classroom has already been addressed in a few papers, most recently Ball et al. (2006), who showed the net impact on grades of classroom experiments in an economics principles class. In contrast, Dufwenberg & Swarthout (2009) found that participating in an experiment had no effect on learning how to solve game-theoretical problems. Nonetheless, field experiments could provide a platform for group learning with respect to the problems under current discussion.

Supporting the idea that field experiments can have pedagogical value, Cárdenas & Carpenter (2005) reported on a series of experiments about cooperation that was repeated in three Colombian villages approximately one year after a series of common-pool resource experiments was run in those locations. Both previous and new participants were included in the subject pool during the second visit. In both series, the exact same protocols and incentives were used. In the second round, not only were the rates of cooperation substantially higher than those observed in the first round, but a similar pattern of cooperation was also observed between both experienced and fresh subjects. The workshops held after the second visits helped us understand the social learning that had taken place in the village following the completion of the first set of experiments. Furthering our understanding were the pregame agreements that were made between villagers once they became aware that the university team was returning to conduct more economic games.

Which actors are included in the workshop experimental design will depend on the particular case: Possible candidates include state officials, private-sector representatives, NGOs, community leaders, or household representatives. These actors may also be participants in an incentivized experiment. At other times, they may be discussants of the results and/or contributors to the next design in the iteration.

4.3. Innovations in the Field and the Laboratory

In exploring the use of creative experimental design to address environmental and development questions, it may be helpful to discuss some examples of innovative proposals that fit well with the ideas proposed in this article. Below, I mention some of these with the idea that the laboratory, especially if brought to the field and understood as a tool-making workshop, could offer opportunities for studying some of the questions critical to these fields.

4.3.1. Innovation 1: introduce ecological dynamics into the game designs. Most of the current environmental applications of economic experiments involve either one-shot or repeated-round experiments, where no dynamic effects occur within the rounds. Moreno & Maldonado (2008) adapted an existing common-pool resources experimental design allowing for dynamic stock effects within rounds: They permitted the option of payoff structures to be determined in each round by the aggregate impact of extraction during the previous round, while continuing to use a hand-run design with fishermen on the Caribbean coast. Cárdenas et al. (2009) adapted simple common-pool resources designs to three specific natural resources where space and time dynamics are crucial: water/irrigation, forests, and fisheries. In these three games, all of which are based on a payoff structure built around a social dilemma, the particular choices and consequences are related to the specific problem of interest and involve certain types of nonlinearities usually observed in all of the respective ecosystems. For instance, in the forest game, the stock of uncut trees determines the growth of the forest in the next round. Likewise, in the irrigation game, the stage during which water is appropriated or extracted happens in a sequential manner, starting with the upstream players who can decide to leave or not leave water available for those downstream. In the fisheries game, players need to decide where to fish, meaning that they have an impact on the aggregate effort at each of the fishing sites, thus affecting the stock of fish available in the next round.

4.3.2. Innovation 2: use nonmonetary but still salient incentives in the experiment. Often, the context or the conditions in the field make it difficult or undesirable to use cash as the saliency vehicle. Furthermore, incentives or values may not be well represented by cash when there are symbolic values attached to decisions or consequences. One good example, with an effective applicability in the economic valuation of the environment, consists of the experiments reported by Boyce et al. (1992), where actual living trees were set up in front of subjects who received an endowment of cash. The players could use the money to buy or sell the trees that were in front of them. The experimenters also explored the (actual) willingness of these subjects to pay to save the trees, which otherwise would be killed by the experimenters (i.e., if not acquired by the subjects). The authors argued that the moral values associated with these commodities may have played a significant role in determining their findings, thereby explaining the disparities between a willingness to accept and a willingness to pay for an environmental amenity.

Jack (2008) has begun to build a bridge between controlled lab experiments conducted in the field and the random interventions approach in an effort to better design reforestation projects for the International Food Policy Research Institute. Using different types of auctions for tree-planting contracts in Malawi, and inspired by a previous study in Indonesia that explored the provision of soil erosion control, Jack et al. (2009) tested different properties observed in the lab regarding behavior at auctions so as to improve the conditions under which tree-planting contracts among farmers may prove more successful.

In another study, conducted in the Sarayacu (a Kichwa community) in the Ecuadorian Amazon, Sirén and colleagues (Sirén et al. 2006) explored to what extent nonhunting income sources affected hunting in a community that derives most of its income from the latter. They devised a simple lottery that was played out for all volunteers in the community, wherein the volunteers had to choose between receiving a prize in the form of gunpowder or chick nets, representative of hunting versus nonhunting strategies (in terms of the acquisition of animal protein), respectively. The use of highly valued items reflective of preferences for hunted or nonhunted meat allowed the researcher to detect the marginal effect of providing alternative meat options on those with a regular employment activity versus those without it.

In a second study currently under way involving the same community, Sirén is studying the cost of hunting by estimating the economic value of the effort involved in walking long distances and carrying a heavy load (such as is required in hunting) (A.H. Sirén, unpublished results). In this case, the design involves asking all volunteering hunters to indicate the minimum amount of money they would like to receive in order to walk a certain distance to bring back a marked and sealed water bucket located in a certain part of the forest. Each hunter has to respond to several possible combinations, and the following day each hunter has to make the actual trip and bring back the water from one of the randomly selected sites.

4.3.3. Innovation 3: invite relevant actors to be part of your experimental framing and to act as redesigners. The possibility of bringing nonstudent subject pools to the lab, whether on campus or in the field, has been explored by many researchers: Carpenter & Seki (2006) invited Japanese fishermen to explore possibilities related to team work in a very competitive setting. Carpenter and colleagues have also been involved in other studies that focus on the behavioral aspects of certain kinds of workplaces, including those reflective of the work space of truck drivers (Burks etal. 2007). Karlan (2005) conducted experiments about trust with participants in a microfinance program in Peru. Barr et al. (2004) conducted an experimental study of Ethiopian nursing students who usually end up moving to civil service jobs in the health sector. Alatas et al. (2006) worked with Indonesian public servants and a control group of students. Another particular case relevant to poverty issues is the study of prosocial preferences among the most vulnerable groups of society. Fong & Luttmer (2009), for instance, conducted experiments about altruism with victims of Hurricane Katrina. Fong (2007) also conducted experiments on altruism with welfare recipients. In a similar vein, Cárdenas & Sethi (2008) and Cárdenas et al. (2008) reported on experiments involving welfare recipients where those making the decisions regarding the transfers are public officials involved in welfare programs (education, child care, nutrition, health, etc.) in Bogota, Colombia. See also Cárdenas & Carpenter (2008) for several experiments surveyed involving common-pool resource users in Colombia.

The idea in all these experiments is to involve people who are more familiar with the task under study. In addition to being experimental subjects, relevant actors could add to the framing and validity of the design in a number of ways. With respect to natural resource management, Moreno & Maldonado (2008) invited park rangers to participate in experiments aimed at studying the exploitation of fisheries within and outside of a marine national park in Colombia. The park rangers showed up in the middle of the session and had the opportunity to talk with the participants—actual fishermen—about the management of the park and the threat posed by the tragedy of the commons, in this case, the overexploitation of the fisheries at the site.

One could go a step further and explore the possibility of having our experimental participants take part in the redesigning of new experiments, as suggested in **Figure 3** or in iterations B-E in **Figure 2**. In a project, the Dynamics of Rules and Commons Dilemmas, funded by the National Science Foundation (for details, see **http://www.public.asu.edu/~majansse/dor/nsfhsd.htm**), researchers revisited the same villages where the initial set of field experiments were conducted, though only after having shown a first analysis of the results to the former participants and other key local actors. Researchers then invited a group of these stakeholders to work over a two-day period on reinventing the game and to come up with a new experimental design to capture components of reality that were missed in the first design. Such an approach runs the risk of generating new designs that produce games with less tractable solutions or with more variables than desired by the experimenter. Nonetheless, the resultant new design is currently being tested as a pilot in these villages and could be the source of a new generation of experiments within the project, one that, it is hoped, will incorporate components that the participants judged as relevant to understanding their reality better.

4.3.4. Innovation 4: create virtual incentivized worlds for studying economic behavior. To date, at least two initiatives exist that use controlled experiments with monetary incentives and that have a direct application to environmental problems. The first is the above-mentioned project the Dynamics of Rules and Commons Dilemmas, which combines different methodological strategies. One of the experimental designs includes a virtual three-dimensional environment representative of forest extraction, an experimental design wherein the participants are engaged in a task of downloading files from the network and congestion occurs because of excessive downloading by those first in the bandwidth. It represents a spatial game where players move over a two-dimensional space that emulates a renewable resource and where regrowth is affected by the surrounding conditions of the resource units left on the ground. Fiore et al. (2009) reported on the second case labeled as Virtual Experiments where a virtual world is created for the purpose of studying risk and the management of wildfires.

4.3.5. Innovation 5: create experiments with multiple economic domains. A major challenge when studying the behavior of the poor, as well as the microeconomic conditions experienced by most users of ecosystems around the developing world, is the multiplicity of the simultaneous economic activities in which these households are usually engaged (Banerjee & Duflo 2009). In many cases, these households are production-consumption units (Singh et al. 1986) that act as both buyers and sellers in the labor, land, and production markets. They derive income from both market- and non-market-based production, in some cases by competing with other neighbors in one domain (e.g., crops production) and cooperating with the same neighbors in another (e.g., water conservation). Yet, the experimental designs brought to the field continue to be simple with regard to the income sources players have and the institutional setting in which economic activities are carried out. Specialization and scale in economic activities are efficiency enhancing, but the diversification of income sources remains an adaptive strategy among the poor, given that insurance, credit, produce, and labor markets are thin and imperfect. New experiments combine—either as a within-subjects design or to account for multiple tasks—different sources of income and maintain control by using a partial or general equilibrium context in the game. An interesting step in this direction is reported by Capra et al. (2009). They explored poverty traps in a controlled lab experiment where players participate in a closed economy as producers and consumers with respect to the larger economy. In their design, the participants' consumption determines the economy's rates of return on their investments. By detecting the most relevant sources of income from monetary and nonmonetary activities in terms of how the poor allocate their assets and labor, one can generate lab and field designs where the players need to make simultaneous decisions that affect their experimental earnings and explore possible interactions among behavior, institutions, and ecosystems.

5. CONCLUDING REMARKS

The use of experiments in the fields of development, environmental, and resource economics has a long and rich history. Random interventions to test the impacts and the adoption of policies and programs have been implemented worldwide. For example, the World Bank has 67 ongoing projects involving random evaluations in Africa alone (Banerjee & Duflo 2009). Replications of field and lab experiments are available across the globe for most of the key behavioral traits of interest. Robust patterns of behavior are now part of the mainstream in the modeling of behavior regarding risk, time, fairness, and the environment. However, the task is not yet complete. Small improvements could yield large payoffs in terms of scientific and policy applications, particularly with respect to the developing world. Let me describe just two.

There is a gap to be filled between policy implementation and the vast work modeling and testing the above-discussed behaviors. Policies and instruments of intervention in the developing world remain in large part based on a model of rational choice that itself is based on complete and self-oriented preference mapping (Venkatachalam 2008)—although the self-oriented perfect maximizer assumption has been discarded for the most part in the theoretical and experimental literature reported here. In addition, the use of randomized interventions provides a rich setting for identifying some certain patterns of behavior. These random interventions could be complemented with lab and/or field experiments, which could help explain the reasons for the patterns of behavior observed in the interventions.

In other words, random interventions can yield insights into what works and what does not, whereas field and lab experiments may uncover why something worked or why it did not. Experiments can be tailored to the interests of stakeholders (agencies, community leaders, and members) to enable the testing of possible alternative explanations to understand the success or failure of interventions.

Despite the vast literature and experience with market-based institutions found in the laboratory, little experimental work has been carried out in the developing world, and even less in the field, concerning how market institutions may address the challenges of development and poverty reduction (for an exception from the lab, see Capra et al. 2009). A few examples of market-based instruments used in environmental protection have been mentioned (Murphy & Stranlund, 2007), although these pertain primarily to industrial societies and reflect student-based experiments. The problems of poverty traps, market power, regulation, and state intervention are a crucial part of the theoretical and empirical work of development economics. The debate on the power and limitations of markets to address growth and poverty remains on the agenda of agencies and academia. However, not much field and experimental work in developing countries settings has been done on how individuals behave within competitive and imperfect markets when addressing issues related to development and the environment. Nonetheless, such policies and programs circle around markets, both perfect and imperfect.

DISCLOSURE STATEMENT

The author is not aware of any affiliations, memberships, funding, or financial holdings that might be perceived as affecting the objectivity of this review.

ACKNOWLEDGMENTS

Comments from an anonymous reviewer and assistance by Miguel Espinosa enriched the present version of this article. The David Rockefeller Center for Latin American Studies at Harvard University and its Robert F. Kennedy Visiting Professorship of Latin American Studies provided an ideal environment for research. A generous grant within the Human and Social Dynamics program at the National Science Foundation supported the author's field research conducted and reported here.

LITERATURE CITED

Alatas V, Cameron L, Chaudhuri A, Erkal N, Gangadharan L. 2006. *Subject pool effects in a corruption experiment: a comparison of Indonesian public servants and Indonesian students.* Work. Pap. Ser. 975, Dep. Econ., Univ. Melbourne

Alpizar F, Carlsson F, Johansson-Stenman O. 2008a. Anonymity, reciprocity, and conformity: evidence from voluntary contributions to a national park in Costa Rica. *J. Public Econ.* 92(5–6):1047–60

Alpizar F, Carlsson F, Johansson-Stenman O. 2008b. Does context matter more for hypothetical than for actual contributions? Evidence from a natural field experiment. *Exp. Econ.* 11(3):299–314

Arrow KJ, Dasgupta P, Goulder LH, Daily G, Heal GM, et al. 2004. Are we consuming too much? *J. Econ. Perspect.* 18(3):147–72

Ashraf N, Camerer CF, Lowenstein G. 2005. Adam Smith, behavioral economist. *J. Econ. Perspect.* 19(3):131–46

Ashraf N, Bohnet I, Piankov N. 2006a. Decomposing trust and trustworthiness. *Exp. Econ.* 9(3):193–208

Ashraf N, Karlan D, Yin W. 2006b. Tying Odysseus to the mast: evidence from a commitment savings product in the Philippines. *Q. J. Econ.* 121(2):635–72

Ball S, Eckel C, Rojas C. 2006. Technology improves learning in large principles of economics classes: using our WITS. *Am. Econ. Rev.* 96(2):442–46

Banerjee AV, Duflo E. 2007. The economic lives of the poor. *J. Econ. Perspect.* 21(1):141–67

Banerjee AV, Duflo E. 2009. The experimental approach to development economics. *Annu. Rev. Econ.* 1: In press

Bardhan P, Udry C. 1999. *Development Microeconomics.* Oxford/New York: Oxford Univ. Press

Barr A. 2003. Trust and expected trustworthiness: experimental evidence from Zimbabwean villages. *Econ. J.* 113(489):614–30

Barr A, Lindelow M, Serneels P. 2004. *To serve the community or oneself—the public servant's dilemma.* Policy Res. Work. Pap. Ser. 3187, World Bank

Barr A, Wallace C, Ensminger J, Henrich J, Barrett C, et al. 2009. *Homo aequalis: a cross-society experimental analysis of three bargaining games.* Econ. Ser. Work. Pap. 422, Dep. Econ., Univ. Oxford

Bettinger E, Slonim R. 2006. Using experimental economics to measure the effects of a natural educational experiment on altruism. *J. Public Econ.* 90(8–9):1625–48

Binswanger H. 1980. Attitudes toward risk: experimental measurement in rural India. *Am. J. Agric. Econ.* 62:395–407

Binswanger H. 1981. Attitudes toward risk: theoretical implications of an experiment in rural India. *Econ. J.* 91(364):867–90

Bohnet I, Zeckhauser R. 2004. Trust, risk and betrayal. *J. Econ. Behav. Organ.* 55(4):467–84

Bouma J, Bulteb E, van Soest D. 2008. Trust and cooperation: social capital and community resource management. *J. Environ. Econ. Manag.* 56(2):155–66

Bowles S. 2004. *Microeconomics: Behavior, Institutions and Evolution.* Princeton, NJ: Princeton Univ. Press

Boyce RR, Brown TC, McClelland GH, Peterson GL. 1992. An experimental examination of intrinsic values as a source. *Am. Econ. Rev.* 82(5):1366–73

Burks SV, Carpenter J, Goette L, Monaco K, Rustichini A, Porter K. 2007. *Using behavioral economic field experiments at a large motor carried: the context and design of the truckers and turnover project.* Work. Pap. 12976, NBER

Camerer CF. 2003. *Behavioral Game Theory: Experiments in Strategic Interaction.* Princeton, NJ: Princeton Univ. Press

Capra M, Tanaka T, Camerer CF, Feiler L, Sovero V, Noussair C. 2009. The impact of simple institutions in experimental economies with poverty traps. *Econ. J.* In press

Carbone E. 2005. Demographics and behaviour. *Exp. Econ.* 8(3):217–32

Cárdenas JC. 2003. Real wealth and experimental cooperation: evidence from field experiments. *J. Dev. Econ.* 70(2):263–89

Cárdenas JC, Candelo N, Gaviria A, Polania S, Sethi R. 2008. *Discrimination in the provision of social services to the poor: a field experimental study.* RES Work. Pap. 3247, Res. Dep., Inter-Am. Dev. Bank

Cárdenas JC, Carpenter J. 2005. *Three themes on field experiments and economic development.* See Carpenter et al. 2005, pp. 71–123

Cárdenas JC, Carpenter J. 2008. Behavioural development economics: lessons from field labs in the developing world. *J. Dev. Stud.* 44(3):337–64

Cárdenas JC, Janssen MA, Bousquet F. 2009. Dynamics of rules and resources: three new field experiments on water, forests and fisheries. In *Handbook on Experimental Economics and the Environment*, ed. J List, M Price. Cheltenham, UK: Edward Elgar. In press

Cárdenas JC, Jaramillo CRH. 2007. *Cooperation in large networks: an experimental.* Work. Pap. 002202, Univ. Andes, CEDE

Cárdenas JC, Ostrom E. 2004. *What do people bring into the game? Experiments in the field about cooperation in the commons.* Agric. Syst. 82(3):307–26

Cárdenas JC, Sethi R. 2009. Resource allocation in public agencies: experimental evidence. *J. Public Econ. Theory.* In press

Cárdenas JC, Stranlund JK, Willis CE. 2000. Local environmental control and institutional crowding-out. *World Dev.* 28(10):1719–33

Cárdenas JC, Stranlund JK, Willis CE. 2002. Economic inequality and burden-sharing in the provision of local environmental quality. *Ecol. Econ.* 40:379–95

Carpenter J, Harrison GW, List JA, eds. 2005. *Field Experiments in Economics*, Vol. 10. Greenwich, CT: JAI Press

Carpenter J, Seki E. 2006. Competitive work environments and social preferences: field experimental evidence from a Japanese fishing community. *Contrib. Econ. Anal. Policy* 5(2):1460

Casey JF, Kahna JR, Rivas AAF. 2008. Willingness to accept compensation for the environmental risks of oil transport on the Amazon: a choice modeling experiment. *Ecol. Econ.* 67(4):552–59

Cassar A, Crowley L, Wydick B. 2007. The effect of social capital on group loan repayment: evidence from field experiments. *Econ. J.* 117(517):F85–106

Chong A, Ñopo H, Cárdenas JC. 2008. *To what extent do Latin Americans trust and cooperate? Field experiments on social exclusion in six Latin American Countries.* RES Work. Pap. 4577, Res. Dep., Inter-Am. Dev. Bank

Danielson AJ, Holm HJ. 2007. Do you trust your brethren? Eliciting trust attitudes and trust behavior in a Tanzanian congregation. *J. Econ. Behav. Organ.* 62(2):255–71

Duflo E. 2005. *Field experiments in development economics.* Mimeogr., Dep. Econ. Abdul Latif Jameel Poverty Action Lab, MIT

Dufwenberg M, Harrison GW. 2008. Peter Bohm: father of field experiments. *Exp. Econ.* 11:213–20

Dufwenberg M, Swarthout JT. 2009. *Play to learn? An experiment.* Exp. Econ. Cent. Work. Pap. 2009-08, Andrew Young Sch. Policy Stud., Georgia State Univ.

Ehmke MD, Shogren JF. 2009. Experimental methods for environment and development economics. *Environ. Dev. Econ.* doi:10.1017/S1355770X08004592

Engle-Warnick J, Escobal J, Laszlo S. 2007. *Ambiguity aversion as a predictor of technology choice: experimental evidence from Peru.* New Econ. Pap., CIRANO

Engle-Warnick J, Laszlo S. 2006. *Learning-by-doing in an ambiguous environment.* New Econ. Pap., CIRANO

Fiore SM, Harrison GW, Hughes CE, Rutström EE. 2009. Virtual experiments and environmental policy. *J. Environ. Econ. Manag.* 57(1):65–86

Fisher A, Wheeler W, Zwick R. 1993. Experimental methods in agricultural and resource economics: How useful are they? *Agric. Resour. Econ. Rev.* 22(2):103–16

Fong C. 2007. Evidence from an experiment on charity to welfare recipients: reciprocity, altruism and the empathic responsiveness hypothesis. *Econ. J.* 117:1008–24

Fong C, Luttmer E. 2009. What determines giving to Hurricane Katrina victims? Experimental evidence on racial group loyalty. *Am. Econ. J. Appl. Econ.* 1(2):64–87

Gaechter S, Herrmann B. 2006. *The limits of self-governance in the presence of spite: experimental evidence from urban and rural Russia.* New Econ. Pap., CIRANO

Gintis H. 2000a. Beyond Homo economicus: evidence from experimental economics. *Ecol. Econ.* 35:311–22

Gintis H. 2000b. *Game Theory Evolving.* Princeton, NJ: Princeton Univ. Press

Gurven M. 2004. Reciprocal altruism and food sharing decisions among Hiwi and Ache hunter-gatherers. *Behav. Ecol. Sociobiol.* 56:366–80

Gurven M, Hill K, Kaplan H, Hurtado A, Lyles R. 2000. Food transfers among Hiwi foragers of Venezuela: tests of reciprocity. *J. Hum. Ecol.* 28(2):171–218

Haider SJ, McGarry K. 2006. Recent trends in income sharing among the poor. In *Working and Poor: How Economic and Policy Changes Are Affecting Low-Wage Workers*, eds. R Blank, S Danziger, R Schoeni. New York: Russell Sage

Harrison G. 1996. *Experimental economics and contingent valuation.* Econ. Work. Pap. 96-10, Div. Res., Coll. Bus. Admin., Univ. South Carolina

Harrison GW, List JA. 2004. Field experiments. *J. Econ. Lit.* 42(4):1009

Henrich J, McElreath R, Barr A, Ensminger J, Barrett C, et al. 2006. Costly punishment across human societies. *Science* 23:1767–70

Hermann B, Thöni C, Gächter S. 2008. Antisocial punishment across societies. *Science* 319 (5868):1362–67

Holm HJ, Danielson A. 2005. Tropic trust versus nordic trust: experimental evidence from Tanzania and Sweden. *Econ. J.* 115(503):505–32

Ibañez M, Carlsson F. 2009. *A choice experiment on coca cropping.* Mimeogr., Dep. Econ., Sch. Bus. Econ. Law, Göteborg Univ.

Jack BK. 2008. *Alternative allocation mechanisms for incentive contracts: tree planting in Malawi.* Presented at Cent. Int. Dev., Harvard Univ.

Jack BK, Leimona B, Ferraro PJ. 2009. A revealed preference approach to estimating supply curves for ecosystem services: using auctions to set payments for soil erosion control in Indonesia. *Conserv. Biol.* 23(2):359–67

Karlan D. 2005. Using experimental economics to measure social capital and predict financial decisions. *Am. Econ. Rev.* 95(5):1688–99

Knetsch J. 1989. The endowment effect and evidence of nonreversible indifference curves. *Am. Econ. Rev.* 79:1277–84

Knetsch J, Sinden JA. 1984. Willingness to pay and compensation demanded: experimental evidence of an unexpected disparity in measures of values. *Q. J. Econ.* 99:507–21

Leider S, Mobius M, Rosenblat T, Do Q-A. 2009. Directed altruism and enforced reciprocity in social networks. *Q. J. Econ.* 124: In press

Levitt SD, List JA. 2007. What do laboratory experiments measuring social preferences reveal about the real world? *J. Econ. Perspect.* 21(2):153–74

List J, Gallet C. 2001. What experimental protocol influence disparities between actual and hypothetical stated values? *Environ. Resour. Econ.* 20(3):241–54

Loewenstein G. 1999. Experimental economics from the vantage point of behavioural economics. *Econ. J.* 109:F25–34

Loomes G. 1999a. Experimental economics: introduction. *Econ. J.* 109:F1–4

Loomes G. 1999b. Some lessons from past experiments and some challenges for the future. *Econ. J.* 109:F35–45

Lopez MC, Murphy JJ, Spraggon JM, Stranlund JK. 2009. *Comparing the effectiveness of regulation and pro-social emotions to enhance cooperation: experimental evidence from fishing communities in Colombia.* Work. Pap., Resour. Econ., Univ. Mass.

Marette S, Roosen J, Blanchemanche S, Verger P. 2008. The choice of fish species: an experiment measuring the impact of risk and benefit information. *J. Agric. Resour. Econ.* 33(1): http://econpapers.repec.org/article/agsjlaare/36701.htm

Marlowe FW, Berbesque JC, Barr A, Barrett C, Bolyantz A, et al. 2008. More 'altruistic' punishment in larger societies. *Proc. R. Soc. Lond. Ser. B* 275:587–90

Moreno R, Maldonado JH. 2008. *Can co-management strategies improve governance in a marine protected area? Lessons from experimental economic games in the Colombian Caribbean.* Presented at 16th Annu. Conf. Eur. Assoc. Environ. Resour. Econ., Gothenburg, Sweden

Murphy JJ, Stevens TH. 2004. Contingent valuation, hypothetical bias and experimental economics. *Agric. Resour. Econ. Rev.* 33(2):182–92

Murphy JJ, Stranlund JK. 2007. A laboratory investigation of compliance behavior under tradable emissions rights: implications for targeted enforcement. *J. Environ. Econ. Manag.* 53(2):196–212

Neill HR, Cummings RG, Ganderton PT, Harrison GW. 1994. Hypothetical surveys and real economic commitments. *Land Econ.* 70(2):145

Ñopo H, Chong A, Cárdenas JC. 2008. *Stated social behavior and revealed actions: evidence from six Latin American countries using representative samples.* RES Work. Pap. 4575, Res. Dep, Inter-Am. Dev. Bank

Oosterbeek H, Sloof R, van de Kuilen G. 2004. Cultural differences in ultimatum game experiments: evidence from a meta-analysis. *Exp. Econ.* 7(2):171–88

Osés-Erasoa N, Viladrich-Grau M. 2007. Appropriation and concern for resource scarcity in the commons: an experimental study. *Ecol. Econ.* 63(2–3):435–45

Ostrom E. 2006. The value-added of laboratory experiments for the study of institutions and common-pool resources. *J. Econ. Behav. Organ.* 61(2):149–63

Ostrom E. 2007. A diagnostic approach for going beyond panaceas. *Proc. Natl. Acad. Sci. USA* 104(39):15181–87

Ostrom E, Janssen MA, Anderies JM. 2007. Going beyond panaceas. *Proc. Natl. Acad. Sci. USA* 104(39):15176–78

Ostrom V. 1980. Artisanship and artifact. *Public Admin. Rev.* 40(4):309–17

Rodríguez-Sicker C, Guzmán RA, Cárdenas JC. 2008. Institutions influence preferences: evidence from a common pool resource experiment. *J. Econ. Behav. Organ.* 67(1):215–27

Rondeau D, Poeb GL, Schulze WD. 2005. VCM or PPM? A comparison of the performance of two voluntary public goods mechanisms. *J. Public Econ.* 89(8):1581–92

Roth A. 2002. The economist as engineer: game theory experimentation, and computation as tools for design economics. *Econometrica* 70(4):1341–78

Sandhua HS, Wrattena SD, Cullenb R, Case B. 2008. The future of farming: the value of ecosystem services in conventional and organic arable land. An experimental approach. *Ecol. Econ.* 64(4):835–48

Shogren JF. 2005. Experimental methods and valuation. In *Handbook of Environmental Economics*, Vol. 2, ch. 19, pp. 969–1027. Amsterdam: Elsevier

Singh I, Squire L, Strauss J, eds. 1986. *Agricultural Household Models—Extensions, Applications and Policy.* Baltimore, MD: Johns Hopkins Univ. Press

Sirén AH, Cárdenas JC, Machoa JD. 2006. The relation between income and hunting in tropical forests: an economic experiment in the field. *Ecol. Soc.* 11(1): artic. 44

Smith VL. 2003. Constructivist and ecological rationality in economics. *Am. Econ. Rev.* 93(3):465–508

Siwan A, Baland J-M. 2002. The economics of ROSCAS and intrahousehold resource allocation. *Q. U. Econ.* 117(3):963–95

Stark O. 1996. On the evolution of altruism. *Nordic J. Polit. Econ.* 23:145–49

Stark O. 1999. *Altruism and Beyond: An Economic Analysis of Transfers and Exchanges Within Families and Groups.* Cambridge, UK: Cambridge Univ. Press

Stiglitz J. 1991. Rational peasants, efficient institutions, and the theory of rural organization: methodological remarks for development economics. In *The Economic Theory of Agrarian Institutions*, ed. P Bardhan. Cambridge, UK: Oxford Univ. Press

Sturm B, Weimann J. 2006. Experiments in environmental economics and some close relatives. *J. Econ. Surv.* 20(3):419–457

Sutherland WJ, Adams WM, Aronson RB, Aveling R, Blackburn TM, Broad S, et al. 2009. One hundred questions of importance to the conservation of global biological diversity. *Conserv. Biol.* In press. doi:10.1111/j.1523-1739.2009.01212.x

Venkatachalam L. 2008. Behavioral economics for environmental policy. *Ecol. Econ.* 67(4):640–45

Vollan B. 2008. Socio-ecological explanations for crowding-out effects from economic field experiments in southern Africa. *Ecol. Econ.* 67(4):560–73

Vyrastekova J, van Soest D. 2003. Centralized common-pool management and local community participation. *Land Econ.* 79:500–14

World Bank. 2001. *World Development Report 2000/20001: Attacking Poverty.* Washington, DC: World Bank

World Bank. 2003. *World Development Report 2003: Sustainable Development in a Dynamic World.* Washington, DC: World Bank

World Bank. 2006. *World Development Report 2006: Equity and Development.* Washington, DC: World Bank

World Bank. 2008. *World Development Report 2008: Agriculture for Development.* Washington, DC: World Bank

World Bank. 2010. *World Development Report 2010: Development in Changing Climate.* Washington, DC: World Bank

Behavior, Environment, and Health in Developing Countries: Evaluation and Valuation

Subhrendu K. Pattanayak[1,2] and Alexander Pfaff[1]

[1]Sanford School of Public Policy, Duke University, Durham, North Carolina 27708;
email: subhrendu.pattanayak@duke.edu, alex.pfaff@duke.edu

[2]Nicholas School of the Environment, Duke University, Durham, North Carolina
27708

Annu. Rev. Resour. Econ. 2009. 1:183–217

The *Annual Review of Resource Economics* is
online at resource.annualreviews.org

This article's doi:
10.1146/annurev.resource.050708.144053

Key Words

policy interventions, water quality, arsenic, indoor air pollution,
diarrhea, malaria, acute respiratory infections, stove, toilets,
bed nets, fuel

Abstract

We consider health and environmental quality in developing
countries, where limited resources constrain behaviors that combat
enormously burdensome health challenges. We focus on four huge
challenges that are preventable (i.e., are resolved in rich countries).
We distinguish them as special cases in a general model of household behavior, which is critical and depends on risk information.
Simply informing households may achieve a lot in the simplest
challenge (groundwater arsenic); yet, for the three infectious situations discussed (respiratory, diarrhea, and malaria), community
coordination and public provision may also be necessary. More
generally, social interactions may justify additional policies. For
each situation, we discuss the valuation of private spillovers (i.e.,
externalities) and evaluation of public policies to reduce environmental risks and spillovers. Finally, we reflect on open questions in
our model and knowledge gaps in the empirical literature including
the challenges of scaling up and climate change.

1. INTRODUCTION

In 400 BC, Hippocrates noted the ecological basis for disease in *On Airs, Waters, and Place*. As elaborated by Wilson (1995), our understanding and control of disease is inadequate without an "ecological" perspective on the life cycles of parasitic microorganisms and associated infectious diseases. Certainly ecology per se has a key role. However, we contend that a broad ecological perspective must include examination of behaviors. Behavioral choice plays central roles in the understanding and control of diseases. Pattanayak & Yasuoka (2008), for example, argued that prevention behaviors respond to disease levels in an exposure-management dynamic. Furthermore, if impacts on others are ignored, private behavior is socially inefficient in the absence of coercion.

In assessing the state of health across the globe, Smith et al. 1999 (p. 583) contend that "many of the critical health problems in the world today cannot be solved without major improvement in environmental quality." A recent updating of this analysis "confirms that approximately one-quarter of the global disease burden, and more than one-third of the burden among children, is due to modifiable environmental factors" (Prüss-Üstün & Corvalan 2006, p. 6).

These assessments suggest three regularities: Children are most vulnerable; environmental disease[1] is concentrated in the poorer countries (**Figure 1**, see color insert); and infectious diseases such as diarrhea, malaria, and acute respiratory infections are a larger share of the global burden than are noncommunicable chronic diseases (Smith et al. 1999) (**Figure 2**, see color insert).

In light of **Figure 1**, we focus on developing countries in our review of environment and health. The question we pose is, What explains the concentration of environmentally driven health burdens in developing countries? Developing countries differ from developed ones in the following ways, at minimum: Average per capita GDP is low, while poverty is high; government and/or market institutions are weaker relative to community processes' influence; most locations are tropical (located between the Tropics of Cancer and Capricorn); and the levels and trends in climate, i.e., rainfall and temperature, as well as urban concentration expose populations to health risks. Thus, some countries simply start poor and with poor environment and health.

However, many of the most important health issues are affected by human behavior and the underlying incentives to act to improve environment and health. For instance, below we consider how incentives differ for infectious diseases and the implications of key externalities for individual, coordinated, and public action. As state action can be particularly productive in such settings, while developing-state governance can be weak, the findings in **Figure 2** may not be surprising.

Thus, starting from these informative global overviews of environmental health, which indicate that economic development matters, and given our focus on behavior, in this paper we attempt the following: Section 2 summarizes the linkages among development, environmental quality, and health from a macroperspective and then in a micromodel of household behavioral choices about whether and how to avoid health risks. Section 3 next describes

---

[1]By environmental, the World Health Organization (WHO) means all physical, chemical, and biological factors external to human and related behavior but excludes environments that cannot reasonably be modified. Thus, traffic risk is included because housing, roads, and land use are choices, whereas the diseases caused by vectors in natural environments such as wetlands are excluded because policy interventions are assumed by the experts supporting the WHO assessment to be infeasible.

four major health challenges in developing countries, providing background and then characterizing them in terms of the micromodel. Section 4 describes examples of research on behavior and policy for each of these four health challenges and then considers the overlap between the evaluation of such policy interventions and the valuation by households of improvements in environmental quality, which lower health risks. Section 5 then considers the basis for public policy in this area, starting with classical externalities then moving to other interactions between households, with a final emphasis on the many spillovers involved in infectious diseases. Finally, Section 6 concludes by listing a few apparent hurdles to come for future analyses that could inform environmental health policy.

2. CONCEPTUAL FRAMEWORK

The findings of prior overviews of global environmental health motivate consideration of at least two scales. First, the global distribution of the environmental health burden is truly striking. Here then, from a macroperspective and bringing in behavioral choice at an aggregate level, we consider not only the differences in countries' or regions' initial endowments mentioned above, but also the simple yet critical trade-offs between consumption and health that may drive behaviors. Second, within this disease burden in developing countries, the dominance of infectious disease is also striking. Thus, from a microperspective, we consider what is common and what is different for infectious diseases by setting out a micro- or household-level model that can be applied to varied settings.

2.1. Macroperspective

A very broad macroframework helps to organize external and endogenous drivers. Our interests lie in the conditions with the least clear predictions in that framework, in which low income discourages prohealth actions while low environmental quality encourages such actions. This describes many poor tropical countries and environmental health challenges.

We consider diarrhea, respiratory infections, and malaria (i.e., ranked first, second, and fourth, respectively, in **Figure 2**) alongside groundwater arsenic ("the largest mass poisoning"). As our goal is for research to inform policy, we further focus on where the environment can be modified yet may not currently be modified within a given development setting. For considering these cases, in Section 2.2 below, we discuss a micro- or household-level model in more detail, including how a household's behavior can impact others, to distinguish these major health issues.

We assume multiple individual wants to illustrate the relationships among development, environment, and health (Gersovitz & Hammer 2003). We assume people like both consumption and health. Health is affected by prevention expenditures as well as one's environment. Quality of the environment is lowered by consumption but it is raised by prevention expenditures. Trade-offs arise because spending money to help environment and health lowers consumption, whereas consumption, which is valued separately, degrades the environment and, thus, health.

Consider the case of high consumption and low environmental quality. High consumption is not a starting point but a result of activities that may also lower environmental quality. Having raised consumption, individuals may value additional consumption less than additional environmental quality. Thus, citizens may be willing to invest in environmental quality or to improve health given environment (e.g., buy water or filters). This seems to be a common recent history for developed countries (e.g., Preston 1996).

Within that history, consider the implications for a nation's health. We see health rises with income (Smith & Ezzati 2005) (**Figure 3**, see color insert) as spending to help environment and to improve health given environment also rises. Yet, earlier in the development path, as economic activities were causing consumption to rise but counter-vailing expenditures were not yet considered worthwhile, health could fall as income rises. Thus at some income trends could shift, though that exact income level responds to multiple parameters (Pfaff & Chaudhuri 2004).

Consider next the opposite case of low consumption and high environmental quali-ty. This could be an exogenous or predevelopment starting point if a country has good environmental quality. Here, citizens may prefer to invest in consumption, as health will be fine given the environment. Should consumption be the only expenditure for some time, environment and thus health will fall. This situation should continue until expenditures on environment and health become worthwhile, which could prevent further falls in, or may even raise, health. This scenario may be the early history of the now-developed countries and may also represent the future of some developing countries.

Finally, a more challenging predevelopment situation is one in which both consumption and environment start low. Health is likely to be low because environmental quality is low and expenditures on health or environment are constrained by low income, i.e., consump-tion cannot easily be reduced to protect the environment and improve health. We note that this could also describe the case of a higher starting environment when even subsistence living rapidly degrades the environment relevant for health.

In this unfortunate (and unfortunately common) setting, the gains from small increases in either consumption or health may be very high and it is hard to predict where resources will go. Because a situation with low consumption and low environment and health is akin to starting at the origin, which is the typical starting point assumed in many economic models, we may expect resources will be allocated to advance consumption, environment, and health in a balanced way. Yet, the details of what is most critical for life will affect trends in environment as well as health.

Looking for support or refutation of this ambiguous prediction, one does see house-holds with low consumption, environment, and health spending a great deal of scarce time collecting potable water in an effort to improve environment and health. Yet, other house-holds let children forage in polluted waste dumps, which can greatly worsen health, to try to raise consumption. In short, all households in this situation are at risk and the details of their options affect behaviors.

2.2. Micromodel of Health-Risk Avoidance

For purposes of discussion, and organization of empirical analysis, it is helpful to have a single explicit model of the choices that households face when exposed to environmental health challenges. The basic economic explanation for household investments of time and other scarce resources to improve health is that investments will occur when their perceived benefits outweigh their perceived costs. To apply this, we must first define concepts common to our four cases.

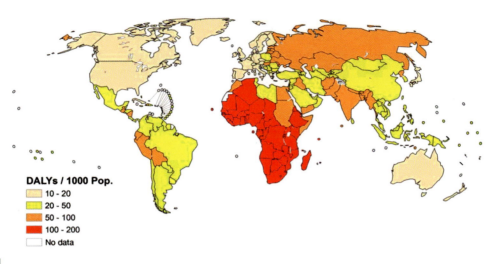

Figure 1

Environmental disease burden; incidence per unit population is shown, i.e., population weights do not emphasize China, India, Brazil, etc. Measured in disability-adjusted life years (DALYs) per 1000 people by World Health Organization subregion. Source: Prüss-Üstün & Corvalan (2006).

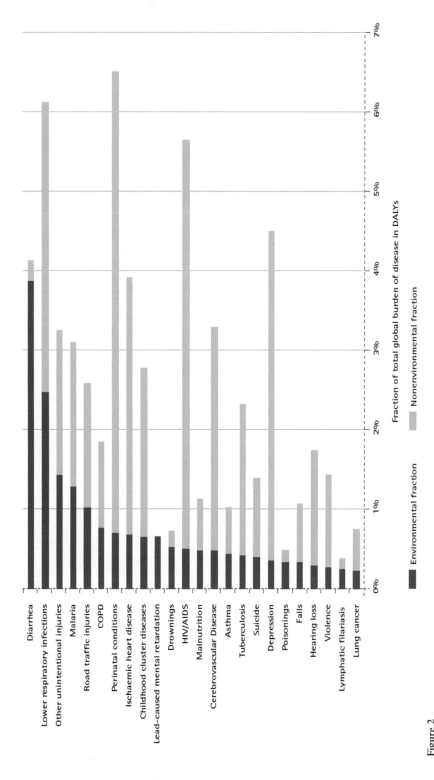

Figure 2

Diseases with the largest environmental contribution. Abbreviations: COPD, chronic obstructive pulmonary disease; DALYs, disability-adjusted life years. Source: Prüss-Üstün & Corvalan (2006).

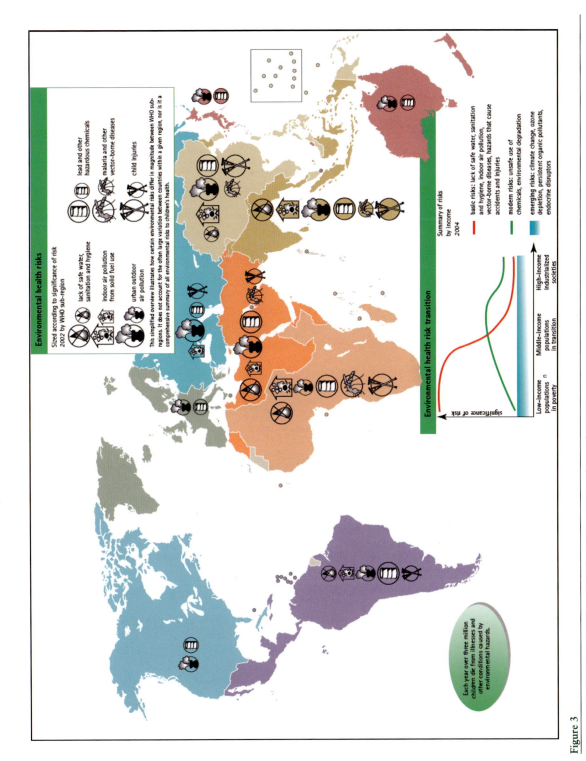

Figure 3

Traditional health hazards and new health risks. Source: Gordon et al. (2004).

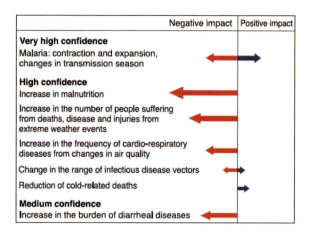

Figure 4

Impacts of climate change on health. For a description of how confidence levels are established, see http://www.ipcc.ch/activity/uncertaintyguidancenote.pdf.

Our household-level model below draws on a category of economic utility maximization theory called household production theory, which describes situations when something that is valued by the household cannot simply be bought off the shelf at some price. In our cases, that something is health. One cannot literally buy a unit of health. Rather, various inputs to health can be applied in an effort to be healthier and thus, it is assumed, also happier. Providing those inputs has costs as well as benefits. Although our focus is health benefits, other benefits of such actions may also matter for the impacts of health policies. The model below draws on Pattanayak et al. (2005, 2008), who adapted the averting behavior models (also called defensive expenditure or coping behavior models) described in Dickie & Gerking (1991) to consider demand for drinking water and sanitation services. See Larson & Gnedenko (1998), McConnell & Rosado (2000), Larson & Rosen (2002), and Dasgupta (2004) for other examples of this type of household and microeconometric behavioral modeling applied to environmental risks in developing countries.

A household maximizes utility by allocating its limited time and income across leisure (l), health (s represents the number of sick days), and a composite consumption good (c). Given the vector of values for l, s, and c, a household's utility will also be a function of preference parameters (θ) characterizing the shape of the utility curve. Empirically, socioeconomic data serve as proxies for these parameters. Preferences commonly cited as relevant are aversion to risk and interest in others' welfare.

A health production function (assumed to be twice differentiable, continuous, and convex) constrains choices and outcomes. s depends on environmental quality (e) and the extent of coping behavior, i.e. avoidance (a) of health risks. e can be a vector of health-relevant characteristics of the environment such as the density of biological or chemical contaminants in water. Optimal a is a choice. It depends on knowledge (k) of different kinds, a vector that includes an awareness of the threat to health from poor quality of the environment and an understanding of the impacts of avoidance. As such, k is typically not free. Avoidance can raise e, for example, when a is the use of a toilet instead of a stream; avoidance can also improve health given the overall quality of the environment, e.g., when a reduces exposure as a result of wearing a mask or drinking bottled water. Community avoidance totals (A), the result of many households employing a, could in turn affect each household. e depends on government actions (G), which respond in part to ambient environmental quality (E). Note that a capital letter signifies an amount that applies equally to and is therefore shared by all households. In purely biophysical terms, $e_E > = 0$; for instance, some of a household's exposure to air pollution (lowering e) results from the ambient air quality common to all households and influenced by regulations. However, behavioral adjustments to E by households, such as the prevalence elasticity idea discussed in Sections 3.4 and 4.4 in which public action crowds out private avoidance, could result in a net $e_E < 0$ correlation. Returning to a household, production of avoidance has costs because it requires inputs of time (t) as well as material (m) along with some of the types of knowledge (k).

Avoidance (a) may contribute not only to health but also directly to utility. For example, women may benefit from the convenience afforded by a latrine or private tube well as a substitute for walking long distances and/or always traveling and defecating in the company of other women. The household budget also constrains choices and outcomes. Expenditures on l and c, as well as on avoidance inputs (t, m, k), must be no greater than the sum of exogenous income (y) and earned income. Income is earned at a wage rate per hour (w) in all hours not spent on leisure (l), avoidance (t), or being sick (s). Materials and knowledge have known market prices (p and r, respectively), and all prices are normalized by a unitary price of consumption (c).

We assume that the time and the health-production constraints are binding and use a full-income constraint below. The Lagrangian for this problem is presented in Equation 1, where μ and λ are Lagrangian multipliers that represent the marginal utility of income and averting behavior.

$$L\{_{l,t,c,k,m,\lambda,\mu}\} = \max \quad u[\theta, l, c, a, s(a, A, G, e\{a, A, G\})] - \lambda[f(a, t, m, k)]$$
$$+ \quad \mu[y - c - pm - rk + w(24 - s - l - t)]. \tag{1}$$

Solution of the first-order conditions from Equation 1 determines optimal sickness (s), consumption (c), and leisure (l) on the basis of the optimal avoidance (a). Time and money are allocated so that their marginal opportunity costs are equal to the marginal utilities generated by efforts to generate consumption and leisure and minimize sickness. The household's choices (l, t, c, m, k) and the resulting a and s will vary with exogenous parameters like the opportunity cost of time (w) and the prices of material (p) and knowledge (r) (i.e., the inputs to avoidance) and the preference parameters (θ) as well as exogenous income (y), government policies (G), and community-averting behavior that affects environmental quality (A independent of a in large communities).

We move directly to consideration of a reduced-form characterization (instead of a structural representation) of the first-order conditions from above. However, we devote extra attention to derivation of optimal avoidance. In doing so, we can rewrite the first-order condition in the following way:

$$u_a + u_s.s_a - \mu.w.s_a = \lambda \cdot f_a. \tag{2}$$

The left-hand side of Equation 2 represents the marginal benefits of avoidance (a). These include direct effects on utility such as psychic benefits (safety, privacy, convenience). They also include health effects as well as productivity gains, recalling that avoidance lowers sickness ($s_a < 0$). As Pattanayak et al. (2008) showed, we can get a clearer intuition for the averting costs by substituting f_a by its constituent elements (f_t, f_m, and f_k) and replacing the Lagrangian multipliers (using the first-order conditions) to obtain

$$\frac{u_a + u_s.s_a}{\mu} - w.s_a = w \cdot a_t + p \cdot a_m + r \cdot a_k. \tag{3}$$

Now the marginal benefits are in money terms (normalized by marginal utility of money) and the marginal costs are the marginal productivity of time (t), materials (m), and knowledge (k) in the production of avoidance (a). Thus, Equation 3 represents the Marshallian interior solution, which states that the household will invest time and money in avoidance up to the level that the costs of the marginal unit of avoidance are equal to the perceived psychic and health benefits.

Starting with the result in the seminal article by Harrington & Portney (1987), this type of model has repeatedly been used to derive a microeconomic measure of the value of improvement in environmental quality. It suggests that four economic concepts taken together—avoidance costs, costs of illness, opportunity costs of lost work days, and monetary value of pain and suffering—indicate the value of a better environment (which may result from either improving environmental quality or reducing the household's exposure to a given environment).

We can see that this is the case within a derivation of the household's willingness to pay (WTP) for improvement in environmental quality (e). This inference is based on a comparative static analysis of the avoidance (a) a household chooses to undertake to improve e or to lower s given the environment. An intuitive explanation suggests that the demand for avoidance activities increases if

1. inputs to avoidance (time, materials, knowledge) are subsidized,
2. technical knowledge of best/better avoidance is enhanced,
3. perceptions of avoidance's nonhealth benefits (dignity, prestige) rise, and
4. knowledge of health benefits of avoidance is better disseminated.

Recent studies suggest the relevance of each of these predictions to how households will respond to various policy interventions (e.g., information provision or subsidized material) and to how the response will vary across households with levels of environmental quality.

3. DISTINGUISHING HEALTH CHALLENGES

Millions are at risk from diarrhea, acute respiratory infections, malaria, and arsenic exposure. Furthermore, each of these major health challenges permits choices that can reduce the risks faced, with some behaviors affecting environmental quality and others reducing exposure. From the macroperspective, each arises primarily when low income constrains the preventive expenditures critical for basic health. From the microperspective, however, there are significant differences among the four challenges we review. In this section, for each challenge, first we provide background on the health problem and then we represent the problem in our model.

3.1. Groundwater Arsenic

A Millennium Development Goal is to halve by 2015 the population without safe drinking water. Arsenic is now recognized as a major contaminant of drinking water in Asia. The many countries affected by arsenic contamination of drinking water include Bangladesh, India, Myanmar, Nepal, Pakistan, Cambodia, China, Lao People's Democratic Republic, and Vietnam (World Bank 1993). Long-term arsenic exposure causes health problems over 5 to 15 years for early adverse health effects and over 20 years or more for cancers. The incidence of symptoms is rising (World Health Organization 2001).

In Bangladesh, starting in the 1970s UNICEF advocated drinking groundwater and facilitated the digging of tube wells. By the early 1990s, more than 90% of the population had switched to groundwater, the vast majority from privately installed tube wells, and infant and child mortality declined from 211 per 1000 in 1980 to 104 per 1000 in 1997 (World Bank 2001) largely due to the fall in waterborne diseases.[2] When the switch to groundwater was being advocated, neither the local government(s) nor UNICEF was aware of the potential of arsenic contamination.

Recent studies suggest that approximately one-third of the tube wells in Bangladesh should be officially considered contaminated (concentrations $> 50\mu gL^{-1}$), with 35 million

---

[2]This may not be entirely due to safer drinking water. Changes in medical treatment, e.g., the use of oral rehydration therapy, and improvements in access to medical care and nutrition may have mattered. However, the decline is almost twice as large as the average decline for low-income countries (World Bank 2001).

people thought to be drinking such contaminated water and 57 million drinking water with arsenic above $10\mu gL^{-1}$. UNICEF estimates that 1.4 million out of 6–10 million tube wells in the country were tested by the end of 2001 and then testing reached over 5 million wells by 2004 as a result of the BAMWSP (Bangladesh Arsenic Mitigation Water Supply Project) unit funded by the World Bank. Thus, many wells remain untested, especially in the cleaner areas. Equally important, new wells are drilled regularly in all areas. Therefore, there is a need for ongoing well tests.

Most arsenic studies have been technical, concentrating on geochemical and engineering aspects. Prevention can take two forms: removing the arsenic, e.g., using either household- or community-level treatment systems, or shifting one's source of drinking water. Removal can be costly and debate about its effectiveness remains (World Bank 2009), although progress is being made. Next, we consider behaviors that can lower exposure and what drives them.

Of the four issues we discuss, arsenic in groundwater presents the simplest situation. In Bangladesh, where it has been considered and addressed extensively, arsenic exposure can be and mostly has been addressed at household level. To start, environmental quality (e) varies by household or, more specifically, by tube well. Often, a single tube well serves one household, which may be an extended family, though many wells also serve a small neighborhood, comprising a few households.

One reason this is a simpler setting is that $e_a = 0$, i.e., avoidance does not affect the level of environmental quality for the household or for that matter other households, at least to first order. The dominant avoidance behavior is to switch to another tube well; other options include buying a filter to place on the well, which is rare, or purchasing clean water, even rarer. All these options show $s_a\,le < 0$ because avoidance changes exposure and sickness, but not arsenic levels.

The spatial heterogeneity of contamination (low e) is considerable. Thus, switching to another well often means using another household's uncontaminated well (usually within 100 m). Drilling a new well in a different location also occurs, and because the older and deeper aquifers are lower in arsenic, higher-cost deep drilling may occur (and cost may be shared so that $s_A < 0$). In a city, public filtration and piping may bring clean water to the household ($s_{E(G)}\,le < 0$).

One critical constraint on avoidance is knowledge ($a_k > 0$). In Bangladesh, a national television campaign provided information in a general way, alerting citizens to the existence of groundwater arsenic as a health threat. This public subsidy to knowledge could have led to a costly household search for a more actionable, household-specific k such as finding the right local government or agency actors and convincing them to come to test household wells. That appears not to have happened, i.e., the costs r of that path to knowledge were too large given the current situation. However, because BAMWSP is no longer conducting free well tests in Bangladesh, households may need to acquire these tests themselves.[3]

What led to avoidance (see Section 4.1 below) was another subsidy to knowledge, i.e., free well tests.[4] Thus, we learn that $a_r < 0$. However, the broad knowledge about arsenic

---

[3]Thornton (2008) considered such a situation in a randomized experiment about the demand for learning HIV status and any subsequent behavior change. Of more than 2700 individuals, less than half attended a clinic to learn their HIV status without any incentive, but even a small incentive increased that share by 50%.

[4]Development economics has recently given more attention to the potential impact of information. However, research on households' responses to information about risks from drinking water exists but has been limited for development settings (e.g., Jalan & Somanathan, 2008).

being unhealthy ($s_e < 0$) complements the household-specific well-test knowledge. Knowing the level of arsenic in the well water will not lead to walking (at cost w) or purchasing (cost p) if no risk is perceived.

3.2. Acute Respiratory Infections

More than 3 billion people in developing countries face health risks associated with biomass use for energy, e.g., the burning of wood, dung, and crop residues (Reddy et al. 1996). The World Health Organization found that ARI caused by indoor smoke already accounts for 3.7% of the burden of disease in developing countries, and current trends suggest that the number exposed to such risks will increase over time (World Health Organization 1997).[5]

Smith et al. (2004) emphasized the combination of high indoor exposure and high indoor pollutant concentration, making indoor air pollution an important factor in terms of health. Total exposure to air pollution occurs largely indoors even if more total pollution is emitted outdoors. Biomass fuels are often used in poorly ventilated places with open fires or inefficient stoves, yielding pollutant levels well above the ambient air pollution levels, even worse than those of dirty cities (Smith 1993). Smith et al. (2004) also emphasized that such indoor exposure to air pollution is not the same for all members of a household. On average, men tend to spend more time outdoors and cook less, while children and women spend more time indoors, thus increasing their exposure.

The severity of the problem has inspired studies evaluating health risks associated with biomass fuel use. Published papers suggest that changing what biomass is used as well as how it is used could reduce health risks. Bruce et al. (1998) found fewer respiratory symptoms when women use *plancha* stoves with enclosed combustion chambers and chimneys, whereas McCracken et al. (2007) found *plancha* stoves impacted blood pressure, an indicator for cardiovascular disease (He et al. 1999). Along these lines, also see research by Bruce et al. (2000, 2004).

Ezzati & Kammen (2002) summarized studies concerning the contributions from biomass and coal smoke to the incidence of acute respiratory infections, middle-ear infection, chronic obstructive pulmonary disorder, lung and other cancers, asthma, tuberculosis, low birth weight, and eye diseases (Smith et al. 2000; Bruce et al. 2000; Ezzati & Kammen 2001a, 2001b), with the main focus on acute lung and respiratory infection, middle-ear infection, and chronic obstructive pulmonary disorder (Bruce et al. 2000, Smith et al. 2000). They noted that, in 2000, 1.5 to 2 million deaths, i.e., 3% to 4% of total mortality, were attributable to these risks.

This type of research has been successful in inspiring projects worldwide to spread the use of and to commercialize emission-reducing stoves. However, such attempts to inspire preventive action on the part of households have been less successful in influencing perceived environmental health risks sufficiently to impact individuals' willingness to bear the costs of prevention. This finding is based on personal communications with researchers and other commentators, leading us to conclude it is an important feature of the policy

---

[5]Given recent attention to mitigating the emissions thought to cause long-run climate change, even though we focus on direct local health impacts, it is worth noting that biomass emissions also become outdoor and atmospheric pollution. This adds externalities even from household prevention (such as switching of fuels) that lowers emissions and thus could add to the basis for public action to facilitate such prevention behaviors.

landscape regarding acute respiratory infection (and a distinguishing feature relative to arsenic exposure).

Characterizing this challenge in the model, a distinguishing feature of it relative to the arsenic problem is that the household-specific environment (e) can be affected by avoidance ($e_a > 0$). Thus, we can change particulate levels in indoor air by changing fuels or combustion efficiency. This suggests that individuals can be affected by others' avoidance. For example, to improve his indoor air, an individual may add a chimney that then relocates particulates to the rest of the neighborhood and thus lowers ambient air quality. Depending on conditions such as wind strength, we see $E_a < 0$. Although individuals' exposure occurs mostly indoors, a significant fraction of personal exposure can result from ambient air quality levels ($e_E > 0$). Thus, given that ambient air quality will be affected by others' avoidance via chimneys ($E_A < 0$), others' avoidance can hurt ($e_A < 0$, but see Section 5 for discussion of the possible positive spillovers from other households being healthy).

Avoidance can also reduce exposure given the quality of the environment ($s_a \,|e < 0$). For air quality, this may be achieved by staying away from stoves while the cooking is taking place. This avoidance has time cost (w) if cooking takes longer at lower temperature to avoid burning while individuals are away. It could also have a direct utility cost ($u_a < 0$) if, for instance, this revised cooking method affects the way traditional food tastes.

In determining whether these costly acts are worthwhile, we found that local knowledge (k) is imperfect. As noted above, we believe efforts to inform households about risk (at $r = 0$) have not driven much avoidance (i.e., to first order $a_r = 0$). Sickness has disutility ($U_s < 0$) but households do not see the relevant linkages (low k about $s_e < 0$ or $e_a > 0$). Thus, little adoption occurs.

Nonetheless, avoidance such as stove adoption occurred. To some extent, this happened because of subsidies such as the distribution of free stoves ($p = 0$). In addition to the potential disutility from prevention, there is also potential (nonhealth) utility gains from avoidance such as piping out smoke, which reduces discomfort from getting smoke in one's eyes ($u_a > 0$). That alone, however, is unlikely to explain why some households have paid for stoves within various distribution programs in which price $p > 0$, even though some amount of subsidy was provided.

Assuming that in the short term the households do not believe in valued health gains, one reason such prevention could be scaled up is the potential for savings in fuel costs. If that is a leading dynamic, then loans (such as microcredit) for purchasing expensive materials, e.g., stoves, may be a leading policy if the stoves do more than pay for themselves in fuel ($y_a > 0$). Such an approach still may not reach everybody, however, and some households may prefer not to pay. Another option currently being pursued is subsidizing the use of better stoves. Such an approach is based on the belief that a global E_a is positive so the globe wants to support stoves.

3.3. Diarrhea

Inadequate water and sanitation infrastructure, coupled with unsafe hygiene behaviors, cause diarrheal diseases, which are blamed for 2 million child deaths annually, approximately half of which are in India. Women, children, and other marginalized subpopulations typically bear the brunt of the burden related to inadequate water sanitation. They lack the political voice and/or the financial capital to force investments in sanitation goods and services in ways that improve their health. Policies have often focused on the supply of health-related technologies. However, there is growing recognition that a lack of demand contributes to policy failures (Figueroa & Kincaid 2007). Thus, if understanding and motivation are not present, expenditures on supply of technologies may have little impact on outcomes.

Reflecting on the choice about where to intervene, public health practitioners disagree about where to focus: at either the source of water or the point of use. Traditionally (as with the arsenic situation), water-source treatment and provision of piped water and sewage have been emphasized (Van der Slice & Briscoe, 1995). However, proponents of supply-led interventions have been frustrated by local governments and community management of water resources. Furthermore, the way people habitually use water can introduce contamination between source and consumption. This suggests the potential value of point-of-use water treatment. Clasen et al. (2007) compared the effectiveness of community-level water-supply interventions against household-level interventions. Their meta-analysis suggests that water treatment at the household level may be more effective in preventing enteric disease, yet they noted that methodological flaws limit comparability of the existing studies of such policies.

Patil & Pattanayak (2007) emphasized the multiplicity of possible intervention points given the complex web of exposure pathways through which fecal-oral pathogens can cause diarrhea. For example, using an F diagram, Wagner & Lanois (1958) illustrated many potential links among feces, food, and health via fingers, flies, fields, and fluids. A suite of avoidance behaviors could disrupt these links. Literature typically classifies these interventions or their outputs as water quantity [source (well, tap) and quantity], water quality (e.g., home water storage and handling), sanitation (e.g., pit latrine), and hygiene (e.g., hand washing). In fact, because of the singular lack of progress with sanitation, 2008 was declared the International Year of Sanitation.

Overall, consensus exists that *Escherichia coli* is the best biomarker for microbiological or (microbial) water quality, which is likely to vary at the household level (e). As discussed above, $s_e < 0$; yet beyond this first derivative, there is little agreement on functional form (e.g., Do e thresholds matter?). As important, there is disagreement about what types and combinations of avoidance actions (a) either change e or prevent low e from causing sickness s [i.e., $s(a)|e$ when a influences exposure]. Because microbes are not observed by the naked eye, it is harder for people to learn about these linkages.

The difficulty of knowing when a clean source water has been contaminated as a result of habits of use suggests the need to pay attention to point-of-use avoidance. As such, source-intervention advocates cite developed-country policies and outcomes in stressing the potentially large $s_{E(G,A)} < 0$, i.e., drops in sickness due to public investments to improve water quality. For example, Cutler & Miller (2004) suggested that water purification alone can explain half of the mortality reduction in United States cities in the first third of the twentieth century. In Section 5, we return to the issue of externalities with additional focus on social spillovers in environmental health problems.

The role of multiplicity of interventions requires further attention. In general, we must expect the marginal impacts of interventions (either on e or on $s|e$) to be affected by other interventions, such as $e_{a1}(a_2, E[A,G])$ or $s_{a1}|e$ ($a_2, E[A,G]$) (Van der Slice & Briscoe 1995, Corey et al. 2007, Patil & Pattanayak 2007). In addition, when households know this or otherwise view practices as substitutes for each other, they may shift their behaviors (e.g., Bennett 2008, Jessoe, 2009).

Different disciplines have focused on various points of the exposure pathway and impacts. Epidemiologists have largely focused on the size and sign of s_a (or S_A for those studying population health outcomes of community interventions), and environmental scientists on e_a. and E_A. Economists have focused on household perceived $u_s.s_e$. and e_a in examining stated WTP for hypothetical improvement in water quality (or the sanitation infrastructure that can provide it) or revealed preferences for water quality in the form of expenses that households incur for avoidance or capitalized value in rental prices. For a brief summary of this literature, see Pattanayak et al. (2009a) or the original papers cited in this summary, including Hope (2006), Larson et al. (2006), Whittington et al. (2002), World Bank (1993), Anselin et al. (2008), North & Griffin (1993), Jalan et al. (2009) and Pattanayak et al. (2005).

Other behavioral empirics focus more directly on the constituents of a and the marginal products a_k, a_m, and a_t (sometimes measured as impacts on sickness s). Thus, the question becomes, Do knowledge, materials, and time statistically and significantly generate avoidance because of interventions that change their costs? The model predicts a_n, a_p, $a_w < 0$, but the magnitudes of all these derivatives remain empirical questions. For example, Jalan & Somanathan (2008) conducted a randomized trial in Delhi, India, that informed households about the fecal contamination of their household's drinking water, and they determined that informed households were more likely to purify their home water compared with control households that did not know the quality of their drinking water. Curtis et al. (2007) offered a parallel example in the case of hand-washing behaviors in Ghana, whereas Pattanayak et al. (2009d) provided an example of toilet construction in Orissa, India.

Other researchers have employed a social marketing strategy to improve the salience of subsidized knowledge. In a study of toilets in Benin, Jenkins & Curtis (2005) showed that "prestige" and "well-being," such as identifying with the urban elite or increasing convenience and comfort, play a key in avoidance of fecal-oral disease transmission. This suggests direct contributions to utility ($u_a > 0$) from avoidance. Cornes & Sandler (1994) argued that focusing exclusively on public or private dimensions may have limits because such an approach fails to recognize impure public good dimensions. They explained, "If the joint products are complementary, then private outputs have a privatizing effect, not unlike the establishment of property rights. As a result, free-riding motives are attenuated" (p. 404). In addition, Heal (2003) explicitly suggested that, through "bundling," private gains can promote the adoption of publicly beneficial actions.

3.4. Malaria

Despite the investment of billions of dollars, approximately one-third of the world (2 billion people) lives in areas infected by malaria, and more people die from it today than did 40 years ago. Re-emerging with its distribution expanded; higher local incidence; and increased severity, duration, and resistance to treatment (Wilcox & Colwell 2003, Greenwood et al. 2005), malaria causes 2 million deaths annually, ranking as the top vector-borne disease. Beyond mortality, malaria causes morbidity through fever, weakness, malnutrition, anemia, spleen diseases, and vulnerability to other diseases.

Response can be broadly grouped into prevention (vector control) and mitigation (treatment). Predominant prevention strategies include the use of insecticide-treated bed nets or indoor residual spraying of insecticides. Vaccinations represent another prevention strategy that could prove beneficial in the long run. Prompt and effective case management (treatment) using chemophrophylaxis has represented the other major strategy in society's efforts to combat malaria. Because the rate of infectious contact is a key factor in disease transmission, prompt individual treatment is an important form of population-level prevention (Wilson 2001).

Additional options derive from the environmental bases for malaria. Breeding sites, survival probability, density, biting rates, and incubation periods all are profoundly impacted by ecosystem changes, particularly land transformation (Pattanayak & Yasuoka 2008). A recent comparative risk assessment suggests that "practices regarding land use, deforestation, water resource management, settlement siting and modified house design" contribute to 42% of cases worldwide (Prüss-Üstün & Corvalan 2006).[6]

Avoidance via management of water and vegetation is gaining support, particularly in light of mosquito resistance to insecticides and antimalarials (Lindsay & Birley 2004). A recent synthesis proposes numerous paths through which forest degradation (including disturbance, fragmentation, and deforestation) can affect malaria infection and disease (Pattanayak et al. 2006a). Mechanisms involve changes in vector ecology (Yasuoka & Levins 2007), mosquito predators, microclimate (Walsh et al. 1993), and behaviors such as irrigation and migration that increase exposure (Wilson 2001). The following are specific ways in which environmental changes can impact the spread of malaria: First, deforestation changes vector ecology. For example, cleared lands are generally more sunlit and prone to the formation of puddles with more neutral pH that can favor specific *Anopheline* larvae development (Patz et al. 2000). Second, deforestation can negatively impact biodiversity, thereby favoring proliferation of malaria-related species by eliminating species such as dragonflies that prey on anophele larvae. Third, deforestation can change local climate and thus affect the spread of disease by raising ground temperatures, which in turn can increase the rate at which mosquitoes develop into adults, the frequency of their blood feeding, the rate at which parasites are acquired, and the incubation of the parasite within mosquitoes (Patz & Olson 2006b, Walsh et al. 1993). Fourth, forest degradation may yield land-use changes that not only result in mosquito populations that have higher rates of malaria transmission, but also lead to increased human contact and transmission (Petney 2001). Finally, deforestation is accompanied by human migration, which aids transmission. Not only do migrants have little previous exposure and lower natural immunity, but administering health services to transient populations is also difficult.

Within our model, household-varying environmental quality (e) is the environmental conditions (or lack thereof) that encourage mosquito breeding, survival, and biting. Then, $s_e < 0$ and $e_a > 0$, e.g., a household can lower sickness by eliminating standing water and by applying oil to water bodies. A review of 24 studies by Keiser et al. (2005) suggests that environmental management can reduce the malaria risk ratio by 88%.

Yet, as with indoor air quality, the ability to change environmental quality raises the question of how avoidance by others affects you. Here, in contrast to indoor air quality, when others change environmental quality is most likely to help. This may be best

---

[6]The fraction amenable to environmental management varied slightly, depending on the region: 36% (25–47%) in the Eastern Mediterranean region, 40% (34–46%) in the Western Pacific region, 42% (28–55%) in Sub-Saharan Africa, 42% (30–54%) in the Southeast Asia region; 50% (38–63%) in the European region, and 64% (51–77%) in the North and South America regions.

expressed in our model as $e_A > 0$, i.e., having others manage their water supply improves conditions such that mosquitoes are less likely to infect you. Economies of scale in environmental management may also exist that are relevant for malaria (e.g., draining swamps or larval control, controlling deforestation), which could lead to public action with $e_{E(G,A)} > 0$ or could lower the cost of household action ($p_A < 0$).

Empirical economics research on vegetation and water management for malaria is rare. Part of the problem is that the k regarding mosquito-parasite ecology and malaria epidemiology is low. This could simply reflect high costs (r) of searching for and obtaining this knowledge and, more generally, the high costs of other inputs (p), particularly those relative to income levels in settings where malaria prevails. Below, we discuss intensive education and communication with respect to rice farmers in Sri Lanka, finding $a_r < 0$ and $a_p < 0$ (presumably because other inputs are effectively subsidized).

Even if households are fully informed, two behavioral tendencies may limit the effectiveness of malaria-prevention strategies. First, as with diarrhea, interactions may exist across interventions as $e_{a1}(a_2, E[A,G])$ or $s_{a1}|e(a_2, E[A,G])$. The effectiveness of environmental management, for instance, could well be conditional on the extent of use of insecticide-treated bed nets and indoor residual spraying of insecticides within the community. If actions are seen as substitutes, correctly or not, then arriving at the best choices will involve coordination.

Second, prevalence elasticity of prevention demand is likely to be positive (see Philipson 2000). The broader literature suggests that public health interventions are characterized by diminishing returns given increasing opportunity costs of prevention and declining demand for prevention as prevalence decreases. The key idea is that, whereas disease prevalence depends on the prevalence of safe behaviors ($s_A < 0$), the choice of safe behaviors is correlated with disease prevalence ($a_S > 0$, at least for lower values of S; very high S may also discourage some actions).

Section 5 focuses explicitly on spillovers, but for the case of malaria, this is fundamental enough to bear mention here. The environmental ($s_E < 0$) and contagious ($s_S > 0$) nature of these risks create classic coordination failure problems related to the optimal provision of local public goods—most notably free riding (or easy riding). Thus, if everyone else in the community manages vegetation and water to reduce mosquito-borne transmission, then an individual's risk of getting malaria falls ($s_E < 0$). Presumably then, any given household might free ride ($a_A < 0$) unless there is some form of community monitoring and enforcement strategies (e.g., informal norms that induce conformity, as within the sanitation case that is described in Section 4.3).

4. EMPIRICAL RESEARCH

Above, we treat each of our four health challenges in a broad manner, with an overview sketch and then a general conceptual characterization, albeit one distinguishing challenges. Here, we present some concrete examples of empirical research illuminating one piece of each of our four environmental health challenges. In each case, we review how specific interventions were studied and then we turn to consideration of how the evaluation of those interventions and the valuation of changes in environmental health risks can facilitate and inform each other.

4.1. Groundwater Arsenic

Continuing on our discussion of the Bangladeshi case, Madajewicz et al. (2007) examined households' responses to having the arsenic levels of their well water tested for free in Araihazar *thana*.[7] Conclusions about the impact of this information are bolstered by the fact that the natural distribution of arsenic across tube wells is independent of socioeconomic processes affecting responses. Here, we distinguish this exogenous arrival of risk information, when all wells are tested and only some are unsafe, from endogenous communication that occurs when households choose to attend an information session about arsenic (also discussed in Madajewicz et al. 2007). In the latter case, those who are seeking health-risk information by making a choice to attend an information session may represent those households who were more likely to take preventive action on their own. In contrast, bad news about well water arsenic is exogenous.

In Araihazar, the well water was tested for approximately 2500 people, and wells were labeled either safe or unsafe. The test results were then reported to the users within the sample. Households in the study site and in four control areas where no well testing was conducted were also exposed to information about arsenic. This information was disseminated by the government through television, radio, and newspapers.

The most striking result was the strong response to the well tests. Even before the information campaign, 60% of people who learned that the well they used was unsafe changed to another well within one year. Only 14% of people whose baseline well was safe changed, and only 8% of people changed in control areas. Controlling for other factors that may affect the decision to switch, learning that a well was unsafe increased the probability that a household changed to another well by 0.37.

As a result of the study, 98% of people in Araihazar can correctly state whether the baseline well is safe. Few people in control areas claim to know the status of their well, even though the television and radio campaigns on arsenic led almost everyone to become generally aware of the arsenic issue. Therefore, the change in behavior in Araihazar appears to be a response to the specific arsenic information about the concentration in individuals' primary drinking wells, not to other factors.

Opar et al. (2006) followed up one year later in the same location but with three times as many households. They found slightly higher impacts of receiving information regarding the well-water tests. This finding helps to address a concern (e.g., see Hanchett 2001) that switching is only temporary. Schoenfeld et al. (2005) then started to explore whether other locations showed similar responses. In a similar, nearby location without an ongoing health-impacts study (which could have inadvertently heightened arsenic sensitivity in the prior study site), they found that approximately one-third of those receiving news of unsafe arsenic levels in their well water switched to a safe source. These findings are significantly lower than the findings near the original health study site, yet they are still significantly higher than those previously found for responses to other health-risk information provisions (see, e.g., Jalan & Somanathan 2008).

In terms of evaluation of an intervention overlapping with valuation of improvements in environmental quality, the groundwater-arsenic setting provides us with a simple scenario. Avoidance was not occurring before the intervention that provided test knowledge,

---

[7]Different approaches to facilitating communal adoption and use of deep wells is being studied in ongoing research under a grant from the National Science Foundation (M. Madajewicz & A. Pfaff, unpublished results) in which Madajewicz is working with nongovernmental organizations on a randomized approach.

because households did not know which wells to avoid. Thus, although the knowledge was free, such that no value-revealing choice was required to make avoidance feasible, having a well test made feasible another value-revealing choice, most typically a costly choice to walk to another well.

If we know to which well a household switches, we can directly measure the change in arsenic exposure (i.e., environmental quality e) that results from avoidance. In addition, by knowing how far away the well is and thus how long it takes to avoid the health risk, we can measure time that can be valued at the wage. This combination of information, a measured costly action that changes e, is not always present in other cases. Very directly, then, this intervention provides an estimate of WTP to avoid the risk. Put another way, this setting is tailor-made to suggest a value of safe water. Having that value plus the fraction of people who switch and the cost of the intervention permits evaluation of the net benefits of publicly subsidizing the testing of arsenic levels in well water.

4.2. Acute Respiratory Infections

Mueller et al. (2009) re-examined data on approximately 3500 Chinese households, following a comparison by Peabody et al. (2005) that found significant effects of improved biomass stoves.[8] Mueller et al. (2009) compared different stoves with an emphasis on how nonrandom provision and adoption of cleaner stoves can confound impact evaluation. We note that randomization of stove distribution is now also being tried to avoid such confounding (McCracken et al. 2007, World Bank 2009). This is a small fraction of existing and ongoing studies, and such work avoids, but does not demonstrate the magnitude of, the bias from nonrandom allocation. Furthermore, household members' choices, such as where to be during cooking, can still confound evaluation of stove impacts.

Much of the existing literature supporting such stove interventions is subject to selection biases (Heckman & Smith 1995) because stove choice may be correlated with health outcomes for reasons other than the impact of the stove itself on health. Any such correlation confounds the accurate estimation of how the cleaner stove impacts health. Cleaner stoves may be more likely to be adopted by households with poor ventilation or by those that already have generally poor health. In each case, nonlinear responses of air quality to emissions and/or of health status to exposure may imply that the adopting households' marginal benefits of lower stove emissions are greater than those of nonadopters. If so, and if the characteristics of poor ventilation (e.g., see Bruce et al. 1998, Dasgupta et al. 2006) and poor prior health are associated with worse health outcomes, then well-intended and reasonable analyses may underestimate the benefits of using a cleaner stove. Yet, for a study looking at this bias in the opposite direction, see Pitt et al. (2006).

Mueller et al. (2009) found that those owning different stoves do in fact differ in terms of their characteristics that affect health outcomes. Such differences across the improved-stove and other-stove groups create bias. To address such bias, matching techniques are applied to control explicitly for group differences in estimating the effects on health outcomes of moving from traditional biomass and coal stoves to improved biomass and clean-fuel stoves. The idea, common in policy evaluation settings, is to

---

[8]Exploring other causes of respiratory infections are Dasgupta et al. (2006), who examined more than 30,000 households in Bangladesh to explain air quality, as well as Boy et al. (2002) and Mishra et al. (2004), who studied thousands of households by focusing on birth weight as a health outcome.

compare like with like, i.e., the outcomes for those with cleaner stoves to the outcomes for similar households with the original stoves.[9] Such comparisons generally raised estimated benefits.

In Nepal, Malla et al. (2008) considered the co-benefits of improved cooking stoves in terms of fuel use, forest and biodiversity, time savings for women and children, and regional climate benefits. They conducted studies in the Syangja, Chitwan, and Rusuwa districts of Nepal, using socioeconomic surveys of approximately 1000 households and pollution monitoring to measure cooking technology, kitchen design, fuel type, fuel-wood consumption, time allocation, particulate matter concentration, health conditions, medical costs, and socioeconomic status.

Statistical comparisons of households across districts differing in sociodemographic and ecoclimatic dimensions show that stoves can reduce particulate matter concentration (10–70%), acute respiratory illnesses (10–30%), medical costs (10–50%), cooking and collection time (20%), fuel-wood consumption (25%), and greenhouse gas emissions (25%). These findings are supported by instrumental variables approaches that revisit such comparisons while accounting for omitted variable bias and endogenous household responses.

Such results suggest a question: If these impacts collectively imply high internal rates of return, why are not more households adopting the improved stove technology? Limited access to capital can be an answer. Malla et al. (2008) found that both credit and peer-pressure (see Section 5.1) are key constraints. Thus, there can be gains from microfinance programs and information-regulatory campaigns.

In our model, inferring a value for improvements in environmental quality within this setting is more complex than was the case for groundwater arsenic. Recall that in Section 3.2, we focus on the case in which households do not perceive the benefit of improving environment quality. Despite the free provision of environmental-health-risk information ($s_e < 0$ and $e_a < 0$), households may not see a sufficient link to health. Although avoidance has occurred, in the form of improved stove use, recall that many stoves were provided for free (not bought by households). With free provision, even if a perfectly random group receives the improved stoves, there are no value-revealing choices made by households that could indicate household WTP for the stoves.

Even when stoves are not free, learning the value of indoor air quality from these choices remains challenging not only because it may be zero but also because other gains (such as lowering fuel cost) explain some of the WTP (Larson & Rosen, 2002). As discussed below, this complication is common for these major health challenges. That is, leading interventions may provide a bundle of changes and thus estimating WTP for changes in environmental quality may be much less straightforward than desired for valuation to support policy evaluation.[10]

---

[9]Matching is used in various settings to identify the effect of policies. For instance, policy-relevant re-evaluations have been carried out for job training (Dehejia & Wahba 1999), health (Hill et al. 2003), and forest conservation (Andam et al. 2008). In these studies, the re-evaluations are used to estimate the effect of the cleaner stoves on self-reported health status.

[10]Whether impacts on other households matter for a household's choice is another important consideration. To learn θ from this case, recall the two effects on the broader world's environmental quality (as discussed previously). In terms of the Clean Development Mechanism, the E in question is the world's atmospheric pollution, and it would be surprising if θ were meaningfully different from zero. In terms of impacts on others in the same village, θ could matter in some cases, but recall that here avoidance via chimney use could actually hurt the environmental quality of one's neighbors. Thus, other-regarding behavior could indicate less avoidance.

Even in the arsenic case, asking about bundles of changes raises the point that women who switched to tube wells from surface water often commented on water color, taste, and temperature as well as privacy. Thus, their avoidance behaviors provided a bundle of gains ($u_a > 0$ being a part). But this further highlights the convenience of the arsenic setting studied above, i.e., inducing switching from well to well, for which many of these bundled changed are fixed.

Yet, even if valuation is challenging in such situations, policy evaluation is not ruled out. As Larson & Rosen (2002) showed, the evaluation of improved stove provisions may involve many parameters (consistent with the discussion above) and can be approached using benefits transfer strategies (Smith et al. 2006). Some of these parameters could be learned by looking at different study sites and then transferred to a policy evaluation site to estimate the benefits of (or WTP for) improvements in air quality. For instance, providing free stoves to a random subset of households may enable researchers to estimate accurately the disease reductions from new stoves ($s_a < 0$, and information may permit learning that $s_e < 0$ as well as $e_a > 0$). Combining these s_a estimates with other u_s estimates enables us to determine whether the benefits of the provision outweigh its costs. This leaves open the question of why a public actor perceives benefits that the household may not. We return to this issue below.

4.3. Diarrhea

A cluster-randomized sanitation campaign in Orissa, India, provided a setting to examine responses to incentives and the resulting environmental health gains (Pattanayak et al. 2008). The study took place in 40 rural villages located in two adjacent blocks, Tihidi and Chandbali, in the Bhadrak district. Twenty villages were randomly selected and assigned to the treatment group, while the other villages served as controls.

The social mobilization campaign drew ideas from a model of community-led total sanitation that contends knowledge alone is not sufficient to generate lasting behavioral change. This models also seeks to generate strong, emotional responses at the community and individual level, culminating in a collective resolve to end open defecation by a community-defined target date by implementing a number of participatory activities. For example, the "walk of shame" activity involving a procession of village members drew attention to the volume and location of feces as well as the impact on the village environment.

Subsidies were offered to poor households because the campaign was implemented within the framework of the Indian government's nationwide Total Sanitation Campaign, which recognizes that low income constrains many households in the study area. Interviews and focus groups revealed that constructing the off-pit latrines promoted under this campaign was prohibitively expensive, and a baseline survey confirmed that cost was the main reason households did not construct latrines.

The intervention took place in the 20 treatment villages between January and May of 2006, and postintervention data were collected in August and September of 2006. A comprehensive household survey was conducted in all 40 villages in 2005 (baseline) and 2006 (follow-up), resulting in a balanced panel of 1050 households (529 treatment and 521 control households). Sample-size calculations indicated that 40 villages with 25 eligible households per village would provide sufficient power to identify differences between treatments and controls in toilet ownership and usage outcomes.

Pre- and postintervention data collection permits a difference-in-difference (DID) estimator to measure the treatment effect. These estimators compare changes in sanitation conditions across the two groups. The standard errors are inflated to correct for the clustered nature of survey data.

DID estimators suggest that the intervention increased latrine uptake by approximately 30%. *E. coli* levels rose from 1.3 to 3.7 colony-forming units per 100 ml in the control villages and declined from 0.9 to 0.1 colony-forming units per 100 ml in the treatment villages. Critically, the number of water sources with *E. coli* contamination increased from four to six in control villages and decreased from nine to two in treatment villages. Intention-to-treat and instrumental variables estimation of impacts of latrine adoption suggests (*a*) two-week diarrhea incidence in children under 5 may have decreased by 5%; (*b*) nutritional status of children under 5, measured by arm circumference, improved by 2%; and (*c*) time spent walking to open defecation site decreased by 72 min per household per day.

The study design permits the examination of two predictions of the model—household responses to free information (delivered in an intensive fashion) and cash subsidies—by stratifying the analysis by households below the poverty line (BPL) (subsidy eligible) and those not BPL (subsidy ineligible) households (Pattanayak et al. 2009d). The authors found a treatment effect of 36% in BPL households and 23% in non-BPL households in the treatment villages compared with their counterparts in control villages. Thus, by differencing the two DID estimates for BPL and non-BPL, they obtained a triple-difference estimate of 13% that suggests that subsidies caused approximately one-third of the impact, whereas the information-only scenario caused approximately two-thirds of the full impact.

However, this setting emphasizes a distinct challenge for valuation, as the water quality did not change significantly. Thus, even though households made costly choices that could in principle reveal their valuation of improved water quality, to first order the findings reveal that households not surprisingly prefer it when they can achieve relatively the same water quality (and health) at lower cost. This is useful for evaluating the provision of the latrine technology but is not nearly as helpful for the valuation of changes in household environmental quality *e*.

Specifically, before the new toilet technology was made available (at a subsidized positive cost), households achieved the health levels they desired by walking to defecate far enough from the village to avoid health consequences. Thus, an effective avoidance strategy had long existed, and the cost of time it requires reflects a household's value of a relatively clean environment. The existing avoidance strategy, then, certainly indicates environmental value.

Yet, water quality did improve to some degree. Given an effective, existing avoidance method, we may ask why, and one possible answer is the drop in the cost of avoidance. With higher cost avoidance, such as walking, many people avoid but some may not. As the cost of avoidance falls with improvements in toilet technology compliance with avoidance norms could reach 100%, thereby improving water quality. Looking for evidence of the relevance of imperfect compliance, we see that Pattanayak et al. (2009d) showed that toilet use increases by 25% among adults and 11% among children, even though toilet ownership increased by 30% on average.

The modest impacts on household health (s_a), in principle, provide some information to estimate values of improved water quality. If an independently reliable estimate of the impact of improved environmental quality (s_e) is available and the only role that a plays in the household economy is the prevention of water-quality risks, then household WTP for e can be $(p_a/s_a.).s_e$.

That said, recalling a theme from Section 4.2, the price paid for the toilet may not help if the technology generates a bundle of utility-yielding services. For example, if privacy or prestige also are associated with the toilet (much as prestige may be associated with a new stove, $u_a > 0$), then the WTP term above overestimates the contributions of this avoidance via water quality.

As with stoves, however, the health-impact information from such studies is still useful to evaluate interventions such as the information and communication campaign. One estimate of household benefits would be the sum of savings in cost of illness and prevention. Whittington et al. (2008) recently conducted such an exercise, with a Monte Carlo simulation to account for uncertainties, and concluded that the benefit/cost ratio significantly and typically exceeds 1 and that these types of interventions are generally viable.

4.4. Malaria

As noted in Section 3.4, Yasuoka et al. (2006) conducted a 20-week pilot education program to improve community knowledge about avoidance, particularly mosquito-control avoidance actions, using participatory and nonchemical approaches in Sri Lanka. In their study, households received free intensive training (knowledge) concerning s_E (the importance of environmental conditions for sickness) and E_a (household actions to manage the environment affecting those conditions). The authors evaluated program effectiveness using before-and-after surveys in two intervention and two control villages, and they found that the participatory education program led to improved knowledge of mosquito ecology and disease epidemiology, changes in agricultural practices, and an increase in environmentally sound measures for mosquito control and disease prevention.

Yasuoka et al. (2006) stated that household malaria history is correlated with malaria prevention but provided no direct estimates of the demand elasticities. In another study, Over et al. (2004) studied the effectiveness of indoor residual spraying of insecticides and insecticide-treated bed nets. They estimated two-stage regressions to account for the potential endogeneity of prevention concerning malaria prevalence, which they attributed to prevalence elasticity. To our knowledge, the existing literature provides little or no empirical evidence on the magnitudes of prevalence elasticity (Gersovitz & Hammer 2003).

However, the study by Pattanayak et al. (2006b) is an exception. They presented an empirical measurement of the prevalence elasticity of malaria prevention behaviors in the eastern ghats of India (Keonjhar district in the state of Orissa, which is a rural forested and malarial region of eastern India). Pattanayak et al. (2006b) examined links between village-level malaria prevalence and household-level prevention behaviors.

Approximately 600 randomly chosen households were interviewed from 20 villages in the towns of Joda and Keonjhar Sadar in the Keonjhar district. Topographical and infrastructure (e.g., road) data were also collected from administrative records and overlaid on the survey data by using a geographic information system. The survey contained many modules including self-reports on individual malaria prevalence, knowledge regarding the illness, and a variety of related prevention and treatment behaviors. Malaria prevalence is defined using data prior to 2005 to break direct simultaneity of household-level prevention behaviors in 2006 and village-level prevalence in prior years. Survey data showed that 34% of individuals in the sample had experienced malaria in the past 5 years (2001–2005), with approximately 75% of households having had someone suffer malaria in the past 2 years.

Seventy-three percent of the households practice at least one preventive behavior. Specifically, these behaviors included the following: 41% sleep under a mosquito net, 33% use repellants (mostly traditional, rather than commercial), 5% rely on public health spraying (indoors as well as outdoors), and only 4% clean drains and avoid standing water. The prevention measures were general, i.e., if households engage in any of the behaviors listed, and specific, i.e. if households sleep under insecticide-treated bed nets (the most popular prevention activity). These statistics also highlight the claim in Yasuoka et al. (2006) that environmental management for malaria is rare and needs incentives.

Regression models show prevention is positively and significantly correlated with prevalence. Controlling for demographic characteristics, caregiver characteristics, malaria knowledge, and socioeconomic factors, prevention decisions are more common when prevalence is higher. Whereas prevalence and prevention are simultaneously determined in other models, here identification is possible if a disease ecology complex enough to escape scientific consensus is not precisely understood by the households (as confirmed by Yasuoka et al. 2006). In this case, ecological factors, including extent of forest stock, irrigated farming, and distance to iron-ore mines, could be considered exogenous to behavior while explaining prevalence (see previous discussion on their links with malaria).[11] Thus, they are potential econometric instruments for prevalence as a determinant of prevention. The first stage finds the instruments to be individually and significantly correlated with village-level malaria prevalence, and overidentification tests confirm exogeneity. The second stage verifies that instrumented prevalence is positively correlated with prevention behaviors.

The explanation of intervention success by Yasuoka et al. (2006) has much in common with the arsenic situation. Yasuoka et al. (2006) contended residents' understanding of mosquito-borne disease rose as a result of community-based education. A twist here is the claim about how to transfer knowledge. In this case, that transfer was a function of a participatory approach involving hands-on experience in using nonchemical measures. Such an emphasis on the form and style of knowledge communication echoes the sanitation intervention.

In short, subsidized knowledge provision (lowering r) causes avoidance. The choice of communication strategies may also be modeled as ways of lowering r further. That said, these interventions may also effectively reduce other costs—for example, by lowering the supply costs of materials due to economies of scale or by offering technical assistance. Alternatively (or in addition), the externally driven campaign lowers transaction and coordination costs by guaranteeing a significant collective response by virtue of informal enforcement and external commitment.

The study by Yasuoka et al. (2006) is limited in allowing us to infer household valuation of the changes in E. The authors contended that success was in part due to a lack of

---

[11]Sachs (2003) discussed the use of tropical ecology indicators as predictors of disease ecology in his cross-country regressions of economic growth on malaria prevalence, but he did not implement his logic using econometric instrumental variables procedures. Carstensen & Gundlak (2006) implemented Sachs' logic and confirmed the usefulness of the instrumental variables approach.

costly materials or extensive inputs, whereas most economists suspect that households with more knowledge would already have been avoiding if this were the case (i.e., if modifying behavior was cheap or costless). Unfortunately, their study does not provide estimates of the changes in the time and material costs of household participation. If this avoidance cost information were available, as in the arsenic scenario, we could estimate household valuation of a lower-malaria environment (E).

In the India example as well, costs (p) of treated bed nets and repellants are not available. With these costs, we could derive what households' WTP (see formula in Section 4.3) for a given improvement in conditions or, given reliable estimates of s_E from either the study or other sources, for a specific reduction in sickness that would generate s_a.

Although these results contribute to the prevalence elasticity findings in developed countries (Philipson 2000), they do not resolve the issue of what is an appropriate role for public health. The results are consistent with Philipson's predictions that because public health investments (G) crowd out private averting behaviors (a), such investments are somewhat self-limiting. If households stop prevention when G lowers S and this significantly affects sickness, it may be necessary to accept endemic disease as a second-best outcome. So, are public health interventions not worthwhile because the disease reduction is lower than it would be if prevalence elasticity were zero and private prevention were held fixed? This is an overly negative view of public interventions because it ignores the fact that households will save the private costs of avoidance, owing to their endogenous private response (a) to public action (G).

5. EXTERNALITIES, SOCIAL INTERACTIONS, AND PUBLIC POLICY

5.1. The Case for Environmental Health Policy in Developing Countries

Up to this point in the article, we have described four major health challenges, discussed prevailing policies and programs, conveyed how these differing challenges and policies can be studied using a single modeling framework, and presented empirical research relevant for policy evaluation, including when evaluation is based on household valuation of environmental quality. We have not yet, however, focused on whether public action is merited. Below we describe interactions that could affect an agency's calculus concerning the decision to intervene.

5.1.1. Classical environmental externalities (policy and bargaining). For economists, externalities may justify interventions in the environmental health arena, such as the promotion of bed nets, toilets, and stoves. Credible and specific estimates of externalities' magnitudes are critical not only for determining the details of public programs but also for deciding whether to act publicly.[12] Limited public funds and concerns regarding efficiency suggest that governments must consider whether intervening is the best course of action.

Consider indoor air quality, noted above as improving with avoidance. Specifically, private air quality (e) improves. Two forms of externalities have been discussed: First, ambient air quality can fall if avoidance means venting via chimneys. Second, if avoidance is purchasing a costly stove to reduce fuel use and emissions, community and global

---

[12]Although the intent-to-treat and instrumental variables estimates of campaign impacts in the sanitation case study (Pattanayak et al. 2008) are indicative of externalities, this is not conclusive because of the contemporaneous nature of these data.

environmental quality may rise owing to household avoidance. In that setting complete internalization of individuals' global spillovers from the mixing of emissions of greenhouse gases cannot be expected, on the basis of households' other-regarding preferences or household-level bargaining. Some form of public intervention to limit emissions, for instance payments for emissions reductions under a program such as the Clean Development Mechanism, will be needed to attain social efficiency.

In contrast, consider the community spillover effects from venting via chimney. Here, what helps the household hurts its neighbors. Although such "dumping" could be taxed, repeated interactions in small villages may yield bargaining over processes, thus eliminating the need for a formal monitoring and monetary regulatory infrastructure. Such a process could involve local information that would make arranging efficient external solutions difficult. As a thought experiment, we can imagine a situation in which households establish coordination mechanisms to vent internal air while staying inside during cooking times, thereby efficiently responding to concavities in ambient air quality degradation. Recall that one reason this thought experiment remains in the realm of speculation is that households do not appear to perceive significant health risks from indoor air quality.

Similar to installing chimneys on stoves, environmental management to discourage mosquitoes affects not only the conditions relevant to the household in question, but also the environmental conditions relevant to other households. In our model, for other households such avoidance behavior likely provides only benefits. In terms of a pure prevention externality, however, we may not expect private decisions to take spillovers into account (Gersovitz & Hammer, 2003). Thus, in deciding on the use of larvicides, households will likely disregard that killing larvae lessens the probability that others will be bitten and infected.

5.1.2. Generic social interactions (public provision and learning). Consider the case of arsenic as represented above, where avoidance helps the household but does not raise environmental quality ($e_a = 0$). In this case, private avoidance required a public subsidy to information. But with knowledge having reached a considerable level and given that well tests and filters can in principle be purchased, it is possible that only poverty or equity will motivate ongoing public actions. Even though equity motivations may seem sufficient, the public well-testing program has ended. Thus, our description of the setting to date suggests privately efficient avoidance may be feasible if private options exist and they credit markets, e.g., are fully functional.

Yet, other characteristics of the problem suggest the value of community action. As noted, deeper wells are less likely to be contaminated with arsenic. They are also more costly, but many households can use a well and can thus share not only use but also installation and maintenance costs. Sharing raises free-rider and classic concerns of raising revenue and allocating effort to provide clean water. Public taxation and provision seem unlikely in rural Bangladesh at this time. Nonetheless, communities may advance health-risk avoidance in this setting, given the significant capacity of nongovernmental organizations in Bangladesh, including those with long-standing rural traditions. For a general discussion of analogous problems of common property resource management, see Ostrom (1990), which essentially is a response to Hardin (1968).

However, there may still be important uninternalized interactions, such as with learning. Although the government conducted a national television campaign and tested and painted wells, Madjajewicz et al. (2007) found many gaps in understanding. Thus, learning from others could have real value (see, e.g., Miguel & Kremer 2004, Munshi & Myaux 2006, Kremer & Miguel 2007, Conley & Udry 2009). This important interaction may be present in any setting including within any of the four major environmental health challenges that we have discussed here.

Returning to the issue of public intervention, such social interactions as described above can change the calculus for evaluation of public action. If avoidance by one household accurately raises the risk perceptions of others, then educating the first household has multiplier benefits.

5.1.3. Interactive private benefits. As noted above, private avoidance benefits could drive household decisions if external benefits are ignored [Heal (2003) advocated exploiting this channel through "bundling," which could apply to cases of either ignored or no externalities]. Many such private gains are purely individual, e.g., if an individual uses a big new free stove as a table rather than for cooking.

Other private benefits may have social or interactive elements. Social marketing of toilets may have contributed significantly to their adoption (and for indoor air quality an advanced stove may confer prestige). Benefits such as feeling one has joined the elite involve comparisons with the behaviors of others. They may yield multiple equilibria and various adoption dynamics. For example, Dickinson & Pattanayak (2009) suggested that low-level equilibrium traps could result from peer effects, particularly if private incentives related to regulations and price signals are weak. To avoid such low-level traps and to exploit multipliers, public policies that create the prestige of avoidance and/or subsidize avoidance by the first movers may be justified.

These alternative forms of public expenditures could be efficient, i.e., cheaper than other subsidies. In the case of $e_a = 0$, i.e., no externality exists, public expenditure would have to be justified (and perhaps funded) by gains across equilibria, such as reducing the mistakes made when households do not completely understand health risks. Then the cost of triggering any private dynamics could be compared with those of free education. Alternatively, a combination of education, learning from others, and private prestige may provide the best approach.

5.1.4. Infectious diseases. For acute respiratory infection, diarrhea, and malaria (as well as all the infectious diseases that dominate in **Figure 2**), externalities expand dramatically, perhaps explaining why the infectious diseases continue to figure prominently in statistics of health burdens. Given that a household's sickness here is part of the environmental conditions generating others' sickness, a new class of actions with infection externalities here exists, i.e., all the actions that keep others healthy when a household member is sick. Those actions could include prevention such as hand washing, as well as mitigation behaviors such as taking medicines to lessen sicknesss—both of which help others.

Unfortunately, private net benefits are likely to be lower than social net benefits from such actions, requiring some form of induced internalization of external gains from actions that curtail infections (Gersovitz & Hammer 2003). Accordingly, community leaders may invest in creating social norms to address both a household's lack of information (private inefficiency) and externalities (social inefficiency) as constraints on the avoidance of infection. Kosher rules and regular hand washing are examples of health-oriented norms.

Within our model, gains from conformity with norms could be seen as private ($u_a > 0$). Written that way, they appear to exclude entirely health or health externalities, as opposed to collateral avoidance benefits. Yet, if created to internalize unperceived or ignored health effects, such norms serve as health regulations, although mechanisms of enforcement could differ for this kind of regulation. They might take the form of public shaming versus monitoring and monetary instruments. Societies may choose between types of regulation on the basis of local feasibility.

5.2. Social Interactions Within a Case Study of Diarrhea

Empirical identification of social interactions is complicated (Manski 1993). Individuals' apparent influence on their neighbors could simply reflect shared characteristics (unobserved correlated effects) or identical exogenous influences (observed exogenous effects). Additional research on the specific mechanism of interaction—in constraints, expectations, or preferences—could not only provide clarification (i.e., Is this interaction related to epidemiology, imitation, conforming, or learning?), but also help to identify the magnitudes of key parameters relevant for policy choice (Manski 1995).

To provide one example, we revisit the sanitation case study. Dickinson & Pattanayak (2009) applied three econometric strategies to examine whether such apparent impacts, or correlations, were caused by social interactions: functional-form assumptions (Brock & Durlauf 2001), exclusion restrictions (Bajari et al. 2006), and an untargeted subpopulation (Moffitt 2001).

In the first approach, average adoption among other households in the village is a variable in a probit regression. This is a simple approach and the identification relies on functional-form assumptions.

In the second approach, neighbor characteristics with no direct effect on the household's adoption decision are critical. Any observed impact of such characteristics on choice of sanitation by the household must be measured through the impact on neighbors' behaviors, which in turn affect the original household. In the first stage, a neighbor's latrine adoption is explained as a function of the excludable characteristics—neighbor's housing materials—or as a robustness check yielding similar results, e.g., monthly expenditure and ownership of consumer durables. This regression generates predicted probabilities of adoption for each household. In the second stage, a household's latrine adoption is regressed on the full set of household and village characteristics expected to affect sanitation as well as the predicted level of adoption among other households in the village.

The third approach examines an intervention in incentives (e.g., prices) for only a subset of the sample. Changes in behavior by those not directly affected by the incentive change may provide evidence of interactions. The sanitation campaign involved a social component that was intended to address social norms as well as a subsidy for latrine adoption. The subsidy was offered only to households below the poverty line. Thus, observed increases in latrine uptake among households above the poverty line suggest that impact was partially due to social interactions. To test this, the adoption of latrines in the excluded group is regressed on own-household characteristics and the percentage of other households in the village that adopted latrines. The percentage of households below the poverty line in a village is an instrument for the percentage who have adopted the latrine.

Across these three econometric approaches, the empirical evidence consistently indicates that latrine adoption among other households in the village had a positive and significant effect on a household's own adoption decision. Thus, an individual's probability of adoption increases by 0.4% for every 1% increase adoption by everyone else in the community. Social effects are twice as large (0.8%) when analyses are limited to villages that were exposed to the communication campaign, indicating that the campaign caused households to place more weight on social components of utility and increased the social pressure to adopt latrines.

Collectively, these suggest that the campaign's impact was achieved by strengthening the social pressure to adopt latrines, and policies that target social drivers of behavior change may be more effective than those that focus only on private incentives such as subsidies. Thus, the social campaign may have increased the effectiveness of subsidies by creating a multiplier effect that shifted social norms.

6. HURDLES LOOKING AHEAD

6.1. Within These Four Health Challenges

Our overarching point is that behavioral choices are critical. This should be clear within each of the four major environmental health challenges we review, yet the findings suggest considerable nuance within and across settings. One common theme is that estimating households' WTP for changes in the quality of the environment is not simple, particularly if the technology that changes quality also delivers other benefits. Risk information and understanding are other common themes. In the simplest setting, policy makers can empower individuals' demand for health by providing risk information (Madajewicz et al. 2007). Yet, in more interactive settings, rational private choice can be prevalence elastic, for instance, even when each individual is fully informed. This suggests that rational individual participation in avoidance behaviors could fall despite the success of a public campaign, as was found for malaria (Pattanayak et al. 2006b).

The likelihood of the existence of many actions featuring externalities within the three infectious settings (respiratory ailments, diarrhea, and malaria) raised the issue of community coordination, particularly in areas where the actions of the state are limited. Incomplete capital (as well as other) markets may also hamper individual initiative. Generally, issues of behavioral interdependence raise ideas about communication via social channels, as in the sanitation case (Pattanayak et al. 2009c). For the highly burdensome infectious diseases, we find a complex frontier stressing social interactions, missing markets, and related responses (Malla et al. 2008).

6.2. The Challenges of Scaling Up

Existing empirical literature on global environmental health tests efficacy and effectiveness in the case in which intervention arrives exogenously. It focuses on the average treatment effect. Above, we also suggest the importance of differences from averages in considering the response heterogeneity implied by all of the different settings, exposure channels, and disease dynamics.

The effort to identify clearly the average treatment effects has led to holding randomized control trials (RCTs) as the "gold standard" for any policy evaluation, at least when political and ethical contexts permit. The parameters identified have clear value. That said, we note that they may not predict the outcomes of actual interventions, for instance those not randomly targeted. Many environmental health programs are and likely will remain nonrandomly targeted by program administrators and/or will be driven by local demands (Pattanayak et al. 2009b).

One nonrandom dynamic for scaling up programs is household choice. We can learn the impact of free well-water arsenic tests but yet not be able to predict what will happen when the funding for such knowledge subsidies ends and households must choose to test their own wells. An RCT could address the latter unknown by focusing on the household demand for information; however, that is best motivated by a concern with nonrandom scaling that is not always present.

More generally, as the causal chain of environment and health is neither short nor simple, external validity of treatment effect estimates is key to answer critical questions about whether interventions are sustainable and scalable (Pattanayak et al. 2009b). Victora et al. (2004) contended, "although some progress can be made by extension and adaptation of RCTs, ...new designs that incorporate adequacy and plausibility approaches must be developed, tried, and taught."[13] Such concerns reflect a larger trend in public health to accelerate the translation of research findings into public health practice through implementation, dissemination, and diffusion research.[14] Translation research that predicts actual scaling of interventions must identify major practical impediments to successful application of strategies in order to enhance the widespread adoption and institutionalization of an intervention. In sum, RCTs usually stop short of such questions.

Looking beyond efficacy trials to permit further comment on scaled-up programs echoes academic (e.g., Heckman & Smith 1995, Deaton 2009) and practitioner (e.g. Ravallion 2007) interest in analysis of participant or program heterogeneity. The idea of "opening the black box of the conditional mean impact" explicitly notes heterogeneity in program delivery, acceptance, and impacts (Ravallion 2007). If the target population chose and received different environment and development packages at the baseline, for example, multiple interventions should be studied (Mueller et al. 2009). Quantile treatment effects represent a semiparametric way to examine treatment heterogeneity (Gamper-Rabindran et al. 2009). We can also estimate heterogeneous effects of intervention via explicit analysis of subgroups, for instance by separating out subgroups of households by poverty status, ethnicity, or household characteristics (Jalan & Ravallion 2003, Pattanayak et al. 2009d).

Our focus on spillovers also suggests limitations on traditional partial equilibrium impact estimation. If varied interactions drive shifts between distinct equilibria following interventions, then assessment could be enhanced via computable general equilibrium models. For instance, the health impacts of climate change could have economy-wide

---

[13]Adequacy relies on documentation of time trends in key indicators after the intervention. Plausibility examines causality by comparing with control groups (historical, geographic, or internal) and addressing confounding factors.

[14]Translation research characterizes the sequence of events (i.e., process) in which a proven scientific discovery (i.e., evidence-based public health intervention) is successfully institutionalized (i.e., seamlessly integrated into established practice and policy). Translation research comprises many complex components that include specialized fields of study, specifically (a) dissemination research: how the targeted distribution of information and intervention materials to a specific public health audience can be successfully executed to increase spread of knowledge and, ultimately, use and impact; (b) implementation research: how a specific set of activities and designed strategies are used to successfully integrate an evidence-based public health intervention within specific settings (e.g., primary care clinic, community center, school); and (c) diffusion research: the systematic study of the factors necessary for successful adoption by a targeted population, which results in widespread use (e.g., state or national level) and includes the uptake of new practices or the penetration of broad-scale recommendations through dissemination and implementation efforts, marketing, laws and regulations, systems research, and policies.

consequences due to labor-productivity effects (Pattanayak et al. 2009c). The empirical toolkit for analyzing shifts at such scale could also include locational equilibrium or sorting models (Sieg et al. 2004, Bayer et al. 2009). By allowing for key behavioral adjustments, such general equilibrium evaluations may suggest significantly different impacts relative to the purely partial equilibrium approaches.

6.3. Additional Challenges

The environmental health economics literature is small, particularly when considering rigorous empirical research in developing countries. Although our list below is neither exhaustive nor mutually exclusive, we believe that at least the following three topics need greater attention.

6.3.1. Nonlinearities.
We start with a catchall of complications: nonlinearities arising at several points in the environmental health arena. First, we must acknowledge the tremendous range of magnitudes of threat or risk faced by individuals and communities across space and the associated nonconvexities, which we do not emphasize in our conceptual model in Section 2 or 3. Thus, we should not expect that understanding of shifts (for example, from zero to low, low to medium, medium to high, and high to extreme exposures) will accurately inform each other.

Starting at the physical level, the body has thresholds of resistance (which vary in the population) that are critical for evaluation. At the level of household decision making, we must consider the extensive margin (as opposed to the focus on the intensive margin in the model in Section 2), for instance an abrupt change in technology (e.g., using an electric stove) or behavior (e.g., sleeping under bed nets). Moving further to the community level, in particular when collective actions are desirable, additional forms of nonlinearity in response arise (see Section 5). For instance, because a household's contribution to the public good is likely to be affected by its expectations of others' actions, multiple equilbria are possible and can be shifted by any number of parameters. Equilibrium shifts can also be caused by a changed distribution of citizen types (e.g., less versus more likely to engage in avoidance), which in turn might have resulted as a function of nonrandom migration of these types (e.g., sorting).

Many of these concerns arise in the mainstream news accounts of environmental refugees initially made homeless by a natural disaster, such as an earthquake, tsunami, or drought, then caught up in a complex interaction among relief, aid, incapacities, and poverty. Climate change projections suggest more extreme stresses in the future: For instance, we may begin to expect the unexpected, such as "100-year" floods, droughts, or other extreme events. Empirical research on health impacts of natural hazards is still limited, despite empirical studies on coping with hazards in developed countries (e.g., Smith et al. 2006). As individuals, communities, and societies may begin to adapt to nonconvexities (perhaps by migrating), more research is needed on the careful assessment of a diverse range of policy instruments such as surveillance, early warning systems, and rainfall insurance. For example, Das & Vincent (2009) analyzed storm-protection benefits of coastal mangroves, using data before and after a super cyclone in Orissa, India, in 1999. They suggested that, although mangroves evidently saved fewer lives than an early warning issued by the government, the retention of remaining mangroves in Orissa is economically justified.

6.3.2. Migration. Consider the specific behavioral response of migration, one of the extreme situations discussed above. Migration has been an important concern for economists, not only because it reflects one of the most important, yet costly, choices exercised by households, but also because it reveals preferences for and values of geographic factors, potentially including the disease environment. In our context, households can engage in a whole menu of prevention and mitigation choices at the intensive margin to confront environmental health risks, e.g., hand washing and using bed nets. In contrast, migrating to escape the contagion represents a prevention choice at the extensive margin.

In a recent theoretical paper, Mesnard & Seabright (2008) developed a dynamic framework in which migration and prevention behavior are endogenous, responding to disease prevalence, migration and treatment costs, and current and anticipated health regulations. They explored how pressure for migration, which responds to differing equilibrium levels of disease prevalence, causes countervailing differences in city characteristics such as land rents. From a policy guidance perspective, the multiple equilibria in such models create a strong rationale for empirical testing of household choices on intensive and extensive margins. Although Timmins (2005) reviewed this migration literature (derived from a new economic geography), no one has empirically examined migration within an environmental and disease context.

6.3.3. Climate change. We close with a discussion of what may be the most profound environmental challenge confronting policy makers today: climate change. To some extent, this is related to the unequal distribution of health impacts of climate change (Haines et al. 2006). In the past 50 years, global mean temperature has risen by 0.6°C, sea level has risen by a mean of 1–2 cm/decade, and ocean heat content has also measurably increased. According to the United Nations Intergovernmental Panel on Climate Change (IPCC), mean global temperatures will increase by 1.4–5.8°C, sea level will rise by 9–88 cm, additional greenhouse gas releases from warmer oceans and warmer soils will increase temperatures by another 2°C, and floods and droughts will increase. Many health outcomes and diseases are sensitive to climate; these include the following:

- Climate change, excessive temperatures, and heat waves can alter arterial pressure, blood viscosity, and heart rate, thereby causing cardiovascular and cerebrovascular diseases among the elderly.
- Thermal stress and temperature-related air pollution (thermal inversion), pollen counts, mold growth, and pollution precursor (nitrogen oxide–based ground-level ozone) can cause a variety of respiratory diseases including asthma, bronchitis, pneumonia, cough, and cold.
- Increasing temperatures, humidity, and rainfall can affect proliferation, density, behavior, variety, viability, and maturation of insect vectors such as mosquitoes (which carry malaria and dengue parasites) as well as ticks and flies.
- Projected floods and droughts are expected to worsen water quantity and quality problems and impact water-washed diseases such as diarrhea and cholera.
- Finally, climate change can indirectly affect nutrition through its impact on agriculture yield, thereby affecting refugee health issues, which are linked to forced population migration.

Patz & Olson (2006a) contended that "changing landscapes can significantly affect local weather more acutely than long-term climate change" because land-cover change can influence microclimatic conditions (e.g., temperature, evapo-transpiration, and surface runoff), which influence the emergence of infectious diseases. **Figure 4** (see color insert) provides the direction and magnitude of health impacts of climate change according to the IPCC, taking into account the number of people impacted and potential adaptive capacity (Confalonieri et al. 2007). This latest health report from the IPCC also suggests the following:

- Health impacts will be greatest in African and Asian countries that already have high disease burdens. Those at greater risk include the urban poor, the elderly and children, traditional societies, subsistence farmers, and coastal populations.
- Adaptive capacity will need to improve everywhere. Although economic development is a major adaptation tool, it will not be sufficient to insulate millions from disease and injury.

Not surprisingly, significant knowledge gaps remain about not just whether major health outcomes will improve, but also how fast, where, when, at what cost, and whether all population groups will be able to share in these developments. Thus, key research priorities include improved empirical analyses of (*a*) health impacts of (and vulnerability to) climate change and (*b*) effectiveness and costs of adaptation. As Malla et al. (2008) contended, in this context, household energy technologies such as improved cook stoves are potentially win-win interventions by reducing respiratory infections and mitigating climate change (because traditional cooking technologies are not only dirty but also inefficient). In sum, adapting to avoid the adverse health impacts of climate change provides a clear and important final example of our paper's theme and title—i.e., the centrality of behavioral choices for understanding people's valuation of environmental risks and the social evaluation of environmental health policies.

DISCLOSURE STATEMENT

The authors are not aware of any affiliations, memberships, funding, or financial holdings that might be perceived as affecting the objectivity of this review.

ACKNOWLEDGMENTS

We are grateful to V. Kerry Smith for encouraging us to work on this review and for extensive helpful comments. As this review draws directly from research each of us has done with others, we also acknowledge various coauthors and the funding from employers and grantors. S.K.P. acknowledges his collaboration with Jui-Chen Yang, Sumeet Patil, Christine Poulos, Katie Dickinson, Dale Whittington, George Van Houtven, Min Malla, Krishna Pant, Jack Colford, and Ben Arnold as well as funding from the World Bank and the Duke Global Health Institute. A.P. acknowledges his collaboration with Shubham Chaudhuri, Malgosia Madajewicz, Lex van Geen, Alisa Opar, Amy Schoenfeld, Kazi Matin, Joseph Graziano, Lori Bennear, Alessandro Tarozzi, and Soumya Balasubramanya on arsenic; and with Shubham Chaudhuri, Howard Nye, Valerie Mueller, Kirk Smith, John Peabody, Darby Jack, and Niels Tomijima on indoor air quality as well as funding from the Earth Institute at Columbia University and the CCBVP at Duke University.

LITERATURE CITED

Andam K, Ferraro PJ, Pfaff A, Sanchez-Azofeifa A, Robalino J. 2008. Measuring the effectiveness of protected area networks in reducing deforestation: a rigorous impact evaluation approach. *Proc. Nat. Acad. Sci. USA* 105(42):16089–94

Anselin L, Lozano-Gracia N, Deichmann U, Lall S. 2008. *Valuing access to water—a spatial hedonic approach applied to Indian cities.* Policy Res. Work. Pap. 4533, World Bank

Bajari P, Hong H, Krainer J, Nekipelov D. 2006. *Estimating Static Models of Strategic Interactions.* Stanford, CA: Stanford Univ. Press

Bayer P, Keohane N, Timmins C. 2009. Migration and hedonic valuation: the case of air quality. *J. Environ. Econ. Manag.* 58(1):1–14

Bennett D. 2008. *Clean water makes you dirty: water supply and sanitation behavior in the Philippines.* Work. Pap., Univ. Chicago

Boy E, Bruce N, Delgado H. 2002. Birth weight and exposure to kitchen wood smoke during pregnancy in rural Guatemala. *Environ. Health Perspect.* 110(11):109–14

Brock WA, Durlauf SN. 2001. Discrete choice with social interactions. *Rev. Econ. Stud.* 68(2):235–60

Bruce N, McCracken J, Albalak R, Schei M, Smith KR, et al. 2004. Impact of improved stoves, house construction, and child location on levels of indoor air pollution exposure in young Guatemalan children. *J. Expo. Anal. Environ. Epidemiol.* 14:S26–33

Bruce N, Neufeld L, Boy E, West C. 1998. Indoor biofuel air pollution and respiratory health: the role of confounding factors among women in highland Guatemala. *Int. J. Epidemiol.* 27:454–58

Bruce N, Perez-Padilla R, Albalak R. 2000. Indoor air pollution in developing countries: a major environmental and public health challenge. *Bull. World Health Organ.* 78:1078–92

Carstensen K, Gundlach E. 2006. The primacy of institutions reconsidered: direct income effects of malaria prevalence. *World Bank Res. Obs.* 20(3):309–39

Clasen T, Schmidt W-P, Rabie T, Roberts I, Cairncross S. 2007. Interventions to improve water quality for preventing diarrhea: systematic review and meta-analysis. *Br. Med. J.* 334(7597):782

Confalonieri U, Menne B, Akhtar R, Ebi KL, Hauengue M, et al. 2007. *Human Health. Climate Change 2007: Impacts, Adaptation and Vulnerability. Contribution of Working Group II to the Fourth Assessment Report of the Intergovernmental Panel on Climate Change,* ed. ML Parry, OF Canziani, JP Palutikof, PJ van der Linden, CE Hanson, pp. 391–431. Cambridge, UK: Cambridge Univ. Press

Conley TG, Udry CR. 2009. Learning about a new technology: pineapple in Ghana. *Am. Econ. Rev.* In press

Corey CG, Yang J-C, Pattanayak SK. 2007. *Seasonal variation in risk factors associated with diarrheal diseases, rural Maharashtra, India.* Work. Pap. 07_01, RTI

Cornes R, Sandler T. 1994. Easy riders, joint production, and public goods. *Econ. J.* 94:580–98

Curtis V, Garbrah Aidoo N, Scott MB. 2007. Masters of marketing: bridging private sector to skills to public health partnerships. *Am. J. Public Health* 97(4):634–41

Cutler D, Miller G. 2004. The role of public health improvements in health advances: the twentieth-century United States. *Demography* 42(1):1–22

Das S, Vincent JR. 2009. Mangroves protected villages and reduced death toll during Indian super cyclone. *Proc. Natl. Acad. Sci. USA* 106:7357–60

Dasgupta S, Huq M, Khaliquuzaman M, Pandey K, Wheeler D. 2006. Indoor air quality for poor families: new evidence from Bangladesh. *Indoor Air* 16:426–44

Deaton A. 2009. *Instruments of development: randomization in the tropics, and the search for the elusive keys to economic development.* Work. Pap.14690, NBER

Dehejia R, Wahba S. 1999. Causal effects in nonexperimental studies: re-evaluating the evaluation of training programs. *J. Am. Stat. Assoc.* 94:1053–62

Dickinson K, Pattanayak SK. 2009. *Social reinforcing in the case of a (very) impure public good.* Work. Pap., Duke Univ.

Ezzati M, Kammen D. 2001a. Indoor air pollution from biomass comubstion and acute respiratory infections in Kenya: an exposure-response study. *Lancet* 358:619–24

Ezzati M, Kammen D. 2001b. Quantifying the effects of exposure to indoor air pollution from biomass combustion on acute respiratory infections in developing countries. *Environ. Health Perspect.* 109(5):481–88

Ezzati M, Kammen D. 2002. Household energy, indoor air pollution, and health in developing countries: knowledge base for effective interventions. *Annu. Rev. Energy Environ.* 27:233–70

Figueroa ME, Kincaid DL. 2007. Social, cultural, and behavioral correlates of household water treatment and storage. In *Household Water Treatment and Safe Storage*, ed. M Sobsey, T Clasen. Geneva: WHO

Ferriman A. 2007. BMJ readers choose the "sanitary revolution" as greatest medical advance since 1840. *Br. Med. J.* 334:111

Gamper-Rabindran S, Timmins C, Khan S. 2009. The impact of piped water provision on infant mortality in Brazil: a quantile panel data approach. *J. Dev. Econ.* In press. doi:10.1016/j.jdeveco.2009.02.006

Gersovitz M, Hammer JS. 2003. Infectious diseases, public policy, and the marriage of economics and epidemiology. *World Bank Res. Obs.* 18:129–57

Gordon B, Mackay R, Rehfuess E. 2004. *Inheriting the World: the Atlas of Children's Health and the Environment.* Washington, DC: WHO

Greenwood BM, Bojang K, Whitty CJM, Targett GAT. 2005. Malaria. *Lancet* 365:1487–98

Haines A, Kovats RS, Campbell-Lendrum D, Corvalan C. 2006. Climate change and human health: impacts, vulnerability, and mitigation. 367:2101–9

Hanchett S, Nahar Q, van Agrhoven A, Geers C, Ferdous Jamil Rezvi MD. 2001. Increasing awareness of arsenic in Bangladesh: lessons from a public education programme. *Health Policy Plan.* 17(4):393–401

Hardin G. 1968. The tragedy of the commons. *Science* 162:1243–48

Harrington W, Portney P. 1987. Valuing the benefits of health and safety regulation. *J. Urban Econ.* 22(1):101–12

He J, Vupputuri S, Allen K, Prerost MR, Hughes J, Whelton PK. 1999. Passive smoking and the risk of coronary heart disease—a meta-analysis of epidemiologic studies. *N. Engl. J. Med.* 340(12):920–26

Heal GM. 2003. Bundling biodiversity. *J. Eur. Econ. Assoc.* 1:553–60

Heckman J, Smith J. 1995 Assessing the case for social experiments. *J. Econ. Perspect.* 9(2):85–110

Hill JL, Brooks-Gunn J, Waldfogel J. 2003. Sustained effects of high participation in an early intervention for low-birth-weight premature infants. *Dev. Psychol.* 39(4):730–44

Hope RA. 2006. Evaluating water policy scenarios against the priorities of the rural poor. *World Dev.* 34(1):167–79

Jalan J, Ravallion M. 2003. Does piped water reduce diarrhea for children in rural India? *J. Econ.* 112(1):153–73

Jalan J, Somanathan E. 2008. The importance of being informed: experimental evidence on demand for environmental quality. *J. Dev. Econ.* 87(1):14–28

Jalan J, Somanathan E, Chaudhuri S. 2009. Awareness and the demand for environmental quality: drinking water in urban India. *Environ. Dev. Econ.* In press. doi: 10.1017/S1355770X08005020

Jessoe KJ. 2009. *Improved source, improved quality? Demand for drinking water quality in rural India.* Work. Pap., Yale Univ.

Jenkins MW, Curtis V. 2005. Achieving the 'good life': why some people want latrines in rural Benin. *Soc. Sci. Med.* 61:2446–59

Kenkel D. 2000. Prevention. In *Handbook of Health Economics*, Vol. 1, ed. AJ Culyer, JP Newhouse. Amsterdam: Elsevier

Kremer M, Miguel E. 2007. The illusion of sustainability. *Q. J. Econ.* 122(3):1007–65

Larson BA, Rosen S. 2002. Understanding household demand for indoor air pollution control in developing countries. *Soc. Sci. Med.* 55(4):571–84

Larson B, Minten B, Razafindralambo R. 2006. Unravelling the linkages between the Millennium Development Goals for poverty, education, access to water and household water use in developing countries: evidence from Madagascar. *J. Dev. Stud.* 42(1):22–40

Lindsay SW, Birley M. 2004. Rural development and malaria control in Sub-Saharan Africa. *EcoHealth* 1:129–37

Madajewicz M, Pfaff A, Graziano J, van Geen A, Hussein I, et al. 2007. Can information alone both improve awareness and change behavior? Arsenic contamination of groundwater in Bangladesh. *J. Dev. Econ.* 84:731–54

Malla MB, Pant KP, Pattanayak SK. 2008. *Climate change, cook stoves, and coughs and colds: evidence from rural Nepal on thinking global, and acting local.* Presented at Am. Public Health Assoc. Meet., San Diego, CA

Manski CF. 1993. Identification of endogenous social effects: the reflection problem. *Rev. Econ. Stud.* 60(3):531–42

Manski CF. 1995. Economic analysis of social interactions. *J. Econ. Perspect.* 14(3):115–36

McCracken JP, Diaz A, Smith KR, Mittleman MA, Schwartz J. 2007. Chimney stove intervention to reduce long-term wood smoke exposure lowers blood pressure among Guatemalan women. *Environ. Health Perspect.* 115(7):996–1001

Mesnard A, Seabright P. 2008. *Migration and the equilibrium prevalence of infectious diseases.* Discuss. Pap. DP6651, CEPR

Miguel E, Kremer M. 2004. Worms: identifying impacts on education and health in the presence of treatment externalities. *Econometrica* 72(1):159–217

Mishra V, Dai X, Smith K, Mika L. 2004. Maternal exposure to biomass smoke and reduced birth weight in Zimbabwe. *Ann. Epidemiol.* 14(1):740–47

Moffitt RA. 2001. Policy interventions, low-level equilibria, and social interactions. In *Social Dynamics,* ed. SN Durlauf, HP Young. Cambridge, MA: MIT Press

Moshammer H, Hutter H-P, Neuberger M. 2006. Gas cooking and reduced lung function in school children. *Atmos. Environ.* 40:3349–54

Mueller V, Pfaff A, Peabody J, Liu Y, Riddell T, Smith KR. 2009. *Who adopts matters: evaluating the health impacts of improved stoves in China using matching methods.* Work. Pap., Duke Univ.

Munshi K, Myaux J. 2006. Social norms and the fertility transition. *J. Dev. Econ.* 80:1–38

North JH, Griffin CC. 1993. Water as a housing characteristic: hedonic property valuation and willingness to pay for water. *Water Resour. Res.* 29(7):1923–29

Opar A, Pfaff A, Seddique AA, Ahmed KM, Graziano JH, van Geen A. 2007. Responses of 6500 households to arsenic mitigation in Araihazar, Bangladesh. *Health Place* 13(1):164–72

Ostrom E. 1990. *Governing the Commons: The Evolution of Institutions for Collective Action.* Cambridge, UK: Cambridge Univ. Press

Over M, Bakote'e B, Velayudhan R, Wilkai P, Graves PM. 2004. Impregnated nets or DDT residual spraying? Field effectiveness of malaria prevention techniques in Solomon Islands, 1993–1999. *Am. J. Trop. Med. Hyg.* 71(Suppl. 2):214–23

Patil SR, Pattanayak SK. 2007. *Behaviors exposed: household production of microbial exposure.* Work. Pap. 07_03, RTI

Pattanayak SK, Dickinson K, Corey C, Sills EO, Murray BC, Kramer R. 2006a. Deforestation, malaria, and poverty: a call for transdisciplinary research to design cross-sectoral policies. *Sustain. Sci. Pract. Policy* 2(2):1–12

Pattanayak SK, Dickinson K, Yang J-C, Patil SR, Poulos C, et al. 2008. *Nature's call: health and welfare impacts of latrines in Orissa, India.* Work. Pap., Duke Univ.

Pattanayak SK, Poulos C, Yang J-C, Patil SR. 2009a. *How valuable are environmental health interventions? Economic evaluation of a water and sanitation project in Maharashtra, India.* Presented at the Assoc. Environ. Resour. Econ. Annu. Work., Berkeley, Calif.

Pattanayak SK, Poulos C, Yang J-C, Patil SR, Wendland KJ. 2009b. Of taps and toilets: quasi-experimental protocols for evaluating community-demand driven projects. *J. Water Health* 7(3):434–51

Pattanayak SK, Poulos C, Yang J-C, Wendland KJ, Van Houtven G. 2006b. *Economics modeling self-protection against infectious disease: towards a theory of the economics of environmental epidemiology.* Work. Pap., Res. Triangle Inst. Int.

Pattanayak SK, Ross MT, Depro BM, Bauch SC, Timmins C, et al. 2009c. *Evaluating the health impacts of climate change and conservation policies using applied CGE.* Work. Pap., Duke Univ.

Pattanayak SK, Yang J-C, Dickinson K, Poulos C, Patil SR, et al. 2009d. Shame or subsidy revisited: social mobilization for sanitation in Orissa, India. *Bull. World Health Organ.* In press. doi: 10.2471/BLT.08.057422

Pattanayak SK, Yasuoka J. 2008. Deforestation and malaria: revisiting the human ecology perspective. In *Forests, People and Health: A Global Interdisciplinary Overview*, ed. CJP Colfer, pp. 197–217. London: Earthscan Publ.

Patz JA, Campbell-Lendrum D, Holloway T, Foley JA. 2005a. Impact of regional climate change on human health. *Nature* 438:310–17

Patz JA, Confalonieri UEC, Amerasinghe FE, Chua KB, Daszak P, et al. 2005b. Human infectious disease agents. In *Ecosystems and Human Well-Being: Current State and Trends*, 1:391–415. Washington, DC: Island Press

Patz JA, Graczyk TK, Geller N, Vittor AY. 2000. Effects of environmental change on emerging parasitic diseases. *Int. J. Parasitol.* 30(12–13):1395–405

Patz JA, Olson SH. 2006a. Climate change and health: global to local influences on disease risk. *Ann. Trop. Med. Parasitol.* 100(5-6):535–49

Patz JA, Olson SH. 2006b. Malaria risk and temperature: influences from global climate change and local land use practices. *Proc. Natl. Acad. Sci. USA* 103(15):5635–36

Peabody JW, Riddell TJ, Smith KR, Liu Y, Zhao Y, Gong J, et al. 2005. Indoor air pollution in rural china: cooking fuels, stoves, and health status. *Arch. Environ. Occup. Health* 60(2):1–10

Petney TN. 2001. Environmental, cultural, and social changes and their influence on parasite infections. *Int. J. Parasitol.* 31(9):919–32

Philipson T. 2000. Economic epidemiology and infectious diseases. In *Handbook of Health Economics*, Vol. 1, ed. AJ Culyer, JP Newhouse. Amsterdam: Elsevier

Pitt M, Rosenzweig M, Hassan MN. 2006. *Sharing the burden of disease: gender, the household division of labor and the health effects of indoor air pollution in Bangladesh and India.* Work. Pap., Cent. Int. Dev.

Preston SH. 1996. *American longevity: past, present, and future.* Policy Brief 7, Syracuse Univ.

Prüss-Üstün A, Corvalan C. 2006. *Preventing Disease Through Healthy Environments. Towards an Estimate of the Environmental Burden of Disease.* Geneva: WHO

Ravallion M. 2007. Evaluating anti-poverty programs. In *Handbook of Development Economics*, ed. TP Schultz, J Strauss, 4:3787–846. Amsterdam: Elsevier

Reddy AKN, Williams RH, Johansson TB, eds. 1996. *Energy After Rio: Prospects and Challenges.* New York: United Nations Publ.

Sachs J. 2003. *Institutions don't rule: direct effects of geography on per capita income.* Work. Pap. 9490, NBER

Sieg H, Smith VK, Banzhaf HS, Walsh R. 2004. Estimating the general equilibrium benefits of large changes in spatially delineated public goods. *Int. Econ. Rev.* 45(4):1047–77

Smith KR, Corvalán CF, Kjellstrom T. 1999. How much global ill health is attributable to environmental factors? *Epidemiology* 10:573–84

Smith KR, Ezzati M. 2005. How environmental health risks change with development: the epidemiologic and environmental risk transitions revisited. *Annu. Rev. Environ. Resour.* 30:291–33

Smith KR, Mehta S, Maeusezahl-Feuz M. 2004. Indoor smoke from household solid fuels. In *Comparative Quantification of Health Risks: Global and Regional Burden of Disease Due to Selected*

Major Risk Factors, ed. M Ezzati, AD Rodgers, AD Lopez, CJL Murray, 2:1435–93. Geneva: WHO

Smith KR, Samet JM, Romieu I, Bruce N. 2000. Indoor air pollution in developing countries and acute lower respiratory infections in children. *Thorax* 55:518–32

Smith VK, Carbone JC, Pope JC, Hallstrom DG, Darden ME. 2006. Adjusting to natural hazards. *J. Risk Uncertain.* 33:37–54

Smith VK, Pattanayak SK, Van Houtven G. 2006. Structural benefits transfer: an example using VSL estimation. *Ecol. Econ.* 60(2):361–71

Thornton RL. 2008. The demand for, and impact of, learning HIV status. *Am. Econ. Rev.* 98(5):1829–63

Timmins C. 2005. Estimable equilibrium models of locational sorting and their role in development economics. *J. Econ. Geogr.* 5:83–100

Van der Slice J, Briscoe J. 1995. Environmental interventions in developing countries: interactions and their implications. *Am. J. Epidemiol.* 141(2):135–44

Victora CG, Habitch JP, Bryce J. 2004. Evidence-based public health: moving beyond randomized trials. *Am. J. Public Health* 94(3):400–5

Wagner EG, Lanoix JN. 1958. *Excreta disposal for rural areas and small communities*. Monogr. Ser. 39, World Health Organ.

Walsh JF, Molyneux DH, Birley MH. 1993. Deforestation: effects on vector-borne disease. *Parasitology* 106(Suppl.) S55–75

Whittington D, Hanemann WM, Sadoff C, Jeuland M. 2008. *Water and sanitation*. Chall. Pap., Copenhagen Consens. Cent., Copenhagen Bus. Sch.

Whittington D, Pattanayak SK, Yang J-C, Bal Kumar KC. 2002. Household demand for improved piped water services: evidence from Kathmandu, Nepal. *Water Policy* 4(6):531–56

Wilcox BA, Colwell RR. 2003. Emerging and reemerging infectious diseases: biocomplexity as an interdisciplinary paradigm. *EcoHealth* 2:244–57

Wilson ME. 1995. Infectious diseases: an ecological perspective. *Br. Med. J.* 311(7021):1681–84

Wilson ML. 2001. Ecology and infectious disease. In *Ecosystem Change and Public Health*, ed. J Aron, JA Patz, pp. 285–91. Baltimore, MD: Johns Hopkins Univ. Press

World Bank. 1993. The demand for water in rural areas: determinants and policy implications. *World Bank Res. Obs.* 8(1):47–70

World Bank. 2001. *World Development Report 2000/2001: Attacking Poverty*. Washington, DC: World Bank

World Bank. 2009. *No smoke without fire: fresh perspectives on indoor air pollution*, Vol. 2. Tech. Rep., World Bank

World Health Organ. 1997. *Health and Environment in Sustainable Development*. WHO/EHG/97.8. Geneva: WHO

World Health Organ. 2005. *Indoor air pollution and health*. Fact sheet 292. http://www.who.int/mediacentre/factsheets/fs292/en/index.html

Yasuoka J, Levins R. 2007. Impact of deforestation and agricultural development on anopheline ecology and malaria epidemiology. *Am. J. Trop. Med. Hyg.* 76(3):450–60

Yasuoka J, Mangione TW, Spielman A, Levins R. 2006. Impact of education on knowledge, agricultural practices, and community actions for mosquito control and mosquito-borne disease prevention in rice ecosystems in Sri Lanka. *Am. J. Trop. Med. Hyg.* 74(6):1034–42

Irreversibility in Economics

Charles Perrings[1] and William Brock[2]

[1]School of Life Sciences, Arizona State University, Tempe, Arizona 85287;
email: Charles.Perrings@asu.edu

[2]Department of Economics, University of Wisconsin-Madison, Madison, Wisconsin
53706: email: wbrock@ssc.wisc.edu

Annu. Rev. Resour. Econ. 2009. 1:219–38

First published online as a Review in Advance on
May 21, 2009

The *Annual Review of Resource Economics* is
online at resource.annualreviews.org

This article's doi:
10.1146/annurev.resource.050708.144103

Key Words

irreversibility, uncertainty, option value, quasi-option value,
entrainment

Abstract

Three independent literatures have contributed to the understanding of irreversibility in economics. The first focuses on the future opportunities forgone by investments with irreversible consequences. The second considers irreversibility (and hysteresis) in the context of the dynamics of systems characterized by multiple equilibria. The third, with roots in complex systems theory, focuses on entrainment—a phenomenon recognized in economics as lock-in or lock-out. This paper disentangles the different strands in the economic analysis of irreversibility in order to identify the core ideas involved and to connect them to arguments in the parallel literatures on sustainability and uncertainty.

1. INTRODUCTION

The treatment of irreversibility in economics has a number of different origins. Indeed, the concept of irreversibility involved in the analysis of entrainment, the dynamics of multiple equilibrium systems, and the forgone opportunities to learn about system dynamics are all different. In this paper, we seek to disentangle the different elements in the analysis of irreversibility in order to identify the common threads in the arguments. At the same time, we seek to clarify the connections between the economic treatment of irreversibility and parallel discussions in other disciplines. Many of the points at issue in the analysis of irreversibility have been addressed in the literature on the stability properties of particular equilibria in ecological systems characterized by multistable states. These same points are also central to the emerging science of sustainability. We show how the treatment of irreversibility in economics relates to the sustainable management of coupled social-ecological systems and, in particular, to the management of the uncertainty associated with evolutionary change in such systems.

Three important but independent literatures have dominated the treatment of irreversibility in economic systems. The literature most familiar to economists stems from seminal papers by Arrow & Fisher (1974) and Henry (1974). These papers established that the economic significance of what Arrow and Fisher called the technical irreversibility of investment decisions lies in the forgone future opportunities—the options lost by the investment. This literature is less concerned with the factors behind technical irreversibility than with understanding its consequences for current decisions.

The second literature has its roots not in economics, but in ecology and focuses on the dynamics of systems that may exist in multiple stable states (Holling 1973). This literature considers irreversibility in the context of the stability properties of different states. Transition to an absorbing state is irreversible. Transition to a persistent state may be slowly reversible. More generally, the degree to which transition to some state is irreversible is implicitly measured by the resilience of the system in that state. The approach has been applied to a number of decision problems involving the economic exploitation of such systems (Carpenter et al. 1999, Mäler et al. 2003).

The third literature, with roots in complex systems theory, starts from the path dependence of many biophysical and social processes. Perhaps the clearest statement of the points at issue in this literature is provided by Ayres (1991), who argues that the phenomena recognized in economics as "lock-in" or "lock-out" are special cases of a more general property of complex dynamical systems—that their future is entrained by their past. Feedback effects serve to entrench or exclude some technologies or social processes, at least for a time. Agents in economic systems have more options than in other systems, given that they are forward looking and form expectations about the future, can form consortiums, and take other actions to "unlock" past choices [see, for example, the debate on the lock-in effects of increasing returns and/or network externalities (Liebowitz & Margolis 1994, Spulber 2008)].

In what follows, we identify the common strands in these literatures in an effort to characterize irreversibility and draw out the implications it has for understanding economic decision making in evolving systems. We then explore the main results from the different literatures and connect these to the emerging field of sustainability science. Because the focus of that field is the capacity of coupled economic and environmental systems to persist over time in states that are deemed desirable (Kates et al. 2001), the reversibility or irreversibility of social and biophysical processes is of central interest. In particular, it has implications for the level of uncertainty in that system, the degree of its predictability, and the time over which predictability extends.

2. CONCEPTS OF IRREVERSIBILITY

Arrow & Fisher (1974) defined an irreversible action as one that is infinitely costly to reverse, but then they immediately noted that the decision problem relating to irreversibility derives from the fact that a wide array of actions that fail this test are nevertheless sufficiently costly to reverse that this should be taken into account in the initial decision. This brings a much larger class of problems into the frame. Henry (1974) was more qualified still. He defined a decision as irreversible "if it significantly reduces for a long time the variety of choices that would be possible in the future." The phrase "for a long time" is, again, strictly relative. A long time in one decision problem may be a short time in another. So the qualification implies that we should be concerned over actions that are costly to reverse within a relevant time frame.

Many of the early papers on irreversibility focused on conservation issues that raise the question of the time frame in an acute way. The decision problem in these cases involves the choice between the preservation of some environmental asset in one form or its conversion to another. Hotelling (1931) established the conditions in which it was optimal to convert natural assets into alternative forms of capital, but, as Clark (1973) and Fisher et al. (1972) noted, the outcome depends heavily on the future value of the resource to be converted and the reversibility of the action involved within the decision maker's time horizon. In practice, most contributors to this literature have been concerned with actions that are difficult to reverse over relatively short periods. Arrow & Fisher (1974) argued, for example, that the choice between preserving a virgin redwood forest for wilderness recreation and clear-cut logging the same forest may be technically reversible, but given the length of time required for regeneration and a positive rate of time preference, it is effectively irreversible. The analysis by Fisher, Krutilla, and Cicchetti (Fisher et al. 1972) of the "irreversible" consequences of dam construction in wilderness areas falls into the same category.

The economic problem of irreversibility—for both Arrow & Fisher (1974) and Henry (1974)—was that it compromised the optimality of decisions made under uncertainty. Henry identified what he termed an "irreversibility effect": a risk-neutral decision maker deciding whether or not to undertake an irreversible investment on the basis of the expected value of the outcomes would "systematically and unduly, favor irreversible decisions" (Henry 1974, p. 1007). Arrow & Fisher (1974) were concerned with the social optimality of that bias, and they found that it would generally be optimal not to undertake an investment if there was some probability that it would be desirable to reverse it in the future. The driver in this case is the additional information to be had from waiting. Inclusion of (a) the option value in preservation and (b) the quasi-option value of the information acquired by waiting reduces the net benefits from development. More particularly, the possibility of acquiring better information about future benefits or costs regarding current actions should reduce levels of irreversible commitment relative to the case where there is no possibility of getting better information (Ulph & Ulph 1997). In this approach, therefore, the value of the options lost through undertaking an irreversible action is equivalent to the expected value of the information that could have been acquired had the action not been undertaken. In particular (rather extreme) conditions, the quasi-option value of irreversible actions taken under uncertainty is the expected value of perfect information (Conrad 2000).

For the literature that built on these foundations, irreversibility came to be equated with the sunk costs of investment, and the focus switched to the value of information either lost (Brennan & Schwartz 1985; Dixit 1992; Pindyck 1991, 2000) or acquired (Roberts & Weitzman 1981) through investment. In other words, irreversibility was considered a product of the fact that capital is not perfectly malleable. Because factories and equipment built for one purpose cannot be instantaneously switched to another purpose (Arrow 1986), this introduces constraints on the disinvestment of capital assets used to exploit resource stocks (Clark et al. 1979, Boyce 1995). Indeed, it simply reflects the difference between short- and long-run supply elasticities in an industry.

Below, we return to the implications of this approach. Note, however, that none of this literature questions the standard assumptions about the convexity of production or preference sets. Indeed, Arrow & Fisher (1974) made a point of asserting that the only effect of irreversibility was to raise the cost of investment. Irreversibility, in the sense in which they use the term, has no implications for the continuity or smoothness of the underlying production functions.

The second literature that bears on this problem focuses on the properties of the biophysical systems involved and starts from the assumption that those systems are (a) complex and (b) nonlinear. They can exist in many possible states, and the transition between states can be both abrupt and irreversible. The literature stems from a seminal paper by Holling (1973), which explored the capacity of ecosystems in one of many possible stable states to absorb perturbations without flipping to some alternate state. Holling referred to this capacity as the resilience of the system in that state (Kinzig et al. 2006, Walker et al. 2004, 2006). Resilience, in this sense, is determined by the size and depth of the basin of attraction corresponding to that state and is measured by the probability that the system will transition to some alternate state, given the existing disturbance regime (Common & Perrings 1992, Perrings 1998).

The measure of irreversibility that falls out of this literature is the probability that a system which transitions from one state to another will return to the original state in some finite time. If that probability is zero, then the transition is strictly irreversible. If the probability is one, it is strictly reversible. More generally, the degree of irreversibility of any transition will reflect the structure of the probability transition matrix as well as the limiting transition probabilities (the elements of that matrix). If the matrix decomposes to include both transient and absorbing states, then any transition into an absorbing state is irreversible (Perrings 1998). Note that, because the transition probabilities can be identified for any time horizon, the return transition probability is a measure of irreversibility over that horizon.

The relevance of Holling's work for understanding the dynamics of economic systems has since been extensively explored, both with respect to the general properties of nonlinear dynamical systems (Common & Perrings 1992, Brock & Starrett 2003, Brock et al. 2002, Dasgupta & Maler 2004) and the properties of specific systems (Carpenter et al. 1999, Mäler et al. 2003, Rondeau 2001, Horan & Wolf 2005, Perrings & Walker 2005). The specifics of this analysis are discussed below, but the concept of irreversibility it contains is the same as that implicit in Holling (1973), i.e., it is a property of the resilience of states to which the system transitions. The degree of resilience in this work tends to be measured through the return time to the original state, and it is frequently approximated by the extent of hysteretic effects.

The last concepts of irreversibility we discuss derive from another property of complex systems: that of path dependence or entrainment. This is closely related to the concept of irreversibility that falls out of the stability of particular equilibria. Field effects that concentrate activities, expectations, or beliefs, for example, may lock economic systems into particular technologies or preferences (Arthur 1989, Aoki 1996), though the ex-post evidence for lock-in in some frequently cited cases has been disputed (Liebowitz & Margolis 1994, Spulber 2008). Whereas some common examples of field effects, such as speculative bubbles, may be relatively short-lived, many examples of technological lock-in and even more examples of social customs are more long lasting. Social customs can be thought of as field effects that tend to retard change and, where codified into law or reinforced by institutions, can significantly reduce the probability of transition into alternate states. Holling (1973, 1986) argued that the vulnerability of ecological systems to perturbations depends on where they are in a cycle of states that corresponds, loosely, to the birth, growth, maturity, death, and rebirth of the system. Ecoystems that are in a mature, highly connected, brittle state (what he called the K phase) are less resilient than ecosystems in a newly emerging, rapidly growing state (what he called the r phase). But transition into a particular sequence may imply that the system is locked into that sequence until it becomes more vulnerable to exogenous shocks.

The concept of irreversibility that falls out of this is relatively weak, but it is more than just a notion that time is a one-way street. Wherever the dynamics of a system are entrained, the scope for reversing the process and the costs of doing so are diminished. Ayres (1991) characterized the phenomenon as hyperselection in the neighborhood of alternative attractors: A transient stage of evolution enables a system to "choose" between disjoint "attractors," which are thus equated with "lock-in." This reflects Arthur's (1989) perception that selection of one among a number of paths may be accidental, and yet that path may be evolutionarily dominant for a considerable period of time. Holling (1986, 1992) and Gunderson & Holling (2002) addressed the same phenomenon in terms of system reorganization—or transition between stable states—once its structure has collapsed under external shock or stress.

This has some similarities to sunk-costs effects, in the sense that the nonmalleability of capital does entrain production decisions, but notice that the emphasis in this literature is on the role of investment in shifting the whole system from one basin of attraction to another. Investment in new technologies and the attendant field effects induce the evolution of the system at moments when a number of alternative paths are open (Arthur 1989). They drive macro, system-level, change. The sunk-cost effect experienced by firms influences their investment decisions, but it is not sufficient to explain irreversibility as a macrophenomenon. To be sure, the benefits of delaying investment may lie in information on field effects—on which standard or technology is likely to "win", for example—but the evolutionary drivers are the factors that tip the system one way or another during transient states. All investment is associated with sunk costs, but whether or not they matter depends on the uncertainty associated with investment. The option and quasi-option value of particular investment decisions are sensitive to the evolutionary state of the system. In rapidly evolving systems, where investment may induce transition to states for which there are few or no historical precedents, the uncertainty associated with the investment is likely to be very high, and the irreversibility effect identified by Arrow & Fisher (1974) and

Henry (1974) is likely to be pronounced. More than 50 years ago, Shackle (1955) referred to such decisions as "crucial." They are potentially transformative decisions without precedent. They involve fundamental uncertainty, in the sense that there are insufficient historical precedents to identify either the set of possible outcomes associated with the decision or the probabilities attached to each of those outcomes. In other words, they are beyond conventional risk analysis.

Van den Berg & Gowdy (2000), in reviewing the application of evolutionary theories in economics, noted that "evolution can be characterized as disequilibrium and qualitative (structural) change that is irreversible and unpredictable, can be gradual and radical, and is based on microlevel diversity (variation) and selection, as well as macro-level trends and shocks ('large-scale accidents')" (p. 38). Economic models that leave room for evolution—i.e., that admit the diversity among economic agents that allows selection (or sorting) to take place—have tended to adopt an incrementalist Darwinian approach to economic development (Hirshleifer 1985), but the kind of discontinuous change that follows transitions between stability domains is closer to what biologists refer to as punctuated equilibrium (Eldredge & Gould 1972). In punctuated equilibrium, periods of stability are interspersed with periods of rapid change, similar to the processes described by Holling (1973, 1986). In evolutionary terms, this is induced by macroselection processes superimposed on the microevolution that stems from individual selection (Gould & Eldredge 1993). This has also led biologists to distinguish between selection and sorting, in which the causal aspect of individual selection is contrasted with the random events that drive sorting at macroscales. We argue below that if the transition between states is a function of random perturbations in the neighborhood of the thresholds or unstable manifolds of a system that can exist in multiple stable states, then individual actions that move the system closer to a threshold in any particular state will affect the probability of transition between states. Evolution of the system is not independent of the behavior of individual agents. Moreover, as Norgaard (1984) observed, evolutionary pressures in the biophysical system interact with evolutionary pressures in the social system.

So, what are the common threads in the various literatures on irreversibility? Four elements in the concept of irreversibility are general. First, irreversibility is a measure of the difficulty of returning to an initial state within an economically meaningful time frame following some perturbation. In the economic literature, perturbation has generally been interpreted as investment. Yet, even in 1974, Arrow and Fisher cited the impact of carbon emissions on climate change as an example of irreversibility, and most empirical studies have focused on environmental change.

Second, the focus on return time makes it possible to evaluate the "reversibility" of perturbations both within and across stability domains. Indeed, many of the examples of irreversibility cited in the literature are not irreversible in any strict sense but are simply examples of variables that are slow relative to the time horizon of the decision maker. There are, in fact, two measures of resilience in ecological theory: Aside from Holling's measure of the strength of the perturbation a system can absorb without transitioning to a new stability domain, there is a second measure [due to Pimm (1984)] that is the speed of return to equilibrium. Both measures are relevant in this context.

Third, irreversibility is a consequence of entrainment or path dependence. At its simplest, this means that perturbations induce positive feedback effects, at least over the relevant time horizon. The link between this aspect of irreversibility and the stability of equilibria is direct. Irreversible decisions are necessarily destabilizing. They are also a driver of evolutionary change, both within the economic system and within the biophysical systems on which the economy depends.

Fourth, irreversibility poses a meaningful problem only when it alters the decisions that individuals or societies would choose to make. In the economic literature, this has been identified with the scope for reducing the associated uncertainty. That is, there is a quasi-option value to deferring (or accelerating) an investment decision. The seminal work on this is by Dixit & Pindyck (1994).

3. MODELS OF IRREVERSIBILITY

Epstein (1980) completed the basic results on irreversibility and learning introduced by Arrow & Fisher (1974) and Henry (1974). We summarize these using the variant of the Epstein model developed by Ulph & Ulph (1997). They took a decision problem involving two periods: present and future. In the first period, the state of the world and the payoff associated with that state are known. In the second period, there are S possible states of the world, each of which yields an uncertain payoff, $\theta_i, i = 1, \ldots, S$. Uncertainty is reflected in the prior probability of state i occurring given by $p_i > 0, \sum_{i=1}^{S} p_i = 1$. The decision problem involves choice of actions x in period 1 and y in period 2 so as to maximize the expectation of a concave benefit function, $W(x, y, \theta)$.
Let

$$J(x, p; k) := \max_{y \in Y_{kx}} \{ \sum_{i=1}^{i=S} p_i W(x, y, \theta_i) \}.$$

Here, $Y_{kx} := \{y | y \geq kx\}$, with $k = 0$ if the effects are reversible and $k = 1$ if they are irreversible. Note that irreversibility is taken to mean that a decision variable in the future period is constrained by the choice of a decision variable in the current period. In other words, y is constrained more by x in the irreversible case ($k = 1$) than in the reversible case ($k = 0$). The main focus of Ulph & Ulph (1997) is to locate interpretable sufficient conditions so that if an irreversibility effect applies, (i.e., $k = 1$), then the optimal choice of x will be reduced relative to the case where there is no irreversibility effect (i.e., $k = 0$).

It turns out that whether or not an irreversibility effect applies depends on whether or not the decision maker is able to learn about the system by waiting. Take the polar cases first. If there is no scope for learning, decision makers remain ignorant about the state of the world in the future and face the same decision problem in period 2 that they face in period 1. In this case, action y will be the same irrespective of which state of the world eventuates. If, on the other hand, the decision maker is able to acquire complete information about the states of the world in period 2 before choosing y, then they are able to condition y on the state that actually eventuates. Now suppose that the choice of y is constrained by the choice of x. The polar cases are as follows: y is independent of x, and y is completely determined by x. In the first case, there is no entrainment, and the decision reached in period 1 is completely reversible. In the second case, y is entrained, and the decision taken in period 1 is irreversible. The cases treated by Ulph & Ulph (1997) are defined by $Y_{kx}, k = 0,1$.

The first point to make about this model is that the irreversibility effect is strictly a function of learning. Denoting the polar cases on learning N and L, Ulph & Ulph (1997) noted that sufficient conditions for the irreversibility effect to hold, i.e., for $x^N \geq x^L$, depend only on how uncertainty is resolved over time.

Recalling that $J(x, p; k) := Max_{y \in Y_{kx}}\{\sum_{i=1}^{S} p_i W(x, y, \theta_i)\}$, Epstein (1980) demonstrated (a) that if $J_x(x, p; k)$ is convex in p, then $x^N \leq x^L$ and that if it is concave in p, then $x^N \geq x^L$ and (b) that this is independent of whether or not the changes induced by x are irreversible. Here, $J_x(x, p; k)$ denotes the partial derivative of J w.r.t. x. In other words, the sufficient condition for an "irreversibility effect" to apply does not at all depend on irreversibility, but on how information is acquired. It is not surprising in these circumstances that both cases are feasible, depending on whether action now (Roberts & Weitzman 1981) or waiting (Pindyck 1991) yields the better information about future states of nature.

Ulph & Ulph (1997) also noted that all of the early models of the irreversibility effect (Arrow & Fisher 1974, Henry 1974, Freixas & Laffont 1984) assume intertemporal separability in the effect—i.e., no entrainment. To see whether irreversibility in this sense induces an irreversibility effect, they reformulated the problem to address the question of emissions in two periods and their impact on climate change. The payoff function now takes the form $W(x, y, \theta) = W^1(x) + W^2(y - x) - \theta D(y)$, with W^1 and W^2 and strictly increasing and concave and $D(y)$ is strictly increasing and convex. By symmetry with the Epstein (1980) result, they showed that if the partial derivative w.r.t. x of the cost function $C_x(x, \theta, k) = Min_y\left(\theta D(y) - W^2(y - x)\right)$ is convex in θ, then $x^N \geq x^L$ and that if it is concave in θ, then $x^N \leq x^L$. As in the Epstein result, this is independent of whether the problem is irreversible and merely reflects the value of information and the way that information is acquired.

For the cost function $C(x, \theta, k) = Min_y\left(\theta D(y) - W^2(y - x)\right)$, the irreversibility effect implies that $x^{Nk} \geq x^{Lk}$. The marginal cost of irreversible first-period emissions is strictly greater than the marginal cost of reversible first-period emissions. However, they showed that first-period reversible emissions are at least as great as first-period irreversible emissions both where there is learning and where there is no learning, i.e., $x^{Nk} \geq x^{Lk}, k = 0, 1$.

Defining the expected damage cost associated with first-period decisions with reversible and irreversible effects, and with and without learning, as $C_x(x, \bar{\theta}, 0)$, $C_x(x, \bar{\theta}, 1), \sum_{i-1}^{n} \pi_i \bar{C}_x(x, \theta_i, 0), \sum_{i-1}^{n} \pi_i \bar{C}_x(x, \theta_i, 1)$, Ulph & Ulph (1997) argued (recalling that $0 \leq \theta_1 < \theta_2 < \ldots < \theta_S$)

$$\text{for } x \leq \tilde{x}(\theta_1), C_x(x, \bar{\theta}, 1) = \sum_{i-1}^{n} p_i \bar{C}_x(x, \theta_i, 1), \text{ and} \tag{1}$$

$$\text{for } x \leq \tilde{x}(\bar{\theta}), C_x(x, \bar{\theta}, 1) \leq \sum_{i-1}^{n} p_i \bar{C}_x(x, \theta_i, 1). \tag{2}$$

From Equation 1, if choice of x is such that the irreversibility constraint is binding in the state of the world with lowest damage cost, then it will be binding in all states of the world, and marginal costs with learning and irreversibility are the same as marginal costs with no learning and irreversibility (because choice of second-period emissions is fixed by the irreversibility constraint). From Equation 2, if emissions are irreversible and if the choice of x is such that the irreversibility constraint bites at the expected level of damage costs, then marginal costs with learning must be at least as great as marginal costs with no learning. From this, Ulph & Ulph (1997) offered the following sufficient condition for an irreversibility effect: If $x^{N1} \leq \tilde{x}(\bar{\theta})$, then $x^{N1} \geq x^{L1}$ with the corollary that if $x^{N1} \leq \tilde{x}(\theta_1)$, then $x^{N1} = x^{L1}$. The proposition states that if there is no learning but there is irreversibility, then the irreversibility effect will hold: First-period emissions with learning will be no higher than first-period emissions with no learning. The corollary states that if there is irreversibility (in all states of the world), then the optimal choice of first-period emissions is independent of whether there is learning.

The treatment of the irreversibility of underlying processes in all of these models is rudimentary, because the objective was primarily to uncover the consequences of learning with and without entrainment. Subsequent contributions have explored the significance of different types of learning—whether active or passive (Chavas & Larson 1994, Chavas & Mullarkey 2002)—and have elaborated the quasi-option value in information flows (Hanemann 1989; Fisher & Hanemann 1986, 1990), but they have not qualified the basic insights that flow from Arrow & Fisher (1974) and Henry (1974).

Applications to particular systems have introduced more realism into the underlying dynamics of the system but with limited entrainment of investment. Clark et al. (1979) explored the implications of the nonmalleability of capital in a Schaefer fishery and found that nonmalleability primarily influenced the smoothness with which the long-run equilibrium capital stock is approached. Specifically, the initial development of the fishery generates overcapitalization relative to the long-run optimum, which is followed by contraction of that stock through depreciation until the long-run equilibrium stock is attained. Variants of the same approach have generated different investment paths (e.g., Boyce 1995), but the stickiness of investment has remained an essential part of the story.

The irreversibility of changes in the underlying biophysical system is the subject of a growing literature in economics. Although there is no standard reference for this work, the "shallow-lake" problem has come to be seen as an archetype and has attracted considerable attention (Carpenter et al. 1999, Mäler et al. 2003). We accordingly use that problem to illustrate the principal results. The problem has the convenient properties that the system can exist in one of two states, oligotrophic or eutrophic, and that whether it is one or the other state is a function of a single variable, nutrient loading—which may be a product of a number of different economic activities. Irreversibility (and hysteresis) in the model is the result of a typical "cusp catastrophe" of the sort illustrated in **Figure 1**.

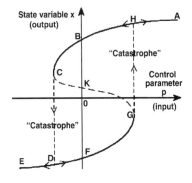

Figure 1

Equilibrium values for the state variable x for different values of the "control" parameter p.
Source: Göcke (2002).

In the shallow-lake model, nutrient dynamics are described through a conveniently simple differential equation:

$$\frac{dP}{dt} = \ell - sP + \frac{rP^q}{m^q + P^q},$$

where P is the concentration of phosphorus in the water column, ℓ is the rate of phosphorus loading, s is the rate of phosphorus loss (through sedimentation, outflow, and sequestration in biomass of consumers or benthic plants), r is the maximum rate of recycling of phosphorus from sediments or by consumers, and q determines the shape of the (sigmoidal) curve describing phosphorus fluxes. The concentration at which phosphorus recycling reaches half the maximum rate is m.

Depending on the parameter values, phosphorus loading can lead to changes that are reversible, hysteretic, or irreversible (**Figure 2**). Note that in this case the existence of the two states is known. Uncertainty relates only to the precise value of the parameters that will, in a given set of environmental conditions, induce a transition between the states.

Carpenter et al. (1999) established that the system will be optimally managed close to the threshold between the states—what they call the edge of hysteresis. They noted that the effect of uncertainty about the transition probabilities should, in hysteretic and irreversible lakes, induce a precautionary response—equivalent to an irreversibility effect. That is, uncertainty about the values of P, ℓ, and r that induce a transition from an oligotrophic to a eutrophic state should cause lake users to adopt lower phosphorus loads than would be optimal under complete information. Although the irreversibility effect is not directly addressed in the model, it is easy to see how uncertainty about the value of b is directly equivalent to uncertainty about θ in Ulph & Ulph (1997) and how it would affect the nutrient-loading decision with and without learning.

The shallow-lake model has also served as the focus for a set of dynamic models of learning. Recent work by Dechert et al. (2007) studied optimal Bayesian learning about the parameter b when it is unknown but is known to lie in a finite set $B := \{b_1, \ldots, b_n\}$ of possible values. This problem can become challenging if n is large because the state vector

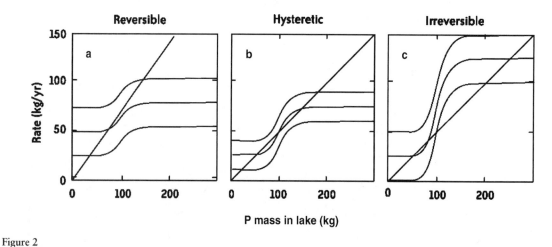

Figure 2

P sources (*sigmoid curves*) and sinks (*diagonal lines*) for (*a*) reversible lakes, (*b*) hysteretic lakes, and (*c*) irreversible lakes. Source: Carpenter et al. (1999).

must now be expanded to include the current vector of prior probabilities $\{p_{1t}, \ldots, p_{nt}\}$ on $\{b_1, \ldots, b_n\}$ as well as the state x_t of the lake at each date t. Dechert et al. (2007) built on the stochastic-lake problem of Dechert & O'Donnell (2006) to locate sufficient conditions for convergence of optimal Bayesian learning to the true value of b even when discounting is present. Discounting tends to lower the chance of convergence of Bayesian learning to the truth in this kind of problem. However, the effect of the interaction between discounting and the detailed structure of the problem on the speed of learning cannot be evaluated in two-period or even multiperiod deterministic models. We see this as a very important and wide open research area.

Subsequent papers have established that the transition probabilities between states in the shallow-lake model are highly sensitive to institutional conditions. Mäler et al. (2003), for example, optimized a welfare function of the form

$$\sum_i \ln a_i - ncx^2,$$

where n is the number of communities impacting the lake. This is subject to a transformation of the phosphorus-loading equation used by Carpenter et al. (1999):

$$\dot{x}(t) = a(t) - bx(t) + \frac{x(t)^2}{x(t)^2 + 1}, x(0) = x_0,$$

where $x = P/m$, $a = \ell/r$, $b = sm/r$, the time scale is rt/m, and $c > 0$ is the loss of ecological services relative to the value of the lake as a waste sink for phosphorus. They selected parameter values such that the lake will settle in an oligotrophic state but close to the threshold of transition to a eutrophic state.

In the absence of cooperation between the communities, the outcome is a Nash equilibrium in which the steady-state phosphorus loading is a solution to

$$b - \frac{2x}{(x^2 + 1)^2} - \frac{1}{n} 2cx \left(bx - \frac{x^2}{x^2 + 1} \right) = 0.$$

For $n = 2$, there are three solutions, two of which are Nash equilibria. One lies between the full cooperative outcome and the threshold, implying that the lake is managed even closer to the latter. The second has the lake in a eutrophic state (with welfare well below either the cooperative or the "oligotrophic" noncooperative cases). Which solution dominates depends on the initial phosphorus loading: A high loading will lead to a eutrophic steady state; a low loading will lead to an oligotrophic steady state. Moreover, because the distance to that threshold is lower in the noncooperative than it is in the cooperative case, the probability that the system will transition to a eutrophic state is higher in the noncooperative case.

The interdependence between the social and biophysical systems is reflected in the notion of coevolution (Norgaard 1984) in which the path dependence of a coupled system reflects the dynamics of both constituent parts and their interactions. Indeed, entrainment in the shallow-lake case follows from the impact of noncooperative behavior of those responsible for the pollution of the lake on the probability of transition between lake states.

More generally, let us reconsider the case where there are S possible states of the world, and suppose that the state of the system at time t, x_t, takes value i with probability $p_i = p(x_t = i)$. Entrainment implies that this probability is influenced by the choice of the actions available to the decision maker(s), u_t. If we call the set of actions over time a "policy," this defines as a sequence of functions that determines a probability law for the process $(x_t)_{t \geq 0}$ (Perrings 1998, 2001):

$$p^u(x_{t+1} = i_{t+1} | x_0 = i_0, \ldots, x_t = i_t) = p_{it, it+1}(u_t(i_0, \ldots, i_t)).$$

Thus, the optimal policy is that which maximizes the expected present value of the appropriate index of well-being:

$$W^u(i) = E^u \sum_{t=0}^{T} W(x_t, u_t(x_0, \ldots, x_{t-1})).$$

So the entrained trajectory of the system is $x_t = f(x_0, u_1, \ldots, u_{t-1})$. Note that the time taken for a system perturbed from a subset of the state space, S_A, to return to that state—the first return time—is $\sigma_A = \min(t \geq 1 : x_t \in S_A)$.

Not all states are reachable from x_0. If we define the set of states that are reachable from x_0 at time t as $S^t(x_0)$ and the set of all states that are ultimately reachable as $S^\infty(x_0)$, we can tighten the concept of irreversibility considerably. Specifically, if all states in S can be reached from x_0, then no action in a policy is irreversible. Technically, this implies that the probability transition matrix governing the evolution of the system, $\mathbf{P} = (p_{ij}, i, j \in S)$, will be irreducible. If $S^t(x_0) < S^\infty(x_0)$, implying that not all states that are ultimately reachable are reachable at time t, then some actions in a policy may be irreversible within that time frame. This is the example of the felling redwoods cited by Arrow & Fisher (1974). If not all states are ultimately reachable from x_0, then $\mathbf{P}$ will be reducible—and it can be written in normal form as

$$
\mathbf{P} =
\left[
\begin{array}{ccc|ccc}
\mathbf{P}_{11} & \cdots & 0 & 0 & \cdots & 0 \\
\vdots & \ddots & \ddots & \vdots & \ddots & \vdots \\
0 & \cdots & \mathbf{P}_{mm} & 0 & \cdots & 0 \\
\hline
\mathbf{P}_{m+1} & \cdots & \mathbf{P}_{m+1\,m} & \mathbf{P}_{m+1\,m+1} & \cdots & 0 \\
\vdots & \ddots & \vdots & \vdots & \ddots & \vdots \\
\mathbf{P}_{s1} & \cdots & \mathbf{P}_{sm} & \mathbf{P}_{sm+1} & \cdots & \mathbf{P}_{ss}
\end{array}
\right].
$$

In this case, the first m states are "closed": In effect, if x_0 corresponds to any of these states, the system will remain within that state. If x_0 corresponds to any of the remaining states, it will be able to reach alternative states with some probability. If $\mathbf{P}$ is decomposable in this way, the state space can be partitioned into two groups, S_m and S_{s-m}, where S_m is the set of closed blocks on the principal diagonal of the probability transition matrix. Separating the welfare functions corresponding to the two groups of states, W_m, W_s, we can write the expected net benefits of the control policy that determines the probability law for this system as

$$W^u(i) = E^u \left[\sum_{t < \tau} W_s \left(x_t, u_t(x_0, \ldots, x_{t-1}) \right) + W_m(x_\tau) \right],$$

where τ is the hitting time of W_m. That is, we can separate benefit streams associated with both reversible and irreversible states. Depending on the payoff associated with each of the states, the policy will be chosen to either shorten or lengthen the hitting time τ. In other words, the decision to slow or accelerate evolution toward an irreversible state will depend on the expected payoffs associated with that state.

Note that uncertainty about the impact of the policy on transition probabilities will have the same effect in this case as in the cases considered by Epstein (1980). If probing the system generates information about its dynamics, then the optimal policy will intensify the stressor (*sensu* Roberts & Weitzman 1981). If waiting reveals information about the system, allowing passive Bayesian learning, then the optimal policy will reflect a classical irreversibility effect (*sensu* Arrow & Fisher 1974). In both cases, however, the real impact of irreversibility will be to build the locked-in payoffs associated with irreversible states into the optimal policy.

4. IRREVERSIBILITY AND SUSTAINABILITY

Above, we highlight the close relationship between the issues raised in the literature on irreversibility and the emerging sustainability science. At the most general level, Kates et al. (2001) defined sustainability science as the science of the interactions between nature and society across both space and time. A similarly general measure of the sustainability of coupled systems is their capacity to maintain the flow of services on which people depend over time. This implies that the option and quasi-option values that are the focus of the irreversibility literature are nondeclining (Dasgupta 2001). Although the existence of a stable equilibrium (a steady state) may be sufficient to assure the sustainability of some dynamical system by this criterion, it is not a necessary condition. Nor is it necessarily attainable in an evolutionary system subject to selective and sorting pressures, irreversible changes, and fundamental uncertainty.

Recalling that irreversibility implies loss of stability, if the coupled system is only partially observable and controllable, then policies that perturb the unobserved and uncontrolled parts of the system may be destabilizing, i.e., may have unforeseen and potentially unforeseeable positive feedbacks on the economic system. In this case, the most that may be achieved is the "stabilization" of the system, i.e., the regulation of stresses on the uncontrolled part of the system to maintain stability given uncertainty about that part of the system (Perrings 1991). Stabilization strategies apply both to protect a system in a desired state and to avoid transition into an alternative undesired but irreversible or at least hysteretic state. So they fit the shallow-lake problem. But they are also strategies for maintaining stability (avoiding irreversible change) in systems that are imperfectly understood—they are not strategies for learning.

The scientific problem posed by the maintenance of sustainability in imperfectly observed or controlled complex coupled systems is to learn the dynamics of those systems without compromising their ability to deliver valued services (Perrings 2007). Most technological or policy innovation represents an experiment undertaken in largely uncontrolled conditions—a perturbation of the system that may be bounded by the scale of the experiment, but which is generally not isolated. Indeed, the more integrated the global system, the harder it is to isolate the subjects of such experiments. Many current environmental "experiments" are far from bounded—climate change and biodiversity loss among them. Both are irreversible, and both have the capacity to transform existing life-support functions of the biosphere. Yet, if technological or policy experiments are to yield a better understanding of the system dynamics without risking system stability or system sustainability, then they do need to be bounded. The most secure option in the case of economic systems—or coupled ecological-economic systems—is the development of models, along with criteria for model selection. Although there are few models of macro-environmental and -social processes, there exist reasonable selection mechanisms to discriminate between models on the basis of their fit to the data, predictive capacity, or the loss associated with decision-model error. Bayesian model updating on measures of output dispersion—the variation in the loss function associated with a decision rule applied to different models—is one such mechanism (Brock & Carpenter 2006).

The policy problem posed by sustainability is to assure that the irreversible changes induced by policies do not reduce the value of the system assets, especially the value of the options to use those assets in the future. In an evolutionary system, this implies maintenance of future evolutionary potential. There are two related criteria identified in the literature for this. The first is the maintenance of diversity. Evolutionary potential depends on selection and sorting, and both depend on diversity—among species, populations, cultures, institutions, technologies, and policy options (van den Berg & Gowdy 2000). Yet, diversity is threatened by the homogenizing force of competitive exclusion, which becomes more effective the more spatially integrated the system becomes. The aspect of irreversible loss of diversity that has attracted the most attention from economists is the loss of biological diversity, but the loss of diversity in other dimensions of the system similarly restricts its evolutionary potential. The displacement of local firms and local products and the displacement of alternative technologies and knowledge systems has the same effect. Indeed, that is the original concern over the phenomenon of lock-out—the exclusion of certain technological options as a result of the dominance of one (Arthur 1989). Nor is it sufficient to protect diversity in one dimension only, because the effect—particularly at the macro level—depends on the interaction between different types of diversity (Levin et al. 1998).

The second criterion identified in the literature depends not only on diversity, but also on the capacity of the system to respond constructively and creatively to external shocks. The capacity to respond to shocks without losing function defines system resilience. This is an area of explosive growth in the literature starting from the seminal contribution of Walters (1986). The link between loss of resilience and irreversibility is discussed above, but it is worth repeating that, because loss of resilience signals the transition of a system from one stability domain to another, such loss is generally associated with either irreversible or hysteretic change. This says nothing about the desirability or otherwise of that change, which depends on the payoffs associated with the system in either state. The desirability of maintaining adaptive capacity depends on the desirability of the reference state—or sequence of states. So an optimal policy in a desirable state would be one that reduces the probability that the system will flip into a less desirable state, and this is equivalent to assuring that it can adapt to the external stresses and shocks it faces.

5. IRREVERSIBILITY AND PRECAUTION

Consider the connection between irreversibility and a principle that is generally considered to be conservative: the precautionary principle. A widely held interpretation of the principle is that where the costs of current activities are uncertain but potentially both high and irreversible, then a precautionary response requires action before the uncertainty is resolved. Implicitly, it applies where the costs of inaction may exceed the costs of anticipatory action, but where there are insufficient data to form an expectation about the payoff (Taylor 1991). This principle was adopted at the 1992 Rio Conference as Principle 15: "[W]here there are threats of serious or irreversible damage, lack of full scientific certainty shall not be used as a reason for postponing cost-effective measures to prevent environmental degradation" (Gollier 2001). It is also enacted into law in a number of European countries. In French law, for example, it is defined as follows: "[T]he absence of certainty, given our current scientific knowledge, should not delay the use of measures preventing a risk of large and irreversible damages to the environment, at an acceptable cost" (Gollier et al. 2000). Notice the key role of irreversibility in both of these statements.

Application of the principle in the past has been extremely inconsistent. Harremoës et al. (2001) showed that in several cases where early scientific results indicated the potential for widespread, significant, and irreversible consequences, but where there was no basis for estimating a probability distribution of outcomes—e.g., halocarbons, polychlorinated biphenyls, and methyl tert-butyl ether (MTBE)—policy makers failed to respond. This partly reflects more widespread distortions in people's perceptions of certain types of risks. Empirically, decision makers generally underestimate risks from frequent causes and overestimate risks from infrequent causes (Pigeon et al. 1992, Starmer 2000). For example, insurers faced with low-probability, high-loss risks systematically quote rates that exceed the expected losses (Katzman 1988). To capture this, the weighted expected utility approach supposes that there exists an estimate of the probability distribution of outcomes that is known to the decision maker, but that the decision maker then weighs the various outcomes of their actions. It has, for example, been argued that decision makers weigh outcomes relative to some reference point (Starmer 2000). Decision makers' weighted preferences over outcomes can be represented by the function

$$W^u(i,p,\psi) = \sum_{t=0}^{T}\sum_{i=1}^{S} p_{it}g(\psi_t)\,W_{it}(x_t, u_t(x_0, \ldots, x_{t-1})),$$

where $g(\psi_t)$ is the weighting function that depends on the state of knowledge at time t, Ψ_t. If the weights attaching to all outcomes are identical, implying that the decision maker has no reason to discriminate between outcomes, this reduces to standard expected utility. If the weights are inversely related to the decision makers' confidence in the science behind particular estimates, then extreme, unique, rare, and irreversible events with few historical precedents will attract greater weight than they might objectively deserve. Uncertainty aversion of this sort will induce a response that looks precautionary.

For the most part, the irreversibility affect discussed above makes no assumption about either risk or uncertainty aversion, and it has been interpreted as a precautionary response. But note that we do need something like weighted expected utility to explain the more classically precautionary responses to novel threats. In the context of the irreversibility problem, identification of outcomes that are both potentially irreversible and potentially high cost can increase the value of additional information to the point that decision makers are prepared to carry a significant cost in terms of forgone output in order to acquire that information.

Although much has been done to clarify the theoretical points at issue in the precautionary principle (Gollier et al. 2000, Heal & Kristom 2002, Gollier & Treich 2003), significant questions remain about how to operationalize it—especially about how to discipline application of the principle by data and theory and to respect the true level of uncertainty that policy makers face. One option is to adapt recent work on Bayesian model averaging and model uncertainty to environmental issues. Brock et al. (2003, 2007) developed this approach in the context of monetary policy and growth policy. Their conclusion is that the "true" level of uncertainty is typically understated when a commitment (implicit or explicit) is made to one estimated model, albeit with the usual econometric measures of uncertainty reported for the estimated coefficients. Ludwig et al. (2005) noted that that there are two main sources of model uncertainty in environmental accounting applications: (a) model uncertainty in the discounting process and (b) model uncertainty in the underlying socioecosystem dynamics. The former reflects intense debates about the appropriate rate at which to discount far-future relative to near-future effects—what may be referred to as theory uncertainty (consider the debates in Chichilnisky 1996; Heal 1998; Weitzman 1998; Gollier 2001, 2002).

Brock et al. (2003) argued that one should approach model uncertainty through the following hierarchy: (step 1) theory uncertainty, (step 2) model uncertainty given each theory, (step 3) proxy uncertainty in the empirical counterparts of the theoretic objects in each theory. The idea is that each step leads to a class of models and each model contains relationships among theoretic objects. Thus, the empirical researcher must produce proxies for the theoretic objects contained in each theory. For example, Ludwig et al. (2005) cited a set of empirical studies of discounting processes and ecosystem dynamics that would go into a proper Bayesian model averaging study. However, Ludwig et al. (2005) sketched only how this might be done and illustrated by sketching a potential application for three problems: (a) What population size is optimal for a harvested resource? (b) Should North Atlantic Right Whales be protected? (c) How much phosphorus should be discharged into a lake? Extinction is irreversible for the first two problems, and the lake may be flipped into an essentially irreversible state in the third case.

Brock et al. (2007) argued that the scientific team should create a display that they call "action dispersion" and "value dispersion" plots where for each estimated model, the optimal action and optimal value of that action conditional upon the given model is displayed with data-disciplined Bayesian posterior probabilities. Brock et al. (2007) argued that the policy makers then can impose their own attitudes toward uncertainty and risk on these plots and make the policy choice as representative of the public. Ludwig et al. (2005) gave an argument that such a process tends to lead to precaution against irreversible actions for two reasons. The first is that the far-distant future has some probability of getting a large weight due to theory uncertainty and model uncertainty in the discounting process. The second is that the worst-case scenario of a totally irreversible possibility gets some probability due to theory uncertainty and model uncertainty in the underlying socioecosystem dynamics.

How should policy makers use the data/theory-disciplined display of action dispersion plots discussed above, which gives them an estimate of the "true" measure of the uncertain consequences for social value of their potential actions? Lempert & Collins (2007) presented an interesting approach and comparison of robust, optimum, and precautionary approaches. In the above discussion, we stress the problems with committing to a particular model and optimizing conditional on estimates of that model (even if one assures robustness to estimation uncertainty of that particular model). The problem with this commonly used approach is that it is too "brittle" in case the model specification is wrong. Hence, we argue that the Bayesian model uncertainty approach discussed above is a possible remedy to this "excessive brittleness" problem. But an excessively precautionary approach would be to maximize against the worst-case scenario, which represents the worst-case model that has positive posterior probability in the Bayesian model uncertainty approach. Because the maximin approach to assuring robustness seems too precautionary and, hence, may fall victim to the flaws pointed out by Gollier (2001), recent research has approached the problem via minimax regret (Iverson 2008). Minimax regret approaches to assuring the robustness of decision making choose the action that minimizes a measure of maximum regret over all models that have positive posterior probability in a Bayesian model uncertainty application. Variations on maximin and minimax regret in Bayesian model uncertainty applications "trim" away models that have positive but "small" posterior probability (Brock et al. 2007, Iverson 2008).

6. CONCLUDING REMARKS

The economic treatment of irreversibility discussed in this paper centers on two core ideas. The first is that the foregone options associated with any action that entrains the future should be taken into account in deciding that action (i.e., it has option value). The second is that, in a system that is imperfectly understood, the information offered by foregone options should also be taken into account (i.e., it also has quasi-option value). When combined with the wider literature on the nature of irreversibility in complex, evolving systems, these ideas provide a straightforward way of analyzing strategies that affect the transition probabilities for a system in any given state. Although they provide a compelling logic for the conservation of many environmental resources, irreversibility does not necessarily indicate a conservative policy. Whether a policy is optimally stabilizing or destabilizing depends on (a) the value of the system in alternate stable states and (b) the way that uncertainty about future states is best resolved. The cases that motivated Fisher et al. (1972) and Arrow & Fisher (1974) indicated that the socially optimal outcome would be more conservative than the privately optimal outcome, but that need not be true in all cases.

Indeed, the inconsistency of policies to address irreversible environmental change suggests that there is still much to do. Although economics has made significant progress in the theory of uncertainty management in dynamic coupled socioecological systems facing irreversible change, more needs to be done to develop a coherent framework for policy implementation.

DISCLOSURE STATEMENT

The authors are not aware of any affiliations, memberships, funding, or financial holdings that might be perceived as affecting the objectivity of this review.

LITERATURE CITED

Aoki M. 1996. *New Approaches to Macroeconomic Modeling*. Cambridge, UK: Cambridge Univ. Press

Arrow KJ. 1986. Optimal capital policy with irreversible investment. In *Value, Capital and Growth*, ed. JN Wolfe, pp. 1–20. Edinborough: Edinborough Univ. Press

Arrow KJ, Fisher A. 1974. Environmental preservation, uncertainty and irreversibility. *Q. J. Econ.* 88 (2):312–19

Arthur B. 1989. Competing technologies, increasing returns and lock-in by historical events. *Econ. J.* 99:116–31

Ayres R. 1991. Evolutionary economics and environmental imperatives. *Struct. Change Econ. Dyn. 2* (2):255–73

Boyce J. 1995. Optimal capital accumulation in a fishery: a non-linear irreversible investment model. *J. Environ. Econ. Manag.* 28:324–39

Brennan MJ, Schwartz ES. 1985. A note on the geometric mean index. *J. Financ. Quant. Anal.* 20 (1):119–22

Brock W, Durlauf S, West K. 2003. Policy analysis in uncertain economic environments. *Brookings Pap. Econ. Act.* 1:235–322

Brock W, Durlauf S, West K. 2007. Model uncertainty and policy evaluation: some theory and empirics. *J. Econ.* 136(2):629–64

Brock WA, Carpenter S. 2006. Rising variance: a leading indicator of ecological transition. *Ecol. Lett.* 9:311–18

Brock WA, Mäler K-G, Perrings C. 2002. Resilience and sustainability: the economic analysis of non-linear dynamic systems. In *Panarchy: Understanding Transformations in Systems of Humans and Nature*, ed. LH Gunderson, CS Holling, pp. 261–91. Washington, DC: Island Press

Brock WA, Starrett D. 2003. Nonconvexities in ecological management problems. *Environ. Resour. Econ.* 26(4):575–624

Carpenter S, Ludwig D, Brock W. 1999. Management of eutrophication for lakes subject to potentially irreversible change. *Ecol. Appl.* 9:751–71

Chavas J-P, Larson BA. 1994. Economic behavior under temporal uncertainty. *South. Econ. J.* 61 (2):465–77

Chavas J-P, Mullarkey D. 2002. On the valuation of uncertainty in welfare analysis. *Am. J. Agric. Econ.* 84(1):23–38

Chichilnisky G. 1996. An axiomatic approach to sustainable development. *Soc. Choice Welfare* 13:219–48

Clark CW. 1973. The economics of overexploitation. *Science* 181:630–34

Clark CW, Clarke FH, Munro GR. 1979. The optimal exploitation of renewable resource stocks: problems of irreversible investment. *Econometrica* 47(1):25–47

Common M, Perrings C. 1992. Towards an ecological economics of sustainability. *Ecol. Econ.* 6:7–34

Conrad JM. 2000. Wilderness: options to preserve, extract or develop. *Resour. Energy Econ.* 22:205–19

Dasgupta P. 2001. *Human Well-Being and the Natural Environment*. Oxford, UK: Oxford Univ. Press

Dasgupta P, Maler K-G, eds. 2004. *The Economics of Non-Convex Ecosystems*. Dordrecht/Boston/London: Kluwer Acad.

Dechert W, O'Donnell S. 2006. The stochastic lake game: a numerical solution. *J. Econ. Dyn. Control* 30:1569–87

Dechert W, O'Donnell S, Brock W. 2007. Bayes' learning of unknown parameters. *J. Differ. Equ. Appl.* 13(2-3):121–33

Dixit AK. 1992. Investment and hysteresis. *J. Econ. Perspect.* 6:107–32

Dixit AK, Pindyck RS. 1994. *Investment Under Uncertainty*. Princeton, NJ: Princeton Univ. Press

Eldredge N, Gould SJ. 1972. Punctuated equilibria: an alternative to phyletic gradualism. In *Models in Paleobiology*, ed. TJM Schopf, pp. 82–115. San Francisco, CA: Freeman

Epstein LG. 1980. Decision making and the temporal resolution of uncertainty. *Int. Econ. Rev.* 21:269–83

Fisher AC, Hanemann WM. 1986. Environmental damages and option values. *Nat. Resour. Model.* 1:111–24

Fisher AC, Hanemann WM. 1990. Information and the dynamics of environment protection: the concept of the critical period. *Scand. J. Econ.* 92:399–414

Fisher AC, Krutilla JV, Cicchetti CJ. 1972. The economics of environmental preservation: a theoretical and empirical analysis *Am. Econ. Rev.* 62(4):605–19

Freixas X, Laffont J-J. 1984. On the irreversibility effect. In *Bayesian Models in Economic Theory*, ed. M Boyer, R Kihlstrom, pp. 381–412. Dordrecht: Elsevier

Göcke M. 2002. Various concepts of hysteresis in applied economics. *J. Econ. Surv.* 16(2):167–88

Gollier C. 2001. *The Economics of Risk and Time*. Cambridge, MA: MIT Press

Gollier C. 2002. Discounting an uncertain future. *J. Public Econ.* 85:149–66

Gollier C, Jullien B, Treich N. 2000. Scientific progress and irreversibility: an economic interpretation of the "Precautionary Principle." *J. Public Econ.* 75:229–53

Gollier C, Treich N. 2003. Decision making under scientific uncertainty: the economics of the precautionary principle. *J. Risk Uncertain.* 27(1):77–103

Gould SJ, Eldredge N. 1993. Punctuated equilibrium comes of age. *Nature* 366(6452):223–27

Gunderson LH, Holling CS. 2002. *Panarchy: Understanding Transformations in Systems of Humans and Nature*. Washington, D.C: Island Press

Hanemann WM. 1989. Information and the concept of option value. *J. Environ. Econ. Manag.* 16:23–37

Harremoës P, Gee D, MacGarvin M, Stirling A, Keys J, et al., eds. 2001. Late lessons from early warnings: the precautionary principle. *Environ. Issue Rep. 22*, Eur. Environ. Agency, Copenhagen, Denmark

Heal G. 1998. *Valuing the Future: Economic Theory and Sustainability*. New York: Columbia Univ. Press

Heal G, Kristom B. 2002. Uncertainty and climate change. *Environ. Resour. Econ.* 22:3–39

Henry C. 1974. Investment decisions under uncertainty: the "Irreversibility Effect." *Am. Econ. Rev.* 64(6):1006–12

Hirshleifer J. 1985. The expanding domain of economics. *Am. Econ. Rev.* 75:53–68

Holling CS. 1973. Resilience and stability of ecological systems. *Annu. Rev. Ecol. Syst.* 4:1–23

Holling CS. 1986. The resilience of terrestrial ecosystems: local surprise and global change. In *Sustainable Development of the Biosphere*, ed. WC Clark, RE Munn. Cambridge, UK: Cambridge Univ. Press

Holling CS. 1992. Cross-scale morphology geometry and dynamics of ecosystems. *Ecol. Monogr.* 62:447–502

Horan R, Wolf C. 2005. The economics of managing infectious wildlife disease. *Am. J. Agric. Econ.* 87(3):537–51

Hotelling H. 1931. The economics of exhaustible resources. *J. Polit. Econ.* 39(2):137–75

Iverson T. 2008. *Cooperation amid controversy: decision support for climate change policy*. Work. Pap., Dep. Econ., Univ. Wisconsin-Madison

Kates RW, Clark WC, Corell R, Hall JM, Jaeger CC, et al. 2001. Sustainability science. *Science* 292:641–42

Katzman MT. 1988. Pollution liability insurance and catastrophic environmental risk. *J. Risk Insur.* 55:75–100

Kinzig AP, Ryan P, Etienne M, Elmqvist T, Allison H, Walker BH. 2006. Resilience and regime shifts: assessing cascading effects. *Ecol. Soc.* 11(1): artic. 13

Lempert R, Collins M. 2007. Managing the risk of uncertain threshold responses: comparison of robust, optimum, and precautionary approaches. *Risk Anal.* 27(4):1009–26

Levin SA, Barrett S, Aniyar S, Baumol W, Bliss C, et al. 1998. Resilience in natural and socioeconomic systems. *Environ. Dev. Econ.* 3(2):222–34

Liebowitz S, Margolis S. 1994. Network externalities: an uncommon tragedy. *J. Econ. Perspect.* 8(2):133–50

Ludwig D, Brock W, Carpenter S. 2005. Uncertainty in discount models and environmental accounting. *Ecol. Soc.* 10(2): artic. 13

Mäler K, Xepapadeas A, de Zeeuw A. 2003. The economics of shallow lakes. *Environ. Resour. Econ.* 26:603–24

Norgaard R. 1984. Coevolutionary development potential. *Land Econ.* 60(2):160–73

Perrings C. 1991. Ecological sustainability and environmental control. *Struct. Change Econ. Dyn.* 2:275–95

Perrings C. 1998. Resilience in the dynamics of economy-environment systems. *Environ. Resour. Econ.* 11(3-4):503–20

Perrings C. 2001. Modelling sustainable ecological-economic development. In *International Yearbook of Environmental and Resource Economics*, ed. H Folmer, T Tietenberg, pp.179–201. Cheltenham, UK: Edward Elgar

Perrings C. 2007. Going beyond panaceas: future challenges. *Proc. Natl. Acad. Sci. USA* 104:15179–80

Perrings C, Walker BH. 2005. Conservation in the optimal use of rangelands. *Ecol. Econ.* 49:119–28

Pigeon N, Hood C, Jones D, Turner B, Gibson R. 1992. Risk perception. In *Risk: Analysis, Perceptions and Management*. London: R. Soc.

Pimm SL. 1984. The complexity and stability of ecosystems. *Nature* 307:321–26

Pindyck RS. 1991. Irreversibility, uncertainty and investment. *J. Econ. Lit.* 29(3):1110–48

Pindyck RS. 2000. Irreversibilities and the timing of environmental policy. *Resour. Energy Econ.* 22:223–59

Roberts K, Weitzman ML. 1981. Funding criteria for research, development, and exploration projects. *Econometrica* 49(5):1261–88

Rondeau D. 2001. Along the way back from the brink. *J. Environ. Econ. Manag.* 42:156–82

Shackle GLS. 1955. *Uncertainty in Economics*. Cambridge, UK: Cambridge Univ. Press

Spulber D. 2008. Unlocking technology: antitrust and innovation. *J. Compet. Law Econ.* doi:10.1093/joclec/nhn016

Starmer C. 2000. Development in non-expected utility theory: the hunt for a descriptive theory of choice under risk. *J. Econ. Lit.* 38:332–82

Taylor P. 1991. The precautionary principle and the prevention of pollution. *ECOS* 124:41–46

Ulph A, Ulph D. 1997. Global warming, irreversibility and learning. *Econ. J.* 107(442):636–50

van den Berg CJM, Gowdy JM. 2000. Evolutionary theories in environmental and resource economics: approaches and applications. *Environ. Resour. Econ.* 17:37–57

Walker BH, Gunderson LH, Kinzig AP, Folke C, Carpenter SR, Schultz L. 2006. A handful of heuristics and some propositions for understanding resilience in social-ecological systems. *Ecol. Soc.* 11(1): artic. 13. http://www.consecol.org/vol11/iss1/art13/.

Walker BH, Holling CS, Carpenter SR, Kinzig AP. 2004. Resilience, adaptability, and transformability. *Ecol. Soc.* 9(2): artic. 5

Walters C. 1986. *Adaptive Management of Renewable Resources*. New York: Macmillan

Weitzman M. 1998. Why the far-distant future should be discounted at the lowest possible rate. *J. Environ. Econ. Manag.* 36:201–8

Whither Hotelling: Tests of the Theory of Exhaustible Resources

Margaret E. Slade

Department of Economics, The University of British Columbia, Vancouver, British Columbia, V6T 1Z1, Canada, email: m.slade@mac.com

Henry Thille

Department of Economics, The University of Guelph, Guelph, Ontario, N1G 2W1 Canada, email: hthille@uoguelph.ca

Annu. Rev. Resour. Econ. 2009. 1:239–59

First published online as a Review in Advance on June 25, 2009

The *Annual Review of Resource Economics* is online at resource.annualreviews.org

This article's doi:
10.1146/annurev.resource.050708.144223

Key Words

Hotelling model, optimal extraction, empirical tests, oil and gas, nonfuel minerals

Abstract

We review the empirical literature that extends and tests the Hotelling model of the optimal depletion of an exhaustible resource. The theory is briefly described to set the stage for the review of empirical tests and applications. Those tests can be roughly divided into two broad categories—descriptive and structural—and we discuss the strengths and weaknesses of each before presenting the empirical studies of optimal extraction under conditions of exhaustibility. We also discuss some econometric pitfalls that applied researchers face when attempting to test the model.

1. INTRODUCTION

A survey of Hotelling's (1931) model of resource extraction and tests of that theory is particularly appropriate, as Hotelling's model has dominated the economics of exhaustible resources for many decades. Not only was Hotelling the first to derive the implications of finite reserves for the evolution of prices and consumption under an optimal plan, but he also showed that competitive markets will achieve the planner's solution. This rosy picture is, of course, a special case of the first theorem of welfare economics, which states that competitive markets are Pareto efficient.

One could therefore conclude that, because the market will solve the resource-extraction problem, we should forget about it. Unfortunately, this is not the case. Indeed, many aspects of real-world markets, such as imperfect competition, non-neutral taxation, and the absence of property rights, can lead to severe intertemporal distortions. Although most of those complications were not considered by Hotelling, his model can easily be altered to assess many interesting and realistic features of fuel and nonfuel mineral markets. Our survey discusses how this can be done.

Although we discuss the theory and derive simple models of optimal extraction, we emphasize empirical tests of that theory (for a recent review of the theory, see Gaudet 2007). In particular, we look at studies that use data in an attempt to assess how well the Hotelling model predicts observed outcomes. Those studies range from simple descriptive exercises to more complex structural models of optimal extraction in a dynamic setting. We do not attempt to provide a complete survey of the literature on optimal extraction, especially the numerous theoretical models. Instead, we indicate some of the more influential articles when doing so aids the exposition and apologize to any who feel that their papers have been neglected.

The organization of the paper is as follows: In the next section, we discuss some aspects of the history of the economics of exhaustible resources. We do this to explain why interest in the subject has waned in recent years and to convince the reader that Hotelling still has something to say to us. In Section 3, we derive the Hotelling model and some of its more important variants. We do this because the empirical tests that we discuss are theory driven. In particular, even the simplest descriptive studies are attempts to assess the theoretical predictions. Section 4 discusses some of the econometric pitfalls that empiricists face when attempting to test the Hotelling model. These include problems that are associated with determining if market prices are stationary, dealing with endogeneity, and measuring shadow prices. Sections 5 and 6, which are the heart of the paper, discuss empirical tests of the simple Hotelling model and some of its more tested variants. We say "tested" rather than "interesting" because we are limited in our coverage by the literature. In other words, some aspects of the Hotelling model have been tested more than others, which means that evidence supporting or rejecting some theories is scant. Furthermore, we limit attention to studies that deal explicitly with exhaustibility as opposed to extraction more generally. Finally, Section 7 contains concluding remarks and suggestions for future research.

2. BACKGROUND

Hotelling's classic article, which was published in 1931, inaugurated the theory of the optimal extraction of an exhaustible resource and exhaustible-resource economics more generally. Moreover, perhaps more than any other article, it has dominated a subdiscipline of economics. Nevertheless, it was not until the 1970s that theorists began to take serious note. At that time, many researchers who had previously shown little interest in the subject developed more sophisticated models that modified the basic Hotelling assumptions to include realistic features of the world.

Although Hotelling derived several variants of his model—in particular he solved the monopolist's extraction problem and he considered extraction costs that increase as the resource base is depleted—since that time, other researchers have introduced additional complicating factors, of which we mention a few. General equilibrium effects have been included by embedding the Hotelling model in a model of aggregate growth (Stiglitz 1974, Solow & Wan 1976). Exploration has been modeled by allowing augmentation of the resource base through discoveries (Pindyck 1978). Uncertainty about the size of reserves (Gilbert 1979) or future demand and costs (Pindyck 1980) has been introduced. Durability effects have been included by allowing recycling and stockpiling (Levhari & Pindyck 1981). Imperfect competition among producers has been considered in the context of a dominant-firm model (Gilbert 1978) and a cartel (Salant 1976). Taxation effects have been modeled by introducing distortions due to non-neutral tax policy (Sweeney 1977, Dasgupta et al. 1980). Finally, technical change has been examined by considering cost-lowering technological improvements (Slade 1982).

Despite the explosion of interest in the theory of exhaustible resources, as is typical in economics, empirical tests of the theoretical models lagged behind. Nevertheless, in the 1980s, a number of researchers published papers containing tests of both the simple model and some of its more realistic variants (e.g., Heal & Barrow 1980, Smith 1981, Slade 1982, Farrow 1985, Miller & Upton 1985a).

By the 1990s, however, interest in the subject began to wane, and by 2000, the flow of new theories and tests had been reduced to a trickle. Furthermore, although it was common in the 1980s for economics departments to offer courses in the economics of exhaustible resources, most such courses are now offered by resource, agricultural, or mineral economics departments, if at all. It is thus safe to say that mainstream economics has neglected Hotelling, at least his theory of extraction.[1] In this section, we discuss why interest blossomed in the 1970s and waned 20 years later.

A major event, or sequence of events, accounts for the outpouring of theoretical and empirical research on the optimal depletion of an exhaustible resource—the energy-price shocks that began in the early 1970s and culminated at the end of that decade. Prior to that time, the real price of crude oil had remained relatively constant for decades. However, between 1972 and 1981, the real price increased fivefold, from just under 14 to 71 2008 dollars per barrel. At that time, the industrialized world, which was totally unprepared for such an occurrence, began to think seriously about resource depletion and the limits to growth.

We are now in the throes of another set of oil-price shocks. In fact, the situation is even more dramatic this time. Indeed, the yearly average real price of crude oil rose from a low of $13 per barrel in 1998, lower than the price in 1946 or at any time since then, to an all-time high of $145 in July 2008, an 11-fold increase in just one decade; it then fell precipitously as the global economy cooled. Will this trigger a renaissance in the theory of exhaustible resources? We think not.

---

[1]Of course, Hotelling wrote other seminal papers in, e.g., industrial organization (Hotelling 1929) and public economics (Hotelling 1938), which are outside the focus of this article.

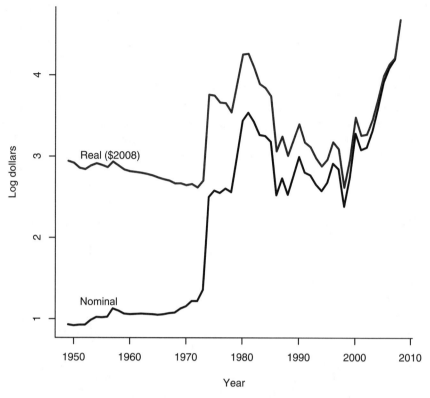

Figure 1

Annual crude-oil prices (log scale).

One reason why interest in the Hotelling model has waned is that it is a very long-run model and attention has shifted to the here and now. Commodity, and in particular oil, markets have been so volatile in recent years that it is difficult to focus on long-run trends. To illustrate this point, we present as an example some historical statistics for U.S. crude-oil prices[2] in **Figures 1** and **2**. In **Figure 1,** we plot the log of annual average nominal and real (2008 dollar) price for the period 1949–2008. Even though the averaging process removes much variation in the data, it is clear that the price behaves very differently in the periods before and after the early 1970s. To examine price volatility in more detail, in **Figure 2** we plot the annual coefficient of variation of the monthly average crude-oil price for the period from January 1974 to August 2008. To our knowledge, monthly data do not exist prior to this period. Although there are episodes of relatively high volatility throughout the period, the trend in volatility is clearly upward. Under such circumstances, it is difficult to plan or to make sensible investment decisions. The lack of interest in thinking about the very long run is therefore not surprising.

---

[2]The annual price is the "crude-oil domestic first purchase price" provided by the U.S. Energy Information Administration (2008). To this, we add the difference between imported and domestic refinery acquisition prices to the first purchase price for the 1974–1982 period to allow for the effects of price controls implemented in the United States at that time.

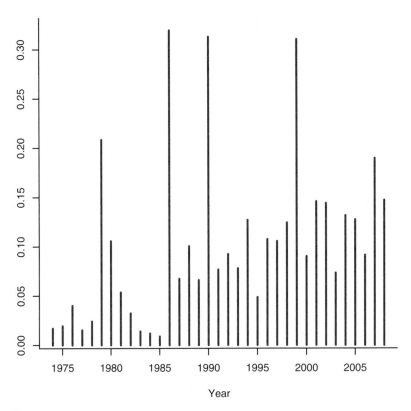

Figure 2

Annual coefficient of variation of crude-oil price.

Although they are the most publicized, crude-oil markets are not alone in their volatility. For example, copper prices rose from less than $1 per pound in 2003 to more than $4 five years later. Furthermore, like oil, the rise was not steady but was characterized by peaks and troughs. Attention has therefore shifted to assessing the consequences of high prices and predicting the occurrence of high-price periods. In particular, the links between oil prices and the macro economy have received much attention (e.g., Hamilton 1983) owing to the presumption that high prices are linked to recessions and are thus "bad."

Are we running out of cheap sources of energy and nonfuel minerals? On the one hand, many of the reserves that were easiest and cheapest to extract have been depleted. On the other hand, technological improvements have meant that extraction of previously uneconomic resources is now possible. Nevertheless, it seems imperative to have a long-run plan that encompasses diminished supplies of fuel and nonfuel minerals and to seek reasonable substitutes for those commodities. Unfortunately, excessive volatility makes sensible planning difficult.

To illustrate, consider consumer reaction to the oil-price shocks that occurred in the 1970s. At first, consumers were interested in buying smaller more fuel-efficient cars. However, as the price returned to "normal" levels, interest in efficiency dwindled, and even though the average new car has a much better mileage rating today than it did several decades ago, an inordinate number of sports utility vehicles are driven almost exclusively on city streets. Had high prices been sustained, through taxation or other means, it is likely that the stock of cars in North America would more closely resemble the stock in Europe. Furthermore, the revenue from taxation could have been invested in developing new technologies and substitute materials.

These are ideas to keep in mind when reading our survey. In particular, we should not let extreme price volatility trick us into taking a short-run view. It seems inevitable that relative prices of exhaustible resources will rise at some future time, not just in the short run but on a permanent basis. Furthermore, as Hotelling demonstrated, high prices need not be "bad" but instead can result from an optimal plan. We now turn from history to the theory of long-run price movements and tests of that theory.

3. THE BASIC HOTELLING MODEL AND SOME EXTENSIONS

3.1. The Basic Model

The simple Hotelling model can be derived with the help of optimal control theory. Consider a mine owner who extracts an exhaustible resource that is sold in a competitive market. Let the market price, quantity extracted, and reserves remaining in time t be $p(t)$, $q(t)$, and $R(t)$, respectively, and the constant discount rate be r. The extraction-cost function is assumed to depend on the rate of extraction, with $C(0) = 0$, $C'(q(t)) \geq 0$, and $C''(q(t)) > 0$. In other words, extraction costs are convex.

The producer's objective function, J, is his discounted profit stream,

$$J = \int_0^\infty e^{-rt}\pi(q(t))dt = \int_0^\infty e^{-rt}[p(t)(q(t) - C(q(t)))]dt, \qquad (1)$$

and he chooses a time path for extraction to maximize J, subject to the constraints $\dot{R}(t) = -q(t)$, $q(t) \geq 0$, $R(t) \geq 0$, and $R(0) = R_0$, where a dot over a variable denotes a time derivative. In other words, extraction depletes reserves, both must be nonnegative, and initial reserves are R_0. The current-value Hamiltonian for this problem is $H = pq - C(q) + \lambda\dot{R} = pq - C(q) - \lambda q$, where λ is the shadow price on the resource constraint and the time argument has been suppressed. Among the necessary conditions for the solution to this dynamic optimization problem are the following three first-order conditions:

$$H_q = p - C_q - \lambda = 0 \quad or \quad \lambda = p - C_q, \qquad (2)$$

$$\dot{\lambda} = r\lambda \quad or \quad \frac{\dot{p} - \dot{C_q}}{p - C_q} = r, \qquad (3)$$

and

$$\dot{R} = -q, \qquad (4)$$

where a subscript on a function denotes a partial derivative.

The initial first-order condition says that the shadow price on the resource constraint is the profit on the marginal unit. In other words, an extra unit of the resource would yield a marginal profit equal to the market price net of marginal extraction cost. The second condition is the famous r-percent rule, which states that the shadow price must rise at the rate of interest, r. Because the producer discounts the future at the rate r, the shadow price is constant in present-value terms, which ensures that, at the margin, the producer is indifferent between extracting one unit today or at some time in the future. Finally, the third condition says that the constraint on the rate of depletion is satisfied.

Let us consider the second first-order condition further. First, Hotelling derived his r-percent rule under the assumption of zero extraction cost [i.e., $C(q) = 0$]. Under that assumption, the shadow price equals the market price, and both rise at the rate of interest. The producer, however, is a price taker with constant (zero) marginal costs. This means that the producer cannot choose q so as to equate his marginal profit with the shadow price. Instead, the industry price must evolve so as to make Equation 2 true. In other words, aggregate consumption or industry demand in period t, $D(p(t))$, must equal aggregate production in that period, $Q(p(t))$. The production of individual firms, however, is not well defined (which is true of any competitive industry with constant marginal cost).

Second, Equation 3 determines the rate of change of price, not its level. In particular, Equations 2, 3, and 4 define a pair of differential equations, for which two boundary conditions are required to determine a particular solution. The initial stocks define one boundary condition ($R(0) = R_0$). Under complete exhaustion of the resource, the other boundary condition is that all stocks are extracted. The level of price is then determined by the equality of cumulative consumption and cumulative production over the lifetime of the industry, a relationship that can be expressed as

$$\int_0^\infty D(p(t))dt = \int_0^\infty Q(p(t))dt = \mathbf{R}_0, \tag{5}$$

where $\mathbf{R}_0$ denotes aggregate industry reserves in period 0.

Finally, Hotelling showed that the monopolist's problem is similar. One merely substitutes marginal revenue for price in the first-order conditions. To illustrate, the shadow price λ, or marginal value, becomes marginal revenue net of marginal cost, which increases at the rate of interest.

3.2. Depletion

To understand how the simple model can be modified to include realistic features of resource markets, consider first the possibility that extraction costs depend not only on current extraction, but also on remaining reserves. The new cost function, which is $C(q, R)$ with $C_R < 0$, captures the notion that the best or cheapest ores will be extracted first. Depletion thus involves moving to successively higher-cost ores. Although least cost first is assumed here, it is an optimal plan in many models (e.g., Solow & Wan 1976).

When depletion is introduced, Equations 2 and 4 are unchanged. Equation 3, however, becomes

$$\dot{\lambda} = r\lambda + C_R \quad or \quad \frac{\dot{p} - \dot{C}_q}{p - C_q} = r + \frac{C_R}{\lambda}. \tag{6}$$

Because $C_R < 0$, the shadow price increases at a slower rate in Equation 6 than it does in Equation 3. This is true because extraction today leads to higher costs tomorrow, and the owner internalizes this externality.

We now have two predictions that can be taken to data—shadow prices should increase either at the rate of interest or at a slower rate. However, casual inspection of price data reveals that, for many commodities, prices have fallen over long periods, and the models that we have derived thus far cannot explain falling prices. There are, however, simple and realistic assumptions under which market prices can fall. We discuss three of these, using models that incorporate exploration, technical change, and recycling.

3.3. Exploration

We have thus far assumed that reserves are known in period 0 and that they cannot be augmented. However, oil and mining companies spend vast amounts on exploration in an attempt to find new deposits. Furthermore, if the extraction cost function is of the form $C(q, R)$, with $C_R < 0$, new discoveries, by augmenting the reserve base, lower costs. We examine this model formally, paying particular attention to the effect of exploration on market prices.

Suppose that we amend the previous model by adding a stock of cumulative discoveries, D, with rate of change $\dot{D}$. The firm can exert an exploratory effort e at cost $C^2(e)$, which is assumed to be convex. New additions, or equivalently the rate of change of discoveries, evolve according to the rule $\dot{D} = f(e, D)$, with $f_e > 0$ and $f_D > 0$. In other words, exploratory effort leads to additional discoveries, but the rate at which deposits are found falls as cumulative discoveries increase. This is true because exploration is sampling without replacement—once a deposit has been found, it cannot be found again. Finally, the equation for the evolution of reserves, which must be amended to include new discoveries, becomes $\dot{R} = f(e, D) - q$.

Although not necessary, it is simpler to work with an extraction cost function of the form $C(q, R) = C^1(R)q$. With this cost function, marginal cost is constant within a period but changes as reserves are discovered and/or depleted. Under these assumptions, one can show that (see, e.g., Pindyck 1978)

$$\dot{p} = r[p - C^1(R)] + C^{1'}(R)f(e, D) = r(p - C_q) + C_{qR}\dot{D}. \tag{7}$$

To understand the implications of exploration for prices, one must compare Equation 7 to the constant marginal cost, no-exploration case. One can show that the comparable equation for that case is

$$\dot{p} = r(p - C_q). \tag{8}$$

With Equation 8, market prices increase over time. Equation 7, however, contains a second term, $C_{qR}\dot{D}$. New discoveries, $\dot{D}$, cannot be negative. However, when marginal extraction costs rise as reserves are depleted (i.e., $C_{qR} < 0$) as assumed, the second term is negative.

Pindyck (1978) argued that costs initially fall rapidly, because cumulative discoveries are small and exploratory effort is very productive. Later, however, when most deposits have been found, costs fall slowly, if at all. This can give rise to U-shaped price paths, and there have been numerous tests of that hypothesis.

3.4. Technical Change

The evolution of an industry or an economy is characterized by two important factors—growth and technical change—and in our view, the latter is more important. Indeed, new techniques and processes have revolutionized our world, and the fuel and nonfuel mineral industries are no exceptions. We therefore examine how changes in technology affect the evolution of an exhaustible-resource industry, paying particular attention to the effect on market prices.

We assume that technical change enters the extraction cost function, which becomes $C(q, R, t)$, with $C_t < 0$. In other words, costs fall over time as technology improves. Although not necessary, the analysis is facilitated by assuming that technical change is Hicks neutral and that there are constant returns to scale in production. Under those assumptions, the cost function takes the form $C(q, R, t) = h(t)C^1(R)q$, and the new first-order conditions yield

$$\dot{p} = r(p - C_q) + C^1(R)h'(t) = r(p - C_q) + C_{qt} \qquad (9)$$

(see Slade 1982). Compared with Equation 8 (the equation for the rate of change of price in the absence of technical change), Equation 9 contains an additional term that represents the rate at which marginal costs fall as a result of changes in technology. In particular, because this term is negative, prices can fall. Slade (1982) argued that such is apt to be the case early on when scarcity rents (λ) are small. However, as reserves are depleted, prices eventually rise, leading to U-shaped price paths.

3.5. Durability, Recycling, and Inventories

Unlike mineral fuels, which once consumed cannot be reused, many nonfuel minerals can be recycled. Indeed, commodities like gold are rarely discarded. This implies that the stock of the commodity that is in circulation—rather than the flow of current extraction—is important. Furthermore, that stock depreciates only slowly.

One can model this situation formally by introducing a new state variable, S, representing the stock in circulation, with $\dot{S} = q - \delta S$ and $S(0) = 0$, where δ is the depreciation rate or rate at which the stock is lost. Following Levhari & Pindyck (1981), we also introduce an inverse-demand relationship, $f(S)$, the marginal value of the flow of services from holding one unit of the stock, with $f'(S) < 0$. In other words, the marginal value is greater when the stock is smaller.

In equilibrium, the marginal value of holding a unit should equal the marginal cost, which has three terms: the opportunity cost of the cash investment, rp; the monetary value of the depreciation, δp; and the capital gain, $\dot{p}$ (which is a negative cost). Thus, $f(S) = p(r + \delta) - \dot{p}$, which can be rearranged to obtain

$$\dot{p} = -f(S) + p(r + \delta). \qquad (10)$$

Levhari & Pindyck (1981) argued that, because S increases initially but falls eventually, the price path is U shaped. However, if the cost function is $C(q)$, the shadow price obeys the r-percent rule.

Finally, although many fuels cannot be recycled, both fuel and nonfuel minerals can be stored, and inventory holding is an important aspect of commodity markets. Bresnahan & Suslow (1985) showed that, if storage costs are zero and inventories are positive, the market price will follow the r-percent rule, at least in the short run. Indeed, this is an equilibrium condition in the asset market.

Although this section emphasizes the behavior of market and shadow prices, the pattern of extraction is interesting as well. In simple models, q falls monotonically to zero. In more complex models, however, the extraction profile can be nonmonotonic. We emphasize prices because price is the variable that has received closest scrutiny in the empirical literature.

4. ECONOMETRIC ISSUES

There are many econometric pitfalls that the applied researcher must deal with in attempting to test the Hotelling model. Unfortunately, the treatment of those problems in the research we discuss below is not always satisfactory. Rather than point to flaws in individual papers, however, we discuss three topics that pose problems in many applications: the assumption of stationarity (nonstationarity), the issue of endogeneity, and the measurement of shadow prices.

4.1. Nonstationarity

A time series, x, is said to be stationary if the dependence between x_t and x_{t-j} depends on the distance between observations, j, but not on location, t, implying that the mean and variance do not change over time. Many time series have a single unit root, which means that the first difference, $x_t - x_{t-1}$, is stationary. Unfortunately, when one runs regressions that involve nonstationary variables and does not difference those variables, the results obtained, such as tests of significance, are incorrect, and spurious relationships can be found.

This problem is important when attempting to assess trends in time-series data such as prices. To illustrate, consider the time-series model with a linear trend

$$p_t = \alpha_0 + \alpha_1 t + z_t, \qquad z_t = \beta z_{t-1} + \varepsilon_t. \qquad (11)$$

When $\beta = 1$ ($\beta < 1$), p is nonstationary (stationary). Unfortunately, it is difficult to distinguish between these possibilities when β is close to 1, as is often the case for commodity prices, and researchers have taken different stances on this issue.

We believe that many commodity prices are stationary. Our belief is not based on tests for unit roots, but rather on variance-ratio tests that reveal the extent to which price shocks are persistent or transitory [for coal, crude oil, and natural gas, see Pindyck (1999); for copper, see Slade (2001)]. Those tests show that many prices are mean reverting to a trend, but that the rate of mean reversion is very slow and the trend can shift over time. However, many researchers would disagree with us and claim that commodity prices have a unit root and must therefore be differenced.

There is also a theoretical basis for our objection to the unit-root approach to examining the time-series properties of commodity prices in the context of Hotelling's model. The predictions of Hotelling's model and most extensions point to nonstationary price behavior. The issue is clear from the simplest of Hotelling's specifications in which $\dot{p}/p = r$. Converting this to a discrete-time, time-series model, we have

$$p_t = (1 + r)p_{t-1} + z_t,$$

which is nonstationary [as $(1 + r) > 1$], but at the same time, it is not a unit-root process.[3] Standard unit root tests for whether $\beta < 1$ or $\beta = 1$ are not designed to handle the explosive autoregressive case predicted by theory. They are also not designed to distinguish a unit root in z_t from the nonstationarity caused by eventual exhaustion of the resource.

Finally, theory predicts that certain types of shocks, such as to the level of reserves, have permanent effects, as the entire price path is affected by such shocks. Other shocks,

---

[3]If shocks are multiplicative in this model, $ln(p(t))$ has a unit root. However, most researchers work with price levels.

such as strikes or business-cycle fluctuations, may be of a temporary nature but, to the extent to which they affect output and hence remaining reserves, can have long-term price effects. The relative importance of permanent and transitory shocks is then an empirical issue. However, we do not expect unit-root tests to shed much light on these issues.

4.2. Endogeneity

Endogeneity is a ubiquitous problem in applied work, and tests of the Hotelling model are no exception. To illustrate this problem, consider estimating an extraction cost function. Suppose that this function is $C(q, R, t, v)$, where q is output, R is remaining reserves, t is time, and v is a vector of factor prices. The endogeneity problem arises when trying to estimate the cost function to obtain estimates of marginal cost (C_q and C_R) required for testing the Hotelling rule, because q is generally endogenous.

The standard solution to the endogeneity problem is to find a set of variables (instruments) that are correlated with the endogenous right-hand-side variable but not with the error in the estimating equation. Often, the instruments are lagged endogenous variables that are assumed to be predetermined. This solution fails when considering extraction cost functions because, with finite or increasing-cost reserves, extraction today affects extraction in all future time periods, implying that lagged endogenous variables are not predetermined.

Another possible solution to the endogeneity problem is to look for contemporaneous variables that are good instruments. In particular, when estimating a cost function, it is customary to look for demand-side variables that shift q. To determine if this is a legitimate remedy here, one must consider what the error represents. Typically, it contains unobserved or omitted factor prices. Unfortunately, as with output prices, factor prices are apt to be correlated with demand-side variables such as industrial production, which means that demand shifters are often not valid instruments. Although the endogeneity problem is not insurmountable, it requires ingenuity in finding appropriate instruments.

4.3. Measuring Shadow Prices

If extractive firms purchased unextracted ore from its owner during each period in a competitive environment, we would observe a competitive-market price for the *in situ* resource. Of course, this rarely happens; usually, vertically integrated mining firms own the rights to extract from a large deposit and do not regularly purchase the ore input. Consequently, an important variable for tests of the Hotelling model, λ, is rarely observed and must be inferred, usually by applying the definition obtained from a particular theoretical model (a situation analogous to the issue of determining the user cost of capital).

With most of the models discussed in the previous section, the shadow price, λ, is the market price, p, net of marginal cost, C_q. Market prices are observable and pose no measurement problem.[4] However, it is difficult, if not impossible, to measure true marginal cost. In particular, determining which inputs are variable and which are fixed is not always obvious. To illustrate, labor is usually considered to be variable. However, many workers in extractive industries are employed under contract rather than on a day-to-day

---

[4]This depends on how far down the supply chain the commodities are observed. The more processed the commodity on which we observe price, the more complicated the cost function is that must be determined to compute λ.

basis, which implies that a substantial portion of the work force is quasi fixed and should be excluded from marginal-cost calculations.

This problem is not unique to the Hotelling model, and various solutions have been adopted in the literature. We discuss one solution and indicate why it is inappropriate here. Industrial Organization economists frequently must estimate marginal costs, and many have given up on direct measures. Instead, they retrieve marginal costs (either numbers or functions) from first-order conditions for equilibrium in the market. With structural tests of the Hotelling model, in contrast, the equilibrium condition is the object of the tests; assuming that it holds is therefore inappropriate.

5. TESTS AND EVALUATION OF THE HOTELLING MODEL

5.1. General Comments

As discussed in Section 3, the basic Hotelling model predicts that, in the absence of extraction cost, the market price p of an exhaustible-resource commodity will rise at the rate of interest r, $\dot{p}/p = r$. When marginal extraction cost is nonzero, the shadow price or marginal profit, $\lambda = p - C_q$, rises at the rate of interest, $\dot{\lambda}/\lambda = r$. Moreover, when extraction costs depend on the level of reserves remaining (R), the shadow price rises at a rate that is less than the rate of interest. This lower rate of shadow-price appreciation, which is given by $\dot{\lambda}/\lambda = r + C_R/\lambda$, reflects the user cost associated with deterioration of the quality of ore mined in the future. Furthermore, several factors yield U-shaped price paths that decline initially but rise eventually. Finally, when markets are imperfectly competitive, one must replace price in the above equations with marginal revenue. These are some of the predictions that have been taken to data.

The tests that have been performed have mainly been of two sorts: descriptive and structural. The first class assesses outcomes that are associated with the market equilibrium without having to specify the nature of that equilibrium. Its advantage is that there is no need to commit to a specific model. Instead, one can assess which models are consistent with the data and which are not. Its shortcoming is that one cannot perform formal tests. The second class tests a specific model by estimating structural equations. Its strength is that formal tests can be performed. Its shortcoming is that it imposes more structure (e.g., on the cost function and the nature of competition in the market), and this structure may be inappropriate. We report findings from both classes.

5.2. Descriptive Studies

Most descriptive studies have examined the behavior of mineral commodity prices. Moreover, because the predictions of Hotelling's model are long run, many tests make use of a century or more of data on the prices of different fuel and nonfuel minerals.

Barnett & Morse (1963) were the first to analyze mineral commodity prices formally. They looked at relative price trends in an attempt to uncover evidence of natural-resource scarcity, and they concluded that, because real prices had fallen over time, scarcity was not a problem. Other researchers who have examined price trends, however, are not in complete agreement with Barnett and Morse. For example, Smith (1978) looked at the stability of the coefficients of estimated price-trend relationships and decided that the data are too volatile to support definitive conclusions.

Those studies set the stage for more formal descriptive assessments. For example, Heal & Barrow (1980) related metal price movements to interest rates and found that the results do not support the Hotelling model. In particular, they discovered that changes in interest rates, not interest-rate levels, predict prices (for more on the relationship between interest rates and prices, see Smith 1981, Agbeyegbe 1989).

Many researchers have assessed the possibility that price paths can be U shaped. Slade (1982), who was among the first to study this issue, based her descriptive tests on the idea that price declines could be due to technical change, as in Equation 9. Although she found that fitted linear trends were negative for many commodities, quadratic trends revealed evidence of upturns in the real prices of mineral commodities that began in the 1970s.

Subsequently, many other researchers examined the issue of quadratic trends and reached a variety of conclusions. The principal factor that differs across studies, which could account for the different conclusions drawn, is the econometric technique used. For example, Moazzami & Anderson (1994), who estimated an error-correction model, found evidence of U-shaped price paths, whereas Berck & Roberts (1996), who estimated both difference and trend-stationary models, found evidence of U shapes under the former but not the latter. Finally, Pindyck (1999) found U shapes when estimating a model in which prices revert to a quadratic trend that shifts over time, and Lee et al. (2006) found structural breaks in deterministic trends. The evidence is thus mixed. Nevertheless, the idea that real prices have risen in recent years receives stronger support.

Many possible further refinements could also be undertaken. For example, as **Figures 1** and **2** suggest, not only do trends shift over time, but variances are also nonconstant. Indeed, periods of both high and low volatility suggest using an ARCH or GARCH model (see, e.g., Engle 1982, Bollerslev 1986).

5.3. Structural Models

More formal tests of the Hotelling model rely on estimates of some combination of an industry-wide demand function; a production, profit, or cost function for the extractive firm or industry; and a first-order condition (e.g., an Euler equation) that is associated with dynamic-profit maximization. Examples include Stollery (1983), Farrow (1985), Halvorsen & Smith (1984, 1991), Young (1992), and Chermak & Patrick (2001).

There are many possible ways that the estimated structural equations can be used to test the Hotelling model. We list three here:

1. One can estimate a cost function to obtain C_q and use it in conjunction with market prices (or marginal revenue obtained from an estimated demand function if imperfect competition is suspected) to calculate shadow prices, λ. It is then possible to test if those shadow prices increase at the rate of interest, or at a slower rate if the cost function depends on remaining reserves, or if they fall. A modified version of this approach is taken by Stollery (1983), who found support for the Hotelling model with a discount rate of 15%.

2. One can augment the first method to include a first-order condition such as Equation 6. When this is done, the model can be tested by examining whether estimated parameters such as $\hat{r}$ make sense from an economic point of view as well as whether estimated shadow prices behave as predicted by the particular theory that is being tested. Farrow (1985), Halvorsen & Smith (1984, 1991), Young (1992), and Chermak & Patrick

(2001) took this approach. The results of these structural tests are quite mixed, with researchers finding falling shadow prices and/or negative interest rates. Most interpret these findings as unsupportive of the Hotelling model.

3. One could estimate the building blocks, demand and cost, and use those equations to solve for the market equilibrium that is implied by dynamic profit maximization. It would then be possible to test if observed price and output paths lie within the confidence intervals that surround the paths predicted by the model. As far as we know, this has not be done.

A few comments are in order. First, most researchers who have estimated cost or profit functions for individual mines or mining industries assume that the technology of mining involves extracting unprocessed ore, n, which is combined with other inputs to produce metal, q. In other words, both mining and refining are modeled. n, which is transferred inside a vertically integrated firm, is treated as a quasi-fixed factor in the production of q. Once the firm's technology is known, shadow prices or rental rates, λ, can be approximated by one of two methods. They can be calculated as the difference between price and marginal cost, $p - C_q$ (as in Stollery 1983, Farrow 1985, Young 1992), or as the shadow price of the unpriced ore to the vertically integrated metal producer, $-C_n$ (as in Halvorsen & Smith 1984, 1991; Chermak & Patrick 2001). These two estimates of λ, however, do not measure the same thing. The first is the shadow price of one unit of contained metal *in situ*, whereas the second is the shadow price of one unit of ore of the current grade *in situ*.

Second, rejection of the Hotelling model is not an absolute rejection. Instead, it is a rejection of a particular variant. For example, falling shadow prices (which are equivalent to finding negative interest rates) are inconsistent with simple versions of Hotelling's model but not with other formulations.

Finally, the first-order conditions that we derived above are expressed in continuous time. For estimation purposes, however, one normally converts those equations into discrete-time analogs. When this is done, the discrete-time equations contain expected values of future realizations of variables. It is standard to assume that expectations are formed rationally (i.e., that decision makers use all currently available information in forming their forecasts). Estimation, therefore, often makes use of Generalized Method of Moments, which is an instrumental-variables technique. Unfortunately, the difficulties that are associated with finding appropriate instruments are at least as great here as those mentioned above.

5.4. Methods That Use Market Prices

The studies described above are based on proxies for shadow prices that rely on econometric estimation. An alternative that is sometimes possible makes use of market proxies that rely on sales of undeveloped resources or assets of mining companies.

The model proposed and estimated by Miller & Upton (1985a) provides the best-known market-based application. They exploited a less widely known implication of Hotelling's analysis, which they called the Hotelling Valuation Principle (HVP). Specifically, they showed that, in a competitive market, the value of reserves in any currently operating, optimally managed mineral deposit should depend solely on the current spot price net of marginal-extraction cost, regardless of when the reserves will be extracted.

They tested their model using stock-market valuations of the oil and gas reserves of a sample of U.S. companies and found that the data are consistent with their principle. Some subsequent tests, however, have found that the HVP overvalues mineral assets (see, e.g., Miller & Upton 1985b, Cairns & Davis 1998).

Not all market-determined shadow prices are based on stock-market valuations. Some resources are sold in the ground; thus, there is a market price for the unextracted resource. This is true, for example, of timber, which is sold unharvested. Livernois et al. (2006) examined old-growth timber, which is nonrenewable, and used stumpage price bids [which Johnson & Libecap (1980) suggested as proxies for shadow prices] in timber auctions as their measure of shadow prices. Their structural tests are fairly supportive of Hotelling's model.

Finally, Adelman & Watkins (2005, 2008) used transactions involving oil reserves to compute implied values for shadow prices and argued that the shadow prices thus obtained are lower than expected. There is not a discernible upward trend in their data. However, the time series is not long, beginning only in 1982.

On the basis of the limited evidence to date, tests that use market-based proxies for shadow prices appear to lead to conclusions that are more optimistic than do those that use econometrically estimated proxies.

6. APPLICATIONS OF THE HOTELLING MODEL

Many empirical researchers have examined the behavior of market and shadow prices in order to test the validity of the Hotelling model. There are other issues, however, that are also important but have received much less attention. Some of these are not tests but are instead applications. In other words, the Hotelling model is used as a tool in the evaluation of some other issue. In this section, we examine some of those applications, using one or two studies to illustrate possible approaches to each problem. As before, we limit attention to research that is framed in the context of exhaustibility. To illustrate, many applied economists have examined the effects of tax policy on resource extraction. Most of that work, however, is not set in the context of finite reserves and is therefore not discussed here.

6.1. Exploration

Incorporating exploration into a Hotelling model yields further testable hypotheses. In particular, as suggested by Devarajan & Fisher (1982), one can manipulate the first-order conditions from a model that incorporates exploration to obtain an alternative measure of scarcity rent or the shadow price on the resource constraint. This proxy is full marginal discovery cost, which includes not only the direct marginal cost of discovering an extra unit of reserves, but also the scarcity rent on exploration prospects.[5]

Devarajan & Fisher (1982) used data on pre-OPEC oil and gas discovery costs in the United States to assess this relationship and found that direct discovery costs rose prior to the 1970s. They interpreted the positive trend as a leading indicator of impending scarcity. Lasserre (1985) performed a similar analysis with better data on discovery costs for oil

---

[5]The model with exploration contains two shadow prices. Using the notation from Section 3, λ_1, the multiplier on the constraint $\dot{R} = -q + \dot{D}$, is the scarcity rent on the resource *in situ*, whereas λ_2, the multiplier on the constraint $\dot{D} = f(w, D)$, is the rent on exploration prospects.

in Alberta, Canada. In particular, he used information on bonuses as a proxy for the rent on exploration prospects—the second component of full marginal discovery cost. He concluded that not only had direct discovery cost been rising, but also bonus money was a significant (approximately 20%) and rising proportion of full marginal cost, a further confirmation of impending scarcity.

6.2. Scarcity and Growth

The link between resource scarcity and economic growth, in particular whether finite stocks of exhaustible resources will constrain growth, is a controversial question that has been debated by many: Neoclassical economists have taken more optimistic views that rely on substitution possibilities and technical change to relax the resource constraint (see, e.g., Stiglitz 1974), whereas neo-Malthusians assume more pessimistic positions, relying instead on the laws of thermodynamics to argue that sustained growth is neither possible nor desirable (see, e.g., Georgescu-Roegen 1971, Daly 1974). It is, therefore, not surprising that empiricists have also attempted to evaluate possible constraints on growth due to exhaustibility.

Although not made explicit in the studies, the early focus on demand and substitution between man-made capital (K) and exhaustible resources (R) (e.g., Berndt & Wood 1975) can be seen as an attempt to evaluate growth possibilities. Indeed, Stiglitz (1974) showed that the feasibility of sustainable growth depends crucially on the size of the elasticity of substitution between K and R. Unfortunately, the findings of the demand studies were not optimistic, with substitution possibilities estimated to be limited or nonexistent, which is not surprising for many raw material commodities.

More recently, empirical researchers have embedded partial-equilibrium Hotelling models in steady-state growth contexts to test if observed price patterns can be reproduced by estimated models. For example, Lin & Wagner (2007) derived conditions on the parameters of their model that imply that there will be no trend in resource commodity prices. Their model, which incorporates technical progress and depletion effects on the supply side, yields restrictions on the rate of technical change, the cost-increasing effect of depletion, and the rate of growth and price elasticity of demand that must be satisfied for prices to remain constant in real terms. They tested those restrictions using data on 14 minerals and found that approximately half satisfy their condition.

6.3. Pricing Risk

The tests that we have presented thus far either are embedded in a world of certainty or involve risk-neutral agents. It is standard, however, for risk-averse investors to trade off risk and return, and mining investment decisions are no exceptions. Therefore, having a model that prices risk as well as exhaustibility is desirable. Slade & Thille (1997) developed such a model and estimated it using data for a panel of Canadian copper mining firms. Specifically, they derived the rate of return that investors require to hold mining assets when the rate of technical change of the cost function is an exogenous risky process. Their model, which incorporates a capital-asset-pricing model [CAPM; for a discussion of the CAPM, see Brennan (1987)] into a Hotelling model of optimal extraction, yields a first-order condition for the expected rate of shadow-price appreciation of the form

$$\frac{\frac{E(d\lambda)}{dt}}{\lambda} = r + \frac{C_R}{\lambda} + \beta(r^m - r). \qquad (12)$$

Comparing Equations 6 and 12, we see that the latter contains an additional term, which is the risk premium from the CAPM. Slade & Thille (1997) found that neither the coefficient restrictions that are implied by the Hotelling model nor those implied by the CAPM are rejected by the data. Moreover, their estimate of β is negative, which means that mining assets are good hedges against poor performance of financial assets. The degree of risk diversification that is implied by their estimate, however, seems too large to be the whole story. For more on combining the Hotelling model with the CAPM, see Young & Ryan (1996).

6.4. Strategic Behavior

A priori, whether imperfect competition distorts extraction profiles and, if it does, whether the gains from cartelization are large or small are unclear. For example, Stiglitz (1976) demonstrated that, with constant demand elasticity and zero extraction costs, monopoly and competitive price (and thus profit) paths are identical. Furthermore, if reserves are homogeneous and finite, monopoly and competitive price (and thus profit) paths must cross. Under such circumstances, there is little scope for monopoly profits. However, when depletion effects are introduced, total recovery can depend on market structure and monopoly profits can be higher everywhere. The relevant question is then, How profitable is cartel formation for a given industry?

Pindyck (1977) addressed this question using a model of a cartel with a competitive fringe. Pindyck calibrated his model for the oil industry (with cartel OPEC), the bauxite industry (with cartel IBA, International Bauxite Association), and the copper industry (with cartel CIPEC, Intergovernmental Council of Copper-Exporting Countries). Comparing the cartel and competitive solutions for each industry, he concluded that the gains from cartelization are large for the first two but small for the third. These differences are accounted for by the market share of the cartel in each industry as well as by the speeds of adjustment of consumer demand and fringe supply. Indeed, not only do the cartels in the first two industries account for larger fractions of their respective markets, but adjustments to changed conditions are also slower in those markets, allowing for greater short-term gains.[6]

Turning their attention to a different issue, Ellis & Halvorsen (2002) looked at decomposing the gap between price and marginal cost into two components: the rent that is associated with exhaustibility and the rent that is associated with market power. They estimated their model for the largest firm in the nickel industry and found that monopoly power accounts for the lion's share of the gap.

These researchers conclude that, at least in some industries, not only are substantial monopoly profits earned, but distortions relative to competitive trajectories can also be large. However, the conditions that facilitate the successful exercise of market power vary by industry.

---

[6]Salant (1982) calibrated a model of the world oil industry that allows for several Cournot players that can be cartels (e.g., OPEC) or non-OPEC countries (e.g., Mexico) and a competitive fringe of small players.

6.5. Resource Taxation

Mining industries are subject to many forms of taxation and government regulation—including royalties, severance taxes, depletion allowances, and price controls—most of which are distortionary. Furthermore, those taxes can be levied at any stage of production (e.g., mining, refining, or fabrication), and they can be economically large. For example, depletion allowances were set at one-third of total revenues, and price controls in the United States kept domestic prices below one-half of world prices.

As with monopoly power, if reserves are homogeneous and finite, taxes can move extraction only from one period to another—the extraction path tilts but the area under that path remains constant. However, when costs rise with cumulative extraction, ultimate recovery can be distorted. Under those circumstances, it is especially important to evaluate the size of distortions for particular deposits and industries.

Slade (1984) developed a model of an extractive firm in a competitive industry that incorporates both various stages of production in the vertically integrated firm and varying grades of ore mined. The model is estimated for a U.S. copper-mining firm that owned only one mine. Company annual reports therefore provide time-series data for that mine. After estimation, the firm's optimal intertemporal behavior is determined under various assumptions about taxation and government controls. Comparisons of those solutions with the tax-free situation can then be used to evaluate the magnitude and time pattern of distortions. The effects that are uncovered include extraction paths that cross as well as changes in cumulative ore extraction and metal production. However, the latter two effects dominate. Moreover, tax policy can change ultimate ore extraction and metal-processing intensity in opposite directions, and the directions of those changes depend on the stage of production at which the tax is levied. Finally, the size of distortions is estimated to be large. To illustrate, in the simulations, a 10% royalty causes an 8% decline in cumulative metal production over the lifetime of the mine.

To summarize, in this section, we have discussed further tests and applications of the Hotelling model. Unfortunately, there are many interesting issues that we have not covered. Our neglect of those issues is not due to their lack of importance; it is due instead to lack of coverage in the empirical literature or to coverage that does not fit well with the goals of our survey.

7. CONCLUSIONS

In this article, we attempt to survey the large empirical literature that tests and applies the Hotelling model. As the evidence shows, many ways of doing this exist (i.e., many economic and econometric models), each with strengths and weaknesses. In concluding, we emphasize two points that we feel transcend specific models and tests.

- Distortions relative to the planner's solution can be large. These can result from imperfect competition, distortionary taxation, risk aversion, and/or the inappropriate assignment of property rights, among other things. It is not clear, however, if those departures are sufficient to warrant government intervention, which is also distortionary. Resolving this issue requires careful consideration of the circumstances in each market.
- The often-cited fact that the Hotelling model is frequently rejected by the data (see, e.g., Krautkraemer 1998) must be interpreted with caution. Indeed, rejection usually means failure of a simple variant, and incorporating real-world detail can considerably im-

prove performance. Furthermore, given substantial differences across markets and firms, a one-size-fits-all modeling approach and/or the use of very aggregate data are unlikely to be illuminating.

Is empirical testing of the Hotelling model a dead issue? We think not. However, it is imperative to distinguish between short-run volatility and long-run trends. In other words, we must be able to separate the signal from the noise. There are many reasons why mineral commodity prices are so volatile, including inelastic demand and supply at high prices as well as strong links with industrial production and the overall performance of the economy.

A further reason is related to the discrete and lumpy nature of many decisions. For example, the Hotelling model is based on the assumption that q is chosen continuously and costlessly. In reality, however, there are substantial costs associated with mine entry, exit, and temporary openings and closings, and those costs, combined with investment delays, introduce considerable inertia into production decisions. One possible approach to modeling the discrete and lumpy nature of extraction and the associated price and supply volatility is to combine the theory of real options (see, e.g., Brennan & Schwartz 1985) with a Hotelling model of depletion.

Technical change is another factor that can be discrete and lumpy. In particular, not only can it result in substantial cost savings, but it can also change deposits from uneconomic resources to economic reserves. For example, fluid catalytic cracking drastically reduced petroleum refining costs, and the advent of froth flotation transformed many uneconomic sulfide ores into valuable reserves. Nevertheless, in most extant studies, technical change is modeled as a smooth process or as a sequence of small events.

Finally, exploration and discovery of previously unknown deposits are important for modeling depletion (or the lack thereof). However, there has been little empirical work that incorporates models of exploration and discovery into a Hotelling framework.

DISCLOSURE STATEMENT

The authors are not aware of any affiliations, memberships, funding, or financial holdings that might be perceived as affecting the objectivity of this review.

ACKNOWLEDGMENTS

We thank Diderik Lund for useful comments on a draft of this paper.

LITERATURE CITED

Adelman MA, Watkins GC. 2005. *Oil and natural gas reserve prices: addendum to CEEPR Working Paper 03-016, including results for 2003 and revisions to 2001*. Work. Pap. 05-013, CEEPR

Adelman MA, Watkins GC. 2008. Reserve prices and mineral resource theory. *Energy J.* 29:1–16

Agbeyegbe TD. 1989. Interest rates and metal price movements: further evidence. *J. Environ. Econ. Manag.* 16:184–92

Barnett HJ, Morse C. 1963. *Scarcity and Growth*. Baltimore, MD: Johns Hopkins Univ. Press

Berck P, Roberts M. 1996. Natural-resource prices: Will they ever turn up? *J. Environ. Econ. Manag.* 31:65–78

Berndt E, Wood D. 1975. Technology, prices, and the derived demand for energy. *Rev. Econ. Stat.* 57:259–68

Bollerslev T. 1986. Generalized autoregressive conditional heteroskedasticity. *J. Econ.* 31:307–27

Brennan MJ. 1987. Capital asset pricing model. In *The New Palgrave Dictionary of Economics*, ed. J Eatwell, M Milgate, P Newman, pp. 336–41. London: Macmillan

Brennan MJ, Schwartz E. 1985. Evaluating natural-resource assets. *J. Bus.* 58:135–57

Bresnahan TF, Suslow VY. 1985. Inventories as an asset: the volatility of copper prices. *Int. Econ. Rev.* 26:409–24

Cairns RD, Davis GA. 1998. On using current information to evaluate hard rock mineral properties. *Rev. Econ. Stat.* 80:658–63

Chermak JM, Patrick RH. 2001. A microeconomic test of the theory of exhaustible resources. *J. Environ. Econ. Manag.* 42:82–103

Daly H. 1974. The economics of the steady state. *Am. Econ. Rev.* 64:15–21

Dasgupta P, Heal G, Stiglitz J. 1980. The taxation of exhaustible resources. In *Public Policy and the Tax System*, ed. GA Hughes, GM Heal, pp. 150–72. London: George Allen Unwin

Devarajan S, Fisher A. 1982. Exploration and scarcity. *J. Polit. Econ.* 90:1279–90

Ellis GM, Halvorsen R. 2002. Estimation of market power in a nonrenewable resource industry. *J. Polit. Econ.* 110:883–99

Engle RF. 1982. Autoregressive conditional heteroscedasticity with estimates of variance of United Kingdom inflation. *Econometrica* 50:987–1008

Farrow S. 1985. Testing the efficiency of extraction from a stock resource. *J. Polit. Econ.* 93:452–87

Gaudet G. 2007. Natural resource economics under the rule of Hotelling. *Can. J. Econ.* 40:1033–59

Georgescu-Roegen N. 1971. *The Entropy Law and the Economic Process*. Cambridge, MA: Harvard Univ. Press

Gilbert R. 1978. Dominant firm pricing policy in a market for an exhaustible resource. *Bell J. Econ.* 9:385–95

Gilbert R. 1979. Optimal depletion of an uncertain stock. *Rev. Econ. Stud.* 46:47–57

Halvorsen R, Smith T. 1984. On measuring natural-resource scarcity. *J. Polit. Econ.* 92:954–64

Halvorsen R, Smith T. 1991. A test of the theory of exhaustible resources. *Q. J. Econ.* 106:123–40

Hamilton JD. 1983. Oil and the macroeconomy since World War II. *J. Polit. Econ.* 91:228–48

Heal G, Barrow M. 1980. The relationship between interest rates and metal-price movements. *Rev. Econ. Stud.* 47:161–82

Hotelling H. 1929. Stability in competition. *Econ. J.* 39:41–57

Hotelling H. 1931. The economics of exhaustible resources. *J. Polit. Econ.* 39:137–75

Hotelling H. 1938. The general welfare in relation to problems of taxation and of railroad and utility rates. *Econometrica* 6:242–69

Johnson RN, Libecap GD. 1980. Efficient markets and Great Lakes timber: a conservation issue reexamined. *Explor. Econ. Hist.* 17:372–85

Krautkraemer JA. 1998. Nonrenewable resource scarcity. *J. Econ. Lit.* 36:2065–107

Lasserre P. 1985. Discovery costs as a measure of rent. *Can. J. Econ.* 18:474–83

Lee J, List JA, Strazicich MC. 2006. Nonrenewable resource prices: deterministic or stochastic trends? *J. Environ. Econ. Manag.* 51:354–70

Levhari D, Pindyck RS. 1981. The pricing of durable exhaustible resources. *Q. J. Econ.* 96:365–78

Lin CCY, Wagner G. 2007. Steady-state growth in a Hotelling model of resource extraction. *J. Environ. Econ. Manag.* 54:68–83

Livernois J, Thille H, Zhang X. 2006. A test of the Hotelling rule using old-growth timber. *Can. J. Econ.* 39:163–86

Miller MH, Upton CW. 1985a. A test of the Hotelling valuation principle. *J. Polit. Econ.* 93:1–25

Miller MH, Upton CW. 1985b. The pricing of oil and gas: some further results. *J. Financ.* 40:1009–18

Moazzami B, Anderson FJ. 1994. Modeling natural-resource scarcity using the error-correction approach. *Can. J. Econ.* 27:801–12

Pindyck RS. 1977. Cartel pricing and the structure of the world bauxite market. *Bell J. Econ.* 8:343–60

Pindyck RS. 1978. The optimal exploration and production of nonrenewable resources. *J. Polit. Econ.* 86:841–61

Pindyck RS. 1980. Uncertainty and exhaustible-resource markets. *J. Polit. Econ.* 88:1201–25

Pindyck RS. 1999. The long-run evolution of energy prices. *Energy J.* 20:1-27

Salant SW. 1976. Exhaustible resources and industrial structure: a Nash-Cournot approach to the world oil market. *J. Polit. Econ.* 84:1079–93

Salant SW. 1982. Imperfect competition in the international energy market: a computerized Nash-Cournot model. *Oper. Res.* 30:252–80

Slade ME. 1982. Trends in natural-resource commodity prices: an analysis of the time domain. *J. Environ. Econ. Manag.* 9:122–37

Slade ME. 1984. Tax policy and the supply of exhaustible resources: theory and practice. *Land Econ.* 60:133–47

Slade ME. 2001. Valuing managerial flexibility: an application of real-option theory to mining investments. *J. Environ. Econ. Manag.* 41:193–233

Slade ME, Thille H. 1997. Hotelling confronts CAPM: a test of the theory of exhaustible resources. *Can. J. Econ.* 30:685–708

Smith VK. 1978. Measuring natural-resource scarcity: theory and practice. *J. Environ. Econ. Manag.* 5:150–71

Smith VK. 1981. The empirical relevance of Hotelling's model for natural resources. *Resour. Energy* 3:105–17

Solow RM, Wan FY. 1976. Extraction costs in the theory of exhaustible resources. *Bell J. Econ.* 7:359–70

Stiglitz JE. 1974. Growth with exhaustible resources. *Rev. Econ. Stud.* 41:123–38

Stiglitz JE. 1976. Monopoly and the rate of extraction of an exhaustible resource. *Am. Econ. Rev.* 66:655–61

Stollery KR. 1983. Mineral depletion with cost as the extraction limit: a model applied to the behavior of nickel prices. *J. Environ. Econ. Manag.* 10:151–65

Sweeney J. 1977. Economics of depletable natural resources: market forces and intertemporal biases. *Rev. Econ. Stud.* 44:125–41

U.S. Energy Info. Admin. 2008. *EIA Annual Energy Review 2007.* Washington, DC: US Gov. http://www.eia.doe.gov/aer/

Young D. 1992. Cost specification and firm behavior in a Hotelling model of resource extraction. *Can. J. Econ.* 25:41–59

Young D, Ryan DL. 1996. Empirical testing of a risk-adjusted Hotelling model. *Resour. Energy* 18:265–89

Recent Developments in the Intertemporal Modeling of Uncertainty

Christian P. Traeger

Department of Agricultural and Resource Economics, University of California, Berkeley, California 94720; email: traeger@berkeley.edu

Annu. Rev. Resour. Econ. 2009. 1:261–85

The *Annual Review of Resource Economics* is online at resource.annualreviews.org

This article's doi:
10.1146/annurev.resource.050708.144242

Key Words

ambiguity, intertemporal, recursive utility, risk aversion, social discount rate, time preference

Abstract

Time and uncertainty constitute essential ingredients to many of the most challenging resource problems. With respect to the time dimension, agents are generally assumed to have a pure time preference as well as a preference for smoothing consumption over time. With respect to risk, agents are generally assumed to be Arrow-Pratt risk averse. The discounted expected utility model assumes that aversion to risk and aversion to intertemporal fluctuations coincide. This review discusses models and concepts that aim at disentangling time and risk attitude and briefly sketches a generalization of risk attitude to situations where uncertainty is not captured by unique probability measures. This paper reviews resource economic applications and relates the concepts to the debate on the social discount rate.

1. INTRODUCTION

Time and uncertainty constitute essential ingredients to many of the most challenging resource problems. Frequently analyzed questions include how an extraction rate changes under an increase in risk, or how a pollution stock changes with an increase of risk aversion. The discounted expected utility standard model is of limited use for answering these questions. It implicitly assumes that aversion to risk coincides with aversion to intertemporal consumption fluctuations. Thus, a separate analysis of how risk aversion and how aversion to intertemporal change affect an economic variable is not possible within this standard framework. Even worse, this confinement of Arrow-Pratt risk aversion to equal the inverse of the elasticity of intertemporal substitution corresponds to an assumption of (intertemporal) risk neutrality. Finally, more often than not, probabilities are unknown in environmental and resource economics and uncertainty does not seem to be captured satisfactorily by the use of unique probability measures. This paper discusses concepts and models that constitute a better framework for analyzing the above questions. It reviews some of the related resource economics literature and explains new decision theoretic modeling frameworks. I motivate these frameworks with an application to the recent debate on the "correct" social discount rate in climate change.

Since the mid-1990s, scattered efforts have been undertaken in the field of resource economics to disentangle the effects of risk aversion from those of the propensity to smooth consumption over time. All of these approaches build on variants of the generalized isoelastic model introduced by Epstein & Zin (1989, 1991) and Weil (1990). In this paper, I review these contributions and present a recent generalization of the isoelastic model (Traeger 2007c, 2007d). In particular, I introduce the related concept of intertemporal risk aversion. The concept points out that the standard model not only confines risk attitude to the propensity to smooth consumption over time, but also contains an implicit assumption of intertemporal risk neutrality. A simple and intuitive way to think about intertemporal risk aversion is as an aversion with respect to utility gains and losses. Here, cardinality of the utility function is derived from the information on intertemporal trade-offs. The according risk measures can also be applied to multicommodity settings and to situations, frequently met in environmental economics, where a natural cardinal scale for the impact assessment is not given. I relate intertemporal risk aversion to the Kreps & Porteus (1978) intrinsic preference for the timing of uncertainty resolution. I explain that intertemporal risk aversion in combination with indifference to the timing of uncertainty resolution in the intrinsic sense (as it prevails in the standard model) can force the pure rate of time preference to zero (Traeger 2007c). As opposed to the discussion on time preference reaching back many decades, the present assumptions are not a priori normative but rely on axioms like stationarity, time consistency, and the von Neumann & Morgenstern (1944) axioms.

A different decision theoretic ambition over the past decades has been to capture uncertainty that is not well described as a unique probability measure and to account for a different perception of and aversion to such uncertainties. These models seem particularly attractive when facing problems such as climate change, lost prospects from a reduction in biodiversity, or ecosystem changes caused by the introduction of invasive species. I summarize a recent model of ambiguity by Klibanoff et al. (2005, 2009) that distinguishes between risk and more general (ambiguous) uncertainty. The model parametrizes different degrees of aversion for risk and uncertainty.

I start out with a combined measure of risk and time that featured most prominently in the recent debate on the cost-benefit analysis of climate change: the social discount rate. The social discount rate summarizes different contributions to the time development of the marginal utility of consumption in a form that is convenient for both theoretic insight and applied evaluation. In Section 2, I point out how considerations of intertemporal risk aversion and of ambiguity aversion yield contributions to the social discount rate that have been neglected in the recent debate (Traeger 2009). In Section 3, I discuss the literature disentangling risk aversion from intertemporal substitutability. Section 4 introduces the concept of intertemporal risk aversion, the preference for the timing of risk resolution, and a framework for modeling ambiguity aversion. I also discuss how axioms with regard to these concepts can affect the choice of the rate of pure time preference.

2. A MOTIVATING EXAMPLE: SOCIAL DISCOUNTING, INTERTEMPORAL RISK AVERSION, AND AMBIGUITY

Following the Stern (2007) review of climate change, few economic parameters have been as hotly debated over the past years as the different contributions to the social discount rate. The social discount rate characterizes in a convenient way how the value of consumption develops over time. It turns out that differing assumptions in social discounting explain the major differences between most integrated assessments of climate change and mitigation policies (Plambeck et al. 1997, Nordhaus 2007, Weitzman 2007). In this section, I highlight how the concepts discussed in this review affect the debate on social discounting in the face of climate change. The application is based on Traeger (2009) and shows the importance of intertemporal risk aversion whenever dealing with risk and time. I also point out how the ambiguity model discussed in Section 4.3 affects the debate and briefly relate it to Weitzman's (2009) dismal theorem.

2.1. Social Discounting, Climate Change, and the Standard Model

Equation 1 characterizes the social discount rate in a standard setting and underlies most of the debate on climate change and discounting:

$$r = \delta + \eta\mu - \eta^2 \frac{\sigma^2}{2}. \tag{1}$$

It extends the classical Ramsey (1928) formula by a stochastic growth rate. The right-hand side of Equation 1 characterizes the individual components of the certainty-equivalent social discount rate.[1] The rate of pure time preference is represented by δ, which captures impatience and is also known as the utility discount rate. The second term expresses devaluation of future consumption caused by the combination of growth and decreasing marginal utility. The parameter η is the inverse of the intertemporal elasticity of substitu-

---

[1]In a complete market without distortions, the social discount rate equals the real rate of interest (Ramsey equation). However, incomplete markets, distortions, and long-time horizons generally prevent the social discount rate from being observed easily on the market. Moreover, individuals can have differing valuation in their political role, e.g., valuing future generations' welfare, from the preferences observed on a market where they optimize individual utility. For a closer discussion, see Hepburn (2006).

tion, which—in the standard model—coincides with Arrow-Pratt risk aversion. It characterizes the percentage decrease in marginal utility from a percentage increase of consumption and expresses aversion to fluctuations over time and with respect to risk. The parameter μ characterizes the expected growth rate. Together, the term $\eta\mu$ characterizes the loss of marginal utility from future consumption because of growth. In fact, most of the debate concentrates on the first two terms because the third term generally turns out to be negligible. It characterizes the effect of Arrow-Pratt risk aversion on the certainty-equivalent discount rate. The parameter σ characterizes the standard deviation of the (assumed to be normally distributed) growth rate. The parameters δ, μ, and σ are in the order of percent, whereas η is in the unit order. Therefore, σ^2 easily makes the third term 10–100 times smaller than the other two, and risk can be neglected in social discounting. Be aware that σ characterizes risk in the sense of volatility. The frequently met usage of the term risk within the climate change debate, incorporating a reduced expected value as a consequence of possible catastrophic events, would partly be captured by the second term of the social discount rate.

The parameter choices of Stern (2007) can be approximated by $\delta = 0.1\%$, $\eta = 1$, and $\mu = 1.3\%$, thus delivering $r = 1.4\%$ under certainty. Whereas Stern's team clearly argues for a normative dimension of these choices, the majority of integrated assessment modelers refuses such a standpoint.[2] As creator of the widespread open-source integrated assessment model DICE and adhering to a strictly positive perspective, Nordhaus is representative of the latter group of integrated assessment modelers. His parameter choices in the recent version of DICE-2007 (Nordhaus 2008) are $\delta = 1.5\%$, $\eta = 2$, and $\mu = 2\%$, thus delivering $r = 5.5\%$ (again under certainty).[3] Introducing uncertainty with a standard deviation of $\sigma = 2\%$ to the model would result in an adjustment of the risk-free rate by 0.02% in the case of Stern and 0.08% in the case of Nordhaus, both of which are negligible. A standard deviation of $\sigma = 2\%$ is used by Weitzman (2009) to approximate the volatility of economic growth without climate change and possible catastrophic risks.

The next section continues the discussion of the effect of uncertainty in the face of climate change. I close with a recent illustration by Nordhaus (2007) of the importance of the social discount rate in climate change evaluation. The author runs the DICE-2007 with both the Stern (2007) ($r = 1.4\%$) parameterization of the social discount rate and the above-cited values of Nordhaus ($r = 5.5\%$). These different parameterizations cause a difference in the optimal reduction rate of emissions in the period 2010–2019 of 53% versus 14% and a difference in the optimal carbon tax of $360 versus $35 per ton of carbon.

2.2. Social Discounting, Climate Change, and Intertemporal Risk Aversion

Equation 1 is based on the intertemporally additive expected utility standard model. The model contains the implicit assumption of intertemporal risk neutrality, implying that aversion to risk is fully captured by aversion to fluctuations over time. These aspects of intertemporal decision making under uncertainty are discussed in detail in this review.

---

[2]Moreover, Dasgupta (2008) points out that, from a normative perspective, an egalitarian choice of $\delta = 0.1\%$ should also call for a higher propensity of intergenerational consumption smoothing $\eta > 1$.

[3]The growth rate is endogenous in the DICE model and has been reconstructed from Nordhaus (2007, p. 694).

Here, I highlight what happens to Equation 1 when these assumptions are relaxed. As shown in Traeger (2009), the new risk-free social discount rate becomes

$$r = \delta + \eta\mu - \eta^2\frac{\sigma^2}{2} - \text{RIRA}\left|1 - \eta^2\right|\frac{\sigma^2}{2}. \tag{2}$$

Now the parameter η denotes aversion only to intertemporal fluctuations. The coefficient RIRA characterizes intertemporal risk aversion. In the one-dimensional setting of Equation 2, it is a function of the intertemporal elasticity of substitution and the Arrow-Pratt coefficient of risk aversion, both of which can now vary independently.

In Section 3.2, I provide a survey of estimates of the relevant parameters underlying Equation 2. The precise estimation of these parameters remains an ongoing challenge, and for an illustration of this point, I rely on Vissing-Jørgensen & Attanasio (2003). The authors give a best guess of $\eta = \frac{2}{3}$ and Arrow-Pratt relative risk aversion RRA = 9.5, which yields a coefficient of relative intertemporal risk aversion RIRA = 26.5.[4] In particular, it follows that $\left|1 - \eta^2\right| = \frac{5}{9}$. The importance of the intertemporal risk aversion term in the social discount rate with respect to the standard risk term is represented by the ratio

$$\frac{\text{RIRA}\left|1 - \eta^2\right|\frac{\sigma^2}{2}}{\eta^2\frac{\sigma^2}{2}} \approx 33.$$

A factor of 33 easily brings the importance of risk back into the social discount rate. Note that, because of the slightly lower η, the standard risk term in Equation 2 is even lower than in the examples discussed above in relation to the climate change debate. However, the effect of intertemporal risk aversion is significantly larger. For a numerical example of the terms in Equation 2, take again an expected growth rate of μ = 2% and a standard deviation of σ = 2%. Then we find a growth effect of $\eta\mu$ = 1.3%, a standard risk effect of 0.01%, and an intertemporal risk aversion effect of 0.3%. For example, with a pure rate of time preference of ρ = 1.5%, the risk-free social discount rate becomes r = 2.5% instead of r = 2.8%. This is a significant, but not yet huge, difference. Now assume that, in the face of climate change, risk increases to σ = 4%. Because of the nonlinearity in the risk terms, the risk effects become 0.4% (standard risk term) and 1.2% (intertemporal risk aversion term), thereby almost canceling the growth effect. Although σ = 4% may seem high for a one-year period, with time horizons typical to climate change mitigation projects the importance of risk can increase significantly.

Interested only in the possible magnitude, I sidestep questions on the correlation between the stochastic process creating overall growth and the potentially random process characterizing payoffs from climate change mitigation projects (for more on this issue, see Weitzman 2007, Traeger 2009). Instead, I use Equation 2 in a simple two-period model extending the time horizon to 50 years. I employ the same values for the preference parameters based on Vissing-Jørgensen & Attanasio (2003). Keeping expected growth at 50μ = 50 · 2% = 100% implies an expectation that future wealth in 50 years is $\frac{x_{50}}{x_0} = \exp(1) \approx 2.7$ times current wealth. Let me pick σ = 0.3, implying that the probability that climate change (or anything else) causes us to be worse off in 50 years than we are today is approximately 0.04%. Then we find a growth effect of $\eta\mu$ = 67% and an intertemporal risk aversion effect of 66%. Together with the standard risk term of 2.5%, the

---

[4]Section 4.1 explains how to calculate the coefficient RIRA in the isoelastic setting underlying Equation 2.

risk contribution more than cancels the growth effect in the social discount rate, and we are essentially left with pure time preference. Note that an increase of the variance to $\sigma = \frac{1}{3}$, implying a 0.13% probability that we will be worse off in 50 years compared with our situation today, makes the intertemporal risk aversion term dominate the growth term by 15%.

2.3. Social Discounting, Climate Change, and Ambiguity Aversion

Recently, Weitzman (2009) argued that in the context of climate change the parameters of the distribution governing the growth process may not be known. Following Weitzman, I adopt a Bayesian setting to capture such a form of second-order uncertainty. Whereas Weitzman sticks with the standard risk model underlying Equation 1, in contrast, I adopt a recent model developed in the decision theoretic literature by Klibanoff et al. (2005, 2009). The model in Klibanoff et al. (2009) contains the standard Bayesian setting as a special case and is presented in Section 4.3. Taking the simplest example of Bayesian second-order uncertainty, I assume that expected growth μ^* is uncertain and described by a normally distributed prior with expected value μ and a standard deviation τ. For simplicity, I keep the standard deviation of the growth process, for a given μ^*, a known parameter σ as in the previous model. In Traeger (2009), I showed that Equation 1 then turns into

$$r = \delta + \eta\mu - \eta^2 \frac{\sigma^2 + \tau^2}{2} - \text{RAA}\left|1 - \eta^2\right| \frac{\tau^2}{2}, \tag{3}$$

where RAA is a coefficient measuring relative ambiguity aversion. For the moment, let me ignore ambiguity aversion and the term containing RAA. The only difference between the remaining part of Equation 3 and Equation 1 is the additional variance τ in the third term on the right-hand side (standard risk term). It is a straightforward consequence of making the growth process more uncertain by introducing a prior (second-order uncertainty) over some parameter of the growth process. In the case of the normal distributions adopted here, the variance simply adds up. From the given example, it is hard to see how adding a Bayesian prior would bring the standard risk term back into the order of magnitude needed to compare with the other characterizing terms of the social discount rate. Instead of a doubling, a factor of 10–100 is needed. The only way to reach this result is by sufficiently increasing the variance of the prior. Effectively, this is what Weitzman (2009) did in deriving what he calls a dismal theorem. He introduced a fat-tailed ignorant prior whose higher moments do not exist. As a consequence, the risk-free social discount rate in Equation 3 goes to minus infinity, implying an infinite willingness to transfer (certain) consumption into the future. Weitzman limited this willingness by the value of a (or society's) statistical life.[5]

Instead of messing with infinity, in Traeger (2009), I follow the more humble task of introducing ambiguity aversion. Experimental evidence has shown that economic agents tend to be more afraid of unknown probabilities than they are of known probabilities (the most famous experiment being suggested by Ellsberg 1961). Klibanoff et al. (2005, 2009) translated the unknown probabilities into second-order uncertainty and, thus, the prior. Then, they

---

[5]Note that Weitzman (2009) put the prior on the variance σ rather than on the expected value of growth. He loosely related the uncertainty to climate sensitivity. Of course, the above is a simplified perspective on Weitzman's sophisticated approach.

introduced a new function whose curvature captures additional aversion to second-order uncertainty.[6] Using an isoelastic function to describe ambiguity aversion,[7] the aversion can be captured by the parameter RAA. In contrast to intertemporal risk aversion, ambiguity aversion does not act on σ, but only on τ. Otherwise, the expression is strikingly similar to the one in Equation 2. Unfortunately, I am not yet aware of estimates for the parameter RAA in the Klibanoff et al. (2005, 2009) model. It will be interesting to see whether ambiguity aversion can also bring uncertainty back into the social discounting debate.

3. DISENTANGLING RISK AVERSION FROM INTERTEMPORAL SUBSTITUTABILITY

It is well known that the intertemporally additive expected utility framework for modeling preferences implicitly assumes that a decision maker's aversion to risk coincides with his aversion to intertemporal fluctuations. Epstein & Zin (1989) and Weil (1990) derived an alternative setting in which these two a priori distinct characteristics of preference can be disentangled. This section presents a slightly more general framework and discusses the special case derived by Epstein & Zin (1989) and Weil (1990) and its applications to resource economics.

3.1. An Intertemporal Model of Risk Attitude

I refer to the "standard model" as the modeling framework where a decision maker evaluates utility separately for every period and for every state of the world and then sums it over states and over time. Formally, let $\chi = (x_0, x_1, x_2, \ldots)$ denote a consumption path and p_χ a probability distribution over the latter. Then, assuming stationary preferences, the decision maker's overall welfare is given by

$$U = E_{p_\chi} \sum_t \beta^t u(x_t),$$

where β is the utility discount factor. The curvature of u captures the decision maker's aversion to consumption fluctuations. Because the same utility function is used to aggregate over time and over risk, the decision maker's aversion to (certain) intertemporal change is the same as his aversion to risk fluctuations corresponding to different states of the world.

A priori, however, risk aversion and the propensity to smooth consumption over time are two distinct concepts. The notion that in an atemporal setting risky scenarios can be evaluated in the form

$$U = E_{p_\chi} u^{vNM}(x)$$

is based on the von Neumann & Morgenstern (1944) axioms. Here, the curvature of u^{vNM} captures risk aversion. For a single commodity setting, the Arrow-Pratt measure of relative risk aversion $RRA(x) = -\frac{u''(x)}{u'(x)}x$ attaches a numeric value to curvature and risk aversion.

---

[6]That is additional to standard risk aversion. As discussed above, standard risk aversion also creates an effect when confronted with a Bayesian prior, but that is captured by τ^2 in the standard risk aversion term.

[7]Isoelastic functions have implicitly been assumed in all the previous equations, i.e., for describing Arrow-Pratt risk aversion, intertemporal substitutability, and intertemporal risk aversion.

A similar set of axioms[8] provides additive separability of preference representations evaluating certain consumption paths. Adding stationarity to the evaluation makes the utility functions in the different periods coincide up to a common discount factor β:

$$U(\chi) = \sum_t \beta^t u^{\text{int}}(x_t), \tag{4}$$

where the concavity of the utility function u^{int} describes aversion to intertemporal consumption volatility. In a one-commodity setting,[9] this aversion to intertemporal volatility can be measured by means of the consumption elasticity of marginal utility $\eta = -\frac{u^{\text{int}''}(x)}{u^{\text{int}'}(x)}x$. The consumption elasticity of marginal utility is the inverse of the intertemporal elasticity of substitution $\sigma = \frac{1}{\eta}$. Note that the measure η exactly corresponds to the Arrow-Pratt measure of relative risk aversion, only in the context of periods rather than risk states. Instead of calling η an aversion measure to intertemporal volatility, it can also be characterized as a measure for a decision maker's propensity to smooth consumption over time.

A priori, the utility functions u^{vNM} and u^{int} are two distinct objects that carry two different types of information. Traeger (2007d) derived this intuition formally. The paper combines the von Neumann-Morgenstern axioms with the assumption that certain consumption paths can be evaluated in the additively separable form (Equation 4). The resulting preference representation features two independent functions that—in a one-commodity setting—can be identified with the functions u^{vNM} and u^{int} noted above. I give an intuitive derivation of the form of such an evaluation for a two-period setting with certain consumption in the first and uncertain consumption in the second period. Let

$$U_1(x_1, x_2) = u^{\text{int}}(x_1) + \beta u^{\text{int}}(x_2) \tag{5}$$

represent preferences over certain (two-period) consumption paths. Let

$$U_2(p) = E_p u^{\text{vNM}}(x)$$

represent preferences over second-period lotteries.[10] Define x_2^p as the second-period certainty equivalent to the lottery p by requiring

$$U_2(x_2^p) = u^{\text{vNM}}(x_2^p) \overset{!}{=} U_2(p) = E_p u^{\text{vNM}}(x)$$
$$\Rightarrow x_2^p = u^{\text{vNM}^{-1}}[E_p u^{\text{vNM}}(x)]. \tag{6}$$

Now use the certainty equivalent to extend the evaluation functional in Equation 5 to a setting of uncertainty by defining

$$U(x_1, p) = U_2(x_1, x_2^p) = u^{\text{int}}(x_1) + \beta u^{\text{int}}(x_2^p)$$
$$= u^{\text{int}}(x_1) + \beta u^{\text{int}}\left(u^{\text{vNM}^{-1}}\left[E_p u^{\text{vNM}}(x) \right] \right).$$

---

[8]There are various alternative sets of axioms aiming at additive separability. The discussion below is based on Traeger (2007d) where I use Wakker (1988) and give a list of other axiomatizations.

[9]Kihlstrom & Mirman (1974) generalized the one-commodity measure by Arrow and Pratt to a multicommodity setting. In their case, risk aversion becomes good specific and corresponds to the concavity of the utility function along a variation of the particular commodity, keeping the others constant. The same concept of a multidimensional measure could be applied to intertemporal substitutability.

[10]Formally, let $\Delta(\cdot)$ be the space of Borel probability measures on some compact metric space. The second-period preferences are defined over elements of $P = \Delta(X)$.

Taking the inverse of u^{vNM} assumes a one-dimensional setting. More general, it holds that u^{vNM} is always a strictly monotonic transformation of u^{int} (Traeger 2007d).[11] Thus defining f by $u^{\text{vNM}} = f \circ u^{\text{int}}$, I can transform Equation 6 into

$$f \circ u^{\text{int}}(x_2^p) \overset{!}{=} E_p f \circ u^{\text{int}}(x)$$
$$\Leftrightarrow u^{\text{int}}(x_2^p) = f^{-1}\left[E_p f \circ u^{\text{int}}(x)\right]$$

and obtain in combination with Equation 5 the representation

$$U(x_1, p) = u^{\text{int}}(x_1) + \beta f^{-1}\left[E_p f \circ u^{\text{int}}(x)\right] \tag{7}$$

for the multicommodity framework.

For a general time horizon, the corresponding preference representation evaluates consumption recursively and is a special case of a model by Kreps & Porteus (1978). Except for the special case discussed in Section 4.2, a recursive evaluation is necessary to preserve time consistency. Rather than aggregating utility streams derived from every possible probability-weighted consumption path, the decision maker trades current consumption benefits against aggregate future welfare in every period. General objects of choice are no longer lotteries over consumption paths, but instead, they are decision trees. Whereas a lottery over consumption paths contains only information of the probability that a particular event takes place in some period t, the decision tree also contains information about which lottery takes place in which period in order to give the overall probability for the event in period t. As discussed in Section 4.2, the evaluation of a lottery in the future may depend not only on the probabilities attached to each of the outcomes, but also on the period in which the risk resolves.

Formally, a decision tree is a recursion of probability distributions over subtrees. General choice objects in the last period are lotteries p_T over consumption x_T. In the penultimate period, certain consumption is denoted by x_{T-1}. However, before uncertainty resolves, the decision maker neither knows x_{T-1} with certainty, nor does he know the probability distribution that he faces at the beginning of period T with certainty. Instead, at the beginning of period $T-1$, he faces a lottery over the tuple (x_{T-1}, p_T), which I will denote by p_{T-1}. Observe that each tuple (x_{T-1}, p_T) corresponds to a subtree. A recursive construction defining p_{t-1} as a lottery over tuples (x_{t-1}, p_t) for all $t \in \{1, ..., T\}$ gives the desired formal representation of a decision tree in the present p_0.[12]

The general recursive evaluation of such a decision tree is as follows. Consumption in the last period of a finite time horizon is simply $u(x_T)$ and then

$$U_{t-1}(x_{t-1}, p_t) = u(x_{t-1}) + \beta f_t^{-1}\left[E_{pt} f_t \circ U_t(x_t, p_{t+1})\right]. \tag{8}$$

The function U_{t-1} represents preferences in period $t-1$ after the uncertainty with respect to $t-1$ has resolved. The certainty stationarity axiom (only) makes the functions u characterizing intertemporal aggregation coincide. The functions f_t and, thus, uncertainty aggregation can generally differ between periods. Note that, so far, each U_t evaluates

---

[11]In the above setting, observe that both $U_1(\bar{x}_1, x_2)$ and $U_2(x_2) = u^{\text{vNM}}(x_2)$ for some fixed $\bar{x}_1$ have to represent the same preferences over X (assuming time consistency). Therefore, the two different representations have to coincide up to an ordinal transformation.

[12]In the notion of Footnote 10, the choice space in period $t-1$ (before $t-1$ uncertainty resolves) is defined recursively as $P_{t-1} = \Delta(X \times P_t)$.

choices between (sub)trees that describe a unique future scenario with no further choices left open for later periods (equivalent to an open-loop evaluation).[13]

Comparing certain consumption paths, the expected-value operator drops out and the functions f_t^{-1} and f_t cancel. Then it is observed that, as in Equation 7, the utility function u in Equation 8 corresponds to the utility function u^{int}, which describes the decision maker's propensity to smooth consumption over time. In contrast, when comparing uncertain consumption scenarios in the last period or degenerate subtrees, it is observed that $f_t \circ u$, respectively $f_t \circ U_t$, corresponds to u_t^{vNM} and, thus, expresses risk aversion in the Arrow-Pratt sense.

Letting the time horizon approach infinity, the decision tree grows infinite. See Epstein & Zin (1989) for a formal definition of such an infinite decision tree. The advantage of the infinite time horizon is that the set of choice objects becomes the same in every period.[14] That is, if P^∞ denotes the set of all infinite decision trees and $p_{t+1}^\infty \in p^\infty$, then the lottery p_t^∞ over tuples (x_t, p_{t+1}^∞) is also an element of P^∞.

3.2. Disentangling Risk Aversion and Intertemporal Substitutability

Epstein & Zin (1989, 1991) and Weil (1990) famously developed a one-commodity special case of the model noted in Equation 8 for the infinite time horizon.[15] Let $u(x) = \frac{x^\rho}{\rho}$, implying a constant intertemporal elasticity of substitution function over certain consumption paths with the consumption elasticity of marginal utility $\eta = 1 - \rho$ and an intertemporal elasticity of substitution of $\sigma = \frac{1}{\eta}$. From now on, the parameter σ always denotes the intertemporal elasticity of substitution (as opposed to the standard deviation in Section 2). Moreover, assume constant relative Arrow-Pratt risk aversion (constant in consumption level and over time) so that $f_t \circ u(x) = x^\alpha$ for all t, implying $f_t(z) = (\rho z)^{\frac{\alpha}{\rho}}$. Then, Equation 8 turns into

$$U(x_{t-1}, p_t) = \frac{x_{t-1}^\rho}{\rho} + \beta \frac{1}{\rho} \left[E_{pt}(\rho U(x_t, p_{t+1}))^{\frac{\alpha}{\rho}} \right]^{\frac{\rho}{\alpha}}, \tag{9}$$

or with a change in normalization (see Traeger 2009),

$$U(x_{t-1}, p_t) = \left((1 - \beta)x_{t-1}^\rho + \beta[E_{pt}(U(x_t, p_{t+1}))^\alpha]^{\frac{\rho}{\alpha}} \right)^{\frac{1}{\rho}}, \tag{10}$$

which is the form employed by Epstein & Zin (1989, 1991). This special case of Equation 8 is the setting predominantly used in the literature to disentangle risk attitude from the

---

[13]Let me point out a similarity between the (necessity of the) recursivity in the open-loop evaluation in Equation 8 and the (necessity of the) recursivity in a feedback dynamic programming equation for the standard model. In a feedback optimization with standard preferences, the value function in the next period depends on the realization of some random variable. That dependence is based on the fact that the realization of the random variable changes real outcomes and optimal choices in the future. In Equation 8, the future value function depends on the realization of the random variables because the decision maker cares whether uncertainty was resolved earlier or later, even if this realization does not change real outcomes and choices. The underlying intrinsic (rather than instrumental) preference for the timing of uncertainty resolution is discussed in Section 4.2. Below, I integrate feedback into the evaluation structure when analyzing applications of the model. For a technically, slightly more demanding, feedback formulation in the abstract decision-tree setting, consult Kreps & Porteus (1978).

[14]Of course, the set of feasible choices can vary between periods.

[15]In Epstein & Zin (1989, 1991) the authors also analyzed a more general isoelastic model where risk aversion does not satisfy the von Neumann-Morgenstern axioms.

propensity to smooth consumption over time. Epstein & Zin (1991) derived a framework for estimating this type of preference in the context of asset pricing.

Their framework has been carried over to various resource applications, and I use it as an example of how to translate the recursive evaluation functional into a standard dynamic programming setting. For this purpose, I have to specify how current states of the world and some stochastic processes generate the uncertain future (i.e., the decision tree p_t). Define a stationary stochastic process $(\tilde{R}_t, \tilde{z}_t)^{\infty}_{-\infty}$ where $R_t \in [\underline{R}, \bar{R}]^K$ is a vector specifying asset returns and $z_t \in \mathrm{IR}^Z$ captures other random information relevant to predicting future probabilities. An example of a resource economics application is obtained by replacing financial assets with livestock (see Section 3.3). I use a tilde to emphasize the random nature of a variable. The state of the system is specified by wealth A_t and the history of realized asset returns and information variables, which I denote as $I_t = (R_t, z_t)^{t-1}_{-\infty} \in \mathbf{I}_t = \times^{t-1}_{i=-\infty}[\underline{R}, \bar{R}]^K \times \mathrm{IR}^Z$. The equation of motion for the agent's wealth is

$$A_{t+1} = (A_t - x_t)\omega_t \tilde{R}_t,$$

where ω_t is a vector whose component $\omega_{k,t}$ characterizes the share of assets invested in the kth asset that has return $\tilde{R}_{k,t}$. In this setting, the probability distribution over future consumption is determined by wealth, the stochastic process $(\tilde{R}_t, \tilde{z}_t)^{\infty}_{-\infty}$, and the (here optimal) choice of the control variables x_t and ω_t. Thus, I can write a more standard dynamic programming equation where the value function is a function of wealth A_t and information I_t rather than of p_t:

$$V(A_t, I_t) = \max_{x_t, \omega_t} \left((1 - \beta)x_t^{\rho} + \beta \mathrm{E}\left[V((A_t - x_t)\omega_t \tilde{R}_t, \tilde{I}_{t+1})^{\alpha} | I_t \right]^{\frac{\rho}{\alpha}} \right)^{\frac{1}{\rho}}.$$

Note that the choices evaluated in future periods are no longer degenerate. Instead, we assume an optimal choice in every period as we recursively evaluate the future (feedback setting).[16]

Without giving an exhaustive summary of estimates that have been derived for the parameters of the generalized isoelastic model, I present some prominent and, in their collection, representative findings. Most existing econometric estimations analyze portfolio choice in financial markets. In their empirical analysis, Epstein & Zin (1991) employed various consumption measures and instruments, and their results suggest $\alpha \approx 0$ and RRA ≈ 1. Most of their values for α fall into the interval $[-.5, .5]$ with a strong accumulation in $[-0.05, 0.05]$. Their estimates of the intertemporal elasticity of substitution σ stretch over the interval $[0.2, 0.9]$. Interestingly, the pure rate of time preference $\delta = -\ln \beta$ is measured to be approximately zero with estimates ranging $[-0.5\%, +0.4\%]$.[17]

Campbell (1996) log-linearized the Euler equations and estimates RRA $\in [2,10]$ for annual observations, although he estimates a much higher coefficient of Arrow-Pratt risk aversion in $[15, 30]$ for monthly data. His explanation for this difference is that an

---

[16]The Bellman equation can be solved using the trial solution $V(A_t, I_t) = A_t\Phi_t(I_t)$. The linearity of the value function in wealth, which also translates into a linear consumption control function in wealth, is a consequence of the particular assumption of isoelasticity of all relevant aggregators. For the calculations and the resulting Euler equations, consult Epstein & Zin (1991).

[17]An estimated zero rate of pure time preference is of particular interest in relation to the discussion in Section 4.4 on how widespread axioms in combination with intertemporal risk aversion can force the pure rate of time preference to zero.

estimation employing annual observations overlooks mean reversion and therefore over-estimates risk and underestimates risk aversion. Note that the equations estimated by Campbell (1996) do not give information on pure time preference. Vissing-Jørgensen & Attanasio (2003) further elaborated Campbell's (1996) approach and found elasticities of substitution for stockholders that are likely to be above 1. For the risk aversion parameter, the authors proposed RRA $\in [5,10]$ for what they considered realistic assumptions.[18] The authors suggested that the pair $\sigma = 1.5$ and RRA $= 9.5$ would perform well in matching the observed riskless rate and the equity premium. In an overview of different estimates of the above preference parameters (not all based on the simultaneous approach taken in the generalized isoelastic model), Giuliano & Turnovsky (2003) suggested $0 < \sigma < 1$ and $R > 2$.

All the above-mentioned papers reject the standard model with its underlying assumption that $\alpha = \rho \Leftrightarrow$ RRA $= \frac{1}{\sigma}$. I conclude that overall there is substantial indication that attitude with respect to substitution over time and risk aversion are not only a priori distinct characteristics of preference, but also differ in manifestation. However, Normandin & St-Amour (1998) presented an empirical analysis that does not reject the intertemporally additive expected utility model. I discuss two more papers estimating intertemporal substitution and risk aversion in the generalized isoelastic framework in the context of resource use in the next section. The estimation of these characteristics remains a challenge for econometric analysis.

3.3. Applications of the Generalized Isoelastic Model in Resource Economics

Knapp & Olson (1996) provided the first application of the general isoelastic model in the context of natural resources. The authors employed the preference structure in models simulating optimal rangeland management and groundwater management in order to disentangle the effects of a propensity to smooth consumption over time from risk aversion. In the rangeland management model, Knapp & Olson (1996) analyzed optimal stocking rates in a model of livestock and stochastic rangeland quality. Analyzing intertemporal substitution in the determinstic case, the authors found that a decrease in intertemporal substitutability smoothes out stocking rates and, thus, smoothes out net returns. In the stochastic model under risk neutrality (fixing $\alpha = 1$), the same decrease in intertemporal substitutability also smoothes out stocking rates, but it decreases the stocking rates less for low values of rangeland quality.[19] An increase in Arrow-Pratt risk aversion lowers the optimal stocking rate, however, this effect is not large. In their second application, Knapp & Olson (1996) modeled optimal (irrigation) pumping from an aquifer stock under stochastic surface water supply. A reduced intertemporal elasticity of substitution increases the withdrawals from the aquifer under adverse conditions (low surface flows/ low hydraulic head) and reduces pumping under beneficial conditions. The intuition is straightforward as such a behavior corresponds to smoothing consumption by boosting it

---

[18]The authors have to make assumptions about the covariance of consumption growth and stock returns, the share of stocks in the financial wealth portfolio, the properties of the expected returns to human capital, and the share of human capital in overall wealth.

[19]Whereas Knapp & Olson (1996) stated that this lower smoothing over the bad states when introducing stochasticity appears to be a result of the error-term assumption at the boundary, an alternative explanation builds on the concept of intertemporal risk aversion introduced in the next section. The choices made by Knapp & Olson (1996) for α and ρ correspond to an intertemporal risk-loving decision maker. Thus, introducing stochasticity can make the decision maker more willing to accept lower consumption in the bad (rangeland quality) states than under certainty.

in relatively poor times and decreasing it in good times. In the limiting distribution (the stochastic version of a steady state), the authors found that the reduced intertemporal elasticity of substitution implies a higher variance of withdrawals, thus causing a higher variance of the hydraulic head, counterbalancing random surface flows. Knapp & Olson (1996) also found that in the groundwater model the Arrow-Pratt risk aversion coefficient has little effect on pumping in general and virtually no effect on the limiting distribution.[20]

Epaulard & Pommeret (2003) solved a theoretical model of resource extraction building on Svensson's (1989) continuous time limit of the generalized isoelastic model (precisely of the form used in Equation 9). The authors modeled extraction of a nonrenewable resource that a linear production technology transforms into consumption. Production technology and resource stock follow a Brownian motion. Epaulard & Pommeret (2003) analyzed the effects of an increase in uncertainty over the future, i.e., an increase in the variances of the stochastic processes describing technology respectively the resource stock. For $\sigma > 1$, the extraction rate increases under an increase in uncertainty, and for $\sigma < 1$, the extraction rate decreases. The underlying reason is that, under risk aversion, an increase in uncertainty implies an effective loss in future wealth triggering a consumption reduction (income effect). However, at the same time, an increase in uncertainty over the future makes the agent want to substitute consumption into the certain current period. For $\sigma > 1$, the latter substitution effect dominates and the agent consumes and extracts more in the current period. For $\sigma < 1$, aversion to intertemporal substitution counteracts the substitution effect sufficiently so that the income effect dominates. Then, the agent reduces consumption and the extraction rate with an increase in risk. The coefficient of Arrow-Pratt risk aversion determines only the magnitude of the effect, but not the direction. Thus, in the model by Epaulard & Pommeret (2003), uncertainty leads only to a more conservative use of the resource if the intertemporal elasticity of substitution is less than unity. The authors also showed that an increase in the expected rate of technological progress decreases the extraction rate of the resource for $\sigma > 1$ and increases the extraction rate for $\sigma < 1$. Thus, for $\sigma > 1$, the expected productivity increase in the future makes the agent save (substitution effect dominates income effect), whereas for $\sigma < 1$, the expected increase in income makes the agent consume more (income effect dominates). As the authors noted, their analysis confirms in a theoretical way the numerical results obtained by Knapp & Olson (1996) that in an optimal use of a natural resource, each preference parameter affects the optimal extraction in a different way.

Ha-Duong & Treich (2004) applied the generalized isoelastic preference structure to a stylized climate change model. First, the authors analyzed a simple two-period model where consumption produces emissions and a stochastic damage in the second period that is proportional to the greenhouse gas stock. Similar to the cake-eating model by Epaulard & Pommeret (2003), the authors found that first-period consumption decreases in RRA if and only if $\sigma < 1$. The authors state simply that $\sigma < 1$ is generally considered the more plausible parameter value. However, more generally, the same intuition in terms of income and substitution effect as in the above cake-eating model—which originates from Weil (1990)—may be used to interpret the result. Moreover, first-period consumption (and thus emissions) increases in aversion to intertemporal substitution whenever consumption is expected to grow, which is an immediate implication of the desire to smooth consumption

---

[20]In light of the concept of intertemporal risk aversion introduced in the next section, note that all parameter constellations analyzed for the limiting distribution correspond to intertemporal risk lovingness.

over time. Second, the authors tested their findings numerically in a stylized four-period climate change model that is calibrated to a scenario produced by the Intergovernmental Panel on Climate Change.[21] An analysis of the relation between optimal taxes and an increase in aversion to risk respectively to intertemporal substitution confirms the theoretical findings. Fixing $\sigma = \frac{2}{3} < 1$, the authors found that an increase in risk aversion increases the optimal tax (reducing emissions). Fixing RRA = 2, the authors found that increasing aversion to intertemporal substitution decreases, in general, the optimal emission tax. Ha-Duong & Treich (2004) concluded that risk aversion and aversion to intertemporal substitution generally have opposite effects on resource control. They pointed out that, as a consequence, the confinement of the standard model that aversion to intertemporal substitution $\frac{1}{\sigma}$ equals relative risk aversion RRA explains why other simulations underestimate the effect of risk aversion.

Howitt et al. (2005) analyzed the management of the Oroville water reservoir in Northern California and showed in a numerical simulation that the observed water-level management can be explained better within the generalized isoelastic model. Relative to the literature, they found a rather low elasticity of intertemporal substitution of $\sigma \leq 0.1$ and a parameter of relative Arrow-Pratt risk aversion of RRA ≈ 1.5. They also found that setting RRA = 0 does not significantly change the quality of their fit and concluded that (Arrow-Pratt) risk aversion does not play a significant role in their example.

Lybbert & McPeak (2008) applied the model to nomadic herders in Kenya. They analyzed two regions that differ in precipitation volatility and modeled large livestock as an asset of relatively lower risk and lower expected value (camels and cattle are less responsive to precipitation volatility and droughts) and small livestock as an asset of higher risk and higher expected value (goats and sheep). The authors followed Campbell (1996) and Vissing-Jørgensen & Attanasio (2003) to estimate the generalized isoelastic preferences corresponding to the herder's livestock management. Lybbert & McPeak (2008) clearly rejected the hypothesis that risk aversion and aversion to intertemporal fluctuations coincide. They find that herders are more averse to risk than to intertemporal fluctuations.[22] The authors pointed out that it can be particularly important to destabilize intertemporal consumption to avoid risk when living close to a poverty trap threshold. Lybbert et al. (2008) inverted this idea and tried to identify such thresholds by analyzing how estimated preference and aversion parameters change in relation to herd size.

4. CONCEPTS OF UNCERTAINTY ATTITUDE

This section returns to the general evaluation functional (Equation 8) and discusses a particular measure for the difference between Arrow-Pratt risk aversion and intertemporal substitutability. This measure has an interesting interpretation of (intertemporal) risk aversion itself. After presenting the axiomatic characterization of and measures for intertemporal risk aversion, this section uses the derived concept to explain Kreps & Porteus's (1978) preference for the timing of uncertainty resolution from a more fundamental perspective. I point out how

---

[21]Climate change impact is a share of production and proportional to the anthropogenic increase of the greenhouse gas stock. Investment is a fixed fraction of production. Exogenous technological progress and the impact of climate change directly affect a Cobb-Douglas production function with capital, energy, and exogenous labor input. Energy input depends on an endogenous energy tax so that a higher tax reduces input and, as a result, production, consumption, emissions, and damage. The stochastic damage is binary.

[22]The authors found an intertemporal elasiticity of substitution for the combined sample of $\sigma = 1.1$ and RRA = 1.09.

the assumption of indifference with respect to such timing preference (as assumed in the standard model) leads to another parametric special case of the general model (different from the generalized isoelastic model). The section also introduces the recent intertemporal ambiguity model by Klibanoff et al. (2005), which was extended by Klibanoff et al. (2009) to the multiperiod setting, that is encountered in the discussion of the social discount rate (see Section 2). The model captures uncertainty in a more general way than by means of unique probability distributions. Finally, I return to the discussion of discounting. While Section 2 discusses how intertemporal risk aversion can affect the contributions to social discounting from changes in marginal utility, it turns out that intertemporal risk aversion can also affect the pure rate of time preference (or utility discount rate) of the decision maker.

4.1. Definition and Measures of Intertemporal Risk Aversion

Section 3.1 elaborates on the intetepretation of u in Equation 8 as characterizing the attitude toward intertemporal consumption fluctuations and the interpretation of $h_t \equiv f_t \circ u$ as characterizing Arrow-Pratt risk aversion. In the latter equation, f_t is a measure for the difference between aversion to intertemporal fluctuations (as characterized by u) and aversion to risk in the Arrow-Pratt sense (as characterized by h_t). For example, f_t concave is equivalent to h_t being a concave transformation of u, which is a defining relation for h_t being more concave than u (Hardy et al. 1964).

An interesting alternative characterization of f is obtained by the following axiom. Let preferences $\succeq$ be represented by Equation 8 over certain paths as well as probability trees of the according length. For two given consumption paths χ and χ', define the best-of-combination path $\chi^{\text{high}}(\chi, \chi')$ by $(\chi^{\text{high}}(\chi, \chi'))_t = \arg\max_{x \in \{\chi_t, \chi'_t\}} u(x)$ and the worst-of-combination path $\chi^{\text{low}}(\chi, \chi')$ by $(\chi^{\text{low}}(\chi, \chi'))_t = \arg\min_{x \in \{\chi_t, \chi'_t\}} u(x)$ for all t. In every period, the consumption path $\chi^{\text{high}}(\chi, \chi')$ picks out the better outcome of χ and χ', whereas $\chi^{\text{low}}(\chi, \chi')$ collects the inferior outcomes. A decision maker is called (weakly)[23] intertemporal risk averse in period t if and only if for all consumption paths χ and χ' holds

$$\chi \sim \chi' \Rightarrow \chi \succeq_t \frac{1}{2}\chi^{\text{high}}(\chi, \chi') + \frac{1}{2}\chi^{\text{low}}(\chi, \chi'). \tag{11}$$

The premise states that a decision maker is indifferent between the certain consumption paths χ and χ'. Then, an intertemporal risk-averse decision maker prefers the consumption path χ (or equivalently χ') with certainty over a lottery that yields with equal probability either a path combining all the best outcomes or a path combination of all the worst outcomes. Traeger (2007c, 2007d) defined the above axioms purely in terms of preferences. That is, the representation in Equation 8 is not assumed but axiomatically derived and χ^{high} and χ^{low} are defined purely in terms of preferences without the use of u. Whereas Traeger (2007d) deals with the general nonstationary setting where the functions f_t and u_t can be time dependent, Traeger (2007c) analyzed simplifications that arise for stationary preferences. These papers also show that Equation 11 holds if and only if (an increasing function) f_t in the representation of Equation 8 is concave.[24]

---

[23] Analogously, a strict intertemporal risk-averse decision maker can be defined by assuming that there also exists some period t^* such that $u(x_{t*}) \neq u(x'_{t*})$ and requiring a strict preference $\succ$ rather than the weak preference $\succeq$ in Equation 11.

[24] Respectively strictly concave for strict intertemporal risk aversion as defined in Footnote 23. For f_t decreasing, Equation 11 holds if and only if f_t is convex. Note that, for f_t decreasing the function $-f_t$ is increasing and represents the same preferences.

Another useful interpretation of intertemporal risk aversion is simply as risk aversion with respect to utility gains and losses. This interpretation is true if preferences are represented in a form such that the aggregation over time in every recursion is additive, as is the case in all representations chosen for this paper [but see Traeger (2007d) for an example of how the same preferences can be represented by making uncertainty aggregation linear at the cost of incorporating a nonlinear aggregation over time]. Then, utility expressed by u and U characterizes how much the decision maker likes a particular outcome x or a particular degenerate situation in the future. If decision makers are intertemporal risk averse, they dislike taking risk with respect to gains and losses of such utility. Note that, in contrast to the Arrow-Pratt measure of risk aversion, the function f_t is always one dimensional. Thus, measures of intertemporal risk aversion can be used as a commodity-independent risk measure also in a multicommodity setting (for the complications that arise when trying to extend the Arrow-Pratt risk measures to the latter setting, see Kihlstrom & Mirman 1974). Even more interestingly, the measures can be applied to contexts frequently met in environmental economics where impacts, e.g., on an ecosystem, do not have a natural cardinal scale (Traeger 2007d). The measure of absolute intertemporal risk aversion is defined as

$$\text{AIRA}_t(z) = -\frac{f_t''(z)}{f_t'(z)},$$

(12)

and the measure of relative intertemporal risk aversion is defined as

$$\text{RIRA}_t(z) = -\frac{f_t''(z)}{f_t'(z)}|z|.$$

Note that the measure of absolute intertemporal risk aversion depends on the choice of unit for utility, and the measure $\text{RIRA}_t(z)$ depends on the choice of zero in the definition of the utility function u. This normalization dependence is analogous to, e.g., the wealth-level dependence of the Arrow-Pratt measure of relative risk aversion.[25] Note that positivity of the measures AIRA_t and RIRA_t defined above indicates intertemporal risk aversion independently of whether f_t is increasing and concave or decreasing and convex (see Footnote 24). In both cases, $-\frac{f''}{f'}$ is positive. Measuring utility in negative units (as in the case where $u = \frac{x^\rho}{\rho}$ for $\rho < 0$) makes z negative. Therefore, the absolute of the variable z is needed to define the relative risk aversion measure (Traeger 2007b). For the generalized isoelastic model of Equation 9 discussed in Section 3, where $f(z) = (\rho z)^{\frac{\alpha}{\rho}}$, one finds a constant coefficient of relative intertemporal risk aversion $\text{RIRA}_t(z) = 1 - \frac{\alpha}{\rho}$ for $\rho > 0$ and $\text{RIRA}_t(z) = \frac{\alpha}{\rho} - 1$ for $\rho < 0$. In both cases, RIRA_t is positive if and only if $\alpha < \rho$ and the decision maker is more averse to risk in the Arrow-Pratt sense than averse to intertemporal fluctuations. It is precisely this model and measure that underlies Equation 2 and the discussion in Section 2.2. Finally, note that in a recursive evaluation of risk, as in Equation 8, the function f_t measures aversion with respect to current-value utility U_t.

---

[25]In the standard model, the Arrow Pratt measure of relative risk aversion $\text{RRA}(x) = \frac{u''}{u'}x$ depends on what is considered the $x = 0$ level. For example, whether breathing fresh air is part of consumption, or whether human capital is part of wealth, changes the Arrow-Pratt coefficient.

4.2. Preference and Indifference for the Timing of Risk Resolution

This section discusses another characteristic of choice that is closely related to the disentanglement of Arrow-Pratt risk aversion from aversion to intertemporal fluctuation. The concept of an intrinsic preference for the timing of risk resolution was introduced by Kreps & Porteus (1978) and allows us to capture a preference for whether uncertainty about a given event in the future resolves now or later. While interesting per se, it is also crucial for understanding how intertemporal risk aversion can force a zero rate of pure time preference. Such an intrinsic preference has to be distinguished from an instrumental preference for an early resolution of uncertainty that is simply born from the fact that an earlier resolution of uncertainty can permit the decision maker to adapt decisions to new information and, thus, improve expected outcomes. The concept of intertemporal risk aversion gives a nice interpretation of the driving forces underlying the intrinsic timing preference of Kreps & Porteus (1978).

Let $\lambda(x_t, p_{t+1}) + (1 - \lambda)(x_t, p'_{t+1})$ denote a lottery in period t that delivers x_t in period t as well as a future described by (the probability tree) p_{t+1} with probability λ and that delivers both the outcome x_t in period t and a future described by p'_{t+1} with probability $(1-\lambda)$. Note that however the lottery turns out, the decision maker consumes x_t in period t. Compare this first lottery to a second one written as $(x_t, \lambda p_{t+1} + (1 - \lambda)p'_{t+1})$. In this second lottery, the uncertainty over the future does not resolve within period t, but only in period $t + 1$. Otherwise both lotteries coincide.

Figure 1 depicts the comparison between two such lotteries for the two-period setting. A decision maker with intertemporally additive expected utility preferences will always be indifferent between the two depicted lotteries. However, in general, a decision maker may, for example, prefer the lottery with the earlier resolution of uncertainty (as depicted in the left-hand side of **Figure 1**). Note that this characterizes an *intrinsic* preference for the timing of uncertainty resolution. There is no choice that the decision maker can take after the resolution of uncertainty. Thus, such a preference is clearly distinct from an instrumental preference for an early resolution of uncertainty, as it also prevails in the standard model. An instrumental preference for early resolution is caused by adapting optimal choice to resolve information leading to better expected outcomes. Examples of motivation for a nontrivial intrinsic preference for the timing of uncertainty resolution include the wish to delay learning about an incurable genetic disorder (Grant et al. 1998) or about the result of an exam just before a vacation (Chew & Epstein 1989). The concept of intertemporal risk aversion gives rise to an insightful interpretation of the approach by Kreps & Porteus (1978) to capturing this timing preference (Traeger 2007a). Formally, a preference for early resolution of uncertainty at consumption level x_t is defined as

$$\lambda(x_t, p_{t+1}) + (1 - \lambda)(x_t, p'_{t+1}) \succeq_t (x_t, \lambda p_{t+1} + (1 - \lambda)p'_{t+1}) \tag{13}$$

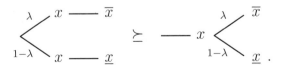

Figure 1

Early versus late resolution of uncertainty.

for all p_{t+1}, p'_{t+1} and $\lambda \in [0, 1]$. **Figure 1** depicts such a preference for the two-period setting. As shown in Traeger (2007a), this relation holds if and only if the expression

$$f_t[u(x_t) + \beta f_{t+1}^{-1}(z)] \tag{14}$$

is convex in z. There are three distinct effects driving a preference for an early resolution of uncertainty. They can best be observed by recognizing that convexity of the expression in Equation 14 is equivalent to $f_{t+1}\left(\frac{z}{\beta}\right)$ being more concave than $f_t[u(x_t) + z]$. First, ignoring β and the constant $u(x_t)$ implies that a decision maker prefers an early resolution of uncertainty if his intertemporal risk aversion increases over time. Second, assume that $f_{t+1} = f_t$ and set $\beta = 1$. Then, for positive measurement of utility $u(x_t) > 0$, a decision maker prefers an early resolution of uncertainty if he exhibits decreasing absolute intertemporal risk aversion (in welfare, not over time). The reason is that in a recursive setting he evaluates the risk resolving in the earlier period at a higher utility level (because $\beta = 1$). Under decreasing *absolute* intertemporal risk aversion, that makes him effectively less risk averse in the first period. Third, for $\beta < 1$ and $u(x_t) = 0$, the decision maker evaluates risk in the future at a higher welfare level than current risk and prefers early resolution of uncertainty if *relative* intertemporal risk aversion increases in welfare. In general, these three effects work together and result in a preference for an early resolution of uncertainty if and only if the expression in Equation 14 is convex. For more details, see Traeger (2007a). For the special case of the generalized isoelastic model, only the second effect is active because the coefficient of relative intertemporal risk aversion is constant over time and over wealth. The model exhibits decreasing absolute intertemporal risk aversion so that a decision maker intrinsically prefers an early resolution of uncertainty whenever he is intertemporal risk averse ($\alpha < \rho$) and prefers a late resolution of uncertainty whenever he is an intertemporal risk lover ($\alpha > \rho$). Because in the generalized isoelastic model a disentanglement of Arrow-Pratt risk aversion and the propensity to smooth consumption over time are immediately linked to an intrinsic preference for the timing of risk resolution, it is a widespread belief that disentanglement is not possible without nontrivial timing preference. However, in general, different combinations of intertemporal risk aversion and timing preference for risk resolution are possible. In particular, Traeger (2007a) showed how it is possible to capture intertemporal risk aversion and disentangle Arrow-Pratt risk aversion from intertemporal substitutability in a model where decision makers are indifferent to the timing of risk resolution (in the intrinsic sense). Indifference may be considered normatively desirable, as decision models with a nontrivial intrinsic preference for the timing of risk resolution imply a willingness to pay for inconsequential information.[26] Models with indifference to the timing of risk resolution imply constant absolute intertemporal risk aversion rather than constant relative intertemporal risk aversion as implied by the generalized isoelastic model. In what follows, I define the according preference representation as another attractive parametric special case of the general model.

---

[26]For a more detailed discussion, see Traeger (2007a). Note that the motivations mentioned for a nontrivial timing preference found in the literature are more convincing without understanding the particular mechanism that drives a preference for late resolution of uncertainty in the Kreps & Porteus (1978) setting. For example, a preference for delaying the knowledge about a genetic disorder is likely due to the fact that such knowledge has an immediate impact on instantaneous (per period) utility, rather than because of the effects related to changes in intertemporal risk aversion over time and over wealth.

Under indifference to the timing of risk resolution, the recursive evaluation of the probability trees can be collapsed to an evaluation of the corresponding distribution over consumption paths p_0^*. To see how the corresponding measure p_0^* can be derived from a probability tree p_0, I refer to Traeger (2007a). However, under indifference to the timing of risk resolution, there is no need to begin with a decision tree and p_0^* may be used as the familiar way of describing uncertainty. The resulting model simplifies to the following evaluation functional (Traeger 2007a, 2007c):

$$-\frac{1}{\xi}\ln E_{p_0^*}\exp\left(-\xi\sum_{t=0}^{T}\beta^t u(x_t)\right). \tag{15}$$

The representation evaluates outcomes in all periods with the stationary utility function u. A consumption path is evaluated by the discounted sum of per period utility. To evaluate an uncertain future, the decision maker weights the aggregate welfare of the possible consumption paths with their respective probabilities and aggregates them using a constant intertemporal risk aversion function $\exp(-\xi \text{ id})$. The renormalization $\frac{1}{\xi}\ln$ serves only to make the expression coincide with Equation 4 in the case of certainty. Note that in difference to the earlier recursive representations, in Equation 15 the function $\exp(-\xi \text{ id})$ aggregates present-value utility rather than current-value utility. Such a representation works only under indifference to the timing of uncertainty resolution. As a result, the coefficient ξ measures absolute intertemporal risk aversion in present-value terms as opposed to the coefficient defined by Equation 12 in relation to the recursive representation in Equation 8. Constructing the recursive analog to the representation in Equation 15, the expression AIRA_t for the corresponding function f_t is $\text{AIRA}_t = \beta^t \xi$. Thus, the coefficient of intertemporal risk aversion measured in current-value terms declines over time at the rate of pure time preference. From the present-value perspective, this decrease in current-value risk aversion corresponds to the decrease in absolute welfare variations at the rate of time preference, which effectively reduces risk aversion with respect to events happening in the future. That provokes a tension with respect to risk stationarity and time consistency, which is discussed in Section 4.4. Overlapping evaluation functionals with the preference representation in Equation 15 also emerged in engineering and made their way into economics in the linear exponential Gaussian control model, also known as risk sensitive control, robust control, or model uncertainty. It is obvious from considering certain trade-offs that the curvature of u measures aversion to intertemporal consumption fluctuations. In Traeger (2007a), I show how to reconstruct the Arrow-Pratt measures of absolute and relative risk aversion from ξ and u.

4.3. Ambiguity Aversion

So far, all models discussed in Sections 3 and 4 have assumed that the uncertainty over tomorrow can be described by a unique probability measure. However, there are applications where these probability distributions (or the risk) is unknown. The decision-theoretic literature has developed different concepts to capture these situations. One way to characterize nonrisk uncertainty is by extending the concept of probabilities to a form of more general set function called capacities. These set functions weight possible events but are not necessarily additive in the union of disjoint events. Because of this nonadditivity, the measure integral aggregating probability-weighted utility in the expected utility framework has to be replaced by the more general Choquet integral. Therefore, this approach to generalizing uncertainty description and evaluation is called Choquet expected utility. A second approach taken in the literature is to define an evaluation functional that expresses beliefs as sets of probability distributions rather than unique probability distributions. The first and simplest such representation goes back to Gilboa & Schmeidler (1989), where a decision maker evaluates a scenario by taking expected values with respect to every probability distribution deemed possible and then identifies the scenario with the minimal expected value in this set. Hansen & Sargent (2001) give conditions under which this approach is equivalent to what is known as robust control or model uncertainty, which also has overlapping representations to the model of constant absolute intertemporal risk aversion presented in Section 4.2. A more general representation of this type is given by Ghirardato et al. (2004), Maccheroni et al. (2006a) and, in an intertemporal framework, Maccheroni et al. (2006b). There are several equivalency results between the Choquet approach and that of multiple priors as well as rank-dependent utility theory where a decision maker uses distorted probabilities in an expected utility approach to increase the weights given to small-probability events. Axiomatically, all these models relax the independence axiom in some way.

Here, I focus on a recent representation result by Klibanoff et al. (2005) and, in a multiperiod setting, by Klibanoff et al. (2009). The authors modeled nonrisk uncertainty (ambiguity) as second-order probability distributions, i.e., probabilities over probabilities. In some sense, this approach to uncertainty is not that different from the model in the previous sections, which did not relax independence. Also, the previous model represented uncertainty in the present as probability distributions over current consumption and future probabilities. In contrast, however, Klibanoff et al. (2009) used second-order probabilities within the same period. Moreover, they introduced a different attitude for evaluating first-respectively second-order uncertainty. Another way to think about the model is as a Bayesian model with parameter uncertainty. Again, the difference from the standard Bayesian model is that parameter uncertainty (second-order uncertainty) is evaluated with a different degree of aversion than the uncertainty arising from the probability distribution characterized by the parameter (first-order uncertainty). Translated into the setting of this review, the recursive evaluation of the future provided by Klibanoff et al. (2009) can be written as

$$V(x_t, I_t) = u(x_t) + \beta \Phi^{-1} \left\{ \int_\Theta \Phi \left[E_{\Pi_\theta(x_{t+1}|x_t, I_t)} V(x_{t+1}, I_{t+1}) \right] d\mu(\theta|x_t, I_t) \right\}.$$

Here, Π denotes first-order or "objective" probabilities. However, these are not known uniquely and depend on a parameter θ that is unknown and subjective. The probability measure μ denotes the prior over the parameter $\theta \in \Theta$.[27] The utility function u corresponds to the utility function of the standard model. It jointly captures aversion to intertemporal substitutability and objective or first-order risk. The function Φ captures additional aversion with respect to second-order uncertainty, which is called ambiguity aversion. Note that, for Φ linear, the model collapses to the standard Bayesian model. If the objective uncertainty measure Π is degenerate, there is a close formal similarity to the model of intertemporal risk aversion.

---

[27]In the axiomatization of the model by Klibanoff et al. (2009), the parameter Θ is finite.

In a one-commodity setting with isoelastic preferences, as underlying the social discounting application in Section 3.3, $u(x) = \frac{x^\rho}{\rho}$ and $\Phi(z) = z^\varphi$. The evaluation functional in the first of two periods can then be written as

$$V(x_1, I_1) = \frac{x_1^\rho}{\rho} + \beta \frac{1}{\rho} \left\{ \int_\Theta \left[E_{\Pi_\theta(y|x_1, I_1)} x_2^\rho \right]^\varphi d\mu(\theta | x_1, I_1) \right\}^{\frac{1}{\varphi}}.$$

This functional form for Φ implies constant relative ambiguity aversion. The corresponding coefficient is defined as RAA $= \frac{\Phi''(z)}{\Phi'(z)} |z|$ which calculates to RAA $= 1 - \varphi$ for $\rho > 0$ and RAA $= \varphi - 1$ for $\rho < 0$. As highlighted in Section 2.3, the fact that RAA acts only on the second-order variance τ is implied by Φ respectively φ only weighting welfare with respect to second-order uncertainty aggregation, here represented by the measure μ. For a recent application of the model by Klibanoff et al. (2005) in the context of climate change and learning, see Lange & Treich (2008).

4.4. Intertemporal Risk Aversion and Pure Time Preference

This section explains how, in combination with widespread axioms, a nontrivial degree of intertemporal risk aversion can imply a zero rate of pure time preference (Traeger 2007c). Starting with the assumption of additive separability of preferences over time, stationarity makes the utility function in different periods coincide up to a single parameter that stays arbitrary. This parameter has been termed pure time preference. Now consider introducing risk and evaluating the risk under the widespread assumption of the von Neumann & Morgenstern (1944) axioms. Moreover, keep intrinsic indifference to the resolution of uncertainty as discussed in Section 4.2 (indifference in Equation 13 and **Figure 1**). This assumption implies that a decision maker strictly prefers an early resolution of uncertainty only if there is a possibility that he obtains information that could be useful for later decisions. The announced result for the discount rate sets in when introducing not only a stationary evaluation of certain consumption paths as in the representation in Equation 15, but also a stationary evaluation of uncertain scenarios.[28] The standard model implicitly assumes intertemporal risk neutrality. As a result, requiring a stationary evaluation of risky scenarios does not add anything to the model. However, in a model that incorporates nontrivial intertemporal risk aversion, a stationary evaluation of risk adds an additional constraint. In effect, the utility functions in different periods that formerly had to coincide only up to a free parameter now have to coincide completely. Thus, time preference must be zero.

The intuition for this result is the following: To avoid having a strict preference for the timing of risk resolution, the decision maker must have a constant coefficient of absolute intertemporal risk aversion that does not change over time in present-value terms. Constancy in present-value terms must hold because the decision maker contemplates in the present about whether the risk over an event in some fixed future period resolves sooner or later. In contrast, when requiring a stationary evaluation of risk, the decision maker

---

[28]Keep in mind that a stationary evaluation does not assume stationarity of the underlying equations of motion. The assumption of a stationary evaluation (of certain consumption paths) is what enables us to capture pure time preference in a single parameter in the first place. The stationarity assumption implies that the best guess for tomorrow's preferences are current preferences. A change of future preferences over part of the consumption set that is caused by a change in some environmental parameters or other welfare contributing factors over time is incorporated in an appropriate (and multidimensional) stationary evaluation functional.

compares how he would decide about a particular risky scenario today and how he would decide about the same scenario shifted one period into the future tomorrow. Thus, the according axiom requires that the coefficient of absolute intertemporal risk aversion is constant over time in *current*-value terms.[29] However, a nontrivial coefficient of intertemporal risk aversion can only be constant over time in present- and current-value terms if the pure rate of time preference is zero. Thus, in such a framework, a time-consistent evaluation requires no discounting of the future for reasons of mere impatience.

I close this section by summarizing a reasoning given in Traeger (2007c) to explain why discounting because of intertemporal risk aversion can also compare with the pure rate of time preference in terms of discounting future utility rather than consumption. One way of understanding intertemporal risk aversion is as risk aversion with respect to utility gains and losses. Thus, if uncertainty increases over time (not calendar time, but the time span that the agent is looking into the future to evaluate the consequences of today's choice options), intertemporal risk aversion effectively discounts the utility of increasingly uncertain future outcomes. However, while pure time preference equally discounts anything happening in the future, discounting for reasons of intertemporal risk aversion effectively puts more weight on consequences in the future that are known with greater certainty. Thus, less-uncertain future scenarios with better long-term outcomes are ranked higher than in the standard discounted expected utility model.

5. CONCLUSIONS

The paper points out two limitations of the standard model for modeling risk aversion in a dynamic setting. First, the model confines Arrow-Pratt risk aversion to coincide with the aversion to intertemporal consumption fluctuations, implying intertemporal risk neutrality. Second, the model cannot capture an attitude for uncertainty that is not characterized by unique probability measures. I discuss resource economics applications of the generalized isoelastic model and present two other recent modeling frameworks that overcome the restrictions of the standard model. All the applications of the generalized isoelastic model in resource economics conclude that risk and risk attitude have a different implication for, e.g., the optimal extraction and control of resources, for stocking rates, and for greenhouse gas emissions than those of the attitude toward intertemporal fluctuations. A recurring pattern is that the income effect of an increase in future risk or risk aversion tends to reduce extractions or emissions, while a substitution effect between current certain consumption and future uncertain consumption counteracts. Some of the models discussed show that for high aversion to intertemporal substitution the income effect dominates, and increasing risk and risk aversion reduce extraction, emissions, and consumption. In contrast, with a high intertemporal elasticity of substitution, the substitution effect dominates, and an increase in risk or risk aversion can imply an increase in current extraction rates and emissions. In all these models, the effects of a change in risk aversion and in aversion to intertemporal substitution differed, sometimes quantitatively

---

[29]Recall that, in the recursive representation of the model in Section 4.1, f_t measures intertemporal risk aversion in current-value terms, i.e., it aggregates over the different realizations of U_t. In the nonrecursive representation in Section 4.2—which is possible only under indifference to the timing of risk resolution—risk aggregation takes place in the present period and the parameter ξ corresponds to the coefficient of absolute intertemporal risk aversion as measured in present-value terms.

and sometimes qualitatively. As a consequence, a detailed analysis of the questions pointed out in the introduction should not rely on the discounted expected utility model.

In addition, I present how the concepts of intertemporal risk aversion and ambiguity affect the social discount rate, a widespread tool for the evaluation of intertemporal trade-offs. Both intertemporal risk aversion and ambiguity aversion contribute an additional term to the social discount rate. The higher the aversion, the lower the certainty equivalent discount rate. Thus, under intertemporal risk aversion and risk, or under ambiguity aversion and uncertainty, projects featuring a certain transfer of consumption into the future are optimal, even with a significantly lower productivity than proposed by the standard model. Finally, the pure rate of time preference was seen to be a contribution to the social discount rate that is in a way special to the discounted expected utility model. In models of intertemporal risk aversion, some of the widespread axioms of the standard model have to be abandoned to allow for consistent decision making under strictly positive pure time preference.

The models presented in this review await an application in any field of environmental and resource economics where time and uncertainty play important roles. These include various considerations in analyzing climate change policies, biodiversity loss, invasive species, classical renewable and nonrenewable resource extraction, and many more. Besides the mere effect of risk and uncertainty and attitude with respect to time and uncertainty, an important challenge will be to systematically analyze the effects of learning with respect to the optimal control of resources and the corresponding policy measures in these models. Moreover, the present discussion features individual decision makers and representative agents. Future analysis in this field will have to examine how heterogeneous agents and their aggregation in complete and incomplete markets affect the findings.

DISCLOSURE STATEMENT

The author is not aware of any affiliations, memberships, funding, or financial holdings that might be perceived as affecting the objectivity of this review.

LITERATURE CITED

Campbell JY. 1996. Understanding risk and return. *J. Polit. Econ.* 104(2):298–345

Chew SH, Epstein LG. 1989. The structure of preferences and attitudes towards the timing of the resolution of uncertainty. *Int. Econ. Rev.* 30(1):103–17

Dasgupta P. 2008. Commentary: the Stern review's economics of climate change. *Natl. Inst. Econ. Rev.* 199:4

Ellsberg D. 1961. Risk, ambiguity and the savage axioms. *Q. J. Econ.* 75:643–69

Epaulard A, Pommeret A. 2003. Optimally eating a stochastic cake: a recursive utility approach. *Resour. Energy Econ.* 25:129–39

Epstein LG, Zin SE. 1989. Substitution, risk aversion, and the temporal behavior of consumption and asset returns: a theoretical framework. *Econometrica* 57(4):937–69

Epstein LG, Zin SE. 1991. Substitution, risk aversion, and the temporal behavior of consumption and asset returns: an empirical analysis. *J. Polit. Econ.* 99(2):263–86

Ghirardato P, Maccheroni F, Marinacci M. 2004. Differentiating ambiguity and ambiguity attitude. *J. Econ. Theory* 118(2):122–73

Gilboa I, Schmeidler D. 1989. Maxmin expected utility with non-unique prior. *J. Math. Econ.* 18(2):141–53

Giuliano P, Turnovsky SJ. 2003. Intertemporal substitution, risk aversion, and economic performance in a stochastically growing open economy. *J. Int. Money Finance* 22(4):529–56

Grant S, Kajii A, Polak B. 1998. Intrinsic preference for information. *J. Econ. Theory* 83:233–59

Ha-Duong M, Treich N. 2004. Risk aversion, intergenerational equity and climate change. *Environ. Resour. Econ.* 28(2):195–207

Hansen LP, Sargent TJ. 2001. Robust control and model uncertainty. *Am. Econ. Rev.* 91(2):60–66

Hardy G, Littlewood J, Polya G. 1964. *Inequalities.* Cambridge, UK: Cambridge Univ. Press. 2nd ed.

Hepburn C. 2006. *Discounting climate change damages: working notes for the Stern review.* Work. Pap., Univ. Oxford

Howitt RE, Msangi S, Reynaud A, Knapp KC. 2005. Estimating intertemporal preferences for natural resource allocation. *Am. J. Agric. Econ.* 87(4):969–83

Kihlstrom RE, Mirman LJ. 1974. Risk aversion with many commodities. *J. Econ. Theory* 8(3):361–88

Klibanoff P, Marinacci M, Mukerji S. 2005. A smooth model of decision making under ambiguity. *Econometrica* 73(6):1849–92

Klibanoff P, Marinacci M, Mukerji S. 2009. Recursive smooth ambiguity preferences. *J. Econ. Theory* 144:930–76

Knapp KC, Olson LJ. 1996. Dynamic resource management: intertemporal substitution and risk aversion. *Am. J. Agric. Econ.* 78(4):1004–14

Kreps DM, Porteus EL. 1978. Temporal resolution of uncertainty and dynamic choice theory. *Econometrica* 46(1):185–200

Lange A, Treich N. 2008. Uncertainty, learning and ambiguity in economic models on climate policy: some classical results and new directions. *Clim. Change* 89:7–21

Lybbert TJ, Just DR, McPeak J. 2008. *Asset dynamics and variability preferences: risk aversion and intertemporal substitution among Kenyan pastoralists.* Work. Pap., Harvard Univ.

Lybbert TJ, McPeak J. 2008. *Risk, intertemporal substitution and early resolution of uncertainty: livestock portfolio allocations and offtake among Kenyan pastoralists.* Work. Pap., Harvard Univ.

Maccheroni F, Marinacci M, Rustichini A. 2006a. Ambiguity aversion, robustness, and the variational representation of preferences. *Econometrica* 74(6):1447–98

Maccheroni F, Marinacci M, Rustichini A. 2006b. Dynamic variational preferences. *J. Econ. Theory* 128(1):4–44

Nordhaus W. 2008. *A Question of Balance: Economic Modeling of Global Warming.* New Haven, CT: Yale Univ. Press

Nordhaus WD. 2007. A review of the Stern review on the economics of climate change. *J. Econ. Lit.* 45(3):686–702

Normandin M, St-Amour P. 1998. Substitution, risk aversion, taste shocks and equity premia. *J. Appl. Econ.* 13(3):265–81

Plambeck EL, Hope C, Anderson J. 1997. The model: integrating the science and economics of global warming. *Energy Econ.* 19:77–101

Ramsey FP. 1928. A mathematical theory of saving. *Econ. J.* 38(152):543–59

Stern N, ed. 2007. *The Economics of Climate Change: The Stern Review.* Cambridge, UK: Cambridge Univ. Press

Svensson LE. 1989. Portfolio choice with non-expected utility in continuous time. *Econ. Lett.* 30:313–17

Traeger C. 2007a. *Disentangling risk aversion from intertemporal substitutability and the temporal resolution of uncertainty.* Work. Pap.

Traeger C. 2007b. *The generalized isoelastic model for many commodities.* Work. Pap.

Traeger C. 2007c. *Intertemporal risk aversion, stationarity and the rate of discount.* Work. Pap.

Traeger C. 2007d. *Wouldn't it be nice to know whether Robinson is risk averse?* Work. Pap.

Traeger C. 2009. *The social discount rate under intertemporal risk aversion and ambiguity.* Work. Pap.

Vissing-Jørgensen A, Attanasio OP. 2003. Stock-market participation, intertemporal substitution, and risk-aversion. *Am. Econ. Rev.* 93(2):383–91

von Neumann J, Morgenstern O. 1944. *Theory of Games and Economic Behaviour.* Princeton, NJ: Princeton Univ. Press

Wakker P. 1988. The algebraic versus the topological approach to additive representations. *J. Math. Psychol.* 32:421–35

Weil P. 1990. Nonexpected utility in macroeconomics. *Q. J. Econ.* 105(1):29–42

Weitzman ML. 2007. A review of the Stern review on the economics of climate change. *J. Econ. Lit.* 45(3):703–24

Weitzman ML. 2009. On modeling and interpreting the economics of catastrophic climate change. *Rev. Econ. Stat.* 91(1):1–19

Rent Taxation for Nonrenewable Resources

Diderik Lund

Department of Economics, University of Oslo, NO–0317 Oslo,
Norway; email: diderik.lund@econ.uio.no

Annu. Rev. Resour. Econ. 2009. 1:287–307

The *Annual Review of Resource Economics* is
online at resource.annualreviews.org

This article's doi:
10.1146/annurev.resource.050708.144216

Key Words

natural resources, rent tax, royalty, oil, minerals, energy

Abstract

The literature on taxation of rents from nonrenewable resources
uses different theoretical assumptions and methods and a variety of
empirical observations to arrive at widely diverging conclusions.
Many studies use models and methods that disregard uncertainty,
investigating distortionary effects of different taxes on whether,
when, and how to explore for, develop, and operate resource deposits. Introducing uncertainty into the analysis opens a range of
challenges and leads to results that cast doubt on the relevance of
studies that neglect uncertainty. There are, however, several ways
to analyze uncertainty regarding companies' behavior, resource
price processes, and diversification opportunities, all with different
implications for taxation. Methods developed in financial economics since the 1980s, though promising, are still not in widespread
use. Additional topics covered in this review are optimal risk sharing between companies and governments, time consistency and
fiscal stability, the relationship between taxes and discount rates,
tax competition, and transfer pricing.

1. INTRODUCTION

In many countries, extraction of nonrenewable natural resources, including petroleum, coal, metals, and other minerals, is an important source of government revenue. Recent overviews by Baunsgaard (2001), Sunley et al. (2003), and Otto et al. (2006) show global use of various taxes specific to these sectors.

To minimize the need for distortionary taxes, economists have recommended maximizing rent taxes, which are supposed to be neutral. A combination of factors makes the design of these taxes, or alternative arrangements for government revenue, very challenging. When resource prices are high, large rents may lead to a strong public demand for government revenue. There is also high uncertainty in prices and geology, and technology is often owned by big multinationals. This situation raises issues about attitudes to risk and asymmetries of information, which are exacerbated by high tax rates.

This paper reviews the literature on rent taxation of nonrenewable resources published since 1975. Sections 1.1 and 1.2 delineate this topic and introduce some theories of companies' behavior, respectively. Sections 2–5 present major strands of the literature. Section 2 considers models in the Hotelling tradition. The question is, How do taxes affect the equilibrium price and extraction paths for a nonrenewable resource? Section 3 focuses on studies directed at policy reforms, some of which have been highly influential, despite attendant weaknesses (which are highlighted). Section 4 discusses various approaches to the analysis of tax effects on companies' decisions. Section 5 shows how auctions have been promoted as an alternative to taxation and presents the possible advantages of combining the two policy tools. Section 6 contains miscellaneous topics, and Section 7 offers concluding remarks.

1.1. Delineation of the Topic

Governments generate revenue from resource activities in various legal and economic forms. A company extracting a nonrenewable resource may have ownership of the resource, or the company may obtain a license to exploit it. The company's resource extraction is subject to taxation. In some cases, this taxation is part of a tax that is levied on the whole company. Taxation here means that payments depend on the realized outcomes of a given activity. If the complete payment is determined independently of realized outcomes, it is not considered taxation. In such cases, a fixed fee may be set by the government, negotiated with companies, or determined through auction. This review covers only parts of the literature on fixed-fee systems.

Because ownership rights are outside the scope of this review, equity participation by governments is not covered, even though the cash flow implications of such arrangements may be interpreted as taxation. However, even without equity participation, governments regulate many aspects of the taxed activity, which has implications for the practical interest in analysis of taxation. If all companies' choices are severely regulated, distortionary taxes may exert little influence on them. In practice, some choices are less restricted than others, but this varies greatly among countries and types of resources. If one wants to exploit the expertise found in private-sector companies, they must be allowed to make important decisions, which creates opportunity for tax distortions.

Royalty here denotes taxes on gross production value. Some of the literature uses royalty more generally to include net profits (or rent) taxes. This may be a matter of definition only, but the difference between taxes and royalties has historical roots related to their justification. According to Watkins (2001), "royalties derive from ownership of resources by the Crown. Thus, a functional distinction can be made between royalties and general tax revenues. In this light, the principles governing taxation do not apply in equal measure to royalty incomes" (p. 29). Philosophical discussions on the justification of taxes or royalties are omitted here, although such justifications may have economic implications, for instance when the United States decides which taxes and royalties are eligible for foreign tax credit.

For analytical simplicity, it is convenient to assume that economies are open with a world market for extracted units of the resource. This allows a distinction between rent taxes and excise taxes. A rent tax is levied on rent realized when the resource is sold at the world market price. Excise taxes, not discussed here, are in addition to the world market price, increasing the consumer price. Pigouvian taxes to correct for externalities are also not discussed.

1.2. Alternative Models of the Behavior of Companies

To predict the effects on the behavior of companies, one needs assumptions about how companies make decisions. Different studies use various assumptions. This section highlights some differences that are particularly relevant to the following sections. I first discuss two alternative assumptions regarding risk. Then I mention an unconventional assumption related to the volume of rents.

The first alternative is to assume risk aversion on the part of companies. The assumption is often that companies maximize von Neumann & Morgenstern (1947) (vN-M) expected utility. Other types of preferences with aversion to risk are found in studies of taxation by, e.g., Domar & Musgrave (1944) and Emerson & Garnaut (1984, sect. 2–5). Most studies in this tradition take no consideration of the diversification possibilities of the company or its shareholders. Variance or some other measure of profit dispersion is sometimes taken as a measure of risk. As a result, three possible complications now arise. First, if the company diversifies, the covariance between one project and the rest of its portfolio takes over as the risk measure. Second, if shareholders diversify, companies will maximize market value (see next paragraph). Third, managers may act in their risk-averse self-interest, neglecting preferences of shareholders (cf. Leland 1978).

The second alternative is to assume that companies maximize market value, in the stated interest of shareholders. The market value is additive, meaning that the value of a linear combination of assets is equal to the same linear combination of separate values of those assets. This follows from theories developed since the 1950s, such as the Arrow-Debreu model of complete markets (Arrow 1953, Debreu 1959), or various models in financial economics, starting with the capital asset pricing model of Sharpe (1964), Lintner (1965), and Mossin (1966). Value additivity implies that variance cannot be a risk measure for each part of a portfolio, whereas covariance can.

For the theoretical study of taxation of companies, and for resource extraction in particular (high tax rates, high risk), the implications of making one of these assumptions are far-reaching. Because companies differ, and no model of financial economics is established as the final truth about financial markets or decision making, there are arguments for both assumptions.

Finally in this section, an assumption that has received some attention recently should be noted. Osmundsen (2005) assumes that oil companies, in order to start a project, require some minimum volume of rent, sometimes called materiality. This assumption also has far-reaching implications: An otherwise neutral rent tax with a low rate will now cause some projects to move from being acceptable to unacceptable.

2. EQUILIBRIUM MODELS

Since Hotelling (1931), the analysis of economics of nonrenewable resources has been based on dynamic, partial equilibrium models of the resource market. The value of an unextracted unit must rise at the exogenous rate of interest. Herfindahl (1967) extends the model to include deposits with different costs, which determine the sequence of extraction.

Dasgupta & Heal (1979, ch. 12) discuss the introduction of taxes in Hotelling (1931) models. The question is, How do different taxes distort the market solution? Some neutrality results are derived. A final section in the chapter considers taxation as a means to correct for tragedy-of-the-commons problems. The main model in the chapter is of a closed economy, or worldwide taxation. All extraction is subject to the same tax. In most actual situations, this is irrelevant as policy advice. A government will consider its country either to be a price taker or, at most, to have some limited market power. Almost all subsequent theoretical studies of resource taxation have assumed exogenous prices; Gaudet & Lasserre (1986) and Lindholt (2008) are exceptions.

Few studies have analyzed resource taxation in intertemporal general equilibrium models, in which the interest rate is also endogenous. Groth & Schou (2007) have a growth model for a closed economy, which encompasses both endogenous and exogenous growth, with both produced and natural capital and a possible externality from resource use, such as global warming. All of the resource will be used in the limit in infinite time. The study shows that the resource use will decline exponentially in the long run, with the decline rate possibly affected by taxation. The model cannot analyze distortions from labor income taxation, as there is no labor-leisure choice. It suffers from the unrealistic feature that the same taxes are applied on all natural capital worldwide. In terms of resource taxation, the model implies that a tax on capital gains on natural capital leads to too little conservation of the resource, thus impeding sustainable growth.

There is some evidence (Krautkraemer 1998, Slade & Thille 2009) against the empirical relevance of Hotelling models and, implicitly, also of Groth & Schou (2007). Another problem with existing equilibrium models is the absence of uncertainty. Unfortunately, no established model of a dynamic equilibrium under uncertainty exists for such a market to extend the Hotelling-Herfindahl tradition. At best, taxation has been treated with an exogenous price process, although not necessarily a credible one (discussed below). Lund (1993) points out why the geometric Brownian motion (GBM) with drift is hardly an equilibrium price process. GBM is nevertheless assumed in four studies discussed below: Ball & Bowers (1983), Lund (1992), Zhang (1997), and Blake & Roberts (2006), who claim (pp. 98–99) that, although unrealistic, the GBM is acceptable for their purpose.

3. COMPARING TAX SYSTEMS, SUGGESTING TAX REFORMS

The basic problem for a country trying to collect resource rent via taxation is that a higher tax rate in one sector is likely to distort decisions by companies. One may simply set a higher tax rate for a corporate income tax (CIT) in this sector. But wedges between rates of return before and after tax increase with CIT rates. In a closed economy, this will be counteracted if interest income and all corporate income are taxed at the same rate [cf. the Johansson-Samuelson theorem (Sinn 1987, p. 119)]. But this does not help in open economies or if one sector has a higher tax rate than the rest of the economy. A higher tax rate with an unmodified tax base implies that projects (or high-cost resource units within projects) that would be seen as profitable under a lower tax can be rejected under the higher tax.

Royalties also distort decisions. Without cost deductions, they make resource units with high costs unprofitable. In actual tax systems, there may be many complicating features, including taxes and deductions at several levels. A first approximation to the high potential for distortions is that a marginal decision on additional costs and income within the same year is distorted by the ratio $(1 - t_y)/(1 - t_c)$, where t_y is the marginal tax rate on income and t_c is the marginal tax rate on cost reductions. These are not statutory rates, but effective rates in an expected, risk-adjusted present-value sense. Clearly, the higher the rates, the more sensitive this ratio will be to small differences in the rates. Thus, there has been interest in economic analyses of how to tax resource rent optimally.

The seminal article for this part of the literature is by Garnaut & Clunies Ross (1975), who propose the Resource Rent Tax (RRT) scheme. It intends to give a deduction equal in present value to the investment itself, typically exceeding most CIT systems' depreciation allowances. A generalization of the idea is found in Boadway & Bruce (1984). Investment, indeed any yearly negative net cash flow, is carried forward for later deduction, along with interest accumulation, as soon as revenues allow. If the tax base in subsequent years is sufficient to allow complete, effective deduction of the carry-forward, this can ensure that only the rent is taxed.

Authorities must determine an interest rate for the accumulation. The intention is that companies be indifferent between receiving the refund immediately or through deductions in subsequent years. Garnaut & Clunies Ross (1975; 1979; 1983 ch. 4) acknowledge that implementation will suffer under information asymmetry. They suggest that the correct rate should be companies' required rate of return. They state that a risk premium will be included, but they have no model or precise discussion of how this is determined. The difficulties of assessing the rate of return, and the various resulting consequences, are the topics of much of the subsequent debate (Sumner 1978, Dowell 1978).

Other authors (Mayo 1979, Ball & Bowers 1983, Lund 1992, Smith 1999) focus on the possibility that the income stream in later years may be insufficient to allow for an effective deduction. Typically, RRT offers no payout if the income stream is too small. Garnaut & Clunies Ross (1979, p. 196) recognize this problem. The tax will reduce realized net value when positive, but it will not subsidize negative outcomes similarly. Mayo (1979) shows that under reasonable assumptions this asymmetry will cause distortions. The implication of the analysis is to prefer a Brown (1948) tax or some other arrangement with payout of negative taxes. (A Brown tax is a proportional tax on nonfinancial cash flow, with immediate payout of negative taxes.) Emerson & Garnaut (1984, p. 140) mention this possibility, but they seem to view negative taxes as impractical. Even then, one may want to increase the likelihood that the loss carry-forward can be effectively deducted. Mayo (1979, p. 208) argues that a company tax base would allow for deductions between projects, the opposite of "ring-fencing" (i.e., that each project/plant/deposit is taxed as a separate unit, without allowing deductions in the same company's profits elsewhere). Although aware of this, Garnaut & Clunies Ross (1979, p. 198) nevertheless advocate project-based taxation, giving priority to avoiding the possibility that companies overinvest when the threshold rate is set too high. Saunders (1987) looks at effects of the cross-field allowance introduced in Britain in 1987. He points out deficiencies of an allowance for 10% cross-field cost relief, introduced in 1987 in the otherwise field-based British Petroleum Revenue Tax (PRT).

The inability to decide on the correct rate for interest accumulation leads to a suggestion to use two or three different rates. If and when a rate of return above a lower threshold is realized, the company starts paying RRT at a relatively low rate. If a rate of return above a higher threshold is realized, the company starts paying at a higher rate. Garnaut & Clunies Ross (1975) give several reasons for applying more than one rate. While addressing the ignorance about actual required rates of return, and the possibility that these differ between projects, they sketch an argument in which risk aversion makes progressivity desirable (Garnaut & Clunies Ross 1975, p. 280). However, despite including risk aversion in the title, Garnaut & Clunies Ross (1975) provide no formal definition of it, only an informal description of a concave objective function (p. 273). This vagueness conceals some problems. Their arguments can be contrasted with alternative approaches that existed at the time.

Domar & Musgrave (1944) show that taxation may encourage risk taking, inducing more investment than under no taxation. They do not use vN-M expected utility, but Mossin (1968), Black et al. (1982), and Fraser (1998) have similar results based on expected utility theory. Their results rely on assumptions about details of the tax structure, in particular loss offset provisions. But Garnaut & Clunies Ross (1975) state without conditions that "risk aversion causes the supply price of investment [the required expected return] to rise if a project is subject to [... various taxes or levies, e.g., ...] proportional taxes on profits" (p. 275). Becasue there is no formal argument, it is difficult to see how they arrived at a different conclusion from that of Domar & Musgrave (1944) as well as Mossin (1968) when assumptions are so similar.

Garnaut & Clunies Ross (1975) also mention other issues: the transfer pricing problem (see Section 6.3 below), the creditability of RRT payments toward taxes in other countries, and the possibility of combining RRT with CIT. Although not unimportant, the two latter topics are excluded from this review. The authors followed up with several other articles, some with other coauthors, and then a book (Garnaut & Clunies Ross 1983) which covers the field with a broad, mostly verbal discussion. The advantage of including many aspects is that hardly anything has been left out. The disadvantage is that it is difficult to arrive at a clear conclusion, neither on the optimal system nor optimal tax rate(s). A similar complaint can be issued about more recent documents from the International Monetary Fund and the World Bank.

For the International Monetary Fund, Baunsgaard (2001, p. 30) concludes that, "It is unlikely to be possible to design one optimal fiscal regime suitable for all mineral projects in all countries. Countries differ, most importantly in regard to exploration, development and production costs; the size and quality of mineral resources; and investor perception of risk. Likewise, projects may differ sufficiently that some flexibility is necessary in deriving an appropriate fiscal regime." The paper includes a table (p. 16), in part adapted from Garnaut & Clunies Ross (1983, p. 332f). It provides a comparative assessment of eight different stylized tax schemes, giving them 8×9 marks on nine different criteria. But "it is not possible to provide an overall quantitative assessment of each tax" from the table (Baunsgaard 2001, p. 16). For the World Bank, Otto et al. (2006, p. 276) conclude, "Countries' geological, economic, social, and political circumstances make each nation unique, and an approach to royalty taxes that is optimal for one nation may be impractical for another."

Kemp (1992) provides a representative paper in the tradition of comparing tax systems. Petroleum taxes in the United Kingdom, Norway, Denmark, and the Netherlands are compared. A set of scenarios for oil prices, as well as extraction and cost data for five representative fields, is constructed on the basis of the author's experience and judgment. After-tax internal rates of return and net present values at a 10% real discount rate are calculated for companies, under the alternative assumptions of no other activity or full tax deductability against other income. There is no analysis of uncertainty, and the high real discount rate applies to all cash flows. The conclusions on average tax rates and progressivity are determined by the choice of these methods (see Section 6.2 below). A curious weakness in the results is that "the Danish system collects a very substantial share of any economic rents to the state," when, in fact, the rent tax in Denmark collected very close to nothing as a result of its generous uplift (Lund 2006).

4. HOW TAXES DISTORT DECISIONS

Whereas Kemp (1992) considers only whether a project is started or not, several studies look at more detailed analyses of distortions to decisions, using a variety of methods. Analyses of marginal tax rates have a general scope, in that they illustrate (non)neutrality without specifying the production possibilities. However, to quantify average tax rates and the effects on extraction output or rent, one must specify production possibilities. Along such lines, several studies leave the exploration phase out of the analysis, some focus on whether and when to start development, and others neglect this and focus on scale of development or time paths of extraction after development.

Boadway et al. (1987) define a marginal effective tax rate as a relative wedge between the rate of return before and after tax for a marginal project. This is a different concept from the two marginal rates t_y, t_c mentioned in the beginning of Section 3, above. Those rates are simply the percentage to be paid of a marginal change in gross income and the percentage to be refunded through deduction of a marginal change in cost. In a two-period version, the Boadway et al. (1987) concept is $(t_y - t_I)/(1 - t_I)$, where t_I is the marginal tax on reduced investment cost one period ahead of the income. The simpler concept was, e.g., used by Smith (1997) to analyze Russian petroleum taxation. For a neutral cash flow tax of 80%, the marginal effective rate would be zero according to the definition of Boadway et al. (1987), whereas the marginal tax rates would be 80% on both income and costs according to the simpler concept.

Boadway et al. (1987) consider a deterministic model of mining and calculate tax rates for various mining assets in the Canadian provinces of Ontario and Quebec. The findings are that many marginal effective rates were negative, so that taxes are distortionary (but in the direction of subsidies) and do poor jobs of collecting rent. Boadway & Keen (2008) extend the discussion. One qualification they mention is that typical analyses of such taxation concentrate only on host country tax rates, neglecting taxation of an international company by its home country as well as taxation of the shareholder.

Krautkraemer (1990) studies the theoretical impact of taxation on ore selection, tilting of the time profile of extraction, and total depletion from a mine. He includes a useful overview of related studies. Slade (1984) estimates a cost function for copper mines, taking both the intertemporal constraint and the processing of ore into the model.

[She admits (p. 146) to ignoring the important exploration phase.] On the basis of the estimated model, she calculates what distortions will occur due to imposition of various taxes and price controls. Taxes will typically lead to intertemporal tilting, less extraction, and less intensive processing (i.e., less final metal output). The second and third of these effects, i.e., effects on total final output, not the tilting, dominate. In terms of tilting, there is the unexpected result that royalty leads to higher extraction in earlier years and lower extraction in later years. Whether the results also hold for petroleum, coal, or other metals is an empirical question. Deacon (1993, p. 173) confirms that tilting is the less important distortion from a royalty on oil.

Inspired by Hotelling (1931), interest has concentrated on the intertemporal profile. An alternative focus on the scale of investment in each project is supported not only by findings in Slade (1984) and Deacon (1993), but also by reference to Campbell (1980). Campbell finds that the most important decision is investment, i.e., installation of extraction capacity. Afterward, operating costs are often so low that extraction takes place at full capacity. Many other studies use either the intertemporal profile or the scale of investment to describe the opportunity set for companies. Sumner (1978) assumes an exogenous total extraction from a field, with companies choosing the constant yearly rate at which to extract. Lund (1992), on the other hand, assumes that companies choose scale of development of an oil field and that total extraction is an increasing, concave function of this, but that the intertemporal profile is constant in relative terms.

Deacon (1993) may have the broadest scope of any of the deterministic tax distortion studies. He estimates and calibrates an optimization model of exploration and extraction by a representative oil company, using data for the contiguous 48 states of the United States from 1859 onward. He considers distortionary effects of CIT (found to be small), royalty (medium), and property tax (severe). Besides several improvements in methods, the inclusion of property taxes is interesting. Whereas most studies neglect property taxes, they turn out to have significant effects.

The remainder of Section 4 covers authors who use models inspired by financial option theory. Generally, they find tax distortions exacerbated by uncertainty, effects that could not be discovered by most of the authors cited above, who neglect uncertainty.

Ball & Bowers (1983) observe that an RRT has imperfect loss offset and that the tax claim is similar to a European call option. Using standard assumptions from financial economics, the authors quantify the market value of the government's tax claim under price uncertainty. Green & Talmor (1985) and Majd & Myers (1985) use a similar approach for the CIT. MacKie-Mason (1990) studies nonlinear taxes with the U.S. depletion allowance as an example. Later contributions with applications to rent taxation include Jacoby & Laughton (1992), Lund (1992), Zhang (1997), Bradley (1998), Blake & Roberts (2006), and Samis et al. (2007).

Besides similar assumptions, the common theme in these studies is valuation of non-linear tax claims, occurring, e.g., as a result of imperfect loss offset or progressive tax schedules. In most cases, the tax claim is convex (for an exception, see MacKie-Mason 1990), implying that the tax claim increases in value with increased uncertainty. Jensen's inequality is all one needs to show this, but the studies are more elaborate, using the risk adjustment method from modern asset pricing (MAP). This is explained in detail in Jacoby & Laughton (1992) and is the topic of a special issue of the *Energy Journal* in 1998 (see Laughton 1998, Salahor 1998). [MAP and related methods are also called market-based valuation, contingent-claims analysis, and derivative assets analysis

(Rubinstein 1987, footnote 1).] The method is used for real options in resource economics, but among the cited authors, only MacKie-Mason (1990) and Zhang (1997) consider this, i.e., managerial flexibility. Both obtain analytical results in stylized models. Jacoby & Laughton (1992), Lund (1992), Bradley (1998), Blake & Roberts (2006), and Samis et al. (2007) analyze taxes with option-like cash flows using Monte Carlo simulations. These differ from typical Monte Carlo simulations in that the simulated price process is not intended to emulate actual prices. When the drift term is reduced, this is known in financial economics as the risk-neutral process. Under standard assumptions, this yields market values of the company's cash flows after tax.

Lund (1992) considers Norwegian petroleum taxes before and after 1987. He finds large tax distortions if measured as deviations in costs, but smaller in net value, because there are decreasing returns to scale within fields. Blake & Roberts (2006) use the same type of production function to analyze petroleum taxes in Alberta (Canada), Papua New Guinea, São Tomé and Principe along with Nigeria, Tanzania, and Trinidad and Tobago. They find strong distortionary effects for the latter two, less for the others.

Zhang (1997) studies the effects of two different taxes on the choices of when and whether to invest in a stylized project. One tax is the RRT; the other is a simplified version of the British PRT. The result is that RRT cannot be neutral, but a stylized PRT can, provided that the uplift is set so as to allow for the option value. It must be assumed that the nonneutrality result for RRT is the result of imperfect loss offset. As explained in Section 6.2 with reference to Fane (1987), a tax will be neutral if the loss offset and other deductions are nonstochastic and the deviation from a constant-rate cash flow tax has a present value of zero at a riskless interest rate. This neutrality also holds in real option models.

Bradley (1998) and Samis et al. (2007) give detailed accounts of the method and apply it to stylized projects, oil and copper/gold, respectively. Both consider two alternative resource price processes, GBM and mean reversion. Both highlight the merits of the method relative to traditional discounted cash flow (DCF) analysis, for which there is no theoretical justification in a world of uncertainty. Emhjellen & Alaouze (2003) also compare these methods, but they ignore the fact that most taxes are nonlinear.

Nakhle (2008) includes both DCF (ch. 5–6) and MAP (ch. 7). She claims without explanation that, compared with DCF, MAP is "controversial" (p. 116), but also "more useful" (pp. 117, 128). In spite of its usefulness, the newer method is "unlikely to capture many sponsors" (p. 148). Apart from chapters 5–7, the book gives an account of the history and politics of petroleum taxation from a U.K. perspective, also comparing against other nations.

5. RISK SHARING: FIXED FEES OR TAXES?

Many contributions consider taxation without mentioning fixed fees as an alternative. Because fixed fees are not a focus here, only the literature that discusses auctions as alternative to, or in combination with, taxation is considered.

Leland (1978) provides a seminal paper with a thorough theoretical analysis of optimal combinations of taxation and fixed fees when both companies and government (the nation) are risk averse or, in extreme cases, risk neutral. Both parties are assumed to maximize vN-M expected utility. At the outset, Leland considers the possibility of perfect markets for state-contingent claims, so that companies would instead maximize market value in the interest of shareholders. He dismisses this idea because a "variety of considerations conspire to make the actual environment diverge from the perfect market paradigm" (Leland 1978, p. 414). He mentions transaction costs, information asymmetries, bankruptcy costs, and managers' self-interests as reasons to assume risk aversion instead.

Leland considers various sets of assumptions on information asymmetries and the effect of taxation on companies' actions. Companies compete to the extent that they get no increase in expected utility as a result of winning a lease. Knowing companies' patterns of behavior, authorities announce payment schedules before the bidding to maximize expected utility for the nation. One result is that only if companies are risk neutral will authorities rely solely on fixed fees. Only if authorities are risk neutral will they rely solely on taxes. If both parties are risk averse to some extent, both types of payments will be used. There are further results on the concavity of the optimal payment schedule, which depends on the relation between risk tolerances of companies and authorities. There are also results on the effects of shifts in the probability distributions of values. With decreasing absolute risk aversion for both parties, a higher value (in expected utility terms) leads to higher optimal tax schedules, also in relative terms.

Emerson & Garnaut (1984) extend Leland (1978) to include more detailed policy recommendations. In addition to Leland's reasons for recommending taxes on rents, they consider sovereign risk, the possibility experienced by companies of unannounced changes in taxes. They claim that the "most nearly ideal system of conditional payments *in current application* is the Resource Rent Tax" (Emerson & Garnaut 1984, p. 140; emphasis in original), in part because tax payments come late, thus reducing sovereign risk.

Fraser (1998) considers vN-M risk-averse firms. Deposit size is uncertain, whereas price is assumed known. [Fraser (2000) considers price uncertainty in a similar model.] He studies how an RRT with imperfect loss offset could be combined with fixed fees, set discretionarily or through auctions. Thus, RRT can lead to over- or underinvestment compared with a no-tax situation. For constant relative risk aversion less than unity, there are interior solutions for the pairs of tax rate and threshold rate which achieve neutrality in this sense. This means that for a given threshold rate the company's optimal investment choice is first an increasing, then a decreasing, function of the tax rate as this goes from zero to unity. The Domar-Musgrave effect dominates for tax rates close to zero, but the concave after-tax profit function dominates for higher tax rates.

Fraser (1998, p. 116) goes on to "investigate the potential for the government to choose the structure of the RRT so as to maximise expected government revenue from the allocation of a mining lease subject to the RRT, while at the same time leaving the firm's preferred level of investment unchanged." The constraint imposed in the last part of this sentence is not well explained. Risk aversion will restrict investment in absence of a tax. It is not clear why authorities would not want to encourage a higher investment level.

Using the results of Leland (1978), Emerson & Garnaut (1984), and Fraser (1998) for policy recommendations entails some problems. Whether risk aversion describes the behavior of these companies better than does market value maximization is unclear. But even then, generating a precise recommendation remains difficult. There is no reason to believe that all companies under one jurisdiction have the same risk aversion at any point in time or that risk aversion does not vary over time. How to measure it, or that of the government, is unclear.

Sunnevåg (2000) observes that a combination of RRT and auctions may be preferable to relying on auctions only, because of political (i.e., sovereign) risk. If only a fixed fee is paid, and realized prices or quantities then turn out favorably, there will be political pressure to capture windfalls. Companies may suspect that this is, in effect, asymmetric, with no compensation for bad outcomes (Lund 1999, p. 218; Sunnevåg 2000, p. 15). It may be more credible to combine a fixed fee with a tax at such a high rate that it captures much of the *ex post* variation. One point not mentioned in the literature is that the very existence of rent taxes may lead bidders to expect asymmetries and thus reduce bids. If so, this is an argument against the combination of fixed fees and rent taxes. If a rent tax is in place from the outset, companies may perceive that this makes it easier for governments to increase its rate in case of large discoveries or price increases. For more on the credibility issue, see Section 6.1 below.

Mead (1994) is a prominent example of an author who considers the alternatives but draws a clear conclusion in favor of cash-bonus bidding alone. The article has several suggestions for improvements in the U.S. system but concludes that a bidding-based system is superior to taxation-based alternatives. Partly theoretical, these arguments are also based on empirical research, in particular Mead et al. (1983), who investigate whether there are indications that auctions of petroleum leases on the U.S. outer continental shelf have not captured the whole rent. Leases were acquired from 1954 to 1969, with production data ending in or before 1979 and with projections made for the subsequent period when needed. The finding is that the average after-tax return on equity was 10.74%, whereas it was 11.8%, on average, in the U.S. manufacturing sector.

Low returns are claimed to indicate that there is sufficient competition, so that lease payments capture the rent. Mead et al. (1983) recognize that oil price increases in the 1970s were not anticipated, so bidding was probably based on expectations well below those that were realized. But in the return calculations, the 1970s count less than earlier years, which saw declining real prices. Whatever the reasons are, the fact that returns are lower than in other sectors in spite of higher risks may be seen (but see Section 6.2 for a discussion of tax effects on after-tax required returns) as indications of a "strong winner's curse" (as noted by Thaler 1988). This is not a good outcome for anyone in the long run. Nevertheless, a test based on one output price path is insufficient to settle the question. Mead (1994) dismisses the argument from Leland (1978) that companies may be so risk averse that they are willing to pay only a low price for leases. Again, the empirical evidence is used in the argument. A more recent account of the U.S. experience is found in Boué (2006). He is critical of the area-wide leasing introduced in the early 1980s and summarizes evidence that tax reductions have weak incentive effects.

Considering risk sharing, another approach exists. Blitzer et al. (1984) ask the same question as do Leland, Emerson and Garnaut, and Fraser, but they rely on different assumptions in their analysis. Instead of using the concept of risk aversion alone, they rely on portfolio theory and, to some extent, financial markets, but with incomplete international diversification. They observe that both countries and the shareholders of companies hold portfolios, but that these are not similar, contrary to predictions in standard finance models. Some authorities act on behalf of countries that are heavily reliant on a few natural resources for much of their national income, whereas other countries import those same resources for the foreseeable future. The covariances between the resource price and the national portfolios have different signs and magnitudes. Shareholders' portfolios also have different national biases, which are held for various reasons. All of this has implications for who is better suited to bear the risk. Blitzer et al. (1984) do not go into detail on tax systems, but instead they look at the broader question of contracts, including contract risks and political risks.

6. OTHER TOPICS

Although the topics below are important, others of similar import have been left out owing to space limitations. There is, e.g., no mention of taxation under imperfect competition, a situation prevalent in many markets for nonrenewable resources.

6.1. Time Consistency, Fiscal Stability, and Progressivity

Many of the cited studies contain passages on the importance of stability in tax systems. Garnaut & Clunies Ross (1981) provide a historical account of this and related issues. Whereas governments may increase taxes after positive outcomes for prices or reserves (windfall profits taxes), they might not decrease them after negative outcomes. High payments that must be paid to authorities up front (typically found under an auction system), in addition to large investments, exacerbate the problem. This situation helps explain why auctions are found most often in stable political environments with perceived reluctance to impose additional taxes.

Boadway & Keen (2008) point out that having companies realize that governments cannot credibly commit to not increasing taxes will lower investment, thereby hurting both parties. This may be overcome by noncarried equity participation by the government (an up-front payment in the opposite direction of the one mentioned above) or by acquiring a reputation for keeping a stable system. Osmundsen (2008) sketches the game-theoretic argument, which allows for an equilibrium without underinvestment in an infinite-horizon game supported by trigger strategies. But these are not unique equilibria, and many conditions need to be satisfied; thus one cannot say that the problem has found its solution. He goes on to consider Norwegian petroleum taxation, finding that "[o]ver the past decade, Norway has shifted to a policy of absolute commitment, where the tax system is unchanging." But he is aware that there may be country-specific problems related to attaining this solution.

In some countries, governments offer explicit fiscal stability clauses in contracts, promising renegotiations or immunity in the event of future tax increases. One problem is the short lifetime of governments compared with that of many resource projects, as highlighted by Daniel & Sunley (2008). They argue that fiscal stability clauses are prone to being overridden by changed circumstances. They mention that clauses are sometimes best seen as smoke screens, which may be circumvented by government actions not covered by the clauses.

When Denmark introduced a fiscal stability clause in 2003, Lund (2003) stressed two potential problems. First, companies paid both CIT and a rent tax. If international competition later forced authorities to lower the CIT rate, a simultaneous increase in the rent tax rate would be prohibited by the clause. Such a pair of tax-rate changes happened in Norway in 1992, and a switch from mobile to immobile tax bases is a well-known prediction in the public economics literature. Second, the clause could complicate the introduction of Pigouvian taxation.

In addition to questions of whether and how a government may commit itself comes the broader issue of political support. There may be considerable unrest if companies earn large after-tax rents ("windfalls") due to resource price increases or large discoveries. This has led some authors (notably those connected to the International Monetary Fund and the World Bank) to recommend progressive taxes. Boadway & Keen (2008, p. 45) argue that "progressive rate schedules may be more robust against political pressures in the event of high return outcomes than are proportional schemes." Similarly, Sunley et al. (2003, pp. 159–60) point out that "[p]roponents argue that the RRT can enhance contract stability because it automatically increases the government share in highly profitable projects." Daniel & Sunley (2008, p. 6) stated [and Land (2008, p. 4) argues similarly] that a "robust fiscal regime is therefore adaptable and progressive."

Possible benefits from progressivity must be weighed against distortionary effects. Using models without uncertainty, Conrad & Hool (1984) show that taxes with variable rates have distortionary effects, and Sumner (1978, p. 9) states that "the basic objection to the resource rent tax is that it cannot simultaneously provide neutrality and progressivity." Under uncertainty, progressivity combined with imperfect loss offset will give the convexity that implies that the tax claim's value increases with higher uncertainty (cf. Section 4, above). Bond & Devereux (1995, pp. 58, 67f) show theoretically that "neutrality with a non-constant tax rate requires that the investment project generates a non-negative tax base in every period." Blake & Roberts (2006, p. 101) find that "the two most distorting systems, Tanzania's and Trinidad's, contain a common fiscal component which attempts to capture more revenues for the host government with increasing production."

6.2. Risk Attitudes and Discount Rates

As mentioned in Section 1.2, there is a fundamental difference between two sets of assumptions regarding companies' behavior under uncertainty. This section discusses these consequences in more detail.

The assumption that companies behave as risk averse implies that almost all tax systems are nonneutral. Most actual taxes are distortionary under conditions of full certainty, typically by having higher marginal tax rates on the revenue side than on savings on various costs [but see Boadway et al. (1987) for examples of the opposite distortion]. Under uncertainty, there will be a counteracting effect of sharing risk with the government, encouraging higher activity. Under some circumstances, this leads to an interior solution to the problem of neutral taxation: A set of tax rates may exist for which the two effects cancel each other out at the margin (Fraser 1998), although this is of little practical interest (Smith 1999).

An assumption that companies maximize market value has markedly different implications. Value additivity is assumed to be standard knowledge in the business community, mentioned by Brealey et al. (2008, p. 968) as one of the seven most important ideas in finance. For tax authorities, it is a crucial question whether taxes should be designed based on the assumption that companies behave according to the textbook. Value additivity has been assumed in analysis of corporate taxation under uncertainty in public economics since Fane (1987). He shows that a Brown (1948) cash flow tax is then neutral, because it acts in cash flow terms as just another shareholder. Maintaining the neutrality is possible if some cash flows (e.g., tax value of deductions) are postponed in time, provided that interest accumulates so as to leave companies indifferent to the postponement. Bond & Devereux (1995), building on Boadway & Bruce (1984), generalize this result.

What interest rate is needed? On the basis of value additivity, the postponement can be valued separately. If it happens with full certainty, the appropriate rate is the riskless interest rate. The tax system is neutral if deviations from a cash flow tax are nonstochastic and have zero net present value at that interest rate. Although this result by Fane (1987) is theoretically uncontroversial, it seems to be disconnected from much of the preceding literature on rent taxation and also from the practice of many companies. In general, practice is to apply one (and the same) discount rate to (all elements of) the net cash flow of a company, regardless of the specific risk of each element (cf. Graham & Harvey 2001). Garnaut & Clunies Ross (1975) have a similar idea: The rate at which deductions (or losses) are allowed to accumulate is ideally the "supply price of investment," which depends on "investors' attitude to risk" (p. 273) among other things. Although RRT deductions are not risk free, it is equally true that they do not have the same risk characteristics as before-tax cash flows.

Most real-world tax deductions are risky, although to different degrees (cf. Lund 2009). Intuitively, a deduction is almost risk free when the net tax base is much larger, depending also on correlations. If the tax code includes one or more specified interest rates, at which losses are carried forward, no practicable suggestion exists for how the rate(s) could depend on project-specific details affecting riskiness of deductions.

In a policy perspective, it may be possible to ensure that the deductions are (perceived as) close to risk free. Summers (1987, p. 298) argues that "[o]n balance, it seems fair to conclude that deprecation tax shields represent an essentially riskless asset." This is usually not the case for all deductions in resource extraction, owing to higher tax rates, high uncertainty, and, in many countries, ring-fencing. The petroleum tax reform suggestions in Norway in 2000 and in Denmark in 2001 tried to get closer to certainty for deductions, and accordingly, they applied a riskless interest rate for carry-forward. Lund (2002a) and Bjerkedal & Johnsen (2005) give details. This could be obtained by no ring-fencing, sale of negative tax positions, or refund of tax values of unused deductions. A possible objection is that apparently wasteful expenditures would be partly subsidized, possibly allowing experimentation paid by reduced taxes, which is useful for companies. This may be prevented by government regulations or equity participation; the latter would also allow governments to learn.

For reform efforts in these countries, it was crucial to apply separate discounting for different cash flow elements. Although the reforms went far to achieve neutrality, this could not be understood by oil companies (or anyone) who applied one discount rate to the net cash flow. Using the finance-theoretic approach, Lund (2002c) shows how this is a mistaken practice when companies operate in jurisdictions that differ (signficantly) in tax rates and investment-related deductions, which companies in resource extraction typically do. Systematic risk (and thus the correct discount rate) of the net after-tax cash flow depends on the tax system. Lund (2002c) gives analytical solutions for stylized linear tax systems, whereas Lund (2009) extends the analytical solutions to nonlinear cases with imperfect loss offset. When taxes are nonlinear in many periods, numerical methods are needed, and risk-adjusted discount rates are no longer practical tools. Jacoby & Laughton (1992) and Bradley (1998) give numerical examples for several realistic cases. Typically, the correct discount rate for the expected net cash flow after tax is less than before tax, and it decreases the tax rate.

Another topic that has received much less attention is whether the interest rate should be an after-tax interest rate. Lund (2002a) shows how the views of the petroleum tax reform commissions in Norway and Denmark differed at this point, and he relates it to the more general literature on taxation of companies and their shareholders. If the marginal investors' alternatives are taxed, an after-tax interest rate should be used (cf. Dasgupta & Heal 1979, equation 12.11; see also Gaudet & Lasserre 1986, p. 242).

6.3. Transfer Pricing and Income Shifting

Rent taxation exacerbates the problem of transfer pricing, which is well known in international taxation, but also occurs between sectors in one country. The problem is one important argument for relying on fixed fees instead of higher tax rates (Mead 1994). To avoid transfer pricing, authorities require use of "arm's length" prices, i.e., prices as they would have been between unrelated parties. Establishing these is easier for resource output than for costs. Costs are made up of numerous inputs, which are often tailor-made. Thus, the problem is bigger on the cost side, borrowing costs and insurance included. Income shifting is broader than transfer pricing and also includes real transfers, such as testing new equipment in a sector with high tax rates, which can also represent a distortion. Using the notation from the beginning of Section 3, one should distinguish among $t_c > t_y$ (overinvestment incentives), $t_c > 1$ (gold plating incentives), and t_c exceeding the t_c of another sector or jurisdiction (transfer incentives).

Osmundsen (1995, 1998) includes principal-agent models, in which authorities impose tax schedules that do not rely on reported costs (see also Dowell 1978, p. 136). This approach follows from the somewhat extreme assumption that traditionally monitored self-reporting of costs contains no useful information. Authorities must regulate under asymmetric information on the basis of only probability distributions of costs. The optimal solution is to present companies with a schedule of payment obligations, conditional on output value. This can be implemented as alternative combinations of fixed fees and royalties. Osmundsen (1998) extends this to a two-period model, inspired also by Gaudet et al. (1995).

Lund (2002b), building on Gordon & MacKie-Mason (1995), has a model in which taxes allow deductions for traditionally reported operating (or investment) costs. Companies can shift income from a jurisdiction with a high marginal tax rate to one with a low rate, but only at a (nontraditional) transfer cost, quadratic in the amount to be shifted. The model is constructed such that, were it not for the possible income shifting, authorities would want a rent tax at a rate arbitrarily close to 100%. Introducing costly income shifting can lead to two different results, depending on model parameters. If the output price and/or the transfer cost is high, relative to operating costs, then royalty is not used, but instead a rent tax is set arbitrarily close to 100%. If not, there will be a combination of rent tax at some lower rate and a royalty. Both the possible reliance on a rent tax alone and a discontinuity in the solution are surprising theoretical results. The model is difficult to apply in practice, as admitted by Lund (2002b).

Boadway & Keen (2008, p. 43) are skeptical of principal-agent contracts in this connection. They claim that a "reasonably good tax audit system" will allow "a profit tax system to collect reasonable rents." Fraser (1999, p. 273) has a third alternative: The "government and the firm negotiated an agreement over the allowable cost per unit of production." This may suffer from asymmetric information problems and needs frequent revisions.

In summary, the arguments for any of the approaches seem incomplete. The theoretical models are stylized, and some empirical research would be welcome to decide how to tackle the problem of income shifting.

6.4. Is Tax Competition a Concern?

Within the literature on taxation in open economies, tax competition among countries has an important role. Whereas mobile factors can escape high tax rates by moving to other countries, immobile factors cannot. This provides a separate, strong reason for imposing higher tax rates on resource extraction, in addition to those that apply to closed economies.

Osmundsen (2005) argues that companies have unique factors of production, such as skills and technology, that they use only where it is most rewarding. He implies that a country is limited in its ability to tax resource extraction by the tax level in other countries competing for the attention of the same companies. Boadway & Keen (2008, p. 48) have reservations about this: One "would expect high rewards to expand the supply of these scarce factors, at least in the medium term, just as one would expect a shortage of oil rigs to lead to an increase in their price."

Lund (2001) asks why a company in (a previous publication of) the model of Osmundsen (2005) undertakes only the projects that give the highest reward after tax to its scarce factors of production. The question is why factors cannot be duplicated. Technology can be duplicated, and the skills of employees can be transferred to others through training. Those skills that cannot are the property of the employee and would not result in profits for the company in a competitive model. Monopsony in the market for engineers may explain part of the problem, but its scale is insufficient to explain much. Dowell (1978, p. 136) also has a discussion of these issues. Another point in Lund (2001) is that the Norwegian experience seems to contradict Osmundsen's model. Comparing Britain and Norway reveals fairly similar offshore petroleum prospects and political and regulatory environments. In spite of higher taxes for long periods (see Kemp 1992), Norway has been able to attract a lot of foreign investment in the sector.

6.5. What Is the Optimal Tax Rate?

Perhaps surprisingly, many studies referenced above pay little attention to the tax level. Governments and companies both regard this as very important, whereas economists who focus on tax neutrality have nothing to say about the optimal tax rate. Zhang (1997, p. 1107) states that "under such a neutral up-lift rate, varying the tax rate has no effect on the development trigger." Although Garnaut & Clunies Ross (1975) are quite policy oriented, their discussion of tax rates (pp. 280–81) is vague. Instead, they argue strongly about neutrality—even more so in Garnaut & Clunies Ross (1979).

Theoretical models with international comparisons (Sections 6.3 and 6.4) lead to recommendations on tax rates. Even for closed economies, there can be interior optima for the tax rate in models that combine fixed fees with taxes (Leland 1978, Fraser 1998).

Boadway & Keen (2008, p. 10) write, "There is another aspect of the international nature of the resource business that is more puzzling. Host countries evidently care very much how their tax systems compare with others, and are often concerned not to offer regimes that are substantially more onerous. Quite why this is so, however, is by no means obvious." Maximization of rent tax revenue would reduce the need for other, distortionary taxes. This also raises doubt about the relevance of analyzing a revenue neutral rent tax reform (Deacon 1993).

Several authors compare the tax level of one jurisdiction with that of others in order to find whether the level is "reasonable." For example, Watkins (2001, p. 28) finds that resource tax regimes in Newfoundland and Nova Scotia "do not suffer by comparison with those in other offshore regions, such as the North Sea and Australia." He adds, "Overall, then, the regimes are sensible." Otto (2000, p. 2) states that "[m]ost governments try to strike a balance between government and investor revenue needs by implementing a 'fair and equitable' system. Unfortunately, no one has yet been able to determine what an ideal fair and equitable system is." It is likely that advice to authorities will be more valuable if it is able to address such issues.

7. CONCLUDING REMARKS

As discussed above, there are important problems related to our lack of knowledge of the objective functions of companies under uncertainty. The economics profession has not found one model of company behavior that is valid for all those which extract nonrenewable resources. In part, this has to do with observable differences between companies, such as small mining operations versus multinational oil companies. Such differences can be modeled. But the different theoretical traditions and various interpretations of empirical evidence also result in the wide variety of policy recommendations in the literature.

Even for a simple problem like the valuation of depreciation tax shields, Summers (1987) finds that companies deviate from the methods that have been suggested in textbooks since the 1970s. He asks how tax policies should respond to the fact that companies seem to make mistakes, but he does not arrive at a definite conclusion. More generally, the question is, What is an optimal tax policy if (a substantial fraction of) companies do not behave according to a neoclassical model? In such cases, the standard theory of optimal taxation no longer works, so many standard results need to be amended.

To end on a positive note, there are some situations in which the same tax policy may be beneficial in relation both to neoclassical companies and others. The companies that behave as risk averse, i.e., not taking advantage of diversification possibilities in capital markets, will typically underexploit investment opportunities and take on too little unsystematic risk. The Domar-Musgrave effect means that a Brown cash flow tax with full, immediate loss offset will encourage investment by these companies. At the same time, this tax is neutral in relation to companies that are well diversified. Lund (2000, sect. 8.2) points out that the tax works in the right direction for both types of companies. Sørensen (2005) has a model of this, which leads to an optimal tax policy. Although the information needed to implement an exactly optimal tax rate may be difficult to obtain, this is at least an example that all is not dark.

DISCLOSURE STATEMENT

The author was a member of the petroleum tax commissions in Norway from 1999 to 2000 and in Denmark in 2001. The views expressed in this review are those of the author, not necessarily those of the commissions or the authorities who appointed him.

ACKNOWLEDGMENTS

Part of this research was undertaken while I was visiting the Haas School of Business at the University of California, Berkeley. I am grateful for their hospitality and for funding from the Nordic Tax Research Council. Thanks to André Anundsen for research assistance.

I am also grateful for valuable comments from Graham Davis, Rob Fraser, Rolf Golombek, Christian Groth, Snorre Kverndokk, Charles McPherson, Asbjørn Moseidjord, David Newbery, Karine Nyborg, Petter Osmundsen, and Atle Seierstad, and during a presentation at IAEE Asia (Perth, 2008). I am solely responsible for any remaining errors and omissions.

LITERATURE CITED

Arrow KJ. 1953 (1964). The role of securities in the optimal allocation of risk-bearing. *Rev. Econ. Stud.* 31(2):91–96 (Transl. from French)

Ball R, Bowers J. 1983. Distortions created by taxes which are options on value creation: the Australian Resources Rent Tax proposal. *Aust. J. Manag.* 8(2):1–14

Baunsgaard T. 2001. *A primer on mineral taxation.* Work. Pap. 01/139, IMF

Bjerkedal N, Johnsen T. 2005. The petroleum tax system revisited. See Glomsrød & Osmundsen 2005, 8:157–75

Black JM, Jones G, Rodriguez F, Woodward RS. 1982. Taxation of high risk ventures: some results using an expected utility approach. *Public Financ.* 37(1):1–17

Blake AJ, Roberts MC. 2006. Comparing petroleum fiscal regimes under oil price uncertainty. *Resour. Policy* 31(2):95–105

Blitzer CR, Lessard DR, Paddock JL. 1984. Risk-bearing and the choice of contract forms for oil exploration and development. *Energy J.* 5(1):1–28

Boadway R, Bruce N. 1984. A general proposition on the design of a neutral business tax. *J. Public Econ.* 24(2):231–39

Boadway R, Bruce N, McKenzie K, Mintz J. 1987. Marginal effective tax rates for capital in the Canadian mining industry. *Can. J. Econ.* 87(1):1–16

Boadway R, Keen M. 2008. *Theoretical perspectives on resource rent tax design.* Presented at the Int. Monet. Fund Conf. Tax. Nat. Resour., Washington, DC

Bond SR, Devereux MP. 1995. On the design of a neutral business tax under uncertainty. *J. Public Econ.* 58(1):57–71

Boué JC. 2006. *A Question of Rigs, of Rules, or of Rigging the Rules?* Oxford, UK: Oxf. Univ. Press

Bradley PG. 1998. On the use of modern asset pricing for comparing alternative royalty systems for petroleum development projects. *Energy J.* 19(1):47–81

Brealey RA, Myers SC, Allen F. 2008. *Principles of Corporate Finance.* Boston, MA: McGraw-Hill/Irwin. 9th ed.

Brown EC. 1948. Business income, taxation, and investment incentives. In *Income, Employment and Public Policy: Essays in Honor of Alvin H. Hansen,* ed. LA Metzler, pp. 300–16. New York: Norton

Campbell H. 1980. The effect of capital intensity on the optimal rate of extraction of a mineral deposit. *Can. J. Econ.* 13(2):349–56

Conrad RF, Hool RB. 1984. Intertemporal extraction of mineral resources under variable rate taxes. *Land Econ.* 60(4):319–27

Daniel P, Sunley EM. 2008. *Contractual assurances of fiscal stability.* Presented at the Int. Monet. Fund Conf. Tax. Nat. Resour., Washington, DC

Dasgupta PS, Heal GM. 1979. *Economic Theory and Exhaustible Resources.* Cambridge, UK: Cambridge Univ. Press

Deacon RT. 1993. Taxation, depletion, and welfare: a simulation study on the U.S. petroleum resource. *J. Environ. Econ. Manag.* 24(2):159–87

Debreu G. 1959. *Theory of Value: An Axiomatic Analysis of Economic Equilibrium.* New Haven, CT: Yale Univ. Press

Domar ED, Musgrave RA. 1944. Proportional income taxation and risk-taking. *Q. J. Econ.* 58(2):388–422

Dowell R. 1978. Resources rent taxation. *Aust. J. Manag.* 3(2):127–46

Emerson C, Garnaut R. 1984. Mineral leasing policy: competitive bidding and the Resource Rent Tax given various responses to risk. *Econ. Rec.* 60(2):133–42

Emhjellen M, Alaouze CM. 2003. A comparison of discounted cashflow and modern asset pricing methods—project selection and policy implications. *Energy Policy* 31(12):1213–20

Fane G. 1987. Neutral taxation under uncertainty. *J. Public Econ.* 33(1):95–105

Fraser R. 1998. Lease allocation systems, risk aversion and the resource rent tax. *Aust. J. Agric. Resour. Econ.* 42(2):115–30

Fraser R. 1999. The state of resource taxation in Australia: "an inexcusable folly for the nation"? *Aust. J. Agric. Resour. Econ.* 43(3):259–78

Fraser R. 2000. Is risk-sharing resource taxation in society's best interests if prices are log-normally distributed? *Resour. Policy* 26(4):219–25

Garnaut R, Clunies Ross A. 1975. Uncertainty, risk aversion and the taxing of natural resource projects. *Econ. J.* 85(338):272–87

Garnaut R, Clunies Ross A. 1979. The neutrality of the Resource Rent Tax. *Econ. Rec.* 55(150): 193–201

Garnaut R, Clunies Ross A. 1981. Relationships between governments and mining investors. *Mater. Soc.* 5(4):437–47

Garnaut R, Clunies Ross A. 1983. *Taxation of Mineral Rents*. Oxford, UK: Oxf. Univ. Press

Gaudet G, Lasserre P. 1986. Capital income taxation, depletion allowances, and nonrenewable resource extraction. *J. Public Econ.* 29(2):241–53

Gaudet G, Lasserre P, Long NV. 1995. Optimal resource royalties with unknown and temporally independent extraction cost structures. *Int. Econ. Rev.* 36(3):715–49

Glomsrød S, Osmundsen P. 2005. *Petroleum Industry Regulation within Stable States*. Aldershot, UK: Ashgate

Gordon RH, MacKie-Mason JK. 1995. Why is there corporate taxation in a small open economy? The role of transfer pricing and income shifting. In *The Effects of Taxation on Multinational Corporations*, ed. M Feldstein, JR Hines Jr, RG Hubbard, 3:67–91. Chicago, IL: Univ. Chicago Press

Graham JR, Harvey CR. 2001. The theory and practice of corporate finance: evidence from the field. *J. Financ. Econ.* 60(2–3):187–243

Green RC, Talmor E. 1985. The structure and incentive effects of corporate tax liabilities. *J. Financ.* 40(4):1095–114

Groth C, Schou P. 2007. Growth and non-renewable resources: the different roles of capital and resource taxes. *J. Environ. Econ. Manag.* 53(1):80–98

Herfindahl OC. 1967. Depletion and economic theory. In *Extractive Resources and Taxation*, ed. M Gaffney, pp. 63–90. Madison, WI: Univ. Wis. Press

Hotelling H. 1931. The economics of exhaustible resources. *J. Polit. Econ.* 39(2):137–75

Jacoby HD, Laughton DG. 1992. Project evaluation: a practical asset pricing method. *Energy J.* 13(2):19–47

Kemp A. 1992. Development risks and petroleum fiscal systems: a comparative study of the UK, Norway, Denmark and the Netherlands. *Energy J.* 13(3):17–39

Krautkraemer JA. 1990. Taxation, ore quality selection, and the depletion of a heterogeneous deposit of a nonrenewable resource. *J. Environ. Econ. Manag.* 18(2):120–35

Krautkraemer JA. 1998. Nonrenewable resource scarcity. *J. Econ. Lit.* 36(4):2065–107

Land BC. 2008. *Resource rent taxation—theory and experience*. Presented at the Int. Monet. Fund Conf. Tax. Nat. Resour., Washington, DC

Laughton DG. 1998. The potential for use of modern asset pricing methods for upstream petroleum project evaluation: Introductory remarks. *Energy J.* 19(1):1–11

Leland HE. 1978. Optimal risk sharing and the leasing of natural resources, with application to oil and gas leasing on the OCS. *Q. J. Econ.* 92(3):413–37

Lindholt L. 2008. *Maximizing the discounted tax revenue in a mature oil province*. Discuss. Pap. 544, Res. Dep. Stat. Norway, Oslo

Lintner J. 1965. The valuation of risk assets and the selection of risky investment in stock portfolios and capital budgets. *Rev. Econ. Stat.* 47(1):13–37

Lund D. 1992. Petroleum taxation under uncertainty: contingent claims analysis with an application to Norway. *Energy Econ.* 14(1):23–31

Lund D. 1993. The lognormal diffusion is hardly an equilibrium price process for exhaustible resources. *J. Environ. Econ. Manag.* 25(3):235–41

Lund D. 1999. Taxation and regulation of an exhaustible natural resource: the case of the Norwegian petroleum. In *Economic Rents and Environmental Management in Mining and Natural Resource Sectors*, ed. E Figueroa, pp. 189–244. Santiago/Edmonton: Univ. Chile, Santiago/Univ. Alberta

Lund D. 2000. Nøytralitet i petroleumsskattleggingen (Neutrality in petroleum taxation). In *Skattlegging av Petroleumsvirksomhet (Taxation of Petroleum Activity)*, Nor. Public Rep. 2000:18, append. 1, pp. 185–226. Oslo: Minist. Financ.

Lund D. 2001. Petroleumsskatt—flere uavklarte spørsmål (Petroleum tax—further undecided issues). *Økonom. Forum* 55(9):34–40

Lund D. 2002a. Petroleum tax proposals in Norway and Denmark. *Energy J.* 23(4):37–56

Lund D. 2002b. Rent taxation when cost monitoring is imperfect. *Resour. Energy Econ.* 24(3):211–28

Lund D. 2002c. Taxation, uncertainty, and the cost of equity. *Int. Tax Public Financ.* 9(4):483–503

Lund D. 2003. Testimony on consequences of a fiscal stability clause in Danish petroleum. In *Høring om de Statsretlige Aspekter af Nordsøaftalen*, pp. 43–47. Copenhagen: Energipolit. Udvalg, Folket. http://www.ft.dk/img20031/udvbilag/lib3/20031_25563/20031_25563.pdf (In Danish)

Lund D. 2006. Neutral company taxation under uncertainty, with some experiences from the petroleum sectors of Norway and Denmark. In *Yearbook for Nordic Tax Research 2006*, ed. R Påhlsson, pp. 116–23. Oslo: Universitetsforlaget

Lund D. 2009. *Marginal versus average beta of equity under corporate taxation*. Memo. 12/2009, Dep. Econ., Univ. Oslo

MacKie-Mason JK. 1990. Some nonlinear tax effects on asset values and investment decisions under uncertainty. *J. Public Econ.* 42(3):301–27

Majd S, Myers SC. 1985. *Valuing the government's tax claim on risky corporate assets*. Work. Pap. 1553, NBER

Mayo W. 1979. Rent royalties. *Econ. Rec.* 55(150):202–13

Mead WJ. 1994. Toward an optimal oil and gas leasing system. *Energy J.* 15(4):1–18

Mead WJ, Moseidjord A, Sorensen PE. 1983. The rate of return earned by lessees under cash bonus bidding for OCS oil and gas leases. *Energy J.* 4(4):37–52

Mossin J. 1966. Equilibrium in a capital asset market. *Econometrica* 34(4):768–83

Mossin J. 1968. Taxation and risk-taking: an expected utility approach. *Economica* 35(137):74–82

Nakhle C. 2008. *Petroleum Taxation. Sharing the Oil Wealth: A Study of Petroleum Taxation Yesterday, Today and Tomorrow.* London, UK: Routledge

Osmundsen P. 1995. Taxation of petroleum companies possessing private information. *Resour. Energy Econ.* 17(4):357–77

Osmundsen P. 1998. Dynamic taxation of non-renewable natural resources under asymmetric information about reserves. *Can. J. Econ.* 31(4):933–51

Osmundsen P. 2005. Optimal petroleum taxation subject to mobility and information constraints. See Glomsrød & Osmundsen 2005, 2:12–25

Osmundsen P. 2008. *Time consistency in petroleum taxation—the case of Norway*. Presented at the Int. Monet. Fund Conf. Tax. Nat. Resour., Washington, DC

Otto J. 2000. *Mining taxation in developing countries. Study prepared for UNCTAD, November.* New York: United Nations

Otto J, Andrews C, Cawood F, Doggett M, Guj P, et al. 2006. *Mining Royalties: A Global Study of Their Impact on Investors, Government and Civil Society.* Washington, DC: World Bank

Rubinstein M. 1987. Derivative assets analysis. *J. Econ. Perspect.* 1(2):73–93

Salahor G. 1998. Implications of output price risk and operating leverage for the evaluation of petroleum development projects. *Energy J.* 19(1):13–46

Samis MR, Davis GA, Laughton DG. 2007. Using stochastic discounted cash flow and real option Monte Carlo simulation to analyse the impacts of contingent taxes on mining projects. *Proc. Proj. Eval., AusIMM, Melbourne, 2007:*127–37 Carlton, VIC: Australas. Inst. Mining Metallurgy

Saunders M. 1987. Oil taxation: the cross-field allowance. *Fisc. Stud.* 8(4):55–68

Sharpe WF. 1964. Capital asset prices: a theory of market equilibrium under conditions of risk. *J. Financ.* 19(3):425–42

Sinn HW. 1987. *Capital Income Taxation and Resource Allocation.* Amsterdam: North-Holland

Slade ME. 1984. Tax policy and the supply of exhaustible resources: theory and practice. *Land Econ.* 60(2):133–47

Slade ME, Thille H. 2009. Whither Hotelling: tests of the theory of exhaustible resources. *Annu. Rev. Resour. Econ.* 1:239–59

Smith B. 1999. *The impossibility of a neutral Resource Rent Tax.* Work. Pap. Econ. Econom. 380, Aust. Natl. Univ. Canberra

Smith JL. 1997. Taxation and investment in Russian oil. *J. Energy Financ. Dev.* 2(1):5–23

Sørensen PB. 2005. Taxation of shareholder income and the cost of capital in an open economy: theory and applications to the Nordic countries. *Nationaløkon. Tidsskr. (Danish J. Econ.)* 143(3):433–47

Summers LH. 1987. Investment incentives and the discounting of depreciation allowances. In *The Effects of Taxation on Capital Accumulation*, ed. M Feldstein, pp. 295–304. Chicago, IL: Univ. Chicago Press

Sumner MT. 1978. Progressive taxation of natural resource rents. *Manchester Sch. Econ. Soc. Stud.* 46(1):1–16

Sunley EM, Baunsgaard T, Simard D. 2003. Revenue from the oil and gas sector: issues and country experience. In *Fiscal Policy Formulation and Implementation in Oil-Producing Countries*, ed. JM Davis, R Ossowski, A Fedelino, 6:153–83. Washington, DC: IMF

Sunnevåg KJ. 2000. Designing auctions for offshore petroleum lease allocation. *Resour. Policy* 26(1):3–16

Thaler RH. 1988. Anomalies: the winner's curse. *J. Econ. Perspect.* 2(1):191–202

von Neumann J, Morgenstern O. 1947. *Theory of Games and Economic Behavior.* Princeton, NJ: Princeton Univ. Press. 2nd ed.

Watkins GC. 2001. Atlantic petroleum royalties: fair deal or raw deal? *Oil Gas Pap.* 2, Atl. Inst. Mark. Stud., Halifax, NS

Zhang L. 1997. Neutrality and efficiency of Petroleum Revenue Tax: a theoretical assessment. *Econ. J.* 107(443):1106–20

Land Use and Climate Change Interactions

Robert Mendelsohn[1] and Ariel Dinar[2]

[1]Forestry and Environmental Studies, Yale University, New Haven, Connecticut 06511; email: robert.mendelsohn@yale.edu

[2]Department of Environmental Sciences, University of California, Riverside, California 92521; email: ariel.dinar@ucr.edu

Annu. Rev. Resour. Econ. 2009. 1:309–32

First published online as a Review in Advance on June 25, 2009

The *Annual Review of Resource Economics* is online at resource.annualreviews.org

This article's doi: doi: 10.1146/annurev.resource.050708.144246

Key Words

carbon emissions, agriculture, forestry, climate impacts

Abstract

Land use and land-use change can result in the emissions of greenhouse gases that cause climate change. Climate change also affects the productivity of land, which in turn leads to further land-use change. This paper explores the growing research on both topics. The land-use emission literature has focused on deforestation (harvests) and ignored the fact that harvests have led to a much younger and therefore growing global forest. Taking this into account, mankind's current and future influence over land use will have a small positive effect on reducing greenhouse gas emissions. Although the literature initially focused on climate impacts alone, when adaptation is taken into account we find that climate change is likely to have benign net global impacts on market sectors related to land use. Climate impacts on nonmarket sectors, however, are much more poorly understood or measured. Furthermore, it is not yet clear whether governments will adapt or maladapt to climate change.

1. INTRODUCTION

This paper reviews the growing literature on the interaction between climate change and land use. There are two distinct strands to this literature. One strand focuses on the impact of land use on greenhouse gas emissions, which then cause climate change. The other strand examines how climate change affects land use.

In the 1990s, deforestation contributed 5.8 $GtCO_2$ (gigatons carbon dioxide equivalent) per year to the atmosphere, which was 20% of global carbon emissions (IPCC 2007c). The remaining 80% came largely from burning fossil fuels. The land-use emissions were caused by deforestation: harvesting old-growth (primary forest) and converting forestland to farmland. This reduced the carbon stored on the land, leading to more carbon in the atmosphere. In addition, agriculture was responsible for methane emissions equal to 3.3 $GtCO_2/y$ and nitrogen dioxide emissions equal to 2.8 $GtCO_2/y$ (IPCC 2007b). These greenhouse gases, in turn, cause climate change (IPCC 2007c). Land-use change may also contribute to warming by changing Earth's albedo (reflectance of light), but this is likely to be a smaller influence.

Climate change also affects land use. The ecological literature suggests that warming will increase plant productivity and lead to a widespread movement of ecosystems toward the poles (Mellilo et al. 1993, Neilson et al. 2005). Land uses, such as forestry and grazing, that depend on specific ecosystems will be affected. Productivity will change and the mix of land uses in different regions will change. This process is dynamic and progresses as climate changes. Climate change may also have an indirect effect as it changes hydrological systems, affecting flows of water available to land owners. Insect and disease vectors may change, thereby affecting farms and forests with new pest problems. Finally, sea-level rise will affect land uses along the coast.

These two links pose two broad challenges. First, what are the best conceptual frameworks for looking at the effects of land use on climate change and for looking at the impact of climate change on land use? Second, how do we measure the actual magnitudes of these effects? Both questions are global and dynamic, which makes obtaining precise answers a daunting task.

This review is organized into two broad sections. The next section deals with the conceptual problems associated with these issues and lays out some promising theoretical approaches. Section 3 discusses attempts to measure the magnitude of the interactions. We begin with the influence of land use on climate and then discuss the impact of climate on land use. Ultimately, society needs to capture both effects simultaneously, but that is beyond the current literature.

2. THEORETICAL MODEL

Humans have altered the global landscape to create cropland, pasture, and living space. A great deal of the productive forests and grasslands have been converted to cropland and pastureland. Cropland now accounts for approximately 10% of all land and pastureland accounts for another 22% (Food and Agriculture Organization 2006). A small fraction has been converted to urban use (1.5%). Furthermore, a large fraction of the remaining forests has been converted to younger secondary forests. This transformation of the landscape has reduced the amount of global carbon held on land and thus contributed to the amount of carbon in the atmosphere. Land-use change has been responsible for approximately 20% of past emissions of CO_2 (IPCC 2007b).

2.1. Land-Use Effects on Climate

Although the burning of fossil fuels accounted for 80% of greenhouse gas emissions in the twentieth century, land use was also a major contributor to greenhouse gas emissions (IPCC 2007b). First, primary (old-growth) forests were converted to secondary (younger) forests in a massive global nonrenewable harvest. Second, forestland was converted to farmland to feed the world's population, which grew rapidly from 1 billion to over 6 billion people. Third, agriculture was a continual source of greenhouse gas emissions as a by-product of production. We examine simple theoretical models for each of these phenomena.

2.1.1. Timber. From the beginning of the industrial revolution through the 1990s, the global forest sector was primarily a nonrenewable resource sector (although renewable forests existed). Old-growth (primary) forests were the source of a large fraction of the harvested timber. In the 1990s, the stock of the old-growth forest dwindled to a point where most forest resources were coming from renewable forests. Today, timber is a renewable resource. The industry has planted the trees they are now harvesting.

Economics has developed a general model to describe how markets use nonrenewable resources (Hotelling 1931) and also specifically how it applies to forestry (Berck 1979, Berck & Bentley 1997). The society's objective is to maximize the present value of the resource given the limitation that only so much stock (S_0) is available:

$$Max \int_{t_0}^{T} P_t Q_t e^{-rt} dt$$
$$s.t. \int_{t_0}^{T} Q_t \leq S_0 \tag{1}$$
$$P_t \leq P_{\max},$$

where P_t is the price of timber in year t, Q_t is the quantity of harvests, and r is the discount rate. There are two constraints: The total amount of harvests over time cannot exceed the stock, and timber prices cannot exceed a maximum price (P_{max}) at which all timber could be produced using renewable forestry. The price of the nonrenewable resource cannot exceed the renewable price because buyers will turn to whatever is cheaper.

The first-order conditions for this problem are

$$dP/dt/P_t = r \text{ and } P_0 = P_{max}e^{-rT} \text{ and } S_T = 0, \tag{2}$$

where P_0 is the initial price of timber and T is the terminal date for nonrenewable harvests. Prices must rise at the interest rate during the period of harvesting, prices must reach P_{max} in year T, and the stock must be completely consumed by year T. The accessible old-growth forest must be completely harvested. That does not mean that every old-growth forest will be cut. Remote old-growth forest that is too expensive to harvest or forests that have been set aside for posterity would remain. This last point is a source of continued confusion and conflict. To the extent that countries do not protect their alleged set-aside forests, old-growth forests will continue to be harvested. If the price of renewable timber rises, some remote old-growth forests become economically attractive to harvest. If governments subsidize roads into old-growth forests, the forests will become part of the stock.

Once the old-growth forest is harvested, the industry turns to a renewable forest. Trees are planted in advance to supply all the needed timber in the future. There is no longer a time trend to timber prices. This has important implications for the role of forestry as a source of carbon. First, renewable forestry is carbon neutral. It will remove as much carbon from the atmosphere as it adds when trees are being harvested. The timber industry will no longer be a driving force of carbon emissions. Second, the carbon per hectare in forests will be considerably lower than in preindustrial times because renewable forestry will keep forests younger. Third, the low stock of carbon per hectare in these forests implies an opportunity to encourage forest owners to increase carbon per hectare through carbon sequestration incentive programs.

2.1.2. Agriculture. Since the beginning of agriculture (approximately 10,000 years ago), humans have been converting forests and grasslands into farmland. Despite improvements in farm productivity, the increase in global demand for food has caused the amount of global farmland to continue to increase. This process can be modeled as a competition among land uses for available space. In particular, one could model the demand for farmland (Q_A) and the demand for forestland (Q_F) given the supply of land (L) that can support forests:

$$\begin{aligned} Q_A &= D_A(P_A, P_L, Z) \\ Q_F &= D_F(P_F, P_L, Z) \\ Q_A + Q_F &= L, \end{aligned} \tag{3}$$

where P_A is the price of agricultural products, P_F is the price of forest products, and Z is a set of demand-shift variables such as population and income. For the moment, we ignore the effect of climate. The market solution leads to a market price for land (P_L) that equilibrates the marginal value (price) of farmland and forestland. The global supply of land available for farmland and agriculture, in turn, affects the price of food and the price of timber.

As population and GDP grow (Z changes), the demand for timberland and farmland shifts upward. Because the demand for agricultural land is relatively price inelastic, an increase in land price causes forests to be converted to farmland. As shown in **Figure 1**, this has led to a substantial increase in the demand for agricultural land. This conversion leads to permanent deforestation and the emission of large amounts of carbon into the atmosphere.

2.1.3. Carbon sequestration policies. Carbon sequestration policies can help mitigate greenhouse gases by storing carbon in the land versus releasing it into the atmosphere (Cacho et al. 2003, Sohngen & Mendelsohn 2003, Richards & Stokes 2004). A sequestration program favors forestry because it stores more carbon than does agriculture. To capture this in the theoretical model, Equation 3 is modified to count storing carbon (C) as an output:

$$\begin{aligned} Q_A &= D_A(P_A, P_L, Z, C) \\ Q_F &= D_F(P_F, P_L, Z, C) \\ Q_A + Q_F &= L. \end{aligned} \tag{4}$$

Technically, one must also include carbon storage in agriculture because farms also store carbon, although not as much as forests do. If the price of (shadow value of storing) carbon is taken into account, more land should be in forests compared with the case discussed above in which carbon is ignored.

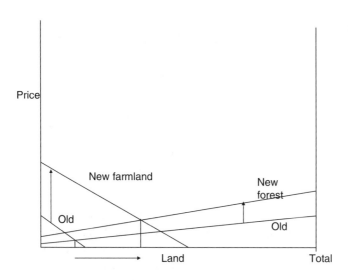

Figure 1

The changing market for global farmland and forestland.

The optimal price of carbon depends on both the damages that greenhouse gases will cause and the cost of mitigating (removing) them (Nordhaus 1991). Society's objective is to choose a path with the least total cost (i.e., to minimize the present value of mitigation and climate damage). The solution to this problem suggests that the price of carbon should increase over time as the stock accumulates in the atmosphere and causes ever increasing amounts of damage. As the price of carbon increases over time, more land should be converted to forest. The net result will be gradually less land available for agriculture and higher food prices.

Higher carbon prices increase the incentive to hold old-growth forests intact, reforest productive lands, and lengthen the rotations of renewable forests. Longer rotations would store more carbon in forests as average tree size would increase. At the current optimal rotation length, the benefits to the forest owner of holding trees in the ground offset the opportunity costs of the timber and the land. From a carbon sequestration perspective, the marginal cost of lengthening the rotation is low, suggesting that the marginal cost of sequestration is also low. However, the marginal cost of sequestration will increase as the trees grow in size and the opportunity cost of holding them increases. The marginal cost of sequestration will also rise as the amount of carbon being stored increases.

2.1.4. Farm emissions. The third substantial source of greenhouse gases from land use is the continued emissions of N_2O and CH_4 from farms (IPCC 2007b). These are by-products of growing crops and livestock, respectively. Currently, these emissions are not regulated and farmers do not have to pay for emitting them. As a result, farmers weighing whether to invest in abatement of these emissions have chosen to minimize abatement costs (i.e., spend no money on abatement).

As greenhouse gas concentrations rise, the price of emitting more greenhouse gases should increase as well. Using regulations or fees, society should encourage farmers to take increasingly stringent steps to mitigate and reduce emissions of N_2O and CH_4 over time. As marginal damages rise, the levels of abatement should also rise.

2.1.5. Biofuels. As part of a mitigation policy, society may also try to replace fossil fuels that emit carbon with biofuels that do not. The logic of biofuels is that they capture the carbon from the atmosphere that they emit when they are burned, making them carbon neutral. Proponents of biofuels sometimes argue that their product will be grown on marginal land that currently has no other purpose so that the biofuels will not displace any other land use. In practice, biofuels are expensive because it is difficult to collect a fuel across a wide landscape (they provide less net fuel). This is especially true for biofuels grown on low-productivity land because even more land is needed to produce the fuel. In practice, almost all existing biofuel plantations have been located on relatively fertile land and have therefore been in direct competition with either forests or cropland.

Figure 2 examines how a biofuels program could affect the market outcome for land. Because the biofuels increase the demand for land, they will increase the price of land. Because the demand for farmland is more inelastic than the demand for forestland, most of this land will come from forestland. In other words, the biofuels program will cause large increases in deforestation. Although the biofuels may be carbon neutral, they may have large negative impacts on carbon emissions because they will displace forestland. This will occur even if biofuel plantations are not built directly on existing forestland. There will also be a small reduction in farmland, which will, in turn, cause a small increase in food prices.

In **Figure 3**, we examine the combination of a biofuels program and a program to prevent deforestation. We assume that the deforestation program provides incentives for landowners to retain existing forests, which results in an increased demand for land to be used for forests. The amount of forestland consequently increases at the expense of biofuel land and farmland. Thus, the overall price of land increases, and both biofuel prices and food prices will rise. In sum, a biofuels program in conjunction with a deforestation program could lead to higher food prices (and greater food scarcity) than could result

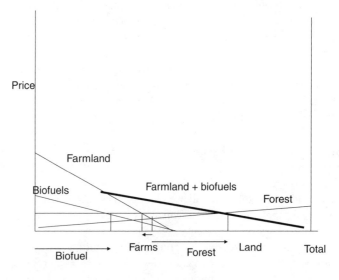

Figure 2

Adding biofuels to a land market for farmland and forestland.

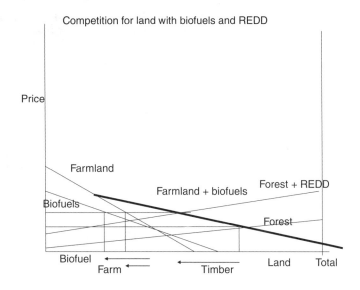

Figure 3

Results of a biofuels program in combination with a forest protection program.

from climate change. A combined forest protection and biofuels program is also likely be very expensive.

2.2. Climate Change Effects on Land Use

The impact of climate change on land and land use (ecosystems) is important. Climate change further impacts the economy by affecting agriculture, forestry, water, and coastal lands. Nonmarket impacts include changes in ecosystems, endangered species, and vector-borne diseases. Although dollar estimates of the magnitude of global damages are controversial, the impacts assigned to the systems noted above are a large fraction of total market impacts (Tol 2002, Mendelsohn & Williams 2004).

Climate change will affect every ecosystem on Earth. In general, warming will cause ecosystems to move poleward and to higher altitudes (Neilson et al. 2005). The shifts in climate will cause some ecosystems to expand and others to shrink. Warming and changes in the hydrological cycle will affect droughts, floods, and the supply of water (flow) (IPCC 2007a). Warming will also cause sea levels to rise, affecting coastal lands (IPCC 2007a). Possible increases in hurricane intensity could further threaten coastal lands (Emanuel et al. 2008).

The forest industry will be directly affected by changes in forest productivity as particularly valuable timber species shift over time and space. In general, a warmer, wetter, CO_2-enriched planet will lead to more extensive and more productive forests (VEMAP 1995, Bachelet et al. 2001a). This change would likely lead to an increase in the supply of forestland. However, in certain locations, forestland may shift to grassland, and trees will be in jeopardy.

Understanding the dynamics of these shifts requires more than just a description of the differences between potential equilibriums. Two prominent changes could occur in each of the impacted ecosystems: In one scenario, the new ecosystem would outcompete in regeneration, thereby leading to a slow and orderly change. In the other scenario, the old ecosystem would be rapidly removed by fire or pest outbreaks. Ecosystem research is beginning to model these dynamics (Bachelet et al. 2001b).

The productivity of agricultural land will also change. Research from both laboratories and the field suggest that crops have a hill-shaped relationship with temperature. The effect of warming will vary for each crop depending upon whether it is currently being grown in a cool location relative to its optimum or a relatively warm location. Looking across all crops, the impacts on farmers will depend on their location. Farmers in places that are cool relative to the most valuable climates will see benefits. Farmers in places that are already too warm will be harmed.

The impact of climate change on land use can be captured by including climate (W) as an explanatory factor in the land-use model (Equation 3) to obtain

$$
\begin{aligned}
Q_A &= D_A(P_L, Z, W) \\
Q_F &= D_F(P_L, Z, P_{Ct}, W) \\
Q_A &+ Q_F = L.
\end{aligned}
\tag{5}
$$

The productivity of land for agriculture and forestry will change as local climate changes. Specifically, warming is likely to increase the productivity of agriculture relative to forestry in cool places but reduce agricultural productivity in relatively warm places. The market will respond to this by expanding agriculture in the cooler locations and expanding forests in the warmer locations. If both forest and agricultural productivity increases (falls), the price of land will rise (fall). Looking across the planet, if the total amount of productive agricultural land increases (falls), food prices will fall (increase).

The model could be further expanded to include unproductive or nonmarket land uses. If market productivity increases, there will be increasing pressure to convert land to market uses, and if market productivity falls, land would shift out of market use. Non-market lands that are not secure (subject to invasion) may be very sensitive to climate effects.

In addition to accounting for land shifting from one use to another, it is also important to realize that land owners will adapt to climate change. The implicit assumption about adaptation is that each user will adjust to improve their situation in each climate scenario. This can be captured with a simple model of a net revenue maximizing actor (landowner). Each landowner wants to maximize the net revenue (π) from her land:

$$
\pi = PQ(I, W, G) - RI,
\tag{6}
$$

where P is the market price of output; Q is a production function that determines output given all the input and exogenous variables; I is a vector of purchased inputs (other than land); W is a vector of climate variables; G is a vector of time invariant geographic, soil, and exogenous economic variables such as distance to market; and R is a vector of input prices. The landowner maximizes net revenues by choosing I, given climate, soil, geography, market prices, and other exogenous socioeconomic conditions.

The resulting input demand functions by the landowner depend on all the exogenous factors:

$$
I = f(R, P, G, W).
\tag{7}
$$

As climate changes, the optimal input choices of the landowner will change. The land-owner will also examine the relative net revenues associated with each output. For example, if warming causes the net revenues of current output (crop type, livestock species, or tree species) to fall, the farmer will shift to a new output that is more suitable for the new conditions.

These adjustments by landowners to climate change are adaptations. Because climate change is dynamic, adaptation should also be dynamic. Although climate change is a global phenomenon, the response to climate change is local. What each farmer and forester should do depends on local conditions, not a global average. Adaptation will resemble a quilt-like response to climate change rather than a uniform blanket response.

Note that adaptation may be problematic if there is not a single landowner. For example, some resources are collectively owned. The incentive for individuals is to maximize their own net revenues, not aggregate net revenue. As a result, common property resources may not adapt well to climate change. Resources that are owned by the government but used by local people may suffer a similar fate. The local user may not have any incentive to protect the long-run value of the resource. Finally, places that are shared universally such as national parks and wildlife preserves are vulnerable because it is difficult for collections of users to act. These "public" resources may not adapt well to climate change. For all these resources, an argument can be made for privatizing the resource or improving government management (Mendelsohn 2006).

2.3. The Interaction Between Land Use and Climate Change Effects

The literature has not yet tackled the complex task of capturing the effect of climate on land as well as that of land on climate simultaneously. As climate changes, it affects land productivity and land uses. These changes may alter the emissions of greenhouse gases from land use and land-use change, which may produce a feedback loop. For example, warming may release methane from the tundra (IPCC 2007c) or warming may increase forest fires, which would then release carbon from existing forest inventories (Lenihan et al. 2003). Climate change may also alter the attractiveness of policy efforts to sequester carbon on land. For example, if warming increases the risk of fire, it may be more difficult to store carbon in forests. In contrast, if climate change increases forest productivity, it may be less expensive to store more carbon in forests. Climate change may alter the effectiveness of land-based carbon mitigation (sequestration) efforts.

Mitigation, in turn, may affect the vulnerability of land to climate if it causes land uses to shift toward more vulnerable activities. For example, a biofuels program may cause landowners to shift away from forestry toward biofuels, which, in turn, may be vulnerable to climate change. Although it is easy to imagine many complex impacts, the critical issue is to measure them to determine which are important in order to capture how the system is behaving.

3. LAND-USE EFFECTS ON CLIMATE

We now discuss the empirical research available to date regarding climate change and land use. The primary source of CO_2 in the atmosphere is the burning of fossil fuels, but in this section, we focus on just the CO_2 emissions attributable to land use. In this regard, the harvesting of old-growth (mature) timber and the conversion of forestland to agriculture are responsible for most of the carbon emissions; cropland is responsible for the nitrogen dioxide emissions; and livestock, water, and solid-waste facilities are responsible for the methane emissions. Remote-sensing projects that measure extent of forest cover over time observe substantial deforestation rates, especially in the tropics. Scientists have projected how much carbon is likely lost given the acreage of forest removed and the carbon per hectare in a typical forest. These extrapolations have led to the assertion that deforestation is responsible for 5.6 GTCO$_2$ per year.

The strength of these studies is that they are firmly rooted in measurement. With the advent of satellites, it is suddenly possible to see Earth's entire surface and make comparisons from one time period to the next. Remote sensing can measure land cover for the entire planet. By comparing the results across time periods, measurements of how land use is changing are possible. One weakness in relying heavily on forest cover to measure carbon, however, is that changes in carbon underneath the canopy cannot be measured. Selective logging or removal of small woody debris can leave the canopy intact but can substantially reduce carbon content. In the above cases, the deforestation estimates may underestimate carbon losses. Measuring only forest canopy will also not capture the substantial increase in carbon associated with a young growing forest. In this case, carbon emissions will be overestimated.

Top-down studies of the amount of CO$_2$ in the atmosphere can help provide a gross check on whether the deforestation estimates lead to under- or overestimates of carbon emissions from land. Over the past two decades, increases of CO$_2$ in the atmosphere have been smaller than emissions from fossil-fuel burning. After taking into account oceanic uptake, there is still another major carbon sink on Earth. By process of elimination, researchers have deduced that the land must have been a net sink of carbon over the past few decades (IPCC 2007c). It is very likely that standing forests have absorbed more carbon than deforestation has released.

The recent role of forests as a sink for CO$_2$ can be explained using the widespread conversion of the world's forests from old-growth forests to secondary (cut) forests. Old-growth forests are in stasis; they grow as much as they decay. On net, they do not absorb much carbon from the atmosphere. However, secondary forests are immature and still growing. Thus, they are a major carbon sink. Taking the consequences of this conversion effect into account, research indicates that human's influence on carbon emissions in terms of land use has been slightly beneficial over the past two decades.

In addition to ignoring the critical role of young forests, natural scientists may also be overestimating the magnitude of future deforestation rates. They have used trends from past deforestation rates to predict the future (IPCC 2007b). They have estimated deforestation rates in previous decades and assumed that they would continue through the current century. However, because of substantial changes in the underlying forces that cause deforestation, there is every reason to believe these trends will not continue. First, the timber sector has become a renewable industry (Sohngen et al. 1999). Forest companies already harvest the timber that they plant in a sustainable way. Only in a few places in the tropics, because of common or public property rights, are forests still harvested unsustainably. Unsustainable harvests are no longer driving the timber industry. Second, the world's population growth is slowing. The pressure to deforest land to obtain farmland is dropping. With the continued growth of agricultural productivity and the slowing of global population growth, it is no longer clear that more cropland will be needed in the future. This implies that deforestation rates should fall.

To capture what will happen to future land use, structural models are needed. These models should capture the underlying processes that lead to deforestation or carbon sequestration. Whereas the abstract models discussed in the theory section (Section 2) describe the market processes that have led to land-use change across the world, structural models need to reflect these market processes using empirically derived parameters. Currently, there are well-developed structural models of agriculture (Adams et al. 1990, 1999) and forestry (Sohngen & Mendelsohn 1998, 2003) for the United States. Farmers choose crops and inputs in response to input and output prices. Output prices are determined by equating supply and demand. Timber companies choose species, management intensity, and harvest ages to maximize profits. Timber prices are determined by equating supply and demand.

One flaw of the national studies is that they cannot predict how imports and exports may change. It is therefore important to model market sectors with global models. There are only a few examples of global land models in agriculture (Fischer et al. 1988, Darwin 1999, Hertel 1999) and forestry (Perez-Garcia et al. 1997; Sohngen et al. 1999, 2002). Because these models are global, they determine prices and land use as endogenous outcomes. The models explore how exogenous driving forces such as population, income, and the remaining stock of old growth affect these endogenous choices over time. The models are also well suited to determine how policy might affect outcomes. Trade restrictions, subsidies, and carbon sequestration programs can all be evaluated with these models (Sohngen et al. 2002, Fischer et al. 2005).

The fact that not all forests and farms are operated by profit-maximizing owners reflects one of the weaknesses of this literature. In many low-latitude countries, the forests are still owned as common property or they are weakly held by the government. Because the people making decisions about the land may not own it, they may opt not to protect the natural capital on the land and may overgraze and overharvest. The models do not reflect this problem. A second weakness of the models is their depiction of the edge between agriculture and forests. In places where farming is either expanding or contracting, agriculture and forests have large impacts on each other. The current models do not do a good job capturing this interaction. Finally, another weakness of global land-use models is the underlying quality of the data used to parameterize them. For example, estimates of the aggregate amount of cropland in Africa vary by more than a factor of four from 71 million ha (Mayaux et al. 2003) to 342 million ha (Friedl et al. 2002).

4. CLIMATE CHANGE EFFECTS ON LAND USE

4.1. Agriculture

Five types of approaches have been developed to study the impact of climate change on agriculture: (*a*) crop simulation models, (*b*) cross-sectional or intertemporal analyses of yields, (*c*) agroeconomic simulation models of farms, (*d*) cross-sectional or panel analyses of net revenues or land values, and (*e*) general equilibrium models. In the following sections, we discuss each of these approaches and highlight their strengths and weaknesses.

Crop simulation models use agronomic functions to capture the interaction between crop growth and climate, soils, and management practices. These models are calibrated to selected locations and usually for a particular management practice. The models predict how yield would change at each location with all else held constant (Rosenzweig & Parry 1994, Parry et al. 2004). The results are then aggregated across locations.

The crop simulation models are attractive because they are built from a deep understanding of agronomic science, are linked with hydrologic and soil conditions, and can capture the effects of CO_2 fertilization. The crop simulation models have been widely applied to examine the impacts of climate change on the major grains including maize, wheat, soybeans, and rice (e.g., Rosenzweig & Parry 1994, Parry et al. 2004).

However, crop simulation models also have important limitations. The models do a poor job with adaptation. A crop simulation model contains a purely agronomic relationship. The model does not capture the behavior of the farmer. The management practice of the farmer is assumed to be exogenous or fixed. Therefore, the models cannot predict how farmers are likely to change their behavior as climate changes. To the extent that adaptation is included in crop simulation studies, it is introduced exogenously by the researcher. For example, the most comprehensive crop simulation studies have assumed that all farmers might add fertilizer to compensate partially for the loss in yields (Rosenzweig & Parry 1994, Parry et al. 2004). The arbitrariness of these examples of adaptation makes them problematic. They are neither targeted at climate change nor motivated by profit maximization.

This limitation in the crop simulation literature can be overcome. Several studies using crop simulation models have examined possible responses by the farmer to climate change. For example, Jin et al. (1994) found that using new rice cultivars and changing planting dates in southern China can substantially increase rice yields. Also in China, You (2001) found that switching from rice to corn has the potential to save 7 billion m^3 of water per year. In Greece, changing planting dates and varieties of maize can increase yields by 10% (Kapetanaki & Rosenzweig 1997). And in Spain, hybrid seeds and altered sowing dates can allow for double cropping of wheat and maize, thus increasing yields and reducing water use (Iglesias & Minguez 1997). Note that these adaptations are designed for local conditions. However, even these examples are not motivated by profit maximization.

A second limitation of the crop simulation models is that they model only one crop at a time. The crop simulation models have not been used to predict how farmers would react as one crop becomes less suitable and another crop becomes more suitable. They do not predict crop switching despite its clear importance in climate change.

A third limitation is that only a small number of crops and locations have been studied. Researchers have targeted the major grains because they are the largest single crops. However, the major grains tend to be grown in cool or temperate climates (with the exception of irrigated rice). Crops that are more suited for warm climates such as fruits and vegetables have been omitted. The studies are consequently biased toward the finding that warming is harmful. Finally, crop simulation models have been calibrated in only a limited number of places. If these locations are not representative of the universe of farms, they can provide misleading predictions.

Another way to measure the sensitivity of yields to climate is to measure how actual yields vary under different climate conditions. For example, one can conduct cross-sectional studies of actual yields across different climate zones. By applying an empirical production function model, one can isolate the effects of climate from other factors influencing yields. The production function approach links water, soil, climate, and economic inputs to crop yields for specific crops. For example, Onyeji & Fischer (1994) considered the impacts of climate change on yields in Egypt with and without adaptation. Gbetibouo & Hassan (2005) applied a cross-sectional approach to estimate a climate sensitivity surface for seven field crops in South Africa. Econometric methods have also been used to predict the climate sensitivity of yields of sorghum and corn in the United States (see review by Sands & Edmonds 2005). The U.S. studies show that future climate change would have a positive effect on sorghum yields but a negative effect on corn yields.

Another way to measure empirically the sensitivity of yields is to examine the effect of weather on yields over time. The first study to do this used the 1930s U.S. dust bowl (Crosson 1993, Easterling et al. 1993). During this brief period, temperatures in the middle parts of the United States were higher and precipitation was slightly lower, leading to unusually dry soil conditions in this region. The study measures the reduction in yields of selected grains during this period compared with periods of normal weather across the region. In a slightly different approach, Deschenes & Greenstone (2007) used panel data to estimate how yields or net revenue change over time. This approach examines how annual weather affects annual production.

The empirical yield function approach, however, has some of the same limitations as the crop simulation approach. Farmers are often assumed to continue growing the same crop with the same technology regardless of the change in climate. The analyses often focus on only a limited set of crops. The full set of adaptations available to farmers is underestimated.

To capture farm behavior, it is important to model the farm and the farming sector, not just the plants. Farm simulation models assume that farmers wish to maximize their profits. One can then determine what farm behavior would lead to profit maximization. One can also determine what farm adaptations would maximize profits in response to climate change. For example, farmers may alter planting times, crop varieties, harvests dates, tillage, and irrigation methods. Taking these into account, the researcher can determine which activity would maximize profit and then trace out actual yields and net revenues for different climates. In practice, using farm simulation models to look at all alternatives is too expensive. So even though they tend to include only a limited number of alternative farming methods, the farm simulation models have begun to address the critical issue of adaptation. However, it is likely that the models do not yet fully capture the full range of adaptations that farmers can practice.

Nonetheless, farm simulation models can capture the behavior of a single farm (Kaiser et al. 1993) or all farms in a country (Adams et al. 1990; 1993; 1999). The single-farm model can describe in detail the alternative choices a farmer might make to maximize profits at a specific location. A national farm sector model can describe how these farm choices vary from place to place and also how farm prices are likely to change (although changes in farm prices require assumptions about changes in other countries).

In practice, most farm simulation models have been estimated for only the United States. The farm simulation models tend to rely on crop simulation models to make the link between changes in climate and CO_2 and crop yields. Mathematical programming methods are used to determine profit-maximizing choices of crops by farmers across the United States (Adams et al. 1990, 1993, 1995, 1999) or on a single farm (Kaiser et al. 1993).

The farm simulation models predict climate change will induce crop switching. With this adaptation, U.S. farms are predicted to benefit from warming (Adams et al. 1990, 1999; Reilly et al. 2001). Rain-fed agricultural yields will rise on average by 89% for cotton, 29% for corn, 80% for soybeans, 24% for wheat, and 11% for rice, and irrigated yields are estimated to rise by 110% for cotton, 4% for corn, 36% for soybeans, 4% for wheat, and 11% for rice (Reilly et al. 2001). Only potato yields are expected to fall.

With the Ricardian technique, net revenue or land value is regressed on climate, soils, and other control variables (Mendelsohn et al. 1994). The technique relies on cross-sectional samples of farms to measure the sensitivity of land value or farm net revenue per hectare to climate. The Ricardian method has frequently been applied to the United States to study the impact of climate as well as other issues. For example, studies have examined the effect of climate on the quantity of cropland (Mendelsohn et al. 1996) and the sensitivity of crop revenue to climate variance (Mendelsohn et al. 1999), water withdrawals (Mendelsohn & Dinar 2003), and degree days (Schlenker et al 2006). Studies have also revealed that rain-fed farms are more sensitive than other farms to climate (Schlenker et al. 2005). All the U.S. studies with the exception of those by Schlenker et al. (2005, 2006) found that U.S. agriculture is climate resilient. Schlenker et al. (2005, 2006) argued that even U.S. agriculture may be sensitive to climate change because a great deal of farmland is rain fed and rain-fed farms are more climate sensitive than other farms. They also argued that the temperature sensitivity of crops increases dramatically above a critical threshold. These criticisms are especially relevant with large changes in temperatures.

The Ricardian method has been applied to a number of other locations. Single-country studies have been conducted in India and Brazil (Mendelsohn & Dinar 1999, Kumar & Parikh 2001, Sanghi & Mendelsohn 2008), Canada (Reinsborough 2003), Sri Lanka (Seo et al. 2005, Kurukulasuriya and Ajwad 2007), Great Britain (Maddison 2000), Israel (Fleischer et al. 2008), and China (Wang et al. 2009). There have also been two continental studies: a study of 11 countries in Africa (Dinar et al. 2008) and a study of 7 countries in Latin America (Mendelsohn et al. 2007). Substantial warming is predicted to cause large losses to crop net revenue in Africa (Kurukulasuriya et al 2006, Kurukulasuriya & Mendelsohn 2008). These same warming scenarios would also be harmful to commercial livestock but beneficial to small landowners (Seo & Mendelsohn 2008a). The increases in livestock net revenue would help offset some of the crop losses. The effects on farmers were expected to vary a great deal across agroecological zones and so they would vary across the African landscape (Seo et al. 2009). The Ricardian study of South America examined farmland values (Mendelsohn et al. 2007). Using Ricardian regressions across all seven countries, Seo & Mendelsohn (2008b) revealed that Latin American farmers were more vulnerable to warming than were African farmers.

One of the principal advantages of the Ricardian technique is that it incorporates efficient adaptations by farmers to climate change. The technique captures how farmers modify their production practices in response to changes in water availability, rainfall pattern, and temperature. However, the Ricardian method cannot measure the impact of changes that do not vary across space. Differences in future technology, CO_2 levels, prices, or agricultural policies may all impact how future farmers react to climate change. Because it holds prices constant, the technique is biased (Cline 1996). Specifically, the Ricardian method overestimates losses and benefits, but the bias is likely small (Mendelsohn & Nordhaus 1999). The Ricardian technique also does not control for irrigation (Darwin 1999, Schlenker et al. 2005). Subsequent studies have tried to address irrigation by including measures of surface water (Mendelsohn & Dinar 2003), by modeling irrigation (Kurukulasuriya & Mendelsohn 2008), and by separating rain-fed from irrigated farms (Schlenker et al. 2005, Kurukulasuriya & Mendelsohn 2008, Seo & Mendelsohn 2008b). Finally, the Ricardian method is a comparative static analysis of long-term equilibrium impacts, and so it does not measure the adjustment costs of moving from one equilibrium to another (Quiggin & Horowitz 1999, Kelly et al. 2005).

The approaches reviewed above are partial equilibrium models of the agriculture sector. However, if changes induced by climate change are large enough, they may affect the entire economy and alter both input and output prices. Computable general equilibrium (CGE) models can predict how large shifts in supply and demand alter prices—changes that the partial equilibrium models miss. The CGE framework can be applied to a single country such as the United States (Scheraga et al. 1993, Jorgenson et al. 2004) or to the entire world (Darwin et al. 1996). Although the partial equilibrium models might capture shifts within the sector such as in crop prices, they invariably miss changes in interest rates or labor prices.

One of the disadvantages of moving to general equilibrium global models is that such models, although theoretically sound, are poorly calibrated. Thus, the underlying inaccuracies in each component of the model may make the results unreliable. Specifically, the CGE models tend not to have reliable measures of the underlying sensitivity of each sector to climate change. The models also need to have reliable estimates of how the different sectors of the economy interact. These inaccuracies are compounded with aggregation. It is very difficult for CGE modelers to predict how climate affects supply in large regions, much less in regions that are poorly studied, such as developing countries. With the bulk of climate damages occurring in developing countries, one must treat CGE results with caution. For example, Darwin et al. (1996) group all the developing countries into a single region despite the wide differences across countries. The CGE models simply do not have the detailed knowledge of land and land uses required to make accurate measurements.

More regionally based studies can help address these shortcomings by verifying assumptions with more detailed country-level analysis. Winters et al. (1998) studied the impact of global climate change on developing countries using a CGE model for three archetype economies representing the poor cereal-importing nations of Africa, Asia, and Latin America. The results suggest that all these developing countries will likely suffer income and production losses but the African country would have the largest income loss.

4.2. Forestry

The impact of climate change on forests has also been measured using a set of different approaches. Climate is expected to change forest productivity and to shift ecosystems over space. The initial quantitative biological studies of climate impacts on forests focused on comparative static analyses (e.g., Mellilo et al. 1993, Haxeltine & Prentice 1996). Equilibrium ecological outcomes were computed for the equilibrium climate from a CO_2-doubled atmosphere. The ecological models predicted that global forests would expand and become slightly more productive and forest ecosystems would shift poleward and to higher elevations. Economic analyses of these initial ecological predictions suggested that climate change would cause a net gain in the U.S. timber sector (Joyce et al. 1995, Sohngen & Mendelsohn 1998). However, to grasp what will happen to the planet, it is necessary to model the entire globe (Perez-Garcia et al. 1997, Sohngen et al. 2002).

Global analyses can capture partial equilibrium price effects that single-country studies cannot. However, the models need to capture adaptation. The forest sector can plant species that will be adapted to the new climate conditions, and this sector can reduce losses from fire or insect attack by harvesting high-risk stocks before they can be destroyed. However, it is difficult to change large forest stocks quickly. It is therefore important to recognize that forest adaptation is dynamic (Sohngen & Mendelsohn 1998, Sohngen et al. 2002).

Forest modeling can be improved. The ecological modeling must become dynamic. Ecology should not be viewed as a comparative static problem but rather a dynamic problem. How will forests evolve over time as climate changes? Will forests change slowly as a result of regeneration effects, or will they change rapidly as a result of fires and insect outbreaks? The newest ecological models are beginning to capture these dynamic effects (Bachelet et al. 2001b).

The economics of timber modeling must also be dynamic (Sohngen & Mendelsohn 1998, Sohngen et al. 2002). The models must be able to capture how prices, planting, and rotation lengths change over time. The behavior of the timber sector in developing countries also needs more careful development. Although the model of a profit-maximizing landowner may fit developed countries, low-latitude forests are more likely commonly owned or poorly operated by governments. The interaction between forests and agriculture needs to be improved. The boundary between what is a forest and a farm is a fluid and dynamic edge. Forest models need to capture both permanent forest conversion and farm abandonment over time. Finally, the models need to capture efforts to set aside land for ecological preservation. Although this can be readily done in developed countries where set-aside land is unlikely to reenter the market, the lands in developing countries that remain set aside are constantly changing. All of these factors can affect how climate change will affect the timber market.

4.3. Water

The natural sciences predict climate change could affect the water sector in several ways. First, higher temperatures are expected to speed up the hydrological cycle, leading to more precipitation and more evaporation (IPCC 2007c). Second, warmer temperatures will increase the amount of rain in winter and will lead to earlier snow melt, causing greater flows in early spring and lower flows in summer (Gleick 1987, Lettenmaier et al. 1992). Third, the geographic pattern of rainfall may change, causing some areas to get wetter and other areas to get dryer (IPCC 2007c). Fourth, the intertemporal pattern of precipitation may also change, possibly leading to more droughts and more floods (IPCC 2007c). Finally, higher temperatures may lead to an increased demand for water (IPCC 2007a). All of these changes have ramifications for the water sector.

Several studies have estimated the impact of climate change on water supply. Because water is very expensive to move among watersheds, the impact of climate change on water must be studied at the watershed level. Early studies predicted large negative impacts because of the expected declines in water supplies (Lettenmaier & Sheer 1991, Nash & Gleick 1993). However, these studies did not allow water allocations to change and so could not estimate economic impacts. More recent analyses have allowed water allocations to adjust as supplies decline (Hurd et al. 1999, Hurd & Harrod 2001, Howitt & Pienaar 2006, Lund et al. 2006). The California study by Lund et al. (2006) and Howitt & Pienaar (2006) also took into account changes in water demand. These new studies predict that falling supplies would still cause damages but the damages would be much smaller. Most of the reductions in water use would come from low-valued irrigation, and higher valued uses should be protected. The reduction in irrigation water, however, has ramifications for land use as farmers have to turn to rain-fed agriculture or must shift the land to livestock or a nonagricultural land use. For example, in California, low-valued irrigation for alfalfa in the Central Valley would be discontinued, allowing adequate water supplies for high-valued irrigation for fruits and vegetables and for urban and industrial users. The alfalfa land, in turn, would shift toward grazing or perhaps residential development.

Water studies still face several challenges. First, how can one calculate national impacts? Individual watershed studies are expensive, so a methodology is needed to go from local watershed estimates to national estimates. Second, most studies have been conducted in the United States with only a few examples from other countries (e.g., Strzepek et al. 1996). Third, the studies sometimes consider the variability in annual and seasonal flow, but they generally do not measure flooding effects. Fourth, none of the studies yet consider changes in hard structures such as dams, canals, and levies. These investments can move water from spring to summer, reduce flooding risks, and increase the overall value of water. Finally, fisheries, marshes, and endangered species may all be affected by changes in water flow and by adaptations. These nonmarket impacts need to be taken into account as well.

4.4. Nonmarket Ecosystems

The agriculture, forestry, and water impacts listed above all consider market impacts. However, climate will also affect terrestrial and aquatic ecosystem services for which there are no markets (IPCC 2007a). The availability of wildlands, open spaces, habitat for desired wildlife and endangered species, fisheries, and running rivers depends on the climate and human use of water and land resources. These resources are not traded in markets because they are shared jointly across many consumers. Markets undersupply such jointly consumed products. In general, we depend on government to help provide these resources.

Climate may have direct effects on many of these ecosystem resources through changes in the net productivity of the ecosystem (IPCC 2007a). Increases (decreases) in local plant productivity, in turn, will likely create more (less) productive habitats for animals. Climate may also affect how humans use these resources. As society adapts to climate, this may change the availability of these resources. For example, if climate change increases (decreases) the productivity of timber in a particular place, the trees will be more (less) attractive to timber management, leading to less (more) wildlands. If water becomes scarcer, farmers may want to withdraw more water, leaving less for the aquatic ecosystem.

Analyses of climate change have made very little progress in assessing the impacts to either aquatic or terrestrial ecosystems (IPCC 2007a). Ecological studies have been able to quantify how ecosystem types may move across the landscape and how plant productivity will change. There is much less research on how animal populations will be affected. But the largest gap concerns societies' responses to these changes. What will market forces do in response to climate change and how will this affect nonmarket services? How will government agencies responsible for protecting ecological services respond? Will they spend vast resources trying to prevent the ecosystems from changing as climate changes? Will they adopt dynamic responses that encourage natural adaptation by plants and animals? Finally and perhaps most importantly, what is the value of the resulting changes in the ecosystem?

4.5. Health

A final subject linked to climate-related changes in ecosystems concerns the impacts on health from vector-borne diseases. Many infectious illnesses such as malaria and dengue fever depend on environmental carriers that are climate sensitive (IPCC 2007a). For example, the malaria-spreading mosquito needs temperatures within a narrow band to have a sufficient growing season to be infectious. If temperatures are too cold, malaria is not a risk. As temperatures warm, however, new territories suddenly become viable malaria zones. The potential number of the resulting new cases is staggering, estimated to be in the hundreds of millions (IPCC 2007a).

Although the health literature regarding climate change largely comes from public health schools, the quantitative literature is surprisingly blind to the role that public health plays in human disease. Malaria is already endemic to the United States, for example, but it has been eliminated through mosquito control and health care. It is unlikely that climate change will lead to thousands of cases of malaria in the United States or other developed nations. Most likely, climate change will simply require additional costs spent controlling the disease. It is less clear what will happen in poorer countries. At the moment, the least developed nations are doing a poor job of controlling vector-borne diseases. As these countries become richer in the future, however, they may do a better job. Furthermore, it remains inexpensive to control most vector-borne diseases. Thus, the obvious health solution is for richer nations to help pay for public health controls rather than let climate change take so many lives.

4.6. Sea-Level Rise

One final effect that climate change will likely have on land use is from rising seas. As warming expands the ocean and melts ice on land, seas are expected to rise (IPCC 2007a). Coastal lands will be at risk of flooding and salt-water intrusion. Nonmarket and low-valued market lands such as farms will likely retreat as seas advance (Ng & Mendelsohn 2006). In contrast, coastal urban land is likely to be protected with hard structures because it is so valuable (Yohe et al 1999, Ng & Mendelsohn 2005).

5. CONCLUSION

Land use and climate are closely linked. Land use has an effect on climate because it affects carbon and other greenhouse gas emissions. Climate affects land use directly by changing productivity and the location of ecosystems as well as indirectly by changing water, pests, and sea level.

The accepted conclusion in the literature is that human influences on forests through deforestation have resulted in carbon emissions equal to 20% of total human emissions in recent decades. However, these predictions ignore the role that the timber industry plays in keeping the forests young. When this latter effect is included, human interference in forests appears to be having a net beneficial effect (reducing carbon emissions).

The scientific literature predicts that human interference in land use will likely worsen over time (IPCC 2007b). However, economic analyses of the causes of deforestation suggest that deforestation rates will likely shrink in the future. Because the timber industry will continue to keep forests young, it is likely that this beneficial effect will continue indefinitely. The economic analyses of land use, therefore, lead to exactly the opposite prediction. It is very likely that human interference with land uses will cause land to remain a net carbon sink in the future.

Regardless of what role the market plays in future land use, it is important to recognize that policy can also influence how land use affects future emissions. Government policies can encourage landowners to sequester carbon in forests and soils, and this should be part of a global mitigation strategy (Sohngen & Mendelsohn 2003, Cacho et al. 2003, Richards & Stokes 2004). However, policy design is critical. Forests that are part or could be part of the global timber market require a global systemic policy. Effective carbon sequestration policies must address the entire global stock. Plans targeted at selected pieces of land or even isolated countries are likely to be ineffective because of leakage (Sathaye & Andrasko 2007, Sohngen & Brown 2008). Countries and plots that are not being regulated will react to the higher price of timber caused by the sequestration plan and harvest more (i.e., reduce their stocks). Leakage can happen anywhere in the world. Monitoring costs, consequently, is a serious issue. Without technological innovations, the cost of accounting for carbon per hectare will be high.

Assuming that a sequestration plan is global, it is relatively inexpensive to secure a small amount of additional carbon in forests. Preventing deforestation of low-valued old growth, slightly lengthening tree rotations in managed stands, and reforesting productive forestland are relatively low cost. However, securing large amounts of carbon will result in policies becoming increasingly expensive. To secure approximately 40 additional $GTCO_2$, prices have to rise only to $17/$TCO_2$ by 2100 (Sohngen & Mendelsohn 2003); to secure 100 $GTCO_2$, prices have to rise to $51/$TCO_2$ (Sohngen & Mendelsohn 2003); but to secure 350 $GTCO_2$, prices have to rise to $400/$TCO_2$ (Sathaye et al. 2007).

The impact literature is quite clear that climate change will have large physical impacts (IPCC 2007a). The ecological literature suggests there will be widespread movement of ecosystems toward the poles and toward higher altitudes. The hydrological literature suggests a speeding up of the hydrological cycle. Many places will see reductions in annual water supplies and earlier runoff. The agronomic literature suggests crop productivity will fall if crops continue to be grown where they are now.

These physical impacts could lead to large social impacts as well (IPCC 2007a). Without adaptation, there will be large losses in the agriculture, forestry, coastal, and water sectors and potential health losses and reductions in the effectiveness of conservation. If society makes no changes to adapt to warming, sea-level rise, and changes in precipitation, climate change will lead to large economic and nonmarket damages (IPCC 2007a). Low-latitude countries are expected to be the hardest hit because they are already too hot and more dependent on climate-sensitive sectors (namely agriculture) (Mendelsohn et al. 2006).

However, it is very likely that people will adapt. Individuals will make changes that make themselves less vulnerable. Governments are likely to make changes that help their own people adapt. The governmental adaptations may not be perfectly efficient, but it is very unlikely that governments at all levels would do nothing. Consequently, one should expect to see that farmers will shift crops so they grow in new conditions, and foresters will plant trees where they will prosper. Water is likely to be reallocated to more valuable uses as it becomes scarcer. Developed coastlines around the world will be protected. New health threats from climate change will be met by relatively inexpensive public health measures. Conservation organizations will learn to cope with a dynamic vision of ecosystems rather than a static model. These adaptations do not eliminate climate impacts from happening, nor are they costless. However, these adaptations reduce the magnitude of the social impacts from climate change dramatically.

Of course, not all climate impacts are well understood. What will happen to sensitive aquatic and terrestrial ecosystems? How will endangered species fare? Will government policies be effective at reducing damages, or may they actually increase these damages? For example, will governments continue to encourage people to live in floodplains and vulnerable coastal lands through subsidized insurance and disaster relief programs? Can we design effective dynamic conservation plans? Are there other impacts that we have not anticipated? Future research and monitoring need to continue so that public and private decision making can be undertaken on the basis of sound knowledge.

DISCLOSURE STATEMENT

The authors are not aware of any affiliations, memberships, funding, or financial holdings that might be perceived as affecting the objectivity of this review.

LITERATURE CITED

Adams R, Fleming R, Chang C, McCarl B, Rosenzweig C. 1993. *A Reassessment of the Economic Effects of Global Climate Change on U.S. Agriculture.* Washington, DC: US EPA

Adams RM, Fleming RA, Chang CC, McCarl BA, Rosenzweig C. 1995. A reassessment of the economic-effects of global climate-change on US agriculture. *Clim. Change* 30(2):147–67

Adams RM, McCarl BA, Segerson K, Rosenzweig C, Bryant KJ, et al. 1999. Economic effects of climate change on US agriculture. See Mendelsohn & Neumann 1999, pp. 18–54

Adams RM, Rosenzweig C, Peart R, Ritchie J, McCarl B, et al. 1990. Global climate change and U.S. agriculture. *Nature* 345:219–24

Bachelet D, Neilson RP, Lenihan JM, Drapek RJ. 2001a. Climate change effects on vegetation distribution and carbon budget in the U.S. *Ecosystems* 4:164–85

Bachelet D, Lenihan JM, Daly C, Neilson RP, Ojima DS, Parton WJ. 2001b. MC1: a dynamic vegetation model for estimating the distribution of vegetation and associated ecosystem fluxes of carbon, nutrients and water. *USDA Tech. Rep.* PNW-GTR-508 1-95, For. Serv. Gen.

Berck P. 1979. The economics of timber: a renewable resource in the long run. *Bell J. Econ.* 10:447–62

Berck P, Bentley W. 1997. Hotelling's theory, enhancement, and the taking of the Redwood National Park. *Am. J. Agric. Econ.* 79:287–98

Cacho O, Hean R, Wise R. 2003. Carbon accounting methods and reforestation incentives. *Aust. J. Agric. Resour. Econ.* 47:153–74

Cline WR. 1996. The impact of global warming on agriculture: comment. *Am. Econ. Rev.* 86:1309–11

Crosson P. 1993. Impacts of climate change on the agriculture and economy of the Missouri, Iowa, Nebraska and Kansas (MINK) region. In *Agricultural Dimensions of Global Climate Change,* ed. H Kaiser, T Drennen. Boca Raton, FL: St. Lucie Press

Darwin R. 1999. The impact of global warming on agriculture: a Ricardian analysis. Comment. *Am. Econ. Rev.* 89:1049–52

Darwin R, Tsigas M, Lewandrowski J, Raneses A. 1996. Land use and cover in ecological economies. *Ecol. Econ.* 17:157–81

Deschenes O, Greenstone M. 2007. The economic impacts of climate change: evidence from agricultural output and random fluctuations in weather. *Am. Econ. Rev.* 97:354–85

Dinar A, Hassan R, Mendelsohn R, Benhin J. 2008. *Climate Change and Agriculture in Africa: Impact Assessment and Adaptation Strategies*. London: EarthScan

Easterling W, Crosson P, Rosenberg N, McKenney M, Katz L, Lemon K. 1993. Agricultural impacts of and response to climate change in the Missouri-Iowa-Nebraska-Kansas (MINK) region. *Clim. Change* 24:23–61

Emanuel K, Sundarajan R, Williams J. 2008. Hurricanes and global warming: results from downscaling IPCC AR4 simulations. *Am. Meteorol. Soc.* 89:347–67

Fischer G, Frohberg K, Keyzer MA, Parikh KS. 1988. *Linked National Models: A Tool for International Policy Analysis*. Dordrecht: Kluwer Acad.

Fischer G, Shah M, Tubiello FN, van Velthuizen H. 2005. Socio-economic and climate change impacts on agriculture: an integrated assessment, 1990–2080. *Philos. Trans. R. Soc. Lond. Ser. B.* 360(1463):2067–83

Fleischer A, Lichtman I, Mendelsohn R. 2008. Climate change, irrigation, and Israeli agriculture: Will warming be harmful? *Ecol. Econ.* 67:109–16

Food Agric. Organ. 2006. *FAOSTAT*. http://faostat.fao.org/Portals/_Faostat/documents/pdf/world.pdf

Friedl MA, Mciver DK, Hodges JCF, Zhang XY, Muchoney D, et al. 2002. Global land cover from MODIS: algorithms and early results. *Remote Sens. Environ.* 83:287–302

Gbetibouo GA, Hassan RM. 2005. Measuring the economic impact of climate change on major South African field crops: a Ricardian approach. *Glob. Planet. Change* 47:143–52

Gleick P. 1987. The development and testing of a water balance model for climate impacts assessment: modeling the Sacramento River. *Water Resour. Res.* 23:1049–61

Haxeltine A, Prentice I. 1996. BIOME3: an equilibrium terrestrial biosphere model based on ecophysical constraints, resource availability, and competition amongst plant functional types. *Glob. Biogeochem. Cycles* 10:693–709

Hertel T, ed. 1999. *Global Trade Analysis: Modeling and Applications*. Cambridge, UK: Cambridge Univ. Press

Hotelling H. 1931. The economics of exhaustible resources. *J. Polit. Econ.* 39:137–75

Howitt R, Pienaar E. 2006. Agricultural impacts. See Smith & Mendelsohn 2006, pp. 188–207

Hurd BH, Callaway JM, Smith JP, Kirshen P. 1999. Economic effects of climate change on US water resources. See Mendelsohn & Neumann 1999, pp. 133–77

Hurd B, Harrod M. 2001. Water resources: economic analysis. In *Global Warming and the American Economy: A Regional Analysis*, ed. R. Mendelsohn. Cheltenham, UK: Edward Elgar

Iglesias A, Minguez MI. 1996. Modeling crop-climate interactions in Spain. Vulnerability and adaptation of different agricultural systems to climate change. *Mitig. Adapt. Strat. Glob. Change* 1:273–88

IPCC (Intergov. Panel Clim. Change). 2007a. *Impacts, Adaptation and Vulnerability*. Cambridge, UK: Cambridge Univ. Press

IPCC (Intergov. Panel Clim. Change). 2007b. *Mitigation of Climate Change*. Cambridge, UK: Cambridge Univ. Press

IPCC (Intergov. Panel Clim. Change). 2007c. *The Physical Science Basis*. Cambridge, UK: Cambridge Univ. Press

Jin Z, Ge D, Chen H, Fang J. 1994. Effects of climate change on rice production and strategies for adaptation in southern China. In *Implications of Climate Change for International Agriculture: Crop Modeling Study*, ed. C Rosenzweig, A Iglesias. Washington, DC: EPA

Jorgenson DW, Goettle RJ, Hurd BH, Smith JB, Chestnut LG, Mills DM. 2004. *U.S. Market Consequences of Global Climate Change*. Washington, DC: Pew Cent. Glob. Clim. Change

Joyce L, Mills R, Heath L, McGuire A, Haynes R, Birdsey R. 1995. Forest sector impacts from changes in forest productivity in the United States. *J. Biogeogr.* 22:703–13

Kaiser HM, Riha SJ, Wilkes DS, Rossiter DG, Sampath RK. 1993. A farm-level analysis of economic and agronomic impacts of gradual warming. *Am. J. Agric. Econ.* 75:387–98

Kapetanaki G, Rosenzweig C. 1996. Impact of climate change on maize yield in central and northern Greece: a simulation study with CERES-maize. *Mitig. Adapt. Strat. Glob. Change* 1:251–71

Kelly DL, Kolstad CD, Mitchell GT. 2005. Adjustment costs from environmental change. *J. Environ. Econ. Manag.* 50:468–95

Kumar KSK, Parikh J. 2001. Indian agriculture and climate sensitivity. *Glob. Environ. Change Hum. Policy Dimens.* 11:147–54

Kurukulasuriya P, Ajwad MI. 2007. Application of the Ricardian technique to estimate the impact of climate change on smallholder farming in Sri Lanka. *Clim. Change* 81:39–59

Kurukulasuriya P, Mendelsohn R. 2008. A Ricardian analysis of the impact of climate change on African cropland. *Afr. J. Agric. Res. Econ.* 2:1–23

Kurukulasuriya P, Mendelsohn R, Hassan R, Benhin J. Diop M, et al. 2006. Will African agriculture survive climate change? *World Bank Econ. Rev.* 20:367–88

Lenihan J, Drapek R, Bachelet D, Neilson R. 2003. Climate change effects on vegetation distribution, carbon, and fire in California. *Ecol. Appl.* 13:1667–81

Lettenmaier D, Brettman K, Vail L, Yabusaki S, Scott M. 1992. Sensitivity of Pacific Northwest water resources to global warming. *Northwest Environ. J.* 8:265–83

Lettenmaier D, Sheer D. 1991. Climate sensitivity of California water resources. *J. Water Resour. Plan. Manag.* 117:108–25

Lund J, Zhu T, Tunaka S, Jenkins M. 2006. Water resource impacts. See Smith & Mendelsohn, pp. 165–87

Maddison D. 2000. A hedonic analysis of agricultural land prices in England and Wales. *Eur. Rev. Agric. Econ.* 27:519–32

Mayaux P, Bartholomé E, Fritz S, Belward A. 2003. *A land-cover map of Africa.* Eur. Comm. Joint Res. Cent., Ispra, Italy

Mellilo J, McGuire A, Kicklighter D, Moore B, Vorosmarty C, Schloss A. 1993. Global climate change and terrestrial net primary productivity. *Nature* 363:234–40

Mendelsohn R. 2006. The role of markets and governments in helping society adapt to a changing climate. *Clim. Change. Spec. Iss.* 78: 203–15

Mendelsohn R, Ávila AFD, Seo SN. 2007. *Incorporation of the Climate Change to the Strategies of Rural Development: Synthesis of the Latin America Results.* Montevideo, Uruguay: PROCISUR

Mendelsohn R, Dinar A. 1999. Climate change, agriculture, and developing countries: Does adaptation matter? *World Bank Res. Obs.* 14:277–93

Mendelsohn R, Dinar A. 2003. Climate, water, and agriculture. *Land Econ.* 79:328–41

Mendelsohn R, Dinar A, Sanghi A. 2001. The effect of development on the climate sensitivity of agriculture. *Environ. Dev. Econ.* 6:85–101

Mendelsohn R, Dinar A, Williams L. 2006. The distributional impact of climate change on rich and poor countries. *Environ. Dev. Econ.* 11:1–20

Mendelsohn R, Neumann JE, eds. 1999. *The Impact of Climate Change on the United States Economy.* Cambridge, UK: Cambridge Univ. Press

Mendelsohn R, Nordhaus W. 1996. The impact of global warming on agriculture. Reply. *Am. Econ. Rev.* 86:1312–15

Mendelsohn R, Nordhaus W. 1999. The impact of global warming on agriculture: a Ricardian analysis. Reply. *Am. Econ. Rev.* 89:1046–8

Mendelsohn R, Nordhaus W, Shaw D. 1994. Measuring the impact of global warming on agriculture. *Am. Econ. Rev.* 84:753–71

Mendelsohn R, Nordhaus W, Shaw D. 1999. The impact of climate variation on US agriculture. See Mendelsohn & Neumann 1999 pp. 55–74

Mendelsohn R., Williams L. 2004. Comparing forecasts of the global impacts of climate change. *Mitig. Adapt. Strat. Glob. Change* 9:315–33

Nash L, Gleick P. 1993. The Colorado River Basin and climatic change: the sensitivity of streamflow and water supply to variations in temperature and precipitation. *US EPA Rep. 230-R-93-009*, Washington, DC

Neilson R, Pitelka L, Solomon A, Nathan R, Midgley G, et al. 2005. Forecasting regional to global plant migration in response to climate change. *Bioscience* 55:749–59

Ng W, Mendelsohn R. 2005. The impact of sea-level rise on Singapore. *Environ. Dev. Econ.* 10:201–15

Ng W, Mendelsohn R. 2006. The impact of sea-level rise on non-market lands in Singapore. *Ambio* 35:289–96

Nordhaus WD. 1991. To slow or not to slow: the economics of the greenhouse effect. *Econ. J.* 101:920–37

Onyeji SC, Fischer G. 1994. An economic analysis of potential impacts of climate change in Egypt. *Glob. Environ. Change Policy Dimens.* 4:281–99

Parry ML, Rosenzweig C, Iglesias A, Livermore M, Fischer G. 2004. Effects of climate change on global food production under SRES emissions and socio-economic scenarios. *Glob. Environ. Change* 14:53–67

Perez-Garcia J, Joyce L, McGuire A, Binkley C. 1997. Economic impact of climate change on the global forest sector. In *Economics of Carbon Sequestration in Forestry*, ed. R Sedjo, R Sampson, J Wisniewski, pp. 123–29. Boca Raton, FL: Lewis Publ.

Quiggin J, Horowitz JK. 1999. The impact of global warming on agriculture: a Ricardian analysis. Comment. *Am. Econ. Rev.* 89(4):1044–45

Reilly J, Tubiello FN, McCarl B, Mellilo J. 2001. Impacts of climate change and variability on agriculture. In *US National Assessment Foundation Document. National Assessment Synthesis Team*. Washington, DC: US Glob. Change Res. Program

Reinsborough MJ. 2003. A Ricardian model of climate change in Canada. *Can. J. Econ.* 36:21–40

Richards K, Stokes C. 2004. A review of forest carbon sequestration cost studies: a dozen years of research. *Clim. Change* 63:1–46

Rosenzweig C, Parry M. 1994. Potential impact of climate change on world food supply. *Nature* 367:133–38

Sands RD, Edmonds JA. 2005. Climate change impacts for the coterminous USA: an integrated assessment. Part 7. Economic analysis of field crops and land use with climate change. *Clim. Change* 69:127–50

Sanghi A, Mendelsohn R. 2008. The impacts of global warming on farmers in Brazil and India. *Glob. Environ. Change* 18:655–65

Sathaye J, Makundi W, Dale L, Chan P, Andrasko K. 2007. GHG mitigation potential, costs and benefits in global forests: a dynamic partial equilibrium approach. *Energy J.* 3:127–72

Schlenker W, Hanemann M, Fischer AC. 2005. Will US agriculture really benefit from global warming? Accounting for irrigation in the hedonic approach. *Am. Econ. Rev.* 95:395–406

Schlenker W, Hanemann WM, Fisher AC. 2006. The impact of global warming on US agriculture: an econometric analysis of optimal growing conditions. *Rev. Econ. Stat.* 81:113–25

Seo N, Mendelsohn R. 2008a. Measuring impacts and adaptation to climate change: a structural Ricardian model of African livestock management. *Agric. Econ.* 38:150–65

Seo N, Mendelsohn R. 2008b. A Ricardian analysis of the impact of climate change on South American farms. *Chil. J. Agric. Res.* 68:69–79

Seo N, Mendelsohn R, Dinar A, Hassan R, Kurukulasuriya P. 2009. A Ricardian analysis of the distribution of climate change impacts on agriculture across agro-ecological zones in Africa. *Environ. Resour. Econ.* In press. doi:10.1007/s10640-009-9270-z

Seo SN, Mendelsohn R, Munasinghe M. 2005. Climate change and agriculture in Sri Lanka: a Ricardian valuation. *Environ. Dev. Econ.* 10:581–96

Smith J, Mendelsohn R, eds. *The Impact of Climate Change on Regional Systems: A Comprehensive Analysis of California*. Northampton, MA: Edward Elgar

Sohngen B, Brown S. 2008. The cost and quantity of carbon sequestration by extending the forest rotation age. *Clim. Policy* 8:435–51

Sohngen B, Mendelsohn R. 1998. Valuing the market impact of large-scale ecological change: the effect of climate change on US timber. *Am. Econ. Rev.* 88:686–710

Sohngen B, Mendelsohn R. 2003. An optimal control model of forest carbon sequestration. *Am. J. Agric. Econ.* 85:448–57

Sohngen B, Mendelsohn R, Sedjo R. 1999. Forest management, conservation and global timber markets. *Am. J. Agric. Econ.* 81:1–13

Sohngen B, Mendelsohn R, Sedjo R. 2002. A global model of climate change impacts on timber markets. *J. Agric. Resour. Econ.* 26:326–43

Strzepek KM, Yates DN, El. Quosy DE. 1996. Vulnerability assessment of water resources in Egypt to climate change. *Clim. Res.* 6:89–95

Tol R. 2002. New estimates of the damage costs of climate change. Part I: benchmark estimates. *Environ. Resour. Econ.* 21:47–73

VEMAP. 1995. Vegetation/ecosystem modeling and analysis project: comparing biogeography and biogeochemistry models in a continental-scale study of terrestrial ecosystem responses to climate change and CO_2 doubling. *Glob. Biogeochem. Cycles* 9:407–37

Wang J, Mendelsohn R, Dinar A, Huang J, Rozelle S, Zhang L. 2009. The impact of climate change on China's agriculture. *Agric. Econ.* 40:323–37

Winters P, Murgai R, Sadoulet E, De Janvry A, Frisvold G. 1998. Economic and welfare impacts of climate change on developing countries. *Environ. Resour. Econ.* 12:1–24

Yohe G, Neumann JH, Marshall P. 1999. The economic damage induced by sea level rise in the United States. See Mendelsohn & Neumann 1999, pp. 178–208

You SC. 2001. Agricultural adaptation to climate change in China. *J. Environ. Sci.* 13:192–97

Urban Growth and Climate Change

Matthew E. Kahn

Institute of the Environment and Department of Economics, University of
California, Los Angeles, California 90095; NBER, Cambridge, Massachusetts
02138; email: mkahn@ioe.ucla.edu

Annu. Rev. Resour. Econ. 2009. 1:333–49

First published online as a Review in Advance on
June 26, 2009

The *Annual Review of Resource Economics* is
online at resource.annualreviews.org

This article's doi:
10.1146/annurev.resource.050708.144249

Key Words

global externality, tragedy of the commons, adaptation, incidence,
cities, global warming

Abstract

Between 1950 and 2030, the share of the world's population that
lives in cities is predicted to grow from 30% to 60%. This urbanization has consequences for the likelihood of climate change and
for the social costs that climate change will impose on the world's
quality of life. This paper examines how urbanization affects
greenhouse gas production, and it studies how urbanites in the
developed and developing world will adapt to the challenges posed
by climate change.

1. INTRODUCTION

Climate change is the leading environmental challenge we face. Climate scientists continue to investigate the amount by which we must reduce global greenhouse gas (GHG) production to mitigate the impacts of climate change (Hansen et al. 2008). They measure the atmospheric concentration of carbon dioxide in parts per million (ppm). "Very roughly, stabilization at 500 ppm requires that emissions be held near the present level of 7 billion tons of carbon per year for the next 50 years, even though they are currently on course to more than double" (Pacala & Socolow 2004).

The fundamental challenge posed by climate change is that GHG emissions represent a global externality. No individual, firm, or nation has an incentive to unilaterally reduce its emissions. Such an action would be costly and would have only a minor impact on reducing aggregate global GHG emissions. Given that the world's population equals roughly 7 billion, global annual average per-capita carbon emissions would need to decline to 1 ton to achieve the aggregate goal described by Pacala & Socolow (2004). To put this target in perspective, if a person drives merely 7817 miles per year using a vehicle whose fuel economy is 25 miles per gallon, then this person would already exceed this target. Each person in the United States is currently producing 18 tons of carbon dioxide per year.

Is city growth exacerbating this problem? Around the world, people are moving to cities. In 1950, 30% of the world's population lived in cities. In 2000, this fraction grew to 47%, and it is predicted to rise to 60% by 2030 (United Nations 2004). This paper melds insights from urban and environmental economics to answer two main questions. First, does urban growth increase or decrease world GHG emissions? In the absence of explicit carbon incentives, we examine how city growth affects GHG production. Second, as climate change takes place, how will different cities in developed and developing nations cope and adapt?

Cities are the engine of capitalist growth. Over time, people move from rural to urban areas as they seek a higher standard of living. In cities, people earn higher incomes and thus have the financial resources to purchase more consumption products ranging from private transportation to larger homes. Urbanization increases the demand for residential and commercial electricity consumption. Although urbanites produce more emissions per capita than do rural residents, they also choose to have fewer children. Urbanization also facilitates discovery and diffusion of new ideas. Although these last two factors suggest that urbanization could actually reduce the world's stock of GHG emissions, up until this point the sheer scale of consumption growth has overwhelmed the beneficial effects of urbanization. One major reason for this is the lack of strong incentives to economize on GHG emissions. In the absence of a global carbon tax, this retards targeted induced innovation intended to reduce GHG emissions.

In the first section of the paper, I investigate how urban growth affects GHG production when there are no explicit carbon mitigation incentives and contrast this with the likely consequences of urban growth on GHG production in a world that adopts aggressive carbon pricing.

No matter how much we reduce the global stock of GHG emissions, we will experience some climate change. The second half of the paper focuses on urban adaptation to climate change. I examine how it will affect urban quality of life in different cities around the world. How will cities adapt to climate change? Which cities will gain and which will lose? As I document below, climate change is predicted to have significant effects on the average temperature and rainfall of major cities throughout the United States. The best models of future temperature and rainfall indicate that over the next 75 years, Southern California's cities such as Los Angeles will suffer a sharp reduction in climate amenity levels while a few cities in Florida will experience improvements in their climate amenity bundle as a result of climate change.

Climate change also poses a set of high-risk, low-probability events for cities (Weitzman 2009). Cities differ with respect to the levels of risk that they will face and their ability to handle these expected blows. Some coastal cities will experience more severe floods while other cities will suffer from worse heat waves. Given that cities differ with respect to the objective risk that climate change poses, what is the optimal role for the federal government in terms of paying for local public goods such as sea walls? Are moral hazard effects a significant concern? For example, could government investment in coastal protection increase the number of "victims" who locate in coastal areas as public investment crowds out private self-protection?

It is important to investigate how city residents expect to cope with climate change. Around the world, the median voter lives in a city. This paper's analysis is useful for understanding how voters in different cities form expectations concerning how climate change will affect their daily life. Self-interested voters are more likely to support aggressive carbon mitigation if they believe that they will significantly suffer under the business as usual scenario (Cragg & Kahn 2009). Expectations of the incidence of climate change play a key role in determining whether voters prioritize climate change as an important policy issue.

2. URBAN GROWTH'S IMPACT ON GREENHOUSE GAS PRODUCTION

Total GHG emissions are equal to income per capita multiplied by population and GHG emissions per dollar of income. This accounting identity highlights the role that scale and composition effects play in determining pollution production. This product can be calculated at any level of geographical aggregation, ranging from a household to a city to a nation to the world. Given that the marginal damage caused by GHG production is independent of where it is produced, we ultimately care about the world's production of GHG emissions. This equation highlights the mitigation challenge. World population is growing and world per-capita income is growing more quickly than population growth.

How does city growth affect a nation's GHG production? Cities are the key engine of economic growth because they economize on the transportation cost of goods, workers, and ideas (Glaeser 1998). Cities facilitate learning as well as the generation and diffusion of new ideas (Duranton & Puga 2001, Audretsch & Feldman 2004). By encouraging specialization and facilitating trade, cities raise our per-capita income (Glaeser & Mare 2001).

Richer consumers spend more on goods and energy, and a by-product of this activity is more GHGs. The income elasticity of the demand for energy is typically found to be between 0.8 and 1.1 (Nordhaus 1979, Gately & Huntington 2001). The aggregate consequences of income growth can be seen in Beijing, China. In 2001, there were 1.5 million vehicles in Beijing. By August 2008, its vehicle total had grown to 3.3 million. Prominent environmental writers such as Jared Diamond are deeply worried about the growth of the middle class in the developing world:

Per capita consumption rates in China are still about 11 times below ours, but let's suppose they rise to our level. Let's also make things easy by imagining that nothing else happens to increase world consumption—that is, no other country increases its consumption, all national populations (including China's) remain unchanged and immigration ceases. China's catching up alone would roughly double world consumption rates. Oil consumption would increase by 106 percent, for instance, and world metal consumption by 94 percent.

If India as well as China were to catch up, world consumption rates would triple. If the whole developing world were suddenly to catch up, world rates would increase elevenfold. It would be as if the world population ballooned to 72 billion people (retaining present consumption rates).

Diamond (2008, p. A21)

Although vehicles are the most salient example, we can expect to see sharp global increases in the consumption of electricity and residential durables ranging from ovens to refrigerators. Cross-national environmental Kuznets curve research (Schmalensee et al. 1998) has demonstrated that per-capita carbon dioxide emissions rise sharply for nations as they make the transition from low income to middle income and then flatten out as national per-capita income increases further. Unlike in the case of urban lead emissions, richer nations do not appear to be much "cleaner" than middle-income nations (Hilton & Levinson 1998).[1] Recent research has examined the relationship between greenhouse gas emissions and per-capita income within major developing countries such as China. Auffhammer & Carson (2008) created a panel data set of 30 Chinese provinces covering the years 1985 to 2004.[2] They found that a province/year's log of GHG emissions is an increasing and concave function of province/year log of per-capita income.

GHG mitigation represents the ultimate global free-rider problem. Unlike in the case of localized externalities such as urban air pollution or urban water pollution, local and national regulatory authorities have little incentive to regulate such emissions. Even for a nation such as the United States, the basic free-rider logic holds. Sunstein (2007) argued that the fundamental problem is that China and the United States produce roughly 45% of the world's GHG emissions, but that as climate change takes place, these two nations will suffer a much smaller percentage of its costs. If these nations expect to experience large losses from climate change, then they would have a private incentive to mitigate their emissions and to work cooperatively.

This logic has not slowed states such as California from unilaterally pursuing climate change mitigation regulation. In 2006, Governor Arnold Schwarzenegger signed the California Global Warming Solutions Act of 2006 (AB 32). This law commits California to reduce

---

[1]Future microeconometric research should investigate why the marginal increase in GHG is a decreasing function of income. One possible explanation is cobenefits. Consider coal-fired power plants. They emit both GHGs and local pollutants. If their GHG production is reduced, then local air quality also improves and the populace immediately enjoys improvements in public health.

[2]It is useful to contrast these results with other environmental Kuznets curve studies (see Kahn 2006). For local pollutants such as lead, we know that, as nations grow richer, emissions rise owing to scale effects of more driving using leaded gasoline. As nations grow richer, they enact regulations that lower pollution per mile of driving, and lead emissions start to decline as a function of national income. Hilton & Levinson (1998) demonstrated for a cross section of nations how both scale and technique effects vary as a function of national income. The early environmental Kuznets curve literature argued that a per-capita income turning point exists such that for richer nations economic development is positively correlated with reduced pollution levels. More recent research has documented that this finding is not robust (Harbaugh et al. 2002).

its GHG emissions to 80% below its 1990 levels by 2050. The California Air Resources Board is the regulatory agency charged with meeting this goal. It has proposed a bundle of regulations including increasing commercial and residential building energy efficiency, forcing electric utilities to supply power with an ever-growing share of power generated by renewable energy sources, and making utilities participate in a cap and trade market. California is responsible for only 5.9% of the nation's GHGs despite the fact that roughly 18% of the nation lives in California (http://www.purdue.edu/eas/carbon/vulcan/research.html). The United States is responsible for 25% of the world's GHG emissions. Holding the rest of the world's GHG emissions constant, an 80% reduction in California's emissions today would reduce the United States' emissions by 1.18% and the world's emissions by 0.3%. This arithmetic highlights that unilateral action yields small aggregate effects.

Urbanization triggers two offsetting forces. Urbanization slows national population growth through changing fertility patterns.[3] This can offset some of the GHG produced as a result of the urban productivity effect. Women have numerous employment opportunities in cities. This encourages women to marry later and delay having their first child. Anticipating that they will live in an urban area with labor market opportunities gives school-age women a greater incentive to invest in their human capital. Given that cities raise women's wages and offer a thick local labor market, women have greater opportunities outside the home. This raises the opportunity cost of having children. Urban land is more expensive than rural land, which provides an incentive for smaller household sizes. Urbanization also facilitates idea generation and diffusion. Proximity enhances the ability of firms to exchange ideas and be cognizant of important new knowledge (Audretsch & Feldman 2004).

3. URBAN ADAPTATION TO CARBON PRICING

The adoption of a credible carbon-trading market, or a carbon tax, could incentivize polluters to change their behavior. These policies could induce innovation to reduce GHG emissions per dollar of output (Metcalf 2007, Stern 2008).[4] Despite the fundamental free-rider problem, regional carbon-trading agreements have been implemented in Europe (see Ellerman & Buchner 2007, Kruger et al. 2007) and in North American's East Coast (http://www.rggi.org/home) and West Coast (http://www.westernclimateinitiative.org/Index.cfm).

If the United States participated in a national cap and trade system, how would cities adapt? Cities differ with respect to their marginal contribution to GHG production. Under the assumption that a ton of carbon dioxide is priced at $43, Glaeser & Kahn (2008) documented that the marginal social cost of moving a household from a high GHG city such as Houston, Texas, to a low GHG city such as San Francisco, California, is roughly $600 per year. Relative to a "green city" such as San Francisco, Houston's humid summer climate requires much more electricity consumption for air conditioning. Houston's cheaper housing encourages households to buy more housing and this increases their energy consumption. Houston's low population density and spread out employment mean that people rely on private vehicles for transportation and few use public transit.

---

[3]For a sociologist's perspective on the causal role of urbanization in explaining differential rural/urban fertility, see the work of White et al. (2005).

[4]Metcalf (2007) based his analysis on a starting tax of $15 per ton of carbon dioxide. This rises over time such that it equals $50 in year 2005 dollars by the year 2050. This is a much smaller number than Stern's (2008) estimate of a marginal social damage cost of $85 per ton of carbon dioxide.

Houston's electricity is generated by dirtier power plants than those which generate San Francisco's electricity. A majority of California's power plants are fired by natural gas rather than the dirtier coal used by other power plants. The study by Glaeser & Kahn (2008) quantifies cross-city differences at a point in time (year 2000). How this ranking of cities would change in the presence of a carbon tax and how these city rankings compare in developing countries such as China and India remain open questions. The baseline carbon production differentials between cities such as San Francisco and Houston indicate that the adoption of carbon pricing would be capitalized into local land prices and wages. All else being equal, San Francisco's rents would rise relative to Houston's.

The durability of residential and commercial buildings introduces differential effects from carbon pricing in booming cities versus declining cities. Consider growing cities in the western United States such as Las Vegas, Nevada, and Phoenix, Arizona. As these cities grow, new residential and commercial buildings will be constructed. Facing a carbon tax, real estate developers will have incentives to produce buildings whose marginal energy consumption is less than the incumbent capital stock's average. Contrast these growing cities with shrinking cities such as Buffalo, New York, and Detroit, Michigan. In such cities with very cold weather and low amenities, there is little new construction. In the face of carbon pricing, two possible outcomes emerge: One possibility is that carbon pricing will accelerate the demolition of older energy-inefficient buildings. This logic is similar to the claim of how higher gas prices affect the scrappage rate of used sport utility vehicles. This is especially likely in cities whose power is generated by coal-fired power plants. Whether real estate owners in declining cities will make significant investments in retrofitting existing buildings to improve their energy efficiency is an open question. This hinges on whether energy efficiency investments are capitalized into real estate prices and what is the short-term present discounted value of electricity expenditure savings. In a booming city, the real estate owner who chooses to retrofit an existing building gains the short-run electricity expenditure savings and will gain from the capitalization effect upon selling the asset. The present discounted value of these two terms will be compared with the cost today of retrofitting the building. Such retrofit costs are unlikely to vary across cities.

Another possibility is that carbon pricing will encourage densification within cities and more people will live closer to the city center. How large could these effects be? The 1970s OPEC oil shocks provided one "natural experiment." Urban economists do not believe that this increase in the price of gasoline pushed many people to live in the center cities. Instead, people responded by purchasing smaller, more fuel-efficient vehicles. Today, urban economists are celebrating the high quality of life in consumer center cities (Glaeser et al. 2001). Recent reductions in crime have dramatically improved center-city quality of life (Levitt 2004). Reyes (2007) predicts that crime rates will continue to decline.[5] Street safety and high gas prices both encourage people to live in new urbanistic walking

---

[5]She argues that urban lead exposure is a key determinant of crime. In a nutshell, she argues that, in the 1950s, an increasing number of households were buying cars fueled by leaded gasoline and driving them around their new suburban homes. Although no individual car driver intended to pollute the air, an unintended consequence of rising leaded-gasoline consumption was elevated lead levels. This created public health problems as exposed children suffered from IQ loss and were more prone to attention deficit disorder. The criminology literature has documented that these two factors increase a person's likelihood of becoming a criminal. Indeed, urban crime levels increased from the 1950s to the 1970s. Then, in the early 1970s, the U.S Environmental Protection Agency started its regulatory efforts. With fewer vehicles using leaded gasoline, ambient lead emissions declined, so children born after 1972 were exposed to less ambient lead. And as they became adults (starting in the early 1990s), they committed fewer crimes relative to earlier cohorts.

communities. Weak urban public schools appear to be the last hurdle discouraging adults with young children from living in center cities.

Carbon pricing would encourage electric utilities to rely less on coal-fired power. Based on year 2004 data from the Environmental Protection Agency's EGRID database, the average emissions factor for coal-fired power plants is 50% higher than the average emissions factor for non-coal-fired power plants (see **http://www.epa.gov/cleanenergy/ energy-resources/egrid/index.html**). U.S. states in regions such as the South East feature high average-emitting power plants. In the presence of carbon pricing, these electric utilities would have a strong incentive to change the composition of their power generation and to green their techniques. A health benefit of these efforts is that local air pollution would decline. A cobenefit of taxing carbon dioxide is that ambient pollution from coal-fired power plants would fall. Major cities close to coal-fired power plants would enjoy an improvement in local ambient air quality as these plants cleaned up their emissions.

Policy makers such as the California Air Resources Board, the agency responsible for meeting the goals set in AB 32, have voiced tremendous optimism that carbon pricing will offer a "free lunch" as households and firms will experience a net reduction in the present discounted value of their electricity expenditures (**http://www.arb.ca.gov/cc/scopingplan/ document/economic_appendix1.pdf**). Such environmental regulators are implicitly embracing a behavioral economics viewpoint that, in the absence of carbon pricing and carbon regulation, households and firms would simply satisfice rather than ruthlessly minimize their electricity expenditures. This claim, which appears to be a close cousin of the Porter Hypothesis, merits further research to test whether real-world consumers and firms need regulatory mandates to push them to make energy efficiency investments that have negative net costs. The California Air Resources Board has also argued that its requirements that electric utilities sharply increase the percentage of their power generated by renewables will catalyze new "green" industry corridors in major cities such as Los Angeles and San Francisco. If firms enjoy sharp learning-by-doing effects such that their costs decline as a function of cumulative experience, then government mandates that require green technologies can help to jump start new urban cores. Whether a new green jobs cluster similar to Silicon Valley emerges remains an open question. If the U.S government adopts anticarbon measures, then this would create a demand-side push that would encourage such green innovation.

4. URBAN ADAPTATION TO CLIMATE CHANGE IN THE UNITED STATES

Even if we could reduce our GHG emissions to zero starting today, we will still experience the consequences of climate change. Relative to a rural agricultural world economy, will we suffer less because we live in cities? Is an urban household insulated from the effects of climate change relative to rural households? Urban households live an indoor life where one's productivity is not a function of outdoor climate. In contrast, farmers know that the quantity and quality of their output are directly related to climate.

Climate change will shift the distribution of temperature and rainfall by varying amounts in different locations. Given that urbanites value quality of life, it is important to consider which cities in the United States will be net "winners" and "losers" as a result of changes in the climate amenity bundle. Quality of life is a key determinant of which cities attract the skilled. The greater number of highly skilled people living in San Francisco than in Detroit must be a function of selective migration rather than any inherent productivity effect from living in San Francisco. From this, we can predict that "consumer cities" with a high quality of life will attract the skilled and thus experience economic growth (Shapiro 2006, Glaeser & Gottlieb 2006, Glaeser et al. 2001).

But this raises the issue, what determines a city's quality of life? Admirers of San Francisco would point to its temperate climate, low pollution levels, amenity beauty, and low crime levels as major attractors. For a city such as San Francisco, climate change will shift its average monthly climate and rainfall. This, in turn, will expose the population to greater air pollution levels as pollutants such as ozone reach their highest levels in the summer heat.

Given the predictability of these climate changes, compensating differentials theory predicts that cities that are now exposed to cooler winters and warmer summers will experience declining home prices and rising wages (Blomquist et al. 1988, Gyourko & Tracy 1991). This logic is based on an open-city model where households can vote with their feet and migrate across cities. If migration costs are zero, spatially tied attributes such as climate will be capitalized into wages and rents such that the marginal household becomes indifferent about living in a "nice" city as opposed to one with a low quality of life. Climate change is likely to change this spatial equilibrium.

To investigate the possible size of these effects, I use county level data from the year 2000 Census of Population and Housing. I estimate some simple hedonic home-price regressions. The dependent variable is the county's average home price. I control for no explanatory variables except for a vector of county climate variables. Provided by Olivier Deschenes, these climate data are also used in other work by Deschenes & Greenstone (2007a,b). In the regressions here, the key explanatory variables are a county's average temperature and average rainfall, both measured in January and July from 1968 to 2000. Table 1 shows one ordinary least squares regressions based on Equation 1.

Table 1   Cross-county hedonic home price regression (year 2000)[a]

	Beta[b]	t-stat
January rainfall (measured in inches)	36339.89	11.37
January rainfall squared	−4236.50	−11.42
January temperature (degrees F)	1608.20	5.53
July rainfall	−22834.13	−5.64
July rainfall squared	1566.56	2.85
July temperature	−6527.14	−13.09
Constant	595167.40	19.97
Observations	3105	
R2	0.282	

[a]Regressions weighted by county for population in year 2000. See Equation 1 in the text. The unit of analysis is a county. The dependent variable is the average home price in the county.
[b]This table reports ordinary least squares regression coefficients (Beta) and each regression coefficient estimate's t-statistic (t-stat).

$$\text{Home Price}_i = \alpha + \beta * \text{Climate}_j + \varepsilon_j. \qquad (1)$$

I take the ordinary least squares estimates of β and use these as index weights. These index weights represent the marginal valuation of winter and summer temperature and rainfall in the year 2000.

Climate researchers have developed two different models of climate change's predicted effects for future temperature and rainfall by month by county: the CCSM Model and the H3A1FI Model (for more details, see Deschenes & Greenstone 2007a,b). These models yield county-level predictions over average temperature and rainfall by month between 2070 and 2099. I average the two sets of county-level predictions and use the average January and July predictions for rainfall and temperature. Define this vector of future county climate conditions as $\text{Climate}_{jlfuture}$ and define the historical county climate conditions as Climate_{jlpast}. I then calculate for each county j, the predicted climate change index:

$$\text{climate change(measured in dollars)} = \beta * (\text{Climate}_{jlfuture} - \text{Climate}_{jlpast}). \qquad (2)$$

The estimate of β is based on estimates of Equation 1 (see **Table 1**, column 1). I calculate this dollar climate hedonic index for each county and then aggregate this to the metropolitan area level using the county's year 2000 population level as the weight. Intuitively, this index, measured in dollars, represents the expected dollar gain in metropolitan area quality of life as a result of climate change. Positive values of this index indicate metropolitan areas whose climate quality of life is expected to improve owing to climate change, and negative values indicate expected climate quality of life losses. In **Table 2**, I report the climate index change for all 53 U.S. metropolitan areas that had more than 1 million

Table 2 Predicted change in the climate bundle amenity (2000 to 2080)[a]

Metropolitan area	MSA code[b]	Predicted change in the MSA's climate index[c]
Las Vegas, Nevada	4120	19971
Fort Lauderdale, Florida	2680	12109
West Palm Beach, Florida	8960	406
Tampa, Florida	8280	−10313
Orlando, Florida	5960	−11068
Phoenix, Arizona	6200	−17586
Portland, Oregon	6440	−20945
New Orleans, Louisiana	5560	−26613
Norfolk, Virginia	5720	−32457
Minneapolis, Minnesota	5120	−39151
Detroit, Michigan	2160	−41211
Rochester, New York	6840	−41702
New York City	5600	−42546
Milwaukee, Wisconsin	5080	−43401

Table 2 (cont.)

Metropolitan area	MSA code[b]	Predicted change in the MSA's climate index[c]
Jacksonville, Florida	3600	−45006
New Haven, Connecticut	5483	−48817
Sacramento, California	6920	−50724
Baltimore, Maryland	720	−50825
Hartford, Connecticut	3283	−51877
Salt Lake City, Utah	7160	−52006
Buffalo, New York	1280	−52587
Philadelphia, Pennsylvania	6160	−53649
Houston, Texas	3360	−53815
San Jose, California	7400	−54637
Cleveland, Ohio	1680	−54663
Boston, Massachusetts	1123	−54687
Washington, D.C.	8840	−54708
Denver, Colorado	2080	−57849
Seattle, Washington	7600	−59214
Chicago, Illinois	1600	−61211
Pittsburgh, Pennsylvania	6280	−61908
Columbus, Ohio	1840	−64360
San Antonio, Texas	7240	−67724
Raleigh, North Carolina	6640	−68573
Charlotte, North Carolina	1520	−71427
Greensborough, North Carolina	3120	−74576
Atlanta, Georgia	520	−75238
Indianapolis, Indiana	3480	−75335
Cincinnati, Ohio	1640	−77526
San Francisco, California	7360	−78052
Austin, Texas	640	−80162
Kansas City, Missouri	3760	−81612
Louisville, Kentucky	4520	−84651
Fort Worth, Texas	2800	−88857
St. Louis, Missouri	7040	−89137

Table 2   (cont.)

Metropolitan area	MSA code[b]	Predicted change in the MSA's climate index[c]
Dallas, Texas	1920	−89643
Nashville, Tennessee	5360	−93787
Memphis, Tennessee	4920	−97437
Oklahoma City, Oklahoma	5880	−98875
Orange County, California	5945	−127702
Los Angeles, California	4480	−128733
Riverside, California	6780	−136823
San Diego, California	7320	−144351

[a]For reference, see Equation 2 in text.
[b]MSA, metropolitan statistical area.
[c]Values are all in year 2000 dollars.

people in the year 2000. As a home owner in Los Angeles, California, I am struck by the bottom rows of the matrix: Los Angeles will suffer one of the largest climate amenity losses due to climate change. A look at the raw data reveals the issue. During the historical time period, Los Angeles was blessed with an average August temperature of 75°F. The climate change models are predicting that this area's mean temperature will rise to 90°F by the late twenty-first century.

Climate change will have a differential impact on major-city quality of life. **Table 2** highlights that all of the cities in Southern California are expected to suffer a sharp climate amenity loss due to climate change. In contrast, cities in Florida will experience an improvement in their climate bundle as winter temperatures increase (an amenity) and summer average temperatures rise relatively little. Only three major U.S. metropolitan areas are expected to experience an improvement in their climate bundle due to climate change. Relative real estate prices will adjust to reflect these underlying changes in climate amenities. These effects could be quite large. The average home price in the year 2000 for Los Angeles County was $286,632.8. Thus, the predicted amenity decline of $128,773 reported in **Table 2** represents more than a 50% decline! The climate models are predicting that Los Angeles will have a similar climate amenity bundle as Jacksonville, Florida, by the year 2070.

Climate is just one dimension of risks that cities face owing to climate change. Warmer summer temperatures will raise urban ozone smog levels, and this will reverse some of the recent gains in big-city smog progress (**http://www.epa.gov/airtrends**). Cities also differ with respect to whether they are located on a coast and thus at risk for flooding. All over the United States, people are moving to the coasts (Rapapport & Sachs 2003). As population increases in coastal areas, resulting in more construction, are assets at risk? Pielke and coauthors (Pielke & Downton 2000, Pielke et al. 2008) have documented that population locational trends have increased the risk that more people and capital will be destroyed by floods and hurricanes.

Data indicate that certain coastal cities now face increased risk of flooding due to climate change—think of New Orleans, Louisiana. But are these low-probability events salient enough and large enough to be capitalized into the cross-city hedonic wage and real estate gradients? Risk perception plays a key role in determining the incidence of the amenity dynamics induced by climate change. If safer, more pleasant cities do not command a real estate premium, then land owners in such cities are not enjoying the rents from this dimension of city quality. Conversely, if at-risk cities feature a sharp capitalization effect, then this could affect population sorting. Such cities may be more likely to attract the poor as well as risk lovers.

Experience has shown that government interventions can help cities self-protect against shocks posed by climate change. Although government cannot change the weather, engineering investments such as improved levees help to reduce the risks posed by storms. In the presence of Knightian uncertainty, how do we estimate the expected present discounted value of the benefits we gain from making such engineering investments versus delaying such an investment? Weitzman (2009) sketched some alarming right-tail, low-probability events associated with climate change.

Government investment in city protection can have important implications for the spatial distribution of investment and human capital across a nation. Kousky et al. (2006) offered a useful framework. They modeled the noncooperative investments of the private sector and a government that both recognize that their investments are complementary. For example, suppose that the private sector must decide whether to make an irreversible investment in a new hotel. The government must decide whether to invest in sea walls that reduce the probability of climate change–induced flood. If the private investor believes that the government will build the sea wall, then the expected benefits of building the hotel increase. Symmetrically, if the government believes that the hotel will be built, then its incentive to build the sea wall also increases as more physical assets are now in need of protection. This scenario presents an implicit moral hazard problem. If people and capital that would have self-protected and located in a "safe city" such as St. Louis, Missouri, now locate in New Orleans because they trust that government will invest and protect them, then the government's activism will crowd out self-protection and more people will be at risk from the climate change shock. If the sea walls have a positive probability of crumbling due to Mother Nature's blows, then the *ex post* costs of government activism can be large.

In terms of political economy, politicians based in at-risk areas (e.g., New Orleans) such as mayors and congressional representatives have strong incentives to attract resources to build up their city (Glaeser & Gottlieb 2008). They will lobby for federal financing of local public goods such as sea walls. Indeed, major public transit infrastructure projects such as urban subway systems receive subsidies of up to 80%. The Boston Big Dig is a famous example. But do such investments encourage efficiency or do they breed moral hazard effects as more people move to coastal areas because they feel safe as a result of government investments? If significant federal resources are used to provide local public goods for specific cities, then this will be a redistribution from tax payers in safe cities to tax payers in at-risk areas. This raises efficiency and equity issues.

An interesting, but potentially costly, game of "chicken" could arise. Suppose that cities such as New Orleans want improved sea walls but they want the federal government to pay for them. These cities have an incentive to delay constructing such capital-intensive projects. If they delay, they can pass the costs on to the federal government. Thus, in the short run, they face more climate risk because they are not prepared should disaster strike. An alternative financing approach would be to tax local land owners. In an economy with low cross-city migration costs, urban land owners bear the incidence of improvements in public goods.

Cities that could suffer from the effects of climate change can use public policies and market incentives to reduce *ex ante* risk taking and reduce the costs of adaptation. Cities can use zoning laws to discourage high-density development in at-risk areas. If property insurance prices reflect actuarial risk, then this would discourage building in flood zones and fire zones. Climate change is likely to increase the frequency and severity of such events. Insurance is a regulated market. Whereas economists may support price discrimination such that at-risk areas feature higher insurance premiums, citizens may complain that this is "price gouging." The government may have to provide insurance policies to the public if private firms think that they cannot earn profits in the face of potential regulation (Ross et al. 2007). If governments do not allow the insurance industry to engage in price discrimination, then the *ex post* costs of adaptation will be higher.

An important open question concerns how the population forms subjective expectations over the likelihood of low-probability "bad states of nature." For example, if coastal residents believe that horrific floods never take place, then they will take no precautions against such events. If urbanites form rational expectations regarding the likelihood of future disasters, then real estate prices will be low in areas that face greater risk. This would induce sorting such that risk lovers and the poor would live in the at-risk areas. However, if the public is unaware of the actuarial risk, then the government has a paternalistic justification for investing in public self-protection. An open issue is whether voters will view such investments positively, or if they need to experience additional salient events such as a Hurricane Katrina before they are willing to support costly self-protection investment? The answer partially hinges on whether voters believe climate scientists. If the public views these scientists as alarmists who have been wrong about past predictions, then the government may respond by underinvesting in public self-protection and the public will also underinvest in private self-protection as they underestimate the true threat posed by climate change.

5. ADAPTATION IN CITIES IN DEVELOPING NATIONS

Cities in least developed countries face two additional adaptation challenges. One is the rural to urban migration accelerated by climate change. The other is the increased risks of disease, pollution exposure, and natural disaster faced by informal urban squatters. The following sections sketch the likely consequences of these patterns and suggest a research agenda.

5.1. Rural to Urban Migration

In developing nations, many more people live in rural areas. Many of these people may move to nearby cities if the income they earn from farming declines owing to climate change. Barrios et al. (2006) report that climatic change, as proxied by rainfall, has affected urbanization in Sub-Saharan Africa but not elsewhere in the developing world. Decolonization, which has removed legislation prohibiting the free internal movement of native Africans, has further strengthened this link. In a Harris-Todaro expected utility framework, climate change provides a push from farming areas as previously profitable areas experience a reduction in profitability. An active agricultural economics literature has examined how farmer profitability varies as a function of climate (see the work of Mendelsohn & Dinar 1999). One optimistic claim is that farmers currently suffer less from climate variability than they did in the past. The simplest static expected-income calculation comparison would yield a locational decision rule stating that a farmer should move to the city given the following:

$$\text{Profits farming} <= (\text{probability find job}) * \text{urban wage} - \text{migration cost} - \text{urban rent.}$$
$$(3)$$

In the short term, climate change will lower farming profits, thereby encouraging urbanization. In the medium term, such migration may have general equilibrium effects. As farmers urbanize, equilibrium urban wages will decline and urban rents will increase. These changes in factor prices will slow migration.

5.2. Risks to Urban Poor

Climate change also poses a set of risks to the urban poor. Heat waves, exposure to high levels of urban smog, and climate-related events such as floods and mudslides all threaten this vulnerable group.[6] In the developing world, city governments are not providing high-quality services. Comparative research has documented that governance quality is worse in poorer nations (La Porta et al. 1999). If local governments do not have the revenue to provide basic services such as clean water and sanitation for a growing urban population, then climate change–induced "environmental refugees" can help to unintentionally trigger local urban quality of life challenges. In such nations, the urban poor face the greatest risks from climate change–induced events such as heat waves and flooding. Relative to richer households, they have less access to medical services and household durables to offset climate exposure (e.g., air conditioning, refrigeration). Facing the land price gradient, the poor choose to live in the lowest quality, least desirable parts of the city where rents are low. The inability of the poor to defend themselves from climate change matters because local governments in developing countries are least likely to have financial resources to provide public goods to protect the local population. Such governments are also likely to be unresponsive to the needs of informal squatters who are unlikely to vote.

International research continues to investigate which cities are the "hot spots" of climate risk. A recent OECD study of 130 cities states that merely 10 cities in the world today account for half of the total world exposure to coastal flooding. These cities include the following: Kolkata and Mumbai in India; Dhaka, Bangladesh; Guangzhou, China; Ho Chi Minh City, Vietnam; Shanghai, China; Bangkok, Thailand; Rangoon, Burma (Myanmar); Miami, Florida, United States; and Hai Phong, Vietnam (Nicholls et al. 2008). Future research should examine whether these cities are investing in self-protection (e.g., sea walls) against flooding or are taking proactive steps to move the population away from areas at the highest risk from flooding.

6. CONCLUSION

Relatively little economic research has focused on cities and climate change. This paper argues that the role of cities in causing climate change and the impact that climate change will have on different types of cities represent first-order issues at the intersection of

---

[6]In recent work, I have documented that richer nations suffer fewer deaths from natural disasters than do poorer nations (see Kahn 2005). I argued that income is associated with a higher quality capital stock, better functioning government, and greater medical resources to treat those affected by natural disasters.

environmental and urban economics. After all, urban growth fuels income growth. As people around the world achieve the "American Dream," an unintended consequence is increased per-capita GHG production. Such scale effects unleashed by capitalism suggest that city growth is causing climate change. But, city growth also helps to slow population growth and accelerate technological innovation and diffusion. In a world without explicit carbon pricing, the net effect of urbanization is GHG growth. This paper offers a set of conjectures for how cities will be affected by the introduction of carbon pricing. The investigation of such incentive pricing in both developed and least-developed cities represents an important topic for future research.

This paper also examines how city quality of life will be affected by climate change. Adaptation to climate change can take place at the individual, city, and national levels. Strategic interactions among these three sectors merit future research. Under plausible scenarios, government *ex ante* investments in self-protection (i.e., sea walls) will crowd out self-protection of private individuals and firms.

DISCLOSURE STATEMENT

The author is not aware of any affiliations, memberships, funding, or financial holdings that might be perceived as affecting the objectivity of this review.

LITERATURE CITED

Auffhammer M, Carson RT. 2008. Forecasting the path of China's CO_2 emissions using province-level information. *J. Environ. Econ. Manag.* 55:229–47

Audretsch D, Feldman MP. 2004. Knowledge spillovers and the geography of innovation. Vol. 4. In *Handbook of Urban and Regional Economics*, ed. JV Henderson, JF Thisse, 4:2713–39. Amsterdam: Elsevier

Barrios S, Bertinelli L, Strobl E. 2006. Climatic change and rural-urban migration: the case of Sub-Saharan Africa. *J. Urban Econ.* 60:357–71

Blomquist G, Berger M, Hoen J. 1988. New estimates of quality of life in urban areas. *Am. Econ. Rev.* 78:89–107

Cragg M, Kahn ME. 2009. *Carbon geography: the political economy of congressional support for legislation intended to mitigate greenhouse gas production.* Work. Pap. 13178, NBER

Deschenes O, Greenstone M. 2007a. *Climate change, mortality and adaptation: evidence from annual fluctuations in weather in the US.* Work. Pap. 13178, NBER

Deschenes O, Greenstone M. 2007b. The economic impacts of climate change: evidence from agricultural output and random fluctuations in weather. *Am. Econ. Rev.* 97(1):354–85

Diamond J. What's your consumption factor? *New York Times.* Jan. 2: Op-Ed. http://www.nytimes.com/2008/01/02/opinion/02diamond.html?_r=1&oref=slogin&pagewanted=print January 2, 2008

Duranton G, Puga D. 2001. Nursery cities: urban diversity, process innovation, and the life cycle of products. *Am. Econ. Rev.* 91(5):1454–77

Ellerman AD, Buchner BK. 2007. The European Union emissions trading scheme: origins, allocation, and early results. *Rev. Environ. Econ. Policy* 1(1):66–87

Gately D, Huntington HG. 2001. *The asymmetric effects of changes in price and income on energy and oil demand.* Work. Pap., Stanford Univ. http://www.stanford.edu/group/EMF/publications/doc/OP50.pdf

Glaeser E, Kahn ME. 2008. *The greenness of cities: carbon dioxide emissions and urban development.* Work. Pap. 14238, NBER

Glaeser E, Kolko J, Saiz A. 2001. Consumer city. *J. Econ. Geogr.* 1(1):27–50

Glaeser EL. 1998. Are cities dying? *J. Econ. Perspect.* 12(2):139–60

Glaeser EL, Gottlieb J. 2006. Urban resurgence and the consumer city. *Urban Stud.* 43(8):1275–99

Glaeser EL, Gottlieb J. 2008. *The economics of place-making policies.* Work. Pap. 14373, NBER

Glaeser EL, Mare DC. 2001. Cities and skills. *J. Labor Econ.* 19(2):316–42

Gyourko J, Tracy J. 1991. The structure of local public finance and the quality of life. *J. Polit. Econ.* 91(4):774–806

Hansen J, Sato M, Kharecha P, Beerling D, Masson-Delmotte V, et al. 2008. *Target atmosphere CO$_2$; where should humanity aim?* Work. Pap., Columbia Univ. http://www.columbia.edu/~jeh1/2008/TargetCO2_20080407.pdf

Harbaugh W, Levinson A, Wilson D. 2002. Re-examining the empirical evidence for an environmental Kuznets curve. *Rev. Econ. Stat.* 84(3):541–51

Hilton FGH, Levinson A. 1998. Factoring the environmental Kuznets curve: evidence from automotive lead emissions. *J. Environ. Econ. Manag.* 35(2):126–41

Kahn ME. 2005. The death toll from natural disasters: the role of income, geography and institutions. *Rev. Econ. Stat.* 87(2):271–84

Kahn ME. 2006. *Green Cities: Urban Growth and the Environment.* Washington, DC: Brook. Inst. Press

Kousky C, Luttmer E, Zeckhauser R. 2006. Private investment and government protection. *J. Risk Uncertain.* 33(1):73–100

Kruger J, Oates WE, Pizer WA. 2007. Decentralization in the EU emissions trading scheme and lessons for global policy. *Rev. Environ. Econ. Policy* 1(1):112–33

La Porta R, Lopez-de-Silanes F, Shleifer A, Vishny R. 1999. The quality of government. *J. Law Econ. Organ.* 15(1):222–79

Levitt SD. 2004. Understanding why crime fell in the 1990s: four factors that explain the decline and six that do not. *J. Econ. Perspect.* 18(1):1673–190

Mendelsohn R, Dinar A. 1999. Climate change, agriculture, and developing countries: does adaptation matter? *World Bank Res. Obs.* 14(2):277–93

Metcalf G. 2007. *A proposal for a U.S carbon tax swap.* Work. Pap. 2007-12, Hamilton Proj., Brook. Inst.

Nicholls RJ, Hanson S, Herweijer C, Patmore N, Hallegette S, et al. 2008. *Ranking port cities with high exposure and vulnerability to climate extremes: exposure estimates.* Work. Pap. 1, OECD Environ.

Nordhaus W. 1979. *The efficient use of energy resources*, Cowles Monogr., Yale Univ. Press

Pacala S, Socolow R. 2004. Stabilization wedges: solving the climate problem for the next 50 years with current technologies. *Science* 305:968–72

Pielke RA Jr, Downton MW. 2000. Precipitation and damaging floods: trends in the United States, 1932–97. *J. Clim.* 13(20):3625–37

Pielke RA Jr, Gratz J, Landsea CW, Collins D, Saunders MA, Musulin R. 2008. Normalized hurricane damage in the United States: 1900–2005. *Nat. Hazards Rev.* 9(1):29–42

Rapapport J, Sachs J. 2003. The United States as a coastal nation. *J. Econ. Growth.* 8:5–46

Reyes JW. 2007. Environmental policy as social policy? The impact of childhood lead exposure on crime. *B.E. J. Econ. Anal. Policy* 7(1): artic. 51

Ross C, Mills E, Hecht S. 2007. *Limiting liability in the greenhouse: insurance risk management strategies in the context of global climate change.* Res. Pap. Ser. 07-18, Sch. Law, Univ. Calif. Los Angeles

Schmalensee R, Stoker T, Judson R. 1998. World carbon dioxide emissions: 1950–2050. *Rev. Econ. Stat.* 80(1):15–28

Shapiro J. 2006. Smart cities: quality of life, productivity, and the growth effects of human capital. *Rev. Econ. Stat.* 88:324–35

Stern N. 2008. The economics of climate change. *Am. Econ. Rev.* 98(2):1–37

Sunstein C. 2007. *The complex climate change incentives of China and the United States*. Work. Pap., SSRN

United Nations. 2004. *World population prospects: the 2004 Revision Population Database*. esa.un. org/unpp

Weitzman M. 2009. On modeling and interpreting the economics of catastrophic climate change. *Rev. Econ. Stat.* 91:1–19

White M, Tagoe E, Stiff C, Adazu K, Smith D. 2005. Urbanization and the fertility transition in Ghana. *Popul. Res. Policy Rev.* 24:59–83

Reduced-Form Versus Structural Modeling in Environmental and Resource Economics

Christopher Timmins

Department of Economics, Duke University, Durham, North Carolina 27708;
email: christopher.timmins@duke.edu

Wolfram Schlenker

School of International and Public Affairs, Department of Economics, Columbia
University, New York, New York 10027; email: wolfram.schlenker@columbia.edu

Annu. Rev. Resour. Econ. 2009. 1:351–80

The *Annual Review of Resource Economics* is online at resource.annualreviews.org

This article's doi:
10.1146/annurev.resource.050708.144119

Key Words

structural modeling, Tiebout sorting, hedonics, bioeconomic systems, general equilibrium, functional form, causality, identification, randomization, quasi-experiments

Abstract

We contrast structural and reduced form empirical studies in environmental and resource economics. Both methodologies have their own context-specific advantages and disadvantages, and should be viewed as complements, not substitutes. Structural models typically require a theoretical model and explicit assumptions about structural errors in order to recover the parameters of behavioral functions. These estimates may be required to measure general equilibrium welfare effects or to simulate intricate feedback loops between natural and economic processes. However, many of the assumptions used to recover structural estimates are untestable. The goal of reduced form studies is, conversely, to recover key parameters of interest using exogenous within-sample variation with as few structural assumptions as possible—reducing reliance on these assumptions assists in establishing causality in the relationship of interest. Reduced-form studies do, however, require assumptions of their own, e.g., the (quasi) randomness of an experiment with no spillover effects on the control group.

1. INTRODUCTION

There is an active debate over the advantages and disadvantages of reduced-form versus structural approaches to empirical modeling. While some subfields of economics rely heavily on structural methods (e.g., industrial organization and, more recently, public finance), others tend toward more reduced-form approaches (e.g., labor and development economics). In this article, we review some of the primary issues that arise in the implementation of each methodological approach and discuss the advantages and disadvantages of each. In so doing, we focus our attention on recent examples in environmental and resource economics.

We feel both methodological approaches have important advantages and disadvantages and that each may be better suited to answering particular types of questions. On the one hand, the structural approach is particularly useful in the presence of feedback loops, or when rational agents can reoptimize in response to large policy shifts. Feedback loops pose difficult endogeneity problems that generally make them more difficult to estimate using reduced-form methods. Counter-factual policy simulations that include out-of-sample predictions by definition require structural parameters that model how people readjust in response to the policy.

Reduced-form studies, on the other hand, are better suited to identifying key high-level response parameters as opposed to primitives in a structural model. Causality and identification are established by focusing on the source of variation, while avoiding reliance on untestable functional-form, distributional, and other modeling assumptions, even though it should be noted that reduced-form studies do require assumptions of their own (Smith 2007).

Each approach therefore fills an important niche. One method may be preferable to the other for a particular empirical question, and the two methods may even be used in conjunction with one another to provide different perspectives on the same question. We would encourage the reader to view the methods as complements rather than as substitutes. For example, reduced-form studies can be used to estimate high-level response parameters of interest, e.g., the effect of environmental amenities (clean air, good weather, etc) on humans (e.g., infant health) or the ecosystem (e.g., crop yields) that are then used in structural models to simulate policy responses by economic agents. Recent work by Chetty (2008) highlights these complementarities.

Before beginning with our review, we start with a few disclaimers. First, we do not attempt a comprehensive review of either literature. Rather, the goal of this article is to highlight the strengths and weaknesses of both structural and reduced-form approaches by discussing a carefully selected set of empirical examples. Second, we do not attempt to describe exhaustively each of the papers that we do cite; instead, we focus our attention on the elements of each paper that are most relevant for explaining the strength or weakness in question. Third, although many of the papers are quite technical (especially those using structural methods), we do not use any math in our exposition. There is really no way to do so in a limited way—even with the short list of papers that we consider, describing the technical details of each would unduly extend this article. Instead, we hope that the description we provide will lead interested readers to explore these papers in more depth. We believe that the papers we have chosen provide good references for those interested in implementing these techniques.

The remainder of this article first discusses structural modeling techniques (Section 2) and then moves on to a description of reduced-form methods (Section 3). The discussion of each method begins with a description of the ways in which it may prove useful to environmental economists. That description is then followed by a more detailed accounting of specific papers that illustrate those advantages. Section 4 provides a brief conclusion.

2. STRUCTURAL MODELS IN ENVIRONMENTAL AND RESOURCE ECONOMICS

In this section, we focus on the role of structural models in the analysis of a wide variety of topics in environmental economics. We first pause to define what applied structural modeling is. Put simply, we consider it to be any empirical model where one recovers the parameters of behavioral functions—e.g., demand and supply equations, indirect utility functions of individuals, or the cost structures of firms. One typically begins with a theoretical model, being explicit about what can and cannot be observed by the researcher. Those elements of the model that cannot be observed are then classified as structural errors. These errors are often associated with unobserved heterogeneity across people or choice alternatives, and they are usually "backed-out" from observed behavior for a particular guess at the values of the behavioral parameters. Exactly how this is done will differ tremendously across applications. It could, for example, require simulating dynamic decision making or, alternatively, solving for the equilibrium of a strategic game. These errors allow for the estimation of behavioral parameters by way of an econometric procedure (e.g., generalized method of moments or maximum likelihood) that provides a criterion function on which to evaluate the quality of any particular vector of parameters.

2.1. The Advantages of Structural Modeling

In this section, we list a number of the key advantages associated with structural estimation techniques. Some brief references are made to papers that exploit these advantages, but detailed discussions of particular applications are left to Section 2.4.

Combining environmental systems with human behavior can lead to models with complicated feedback effects. Very often, environmental economists find themselves modeling equilibrium phenomena. Structural models are able to address explicitly those feedbacks. This can have a number of advantages. For example, many of the covariates in these models will be endogenous (e.g., congestion in a recreation demand or Tiebout sorting model). The structure of the model may suggest instrumental variables strategies to deal with those endogenous variables and recover consistent estimates, where otherwise valid instruments may be hard to find. See, for example, Murdock & Timmins (2007) and Bayer & Timmins (2007), which are discussed in further detail below.

Considering large policies (exactly what we mean by "large" will become clearer in the context of the applications we consider), welfare impacts may need to account explicitly for feedback effects. For example, a change in environmental quality in a neighborhood may induce people to re-sort across neighborhoods in a Tiebout fashion, changing important endogenous local attributes such as racial composition. Other neighborhood attributes (e.g., crime, school quality, traffic, and proximity to open space[1]) may vary with the socioeconomic characteristics of residents as well. In a different context, fish stocks affect

---

[1]See Walsh (2007) and Klaiber & Phaneuf (2009) for examples of models that evaluate open-space policies accounting for the endogeneity of private land conversion decisions in an equilibrium framework.

the allocation of fishing effort, but fishing effort affects those stocks through the harvest. An exogenous change in stocks or the cost of effort will set in motion the re-equilibration of the entire system.

Especially in the environmental context, feedback effects can work through natural/biological systems. Human behavior will impact biological processes (differentially in different places), and biological processes can induce varied, highly nonlinear feedback effects. Structural models allow one to make out-of-sample predictions of the impact of policy when feedback effects and nonlinearities are important. Of course, being able to make such predictions often relies crucially on assumptions one has to make about the functional form of behavioral equations, the distributions of unobservables, and other modeling assumptions. Looking for ways to test the validity of these assumptions (e.g., by investigating a model's ability to predict outcomes that are not used for model identification) is one of the most important areas for future research in structural modeling.

More generally, structural models can be useful when it comes to monetizing welfare effects, which is critical for doing cost-benefit analysis when the sources of benefits are diverse. For example, consider gasoline taxes versus CAFE (corporate average fuel economy) standards (a comparison we return to below). The former will operate mostly through the intensive margin (i.e., how often to drive), whereas the latter operates primarily through the extensive margin (i.e., which car to purchase or, more generally, whether to drive at all). Effects on each margin can have important policy implications. More generally, environmental economists need to combine health effects, amenity effects, effects on the quality of recreational uses, employment effects, etc., to value fully the welfare effects of a policy. Structural modeling allows us to convert many effects into a common denominator (i.e., dollars) through the lens of a utility function and an estimate of the marginal utility of income.

There are a number of other ways in which writing down a structural model can be useful in environmental contexts. First, doing so allows for the explicit modeling of heterogeneity in preferences and budget constraints. This can be important because heterogeneity can impact the effectiveness of a policy and its distributional impacts. Jacobsen (2008), discussed in further detail below, modeled the dynamic interactions between CAFE standards and the used-car market. Doing so, he found that it is not rich, new-car buyers who ultimately bear the costs of the policy, as is typically assumed, but rather the poor, who disproportionately buy used cars.

Second, in many environmental applications, policies affect interlinked decisions—e.g., whether to buy a fuel-efficient appliance or not (the extensive margin) and how much to use it (the intensive margin). Heterogeneity matters in this context as well—in particular, we do not want to treat these decisions as separate, because people who are more likely to buy a more efficient appliance may be disproportionately more or less likely to use it more often. The same structural parameters and sources of heterogeneity enter into both decisions. Bento et al. (2009) showed that this plays an important role in calculating the welfare effects of a gasoline tax.

The difference between the intensive and extensive margins is also important in the analysis of recreation demand (i.e., travel-cost models, which use the time costs and other expenditures incurred when visiting a recreation site to value the attributes that it provides). Typically, any particular recreator does not visit most sites—rather, visitors tend to make a few trips to a small subset of sites. Random-utility models are appropriate for studying decisions over a large number of differentiated alternatives, but they become more difficult to apply when multiple decisions made by the same individual are not independent.[2] In contrast, traditional demand systems cannot handle the many zeros typical in these data. Instead, estimators have been developed that make explicit the use of the Kuhn-Tucker conditions that arise because consumption cannot be negative (Phaneuf et al. 2000).

Finally, structural models may often be able to predict or explain unintended consequences of a policy. The strength of a structural model is its ability to simulate counterfactual scenarios. One is able to "turn off" a piece of the policy environment to see how the world would have played out in its absence. This can be important when the policy interacts in a complicated way with the rest of the economic system (e.g., a pollution-control policy that also functions as a barrier to entry that restricts competition).

2.2. Structural Modeling and Tiebout Sorting

The structural approach is particularly useful in the class of models that rely on Tiebout's idea that, by "voting with their feet," individuals reveal their preferences for local public goods and bads. Originally, such models fell into the category of hedonic analysis, a two-stage procedure that first applies reduced-form empirical methods to estimate a hedonic price function. That hedonic price function is then combined with utility theory, which is used to recover preferences in the form of a marginal willingness-to-pay (WTP) function (Rosen 1974). Although the hedonic technique is widely used in academic, government, and consulting applications, it exhibits several well-known problems, many of which can be addressed by applying structural techniques. We now discuss nine instances where we believe this to be the case.

2.2.1. Omitted variables bias.
If important unobserved local attributes covary with the local attribute of interest, the researcher estimating the first-stage hedonic price function will recover a biased estimate of the marginal value of that attribute (Small 1975). One of the simplest solutions to this problem is to exploit variation in that attribute over time, assuming other attributes remain fixed (i.e., house or neighborhood fixed effects). The reduced-form literature has produced a variety of other approaches to deal with the omitted variables problem (see, for example, Chay & Greenstone 2005), whereas instrumental variables solutions have also been incorporated into structural models (e.g., Bayer et al. 2009).

2.2.2. Identification.
The simple linear-quadratic hedonic model does not identify the marginal WTP function (Brown & Rosen 1982). Solutions to this problem have been found in the use of data from multiple markets or functional form restrictions (Mendelsohn 1985), although more recently Ekeland et al. (2004) showed that the linear-quadratic model is a very special case and that, by being flexible about the first stage, the identification problem goes away. Without careful structural modeling of the individual utility maximization decision (checking to see if second-order conditions are satisfied), however, the flexible first stage can yield misleading estimates (Bishop & Timmins 2008).

---

[2]For example, one may redefine combinations of different choices to be new elements of an expanded choice set. If individuals make relatively few decisions [e.g., where to work and where to live, as in Kuminoff (2008)], this will be feasible. For individuals choosing how to allocate a large number of potential recreation opportunities over many different sites, the size of the redefined choice set will become intractable.

2.2.3. Endogeneity. The individual simultaneously picks both the quantity of an amenity and its hedonic price (assuming that price is allowed to vary with the quantity consumed), meaning that the simple hedonic estimation of the marginal WTP function will yield biased estimates (Bartik 1987, Epple 1987). Valid candidates for instrumental variables can be hard to find. Bishop & Timmins (2008) showed how this problem can be avoided with a structural model of the choice of the attribute subject to a nonlinear budget constraint.

2.2.4. Endogenous attributes. Many attributes of interest are formed by the equilibrium process of individuals sorting in a Tiebout fashion (e.g., crime rates, pollution caused by traffic flows, emissions from production activity). As alluded to above, structural modeling may suggest instrumental variables strategies for many of these attributes. Specific examples are described below.

2.2.5. Re-equilibration. In response to large changes in amenities, people may reoptimize. To model welfare effects, we need to know how they do that. Simply modeling the equilibrium hedonic price function is insufficient. This has been the main area where structural models of Tiebout sorting have proven useful. See, for example, Sieg et al. 2004 and Murdock & Timmins 2007.

2.2.6. Choice set. The hedonic model assumes individuals are free to maximize utility with respect to every attribute that enters into utility (i.e., the choice set is dense). In reality, the choice set may contain "holes"—certain combinations of attributes may be unavailable at any price, and individuals are forced to choose the best option from the discrete set of available opportunities. In contrast to the hedonic framework, structural models of Tiebout sorting typically begin from the premise that individuals maximize utility from a discrete set of available choices (e.g., houses or jurisdictions).

In addition, sorting models give the researcher the ability to model interrelated choice sets (e.g., where to live, how much housing to purchase in that location, and where to work) in a straightforward way (Kuminoff 2008). The decisions made in one of these dimensions can have important implications for how responsive individuals will be to policies designed to influence their behavior in other dimensions.

2.2.7. Dynamics. Hedonic models do not treat individuals as though they are forward-looking. However, given the expense incurred and effort involved in buying a house, we may expect that people will care about more than just the current attributes of the house and its neighborhood—they may base decisions on expectations about how those attributes will evolve over time. In the classic dynamic estimation framework developed by Rust (1987), this would involve a computationally prohibitive state space. Recently developed two-step estimators (Hotz & Miller 1993, Arcidiacono & Miller 2008) have helped to avoid these problems. Bishop (2008) applied these new methods to the sort of intercity sorting problem described by Roback (1982). Bayer et al. (2008b) adapted them for use in describing intracity sorting across houses.

2.2.8. Stickiness. Hedonic models do not generally allow for "stickiness" in individual decision making (e.g., transactions costs in a house-price model or moving costs in a wage-hedonic framework). We logically expect that people relocate only when the utility gain from doing so exceeds those transactions costs. In the wage-hedonic context, research shows that people tend to live close to the region of their birth (Bayer et al. 2009), creating a tension within hedonic theory. In particular, the model assumes that individuals face no impediments to mobility in the formation of the hedonic equilibrium, while assuming that no one would reoptimize in response to a large policy. Sorting models, which model the processes that yield the hedonic equilibrium rather than the equilibrium itself, allow for stickiness to be incorporated explicitly into the hedonic equilibrium. For example, Bayer et al. (2009) modeled long-run migration costs (i.e., location at ages 25–35 relative to birth location), whereas Bishop (2008) also included short-run migration costs (i.e., current location relative to location two years prior) in her modeling of forward-looking agents. Moreover, she included search costs (another form of stickiness) in the manner of Kennan & Walker (2005), by allowing people to have better information about labor markets in the areas where they had lived in recently.

2.2.9. Endogenous outcomes. When sorting over labor markets, as is the case in the wage-hedonic model described by Roback (1982), observed wage distributions provide a distorted representation of underlying (unconditional) wage distributions. This insight is from the Roy (1951) model, where individuals sort across employment sectors based on common returns (i.e., returns to education or experience) and idiosyncratic returns (i.e., individuals tend to go where their individual-specific returns are high, shifting up the conditional wage distribution). The complicating factor is that individuals also sort based on nonwage factors (i.e., amenities). Bayer et al. (2008a) described the problems that arise in identifying the role of these amenities and showed how they (and the wage distributions from which sorting individuals receive draws) can be recovered nonparametrically. Deleire & Timmins (2008) employed a similar approach to model the sorting of workers across occupations that underlies the wage-hedonic measurement of the value of a statistical life, accounting for Roy sorting. This is akin to the classic Roy job-sorting application; the main difference is that people are allowed to care about nonwage job attributes such as fatality risk. Controlling for the biases caused by Roy sorting raises the value of a statistical life estimated by Deleire & Timmins (2008) by as much as a factor of 4, compared with the traditional wage-hedonic estimate.

2.3. Drawbacks of Structural Approaches in Sorting Models

It is worth pausing at this point to mention some of the drawbacks of structural approaches to modeling Tiebout sorting behavior. While able to deal with many of the problems described above, a tractable sorting model requires the researcher to specify a choice set, define limits on mobility, establish parametric restrictions on utility, and impose distributional assumptions on random parameters. These modeling choices are not inconsequential and should be verified whenever possible (e.g., by estimating the model with a subset of the data and checking its ability to predict behavior in the remaining data). Kuminoff (2009) investigated the role played by each of these structural assumptions in identifying nonmarket values.

Structural models used to predict the equilibrium impacts of large policy changes may require even more modeling assumptions. For example, a model of sorting over both labor and housing markets may require additional assumptions such as having the spatial distribution of employers and the supply of heterogeneous housing remain fixed in order to calculate counterfactual labor and housing market equilibria. In the long run, these may be particularly poor assumptions. Although nothing, in principle, prohibits one from relaxing these assumptions, data and computational burdens may make doing so impractical.

2.4. Examples of Structural Estimation in Environmental and Resource Economics

Smith & Wilen (2003) re-examined the effectiveness of marine reserves—spatially delineated closures of fishing areas designed to prevent overexploitation and allow for regrowth of a fish stock. For years, reserves have been thought of as one of the most promising options for managing declining fisheries (as opposed to regulating the length of the fishing season or imposing gear restrictions). This impression, however, has been based largely on models that did not realistically describe how fishermen would respond to the imposition of reserve restrictions. Prior to this paper, models tended to assume that fishermen would reallocate effort evenly over the remaining unregulated fishing grounds. Working with data from the Northern California sea urchin fishery, Smith & Wilen instead used a behavioral model to describe how fishermen would reallocate effort; they then connected that model to a realistic description of biological processes.[3] Factors affecting the decision of whether to fish (and if so, in which patches) include abundance, weather risk, price, travel distance, and the spatial distribution of closures. Both biology and behavior are important to policy conclusions. In particular, in the behavioral model, unattractive patches serve as de facto reserves. In combination with a declining overall effort on the part of fishermen in response to the imposition of a reserve, this leads to an increase in the production of sea urchin eggs. However, whereas the model that naïvely assumes a uniform redistribution of effort in response to a closure predicts an overall increase in harvest, the model that assumes an optimizing reallocation of effort predicts a reduction in total harvest, owing to the reduction in the optimizing level of effort.

Smith & Wilen (2003) provided an example of the importance of marrying behavioral and biological modeling, particularly when making out-of-sample predictions. Simply using the effects of an observed closure on harvests and egg production to predict the effects of a hypothetical closure may not work. Closing a patch that is particularly important for larval growth will have big impacts on stock and harvest. However, closing a patch in which fishermen have little interest will have little impact. The geography of closures matters as well. Because Northern California sea urchin larvae flow from north to south, closing a northern patch will have very different impacts on behavior and harvest outcomes than would closing a southern patch. Alternatively, a closure that reallocates effort to a patch that is important for larval production can be extremely damaging.

Finally, Smith & Wilen (2003) illustrated the importance of controlling for feedback effects in simulating equilibrium outcomes. Those equilibrium effects operate through biological channels. In particular, increased stock abundance from a closure may lead to increased fishing effort on that patch, thereby diminishing stock in the long run and reducing equilibrium effort. In equilibrium, the reallocation of effort will dampen the initial stock effect.

---

[3]From a biological perspective, sea urchins provide an ideal species with which to study these effects, both because they are "patchy" (i.e., sea urchins live in small, spatially delimited groups) and because there are important larval transmission mechanisms that impact growth rates. For both these reasons, spatial effects matter for sea urchins.

Murdock & Timmins (2007) looked instead at the behavior of recreational anglers, with the goal of determining the welfare effects of a "large" policy. This paper follows the established methodological approach of using the trade-offs made by individuals when choosing a recreation site to value site attributes. Along with expected catch, an important (but problematic) site attribute that may affect the recreation decision is congestion, i.e., the number of other anglers one expects to encounter. Congestion is problematic because it is likely to be correlated with site attributes that the researcher cannot observe. Crowded sites are likely to be crowded for a reason—they have attractive features that draw in anglers. The fact that anglers choose sites with attractive unobservables therefore means that they will also tend to choose congested locations. A naïve empirical model concludes from this that they derive utility from congestion.

This conclusion has important implications for valuing the welfare impacts of a large policy change. Murdock & Timmins (2007) considered the effects of closing Lake Winnebago to fishing. Closures (or at least fish consumption advisories) of this sort are typically caused by pollution, e.g., excessive contamination of mercury or polychlorinated biphenyls. Lake Winnebago is the largest lake located entirely inside Wisconsin (measuring approximately 30 by 10 miles in area). It is a popular fishing destination, known particularly for walleye. A closure of this magnitude would send a large number of anglers to substitute sites. A model that understates the congestion costs (or even incorrectly measures the sign of their welfare effect) would not properly account for this impact and would understate the cost of the closure. Properly recovering the unbiased contribution of congestion, Murdock & Timmins (2007) found that the welfare costs of the closure are approximately doubled.

In intuitive terms, congestion externalities can be viewed as a standard endogeneity problem. Even though the angler's decision-making process is described with a random-utility model discrete-choice framework, the solution to the problem can still be expressed in an instrumental variables framework (Berry et al. 1995). The logic of instrumental variables estimation requires a variable that is correlated with the number of other visitors attending a particular site, but uncorrelated with the unobserved attributes of that site. This is where structural modeling enters the picture. With a guess at the parameters of the angler's random-utility function, it is possible to build a prediction of the number of fishermen who would choose each site on the basis of only observable, exogenous attributes (i.e., ignoring congestion and unobservables). By construction, that prediction will be uncorrelated with the unobservable attributes of the location in question, but (assuming observable, exogenous site attributes are consequential in the angler's decision-making process) it will be correlated with the congestion variable. Bayer & Timmins (2007) described this strategy for constructing instruments (which is useful in the cases of congestion, agglomeration, and endogenous neighborhood attributes based on socioeconomic factors and demographics) in more detail.

There are other empirical strategies used in the environmental economics literature to deal with the problem of measuring the spillover impacts of congestion and agglomeration. Hicks et al. (2008) considered the case of commercial fishermen in the Bering Sea, where the effect of congestion on profits may be nonmonotonic. They employed an instrumental variables strategy similar to that used by Murdock & Timmins (2007), but they dealt with a far more complex definition of equilibrium. Phaneuf et al. (2009) demonstrated how the problem can be addressed in the context of the Kuhn-Tucker estimation models described above. Boxall et al. (2005) dealt with a similar problem (modeling congestion in Canadian wilderness canoeing), but they employed a very different remedy for the endogeneity problem. Whereas the approach described above relies on a great deal of choice-set variation to construct powerful instruments, Boxall et al. (2005) showed how an exogenous source of variation can be obtained by combining stated-preference and revealed-preference data. The result is an approach to measuring congestion that is particularly valuable when the choice set is small. Also dealing with a small choice set, von Haefen & Phaneuf (2008) demonstrated how stated-preference data can be combined directly with the empirical strategy described in Murdock & Timmins (2007) to achieve identification. Finally, Pfaff & Robalino (2005) modeled spillover effects in neighbors' decisions about land clearing in Costa Rica. This is another spatially localized form of agglomeration effect. They employed land slope as an instrument, i.e., an exogenous determinant of a neighbor's deforestation decision that can only affect one's deforestation decision through the neighbor's decision. Doing so, they found important evidence of spatial spillovers. This has practical importance for policy makers, as policies designed to reduce deforestation may reduce deforestation activities on plots not directly targeted by those policies.

In no other area of environmental economics are feedback effects more important than when sorting behavior in housing or labor markets is used to value nonmarketed amenities. This is the basis for the hedonic approach, which uses the information in the outcome of the sorting process (i.e., the equilibrium hedonic price function) to value goods ranging from processor speed in computers to human lives, and amenities ranging from air quality to Superfund site proximity. Given the well-known problems with the hedonic method cited in Section 2.3, a new class of estimable Tiebout sorting models has evolved. These models contrast with the traditional hedonic models in that they focus on the process that leads to equilibrium, rather than relying only on the information in the hedonic equilibrium. As a result, many of the problems associated with the traditional hedonic model may be addressed directly.

The first models of local public goods provision and residential location, based on the original ideas of Tiebout (1956), were developed by Epple et al. (1984), Epple & Romer (1991), Fernandez & Rogerson (1996), and Nechyba (1997a, 1997b). An estimation framework for this class of models was then developed by Epple & Sieg (1999). Sieg et al. (2004) used that approach to value air quality in Southern California, paying particular attention to the fact that, were air quality to change nonmarginally, people may find it optimal to live elsewhere (with subsequent changes in the equilibrium prices that clear the housing market). The intuition for the Epple-Sieg estimation strategy is to build a full equilibrium model of the location decisions of heterogeneous households (who differ by income and preferences for public goods), requiring housing prices to adjust to clear the market in every jurisdiction. Two key features of the model facilitate its use. First, all households are assumed to place the same utility weights on different local public goods. For example, no matter whether one has children or not, one puts the same relative weights on air quality and school quality. Everyone is therefore able to agree on a quality ranking for jurisdictions, and all can then make decisions based on how they value jurisdictional quality relative to private consumption. Because of the similarity of this assumption to vertical models of differentiated product demand in industrial organization, this has come to be known as the class of vertical sorting models.

Second, conditional upon having the same preference for jurisdictional quality relative to private consumption, individuals will stratify according to income (i.e., high-income individuals will locate in higher quality jurisdictions). This is a result of a single-crossing property exhibited by utility.[4] The model is closed in the sense that, given a vector of structural parameters, it can predict population, income distributions, housing consumption, and (subject to a normalization) the index of jurisdictional quality in every location. Estimation proceeds by matching elements from the distributions of the first three to observed data. The index of jurisdictional quality can be further decomposed to determine the value individuals place on particular local attributes (e.g., air quality).

In their application, Sieg et al. (2004) considered 103 school districts located in five Southern California counties, and they used data describing housing transactions between 1989 and 1991. They interpolated air quality measures for individual houses, using monitor data for ozone and particulates, and they considered school quality measured by the average math score on the 1992–1993 California Learning Assessment System Grade Level Performance Assessment Test. After recovering structural utility parameters, they used their model to value the welfare improvement associated with the large changes in ozone concentrations in the area between 1990 and 1995 (i.e., a 13.9% average reduction) in both a partial equilibrium (PE) setting (i.e., assuming people do not re-equilibrate) and in a general equilibrium (GE) context (i.e., allowing people to reoptimize in their location choices). In calculating the GE welfare gain, the paper asks the following question: After re-equilibration, how much compensation would everyone need to be given (or have taken away) in order to be returned to her pre-policy level of utility? Calculation of this utility theoretic measure of welfare relies heavily on having recovered estimates of structural utility parameters. It also requires the strong assumption that no individuals are allowed to enter or leave the five counties being considered—i.e., only the decisions of those present at the start of the decade are modeled.

While the average welfare gain in the GE context is only slightly higher than that in the PE context (i.e., $1371 versus $1210), the difference between the two measures can be very large for certain individuals. For example, those in the least expensive school district, who (conditional on income) have revealed a preference for private (relative to public) goods consumption, will have nowhere else to go as the price of housing starts to rise because of improved air quality in their district relative to that in other districts. Assuming these individuals are renters, they are made worse off in the GE model relative to the PE model. Alternatively, those starting in affluent locations with good public goods will do better in the GE framework, as the presence of more quality substitute locations lowers the price they must pay for a home.

Based again on comparisons with the literature on differentiated product demand in industrial organization, the alternative approach to modeling Tiebout sorting behavior is classified as the horizontal approach. Whereas the vertical model required all individuals to agree on a quality index associated with each jurisdiction, the horizontal model allows each individual to potentially place a unique value on each component of the jurisdictional public good. In most applications, individuals are also given an idiosyncratic preference for each jurisdiction. If this preference is drawn from a Type II extreme value distribution, the horizontal location choice model can be written as a logit. If all individuals are allowed to have preferences for each component public good drawn from a random distribution, this is a random parameters logit. If preferences vary only by observable individual attributes, it is described as a heterogeneous parameters logit.

---

[4]In technical terms, single crossing requires the slope of indifference curves in amenity-housing price space to vary monotonically with income, conditional on preferences (and vice versa).

What makes the horizontal sorting model different from a simple multinomial logit model of location choice are the complications imposed by equilibrium. In particular, many of the attributes that are important for location choice are determined in equilibrium by the location-choice process (e.g., neighborhood racial composition, housing services prices, agglomeration or congestion effects in intercity sorting). If these variables are important factors in location choice, then properly estimating how they enter the utility function will be crucial to making accurate GE predictions of the welfare effects of a large policy change. An identification strategy similar to that described in Murdock & Timmins (2007) for recovering the effect of congestion on recreational demand can be employed.

Bayer et al. (2009) used a simpler version of the horizontal model (i.e., one that considers only marginal changes) in a paper that focuses on the role of migration costs in valuing air quality. A casual inspection of Census data describing long-term migration behavior shows that most U.S. residents do not move far from where they were born. For example, between 58% and 79% of household heads were found to be living in the Census division of their birth in the 2000 Census.[5] However, if individuals tend to be born in locations with relatively poor air quality (e.g., the Northeast and Rust Belt), then their failure to move to relatively clean states in the West would bias downward estimates of the disutility associated with pollution, unless these migration costs are modeled explicitly. This paper includes explicit migration costs in the sorting process; doing so nearly doubles the estimate of marginal WTP to avoid a small increase in particulate matter.

Neither the vertical nor the horizontal approach to modeling equilibrium sorting is ideal. On the one hand, the pure vertical model requires all individuals to agree on a relative ranking of jurisdictions based on factors besides housing prices, which is not realistic. Different people will have varying work locations and commuting costs can be important, not to mention the fact that different types of people (e.g., with and without children) will care differentially about public goods (e.g., school quality). On the other hand, horizontal models, which handle these sorts of preference heterogeneity very well, rely to a greater extent on distributional assumptions for identification. In particular, in a vertical model, only neighboring jurisdictions in quality space are potential substitutes, whereas in a horizontal model, every location is one. This feature arises because the horizontal model includes an idiosyncratic preference shock. Because of this shock, every individual has a positive probability of choosing every location.

In the process of building a hybrid model, Kuminoff (2009) explained these trade-offs in clear terms. His Epple-Sieg equilibrium framework nonparametrically bounds individual utility parameters (Epple et al. 2004). By parameterizing the distribution of preference heterogeneity and income, these bounds imply a likelihood function that could be maximized for parameter point identification. Different people can therefore have different relative preferences for the same public goods. Moreover, in common with many horizontal models, Kuminoff (2008) explicitly modeled the fact that individuals choosing over a large geographic area will choose over both housing and labor markets (i.e., where one chooses to live impacts the labor market opportunities available to that individual). In an application to sorting over school districts in Sacramento, California, and the San Francisco Bay Area (close enough that they may be considered to be in the same residential choice set, but far enough

---

[5]The Census Bureau divides the United States into nine divisions: New England, Mid-Atlantic, East North Central, West North Central, South Atlantic, East South Central, West South Central, Mountain, and Pacific.

apart that they constitute separate labor markets), Kuminoff found that incorporating the labor market decision significantly expands the upper bound on possible marginal WTPs for ozone. Many people living in places with high levels of ozone do so because it affords them access to better labor market opportunities. Moreover, by adding preference heterogeneity to the vertical model, the estimated bounds on preference parameters are widened. If one were to use these bounds to carry out maximum likelihood estimation, this would imply that the resulting point estimates would become more sensitive to the assumed distribution of individual preference heterogeneity.

Jacobsen (2008) is an outstanding example of how structural modeling can be used to (a) jointly model multiple interlinked decision processes, (b) explicitly control for the role of heterogeneity in decision making and determine how that heterogeneity affects policy outcomes and incidence, and (c) combine the many complicated effects of policy to arrive at a single welfare estimate that can be used for cost-benefit analysis. Jacobsen (2008) explored the relative effectiveness of CAFE standards and the gasoline tax as tools for reducing gasoline consumption (for an application to digital cameras, which are differentiated only by pixels, see Carranza 2008). Properly modeling these policies requires a model of price setting by imperfectly competitive firms that are differentially affected by tightening CAFE standards. That model must also describe consumers' decisions about which car to buy and how much to drive it. Finally, it needs to account for interactions between the new- and used-car markets.

Modeling the car-purchase and driving decisions is especially important for this application, because most of the benefits of the CAFE standards come on the extensive margin, whereas the gasoline tax matters primarily on the intensive margin. Considering these decisions together is important because of the rebound effect (i.e., after buying a more fuel-efficient car, made less expensive by stricter CAFE standards, the individual may actually choose to drive it more than she would have driven a less fuel-efficient vehicle, thereby reducing the fuel savings).

Incorporating the used-car market turns out to be particularly important, for evaluating both the effectiveness of the CAFE standard and its incidence. When buying a car, consumers have the option of going to either the new- or used-car market. Because of income effects, richer individuals are more likely to purchase a new vehicle. Because the immediate effect of the CAFE standard is to raise new-car prices, the conventional wisdom is that the burden falls mainly on the rich (i.e., a progressive policy). However, modeling the interaction of the new- and used-car markets over time paints a very different picture. Increased CAFE standards today reduce the flow of larger cars to the used market, raising the price of those vehicles and making it more costly for a used-car consumer to buy one. Moreover, the used-car fleet becomes more inefficient as large used cars become more scarce and are less likely to be scrapped.

Finally, looking at the effect of strategic pricing decisions between imperfectly competitive firms, many of the gains of tightened CAFE standards are undone by the fact that violating types (i.e., European importers) find it optimal to sell more large cars to fill the void in the market left by the constrained domestic producers who raise the miles per gallon of their fleet in response to the policy. These firms enjoy increased profits at the expense of the U.S. producers, who bear most of the costs. Accounting for these market equilibrium effects, Jacobsen (2008) found that CAFE standards do a relatively poor job of reducing fuel consumption. Combining all of these effects, the gasoline tax can achieve the same reduction in gasoline use at one-sixth the cost.

2.5. Using Structural Models to Measure the Unintended Consequences of Environmental Policy

We now turn to two papers that use structural models of dynamic decision making to illustrate the unintended consequences of an environmental policy. Very often, dynamic incentives lead to outcomes and policy incidence that differ greatly from that which would be expected on the basis of a simple static analysis. In our first example, Ryan (2006) used a structural model of dynamic decision making to simulate the world in the absence of air quality regulation. He measured the dynamic impacts of the 1990 Clean Air Act Amendments (CAAA) on the producers of Portland cement. Making Portland cement is an extremely polluting activity, and the 1990 CAAA increased the certification requirements for new producers. Although the policy resulted in no immediate changes in variable production costs, the regulation was expected, in the long run, to reduce emissions from the industry. The policy also had the effects, however, of increasing entry costs and reducing entry. These outcomes enabled incumbents to raise prices on consumers.

To measure these unintended consequences, Ryan (2006) required a model of the process governing entry into the industry. Assuming the industry is made up of many small markets, he modeled the strategic pricing, investment, and exit decisions of incumbents, along with the entry decision of a potential new entrant. This is a difficult task because of the dynamic nature of the game played between firms. Typical of the industrial organization literature on dynamic games, Ryan assumed that the price-setting decision is made in a static game played conditional upon dynamic capacity investment decisions. Investment decisions are, however, made given expectations about the investment decisions of rivals. Investment determines capacity, which, in turn, determines production costs. The capital stocks of each firm (both incumbents and potential entrants) are state variables, and solving the game with traditional methods (e.g., Pakes & McGuire 1994) requires the repeated solution to a very high-dimension dynamic programming problem. Because solving this problem even once takes a very long time, embedding it in an estimation algorithm is impractical (i.e., solving it repeatedly for different parameter guesses). Instead, Ryan (2006) employed the estimation algorithm suggested by Bajari et al. (2007) to avoid this problem.

Part of a new wave of two-step estimators (see also Pesendorfer & Schmidt-Dengler 2008, Aguirregabiria & Mira 2007, Pakes et al. 2004), Bajari et al. (2007) recovered the structural parameters governing firms' investment decisions without ever actually solving the dynamic game. The intuition is as follows: First, the researcher recovers simple reduced-form estimates of the firm's policy functions (e.g., how much should the firm invest and when should it exit, conditional upon any set of market circumstances) directly from the data, being careful to impose as little structure on those estimates as possible. The firm's behavioral structural parameters can then be estimated by guessing at values for those parameters and then simulating behavior according to the policy functions. Assuming that the policy functions were indeed optimal, this simulated behavior should yield a larger net present discounted value than would any other policy function (e.g., one defined by making a slight perturbation to the observed policy function). The researcher searches over structural parameters until the observed policy function tends always to generate higher discounted net present value payoffs than any other perturbed policy function. Because the game is never solved (only simulated on the basis of reduced-form policy functions), the "curse of dimensionality" associated with the large state space does not come into play. Ryan (2006) found that the sunk cost of entry rises because of the new certification requirements imposed by the CAAA from $46 million to $58 million.

Having estimated the parameters governing this dynamic game, Ryan (2006) simulated how the industry would have evolved in the absence of the CAAAs in order to determine how strategic play (in particular, entry and subsequent pricing decisions) would be altered. Specifically, he simulated entry and pricing behavior in a typical market after the CAAAs and then did so again while assuming that the post-CAAA sunk entry cost had remained equal to its pre-CAAA level. As a result of the increased entry costs, prices rise by 6%, whereas quantities fall by 16%. With a 90% drop in entry, consumers take a welfare penalty of approximately $29 million, whereas producers benefit from the reduced competition by just under $3 million. Although the impression had been that the CAAAs were a burdensome regulation for all firms, this model of strategic entry and investment behavior suggests otherwise. The barrier to entry imposed by these regulations proved to be a net benefit for incumbent firms, who face less competition in the price-setting game.

Note that the two-step approach to estimating the structural parameters of a dynamic game does have its limitations. In particular, to simulate a counterfactual scenario (e.g., entry in a world in which entry costs had not risen), the solution to the dynamic game does need to be solved (at least once). The size of the state space then becomes an issue. In practice, this limits the number of firms (both incumbents and potential entrants) that can be considered in the simulation to four or five. Beyond this point, the curse of dimensionality caused by the expanding state space makes the problem computationally infeasible. This limit allows for fewer firms in a single market than is typical in many industries. Benkard et al. (2007) have proposed a solution to this problem in which firms ignore the identities of the firms they are playing against.

We conclude this section with a brief discussion of a second paper that uses dynamic estimation techniques to recover the unintended consequences of clean air regulations. Heutel (2008) estimated a model of the decision by power-plant owners to scrap and rebuild as either a coal or noncoal plant, to install a scrubber, or to switch to low-sulfur coal in response to the 1990 CAAAs. Plants built prior to the amendments, however, had been grandfathered (i.e., made exempt) from the rules contained in the New Source Pollution Standards. Scrapping and building a new generator would void their grandfathered status, causing forward-looking plant owners to postpone that decision beyond the time when it would normally be optimal. By recovering the parameters governing these dynamic decision processes, Heutel (2008) simulated how investment behavior would have changed had grandfathered status never been granted: He found that SO_2 emissions would have fallen by 60% by 1995.

3. REDUCED-FORM APPROACHES

Although the term reduced form is used frequently, the underlying definition has evolved over time. The traditional econometrics textbook definition of reduced form refers to simultaneous equations, where the system of equations is solved to eliminate all endogenous variables. The reduced-form model links the dependent variable solely to exogenous variables, which, by definition, are not influenced through feedback loops of the system. For example, both demand and supply equations depend on price as well as on other exogenous demand/supply shifters. The reduced-form model eliminates the price variable and derives the equilibrium quantity solely as a function of the demand/supply shifters, which presumably are exogenous. The emphasis is on eliminating endogenous variables, whereas a structural setup would model and estimate the effect of such variables directly. Modeling such endogenous variables usually requires structural assumptions to identify these variables of interest as well as suitable instruments. The goal of a reduced-form model is to avoid as many structural assumptions as possible. It should be noted that almost all models rely on some assumptions, and reduced-form models require assumptions of their own, e.g., additive separability and conditional independence in dynamic discrete choice settings (Rust 2008).

Using the traditional econometrics textbook definition, a cross-sectional study that relates a variable of interest to exogenous characteristics that vary in space would be considered reduced form. For example, a hedonic model that, following Rosen (1974), estimates the marginal WTP for a public good by linking house prices to different levels of the public good across space at a given point in time would fall under such a classification.

More recently, the definition of reduced form has sometimes been narrowed further and become synonymous with program evaluation or treatment effects, where further emphasis is placed on the identification of the exogenous variables. The researcher is interested not only in limiting the model to exogenous variables, but also in how these variables are assigned. The primary concern is that exogenous variables may be correlated with other confounding variables, and hence the estimated coefficient on the exogenous variable would be biased as it picks up both the direct effect of the exogenous variable and the effect of the collinear variables that are omitted from the analysis. This narrower definition is a natural extension of the aforementioned goal to make the results as independent as possible of structural assumptions. A pure cross-sectional approach requires that all confounding factors be correctly accounted for to derive an unbiased estimate.

Various research designs are used to avoid a potential correlation with the omitted variables. A nonexhaustive list includes the following:

1. A panel setting that can allow a researcher to use fixed effects to capture all time-invariant additive factors, thereby accounting for some baseline differences.
2. Quasi-experiments that are conducted under conditions where the exogenous variables are arguably randomly assigned and orthogonal to other variables of interests. For example, weather is random and not influenced by economic agents: "Good" and "bad" weather outcomes over time should be orthogonal to other controls.
3. In a regression discontinuity framework, a treatment variable gets "switched on" once a threshold is passed. Observations just below the threshold are compared with observations right above the threshold. The important underlying assumption is that there is no stratification at the threshold, and hence observations right below it are similar to the ones right above it, except for the triggered treatment.
4. Randomization, which assigns a treatment deliberately to a subsample of the entire population, while the remaining observations that were not assigned the treatment act as a control group. The randomization of the treatment ensures that it is uncorrelated with other variables and that the coefficient on the treatment variable will be unbiased.

3.1 The Advantages of Reduced-Form Modeling

Before we start our overview of reduced-form studies, it is helpful to remind the reader what can and cannot be accomplished with regression analysis. Freedman (1991) discussed the use of regression models in the social sciences by elaborating the virtues and vices of both structural work and reduced form models. He argued that "causal arguments based on significance test and regression are almost necessarily circular. To derive a regression model we need an elaborate theory that specifies the variables in the system, their causal interconnections, the functional form of the relationships, and the statistical properties of the error terms—independence, exogeneity, etc." (Freedman 1991, p. 292). Such a line of reasoning has more in common with the structural setup, which starts with a broad model that relies only on primitive variables and is guided by theory on the functional form. Freedman then continued, "There is an alternative validation strategy, which is less dependent on prior theory: Take the model as a black box and test it against empirical reality. Does the model predict new phenomena? Does it predict the results of interventions? Are the predictions right?" (p. 293). Such a strategy is more in line with a reduced-form approach. Are reliable predictions feasible with as few assumptions and structural feedback mechanisms as possible? Common themes in reduced-form studies hence are as follows.

3.1.1 Identification. Economics shares the problem of most other social sciences, which all rely predominantly on observational data. For that reason, great care has to be exercised in identifying the parameters of interest to ensure that the regression is not picking up some spurious correlation. A clever identification strategy that establishes some exogenous variation can be more convincing than a model that aims at incorporating all possible confounding variables explicitly. It is difficult to include all possible confounding variables in a structural model and free it from potential omitted variables bias.

3.1.2. Transparency. Reduced-form models make it easier to understand what source of variation explains the source of variation in the dependent variable. They are often simpler to estimate from a statistical perspective, and simplicity is a virtue. It is more straightforward for the reader to see which variables are ultimately responsible for the new outcome.

3.1.3. Predictive power. Examples from macroeconomics literature show that complex equilibrium models perform worse than simple univariate time-series models when predicting future economic outcomes (e.g., Wallis 1989, Granger & Yongil 2003). Errors can feed through structural models and propagate. Both reduced-form and structural models should be judged by how well they can predict empirical phenomena. One important qualification of the goodness-of-fit measures is in order: Generally, testing out-of sample performance is superior to in-sample measures like R-square. The latter can "over-fit" the data. To give an illustrative example of a model with a great in-sample fit that does not extend out of sample, consider the following: Before 2006, Germany won the soccer World Cup if and only if the final was played on a single-digit July date. The R-square of this model is 1 as it gives a perfect prediction of Germany's success. In 2006, Germany hosted the World Cup, and in accordance with this model, the final was played on a single-digit July day. However, although the in-sample prediction was perfect, it did not extend out of sample, as Italy won the World Cup. Although this is an anecdotal story, it illustrates the point that models that can be fit to a set of data and give very good fits do not necessarily provide equally convincing out-of-sample forecasts.

3.1.4. Robustness. Highly nonlinear structural problems require numerical solution techniques to approximate extrema, and it is not always evident that the chosen extreme was indeed the global optimum (Knittel & Metaxoglou 2008).

Freedman (1991) cited the work of Snow (1965) as a prime example of a data-driven reduced-form approach. Snow discovered that cholera is a waterborne disease. Although Snow did not run advanced regressions, he did a lot of "legwork." He realized that one apartment building whose water supply was contaminated with runoff from privies had many more cases than an adjacent building with a clear source. This was a cross-sectional analysis. Subsequently, he discovered that three water companies serviced London. One company received water from the Thames above the major discharge areas, whereas the other two obtained water from sources below the discharge areas. The type of constituents serviced by each company were indistinguishable, yet the cholera rate among the former was much lower than among the latter. In a sense, Snow discovered a quasi-experiment: Because the water agencies served customers throughout London, the subsets were balanced (same type of households, incomes, etc.), and the only difference was the water source. Difference in cholera rates between the different samples could convincingly be linked to the water source. Snow exercised great effort to come up with a plausible identification strategy. Once he had established the hypothesis that cholera was a waterborne disease, he tested it with various data sets to confirm it. Different reduced-form approaches are discussed in further detail in Section 3.2 below.

Chetty (2008) recently contrasted structural and reduced-form approaches and discussed how they can inform one another. Structural models are often needed for welfare analysis, yet some analyses can be answered with the help of a few high-level parameters, i.e., these parameters are sufficient for the analysis. For example, a Harberger deadweight loss triangle of taxation depends solely on the elasticity of demand for a good with respect to a tax, and hence that elasticity is all that is required for a study of the welfare impacts of taxation. There may be various combinations of primitives that all give the same elasticity, but the primitives have no impact on the ultimate welfare estimate. Whenever a welfare analysis can be reduced to a set of sufficient high-level statistics and it does not require the researcher to indentify the underlying primitives of the structural model, reduced-form studies can be especially valuable in identifying them with as few assumptions as possible and a high degree of transparency. An example of a key parameter best suited for reduced-form studies is the effect of any exogenously changing environmental variable on an economic or natural indicator, e.g., the impact of exogenous pollution variation on health, housing values, etc.

3.2. Examples of Reduced-Form Models in Environmental and Resource Economics

The following examples contrast various reduced-form approaches in more depth and briefly discuss the advantages and disadvantages of each approach in identifying key parameters. Readers interested in the latest developments in econometric techniques using reduced-form estimators are referred to Imbens & Wooldridge (2008).

3.2.1. Cross-sectional studies.
A large number of studies in environmental economics use cross-sectional variation in amenities (e.g., pollution levels or access to parks) to derive the WTP for such amenities. Most of these amenities are not directly traded in a market, so indirect methods are the only possible option to derive preferences. Using a sample of houses in St. Louis, Missouri, Ridker & Henning (1967) were among the first to argue that better air quality capitalizes into housing values. If two houses are identical (same

housing attributes, neighborhood characteristics, distance to urban centers/schools, etc.), except that one is in a polluted area while the other is in a clean area, one would expect that the price of the latter should be higher. Rosen (1974) formalized the concept of hedonic bid functions, whose underlying assumptions are outlined in more detail in Section 2.2.

The big empirical challenge when estimating the marginal WTP is to account for all other factors that might differ between various houses. Smith & Huang (1993, 1995) conducted meta-analyses of hedonic studies that estimate the WTP for air quality. Smith & Huang (1993) found that hedonic studies are successful at establishing that pollution impacts housing values. In their follow-up paper (Smith & Huang 1995), they found that the chosen procedure had an important influence on the estimated marginal WTP for improvements in air quality. When the authors regressed the estimated marginal WTP of each study on characteristics of the study, they found that the number of neighborhood control variables is positive and significant, as are dummies for linear, semilog, and log-linear specifications as well as controls for the time the study was conducted. The mean estimate is five times as large as the median, suggesting that outliers can have a large impact. Although none of these is unique to cross-sectional studies, it shows that great care should be taken in the study design and in determining what it can be used for.

In another meta-study, Boyle & Kiel (2001) found that hedonic pricing studies of air quality more frequently have insignificant coefficients or even coefficients with counterintuitive signs compared with studies that value water quality or the distance to undesirable land use. One possible reason is that water quality measures (e.g., turbidity) and the distance to toxic waste sites are easily observable, unlike common air quality measures, such as ozone, that can be observed only with special instruments.

Given these mixed results and empirical challenges, why are researchers employing them? The main reason may be the lack of alternatives combined with the fact that alternatives often require assumptions of their own. The first advantage of reduced-form cross-sectional studies is that they are more easily understood than some structural models, and it is more evident what source of variation is used to explain the variation in the dependent variable. Second, quasi-experiments are not always available. If they are available, they may measure a different parameter than a cross-sectional study or require assumptions of their own (discussed below). Kuminoff & Pope (2009) highlighted the theoretical reasons why a cross-sectional approach and a quasi-experimental approach may give different estimates. The former measures the marginal WTP at a market equilibrium at a single point in time, whereas the latter usually measures the capitalization of a discrete nonmarginal change where equilibrium prices and quantities adjust. Only under certain conditions, e.g., constant prices and the assumption that the marginal WTP is constant over the change, will the two coincide. Because quasi-experimental approaches usually evaluate larger differences that sometimes span an extended period of time, these assumptions are not always met. Third, a cross section may be the only setting that allows researchers to measure how people adapt to changes in long-term averages (discussed in Section 3.2.2).

3.2.2. Panel studies. A panel setting allows the use of fixed effects to account for all time-invariant factors that impact the decision in an additive way. This method is, hence, less susceptible to omitted variables bias than a cross-sectional approach. The source of identification is different: One does not rely on the difference in the average of each unit (individuals, households, or spatial units such as zip codes), but instead one relies on deviation from the mean of each unit to identify the parameters of interest. For example, Currie & Neidell (2005) used the variation in pollution levels over time to identify the impact of several pollutants on infant mortality using zip-code fixed effects as well as year and month fixed effects and the interactions of these fixed effects. Such an approach allows average mortality rates to be different between zip codes and relies only on variation within locations over time (net of seasonality effects of overall yearly time trends) to estimate effect of pollution on mortality.

A fixed-effect regression is equivalent to a joint demeaning of the dependent and independent variables. By definition, time-invariant factors do not evolve over time; therefore, subtracting the constant mean subtracts out the additive influence of such variables. The advantage of implicitly accounting for all time-invariant factors, however, comes at a cost: Deviation from means can have distinct economic implications than differences in means. A panel relies on period-to-period variation and is hence inherently a short-term response, whereas the cross-sectional approach uses differences in long-term averages to which units can adapt. The direction of the difference can go either way, depending on how the set of possible responses varies in the short and long term. If the set of possible responses is wider in the long run (e.g., because additional investments are possible that cannot be accomplished in the short term), the long-run impact should be a larger net benefit (or lower cost). This is the Le Chatelier principle—responses in the long term have fewer constraints than in the short term and hence are less harmful or more beneficial. In contrast, within the environmental area, there may also be short-term responses that cannot be sustained indefinitely (as the resources necessary to do so would be depleted) and hence the short-run impact may give higher net benefits. For example, a one-time bacterial infection can easily be fought by using antibiotics, i.e., the response to a short-term infection is to increase the use of antibiotics. However, continued use of antibiotics makes bacteria resistant, so the use of antibiotics on a long-term basis would not be feasible. Similarly, a drought can be mitigated by pumping groundwater, but continued droughts may require more water than the aquifer holds.

Another difference between the short and long term is that individuals are stuck in the former but can re-sort in the latter. Under Tiebout (1956) sorting, people with a high aversion to a nuisance, e.g., proximity to an industrial facility with emissions in the Toxic Release Inventory, sort to neighborhoods that do not have a facility in close proximity. Banzhaf & Walsh (2008) showed that air quality improvements lead to increased population density, as people migrate to the cleaner neighborhood, and increased average income levels. Such sorting implies that, as they sorted, families in clean areas had different marginal WTP for improvements in air quality. Therefore, deviations from mean levels may differ for at least two reasons. First, individuals with high values for clean areas may re-sort into cleaner areas and hence have a different marginal WTP, even if pollution levels were identical. Second, the marginal WTP may be increasing in the pollution level if damages are convex. Under convex damages, the marginal effect depends on the initial pollution level; hence, the marginal WTP is heterogeneous and determined by initial starting values. Although Banzhaf & Walsh (2008) conducted a reduced-form study that estimates the net effect of re-sorting, it highlights why structural approaches (outlined in the first half of this article) that explicitly incorporate such sorting are a useful tool to evaluate nonmarginal changes in amenities.

To avoid possible sorting responses, it is ideal if the variable whose effect the researcher is interested in measuring is exogenously assigned. Quasi-experiments, discussed next, focus on the exogenous assignment of a treatment on individuals. All other initial controls or initial levels should be balanced, i.e., identical between the treatment and control groups.

3.2.3. Quasi-experiments. It is often impossible to conduct a randomized experiment in the economy, but unique events can act like a natural experiment or quasi-experiment. Such events ideally should assign a "treatment" to a subset of the observations, and this assignment should be random. For an example of a quasi-experiment, consider the relationship between wind direction and pollution. Except within dense city centers with skyscrapers, wind direction is exogenously given and varies daily or hourly in most locations. When examining the effects of pollution, one can compare days on which a location is downwind with days on which it is upwind of the pollution source. All characteristics except the pollution level should be balanced between the two samples. Different outcomes between days with various wind directions can hence be attributed to the pollution.

Chay & Greenstone (2003) used changes in pollution that were induced by a recession to estimate the effect of air pollution on infant health. The authors compared the change in infant mortality rates in the third of the counties with the largest reduction in pollution levels to the third of counties with the smallest change in pollution levels. The idea is that the recession induced exogenous pollution reductions; therefore, all other confounding variables should be balanced between the two groups of counties. The authors tested whether various socioeconomic variables are balanced between these subsamples and found only a small difference in income—so small that it cannot explain the observed differences in the measured response. The estimated relationship between pollution and infant health is much larger and more robust than estimates obtained in a cross section.

Davis (2004) examined the effect a sudden spike in pediatric cancer cases in a town in Nevada had on housing values. The event is the sudden occurrence of an unusually larger number of such cases within a limited time window. He used two towns in Nevada that have very similar pre-event trends in housing prices. The town with the sudden number of cancer cases is the treatment town, whereas the other with no occurrences acts like a control. Because the occurrence of the cancer cases started and ceased unexpectedly and suddenly, this method was similar to assigning a treatment to one town but not to the other. Davis used, among other things, a difference-in-difference estimator by first constructing the difference in housing prices before and after the event in both the treatment and control village. The second difference, or difference-in-difference estimator, takes the difference between the change in the housing price in the treatment village where the cancer cases occurred and compares it to the difference in the control village. The advantage of a difference-in-difference approach is that, by taking the second difference, the analysis subtracts the change in housing prices observed in the control village, thus removing overall price movements that are common throughout Nevada. Davis found a strong and statistically significant reduction in housing prices of approximately 15% in the treatment town compared with the control town following the discovery of the cancer cases. Similar results are obtained in a cross-sectional analysis of housing prices.

Fowlie & Perloff (2008) used the random assignment of firms to one of two compliance cycles of the RECLAIM market for NO_x emissions in Southern California to test whether pollution outcomes are independent of initial permit allocation, as predicted under the Coase theorem. Firms receive facility-specific permit allocation schemes that decreased in a stepwise function over time. Permits are valid for 12-month periods and may be traded between firms. However, regulations prohibit banking, i.e., the trading of permits across time periods. The quasi-experimental design is possible because of the way the permits were issued. Firms were randomly assigned to one of two 12-month cycles, one ending in January and the other ending in July. Since firms are not allowed to shift permits between time periods, the declining permit structure was exogenously given by a random draw. The authors found that the null hypothesis that emissions are independent of initial permit allocation cannot be rejected. The analysis establishes this result convincingly as it relies on exogenous variation in the timing of the permit profile, which is independent of firm characteristics that influence overall permit allocation. Such randomization ensures that the variation is orthogonal to other possible confounding factors.

Another strand of quasi-experimental research designs is the regression discontinuity framework. The idea is to look for a treatment that switches on when a critical threshold value is reached. For this approach to work, there must not be endogenous "bunching" at the threshold level, where individuals can choose whether they will be above or below it. A continuous exogenous distribution around the threshold ensures that an observation just above and just below the threshold should be comparable, except that one receives the treatment while the other does not. For example, Urquiola & Verhoogen (2009) showed that there is bunching around the class size cutoff in schools. Thus, a regression discontinuity design in class size is problematic.

Auffhammer & Kellogg (2009) applied the regression discontinuity method to examine whether gasoline content regulation has an effect on air quality. The authors used the fact that various regulations in the United States are binding for only parts of the year, mostly the summer months as higher temperatures are conducive to ozone formation. The authors then estimated whether days just before and after the phase-in have different pollution levels. These levels should be comparable, especially when days before and after the phase-in each is averaged over several years, as idiosyncratic shocks are averaged out. The authors found that most gasoline content regulations that regulate volatile organic compounds (VOC) do not reduce ozone formation, as these regulations specify only a limit on the total quantity of VOCs emitted, but not which type. Not surprisingly, firms meet the regulation by eliminating the cheapest source of VOCs, which has little or no impact on ozone formation. In contrast, a California law that postulates which VOCs have to be removed does lead to significant improvements in air quality.

A regression discontinuity approach is similar in spirit to an event study approach in finance, where abnormal stock market returns are linked to the event in question. In the event study, the discontinuity does not happen along a state variable (e.g., pollution levels), but rather in time. New information is suddenly made available and financial markets react to the release of this new information. Arbitrage requires that such new information be incorporated immediately. Hamilton (1995) found that firms with the largest emissions, as reported in the Toxic Release Inventory, had negative stock market returns after the information was made initially public. The point estimate for the effect of Toxic Release Inventory emissions is larger for the event date than for the week following the event, suggesting that new information is immediately incorporated in efficient markets. Such methodology is suited for cases in which it is clear when new information becomes available, e.g., sudden catastrophes or unexpected changes. It is important to be able to identify the temporal window when the stock market recognizes the information as "new."

The effect of sudden changes on firms' values has been examined in a wide variety of settings. Fisman (2001) showed that firms connected to Indonesia's former dictator Suharto had abnormal returns when concerns surfaced about his health. Similarly, Jayachandran (2006) examined the event when Senator Jeffords unexpectedly switched party affiliations and tipped the U.S. Senate majority from Republican to Democratic. Firms that predominantly donated to Republicans had negative returns, while firms with larger donations to Democrats had positive returns. Lange & Linn (2008) used the uncertainty surrounding the recount of the 2000 U.S. Presidential election in Florida to estimate the cost of the New Source Review standard under the Clean Air Act. On the one hand, it was believed that Gore would interpret the rule more stringently, which would lead to higher costs for industries with regulated boilers. On the other hand, Bush was expected to interpret the rule more loosely. The sudden back-and-forth between the Florida and U.S. Supreme Court rulings changed the probability that each candidate would capture Florida and win the overall election. As a result, the profit of companies would shift with the predicted winner as the regulation would be more or less severe.

3.2.4. Randomization: field experiments. Whereas quasi-experiments examine events that split the sample into treatment and control groups that are arguably random, field experiments go one step further and deliberately randomize an experiment. By design, a certain fraction of the overall population actually receives one out of a set of treatment options. The most famous examples are medical trials, where a fraction of the patients receive a new drug whose effect is tested and the control sample receives a placebo (usually a sugar pill). The outcome of the sample that received the treatment is then compared with the sample that did not.

In the economic literature, field experiments are prevalent in various other disciplines, notably, development economics and the economics of education. The major advantage of randomized experiments is that, by design, the treatment is uncorrelated with any other controls. As a result, the treatment effect is clearly identified. The statistical tools required in such an analysis are simple and often contain only t-tests to examine whether the means of the treatment and control group are different. Heterogeneous treatment effects can be examined by interacting the treatment variable with other controls. For example, Landry et al. (2006) examined the effects of various fund-raising mechanisms. They first argued that lotteries should raise more money than voluntary donations. Under the former, the donor not only gets the "joy of giving," but also has the possibility of a private payoff. They tested this proposition in a field experiment in North Carolina in which 5000 potential donors were approached with a randomly chosen donation mechanism. As hypothesized, the lottery resulted in higher average donations than voluntary giving. But the authors did not stop at the difference between various donation mechanisms. They also interacted the donation amount with various measures of the beauty of the solicitors to test whether physical attractiveness has an impact on giving. A one standard deviation increase in the beauty measure increased average giving by about the same as the lottery incentive, compared with voluntary donations.

Field experiments allow a researcher to observe human behaviors and attitudes that are difficult to establish in a cross section. For example, there is an ongoing debate in the environmental justice literature as to whether plants locate disproportionately in minority neighborhoods, or whether minorities, which on average are poorer, tend to move to areas with more plants because rents are lower (Wolverton 2008). Establishing a causal link by comparing neighborhoods is very difficult. List (2004) used interactions between various ethnic groups in a field experiment where individuals trade baseball cards to test discrimination. The advantage is that the moderator can influence the racial composition of the buyer and seller. List (2004) found that trading partners from minority groups tend to get lower offers, but a subsequent analysis revealed that these lower offers are not due to animus or taste-based preferences toward the group, but rather statistical discrimination is the cause. In other words, market participants aim at maximizing profit (irrespective of their counterpart's ethnic group) and use race as an indicator of private reservation values.

Although randomized experiments offer a clear form of identification, the researcher also has to ensure that the assigned treatment was eventually implemented. Sometimes, subjects cannot be forced to undergo treatment but can only be offered the option to be treated. A subject's decision to be treated is endogenous to the subject and is based on unobservable characteristics. The researcher has to account for such selection. The intend-to-treat literature addresses such issues.

Moreover, it is important to ensure that there are no spillover effects from the treatment to the control group. This is particularly true if subjects are randomly given additional information or monetary incentives that they could share with their neighbors or relatives in the control group. Such behavior will dilute the measured effect of the treatment, as part of the control group indirectly receives the treatment as well. For example, Ferraro (2009) convinced a water utility in Georgia to add information randomly about a household's water use (compared with the average user) to the water bill. He found that simply providing such information changes the water use of the household, but he did not detect a change in neighbors' consumption, so spillover effects seem not to be a major issue.

Finally, Deaton (2009) recently emphasized that experimental (or quasi-experimental) approaches have sometimes given the false illusion of exogeneity and rest on other assumptions. Moreover, he emphasized that the randomized file experiments have focused too much on whether a particular policy works, and not why it works.

3.2.5. Randomization: lab experiments.
Lab experiments offer a cheaper alternative to field experiments, which are often expensive and administratively cumbersome to implement. Moreover, a lab experiment can create a payoff structure that may not be implemented in the field owing to ethical concerns. For example, Shogren et al. (1994) examined the differences between WTP and willingness to accept (WTA) for market goods as well as nonmarket goods with few substitutes, e.g., health risks. In a laboratory experiment, people were first given a market good (candy) and some income. In an auction, WTP and WTA converged when the same experiment was repeated. Subjects were then given $15 and a free lunch from a local supplier that had a certain percentage of being contaminated with food pathogens. Participants WTP and WTA were subsequently tested for a scanned "safe" lunch with lower probability of food poisoning, and the two measures did not converge over time.

Lab experiments can also be used to test specific implementation issues of various policy settings and whether individuals react as predicted by economic theory. For example, the CAAA of 1990 require the Environmental Protection Agency to conduct annual auctions of emission allowances. The unique feature of this auction rule is that sellers are ranked according to increasing asking prices while buyers are ranked according to decreasing bid prices. The seller with the lowest asking price then receives the bid of the highest bid. There is an incentive to underbid in order to be paired with the highest bidder and thereby receive a higher price. Cason (1995) examined the opposite situation in a laboratory experiment in which buyers with the highest bid pay the lowest asking price. As predicted by theory, buyers bid above their true value, driving up the equilibrium price to inefficient levels.

Although experiments can be tailored to various setups, potential downsides also exist. First, experiments are usually conducted in an artificial setting, often administered via computers, and we learn about how humans cooperate and behave given these recreated incentive structures. Second, subjects are predominantly students who participate in an experiment and hence may not be representative of the overall population. Third, Levitt & List (2007) argued that responses in lab experiments are governed by factors other than monetary calculations, e.g., the specific context, social stigma, moral and ethical considerations, as well as the stakes of the game.

3.2.6. Reduced-form studies: possible challenges. The key strength of reduced-form studies is a clear and transparent identification of a parameter of interest without structural assumptions about feedback loops. Possible challenges are that both long-term feedback effects and spillovers can be important for welfare analyses.

Cohort studies can sometimes address long-term effects after people are able to reoptimize. Such studies rely on an event where an entire cohort of people is subjected to a shock. The cohort's eventual outcome revealed several years later is contrasted to the outcomes of previous and later cohorts. For example, Almond (2006) estimated the long-term effects of the big influenza epidemic of 1918 by contrasting cohorts that were in utero in 1918 to cohorts right before and after the epidemic. He used the 1960–1980 Censuses to examine long-term effects and found that the exposed cohort had higher rates of disability, unemployment, and various other factors even at a much later stage in life.

The second problem of spillover effects is more severe. Treatment-control experiments usually assume that the treatment has no effect on the control group. Imbens & Wooldridge (2008, p. 9) argued that, although this seems justifiable for medical research, interactions between the treatment and control group can be a serious concern in economic studies. For example, a labor market treatment may have spillover effects for the control group by impacting the market-clearing wage rate, even if a person is in the control group. The authors cited some recent advances that see these interactions not as a problem but as an interesting objective of the study. For example, Kling et al. (2007) examined the outcomes of individuals five years after they randomly received housing vouchers, giving them time to re-sort. Imbens & Wooldridge (2008) conceded that "[m]any identification and inferential questions remain unanswered in this literature" (p. 10). This line of research should be expanded in the future.

3.3. Summary

Reduced-form studies are best equipped to identify key high-level parameters of interest. The major advantage is that the identification strategy often requires fewer assumptions and is easier to grasp than structural models with all their embodied feedback loops while trying to estimate underlying primitives. We have discussed how randomization simplifies the task at hand for an econometrician, as all covariates are by design balanced between the treatment and control group. Such randomized experiments offer the most compelling evidence to establish a causal argument between a treatment and an outcome, yet these studies require assumptions of their own. Field experiments offer the most realistic setting, yet some problems involving pollution and health can be simulated only in a hypothetical lab setting for ethical reasons. Cross-sectional studies sometimes offer the best possible setting to test how individuals adapt to long-term differences. For these reasons, both quasi-experiments and cross-sectional studies can give viable insights. As described above, there are theoretical reasons why quasi-experiments that rely on significant nonmarginal changes can give estimates of the marginal WTP that differ from those obtained by cross-sectional studies.

Returning to the article by Freedman (1991) and his discussion of the statistical evidence surrounding the hypothesis that cholera is a waterborne disease, the most convincing fact was that the researcher employed "shoe leather," i.e., he tested various sources of variation and models and found them to agree.

4. CONCLUSIONS

In this article, we have discussed both structural and reduced-form models as well as their strengths and weaknesses. These strengths and weaknesses are not unique to environmental and resource economics; instead, they are common to other subfields in economics. Structural models can allow for feedback loops that are difficult, if not impossible, to implement in a reduced-form setting. A complete welfare analyses may require these structural feedback loops. However, reduced-form studies can offer a clear identification of key high-level response parameters of interest and are better suited at establishing causality. They can also be used to test predictions from economic theory using data-driven approaches that are less dependent on modeling assumptions. We believe both approaches have their own unique advantages. For example, in the case of air quality, reduced-form studies have been used to establish the link between air quality and infant health using variation induced by a recession (Chay & Greenstone 2003) or using panel data that link health outcomes to variation in pollution taking into account location fixed effects as well as temporal fixed effects (Currie & Neidell 2005). Both studies find a robust and consistent relationship between reduction in pollution and infant mortality. The latter study uses more recent data when air quality levels had improved further compared with the first study that uses data in the early 1980s. However, to value the WTP for large reduction in air quality, re-sorting of constituents into cleaner or dirtier neighborhoods can become important. The structural paper by Sieg et al. (2004) models the ability of people in the Los Angeles area to relocate in response to a large reduction in pollution levels, and it shows how relocation would impact estimates of their marginal WTP for that improvement. The horizontal model used by Bayer et al. (2009) alternatively shows how stickiness in the sorting process can lead to a downward bias in WTP as measured by a simple hedonic model.

Generally, the most convincing evidence stems from contrasting various approaches instead of limiting ourselves to only one approach and, in the process, enabling us to discuss why these approaches agree or disagree.

DISCLOSURE STATEMENT

The authors are not aware of any affiliations, memberships, funding, or financial holdings that might be perceived as affecting the objectivity of this review.

LITERATURE CITED

Aguirregabiria V, Mira P. 2007. Sequential estimation of dynamic discrete games. *Econometrica* 75(1):1–53

Almond D. 2006. Is the 1918 influenza pandemic over? Long-term effects of *in utero* influenza exposure in the post-1940 U.S. population. *J. Polit. Econ.* 114(4):672–721

Arcidiacono P, Miller R. 2008. *CCP estimation of dynamic discrete choice models with unobserved heterogeneity.* Work. Pap., Duke Univ.

Auffhammer M, Kellogg R. 2009. *Clearing the air? The effects of gasoline content regulation on air quality.* CSEM Work. Pap. 185, Univ. Calif., Berkeley

Bajari P, Benkard L, Levin J. 2007. Estimating dynamic models of imperfect competition. *Econometrica* 75(5):1331–70

Banzhaf HS, Walsh RP. 2008. Do people vote with their feet? An empirical test of Tiebout's mechanism. *Am. Econ. Rev.* 98(3):843–63

Bartik T. 1987. The estimation of demand parameters in hedonic price models. *J. Polit. Econ.* 95(1):81–88

Bayer P, Keohane N, Timmins C. 2009. Migration and hedonic valuation: the case of air quality. *J. Environ. Econ. Manag.* 58:1–14

Bayer P, Khan S, Timmins C. 2008a. *Nonparametric identification and estimation in a generalized Roy model.* Work. Pap. 13949, NBER

Bayer P, MacMillan R, Murphy A, Timmins C. 2008b. *A dynamic model of demand for houses and neighborhoods.* Work. Pap., Duke Univ.

Bayer P, Timmins C. 2007. Estimating equilibrium models of sorting across locations. *Econ. J.* 117(518):353–74

Benkard L, Weintraub G, Van Roy B. 2007. *Computational methods for oblivous equilibrium.* Res. Pap. 1969, Grad. Sch. Bus., Stanford Univ.

Bento A, Goulder L, Jacobsen M, von Haefen R. 2009. Distributional and efficiency impacts of increased U.S. gasoline taxes. *Am. Econ. Rev.* 99(3):1–37

Berry S, Levinsohn J, Pakes A. 1995. Automobile prices in market equilibrium. *Econometrica* 63(4):841–90

Bishop K. 2008. *A dynamic model of location choice and hedonic valuation.* Work. Pap., Dep. Econ., Duke Univ.

Bishop K, Timmins C. 2008. *Simple, consistent estimation of the marginal willingness to pay function: recovering Rosen's second stage without instrumental variables.* Work. Pap., Dep. Econ., Duke Univ.

Boxall PC, Hauer G, Adamowicz WL. 2005. *Modeling congestion as a form of interdependence in random utility models.* Staff Pap. Ser. 05-01, Dep. Rural Econ., Univ. Alberta

Boyle M, Kiel KA. 2001. A survey of house price hedonic studies of the impact of environmental externalities. *J. Real Estate Lit.* 9(2):117–44

Brown JN, Rosen HS. 1982. On the estimation of structural hedonic price models. *Econometrica* 50(3):765–68

Carranza JE. 2008. *Product innovation and adoption in market equilibrium: the case of digital cameras.* Work. Pap., Univ. Wisc., Madison

Cason TN. 1995. An experimental investigation of the seller incentives in the EPA's emission trading auction. *Am. Econ. Rev.* 85(4):905–22

Chay K, Greenstone M. 2003. The impact of air pollution on infant mortality: evidence from geographic variation in pollution shocks induced by a recession. *Q. J. Econ.* 118(3):1121–67

Chay K, Greenstone M. 2005. Does air quality matter? Evidence from the housing market. *J. Polit. Econ.* 113(2):376–424

Chetty R. 2008. *Sufficient statistics for welfare analysis: a bridge between structural and reduced-form methods.* Mimeogr., Univ. Calif., Berkeley

Currie J, Neidell M. 2005. Air pollution and infant health: What can we learn from California's recent experience? *Q. J. Econ.* 120(3):1003–30

Davis LW. 2004. The effect of health risk on housing values: evidence from a cancer cluster. *Am. Econ. Rev.* 94(5):1693–704

Deaton A. 2009. *Instruments of development: randomization in the tropics, and the search for the elusive keys to economic development.* Work. Pap. 14690, NBER

Deleire T, Timmins C. 2008. *Roy model sorting and non-random selection in the valuation of a statistical life.* Work. Pap. 14364, NBER

Ekeland I, Heckman J, Nesheim L. 2004. Identification and estimation of hedonic models. *J. Polit. Econ.* 112(1.2):S60–109

Epple D. 1987. Hedonic prices and implicit markets: estimating demand and supply functions for differentiated products. *J. Polit. Econ.* 95(1):59–80

Epple D, Romer T. 1991. Mobility and redistribution. *J. Polit. Econ.* 99(4):828–58

Epple D, Filimon R, Romer T. 1984. Equilibrium among local jurisdictions: toward an integrated approach of voting and residential choice. *J. Public Econ.* 24:281–304

Epple D, Sieg H. 1999. Estimating equilibrium models of local jurisdictions. *J. Polit. Econ.* 107(4):645–81

Epple D, Sieg H, Peress M. 2004. *Identification and estimation of discrete-continuous choice models with vertical product differentiation.* Tepper Sch. Bus. Work. Pap. 2003-06, Carnegie Mellon Univ.

Fernandez R, Rogerson R. 1996. Income distribution, communities, and the quality of public education. *Q. J. Econ.* 111(1):135–64

Ferraro PJ. 2009. *Common pool resource management without prices: a large-scale randomized experiment to test the effects of information, moral suasion and social norms.* Work. Pap., Dep. Econ., Georgia State Univ.

Fisman R. 2001. Estimating the value of political connections. *Am. Econ. Rev.* 91(4):1095–102

Fowlie M, Perloff JM. 2008. *Distributing pollution rights in cap-and-trade programs: are outcomes independent of allocation?* Work. Pap., Dep. Agric. Resour. Econ., Univ. Calif., Berkeley

Freedman DA. 1991. Statistical models and shoe leather. *Sociol. Methodol.* 21:291–313

Granger CWJ, Yongil J. 2003. Interactions between large macro models and time series analysis. *Int. J. Financ. Econ.* 8(1):1–10

Hamilton JT. 1995. Pollution as news: media and stock market reactions to the toxic release inventory data. *J. Environ. Econ. Manag.* 28(1):98–113

Heutel G. 2008. *Plant vintages, grandfathering, and environmental policy.* Work. Pap., Harvard Univ.

Hicks R, Horrace W, Schnier K. 2008. *Strategic substitutes or complements? The game of where to fish.* Work. Pap., Cent. Policy Res., Syracuse Univ.

Hotz J, Miller R. 1993. Conditional choice probabilities and estimation of dynamic models. *Rev. Econ. Stud.* 60:497–529

Imbens GM, Wooldridge JM. 2008. *Recent developments in the econometrics of program evaluation.* Work. Pap. 14251, NBER

Jacobsen M. 2008. *Evaluating U.S. fuel economy standards in a model with producer and household heterogeneity.* Work. Pap., Univ. Calif., San Diego

Jayachandran S. 2006. The Jeffords effect. *J. Law Econ.* 49(2):397–425

Kennan J, Walker J. 2005. *The effect of expected income on individual migration decisions.* Work. Pap. 9585, NBER

Klaiber A, Phaneuf D. 2009. *Valuing open space in a residential sorting model of the Twin Cities.* Work. Pap., North Carolina State Univ.

Kling J, Liebman J, Katz L. 2007. Experimental analysis of neighborhood effects. *Econometrica* 75(1):83–119

Knittel CR, Metaxoglou K. 2008. *Estimation of random coefficient demand models: challenges, difficulties and warnings.* Work. Pap. 14080, NBER

Kuminoff N. 2008. *Recovering preferences from a dual-market locational equilibrium*. Presented at Aust. Agric. Resour. Econ. Soc. Conf., 52nd, Canberra

Kuminoff N. 2009. Decomposing the structural identification of non-market values. *J. Environ. Econ. Manag.* 57(2):123–39

Kuminoff NC, Pope JC. 2009. *Capitalization and welfare measurement in the hedonic model*. Work. Pap. 2009-01, Dep. Agric. Appl. Econ., Virginia Tech

Landry CE, Lange A, List JA, Price MK, Rupp NG. 2006. Toward an understanding of the economics of charity: evidence from a field experiment. *Q. J. Econ.* 121(2):747–82

Lange I, Linn J. 2008. Bush vs Gore and the effect of new source review on power plant emissions. *Environ. Resour. Econ.* 40(4):571–91

Levitt SD, List JA. 2007. What do laboratory experiments measuring social preferences reveal about the real world? *J. Econ. Perspect.* 21(2):153–74

List JA. 2004. The nature and extent of discrimination in the marketplace: evidence from the field. *Q. J. Econ.* 119(1):49–89

Mendelsohn R. 1985. Identifying structural equations with single market data. *Rev. Econ. Stat.* 67(3):525–29

Murdock J, Timmins C. 2007. A revealed preference approach to the measurement of congestion in travel cost models. *J. Environ. Econ. Manag.* 53(2):230–49

Nechyba T. 1997a. Existence of equilibrium and stratification in local and hierarchical Tiebout economies with property taxes and voting. *Econ. Theory* 10(2):277–304

Nechyba T. 1997b. Local property and state income taxes: the role of interjurisdictional competition and collusion. *J. Polit. Econ.* 105(2):351–84

Pakes A, McGuire P. 1994. Computing Markov-perfect Nash equilibria: numerical implications of a dynamic differentiated product model. *Rand J. Econ.* 25(4):555–89

Pakes A, Ostrovsky M, Berry S. 2004. *Simple estimators for the parameters of discrete dynamic games (with entry/exit samples)*. Work. Pap. 10506, NBER

Pesendorfer M, Schmidt-Dengler P. 2008. Asymptotic least squares estimators for dynamic games. *Rev. Econ. Stud.* 75(3):901–28

Pfaff A, Robalino J. 2005. *Contagious development: neighbors' interactions in deforestation*. Work. Pap., Duke Univ.

Phaneuf D, Carbone J, Herriges JA. 2009. Non-price equilibria for non-market goods. *J. Environ. Econ. Manag.* 57(1):45–64

Phaneuf D, Kling C, Herriges J. 2000. Estimation and welfare calculations in a generalized corner solution model with an application to recreation demand. *Rev. Econ. Stat.* 82(1):83–92

Ridker RG, Henning JA. 1967. The determinants of residential property values with special reference to air pollution. *Rev. Econ. Stat.* 49(2):246–57

Roback J. 1982. Wages, rents, and the quality of life. *J. Polit. Econ.* 90:1257–78

Rosen S. 1974. Hedonic prices and implicit markets: product differentiation in pure competition. *J. Polit. Econ.* 82(1):34–55

Roy AD. 1951. Some thoughts on the distribution of earnings. *Oxf. Econ. Pap.* 3:135–46

Rust J. 1987. Optimal replacement of GMC bus engines: an empirical model of Harold Zurcher. *Econometrica* 55(5):999–1033

Rust J. 2008. *Structural vs Atheoretic Approaches in Econometrics: Comment*. Work. Pap., Univ. Maryland

Ryan S. 2006. *The costs of environmental regulation in a concentrated industry*. Work. Pap., Dep. Econ., MIT

Shogren JF, Shin SY, Hayes DJ, Kliebenstein JB. 1994. Resolving differences in willingness to pay and willingness to accept. *Am. Econ. Rev.* 84(1):255–70

Sieg H, Smith VK, Banzhaf S, Walsh R. 2004. Estimating the general equilibrium benefits of large changes in spatially delineated public goods. *Int. Econ. Rev.* 45(4):1047–77

Small KA. 1975. Air pollution and property values: further comment. *Rev. Econ. Stat.* 57(1):105–7

Smith M, Wilen J. 2003. Economic impacts of marine reserves: the importance of spatial behavior. *J. Environ. Econ. Manag.* 46(2):183–206

Smith VK. 2007. Reflections on the literature. *Rev. Environ. Econ. Policy* 1(2):300–18

Smith VK, Huang J-C. 1993. Hedonic models and air pollution: twenty-five years and counting. *Environ. Resour. Econ.* 3(4):381–94

Smith VK, Huang J-C. 1995. Can markets value air quality? A meta-analysis of hedonic property value models. *J. Polit. Econ.* 103(1):209–27

Snow J. 1965. *On the Mode of Communication of Cholera.* New York: Hafner. Reprint ed. (Orig. publ. 1855)

Tiebout C. 1956. A pure theory of local expenditures. *J. Polit. Econ.* 64(5):416–24

Urquiola M, Verhoogen E. 2009. Class-size caps, sorting, and the regression discontinuity design. *Am. Econ. Rev.* 99(1):179–215

von Haefen R, Phaneuf D. 2008. Identifying demand parameters in the presence of unobservables: a combined revealed and stated preference approach. *J. Environ. Econ. Manag.* 56(1):19–32

Wallis KF. 1989. Macroeconomic forecasting: a survey. *Econ. J.* 99(394):28–61

Walsh R. 2007. Endogenous open space amenities in a locational equilibrium. *J. Urban Econ.* 61(2):319–44

Wolverton A. 2008. *Effects of socio-economic and input-related factors on polluting plants' location decisions.* Work. Pap. 2008-08, Natl. Cent. Environ. Econ.

Integrated Ecological-Economic Models

John Tschirhart

Department of Economics and Finance, University of Wyoming, Laramie, Wyoming 82071: email: jtsch@uwyo.edu

Annu. Rev. Resour. Econ. 2009. 1:381–407

First published online as a Review in Advance on July 14, 2009

The *Annual Review of Resource Economics* is online at resource.annualreviews.org

This article's doi: 10.1146/annurev.resource.050708.144113

Key Words

biodiversity, ecosystem services, ecosystem externalities, adaptive behavior, mechanistic, Lotka-Volterra

Abstract

Scientific evidence suggests that economic activity is threatening global biodiversity in ways that could severely degrade nature's flow of ecosystem services. Yet, there is relatively little work in economics that addresses biodiversity loss. Some economists have called for better integration of economic and ecological models to address biodiversity and the attendant ecosystem services. Current integrated approaches in economics are discussed, and they take in ecosystem services, ecosystem externalities, and substantial ecological modeling. Much of the modeling uses Lotka-Volterra equations, which are standard in ecology, although there is concern that the equations lack the microfoundations of plant and animal behavior. An alternative approach is to admit microbehavior using economic optimization techniques that build adaptive ecological systems. However, much more effort is needed to assess whether admitting more ecological detail into economic models will be fruitful.

The conservation of natural resources is the fundamental problem. Unless we solve that problem it will avail us little to solve all others.

Theodore Roosevelt address to the Deep Waterway Convention,
Memphis, Tennessee, 4 October 1907

1. INTRODUCTION

Bioeconomic modeling dates back at least to the Faustman forest rotation model and, outside forestry, to the fisheries work of Gordon (1954) and Scott (1955), the theoretical and empirical examination of waterfowl by Hammack & Brown (1974), and Clark's (1976) influential mathematical bioeconomics book. This paper does not survey bioeconomic modeling, but it does discuss a subset of the area labeled ecological-economic modeling. The aim is to draw attention to models in the economic literature that integrate a significant ecological component. Paring down from a survey of bioeconomics narrows the focus considerably, but doing so still leaves a large enough body of work that some of it inevitably will be missed. What is discussed, however, represents interesting analyses that may lead to insights and policies that are not available from less integrated models.

The work discussed is based on the economy-ecosystem interface in **Figure 1** (see color insert), which contains the basic trade-off that anthropogenic activity depends on ecosystem services but generates ecosystem externalities. Biodiversity plays an important role in ecosystem functions from which flow values to humans that economists label direct use, indirect use, and existence (Goulder & Kennedy 1997). These values can be conveniently, if not neatly, divided into the Millennium Ecosystem Assessment's (MEA 2005) classification of ecosystem services: supporting (e.g., soil formation, nutrient cycling), regulating (e.g., climate regulation, water purification), provisioning (e.g., food, wood), and cultural (e.g., recreation, aesthetic). The supporting and regulating services bear the economy's circular flow, whereas the provisioning and cultural ecosystem services are inputs into production and consumption activities. The anthropogenic activity generates ecosystem externalities, which are distinguished from traditional externalities because they involve internal adjustments within ecosystems (Crocker & Tschirhart 1992) (see Ecosystem Externalities, sidebar below). In **Figure 1** the anthropogenic activities creating ecosystem externalities are divided into the five drivers of biodiversity loss that are discussed in the next section.

ECOSYSTEM EXTERNALITIES

Anthropogenic activities use ecosystem services, and the consequent impacts on plants and animals generate ecosystem externalities. That is, following activities, individual plants and animals adapt, species populations alter their paths toward different states, possibly irreversibly (Dasgupta & Mäler 2004, Brock & Xepapadeas 2004), and ecosystem functions and the flow of ecosystem services are altered. If economic agents who receive the altered flows are not compensated, there is said to be an ecosystem externality.

Models covered herein pose an economic problem that includes at least one ecosystem service or the damage to resources providing at least one ecosystem service, at least one ecosystem externality, and an integrated ecological component. An example may help clarify the scope of work. A large percentage of harvesting papers in economics use the following single-species logistic growth function as their ecological component:

$$\dot{N} = rN\left(1 - \frac{N}{K}\right), \qquad (1)$$

where N is the species population density, r is the difference between the per capita birth and death rates or the intrinsic growth rate, K is carrying capacity, and $\dot{N}$ is a time derivative. This function is an extremely simple form of density-dependent growth regulation (Kot2001), and it has been criticized for its lack of biological realism (Getz 1984, Murray 2002) (see Density-Independent Growth, sidebar below). Although lack of realism permeates many ecological and economic models and is not necessarily a shortcoming, the economic work employing Equation 1 is not covered here because it does not include an ecosystem externality. The entire ecosystem beyond the single species is collapsed into K.[1] There is no opportunity to investigate how harvesting impacts biodiversity and ecosystem function, and thereby impacts ecosystem services, beyond the harvest-provisioning service.[2]

DENSITY-INDEPENDENT GROWTH

Density-independent growth implies $(dN/dt)/N$ is independent of N. Whether growth is regulated by density-dependent biotic factors (competition, disease) or density-independent abiotic factors (weather, climate) was debated in ecology from the 1930s to the 1950s, although now both factors are considered important (Kot 2001).

A main theme in this paper is that biological systems are composed of individual organisms that exhibit predictable behavior in response to environmental constraints. Consequently, ecological-economic modeling ought to include those portions of behavior that have a bearing on policies. To this end, and after motivating the need for integrated modeling in Section 2, the structure of the paper is to begin with the most popular ecological models of species interactions and show how they are used in economics. Then the point is made that these models lack behavioral microfoundations of the type economists pioneered with respect to human behavior. Models that develop microfoundations are examined, followed by a discussion of valuing the biodiversity that underpins ecosystem services. The conclusion addresses the usefulness of integration for policy making.

2. MOTIVATION FOR ECOLOGICAL/ECONOMIC MODELS

Late in the twentieth century, Perrings et al. (1995) indicated that biodiversity loss and climate change were the two global environmental transformations that were garnering obsessive public interest, and that of the two, climate change dominated the scientific and policy agenda. The difference today is that climate change also dominates the public

---

[1]Some economists introduce habitat into the growth function [e.g., $K = K(habitat)$ in Equation 1], which is useful for linking a driver of biodiversity loss to economic decisions (Swallow 1990, Skonhoft 1999, Barbier 2003).

[2]Also not covered is the economic forestry literature. Authors have modeled multiple forest ecosystem services (Hartman 1976, Swallow et al. 1990), although the ecological component is usually a standard single-stand model.

interest. Consider two high-profile, exhaustively researched reports that have been published recently: MEA (2005), which reviews biodiversity loss and its consequences for human well-being, and the Nobel Prize–winning report from the Intergovernmental Panel on Climate Change (IPCC 2007). A search for MEA versus IPCC on the *New York Times* Web site reveals 211 results for biodiversity versus 18600 results for climate change. Similar Web-site searches on other information outlets yield the following results: *Time Magazine* (2 versus 387), *The Economist* (2 versus 423), *Der Spiegel* (6 versus 200), *People's Daily* (8 versus 132), *National Geographic* (4 versus 188), *Science* (16140 versus 201730), and *Nature* (39555 versus 159682).

Perrings et al. (1995) speculated that the disproportionate public concern and commitment of resources to climate change versus biodiversity loss are justified if the dire predictions of biologists regarding the latter are wrong. But they reject this speculation, and they are supported by continuing and voluminous evidence of deteriorating ecosystems. Every ecosystem on Earth is significantly impacted by anthropogenic activities in ways that lead to biodiversity loss (Vitousek et al. 1997a), in spite of the fact that economic activities are founded on ecosystem services that flow from biodiversity (Dasgupta 2001).

Consider the five main drivers of biodiversity loss identified in MEA (2005) and listed in **Figure 1**: (*a*) habitat change, (*b*) invasive species, (*c*) pollution, (*d*) overharvesting, and (*e*) climate change. Habitat change follows from humans transforming 50% of Earth's ice-free land surface to agricultural and urban usage (Chapin et al. 2000), appropriating 54% of the available fresh water (Postel et al. 1996) and 40% of vegetation's net primary production (Vitousek et al. 1986). The human population has increased 30% since the latter estimate. Invasive species may be intentionally or unintentionally introduced, often through international trade (Costello & McAusland 2003, Margolis et al. 2005, Mérel & Carter 2008), and they pose significant risks to society (Lodge 2001). Pimentel et al. (2005) estimated annual damages at $120 billion in the United States. In economics, pollution is usually associated with human health, but its impact is so extensive that biogeochemical cycles are being altered. Industrial nitrogen fixation has doubled nitrogen in the environment, which substantially alters ecosystem function (Vitousek et al. 1997b). Historically, overharvesting has been responsible for stunning extinctions such as the passenger pigeon (Conrad 2005), and recent literature describes how overharvesting decimates marine ecosystems. Historical populations of large vertebrates (whales, sharks, turtles, etc.) were "fantastically large" (Jackson et al. 2001), and Worm et al. (2006) projected collapse of all currently harvested marine species by the mid-twenty-first century. Finally, climate change on land is shifting the distribution and abundance of species (Thomas et al. 2004), and at sea, warmer surface water is decreasing marine productivity (Jackson 2008). Thomas et al. (2004) estimated that 15%–37% of species will be committed to future extinction by the mid-twenty-first century.

An alternative reason for the disproportionate emphasis on climate change versus biodiversity loss may be that policy makers and the public have not heard enough from economists. There has been a lively debate on climate change among economists (e.g., Stern 2007, Nordhaus 2007); there has been little debate on biodiversity loss. Regarding the five drivers of biodiversity loss, the debate on climate change has been about discount rates and optimal emissions paths and not on biodiversity. Economists' pollution work is largely about human health and not ecosystem health. Although there is considerable economic work on habitat change regarding land conversion to agriculture in developing countries (e.g., Barbier & Burgess 2001, Barbier 2007) and developed countries (e.g., Langpap et al. 2008), it focuses mostly on institutional incentives, sometimes using indices of ecosystem health, and not on addressing long-term consequences of biodiversity loss. Overharvesting has been by far the most studied driver in the economics literature for over a half century (Gordon 1954, Scott 1955). The literature has been surveyed elsewhere (Wilen 1985, Munro & Scott 1986), and most often it employs single-species, analytically tractable models that biologists have moved away from (Wilen 2000), thereby omitting biodiversity impacts. Recently, economists have turned attention to invasive species where a small literature contains ecological modeling (Shogren & Tschirhart 2005). The invasive-species driver is covered elsewhere (Finnoff & Shogren 2009).

If economists have paid little attention to biodiversity loss, it may stem from a sense of complacency attributable to two popular but mistaken notions. First is the environmental Kuznets curve that portrays an inverted-U relation between economic growth and environmental damage (see Environmental Kuznets Curve, sidebar below). The hypothesis supporting the relation is not compelling if the damage is biodiversity loss, because biodiversity is finite and damages can be irreversible (Arrow et al. 1995). Second is the notion that human and reproducible capital can be substituted for natural capital as the latter becomes scarcer. Although substitutability holds for some natural resources, it does not hold for dwindling biodiversity that implies dwindling ecosystem services, some of which are essential for human existence (Georgescu-Roegen 1975, Clark 1997, Dasgupta, Levin & Lubchenco 2000, Dasgupta 2008).

ENVIRONMENTAL KUZNETS CURVE

The environmental Kuznets curve hypothesis is that in the early stages of a nation's development some environmental damage is acceptable, but as living standards increase, people become more concerned with the environment and create institutions that mitigate the damage. The relation has some empirical support, although mainly for air pollutants, which are narrow measures of environmental quality (Barbier 1997).

In spite of these mistaken notions, some economists have recognized the critical role biodiversity plays in economies. Early on, Daly (1968) pointed out that ecologists abstract from the human economy and study nature's interdependencies, while economists abstract from nature and study human interdependencies. He called for integrating the human economy into the larger economy of nature. For the past two decades, researchers have stressed that ecological and economic systems are jointly determined, because important ecological variables are dependent on economic variables and vice versa. Therefore, in spite of the difficulties, models should integrate ecology and economics to capture important intersystem feedbacks (Amir 1979, Perrings 1987, Crocker & Tschirhart 1987, Costanza et al. 1993, Barbier et al. 1994, Bockstael et al. 1995, Landa & Ghiselin 1999, Settle et al. 2002, Eichner & Pethig 2005, Tilman et al. 2005, Wätzold et al. 2006). Ecological economics, a relatively new field, was founded by ecologists and economists in response to perceived shortcomings in neoclassical resource economics, one of which is the lack of integration between ecology and economics (Costanza & Daly 1987). Government agencies have stressed the need for integration and have funded interdisciplinary work between ecologists and economists.[3]

3. MULTIPLE-SPECIES AND LOTKA-VOLTERRA MODELS

Relationships between interacting species are categorized by how the species impact one another. Six possibilities depend on whether one species impacts another favorably (+), unfavorably (-), or not at all (0): (*a*) neutral (0, 0), (*b*) commensalism (0, +), (*c*) amensalism (0, -), (*d*) mutualism (+, +), (*e*) predator-prey and parasitism (+, -), and (*f*) competition (-, -) (Smith 1995). Predator-prey and competition relations receive the most attention. Ecological models of these relations usually contain two or three species, although they can be extended to many species, and they start with a population-growth function for each species that depends on densities.

The early work of Lotka (1925, 1932) and Volterra (1926) provides the foundation for these models. The simplest structure for the Lotka-Volterra predator-prey model is

$$\dot{N} = rN - bNP \text{ and } \dot{P} = cNP - dP, \tag{2}$$

where N and P are the prey and predator densities, respectively, r and d are per capita rates of growth (in each other's absence prey would grow and the predator decline exponentially), and b and c are rates of change due to the interactions.[4] Growths of the species are density independent. The interaction between predator and prey, NP, is linear and called mass action, a notion borrowed from chemistry that the force between two reactants is proportional to their masses. In essence, an amount of energy, bNP, is taken from the prey of which cNP is captured by the predator. Although solutions to Equation 2 yield stable predator-prey cycles, the system is not structurally stable because small changes in the initial conditions can move the system to very different trajectories (Murray 2002).

The instability and unrealistic exponential growth and decline prompted many extensions to Equation 2. Density-dependent prey growth is often included by appending to Equation 2 the logistic growth function from Equation 1: $\dot{N} = rN(1 - N/K) - bNP$. With this self-limiting prey, instead of stable oscillations, oscillations are transient and converge to steady-state densities that are independent of initial conditions (Gurney & Nisbet 1998).

Another step toward realism is to enrich the functional response that in Equation 2 is simply a linear function of prey density, cNP. As Gurney & Nisbet (1998) noted, "One of the most important interactions between any living organism and its environment is the finding and ingestion of food" (p. 85). Measured as the rate at which predators capture prey and stated as a function of prey, and possibly predator, abundances, functional response represents this interaction. The functional response may depend on how predators expend time to capture and handle prey, and whether they are satiated. Adding a more realistic functional response to Equation 2 yields

---

[3]Examples include programs by the U.S. Environmental Protection Agency (An Interdisciplinary Approach to Examining the Links Between Social Stressors, Biodiversity and Human Health) and the National Science Foundation (Dynamics of Coupled Natural and Human Systems). Additionally, some institutions specifically address biodiversity issues and the need for integration: For examples, see Beijer Institute of Ecological Economics (**http://www.beijer.kva.se/**) and DIVERSITAS (**http://www.diversitas-international.org/**).

[4]Nicholas & Bailey (1935) presented an alternative predator-prey model that uses discrete time and difference equations, but it is conceptually identical to the Lotka-Volterra model (Royoma 1971).

$$\dot{N} = rN(1 - N/K) - b(N)P \text{ and } \dot{P} = cPb(N) - dP, \tag{3}$$

where $b(N)$ is the response (Berryman 1992). The functional response form is subject to much debate, although many models follow Holling (1966) and use forms that are either strictly concave (Type II) or sigmoid (Type III):

$$\text{(II) } b(N) = \frac{mN}{a + N}; \text{(III) } b(N) = \frac{mN^2}{a^2 + N^2}. \tag{4}$$

In Equation 4, m is a maximum attack rate and a is a half-saturation constant. A Type I response is the linear mass-action form in Equation 2. With a Type II functional response, a steady-state solution can be obtained that is independent of initial conditions, provided the predator density can grow when the prey is at its carrying capacity. However, if the prey carrying capacity is above a critical value, the solution is unstable, a result referred to as the "paradox of enrichment" (Gurney & Nisbet 1998).

Another debate surrounding predator-prey modeling is whether the functional response should be written $b(N/P)$, yielding a so-called ratio-dependent predator-prey theory. On the one hand, Arditi & Ginzburg (1989) claimed that this formulation does away with the timescale problem whereby predator search is on a behavioral timescale (hours) and growth is on a reproductive timescale (days, years). Additionally, Gutierrez (1992) offered a physiological basis for ratio-dependent predation. On the other hand, Abrams (1994) argued that there can be no separation of behavioral and reproductive timescales, because predator behavior determines prey death rates. He argued that proponents are confounding functional and numerical response, where the latter is the predator density as a function of prey density.

Economists have used the Lotka-Volterra predator-prey model with self-limiting growth for both predator and prey and the Type I functional response from Equation 2. In this work, either the predator, prey, or both are harvested (Hannesson 1983, Ragozin & Brown 1985, Wilen & Brown 1986, Ströbele & Wacker 1991, Hartwick & Olewiler 1998, Brown et al. 2005), or neither is harvested but the predator density is controlled (Tu & Wilman 1992). Harvest of one species provides a provisioning ecosystem service, and if the other species provides a separate ecosystem service, then the ecosystem externality refers to how harvesting one species affects the other species via the predator-prey relation. When it is explicitly modeled in these papers, harvesting also provides the other species ecosystem service. Analytical results for two-species models are elusive (Brown et al. 2005); simpler models yield clearer results at the expense of ecological reality such as more realistic functional responses. Optimal harvesting depends on how efficiently prey biomass is biologically converted into predator biomass: Lower efficiency means less valuable prey. A higher market price for predators (prey) favors larger (smaller) predator and prey stocks. If predators have low value, optimality may call for their elimination and may include subsidized predator harvests. Alternatively, if predator value is high, optimality may call for no prey harvests. Abiotic perturbations to predator-prey populations require either cutting back on predator harvests or, if the prey is disproportionately negatively impacted, increasing predator harvests.

Bulte & Damania (2003) presented a predator-prey harvesting model containing the more complex Holling Type II functional response in the prey equation; however, the predator equation exhibits logistic growth and does not contain the response. Under open access, they find that if there are multiple equilibria, there is the possibility that heavier predator harvesting can increase the prey density (especially if habitat is fragmented) and ultimately be beneficial to the predator.

The equations for the Lotka-Volterra competition model for two competing species with densities N_1 and N_2 are

$$\dot{N}_1 = r_1 N_1 \left[1 - \frac{N_1}{K_1} \right] - \frac{r_1 a_{12} N_1 N_2}{K_1} \text{ and}$$

$$\dot{N}_2 = r_2 N_2 \left[1 - \frac{N_2}{K_2} \right] - \frac{r_2 a_{21} N_2 N_1}{K_2}, \tag{5a, b}$$

where a_{ij} is the competition coefficient that measures how species j diminishes the growth of species i, $i, j = 1, 2, i \neq j$. Equations 5a and 5b are also attributed to Gause (1934). Both species exhibit self-limiting growth, and the strength of the interference is proportional to the densities (see Competitive Exclusion Principle, sidebar below). For a wide range of a values, one species will drive the other to extinction: Coexistence requires $a_{ij} < K_i / K_j$ (Kot 2001). If the negative signs before the last terms in both equations are positive, the species are in a mutualistic relation. Wacker (1999) investigated the mutualistic version of Equations 5a and 5b and concluded that optimum harvesting is more conservative than with single-species models.

COMPETITIVE EXCLUSION PRINCIPLE

One species extinguishing the other is called the competitive exclusion principle, and it is "one of the foundations of theoretical ecology" (Wangersky 1978, p. 203). The principle is often referred to as Gause's Law (Gause 1934) and has been the subject of extensive debate in ecology (Armstrong & McGehee 1980). It maintains that two or more resource-limited species cannot coexist in a stable environment.

A few economists have used Equations 5a and 5b in harvesting models of competing species, although general results are difficult to obtain and a mix of estimated and arbitrary biological parameters are employed. Conrad & Adu-Asamoah (1986) studied two species of tuna and contrasted open-access and optimum harvests. Not surprisingly, for optimum harvesting, the densities of both species were between their open-access densities and their densities in the absence of all harvesting. Surprisingly, however, the density of Skipjack tuna was greater under open access than under no harvesting, because harvesting has a measurable impact on Yellowfin's competitive ability. Flaaten (1991) investigated harvests of two competing species in a theoretical model and derived a maximum sustainable frontier, or production possibility frontier, that is the counterpart of the maximum sustainable yield in single-species models. The frontier shows the maximum sustainable yields of one species for constant sustainable yields of the other species (May et al. 1979). Flaaten (1991) illustrated that the optimum harvested density for a competing species may be increasing in the discount rate and may be lower than its open-access density, a result that is also possible for predators in a predator-prey model but not in single-species models.

In a twist to the competing-species model, Guttormsen et al. (2008) examined competing phenotypes of a harvested fish in which the equivalent of Equations 5a and 5b is

$$\dot{N}_g + \dot{N}_b = r(N_g + N_b)\left[1 - \frac{N_g + N_b}{K}\right] - d_g(1 - q^2)(N_g + N_b) - d_b q^2(N_g + N_b), \quad (6)$$

where g and b stand for the good and bad phenotype, respectively, d_i is a mortality rate, and $(1 - q)$ and q are the frequencies of the good and bad phenotypes derived from a standard Mendelian genetic model. Good types form schools to reduce mortality and energy use, but schooling is essential for harvesting and the fishery would not be viable without it. In the absence of harvesting, the good type eventually would drive out the bad. However, optimal harvesting may allow positive densities of the bad type to persist.

Lotka-Volterra equations may also be applied to spatial modeling wherein species are mobile between geographically separate areas or patches. For example, for a predator-prey system in two patches, $j, k = 1, 2, j \neq k$, Gurney & Nisbet (1998) explained the system as follows:

$$\dot{N}_k = r_k N_k(1 - N_k/K_k) - bN_k P_k \text{ and}$$
$$\dot{P}_k = \varepsilon bN_k P_k - dP_k + \sigma(P_j - P_k). \quad (7a, b)$$

The key difference from the basic predator-prey model is the last term in the predator equation in which σ is the probability per unit time that a predator will move to another patch. Admitting spatial considerations is ecologically realistic because environments are not homogeneous, species growth rates and carrying capacities may vary across patches, and organisms may spread from high- to low-density habitat.

Economists have used variants of Equations 7a and 7b, including stochastic versions, and the work is important for bringing spatial elements into economic modeling (Bockstael 1996, Wilen 2007). Smith & Crowder (2005) modeled blue crab predators that follow prey between two patches in a North Carolina estuary. Nitrogen loading from agriculture is an ecosystem externality that differentially harms the prey between patches, thereby impacting the blue crab harvests. The authors estimated the net benefits of reducing nitrogen loading. Other economists omit the predator-prey relation in Equations 7a and 7b and consider one mobile, harvested species (Brown & Roughgarden 1997, Conrad 1999, Sanchirico & Wilen 1999, 2005, Bhat & Huffaker 2007, Costello & Polaksy 2008). Particular emphasis is on establishing marine reserves closed to fishing and whether such reserves can increase profits. The ecosystem externality is the spatial externality where harvesting in one patch impacts the economic returns in other patches through fish migration, larvae drift, or other ecological changes (Costello & Polaksy 2008).

In terrestrial systems, the Lotka-Volterra competition as noted in Equations 5a and 5b has been used to model plant competitors that are subject to pressure from livestock that provide a grazing ecosystem service. Huffaker & Cooper (1995) investigated competition between native grass and less nutritious invasive grass, with fast dynamics represented by grazing and slow dynamics by plant competition. Perrings & Walker (1997) investigated competition between grasses and woody vegetation subject to periodic fires. Terms are added in Equations 5a and 5b to capture the fire regime where fire reduces the woody vegetation and allows more grass for grazing. Stocking is a control variable in both papers, and both emphasize that grazing can cause the rangeland to flip from a grass-dominated system to one dominated by invasive grass or woody plants. Janssen et al. (2004) offered a more ecologically detailed grazing model using stochastic rainfall and stocking as well as fire suppression as control variables. Grass competes with woody shrubs, but the grass is divided into roots and shoots. The shoot biomass competes with shrubs and is consumed by grazers. The manager must balance fire suppression by allowing more grass forage and by using grass as fuel for a fire that will reduce shrub biomass. Again, the rangeland can flip between grass- and shrub-dominated systems, and rainfall uncertainty calls for a precautionary management strategy.

Using a very different ecological model, Finnoff et al. (2008) also addressed the grazing problem. The Lotka-Volterra approach is replaced by individual native and invasive grass plants that optimize net energy from photosynthesis by competing for light and that respond differentially to anthropogenically elevated nitrogen levels. Individual optimization introduces microfoundations into population dynamics by suggesting a mechanism for competition and predation.

4. MECHANISTIC COMPETITION MODELS

The Lotka-Volterra competition model has been criticized for being phenomenological as opposed to mechanistic (Schoener 1976; Tilman 1982, 1987). In economic terminology, the model lacks microfoundations because it provides only a description of the outcome of competition instead of an actual competitive mechanism grounded in physiological processes. Additionally, the competition coefficients in Equations 5a and 5b change as competitor densities change (Schoener 1976, Abrams 1977). Therefore, inferences about competitive processes drawn from the Lotka-Volterra model are limited. One alternative is to use exploitation competition models in which two or more competitors share a common resource. A dynamic equation describes the resource, which can be either abiotic such as nitrogen or biotic such as a common prey. Tilman (1987) cited authors in the 1960s and 1970s for introducing more mechanistic models of competition that include the process by which competition occurs as well as information on the physiology, morphology, and/or behavior of individual species. Extending MacArthur (1972), Tilman (1982, 1988) introduced a mechanistic competitive model to generalize previous work and to introduce competition more explicitly at the species level. The "resource-ratio theory" of interactions based on species' use of shared resources has been very influential and has fostered at least 1333 papers in which the authors cite Tilman's approach (Miller et al. 2005).

Brock & Xepapadeas (2002, 2003) integrated resource-ratio theory into economic models, and in doing so, not only do they derive results that extend previous economic analyses, but they also generalize Tilman's model (Brock et al. 2009). The authors considered multiple patches of land, each of which contains multiple plant species that are competing for a limiting resource. Humans enjoy provisioning ecosystem services by harvesting species on the patches, and they also enjoy cultural ecosystem services because they derive utility from the nonconsumptive use of biodiversity on each patch. The authors considered two programs: a private optimal management program (POMP) in which humans do not account for the effect harvesting has on biodiversity and a social optimal management program (SOMP) in which humans do account for the effect. In a POMP, harvesting generates an ecosystem externality, but in a SOMP, the ecosystem externality is internalized.

The ecology that Brock & Xepapadeas (2002, 2003) integrate into their economic problem can be summarized as follows: On each patch of land there are n species that are competing for a single limiting resource. A resource might be nitrate, water, or any other factor that is required by the organisms, exogenously supplied, and depleted by use. The competition equations are

$$\dot{B}_{ic} = B_{ic}[g_{ic}(R_c) - d_{ic}] \text{ and } \dot{R}_c = S_c - aR_c - \sum_{i=1}^{n} w_i B_{ic} g_{ic}(R_c), \quad (8\text{a,b})$$

where B_{ic} is the biomass of species i on patch c, R_c is the amount of resource on patch c with natural supply rate S_c, g_{ic} is the biomass growth that depends on availability of the resource, d_{ic} is the species natural death rate, α is the natural rate of resource deterioration, and w_i is the usage of the resource by species i. An equilibrium of this system is defined by $\dot{B}_{ic} = \dot{R}_c = 0$ for all i and c. Letting $\dot{R}_{ic}^*$ be the resource level for species i in patch c at which the species' growth and death rates are equal, the authors showed that the species with the lowest $\dot{R}_{ic}^*$ will displace all other species. The mechanism for displacement is that the biomass of the surviving species will increase until it drives the amount of available resource so low that other species cannot survive. This result reproduces part of the competitive exclusion principle.

In Brock & Xepapadeas (2002), the provisional ecosystem services are defined as

$$V(\bar{H}_c(t)) = \sum_{i=1}^{n} p_i(y) H_{ic}(t), \quad (9)$$

where H_{ic} is the harvest of species i from patch c, p_i is the market price of the harvested species net of costs, and $\bar{H}_c$ is a vector of the harvests. For each harvested species, the harvest must be subtracted from the right side of Equation 8a to account for the loss of biomass. The cultural ecosystem service is defined as

$$U(\bar{B}_c(t)) = \sum_{i=1}^{n} s_{ic} B_{ic}(t), \quad (10)$$

where s_{ic} is a constant social benefit for the nonmarketed flow of services that depend on the biomass of the species in each patch.

In the POMP, the discounted present value of Equation 9 is maximized with harvests as control variables and biomasses and the limiting resource as state variables. The steady-state solutions are characterized in terms of the pattern of species specialization, that is, which conditions determine whether a monoculture is optimum in each patch. Specialization is optimal in the species that yields the highest steady-state, present value of profits. The conditions that determine the pattern of specialization depend on both economic parameters, including the discount rate and price of the marketed harvest, and ecological parameters, including growth and death rates, the resource supply and deterioration rates, and the usage of the resource by the species. The bottom line is that nature and humans will not necessarily choose the same specialization pattern. In particular, the ecosystem chooses according to the resource ratio theory that states the surviving species will have the lowest $\dot{R}_{ic}^*$ d_i/g_i. Not surprisingly, nature favors species with low death and high growth rates. Alternatively, to form monocultures, humans choose the species with high values of p_i/w_i. In essence, humans are looking for the biggest "bang for their buck" by choosing species with a high market value per unit of limiting resource that the species absorbs.

In the SOMP, the discounted present value of Equations 9 plus 10 is maximized so that both provisioning and cultural services are recognized. In this case, specialization depends not only on p_i/w_i but also on s_i/w_i so that the social benefit of the species matters. Depending on parameter values, it is possible that nature, the POMP, and the SOMP will each yield different patterns of specialization. Brock & Xepapadeas (2002) pointed to "biomimicry" as a possible outcome wherein the SOMP corresponds to nature's outcome but differs from the POMP. This case can occur when farmers, who typically practice specialization in the highest valued crops, are encouraged to farm closer to nature because other crops might yield nonmarket ecosystem services. The POMP generates ecosystem externalities because species adapt to specialization patterns by producing biomasses that yield suboptimal societal welfare. Taxes can provide incentives to move from the POMP to the SOMP.

5. MECHANISTIC PREDATOR-PREY AND COMPETITION MODELS WITH ADAPTIVE BEHAVIOR

The criticism that Lotka-Volterra competition models are phenomenological as opposed to mechanistic has also been levied against Lotka-Volterra predator-prey models. Abrams (1982, 1994) argued that real predator functional responses are likely to be more flexible than modeled, because predators occupy environments in which the benefits and costs of predation differ. Therefore, predators probably have some mechanism for adapting foraging strategies, whereas ratio-dependent, functional response models do not take such adaptations into account. Omitting adaptive behavior is particularly problematic in models with two or more prey where predators can potentially substitute, or switch in ecological terms, between prey. Eichner & Pethig (2003) developed a more mechanistic predator-prey model in which each species maximizes biomass that is determined by consumption of prey, losses to predators, and the cost of hunting. To emphasize the role of scarcity in ecosystems, prices of hunting are used as scarcity indicators. The price of capturing prey is either positive, indicating the prey is scarce, or zero, indicating the prey is free, in which case the predator is satiated. Prices are also endogenous and depend on populations. Using a three-species food chain, the authors identified eight regimes differentiated by whether the three prices are zero or positive. Population dynamics depend on optimum biomasses attained by the species, and species growth equations differ depending on satiation. This contrasts to Lotka-Volterra equations with population-independent parameters.

Asserting that species optimize adds a mechanism to predator-prey modeling, although in reality individuals, not species, optimize. Admitting adaptive predator behavior via individual optimum foraging is a further step toward a more realistic mechanism. Inspired by economic consumer theory, optimum foraging is a well-established area of ecology (Stephans & Krebs 1986); however, as Amir (1979) and Abrams (1999) indicated, most studies employing optimum foraging ignore population dynamics and most studies of population dynamics ignore optimum foraging.

Given ecologists' criticism of Lotka-Volterra equations as lacking competitive or predation mechanisms, and given that the alternative resource-ratio theory is based on species behavior instead of individual behavior, there is opportunity for introducing more microfounded mechanisms. This is the motivation for approaches that integrate economic methods into ecology. The methods encompass adaptive behavior by individual organisms, similar to optimum foraging, and aggregate stories emerge from individual decisions. Individual choices are endogenous and not restricted a priori with specific functional forms for switching behavior and functional responses (see Predator Switching, sidebar below). Competition is not described by species-specific constant coefficients that specify resource usage, but rather by endogenous prices as signals of resource scarcity. And instead of dissimilar predator and prey growth equations, the same equations apply to all species (Getz 1984). Note that most of these features are common in economics models. Indeed, ecologists and economists often have noted similarities between economic and ecological systems (see Rapport 1971, Tullock 1971, Hannon 1973, 1976, Rapport & Turner 1977, Hirshleifer 1977, Amir 1979, Bloom et al. 1985, Finnoff & Tschirhart 2007).

PREDATOR SWITCHING

Predator switching behavior is similar to consumer substitution. However, unlike economic models where substitution depends on prices, within ecology, switching is not modeled as a function of predation costs. Instead switching is a function of prey densities and occurs when the ratio of prey consumptions varies from the ratio of prey densities. Switching based on densities seems behaviorally less plausible than switching based on predation costs, because predators are unlikely to inventory densities in choosing an optimal diet.

Tschirhart (2000) introduced a general equilibrium ecosystem model (GEEM) that includes these features. GEEM is a modified version of an economic general equilibrium model in which industries are replaced by species, firms are replaced by individual plants and animals, individuals are assumed to behave as if they are optimizing net energy intake, and energy is the currency. Demand and supply are replaced by predator-prey relations, and predators (plants) engage in intra- and interspecies competition for prey (sunlight). A major difference between the GEEM and economic models is that demanders and suppliers do not engage in voluntary exchange: In predator-prey relations, there is an involuntary transfer of energy and biomass from prey to predators. The modeling significance of the difference is discussed in Tschirhart (2003). GEEM dynamics involve individuals converting their optimum net energies into offspring, a common ecological notion (Schoener 1986), which is not unlike firms entering or exiting fisheries depending on profits (Smith 1969, Wilen 1976, Amundsen et al. 1995).

As an ecological model, the GEEM is more mechanistic and provides microfoundations for population dynamics by deriving dynamic equations from optimal foraging. Building from microfoundations is also the theme in Eichner & Pethig (2006a, 2006b) and Christiaans et al. (2007), who also modeled individuals as optimizers and, as in the GEEM, used endogenous prices as scarcity indicators. They draw more heavily than the GEEM upon the similarities between demand-supply and predator-prey relations, because an individual's biomass supplies to predators are seen as a voluntary exchange. In contrast to the GEEM, individual organisms are not depicted as firms maximizing net energy (profit), but as consumers maximizing biomass (utility), subject to a constraint. In the firm analogy, predation is a cost to the individual, whereas in the utility analogy, predation is a source of income to a predator, which, along with an endowment, the predator spends on consuming prey. The latter interpretation may be problematic for empirical work if the income and endowment are not well matched to ecological data; nevertheless, the authors' results illuminate the power of the individual-optimization approach. They start with the following problems:

$$\max B^y(d_r, s_y, y) \text{ subject to } \omega_y + p_y s_y = p_r d_r \text{ and} \tag{11}$$

$$\max B^x(d_x, x) \text{ subject to } \omega_x = p_y d_y, \tag{12}$$

where B^i is the offspring to an individual prey ($i = y$) or predator ($i = x$), x and y are densities, p terms are prices, ω_i are endowments, and d and s terms are demands and supplies, respectively. Eichner & Pethig (2006a, 2006b) and Christiaans et al. (2007) ask whether there is a form for B^i that will yield reasonable predator-prey equations. They answer by deriving Lotka-Volterra equations with Holling Type II functional responses for top predators, but for prey species the growth equations differ structurally from their Lotka-Volterra counterparts. The system converges to steady state without exhibiting oscillating behavior as in Lotka-Volterra models, because the endogenous prices have a dampening effect on population swings.

Amir (1979) maintained the importance of general equilibrium analysis for addressing interactions between ecosystems and economies. Eichner & Pethig (2009) forcefully extended this theme by inserting their individual-optimization approach into a theoretical general dynamic analysis that includes the economy and the multispecies ecosystem as interdependent subsystems. Humans harvest biomass and convert land from habitat to economic uses, and both activities generate ecosystem externalities that have intertemporal impacts on ecosystem services. Both subsystems possess the same level of structural detail including markets for land and biomass as well as decentralized competitive mechanisms that yield an efficient joint system, so long as tax-subsidy schemes are employed. In the absence of such schemes, human private property rights over species habitat are insufficient to ensure efficient outcomes. The analysis also ties together shadow prices in the ecosystem with economic prices to determine values for all ecosystem components.

The GEEM applies general equilibrium concepts to ecosystems that are discussed below; therefore, its basic structure is briefly summarized here. The objective function of an individual animal in species j is in power units (Watts or kilocalories/time):

$$R_j = \sum_{k=1}^{j-1} (e_k - e_{jk}) x_{jk} - r^j(x_{j1}, \ldots, x_{j,j-1}) - b_j - e_j \sum_{k=j+1}^{s} y^{jk}(x_{j1}, \ldots, x_{j,j-1}, e_{kj}). \tag{13}$$

The first term on the right side is the inflow of energy from prey species (including plants). The choice variables or demands, x_{jk}, are the prey biomasses consumed, e_k are the energies embodied in the biomasses, and e_{jk} are the energies spent capturing biomasses. These latter energies are essentially energy prices; there is one price in each predator and prey relation. As in economic computable general equilibrium (CGE) models, prices play a central role. Individuals are assumed to be price takers, because each is only one among many individuals in a predator species capturing one of many individuals in a prey species.

The second and third terms represent respiration energy lost to the atmosphere, which, following Gurney & Nisbet (1998), is divided into a variable component, $r^j(\cdot)$, that depends on energy intake and includes reproduction, defending territory, etc., and a fixed component or basal metabolism. The fourth term is the outflow of energy to predators of species j. The e_j is the embodied energy in individual j's biomass, and y^{jk} is the biomass supplied to j's predators in species k. The biomass supply function depends on the individual's demands, because the more the individual feeds, the more it is exposed and the more biomass it supplies to predators. This trade-off between foraging gains and losses is called predation risk.

The animal's biomass consumption of species i is characterized by Kuhn-Tucker conditions:

$$\partial R_j / \partial x_{ji} = (e_i - e_{ji}) - \partial r^j / \partial x_{ji} - \sum_{k=j+1}^{s} \partial y^{jk} / \partial x_{j1} \leq 0 \quad , \text{and} \tag{14}$$

$$[\partial R_j / \partial x_{ji}] x_{ji} = 0 \qquad x_{ji} \geq 0$$

$$N_j x_{ji} - N_i y^{ji} \leq 0 \tag{15}$$

$$e_{ji} [N_j x_{ji} - N_i y^{ji}] = 0 \quad e_{ji} \geq 0$$

Conditions noted in Equation 14 imply that if the predator j consumes the ith prey, then the marginal energy gained equals the sum of marginal energy losses to predation and respiration. Alternatively, if the marginal energy gained is less than the sum, the ith prey is not consumed. The marginal gain/marginal loss ratios are equal across prey species. Conditions noted in Equation 15 are the demand/supply condition between the jth and i^{th} species, where N_k is the density of species $k = i, j$. If demand is less than supply, the energy price paid by the predator is zero, or in other words, the prey is a free good and the predator is satiated in that prey. In this case, there is said to be no competition among species j predators for species i. Alternatively, a positive price implies demand equals supply and nonsatiation.

For each reproductive period and for given species densities, Equations 14 and 15 yield all species demands and energy prices. The densities then are updated to start the next period. The update equation for species j is

$$N_j^{t+1} - N_j^t = N_j^t \left\{ \left[pred_j^t \left[1 - \frac{1}{s_j} \right] + \frac{1}{s_j} \right] \left[\frac{R_j^t \left(\bar{x}_j^t(\bar{N}), \bar{e}_j^t(\bar{N}) \right) + r^j}{r_{ss}^j} - 1 \right] \right\}, \tag{16}$$

where s_j is the average individual life span, r_{ss}^j is the steady-state variable respiration, $pred$ is the predation rate, and the t superscript denotes the time period. The bar notation indicates vectors; thus, the individual's optimum net energy is a function of prices and its optimum consumptions, both of which are functions of all densities. This functional relationship reflects the general equilibrium nature of the model, although it is not possible to solve analytically for the consumptions and prices when there is more than one trophic level. Therefore, it is not possible to determine analytically steady-state stability.[5]

---

[5]Parameterizing the GEEM with real data and many species has invariably yielded stable equilibriums, but Christiaans et al. (2006) showed that the dynamics are complex. Using a one predator–one prey GEEM model, they rigorously derived conditions for global asymptotic stability and local asymptotic stability and instability.

The GEEM has been applied to both metaphoric and real ecosystems with or without connections to economies. The data to examine real systems are mostly individual plant and animal physiological parameters that are available but scattered across the ecological literature. In applications excluding humans, the GEEM has been used to derive conditions for the coexistence of competing plant species (Tschirhart 2002), to derive functional and numerical responses and switching behavior of killer whales (Tschirhart 2004), and to predict the mediating effect of a predator on prey competitors (Kim et al. 2007). In the latter case, early in the twentieth century, invasive house mice competed with California native mice for forage. When citizens exterminated the mice predators, the house mice outcompeted the native mice, which resulted in what was arguably the most dramatic rodent outbreak ever reported in North America.

The impetus for developing the GEEM is to integrate it with economic models. To that end, the economic-ecological GEEM have been applied to the Alaskan economy and marine ecosystem (Finnoff & Tschirhart 2003a, 2003b). **Figure 2** (see color insert) illustrates the most recent version of the links between the systems. In this example, pollock harvesting generates an ecosystem externality by diminishing marine mammal populations and thereby reducing profits in the recreation industry.

The point of building CGE models is to draw on the basic microbehavior of interacting agents to inform tax, trade, environmental, or other policies that are expected to impact economic prices and thereby change the flow of real goods, factors of production, consumer incomes and their distribution, and ultimately welfare. The general equilibrium structure may sometimes reveal insights that would not be forthcoming in partial equilibrium analyses. The same can be said for an integrated CGE-GEEM model, although the insights may involve internal ecosystem adjustments that would not be available in one or two species models.

For example, in the ecosystem in **Figure 2**, growth curves for each species can be derived. **Figure 3** illustrates the growth curve for cod, a harvested species and an important predator and prey species in the food web. At each cod density, the curve shows a steady-state cod harvest, whereas all other species are at steady-state levels that support the harvest. The curve begins at the origin with a linear segment over which growth is density independent, then moves into piecewise, strictly convex segments over which growth is density dependent. The shape is explained by the cods' predatory behavior: When growth is density independent, the prices for all five prey species are zero and cod are satiated. As the cod population grows, at each connection point between adjoining segments, one prey's price turns positive and cod substitute or switch from this costly prey to prey that are still "free" (Finnoff & Tschirhart 2008b). The density-independent portion of the curve was anticipated in individual-optimization theoretical models for a single species (Pethig & Tschirhart 2001) and for a three-species food chain (Eichner & Pethig 2006a, 2006b). Although overall the growth curve is reminiscent of the logistic growth curve, the obvious differences yield a nonconvex harvest function. The nonconvexity is due to biological processes and distinct from the familiar nonconvex harvest function associated with growth curves that exhibit critical depensation (Clark 1976, Dasgupta & Mäler 2004).

Another example of insights unavailable in one or two species models is brought out in the economy-ecosystem model in **Figure 2**. In 2001, the National Marine Fisheries Service offered alternative management strategies that specified reduced pollock catch

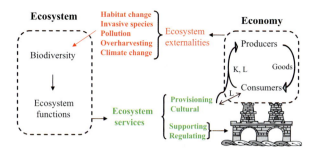

Figure 1

Linkages within and between the economic and ecological systems. For an alternative version of this figure, see Barbier et al. (1994).

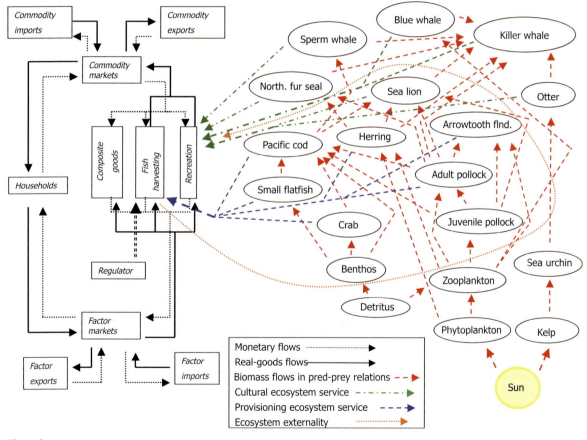

Figure 2

System integrating ecological (general equilibrium ecosystem model, GEEM) and economic (computable general equilibrium model, CGE) models of an Alaskan marine ecosystem and the state economy. Indicated are the predator-prey relations (*red arrows*); ecosystem linkages to the CGE model of the economy (*blue and green arrows*); and the externality from the harvesting industry, cascading through the ecosystem and ending in the recreation industry (*dotted orange arrow*). Seven interspecies competitive relations, five harvested species including age-structured pollock supplying provisioning ecosystem services, and six mammal species supplying cultural ecosystem services via tourism or recreation are included. Phytoplankton and kelp "prey" on the sun, which is the source of all ecosystem energy. Source: Finnoff & Tschirhart (2008a).

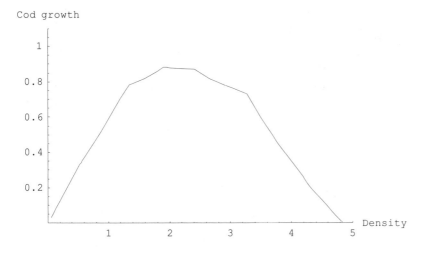

Figure 3

Growth curve for cod with cod predator and prey species held at steady-state values that change with cod steady-state harvests. The curve is made up of an initial linear segment followed by piecewise strictly convex segments.

limits and no fishing zones to protect endangered sea lions. The justification was that reduced limits would increase pollock populations, and because sea lions prey on pollock this would shore up their populations. Simulations of the model in **Figure 2** suggest another possibility. Decreased harvests of adult pollock increase their population, which increases the price individual adults pay to cannibalize juvenile pollock. There is a negative functional response, or lower adult consumption, but a positive numerical response because more adults are consuming juvenile pollock. Additionally, the higher price lowers an individual adult's energy and the adult produces fewer offspring. The net result of these countervailing forces is a lower juvenile population. The lower price sea lions pay for the greater adult population is more than offset by the higher price they pay for the smaller juvenile population, and sea lion net energy and population decrease instead of increase as expected. In addition, sea lions are more heavily preyed upon by killer whales: Because these predators also consume adult pollock, when the pollock are more plentiful after reduced harvests, the killer whales show a positive numerical response and their greater numbers consume more sea lions.

The result that reduced pollock harvesting may reduce sea lion populations was also obtained by Trites et al. (1999) using an ECOPATH with ECOSIM (EwE) model (see ECOPATH, sidebar below). Unfortunately, limited information about trophic interactions makes verification of EwE, GEEM, or other multispecies models difficult (Hollowed et al. 2000). Nevertheless, the trophic interactions are important for the many government agencies that have moved in recent years from single-species management to an ecosystem approach to management (Sutinen 2007). The aspiration is to integrate EwE with sophisticated economic models, similar to the above attempt of linking a GEEM to a CGE model, to determine whether either approach yields enough additional insights over traditional single-species, single-industry models to warrant the additional effort.

ECOPATH

NOAA sites Ecopath as one of its top-ten breakthroughs, along with its Climate Model and other works (**http://www.ecopath.org/**). New ECOPATH versions and its dynamic extension, ECOSIM (Walters et al. 1997), calculate energy flows under mass-balance assumptions and have been applied to numerous ecosystems, mostly aquatic. EwE may contain hundreds of predator-prey and competitive relations among hundreds of species, and it is the most widely used approach for assessing ecosystem effects of fishing (Plagányi & Butterworth 2004). ECOPATH can be likened to a one-period calculation in a GEEM, and ECOSIM adds the dynamic part of a GEEM. EwE is not behavioral as it does not rely on individual optimization; therefore, it does not replicate predator switching or endogenous functional responses. Also, it does not connect success in optimization to reproduction, relying instead on fixed ratios for reproduction to total biomass (Plagányi & Butterworth 2004). A rough analogy is that EwE is to a GEEM as input-output analysis is to a CGE. Another approach is to integrate input-output ecological and economic models (Hannon et al. 1991, Jin et al. 2003).

6. BIODIVERSITY LOSS

Because economic activities create ecosystem externalities that diminish biodiversity and, in turn, diminish ecosystem services, a natural role for economists is to examine the trade-offs between consuming ecosystem services and generating ecosystem externalities. A somewhat less natural role is to address the question of whether society has a moral imperative to conserve biodiversity. Does all value from nature originate with human preferences, or as environmental ethicists argue, is there intrinsic value in nature that transcends consumptive or nonconsumptive values to humans? Eichner & Pethig (2006c) tackled this question using an economic-ecological model in which humans allocate land to a consumer good or to species habitat, and species are a second input into the consumer good. The authors employed their individual-offspring-maximization approach described above, where individuals consume prey and require habitat. The welfare function is either anthropocentric (only human utility matters), biocentric (only nonhuman utility determined by individual biomasses and densities matters), or nonanthropocentric (both human and nonhuman utilities matter). For biocentricity, a welfare maximum has all economic activity going to zero, because nonhumans can exist without humans, whereas the reverse is not true. The nonanthropocentric solution yields a greater habitat protection than does the anthropocentric solution; but greater habitat is also achieved with higher weights on the existence of nonhuman species in the human utility function. This result can be interpreted as a justification for the standard economic anthropocentric approach, provided the weights on nonhuman populations are correct.

If trade-offs between consuming ecosystem services and generating ecosystem externalities indicate more biodiversity is desirable, then conservation should be efficient, which is the subject of various theoretical and applied studies. Brock & Xepapadeas (2003) used a Tilman competition model as described in Section 4 to investigate optimum biodiversity in an agricultural system: Two crops compete for a limiting resource, and three pests are distinguished by genotype. One crop kills two of the pests, while the other crop kills no pests. The pests' propagation depends on how much land is cultivated in each crop. The economic problem is to maximize the value of harvests given the plant competition and pest propagation. There is a trade-off between specializing in a single crop today at the expense of a smaller gene pool tomorrow. In a SOMP, this trade-off is taken into account, whereas in a POMP the agriculturalists believe their crop choices have negligible impacts on the pests' gene pool so the impacts are ignored. The difference between the Bellman state value function for the SOMP and optimum diversity, and for the POMP and suboptimum diversity, yields the value of biodiversity.

The study by Brock & Xepapadeas (2003) is an agriculture story more than a biodiversity story. The ecosystem service is crop output, but agriculture is a highly managed system that has replaced whatever ecosystem existed prior to cultivation. The work omits perhaps the most important ecosystem externalities associated with agriculture: Agriculture productivity "is a success story of enhanced production of one key ecosystem service, [that] has come at high and growing costs in terms of trade-offs with other ecosystem services," owing to land-cover change and nutrient runoff (MEA 2005, p. 8).

Nevertheless, the work is an exceptional example of rigorously integrated economic and biological modeling, and the authors noted that the methodology is general enough for application to other ecosystems. The authors also made the point that, by integrating biodiversity with an economic model, its value can be ascertained by the services it provides, in contrast to assuming that biodiversity is desirable in its own right so that the problem is one of measuring it and conserving it at least cost. Other noteworthy examples include the following: Weitzman (1992) and Solow et al. (1993) defined diversity using pairwise distances between species, which can then be used to prioritize conservation plans. Ando et al. (1998) used land prices for finding least-cost solutions for conserving suites of species. Wätzold & Drechsler (2005) incorporated a species area curve to investigate uniform versus spatially heterogeneous compensation payments. Polasky et al. (2005) used habitat preferences, area requirements, and dispersal ability to demonstrate that an economic-ecology model can lower costs and improve conservation relative to models that assume all economic activity (biological activity) takes place outside (inside) nature reserves.

In another study, Eichner & Pethig (2006d) used their integrated economic-ecology dynamic modeling approach to show that species populations that enter a welfare function as proxies for ecosystem services are also public goods and as such are undersupplied in a laissez-faire economy. In a steady-state analysis, Eichner & Tschirhart (2007) came to a similar conclusion, although they used an integrated economic-GEEM model and defined and estimated a measure of naturalness as a proxy for nonconsumptive, cultural ecosystem services. This measure, labeled divergence from natural biodiversity, enters the welfare function on the basis of the notion that humans prefer ecosystems to be free of anthropogenic intervention, all other things being equal.

Divergence from natural biodiversity is one possible index of biodiversity, of which there are many in the ecological literature (Magurran 2003). Species richness, which is the number of species, is the simplest but it has serious limitations (MEA 2005, p. 20). The Shannon index is the most widely used and it heavily weights species evenness, but it does not reflect changes in species' overall abundances (Buckland et al. 2005). Economists have contributed to developing biodiversity measures (Solow et al. 1993, Weitzman 1992), because they need something tangible to set alongside other goods to assess trade-offs. For example, Nalle et al. (2004) examined the trade-off between timber production and species conservation using species temporal geometric mean populations as a biodiversity measure. Similarly, Conrad & Salas (1993) used the measure $\Pi N_{jt}/K_j$ over all species j in period t to examine trade-offs between timber production and Monarch butterfly preservation in Mexico.

7. CONCLUSION

In his seminal paper, Gordon (1954) indicated that there was virtually no economic fisheries research. Consequently, the biologists responsible for the great bulk of fisheries research up to that time were forced to extend their efforts into economics. This state changed as economists, ever the imperialists, saw the opportunity and need to insert economic reasoning and human behavior into the management of important nonrenewable resources. Early bioeconomic models employed the simplest biology, which was fitting because the emphasis was on the economics of the problem. Significant insights followed regarding the costs of open access, gear restrictions, and over capacity, and they culminated with an embrace of individual transfer quotas. Through most of the literature, however, economic models did not move much beyond the simple "stick-figure portrayals" of nonhuman life (Brown 2000) and ignored the technical interdependence of ecosystems. Meanwhile, in ecology "the field of population dynamics moved beyond the logistic growth model towards models with many parameters that are more closely tied to observable quantities in nature" (Smith & Crowder 2005).

Emphases in the above studies have been both on integrating ecology and economics and on introducing into ecological models economic optimization methods as mechanism. The latter emphasis can lead to closer connections between ecological and economic processes that favor credibility and allow resource economists to reach a broader scientific audience, thereby strengthening communications across disciplines. As most integrated models now stand, there is a noteworthy distinction between economic and ecological practices. Finnoff et al. (2008) indicated that if the Lotka-Volterra equations in Equations 3 and 5 were used to explain changes in the numbers of firms in several industries, where the N and P terms represent the number of firms, the conclusions would be unsatisfying. The equations state that the change in the number of firms in one industry depends on the number of firms in that and other industries. From a microeconomics perspective, this explanation completely omits firm behavior. Economists ask what types of firm behavior lead to more or fewer firms in the industries, because without that knowledge they would not know how incentives can be used to influence behavior and impact policy. Similarly, when the Lotka-Volterra model refers to plants and animals, it does not explain the mechanisms that drive species behavior and leaves us without guidance as to what policies might influence that behavior.

The issues are whether relatively simple ecology combined with sophisticated economics continues to be sufficient for addressing renewable resource problems or whether the ecology that economist integrate needs to be sophisticated as well. Certainly the problems of the twenty-first century differ from just a half century ago. At the time of Gordon's seminal paper, the notion that the ocean's bounty was limitless had not fully fallen out of favor. Today the MEA and many experts paint a rather bleak picture for the planet's biological resources owing to the ecosystem externalities generated by human activity. The point of distinguishing between traditional and ecosystem externalities is that the former can be understood only by digging into the technical interdependence of ecosystems. Maybe economists can leave the digging to ecologists and model only the end result of the externality. However, in other realms, economists do dig into noneconomic processes, such as incorporating enough atmospheric chemistry to model acid precipitation or incorporating enough geological engineering to model the net benefits of enhanced oil recovery. In some ways, integrating ecology should be more familiar to economists than integrating physical or chemical processes, because ecosystems are composed of sentient beings that behave as if they are making decisions that are amenable to economic methods.

DISCLOSURE STATEMENT

The author is not aware of any affiliations, memberships, funding, or financial holdings that might be perceived as affecting the objectivity of this review.

ACKNOWLEDGMENTS

I am grateful to Ed Barbier, Rüdiger Pethig, and Jay Shogren for helpful comments, and I apologize to the many investigators whose work is not cited owing to space constraints.

LITERATURE CITED

Abrams PA. 1977. Density-independent mortality and interspecific competition: a test of Pianka's niche overlap hypothesis. *Am. Nat.* 111:539–52

Abrams PA. 1982. Functional response of optimal foragers. *Am. Nat.* 120(3):382–90

Abrams PA. 1994. The fallacies of "ratio-dependent" predation. *Ecology* 75(6):1842–50

Abrams PA. 1999. The adaptive dynamics of consumer choice. *Am. Nat.* 153:83–97

Amir S. 1979. Economic interpretations of equilibrium concepts in ecological systems. *J. Soc. Biol. Struct.* 2:293–314

Amundsen ES, Bjørndal T, Conrad JM. 1995. Open access harvesting of the Northeast Atlantic minke whale. *Environ. Resour. Econ.* 6:167–85

Ando A, Camm J, Polasky S, Solow A. 1998. Species distributions, land values and efficient conservation. *Science* 279(27):2126–28

Arditi R, Ginzburg LR. 1989. Coupling in predator-prey dynamics: ratio dependence. *J Theor. Bio.* 139:311–26

Armstrong RA, McGehee R. 1980. Competitive exclusion. *Am. Nat.* 115(2):151–70

Arrow K, Bolin B, Costanza R, Dasgupta P, Folke C, et al. 1995. Economic growth, carrying capacity, and the environment. *Science* 268:520–21

Barbier EB. 1997. Introduction to the environment Kuznets curve special issue. *Environ. Dev. Econ.* 2(4):369–82

Barbier EB. 2003. Habitat-fishery linkages and mangrove loss in Thailand. *Contemp. Econ. Policy* 21(1):59–77

Barbier EB. 2007. The economics of land conversion, open access and biodiversity loss. In *Biodiversity Economics: Principles, Methods and Applications*, ed. A Kontoleon, U Pascual, T Swanson, pp. 59–91. Cambridge, UK: Cambridge Univ. Press

Barbier EB, Burgess JC. 2001. The economics of tropical deforestation. *J. Econ. Surv.* 15(3):413–32

Barbier EB, Burgess JC, Folke C. 1994. *Paradise Lost?* London: Earthscan

Berryman AA. 1992. The origins and evolution of predator-prey theory. *Ecology* 73(5):1530–35

Bhat MG, Huffaker RG. 2007. Management of a transboundary wildlife population: a self-enforcing cooperative agreement with renegotiation and variable transfer payments. *J. Environ. Econ. Manag.* 53:54–67

Bloom AJ, Chapin FSIII, Mooney HA. 1985. Resource limitation in plants—an economic analogy. *Annu. Rev. Ecol. Syst.* 16:363–92

Bockstael N. 1996. Modeling economics and ecology: the importance of a spatial perspective. *Am. J. Agric. Econ.* 78:1168–80

Includes trade-offs among five ecosystem services in a mangrove ecosystem.

Bockstael N, Costanza R, Strand I, Boynton W, Bell K, Wainger L. 1995. Ecological economic modeling and valuation of ecosystems. *Ecol. Econ.* 14(2):143–59

Brock W, Finnoff D, Kinzig AP, Pascual U, Perrings C, et al. 2009. Modeling biodiversity and ecosystem services in coupled ecological-economic systems. In *Biodiversity and Human Impacts*, ed. S Naeem, D Bunker, A Hector, M Loreau, C Perrings. Oxford: Oxford Univ. Press

Brock WA, Xepapadeas A. 2002. Optimal ecosystem management when species compete for limiting resources. *J. Environ. Econ. Manag.* 44:189–220

Brock WA, Xepapadeas A. 2003. Valuing biodiversity from an economic perspective: a unified economic, ecological, and genetic approach. *Am. Econ. Rev.* 93:1597–614

Brock WA, Xepapadeas A. 2004. Management of interacting species: regulation under nonlinearities and hysteresis. *Resour. Energy Econ.* 26:137–56

Brown G. 2000. Renewable natural resource management and use without markets. *J. Econ. Lit.* 38:875–914

Brown G, Berger B, Ikiara Brett M. 2005. A predator-prey model with an application to Lake Victoria fisheries. *Mar. Resour. Econ.* 20:221–47

Brown G, Roughgarden J. 1997. A metapopulation model with private property and a common pool. *Ecol. Econ.* 22:65–71

Buckland ST, Magurran AE, Green RE, Fewster RM. 2005. Monitoring change in biodiversity through composite indices. *Philos. Trans. Royal Soc. Biol. Sci.* 360(1454):243–54

Bulte EH, Damania R. 2003. Managing ecologically interdependent species. *Nat. Resour. Model.* 16:21–38

Chapin FS III, Zavaleta ES, Eviner VT, Naylor RL, Vitousek PM, et al. 2000. Consequences of changing biodiversity. *Nature* 405:234–42

Christiaans T, Eichner T, Pethig R. 2006. On the dynamics of Tschirhart's predator-prey model. *Ecol. Model.* 197:52–58

Christiaans T, Eichner T, Pethig R. 2007. A micro-level 'consumer approach' to population dynamics. *Nat. Resour. Model.* 20:279–322

Seminal and comprehensive textbook for bioeconomic modeling of renewable resources.

Clark C. 1976. *Mathematical Bioeconomics: The Optimal Management of Renewable Resources.* New York: Wiley. 1st ed. (2nd ed. 1990)

Clark C. 1997. Renewable resources and economic growth. *Ecol. Econ.* 22(3):275–76

Conrad JM. 1999. The bioeconomics of marine sanctuaries. *J. Bioecon.* 1(2):205–18

Conrad JM. 2005. Open access and extinction of the passenger pigeon in North America. *Nat. Resour. Model.* 18(4):1–19

Conrad JM, Adu-Asamoah R. 1986. Single and multispecies systems: the case of tuna in the Eastern Tropical Atlantic. *J. Environ. Econ. Manag.* 13:50–68

Conrad JM, Salas G. 1993. Economic strategies for coevolution: timber and butterflies in Mexico. *Land Econ.* 69(4):404–15

Costanza R, Daly HE. 1987. Toward an ecological economics. *Ecol. Model.* 38:1–7

Costanza R, Wainger L, Folke C, Mäler K. 1993. Modeling complex ecological economic systems. *BioScience* 43(8):545–55

Introduces the concept of ecosystem externalities that involve internal adjustments in ecosystems.

Costello C, McAusland C. 2003. Protectionism, trade, and measures of damage from exotic species introductions. *Am. J. Agric. Econ.* 85(4):964–75

Costello C, Polasky S. 2008. Optimal harvesting of stochastic spatial resources. *J. Environ. Econ. Manag.* 56:1–18

Crocker TD, Tschirhart J. 1987. Economic value of ecosystems. *Trans. Am. Fish. Soc.* 116:469–78

Crocker TD, Tschirhart J. 1992. Ecosystems, externalities and economies. *Environ. Resour. Econ.* 2:551–67

Daly HE. 1968. On economics as a life science. *J. Polit. Econ.* 76(3):392–406

Dasgupta P. 2001. *Human Well-Being and the Natural Environment.* Oxford: Oxford Univ. Press

Dasgupta P. 2008. Nature in economics. *Environ. Resour. Econ.* 39:1–7

Dasgupta P, Levin S, Lubchenco J. 2000. Economic pathways to ecological sustainability. *BioScience* 50(4):339–45

Dasgupta P, Mäler KG. 2004. The economics of non-convex ecosystems: introduction. In *The Economics of Non-Convex Ecosystems*, ed. P Dasgupta, KG Mäler, pp. 1–28. Dordrecht: Kluwer Acad.

Eichner T, Pethig R. 2003. The impact of scarcity and abundance in food chains on species population dynamics. *Nat. Resour. Model.* 16:259–303

Eichner T, Pethig R. 2005. Ecosystem and economy: an integrated dynamic general equilibrium approach. *J. Econ.* 85:213–49

Eichner T, Pethig R. 2006a. An analytical foundation of the ratio-dependent predator-prey model. *J. Bioecon.* 8:121–32

Eichner T, Pethig R. 2006b. A microfoundation of predator-prey dynamics. *Nat. Resour. Model.* 19:279–322

Eichner T, Pethig R. 2006c. Efficient nonanthropocentric nature protection. *Soc. Choice Welfare* 26:47–74

Eichner T, Pethig R. 2006d. Economic land use and biodiversity with microfounded population dynamics. *J. Environ. Econ. Manag.* 52:707–20

Eichner T, Pethig R. 2009. Pricing the ecosystem and taxing ecosystem services: a general equilibrium approach. *J. Econ.Theory.* In press. doi:10.1016/j.jet.2009.01.008

Eichner T, Tschirhart J. 2007. Efficient ecosystem services and naturalness in an ecological/economic model. *Environ. Resour. Econ.* 37(4):733–55

Finnoff D, Shogren JF. 2009. *Choosing the risks of invasive species.* Work. Pap., Univ. Wyoming

Finnoff D, Tschirhart J. 2003a. Protecting an endangered species while harvesting its prey in a general equilibrium ecosystem model. *Land Econ.* 79:160–80

Finnoff D, Tschirhart J. 2003b. Harvesting in an eight species ecosystem. *J. Environ. Econ. Manag.* 45 (3):589–611

Finnoff D, Tschirhart J. 2007. Using oligopoly theory to examine individual plant versus community optimization and evolutionary stable objectives. *Nat. Resour. Model.* 20(1):61–86

Finnoff D, Tschirhart J. 2008a. Linking dynamic ecological and economic general equilibrium models. *Resour. Energy Econ.* 30:91–114

Finnoff D, Tschirhart J. 2008b. *Growth functions for multiple species with predator saturation and switching.* Work. Pap., Univ. Wyoming

Finnoff D, Strong A, Tschirhart J. 2008. A bioeconomic model of cattle stocking on rangeland threatened by invasive plants and nitrogen deposition. *Am. J. Agric. Econ.* 90(4):1074–90

Flaaten O. 1991. Bioeconomics of sustainable harvest of competing species. *J. Environ. Econ. Manag.* 20:163–80

Gause GF. 1934. *The Struggle for Existence.* Baltimore, MD: Williams & Wilkins

Georgescu-Roegen N. 1975. Energy and economic myths. *South. Econ. J.* 42:347–81

Getz WM. 1984. Population dynamics: a per capita resource approach. *J. Theor. Biol.* 108:623–43

Gordon HS. 1954. The economic theory of a common property resource: the fishery. *J. Polit. Econ.* 62:124–42

Goulder LH, Kennedy D. 1997. Valuing ecosystem services: philosophical bases and empirical methods. In *Nature's Services*, ed. G Daily. Washington, DC: Island Press

Gurney WSC, Nisbet RM. 1998. *Ecological Dynamics.* New York: Oxford Univ. Press

Gutierrez AP. 1992. Physiological basis of ratio-dependent predator-prey theory: the metabolic pool model as a paradigm. *Ecology* 73(5):1552–63

Guttormsen AG, Kristofersson D, Nævdal E. 2008. Optimal management of renewable resources with Darwinian selection induced by harvesting. *J. Environ. Econ. Manag.* 56:167–79

Hammack J, Brown GM. 1974. *Waterfowl and Wetlands: Toward Bioeconomic Analysis.* Baltimore, MD: Johns Hopkins Univ. Press

In an economic-ecological general equilibrium framework, examines the trade-off between land used for habitat versus that used for economic production.

Links a dynamic computable general equilibrium economic model with an adaptive general equilibrium ecosystem model.

Hannesson R. 1983. Optimal harvesting of ecologically interdependent fish species. *J. Environ. Econ. Manag.* 10:329–45

Hannon B. 1973. The structure of ecosystems. *J. Theor. Biol.* 41:535–46

Hannon B. 1976. Marginal product pricing in the ecosystem. *J. Theor. Biol.* 56:253–67

Hannon B, Costanza R, Ulanowicz R. 1991. A general accounting framework for ecological systems: a functional taxonomy for connectivist ecology. *Theor. Popul. Biol.* 40:78–104

Hartman R. 1976. The harvesting decision when a standing forest has value. *Econ. Inq.* 16:52–58

Hartwick JM, Olewiler ND. 1998. *The Economics of Natural Resource Use*. New York: Addison-Wesley

Hirshleifer J. 1977. Economics from a biological view point. *J. Law Econ.* 20:1–52

Holling CS. 1966. The functional response of invertebrate predators to prey density. *Mem. Entomol. Soc. Can.* 48:1–86

Hollowed AB, Bax N, Beamish R, Collie J, Fogarty M, et al. 2000. Are multispecies models an improvement on single-species models for measuring fishing impacts on marine ecosystems? *ICES J. Mar. Sci.* 57:707–19

Huffaker R, Cooper K. 1995. Plant succession as a natural range restoration factor in private livestock enterprises. *Am. J. Agric. Econ.* 77:901–13

IPCC (Intergovernmental Panel on Climate Change). 2007. *Climate Change 2007: Synthesis Report*. Contribution of Working Groups I, II and III to the Fourth Assessment Report, IPCC, Geneva, Switzerland, 104pp.

Jackson JBC. 2008. Ecological extinction and evolution in the brave new ocean. *Proc. Natl. Acad. Sci. USA* 105:11458–65

Jackson JBC, Kirby MX, Berger WH, Bjorndal KA, Botsford LW, et al. 2001. Historical overfishing and the recent collapse of coastal ecosystems. *Science* 293(5530):629–38

Janssen MA, Anderies JM, Walker BH. 2004. Robust strategies for managing rangelands with multiple stable attractors. *J. Environ. Econ. Manag.* 47:140–62

Jin D, Hoagland P, Dalton TM. 2003. Linking economic and ecological models for a marine ecosystem. *Ecol. Econ.* 46:367–85

Kaplan JD, Smith MD. 2001. Optimal fisheries management in the presence of an endangered predator and harvestable prey. *Proc. 10th Bienn. Conf. Int. Inst. Fish. Econ. Trade*. Corvallis, OR: IIFET

Kim SH, Buskirk S, Tschirhart J. 2007. Reconstructing past ecosystem processes with general equilibrium models: house mice in Kern County, California, 1926–1927. *Ecol. Model.* 209:235–48

Kot M. 2001. *Elements of Mathematical Ecology*. Cambridge, UK: Cambridge Univ. Press

Landa JT, Ghiselin MT. 1999. The emerging discipline of bioeconomics. *J. Bioecon.* 1(1):5–12

Langpap C, Hascic I, Wu JJ. 2008. Protecting watershed ecosystems through targeted local land use policies. *Am. J. Agric. Econ.* 90(3):684–700

Lodge DM. 2001. Responses of lake biodiversity to global changes. In *Future Scenarios of Global Biodiversity*, ed. FS Chapin III, OE Sala, E Huber-Sannwald, pp. 277–312. New York: Springer Verlag

Lotka AJ. 1925. *Elements of Physical Biology*. Baltimore, MD: Williams & Wilkins

Lotka AJ. 1932. The growth of mixed populations, two species competing for a common food supply. *J. Wash. Acad. Sci.* 22:461–69

MacArthur RH. 1972. *Geographical Ecology: Patterns in the Distribution of Species*. Princeton, NJ: Princeton Univ. Press

Magurran AE. 2003. *Measuring Biological Diversity*. Malden, MA: Blackwell

Margolis M, Shogren JF, Fischer C. 2005. How trade policies affect invasive species control. *Ecol. Econ.* 52(3):305–14

May RM, Beddington JR, Clark CW, Holt SJ, Laws RM. 1979. Management of multispecies fisheries. *Science* 205(4403):267–77

MEA (Millenium Ecosystem Assessment). 2005. *Ecosystems and Human Well-being: Biodiversity Synthesis*. Washington, DC: World Resour. Inst.

Uses species optimization and highlights marginal concepts similar to economic systems.

Admits more detail in plant competition with separate growth functions for roots versus shoots.

Maximum sustainable yield should not be used in multispecies fisheries because it ignores ecological interactions.

Mérel PR, Carter CA. 2008. A second look at managing import risk from invasive species. *J. Environ. Econ. Manag.* 56:286–90

Miller TE, Burns JH, Munguin P, Walters EL, Kneitel JM, et al. 2005. A critical review of twenty years' use of the resource-ratio theory. *Am. Nat.* 165:439–48

Munro GR, Scott AD. 1986. The economics of fisheries management. In *Handbook of Natural Resource and Energy Economics*, ed. AV Kneese, JL Sweeney, 2:623–76. Amsterdam: North-Holland

Murray JD. 2002. *Mathematical Biology: I. An Introduction*. New York: Springer. 3rd ed.

Nalle DJ, Montgomery CA, Arthur JL, Polasky S, Schumaker NH. 2004. Modeling joint production of wildlife and timber. *J. Environ. Econ. Manag.* 48:997–1017

Nicholas AJ, Bailey VA. 1935. The balance of animal populations: Part I. *Proc. Zool. Soc. Lond.* 3:551–98

Nordhaus W. 2007. Critical assumptions in the Stern review on climate change. *Science* 317 (5835):201–2

Perrings C. 1987. *Economy and Environment*. Cambridge, UK: Cambridge Univ. Press

Perrings C, Walker B. 1997. Biodiversity, resilience and the control of ecological-economic systems: the case of fire-driven rangelands. *Ecol. Econ.* 22:73–83

Perrings C, Mäler KG, Folke C, Holling CS, Jansson BO. 1995. Introduction: framing the problem of biodiversity loss. In *Biodiversity Loss: Economic and Ecological Issues*, ed. C Perrings, KG Mäler, C Folke, CS Holling, BO Jansson, pp. 1–18. Cambridge, UK: Cambridge Univ. Press

Pethig R, Tschirhart J. 2001. Microfoundations of population dynamics. *J. Bioecon.* 3:27–49

Pimentel D, Lach L, Zuniga R, Morrison D. 2005. Update of the ecological and economic costs of non-indigenous species invaders in the U.S. *Ecol. Econ.* 52(3):273–88

Plagányi ÉE, Butterworth DS. 2004. A critical look at the potential of ECOPATH with ECOSIM to assist in practical fisheries management. *Afr. J. Mar. Sci.* 26:261–87

Polasky S, Nelson E, Lonsdorf E, Fackler P, Starfield A. 2005. Conserving species in a working landscape: land use with biological and economic objectives. *Ecol. Appl.* 15(4):1387–401

Postel SL, Daily GC, Ehrlich PR. 1996. Human appropriation of renewable fresh water. *Science* 271:785–88

Ragozin DL, Brown G Jr. 1985. Harvest policies and nonmarket valuation in a predator-prey system. *J. Environ. Econ. Manag.* 12:155–68

Rapport DJ. 1971. An optimization model of food selection. *Am. Nat.* 105:575–87

Rapport DJ, Turner JE. 1977. Economic models in ecology. *Science* 195:367–73

Royoma T. 1971. A comparative study of models for predation and parasitism. *Res. Popul. Ecol.* 1 (Suppl.):1–91

Sanchirico J, Wilen J. 1999. Bioeconomics of spatial exploitation in a patchy environment. *J. Environ. Econ. Manag.* 37:129–50

Sanchirico J, Wilen J. 2005. Optimal spatial management of renewable resources: matching policy scope to ecosystem scale. *J. Environ. Econ. Manag.* 50:23–46

Scott AD. 1955. The fishery: the objective of sole ownership. *J. Polit. Econ.* 63:116–24

Settle C, Crocker TD, Shogren JF. 2002. On the joint determination of biological and economic systems. *Ecol. Econ.* 42:301–11

Schoener TW. 1976. Alternatives to Lotka-Volterra competition: models of intermediate complexity. *Theor. Popul. Biol.* 10:309–33

Schoener TW. 1986. Mechanistic approaches to community ecology: a new reductionism? *Am. Zool.* 26:81–106

Shogren JF, Tschirhart J. 2005. Integrating ecology and economics to address bioinvasions. *Ecol. Econ.* 52(3):267–73

Skonhoft A. 1999. On the optimal exploitation of terrestrial animal species. *Environ. Resour. Econ.* 13:45–57

An early demonstration of how simple consumer choice theory can be applied to animal behavior.

Provides an empirical example of how economic outcomes are altered when ecology is integrated into a model.

Smith M, Crowder LB. 2005. *Valuing ecosystem services with fishery rents: a lumped-parameter approach to hypoxia in the Neuse River Estuary.* Presented at Link. Econ. Ecol. Models Environ. Policy Anal. Work., Santa Fe, New Mexico

Smith RL. 1995. *Ecology and Field Biology.* New York: Harper-Collins. 5th ed.

Smith VL. 1969. On models of commercial fishing. *J. Polit. Econ.* 77(2):181–98

Solow A, Polasky S, Broadus J. 1993. On the measurement of biological diversity. *J. Environ. Econ. Manag.* 24:60–68

Stephens DW, Krebs JR. 1986. *Foraging Theory.* Princeton, NJ: Princeton Univ. Press

Stern N. 2007. *The Economics of Climate Change: The Stern Review.* Cambridge, UK: Cambridge Univ. Press

Ströbele WJ, Wacker H. 1991. The concept of sustainable yield in multi-species fisheries. *Ecol. Model.* 53:61–74

Sutinen JG. 2007. *Socioeconomics and the ecosystem approach to management of marine resources.* Presented at Work. Econ. Ecosyst. Based Fish. Manag., Chesapeake Bay

Swallow S. 1990. Depletion of the environmental basis for renewable resources: the economics of interdependent renewable and nonrenewable resources. *J. Environ. Econ. Manag.* 19:281–96

Swallow SK, Parks PJ, Wear DN. 1990. Policy-relevant nonconvexities in the production of multiple forest benefits. *J. Environ. Econ. Manag.* 19:264–80

Thomas CD, Cameron A, Rhys EG, Bakkenes M, Beaumont LJ, et al. 2004. Extinction risk from climate change. *Nature* 427:145–48

Tilman D. 1982. *Resource Competition and Community Structure.* Princeton, NJ: Princeton Univ. Press

Tilman D. 1987. The importance of the mechanisms of interspecific competition. *Am. Nat.* 129:769–74

Tilman D. 1988. *Plant Strategies and the Dynamics and Structure of Plant Communities.* Princeton, NJ: Princeton Univ. Press

Tilman D, Polasky S, Lehman C. 2005. Diversity, productivity and temporal stability in the economies of humans and nature. *J. Environ. Econ. Manag.* 49:405–26

Trites AW, Livingston PA, Mackinson S, Vasconcellos MC, Springer AM, Pauly D. 1999. Ecosystem change and the decline of marine mammals in the Eastern Bering Sea: testing the ecosystem shift and commercial whaling hypotheses. *Fish. Cent. Res. Rep. 7,* Univ. Br. Columbia

Tschirhart J. 2000. General equilibrium of an ecosystem. *J. Theor. Biol.* 203:13–32

Tschirhart J. 2002. Resource competition among plants: from optimizing individuals to community structure. *Ecol. Model.* 148:191–212

Tschirhart J. 2003. Ecological transfers parallel economic markets in a general equilibrium ecosystem model. *J. Bioecon.* 5:193–214

Tschirhart J. 2004. A new adaptive system approach to predator-prey modeling. *Ecol. Model.* 176:255–76

Tu PNV, Wilman EA. 1992. A generalized predator-prey model: uncertainty and management. *J. Environ. Econ. Manag.* 23:123–38

Tullock G. 1971. The coal tit as a careful shopper. *Am. Nat.* 105:77–80

Vitousek PM, Ehrlich PR, Ehrlich AH, Matson PA. 1986. Human appropriation of the products of photosynthesis. *BioScience* 36:368–73

Vitousek PM, Mooney HA, Lubchenco J, Melillo JM. 1997a. Human domination of Earth's ecosystems. *Science* 277:494–99

Vitousek PM, Aber J, Howarth RW, Likens GE, Matson PA, et al. 1997b. Human alteration of the global nitrogen cycle: causes and consequences. *Issues Ecol.* 1:1–16

Volterra V. 1926. Fluctuations in the abundance of a species considered mathematically. *Nature* 118:558–60

Wacker H. 1999. Optimal harvesting of mutualistic ecological systems. *Resour. Energy Econ.* 21:89–102

Walters C, Christensen V, Pauly D. 1997. Structuring dynamic models of exploited ecosystems from trophic mass-balance assessments. *Rev. Fish Biol. Fish.* 7:139–72

Wangersky PJ. 1978. Lotka-Volterra population models. *Annu. Rev. Ecol. Syst.* 9:189–218

First to model entry and exit of firms in fisheries, a technique conspicuously ignored from most economic analyses.

Wätzold F, Drechsler M. 2005. Spatially uniform versus spatially heterogeneous compensation payments for biodiversity-enhancing land-use measures. *Environ. Resour. Econ.* 31:73–93

Wätzold F, Drechsler M, Armstrong CW, Baumgärtner S, Grimm V, et al. 2006. Ecological-economic modeling for biodiversity management: potential, pitfalls, and prospects. *Conserv. Biol.* 20(4):1034–41

Weitzman M. 1992. On diversity. *Q. J. Econ.* 107(2):363–405

Wilen JE. 1976. *Common property resources and the dynamics of overexploitation: the case of the North Pacific fur seal.* Resour. Pap. 3, Univ. Br. Columbia

Wilen JE. 1985. Bioeconomics of renewable resource use. In *Handbook of Natural Resource and Energy Economics*, ed. AV Kneese, JL Sweeney, 1:61–124. Amsterdam: Elsevier Sci.

Wilen JE. 2000. Renewable resource economists and policy: What differences have we made? *J. Environ. Econ. Manag.* 39:306–27

Wilen JE. 2007. Economics of spatial-dynamic processes. *Am. J. Agric. Econ.* 89(5):1134–44

Wilen JE, Brown GM. 1986. Optimal recovery paths for perturbations of trophic-level bioeconomic systems. *J. Environ. Econ. Manag.* 13:225–34

Worm B, Barbier EB, Beaumont N, Duffy JE, Folke C, et al. 2006. Impacts of biodiversity loss on ocean ecosystem services. *Science* 314(5800):787–90

RELATED RESOURCES

Abrams PA. 1990. The effects of adaptive behavior on the Type-2 functional response. *Ecology* 71 (3):877–85

Armsworth PR, Roughgarden JE. 2003. The economic value of ecological stability. *Proc. Natl. Acad. Sci. USA* 100(12):7147–51

Gutierrez AP. 1996. *Applied Population Ecology: A Supply-Demand Approach.* New York: Wiley & Sons

Holt RD. 1983. Optimal foraging and the form of the predator isocline. *Am. Nat.* 122(4):521–41

Regev U, Gutierrez AP, Schriber SJ, Zilberman D. 1998. Biological and economic foundations of renewable resource exploitation. *Ecol. Econ.* 26:227–42

Van Kooten GC, Bulte EH. 2000. *The Economics of Nature.* Oxford: Blackwell

Integrating Ecology and Economics in the Study of Ecosystem Services: Some Lessons Learned

Stephen Polasky

Department of Applied Economics and Department of Ecology, Evolution, and Behavior, University of Minnesota, St. Paul, Minnesota 55108; email: polasky@umn.edu

Kathleen Segerson*

Department of Economics, University of Connecticut, Storrs, Connecticut 06269; email: kathleen.segerson@uconn.edu

Annu. Rev. Resour. Econ. 2009. 1:409–34

The *Annual Review of Resource Economics* is online at resource.annualreviews.org

This article's doi: 10.1146/annurev.resource.050708.144110

1941-1340/09/1010-0409$20.00

*Corresponding author.

Key Words

ecosystem services, valuation, ecological modeling, Millennium Ecosystem Assessment

Abstract

This paper discusses both the opportunities for and the challenges associated with integrating economics and ecology in the study of ecosystem services. We distinguish between integration in positive versus normative analysis. There is rapid growth in positive research that combines the two disciplines to provide insight and better understanding of the bidirectional linkage between economic and ecological systems. This research is a crucial part of addressing growing large-scale environmental challenges. This integration is equally important, but potentially much more difficult, in normative analysis, especially when interdisciplinary groups include individuals with different views regarding appropriate normative criteria. In such cases, reaching consensus can be difficult and slow, even when the practical implications of the different perspectives (i.e., the general policy prescriptions they imply) are the same. We suggest an approach for increasing the scope for collaboration among economists and ecologists in normative analysis.

1. INTRODUCTION

Although ecology and economics have a long history of sharing ideas and reciprocal influence, dating back to Malthus, Darwin, and Marshall (Rapport & Turner 1977), the past decade or so has seen a growing recognition of both the rewards and the challenges of conducting interdisciplinary research that draws from these two disciplines. Recent interest in integrating ecology and economics stems in large part from the growing appreciation of the important role that ecosystems play in providing goods and services that contribute to human welfare and from the growing recognition of the impact of human actions on ecosystems and on the flow of these services from very local to global scales (e.g., Daily 1997). These impacts include not only traditional air and water pollution (such as sulfur dioxide emissions, ground-level ozone, and eutrophication), but also climate change, global changes in the nitrogen cycle, deforestation, loss of wetlands, and reductions in biodiversity. The need to understand and address these problems has led to calls for more closely integrating natural and social sciences, particularly ecology and economics, as part of an effort to ensure that human actions do not damage ecological processes necessary to support the continued flow of ecosystem services on which the welfare of present and future generations depends (Millennium Ecosystem Assessment 2005).

Economists have long acknowledged and studied the goods and services provided by nature—or, more precisely, provided by combining inputs from nature with other inputs such as labor, leisure time, and capital. However, the focus has typically been on single resources or services stemming from the use of natural resource–based inputs (such as land, fish or forest stocks, minerals, and energy resources) in the production of commercial products, or on nonmarket goods and services provided by natural environments (such as clean air, clean water, aesthetics, and recreation). Only recently have economists begun to work with ecologists to study the broader set of services provided by ecosystems and their impacts on human welfare. This reflects an increased appreciation of the complexity and interconnectedness of nature (or "natural capital"), the pervasiveness of joint production in nature, and the crucial role of intermediate services in sustaining the provision of the final services or endpoints that have historically been the focus of economic research.

At the same time, viewing ecosystems services as valuable to humans raised the possibility of creating incentives to provide these services by, for example, creating markets or related mechanisms through which individuals, businesses, governments, or nonprofit organizations could pay for (effectively, purchase) these services. Although the United States and other countries have a long history of paying for conservation (see, for example, Claassen et al. 2008), the recent interest in creating markets for ecosystem services has given the notion of payments for ecosystem services a new appeal and prominence in policy debates (Bulte et al. 2008, Daily & Ellison 1999, Heal 2000, Jack et al. 2008). For example, in December 2008, the U.S. Department of Agriculture announced the formation of a new Office of Ecosystem Services and Markets. Designing and understanding markets for ecosystem services require integrated knowledge of the production of these services (from ecology), the values of these services, and the incentives created by alternative market designs (from economics).

This paper draws on our recent experiences serving on various interdisciplinary committees charged with understanding ecosystem services. We discuss both the opportunities for and the challenges associated with integrating economics and ecology to address environmental issues. We distinguish between integration in positive analysis (understanding and predicting behavior and outcomes) versus normative analysis (evaluating and ranking outcomes), because the challenges of integration vary in these different types of analyses. In the context of ecosystem services, positive analyses include research characterizing the linkages between incentives and human decisions (e.g., responses to incentives created by markets or policies), the effect of such decisions on ecosystems, and the development of ecological production functions that can map ecosystem structure and function to the flow of services. In addition, it includes generating information about the trade-offs people are willing to make to protect ecosystems and the flow of services from them. This information can then be used in normative analyses, which involve evaluating policy or management options. One approach to normative analysis is to use integrated ecological-economic models to estimate the net benefits associated with different options. Under a strict benefit-cost decision rule, the efficiency rankings that these analyses generate would determine policy prescriptions. More generally, this analysis would provide input into policy decisions that would reflect not only economic efficiency but other considerations such as intra- and intertemporal equity (Arrow et al. 1996). However, as we note below, even this more general approach to normative analysis is not universally accepted.

Our primary message can be summarized as follows: Given the inextricable linkages between humans and ecosystems, much can be learned from interdisciplinary analyses that bring insights from ecology and economics to the study of pressing environmental problems. In addition, ecology and economics share many similarities that make their integration natural and allow useful crossfertilization of ideas, concepts, and results. Nonetheless, integrating the two disciplines poses challenges. In some cases, the difficulties stem primarily from limitations in current ecological and economic methods, data, and models that inhibit effective joint understanding and integration. These limitations will lessen as the amount of joint research between ecologists and economists increases.

More profound difficulties arise in normative analysis involving policy prescriptions. In our view the primary source of these difficulties is twofold: (a) differences in views on the sources or nature of value and (b) differences in views on the social choice rule that should be used to rank policy options or outcomes. Economists define value in terms of trade-offs that individuals are willing to make, but this definition is not universally accepted outside of economics. For example, an alternative approach based in environmental ethics recognizes an intrinsic value of nature that is not defined in terms of trade-offs and is separate from concerns about human welfare. These different views regarding the source(s) and nature of value generally give rise to varying views about social choice rules. In some cases these differences will be irreconcilable. For example, collaboration in normative analysis is nearly impossible between an ecologist who believes policy options should be ranked solely on the basis of intrinsic rights or biophysical impacts and an economist who believes in the importance of evaluating trade-offs based on preferences of individuals in society. The ecologist's view would render the assessment of trade-offs irrelevant, whereas the economist's view would not grant legitimacy to a policy ranking based solely on the beliefs or implicit preferences of the ecologist.

Nonetheless, even in policy evaluation contexts without complete agreement, we suggest that substantial progress can be made in integrating ecology and economics in the normative analysis of ecosystem services. The essential component necessary for collaboration in these contexts is agreement among researchers on the relevance of evaluating the trade-offs individuals are willing to make to protect ecosystems or to secure ecosystem services, as reflected in their revealed and stated choices, and an agreement to focus the collaborative effort on assessing those trade-offs. Importantly, such an approach does not require agreement on (a) the motivations that underlie the trade-offs individuals are willing to make (i.e., the reasons that people want to protect ecosystems) or (b) what considerations beyond an assessment of trade-offs should enter into public policy decisions. By recasting the discussion to focus on the relevance and assessment of trade-offs, we believe that economists and ecologists will be able to find greater common ground for collaboration in normative analysis, even if they hold very disparate views on these other issues, and as a result will be able to make greater progress in efforts to evaluate policies designed to protect ecosystems and the services they provide.

2. THE CONCEPT OF ECOSYSTEM SERVICES

In the simplest economic terms, ecosystem services are analogous to other goods and services within the economy, all of which are produced through a combination of inputs and directly or indirectly generate utility. The production of ecosystem services can be represented by an "ecological production function," which is conceptually analogous to the standard production function used in economics to describe how inputs are combined to produce intermediate or final outputs. Although conceptually simple, the implementation of this concept, and what is included in it, often requires detailed and integrated understanding of ecology and economics.

We adopt a broad definition of the term ecosystem services that includes both intermediate and final services. Thus, following the Millennium Ecosystem Assessment (2005), we include not only food, fuelwood, fiber, biochemicals, genetic resources and fresh water (provisioning services), but also flood protection, climate regulation, human disease regulation, water purification, air quality maintenance, pollination, and pest control (regulating services); aesthetic, spiritual, cultural, educational, and recreational values of nature (cultural services); and the underlying services that support them, such as soil formation, nutrient cycling, and primary productivity (supporting services). Provisioning and cultural services are typically, though not always, outputs that directly affect human well-being. In contrast, regulating services are typically intermediate services, which are in turn inputs into other production processes. For example, pollination and pest-control services are inputs into the production of agricultural outputs. Supporting services, in economic terms, are akin to the infrastructure that provides the necessary conditions under which inputs can be usefully combined to provide intermediate and final goods and services of value to society. The Millennium Ecosystem Assessment definition of ecosystem services is useful in that it highlights the many ways in which ecosystems support human well-being.

3. INTERDISCIPLINARY EFFORTS TO STUDY ECOSYSTEM SERVICES

Although the term ecosystem services is relatively new, interest in combining economics and biological sciences to manage human interactions with nature has an extensive history. Combining biological growth models with an economic framework to define optimal use of natural resources dates back (at least) to Faustmann in 1849, who solved for the optimal forest rotation. The modern bioeconomic models of fisheries arose in the 1950s with seminal contributions from Gordon (1954), Scott (1955), and Schaefer (1957). There has been long-standing interest by economists in using insights from biological science, particularly the theory of evolution, in economics (e.g., Alchian 1950). Similarly, there has also been a long-standing interest by ecologists in using insights from economics to study biology and ecology. For example, microeconomic tools have been used to study optimal foraging and competition for scarce resources (e.g., Tilman et al. 2005, Vermeij 2004).

Despite this long history, the current interest in combining ecology and economics reflects a new level of concern, prompted by increasing recognition of the scale of the impact of human systems on the natural environment and the services it provides. With a global population approaching 7 billion people and the prospect of reaching 9 to 10 billion 50 years hence, as well as a large and growing global economy dependent on the use of fossil fuels, human activity is causing environmental changes not only locally but also globally (Millennium Ecosystem Assessment 2005). In addition, awareness of the critical importance of ecosystem services for human welfare has increased. The publication of the book *Nature's Services: Societal Dependence on Natural Ecosystems* (Daily 1997) and an article in *Nature* on the value of global ecosystem services (Costanza et al. 1997) did much to raise the profile of ecosystem services. A further boost was given by the Millennium Ecosystem Assessment (2005), which focused on the link between ecosystems and human well-being. Many ecologists saw work on ecosystem services as a means of putting ecosystem protection on a more equal footing with other (mainly commercial) interests and hence embraced it as a means of justifying ecosystem protection not just for its own sake but also for its contributions to human welfare.

Much of the work on valuing ecosystem services over the past several decades, especially at large regional or global scales, has been led by ecologists, and some of this work has been inconsistent with fundamental economic principles. Perhaps the most notable example of this is the paper by Costanza et al. (1997), which applied estimates of per hectare value derived from local-scale studies to all hectares of a given habitat type to generate an estimate of total economic value at a global scale. Summing up estimates across all habitat types, Costanza et al. (1997) estimated that global ecosystem services were worth $33 trillion annually, far more than global GNP ($18 trillion at that time). Bockstael et al. (2000), Pearce (1998), and Toman (1998), among others, have pointed out serious problems with this approach. Estimates from studies conducted at a local scale measure willingness to pay conditional on the premise that habitat in other places remains unchanged. When these estimates are scaled up to a regional or global scale, this condition is violated. In addition, if accurately conceived and measured, willingness to pay cannot exceed ability to pay (income or GNP) estimates. These flaws in early efforts to put a dollar value on global ecosystem services highlight the critical need for collaboration between ecologists and economists to ensure that assessments of ecosystem services and their value are scientifically sound.

Interest in the role and value of ecosystem services spurred several important national or international efforts to understand better the linkages between human systems and ecosystems. An example of such an effort is the Millennium Ecosystem Assessment, which was designed to "assess the consequences of ecosystem change for human well-being and to establish the scientific basis for actions needed to enhance the conservation and sustainable use of ecosystems and their contributions to human well-being" (Millennium Ecosystem Assessment 2005, p. v). This effort pointed to several key information/knowledge gaps, including the need for better information on the value of ecosystem services and greater integration of ecological and economic studies (Carpenter et al. 2006).

In addition, in 2002, the National Academy of Sciences (NAS) convened a panel composed primarily of economists and ecologists to evaluate economic methods for assessing the value of aquatic and related terrestrial ecosystems. The panel's report (National Research Council 2005) highlights the importance of valuing ecosystem services and the need for an integration of ecology and economics for that purpose. It concludes that the ability to value changes in ecosystem services varies significantly across contexts, for at least two reasons. First, the link between ecosystem structure and functions and the resulting provision of ecosystem services is better understood in some contexts than others. Second, in practice, some sources of value are easier to estimate than others. Valuation is especially challenging in contexts where there are multiple, interrelated services affected by a particular action or policy and where nonuse values are particularly important.

Following the establishment of the NAS panel, in 2003 the U.S. Environmental Protection Agency's Science Advisory Board initiated a study on Valuing the Protection of Ecological Systems and Services. The composition of the Science Advisory Board committee (known as C-VPESS) was broader than that of the NAS committee and included experts in economics and ecology as well as in decision science, engineering, law, philosophy, political science, and psychology. The committee's charge was also broader. C-VPESS set out to assess the state of the art and science in valuing the protection of ecological systems as well as ecosystem services, and unlike the NAS panel, it was not limited to considering valuation solely from an economic perspective. In addition, it was charged with specifically addressing ecological valuation needs and opportunities at the EPA. Because of differing views on the sources and nature of value, as well as the appropriate role of different valuation methods, the committee took five years to complete its work and to come to a reasonable consensus or, on some issues, a reasonable compromise regarding a proposed approach to ecological valuation. In its final report (U.S. Environmental Protection Agency 2009), the committee outlined an approach to valuation that included not only the use of economic valuation methods but also a role for other noneconomic approaches to valuation.

The Natural Capital Project, a joint venture among Stanford University, The Nature Conservancy, and the World Wildlife Fund, was launched in 2006. Unlike the NAS and C-VPESS committees, which focused on assessing the state of the art, the Natural Capital Project had a goal of "mainstreaming" ecosystem services into everyday decisions. A major thrust of the project has been to develop an integrated dynamic landscape model capable of predicting how various decisions will affect the joint provision of ecosystem services and species conservation (see Daily et al. 2009).

Our experiences with the Millennium Ecosystem Assessment, NAS panel, C-VPESS, and the Natural Capital Project have shaped our perspective on the opportunities for and challenges associated with combining economics and ecology in efforts to understand and address links between human and natural systems. The following sections draw from our collective experience and provide our perspective on these opportunities and challenges.

4. ECOLOGICAL AND ECONOMIC SYSTEMS

On the surface, ecology and economics appear to be quite different because of the difference in subject matter to which they are typically applied. Ecology studies the interactions of organisms with their (natural) environment. Economics studies the interaction of individuals, firms, and government in the (human) economy. However, the formal structures of the two disciplines are quite similar. Ecosystems and markets are composed of interacting (largely self-interested) agents whose actions jointly determine system outcomes, which evolve over time through conscious search for better opportunities or unconscious natural selection (Tilman et al. 2005). In **Table 1**, we provide a translation of parallel concepts and terms in ecology and economics. Similarities between the basic structures of the two fields make it relatively easy for an economist to understand ecology, and vice-versa. However, just as in learning a foreign language, learning to translate terms from one field to the other requires some time and effort. Translating between ecology and economics, however, is like translating between two languages from the same language family that share a common structure (e.g., French and Spanish) rather than translating between two languages with fundamentally different structures (e.g., English and Chinese).

The similarities between economic and ecological systems have led to productive cross-fertilization. For example, the basic principles of competition in the presence of resource scarcity developed in economics have been applied to the study of the foraging behavior of species. Likewise, principles from ecology relating to evolution and survival of species have been applied to economic systems where firms seek to adapt and survive in the long run (Tilman et al. 2005). These models do not seek to integrate economics and ecology; rather, they seek to apply concepts/insights from one discipline to the other.

The one area without a fairly direct translation between ecology and economics is normative analysis. Ecology is a positive science and does not have an analog to the normative framework of welfare economics. Nonetheless, ecologists sometimes advocate policy positions based on their personal views. These views then become implicit normative criteria for evaluating policy options. Other environmental disciplines have explicit normative criteria. For example, the mission of conservation biologists is to conserve the Earth's biological diversity. Policy outcomes can be ranked on the basis of how well they achieve this goal. Although the preferences of individuals or objectives such as conserving biodiversity might ultimately point in the same direction as an analysis based on an evaluation of social trade-offs, i.e., toward greater ecosystem protection, the degree of the prescribed protection will generally be different. For example, the potential threats to

Table 1 Comparing ecology and economics

Feature	Ecology	Economics
Subject matter focus	Nature's economy	Human economy
Organizing systems	Ecosystems	Markets
Agents	Organisms	Individuals and firms
Forms of interactions among agents	Competitive and cooperative interactions in producer-consumer networks	Competitive and cooperative interactions among producers and consumers
Typical behavioral assumption	Maximize fitness/survival	Maximize utility/profit
Dynamics	Mutation and natural selection causing evolution	Innovation and entry/exit
Normative framework	None	Welfare economics

ecological systems posed by global climate change have led some natural scientists to advocate establishing stricter limits on atmospheric concentrations of greenhouse gases than those implied by most economic analyses (e.g., Nordhaus & Boyer 2000, Tol 2005; but see Stern 2007 for a different view).

Although it is useful to compare and contrast concepts from economics and ecology to highlight the potential for crossfertilization, the study of ecosystem services requires an explicit integration of the two disciplines. The remainder of this article discusses this integration.

5. INTEGRATING ECOLOGY AND ECONOMICS: AN OVERVIEW

A major impetus to integrate ecology and economics stems from the recognition of the important role that ecosystems play in providing goods and services that contribute to human welfare and of the impact that human actions have on ecosystems and the flow of services from very local to global scales. **Figure 1**, which builds on a figure developed in the Natural Capital Project (Daily et al. 2009), depicts a framework for integrating economics and ecology in the study of ecosystem services.

Starting from the top left oval, **Figure 1** highlights the fact that public policy decisions create incentives that affect the private decisions by firms and individuals (Link 1), which in turn result in actions that affect ecosystems (Link 2). These impacts include the effects of land clearing and habitat modification, changes in species populations from harvesting activities (hunting and fishing), changes in nutrient flows from fertilizer application and runoff, changes in the hydrological cycle from water withdrawals and operation of dams, changes in local air and water quality from discharge of pollutants, and changes in global climate from emissions of greenhouse gases. An understanding of the link between human decisions and ecosystem structure and function requires positive analysis integrating

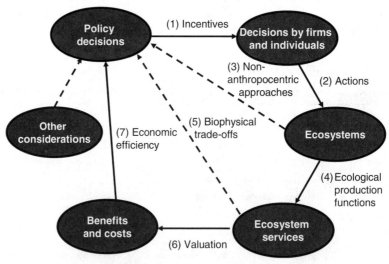

Figure 1

Framework for integrating economics and ecology in the study of ecosystem services. Solid lines indicate the links where the integration of the two disciplines can play a critical role.

economics and ecology. Under a social choice rule where policy rankings are based solely on impacts on the ecosystem (as, for example, under a nonanthropocentric approach—see Section 8), this analysis would form the basis for policy evaluation and social choice (Link 3). Thus, for ecologists who advocate a social choice rule of this type, consideration of the effect of these ecosystem changes on humans is irrelevant. As a result, the potential for collaboration between economists and ecologists who hold this view is limited to positive impact analyses (Links 1 and 2), without any role for collaborative normative analysis based on a consideration of ecosystem services or trade-offs.

Of course, a fundamental element of the ecosystem services paradigm is the recognition that changes in ecosystem structure or function, in turn, influence the provision of ecosystem services enjoyed by humans (Link 4). Ecological production functions can be used to understand how various ecosystem services are produced and how changes in ecosystem conditions affect the provision of these services. The basic understanding required for developing ecological production functions comes from ecology and other natural sciences. The framework and endpoints, however, come from economics. The cooperation between ecologists and economists to develop ecological production functions is analogous to the cooperation between engineers and economists to define production functions in industrial processes. Ecological production functions can in turn be used to identify biophysical trade-offs that are analogous to the marginal rates of transformation embodied in production possibility frontiers. There is considerable scope for collaborative research between economists and ecologists in identifying relevant biophysical trade-offs. Some analysts may prefer to base policy decisions on consideration of impacts on the flow of various ecosystem services, recognizing the potential for trade-offs in those flows (Link 5) rather than assessing them in terms of the public's preferences. As with ecologists who adhere to a nonanthropocentric approach, there is little hope of collaboration on normative analysis between economists and ecologists who hold this view.

Link 6 in **Figure 1** captures the contribution of ecosystem services to human welfare. A fundamental principle of economics is that these contributions can be represented as the benefits of an increase in the flow of ecosystem services or the cost of a decrease in flows, where benefits and costs reflect the preferences of the individuals affected by the change. The value of the change in the flow of an ecosystem service, as defined in economics, is measured in terms of the trade-offs that those individuals are willing to make, regardless of their underlying motivations. Both market and nonmarket valuation methods can be used to estimate these trade-offs (see further discussion below). Information about the benefits and costs of changes in the flow of ecosystem services can then be used to assess the net benefits associated with alternative policy options or outcomes. Although few economists believe that information about the net benefits of alternatives should be the sole basis for social choice, nearly all believe that it should be an important consideration in public policy decisions (Arrow et al. 1996). The potential for collaborative work by ecologists and economists in normative analysis based on aggregate net benefits hinges on acceptance of this premise. Ecologists who believe that trade-offs are important, and that they should be assessed based on the public's preferences, can work with economists both on estimating the trade-offs individuals are willing to make (i.e., valuation— Link 6) and on net benefit analyses (Link 7), even if the economists and ecologists hold different views about the motivations underlying those trade-offs or the other considerations (such as distributional equity or process-related issues) that should also be considered when making policy choices.

In the following sections, we discuss in further detail the opportunities and challenges of integrating economics and ecology that are reflected in **Figure 1**. We first discuss issues involved in positive analysis (understanding decisions and their effect on ecosystems and the services they provide). We then turn to the more difficult issues involved in normative analysis (valuing those changes and using information about values to assess alternative policy options or outcomes).

6. ANALYSIS OF INCENTIVES AND CONSEQUENCES OF DECISIONS ON ECOSYSTEMS

Economics is a behavioral science. Understanding choices and how choices change under different policies or market conditions is a central focus of economic analysis. Environmental economics analyzes incentives created by various environmental policies, such as taxes and cap-and-trade mechanisms. For the most part, this analysis has been directed at policies to achieve environmental improvement by reducing emissions of pollutants (e.g., Baumol & Oates 1988, Hanley et al. 1996). Increasingly though, environmental economists are asked for analysis of policies to create incentives to provide ecosystem services. Much of what we know about the effects of policies for pollution control is directly applicable to understanding policies to promote the provision of ecosystem services.

The standard set of environmental policy tools can be applied to the provision of ecosystem services. Price mechanisms, typically in the form of subsidies for provision of services (payments for ecosystem services), are the most common policy approaches. Examples of such programs include Costa Rica's program *Pago por Servicios Ambientales*, which pays landowners for carbon sequestration, habitat conservation, water quality, and aesthetics (Pagiola 2008). In the United States, the Conservation Reserve Program pays farmers to set land aside for conservation. Originally the Conservation Reserve Program was directed primarily toward preventing soil erosion, but it is now also being used to promote habitat conservation, water quality improvement, and other environmental benefits (see Claassen et al. 2008). Taxes on activities that degrade ecosystems and lessen the provision of services are also possible, but they are not often used in practice. The strong preference for using positive rewards rather than negative sanctions to provide ecosystem services stems largely from the necessity of working with many private landowners and the political difficulties of imposing and enforcing sanctions.

It is also possible to use quantity mechanisms, such as cap-and-trade, for the provision of ecosystem services. For example, programs such as wetland banking or tradable development rights can be used to maintain or ensure a given level of ecosystem protection (Boyd et al. 2001, National Research Council 2001). These programs set a quantity limit (cap) on the total amount of habitat destruction that can occur, but they allow trade in permits among landowners. Such policies can be set up to require no net loss, so that any habitat destruction must be offset by the restoration of habitat somewhere else (as in wetland banking).

Though most of the positive analysis of incentives for the provision of ecosystem services is like that in other areas of environmental economics, there are several issues that are novel or require greater attention when used in this context. Among issues that gain a higher profile when applied to ecosystem services are land use and management as well as the spatial and temporal dimensions of policies and responses.

Economists have developed econometric models that predict land use and land-use change based on the economic returns from alternative potential uses (e.g., Feng et al. 2006, Lubowski et al. 2006). These models are often based on econometric specifications of discrete choice models (Train 2003) and estimates of economic returns based on observables characteristics of the land (Lubowski 2002). Furthermore, this type of model can be used to predict land-use change in response to policies, such as payments for ecosystem services, which result in changes to the economic returns on alternative land uses (e.g., Lewis & Plantinga 2007, Nelson et al. 2008). Other studies of land use and land-use change have also incorporated the impacts of neighborhood effects on the relative utility of alternative decisions (e.g., Irwin & Bockstael 2002, 2004).

The provision of ecosystem services often depends on the spatial pattern of the decisions of many landowners. For example, species conservation outcomes are typically a function of the spatial pattern of habitat across a landscape. An important issue in such contexts is coordinating decisions across many landowners. Recent papers have investigated improving conservation solutions by making payments to landowners a function of decisions of all landowners in a neighborhood (e.g., Parkhurst et al. 2002, Parkhurst & Shogren 2007). This literature shows that it is possible to coordinate landowner decisions by making payoffs contingent on neighbors' decisions. In addition, empirical studies and simulations show that using biological information to target incentives can improve performance (e.g., Lewis et al. 2009, Nelson et al. 2008).

7. FROM ECOSYSTEMS TO SERVICES: ECOLOGICAL PRODUCTION FUNCTIONS AND ECOSYSTEM SERVICES

Beyond estimating how policies and market conditions affect choices that impact ecosystems, other necessary steps in the analysis of ecosystem services involve linking impacts to understanding ecosystem processes and further linking these processes to the provision of ecosystem services. In this section, we focus on the translation required from a primarily ecological focus on ecosystems to information about the provision of ecosystem services, i.e., the ecological production function.

The field of bioeconomics developed an extensive literature on the translation from biological systems to the provision of an economic good long before the term ecosystem service was in common usage. Starting from the 1950s, fisheries biologists and economists worked jointly to develop models of the economic returns from fish harvesting (for a review of bioeconomic models of fisheries and other renewable resources, see Clark 1990). Much of this work focused on a single good or service (e.g., fish harvest) and typically assumed a simple biological growth function (e.g., logistic growth). Over the past 30 years, the bioeconomic framework has been used to show how changes in ecosystems lead to changes in productivity through changes in the biological growth function (e.g., Barbier 1994, 2000, 2003; Barbier & Strand 1998; Barbier et al. 2002; Bell 1997; Ellis & Fisher 1987; Freeman 1991; Lynne et al. 1981; Swallow 1994).

A different strand of analysis starts from land use and habitat type to predict the provision of services. For example, there is a large natural science literature on the amount of carbon stored in a landscape as a function of land cover and land use (e.g., Brown & Schroeder 1999, Cairns et al. 2000, Canadell & Raupach 2008, Nascimento & Laurance 2002). Similarly, agricultural and timber production models use soil quality and the quantity of various inputs (e.g., fertilizer, water) to predict yield. Several papers have used this approach to model agricultural and timber returns across space in conservation and ecosystem service assessments (e.g., Naidoo & Adamowicz 2006; Naidoo & Iwamura 2007; Polasky et al. 2005, 2008; and for a review, see Naidoo et al. 2006).

It is important to distinguish between an approach using land use and land cover to generate spatially explicit maps of particular ecosystem services based on ecological production functions, as done in the papers mentioned above, versus an approach to valuation of ecosystem services based on habitat types and benefit transfer. As noted above, Costanza et al. (1997) used estimates of the value of ecosystem services per hectare at specific locations within a habitat type, and they multiplied these estimates by the total amount of the habitat type to generate global estimates of value for ecosystem services. Other recent papers have used a similar approach to generating estimates of the value of ecosystem services (e.g., Ingraham & Foster 2008, Troy & Wilson 2006, Turner et al. 2007). Assuming a constant per hectare value of ecosystem services by habitat type ignores issues of rarity, spatial configuration, size, habitat quality and condition, and demand for ecosystem services generated by the number of nearby people or their preferences, all of which should matter in the determination of both the quantity of services produced and the value of those services (Nelson et al. 2009). For example, for ecosystem services such as storm protection along coastlines, Barbier et al. (2008) and Koch et al. (2009) examined the details of the pattern and amount of habitat, including temporal and spatial variation, to show why ecosystem service provision is unlikely to be linearly related to the amount of habitat.

Recent work integrating ecological production functions into an economic framework has made several important advances. First, models have become spatially explicit. In a series of papers, Sanchirico & Wilen (1999, 2001, 2005) developed a bioeconomic model with distinct habitat patches and dispersal of a harvested species between patches. Other papers have developed spatially explicit models of ecosystem services as a function of land use and land cover (e.g., Lewis & Plantinga 2007, Nelson et al. 2008, 2009, Polasky et al. 2005, 2008). Second, models have expanded beyond a single service focus to consider provision of the bundle of ecosystem services jointly produced by the ecosystem (e.g., Antle & Stoorvogel 2006; Boody et al. 2005; Coiner et al. 2001; Naidoo & Ricketts 2006; Nelson et al. 2008, 2009). Such work allows an analysis of the production possibility frontier for services and the trade-offs in provision among services (e.g., Jackson et al. 2005; Nelson et al. 2008, 2009; Polasky et al. 2008).

8. TOWARD NORMATIVE ANALYSIS: VALUING CHANGES IN ECOSYSTEM SERVICES

As noted above, a critical problem motivating recent interest in integrating ecology and economics is the recognition of the need to incorporate more fully the value of ecosystem services into policy decisions. By not valuing changes in these services in formal policy evaluations (e.g., benefit-cost analyses), ecosystem services are effectively assigned a value of zero (Daily et al. 2000). All the interdisciplinary efforts discussed in Section 3 emphasize the importance of valuing ecosystem services to better inform decision making. In this section, we discuss recent efforts to combine economics and ecology in the valuation of ecosystem services. However, as also noted, valuation that is closely tied to policy evaluation raises issues about the sources and nature of value as well as the appropriate basis for evaluating alternatives, which can be significant roadblocks to collaboration between economists and researchers from other disciplines, including ecology. This section also discusses some of these issues and the challenges they present.

The valuation of the change in ecosystem services resulting from a particular policy choice includes three basic components: (a) identification of the services provided by the ecosystems that are affected by the policy choice, (b) prediction of the changes in the flow of these services measured in biophysical terms, and (c) estimation of the value of these predicted changes measured in terms of human welfare (National Research Council 2005). The first two components rely primarily on positive analysis of the sort described in the preceding sections, including use of economic models that predict how policy choices affect ecosystems through changes in incentives and decisions as well as the use of ecological models that predict how changes in ecosystems affect the provision of ecosystem services (see Links 1, 2, and 4 in **Figure 1**). However, the third component, estimating value, requires the adoption and application of a specific concept of value.

The literature on environmental values identifies a number of different concepts along various dimensions of value: (a) intrinsic and instrumental, (b) anthropocentric and biocentric (or ecocentric), and (c) utilitarian and deontological (Rolston 1991). Something has intrinsic value if it is valued as an end in itself, whereas it has instrumental value if it is valued as a means to achieve a desired objective. For anthropocentric values, only humans have intrinsic value, whereas for biocentric (ecocentric) values, the natural world beyond humans has intrinsic value. Utilitarian values are defined in terms of how they contribute to the desired objective, which for anthropocentric values is assumed to be the maximization of human utility or welfare. In contrast, under deontological approaches, values are based on rights and obligations rather than consequences or contributions to an objective.

In welfare economics, values are defined in instrumental anthropocentric utilitarian terms and reflect trade-offs individuals are willing to make. In the context of valuing ecosystem services, values reflect the willingness of the affected individuals to trade the increase or decrease in ecosystem services for a decrease or increase in other goods and services. When values are expressed in monetary terms, they are measured in terms of compensating or equivalent variation, typically measured as willingness to pay or willingness to accept (Just et al. 2004). Compensating (equivalent) variation is defined as the amount of money that would exactly compensate individuals for a given change, i.e., allow them to maintain the same level of utility as before (after) the change.

The concept of ecosystem services fits easily within the anthropocentric framework underlying this concept of value, because it is based on the notion that ecosystems contribute to human welfare and hence have instrumental value. In addition, it is conceptually straightforward to combine ecology and economics to value ecosystem services using economic valuation techniques. Ecology provides the understanding of ecological systems necessary to construct ecological production functions that are used to predict changes in the flow of these services, and economics defines services and provides methods for estimating the value of changes in these services.

There is a vast literature within economics on the valuation of market and nonmarket goods (see Freeman 2003), which includes applications to valuing ecosystem services. In fact, most of the methods of valuing the environment developed by economists are directly applicable to valuing ecosystem services. As noted above, ecological inputs can be valued in the same way that other inputs (such as labor and capital) are valued. For example, because wetlands can serve as a breeding ground and nursery for marine populations such as shrimp and crabs, the quantity and/or quality of wetlands can be viewed as an input affecting the productivity of the fishery. Several studies have estimated the value of the contribution of coastal wetlands to increased productivity of commercial or recreational fisheries (e.g., Barbier 1994, 2000, 2003; Barbier & Strand 1998; Barbier et al. 2002; Batie & Wilson 1978; Bell 1997; Ellis & Fisher 1987; Freeman 1991; Lynne et al. 1981; Swallow 1994). Other ecosystem services provided by wetlands that have been valued in a similar way include increased productivity of waterfowl (Hammack & Brown 1974), storm protection (Barbier et al. 2008, Costanza et al. 2008, Sathirathai & Barbier 2001), groundwater recharge (Acharya 2000, Acharya & Barbier 2000, 2002), and water quality improvements (Breaux et al. 1995, Kahn 1987, Kahn & Kemp 1985, McConnell & Strand 1989, Wu et al. 2000). A number of other papers have applied hedonic property price models or contingent valuation to estimate the value of wetlands (e.g., Bin & Polasky 2005, Boyer & Polasky 2004, Doss & Taff 1996, Earnhart 2001, Hammitt et al. 2001, Hoehn et al. 2002, Mahan et al. 2000, Morrison et al. 1999, Woodward & Wui 2001).

Use of an integrated ecological-economic model for valuation allows for a more realistic prediction of changes in the flow of ecosystem services that result from a given policy alternative. It also allows for an examination of the complementarity or trade-offs associated with the provision of various ecosystem services. Integrated models have been applied in a variety of contexts, including eutrophication (Batabyal et al. 2003, Carpenter et al. 1999, Hart 2003, Iwasa et al. 2007), habitat protection and restoration (Ando et al. 1998; Balmford et al. 2000; Montgomery et al. 1994, 1999; Naidoo et al. 2006; Nalle et al. 2004; Polasky et al. 2005, 2008; Wu et al. 2003), biodiversity (Brock & Xepapadeas 2003, Polasky & Solow 1995, Simpson et al. 1996), and the joint provision of multiple ecosystem services (e.g., Antle & Stoorvogel 2006; Coiner et al. 2001; Naidoo & Ricketts 2006; Nelson et al. 2008, 2009).

The existing literature illustrates the potential for applying standard economic valuation methods to the valuation of ecosystem services. However, attempts to apply economic valuation methods to a broad set of interrelated services, both intermediate and final, face a number of practical difficulties that arise in either predicting changes in service flows or estimating the associated values. Among the more important practical difficulties in assessing the value of ecosystem services are the following (National Research Council 2005, US Environmental Protection Agency 2009):

- Limited understanding of the structure and functions of the relevant ecosystem(s), including important dynamics, nonlinearities and threshold effects, irreversibilities, and interconnections
- Lack of multiproduct, ecological production functions to quantitatively map ecosystem structure and function to a flow of services that can then be valued
- Limited public understanding of the services, and ultimately the contributions to welfare, provided by ecosystems
- Reliance on valuation methods that do not adequately capture the role of important underlying ecological relationships

Despite these challenges, at least at a conceptual level, economics and ecology can be integrated to measure the value of ecosystem services using the economic concept of value, as illustrated by the studies referenced above. However, in interdisciplinary contexts, philosophical differences often arise over the sources of value and the appropriate way to measure it. Although well-accepted within neoclassical economics, the welfare economic approach to defining and estimating values discussed above is not universally endorsed (Goulder & Kennedy 1997, Norton & Noonar 2007, Turner 1999, Winkler 2006). Key areas of divergence in views about defining values relate to the questions addressed in the following sections.

8.1. Should Values Be Defined in Anthropocentric Terms?

This question is essentially about who/what has intrinsic value. Some people believe that the natural world has value apart from how it contributes to human welfare. Under this biocentric or ecocentric view, all species may have intrinsic value or the condition of the ecosystem as a whole (health, integrity, resilience) may have intrinsic value (Callicott 1989, Light & Rolston 2003, Norton 1987). Although anthropocentric and nonanthropocentric systems of value can lead to similar policy prescriptions (see further discussion below), they are fundamentally different approaches. Even the concept of existence value, which economists sometimes describe as capturing the intrinsic value of nature, is still fundamentally defined from an anthropocentric perspective because it is based on human preferences (Edwards 1992). Examples of alternative definitions of value that are not explicitly based on human preferences include values defined in terms of energy content or contributions to a prespecified conservation goal such as biodiversity preservation or sustainability (Costanza 2000, 2004; Grossman & Comer 2004; Winkler 2006). If the underlying motivation for these goals is their importance for humans, the associated value concepts are anthropocentric. If alternatively, the motivation is based on intrinsic values of nature, they should be interpreted as biocentric or ecocentric concepts of value.

8.2. Should Values Be Defined in Utilitarian or Deontological Terms?

Even with agreement on an anthropocentric approach to value, the notion of defining values in terms of consequences or contributions to human welfare, rather than rights or moral obligations, is not universally accepted (Anderson 1993; Spash 1997, 2006). For example, some might argue that a given ecosystem should be protected because all people have a right to the services it provides (e.g., access to clean water or clean air). Although in principle the utilitarian approach allows for the possibility of lexicographical preferences, under which some considerations "trump" all others, in general it implies substitutability between ecosystem services and other goods and services that also contribute to utility. For example, the economic (utilitarian) concept of the existence value of a species is not defined in terms of its intrinsic right to exist but rather in terms of the amounts of other goods and services that an individual is willing to give up to ensure its existence. Deontological rights-based approaches do not embody principles of substitutability and acceptable trade-offs, except when there is a conflict between rights.

8.3. Who Should Determine Value When the Public Does Not Have Full Information?

Consumer sovereignty assumes that individuals are the best judges of what is in their own best interest and that their preferences are valid regardless of how they are viewed by others. Under consumer sovereignty, public preferences rather than those of a set of experts or government officials determine the relevant values (National Research Council 1996).

However, the public may not understand or "appreciate" the contributions of ecosystems. For example, the public might not understand the importance of microorganisms that contribute to soil formation and hence, if asked, might assign a value of zero to changes in their abundance. This type of answer can cause some to suggest that expert judgment, rather than public values, should be the basis for policy decisions. The economic approach to this information problem would not be to substitute expert judgment for public values; rather, it would be either to provide the public with the scientific information necessary to understand the contributions provided by the microorganisms, or to recast the valuation question in terms of final services that the public does understand and value (e.g., seek to estimate the value of the change in water quality, crop yield from improved soil fertility, or other final services resulting from changes in microorganism abundance).

8.4. Are Preferences over Ecosystem Services Well-Defined or Constructed?

A foundational assumption of economics is that individuals are rational and have well-defined preferences over bundles of goods and services, which they reveal consistently in a number of ways (e.g., through behavior or surveys). An alternative view within parts of psychology and decision science is that preferences are constructed through a cognitive process, particularly for complex and unfamiliar goods (Lichtenstein & Slovic 2006). This view implies that different contexts or settings can yield varying, and sometimes inconsistent, rankings of alternatives. These alternative views imply not only fundamentally different theoretical constructs for value but also a different set of methods that are deemed appropriate for value elicitation (Gregory et al. 1993).

8.5. Are Values Associated Only with Changes in Services?

In economics, the concept of a change is fundamental to defining values. Economists measure the value of a change from a baseline (prepolicy) level of some price or quantity variable to an alternative (postpolicy) level (Just et al. 2004). However, within some realms, values are conceived as a set of principles, concepts, or beliefs that guide decisions and evaluations (see, for example, Dietz et al. 2005, Hitlin & Piliavin 2004). In addition, even when defined in terms of contributions to human welfare, some valuation studies have sought to estimate the value of an entire ecosystem or even the set of ecosystems that make up a given landscape at a local, regional, or global scale (Costanza et al. 1997). Valuing an entire ecosystem is consistent with an economic approach if the value of the ecosystem is based on a comparison of human welfare with and without the ecosystem. However, typically, eliminating the ecosystem(s) is neither a policy-relevant change (Daily et al. 2000), nor a sensible comparison (Toman 1998). Even if it were, the standard economic valuation methods, which were derived primarily in the context of marginal analysis, would not likely adequately capture the associated value.

8.6. What Is the Relevant Baseline?

Although economic values are defined in terms of a change from some current or alternative level, they do not embody any judgment about whether that level is "good" or "bad," or about the process by which the level was reached (in particular, whether it is higher or lower than some other reference level). However, when an ecosystem is already degraded, some might advocate a baseline defined in terms of an historical level that was deemed "acceptable" (e.g., the system 50 or 100 years ago), or perhaps even a "pristine" level (the system prior to human contact). This can reflect an implicit goal of restoration to that baseline. Defining the baseline may also be tied to views on entitlements or rights such as a view that the public has the right to clean water or a pristine habitat.

The debates surrounding the above issues reflect different views about the sources and nature of value. Focusing on these differences can lead to lengthy debates that generally cannot be resolved through scientific inquiry. In fact, much of the discussion and debate that occupied the C-VPESS for five years in its effort to produce a consensus report surrounded these issues. In contrast, the NRC committee, whose charge explicitly focused on the economic approach to valuation, avoided these debates and as a result reached consensus much more quickly.

9. POLICY EVALUATION FOR COMBINED ECOLOGICAL-ECONOMIC SYSTEMS

A key motivation for conducting valuation of ecosystem services is to improve public policy decisions. This requires evaluation of policy options using some criteria. Different criteria can be used, and these often reflect various views about why people do or should value protection of ecosystem services.

The standard economic efficiency approach to policy evaluation (Link 7 in **Figure 1**), as embodied in benefit-cost analysis, uses net benefits based on estimates of market and nonmarket values to evaluate alternatives. An economically efficient policy is one that maximizes the aggregate net benefits of individuals in society. Efficiency does not require that all people are actually better off compared with the baseline, only that the gains exceed the losses so that the "winners" from the policy change could, in principle, compensate the "losers" in a way that would make everyone better off. Economists generally recommend using benefit-cost analysis as an input into societal decision making rather than as a decision rule, because other considerations not reflected in measures of aggregate net benefits, such as equity considerations, are also important in social choice (Arrow et al. 1996).

There is now a large literature that has applied standard benefit-cost principles to evaluate policy options using integrated ecological-economic models: e.g., Carpenter et al. (1999) on lake eutrophication; Barbier et al. (2008) on coastal protection; Archer & Shogren (2001) on pesticide use; Settle & Shogren (2006) on the introduction of non-native species; Wu et al. (2003) on restoration of salmon habitat; Costello & Polasky (2008), Eichner & Tschirhart (2007), and Sanchirico & Wilen (1999, 2001, 2005) on harvesting marine species. The explicit incorporation of ecological relationships within a benefit-cost analysis will generally highlight the importance of considering uncertainty, irreversibility, risk aversion, and threshold effects, all of which are concerns often raised by ecologists. These considerations can be incorporated through the use of expected utility theory based on appropriately specified utility functions that incorporate risk aversion and probability distributions that incorporate threshold effects and nonlinear dynamics. In addition, the concept of (quasi) option value incorporates irreversibility and uncertainty into an economic efficiency paradigm (Arrow & Fisher 1974, Dixit & Pindyck 1994). Option-value arguments, which place value on avoiding irreversible decisions until uncertainty is resolved, are similar to noneconomists' calls for the use of the precautionary principle, which places a high burden of proof on proponents of actions that might cause irreversible harm (for an economic evaluation of the precautionary principle, see Gollier et al. 2000, Gollier & Treich 2003). Similar arguments can be made for "safe minimum standards" (Ciriacy-Wantrup 1952) to avoid decisions that might result in crossing a threshold with serious negative consequences. Arguments for other risk-averse approaches to decision making can be justified if the uncertainty about the ecological-economic systems is so profound that probability functions over potential outcomes cannot be defined in any meaningful way (termed Knightian uncertainty) (for a recent discussion, see Margolis & Naevdal 2008).

Concerns about ecosystem degradation and resource depletion have also generated calls for using sustainability as a broad normative goal (see, e.g., Arrow et al. 2004, Costanza 1991). Sustainability is generally defined as meeting the "needs of the present without compromising the ability of future generations to meet their own needs" (World Commission on Environment and Development 1987). Although the specific interpretation of this goal can vary (e.g., Pezzey & Toman 2002), sustainability is often viewed as an alternative to standard economic efficiency as a normative goal (e.g., Arrow et al. 2004, Ayres 2008, Costanza 1991). However, Heal (1998) derived sustainability as an efficient outcome when society places a positive value on the very long run and people intrinsically value environmental assets. Including environmental stocks in the utility function can also yield a sustainable solution to an otherwise standard model of the efficient use of an exhaustible resource (Krautkraemer 1985). As these works show, a potentially fruitful approach is to characterize cases in which efficient paths are also sustainable.

Because of the complexity of joint ecological-economic systems, some natural scientists prefer to think about system resilience rather than any deliberate attempt to maximize expected net benefits (e.g., Gunderson & Holling 2002). One definition of resilience is the ability of a system to withstand shocks without fundamentally changing the character of the system (for a more complete set of definitions of resilience, see **http://www.resalliance. org**). Under the resilience approach, actions are desirable if they increase an ecological system's ability to tolerate disturbances or promote flexible human response through learning or adaptation. The resilience approach is a general philosophy of what types of system properties are important, but it does not have well-developed decision-making rules (analogous, for example, to maximizing expected utility).

Despite the differing principles or philosophies that can underlie various decision rules, the various rules can lead to policy prescriptions that are similar, at least qualitatively. For example, Eichner & Pethig (2006) showed that protection of nature can be justified through a variety of channels, using both anthropocentric and non-anthropocentric social welfare functions. Likewise, Arrow et al. (2004) argued that some policies designed to promote efficiency, such as those designed to correct the underpricing of natural resources, can contribute to both efficiency and sustainability goals. Perrings (1995) showed that improvement in ecological resilience increases the likelihood that economic development will be sustainable.

Thus, different perspectives on appropriate normative criteria may have little practical difference in terms of decision making. For example, a person with anthropocentric nonuse values such as existence value and a person with biocentric values may favor similar management alternatives, despite the differences in their underlying motivations. In each case, the person may place much weight on the conservation of biodiversity and ecosystems. Nonetheless, the process of getting to a common policy prescription can be challenging when individuals apply different evaluation criteria and when the debate focuses not on the commonality of the final prescription, but rather on the ideological differences underlying the various ways of reaching that end.

10. INCREASING THE SCOPE FOR COLLABORATION IN NORMATIVE ANALYSIS

The previous sections overview some of the challenges that can arise in valuing ecosystem services for use in policy evaluations. The process of trying to overcome these challenges can be long, frustrating, and discouraging for the parties involved. However, we believe that we could take a significant step toward this end by recasting or reframing the discussion. We suggest the following in the spirit of providing a practical rather than a purist approach.

As noted above, much of the debate over normative analysis of ecosystem services ultimately stems from differing views about why ecosystems are important and should be protected. Views that do not consider the benefits of ecosystems to human well-being (see Links 3 and 5 in **Figure 1**) cannot be reconciled with an economic efficiency approach to policy evaluation; hence, they preclude integration of economics and ecology in normative analyses. However, as the review above suggests, there is considerable potential for integrating economics and ecology in valuing ecosystem services and incorporating those values into policy evaluations that consider trade-offs and economic efficiency (Links 6 and 7 in **Figure 1**). As a step toward this goal, we suggest that, rather than focusing on why individuals value nature and protection of ecological systems, economists and ecologists seeking to collaborate on normative analyses should focus on reaching agreement on the basis of the following premises:

1. Evaluation of trade-offs is an important consideration in evaluating policy options.
2. Trade-offs should be assessed on the basis of what affected individuals are willing to give up to secure, or demand in exchange for foregoing, an ecological improvement, regardless of why they are willing to make these exchanges.
3. Individuals can reveal the exchanges or trade-offs they are willing to make through actual and/or stated choices.

Acceptance of these premises would not require adoption of a particular individual value system or adherence to a set of philosophical or ethical principles relating to people's values. In addition, it would not require agreement about why individuals want to protect ecosystems and would be willing to give up other goods and services toward that end. For these reasons, we believe it would be easier to get agreement among an interdisciplinary group of researchers on these premises than to resolve all of the issues and debates that can hamper collaborative efforts, as discussed in the previous section. We believe that refocusing the discussion around the relevance and assessment of trade-offs could allow interdisciplinary groups of people with differing views to move forward in integrating ecology and economics in normative analyses.

11. CONCLUSION

In this paper, we draw on our collective experience with interdisciplinary committees working on ecosystem services to reflect on both the opportunities and challenges associated with integrating economics and ecology in this context. In terms of positive analysis, there is rapid growth in research that combines the two disciplines to provide insight and better understanding of the bidirectional linkage between economic and ecological systems. This research is a crucial part of addressing the growing large-scale environmental challenges facing the world today. The integration of ecology and economics is equally important, but potentially much more difficult, in normative analyses, because of different views regarding why people value nature and the criteria that should be used in making policy decisions relating to ecosystem protection. Some of these differences are irreconcilable, even though the policy prescriptions implied by the different perspectives can be very similar. Nonetheless, we believe there is still considerable room for collaboration among economists and ecologists in normative analysis, even when they do not fully agree on these two issues. Successful collaboration does not require full agreement on individuals' underlying motivations or appropriate social choice rules. Rather, it requires agreement that the trade-offs that affected individuals are willing to make to preserve or enhance ecosystem services are relevant for public policy decisions and that those trade-offs are reflected in the choices individuals make. Researchers who can agree on these basic premises and then focus collaborative efforts on the study of trade-offs should be able to collaborate successfully on normative analyses, even if they hold disparate views on other issues. Our hope is that such an approach will expand the scope for collaboration by highlighting common ground rather than philosophical and other differences and thus help in moving forward interdisciplinary research on ecosystem services.

DISCLOSURE STATEMENT

The authors are not aware of any affiliations, memberships, funding, or financial holdings that might be perceived as affecting the objectivity of this review.

ACKNOWLEDGMENT

We thank V. Kerry Smith for very useful comments on an earlier draft of this article, which greatly improved its contents.

LITERATURE CITED

Acharya G. 2000. Approaches to valuing the hidden hydrological services of wetland ecosystems. *Ecol. Econ.* 35:63–74

Acharya G, Barbier EB. 2000. Valuing groundwater recharge through agricultural production in the Hadejia'Jama'are wetlands in Northern Nigeria. *Agric. Econ.* 22:247–59

Acharya G, Barbier EB. 2002. Using domestic water analysis to value groundwater recharge in the Hadejia'Jama'are Floodplain in northern Nigeria. *Am. J. Agric. Econ.* 84:415–26

Alchian AA. 1950. Uncertainty, evolution, and economic theory. *J. Polit. Econ.* 58:211–21

Anderson JC. 1993. Species equality and the foundations of moral theory. *Environ. Values* 2:347–65

Ando A, Camm J, Polasky S, Solow A. 1998. Species distributions, land values, and efficient conservation. *Science* 279:2126–28

Antle JM, Stoorvogel JJ. 2006. Incorporating systems dynamics and spatial heterogeneity in integrated assessment of agricultural production systems. *Environ. Dev. Econ.* 11:39–58

Archer DW, Shogren JF. 2001. Risk-indexed herbicide taxes to reduce ground and surface water pollution: an integrated ecological economics evaluation. *Ecol. Econ.* 38:227–50

Arrow KJ, Cropper ML, Eads GC, Hahn RW, Lave LB, et al. 1996. Is there a role for benefit-cost analysis in environmental, health, and safety regulation? *Science* 272:221–22

Arrow K, Dasgupta P, Goulder L, Daily G, Ehrlich P, et al. 2004. Are we consuming too much? *J. Econ. Perspect.* 18:147–72

Arrow KJ, Fisher AC. 1974. Environmental preservation, uncertainty, and irreversibility. *Q. J. Econ.* 88:312–19

Ayres RU. 2008. Sustainability economics: Where do we stand? *Ecol. Econ.* 67:281–310

Balmford A, Gaston KJ, Rodrigues ASL, James A. 2000. Integrating conservation costs into international priority setting. *Conserv. Biol.* 11:597–605

Barbier EB. 1994. Valuing environmental functions: tropical wetlands. *Land Econ.* 70:155–73

Barbier EB. 2000. Valuing the environment as input: applications to mangrove-fishery linkages. *Ecol. Econ.* 35:47–61

Barbier EB. 2003. Habitat-fishery linkages and mangrove loss in Thailand. *Contemp. Econ. Policy* 21:59–77

Barbier EB, Koch EW, Silliman BR, Hacker SD, Wolanski E, et al. 2008. Coastal ecosystem-based management with non-linear ecological functions and values. *Science* 319:321–23

Barbier EB, Strand I. 1998. Valuing mangrove-fishery linkages: a case study of Campeche, Mexico. *Environ. Resour. Econ.* 12:151–66

Barbier EB, Strand I, Sathirathai S. 2002. Do open access conditions affect the valuation of an externality? Estimating the welfare effects of mangrove-fishery linkages in Thailand. *Environ. Resour. Econ.* 21:343–67

Batabyal AA, Kahn JR, O'Neill RV. 2003. On the scarcity value of ecosystem services. *J. Environ. Econ. Manag.* 46:334–52

Batie SS, Wilson JR. 1978. Economic values attributable to Virginia's coastal wetlands as inputs in oyster production. *South. J. Agric. Econ.* 10:111–8

Baumol WJ, Oates WE. 1988. *The Theory of Environmental Policy.* New York: Cambridge Univ. Press. 2nd ed.

Bell FW. 1997. The economic value of saltwater marsh supporting marine recreational fishing in the Southeastern United States. *Ecol. Econ.* 21:243–54

Bin O, Polasky S. 2005. Evidence on the amenity value of wetlands in a rural setting. *J. Agric. Appl. Econ.* 37:589–602

Bockstael N, Freeman AM III, Kopp RJ, Portney PR, Smith VK. 2000. On measuring economic values for nature. *Environ. Sci. Technol.* 34:1384–89

Boody G, Vondracek B, Andow DA, Krinke M, Westra J, et al. 2005. Multifunctional agriculture in the United States. *Bioscience* 55:27–38

Boyd J, King D, Wainger L. 2001. Compensation for lost ecosystem services: the need for benefit-based transfer ratios and restoration criteria. *Stanford Environ. Law J.* 20:393–412

Boyer T, Polasky S. 2004. Valuing urban wetlands: a review of non-market valuation studies. *Wetlands* 24:744–55

Breaux AM, Farber S, Day J. 1995. Using natural coastal wetlands systems for wastewater treatment and economic benefit analysis. *J. Environ. Manag.* 44:285–91

Brock WA, Xepapadeas A. 2003. Valuing biodiversity from an economic perspective: a unified economic, ecological and genetic approach. *Am. Econ. Rev.* 93:1597–614

Brown S, Schroeder PE. 1999. Spatial patterns of aboveground production and mortality of woody biomass for eastern US forests. *Ecol. Appl.* 9:968–80

Bulte EH, Lipper L, Stringer R, Zilberman D. 2008. Payments for ecosystem services and poverty reduction: concepts, issues, and empirical perspectives. *Environ. Dev. Econ.* 13(3):245–54

Cairns MA, Haggerty PK, Alvarez R, De Jong BHJ, Olmsted I. 2000. Tropical Mexico's recent land-use change: a region's contribution to the global carbon cycle. *Ecol. Appl.* 10:1426–41

Callicott JB. 1989. *In Defense of the Land Ethic: Essays in Environmental Philosophy.* Albany, NY: SUNY Press

Canadell JG, Raupach MR. 2008. Managing forests for climate change mitigation. *Science* 320:1456–57

Carpenter S, Defries R, Dietz T, Mooney HA, Polasky S, et al. 2006. Research needs revealed by the Millennium Ecosystem Assessment. *Science* 314:257–58

Carpenter SR, Ludwig D, Brock WA. 1999. Management of eutrophication for lakes subject to potentially irreversible change. *Ecol. Appl.* 9:751–71

Ciriacy-Wantrup SV. 1952. *Resources Conservation: Economics and Policy.* Berkeley, CA: Univ. Calif. Press

Claassen R, Cattaneo A, Johansson R. 2008. Cost-effective design of agri-environmental payment programs: U.S. experience in theory and practice. *Ecol. Econ.* 65:737–52

Clark C. 1990. *Mathematical Bioeconomics.* New York: Wiley. 2nd ed.

Coiner C, Wu J, Polasky S. 2001. Economic and environmental implications of alternative landscape designs in the Walnut Creek Watershed of Iowa. *Ecol. Econ.* 38:119–39

Costanza R, ed. 1991. *Ecological Economics: The Science and Management of Sustainability.* New York: Columbia Univ. Press

Costanza R. 2000. Social goals and the valuation of ecosystem services. *Ecosystems* 3:4–10

Costanza R. 2004. Value theory and energy. In *Encyclopedia of Energy*, Vol. 6, ed. C Cleveland, pp. 337–46. Amsterdam: Elsevier Sci.

Costanza R, d'Arge R, de Groot R, Farber S, Grasso M. 1997. The value of the world's ecosystem services and natural capital. *Nature* 387:253–60

Costanza R, Pérez-Maqueo O, Martinez ML, Sutton P, Anderson SJ, Mulder KV. 2008. The value of coastal wetlands for hurricane protection. *AMBIO J. Hum. Environ.* 37:241--48

Costello C, Polasky S. 2008. Optimal harvesting of stochastic spatial resources. *J. Environ. Econ. Manag.* 56:1–18

Daily GC, ed. 1997. *Nature's Services: Societal Dependence on Natural Ecosystems.* Washington, DC: Island Press

Daily G, Ellison K. 1999. *The New Economy of Nature: The Quest to Make Conservation Profitable.* Cheltenham, UK: Edward Elgar

Daily G, Polasky S, Goldstein J, Kareiva PM, Mooney HA, et al. 2009. Ecosystem services in decision-making: time to deliver. In *Frontiers in Ecology and the Environment*. In press

Daily GC, Söderqvist T, Aniyar S, Arrow K, Dasgupta P, et al. 2000. The value of nature and the nature of value. *Science* 289:395–96

Dietz T, Fitzgerald A, Shwom R. 2005. Environmental values. *Annu. Rev. Environ. Resour.* 30:335–72

Dixit AK, Pindyck RS. 1994. *Investment under Uncertainty.* Princeton, NJ: Princeton Univ. Press

Doss CR, Taff SJ. 1996. The influence of wetland type and wetland proximity on residential property values. *J. Agric. Resour. Econ.* 21:120–29

Earnhart D. 2001. Combining revealed and stated preferences methods to value environmental amenities at residential locations. *Land Econ.* 77:12–29

Edwards S. 1992. Rethinking existence values. *Land Econ.* 68:120–22

Eichner T, Pethig R. 2006. Efficient non-anthropocentric nature protection. *Soc. Choice Welfare* 26:47–74

Eichner T, Tschirhart J. 2007. Efficient ecosystem services and naturalness in an ecological/economic model. *Environ. Resour. Econ.* 37:733–55

Ellis GM, Fisher AC. 1987. Valuing the environment as input. *J. Environ. Manag.* 25:149–56

Feng H, Kurkalova LA, Kling CA, Gassman PW. 2006. Environmental conservation in agriculture: land retirement vs. changing practices on working land. *J. Environ. Econ. Manag.* 52:600–14

Freeman AM. 1991. Valuing environmental resources under alternative management regimes. *Ecol. Econ.* 3:247–56

Freeman AM. 2003. *The Measurement of Environmental and Resource Values.* Washington, DC: Resour. Future

Gollier C, Treich N. 2003. Decision-making under scientific uncertainty: the economics of the Precautionary Principle. *J. Risk Uncertain.* 27:77–103

Gollier C, Treich N, Jullien B. 2000. Scientific progress and irreversibility: an economic interpretation of the precautionary principle. *J. Public Econ.* 75:229–53

Gordon HS. 1954. The economic theory of a common-property resource: the fishery. *J. Polit. Econ.* 62:124–42

Goulder LH, Kennedy D. 1997. Valuing ecosystem services: philosophical bases and empirical methods. In *Nature's Services: Societal Dependence on Natural Ecosystems*, ed. GC Daily, pp. 23–47. Washington, DC: Island Press

Gregory R, Lichtenstein S, Slovic P. 1993. Valuing environmental resources: a constructive approach. *J. Risk Uncertain.* 7:177–97

Grossman DH, Comer PJ. 2004. Setting priorities for biodiversity conservation in Puerto Rico. *NatureServ Techn. Rep.*, Arlington, VA

Gunderson LH, Holling CS. 2002. *Panarchy: Understanding Transformations in Human and Natural Systems.* Washington, DC: Island Press

Hammack J, Brown GM Jr. 1974. *Waterfowl and Wetlands: Toward Bioeconomic Analysis.* Baltimore, MD: Resour. Future/Johns Hopkins Univ. Press

Hammitt JK, Liu JT, Liu JL. 2001. Contingent valuation of Taiwanese wetlands. *Environ. Dev. Econ.* 6:259–68

Hanley N, Shogren JF, White B. 1996. *Environmental Economics in Theory and Practice.* New York: Oxford Univ. Press

Hart R. 2003. Dynamic pollution control—time lags and optimal restoration of marine ecosystems. *Ecol. Econ.* 47:79–93

Heal G. 1998. Interpreting sustainability. In *Sustainability: Dynamics and Uncertainty*, ed. G Chichilnisky, G Heal, A Vercelli, pp. 3–22. Dorrecht: Kluwer Acad.

Heal G. 2000. *Nature and the Marketplace: Capturing the Value of Ecosystem Services.* Washington, DC: Island Press

Hitlin S, Piliavin JA. 2004. Values: reviving a dormant concept. *Annu. Rev. Sociol.* 30:359–93

Hoehn JP, Lupi F, Kaplowitz MD. 2002. The economic equivalency of drained and restored wetlands in Michigan. *Am. J. Agric. Econ.* 84:1355–61

Ingraham MW, Foster SG. 2008. The value of ecosystem services provided by the U.S. National Wildlife Refuge System in the contiguous U.S. *Ecol. Econ.* 67:608–18

Irwin EG, Bockstael NE. 2002. Interacting agents, spatial externalities, and the endogenous evolution of residential land use pattern. *J. Econ. Geogr.* 2:31–54

Irwin EG, Bockstael NE. 2004. Land use externalities, growth management policies, and urban sprawl. *Reg. Sci. Urban Econ.* 34:705–25

Iwasa Y, Uchida T, Yokomizo H. 2007. Nonlinear behavior of the socio-economic dynamics for lake eutrophication control. *Ecol. Econ.* 63:219–29

Jack BK, Kousky C, Sims KRE. 2008. Designing payments for ecosystem services: lessons from previous experience with incentive-based mechanisms. *Proc. Natl. Acad. Sci. USA* 105:9465–70

Jackson RB, Jobbagy EG, Avissar R, Roy SB, Barrett DJ, et al. 2005. Trading water for carbon with biological sequestration. *Science* 310:1944–47

Just RE, Hueth DL, Schmitz A. 2004. *The Welfare Economics of Public Policy: A Practical Approach to Project and Policy Evaluation.* Cheltenham, UK/Northampton, MA: Edward Elgar

Kahn JR. 1987. Measuring the economic damages associated with terrestrial pollution of marine ecosystems. *Mar. Resour. Econ.* 4:193–209

Kahn JR, Kemp WM. 1985. Economic losses associated with the degradation of an ecosystem: the case of submerged aquatic vegetation in the Chesapeake Bay. *J. Environ. Econ. Manag.* 12:246–63

Koch EW, Barbier EB, Silliman BR, Reed DJ, Perillo GME, et al. 2009. Non-linearity in ecosystem services: temporal and spatial variability in coastal protection. *Front. Ecol. Environ.* 7:29–37

Krautkraemer J. 1985. Optimal growth, resource amenities, and the preservation of natural environments. *Rev. Econ. Stud.* 52:153–70

Lewis DJ, Nelson E, Plantinga AJ, Polasky S. 2009. *The efficiency of voluntary incentive policies for preventing biodiversity loss.* Work. Pap., Dep. Agric. Appl. Econ., Univ. Wisc.-Madison

Lewis DJ, Plantinga AJ. 2007. Policies for habitat fragmentation: combining econometrics with GIS-based landscape simulations. *Land Econ.* 83:109–27

Lichtenstein S, Slovic P. 2006. *The Construction of Preferences.* New York: Cambridge Univ. Press

Light A, Rolston III H, eds. 2003. *Environmental Ethics: An Anthology.* Chichester, UK: Blackwell

Lubowski RN. 2002. *Determinants of land-use transitions in the United States: econometric analysis of changes among the major land-use categories.* Ph.D. thesis. Harvard Univ., Cambridge, MA

Lubowski RN, Plantinga AJ, Stavins RN. 2006. Land-use change and carbon sinks: econometric estimation of the carbon sequestration supply function. *J. Environ. Econ. Manag.* 51:135–52

Lynne GD, Conroy P, Prochaska F. 1981. Economic valuation of marsh areas for marine protection. *J. Environ. Econ. Manag.* 8:175–81

Mahan BL, Polasky S, Adams R. 2000. Valuing urban wetlands: a property price approach. *Land Econ.* 76:100–13

Margolis M, Naevdal E. 2008. Safe minimum standards in dynamic resource problems: conditions for living on the edge of risk. *Environ. Resour. Econ.* 40:401–23

McConnell KE, Strand IE. 1989. Benefits from commercial fisheries when demand and supply depend on water quality. *J. Environ. Econ. Manag.* 17:284–92

Millennium Ecosystem Assessment. 2005. *Ecosystems and Human Well-Being. Synthesis.* Washington, DC: Island Press

Montgomery CA, Brown GM, Adams DM. 1994. The marginal cost of species preservation: the northern spotted owl. *J. Environ. Econ. Manag.* 26:111–28

Montgomery CA, Pollak RA, Freemark K, White D. 1999. Pricing biodiversity. *J. Environ. Econ. Manag.* 38:1–19

Morrison M, Bennett J, Blamey R. 1999. Valuing improved wetland quality using choice modeling. *Water Resour. Res.* 35:2805–14

Naidoo R, Adamowicz WL. 2006. Modeling opportunity costs of conservation in transitional landscapes. *Conserv. Biol.* 20:490–500

Naidoo R, Balmford A, Ferraro PJ, Polasky S, Ricketts TH, et al. 2006. Integrating economic cost into conservation planning. *Trends Ecol. Evol.* 21:681–87

Naidoo R, Iwamura T. 2007. Global-scale mapping of economic benefits from agricultural lands: implications for conservation priorities. *Biol. Conserv.* 140:40–49

Naidoo R, Ricketts TH. 2006. Mapping the economic costs and benefits of conservation. *PLoS Biol.* 4:2153–64

Nalle DJ, Montgomery CA, Arthur JL, Polasky S, Schumaker NH. 2004. Modeling joint production of wildlife and timber in forests. *J. Environ. Econ. Manag.* 48:997–1017

Nascimento HEM, Laurance WF. 2002. Total aboveground biomass in central Amazonian rainforests: a landscape-scale study. *For. Ecol. Manag.* 168:311–21

National Research Council. 1996. *Understanding Risk: Informing Decisions in a Democratic Society.* Washington, DC: Natl. Acad. Press

National Research Council. 2001. *Compensating for Wetland Losses under the Clean Water Act.* Washington, DC: Natl. Acad. Press

National Research Council. 2005. *Valuing Ecosystem Services: Toward Better Environmental Decision-Making*. Washington, DC: Natl. Acad. Press

Nelson E, Polasky S, Lewis DJ, Plantinga AJ, Lonsdorf E, et al. 2008. Efficiency of incentives to jointly increase carbon sequestration and species conservation on a landscape. *Proc. Natl. Acad. Sci. USA* 105:9471–76

Nelson EN, Mendoza GM, Regetz J, Polasky S, Tallis H, et al. 2009. Modeling multiple ecosystem services, biodiversity conservation, commodity production and tradeoffs at landscape scales. *Front. Ecol. Environ.* In press

Nordhaus WD, Boyer JG. 2000. *Warming the World: Economic Models of Global Warming*. Cambridge, MA: MIT Press

Norton BG. 1987. *Why Preserve Natural Variety?* Princeton, NJ: Princeton Univ. Press

Norton BG, Noonar D. 2007. Ecology and valuation: big changes needed. *Ecol. Econ.* 63:664–75

Pagiola S. 2008. Payments for environmental services in Costa Rica. *Ecol. Econ.* 65:712–24

Parkhurst GM, Shogren JF. 2007. Spatial incentives to coordinate contiguous habitat. *Ecol. Econ.* 64:344–55

Parkhurst GM, Shogren JF, Bastian C, Kivi P, Donner J, et al. 2002. Agglomeration bonus: an incentive mechanism to reunite fragmented habitat for biodiversity conservation. *Ecol. Econ.* 41:305–28

Pearce D. 1998. Auditing the earth. *Environment* 40:23–28

Perrings C. 1995. Ecological resilience in the sustainability of economic development. *Econ. Appl.* 48:121–42

Pezzey JCV, Toman MA. 2002. Progress and problems in the economics of sustainability. In *The International Yearbook of Environmental and Resource Economics 2002/2003*, ed. T Tietenberg, H Folmer, pp. 165–232. Cheltenham, UK: Edward Elgar

Polasky S, Nelson E, Camm J, Csuti B, Fackler P, et al. 2008. Where to put things? Spatial land management to sustain biodiversity and economic returns. *Biol. Conserv.* 141:1505–24

Polasky S, Nelson E, Lonsdorf E, Fackler P, Starfield A. 2005. Conserving species in a working landscape: land use with biological and economic objectives. *Ecol. Appl.* 15:1387–401

Polasky S, Solow A. 1995. On the value of a collection of species. *J. Environ. Econ. Manag.* 29:298–303

Rapport DJ, Turner JE. 1977. Economic models in ecology. *Science* 195:367–73

Rolston H. 1991. Environmental ethics: values in and duties to the natural world. In *Ecology, Economics and Ethics: The Broken Circle*, ed. FH Bormann, SR Kellert. New Haven, CT: Yale Univ. Press

Sanchirico J, Wilen J. 1999. Bioeconomics of spatial exploitation in a patchy environment. *J. Environ. Econ. Manag.* 37:129–50

Sanchirico J, Wilen J. 2001. A bioeconomic model of marine reserve creation. *J. Environ. Econ. Manag.* 42:257–76

Sanchirico J, Wilen J. 2005. Optimal spatial management of renewable resources: matching policy scope to ecosystem scale. *J. Environ. Econ. Manag.* 50:23–46

Sathirathai S, Barbier EB. 2001. Valuing mangrove conservation in Southern Thailand. *Contemp. Econ. Policy* 19:109–22

Schaefer MB. 1957. Some considerations of population dynamics and economics in relation to the management of marine fishes. *J. Fish. Res. Board Can.* 14:669–81

Scott A. 1955. The fishery: the objectives of sole ownership. *J. Polit. Econ.* 63:116–24

Settle C, Shogren JF. 2006. Does integrating economic and biological systems matter for public policy? The case of Yellowstone Lake. *B.E. J. Econ. Anal. Policy* 6:1–46

Simpson D, Sedjo R, Reid J. 1996. Valuing biodiversity for use in pharmaceutical research. *J. Polit. Econ.* 104:163–85

Spash CL. 1997. Ethics and environmental attitudes with implications for economic valuation. *J. Environ. Manag.* 50:403–16

Spash CL. 2006. Non-economic motivation for contingent values: rights and attitudinal beliefs in willingness to pay for environmental improvements. *Land Econ.* 82:602–22

Stern N. 2007. *Stern review on the economics of climate change. Executive summary.* HM Treasury, London. http://www.hm-treasury.gov.uk/sternreview_index.htm

Swallow SK. 1994. Renewable and nonrenewable resource theory applied to coastal agriculture, forest, wetland and fishery linkages. *Mar. Resour. Econ.* 9:291–310

Tilman D, Polasky S, Lehman C. 2005. Diversity, productivity and temporal stability in the economies of humans and nature. *J. Environ. Econ. Manag.* 49:405–26

Tol RSJ. 2005. The marginal damage costs of carbon dioxide emissions: an assessment of the uncertainties. *Energy Policy* 33:2064–74

Toman M. 1998. Why not to calculate the value of the world's ecosystem services and natural capital. *Ecol. Econ.* 25:57–60

Train KE. 2003. *Discrete Choice Methods with Simulation.* New York: Cambridge Univ. Press

Troy A, Wilson MA. 2006. Mapping ecosystem services: practical challenges and opportunities in linking GIS and value transfer. *Ecol. Econ.* 60:435–49

Turner RK. 1999. The place of economic values in environmental valuation. In *Valuing Environmental Preferences*, ed. I Bateman, KG Willis, pp. 17–42. London: Oxford Univ. Press

Turner WR, Brandon K, Brooks TM, Costanza R, Fonseca GAB, et al. 2007. Global conservation of biodiversity and ecosystem services. *Bioscience* 57:868–73

US Environmental Protection Agency. 2009. *Valuing the protection of ecological systems and services.* EPA Sci. Advis. Board Rep., Washington, DC

Vermeij GJ. 2004. *Nature: An Economic History.* Princeton, NJ: Princeton Univ. Press

Winkler R. 2006. Valuation of ecosystem goods and services: part 1. An integrated dynamic approach. *Ecol. Econ.* 59:82–93

Woodward RT, Wui YS. 2001. The economic value of wetland services: a meta-analysis. *Ecol. Econ.* 37:257–70

World Commission Environment Development. 1987. *Our Common Future.* New York: Oxford Univ. Press

Wu J, Adams RM, Boggess WG. 2000. Cumulative effects and optimal targeting of conservation efforts: steelhead trout habitat enhancement in Oregon. *Am. J. Agric. Econ.* 82:400–13

Wu J, Skelton-Groth K, Boggess WG, Adams RM. 2003. Pacific salmon restoration: trade-offs between economic efficiency and political acceptance. *Contemp. Econ. Policy* 21:78–89

The Economics of Urban-Rural Space

Elena G. Irwin,[1][*] Kathleen P. Bell,[2]
Nancy E. Bockstael,[3] David A. Newburn,[4]
Mark D. Partridge,[1] and JunJie Wu[5]

[1]Department of Agricultural, Environmental and Development Economics,
Ohio State University, Columbus, Ohio 43210; email: irwin.78@osu.edu,
partridge.27@osu.edu

[2]School of Economics, University of Maine, Orono, Maine 04469;
email: kpbell@maine.edu

[3]Department of Agricultural and Resource Economics, University of Maryland,
College Park, Maryland 20742; email: nbockstael@arec.umd.edu

[4]Department of Agricultural Economics, Texas A&M University, College Station,
Texas 77843; email: danewburn@ag.tamu.edu

[5]Department of Agricultural and Resource Economics, Oregon State University,
Corvallis, Oregon 97331; email: JunJie.Wu@oregonstate.edu

Annu. Rev. Resour. Econ. 2009. 1:435–59

First published online as a Review in Advance on
June 25, 2009

The *Annual Review of Resource Economics* is
online at resource.annualreviews.org

This article's doi:
10.1146/annurev.resource.050708.144253

*Corresponding author

Key Words

land use, exurban, sprawl, rural-urban interdependence, natural
amenities, spatial heterogeneity, environmental impacts

Abstract

The emergence of urban-rural space, as evidenced by the expansion of
low-density exurban areas and growth of amenity-based rural areas, is
characterized by the merging of a rural landscape form with urban
economic function. Changing economic conditions, including waning
transportation and communication costs, technological change and
economic restructuring, rising real incomes, and changing tastes for
natural amenities, have led to this new form of urban-rural interdependence. We review the recent research on the causes and consequences of this growth at regional and metropolitan scales, discuss
advances in empirical and theoretical economic models of urban land-
use patterns at spatially disaggregate scales, and highlight research on
environmental impacts and the efficacy of growth controls and land
conservation programs that seek to manage this growth. The paper
concludes with future research questions and needs. These include
spatially disaggregate and accurate data, improved causal inference
and structural modeling, and dynamic models that incorporate multiple sources of spatial and agent heterogeneity and interactions.

1. INTRODUCTION

The classification of urban versus rural has been a long-standing and, until recently, well-accepted taxonomy of people, places, and economic function. Urban areas are defined by more densely settled areas with a concentration of people and jobs in nonprimary production industries. Rural areas are the converse: sparsely settled regions with small towns interspersed and a majority of people and jobs in primary production industries. Such a dichotomy, although a reasonable characterization of people and landscapes for centuries, is no longer valid in many regions of the world, particularly in North America and Europe (**Figures 1 and 2**, see color insert). These changes are witnessed by the increasing proportion of low-density exurban areas—places that are functionally tied to urban areas in terms of employment, housing, and consumption, but that lie outside urban boundaries—and by the shifting mix of economic functions found in so-called rural places. Increasingly, we observe places that are "rural" based on their location and landscape form, but nonetheless partially "urban" in their higher-order economic functioning and composition. Examples include natural amenity-rich rural towns that are home to higher-order businesses and large expanses of low-density exurban landscapes in which the majority of residents commute to proximate suburban or urban employment locations. Such places are neither fully urban nor fully rural, but rather a blend of rural form with some degree of urban function. We refer to such regions as urban-rural space to emphasize the fact that urban and rural are no longer distinct geographic entities, but rather end points of an economic and geographic continuum along which a range of places are arrayed that vary in their mix of urban and rural elements.

The emergence of urban-rural space raises critical economic and environmental policy questions. According to Brown et al. (2005), the amount of land at urban densities (more than one house per acre) increased from less than 1% to nearly 2% between 1950 and 2000 while the amount of exurban land (between 1 and 40 acres per house) increased from approximately 5%–25% in this same time period. Because urban and urbanizing land generate a disproportionate share of environmental impacts, this dramatic increase in exurban land area poses pressing management challenges for ecosystem services. Increased urban-rural interdependence raises important regional economic concerns as well. Commuting distances provide a measure of the geographic extent of urban-rural labor markets and markets for urban production. In a study of U.S. and Canadian urban-rural space, Partridge & Olfert (2009) found that commuting distances from urban centers into surrounding rural fringe can extend out for 100 miles or more. Such a level of interdependence has major implications not only for regional economic development policies, but also a host of governance issues that revolve around the need to collaborate on infrastructure, public service delivery, and sharing of costs and revenues to reflect the mutual dependence in a given region (Partridge & Olfert 2009).

Changing economic conditions have spurred this urban-rural transformation. Waning transportation and communication costs have enabled a nontrivial proportion of people to commute to urban and suburban employment. Rising real incomes, changing tastes for open space, technological change, and economic restructuring have resulted in the growth of many exurban and rural regions that, once lagging behind urban areas, are now growing rapidly. These changes have spurred a variety of new research questions, some deriving from long-standing questions in urban and regional economics and others spurred by greater attention from environmental economists. Key questions include the following:

Exurban: low-density areas outside urban areas, but with a high degree of economic and social dependence on proximate urban and suburban areas

Rural: areas of countryside far from urban areas with low population density; defined by U.S. Census Bureau as nonurban areas

Suburban: areas immediately around cities that are densely settled; traditionally residential, but many modern suburbs include office, retail, and commercial clusters

Urban: towns and cities; areas that exceed a population size or density threshold as defined by the U.S. Census Bureau

Urban-rural space: areas whose landscapes appear largely rural, but are substantially economically and socially tied to urban areas; includes exurban and amenity-based rural areas

- How have declining transportation and communication costs influenced urban-rural space?
- What are the spillover effects of urban agglomeration on urban-rural space?
- How have household preferences and rising real incomes shaped urban-rural space?
- What are the implications of labor-saving technological change and rural economic restructuring for urban-rural space?
- What is the role of environmental amenities in shaping urban-rural space?
- How do local land-use and growth management policies influence land-use patterns in urban-rural space?
- What are the impacts of urban-rural growth on ecosystem services and climate change?

The purpose of this paper is to review selected recent research (specifically, selected papers published within the past 5–10 years and some unpublished manuscripts) that has contributed new theoretical insights, empirical findings, or methodological advances to the economics of urban-rural space. The geographic focus of our review is on North America and, to a lesser extent, Europe, because the integration of urban function and rural form in these areas has been the most prevalent. Economic globalization has led to rapid urbanization in many countries, most notably China, and suburbanization is a worldwide phenomenon. However, although the geographic extent of urban influence has certainly increased in developing countries, this is not the same kind of transformation of urban and rural space—in terms of the extent of exurban development and amenity-led rural growth—that is present in North America and Europe and that is the focus of our discussion here.

The remainder of the paper is structured as follows. Sections 2–5 review selected recent and significant literature and are structured according to the main themes suggested by the research questions above: the role of urban-rural economic restructuring, determinants of urban-rural land-use patterns, environmental interactions, and policy evaluation. The final section discusses future research challenges and needs.

2. URBAN-RURAL ECONOMIC RESTRUCTURING

Decades-long economic restructuring of urban and rural areas has fostered much of the urban-rural interdependence that is evident today. Historically, technological change and declining costs of transporting goods generated productivity advantages for urban areas. Urban advantages were reinforced by labor-saving technological change in the natural resource and agriculture sectors that, along with trade liberalization and global competition, have led to job loss and wholesale out-migration in rural communities unable to establish an alternative economic base (Deller et al. 2001, Partridge et al. 2007). Urbanization trends have been strengthened more recently by global economic trends, including the rise of professional services requiring large markets, increased demand for urban amenities, the concentration of more-educated workers in urban areas, and the growth of the "knowledge economy" (McCann 2007, Partridge & Olfert 2009).

Coincident with this broad urbanization trend, urban decentralization within metropolitan areas has resulted in more expansive cities with substantial suburban and exurban settlement areas. Transportation and technological change are dominant factors in the suburbanization of first people and then jobs, which increased dramatically in the twentieth century with the advent of automobiles and extensive highway construction

Amenity-led growth: population and firms relocate from urban to nonurban locations, attracted by environmental or rural amenities (e.g., nice climate, scenic landscapes, mountains, lakes, forests, oceans).

Land use: the economic and social purposes for which land is used or managed, e.g., uses include residential, commercial, agricultural, private conservation, public park, undeveloped

(Glaeser & Kahn 2004). More recent changes include the emergence of suburban subcenters (Anas et al. 1998), including edge cities—former "bedroom communities" that transformed into places with more jobs than people. Whereas higher-ordered services have continued to cluster in these subcenters, other employment is dispersed throughout metropolitan areas and manufacturing has increasingly relocated to exurban and rural green fields (Desmet & Fafchamps 2005).

These large-scale economic shifts and changes in urban spatial structure have prompted a variety of research. Here we focus on several key elements of urban-rural restructuring, many of which highlight the importance of distance in shaping urban-rural space.

Metropolitan area:
large region (often
multiple counties)
consisting of a large
urban center and its
economic zone of
influence; often
includes smaller
adjacent cities and
towns

2.1. Highways and Automobiles

Declining transportation costs are one of the primary explanations for suburbanization given by urban economists (e.g., Mieszkowski & Mills 1993), and most researchers agree that it is difficult to overstate the historical importance of the automobile in fostering decentralization (Glaeser & Kahn 2004, Nechyba & Walsh 2004). However, until recently, few empirical papers had rigorously analyzed this relationship. Recent findings show that highway construction and automobile subsidies have played a dominant role in urban decentralization, particularly in the United States. Baum-Snow (2007) used exogenous variation in planned portions of the interstate highway system to investigate urban decentralization between 1950 and 1990 within the United States. He found that each interstate highway passing through a central city reduces its population by approximately 18%, thereby contributing hugely to suburbanization. Brueckner (2005) and Su & DeSalvo (2008) showed theoretically that automobile subsidies contribute to excessive spatial growth of cities. Su & DeSalvo (2008) tested this hypothesis using data on public transit and highway spending and other characteristics from 201 urbanized areas in the United States. Their results show that the spatial size of the urbanized area shrinks with an increase in transit subsidies and increases at a decreasing rate with auto subsidies.

Cox et al. (2008) pointed out several weaknesses in the Baum-Snow (2007) paper. First, the large marginal effect of highways in Baum-Snow (2007) may be partly due to other correlations because he did not adequately address competing theories, such as other variables related to fiscal-social issues (e.g., crime, school quality, taxes) and other road infrastructure (e.g., state and local highways). Second, Cox et al. (2008) investigated urban decentralization in European cities and found counter examples in which decentralization occurred in cities without any new highways. However, they did not control for spatial size of the central core nor did they provide evidence that highways can reasonably be treated as exogenous. Further studies are therefore warranted to provide a cross comparison on the effect of highways in both European and American cities. Although the aggregate scale of these studies is useful for analyzing broad trends in urban decentralization, additional work is also needed to investigate the influence of roads on fine-scale, spatial land-use patterns.

2.2. Urban Growth Spillovers

In the wake of new technologies, much of the popular wisdom proclaimed that "distance is dead." Empirical evidence, however, suggests this is overly simplistic. Rather than a pure substitution effect, research shows that these technologies often have extensive urban agglomeration effects and have facilitated more face-to-face contact (Gasper & Glaeser 1998). How have technological change and transportation improvements impacted growth in urban-rural areas? Even if urban agglomeration economies are strengthened by new technologies, low transportation costs and the rise of telecommuting could offset these urban advantages and give rise to greater job and population growth in exurban and rural areas (Safirova 2002).

Partridge et al. (2008a,c; 2009) and Wu & Gopinath (2008) represent the most comprehensive investigations of the death-of-distance hypothesis across the entire urban-rural continuum. Partridge et al. (2008a,c; 2009) examined factor prices, population, and economic growth. Their point of departure is a classic central place theory of urban hierarchy in which cities are distinguished on the basis of their population and economic function. Each successively "higher-tiered" urban center adds higher-ordered economic functions, including cultural and other household amenities and business services. A small city may have only grocery stores, gas stations, and basic restaurants. The very top of the urban hierarchy has the full range of services including sophisticated financial advisors, patent attorneys, and business consultants (e.g., New York or Chicago). Thus, Partridge et al. (2008a,c; 2009) showed that remoteness should be measured across many dimensions over the entire spectrum of the urban hierarchy.

Using data from the U.S. county level, Partridge et al. (2008a,b; 2009) found that rural communities are penalized in terms of lower job and population growth for being more remote from a metropolitan area of any size, with the penalty rising for remoteness from successively larger urban centers up the urban hierarchy. However, distance penalties from large urban centers are actually the greatest for small- and medium-sized cities, suggesting that technological improvements are disadvantaging their service-industry firms when they lack close access to large cities. Thus, it is not rural communities that are most adversely affected by remoteness. Although labor-saving technological change is reducing primary-sector employment that is concentrated in rural communities, Partridge et al. (2008b) noted that these base industries are not as dependent on access to higher-ordered business services found in larger urban communities.

Wu & Gopinath (2008) examined the relative contributions of natural amenities, accumulated human and physical capital, and economic geography to the spatial variations in economic development across U.S. counties. They found that remoteness is the primary factor affecting spatial variations in economic development, accounting for 76% and 85% of the predicted differences in average wage and employment density between the top and bottom 20% of counties' wage and employment growth, respectively.

In contrast to rural remote areas, the growth of urban areas has benefited proximate rural places by improving access to urban markets and amenities. Previous research (Henry et al. 1997) demonstrated two effects: the spread of urban growth into the countryside that creates rural employment and growth and backwash effects that pull rural assets and people to the city. Recent empirical work suggests that spread effects dominate and that their geographical extent is quite large. For example, Partridge et al. (2007) found that urban growth creates positive population growth spillovers into Canadian rural communities for almost 200 kilometers. Likewise, Schmitt et al. (2006) showed that urban spread effects have dominated French rural-urban development.

2.3. Amenity-Led Rural Growth

The rising importance of natural amenities—pleasant landscapes; comfortable climate; proximity to lakes, oceans, forests, hills, and mountains—is largely a consequence of the changes in transportation and technology that have loosened the constraints of distance. Along with rising real incomes and improvements in heating and cooling technologies, these changes have generated substantial increases in the demand for natural amenities in rural areas.

Earlier work on natural amenities and rural growth focused on associations between natural features and population growth at a county level (e.g., McGranahan 1999) and on the relationship between growth and other complementary features of rural places (e.g., Deller et al. 2001, Kim et al. 2005). More recently Partridge et al. (2008b) used geographically weighted regression, an empirical method that accounts for local spatial heterogeneity, to examine differences in the association between amenities and growth. They found substantial differences across U.S. counties, e.g., mountains are more favorably related to population growth in the western United States and lakes have a higher positive association with growth in the arid southern Great Plains. Other research shows that proximity to amenities also matters. Following Roback (1982) and subsequent work that estimated compensating differentials in housing prices and wages to value locational amenities, Schmidt & Courant (2006) examined how access to "nice places" (national parks, seashores, and historical places) influences housing values. They found widespread geographical effects that extend hundreds of miles and evidence of a disamenity effect generated by lack of proximity. In examining the extent of amenity migration, Ferguson et al. (2007) found that amenity migration is more limited in Canada as compared with that in the United States. Likewise, Cheshire & Magrini (2006) found that migration to nice weather occurs primarily within, not between, countries.

The empirical work highlighted here and in Section 2.2 represents an improvement over previous literature in that it takes a spatially explicit approach to examine spillover, proximity, and amenity effects. However, the methods are insufficient for separating multiple sources of spatial autocorrelation; thus, additional work is needed to identify causality. Questions also remain as to how to identify separately the effects of highly correlated amenities. Deller et al. (2001) and Kim et al. (2005) used factor analysis, but although this approach has an appealing statistical basis, it lacks ease of interpretation. Other studies use the individual amenity variables (e.g., McGranahan 2008; Partridge et al. 2008a,c), but great care is necessary to ensure that results are robust to multicollinearity. Lastly, most empirical models that have examined urban spillovers and rural amenity effects lack a structural approach. Many empirical regional growth models are based on the Carlino-Mills model (Carlino & Mills 1985), a reduced-form stock-adjustment model of population and employment change. These models are not derived from a structural demand-supply framework and therefore often suffer endogeneity and identification problems.

2.4. Environmental Amenities and Housing Sorting

The empirical literature on residential location choice indicates that households sort themselves within metropolitan areas on the basis of local public goods, such as schools and crime, and other aspects of neighborhood quality. A substantial literature on "flight from blight" theorizes that suburbanization, on the one hand, is largely the result of households being "pushed" outward by the fiscal and social problems associated with the city. On the other hand, desirable features in the suburbs "pull" mobile households from the city, playing a potentially important role in urban expansion (Nechyba & Walsh 2004).

Building on the equilibrium properties of a Tiebout economy—in which heterogeneous households sort themselves according to their demand for local public goods—urban and environmental economists have used empirical locational equilibrium models (Epple & Sieg 1999) to examine the role of urban and natural amenities in household location decisions (e.g., Bayer et al. 2009, Smith et al. 2004). Walsh (2007) extended the locational equilibrium model developed by Epple and Sieg (1999) to consider the case in which endogenous local public goods, namely open space, are the result of land market outcomes. He found evidence that open space provides positive amenities at high levels of development, but negative amenities at low levels of development, suggesting that households trade off open space with the advantages of urban development. Wu & Cho (2003), also building on Epple and Sieg (1999), estimated households' preferences for alternative environmental amenities in the Portland, Oregon, metropolitan area. They showed that estimated structural parameters are biased if environmental amenities are ignored.

Recent work by Wu extends the theoretical literature on household sorting by developing an integrated model that emphasizes the importance of environmental amenities and public services in the formation of development patterns. Wu (2006) used such a model to examine the causes of urban sprawl and economic segregation and found that the spatial distribution of amenities is a major determinant of urban spatial structure. Wu (2009) developed a similar framework to examine how urban and suburban communities evolve differently with changes in local economic fundamentals such as rising income or falling commuting costs in a metropolitan area; he also highlighted the importance of environmental amenities and the economy of scale in the provision of public services as determinants of urban spatial structure.

3. URBAN-RURAL LAND-USE PATTERNS

Urban-rural land-use patterns cannot be studied without some notion of geographic space. This leads to both conceptual and methodological challenges. Conceptually, a key challenge is to identify the relevant spatial scale(s) and to account for interactions of processes that operate at lower (i.e., more local) and higher (i.e., more aggregate) scales. An implication of such interactions is that many of these processes are codetermined, suggesting obvious challenges for theoretical modeling and empirical identification. Methodologically, spatial correlations in the data introduce additional problems that can further hamper causal inference. Statistically significant spatial interactions can simply be the result of nonsubstantive spatial correlation. This problem is made worse when the spatial scale of the underlying process does not correspond to the scale at which the process is observed, a common occurrence due to aggregate data limitations.

Recent advances in urban land-use modeling have addressed many of the challenges involved in incorporating space. These models have taken advantage of the increasing availability of spatially detailed, microdata, e.g., at the scale of land parcels, and used new econometric methods that address concerns over spatial dependence, endogeneity, and identification. In so doing, they have defined a new frontier in urban and regional economics: spatial economic models that incorporate multiple sources of spatial heterogeneity. Although the majority of these models are empirical, the recent literature has also made theoretical contributions that have extended the simple monocentric model, with its highly stylized definition of space as simply distance to a single urban center, by incorporating alternative sources of spatial variation. These studies, as we review below, have generated new theoretical insights into the underlying market and institutional mechanisms that influence spatially heterogeneous land-use patterns and how, for example, policy interacts with these market forces to influence resulting patterns. As with many of the econometric studies, in which spatial simulation is used to extend the econometric results to spatial prediction, they illustrate the utility of moving beyond strictly analytical models to models that use spatial simulation to extend traditional model results. Such methodological innovations are critical for economic models in which spatial hetoergeneity and land-use dynamics are important considerations (Irwin 2009).

3.1. Urban-Rural Land Markets and Development Patterns

The demand and supply of urban-rural land has changed rapidly in the past few decades. New demand by migrating households and firms has led to rapid increases in the market value of land parcels, reflecting capitalization of their future development potential. Plantinga et al. (2002) used U.S. county-level data from 1997 to decompose current farmland prices into their agriculture and development components. They found that the average discounted value of future development is approximately 10% of the total agricultural land value in the United States, but it is as high as 80% in some rapidly urbanizing states. Using similar data, Livanis et al. (2006) found evidence that proximity to urban areas also bids up farmland values because of higher anticipated agricultural rents, e.g., as a result of increased urban market access.

Land ownership and land use are often at odds with each other in these urban-rural regions. Farmland may be rented for agricultural production while being owned by a land speculator or development company that is waiting for the right time to develop. The fact that development is irreversible and can be delayed and that uncertainty exists over future payoffs makes development analogous to the exercise of an option (Dixit & Pindyck 1994). In the presence of uncertainty, the option of waiting has value, so that the expected returns necessary to induce immediate development are higher than those without uncertainty. In the land-use context, the volatility inherent in future returns to farming or residential development can influence the option value of postponing.

When rural land is developed, it typically results in a fragmented pattern of interspersed developed and undeveloped land, often referred to as scattered, low-density, sprawl, or leapfrog development. Measuring urban-rural land-use patterns requires spatial data that are not only highly disaggregate, but also accurate. Although the physical characteristics of land cover are more readily quantified from satellite imagery, land use defines patterns of human activity. Burchfield et al. (2006) used fine-scale remotely sensed land cover data for all U.S. metropolitan areas to measure sprawl and found that the pattern of residential land use between the mid-1970s and early 1990s was qualitatively unchanged. However, because the mismatch between land cover and land use is particularly acute in low-density areas, their analysis systematically misses new exurban development. Using more accurate data from 1973 and 2000 from Maryland, Irwin & Bockstael (2007) investigated change in urban-rural fragmentation gradients over time. They found large and significant increases

Land cover: the physical and biological cover over the surface of the earth, including water, vegetation, bare soil, and impervious surfaces

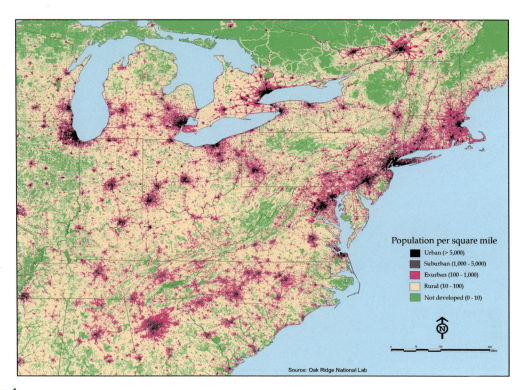

Figure 1

Population density pattern in the eastern United States and southeastern Canada using 2003 Landscan data on estimated population per square mile.

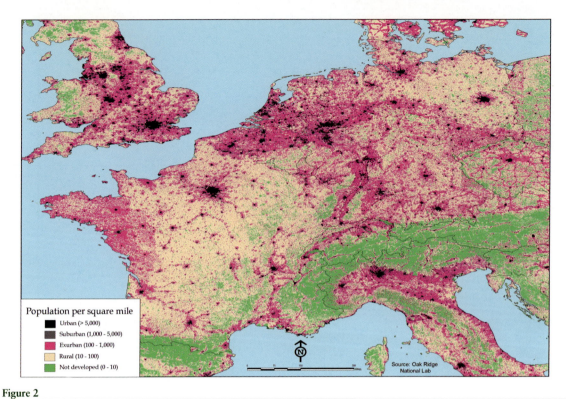

Figure 2

Population density pattern in western Europe using 2003 Landscan data on estimated population per square mile.

in fragmentation and little support for the basic urban economic theory that, in a growing city, outward sprawl is balanced by infill development [this theory is based on the mono-centric model and characterizes leapfrog development as the result of dynamically efficient land developers who wait to develop more-valued land closer to the city (Ohls & Pines 1975)]. Although proximity to cities is clearly a factor, recent empirical and theoretical research has suggested the importance of other processes—including open space, sewer and water infrastructure, and local growth controls—in generating these fragmented development patterns.

3.2. Attraction of Open Space

Open space: land that has not had improvements such as buildings and other structures added to it; includes farmland, forests, parks

A number of hedonic studies have found evidence of positive open space spillover effects that increase the value of proximate houses (see The Value of Open Space to Homeowners, sidebar below). These findings suggest that if neighboring open space is sufficiently valued, then developers may account for this in making their location and timing decisions by choosing locations with adjacent open space. New residential developments should then "repel" one another, creating a more dispersed development pattern. Irwin & Bockstael (2002) are the first to suggest this alternative explanation of scattered residential development and provided empirical evidence of negative effects from neighboring development. Using parcel-level land-use data from Maryland, they estimated residential development as a function of parcel and locational attributes, including spatial externalities from surrounding land uses. The empirical challenge is to distinguish between endogenous interactions (i.e., parcels' development outcomes affect each other), spatial correlation in observables, and spatial correlation in unobservables, which induces spatial error autocorrelation. Irwin & Bockstael (2002) used a bounding strategy that identifies the direction, but not the magnitude, of the spillover effect. They found that the residential development pattern that is predicted when negative development spillovers accounted are for is qualitatively much more similar to the observed pattern than that of predictions that omit these spillovers.

THE VALUE OF OPEN SPACE TO HOMEOWNERS

Spatial hedonic studies have revealed that both the type and configuration of neighboring open space influence exurban and suburban housing values. Examples include Irwin (2002), who found that the type of open space and its ownership status matters; Geoghegan et al. (1997), who showed that the fragmentation of surrounding land uses matter and that these effects are scale dependent; and Walsh (2007) who considered the general equilibrium and welfare effects of open space policies. Identifying open space effects is complicated by general equilibrium effects (Walsh 2007) and the potential endogeneity of open space and unobserved spatial variation that are likely correlated with open space variables (Irwin & Bockstael 2001). Many studies have sought to control for these problems by using standard spatial econometric techniques, including the canonical spatial autoregressive model (Anselin 1988). However, Bell & Bockstael (2000) demonstrated that different, maintained assumptions regarding the spatial error structure (imposed via the spatial weights matrix) can result in substantial differences in parameter estimates. Natural experiments offer an alternative and potentially less restrictive means to identifying land-use spillovers (Carrion-Flores & Irwin 2009). Other approaches to valuing open space include stated-preference methods (for a comprehensive review, see McConnell & Walls 2006).

Wu & Plantinga (2003) explored open space spillovers by extending the monocentric model to a theoretical model that accounts for additional rent gradients from open space. Open space is exogenous, and the focus is on the conditions under which trade-offs between transportation costs and open space spillovers will generate leapfrog development. Newer theoretical work has explicitly considered the underlying market and institutional mechanisms that lead to the provision of either private (Turner 2005, Caruso et al. 2007) or public (Tajibaeva et al. 2008) open space and the implications for fragmented urban patterns. This research has contributed to a better understanding of how the pattern of open space is created as a result of land markets [and interactions with policy in the case of Tajibaeva et al. (2008)] and the economic processes that underlie scattering of residential development.

An implication of open space externalities is that the resulting pattern is not dynamically efficient. Parker (2007) considered the general implications of distance-dependent spatial externalities (so-called edge-effect externalities). She found that distance between the externality generator and recipient is too small and that standard market failures occur as a result. In the absence of spatial externalities, Wu (2006) showed that spatially heterogeneous amenities can generate efficient patterns of leapfrog development when travel costs fall below a certain level or income rises above a certain level.

3.3. Sewer and Water Infrastructure

Both urban and suburban development require municipal sewer and water service lines to be extended to an area before higher density development (more than one dwelling unit per acre) is possible. Meanwhile, exurban development (one or fewer dwellings unit per acre) is almost invariably serviced by privately provided septic systems and groundwater wells that, owing to health concerns, must be adequately separated from each other. This difference generates a discrete break in the residential density associated with suburban versus exurban development, suggesting that suburban and exurban development are fundamentally different.

Newburn & Berck (2006) estimated a spatially explicit residential land-use change model in Sonoma County, California, which includes multiple density classes. Their results indicate that recent development at suburban densities is largely constrained to existing incorporated cities and their annexation regions. In contrast, development at exurban densities leapfrogged well beyond these places into unincorporated areas. The policy implication is that urban growth boundaries (UGBs), e.g., limits on extending sewer and water infrastructure, may curb urban and suburban development, but they are ineffective at guiding exurban development.

Building on their empirical results, D.A. Newburn & P. Berck (unpublished manuscript) analyzed a theoretical spatial dynamic model with two production technologies for residential development—municipal sewer service for suburban development and septic systems for exurban development. In outlying agricultural areas, the additional sewer extension costs can significantly reduce the value of agricultural land in suburban use. Exurban development, although at lower density, can occur immediately and requires only the onsite conversion costs of septic systems. Hence, the willingness to pay for exurban development may exceed the agricultural landowner's reservation price on future suburban development for a range of distances from the city boundary. The result is a "feasible zone" for exurban leapfrog development and another fundamental reason for exurban scattered development.

3.4. Unintended Effects of Policy on Sprawl

Local growth controls designed to restrict the allowable density or timing of development in specific locations can unintentionally exacerbate sprawl. Fischel (1985) hypothesized that large-lot residential zoning, designed to discourage development by constraining density, promoted rather than deterred sprawl. McConnell et al. (2006) tested this hypothesis using residential subdivision data from Calvert County, Maryland. They found little evidence in support of this hypothesis. Instead, they found that many factors other than zoning contributed to subdivision density and that, in the absence of zoning, an estimated 10% more residential lots would have been developed.

Cunningham (2007) employed real options theory to evaluate the intended and unintended consequences of the UGB adopted by Seattle, Washington, in 1990, which imposes density restrictions outside the boundary. The author argued that, although initially suppressing the likelihood that land outside the UGB will be converted to residential use, the actual adoption of the growth-control strategy reduces price volatility by limiting uncertainty over future profitability. The ultimate effect is to eliminate the real option value of delaying development, thus reducing the effectiveness of the UGB.

Spatial externalities generated by a spatially delineated regulation are another form of unintended policy effects. Irwin & Bockstael (2004) considered how landowners respond to a clustering policy that concentrates development but also mandates that an open space area be established within the subdivision. They found that the creation of open space, as required in the clustering policy, hastens the rate of development of neighboring parcels. Hence, the clustering policy protects open space on an individual parcel level, but it can lead to increasingly fragmented development patterns on a landscape or regional level.

Towe & Bockstael (2005) and Towe (2008) evaluated the potential for such effects associated with an agricultural land preservation program in Maryland. Towe treated this as a selection problem in that developable parcels that have preserved neighbors are likely to possess, on average, characteristics different from those of parcels without such neighbors, so that these different characteristics may alter the likelihood of development. A noncorrected comparison of treated and nontreated parcels shows no difference in development rates, but an approach that corrects for selection bias reveals that treated parcels are more than three times as likely to be developed.

4. ENVIRONMENTAL INTERACTIONS

Despite the clear benefits of low-density, fragmented urban-rural growth—including larger lots, greater access to open space, and, on average, shorter commute times—land markets are rife with market failures. Brueckner (2000) cited three market failures that have led to excessive spatial growth of cities and loss of rural land: undervalued open space benefits, congestion externalities, and public service costs that are not fully internalized by private developers. Environmental externalities, including climate change and ecological impacts, constitute additional market failures. Here we review recent selected findings on these environmental impacts and their associated policy responses.

4.1. Climate Change Impacts and Responses

Urban spatial structure influences greenhouse gas emissions by shaping both transport activities and energy consumption in cities. In examining the relationship between urban

Growth controls: regulations designed to restrict the allowable density or timing of land development, e.g., urban growth boundaries, minimum lot zoning, land easement purchases

form and household travel behavior, recent studies have recognized the endogeneity problem that arises if households sort themselves into neighborhoods that support their transportation choices. Bento et al. (2005), in a study that accounts for this and uses 1990 data on U.S. household commuting trips in 114 urban areas, found that greater population centrality, lower road density, and greater spatial evenness in the distribution of jobs relative to housing decreases annual household vehicle miles traveled by reducing a household's likelihood of driving and shortening the average trip length. Other research has provided evidence that lower greenhouse gas emissions are generated when households live in higher density places (e.g., Grazi et al. 2008, Vance & Hedel 2008), but because urban decentralization has resulted in a decline in commuting, some are less convinced that this result always holds (Glaeser & Kahn 2004). The relative greenhouse gas contribution of exurban areas, where households are much fewer but also much more spread out and fully car dependent, remains largely unstudied. Equally unknown is how urban-rural growth may adapt in response to climate change impacts, either directly or, more likely, indirectly through policies that seek to mitigate urban land-use impacts or increase the returns to agricultural or forest land uses.

In contrast to the dearth of exurban studies, a substantial amount of research has focused on responses of the agricultural and forest sectors to climate change amid urbanizing rural landscapes (U.S. Environmental Protection Agency 2005, Easterling et al. 2007, Smith et al. 2007, Nabuurs et al. 2007). Recent work models not only land-use and management responses, but also the impacts of these responses on ecosystem services. Using a time series of Natural Resources Inventory plot data, Nelson et al. (2008) coupled an econometric model of land-use decisions with models of carbon sequestration and species conservation, and they revealed the challenges of designing policies under great uncertainty, landscape heterogeneity, and landscape interactions. Integrating an econometric model of field-level agricultural production decisions with a biogeochemical ecosystem model, Antle et al. (2004) demonstrated that vulnerability to climate change is dependent on the potential for economic adaptation. Using a panel data set tracking 844,000 sample points from the National Resources Inventory, Lubowski et al. (2006) modeled landowner responses to carbon sequestration policies at a national scale and concluded that forest-based carbon sequestration policies are worthy of inclusion in a cost-effective suite of U.S. climate policies. Additional studies provide a mixed assessment of the environmental impacts of carbon sequestration strategies (Jackson et al. 2005, Pattanayak et al. 2005, Nelson et al. 2008). Because the majority of these studies cite data gaps, uncertainties, and sensitivities of results to scale, there is ample room for further consideration of land-use responses to climate change. Future research will undoubtedly revisit assumptions regarding private land owner expectations and decision-making inertia.

4.2. Ecological Impacts and Optimal Conservation Targeting

Ecologists recently have found that the environmental impacts from exurban development (approximately 1–20 acre lots) are substantial and pose a greater threat to the preservation of biodiversity than do urban and suburban development (for a detailed review, see Hansen et al. 2005). Many of these effects were missed previously because of poor data (e.g., Landsat satellite imagery) that failed to identify exurban development. Increasing use of parcel-level data and aerial photographs has provided better spatial data to assess the ecological response to variations in residential density. Using parcel data for watersheds in coastal California, Lohse et al. (2008) analyzed the relative impacts of urban, exurban, and cropland uses on stream habitat conditions for endangered salmonid species. Exurban development and agriculture both were found to have a much larger overall impact on sediment levels in tributaries used for spawning than did urban development.

The ecological effects of clustering polices that concentrate housing and create public open space within subdivisions have recently been analyzed. This spatial configuration is assumed to allow the developer to internalize open space benefits, while providing significant additional benefits to plant and wildlife species. Lenth et al. (2006) compared field-level observations of biodiversity (e.g., songbirds, mammals, plants) within clustered developments, dispersed developments, and undeveloped areas (i.e., regional parks as the control group) in Colorado. In a surprising result, the majority of biodiversity metrics analyzed did not differ between the clustered and dispersed developments. Both types of subdivisions had significantly higher densities of nonnative and human-commensal species and significantly lower densities of native and human-sensitive species than were found in the undeveloped areas. The reason is that edge-effect externalities from development can extend to more than 100 meters from individual houses, thereby leaving a relatively small amount of core habitat within the subdivision's open space area. Taken together, this study and Irwin & Bockstael (2004) indicate that clustering policies at the scale of individual subdivisions may lead to perverse outcomes. Instead, conservation policies should take a landscape perspective that addresses issues of ecological thresholds and spatial scale.

Recent research on conservation targeting emphasizes these points as well. Wu & Boggess (1999) developed a theoretical framework to allocate conservation funds optimally when ecological thresholds are present. They found that the optimal targeting solution is to concentrate the funds into one watershed when the budget is small and that spreading the funds equally may lead to the minimum level of environmental benefits.

Given the dynamic nature of land conservation, Newburn et al. (2006) emphasized the importance of accounting for the likelihood of future land conversion. They argued that, because land costs and likelihood of future development are typically positively correlated, a static targeting approach that includes ecological benefits and land costs, but omits the likelihood of future conversion, will likely be biased toward low-cost sites that have de facto conservation (e.g., steep slopes). In such cases, spending will be inefficient.

Other recent studies have wrestled with the challenge that conservation often relies on voluntary landowner actions. Decisions to participate in conservation programs or to sell easements depend on individual reservation prices that vary systematically over space but are typically unknown to the policy maker. Lewis et al. (2009b) combined this characterization of policy makers' uncertainty with the notion that the marginal net benefits of increasing forest size are likely to be convex owing to habitat thresholds. Their results suggest that strategies that target all or none of the land are superior to applying a uniform incentive that may otherwise be assumed optimal. Lewis et al. (2009a) estimated landowners' willingness to accept payments in exchange for conservation actions. Using an econometric land-use model to derive the probability distribution of reservation prices, the authors showed that, whereas incentive-based conservation policies cannot achieve gains equal to those from direct landscape control, alternative designs for incentive-based policies, such as those that achieve contiguous habitat, are advantageous. However, uncertainty and irreversibility increase the hurdle costs on land-use conversion decisions (Schatzki 2003), and these factors on the risk premium are not explicitly included in this method.

5. POLICY EVALUATION

The evaluation of land-use policy effects centers on attempts to test empirically whether land-use regulations (either specific or in the aggregate) have had an effect on development. Perhaps the greatest contribution of recent literature is the recognition that land-use policies, and in particular growth-control policies, cannot be treated as exogenous. In this section, we review recent empirical literature that has addressed this challenge and recent theoretical contributions to the welfare analysis of growth controls.

5.1. Growth-Control Effects

Growth controls include such diverse regulations as UGBs, adequate public facility ordinances (APFOs), variable minimum lot zoning, clustering requirements, and purchase of or trade in development rights. Recent work that has addressed endogeneity problems includes Burge & Ihlandfeldt (2006), for example, who used panel data on Florida communities to investigate whether housing construction is affected by development fees. They used fixed-time and -area effects to account for the endogeneity problem and found that development fees do not reduce new housing construction, but instead actually increase it by increasing the proportion of housing projects that can be approved by localities.

Although this work and others (e.g., Ihlandfeldt 2007, Mayer & Somerville 2000) address the endogeneity problems, the analysis uses aggregate data. Controls are often nonuniformly applied across space, however, and are often designed to displace development instead of necessarily reducing the total amount. Several recent papers have looked at specific policies at a spatially disaggregated level. This disaggregate setting provides the additional advantage of facilitating the use of matching methods, which permit policy adoption to be characterized as a nonrandom "treatment" problem. These methods provide a means of linking treated observations with untreated counterfactuals and of omitting those for which counterfactual observations cannot be found. The result is a nonparametric measure of the average treatment effect on the treated observations.

McMillen & McDonald (2002) provided one of the first applications of matching in the land-use policy literature with their investigation of how endogenous residential zoning influenced land values in the early twentieth century in Chicago. More recently, Bento et al. (2007) considered the effect of an APFO in Howard County, Maryland. APFOs allow a local government to temporarily deny new development permits in districts where public facilities (e.g., schools, roads) lag behind population growth. Using propensity score matching methods (Heckman et al. 1998), Bento et al. (2007) found that APFOs were effective in reducing new housing in the first two years. Lynch & Liu (2007) also used propensity score matching to evaluate the consequences of Maryland's Rural Legacy program, which seeks to preserve contiguous blocks of rural land through voluntary easement purchase. The authors conclude that the Rural Legacy designation led to more preserved land in the Rural Legacy areas, but it did nothing to reduce new development in those areas.

An alternative means of addressing selection problems relies on natural discontinuities in space. Jaegar et al. (2008) used a regression discontinuity design (Imbens & Lemieux 2007) to study the effect of the UGB of Portland, Oregon, on vacant land prices. The method requires restricting observations to those in the immediate proximity and on either side of a spatially delineated policy boundary of interest, which represents the threshold where the discontinuity in treatment arises. The analysis by Jaegar et al. of Portland's UGB indicates that it is locally binding on one side, but not elsewhere, and provides no evidence of positive price effects from being inside the UGB.

Because these papers employ highly spatially disaggregate data, they are particularly well suited to studying the impact of growth controls on the spatial distribution of new development. The approach has its shortcomings, however. If important conditioning factors are unmeasured, then the best mechanical attempts at matching will fail to address the problem. And, although matching the spatial scale of analysis to the scale of the policy is compelling, the results for a specific policy in one region cannot be generalized to other regions.

5.2. Land Conservation and Preservation Programs

Growth controls include public-sector efforts to purchase development easements from owners of potentially developable land. Easement purchases are also made by private nonprofit conservation trusts whose easement purchases in some U.S. states exceed those of the public sector. Recent work on the effectiveness of land conservation programs has considered the potential interaction effects between government and nongovernmental land conservation. Albers et al. (2008b) explored the relationship between the location of publicly and privately conserved land at the township scale for three states. Given that the spatial configuration of conserved land is important in determining ecological benefits, the authors argued that better public conservation decisions can be made if the attraction or repulsion effects of public actions on private land trusts can be anticipated. In a related paper, Albers et al. (2008a) simulated spatial patterns of land conservation in a game-theoretic context. Outcomes differ depending on budget levels, assumptions about public and private sector conservation objectives, and amount of coordination between public and private agencies.

Walsh (2007) argued that, although individuals may value open space, the long-term social welfare consequences of land preservation depend on the locational distribution of the landscape amenities because the specific location of open space matters. The outcome depends on endogenous adjustments in private decisions, both in terms of housing location and lot sizes, in response to public policies. Using a locational equilibrium model to estimate heterogeneous preferences for open space in Wake County, North Carolina, Walsh showed that increasing public preservation can reduce privately supplied open space (yard space) and that the same amount of public funding for preservation can generate vastly different social benefits depending on the spatial distribution of preservation. Lichtenberg et al. (2007) analyzed the effects of land-use regulations on the provision of open space at a much smaller scale (within residential subdivisions) in central Maryland. They attempted to understand how developers make trade-offs between providing various types of open space when faced with regulatory constraints. Using a tobit model, they found that requiring developers to provide larger lots induces them to substitute private open space for shared public open space.

Using a real options framework, Towe (2008) and Towe et al. (2008) investigated the role of uncertainty and irreversible residential development in the face of an agricultural land preservation program using data on land development in Howard County, Maryland. Development and preservation constitute alternative irreversible land-use options for these landowners. Theoretical results suggest that the existence of multiple options will delay decisions and the delay will to be greater the closer in size and more highly correlated are the returns from the alternative options. Using a duration model, the authors found a statistically significant delay in development timing for land that qualifies for preservation, even if it is ultimately developed rather than preserved. Thus, the effects of agricultural preservation programs aimed at conserving farmland may be greater than the actual acreage enrolled, in that the very presence of the program slows the timing of conversion to residential use.

5.3. Efficiency of Antisprawl Policies

Recent work by Anas & Rhee (2006, 2007) has challenged long-standing theoretical results regarding the efficiency of policies that correct negative congestion externalities. Previous analyses based on the monocentric model have argued that, in the absence of any other market failures, not-too-stringent UGBs that force cities to be more compact are a second-best policy to congestion tolls (e.g., Pines & Sadka 1985, Brueckner 2000). Using a model in which employment is dispersed and households make residential and employment location decisions, Anas & Rhee (2006, 2007) refuted this claim by demonstrating the limited conditions under which UGBs are welfare increasing. They found that, contrary to the standard monocentric result that optimal congestion tolls reduce the spatial extent of cities, efficient tolling may cause additional suburbanization when employment is dispersed because some households will reduce their commute distance by choosing suburban employment. Under such conditions, they concluded that any constraint on outward city growth will be welfare reducing. Empirical analysis by Cheshire & Sheppard (2002) corroborates this theoretical prediction. Using sales data from a highly regulated urban area in the United Kingdom, they found evidence that, despite the positive open space benefits created by these policies, their opportunity cost in terms of forgone residential development is far higher. However, these conclusions, including those by Anas & Rhee (2006, 2007), account for only a subset of externalities and thus cannot be interpreted as a full assessment of costs and benefits.

Focusing solely on undervalued open space benefits, Bento et al. (2006) examined the efficiency and distributional effects of several antisprawl policies. They showed that a land development tax and UGB are equivalent in their overall efficiency but have different distributional effects across space. Thus, whether or not a policy is welfare improving depends on whether the landowner is located in the urban core, suburbs, or rural area. In follow-up work, A.M. Bento, S.F. Franco & D. Kaffine (unpublished manuscript) expanded upon the set of market failures to include urban decay, which is generated by depreciated housing in the city core and which creates additional development pressure on land at the urban fringe. They showed that a development tax whose revenues are recycled by providing subsidies to improve blighted core housing creates additional efficiencies in terms of open space provision by reducing demand for fringe land. Although open space plays an important role in these studies, its treatment is highly stylized, e.g., it only exists outside the city and its effects are not distant dependent. This ignores the welfare effects of open space provision within urban areas, which can be quite large (Walsh 2007), and the implications of spatially heterogeneous open space spillovers, which can have substantial effects on urban land-use patterns (Irwin & Bockstael 2002).

6. RESEARCH CHALLENGES

Although recent research has made meaningful advances in answering both positive and normative questions regarding urban-rural space, many pressing questions remain (see Future Issues, section below). Making meaningful progress on these questions will require additional theoretical, empirical, and methodological advances. These include, but are not necessarily limited to, the following.

6.1. Structural Modeling and Causal Inference

Economists are well accustomed to structural models that explicitly link individual behaviors and aggregate outcomes. Such models are critical for sorting out the hypothesized directions of causality among variables and specifying empirical structural models. Much of the current empirical work relies on reduced-form models, and additional structural modeling is needed to better identify the potential causal linkages among the many interdependent processes that influence urban-rural growth. For example, although we know many of the demographic and economic factors that are correlated with exurban and amenity-led growth, more work is needed to uncover the actual migration mechanisms. The methods used in Bayer et al. (2009), Smith et al. (2004), and Walsh (2007) are examples of empirical structural modeling.

Related to the need for empirical structural models that can untangle the direction of causality, rigorous empirical methods that go beyond traditional regression analyses are also needed to identify causal effects. The need here is not so much for new empirical methods, but rather for increased use among researchers of existing methods that permit causal inference. Much of the current literature suffers from a lack of rigorous empirical work that convincingly solves the problems of identification and selection that often arise in policy evaluation and applied spatial analysis. This is often due to data limitations, e.g., aggregate spatial data that are measured with error and that prohibit distinguishing causation from correlation. However, even with spatially disaggregate data that are defined at the same scale at which the process occurs, traditional regression and even standard spatial econometric models are often insufficient for testing causality (Carrion-Flores & Irwin 2009). Quasi-experimental techniques that use such approaches as matching methods and regression discontinuity designs should be more widely applied to address the selection problems embedded in most policy evaluation. We also view computer lab and field experiments, in which the researcher purposefully controls the experimental design to test the treatment effect, as useful methods that should be more widely adopted.

6.2. Accounting for Scale-Dependence and Cross-Scale Interactions

Recent work, including work reviewed here, demonstrates the importance of local spatial heterogeneity and microlevel interactions in household location and landowner decisions. Other research illustrates the importance of heterogeneous households and the role of household sorting in neighborhood formation and endogenous local public goods. At aggregate regional scales, transportation and commuting costs still matter greatly. Thus, many processes that are relevant to urban-rural dynamics appear to be scale dependent, i.e., the underlying causal mechanisms that influence land-use and location patterns are different depending on the spatial (and temporal) scale of analysis. What are the implications of these scale-dependent processes for modeling, and how are spatial and agent heterogeneity represented? Do land-use spillovers matter only at very local scales, for example, or do their effects aggregate up to influence land markets at neighborhood and regional scales? What other microaspects of agents or landscapes matter, and what are their effects relative to large-scale influences such as transportation costs and economic restructuring? At present, we know relatively little about how microlevel processes and heterogeneity influence aggregate outcomes—including land markets, land-use patterns, and policy choices—and, in turn, how these microeffects are mediated by higher-scale processes. For example, how do the attraction effects of open space depend on transportation costs, and how will higher energy prices modify these effects?

Studying these cross-scale interactions requires moving beyond single-scale models, e.g., the monocentric model in which central city distance is the single spatially heterogeneous feature, to models that account for multiple sources of heterogeneity and interactions across local, neighborhood, and regional scales. Such models are often not analytically tractable, however; thus, researchers must trade off generalizability and model realism. Geographic cellular automata combined with agent-based models offer a promising simulation-based approach for linking spatially explicit analysis with structural models of heterogeneous agent behavior (Parker et al. 2003). Such models have gained tremendous popularity in geography and other disciplines for modeling land-use dynamics, and initial progress has been made on models that incorporate microeconomic features (e.g., Caruso et al. 2007, Filatova et al. 2008, Miller et al. 2004). This framework offers much promise for combining spatially explicit analysis with structural economic models of land use and land markets, although many challenges remain (Irwin 2009, Parker & Filatova 2009).

6.3. Integrated Ecological and Economic Modeling

An impressive amount of work has occurred in integrating ecological and economic spatial models. Given the spatially heterogeneous responses of ecological functions to land-use change, a spatially explicit approach is critical (Bockstael 1996). Econometric models with spatially heterogeneous data and spatial simulation have proven very useful, and agent-based modeling offers another promising approach in this regard. We also emphasize the need for research on dynamic structural models that do not rely on a static equilibrium assumption. Urban-rural systems are often characterized as markets in equilibrium, but spatially delineated labor and land markets may be more appropriately viewed as markets moving toward long-run equilibrium that continually absorb shocks in a dynamically changing environment. Spatial interactions imply these systems exhibit path dependence, nonlinear feedbacks (e.g., urban agglomeration effects), and multiple equilibria. In such cases, economic or ecological shocks can push the system into undesirable domains of attraction. Thus, an understanding of not only dynamic equilibrium, but also system resilience (the ability of the system to maintain its structure in the face of external change) and how resilience is influenced by individual behaviors and policies is important. Such a modeling framework may be necessary for understanding the sustainability of cities, regions, and rural places (Chen et al. 2009).

6.4. Prediction and Policy Scenarios

If policy evaluation is one objective of research, then important questions are whether and how much complexity in modeling is required to generate useful policy recommendations (Nelson et al. 2008). Although we know something about the theoretical and methodological strengths and weaknesses of our models, we know less about their relative usefulness in policy design. Additional work is needed to evaluate the modeling components that are most critical for generating effective policy analysis. One needed advance is better accounting of uncertainty in model forecasts. Lewis (2008) provided a promising example of a joint econometric-simulation framework that accounts for empirical distributions of the spatial pattern of land use.

We conclude by noting that all of these advances depend critically on the availability of accurate, spatial microdata over time. Many of the limitations of the current literature are due either to aggregate data that miss important spatial variations, cross-sectional data that prohibit causal identification, or inaccurate spatial data that misrepresent critical features of the landscape. The increasing availability of geocoded tax assessment records of individual land parcels is promising in this regard, but additional microdata, e.g., on households and firms, are also critical for achieving these modeling goals.

SUMMARY POINTS

1. Urban function is no longer limited to cities and suburbs. In many regions of North America and Europe, an increasing proportion of the population in seemingly rural areas is economically and socially tied to urban areas.

2. Ongoing economic restructuring, caused by falling transportation costs, new communications technologies, and increased global competition, has simultaneously strengthened urbanization and spurred urban decentralization.

3. Urban growth has penalized more remote rural areas in terms of lower job and population growth. The exceptions are amenity-rich rural areas, particularly those in the United States, that have grown rapidly as a result of rising real incomes and changes in transportation and technology.

4. Household demand for open space, lack of municipal services, and unintended policy effects have contributed to scattered patterns of exurban development.

5. Growth controls and land preservation often achieve their targeted goal of constraining or preventing land development in designated areas, but they have also had unintended consequences, such as land preservation crowding out private land conservation and generating spatial spillovers that exacerbate sprawl and increase ecological damages.

FUTURE ISSUES

1. What are the implications of increased economic and social integration of urban function and rural form for the growth and sustainability of cities, regions, and rural places? How should policies be adapted to manage these changes better? Will other countries, especially developing countries, experience the same extent of urban-rural transformation as North America and Europe?

2. How will rising energy costs, transportation changes, and further advances in communications technologies influence the economics of urban-rural space? What are the potential effects of biofuel markets and policies on urban-rural land-use patterns and environmental quality? How will urban-rural growth respond to climate change and to adaptation and mitigation policies aimed at

managing interactions with land use? What are the impacts of urbanization and amenity-led growth on local ecosystems, and what are the implications for the sustainability of cities, regions, and rural places?

3. What is the full range of the spatially explicit costs and benefits of urban-rural growth, and what are the implications for optimal growth-control policies and land-preservation targeting?

DISCLOSURE STATEMENT

The authors are not aware of any affiliations, memberships, funding, or financial holdings that might be perceived as affecting the objectivity of this review.

ACKNOWLEDGMENTS

We apologize to researchers whose work we were unable to include. Given the space limitations of the article, we necessarily had to focus on selected topics and themes. Research by the authors has been supported by grants from the James S. McDonnell Foundation, National Aeronautics and Space Administration, National Oceanic and Atmospheric Administration, National Science Foundation Biocomplexity Program, Ohio Sea Grant Program, U.S. Department of Agriculture, U.S. Environmental Protection Agency, and the U.S. Forest Service Northern and Pacific Northwest Research Stations.

LITERATURE CITED

Albers HJ, Ando AW, Batz M. 2008a. Patterns of multi-agent land conservation: crowding in/out, agglomeration, and policy. *Resour. Energy Econ.* 30(4):492–508

Albers HJ, Ando AW, Chen X. 2008b. Spatial-econometric analysis of attraction and repulsion of private conservation by public reserves. *J. Environ. Econ. Manag.* 56:33–49

Anas A, Arnott R, Small K. 1998. Urban spatial structure. *J. Econ. Lit.* 36:1426–64

Anas A, Rhee HJ. 2007. When are urban growth boundaries not second-best policies to congestion tolls? *J. Urban Econ.* 61(2):263–86

Anas A, Rhee HJ. 2006. Curbing excess sprawl with congestion tolls and urban boundaries. *Reg. Sci. Urban Econ.* 36(4):510–41

Anselin L. 1988. *Spatial Econometrics: Methods and Models.* Dordrecht: Kluwer Acad.

Antle JM, Capalbo SM, Elliott ET, Paustian KH. 2004. Adaptation, spatial heterogeneity, and the vulnerability of agricultural systems to climate change and CO_2 fertilization: an integrated assessment approach. *Clim. Change* 64(3):289–315

Baum-Snow NA. 2007. Did highways cause suburbanization? *Q. J. Econ.* 122(2):775–805

Bayer P, Keohane N, Timmins C. 2009. Migration and hedonic valuation: the case of air quality. *J. Environ. Econ. Manag.* In press

Bell KB, Bockstael NE. 2000. Applying the generalized-moments estimation approach to spatial problems involving micro-level data. *Rev. Econ. Stat.* 82(1):72–82

Bento AM, Cropper ML, Mobarak AM, Vinha K. 2005. The effects of urban spatial structure on travel demand in the United States. *Rev. Econ. Stat.* 87(3):466–78

Bento AM, Franco SF, Kaffine D. 2006. The efficiency and distributional impacts of alternative anti-sprawl policies. *J. Urban Econ.* 59(1):121–41

Bento AM, Towe C, Geoghegan J. 2007. The effects of moratoria on residential development: evidence from a matching approach. *Am. J. Agric. Econ.* 89(5):1211–18

Bockstael NE. 1996. Modeling economics and ecology: the importance of a spatial perspective. *Am. J. Agric. Econ.* 78:1168–80

Brueckner JK. 2000. Urban sprawl: diagnosis and remedies. *Int. Reg. Sci. Rev.* 23(2):160–71

Brueckner JK. 2005. Transport subsidies, system choice, and urban sprawl. *Reg. Sci. Urban Econ.* 35(6):715–33

Brown DG, Johnson KM, Loveland TR, Theobald DM. 2005. Rural land use trends in the contemporaneous United States 1950–2000. *Ecol. Appl.* 15(6):1851–63

Burchfield M, Overman HG, Puga D, Turner MA. 2006. Causes of sprawl: a portrait from space. *Q. J. Econ.* 121:587–633

Burge G, Ihlanfeldt K. 2006. Impact fees and single-family home construction. *J. Urban Econ.* 60:284–306

Carlino GA, Mills ES. 1985. The determinants of county growth. *J. Reg. Sci.* 27(1):39–54

Carrion-Flores C, Irwin EG. 2009. Identifying spatial interactions in the presence of spatial error autocorrelations: an application to land use spillovers. *Resour. Energy Econ.* Forthcoming

Caruso G, Peeters D, Cavailhès J, Rounsevell M. 2007. Spatial configurations in a periurban city. A cellular automata-based microeconomic model. *Reg. Sci. Urban Econ.* 37(5):542–67

Chen Y, Irwin EG, Jayaprakash C. 2009. Dynamic modeling of environmental amenity-driven migration with ecological feedbacks. *Ecol. Econ.* In press

Cheshire P, Magrini S. 2006. Population growth in European cities: Weather matters—but only nationally. *Reg. Stud.* 40:23–37

Cheshire P, Sheppard S. 2002. The welfare economics of land use planning. *J. Urban Econ.* 52:242–69

Cox W, Gordon P, Redfearn C. 2008. Highway penetration of central cities: not a major cause of suburbanization. *Econ. J. Watch* 5(1):32–45

Cunningham C. 2007. Growth controls, real options, and land development. *Rev. Econ. Stat.* 89 (2):343–58

Deller SC, Tsung-Hsiu T, Marcouiller DW, English DBK. 2001. The role of amenities and quality of life in rural economic growth. *Am. J. Agric. Econ.* 83(2):352–65

Desmet K, Fafchamps M. 2005. Changes in the spatial concentration of employment across US counties: a sectoral analysis 1972–2000. *J. Econ. Geogr.* 5(3):261–84

Dixit A, Pindyck S. 1994. *Investment Under Uncertainty.* Princeton, NJ: Princeton Univ. Press

Easterling W, Aggarwal P, Batima P, Brander K, Erda L, et al. 2007. Food, fibre and forest products. In *Climate Change 2007: Impacts, Adaptation and Vulnerability. Contribution of Working Group II to the Fourth Assessment Report of the Intergovernmental Panel on Climate Change,* ed. ML Parry, OF Canziani, JP Palutikof, PJ van der Linden, CE Hanson, pp. 273–313. Cambridge, UK: Cambridge Univ. Press

Epple D, Sieg H. 1999. Estimating equilibrium models of local jurisdictions. *J. Polit. Econ.* 107 (4):645–81

Ferguson M, Ali K, Olfert MR, Partridge MD. 2007. Voting with their feet: jobs versus amenities. *Growth Change* 38(1):77–110

Fischel WA. 1985. *The Economics of Zoning Laws: A Property Rights Approach to American Land Use Controls.* Baltimore, MD: John Hopkins Univ. Press

Filatova T, Parker D, van der Veen A. 2009. Agent-based urban land markets: agent's pricing behavior, land prices and urban land use change. *J. Artif. Soc. Soc. Simul.* In press

Gasper J, Glaeser E. 1998. Information technology and the future of cities. *J. Urban Econ.* 43:136–56

Geoghegan J, Wainger LA, Bockstael NE. 1997. Spatial landscape indices in a hedonic framework: an ecological economics analysis using GIS. *Ecol. Econ.* 23:251–64

Glaeser E, Kahn ME. 2004. Sprawl and urban growth. In *Handbook of Regional and Urban Economics. Volume 4: Cities and Geography*, ed. V Henderson, J Thisse. Amsterdam: North-Holland

Grazi F, van den Bergh JCJM, van Ommeren JN. 2008. An empirical analysis of urban form, transport, and global warming. *Energy J.* 29(4):97–122

Hansen AJ, Knight RL, Marzluff J, Powell S, Brown K, et al. 2005. Effects of exurban development on biodiversity: patterns, mechanisms, research needs. *Ecol. Appl.* 15:1893–905

Heckman J, Ichimura H, Smith J, Todd P. 1998. *Characterizing selection bias using experimental data.* Work. Pap. 6699, NBER

Henry MS, Barkley DL, Bao S. 1997. The hinterland's stake in metropolitan area growth. *J. Reg. Sci.* 37(3):479–501

Ihlanfeldt K. 2007. The effect of land use regulation on housing and land prices. *J. Urban Econ.* 61:420–35

Imbens G, Lemieux T. 2007. *Regression discontinuity designs: a guide to practice.* Work. Pap. 13039, NBER

Irwin EG. 2002. The effects of open space on residential property values. *Land Econ.* 78(4):465–80

Irwin EG. 2009. *New directions for urban economic models of land use change: incorporating spatial heterogeneity and transitional dynamics.* Presented at the *J. Reg. Sci.* 50th Anniv. Symp., New York City, NY

Irwin EG, Bockstael NE. 2001. The problem of identifying land use spillovers: measuring the effects of open space on residential property values. *Am. J. Agric. Econ.* 83(3):698–704

Irwin EG, Bockstael NE. 2002. Interacting agents, spatial externalities and the endogenous evolution of land use patterns. *J. Econ. Geogr.* 2(1):31–54

Irwin EG, Bockstael NE. 2004. Land use externalities, open space preservation, and urban sprawl. *Reg. Sci. Urban Econ.* 34:705–25

Irwin EG, Bockstael NE. 2007. The evolution of urban sprawl: evidence of spatial heterogeneity and increasing land fragmentation. *Proc. Natl. Acad. Sci. USA* 104(52):20672–77

Jackson RB, Jobbágy EG, Avissar R, Roy SB, Barrett DJ, et al. 2005. Trading water for carbon with biological carbon sequestration. *Science* 310:1944–47

Jaegar W, Grout C, Plantinga A. 2008. *Evidence of the effects of Oregon's land use planning system on land prices.* Policy Work. Pap. WP08WJ1, Lincoln Land Inst.

Kim KK, Marcouiller DW, Deller SC. 2005. Natural amenities and rural development: understanding spatial and distributional attributes. *Growth Change* 36:273–97

Lenth B, Knight R, Gilbert W. 2006. Conservation value of clustered housing development. *Conserv. Biol.* 20(5):1445–56

Lewis DJ. 2008. *An economic framework for forecasting land-use and ecosystem change.* Presented at the Spat. Econ. Work., Univ. Wyoming, Laramie

Lewis DJ, Plantinga AJ, Nelson E, Polasky S. 2009a. *The efficiency of voluntary incentive policies for preventing biodiversity loss.* Staff Pap. 533, Dep. Agric. Appl. Econ. Univ. Wisc.

Lewis DJ, Plantinga AJ, Wu J. 2009b. Targeting incentives to reduce habitat fragmentation. *Am. J. Agric. Econ.* In press

Lichtenberg E, Tra C, Hardie I. 2007. Land use regulation and the provision of open space in suburban residential subdivisions. *J. Environ. Econ. Manag.* 54:199–213

Livanis G, Moss CB, Breneman V, Nehring RF. 2006. Urban sprawl and farmland markets. *Am. J. Agric. Econ.* 88(4):915–29

Lohse, KA, Newburn DA, Opperman JJ, Merenlender AM. 2008. Forecasting relative impacts of land use on anadromous fish habitat to guide conservation planning. *Ecol. Appl.* 18:467–82

Lubowski RN, Plantinga AJ, Stavins RN. 2006. Land-use change and carbon sinks: econometric estimation of the carbon sequestration supply function. *J. Environ. Econ. Manag.* 51 (2):135–52

Lynch L, Liu X. 2007. Impact of designated preservation areas on rate of preservation and rate of conversion: preliminary evidence. *Am. J. Agric. Econ.* 89(5):1205–10

Mayer C, Somerville C. 2000. Land use regulation and new construction. *Reg. Sci. Urban Econ.* 30:639–62

McCann P. 2007. Sketching out a model of innovation, face-to-face interaction and economic geography. *Spat. Econ. Anal.* 2(2):117–34

McConnell V, Walls M. 2006. *The value of open space: evidence from studies of non-market benefits.* Discuss. Pap. 03-08, Resour. Future

McConnell V, Walls M, Kopits E. 2006. Zoning, TDRs and the density of development. *J. Urban Econ.* 59:440–57

McGranahan DA. 1999. *Natural amenities drive rural population change.* Agric. Econ. Rep. 781, Food Rural Econ. Div., Econ. Res. Serv., US Dep. Agric.

McGranahan DA 2008. Landscape influence on recent rural migration in the U.S. *Landsc. Urban Plan.* 85:228–40

McMillen D, McDonald J. 2002. Land values in a newly zoned city. *Rev. Econ. Stat.* 84(1):62–72

Mieszkowski P, Mills ES. 1993. The causes of metropolitan suburbanization. *J. Econ. Perspect.* 7:135–47

Miller E, Hunt JD, Abraham JE, Salvini PA. 2004. Microsimulating urban systems. *Comput. Environ. Urban Syst.* 28: 9-44

Nabuurs GJ, Masera O, Andrasko K, Benitez-Ponce P, Boer R, Dutschke M, et al. 2007. Forestry. In *Climate Change 2007: Mitigation. Contribution of Working Group III to the Fourth Assessment Report of the Intergovernmental Panel on Climate Change*, ed. B Metz, OR Davidson, PR Bosch, R Dave, LA Meyer. Cambridge, UK: Cambridge Univ. Press

Nechyba TJ, Walsh RP. 2004. Urban sprawl. *J. Econ. Perspect.* 18:177–200

Nelson E, Polasky S, Lewis DJ, Plantinga AJ, Lonsdorf E, White D, et al. 2008. Efficiency of incentives to jointly increase carbon sequestration and species conservation on a landscape. *Proc. Natl. Acad. Sci. USA* 105(28):9741–46

Newburn DA, Berck P. 2006. Modeling suburban and rural residential development beyond the urban fringe. *Land Econ.* 82(4):481–99

Newburn DA, Berck P, Merenlender AM. 2006. Habitat and open space at risk of land-use conversion: targeting strategies for land conservation. *Am. J. Agric. Econ.* 88(1):28–42

Ohls J, Pines D. 1975. Discontinuous urban development and economic efficiency. *Land Econ.* 3:224–34

Parker DC. 2007. Revealing "space" in spatial externalities: edge-effect externalities and spatial incentives. *J. Environ. Econ. Manag.* 54(1): 84–99

Parker DC, Filatova T. 2009. A conceptual design for a bilateral agent-based land market with heterogeneous economic agents. *Comput. Environ. Urban Syst.* In press

Parker DC, Manson SM, Janssen MA, Hoffman MJ, Deadman P. 2003. Multi-agent systems for the simulation of land-use and land-cover change: a review. *Ann. Assoc. Am. Geogr.* 93(2):314–37

Partridge MD, Bollman R, Olfert MR, Alasia A. 2007. Riding the wave of urban growth in the countryside: spread, backwash, or stagnation. *Land Econ.* 83(2):128–52

Partridge MD, Rickman DS, Ali K, Olfert MR. 2008a. Employment growth in the American urban hierarchy: long live distance. *Berkeley J. Macroecon.* 18(1): artic. 10. **http://www.bepress.com/bejm/vol8/iss1/art10**

Partridge MD, Rickman DS, Ali K, Olfert MR. 2008b. The geographic diversity of U.S. nonmetropolitan growth dynamics: a geographically weighted regression approach. *Land Econ.* 84:241–66

Partridge MD, Rickman DS, Ali K, Olfert MR. 2008c. Lost in space: population dynamics in the American hinterlands and small cities. *J. Econ. Geogr.* 8:727–57

Partridge MD, Rose Olfert M. 2009. Dissension in the countryside: bridging the rural-urban divide with a new rural policy. In *Globalization and the Rural-Urban Divide*, ed. M Gopinath, H Kim. Seoul: Seoul Natl. Univ. Press. In press

Pattanayak SK, McCarl BA, Sommer AJ, Murray BC, Bondelid T, et al. 2005. Water quality co-effects of greenhouse gas mitigation in U.S. agriculture. *Clim. Change* 71:341–72

Pines D, Sadka E. 1985. Zoning, first-best, second-best, and third-best criteria for allocating land for roads. *J. Urban Econ.* 17(2):167–83

Plantinga AJ, Lubowski RN, Stavins RN. 2002. The effects of potential land development on farmland prices. *J. Urban Econ.* 52:561–81

Roback J. 1982. Wages, rents, and the quality of life. *J. Polit. Econ.* 90(6):1257–78

Safirova E. 2002. Telecommuting, traffic congestion, and agglomeration: a general equilibrium model. *J. Urban Econ.* 52:26–52

Schatzki T. 2003. Options, uncertainty and sunk costs: an empirical analysis of land use change. *J. Environ. Econ. Manag.* 46(1):86–105

Schmidt L, Courant PN. 2006. Sometimes close is good enough: the value of nearby environmental amenities. *J. Reg. Sci.* 46:931–51

Schmitt B, Henry MS, Piguet V, Hilal M. 2006. Urban growth effects on rural population, export and service employment: evidence from eastern France. *Ann. Reg. Sci.* 40:779–801

Smith P, Martino D, Cai Z, Gwary D, Janzen HH, et al. 2007. Agriculture. In *Climate Change 2007: Mitigation. Contribution of Working Group III to the Fourth Assessment Report of the Intergovernmental Panel on Climate Change*, ed. B Metz, OR Davidson, PR Bosch, R Dave, LA Meyer. Cambridge, UK/New York: Cambridge Univ. Press

Smith VK, Sieg H, Banzhaf HS, Walsh RP. 2004. General equilibrium benefits for environmental improvements: projected ozone reductions under EPA's Prospective Analysis for the Los Angeles air basin. *J. Environ. Econ. Manag.* 47(3): 559-584

Su Q, DeSalvo JS. 2008. The effect of transportation subsidies on urban sprawl. *J. Reg. Sci.* 48 (3):567–94

Tajibaeva L, Haight RG, Polasky S. 2008. A discrete-space urban model with environmental amenities. *Resour. Energy Econ.* 30(2):170–96

Towe C. 2008. *Impacts of an incentive based land use policy: an evaluation of reservation easements.* PhD thesis. Univ. Maryland

Towe C, Nickerson C, Bockstael NE. 2008. An empirical examination of the timing of land conversions in the presence of farmland preservation programs. *Am. J. Agric. Econ.* 90 (3):613–26

Towe C, Bockstael NE. 2005. *Testing the effect of neighboring open space on development using a real options model and propensity score matching techniques.* Presented at the INRA Work., Role Open Space Green Amenities Resid. Moves Cities, Dijon, France

Turner MA. 2005. Landscape preferences and patterns of residential. *J. Urban Econ.* 57:19–54

US Environ. Prot. Agency. 2005. *Greenhouse gas mitigation potential in U.S. forestry and agriculture.* Work. Pap. 430-R-05-006, Off. Atmos. Programs, EPA

Vance C, Hedel R. 2008. On the link between urban form and automobile use: evidence from German survey data. *Land Econ.* 84(1):51–65

Walsh R. 2007. Endogenous open space amenities in a locational equilibrium. *J. Urban Econ.* 61 (2):319–44

Wu J. 2006. Environmental amenities, urban sprawl, and community characteristics. *J. Environ. Econ. Manag.* 52:527–47

Wu J. 2009. Economic fundamentals and urban-suburban disparities. *J. Reg. Sci.* In press

Wu J, Boggess WG. 1999. The optimal allocation of conservation funds. *J. Environ. Econ. Manag.* 38:302–21

Wu J, Cho SH. 2003. Estimating households' preferences for environmental amenities using equilibrium models of local jurisdictions. *Scott. J. Polit. Econ.* 50(May):189–206

Wu J, Gopinath M. 2008. What causes spatial variations in economic development in the United States? *Am. J. Agric. Econ.* 90(2):392–408

Wu J, Plantinga AJ. 2003. The influence of public open space on urban spatial structure. *J. Environ. Econ. Manag.* 46(2):288–309

RELATED RESOURCES

Berube A, Singer A, Wilson J, Frey W. 2006. *Finding exurbia: America's fast-growing communities at the metropolitan fringe*. Work. Pap., Brook. Inst. http://www.brookings.edu/reports/2006/10metropolitanpolicy_berube.aspx

Bogart WT. 1998. *The Economics of Cities and Suburbs*. New Jersey: Prentice Hall

Daniels T. 1999. *When City and Country Collide*. Washington, DC: Island Press

Glaeser E. 1998. Are cities dying? *J. Econ. Perspect.* 12(2):139–60

Heimlich RE, Anderson WD. 2001. *Development at the urban fringe and beyond: impacts on agriculture and rural land*. Agric. Econ. Rep. 803. Econ. Res. Serv., US Dep. Agric. http://www.ers.usda.gov/publications/aer803/aer803.pdf

Henderson V, Thisse J, eds. 2004. *Handbook of Regional and Urban Economics. Volume 4: Cities and Geography*. Amsterdam: North-Holland

Ohio State Univ. *Exurban change program*. http://exurban.osu.edu/

Ohio State Univ. *Swank program in rural-urban policy*. http://aede.osu.edu/programs/swank/

O'Sullivan. A. 2003. *Urban Economics*. New York: McGraw Hill. 5th ed.

USDA Econ. Res. Serv. *A variety of land use, natural resources, rural economy reports and data*. http://www.ers.usda.gov

USDA Forest Serv. *Forests on the edge project*. http://www.fs.fed.us/openspace/fote/

Pricing Urban Congestion*

Ian W.H. Parry

Resources for the Future, Washington, D.C. 20036; Web site: http://www.rff.org/
parry.cfm; email: parry@rff.org

Annu. Rev. Resour. Econ. 2009. 1:461–84

First published online as a Review in Advance on
June 5, 2009

The *Annual Review of Resource Economics* is
online at resource.annualreviews.org

This article's doi:
10.1146/annurev.resource.050708.144226

Key Words

traffic congestion, externality, peak-period fee, congestion toll
incidence

Abstract

This paper reviews literature on the optimal design of pricing
policies to reduce urban automobile congestion. The implications
of a range of complicating factors are considered; these include
traffic bottlenecks, constraints on which roads and freeway lanes
in the road network can be priced, driver heterogeneity, private toll
operators, other externalities besides congestion, and interactions
between congestion taxes and the broader fiscal system. I also
briefly discuss the incidence of congestion taxes and experience
with this policy in the United States and elsewhere. Although the
economics literature on congestion pricing has advanced considerably over the past 20 years, research is still needed on the empirical
measurement of second-best efficient tolls for urban centers and
whether alternative design features have substantial implications
for efficiency. More research is also needed on the design of
schemes to promote feasibility by compensating adversely affected
groups with minimal loss in economic efficiency.

1. INTRODUCTION

Given relentless growth in population and real income, expanding demand for automobile travel in the United States continues to outpace road construction, causing worsening urban congestion. Between 1980 and 2003, for example, urban vehicle miles traveled increased by 111%, against an increase in lane-mile capacity of only 51% (Bureau of Transportation Statistics 2006, tables 1.6 and 1.33). According to Schrank & Lomax (2007), the average traveler across the 437 largest urban areas in the United States lost 38 h to traffic delays in 2005, up from 14 h in 1982. Delays are most severe in Los Angeles, where the average traveler lost 72 h to congestion in 2005. The next most congested cities, with average delays of approximately 60 h per year, were San Francisco, California; Washington, D.C.; Atlanta, Georgia; Dallas, Texas; and Houston, Texas (Schrank & Lomax 2007, table 1). Nationwide, Schrank & Lomax (2007) put the annual costs of congestion, including wasted fuel, at $78.2 billion in 2005, up from $16.2 billion in 1982 (in 2007 dollars).[1]

Despite higher fuel prices, the trend of rising urban congestion is set to continue. The Department of Transportation (2008) projects an increase in automobile vehicle miles of 50% between 2010 and 2030. Meanwhile, because of environmental constraints, neighborhood opposition, and high land acquisition costs, new road construction is increasingly difficult. In any case, expanding capacity is partly self-defeating as it encourages new driving trips (see, for example, Downs 1992, Standing Advisory Committee on Trunk Road Assessment 1994, Goodwin 1996, Mackie 1996, Noland 2001, Litman 2006).

The limitations of other traditional approaches have also become apparent. Expanding transit and subsidizing fares has limited impacts on automobile congestion, given relatively modest own-price elasticities for transit.[2] In fact, the convenience of auto travel, particularly relative to traditional hub-and-spoke rail networks, may be increasing as places of work become more dispersed, rather than concentrated in the downtown area. Fuel taxes have limited effect as they do not differentiate between urban and rural driving or between peak and off-peak travel, and much of the long-run behavioral response comes from improved fuel economy rather than reduced vehicle mileage. Furthermore, political opposition to fuel taxes is intense in the United States, where auto and oil companies have substantial political influence and where per capita gasoline consumption is several times higher than in Western Europe.

It is therefore not surprising that U.S. policy makers are looking for more effective congestion policies (e.g., De Corla-Souza 2004, National Surface Transportation Policy 2007, Department of Transportation 2006). In theory, peak-period road pricing (sometimes called value pricing) is the ideal policy in this regard because it exploits all behavioral responses for reducing congestion, such as reduced overall travel; increased

---

[1]This figure omits some broader costs of congestion, such as the costs of people deviating from their preferred travel times to avoid the rush-hour peak. Conversely, there are limits to the costs of congestion as people cut back on peak period trips, change housing and job location, etc., as congestion becomes more severe.

[2]A typical estimate for the own-price elasticity for transit is approximately -0.4 (Pratt et al. 2000). Nonetheless, urban transit fares are heavily subsidized. Fare subsidies for the 20 largest transit authorizes in the United States, expressed as the difference between agency operating costs and revenues from passenger fares, vary from 30% to 90% of operating costs for rail systems and from 60% to 90% for bus systems (Parry & Small 2008, table 1). Despite these subsidies, transit accounted for only 4.4% of nationwide commuting trips in 2005, whereas automobiles made up 88.4% (Bureau of Transportation Statistics 2006, table 1-38). Improving service quality (e.g., increasing transit speed, reducing wait times at stops, and improving transit access) may be more effective in deterring automobile use (Litman 2007a).

carpooling; and shifting trips to off-peak periods, to transit, and to less congested routes. Moreover, the feasibility of peak-period pricing has greatly improved with recent developments in electronic metering technology. Fees can now be deducted electronically by in-vehicle transponders, thus reducing bottlenecks at manual tollbooths, or by direct billing with onboard global-positioning systems. Congestion fees may also help bridge the growing funding gap for financing upgrades of the aging transportation infrastructure, given that real fuel-tax revenue per automobile mile has declined with greater fuel economy and the failure of nominal tax rates to keep pace with inflation (Transportation Research Board 2006).

Although there are few successful congestion pricing schemes in the United States so far, it is most likely that congestion pricing will become more appealing as urban travel speeds continue to deteriorate. The relative success of area license fees in London further suggests that public opposition is not insurmountable. Thus, guidance from transportation economists on how congestion pricing policies should be designed, and in ways to reduce public opposition, could not be more timely.

Unfortunately, even at a conceptual level, designing taxes to reduce congestion can be far more complicated than addressing other externalities like household garbage, drunk driving, and smokestack pollution. Real-time variation in the toll rate within the peak period is needed to optimize road capacity by partially flattening the distribution of trip departure times. Moreover, because of political or other constraints, congestion pricing is emerging piecemeal, typically on one lane of one highway at a time. In assessing the appropriate toll, account must be taken of changes in congestion on parallel (unpriced) freeway lanes and on other links in the urban network, as the toll induces drivers to alter their travel routes.

The congestion pricing literature has advanced considerably over the past 20 years, providing valuable insights on various design issues. More research is needed, however, on the empirical measurement of efficient tolls for major urban centers and on the efficiency implications of design features—such as toll variation within the peak period, supplementary pricing on other links in the network, and toll exemption provisions (e.g., for taxis or clean-fuel vehicles). Moreover, not much literature addresses the design of compensation schemes to advance political feasibility, without substantial loss of economic efficiency.

Drawing on several other reviews, this paper distills some key findings from the congestion pricing literature and issues in need of further study, and discusses experience with congestion tolls to date and prospects for more widespread policy implementation in the United States.[3] Section 2 briefly discusses alternative models of congestion. Section 3 discusses complicating factors in the design of congestion tolls. Section 4 considers practical obstacles to, and prospects for improving the feasibility of, congestion pricing. Section 5 summarizes experience with congestion pricing to date. Section 6 offers concluding thoughts.

---

[3]Other recent reviews include Arnott et al. (2005, ch. 1), Lindsey (2006, 2007), Litman (2008), Santos (2004a), and Small & Verhoef (2007). As Arnott et al. (2005) emphasized, economists need to examine policies that may complement congestion pricing, such as appropriately pricing freight and mass transit, staggering work hours for government employees, encouraging biking and walking, and improving the design of roads and intersections to improve traffic flow. Reforming the pricing of parking space is especially important, given that owner- and employer-provided public parking is currently heavily subsidized (Shoup 2005). These broader policies, however, are beyond the scope of this article.

2. ALTERNATIVE APPROACHES TO MODELING CONGESTION

In this section, I outline the two main theoretical approaches to modeling congestion: (*a*) the static, speed/flow model of highway congestion and (*b*) the dynamic model of traffic bottlenecks. I also comment on empirical implementation of these models.

2.1. Basic Model of Highway Congestion

Beckmann et al. (1956), Walters (1961), and Vickrey (1963) developed the basic model of highway congestion, and Hau (2005a,b) provides a recent exposition and various extensions to the basic model. Here, I begin with the basic model of congestion along a uniform segment of an urban freeway. This model makes a number of simplifying assumptions (the implications of relaxing them are discussed below):

- No traffic bottlenecks at highway entry and exit points or intersections
- A uniform flow of incoming traffic across the period
- Uniform traffic flows, and congestion tolls, across all lanes of the freeway
- All motorists have the same value of travel time
- No linkages with congestion on other network links
- No interactions between congestion tolls and distortions in the broader economy
- No consideration of recycling congestion toll revenues

2.1.1. Basic traffic-engineering relationships.

Underlying the model is the fundamental diagram of traffic congestion (shown in **Figure 1**). The upper-left quadrant indicates the relation between vehicle density (*D*)—that is, the average number of vehicles along the highway at a given time—and average speed (*S*). Speed declines with higher density because drivers slow down to maintain a comfortable separation from the vehicle ahead given shorter distances between vehicles. Traffic volume, or flow (*V*), is the number of vehicles passing through the highway segment per unit of time. Volume (vehicles/hour) is the product of density (vehicles/mile) and speed (miles/hour). Higher density is initially associated with higher vehicle flows, or completed highway trips per hour (lower-right quadrant of **Figure 1**). However, at some point, the contribution of an extra vehicle to traffic flow is offset by the reduction in flow attributable to existing vehicles traveling at slightly slower speeds to accommodate more traffic. This point represents the maximum carrying capacity. Beyond this point, the highway is said to experience hypercongestion, because additional vehicle density reduces the overall vehicle flow. This implies an inverted-U relation between speed and volume (the upper-right quadrant of **Figure 1**).

Table 1 shows the approximate relationship between density, speed, and volume under ideal highway conditions (e.g., with no intersections and bends). The flow peaks at roughly 1850–2000 vehicles/hour/lane of highway at speeds of approximately 30–46 mph (i.e., at a particular point on the highway, one vehicle passes approximately every 2 s).

2.1.2. Basic economic analysis.

The traditional economic analysis of congestion tolls uses these relationships to plot average and marginal travel cost, as a function of vehicle flow, against travel demand (depicted in **Figure 2**). Here, the average cost (*AC*) of highway trips/hour is

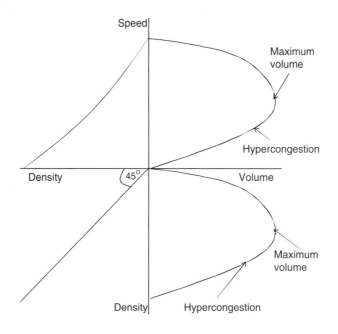

Figure 1

The fundamental diagram of traffic congestion.

Table 1 Typical density, speed, and flow relationships under optimal highway conditions[a]

Density (vehicles/mile)	Speed (mile/hour)	Volume (vehicles/hour)
<12	>60	<700
12–20	57–60	700–1100
20–30	54–57	1100–1550
30–42	46–54	1550–1850
42–67	30–46	1850–2000
>67	<30	Unstable

[a]Source: Homburger et al. (1992).

$$AC = c_m + VOT \cdot T(V), \qquad (1)$$

where c_m denotes the money cost per trip before any toll, reflecting, for example, fuel costs, vehicle wear and tear, possible parking fees, etc.[4] *VOT* [value of (travel) time] represents the amount drivers would be willing to pay to save one hour of travel time (see below). $T(V)$ is the time per trip (the inverse of speed), which rises with increasing traffic/hour on the highway. The average cost curve in **Figure 2** bends backward after the

---

[4]I omit the possibility that congestion could lower fuel economy and thus raise fuel costs per trip. A typical assumption is that vehicle fuel consumption increases by 30% under heavily congested conditions, though there is considerable uncertainty over this figure (see, e.g., Greenwood & Bennett 1996; Small & Gómez-Ibáñez 1999, sect. 3.2).

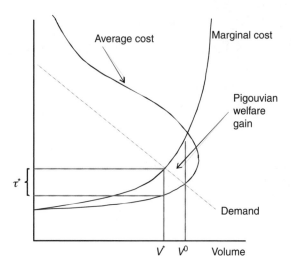

Figure 2

Traditional model of optimal congestion tolls.

maximum traffic flow is exceeded. This reflects the hypercongested portion of the speed-flow curve in **Figure 1**, where additional vehicles increase delays to other drivers by enough to reduce the overall traffic flow. However, as discussed below, a dynamic analysis is needed to study hypercongestion, which is a transitory phenomenon. For the demand curve in **Figure 2**, the equilibrium traffic flow with no toll is V^0, because motorists use the highway until the average cost per trip equals the benefit (or height of the demand curve).

Multiplying AC by V and differentiating gives the marginal social cost (MC):

$$MC = AC + MEC; \quad MEC = VOT \cdot VT'(V). \tag{2}$$

The marginal cost exceeds the average cost by the marginal external cost of congestion (MEC), which equals the increase in travel time attributable to extra congestion from one more trip, times the number of trips/hour, times VOT.

The socially efficient traffic flow for the demand curve in **Figure 2** is V^*, where the marginal social cost of an extra trip equals the marginal benefit. This flow could be induced by levying the Pigouvian congestion toll, τ^* in **Figure 2**, equal to the gap between MC and AC at this point, or $wV^*T'(V^*)$. Note that this toll is less than MEC at the pretoll traffic flow because MEC declines with the reduction in traffic flow.[5] The welfare gain from the Pigouvian toll is the gap between the marginal social cost curve and the demand curve, integrated over the reduction in traffic flow.

Revenue raised by the Pigouvian toll is τ^*V^*. Before any revenue recycling, all drivers are worse off under the toll (assuming they have the same VOT) which is a challenge for political feasibility (see below). For motorists who continue to use the highway, average costs increase because the toll exceeds the VOT savings, whereas drivers who are diverted from the road to their next best alternative are also worse off.

---

[5]According to Litman (2007b, pp. 5.5–5.10), optimal tolls would reduce traffic volume to roughly 1500 vehicles/lane/hour on highways and 800 on urban arterials.

2.2. Bottleneck Model

Although the basic speed-flow model is a useful starting point for analyzing situations when traffic conditions do not change quickly, or when the focus is on average traffic levels over extended periods, it has two main shortcomings (Small and Chu 2003). First, it cannot accommodate the possibility of hypercongestion. Yet, hypercongestion is a real phenomenon at various choke points in the road network (e.g., at stoplights, at highway entry or exit points) where large queues form and then clear during rush hour. In fact, for some of the world's most congested cities, such as Bangkok, Athens, Rome, and Jakarta, most of the road network is hypercongested most of the time. Second, the traditional model captures only one behavioral response, that is, whether to drive on the congested highway. In reality, within the peak period, drivers can change their departure time to avoid the point at which congestion is most severe. Thus, traffic inflow to the highway per unit of time is endogenous not fixed. The bottleneck model of congestion was developed to address these two shortcomings (e.g., Vickrey 1969; Arnott et al. 1991, 1993, 1994).

In bottleneck models, motorists have a preferred arrival time and incur a rising cost for early or late arrival (e.g., workers with fixed work schedules). Drivers choose their trip departure time to trade off these "schedule delay" costs against travel-time savings from leaving before, or after, the rush-hour peak. In the simplest setting, one bottleneck permits a maximum throughput of vehicles/hour. As the inflow rises above the maximum outflow, a queue forms, peaking and then progressively declining as the end of the peak period is approached.

The optimal toll in the basic model rises over the first part of the peak period and then falls, keeping traffic inflow equal to capacity outflow. This dynamic toll thus "flattens" the peak by inducing some people to depart earlier, if they leave before the peak, others to leave later, if they depart after the peak, and still others to use alternate routes or avoid driving all together. In contrast to the speed-flow model, the optimal toll eliminates congestion entirely because there is no queuing when traffic inflow is at or below choke-point capacity.

The inverted-U schedule for the optimal congestion toll during the peak period is an important policy insight from the bottleneck model. Numerical simulations in Arnott et al. (1993) suggest that more than half of the welfare gains from congestion pricing may come from trip rescheduling within the peak, rather than avoidance of peak travel altogether.

Another insight is that the costs of congestion are greater than the extra travel time alone. They also include schedule-delay costs, because people deviate from their preferred arrival times to save time during their trip (Arnott et al. 1994, Small & Chu 2003). However, the extent to which schedule-delay costs are picked up in empirical estimates of the VOT, and therefore are incorporated in estimates of congestion costs, is unclear.

A third insight is that the welfare gains from bottleneck pricing can be roughly the same as the toll revenue collected, unlike in the traditional model, where welfare gains are typically much smaller than revenue transfers. Because it is optimal to eliminate bottleneck queues completely rather than partly, welfare gains are first order, unlike in the static model where they are second order. In principle, this should reduce public opposition to tolls designed to alleviate specific bottlenecks in the road network.

Hybrid models combining elements of both traditional and bottleneck models have also been developed. For example, Mun (1994) developed a dynamic model of travel between two distant points with a queue in the middle that forms and eventually clears during the peak period. Travel time is determined by the standard speed-flow relation on either side of the bottleneck, but it also includes wait times from queuing. The model thus captures hypercongestion at a choke point, but over the entire peak period, the average travel cost curve always increases in traffic flow. In hybrid models, the optimal toll has both a static component analogous to the Pigouvian tax and a dynamic component to address the bottleneck (Arnott & Kraus 1998, equation 20).

2.3. Empirical Implementation of the Basic Model

Most empirical assessments of optimal congestion tolls use the speed-flow approach, which is the model I focus on here.[6] Implementing the basic speed-flow model of congestion charges requires three pieces of information: the VOT, the speed-flow functional relationship, and the demand response to tolling.

2.3.1. Value of travel time.
If people value the pure disutility from an extra hour of work and an extra hour of travel time equally, then the VOT would reflect the net-of-tax wage. More generally, travel may be valued at less than the net wage if, for example, people prefer to be in a car rather than at work, or vice versa, if they prefer the work environment to being in a car.

There is a large empirical literature on the VOT. Some studies use revealed preference methods (e.g., estimating willingness to pay auto fuel and parking costs to save time over an alternative, slower travel mode), whereas others use stated preference methods (e.g., directly asking people what toll they would be willing to pay for a faster commute). Stated-preference studies (e.g., Calfee & Winston 1998) often yield a much lower VOT than do revealed-preference approaches. Brownstone & Small (2005) suggested that this may be due to survey respondents' overestimating the actual time savings from travel options with higher monetary costs.

Given the difficulty of controlling for schedule-delay costs, the extent to which people's estimated willingness to pay for shorter travel times also reflects the advantages of their being able to schedule trips closer to their preferred times is unclear. Another cost of travel delay is the added uncertainty over arrival times when trip times are stochastic, which matters when the cost of being late by a given margin exceeds the cost of being early by the same margin. In response to this uncertainty, people may leave earlier than they would otherwise prefer. However, it is also unclear to what extent the cost of this "buffer time" is reflected in existing estimates of the VOT (Small & Verhoef 2007, p. 54).

Most literature reviews recommend a VOT for personal auto travel equal to approximately half the gross market wage, or somewhat less than the net-of-tax wage (e.g., Waters 1996, U.S. Department of Transportation 1997, Mackie et al. 2003). The recommendation suggests, for example, that if the gross hourly wage for urban areas is $20 (Bureau of Labor Statistic 2006, table 1), then the time cost for driving 1 mile when the road speed is 30 mph will be 33 cents. For comparison, if the vehicle fuel economy is 20 miles per gallon and the retail gasoline price is $3.50 per gallon, then fuel costs per mile are 15 cents. Commuting trips are also valued somewhat more highly than leisure, shopping, and other trips, partly

---

[6]Sometimes, delays at bottlenecks, averaged over the peak period, are taken into account when calibrating speed-flow curves. Quantitative assessments of optimal tolls based on bottleneck models typically must postulate a distribution for schedule delay costs, because there are no direct data to measure them. Numerically solving these models is challenging, given that bottleneck congestion is inherently a disequilibrium phenomenon (for more discussion, see de Palma & Marchal 2001).

because of penalties for late arrival at work. Trips made in the course of work are typically valued at the gross wage, as they reflect the VOT to the employer (Department for Transport 2007). Moreover, as a possible result of stress and frustration, the VOT may be substantially higher under heavily congested, compared with free-flowing, conditions (e.g., MVA Consultancy et al. 1987, Wardman 2001, Steer Davies Gleave 2004). As regards the VOT/income elasticity, Mackie et al. (2003) recommend a value of 0.8.

2.3.2. Speed-flow curves.

The most commonly used functional form relating travel time per mile (the inverse of speed) to traffic flow (where these are observed from time-lapse satellite data or ground-based traffic counts) is

$$T = T_f\{1 + \alpha V^\beta\}, \tag{3}$$

where α and β are parameters and T_f is time per mile when traffic is free flowing. A typical value for the exponent β is $2.5-5.0$. With $\alpha = 0.15$ and $\beta = 4.0$, Equation 3 is the Bureau of Public Roads formula, which is widely used in traffic-engineering models (for a review of the literature on speed-flow curves, see Lindsey & Verhoef 2000).

Differentiating Equation 3 and substituting in Equation 2 give

$$MEC = VOT \cdot \beta \cdot AD, AD = T - T_f, \tag{4}$$

where AD (average delay) represents the excess of time per mile over that under free-flow traffic conditions. Using this formula, Parry & Small (2009) valued the marginal external cost of congestion at 28.0 cents/vehicle-mile for peak automobile travel in metropolitan Washington, D.C., in 2002. **Table 2** extrapolates this estimate to various other large cities, on the basis of travel delay per mile of travel in that city relative to that for Washington, D.C. (see Schrank & Lomax 2007). These rough estimates vary from 33.7 cents/mile in Chicago, Illinois, to 23.5 cents/mile in Detroit, Michigan. These figures may mask considerable variation in marginal external costs across individual links in the network as well as across points in time within the peak period. For example, for peak travel in Twin Cities, Minnesota, Mohring (1999) estimated marginal congestion costs that vary from less than 2.5 cents to more than 50 cents/vehicle-mile, across road classes.

Accurately estimating the parameters of speed-flow relations for specific roads can be tricky, however. For example, the relation will vary with highway gradient, bends, presence of hard shoulders, frequency of stop lights and intersections, etc., so estimates may not transfer across different roads. Furthermore, estimating the point of maximum flow can be challenging because of considerable scatter in observed speed and flow data (Small & Verhoef 2007, ch. 3), and estimates of the speed-flow curve for specific highway segments are sensitive to bottlenecks near that segment.

2.3.3. Demand responses.

Calculating Pigouvian congestion tolls, as opposed to the marginal external cost at prevailing travel flows, requires simultaneously solving for the marginal external cost and the demand for travel as the highway is priced. Demand responses are also needed to assess the net benefits from congestion tolling.

There is a large empirical literature on the overall responsiveness of driving practices to price fluctuations, usually measured by fuel prices or fuel costs per mile. Aggregate cross-sectional studies compare travel behavior across metropolitan areas, or sometimes across different zones within an urban area. Other studies use time-series data, though the results

Table 2 Marginal external congestion costs for selected urban centers[a]

Urban area	Annual person hours of delay[b]	Marginal external congestion cost[c]
Los Angeles, California	490,552	32.4
New York, New York	384,046	31.7
Chicago, Illinois	202,835	33.7
Dallas, Texas	152,129	25.9
Miami, Florida	150,146	28.7
Atlanta, Georgia	132,296	24.7
San Francisco, California	129,919	28.1
Washington, D.C.	127,394	28.0
Houston, Texas	124,131	25.4
Detroit, Michigan	115,547	23.5
San Diego, California	90,711	25.9
San Jose, California	50,038	26.0
Orlando, Florida	40,595	24.4

[a]Sources: Schrank & Lomax (2007), Parry & Small (2009).
[b]Measured across all times of day (thousands of hours).
[c]Measured for peak auto travel (cents/vehicle mile).

can be sensitive to the specification for autocorrelation. A rough rule of thumb is that the elasticity of vehicle miles with respect to fuel prices is between -0.1 and -0.3 (e.g., Goodwin 1992, Goodwin et al. 2004).

However, estimating the potential demand response to peak-period pricing of a link in a road network, as opposed to a uniform increase in the price of all driving, is problematic. Typically, this can be done only after the response to pricing that link has been observed. *Ex ante*, studies may extrapolate estimates of the degree of substitution in demand between priced and unpriced routes from studies of other, previously implemented, congestion pricing policies in other cities, making some adjustment for differences in the proximity of other roads to the priced road across cities.

3. COMPLICATING FACTORS IN THE DESIGN OF CONGESTION TOLLS

Although the speed-flow model is the basis for most empirical assessments of optimal congestion tolls, other assumptions—besides the absence of bottlenecks—are often unrealistic. I now discuss literature that relaxes these other assumptions.

3.1. Limited Pricing Across Freeway Lanes

To date, in the United States, part of the political deal-making needed to implement congestion pricing on freeways has involved leaving motorists with the option of an unpriced, though more congested, alternative lane on the freeway. Suppose, first, that all drivers are homogeneous and a toll is applied to one of two parallel freeway lanes. Because the lanes are perfect substitutes, traffic from one lane will move to the other until the average cost of the unpriced (but more congested) lane equals the average cost of its priced (but less congested) counterpart. In an extreme case, where the demand for travel on the freeway is perfectly inelastic, all the reduction in traffic on the priced lane is shifted onto the other lane and the toll reduces welfare.[7] More generally, with some elasticity in demand for freeway travel, some drivers diverted from the priced lane will give up using the freeway altogether. Nonetheless, accounting for the partial shifting of drivers onto the congested alternative greatly reduces the optimal level, as well as welfare gains, from the single-lane toll. Welfare gains from tolling one lane (initially carrying half of the freeway traffic) are well below half of the potential welfare gains from pricing both lanes. For example, Verhoef et al. (1996) estimated the potential welfare gains from a single-lane toll at only 10% of those from first-best tolls applied to both routes (see also Braid 1996, Liu & MacDonald 1998).

3.2. Driver Heterogeneity

In reality, the VOT differs greatly among drivers, which affects the optimal set of freeway tolls and welfare gains from single-lane tolls. With driver heterogeneity, the best pricing scheme is not a uniform toll across all lanes, but rather differentiated tolls that allow drivers to sort themselves into lanes that are more or less congested, depending on their VOT. Surprisingly however, studies allowing for differences in the VOT find the efficiency gains from differentiated tolling may not be large. For example, Verhoef & Small (2004) and Parry (2002) estimated that uniform tolls may generate more than 90% of the potential welfare gains from the first-best, differentiated set of lane tolls. This is because in the first-best outcome the difference between the tolls, or among marginal external congestion costs across different lanes, is modest. Although people in the high-toll lane have a higher VOT, which raises the marginal external cost of congestion for that lane, the fact that there are fewer drivers in that lane—thus, there is less congestion—partly counteracts the higher cost.

In contrast, the welfare effects of single-lane tolls are substantially enhanced when account is taken of the possibilities for drivers with a high and low VOT to sort into priced and unpriced lanes. Small & Yan (2001) estimated the efficiency gains from single-lane tolls could be three times as large, when driver heterogeneity is taken into account (though the welfare gains are still below half of those from first-best pricing of both freeway lanes). This reflects greater gains from reducing congestion in the priced lane (where drivers have a high VOT) and smaller losses from extra congestion in the unpriced lane (where drivers have a low VOT).[8]

---

[7]In effect, the reduction in congestion from the first vehicle diverted off the priced lane will be exactly offset by added congestion on the unpriced lane. Because marginal congestion costs are now (slightly) higher on the unpriced lane, any further diversion of traffic between lanes will increase total congestion costs and lower welfare.

[8]Heterogeneity in the size of passenger vehicles is less important than driver heterogeneity because differences in the amount of road space taken up by cars versus light-duty trucks (pickups, sport utility vehicles, minivans) are modest relative to average headways between vehicles on the road. Estimated differences in the marginal external costs of congestion for different types of passenger vehicles are therefore not large (Federal Highway Administration 1997, table 5-23). Heavy-duty trucks, however, take up more than twice the road space of passenger cars, implying they should have a separate, and higher, toll.

3.3. Network Effects

Generally, a congested freeway segment is just one link in a road network covering an urban center. By diverting drivers from the freeway, congestion tolls may exacerbate congestion on substitute roads elsewhere in the system or may reduce it on complementary roads feeding into the priced segment. Ideally, congestion on other roads would also be internalized through tolling; in which case, (small) changes in traffic on those roads have no efficiency effects. More realistically, there will not be comprehensive pricing of all other congested roads because of political constraints and perhaps because of high monitoring costs associated with pricing crisscrossing city streets. Under these conditions, the second-best toll differs from the Pigouvian toll, the greater the marginal congestion costs on other roads (net of any toll on those roads), and the greater the portion of drivers diverted off the priced freeway that moves to other roads, as opposed to those who cancel their trip or substitute to the off-peak period (MacDonald 1995, Verhoef 2002).

General statements about the sign of an adjustment to the second-best toll—let alone the magnitude—to account for network effects are difficult, however. This is because the availability of substitute routes and extent of complementary feeder roads are both highly case specific. What is needed is a carefully calibrated computational model of the particular road network under study that realistically captures the main substitution possibilities.

Typically, economically based network models disaggregate an urban system into travel zones where each zone consists of stylized links (such as inbound, outbound, and circumferential) representing an aggregation of arterials and side streets within the zone. Other links, such as freeway segments and bridges, may be represented separately. On the demand side, households are aggregated into groups, perhaps by income class. A decision tree involving the choice of whether to take a trip and, if so, then including which destination, mode, time of day, and route may be used to determine travel demand.

However, few economic-network models exist, given the daunting amount of researcher time and data collection required to develop, calibrate, run, and update them.[9] One such model, developed by Safirova and coauthors, has been applied to metropolitan Washington, D.C. (e.g., Houde et al. 2007). Proost and colleagues have also developed other models for various European cities (e.g., de Borger & Proost 2001). The SATURN model has been used to examine alternative cordon tolls in certain U.K. cities (e.g., May & Milne 2000, May et al. 2002, Santos & Newbery 2002). METROPOLIS, a disequilibrium, dynamic model of bottleneck congestion developed by de Palma and coauthors, has also been applied to European cities (e.g., de Palma & Marchal 2001). The limited results available suggest the empirical significance of network effects and, hence, the potential usefulness of such models (e.g., Safirova & Gillingham 2003).

But even within sophisticated network models, neither the link- (or zone-)specific speed-flow curves, nor the own- and cross-price elasticities of travel demand by road and time of day, can be known precisely. Policy makers may therefore need to rely on trial-and-error approaches where tolls are initially set on the basis of existing models and then

---

[9]Traffic-engineering models of road networks are far more common than economic models and are widely used in forecasting future traffic flows and the traffic impacts of policies such as infrastructure upgrades. Engineering models do not provide welfare-based measures of congestion costs, however, and often do not integrate demand-side behavioral responses to tolls and changes in congestion. Thus, they cannot be used to estimate the welfare effects, and economically efficient levels, of congestion tolls.

revised as models are updated in response to observed, policy-induced changes in travel patterns (e.g., Yang et al. 2004).

3.4. Tolling to Open Up Underutilized Road Capacity

So far, I have compared congestion tolls against a baseline with no policies. However, in some metropolitan areas, certain freeway lanes are restricted to high-occupancy vehicles (HOVs). Converting these lanes to high-occupancy toll (HOT) lanes, where drivers of single-occupant vehicles can pay to use the lane, has several beneficial effects. Unlike in the basic speed-flow model, those paying the toll are better off (they would not pay the toll unless they value the travel-time savings more than the toll). Drivers remaining on the unpriced alternative lane benefit from reduced congestion because single-occupant vehicles switch to the HOT lane. The government also gains tax revenues. The only losers are passengers of HOVs, who suffer from a decline in speed on the HOT lane, though this slowdown may be limited if the toll is high enough to retain reasonable traffic flow. For Washington, D.C., Safirova et al. (2004) estimated the welfare gains from HOV to HOT lane conversion are almost as large as those from more comprehensive pricing covering all lanes of all freeways that currently have HOV lanes.

3.5. Tolling by Private Operators

Private toll roads have been around for some time in Europe and the Pacific Rim and are emerging in the United States (Gómez-Ibáñez & Meyer 1993). If monopoly operators are free to maximize profits, however, the toll will be set above the socially efficient level (Small & Verhoef 2007, ch. 6). Although the operator internalizes congestion by accounting for the increased willingness of drivers to pay for highway use as congestion falls, an additional markup is imposed to exploit monopoly power. The more inelastic the demand for highway travel, that is, the more limited the availability of alternative roads, the greater the markup is. In addition, the divergence between the monopoly toll and the second-best optimal toll is greater if drivers diverted by the toll add to congestion on parallel unpriced lanes of the freeway or on other roads. Under some conditions, the monopoly toll may actually reduce welfare relative to the case of no tolls (Verhoef & Small 2004). Therefore, without a competitive bidding process for toll rates, which would undermine the monopoly markup, there is a case for imposing maximum toll regulations, though the *ex ante* measurement of the efficient toll ceiling may be challenging to obtain before observing behavioral responses to the toll.

3.6. Interactions with Other Externalities

Congestion tolls affect other highway externalities, and to the extent that these externalities are not internalized through other policies, they should be factored into assessments of the welfare effects and, arguably, the optimal levels, of congestion tolls. But do these adjustments make much practical difference? Averaged over urban and rural areas, and over time of day, these other externalities, though not as large as congestion, still appear to be significant. Nationwide, marginal congestion costs have been put at the equivalent of approximately 5–7 cents per vehicle mile (e.g., Federal Highway Administration 1997, 2000). Estimated traffic accident externalities for the United States are almost as large, around 2–7 cents (e.g., Federal Highway Administration 1997, Miller et al. 1998, Parry 2004). The Federal Highway Administration (2000) estimated nationwide local pollution damages at 1.7 cents per mile for 2000, though emission rates are declining over time with more stringent emissions standards for new vehicles.[10] These other externalities are partly counteracted by federal and state fuel taxes, which amount to approximately 40 cents per gallon (or 2 cents per vehicle mile).

However, the key point here is that, to a far greater extent than other externalities, congestion is highly specific to region and time of day. The marginal external congestion costs for peak travel shown in **Table 2** are large relative to the above figures for pollution and accidents, net of fuel taxes. Thus, accounting for other externalities should have a modest effect on the welfare effects of urban, peak-period tolls.

3.7. Interactions with the Broader Fiscal System

Congestion taxes can interact with distortions the broader fiscal system creates elsewhere in the economy. Most importantly, federal and state income taxes and payroll taxes combine to drive a substantial wedge between the effective gross wage firms pay (which, in a flexible market, reflects the value marginal product of labor) and the net wage households receive (which reflects the marginal value of forgone nonmarket time). Therefore, to the extent that a new policy causes an increase or decrease in labor supply, it will induce an efficiency gain or loss in the labor market. In fact, the welfare effects of even tiny changes in labor supply can be empirically important relative to those of reducing congestion, given the large labor tax wedge and the huge size of the labor market in the overall economy.

Congestion tolls can affect the labor market two ways. First, revenues may be used to lower the burden of labor taxes, producing an efficiency gain. Second, tolls levied on heavily used commuter roads reduce the returns to work effort—net of commuting costs—and may deter labor force participation at the margin. This deterrence effect, however, is partly dampened because the reduction in congestion lowers the time cost of commuting. According to Parry & Bento (2001), the net impact of a Pigouvian congestion tax, with revenues used to reduce labor taxes, is to increase labor supply, and welfare gains in the labor market are roughly the same size as those from correcting the externality.

However, the critical issue here is the importance of using congestion tax revenues in a socially productive way, either to offset reductions in distortionary taxes or, more generally, to finance public-spending projects that yield comparable efficiency gains. In fact, if revenue recycling does not lead to significant efficiency gains, the externality-correcting tax may lower overall social welfare, as the gains from correcting the externality may be outweighed by the efficiency losses in the labor market (Parry & Bento 2001). This point needs to be heeded when political feasibility may necessitate either some use of toll revenues to finance compensation schemes for motorists or earmarking of revenues for transportation enhancements.

---

[10] Mainstream estimates of global-warming damages, though highly contentious, are modest relative to these other externalities. Most estimates of these damages are in the order of approximately $5 to $25 per ton of CO_2 (e.g., Aldy et al. 2009). Burning a gallon of gasoline produces 0.0024 tons of carbon, or 0.0088 tons of CO_2, and approximately 1/23 gallons are consumed per vehicle mile driven (National Research Council 2002; Federal Highway Administration 2006, table VM-1). Therefore, a $10 price on CO_2 amounts to approximately 0.4 cents per mile. An additional highway externality is road damage. However, it is standard to attribute this largely to heavy-duty trucks rather than light-duty vehicles. This is because pavement wear and tear is a rapidly rising function of a vehicle's axle weight.

The importance of judicious revenue use is suggested by **Figure 2**. Given that travel demand is inelastic, the amount of revenue can easily be several times larger, and conceivably an order of magnitude larger, than the Pigouvian welfare gains from correcting the externality. Using the central values for labor supply elasticities from the empirical labor economics literature, Parry & Bento (2001) noted the efficiency gain from using $1 of revenue to cut labor taxes, as opposed to financing lump-sum transfers, is $0.25. Thus, the potential gain from revenue recycling (0.25 times the amount of revenue) can easily be as large as, or perhaps much larger than, the welfare gains from congestion reduction.

3.8. Freeway Tolls Versus Cordon Tolls and Area Licenses

An alternative to pricing individual freeways is to implement a cordon toll where drivers pay as they pass points in the road network, where these points connect to form a cordon around a city or city center. Another version of this policy is the area license in which case drivers must pay even if the trip starts and terminates within the area, without crossing the border. These schemes have potential appeal for old European cities where the downtown areas are a mass of higgledy-piggledy streets that would be impractical to price individually. They have also been proposed for some U.S. cities, most notably New York City.

However, cordon-pricing and area-license schemes are inefficient in that they impose the same fee regardless of trip distance. They can also exacerbate congestion elsewhere in the road network, as people change their routes to bypass the pricing region. Despite this, well-designed cordon tolls and area licenses may still capture a large portion of the efficiency gains from more comprehensive pricing (e.g., Akiyama et al. 2002, May et al. 2004, Safirova et al. 2004, Santos 2004b, Verhoef 2002). In particular, efficiency can be improved by varying the toll with driving direction and time of day, by appropriate placement of the pricing boundary, and possibly by using multiple pricing rings.

3.9. Summary

The conceptual framework for designing congestion taxes is well developed, in that we have a reasonable grasp of the potentially important factors to consider when assessing the optimal levels, and welfare effects, of pricing schemes. The importance of network effects, bottlenecks, existing HOV lanes, etc., varies considerably across cities, however. Optimal policies therefore need to be assessed on a case-by-case basis, requiring individually calibrated models on local traffic flows, speed-flow relations, and behavioral responses to tolling.

In fact, more work is needed on empirical models for policy analysis of different urban centers. This includes developing network models that realistically capture changes in congestion throughout the entire road system. In addition, more aggregated simulation models can also play a valuable role in interpreting numerical results from computational models and in roughly gauging the empirical importance of other factors difficult to capture in a detailed network model, such as toll variation within the peak period and impacts on distorted labor markets. Research is also needed on schemes that may help overcome political opposition to congestion pricing and on the efficiency or feasibility trade-offs involved in creating broad coalitions of net beneficiaries from the policy. I now turn to these issues.

4. PRACTICAL OBSTACLES TO CONGESTION PRICING

In the past, opposition to congestion tolls in the United States from the public and elected officials has been strong. However, the development of electric metering technologies has, to some degree, addressed two of the traditional concerns: implementation difficulties and abuse of information collected on individuals' driving habits.

The administrative costs of electronic debiting from smart cards, such as E-Z passes, are minimal and vehicles may not even need to slow down as they pass transponder points. Under a global-positioning system, motorists' driving behavior is monitored by satellite and bills may be periodically mailed to households on the basis of their mileage on congested roads, again at low administrative cost.[11] Under this system, privacy is more of a concern and would need to be addressed through strict legal requirements on information-collection agencies. With electronic debiting from prepaid smart cards, privacy concerns are largely redundant because there is no need to record the vehicle's tag number.

Two especially challenging obstacles to congestion pricing remain, however. First, motorist opposition may be intense if the new charges outweigh their VOT savings. Second, congestion pricing may be unfair from the perspective of vertical equity, given that everyone faces the same tax rate regardless of income. These issues are intertwined because they both depend on the incidence of congestion tolls.

4.1. Congestion-Toll Incidence

Conceptually, leaving aside network effects, the incidence of congestion tolls is straight-forward. Consider the highly simplified setting represented in **Figure 3**, where D_i denotes the demand for mileage (per unit of time) on an isolated, congested freeway by income group i, where $i = L$ (low-income) or H (high-income). $AC_i^0 = c_m + VOT_i \cdot T$ denotes the average cost per mile of travel for income group i that, following Equation 1, consists of the monetary cost (before any toll), plus the product of the VOT for income group i, and the time per mile T (assume $VOT_H > VOT_L$). Suppose a toll of τ per mile is introduced. The cost per mile to income group i is now

$$AC_i^0 + \tau - VOT_i \cdot \Delta T, \tag{5}$$

where ΔT is the reduction in travel time per mile due to reduced congestion. The burden of the policy (or consumer surplus loss) to income group i, denoted B_i, is the shaded trapezoid in **Figure 3** and can be expressed as

$$B_i = (\tau - VOT_i \cdot \Delta T)M_i^0 - \frac{1}{2}(M_i^0 - M_i^1)(\tau - VOT_i \cdot \Delta T), \tag{6}$$

where M_i^0 and M_i^1 denote mileage for income group i before and after the toll, respectively. The two terms in Equation 6 are the first-order burden of the toll and the second-order reduction in the burden as people reduce freeway driving to avoid the toll, respectively.[12]

---

[11]Although technologies are constantly improving, flaws still need to be addressed. For example, under a global-positioning system, the signal from a vehicle is sometimes lost in the presence of tall buildings or other obstructions.

[12]Note that, for the low-income group, the more elastic their demand, the smaller the burden of the toll, because the elasticity reflects more ways to avoid the toll. Thus, the popular argument that tolls are unfair because they may push low-income drivers off the priced highway is somewhat misleading. The above analysis takes drivers' VOT as given. As noted above, however, the VOT may fall as tolls reduce the severity of congestion. This enhances the possibility that some drivers may be better off prior to recycling of the toll revenues (e.g., Santos & Bhakar 2006).

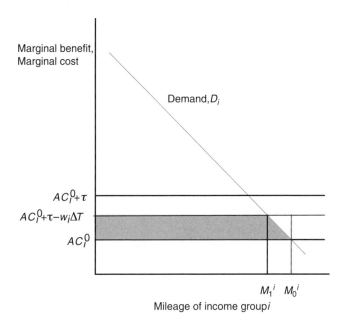

Marginal benefit,
Marginal cost

Demand,D_i

$AC_l^0 + \tau$

$AC_l^0 + \tau - w_i \Delta T$

AC_l^0

$M_1{}^i$ $M_0{}^i$

Mileage of income group i

Figure 3

Incidence of congestion tolls.

Suppose that the proportionate reduction in driving is relatively small; then the burden, relative to income I_i, is approximately

$$\frac{B_i}{I_i} \approx \frac{(\tau - VOT_i \cdot \Delta T) M_i^0}{I_i}. \tag{7}$$

Conceivably, the high-income group could be better off under the toll, even before any revenue recycling, if they value the travel-time savings more than the toll payment. In contrast, the low-income group must be worse off because the toll must reduce the aggregate demand for travel on the freeway. The congestion toll is highly likely to be regressive, in that the burden-to-income ratio is greater for low-income households, or, $B_L/I_L > B_H/I_H$ (e.g., Cohen 1987, Glazer 1981, Small 1983). For the policy to be progressive, $VOT_H \cdot \Delta T < \tau$ and M_H^0/I_H would have to exceed M_L^0/I_L by a large enough margin to outweigh the smaller net-cost increase for the high-income group. That is, the income elasticity of mileage would need to be well above unity. Evidence suggests, however, that the income elasticity is around unity or below (e.g., Pickrell & Schimek 1997).[13]

In general, a more comprehensive incidence analysis should account for the distributional burden of changes in congestion elsewhere in the road network in response to the pricing of one link. The possible long-term impacts on homeowners and workers from induced changes in property values and wages should also be included. Ideally, burdens would be measured against some measure of lifetime income, rather than of annual income, because the former is a better measure of individuals' long-term consumption

---

[13]Note that I am defining a "regressive" and "progressive" policy in a different way from the usual use of these terms in discussions of tax policy. This is because I am defining the burden net of a time-savings benefit that is valued differently by different groups.

possibilities. Measuring against lifetime income tends to weaken the degree of regressivity (e.g., Poterba 1989). Despite these complications, congestion tolls are still likely to impose a disproportionately large burden on lower-income drivers. On the grounds of distributional equity and political feasibility, particular attention needs to be paid to compensating these groups.

4.2. Recycling Possibilities

As noted above, recycling congestion tax revenues in income tax reductions can yield relatively large welfare gains. If congestion tolls were implemented nationwide at the federal level, or (far more likely) at the local level, this could be achieved through accompanying legislation requiring automatic reductions in other taxes to keep total revenue constant. The drawback would be a large disconnect between relatively large numbers of people benefitting slightly from broad tax cuts and relatively few motorists bearing the brunt of the new toll. However, as evident from **Figure 3**, some of the toll revenue can be retained for broader tax reductions, given that compensation needed to prevent motorists being made worse off is less than the toll revenue collected.

These considerations suggest the attraction of proposals targeting some of the toll revenue at local transportation projects to help to compensate motorists, such as expanding other travel options like transit and bike paths (e.g., Small 1992). This approach need not entail significant loss of economic efficiency if these projects generate comparable welfare gains to those from cutting distortionary taxes. Another possibility for compensation is some toll rebate for low-income drivers, though this would partly undermine the overall effectiveness of the toll. More research is badly needed on the distributional and efficiency impacts of alternative packages of revenue uses for prospective congestion pricing schemes.

4.3. Policy Experience to Date

Introduced in 1975, the first attempt to use road pricing for congestion reduction was Singapore's area license (day pass). The scheme dramatically reduced congestion and raised travel speeds within the restricted zone, but congestion initially increased substantially outside of the zone, suggesting that the license price may have been excessive from a second-best perspective (Small & Gómez-Ibáñez 1998). In part, this problem was later addressed through supplementary tolls on major roads leading up to the restricted zone. Additionally, in 1998, Singapore replaced the area licensing with a toll debited electronically from smart cards on certain links, with the objective of maintaining an average speed of 30–40 mph on expressways and 12–18 mph on major roads (Santos 2005). Charges rise and fall in 30-min steps during peak periods, based on congestion levels observed in the previous quarter.

Norway experimented with cordon tolling, though with little impact on congestion because the stated objective of the policy was to raise transportation revenue rather than deter congestion (e.g., Tretvick 2003, Ramjerdi et al. 2004). In London, congestion pricing has been given a large boost following its relatively successful implementation. An area-licensing scheme was introduced in 2003; initially, it covered 8 square miles of central London and was later expanded westward to incorporate Kensington and Chelsea. The fee for entering the charging area was first set at £5 ($9) and later raised to £8. Collection is by video cameras at checkpoints into and within the priced area that record each vehicle's license plate—drivers who have not prepaid are mailed a penalty amounting to £60 or more. In the first two years, the policy reduced congestion by 30% within the priced zone, without causing excessive congestion elsewhere in the network (Transport for London 2004). This is in large part because at least half of the diverted auto trips reflected people switching to mass transit, and only approximately one-quarter were diverted to other roads in the network (Small & Verhoef 2007, p. 151). However, by 2008, average speeds had fallen back to precharging levels as a result of a high number of road works and an increase in traffic from vehicles exempt from the charge (Santos 2008, Transport for London 2008).

Congestion pricing is gaining some, albeit limited, momentum in the United States, with federal funding for pilot schemes under the Value Pricing Program and the reduction of regulatory obstacles to freeway pricing (De Corla-Souza 2004). One type of scheme is the conversion of HOV to HOT lanes, for example, on I-15 in San Diego, California (Brownstone et al. 2003). Another scheme uses tolls to fund new infrastructure, such as the lanes opened on SR-91 in Orange County, California, in 1995.

5. CONCLUSION

Congestion pricing schemes implemented to date have demonstrated their potential to improve urban travel speeds, though appropriate design features can be critical (Santos 2004a, part II). Such features include sizeable and time-varying fees as well as pricing other parts of the road network if congestion-displacement effects are important. Another lesson is the possible need for price ceilings on fees private operators charge. For example, the SR-91 toll lanes reverted to public ownership in 2003 because excessive pricing by the private operator caused unexpectedly severe congestion on parallel, unpriced lanes.

In terms of feasibility, a number of factors, besides forceful political leadership, favored the introduction of congestion pricing in London (Leape 2006, Santos & Fraser 2006). One was the high level of public and business concern about traffic jams. Before the charge, for instance, the average driving speed in Central London was less than 10 mph. Opposition to the scheme was also weakened by a range of exemptions. Taxis are exempt and residents in the charging zone pay only 10% of the fee. Public support, particularly among commuters least able to afford the charge, was garnered by requiring that toll revenues be used to improve public transport. London motorists were also more receptive to video-camera surveillance, because this had previously helped reduce street crime.

Other urban centers in the United Kingdom and United States have yet to follow London's lead, presumably because favorable factors for the introduction of radical congestion pricing schemes have not yet come to a head. These circumstances could easily change down the road, however, as urban travel speeds continue to deteriorate. In fact, at a national level in the United Kingdom, there is serious debate about replacing fuel taxes with a nationwide charge on vehicle miles that would vary across regions and time of day (Department for Transport 2004).

In short, it is an exciting time to be a transportation economist, with political and public opinion beginning, albeit perhaps only gradually, to come around to the idea of congestion pricing. The pricing schemes that eventually emerge may deviate substantially from an economist's ideal—for example, charges may vary little across time of day, many vehicles and drivers may be exempt, and some toll revenues may be dissipated in wasteful spending. But we can envision policy refinement over time—for example, variable fees may be introduced in stages, exemptions may be "bought out" over time through one-off compensation payments, and requirements for efficient revenue uses may be phased in (e.g., revenue-neutrality provisions or requirements that funded projects pass a cost-benefit assessment).

Economists have their work cut out in empirically assessing the optimal design of, and efficiency gains from, congestion pricing. At the same time, they need to better reconcile efficiency and feasibility, particularly in the design of compensation schemes that avoid large burdens on politically influential motorist groups, at minimum cost in terms of forgone economic efficiency.

DISCLOSURE STATEMENT

The author is not aware of any affiliations, memberships, funding, or financial holdings that might be perceived as affecting the objectivity of this review.

ACKNOWLEDGMENT

I am very grateful to Todd Litman, Georgina Santos, and Kenneth Small for very helpful comments on an earlier draft.

LITERATURE CITED

Akiyama T, Mun S-I, Okushima M. 2002. Second-best congestion pricing in urban space: cordon pricing and its alternatives. *Rev. Netw. Econ.* 3:401–14

Aldy J, Krupnick AJ, Newell RG, Parry IWH, Pizer WA. 2009. *Designing climate mitigation policy.* Discuss. Pap., Resour. Future

Arnott R, Kraus M. 1998. When are anonymous congestion charges consistent with marginal cost pricing? *J. Public Econ.* 67:418–42

Arnott R, de Palma A, Lindsey R. 1991. Does providing information to drivers reduce traffic congestion? *Transp. Res. A* 25:309–18

Arnott R, de Palma A, Lindsey R. 1993. A structural model of peak-period congestion: a traffic bottleneck with elastic demand. *Am. Econ. Rev.* 83:161–79

Arnott R, de Palma A, Lindsey R. 1994. The welfare effects of congestion tolls with heterogeneous commuters. *J. Transp. Econ. Policy* 18:139–61

Arnott R, Rave T, Schöb R. 2005. *Alleviating Urban Traffic Congestion.* Cambridge, MA: MIT Press

Beckmann MJ, McGuire CB, Winsten CB. 1956. *Studies in the Economics of Transportation.* New Haven, CT: Yale Univ. Press

Braid RM. 1996. Peak-load pricing of a transportation route with an unpriced substitute. *J. Urban Econ.* 40:179–97

Brownstone D, Ghosh A, Golob TF, Kazimi C, Van Amelsfort D. 2003. Drivers' willingness-to-pay to reduce travel time: evidence from the San Diego I-15 congestion pricing pilot. *Transp. Res. A* 37:373–87

Brownstone D, Small KA. 2005. Valuing time and reliability: assessing the evidence from road demonstrations. *Transp. Res. A* 39:279–93

Bureau of Labor Statistics. 2006. *National Compensation Survey: Occupational Wages in the United States, June 2005. Bulletin 2581.* Washington, DC: US Dep. Labor

Bureau of Transportation Statistics. 2006. *National Transportation Statistics*. Washington, DC: US Dep. Transp. http://www.bts.gov/publications/national_transportation_statistics/2006/index. html

Calfee J, Winston C. 1998. The value of automobile travel time: implications for congestion policy. *J. Public Econ.* 69:83–102

Cohen Y. 1987. Commuter welfare under peak period congestion: Who gains and who loses? *Int. J. Transp. Econ.* 14:239–66

de Borger B, Proost S. 2001. *Reforming Transport Pricing in the European Union*. Northampton, MA: Edward Elgar

De Corla-Souza P. 2004. Recent U.S. experience: pilot projects. In *Road Pricing: Theory and Practice*, Vol. 9, *Research in Transportation Economics*, ed. G Santos, pp. 179–206. San Diego, CA: Elsevier

de Palma A, Marchal F. 2001. *Real-cases applications of the fully dynamic METROPOLIS tool-box: an advocacy for large-scale mesoscopic transportation systems*. Work. Pap. 2001-18, THEMA, Univ. de Cergy-Pontoise. http://www.u-cergy.fr/IMG/2001-18DePalma.pdf

Department for Transport. 2004. *Feasibility Study of Road Pricing in the UK—Report*. London, UK: Dep. Transp.

Department for Transport. 2007. *Transport Analysis Guidance: Values of Time and Operating Costs*. London, UK: TAG Unit 3.5.6. http://www.webtag.org.uk/webdocuments/3_Expert/5_Economy_ Objective/3.5.6.htm.

Downs A. 1992. *Stuck in Traffic: Coping with Peak-Hour Traffic Congestion*. Washington, DC: Brookings Inst. Press

Federal Highway Administration. 1997. *1997 Federal Highway Cost Allocation Study*. Washington, DC: Dep. Transp.

Federal Highway Administration. 2000. *Addendum to the 1997 Federal Highway Cost Allocation Study Final Report*. Washington, DC: Dep. Transp.

Federal Highway Administration. 2006. *Highway Statistics 2005*. Washington, DC: Dep. Transp.

Glazer A. 1981. Congestion tolls and consumer welfare. *Public Financ.* 36:77–83

Gómez-Ibáñez JA, Meyer JR. 1993. *Going Private: The International Experience with Transport Privatization*. Washington, DC: Brookings Inst.

Goodwin PB. 1992. A review of new demand elasticities with special reference to short- and long-run effects of price changes. *J. Transp. Econ. Policy* 26:155–69

Goodwin PB. 1996. Empirical evidence on induced traffic: a review and synthesis. *Transportation* 23:35–54

Goodwin PB, Dargay J, Hanly M. 2004. Elasticities of road traffic and fuel consumption with respect to price and income: a review. *Transp. Rev.* 24:275–92

Greenwood ID, Bennett CR. 1996. The effects of traffic congestion on fuel consumption. *Road Transp. Res.* 5:18–31

Hau T. 2005a. Economic fundamentals of road pricing: a diagrammatic analysis, part I—fundamentals. *Transportmetrica* 1:81–115

Hau T. 2005b. Economic fundamentals of road pricing: a diagrammatic analysis, part II—relation of assumptions. *Transportmetrica* 1:119–49

Homburger WS, Kell JH, Perkins DD. 1992. *Fundamentals of Traffic Engineering*, Berkeley, CA: Inst. Transp. Stud.

Houde S, Safirova EA, Harrington W. 2007. *Washington START transportation model*. Discuss. Pap. 07–43, Resourc. Future

Leape J. 2006. The London congestion charge. *J. Econ. Perspect.* 20:157–76

Lindsey R. 2006. Do economists reach a conclusion on road pricing? The intellectual history of an idea. *Econ. J. Watch* 3(2):292–379

Lindsey R. 2007. *Congestion relief: assessing the case for road tolls in Canada*. Issue 248, CD Howe Inst. Comment.

Lindsey R, Verhoef ET. 2000. Congestion modeling. In *Handbook of Transport Modeling*, ed. KJ Button, DA Hensher, pp. 353–73. Amsterdam: Pergamon

Litman T. 2006. *Smart Congestion Reductions: Reevaluating the Role of Highway Expansion for Improving Urban Transportation*. Victoria, BC: Vic. Transp. Policy Inst. http://www.vtpi.org/cong_relief.pdf

Litman T. 2007a. *Smart Transportation Investments II: Reevaluating the Role of Public Transit for Improving Urban Transportation*. Victoria, BC: Vic. Transp. Policy Inst. http://www.vtpi.org/cong_reliefII.pdf

Litman T. 2007b. *Transportation Cost and Benefit Analysis—Congestion Costs*. Victoria, BC: Vic. Transp. Policy Inst. http://www.vtpi.org

Litman T. 2008. *TDM Encyclopedia*. Victoria, BC: Vic. Transp. Policy Inst. http://www.vtpi.org/tdm/index.php

Liu LN, MacDonald JF. 1998. Efficient congestion tolls in the presence of unpriced congestion: a peak and off-peak simulation model. *J. Urban Econ.* 44:352–66

MacDonald J. 1995. Urban highway congestion: an analysis of second-best tolls. *Transportation* 22:353–69

Mackie P. 1996. Induced traffic and economic appraisal. *Transportation* 23:103–19

Mackie PJ, Wardman M, Fowkes AS, Whelan G, Nellthorp J, Bates J. 2003. *Value of Travel Time Savings in the UK: Summary Report*. Leeds, UK: Inst. Transp. Stud./Univ. Leeds

May AD, Liu R, Shepherd SP, Sumalee A. 2002. The impact of cordon design on the performance of road pricing schemes. *Transp. Policy* 9:209–20

May AD, Milne DS. 2000. Effects of alternative road pricing systems on network performance. *Transp. Res. A* 34:407–36

May AD, Shepherd S, Sumalee A. 2004. Optimal locations and charges for cordon schemes. See Santos 2004a, pp. 61–86

Miller TR, Levy DT, Spicer RS, Letina DC. 1998. Allocating the costs of motor vehicle crashes between vehicle types. *Transp. Res. Rec.* 1635:81–7

Mohring H. 1999. Congestion. In *Essays in Transportation Economics and Policy: A Handbook in Honor of John R. Meyer*, ed. JA Gómez-Ibáñez, WB Tye, C Winston, pp. 181–222. Washington, DC: Brookings Inst.

Mun S-I. 1994. Traffic jams and the congestion toll. *Transp. Res. B* 28:365–75

MVA Consultancy, ITS Univ. Leeds, TSU Univ. Oxford. 1987. *Value of Travel Time Savings*. Newbury, Berks.: Policy J.

National Research Council. 2002. *Effectiveness and Impact of Corporate Average Fuel Economy (CAFE) Standards*. Washington, DC: Natl. Acad. Press

Noland R. 2001. Relationships between highway capacity and induced vehicle travel. *Transp. Res. A* 35:47–72

National Surface Transportation Policy. 2007. *Transportation for Tomorrow: Report of the National Surface Transportation Policy and Revenue Study Commission*. Washington, DC: Natl. Surf. Transp. Policy Revenue Study Comm. http://www.transportationfortomorrow.org/final_report

Parry IWH. 2002. Comparing the efficiency of alternative policies for reducing traffic congestion. *J. Public Econ.* 85:333–62

Parry IWH. 2004. Comparing alternative policies to reduce traffic accidents. *J. Urban Econ.* 56:346–68

Parry IWH, Bento AM. 2001. Revenue recycling and the welfare effects of road pricing. *Scand. J. Econ.* 103:645–71

Parry IWH, Small KA. 2009. Should urban transit subsidies be reduced? *Am. Econ. Rev.* Forthcoming

Pickrell D, Schimek P. 1997. Trends in personal motor vehicle ownership and use: evidence from the nationwide personal transportation survey. *Proc. Nationwide Pers. Transp. Surv. Symp. Search. Solut. Policy Discuss. Ser. No. 17*, pp. 85–127. Washington, DC: US Fed. Highw. Admin.

Poterba JM. 1989. Lifetime incidence and the distributional burden of excise taxes. *Am. Econ. Rev. Pap. Proc.* 79:325–30

Pratt RH, Texas Transp. Inst., Cambr. Syst., Parsons Brinkerhoff Quade Douglas, SG Assoc., et al. 2000. *Traveler Response to Transportation System Changes: Interim Handbook. TCR Web Doc. 12.* Washington, DC: Natl. Res. Counc. Transp. Res. Board

Ramjerdi F, Minken H, Østmoe K. 2004. Norwegian urban tolls. See Santos 2004a, pp. 237–49

Safirova E, Gillingham K. 2003. *Measuring marginal congestion costs of urban transportation: Do networks matter?* Discuss. Pap. 03–56, Resourc. Future

Safirova EA, Gillingham K, Parry I, Nelson P, Harrington W, Mason D. 2004. Welfare and distributional effects of HOT lanes and other road pricing policies in metropolitan Washington, DC. See Santos 2004a, pp. 179–206

Santos G, ed. 2004a. *Road Pricing: Theory and Evidence,* Vol. 9, *Research in Transportation Economics.* San Diego, CA: Elsevier

Santos G. 2004b. Urban congestion charging: a second-best alternative. *J. Transp. Econ. Policy* 38:345–69

Santos G. 2005. Urban congestion charging: a comparison between London and Singapore. *Transp. Rev.* 25:511–34

Santos G. 2008. The London congestion charging scheme. In *Brookings Wharton Papers on Urban Affairs: 2008,* ed. G Burtless, J Rothenberg Pack, pp. 177–234. Washington, DC: Brookings Inst.

Santos G, Bhakar J. 2006. The impact of the London congestion charging scheme on the generalised cost of car commuters to the city of London. *Transp. Policy* 13:22–33

Santos G, Fraser G. 2006. Road pricing: lessons from London. *Econ. Policy* 21:264–310

Santos G, Newbery D. 2002. *Estimating urban congestion charges.* Discuss. Pap. 3176, CEPR

Schrank D, Lomax T. 2007. *The 2007 Urban Mobility Report.* College Station, TX: Texas Transp. Inst./Texas A&M Univ.

Shoup DC. 2005. *The High Cost of Free Parking.* Chicago, IL: Am. Plan. Assoc. Plan. Press

Small KA. 1983. The incidence of congestion tolls on urban highways. *J. Urban Econ.* 13:90–111

Small KA. 1992. Using the revenues from congestion pricing. *Transportation* 19:359–81

Small KA, Chu X. 2003. Hypercongestion. *J. Transp. Econ. Policy* 37:319–52

Small KA, Gómez-Ibáñez JA. 1998. Road pricing for congestion management: the transition from theory to policy. In *Road Pricing, Traffic Congestion and the Environment: Issue of Efficiency and Social Feasibility,* ed. KJ Button, ET Verhoef, pp. 213–46. Cheltenham, UK: Edward Elgar

Small KA, Gómez-Ibáñez JA. 1999. Urban transportation. In *Handbook of Regional and Urban Economics,* Vol. 3, ed. P Cheshire, ES Mills, pp. 1937–99. Amsterdam: North-Holland

Small KA, Verhoef E. 2007. *The Economics of Urban Transportation.* New York: Routledge

Small KA, Yan J. 2001. The value of "value pricing" roads: second-best pricing and product differentiation. *J. Urban Econ.* 49:310–36

Standing Advisory Committee on Trunk Road Assessment. 1994. *Trunk Roads and the Generation of Traffic. Department of Transport.* London: HMSO

Steer Davies Gleave. 2004. The effect of road congestion on rail demand. *Rep. Passeng. Demand Forecast. Counc.,* Assoc. Train Oper. Co., London, UK

Transport for London. 2004. *Congestion Charging Impacts Monitoring: Second Annual Report.* London, UK: Transp. Lond.

Transport for London. 2008. *Central London Congestion Charging: Impacts Monitoring. Sixth Annual Report.* London, UK: Transp. Lond. ww.tfl.gov.uk/roadusers/congestioncharging/6722.aspx

Transportation Research Board. 2006. *The Fuel Tax and Alternatives for Transportation Funding.* Washington, DC: Natl. Res. Counc.

Tretvick T. 2003. Urban road pricing in Norway: public acceptability and travel behaviour. In *Acceptability of Transport Pricing Strategies,* ed. J Schade, B Schlag, pp. 77–92. London, UK: Pergamon

US Department of Transportation. 1997. *The Value of Travel Time: Departmental Guidance for Conducting Economic Evaluations.* Washington, DC: Dep. Transp.

US Department of Transportation. 2006. *National Strategy to Reduce Congestion on America's Transportation Network.* Washington, DC: Dep. Transp.

US Department of Transportation. 2008. *Transportation Vision for 2030: Ensuring Personal Freedom and Economic Vitality for a Nation on the Move*. Washington, DC: Dep. Transp. Res. Innovative Technol. Admin.

Verhoef ET. 2002. Second-best congestion charging in general networks. Heuristic algorithms of finding second-best optimal toll levels and toll point. *Transp. Res. B* 36:707–29

Verhoef ET, Nijkamp P, Rietveld P. 1996. Second-best congestion pricing: the case of an untolled alternative. *J. Urban Econ.* 40:279–302

Verhoef ET, Small KA. 2004. Product differentiation on roads: constrained congestion pricing with heterogeneous users. *J. Transp. Econ. Policy* 38:127–56

Vickrey W. 1963. Pricing in urban and suburban transport. *Am. Econ. Rev.* 53:452–65

Vickrey W. 1969. Congestion theory and transport investment. *Am. Econ. Rev. Pap. Proc.* 59:251–61

Walters A. 1961. The theory and measurement of private and social costs of highway congestion. *Econometrica* 29:676–97

Wardman M. 2001. A review of British evidence on time and service quality valuations. *Transp. Res. E* 37:107–28

Waters WGII. 1996. Values of time savings in road transport project evaluation. In *World Transport Research: Proceedings of 7th World Conference on Transport Research*, Vol. 3., ed. D Hensher, J King, T Oum, pp. 213–33. Oxford, UK: Pergamon

Yang H, Meng Q, Lee D-H. 2004. Trial-and-error implementation of marginal-cost pricing on networks in the absence of demand functions. *Transp. Res. B* 38:477–93

The Economics of Endangered Species

Robert Innes[2] and George Frisvold[1]

[1]Department of Agricultural and Resource Economics, University of Arizona, Tucson, Arizona 85721; email: frisvold@ag.arizona.edu

[2]School of Social Sciences, Humanities and Arts, University of California, Merced, California 95344; email: rinnes@ucmerced.edu

Annu. Rev. Resour. Econ. 2009. 1:485–512

First published online as a Review in Advance on July 9, 2009

The *Annual Review of Resource Economics* is online at resource.annualreviews.org

This article's doi:
10.1146/annurev.resource.050708.144207

Key Words

takings, preemption, regulation, deforestation, biodiversity, land use

Abstract

Because habitat conversion is the greatest threat to species, this article focuses on economic incentives for private land users to protect habitat. Habitat protection policies that fail to account for private incentives often have unintended negative consequences. Private incentives for habitat protection depend on many factors: whether landowners are compensated for the costs of habitat protection, the design of compensation mechanisms, underlying property rights and security of tenure, the structure of conservation contracts, and whether markets can be created that internalize external benefits of habitat protection. In developing countries, agricultural price, credit, tax, and land tenure policies have important effects on the demand for habitat conversion. Private landowners often can provide crucial information about costs of habitat protection and species or habitat values on their property. Policies that encourage self-reporting of this information can greatly improve the cost effectiveness of policies to identify and acquire sites for species protection.

1. INTRODUCTION

The protection of endangered species is of paramount public interest for a variety of reasons. A given species may be of value to food chains that support human food supplies. A species may be integral to ecological systems. Such systems, and biodiversity in general, are invaluable both intrinsically and to human life, with intricate webs of linkages to food, health, recreation, and welfare, both physical and spiritual. Few of these values are priced in markets. Many take the form of existence (nonuse) values, the measurement of which occupies a vast literature in economics (Smith 1996). Because the value of endangered species to society is not captured by private actors who make decisions that crucially affect their fate (and that of natural environments in general), there are externalities present that imply a public interest in molding private incentives to account for the external effects.

The economic literature on externalities associated with endangered species has focused on two main problems (Swanson 1994). The first is overharvesting. When species are found in an open access regime, extraction rates will be higher than is economically efficient and species may be harvested to extinction. Species have value, but ill-defined property rights, and short-run private incentives combine to threaten them. Overharvesting and its policy remedies have been studied extensively in fisheries economics (dating back to Gordon 1954 and including important early work by Clark 1973, 1976; Spence 1975; Clark & Munro 1978; Clark et al. 1979; Berck 1979). Economists have also devoted attention to overharvesting of terrestrial species such as big-game animals (e.g., Barbier et al. 1990). A related literature studies the effects of trade bans on poaching of endangered species (Barbier 2000; Barnes 1996; Bulte et al. 2003; Bulte & van Kooten 1996, 1999; Burton 1999; Fischer 2004; Kremer & Morcom 2000, 2003; Missios 2004).

The other major threat to species—and the focus of this article—is habitat conversion. There is general consensus that habitat conversion is the main source of species loss globally (Raven 1980, Wilson 1988, McNeely et al. 1990, Watson et al. 1995) and that habitat conservation on private lands is at the heart of species preservation in the United States and other advanced economies (Innes et al. 1998). The problem of habitat conversion is particularly acute in tropical forests that are home to a significant share of the world's species and are undergoing rapid conversion. Habitat conversion is fundamentally a land-use problem. Species are threatened because their habitats have a higher private value in agriculture, housing, or some other economic use.

In this article, we focus on two related aspects of habitat conservation: incentives for species preservation on defined private lands (arguably the case most relevant for advanced economies) and incentives for habitat conversion by farmers on the agricultural frontier (arguably the case most relevant to developing countries). We caution the reader at the outset that our focus generally sidesteps important literatures on benefits derived from ecosystem services, biodiversity, and different/marginal species (see Weitzman 1998, in particular, and work on the value of marginal species by Simpson et al. 1996, Rausser & Small 2000, Costello & Ward 2006). We also generally abstract from the political economy of endangered species management—including work on the allocation of budget resources to predominantly "cute" species (Metrick & Weitzman 1996, Ando 1999)—and the role of private politics and ecolabeling in the promotion of species conservation, such as in the dolphin-safe tuna campaign (Baron 2006, Innes 2006, Kirchhoff 2000). Whereas these literatures raise central questions on which species should be protected, and to what extent, we focus primarily on the question of how to protect, given an underpinning premise that species' habitat can have significant external value.

2. HABITAT PROTECTION INCENTIVES ON PRIVATE LANDS

At the forefront of the debate on endangered species policy in the United States is the conservation of species and habitat on private land. Roughly 90% of plant and animal species listed as endangered or threatened are on private property (Brown & Shogren 1998), and over half of listed species have 80% or more of their habitat on private land (U.S. Fish and Wildlife Service 1997). Private costs of habitat protections are substantial. In the Pacific Northwest, for example, salmon and steelhead protections limit development and water use, and habitat of the northern spotted owl limits timber harvesting.

Section 9 of the U.S. Endangered Species Act governs species on private lands, proscribing the "taking" of any endangered animal. A taking has been interpreted to include damage to essential habitat (an interpretation upheld by the U.S. Supreme Court in *Babbitt v. Sweet Home Chapter of Communities for a Great Oregon*, 1995). No compensation is required when private land use is restricted to protect habitat, and horror stories abound about government excesses in implementation of Section 9 (Lambert & Smith 1994, Stroup 1995).

From an economic point of view, the important questions raised, in the context of habitat protection policy, concern the incentives that landowners have to manage their property and incentives that the government has to regulate property use in order to mitigate the negative externalities associated with habitat degradation. Landowners make a variety of decisions that affect social welfare, including the investments in private uses for their land, conservation choices that can affect potential habitat values, and provision of information about species or habitat values on their property that can be invaluable in determining its best use. Government regulators make decisions about which properties to regulate for habitat protection and what conservation measures they should require on regulated lands. Private incentives are driven by the provision or absence of compensation, the design of compensation, the design of rights (such as the ability to exclude biological surveyors from one's land and the burden of proof for enforcement of regulation), and the structure of potential conservation contracts that may be offered to landowners. Beyond government's presumed interest in promoting social welfare by mitigating externalities, its incentives can be driven by statutory or constitutional requirements for compensation (or the lack of such requirements), costs of compensation, and the design of rights. In what follows, we survey the economics literature on these incentive issues and implications for the design of government policy.

The starting point is the literature on government "takings" of private property. The takings rubric derives from the Fifth Amendment to the U.S. Constitution, which prohibits a government taking of private property without just compensation. When prohibiting the taking of a species, is the government taking private property? Case law appears clear that regulation of species does not qualify as a property taking that compels compensation (Meltz 1994). However, even if not obligatory, compensation may nonetheless be desirable.

Economists' first reaction to the compensation issue is often an appeal to the logic of Coase (1960). Property rights can define whether the landowner must pay the government in order to avoid a taking, or conversely, the government must pay the landowner when it takes the property. Either way, the two parties will bargain with one another to an efficient outcome, so that the question of who compensates whom is only a matter of distribution—who gets what, but not how much economic surplus is obtained overall.

Problems of timing and observability confound this logic. Landowners make decisions before negotiations take place because, for example, potential habitat values are not known at the time of private investment decisions. Alternately, conservation decisions may be unobservable and, hence, not something that can be stipulated in a bargain.

Also confounding Coasian logic are problems of entry and exit that are well known in the law and economics (Shavell 1980) as well as the environmental economics (Collinge & Oates 1982) fields. Bargaining cannot take place with those who have not yet entered an activity or land use; as a result, anticipated rents derived from a given property rights regime create entry incentives that cannot be accounted for in the bargaining process. That is, property rights matter for efficiency. For example, suppose that private investments are subject to the protections of nuisance law, so that others who harm the private activity must pay for the harm done, but that private damages to public resources (such as wildlife) are not subject to nuisance law. Then, private activities that harm a public resource are not taxed for the harm, and the public must instead compensate the private agents not to harm the resource. For a given set of activities (and resources), the logic of Coase implies that efficient nuisance-avoidance outcomes will be negotiated. However, investment decisions—that is, investments in private activities and public resources—are not the subject of bargaining, and they are distorted by the asymmetric property rules: Public resources will be undersupplied and private ones will be oversupplied. [For recent work on "coming to the nuisance" and effects of property rules on investment and location decisions, see Pitchford & Snyder (2003) and Innes (2009).]

2.1. Takings

The starting point in the takings literature is Blume et al. (1984), who consider a two-date single parcel model. At time 1, the landowner makes an investment choice I that determines the land's private use value at time 2, $b(I)$. At time 2, the government observes a potential public use of the land—habitat for an endangered species, for example—that is incompatible with the private use. This public-use value, s, is assumed to be either high (with probability a) or low [with probability $(1 - a)$]. In this setting, the government either takes the land completely, which renders the private investment worthless, or leaves the land completely in private hands. When s is high [higher than $b(I)$], the government efficiently takes the land. Hence, the societal return on private investment is $b(I)$ with probability $(1 - a)$ and zero with probability a. As this is precisely the return earned by landowners when they are paid zero compensation for a taking, efficient investment choices are achieved with compensation that is either zero or lump sum (invariant to I). Conversely, compensation tied to the private value $b(I)$ distorts investment choices; the landowner then fails to consider the full societal loss of the investment value in the event of a taking and overinvests.

This stark benchmark motivates substantial subsequent research to identify motives for positive compensation. First is the presence of landowner risk aversion. Absent compensation, the return distribution to the land investment I is very risky: either $b(I)$ with some probability or zero with the complementary probability (when a taking occurs). Compensation reduces the riskiness of this distribution, essentially providing free insurance to the landowner. Blume & Rubinfeld (1984) argue, therefore, that when landowners are risk averse, the government is risk neutral, and there is no insurance market for takings risks, then compensation improves risk sharing and can therefore enhance efficiency. Central to this argument is the absence of an insurance market. There are two possible reasons for the failure of private insurance:

1. Adverse selection: Landowners may have better information about the likelihood of a taking, giving rise to a "market for lemons" in insurance (Akerlof 1970).
2. Political economy: Landowners may be able to lobby successfully for compensation in the event of a taking; if so, one equilibrium outcome is for no landowner to buy (expensive) insurance, and all to successfully lobby the government for compensation.

Farber (1992) and Kaplow (1986) argue that both possible explanations for insurance market failure are not compelling; insurance companies will have information at least as good as landowners will and are likely to have more political power than landowners.

2.2. Preemption

Even absent risk aversion, landowners make decisions that affect the costs of taking land for habitat, the benefits, or both. They can raise costs by preemptively developing their land and lower benefits by altering their management practices to reduce conservation. Theoretical models for regulatory preemption, drawing upon early arguments by Stroup (1997), are developed in Innes (1997, 2000b). Innes (1997) considers a two-period multi-parcel model of land development in which, during the first period (*ex ante*), some land (but not all) is optimally developed and, during the second period (*ex post*), the government observes the value of taking land for a public use (such as habitat or dune restoration, as in the case of *Lucas v. South Carolina*, 1992) and decides how much land to take for this purpose. *Ex post*, it is efficient for the government to take the cheapest (undeveloped) land first. Hence, if a taking (of undeveloped land) is uncompensated, landowners have a powerful incentive to preemptively develop their land *ex ante*, thereby significantly reducing their risk of expropriation. Compensation cures this inefficient incentive for excessive development.

Alternately, preemption may take the form of different management practices, such as harvesting timber in shorter rotations to avoid habitat creation or even overt efforts to "shoot, shovel, and shut up." The case of Benjamin Cone is illustrative. To protect habitat of the red-cockaded woodpecker, a bird that makes its home in old-growth pine forests in the southeastern United States, Cone was prohibited from logging 1560 acres of his land in Greensboro, North Carolina, in the early 1990s. His reaction (Sugg 1993) was, "I cannot afford to let those woodpeckers take over the rest of my property. I'm going to a 40-year rotation instead of a 75–80-year rotation."

Landowners can thus affect the probability distribution of the public use value (s) with their choice of conservation effort (Innes 2000a). Implicitly, these effects may include irreversibilities, for example, the negation of any positive habitat value when private-use investment is sufficiently large. Such effects, as well as information benefits of delayed development in more general dynamic frameworks, yield option values of conservation that motivate less development (Arrow & Fisher 1974). One way to elicit efficient choices of conservation in these cases is to pay Pigovian compensation, namely, pay the landowner the actual public value s whenever the land is taken (Hermalin 1995). The landowner then faces the complete societal distribution of returns: the private value (b) when it is less than the public-use value (b > s) and the public-use value otherwise (s > b).

However, Pigovian compensation is extraordinarily costly to the government. From an efficiency perspective, this cost is important because, in practice, the government must raise tax revenue to meet the cost and taxes are almost always distortionary. Income taxes distort labor/leisure choices, corporate profit taxes distort investment decisions, sales taxes distort choices between taxed and untaxed goods, and so on. Fullerton (1991) estimates that deadweight costs of taxes are between 7 and 25 cents on the dollar. [Measurement of this excess burden is complex, linked to provision of environmental goods, and the subject of a growing literature; for recent treatments, see Carbone & Smith (2008) and Bovenberg & Goulder (1996).]

With costs of compensation, the government will want to elicit efficient conservation choices at minimum possible cost to the Treasury. This can be done with negligence compensation of the type proposed first by Miceli & Segerson (1994). Specifically, let compensation be a fixed positive payment p if and only if the landowner exercises at least a given amount of conservation effort c; otherwise, compensation is zero. Moreover, let the payment p be just sufficient so that, by exercising effort c and receiving payment p in the event of a taking, landowners obtain the same expected payoff as when they face a pure no-compensation rule. Then, landowners are willing to exert the requisite effort c, and the government's cost of eliciting that effort (p) is at a minimum. A final twist is that, because the required payment (p) falls when the target level of conservation c is lowered, it is efficient to set c lower than would be efficient absent any costs of compensation.

Economists have recently uncovered empirical evidence of both forms of regulatory preemption. Margolis et al. (2008) showed that landowners preemptively developed their property because they anticipated their property would be designated as critical habitat for the cactus ferruginous pygmy owl near Tucson, Arizona. Similarly, Zhang (2004) and Lueck & Michael (2003) showed that prospects for habitation by the endangered red cockaded woodpecker accelerated timber harvesting in the southeastern United States.

2.3. Information

2.3.1. Information acquisition.
The potential value of a given property as species habitat is often not known until a biological survey has been conducted. This introduces another margin of efficiency: costly information acquisition. Polasky & Doremus (1998) modeled this decision and its implications for the optimal design of (a) compensation (Must the landowner pay the government to avoid a taking or vice versa?) and (b) the burden of proof (Must the landowner prove that a taking is inefficient in order to avoid the taking, or must the government prove that the taking is efficient?).

Let s be the true value of the public use, known only if a survey is conducted; absent a survey, s has the expected value $E(s)$. Now consider when a taking is not efficient absent information, $E(s) < b$. Then the societal benefit of a survey is any positive net gain from a taking that would not otherwise occur, $s - b > 0$. Moreover, the government obtains these benefits, pays the survey costs, and thus surveys efficiently, when it has both the burden of proof and the compensation obligation. These rules have the added advantage of eliciting landowner cooperation in conducting the survey, which can either lower survey costs or, in some cases, be necessary for performing the survey at all.

Conversely, however, when $E(s) > b$, then the net societal benefit of a survey is any net positive gain from avoiding a taking that would otherwise occur, $b - s > 0$. Here, landowners obtain these benefits, pay survey costs, and survey efficiently, when they have both burden of proof and the compensation obligation.

In Polasky & Doremus (1998), the optimal location of the burden thus depends crucially on the *ceteris paribus*, whether a taking would otherwise occur (implying that the government should have the property right) or would otherwise not occur (implying that the landowner should have the property right).

2.3.2. Information self-reporting. Some information about endangered species is often available to landowners even absent costly survey efforts; they may observe the presence of an endangered creature, for example. When landowners know that their property has become habitat, they have at least three options: (a) "shoot, shovel and shut up" (SSS), effectively destroying the habitat; (b) ignoring the discovery and proceeding (unmaliciously) as they would have done otherwise, which may or may not destroy habitat; or (c) reporting the discovery to the Fish and Wildlife Service and working with them to protect the habitat. Assuming species protection is a desired social objective—in the sense that the value of habitat is greater than the value of a competing use—these choices confront regulators with an enforcement problem.

Related enforcement problems have been studied in the self-reporting literature, beginning with Kaplow & Shavell (1994) and Malik (1993). This literature identifies a number of advantages of regulatory strategies that elicit self-reporting from regulated entities (for a survey, see Innes 2001a). Kaplow & Shavell (1994) and Malik (1993) showed that self-reporting enables regulators to achieve a given probability of government monitoring/ inspection (for regulatory violations) at lower cost; the reason is that self-reporters do not need to be monitored. Kaplow & Shavell (1994) further showed that self-reporting economizes on the use of imprisonment, a very costly sanction, because self-reporters can be confronted with an equivalent average sanction that is purely monetary. Innes (1999) showed that self-reporting strategies promote socially advantageous post-violation remediation; in the present context, self-reporting promotes habitat preservation. Innes (2000b) argued that, when violators have heterogeneous probabilities of apprehension, self-reporting can be used to tie sanctions more closely to harm caused (species benefits in the present context); this encourages more efficient *ex ante* measures for harm avoidance. Finally, Innes (2001b) showed that self-reporting can be used to avoid costly avoidance efforts—efforts to avoid apprehension, such as an SSS strategy.

To illustrate the application of some of these arguments to endangered species, suppose the following:

1. Species preservation requires the protection of government regulators and yields a benefit V.
2. A competing private use yields benefit D.
3. An SSS strategy destroys species habitat at zero direct cost to the landowner.
4. The property is species habitat with probability $p\varepsilon(0,1)$, and the landowner knows when the property is habitat.
5. The government's cost of an audit is m, and it audits a property with endogenous probability p.
6. The probabilities that an audit discovers SSS and present species are $s < 1$ and $q \geq s$, respectively;

7. The government can levy fines for SSS or an unreported species, respectively, of f_s and f_N, both limited by a maximum sanction f^*, and it can compensate self-reporters C.
8. The social cost of funds is $\lambda \varepsilon [0,1)$.
9. Finally, benefits of habitat exceed costs, $V > (1+\lambda)D$.

Assume a species has been discovered by the landowner. Under an SSS strategy, the landowner obtains the payoff $B_{ss} = D - \rho s f_s$. Under a nonreporting strategy, he obtains the payoff $B_{NR} = D(1-\rho q) - \rho q f_N$. And under a self-reporting strategy, he obtains $B_{SR} = C$. Subject to $f_s \leq f^*$, an enforcement regime elicits self-reporting at minimum cost C by satisfying

$$B_{SR} = B_{NR} = B_{ss} \leftrightarrow f_s = f^*, f_N = (sf/q) - D \equiv f, C = D(1 - \rho q) - \rho q f. \qquad (1)$$

The government's cost of monitoring per landowner is $\rho(1-p)m$ under self-reporting, namely, the cost of monitoring nonreporting landowners with probability ρ. With non-reporting, this cost is ρm. Welfare under a self-reporting policy that satisfies Equation 1 is thus

$$W_{SR} = p\{V - \lambda C\} - \rho(1-p)m + (1-p)D = p\{V - \lambda D + \lambda \rho q(D+f)\} - \rho(1-p)m + (1-p)D, \qquad (2)$$

namely, the benefit of species protection (V) less social costs of compensation (λC) when a species arrives on the property (probability p), less costs of monitoring, plus benefits of development when a species does not arrive on the property [probability $(1-p)$]. Similarly, under a nonreporting policy (that satisfies $B_{NR} = B_{ss}$ in Equation 1 but sets $C < B_{NR}$),

$$W_{NR} = p\{D(1 - \rho q) + \rho q(V + \lambda f)\} - \rho m + (1 - p)D. \qquad (3)$$

And under an SSS policy (where $B_{NR} \leq B_{ss}$),

$$W_{ss} = D + \lambda \rho s f_s - \rho m. \qquad (4)$$

Because the SSS policy is socially destructive, we have (for any given ρ)

$$W_{NR} - W_{ss} = p\rho\{q(V - D) + \lambda(qf - sf_s)\} \geq p\rho q(V - (1+\lambda)D) > 0, \qquad (5)$$

where the inequality follows from the definition of f and $f_s \leq f^*$. Because self-reporting yields both enforcement economies (the Kaplow-Shavell-Malik effect) and certainty in species preservation [the Innes (1999) effect], we also have (for given ρ):

$$W_{SR} - W_{NR} = p(1 - \rho q)(V - (1 + \lambda)D) + \rho p m > 0.$$

In sum, a policy that elicits self-reporting of species at minimum cost—the policy defined in Equation 1—is optimal.[1]

2.4. Voluntary Conservation Agreements

The compensation/takings literature is based on two key premises: (a) Ex ante (at time 1), landowners make a noncontractible decision that affects the ex post (future) distribution of returns to land in private and public uses, and (b) ex post (time 2), the government

---

[1]Linearity of W_{SR} in ρ implies a corner solution for the monitoring rate. However, if costs per audit exhibit diminishing returns in ρ ($m = m(\rho)$, where $m' > 0$), then there can be an interior solution.

makes a 0-1 takings decision, and landowner compensation may be paid. Recent work on voluntary conservation agreements (VCAs) instead assumes that *ex ante* conservation decisions are contractible and regulated with some probability.

Segerson & Miceli (1998) provided the starting point for this new literature. In a single period model, a voluntary landowner conservation choice, c_{v1}, costs $a_v c_{v1}$, and a mandated conservation level, c_{m1}, costs $a_m c_{m1}$, where $a_v \leq a_m$ (there are nonnegative costs of enforcing mandates). Benefits of conservation (gross of costs) are $B_1(c)$. Absent a VCA, regulation occurs with probability p. When regulation occurs, the government maximizes social welfare, $c_m^* = \text{argmax } B_1(c) - a_m c$. A VCA can be signed *ex ante*, before it is known whether regulation would otherwise occur; when signed, the VCA displaces any regulation and, in its simplest form, stipulates a conservation level c_{v1} and no compensation or cost sharing.

In this setting, regulation suffers from two inefficiencies: (*a*) Costs of conservation can be higher than with regulation, $a_v < a_m$, and (*b*) regulation can occur with probability less than 1. If neither of these premises holds, so that $a_v/a_m = p = 1$, then regulation is efficient and there is no motive for a VCA. However, if $p < 1$ and/or $a_v < a_m$, then, as Segerson & Miceli (1998) show, a simple (no compensation) VCA will be signed and will enhance efficiency to an extent that generally rises with the relative bargaining power of the regulator. Although proof of this result is somewhat subtle, the intuition is that there are efficiency benefits of locking in a certain (nonstochastic) conservation level—versus the lottery $(0, c_m^*)$—that enable mutual gains from the VCA. Allowing for compensation/cost-sharing inducements for landowners to sign VCAs, even with a positive social cost of funds, can only increase the scope for a VCA to enhance efficiency.

Langpap & Wu (2004) extended this analysis in some important directions. First, they considered a two-period model with second-period uncertainty about benefits of conservation, $B_2(c_2, w)$, where w is random. Second, they considered irreversibilities in conservation, which they modeled with the constraint $c_2 \leq c_1$. Third, they considered a "no-surprise" clause of a VCA, which guarantees landowners that they will be required to meet a fixed (contractually stipulated) time-2 conservation target, c_{v2}, and no more (or less). Conservation irreversibilities give rise to added costs of regulatory mandates because regulators are assumed to be myopic, ignoring the option value of a higher c_1 in permitting higher levels of c_2. No-surprise clauses add a cost to VCAs because they deny regulators the flexibility to tailor *ex post* (time-2) conservation requirements to *ex post* circumstances (the realization of w); however, they also add the benefit of voluntary (versus mandatory) conservation in time 2, which is advantageous when costs of voluntary conservation are lower ($a_v < a_m$). Absent irreversibility, and with a no-surprises clause, benefits of a VCA (due to $p < 1$ and $a_v < a_m$) must offset their costs in lost time-2 conservation flexibility in order for a VCA to enhance efficiency (and thus be signed).

Because VCAs are not always advantageous, Langpap & Wu (2004) can characterize when they are more likely to arise, implications that Langpap's (2006) empirical work broadly supports. In particular, a VCA is more likely to arise when the probability of regulation is lower (although this also induces a lower level of conservation), when the cost advantage of voluntary (versus mandatory) conservation is larger, and when a no-surprises clause is present. The latter conclusion is unexpected given the assumed cost of no surprises in reduced (time-2) conservation flexibility; it is driven by an assumed form of surprises in Langpap & Wu (2004) that is particularly inefficient.

Two limitations of the analysis by Langpap & Wu (2004) are apparent. First, as Innes et al. (1998) observe, a no-surprises clause effectively requires that the government compensate for departures from the contractual conservation level. Admitting compensation vitiates the cost of a VCA in lost conservation flexibility without sacrificing cost economies of voluntary (versus mandatory) conservation. Second, however, compensation (redistribution from taxed agents to compensated agents) has social costs that need to be taken into account.

Absent social costs of compensation, a VCA with a no-surprises clause is always optimal. A no-surprises clause compels compensation for an *ex post* departure from a prespecified conservation target. (Note that the compensation may be a tax if the *ex post* c_2 is less than the agreed target.) The compensation induces voluntary (versus mandatory) time-2 conservation, with attendant cost savings ($a_v < a_m$). Because the compensation is free, the government can achieve first-best conservation levels using the VCA:

$$c_1^*, \{c_2^*(w)\} = \mathrm{argmax}\, \{(B_1(c_1) - a_v c_1) + \int_w (B_2(c_2, w) - a_v c_2)g(w)dw\}.$$

Although the optimization here ignores irreversibilities, it need not do so; however, the government must, of course, be forward-looking (not myopic) when designing the VCA in order to account for the positive option value of higher time-1 conservation (Arrow & Fisher 1974). With $p < 1$ and $a_v < a_m$, pure (mandatory) regulation cannot achieve this optimum, even when allowing (plausibly) for nonmyopic government decisions.

As the literature on VCAs now stands, the broad conclusions are that VCAs can enhance efficiency; that no-surprise clauses, with compensation for *ex post* departures from preagreed conservation levels, are advantageous; and that the background threat of regulation enhances the ability of a VCA to achieve desired conservation at minimal cost to the government Treasury. Further work is needed to study the optimal design and effects of VCAs when there are positive social costs of compensation (due to deadweight costs of taxation), a nonbenevolent regulator, and potential asymmetric information.

Allowing for a nonbenevolent regulator adds an important dimension to the problem. Amacher & Malik (1996, 1998) studied bargaining between a regulator and a polluter over pollution regulation, where the regulator's objective function is a potential object of supergovernmental choice. An overarching conclusion from this work is that efficiency can be enhanced by endowing the regulator with a proenvironment objective function. In the present context, nonbenevolent (proconservation) regulator preferences affect not only the background threat of regulation—increasing a landowner's incentive to sign a given VCA—but also the structure of bargaining over the design of a VCA. Effects and efficiency properties of nonbenevolent preferences are likely to hinge on the extent of regulator bargaining power and the social cost of funds. For example, if regulators have all the bargaining power (because they are able to make take-it-or-leave-it VCA offers) and the social cost of funds is low, then proenvironment regulator preferences are likely to tilt outcomes too far in favor of species and against landowners.

Asymmetric information becomes important in designing VCAs when there is a positive social cost of funds. Smith & Shogren (2002) studied a specific problem of VCA design under asymmetric information, with the government offering VCA menus that have two parts: a landowner's acreage contribution to habitat (a_i) and an associated government payment (T_i). Landowners are of two types: developers, who have a high opportunity cost of habitat acreage, and preservers, who have a low opportunity cost (because they place a higher private value on preserved habitat). Landowners know their own type, but the government does not.

While Smith & Shogren (2002) studied a version of this problem with economies of agglomeration across landowners, let us consider a simplified environment [patterned after Lewis (1996) and others] in which the government obtains benefits of any given landowner's acreage contribution $B(a)$, but faces two constraints: (*a*) the landowner must be willing to contribute the acreage in return for the corresponding compensation (the participation constraint) and (*b*) among the two (developer and preserver) contracts offered by the government, each landowner type must prefer his/her own contract (incentive compatibility). A problem can arise because, absent information constraints, it is optimal for the developer to be offered a contract with a lower acreage contribution (because his costs of acreage are higher) and a higher payment per acre (in order to elicit participation). This is a problem because the preserver often prefers the developer's small habitat/high payment contract to his own. If the social cost of government funds is zero, this problem can be corrected by simply offering the preserver a higher payment (so that he is "more than willing" to participate). However, because government funds are costly, a second-best solution involves lowering both the developer's acreage contribution and his payment level so as to preserve his participation incentive. Because the acreage reduction is more beneficial to the developer than to the preserver, this change reduces the preserver payment needed for him to prefer his contract, and this saves government funds. In sum, asymmetric information motivates a lower conservation level/acreage contribution for landowners that have a high cost of conservation.

2.5. Endangered Species Incentives on Private Lands

The broad message from this literature is that society's interest in habitat preservation is well served by government strategies to provide landowners with positive conservation incentives, backed by the threat of sanctions for bad behavior. Positive incentives can include carefully designed compensation programs for habitat conservation and conservation agreements with no-surprise clauses. Also important are incentives for self-reporting of species on private lands, which require rewards for self-reports rather than the economic penalties that characterize present endangered species laws in the United States.

Omitted from this discussion are the constitutional issues raised by governmental (versus landowner) incentives. When the government is not benevolent (the case that motivates the Fifth Amendment restrictions in the United States), what constitutional/ supergovernmental restrictions are needed to promote efficient regulatory conduct? We have largely sidestepped this issue here because, at least in the United States, endangered species protections are generally outside the scope of the Constitution. However, we refer the reader to Fischel & Shapiro (1989), Innes (1997), and, more recently, Brennan & Boyd (2006) for subtleties that arise in the design of supergovernmental restraints, including potential economic costs of pure compensation requirements (Innes 1997) and the need to tailor restraints to the nature of government biases (Brennan & Boyd 2006).

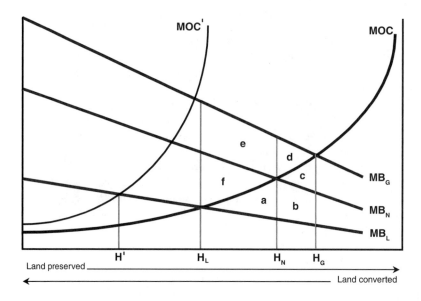

Land preserved
Land converted

Figure 1

The local, national, and global incentives for habitat conversion and preservation. From left to right, the figure shows the marginal benefits of preserving more land, such as a tropical forest. MB_G, MB_N, and MB_L are the marginal benefits of preserving the habitat for the world, for the country where the habitat is located, and for local residents, respectively; H_G, H_N, and H_L represent the hectares of habitat the global community, the country where the habitat is located, and local inhabitants, respectively, would choose to preserve. MOC is the marginal cost to the local residents of preservation. From right to left, the MOC curve maps out land conversion's marginal benefits to local inhabitants.

3. HABITAT CONVERSION INCENTIVES ON THE AGRICULTURAL FRONTIER

Now consider incentives for habitat protection in developing countries. **Figure 1** illustrates the local, national, and global incentives for habitat conversion or preservation.[2] The marginal benefit curve for local residents is MB_L. Nearby forestland can provide fuel, forage, plants and animals for food, traditional medicines, or other goods of local value. Although preserving the land in forests provides a flow of benefits, there is a marginal cost to the local residents of preservation, MOC. This is the marginal opportunity cost of not converting the land to pasture or crop production. Given the marginal benefits of land conversion, local inhabitants would choose to preserve land up to H_L.

Figure 1 reflects a basic incentive problem. The marginal benefits to the country where the habitat is located are MB_N. The unconverted forestland can provide a number of national public goods to the country—such as watersheds, erosion control, or ecotourism revenues—not captured directly by local inhabitants. The government would desire to preserve $H_N > H_L$, but moving there would reduce local welfare by the area a. Nationally, the willingness to pay for such a move would be $a + f$. If transactions costs were not too large, the government could improve national welfare by compensating local residents and shifting toward H_N.

---

[2]This graphical approach could easily apply to freshwater habitats where diversions of instream flows for agriculture or hydropower could threaten aquatic species.

Externalities also exist at the international level. Global benefits from preservation would include the expected value of crop germplasm or medicinal plants. Other benefits would be existence values placed on forests or rare species (Brown 1987) or rainforests as carbon sinks to limit global warming (Sandler 1993). Global benefits would also incorporate some measure of option value (Arrow & Fisher 1974, Fisher & Hanemann 1990). Extinction of a species today irreversibly precludes its use at some future date.

The global marginal benefits of preserving the habitat are MB_G, where global benefits are the sum of national and international preservation benefits. The global optimum level of preservation, H_G, is greater than what the national government would be willing to supply. Global gains from increasing preservation from H_L to H_G equal area $a + b + c + d + e + f$, yet this would come at a cost of $a + b + c$ to local inhabitants.

The marginal opportunity cost of habitat preservation, MOC, also represents the demand for habitat conversion. Not surprisingly, factors that affect the demand for agricultural land are crucial to explaining tropical deforestation and habitat loss. Opportunity costs are not static. Rather, they can shift to the left (to MOC') in response to market, technological, demographic, or policy changes that increase the demand for agricultural land on the frontier. For example, MOC' might represent the marginal opportunity cost of preservation if the government provides subsidies for land clearing, whereas MOC represents costs without subsidies.

Policies to protect habitat can be examined in terms of movements along or shifts in the marginal benefit or marginal opportunity cost curves shown in **Figure 1**. Establishing biological reserves involves designating a particular level of habitat (say, H_N). Local inhabitants may or may not be compensated for loss of access to land and resources. Bioprospecting contracts, ecotourism development, or marketing of ecofriendly forest products attempt to increase local marginal benefits of preservation (MB_L) by creating markets for goods and services compatible with maintaining habitat.

Direct payment programs subsidize local inhabitants directly to protect habitat. In **Figure 1**, local inhabitants have an economic incentive to preserve H_L hectares of habitat. National benefits, however, are maximized at a greater level of preservation, H_N. Increasing preservation from H_L to H_N would increase national benefits by $a + f$, but it would impose a net cost of a on local inhabitants. A direct payment scheme could pay local inhabitants a or more in exchange for their increasing preservation from H_L to H_N.

Integrated conservation and development projects (ICDPs) seek to shift up MB_L by developing income-generating activities that rely on habitat protection. They may also attempt to encourage nonagricultural employment or labor-using technical change in agriculture to shift MOC to the right. Ferraro & Simpson (2002) refer to this as "conservation by distraction."

3.1. Selecting Biological Reserves

A common policy to preserve biological diversity is to establish biological reserves, areas where habitat conversion is prohibited and economic extraction of biological resources is prohibited or limited. Conservation biologists and environmental nongovernmental organizations have devoted considerable attention to the problem of setting priorities for which sites to preserve (see extensive references in Polasky et al. 2001, Costello & Polasky 2004, Murdoch et al. 2007). Many identify biodiversity hot spots—areas with significant biodiversity, but facing intense conversion pressure. Biological approaches to site selection have focused on maximizing the number and diversity of species protected without considering differences in the opportunity costs across sites. Ando et al. (1998) and Polasky et al. (2001), however, argued that considering differences in opportunity costs greatly enhances the cost effectiveness of habitat protection. They assumed private landowners would be compensated for land placed in preserves. Murdoch et al. (2007) found that (*a*) opportunity costs in different locations can vary by orders of magnitude, (*b*) site biodiversity and opportunity costs may not be highly correlated, and, consequently, (*c*) priority areas selected considering costs can be quite different from those selected ignoring costs. These studies suggest that accounting for differences in opportunity costs can greatly increase biodiversity preserved per dollar spent—an important consideration for government agencies or nongovernmental organizations operating with limited budgets. Costello & Polasky (2004) extended the site-selection problem to a dynamic setting where annual budget constraints imply sites must be chosen sequentially and where habitat conversion risks change over time. They used empirically based numerical simulations to demonstrate how front-loading conservation spending and site selection to earlier periods can significantly improve biodiversity protection.

These site-selection studies, applied to developed countries, assume landowners will be compensated for the opportunity cost of habitat preservation. In developing countries, areas have often been designated as preserves with no such compensation. In **Figure 1**, this is equivalent to a national government setting the level of habitat at H_N, imposing a cost on local inhabitants of *a*. In a developing country context, this "fences and fines" approach raises equity concerns and entails significant enforcement costs (Brandon & Wells 1992). The remoteness of many biodiversity-rich areas often makes enforcement of onerous land-use restrictions infeasible.

3.2. Demand for Habitat Conversion

The marginal opportunity cost of habitat preservation, *MOC*, also represents the demand for habitat conversion. A large body of literature has considered household-level incentives to convert tropical habitats for agricultural production (for surveys, see Angelsen & Kaimowitz 1999, Barbier & Burgess 2001).

3.2.1. Agricultural output prices. Several studies found a positive association between agricultural output prices and deforestation/agricultural land expansion (Binswanger et al. 1987, Panayotou & Sungsuwan 1994, Elnagheeb & Bromley 1994, Barbier & Burgess 1996, Deininger & Minten 1999).

3.2.2. Agricultural credit. Many studies also found a positive association between greater access to credit and deforestation (Ozorio de Almeida & Campari 1995, Barbier & Burgess 1996, Pfaff 1997, Deininger & Minten 2002, Binswanger 1991), although Godoy et al. (1997) found a negative association.

3.2.3. Tax incentives. Binswanger (1991), Thiesenhusen (1991), and Schneider (1994) emphasized the role of tax, credit, and land-settlement policies in encouraging land clearing for crop and livestock production in Brazil. Binswanger (1991) considered how various Brazilian tax provisions combined to encourage deforestation in the Brazilian Amazon.

These included treatment of agricultural income, land taxes, capital gains and commodity taxes, and tax schemes for large-scale livestock ranches. These tax policies (combined with other market distortions) accelerated the demand for habitat conversion. Furthermore, they especially encouraged land-extensive cattle production, amplifying the adverse environmental effects of deforestation. Such distortions cause a shift in the marginal opportunity cost of preservation curve from MOC to MOC' (**Figure 1**). With the distortions, land in habitat is reduced to H'. One way to increase local incentives for conservation is simply to remove these distortions.

3.2.4. Wages and employment. Several studies suggested that higher rural wages and employment levels discourage deforestation by making the required labor input more costly (Holden 1993, Ruben et al. 1994, Bluffstone 1995, Barbier & Burgess 1996, Godoy et al. 1997, Pichon 1997, Deininger & Minten 2002). Others, however, noted that increasing ecotourism wages and employment could encourage in-migration, which places pressure on local resources (Wunder 2000, Taylor et al. 2003, Kiss 2004).

3.2.5. Tenurial security. Several studies have documented how tenurial insecurity reduces incentives for soil conservation and intensive cultivation and encourages land clearing in tropical areas (Feder & Onchan 1987, Thiesenhusen 1991, Panayotou & Ashton 1992, Southgate et al. 1991, Pichon 1997). Other studies have considered the general impact of political instability and weak property protection on deforestation (Deacon 1994, 1999; Godoy et al. 1997; Alston et al. 1999, 2000). Here, the main impact is not through increasing demand for agricultural land. Rather, legal insecurity reduces expected returns for sustainable use of forest resources (the MB_L curve shifts downward). In some cases, settlers in forest frontier areas can most readily gain legal title to land by clearing it. Thus, the attempt to secure property rights accelerates habitat conversion (Binswanger 1991, Southgate et al. 1991, Peuker 1992, Mendelsohn 1994, Schneider 1994, Sunderlin & Rodriquez 1996, Angelsen 1999).

3.2.6. Agricultural input prices, and technology. The hypothesized and estimated impacts of changing agricultural technologies and input prices are complex (Angelsen & Kaimowitz 1999, Barbier & Burgess 2001). Other inputs may substitute for or complement converted agricultural land, whereas technical change could be either land using or land saving. De Janvry (1981) and Binswanger (1991) noted that policies encouraging labor-saving mechanization in Latin American agriculture limit labor absorption and encourage migration to frontier areas. However, the impacts of other technology and price changes (e.g., seed, irrigation, fertilizers, etc.) are less certain.

3.2.7. Population growth, poverty, and landholding inequality. Extensive literature addresses links among population growth, poverty, and deforestation, the leading mechanisms for habitat destruction. There is a long-lived debate between, on the one hand, "Malthusians," who conjecture a downward spiral in which population growth depletes natural resources, thereby fueling more population growth and the ultimate collapse of the natural environment (e.g., Ehrlich et al. 1993), and, on the other hand, "Boserupians," who conjecture that resource scarcity fuels innovation that conserves resources and increases the material services that they deliver (Boserup 1965, Simon 1996). There is, however, general consensus that population decisions and environmental change both affect one another. Population growth fuels exploitation of open access natural resources (Brander & Taylor 1998), and environmental degradation fuels demand for children in at least two ways: by attenuating the need for children to manage livestock and fetch water and fuelwood (Nerlove 1991, Dasgupta 1995) and by worsening health status (and raising child and adult mortality), thereby increasing the demand for children for income support (Rosenzweig & Stark 1997). Mitigating this "vicious cycle" are incentives for out-migration from degraded rural environments (Chopra & Gulati 1997, Amacher et al. 1998) and community action to reverse environmental decline. Household production models can generate this sort of vicious cycle, even when accounting for out-migration incentives, but can also predict Boserupian responses to degraded environments, all under a premise of open access to environmental resources (Bhattacharya & Innes 2008).

Foster and Rosenzweig (2003) present a competing view in which forests are privately held and population growth, by fueling demand for forest products, leads to afforestation. Central to their argument is a different property rights regime (private versus open access) than generally thought to dominate environment-related decisions in developing countries.

Ultimately, the nature of reciprocal effects is an empirical issue. Substantial evidence documents the negative effects of population growth on environmental health in developing countries, both in cross-national studies and within-nation cross sections (for surveys, see Panayotou 2000, Bhattacharya & Innes 2008). A smaller literature documents links between resource scarcity and fertility (Loughran & Pritchett 1997, Aggarwal et al. 2001, Filmer & Pritchett 2002) as well as between resource scarcity and migration (Chopra & Gulati 1997, Amacher et al. 1998). Accounting for the joint endogeneity of environmental and population outcomes, Bhattacharya & Innes (2008) reported evidence from rural India that supports predictions of the open access, household production model.

Literature and evidence on the poverty-environment nexus are more limited. Forster (1992) and Thiesenhusen (1991) argued that the main causes of tropical deforestation are rural poverty and inequitable land distribution—conditions that drive peasants onto ecologically fragile frontier areas. These studies considered landholding over a broad geographical area, taking into account the distribution of land between large commercial operations and small-scale producers. Other studies have considered landholding inequality within the class of smallholders in more localized settings. Among this class of traditional, small-scale producers, landholding inequality can make collective action more difficult by discouraging cooperation to conserve resources (Dayton-Johnson 2000). Yet, such inequality may mean that larger landholders within this group (a) capture most of the gains from conservation and (b) are better able to impose their preferences on others. The net effect of inequality will depend on these countervailing forces. Zapata-Rios et al. (2005) found evidence that inequality accelerates deforestation in Bolivia; Alix-Garcia (2007) found the opposite result in Mexico.

A number of authors have argued that indigenous (and poor) communities often conserve local environmental resources in spite of their poverty and that, contrary to the conventional view that poverty drives environmental degradation in developing countries (Duraiappah 1998), the rapacious rich are at least equally to blame for overexploitation of natural resources (Tiffen et al. 1994, Ravnborg 2003, Swinton & Quiroz 2003). Consistent with this view, Narain et al. (2008) recently reported evidence from rural India that both poor and nonpoor households may rely heavily on common property and natural resource extraction. Dasgupta et al. (2005) found negative but insignificant effects of initial poverty on deforestation in Cambodia. A vast literature on the environmental Kuznets curve (for a review, see

Caviglia-Harris et al. 2009) has found conflicting evidence on effects of average incomes on different environmental outcomes, but it does not study environmental effects of income distribution beyond the average. None of this literature distinguishes between the initial income distribution and changes in the income distribution. Nor does it account for the joint determination between environmental degradation or improvement and changes in income for the poor and nonpoor. In their attempt to do so with data from rural India, Bhattacharya & Innes (2009) found evidence for negative effects of initial poverty on forestation and positive effects of increased incomes for all groups (poor and nonpoor), while providing further evidence of the dependence of the poor on environmental/forest resources.

Overall, this literature suggests reason for continued policy interest in population-poverty-environment linkages for the protection of species' habitat. Although much more research is called for, there is evidence that improving the economic well-being of the poor with programs that promote improved health and educational outcomes will reduce incentives for population growth and for exploitation of native forests. Similarly, programs that directly improve the local natural environment, both by reducing incentives for population growth and by directly improving the economic status of the poor, may help stem environmental decline.

3.3. Bioprospecting and Conservation Incentives

Bioprospecting is the search among living organisms for compounds that have commercial value as active ingredients in pharmaceuticals, pesticides, and other products. Natural products, derived from plants and animals, remain a basic source of many pharmaceuticals. Soejarto & Farnsworth (1989) estimated one-quarter of prescription drugs contained some natural products. Natural products remain a major source of drug discovery, either directly or as blueprints for novel chemicals. Newman & Cragg (2007) estimated 63% of the 973 small-molecule drugs approved worldwide from 1981 to June 2006 were based on natural products.

Whereas many biologists and environmentalists have seen bioprospecting agreements as avenues to improve incentives for habitat conservation, economists generally have been more skeptical. Simpson et al. (1996) argued that, although biodiversity is valuable overall, what matters for bioprospecting is the value of a marginal species. They argued that the marginal value of habitat would be low ($21/hectare). When several species produce the same chemical compound, the probability of discovering the compound's value is high, but discovery in one species will render other species redundant as a source of that compound. In cases where a compound is rarely found, the probability of finding a useful lead will be quite small.

Rausser & Small (2000), in contrast, found that marginal values of habitat for bioprospecting could be large (more than $9000/hectare). In such cases, private bioprospecting contracts could create incentives to conserve biological diversity. Rausser & Small (2000) attributed this difference to the role of the information search process. Simpson et al. (1996) assumed a random-search process. Rausser & Small (2000) assumed prospectors can use scientific information to search more efficiently, raising the marginal value of new searches.

Costello & Ward (2006) examined the role of information and search processes on marginal values of biodiversity-rich habitats, explicitly comparing the models and results of Simpson et al. (1996) and Rausser & Small (2000). Using the numerical values assumed in both studies, they calculated the marginal value of land in biodiversity hot spots for both random searches (as in Simpson et al. 1996) and optimal searches (as in

Rausser & Small 2000). They found use of information in the search process did raise marginal values, but the increase accounted for only 4% of the difference in the results of the two studies. The bulk of the difference came from varying assumptions about other parameter values used in the models. Costello & Ward (2006) then derived ranges of estimates of the marginal value of habitat using ranges of parameter values from existing literature. Based on this exercise, their results support the assertion by Simpson et al. (1996) that the marginal value of land under bioprospecting would be low and insufficient to counter conversion incentives.

Other studies focused on different aspects of bioprospecting problems, but they reached similar conclusions. Barrett & Lybbert (2000) emphasized the difficulties of transferring bioprospecting gains to the poor in tropical countries who are making land-clearing decisions. Even if bioprospecting can increase marginal benefits at the national level (a shift out in MB_N in **Figure 1**), incentives may not change at the local level (no change in MB_L). Frisvold & Condon (1994), rather than focus on the absolute value of bioprospecting gains, argued that opportunity costs of preservation are large relative to bioprospecting gains and that costs are growing significantly over time. In terms of **Figure 1**, the MOC curve is steep and shifting to the left rapidly, so internalizing external benefits of habitat may have little effect on conservation. Frisvold & Day-Rubenstein (2008) presented an *ex post* study of the anticancer drug taxol, derived from yew tree species. They illustrated how bioprospecting can exchange one extinction threat (habitat conversion, because a species is not valued) for another (overexploitation, because the resource is harvested under open access). The case of taxol illustrates that creating market demand for genetic resources without clearly defining property rights over them can lead to resource depletion rather than conservation. To date, 64 plant species have been listed as threatened under Convention on International Trade in Endangered Species of Wild Fauna and Flora expressly because of the threat of overharvest for medicinal uses (Schippman 2001).

3.4. Integrated Conservation and Development Projects, Ecotourism, and Green Products

ICDPs are usually directed at populations adjacent to biological reserves, parks, or other protected areas in developing countries. These projects aim to develop local income-generating activities that (*a*) are based on marketing goods or services compatible with sustainable use of resources in or near protected areas or (*b*) provide an alternative to habitat conversion (Brandon & Wells 1992). ICDPs, thus, try to combine conservation with antipoverty and rural development goals. Designing a single program to achieve multiple objectives well is difficult. For example, providing employment opportunities near protected areas might reduce poverty, but it may also draw migrants to the area. Increasing local incomes need not discourage land conversion. Brandon & Wells (1992) pointed out that there is little support for assumptions that poor households will cease economic activity (such as land clearing) once an income target is reached. Local residents may actually invest additional income into expansion of agricultural activities (Kiss 2004).

ICDPs frequently have components to encourage ecotourism. The U.S. Agency for International Development, the World Bank, and conservation nongovernmental organizations have supported numerous community-based ecotourism projects (Kiss 2004). Few of these projects have undergone rigorous study or evaluation (Taylor et al. 2003, Kiss 2004).

Kiss (2004) concluded that, in remote, biodiversity-rich areas, tourism revenues are seldom large enough to shift land use patterns significantly. However, they may play a role in protecting small, critical habitats such as migration corridors.

Ecotourism can have unanticipated negative consequences. Tourist demand for food can increase local incentives to convert forests to agriculture (Wunder 2000). Although, as noted above, higher wages have been associated with less deforestation, Taylor et al. (2003) suggested that higher wages have encouraged in-migration to the Galapagos Islands. They call this a "tourism-income-population growth spiral" that can place burdens on local resources.

There have also been attempts to develop markets for "green" products such as shade-grown coffee or tagua nuts (Ferraro et al. 2005). Again, the goal is to shift up the local marginal benefit curve of habitat preservation, MB_L. The idea is to bundle a private good (e.g., coffee) with a public good (habitat conservation). Cornes & Sandler (1996) referred to this as an "impure" public good. Marketing of green products often includes some sort of third-party certification of the environmental benefits created by production or sale of products. An important policy question is whether such certification programs do in fact enhance conservation (Fischer et al. 2005). As with studies of bioprospecting and ecotourism, economists have questioned the scope for green-product marketing to increase marginal benefits of habitat protection significantly (Stevens et al. 1998, Swallow & Sedjo 2000, Hardner & Rice 2002, Sedjo & Swallow 2002, Fischer et al. 2005).

3.5. Direct Payments for Conservation

ICDPs, bioprospecting, and ecotourism/green markets all aim to shift up the local benefit curve from habitat preservation (MB_L in **Figure 1**). Some studies suggest that, rather than follow this indirect approach, paying for habitat preservation directly may be preferable (Simpson & Sedjo 1996, Ferraro & Simpson 2002, Ferraro & Kiss 2002, Ferraro et al. 2005). In **Figure 1**, this amounts to paying local inhabitants at least $a + b + c$ to increase preservation to H_G rather than institute an indirect program to shift up MB_L. Empirically based numerical simulations suggest direct payments can be significantly more cost effective (Ferraro & Simpson 2002, Ferraro et al. 2005). Yet, implementation of direct payments in developing countries has been limited, and there is a lack of rigorous *ex post* evaluation of such programs. Research on design and implementation of VCAs in developed countries (discussed above) may provide insights to further study in developing countries.

4. CONCLUSIONS

Habitat conversion is the major cause of species endangerment. In advanced economies, private landowners are often the ones making immediate decisions that affect habitat, including outright conversion of native environments to agricultural or other development uses, investments that enhance or detract from habitat values, or providing information about species or habitat values on their property. In developing economies, incentives to private landowners may also be important, particularly in the establishment of biological reserves. However, in addition, vital to habitat preservation or conversion are incentives faced by local residents to expand the agricultural frontier into primitive forestlands. In this article, we review literature and arguments related to the incentives facing private actors in these two stereotypic situations.

By examining incentives to private landowners for habitat conservation, related literature identifies a number of negative effects of uncompensated government mandates, including creating incentives for early land development that destroys potential habitat, noxious SSS behavior that kills individual endangered species, and deterring valuable information collection and reporting about species' status and potential habitat values on private lands. From the policy perspective, a lesson from this work is that positive incentives ("carrots") in tandem with a background threat of regulation ("sticks") can have salutary effects on the public's overall species conservation objectives by providing rewards to self-reporting of species-related information, compensating landowners for regulatory or complete takings of their property in order to protect species, and a careful design of no-surprises VCAs.

Incentive issues on the agricultural frontier are complex, encompassing many macroeconomic linkages. For example, population growth, poverty, and the design of property rights are at the heart of incentives for environmental exploitation by rural residents of poor countries. The literature broadly suggests multidirectional linkages among the environment, population growth, and poverty, with general (but not completely uncontroverted) evidence that population growth and poverty tend to increase deforestation that destroys species habitat. These conclusions suggest the importance, for example, of health and education policy that improves infant and adult health outcomes and educational achievement, thereby alleviating poverty and reducing incentives for population growth, both of which can reduce incentives for forest exploitation on the frontier. They also suggest the importance of direct poverty alleviation programs and ICDPs designed to protect local environments in tandem with vesting the local poor with an economic stake in the preservation of these environments by using such measures as entitlements to some nontimber forest products and rents from ecotourism. The latter policies target the opposite direction of causation in the "vicious cycle" of degradation, with degradation fueling proximate causes of further degradation, including population growth and poverty.

Often missing from academic analyses of these issues is a distinction between different types of environmental/forest resources. In particular, private forests cultivated for timber sales often are ecologically simplified plantations that offer only limited benefits in terms of biodiversity. In contrast, native forests may offer rich rewards in species diversity and habitat. Such a distinction is potentially crucial in the design of policy to promote ecological wealth. For example, Foster & Rosenzweig (2003) stressed the benefits of population growth in spurring demand for marketed forest products that drive increased supplies of private forestlands. While their logic hinges on well-defined property rights (as opposed to open or near-open access resources) that often are lacking in the rural environments of developing economies (Bhattacharya & Innes 2008), it ignores differential ecological benefits of private versus native forests.

Extant literature suggests limits on the scope for bioprospecting agreements to spur species/habitat conservation, in part owing to the *ex post* erosion of rents from overexploitation of a valued but essentially open access species (Frisvold & Day-Rubinstein 2008). In addition, strengthening of property rights need not always help in habitat protection; rather, protecting biologically sensitive or valuable lands by denying property rights to those that clear them (versus allowing land clearing to be the road to title) and penalizing those that clear or poach on these lands can promote protection in principle. A key component of such a strategy, however, must be local support for conservation, as local communities are essential to enforcement of sanctions, and local support requires vesting local communities with an economic stake in conservation (with ICDPs, for example).

Finally, we have said little about incentives for public-sector action to protect species and habitat. Such incentives are front and center to preservation of the world's native tropical forests that house vast treasures of biological wealth and reside principally in countries such as Brazil and Indonesia that have, at times, promoted forest-clearing policies at complete odds with global interests in biodiversity and carbon-sink conservation. This important subject relates to a variety of key literatures, including those on environmental federalism (Oates & Schwabb 1988, Wellisch 1995, Kunce & Shogren 2005), the design of constitutional restraints (Fischel & Shapiro 1989, Innes 1997, Brennan & Boyd 2006), the design of international environmental agreements (Barrett 2003), and the political economy of environmental protection (Damania et al. 2003). Applying (and integrating) this literature to biodiversity protection is an important challenge for future research.

SUMMARY POINTS

1. The economic literature on endangered species focuses on two main threats: overharvesting and habitat conversion. The consensus is that habitat conversion is the main source of species loss.

2. Habitat conversion is fundamentally a land-use problem. Species are threatened because their habitats have a higher private value in another economic use. Landowner decisions that affect social welfare include investments in private land uses, conservation choices that affect habitat values, and providing information about habitat values on their property.

3. A broad message from economics literature is that society's interest in habitat preservation is well served by government strategies to provide landowners with positive conservation incentives, backed by the threat of sanctions for bad behavior. Positive incentives for habitat conversion include compensation and conservation agreements with no-surprise clauses.

4. Also important are policies that reward self-reporting of species on private lands rather than the economic penalties that characterize present endangered species laws in the United States.

5. Policies to protect habitat in developing countries include creation of markets for goods and services compatible with maintaining habitat, direct payments to protect habitat, and encouraging nonagricultural employment or labor-using technical change in agriculture to reduce demand for land conversion.

6. Major factors stimulating demand for agricultural land and habitat conversion in developing countries include agricultural output prices; agricultural credit; tax policies; rural wages; and employment, security of tenure, and landholding inequality.

7. Policies to create markets for goods and services compatible with protecting habitat, such as bioprospecting, ecotourism, or green product promotion, have not received sufficient, rigorous, *ex post* evaluation to determine if they do in fact provide significant conservation incentives.

DISCLOSURE STATEMENT

The authors are not aware of any affiliations, memberships, funding, or financial holdings that might be perceived as affecting the objectivity of this review.

LITERATURE CITED

Aggarwal R, Netanyahu S, Romano C. 2001. Access to natural resources and the fertility decision of women: the case of South Africa. *Environ. Dev. Econ.* 6:209–36

Akerlof G. 1970. The market for lemons: qualitative uncertainty and the market mechanism. *Q. J. Econ.* 84:488–500

Alix-Garcia J. 2007. A spatial analysis of common property deforestation. *J. Environ. Econ. Manag.* 53:141–57

Alston LJ, Libecap GD, Mueller B. 1999. *Titles, Conflicts and Land Use: The Development of Property Rights and Land Reform in the Brazilian Amazon Frontier.* Ann Arbor, MI: Univ. Mich. Press

Alston LJ, Libecap GD, Mueller B. 2000. Land reform policies, the sources of violent conflict, and implications for deforestation in the Brazilian Amazon. *J. Environ. Econ. Manag.* 39:162–88

Amacher G, Cruz W, Grebner D, Hyde W. 1998. Environmental motivation for migration: population pressure, poverty and deforestation in the Philippines. *Land Econ.* 74:92–101

Amacher G, Malik A. 1996. Bargaining in environmental regulation and the ideal regulator. *J. Environ. Econ. Manag.* 30:233–53

Amacher G, Malik A. 1998. Instrument choice when regulators and firms bargain. *J. Environ. Econ. Manag.* 35:225–41

Ando A. 1999. Waiting to be protected under the Endangered Species Act: the political economy of regulatory delay. *J. Law Econ.* 42:29–60

Ando A, Camm J, Polasky S, Solow A. 1998. Species distributions, land values, and efficient conservation. *Science* 279:2126–28

Angelsen A. 1999. Agricultural expansion and deforestation: modelling the impact of population, market forces, and property rights. *J. Dev. Econ.* 58:185–218

Angelsen A, Kaimowitz D. 1999. Rethinking the causes of deforestation: lessons from economic models. *World Bank Res. Obs.* 14:73–98

Arrow K, Fisher A. 1974. Environmental preservation, uncertainty, and irreversibility. *Q. J. Econ.* 88:312–19

Barbier EB. 2000. Biodiversity, trade and international agreements. *J. Econ. Stud.* 27:55–74

Barbier EB, Burgess JC. 1996. Economic analysis of deforestation in Mexico. *Environ. Dev. Econ.* 1(2):203–39

Barbier EB, Burgess JC. 2001. The economics of tropical deforestation. *J. Econ. Surv.* 15:413–33

Barbier EB, Burgess JC, Swanson TM, Pearce DW. 1990. *Elephants, Economics, and Ivory.* London: Earthscan Publ.

Barnes JI. 1996. Changes in the economic use value of elephant in Botswana: the effect of international trade prohibition. *Ecol. Econ.* 18:215–30

Baron D. 2006. *A positive theory of moral management, social pressure, and corporate social performance.* Work. Pap., Grad. Sch. Bus., Stanford Univ.

Barrett CB, Lybbert TJ. 2000. Is bioprospecting a viable strategy for conserving tropical ecosystems? *Ecol. Econ.* 34:293–300

Barrett S. 2003. *Environment and Statecraft: The Strategy of Environmental Treaty-Making.* Oxford: Oxford Univ. Press

Berck P. 1979. Open access and extinction. *Econometrica* 47:877–82

Bhattacharya H, Innes R. 2008. An empirical exploration of the population-environment nexus in India. *Amer. J. Agri. Econ.* 90: 883–901

Bhattacharya H, Innes R. 2009. *Is there a poverty-environment nexus in rural India?* Work. Pap., Univ. Utah/Univ. Arizona

Binswanger HP. 1991. Brazilian policies that encourage deforestation in the Amazon. *World Dev.* 19:821–9

Binswanger HP, Mundlak Y, Yang MC, Bowers A. 1987. On the determinants of cross-country aggregate agricultural supply. *J. Econom.* 36:111–31

Bluffstone RA. 1995. The effect of labor market performance on deforestation in developing countries under open access: an example from rural Nepal. *J. Environ. Econ. Manag.* 29:42–63

Blume L, Rubinfeld D. 1984. Compensation for takings: an economic analysis. *Calif. Law Rev.* 72:569–624

Blume L, Rubinfeld D, Shapiro P. 1984. The taking of land: When should compensation be paid? *Q. J. Econ.* 99:71–92

Boserup E. 1965. *The Conditions of Agricultural Growth.* Chicago, IL: Aldine

Bovenberg L, Goulder L. 1996. Optimal environmental taxation in the presence of other taxes: general equilibrium analysis. *Am. Econ. Rev.* 86:985–1000

Brander J, Taylor S. 1998. The simple economics of Easter Island: a Ricardo-Malthus model of renewable resource use. *Am. Econ. Rev.* 88:119–38

Brandon KE, Wells M. 1992. Planning for people and parks: design dilemmas. *World Dev.* 20:557–70

Brennan T, Boyd J. 2006. Political economy and the efficiency of compensation for takings. *Contemp. Econ. Policy* 24:188–202

Brown G. 1987. Valuation of genetic resources. In *The Preservation and Valuation of Biological Resources,* ed. G Orians, G Brown, W Kunin, J Swierzbinski. Seattle, WA: Univ. Wash. Press

Brown G, Shogren J. 1998. Economics of the Endangered Species Act. *J. Econ. Perspect.* 12:3–20

Bulte EH, Horan RD, Shogren JF. 2003. Elephants. Comment. *Am. Econ. Rev.* 93:1437–45

Bulte EH, van Kooten GC. 1996. A note on ivory trade and elephant conservation. *Environ. Dev. Econ.* 1:433–43

Bulte EH, van Kooten GC. 1999. Economic efficiency, resource conservation and the ivory trade ban. *Ecol. Econ.* 28:171–81

Burton M. 1999. An assessment of alternative methods of estimating the effect of the ivory trade ban on poaching effort. *Ecol. Econ.* 30:93–106

Carbone J, Smith VK. 2008. Evaluating policy interventions with general equilibrium externalities. *J. Public Econ.* 92:1254–74

Caviglia-Harris J, Chambers D, Kahn J. 2009. Taking the "U" out of Kuznets: a comprehensive analysis of the EKC and environmental degradation. *Ecol. Econ.* 68:1149–59

Chopra K, Gulati S. 1997. Environmental degradation and population movements: the role of property rights. *Environ. Res. Econ.* 9:383–408

Clark C. 1976. *Mathematical Bioeconomics: The Optimal Management of Renewable Resources.* New York: John Wiley

Clark C. 1973. Profit maximization and the extinction of animal species. *J. Polit. Econ.* 81:950–61

Clark C, Munro G. 1978. Renewable resources and extinction: note. *J. Environ. Econ. Manag.* 5:23–29

Clark C, Clark F, Munro G. 1979. The optimal exploitation of renewable resource stocks: problems of irreversible investment. *Econometrica* 47:25–29

Coase R. 1960. The problem of social cost. *J. Law Econ.* 3:1–44

Collinge R, Oates W. 1982. Efficiency in pollution control in the short and long runs: a system of rental emission permits. *Can. J. Econ.* 15:346–54

Cornes R, Sandler T. 1996. *The Theory of Externalities, Public Goods and Club Goods.* New York: Cambridge Univ. Press. 2nd ed.

Costello C, Ward M. 2006. Search, bioprospecting, and biodiversity conservation. *J. Environ. Econ. Manag.* 52:615–36

Costello C, Polasky S. 2004. Dynamic reserve site selection. *Resour. Energy Econ.* 26:157–74

Damania R, Fredriksson P, List J. 2003. Trade liberalization, corruption, and environmental policy formation: theory and evidence. *J. Environ. Econ. Manag.* 46:490–512

Dasgupta P. 1995. The population problem: theory and evidence. *J. Econ. Lit.* 33:1879–902

Dasgupta S, Deichmann U, Meisner C, Wheeler D. 2005. Where is the poverty-environment nexus? Evidence from Cambodia, Lao PDR and Vietnam. *World Dev.* 33(4):617–38

Dayton-Johnson J. 2000. Determinants of collective action on the local commons: a model with evidence from Mexico. *J. Dev. Econ.* 62:181–208

Deacon, RT. 1994. Deforestation and the rule of law in a cross-section of countries. *Land Econ.* 70:414–30

Deacon RT. 1999. Deforestation and ownership: evidence from historical accounts and contemporary data. *Land Econ.* 75:341–59

Deininger K, Minten B. 1999. Poverty, policies, and deforestation: the case of Mexico. *Econ. Dev. Cult. Change* 47:313–44

Deininger K, Minten B. 2002. Determinants of deforestation and the economics of protection: an application to Mexico. *Am. J. Agric. Econ.* 84:943–60

de Janvry A. 1981. *The Agrarian Question and Reformism in Latin America.* Baltimore, MD: Johns Hopkins Univ. Press

Duraiappah AK. 1998. Poverty and environmental degradation: a review and analysis of the nexus. *World Dev.* 26(12):2169–79

Ehrlich P, Ehrlich A, Daily G. 1993. Food security, population, and environment. *Popul. Dev. Rev.* 19:1–32

Elnagheeb AH, Bromley DW. 1994. Extensification of agriculture and deforestation: empirical evidence from Sudan. *Agric. Econ.* 10:193–200

Farber D. 1992. Economic analysis and just compensation. *Int. Rev. Law Econ.* 12:125–38

Feder G, Onchan T. 1987. Land ownership security and farm investment in Thailand. *Am. J. Agric. Econ.* 69:311–20

Ferraro PJ, Kiss A. 2002. Getting what you paid for: direct payments as an alternative investment for conserving biological diversity. *Science* 268:1718–19

Ferraro PJ, Simpson RD. 2002. The cost-effectiveness of conservation payments. *Land Econ.* 78:339–53

Ferraro PJ, Uchida T, Conrad JM. 2005. Price premiums for eco-friendly commodities: Are 'green' markets the best way to protect endangered ecosystems? *Environ. Resour. Econ.* 32:419–38

Filmer D, Pritchett L. 2002. Environmental degradation and the demand for children: searching for the vicious circle in Pakistan. *Environ. Dev. Econ.* 7:123–46

Fischel W, Shapiro P. 1989. A constitutional choice model of compensation for takings. *Int. Rev. Law Econ.* 9:115–28

Fischer C. 2004. The complex interactions of markets for endangered species products. *J. Environ. Econ. Manag.* 48:926–53

Fischer C, Aguilar F, Jawahar P, Sedjo R. 2005. *Forest certification: toward common standards?* Discuss. Pap. 05-10, Resour. Future

Fisher A, Hanemann M. 1990. Option value: theory and measurement. *Eur. Rev. Agric. Econ.* 17:167–180

Forster N. 1992. Protecting fragile lands: new reasons to tackle old problems. *World Dev.* 20:571–85

Foster A, Rosenzweig M. 2003. Economic growth and the rise of forests. *Q. J. Econ.* 118:601–37

Frisvold G, Condon P. 1994. Biodiversity conservation and biotechnology development agreements. *Contemp. Econ. Policy* 12:1–9

Frisvold G, Day-Rubenstein K. 2008. Bioprospecting and biodiversity conservation: What happens when discoveries are made? *Ariz. Law Rev.* 50:545–76

Fullerton D. 1991. Reconciling recent estimates of the marginal welfare cost of taxation. *Am. Econ. Rev.* 81:302–8

Godoy R, O'Neill K, Groff S, Kostishack P, Cubas A, et al. 1997. Household determinants of deforestation by Amerindians in Honduras. *World Dev.* 25:977–87

Gordon HS. 1954. The economic theory of a common-property resource: the fishery. *J. Polit. Econ.* 62:124–42

Hardner J, Rice R. 2002. Rethinking green consumerism. *Sci. Am.* 286:89–95

Hermalin B. 1995. An economic analysis of takings. *J. Law Econ. Organ.* 11:518–37

Holden S. 1993. Peasant household modeling: farming systems evolution and sustainability in Northern Zambia. *Agric. Econ.* 9:241–67

Innes R. 1997. Takings, compensation and equal treatment of owners of developed and undeveloped property. *J. Law Econ.* 40:403–32

Innes R. 1999. Remediation and self-reporting in optimal law enforcement. *J. Public Econ.* 72:379–93

Innes R. 2000a. The economics of takings and compensation when land and its public use value are in private hands. *Land Econ.* 76:195–212

Innes R. 2000b. Self-reporting and optimal law enforcement when violators have heterogeneous probabilities of apprehension. *J. Legal Stud.* 29:287–300

Innes R. 2001a. Self-enforcement of environmental law. In *The Law and Economics of the Environment*, ed. A Heyes. Cheltenham, UK: Edward Elgar

Innes R. 2001b. Violator avoidance activities and self-reporting in optimal law enforcement. *J. Law Econ. Organ.* 17:239–56

Innes R. 2006. A theory of consumer boycotts under symmetric information and imperfect competition. *Econ. J.* 116:355–81

Innes R. 2009. Coming to the nuisance: revisiting *Spur* in a model of location choice. *J. Law Econ. Organ.* In press

Innes R, Polasky S, Tschirhart J. 1998. Takings, compensation and endangered species protection on private lands. *J. Econ. Perspect.* 12:35–52

Kaplow L. 1986. An economic analysis of legal transitions. *Harv. Law Rev.* 99:509–617

Kaplow L, Shavell S. 1994. Optimal law enforcement with self-reporting of behavior. *J. Polit. Econ.* 102:583–606

Kirchhoff S. 2000. Green business and blue angels: a model of voluntary overcompliance with asymmetric information. *Environ. Resour. Econ.* 15:403–20

Kiss A. 2004. Is community-based ecotourism a good use of biodiversity conservation funds? *Trends Ecol. Evol.* 19:232–37

Kremer M, Morcom C. 2000. Elephants. *Am. Econ. Rev.* 90:212–34

Kremer M, Morcom C. 2003. Elephants. Reply. *Am. Econ. Rev.* 93:1446–48

Kunce M, Shogren J. 2005. On interjurisdictional competition and environmental federalism. *J. Environ. Econ. Manag.* 50:212–24

Lambert T, Smith R. 1994. *The Endangered Species Act: time for a change.* Policy Study 199, Cent. Study Am. Bus., Wash. Univ., St. Louis, MO

Langpap C. 2006. Conservation of endangered species: Can incentives work for private landowners? *Ecol. Econ.* 57:558–72

Langpap C, Wu J. 2004. Voluntary conservation of endangered species: When does no regulatory assurance mean no conservation? *J. Environ. Econ. Manag.* 47:435–57

Loughran D, Pritchett L. 1997. *Environmental scarcity, resource collection, and the demand for children in Nepal.* Work. Pap., World Bank

Lueck D, Michael J. 2003. Preemptive habitat destruction under the Endangered Species Act. *J. Law Econ.* 46:27–60

Lewis T. 1996. Protecting the environment when costs and benefits are privately known. *Rand J. Econ.* 27:819–47

Malik A. 1993. Self-reporting and the design of policies for regulating stochastic pollution. *J. Environ. Econ. Manag.* 24:241–57

Margolis M, Osgood D, List J. 2008. *Is the Endangered Species Act endangering species?* Work. Pap., Columbia Univ.

McNeely JA, Miller KR, Reid WV, Mittermeier RA, Werner TB. 1990. *Conserving the World's Biological Diversity.* Washington, DC: IUCN, World Resour. Inst., Conserv. Int., World Wildl. Fund. World Bank

Meltz R. 1994. *The Endangered Species Act and constitutional takings.* Presented at Conf. Regul. Tak. Resour., Nat. Resour. Law Cent., Univ. Colo. Sch. Law

Mendelsohn R. 1994. Property rights and tropical deforestation. *Oxf. Econ. Pap.* 46:750–56

Metrick A, Weitzman M. 1996. Patterns of behavior in endangered species preservation. *Land Econ.* 72:1–16

Miceli T, Segerson K. 1994. Regulatory takings: When should compensation be paid? *J. Legal Stud.* 23:749–76

Missios PC. 2004. Wildlife trade and endangered species protection. *Aust. J. Agric. Resour. Econ.* 48:613–27

Murdoch W, Polasky S, Wilson KA, Possingham HP, Kareiva P, Shaw R. 2007. Maximizing return on investment in conservation. *Biol. Conserv.* 139:375–88

Narain U, Gupta S, Veld KV. 2008. Poverty and the environment: exploring the relationship between household incomes, private assets and natural assets. *Land Econ.* 84:148–67

Nerlove M. 1991. Population and the environment: a parable of firewood and other tales. *Am. J. Agric. Econ.* 73:1334–47

Newman D, Cragg GM. 2007. Natural products as sources of new drugs over the last 25 years. *J. Nat. Prod.* 70:461–77

Oates W, Schwab R. 1988. Economic competition among jurisdictions: efficiency enhancing or distortion inducing. *J. Public Econ.* 35:333–54

Ozorio de Almeida AL, Campari JS. 1995. *Sustainable Settlement in the Brazilian Amazon.* New York: Oxford Univ. Press

Panayotou T. 2000. *Population and environment.* CID Work. Pap. 54, Harvard Univ.

Panayotou T, Ashton P. 1992. *Not By Timber Alone: Economics and Ecology of Sustaining Tropical Forests.* Washington, DC: Island Press

Panayotou T, Sungsuwan S. 1994. An econometric analysis of the causes of tropical deforestation: the case of Northeast Thailand. In *The Causes of Tropical Deforestation: The Economic and Statistical Analysis of Factors Giving Rise to the Loss of the Tropical Forests*, ed. K Brown, DW Pearce. London: Univ. Coll. London Press

Peuker A. 1992. Public policies and deforestation: a case study of Costa Rica. *World Bank Rep.* 14, Latin Am. Caribb. Tech. Dep. Reg. Stud. Program, Washington, DC

Pfaff A. 1997. *What drives deforestation in the Brazilian Amazon? Evidence from satellite and socioeconomic data*. Work. Pap. 1772, Policy Res. Dep., World Bank

Pichon FJ. 1997. Colonist land-allocation decisions, land use, and deforestation in the Ecuadorian Amazon frontier. *Econ. Dev. Cult. Change* 44:127–64

Pitchford R, Snyder C. 2003. Coming to the nuisance: an economic analysis from an incomplete contracts perspective. *J. Law Econ. Organ.* 19:491–516

Polasky S, Camm JD, Garber-Yonts B. 2001. Selecting biological reserves cost-effectively: an application to terrestrial vertebrate conservation in Oregon. *Land Econ.* 77:68–78

Polasky S, Doremus H. 1998. When the truth hurts: endangered species policy on private land with imperfect information. *J. Environ. Econ. Manag.* 35:22–47

Rausser G, Small A. 2000. Valuing research leads: bioprospecting and the conservation of genetic resources. *J. Polit. Econ.* 108:173–206

Raven P. 1980. *Research Priorities in Tropical Biology*. Washington, DC: Natl. Res. Counc.

Ravnborg H. 2003. Poverty and environmental degradation in the Nicaraguan hillsides. *World Dev.* 31(11):1933–46

Rosenzweig M, Stark O. 1997. *Handbook of Population and Family Economics*. Amsterdam: Elsevier

Ruben R, Kruseman G, Hengsdijk H. 1994. Farm household modeling for estimating the effectiveness of price instruments on sustainable land uses in the Atlantic Zone of Costa Rica. *DLV Rep. 4*, Wageningen Agric. Univ., The Netherlands

Sandler T. 1993. Tropical deforestation: markets and market failures. *Land Econ.* 69:225–33

Schippman U. 2001. *Medicinal plants significant trade study*. CITES Proj. S-9109, Doc. PC9 9.13 (rev.), Bundesamt Naturshutz, CITES Sci. Auth., Bonn, Germany

Schneider RR. 1994. Government and the economy on the Amazon frontier. *World Bank Rep. 34*, Latin Am. Caribb. Tech. Dep. Reg. Stud. Program, Washington, DC

Sedjo RA, Swallow SK. 2002. Voluntary eco-labeling and the price premium. *Land Econ.* 78:272–84

Segerson K, Miceli T. 1998. Voluntary environmental agreements: good or bad news for environmental protection? *J. Environ. Econ. Manag.* 36:109–30

Shavell S. 1980. Strict liability vs. negligence. *J. Legal Stud.* 9:1–25

Simon J. 1996. *The Ultimate Resource 2*. Princeton, NJ: Princeton Univ. Press

Simpson RD, Sedjo RA. 1996. Paying for the conservation of endangered ecosystems: a comparison of direct and indirect approaches. *Environ. Dev. Econ.* 1:241–57

Simpson RD, Sedjo RA, Reid JW. 1996. Valuing biodiversity for use in pharmaceutical research. *J. Polit. Econ.* 1041:163–85

Smith R, Shogren J. 2002. Voluntary incentive design for endangered species protection. *J. Environ. Econ. Manag.* 43:169–87

Smith VK. 1996. *Estimating Economic Values for Nature: Methods for Non-Market Valuation*. Cheltenham, UK: Edward Elgar

Smith VL. 1975. The primitive hunter culture, Pleistocene extinction, and the rise of agriculture. *J. Polit. Econ.* 83:727–55

Soejarto D, Farnsworth N. 1989. Tropical rainforests: potential sources of new drugs. *Perspect. Biol. Med.* 32:244–56

Southgate D, Sierra R, Brown L. 1991. The causes of tropical deforestation in Ecuador: a statistical analysis. *World Dev.* 19:1145–51

Spence M. 1975. Blue whales and applied control theory. In *System Approaches and Environmental Problems*, ed. H Goettinger. Gottingen: Vandenboeck

Stevens J, Ahmad M, Ruddell S. 1998. Forest products certification: a survey of producers and manufacturers. *For. Prod. J.* 48:43–52

Stroup, R. 1995. *The Endangered Species Act: making innocent species the enemy*. PERC Policy Ser. PS-3, Montana State Univ.

Stroup R. 1997. The economics of compensating property owners. *Contemp. Econ. Policy.* 15:55–65

Sugg I. 1993. Ecosystem Babbitt-babble. *Wall Street Journal*, 2 April: A12

Sunderlin WD, Rodriguez. JA. 1996. *Cattle, broadleaf forests and the agricultural modernization law of Honduras*. Occas. Pap. 7, Cent. Int. For., Jakarta

Swallow S, Sedjo R. 2000. Eco-labelling consequences in general equilibrium: a graphical assessment. *Land Econ.* 76:28–36

Swanson TM. 1994. The economics of extinction revisited and revised: a generalised framework for the analysis of the problems of endangered species and biodiversity losses. *Oxf. Econ. Pap.* 46:800–21

Swinton S, Quiroz R. 2003. Is poverty to blame for soil, pasture and forest degradation in *Peru's* Altiplano? *World Dev.* 31(11):1903–19

Taylor JE, Dyer GA, Stewart M, Yunez-Naude A, Ardila S. 2003. The economics of ecotourism: a Galapagos Islands economy-wide perspective. *Econ. Dev. Cult. Change* 51:977–97

Thiesenhusen W. 1991. Implications of the rural land tenure system for the environmental debate: three scenarios. *J. Dev. Areas* 26:1–24

Tiffen M, Mortimore M, Gichuki F. 1994. *More People, Less Erosion: Environmental Recovery in Kenya*. Wiley: New York

US Fish Wildlife Service. 1997. *News release*, June 6

Watson RT, Heywood VH, Baste I, Dias B, Gamez R, et al. 1995. *Global Biodiversity Assessment: Summary for Policy-Makers*. Cambridge, UK: Cambridge Univ. Press

Weitzman M. 1998. The Noah's ark problem. *Econometrica* 66:1279–98

Wellisch D. 1995. Locational choices of firms and decentralized environmental policy with various instruments. *J. Urban Econ.* 37: 290–310

Wilson EO. 1988. *Biodiversity*. Washington, DC: Natl. Acad. Press

Wunder S. 2000. Ecotourism and economic incentives—an empirical approach. *Ecol. Econ.* 32:465–79

Zapata-Rios O, Vadez V, Godoy R, Reyes-García V, Huanca T, Leonard WR. 2005. *Income inequality and deforestation: evidence from a small-scale, pre-industrial society in the Bolivian Amazon*. Work. Pap. 14, Tsimane Amazon. Panel Study, Brandeis Univ.

Zhang D. 2004. Endangered species and timber harvesting: the case of red-cockaded woodpeckers. *Econ. Inq.* 42:150–65

On the Economics of Water Allocation and Pricing

Yacov Tsur

Department of Agricultural Economics and Management, The Hebrew University of Jerusalem, 76100, Israel; email: tsur@agri.huji.ac.il

Annu. Rev. Resour. Econ. 2009. 1:513–35

First published online as a Review in Advance on May 21, 2009

The *Annual Review of Resource Economics* is online at resource.annualreviews.org

This article's doi:
10.1146/annurev.resource.050708.144256

Key Words

scarcity, pricing, optimal allocation, water economy

Abstract

I present the economic principles of water allocation and pricing in a schematic water economy representing a wide range of real-world situations. The water policy has inter- and intratemporal components. The former determines extractions from the naturally replenished sources, given the stochastic nature of recharge processes. The latter is concerned mainly with the allocation of the extracted and produced water among the end users. The optimal water prices associated with the intratemporal allocation task are derived. Implementation of the optimal policy is discussed.

1. INTRODUCTION

Population growth and rising living standards have led to a rapid increase in the demand for water. However, the annual supply of renewable fresh water in any particular location is, on average, constant. As a result, water has become scarce in many parts of the world. Adding the prevalence of deteriorating water quality and the increased awareness for water-related environmental and social problems helps to understand why water allocation has become a critical policy challenge. A water policy is concerned with efficient use of the existing water sources and a balanced planning and development of new sources. This work presents the underlying economic principles.

Water economies vary in many respects, including hydrology (water sources), precipitation, climate, physical infrastructure, water rights, and social institutions (see examples in Parker & Tsur 1997, Dinar 2000, Saleth & Dinar 2004), and a water policy must be tailored to the relevant conditions in each case. The focus here is on the principles shared by many water policies, in spite of the idiosyncrasies of the water economy to which they are applied. I begin by describing the components composing water economies (Section 2) and continue to define feasible and optimal water allocation (Section 3). A water policy consists of inter- and intratemporal components. The former determines the limits on extractions from the naturally replenished sources, given the stochastic fluctuations caused by precipitation. The latter deals with the allocation of the available water supply among the end users. My focus here is on the intratemporal allocation decisions. (The intertemporal problem is defined and briefly discussed in Appendix B, below.)

Once the components of a water policy have been laid out and the optimal water allocation specified, the ultimate task of implementation arises; this task crucially depends on the idiosyncrasies of the water economy under consideration. In California's water economy, for example, the complex riparian-appropriative water rights system coupled with a variety of water permits (Parker 1997) limit the effectiveness of water pricing and promote various trading schemes. In Israel, the water resources are owned by the state (Yaron 1997) and allocation policies rely on pricing and quota schemes. In such cases, the optimal water prices (defined in Section 4) are necessary for implementing the optimal allocation policy, and this form of regulation raises a variety of agency problems associated with asymmetric information, which are briefly discussed (Section 5).

I note at the outset that this effort does not attempt to survey the wide range of water allocation issues, nor is an attempt made to cover the huge literature on this topic. Moreover, this review is clearly biased toward water economies in which pricing is an effective policy tool. With these qualifications in mind, I set to lay out the main principles of water allocation policies in a concise and coherent fashion and with a view toward actual implementations.

2. THE WATER ECONOMY

A water economy consists of (*a*) the physical resource base (precipitation, rivers, lakes, aquifers), (*b*) consumers and users (irrigators, households, industry), (*c*) suppliers and the associated infrastructure (extraction-conveyance-treatment infrastructure), and (*d*) regulatory and institutional infrastructure (water laws and property rights, prices and quotas, water institutions). I begin with a schematic description of these components.

2.1. Water Resources

There are M (possibly interconnected) naturally replenished water sources (rivers, lakes, reservoirs, aquifers) whose stocks at time t are represented by $Q_t = (Q_t^1, Q_t^2, \ldots, Q_t^M)'$. The water stocks evolve in time according to

$$Q_{t+1}^m = Q_t^m + R^m(Q_t) + x_{t+1}^m - g_{t+1}^m, \quad m = 1, 2, \ldots, M, \tag{2.1}$$

where $R^m(\cdot)$ represents deterministic recharge, x_t^m is stochastic recharge, and $g_{t+1}^m \in A^m(Q_t, x_t)$ is the rate of extraction from source m with $A^m(Q_t, x_t)$ denoting the set of admissible extractions, which depends on hydrological constraints.

Recharge at time t emanates from current precipitation and from subsurface flows. The latter depends on current and past precipitation. Precipitation may vary spatially across the water basin. Accordingly, the basin is divided into $N \geq 1$ subregions and w_t denotes the N-dimensional vector whose elements w_t^n are the precipitation in subregion $n = 1, 2, \ldots, N$ during period t. The w_t, $t = 1, 2 \ldots$, are i.i.d. draws from an N-dimensional distribution F_w defined over a nonnegative support.

Current and past precipitations generate the $M \times 1$ stochastic recharge vector $x_t = (x_t^1, x_t^2, \ldots, x_t^M)'$ according to

$$x_{t+1} = \Lambda w_{t+1} + \Gamma x_t, \tag{2.2}$$

where Λ and Γ are $M \times N$ and $M \times M$ matrices, respectively, of (known) coefficients. The mth row of Λ represents the immediate effect of precipitation on stock m's recharge, whereas the mth row of Γ represents the (diminishing) effects of past precipitation. In light of Equation 2.2, the water stocks evolution (Equation 2.1) can be rendered as

$$Q_{t+1} = Q_t + R(Q_t) + \Gamma x_t + \Lambda w_{t+1} - g_{t+1}, \tag{2.3}$$

where $R(Q) = (R^1(Q), R^2(Q), \ldots, R^M(Q))'$ and $g_{t+1} = (g_{t+1}^1, g_{t+1}^2, \ldots, g_{t+1}^M)'$. The extraction quotas g_{t+1} are restricted to lie in the admissible set $A_t = (A_t^1, A_t^2, \ldots, A_t^M)'$, where $A_t^m = A^m(Q_t, x_t)$, $m = 1, 2, \ldots, M$.

Two types of produced sources may also be available: desalinated water (of brackish sources or seawater) and recycled (treated sewage) water. Desalination is referred to as source $M + h$, $h = 1, 2, \ldots, H$, where H is the number of desalination plants.

Recycled water has two distinctive features that separate it from the other sources. First, exogenous (health and environmental) regulations often require treating sewage water, disregarding whether it will later be reused. Second, the same regulations often forbid mixing treated effluent with potable water, implying that reusing the treated water requires separate conveyance and distribution systems. These properties affect the pricing of recycled water, discussed below.

2.2. Consumers and Users

The basin contains S private sectors (urban, agriculture, industry) and a few public sectors (parks, estuaries, wilderness areas) scattered spatially in L locations (districts, regions, municipalities). Let us consider a single public sector, called the environment (e.g., instream water), indexed $S + 1$.[1] The inverse water demand of sector $s = 1, 2, \ldots, S$,

---

[1]Water allocated to the environment has features of a public good; hence, the analysis of this sector differs from that of the S private sectors.

in location $l = 1, 2, \ldots, L$, is denoted $D^{sl}(\cdot)$: When the water price (dollars per m³, say) is $D^{sl}(q)$, sector s in location l demands the water quantity q. (Water demands are assumed stationary; extensions needed to account for nonstationary effects, e.g., economic and demographic growth, are mentioned in the concluding section.)

2.2.1. Agricultural (irrigation) demand. The number of agricultural sectors depends on the level of aggregation and may contain, for example, orchards, vegetables, fiber (cotton), cereals, other field crops, and livestock. Agricultural sector s in location l has J activities (crops), indexed $j = 1, 2, \ldots, J$. Let $y_j(q)$ denote crop j's water-yield value function, not including the water cost.[2] The corresponding inverse demand for irrigation water is given by $y_j'(\cdot) \equiv \partial y_j(\cdot)/\partial q$. To see this, note that when the price of water is p_w, profit is $y_j(q) - p_w q$ and the water input that maximizes profit satisfies $y_j'(q) = p_w$. Thus, the water demand at that price is $y_j'^{-1}(p_w)$. Typically, $y_j(\cdot)$ is increasing and strictly concave, so that $y_j'(\cdot)$ is decreasing and its inverse exists. The water demand of agricultural sector s in location l is $q_{sl}(p_w) = \sum_j y_j'^{-1}(p_w)$ and the corresponding inverse demand is $D^{sl}(\cdot) = q_{sl}^{-1}(\cdot)$. The diminishing marginal productivity of water implies that $D^{sl}(\cdot)$ is decreasing (see details in Tsur et al. 2004, Tsur 2005).

2.2.2. Industrial demand. Industrial sectors contain nonagricultural production activities that use water as an input of production. As above, the number of industrial sectors depends on the level of aggregation and the sectors are defined according to how water is used in the production process. The inverse water demand of industrial sector s in location l, $D^{sl}(\cdot)$, is derived in the same way as the agricultural water demand, with industrial activities instead of agricultural activities (for a detailed analysis, see Renzetti 2002a).

2.2.3. Residential demand. The utility of household i depends on the per capita consumption of water ($\tilde{q}$) and other goods ($\tilde{z}$). The (per member) demands for $\tilde{q}$ and $\tilde{z}$ are the outcome of

$$v_i(p_w, p_z, y_i, n_i) = \max_{\{\tilde{q}, \tilde{z}\}} u_i(\tilde{q}, \tilde{z}) \; s.t. \; (p_w \tilde{q} + p_z \tilde{z}) n_i \leq y_i, \tag{2.4}$$

where y_i is the household's income, n_i is the household's size (number of members), and (p_w, p_z) are the prices of $(\tilde{q}, \tilde{z})$. Household i's (per capita) water demand is denoted $\tilde{q}_i(p_w, p_z, y_i, n_i)$, the residential water demand in location l is (retaining only the water price argument)

$$q_{sl}(p_w) = \sum_{i \in \text{location } l} n_i \tilde{q}_i(p_w, p_z, y_i, n_i),$$

and the corresponding inverse water demand is $D^{sl}(\cdot) = q_{sl}^{-1}(\cdot)$. The residential sector includes water use for human needs (including water consumed in service, public, and commercial institutions) and private gardening (water use in public urban parks is included in the environmental sector, discussed below, owing to its public-good feature). With some

---

[2]These functions are defined as follows: Let $\tilde{y}_j(q, b, z)$ denote crop j production function, where q is water input, b is a vector of fixed inputs (e.g., land and family labor), and z is a vector of purchased inputs (labor, fertilizers, pesticides, machinery) with price vector r. Then, $y_j(q) = \max_z \{p_j \tilde{y}(q, z, b) - rz\}$ s.t. $b \leq \bar{b}$, where the output price p_j, the fixed inputs constraint $\bar{b}$, and the input prices r are suppressed as arguments [see empirical estimation in Letey et al. (1985)].

added complication, it is possible to consider private gardens as an additional residential sector [detailed accounts can be found in Baumann et al. (1998), Renzetti (2002b)].

2.2.4. Environmental water.

Environmental sectors include public urban parks and in-stream water in wilderness areas and estuaries. They differ from the sectors discussed above because of their public-good features. I briefly outline how to incorporate environmental water, assuming for simplicity a single environmental sector indicated as sector $E \equiv S + 1$. Let $q^{\bullet El}$ represent allocation of environmental water in location l. Household's i demand for $q^{\bullet El}$ is measured in terms of the household's willingness to pay (WTP) to preserve $q^{\bullet El}$ against the alternative in which $q^{\bullet El} = 0$ and the environmental water allocations in all other locations, $q^E_{-l} \equiv (q^{\bullet E1}, q^{\bullet E2}, \ldots, q^{\bullet El-1}, q^{\bullet El+1}, \ldots, q^{\bullet EL})$, are unchanged. Suppose that the utility household i derived from $q^E \equiv (q^E_{-l}, q^{\bullet El})$ is represented by the additive term $u^E_i(q^E)$, which is added to $v_i(p_w, p_z, y_i, n_i)$ of Equation 2.4. Household i's WTP for $q^{\bullet El}$ when environmental water allocation is q^E, denoted $WTP^l_i(\mathbf{q}^E)$, is defined by

$$v_i(p_w, p_z, y_i - WTP^l_i(\mathbf{q}^E), n_i) + u^E_i(q^E) = v(p_w, p_z, y_i, n_i) + u^E_i(q^E_{-l}, 0). \tag{2.5}$$

This WTP represents household i's demand for environmental water.

Estimating the WTP for environmental water belongs to the area of valuing natural amenities, on which a large (and growing) body of literature exists (for recent contributions, see Freeman 2003, Bockstael & McConnell 2007). Examples include Loomis et al. (1991), Dudley & Scott (1997), and Xabadia et al. (2004)—the latter includes negative environmental effects.

2.2.5. Consumers (users) surplus.

The gross surplus (not including the water cost) sector s in location l derived from consuming the water quantity q is

$$B^{sl}(q) = \int_0^q D^{sl}(\alpha) d\alpha, \ s = 1, 2, \ldots, S, \ l = 1, 2, \ldots, L. \tag{2.6}$$

Because $D^{sl}(\cdot)$ is positive and decreasing, $B^{sl}(\cdot)$ is increasing and strictly concave. The surplus generated by q^{El} is the sum of the $WTP^l_i(q^E)$ over all households i in the economy,

$$B^{El}(\mathbf{q}^E) \equiv B^{S+1,l}(\mathbf{q}^{S+1}) = \sum_i WTP^l_i(\mathbf{q}^E), \ l = 1, 2, \ldots, L$$

and the surplus generated by $\mathbf{q}^E$ is

$$B^E(\mathbf{q}^E) \equiv B^{S+1}(\mathbf{q}^{S+1}) = \sum_{l=1}^L B^{El}(\mathbf{q}^E). \tag{2.7}$$

2.3. Water Supply

Water supply entails extraction-production, conveyance, treatment, and distribution. Each activity requires capital, labor, energy, and material inputs. The capital cost constitutes the bulk of the fixed cost (some labor costs, such as management and accounting, may also be independent of the water supply rate, hence included in the fixed cost), whereas the costs of the other inputs make up the variable cost. There is a large literature on the optimal design and management of water supply systems (see, e.g., Chakravorty & Roumasset 1991, Chakravorty et al. 1995). Here, I briefly discuss the various components, as they are used to formulate the optimal pricing rules discussed below.

2.3.1. Capital cost. The capital stock of each activity is measured in terms of the full cost of installing the infrastructure (pipes, pumps, canals, etc.) necessary to carry out the activity. The notation used for the various capital stocks is presented in **Table 1**. A capital stock determines the capacity of the associated supply activity, i.e., the maximal quantity of water that can be supplied during a year, but otherwise it has no effect on the water supply rate. I denote these capacity functions by $F(\cdot)$ with the same subscripts and superscripts as those of the associated capital stock. For example, $F_e^m(k)$ is the maximal annual amount of water that can be extracted from source m when $K_e^m = k$.

Water treatment may occur (*a*) at the source (upon extraction, before conveyance), (*b*) in conjunction with basin-wide conveyance, or (*c*) upon reaching location l. At-the-source treatment occurs in conjunction with extraction and the extraction capital includes in-source treatment capital as well. Likewise, basin-wide treatment is carried out in conjunction with basin-wide conveyance, and K_c also includes the treatment capital. Treatment in location l can be carried out centrally for all sectors, using capital K_{tr}^l, or separately for each sector, in which case the distribution capital K_d^{sl} includes treatment capital as well. Which design is more cost effective depends on the nature of the location. For example, locations that are predominantly urban may prefer to treat all water to a drinking quality, whereas locations that are predominantly agricultural may prefer separate treatment systems for urban (drinking quality) and agricultural users.

Water is conveyed from source m to location l in one of two ways: either directly, using the infrastructure K_c^{ml} designated solely for that purpose, or via the basin-wide conveyance facility K_c. Let J^l denote the set of sources that can supply water directly to location l: If $m \in J^l$, then water from m to l is conveyed via K_c^{ml}; if $m \notin J^l$, then water from m to l is conveyed via the basin-wide conveyance facility K_c if location l has access to K_c. Notice that K_c^{ml} can be used only to deliver water from m to l. If a conveyance facility serves more then one source-location (ml) combination, it is included in K_c.[3] Some locations may not have access to K_c and can receive water only from sources $m \in J^l$. Let J_c denote the set of locations that have access (are connected) to the basin-wide conveyance facility K_c.

Sewage activity refers to the mandatory collection and treatment of water from urban and industrial sectors, disregarding whether the treated water will be reused later. Let J^{sew} denote the set of sectors that are connected to the sewage system. Typically, the sewage infrastructure in location l (K_{sew}^l) serves all sectors connected to the sewage system, i.e., all $s \in J^{sew}$; hence, it is not sector specific (the variable costs of sewage treatment do vary across sectors—see **Table 2** below).

Recycling is the activity of reusing the treated sewage water, which requires further treatment, conveyance, and distribution to end users. Some sectors (e.g., residential) are not allowed to use recycled water, so let J^{rec} represent the set of all sectors that can use recycled water. Because recycled water cannot be mixed with drinking water, it requires a distribution system of its own. The recycling infrastructure, K_{rec}^{sl}, includes treatment, conveyance, and a distribution facility.

The annual cost of capital is the interest and depreciation on the (current-value) capital stock, which constitutes the bulk of the fixed cost of water supply. For example, with r and δ representing the interest and depreciation rates, respectively, the annual capital cost associated with extraction from source m is $(r + \delta)K_e^m$.

---

[3]In general, more than one conveyance system delivers water to multiple source-location combinations. Here, I assume a single K_c system. Allowing for multiple K_c systems will add details but change none of the results.

Table 1   Capital notation

Capital	Capacity	Activity
K_e^m	F_e^m	Extraction from $m = 1, 2, \ldots, M$
$K_{des}^h \equiv K_e^{M+h}$	$F_{des}^h \equiv F_e^{M+h}$	Desalination plant $h = 1, 2, \ldots, H$
K_c	F_c	Basin-wide conveyance
K_c^{ml}	F_c^{ml}	Conveyance from $m \in J^l$ to l
K_{tr}^l	F_{tr}^l	Treatment, location l
K_d^{sl}	F_d^{sl}	Distribution in l to s
K_{sew}^l	F_{sew}^l	Sewage, location l
K_{rec}^{sl}	F_{rec}^{sl}	Recycling to $s \in J^{rec}$ in l

Table 2   Variable costs

Notation	Variable cost of (activity)
C_e^m	Extraction (and possibly treating), source $m = 1, 2, \ldots, M$
$C_{des} \equiv C_e^{M+h}$	Desalination, plant $h = 1, 2, \ldots, H$
C_c^{ml}	Conveyance from source $m \in J^l$ to location l
C_c	Basin-wide conveyance: relevant for conveyance from $m \notin J^l$ to l
C_{tr}^l	Treatment before distribution in location l
C_d^{sl}	Distribution (and possibly treatment) in location l to sector s
C_{sew}^{sl}	Sewage collection and treatment, sector $s \in J^{sew}$ in location l
C_{rec}^{sl}	Recycling: treating, conveying, and distributing to sector $s \in J^{rec}$ location l

2.3.2. Variable cost. The variable costs of supply are due to energy, labor, and material inputs (see **Table 2**). Supplying a m^3 per year to sector $s \in J^{sew}$ in location l from source $m \in J^l$ entails the variable cost

$$\underbrace{C_e^m(a)}_{\text{extraction}} + \underbrace{C_c^{ml}(a)}_{\text{conveyance}} + \underbrace{C_{tr}^l(a)}_{\text{treatment}} + \underbrace{C_d^{sl}(a)}_{\text{distribution}} + \underbrace{C_{sew}^{sl}(a)}_{\text{sewage}}.$$

For $m \notin J^l$ and $l \in J_c$, C_c replaces C_c^{ml}, and $C_{sew}^{sl} = 0$ for $s \notin J^{sew}$. The variable cost of supplying a m^3 per year from desalination plant h to sector s in location l is

$$C_e^{M+h}(a) + C_c^{M+h,l}(a) + C_d^{sl}(a) + C_{sew}^{sl}(a),$$

with the obvious modifications if $M + h \notin J^l$ or $s \notin J^{sew}$. The current state of desalination technology leaves ample room for cost reduction due to technical change (see Tsur & Zemel 2000).

Because mixing recycled water with water derived from the other $M + H$ sources is not allowed, recycled water requires conveyance and distribution systems of its own, which are included in the recycled capital K_{rec}^{sl} (**Table 1**). The variable cost of recycled water supply at the rate a to sector s in location l is $C_{rec}^{sl}(a)$. The regulator, or water authority, oversees and implements the water allocation policy defined next.

3. WATER POLICY

At the beginning of year t, after the precipitation w_t, hence recharge x_t, has been realized, the water state $Z_t = (Q_t, x_t)$ is observed (see Equations 2.2 and 2.3). Given Z_t, the policy decisions for year t entail the following: (a) extraction quotas g_t^m, $m = 1, 2, \ldots, M$, for the M naturally replenished sources, and production of desalinated and recycled water; (b) allocation of the extracted and produced (desalinated and recycled) water among the end users; and (c) investment in the capital infrastructure that determines the capacity of the various supply activities.

The extraction allotments g^m, $m = 1, 2, \ldots, M$, should be determined within an intertemporal decision framework that accounts for hydrological considerations associated with sustaining the water sources in the long run given the stochastic nature of precipitation and the ensuing recharge processes. This task is discussed in Appendix B, below. The existing literature follows the pioneering work of Burt (1964) and includes the works of Tsur (1990), Tsur & Graham-Tomasi (1991), Provencher & Burt (1994), and Knapp & Olson (1995). This area is still underexplored, and the present effort does not change this state of affairs. My focus here is on water allocation and capital infrastructure investment.

3.1. Water Allocation

An annual (intratemporal) water allocation is defined in terms of q^{msl}: The amount of water supplied from source m to sector s in location l, $m = 1, 2, \ldots, M + H + 1$, $s = 1, 2, \ldots, S + 1$ and $l = 1, 2, \ldots, L$, where $m = M + H + 1$ represents the recycling source and $s = S + 1$ is the environment sector. A water allocation $\{q^{msl}\}$ generates the following subaggregate allocations:

$$q^{m\bullet\bullet} = \sum_{s=1}^{S+1} \sum_{l=1}^{L} q^{msl} \text{(extraction-production from } m\text{)}, \tag{3.1a}$$

$$q^{\bullet\bullet l} = \sum_{m=1}^{M+H} \sum_{s=1}^{S+1} q^{msl} \text{(allocation to } l\text{)}, \tag{3.1b}$$

$$q^{m\bullet l} = \sum_{s=1}^{S+1} q^{msl} \text{(allocation from } m \text{ to } l\text{)}, \tag{3.1c}$$

$$q_c = \sum_{l \in J_c} \sum_{m \notin J^l} q^{m\bullet l} \text{(basin-wide conveyance)}, \tag{3.1d}$$

$$q^{\bullet sl} = \sum_{m=1}^{M+H} q^{msl} \text{(allocation to } s \text{ in } l\text{)}, \tag{3.1e}$$

$$q^l_{sew} = \sum_{s \in J^{sew}} (q^{\bullet sl} + q^{M+H+1sl}) \text{ (sewage in } l), \qquad (3.1f)$$

and

$$q_{rec} = \sum_{s \in J^{rec}} \sum_{l=1}^{L} q^{M+H+1sl} \text{(total recycled water).} \qquad (3.1g)$$

3.2. Investment Decisions

I consider a mature water economy for which the bulk of the capital (infrastructure, pumps, pipelines) has already been invested, and the intratemporal capital decisions entail replacement of the depreciated capital and, possibly, investment in new capital to meet a growing demand. The decisions entail the investment rates in any of the capital stocks listed in **Table 1**.

3.3. Feasible Allocation

An annual water allocation is feasible if all the q^{msl} components are nonnegative, $q^{M+H+1sl} = 0$ for $s \notin J^{rec}$ (exogenous recycled water use restrictions), and the subaggregate allocations satisfy

$$q^{m\bullet\bullet} \leq g^m, \ m = 1, 2, \ldots, M \text{(extraction quotas)}, \qquad (3.2a)$$

$$q^{m\bullet\bullet} \leq F_e^m(K_e^m), m = 1, 2, \ldots, M + H \text{(extraction-production capacity)}, \qquad (3.2b)$$

$$q_c \leq F_c(K_c) \text{(basin-wide conveyance capacity)}, \qquad (3.2c)$$

$$q^{m\bullet l} \leq F_c^{ml}(K_c^{ml}) \text{ for } m \in J^l \ \forall l(m \text{ to } l \text{ conveyance capacity)}, \qquad (3.2d)$$

$$q^{\bullet\bullet l} \leq F_{tr}^l(K_{tr}^l) \ \forall l \text{(treatment in } l \text{ capacity)}, \qquad (3.2e)$$

$$q^{\bullet sl} \leq F_d^{sl}(K_d^{sl}) \ \forall (l, s) \text{(distribution to } s \text{ in } l \text{ capacity)}, \qquad (3.2f)$$

$$q^l_{sew} \leq F^l_{sew}(K^l_{sew}) \ \forall l \text{(sewage in } l \text{ capacity)}, \qquad (3.2g)$$

$$q^{M+H+1sl} \leq F_{rec}^{sl}(K_{rec}^{sl}), \ s \in J^{rec}, \forall l \text{(recycled to } sl \text{ capacity)}, \qquad (3.2h)$$

and

$$q_{rec} \leq (1 - \alpha_{rec}) \sum_{l=1}^{L} q^l_{sew} \text{(total recycling)}, \qquad (3.2i)$$

where α_{rec} is the fraction of water loss due to sewage treatment and recycling.

The capital investments are nonnegative and cannot exceed some exogenous bounds (affordable expenditures):

$$K_t - K_{t-1}(1 - \delta) \geq 0 \text{ (irreversible capital)}, \qquad (3.2j)$$

and

$$K_t - K_{t-1}(1 - \delta) \leq \bar{I}\,(\text{affordable investment}), \tag{3.2k}$$

where δ is the depreciation rate and $\bar{I}$ is the exogenous upper bound on investment. Constraints 3.2j and 3.2k apply to each capital stock in **Table 1**.

3.4. Optimal Allocation

An allocation generates the aggregate (gross) surplus

$$\sum_{s=1}^{S}\sum_{l=1}^{L}B^{sl}(q^{\bullet sl}) + \sum_{l=1}^{L}\sum_{s\in J^{rec}}B^{sl}(q^{M+H+1sl}) + B^{E}(q^{E}) \tag{3.3}$$

and inflicts the variable cost

$$\overbrace{\sum_{m=1}^{M+H}C_e^m(q^{m\bullet\bullet})}^{\text{extraction-production}} + \overbrace{\sum_{l=1}^{L}\sum_{m\in J^l}C_c^{ml}(q^{m\bullet l})}^{\text{conveyance } m \text{ to } l} + \overbrace{C_c(q_c)}^{\substack{\text{basin-wide conveyance}}} + \overbrace{\sum_{l=1}^{L}C_{tr}^l(q^{\bullet\bullet l})}^{\text{treatment in } l}$$

$$+ \underbrace{\sum_{s=1}^{S+1}\sum_{l=1}^{L}C_d^{sl}(q^{\bullet sl})}_{\text{distribution to } s \text{ in } l} + \underbrace{\sum_{l=1}^{L}\sum_{s\in J^{sew}}C_{sew}^{sl}(q^{\bullet sl})}_{\text{sewage}} + \underbrace{\sum_{s\in J^{rec}}\sum_{l=1}^{L}C_{rec}^{sl}(q^{M+H+1sl})}_{\text{recycled water to } s\in J^{rec} \text{ in } l} \tag{3.4}$$

and the capital cost (the interest and depreciation on the aggregate capital stock)

$$(r+\delta)\left\{\sum_{m=1}^{M+H}K_e^m + \sum_{l=1}^{L}\sum_{m\in J^l}K_c^{ml} + K_c + \sum_{l=1}^{L}K_{tr}^l + \sum_{l=1}^{L}\sum_{s=1}^{S+1}K_d^{sl} + \sum_{l=1}^{L}K_{sew}^l + \sum_{s\in J^{rec}}\sum_{l=1}^{L}K_{rec}^{sl}\right\}. \tag{3.5}$$

Net annual benefit equals the aggregate surplus minus the variable cost minus the capital cost. The optimal allocation is the feasible allocation that maximizes the net annual benefit.

The capital cost (Equation 3.5) ought to be explained. Recall that I consider a mature water economy—one in which the capital infrastructure has reached a steady state (with a possible growth trend). Therefore, the cost of a capital stock K (recall that K measures the cost of installing the infrastructure at current prices) consists of the cost of financing K, i.e., the interest payment rK, plus the replacement cost δK due to depreciation.

4. OPTIMAL PRICING

I characterize the water prices that implement the optimal allocation for the private sectors $s = 1, 2\ldots, S$, assuming the environmental allocations $q^{mS+1l} \equiv q^{mEl}$, $m = 1, 2, \ldots, M + H + 1$, $l = 1, 2, \ldots, L$, are given.[4] Derivations and technical details are presented in Appendix A, below. Sector s in location l constitutes an end user, called user sl. There are $S \times L$ such users. The water price that user sl faces is specified in terms of intermediate prices associated with extraction and desalination, conveyance,

---

[4]Due to the public-good nature of environmental water, its allocation cannot use pricing and will not be further discussed here.

distribution treatment in each location, and sewage collection treatment. I discuss each in turn.

4.1. Extraction-Production

The extracting firms pay (the regulator) an abstraction fee for each water unit (m^3) pumped from a naturally replenished source. This charge, denoted Δ^m, varies across the M sources and represents the scarcity of water at that source. $\Delta^m = 0$ if $g^m \geq F_e^m(K_e^m)$, i.e., if the extraction quota is not binding; otherwise, it is determined such that extraction from source $m = 1, 2, \ldots, M$ does not exceed the quota g^m. No scarcity rent is imposed on desalination (for all practical purposes, the sea is an unlimited water source), so $\Delta^{M+b} = 0$ for $h = 1, 2, \ldots, H$.

After extraction and in-source treatment the water price is

$$p_e^m = \Delta^m + c_e^m + \frac{r+\delta}{f_e^m}, \quad m = 1, 2, \ldots, M+H, \tag{4.1}$$

where $c_e^m \equiv C_e^{m'}(q^{m \bullet \bullet})$ is the marginal cost of extraction (production) from source m and $f_e^m \equiv F_e^{m'}(K_e^m)$ is the marginal product of extraction (production) capital at source m, i.e., the increase in the extraction capacity associated with a marginal (unit) increase in the extraction capital (all derivatives are evaluated at the optimal water and capital allocation).

The $(r+\delta)/f_e^m$ term in Equation 4.1 is the marginal cost of extraction (production) capital per unit water. To see this, note that, when source m's extraction capacity constraint is binding, f_e^m is the increase in water extraction associated with a marginal (unit) increment in the extraction capital K_e^m. Thus, $1/f_e^m$ is the incremental capital per unit water, which when multiplied by $(r+\delta)$ gives the annual cost of the incremental capital per unit water.

4.2. Conveyance

The intermediate conveyance price is the marginal cost of conveying water from source m to location l:

$$p_c^{ml} = \begin{cases} c_c + \dfrac{r+\delta}{f_c(K_c)} & \text{if } m \notin J^l \text{ and } l \in J_c \\[2ex] c_c^{ml} + \dfrac{r+\delta}{f_c^{ml}(K_c^{ml})} & \text{if } m \in J^l \end{cases}, \quad l = 1, 2, \ldots, L, \; m = 1, 2, \ldots, M+H, \tag{4.2}$$

where $c_c \equiv C_c'(q_c)$, $c_c^{ml} \equiv C_c^{ml'}(q^{m \bullet l})$, $f_c \equiv F_c'(K_c)$, and $f_c^{ml} \equiv F_c^{ml'}(K_c^{ml})$ (all derivatives evaluated at the optimal allocation). Note that if $m \notin J^l$ (i.e., no facility is solely designated to convey water from m to l) and $l \notin J_c$ (i.e., l has no access to the basin-wide conveyance facility), then it is impossible to convey water from m to l and p_c^{ml} does not exist.

4.3. Treatment and Distribution in Location l

Upon reaching location l, the water is treated and distributed to the various sectors. The marginal cost of this operation is

$$p_d^{sl} = c_d^{sl} + \frac{r+\delta}{f_d^{sl}} + c_{tr}^l + \frac{r+\delta}{f_{tr}^l}, \qquad (4.3)$$

where $c_d^{sl} \equiv C_d^{sl\prime}(q^{\bullet sl})$, $f_d^{sl} \equiv F_d^{sl\prime}(K_d^{sl})$, $c_{tr}^l = C_{tr}^{l\prime}(q^{\bullet\bullet l})$, and $f_{tr}^l \equiv F_{tr}^{l\prime}(K_{tr}^l)$ (all derivatives evaluated at the optimal allocation). The first and second terms on the right-hand side of Equation 4.3 represent the marginal cost of distribution to sector s in location l and may also include treatment costs if water is treated separately for sector s. The third and fourth terms represent cost of treatment before the water enters the distribution system. In locations that do not perform central treatment, the last two terms vanish.

4.4. Sewage

The prices considered so far are associated with supplying water from the various sources to end users. The sewage of some sectors, i.e., $s \in J^{sew}$ (urban and industrial sectors), must be collected and treated. The marginal cost of this operation is

$$p_{sew}^{sl} = c_{sew}^{sl} + \frac{r+\delta}{f_{sew}^l} \quad \text{for } s \in J^{sew} \text{ and } \forall l, \qquad (4.4)$$

while $p_{sew}^{sl} = 0$ for $s \notin J^{sew}$, where $c_{sew}^{sl} \equiv C_{sew}^{sl\prime}(q^{\bullet sl})$ and $f_{sew}^l \equiv F_{sew}^{l\prime}(K_{sew}^l)$.

4.5. Recycling

Recycling occurs when the treated sewage water is delivered to user sl, which often entails further treatment to the quality required by the receiving sector. The marginal cost of recycling is

$$p_{rec}^{sl} = c_{rec}^{sl} + \frac{r+\delta}{f_{rec}^{sl}} \quad \text{for } s \in J^{rec} \text{and } \forall l, \qquad (4.5)$$

where $c_{rec}^{sl} \equiv C_{rec}^{sl\prime}(q^{M+H+1sl})$ and $f_{rec}^{sl} \equiv F_{rec}^{sl\prime}(K_{rec}^{sl})$.

4.6. End-User Prices

I now formulate the optimal end-user prices. To that end, let I^{sl} be the set of all water sources aside from recycling for which $q^{msl} > 0$ under the optimal allocation:

$$I^{sl} = \{m \in \{1, 2, \ldots, M+H\} \mid q^{msl} > 0\}. \qquad (4.6)$$

It is easy to detect the exclusion of a particular source from I^{sl}. Let

$$\hat{p}^{sl} \equiv D^{sl}(0), \quad s = 1, 2, \ldots, S, \quad l = 1, 2, \ldots, L, \qquad (4.7)$$

represent the maximal water price below which sector s in location l (i.e., user sl) demands a positive amount of water (this is the price that user sl will pay for the first water unit). Then, $q^{msl} = 0$ when the water price of source m is equal to or exceeds $\hat{p}^{sl}$, implying that $m \notin I^{sl}$. The $\hat{p}^{sl}$ of the urban sectors are much higher than those of the agricultural sectors, and those of the industrial sectors are typically in between.

The I^{sl} sets of some urban sectors contain all sources (otherwise, water from the excluded sources will never be demanded and such sources should not be included in the list of water sources), whereas those of the agricultural sectors typically contain subsets of the $M + H$ sources, e.g., the desalination sources will be excluded from the I^{sl} of most agricultural sectors in most locations. Let M^{sl} indicate the number of sources included in I^{sl}, so $M^{sl} \leq M + H$ with equality holding for at least one end user sl.

Let

$$\bar{p}^{sl} = \frac{1}{M^{sl}} \sum_{m \in I^{sl}} (p_e^m + p_c^{ml}) \tag{4.8}$$

represent the average marginal cost of supplying water to user sl, averaged over the $M + H$ sources (excluding recycling) from which user sl demands water (i.e., over the sources included in I^{sl}).

The optimal $S \times L$ end-user prices can now be specified as follows:

$$p^{sl} = \bar{p}^{sl} + p_d^{sl} + p_{sew}^{sl}, \quad s = 1 \dots, S, \, l = 1, \dots, L. \tag{4.9}$$

Equation 4.9 implies that the end-user prices p^{sl} are not directly affected by the cost of water derived from sources that are irrelevant to user sl, i.e., excluded from the I^{sl} set. For example, the cost of desalination should not directly affect the price of irrigation water in agriculture sectors for which $\hat{p}^{sl} \leq p_e^{M+h} + p_c^{M+hl}$, $h = 1, 2, \dots, H$ (which is the case in Israel for all agricultural sectors). However, the desalination price will affect the price of irrigation water indirectly via its effect on water scarcity. A higher desalination cost reduces the scale of desalination, thereby increasing the scarcity prices, Δ^m, $m = 1, 2, \dots, M$, of the natural water sources.

As recycled water ($m = M + H + 1$) uses separate treatment and conveyance facilities, it is priced separately from water derived from the other $M + H$ sources. The end-user prices of recycled water are

$$p_{rec}^{sl} + p_{sew}^{sl} \text{ for } s \in J^{rec}, \tag{4.10}$$

where p_{rec}^{sl} and p_{sew}^{sl} are defined in Equations 4.5 and 4.4, respectively.

4.7. Supply Stages and Intermediate Prices

The supply process can be viewed as proceeding along the following stages: The extracting firms are restricted not to exceed the extraction allotments $g_t = (g_t^2, g_t^2, \dots, g_t^M)$, determined by the regulator. Alternatively, the regulator can charge the extraction fees Δ^m, $m = 1, 2, \dots, M$, determined such that the extraction firms will not extract beyond the extraction quotas. The extracted (and produced) water is "sold" to the conveyance firms at price p_e^m. The conveyance firms deliver the water to the L locations, charging location l the price

$$p^l = \frac{1}{q^{\bullet \bullet l}} \sum_{s=1}^{S} \bar{p}^{sl} q^{\bullet sl}, \, l = 1, 2, \dots, L, \tag{4.11}$$

where $\bar{p}^{sl}$, $q^{\bullet \bullet l}$, and $q^{\bullet sl}$ are defined in Equations 4.8, 3.1b, and 3.1e, respectively.[5] Location l's water authority treats and distributes the water to end users in its location and then

---

[5]The water proceeds of location l's water authority are $\sum_s \bar{p}^{sl} q^{\bullet sl} + \sum_s (p_d^{sl} + p_{sew}^{sl}) q^{\bullet sl}$. The second sum is used to cover the cost of treatment, distribution, and sewage collection in the location. The first sum is used to "buy" the water quantity $q^{\bullet \bullet l}$ from the conveyance firms, which is the same as buying that quantity at price p_c^l.

collects and treats the sewage, charging end users the price p^{sl}. The intermediate prices associated with each stage are summarized in **Table 3**.

5. REGULATION

Water economies are fraught with market failures, including increasing returns to scale associated with the supply infrastructure, common resources (e.g., aquifers and reservoirs shared by many users), supply and demand uncertainty due to stochastic precipitation, and external effects associated with environmental (in-stream) and irrigation (agricultural landscape) water. As a result, market mechanisms on their own are unlikely to yield efficient allocation (involving the water prices defined above), and some regulation is needed. It is helpful to distinguish between the regulation of supply and demand. The first determines the amount of water available annually by setting the extraction quotas from the M natural sources (i.e., g_t^m, $m = 1, 2, \ldots, M$) and the rate of water production (desalination and recycling). The second entails allocating this amount of water among the various users. Supply regulation is discussed in Appendix B, below. The remainder of this section deals with demand regulation.

Regulation may be direct, involving prices, quotas, or a combination of the two, or indirect, based on a water market of some sort. Depending on the level of the regulatory body (state, region, county, district), it may be confined either to intrasectoral allocation, e.g., within an irrigation district or a municipality, or to intersectoral allocation, e.g., between irrigation districts and municipalities [see Sunding et al. (2002) and Diao et al. (2008) for a discussion on trade-offs due to water relocation between sectors]. The policy tools available to the regulator, as well as the degrees of freedom in using each tool, vary from case to case according to the economic, cultural, political, institutional, and legal structure (see Rausser & Zusman 1991, Zusman 1997, Dinar 2000, Saleth & Dinar 2004, Tsur et al. 2004, Fischhendler & Zilberman 2005, Griffin 2006, and references therein).

The set of policy tools feasible in any particular situation may evolve over time. This often happens when the increasing water demand (due, e.g., to population growth) exacerbates water scarcity and stresses the need for more efficient water allocation. A typical response is a move from allocation based on ad hoc arrangements, such as historical water rights, to more efficient allocation schemes involving water pricing and trading (McCann & Zilberman 2000, Musgrave 2000, Zilberman & Schoengold 2007). In such cases, the optimal prices (listed in **Table 3**) are instrumental for regulation. Calculating these prices in actual practice requires information (on water demands and supply costs) rarely available to water authorities. The regulation task, it turns out, is greatly simplified under the special case of supply technologies involving constant returns to scale, thereby giving rise to linear prices.

Table 3 Water prices along the supply stages

Price	Received by	Paid by
Δ^m	Regulator	Source m's extraction firm
p_e^m	Source m's extraction firm	Conveyance firms
p_c^l	Conveyance firms	Location l's water authority
p^{sl}	Location l's water authority	User sl

5.1. Linear Prices

Suppose that the capacity and variable cost functions listed in **Tables 1** and **2** are of the form $C(a) = ca$ and $F(K) = fK$, where c and f are (scalar) parameters (each activity listed in **Tables 1** and **2** has its own f and c parameters). In such a case, the marginal cost c equals the average cost independent of the supply rate, and the marginal capacity f equals water supply per unit capital independent of the capital stock. Thus, the optimal water prices (listed in **Table 3**) are independent of the water allocation and can be determined solely by the c and f parameters. Moreover, the water proceeds cover exactly the full cost (variable and fixed) of water supply (i.e., full cost recovery for water suppliers).

The regulator, however, is unlikely to know the true values of the c and f parameters. The information available to the regulator typically comes from activity reports (e.g., balance sheets) of water supply firms, giving rise to agency problems, such as when the firms, knowing that their reported information may be used against them (i.e., to determine efficient prices), are likely to misrepresent true costs. The literature offers a variety of methods to overcome or mitigate such problems (for relevant contributions, see Laffont & Tirole 1986, 1993). One example is to set a price cap based on observed (reported) average costs with a period of gradual reduction to a target (lower) price. Firms that outperform the curve (i.e., become efficient faster) can keep the extra profits, whereas firms that trail the curve will be replaced. When feasible, auctions should be used to choose the operating firms, including the desalination firm or the firm that will build and operate an irrigation project.

5.2. Linear Prices as Second-Best Regulation

The pervasiveness of scale economies in water supply technologies renders unlikely the linearity of the variable cost and capacity functions $C(\cdot)$ and $F(\cdot)$. In such cases, the average costs differ from the marginal costs, and both vary with the water allocation. Hence, the task of calculating the optimal prices requires information on the water demands of all end users and the supply costs of all supply firms and quickly becomes intractable. Moreover, aside from the information issue, under the optimal, marginal cost prices, the water proceeds do not cover the full cost of water supply. Imposing the constraint that the water proceeds cover the supply cost implies departure from the optimal, marginal cost pricing rule. The Ramsey (1927) rule specifies a departure that maximizes aggregate consumer surpluses subject to balanced supply budgets (see, e.g., Wilson 1993, ch. 5). This rule requires information on the demand elasticities of all sectors. Lacking this information, the regulator may resort to a simple average cost pricing, by setting all c and f of the various prices at the associated average costs. This simple average cost pricing rule entails full cost recovery (i.e., it balances the budgets of the supply firms) but is suboptimal to the Ramsey pricing rule. Given the information limitation, it is viewed as second-best pricing.

5.3. Decentralized Regulation

The pricing problems discussed above stem from the so-called asymmetric information—when consumers and suppliers have private information that they may not disclose (for water-related discussions, see Smith & Tsur 1997, Tsur 2000). Decentralization, namely delegating decisions to consumers and suppliers, is often an effective way to overcome or mitigate such problems. Water markets are examples of decentralized mechanisms. Trading can be in water, water rights, or water quotas; it may be formal or informal; and it can be carried out within and between sectors (e.g., irrigation associations and urban districts) as well as within and between time periods (Howitt 1994). The wide range of observed market designs stems from the wide range of institutional, hydrological, and physical settings affecting the operation of water markets (see Easter et al. 1998, 1999; Dudley 1999; Zilberman & Schoengold 2005, 2007; and references therein). All these market designs serve to alleviate problems associated with asymmetric information.

6. CONCLUDING REMARKS

The above is a bare-bones account of the basic principles of water allocation and pricing. Any real-world situation presents a myriad of factors that limits the set of feasible policy tools and requires departure from these basic principles. Political and legal constraints have also been briefly discussed. The asymmetric information problem is discussed in Section 5. I close by mentioning additional, frequently encountered considerations:

- **Subsistence water.** Water for basic needs (drinking, cooking, hygiene) is considered by many as a human right to which all are entitled, regardless of supply costs or households' budget constraints. In actual practice, this view is expressed via block-rate pricing of residential water, with a low (or even zero) price for the subsistence block (for basic water needs, see Gleick 1996).
- **Implementation costs.** The prices formulated above are volumetric and require metered water or some other way to infer the volume of water consumed. Volumetric pricing entails implementation costs, associated with installing and maintaining water meters, monitoring water use and collecting fees. These costs are high relative to other pricing methods (which may explain why, worldwide, the bulk of irrigation water is unmetered; see Bos & Wolters 1990). When implementation costs are included in the welfare calculations, other pricing methods, such as area pricing, may outperform volumetric prices (for some examples regarding irrigation water, see Tsur & Dinar 1997).
- **Nonstationary demand.** Water demands increase in time as a result of demographic and economic growth. On the supply side, the recharge processes of the natural sources $m = 1, 2, \ldots, M$, although fluctuating from year to year, are stationary. Driven by the hydrological base and the stationary recharge processes, the extraction quotas $g_t = (g_t^1, g_t^2, \ldots, g_t^M)$ from the M natural sources cannot grow beyond certain limits. Eventually, the growing demand will have to be met by produced (desalinated and recycled) water. Water-abundant or sparsely populated regions do not need the produced sources (at least not in the near term). But many water-scarce or densely populated regions currently need these sources, and the number of such regions increases every year.
- **Public-good features.** Water used in some private sectors may also have public-good effects. Examples include landscape amenities of irrigated farmland and private urban gardens (McConnell 1989, Drake 1992). Fleischer & Tsur (2009) showed that the landscape amenity of a particular (irrigated) agricultural sector (a crop or a group of crops) increases the value of the marginal product of land, hence also of water, for this sector. In such cases, the social water demand (that accounts for the external landscape effects) lies above the private water demand $D^{sl}(\cdot)$ (defined in Section 2.2.1).

The optimal water prices for this sector should be determined according to the social demand schedule rather than the private schedule $D^{sl}(\cdot)$, and the ensuing optimal allocation entails more water to agricultural crops compared with the allocation based on the private demand $D^{sl}(\cdot)$. Such effects may justify subsidizing irrigation water for certain agricultural sectors, e.g., by setting a lower price up to a certain quantity of water (i.e., a form of block-rate pricing).

- **General equilibrium considerations.** The present analysis is of a partial equilibrium type, in that I assume that the rest of the economy is exogenous to the water economy. For example, the price of capital (the interest rate r) is assumed to be given exogenously. Often, the water economy constitutes a substantial part of the entire economy, to the extent that the water policy may have feedback effects with a number of economy-wide variables, such as the price of capital and labor. In such cases, economy-wide considerations can have significant ramifications on water regulation (see, e.g., Tsur et al. 2004, Diao et al. 2008).

APPENDICES

APPENDIX A: DERIVATION OF THE OPTIMAL PRICES

Environmental water allocations are assumed exogenous and set at zero for convenience. I seek the water allocation $\{q^{msl}\}$ and the capital allocation $\{K_e^m, K_c^{ml}, K_c, K_{tr}^l, K_d^{sl}, K_{sew}^l\}$, $m = 1, 2, \ldots, M+H+1$, $s = 1, 2, \ldots, S$, $l = 1, 2, \ldots, L$, that maximize

$$
\begin{aligned}
&\sum_{l=1}^{L}\sum_{s=1}^{S} B^{sl}(q^{\bullet sl}) + \sum_{l=1}^{L}\sum_{s\in J^{rec}} B^{sl}(q^{M+H+1sl}) - \left\{ \sum_{m=1}^{M+H} C_e^m(q^{m\bullet\bullet}) + \sum_{l=1}^{L}\sum_{m\in J^l} C_c^{ml}(q^{m\bullet l}) + C_c(q_c) \right.\\
&+ \sum_{l=1}^{L} C_{tr}^l(q^{\bullet\bullet l}) + \sum_{s=1}^{S}\sum_{l=1}^{L} C_d^{sl}(q^{\bullet sl}) + \sum_{l=1}^{L}\sum_{s\in J^{sew}} C_{sew}^{sl}(q^{\bullet sl}) + \left.\sum_{l=1}^{L}\sum_{s\in J^{rec}} C_{rec}^{sl}(q^{M+H+1sl}) \right\}\\
&-(r+\delta)\left\{ \sum_{m=1}^{M+1} K_e^m + \sum_{l=1}^{L}\sum_{m\in J^l} K_c^{ml} + K_c + \sum_{l=1}^{L} K_{tr}^l + \sum_{l=1}^{L}\sum_{s=1}^{S} K_d^{sl} + \sum_{l=1}^{L} K_{sew}^l + \sum_{s\in J^{rec}}\sum_{l=1}^{L} K_{rec}^{sl} \right\},
\end{aligned}
$$

$$\tag{A.1}$$

subject to the feasibility constraints (Equation 3.2), exogenous constraints regarding water quality (affecting treatment requirement and recycled water allocation), and nonnegativity of the water allocations, given the previous year's capital stocks (the subaggregate allocations are specified in Equations 3.1a–g).

Notice that, given the previous year's capital stocks, the capital decisions entail only this year's investments. Notice also that planning idle capacity in any of the capital stocks is not optimal (because it increases the cost without any benefit compensations). In actual practice, the extraction allotments $g_t = (g_t^1, g_t^2, \ldots, g_t^M)$ vary from year to year (due to fluctuating precipitation), and the capital infrastructure is set according to some average allotment vector $\bar{g}$.[6] I consider Equation A.1 for an average year in which $g_t = \bar{g}$, so Equation 3.2b is binding. Because Equation 3.2a represents the same constraints as Equation 3.2b, it can be ignored. I also assume that Equations 3.2j and 3.2k are nonbinding.

---

[6]The optimal $\bar{g}$ according to which the extraction capital stocks are determined must be specified within an intertemporal decision problem, which is not pursued here.

I use the following notation:

$$c_c^{ml} = \begin{cases} C_c'(q_c) & \text{if } m \notin J^l \text{ and } l \in J_c \\ C_c^{ml'}(q^{m \bullet l}) & \text{if } m \in J^l \end{cases} . \tag{A.2}$$

Recall that J^l is the set of sources from which water is delivered directly to location l via the infrastructure K_c^{ml}. If location l receives water from a source $m \notin J^l$, it is done via the basin-wide conveyance infrastructure K_c, provided l has access to K_c, i.e., $l \in J_c$.

$$c_{sew}^{sl} = \begin{cases} C_{sew}^{sl'}(q^{\bullet sl}) & \text{if } s \in J^{sew} \\ 0 \end{cases} ; \tag{A.3}$$

$$c_{rec}^{sl} = \begin{cases} C_{rec}^{sl'}(q^{M+H+1sl}) & \text{if } s \in J^{rec} \\ 0 \end{cases} . \tag{A.4}$$

In general, lower-case $c(\cdot)$ indicates the marginal cost (derivative) of the corresponding cost function $C(\cdot)$, and lower-case $f(\cdot)$ stands for the marginal product (derivative) of the corresponding capacity function $F(\cdot)$. μ_e^m is the shadow price of Equation 3.2b; μ_c^{ml} is the shadow price of Equation 3.2c or 3.2d for $\{m \notin J^l \text{ and } l \in J_c\}$ or $\{m \in J^l \text{ and } \forall l\}$, respectively; μ_{tr}^l is the shadow price of Equation 3.2e; μ_d^{sl} is the shadow price of Equation 3.2f; μ_{sew}^l is the shadow price of Equation 3.2g; and μ_{rec}^{sl}, $s \in J^{rec}$, is the shadow price of Equation 3.2h. I assume that Equation 3.2i is nonbinding.

Necessary conditions for optimum include

$$D^{sl}(q^{\bullet sl}) - c_e^m(q^{m \bullet \bullet}) - c_c^{ml} - c_{tr}^l(q^{\bullet \bullet l}) - c_d^{sl}(q^{\bullet sl}) - c_{sew}^{sl}$$
$$- (\mu_e^m + \mu_c^{ml} + \mu_{tr}^l + \mu_d^{sl} + \mu_{sew}^{sl}) \le 0, \quad m = 1, 2, \ldots, M + H, \ \forall(s, l) \tag{A.5}$$

equality holding if $q^{msl} > 0$, where $\mu_{sew}^{sl} = \mu_{sew}^l$ or 0 for $s \in J^{sew}$ or $s \notin J^{sew}$, respectively. For $m = M + H + 1$ (recycled water),

$$D^{sl}(q^{M+H+1sl}) - c_{sew}^{sl} - c_{rec}^{sl} - \mu_{sew}^{sl} - \mu_{rec}^{sl} \le 0, \ s \in J^{rec}, \tag{A.6}$$

equality holding if $q^{M+H+1sl} > 0$.

$$\mu_e^m = \frac{r + \delta}{f_e^m(K_e^m)} \tag{A.7}$$

if Equation 3.2b is binding; otherwise, $\mu_e^m = 0$.

$$\mu_c^{ml} = \begin{cases} \dfrac{r + \delta}{f_c(K_c)} & \text{if } m \notin J^l, \ l \in J_c, \text{ and Equation 3.2c is binding} \\[3mm] \dfrac{r + \delta}{f_c^{ml}(K_c^{ml})} & \text{if } m \in J^l, \text{ and Equation 3.2d is binding} \end{cases} , \tag{A.8}$$

and $\mu_c^{ml} = 0$ if Equation 3.2c or 3.2d is not binding (recall that if $m \notin J^l$ and $l \notin J_c$, then no water can be delivered from m to l and μ_c^{ml} does not exist).

$$\mu_{tr}^l = \frac{r + \delta}{f_{tr}^l(K_{tr}^l)} \tag{A.9}$$

if Equation 3.2e is binding; otherwise, $\mu_{tr}^l = 0$.

$$\mu_d^{sl} = \frac{r + \delta}{f_d^{sl}(K_d^{sl})} \tag{A.10}$$

if Equation 3.2f is binding; otherwise, $\mu_d^{sl} = 0$.

$$\mu_{sew}^{sl} = \begin{cases} \dfrac{r + \delta}{f_{sew}^l(K_{sew}^l)} & \text{if } s \in J^{sew} \text{ and } (3.2g) \text{ is binding;} \\[3mm] 0 \end{cases} \tag{A.11}$$

$$\mu_{rec}^{sl} = \begin{cases} \dfrac{r + \delta}{f_{rec}^{sl}(K_{rec}^{sl})} & \text{if } s \in J^{rec} \text{ and } (3.2h) \text{ is binding} \\[3mm] 0 \end{cases}. \tag{A.12}$$

No slack capital under the optimal allocation implies binding capacity constraints, and we can define (all functions are evaluated at the optimal allocation)

$$p_e^m \equiv c_e^m + \mu_e^m + \Delta^m = c_e^m + (r + \delta)/f_e^m + \Delta^m, \tag{A.13a}$$

giving rise to Equation 4.1;

$$p_c^{ml} \equiv c_c^{ml} + \mu_c^{ml} = \begin{cases} c_c + \dfrac{r + \delta}{f_c(K_c)} & \text{if } m \notin J^l \text{ and } l \in J_c \\[3mm] c_c^{ml} + \dfrac{r + \delta}{f_c^{ml}(K_c^{ml})} & \text{if } m \in J^l \end{cases}, \tag{A.13b}$$

as specified in Equation 4.2;

$$p_d^{sl} \equiv c_{tr}^l + c_d^{sl} + \mu_{tr}^l + \mu_d^{sl} = c_{tr}^l + c_d^{sl} + \frac{r + \delta}{f_{tr}^l} + \frac{r + \delta}{f_d^{sl}}, \tag{A.13c}$$

as in Equation 4.3;

$$p_{sew}^{sl} \equiv c_{sew}^{sl} + \mu_{sew}^{sl} = \begin{cases} c_{sew}^{sl} + \dfrac{r + \delta}{f_{sew}^l(K_{sew}^l)}; & \text{otherwise } s \in J^{sew} \\[3mm] 0 \end{cases} \tag{A.13d}$$

as in Equation 4.4; and

$$p_{rec}^{sl} \equiv c_{rec}^{sl} + \mu_{rec}^{sl} = c_{rec}^{sl} + \frac{r + \delta}{f_{rec}^{sl}(K_{rec}^{sl})} \quad \text{for } s \in J^{rec} \tag{A.13e}$$

as in Equation 4.5.

With I^{sl} as the set of all water sources m for which $q^{msl} > 0$ under the optimal allocation, Equation A.5 holds as equality for all $m \in I^{sl}$. Summing Equation A.5 over all $m \in I^{sl}$ and dividing by M^{sl} (the number of water sources in I^{sl}) give

$$D^{sl} = \bar{p}^{sl} + p_d^{sl} + p_{sew}^{sl}, \tag{A.14}$$

where $\bar{p}^{sl}$ is defined in Equation 4.8. Evaluated at the optimal allocation, D^{sl} is the optimal water price for sector s in location l, thereby verifying Equation 4.9. Given Equation A.6, if $q^{M+H+1} > 0$,

$$D^{sl}(q^{M+H+1sl}) = c^{sl}_{rec}(q^{M+H+1sl}) + c^{sl}_{sew} + \mu^{sl}_{rec} + \mu^{sl}_{sew} = p^{sl}_{rec} + p^{sl}_{sew} \quad s \in J^{rec};$$

thus Equation 4.10 is verified. Note that the left-hand side of this equation is the demand price when a positive amount of recycled water is consumed.

APPENDIX B: OPTIMAL EXTRACTION

The water state at period t is represented by

$$Z_t = (Q_t, x_t), \tag{B.1}$$

where x_t is the M-dimensional vector of stochastic recharge defined in Equation 2.2, and Q_t is the M-dimensional vector of water stocks defined in Equation 2.3 or 2.1. Given $Z_t = Z \equiv (Q, x)$ and $g_{t+1} = g$, Equation 2.1 implies that Z_{t+1} is restricted to lie in the M-dimensional subset defined by

$$Z_{(Z,g)} = \{\tilde{Z} \equiv (\tilde{Q}, \tilde{x}) \mid \tilde{Q} - \tilde{x} = Q + R(Q) - g\}. \tag{B.2}$$

From Equation 2.2, we learn that, given $x_t = x$, the density of x_{t+1} evaluated at $\tilde{x}$ is $f_\xi(\tilde{x} - \Gamma x)$, where $\xi \equiv \Lambda w$ and f_ξ is the pdf of ξ induced by the pdf of w, f_w. Then, the pdf of Z_{t+1}, conditional on $Z_t = Z$ and $g_{t+1} = g$, evaluated at $\tilde{Z} \equiv (\tilde{Q}, \tilde{x})$ can be specified as

$$f(\tilde{Z} \mid Z, g) = \begin{cases} f_\xi(\tilde{x} - \Gamma x)/Pr(\tilde{Z} \in Z_{(Z,g)}) & \text{if } \tilde{Z} \in Z_{(Z,g)} \text{ otherwise.} \\ 0 \end{cases} \tag{B.3}$$

$f(\tilde{Z} \mid Z, g)$ is the transition density of the state process.

Let $B(Z_{t-1}, g_t)$ denote year t's annual net benefit, where the dependence on Z_{t-1} comes from the feasibility restriction $g_t \in A(Z_{t-1})$.[7] Given Z_0, the precipitation series $\{w_t\}_{t=1,2,...}$ generates $\{x_t\}_{t=1,2...}$ via Equation 2.2, which together with the policy $\{g_t\}_{t=1,2,...}$ generates $\{Q_t\}_{t=1,2,...}$ via (2.3), giving rise to the (random) payoff

$$\sum_{t=1}^{\infty} \beta^t B(Z_{t-1}, g_t),$$

where $\beta \in (0,1)$ is a constant discount factor. The value function, $v(Z)$, is the maximal expected payoff over all admissible extraction policies $\{g_t \in A(Z_{t-1})\}_{t=1,2...}$, conditional on $Z_0 = Z$:

$$v(Z) = \max_{\{g_t \in A(Z_{t-1})\}} E\left\{ \sum_{t=1}^{\infty} \beta^t B(Z_{t-1}) \mid Z_0 = Z \right\}. \tag{B.4}$$

Then, $v(\cdot)$ satisfies the optimality equation

$$v(Z) = \max_{g \in A(Z)} \left\{ B(Z, g) + \beta \int v(\tilde{Z}) f(\tilde{Z} \mid Z, g) d\tilde{Z} \right\}. \tag{B.5}$$

A stationary Markov extraction policy $g(Z)$ is a rule assigning an admissible g to any $Z \in Z$. The optimal policy $g^*(Z)$ is the extraction rule that maximizes the right-hand side

---

[7] An additional dependence of $B(\cdot)$ on the water stocks Q occurs when the latter affects extraction costs.

of Equation B.5. An important line of research entails studying the properties of the optimal extraction policy, such as existence and uniqueness of $g^*(\cdot)$ as well as convergence of the optimal state process to a steady-state distribution under various recharge processes, water demand forms, and supply technologies [Puterman (2005) is useful for this task].

DISCLOSURE STATEMENT

The author is not aware of any affiliations, memberships, funding, or financial holdings that might be perceived as affecting the objectivity of this review.

ACKNOWLEDGMENTS

I benefited from discussions with Ariel Dinar, Oded Fixler, Alex Kushnir, Arie Leizarowitz, Uri Shani, and Amos Zemel. Helpful comments of an Associate Editor of the *Annual Review of Resource Economics* and two anonymous reviewers are gratefully acknowledged. Financial support was provided by Israel's Water Authority.

LITERATURE CITED

Baumann DD, Boland JJ, Hanemann WM. 1998. *Urban Water Demand Management and Planning.* New York: McGraw-Hill

Bockstael NE, McConnell KE. 2007. *Environmental and Resource Valuation with Revealed Preferences.* New York: Springer

Bos M, Wolters W. 1990. Water charges and irrigation efficiencies. *Irrig. Drain. Syst.* 4:267–78

Burt O. 1964. The economics of conjunctive use of ground and surface water. *Hilgardia* 36:31–111

Chakravorty U, Hochman E, Zilberman D. 1995. A spatial model of optimal water conveyance. *J. Environ. Econ. Manag.* 29:25–41

Chakravorty U, Roumasset J. 1991. Efficient spatial allocation of irrigation water. *Am. J. Agric. Econ.* 73:165–73

Diao X, Dinar A, Roe T, Tsur Y. 2008. A general equilibrium analysis of conjunctive ground and surface water use with an application to Morocco. *Agric. Econ.* 38:117–35

Dinar A, ed. 2000. *The Political Economy of Water Pricing Reforms.* Cambridge, UK: Oxford Univ. Press

Dinar A, Zilberman D, eds. 1991. *The Economics and Management Of Water And Drainage In Agriculture.* Dordrecht: Kluwer Acad.

Drake L. 1992. The non-market value of the Swedish agricultural landscape. *Eur. Rev. Agric. Econ.* 19:351–64

Dudley NJ. 1999. Water resource sharing from a microeconomic perspective. *Camb. Rev. Int. Aff.* 12:239–53

Dudley N, Scott B. 1997. Quantifying trade-offs between in-stream and off-stream uses under weather uncertainty. See Parker & Tsur 1997, pp. 299–315

Easter KW, Rosegrant MW, Dinar A, eds. 1998. *Markets for Water: Potential and Performance.* Dordrecht: Kluwer Acad.

Easter KW, Rosegrant MW, Dinar A. 1999. Formal and informal markets for water: institutions, performance, and constraints. *World Bank Res. Obs.* 14:99–116

Fischhendler I, Zilberman D. 2005. Packaging policies to reform the water sector: the case of the Central Valley Project Improvement Act. *Water Resour. Res.* 41:1–14

Fleischer A, Tsur Y. 2009. The amenity value of agricultural landscape and rural-urban land allocation. *J. Agric. Econ.* 60:132–53

Freeman AM. 2003. *The Measurement of Environmental and Resource Value: Theory and Methods.* Washington, DC: RFF Press. 2nd ed.

Gleick PH. 1996. Basic water requirements for human activities: meeting basic needs. *Water Int.* 21:83–92

Griffin RC. 2006. *Water Resource Economics: The Analysis of Scarcity, Policies, and Projects.* Cambridge, MA: MIT Press

Howitt RE. 1994. Empirical analysis of water market institutions: the 1991 California water market. *Resour. Energy Econ.* 16(4):357–71

Knapp K, Olson L. 1995. The economics of conjunctive groundwater management with stochastic surface supplies. *J. Environ. Econ. Manag.* 28:340–56

Laffont J-J, Tirole J. 1986. Using cost observation to regulate firms. *J. Polit. Econ.* 94(3):614–41

Laffont J-J, Tirole J. 1993. *A Theory of Incentives in Procurement and Regulation.* Cambridge, MA: MIT Press

Letey J, Dinar A, Knapp KC. 1985. Crop-water production function model for saline irrigation waters. *Soil Sci. Soc. Am. J.* 49:1005–9

Loomis J, Hanemann M, Kanninen B, Wegge T. 1991. Willingness to pay to protect wetlands and reduce wildlife contamination from agricultural drainage. See Dinar & Zilberman 1991, pp. 411–30

McCann RJ, Zilberman D. 2000. Governance rules and management decisions in California's agricultural water districts. See Dinar 2000, ch. 4, pp. 79–104

McConnell KE. 1989. Optimal quantity of land in agriculture. *Northeast. J. Agric. Resour. Econ.* 18:63–72

Musgrave W. 2000. The political economy of water price reform in Australia. See Dinar 2000, ch. 14, pp. 299–320

Parker DD. 1997. California's water resources and institutions. See Parker & Tsur 1997, ch. 5, pp. 45–54

Parker DD, Tsur Y, eds. 1997. *Decentralization and Coordination Of Water Resource Management.* Dordrecht: Kluwer Acad.

Provencher B, Burt O. 1994. Approximating the optimal groundwater pumping policy in a multi-aquifer stochastic conjunctive use setting. *Water Resour. Res.* 30:833–43

Puterman ML. 2005. *Markov Decision Processes: Discrete Stochastic Dynamic Programming.* New York: Wiley

Ramsey F. 1927. A contribution to the theory of taxation. *Econ. J.* 37:47–61

Rausser CG, Zusman P. 1991. Organizational failure and the political economy of water resource management. See Dinar & Zilberman 1991, pp. 735–58

Renzetti S. 2002a. *The Economics of Industrial Water Use.* Dordrecht: Kluwer Acad.

Renzetti S. 2002b. *The Economics of Water Demands.* Dordrecht: Kluwer Acad.

Saleth MR, Dinar A. 2004. *The Institutional Economics of Water.* Cheltenham, UK: Edward Elgar

Smith R, Tsur Y. 1997. Asymmetric information and the pricing of natural resources: the case of unmetered water. *Land Econ.* 73:392–403

Sunding D, Zilberman D, Howitt R, Dinar A, MacDougall N. 2002. Measuring the costs of allocating water from agriculture: a multi-model approach. *Nat. Resour. Model.* 15:201–25

Tsur Y. 1990. The stabilization role of groundwater when surface water supplies are uncertain: the implications for groundwater development. *Water Resour. Res.* 26:811–18

Tsur Y. 2000. Water regulation via pricing: the role of implementation costs and asymmetric information. See Dinar 2000, ch. 5, pp. 105–20

Tsur Y. 2005. Economic aspects of irrigation water pricing. *Can. Water Resour. J.* 30:31–46

Tsur Y, Dinar A. 1997. The relative efficiency and implementation costs of alternative methods for pricing irrigation water. *World Bank Econ. Rev.* 11:243–62

Tsur Y, Dinar A, Roe TL, Doukkali RM. 2004. *Pricing Irrigation Water: Principles and Cases from Developing Countries.* Washington, DC: RFF Press

Tsur Y, Graham-Tomasi T. 1991. The buffer value of groundwater with stochastic surface water supplies. *J. Environ. Econ. Manag.* 21:201–24

Tsur Y, Zemel A. 2000. R&D policies for desalination technologies. *Agric. Econ.* 24:73–85

Wilson RB. 1993. *Nonlinear Pricing*. Cambridge, UK: Oxford Univ. Press

Xabadia A, Goetz R, Zilberman D. 2004. Optimal dynamic pricing of water in the presence of waterlogging and spatial heterogeneity of land. *Water Resour. Res.* 40:1–11

Yaron D. 1997. The Israel water economy: an overview. See Parker & Tsur 1997, ch. 2, pp. 9–22

Zilberman D, Schoengold K. 2005. The use of pricing and markets for water allocation. *Can. Water Resour. J.* 30:47–54

Zilberman D, Schoengold K. 2007. The economics of water, irrigation and development. In *Handbook of Agricultural Economics*, Vol. 3, ed. R Evenson, P Pingali, ch. 17. St. Louis, MO: Elsevier

Zusman P. 1997. Informational imperfections in water resource systems and the political economy of water supply and pricing in Israel. See Parker & Tsur 1997, pp. 133–54

The Economics of Agricultural R&D

Julian M. Alston,[1] Philip G. Pardey,[2]
Jennifer S. James,[3] and Matthew A. Andersen[4]

[1]Department of Agricultural and Resource Economics and Director of the
Robert Mondavi Institute Center for Wine Economics, University of California,
Davis, California 95616; email: julian@primal.ucdavis.edu

[2]Department of Applied Economics, University of Minnesota and
Director of the International Science and Technology Practice and
Policy Center, St. Paul, Minnesota 55108; email: ppardey@umn.edu

[3]Department of Agribusiness, California Polytechnic State University,
San Luis Obispo, California 93407; email: jsjames@calpoly.edu

[4]Department of Agricultural and Applied Economics, University of Wyoming,
Laramie, Wyoming 82071; email: mander60@uwyo.edu

Annu. Rev. Resour. Econ. 2009. 1:537–65

The *Annual Review of Resource Economics* is
online at resource.annualreviews.org

This article's doi:
10.1146/annurev.resource.050708.144137

Key Words

rates of return, attribution, R&D lags, spillovers, distribution,
treadmill

Abstract

Agricultural research has transformed agriculture and in doing so
contributed to the transformation of economies. Economic issues
arise because agricultural research is subject to various market failures, because the resulting innovations and technological changes
have important economic consequences for net income and its distribution, and because the consequences are difficult to discern and
attribute. Economists have developed models and measures of the
economic consequences of agricultural R&D and related policies in
contributions that relate to a very broad literature ranging across
production economics, development economics, industrial organization, economic history, welfare economics, political economy, econometrics, and so on. A key general finding is that the social rate of
return to investments in agricultural R&D has been generally high.
Specific findings differ depending on methods and modeling assumptions, particularly assumptions concerning the research lag distribution, the nature of the research-induced technological change, and
the nature of the markets for the affected commodities.

1. INTRODUCTION

Agricultural research has transformed agriculture and in doing so has contributed to the transformation of whole economies. Economic and policy issues arise because agricultural research is subject to various market failures, because the resulting innovations and technological changes have important economic consequences for net income and its distribution among individuals and among factors of production, and because the consequences are difficult to discern. These issues have been studied by economists and documented in a literature on the economics of agricultural research and development (R&D) that began as such in the 1950s, with work by T.W. Schultz and others.

Over the ensuing half century or so, economists have developed models and measures of the economic consequences of agricultural R&D and related policies in contributions that relate to a very broad literature, drawing on and at times contributing to the full range of subfields of economics.[1] For instance, some contributions extend back to the foundations of production economics, the measures of inputs and outputs, and their relationships to one another, as we attempt to obtain better measures of productivity. Others relate to the modern literature on industrial organization as we attempt to understand the role of market power of firms with intellectual property rights to inventions. Yet others relate to income distribution in multimarket settings, whether in the context of rich-country agriculture and concerns for displaced labor or in developing countries where a general equilibrium approach is necessitated by the role of agriculture in the economy as a whole. At some level, then, to understand the economic literature on agricultural R&D requires an appreciation of its relationship to the major subfields of economics (such as econometrics, labor economics, public economics, production economics, economic history, industrial organization, or operations research) to which it contributes and from which it draws ideas, methodological approaches, and tools and techniques. Within the constraints of this review, however, for the most part we treat the literature on the economics of agricultural R&D in isolation, only occasionally drawing attention to the linkages to the broader literature.

In this review, we focus on the role of methods used by economists and their implications for findings about research impacts. We cover the mainstream issues and the bulk of the published work on the economics of agricultural R&D, dealing with conceptual models of the impacts of agricultural research, data and methods for measuring the impacts, the resulting measures of the impacts, and the meaning of those measures.

Section 2 is organized around supply and demand models of the size and distribution of research impacts among producers, consumers, and others in the marketing chain. Much of the literature in this area has concerned the role of modeling assumptions in determining the findings—in particular, assumptions about the nature of research-induced technological changes and how they are represented in the model, as well as assumptions about the form of competition, and related issues. We present the main ideas from that literature and attempt a synthesis.

An important and often underappreciated type of economic research is contributed by studies that describe research institutions and quantify research investments or by

---

[1]Griliches (2001) observed that, "Current work on the role of public and private research in productivity growth has deep roots in the early work of agricultural economics. The first micro-production function estimates (Tintner 1944), the first detailed total-factor productivity (TFP) calculations (Barton & Cooper 1948), the first estimates of returns to public research and development (R&D) expenditures (Griliches 1958, Schultz 1953), and the first production function estimates with an added R&D variable (Griliches 1964) all originated in agricultural economics" (p. 23).

studies that develop measures of agricultural outputs, inputs, and productivity, and thereby provide data for econometric and other modeling studies. Section 3 documents some key contributions of this type and touches on some enduring issues related to the data.

Section 4 discusses a different set of methodological questions that arise in modeling agricultural innovation. In particular, the treatment of (spatial) spillovers and research lag structures can be seen both as elements of the general attribution problem raised by Alston & Pardey (2001) and as sources of specification bias with implications for the interpretation of findings. A related literature linking innovation processes to technology development and economic impacts deals with the rate, extent, and nature of technology adoption and diffusion processes.

Section 5 reports key findings about the impacts of agricultural research in terms of its consequences for the rate of technological change (or productivity growth) and its factor bias as well as the rate of return to the investments. The rate of return evidence generally indicates that agricultural research has generated very large dividends. It supports the view that agriculture is characterized by market failures associated with incomplete property rights over inventions and that, in spite of the significant government intervention to correct the market failure, nations have continued to underinvest in agricultural research. Section 6 summarizes and concludes the review.

2. MODELS OF THE SIZE AND DISTRIBUTION OF RESEARCH BENEFITS

Agricultural economists have used supply and demand models of commodity markets to represent agricultural research impacts, beginning with Schultz (1953) and Griliches (1958), with important subsequent contributions by Petersen (1967), Duncan & Tisdell (1971), Duncan (1972), Akino & Hayami (1975), and Scobie (1976), among others.[2,3] In a standard model of research benefits, research causes the commodity supply curve to shift down and out against a stationary demand curve, giving rise to an increase in quantity produced and consumed as well as a lower price. The benefits are assessed using Marshallian measures of research-induced changes in consumer surplus for consumer benefits and of research-induced changes in producer surplus for producer benefits.

The total gross annual research benefits (GARB) depend primarily on the size of the research-induced supply shift (expressed as a vertical shift by an amount equal to a proportion, k, of the initial price) and the scale of the industry to which it applies. Hence, Griliches (1958) proposed the approximation $GARB = kPQ$, where P is the commodity price and Q is the annual quantity to which the supply shift applies.[4] Some issues in the literature relate to the methods used for measuring the primary determinant of total measured benefits—the research-induced reduction in the industry-wide unit cost of production as represented by the supply shift, k—for instance, those based on adoption rates combined

---

[2]Although this seems to be a natural approach for technologies embodied in particular inputs, like seeds, it is less well-suited to many other kinds of agricultural R&D. An alternative approach may be to use a model of supply and demand for agricultural science.

[3]Some studies leave this model implicit when inferring a rate of return to research from the parameters of an econometric model of production (e.g., Evenson 1967) or when using short-cut approximations to measure benefits (e.g., Griliches 1958).

[4]As noted by Alston et al. (1995, pp. 60–61), and more recently elaborated by Oehmke & Crawford (2002), the elasticity of supply can have important implications for measures of research benefits if it is used to translate an assumed horizontal shift into a vertical shift, or vice versa.

with changes in experimental yields or commercial yields or others based on changes in total factor productivity. Other important issues are the size and structure of the market to which the shift factor pertains as well as the time-varying magnitude of the shift.

The distribution of the benefits between producers and consumers depends on the relative elasticities of supply and demand, the nature of the research-induced supply shift, and, less importantly, on the functional forms of supply and demand (see Alston et al. 1995). The nature of the research-induced supply shift has been controversial because it matters for results and is not easy to observe. Lindner & Jarrett (1978, 1980), Rose (1980), and Wise & Fell (1980) discussed the underlying conditions for and likelihood of parallel, pivotal, convergent, and divergent supply shifts driven by research. They also considered the implications of the alternatives for the size and distribution of total research benefits (see also Voon & Edwards 1991, Oehmke & Crawford 2002, among others). One point demonstrated by this literature was that the assumption of a linear supply function that is inelastic in the neighborhood of the equilibrium implies a positive intercept on the quantity axis, which is both implausible and a source of awkwardness when measuring the benefits from research-induced supply shifts that require extrapolating supply back to the origin. A similar problem arises with constant elasticity supply models (the main alternative to the linear model in this literature), which also become implausible at low prices and quantities.

One solution to this set of problems is to assume an alternative functional form for the supply function, as illustrated in **Figure 1**, where D_0 represents the demand for U.S. agricultural output and S_0 represents the supply.[5] Suppose a research-induced technical change causes supply to shift down in parallel to S_1 and, as a result, quantity produced and consumed increases from Q_0 to Q_1 and price falls from P_0 to P_1. Accepting Harberger's (1971) postulates so that changes in economic surplus are the relevant welfare measures, the total benefits from the research-induced supply shift are equal to the area between the two supply curves, behind the demand curve, and this is equal to area (B + C + E + F + G). Of that total, the consumer benefit is equal to area (A + B + F) and the producer benefit is equal to area (C + G) given the assumption of a vertically parallel supply shift, which means area A is equal to area E. These shares of the total benefits are distributed according to the elasticities of supply (ε) and demand (η, representing the absolute value), where the producer share is approximately $\eta/(\eta + \varepsilon)$ and the consumer share is approximately $\varepsilon/(\eta + \varepsilon)$. Alternatively, suppose research causes a pivotal supply shift (i.e., holding the price intercept constant at b) that would have the same price and quantity effects. The total research benefits are now only roughly one-half of those from a parallel shift, but the consumer benefits are the same as from the corresponding parallel shift such that the producer benefits must be smaller, possibly negative.

To illustrate the role of elasticities in conjunction with the nature of the supply shift in determining the size and distribution of research benefits we use an algebraic representation of the model depicted in **Figure 1**, as follows:

$$P = (1 - k_1)b + (1 - k_2)BQ^\beta \text{ (supply)};\qquad(1)$$

[5]This supply function nests linear and constant elasticity models as special cases and has the virtue of a positive price intercept (or shutdown price) while permitting supply to be inelastic in the vicinity of the equilibrium (see Lynam & Jones 1984, Pachico et al. 1987, Alston & Wohlgenant 1989).

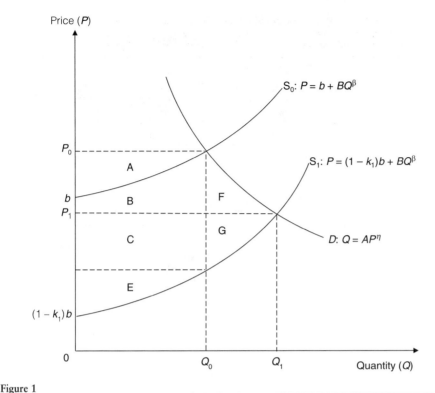

Price (P)

$S_0: P = b + BQ^\beta$

P_0

A

$S_1: P = (1 - k_1)b + BQ^\beta$

b
P_1

B

F

C

G

$D: Q = AP^\eta$

E

$(1 - k_1)b$

0

Q_0

Q_1

Quantity (Q)

Figure 1

Price, quantity, and welfare effects of agricultural R&D.

$$Q = AP^\eta \text{ (demand).} \tag{2}$$

This model nests as special cases both the linear supply model ($\beta = 1$) and the constant elasticity supply model ($b = 0$) and can combine these functional form alternatives with alternative types of supply shifts by using alternative combinations of values for k_1 (which implies parallel shifts in the price direction) and k_2 (which implies multiplicative shifts in the quantity direction); B and A are "slope" parameters. Although it cannot be solved analytically in its general form for the equilibrium price and quantity, this model can be solved numerically given particular values of parameters. **Table 1** shows the resulting estimates of producer benefits as a share of total benefits for three different kinds of 1% shifts down of the supply function: (*a*) vertically "parallel" ($k_1 = 0.01$, $k_2 = 0$); (*b*) "pivotal" (or multiplicative in the quantity direction, $k_1 = 0$, $k_2 = 0.01$); and (*c*) "proportional" (or multiplicative in the price direction, $k_1 = k_2 = 0.01$)—essentially combining a parallel shift and a pivotal shift. This range of parameters, which implies values for the elasticity of supply at the initial equilibrium ranging from 0.33 to 2.0, is combined with demand elasticities from 0.5 to ∞.[6]

---

[6]Small elasticities of demand are appropriate for most agricultural commodities in the context of a closed economy model. But larger elasticities are appropriate for traded (or tradable) goods, and in many cases, either countries are small countries in trade (facing excess demand elasticities for domestic output approaching infinity) or they would be but for trade barriers. More elaborate models are required to partition the "consumer surplus" in **Figure 1** among nations and to deal with the consequences of trade-distorting policies in such cases.

Table 1 Producer shares (percentage) of research benefits and their determinants[a]

Supply function parameters			Demand elasticity (absolute value)				
β	b	Elasticity (ε)	0.5	1.0	1.5	2.0	4.0
Parameter values			Producer shares of benefits (percent)				
Pivotal supply shift: $k_1 = 0.00$, $k_2 = 0.01$							
4.00	0.25	0.33	−100	−25	9	29	62
4.00	0.50	0.50	−150	−67	−25	0	44
4.00	0.75	1.00	−234	−150	−100	−67	0
2.00	0.25	0.67	−71	−20	8	25	57
2.00	0.50	1.00	−100	−50	−20	0	40
2.00	0.75	2.00	−140	−100	−72	−50	0
Proportional supply shift: $k_1 = 0.01$, $k_2 = 0.01$							
4.00	0.25	0.33	0	37	55	64	81
4.00	0.50	0.50	17	44	58	67	82
4.00	0.75	1.00	17	38	50	59	75
2.00	0.25	0.67	−14	20	38	50	71
2.00	0.50	1.00	0	25	40	50	70
2.00	0.75	2.00	4	20	32	40	60
Parallel supply shift: $k_1 = 0.01$, $k_2 = 0.00$							
4.00	0.25	0.33	60	75	82	86	92
4.00	0.50	0.50	50	67	75	80	89
4.00	0.75	1.00	34	50	60	67	80
2.00	0.25	0.67	43	60	69	75	86
2.00	0.50	1.00	33	50	60	67	80
2.00	0.75	2.00	20	34	43	50	67

[a]Entries in this table are measures of producer benefits as a percentage of the total benefits from the supply shift. The parameter b represents the shutdown price as a fraction of the initial price, and the parameter β is the exponent of the quantity in the price-dependent supply response function, such that a larger value of β tends to imply a smaller supply elasticity, as does a smaller value of b.

With a linear model, producers lose from a pivotal shift either if demand is inelastic or if demand is elastic but less elastic than supply. Somewhat similar results are found here for the nonlinear model. Producers do not benefit from a pivotal shift unless demand is elastic, and much more elastic than supply. In contrast, with a parallel research-induced supply shift, producers gain a substantial share of the benefits, especially if supply is relatively inelastic. And, with the proportional shift, although the producer share of benefits is smaller than for the parallel shift, it is still in the range of 30–60% of total benefits given the more likely values for the supply and demand elasticities.

The possibility of losses to producers in aggregate is often discounted, on the grounds either that demand is relatively elastic or that a parallel research-induced supply shift is relatively likely (or that the pivotal shift seems comparatively unlikely), but concrete empirical evidence on that issue has been elusive to date. Thus, even when we can be assured of benefits to the nation, some uncertainty remains about the distribution of benefits between producers and consumers.[7]

2.1. Distribution of Benefits Among Producers

Another issue is distribution of producer benefits among producers. Even if we can be assured that producers as a whole would benefit, those who do not adopt the new technology will not gain and may even be made worse off (if the adoption by others leads to price reductions), so individual producers or groups of producers may be uncertain about their benefits from a given research investment because of uncertainty over what technology may be developed and who will adopt it and when. Timing issues are also important. The lags between investing in agricultural research and reaping benefits are very long—recent results from Alston et al. (2009), reinforced with evidence presented by Alston et al. (2008), suggest lags as long as 10–15 years before important benefits begin to be realized, with streams of benefits extending for 40 years and more after the initial investment. This means that the distributional question has an intergenerational dimension to add to the other dimensions related to factor ownership and adoption patterns.

In addition to issues about the distribution of benefits and costs between adopters and nonadopters, there may be further distributional issues associated with how the "producer surplus" is distributed among factor suppliers: Do land owners benefit at the expense of suppliers of farm labor, including farm operators, or vice versa? To illustrate the key ideas, we can divide the total surplus into benefits accruing to "farmers" (i.e., the suppliers of land and managerial inputs used in agricultural production) and "others" (i.e., the suppliers of other inputs, including off-farm labor, purchased by farmers and other agribusiness inputs used in activities beyond the farm gate). Following Alston et al. (1995, pp. 246–50), we can measure these outcomes using a variant of the Muth (1964) two-factor, single-commodity market in which research gives rise to factor-augmenting changes in technology, which imply shifts in factor demand and product supply. Here, producer benefits correspond to producer surplus measured off the supply function for the factor supplied by farmers, and under the maintained assumption of competition, national benefits are given by the sum of changes in producer surplus across factor suppliers plus consumer surplus in the output market.

---

[7]All of this discussion abstracts from the dynamics of supply response to price, which means that the elasticity of supply (and, in some cases, the elasticity of demand) becomes greater with increases in the length of run. The dynamics of supply response to price—either alone or in combination with the spatial dynamics of the research-innovation-adoption process—mean that the pattern of research benefits evolves over time in complex ways that vary from case to case. A consideration of these dynamic aspects adds to the ambiguity of results derived from relatively simple comparative static analysis.

In this setting, it is not necessary to extrapolate any of the functions back to the origin to measure the changes in welfare associated with technical changes specified in this way. Local approximations to the functions are adequate for measuring the impacts of the small displacements involved. By measuring producer welfare impacts in the factor markets, we avoid the problem of having to specify the nature of the research-induced shift in the commodity supply function. Even so, we cannot avoid the fact that the measure of research benefits will depend on the assumed nature of the research-induced technical changes, which, with other assumptions, will implicitly define the nature of the shift of the commodity supply function. A difference is that we may have a reasonable intuitive basis for assuming a particular type of technological change (e.g., factor augmenting, neutral, or biased) in situations where we do not have such a basis for assuming a particular form of research-induced product supply shift.

In fact, however, the very specification of technology defined at the industry level or the use of a representative firm model will condition distributional findings: The approach generally entails technological changes that are consistent with multiplicative shifts of supply functions and the associated implications for distribution of benefits. For instance, if simple models such as the Cobb-Douglas model or the Constant Elasticity of Substitution model are used to represent the production function, factor-augmenting technological change (whether neutral across all factors or biased to augment just one factor) or the inclusion of research as a separate input will imply proportional (pivotal or otherwise divergent) supply curve shifts. More flexible functional forms for the production function may imply different types of technological possibilities, but such functions may prove difficult to work with. The same issues arise if, rather than a production function, we begin by specifying a cost or profit function, and we derive the implied output supply functions. Martin & Alston (1997) exemplify this approach to discussing the effects of R&D on market outcomes. Here, as they showed, parallel shifts can be derived but only if technological change enters the profit or cost function as a separate input. If the R&D is factor augmenting, or has the effect of reducing the cost for "effective" inputs, however, a multiplicative supply shift is implied.

If an industry is made up of diverse individual firms, it may not be well represented by an approach that implicitly or explicitly assumes an industry technology or a representative firm. Wohlgenant (1997) illustrated the roles of entry and exit of firms, variety in cost conditions among firms, and differential rates of adoption in determining the nature of the shift of the industry supply function (see also Foster & Rausser 1993). Consider an industry made up of heterogeneous firms in which firm entry and exit are key components of adjustment along the industry supply curve in response to price changes. A rising industry supply curve may reflect progressive increments in firms' reservation prices for entry, indicating variations in their opportunity costs of the quasi-fixed factors earning quasi-rents that make up producer surplus. A factor-augmenting technical change could give rise to proportional shifts in individual firm supply functions (in the context of the types of production, cost, or profit functions discussed above), while leaving their reservation prices unaffected, and the resulting shift in the industry supply function may be approximately proportional or pivotal as well. In contrast, similar per-unit reductions in reservation prices across firms would imply an approximately parallel industry supply curve shift, such that marginal and average costs would fall by the same amount per unit. More generally, technical changes may involve combinations of effects on the slopes and intercepts of individual firm supply functions as well as differential effects on different types of firms. Thus, research-induced technological change may plausibly give rise to supply curve shifts that are divergent, convergent, or parallel—depending on the nature of the industry, its technology, and the technological change—in ways that make the issue difficult to judge either *ex ante* or *ex post*. Because specification choices are unavoidable, it makes sense to be aware of the implications of the main alternative specifications for findings about the distribution of research benefits.

2.2. Extensions to the Basic Model

Measures of the size and distribution of research benefits will be affected by various complications that can be introduced to extend the basic model represented in **Figure 1**. The introduction of international trade is a straightforward elaboration of the simple model, from which we can obtain measures of welfare impacts for different spatial or market aggregates.[8] It becomes slightly more complicated when we allow for technological spillovers in the same model. More elaborate and complex multimarket models are implied if we want to disaggregate the market structure either (*a*) vertically in order to represent different stages of the marketing chain or (*b*) horizontally in order to represent different geopolitical or spatial markets for a given product or different products (including different qualities of the same product). Alston et al. (1995) laid out the basic theory for these approaches, and a number of studies have reported specific applications (among the many examples are Mullen et al. 1989, Freebairn 1992, Frisvold 1997, Wohlgenant 1997, Davis & Espinoza 1998, and Zhao et al. 2000).

A further dimension for extension to the basic model is to allow for the case of proprietary technology. The basic model treats the technological change as essentially exogenous, a reasonable treatment for the case of public research from which the results are freely accessible, which is the stereotypical application. However, this model is not appropriate for proprietary technology resulting from private research over which the inventor has (often monopoly) property rights, such as the fruits of modern biotechnology. In an important contribution, Moschini & Lapan (1997) extended the basic model to deal with proprietary research that could lead to a drastic innovation or a nondrastic innovation that would be priced in either case so as to entirely eliminate the pre-existing technology. A number of subsequent studies have extended the ideas, but these types of conceptual developments have not been incorporated much in the applied work to date, and very little evidence is available on the distribution of benefits from private research between technology developers and providers, on the one hand, and others including farmers, consumers, and agribusiness.[9]

---

[8]A significant complication in evaluating the supply-shifting consequences of agricultural research is that, because of the biological basis of agricultural production, many agricultural technologies have distinctive location-specific attributes. The specific location of firms may well affect their decisions about adoption of technology and the resulting factor demand and output supply responses to R&D, with implications for the aggregate industry-wide responses, even within a given spatial or market aggregate. Substantive efforts are under way to calibrate measured supply shifts in ways that take explicit account of these spatial heterogeneities (for example, see **http://www.HarvestChoice.org**).

[9]Moschini & Lapan (1997) treated the research effort and the research result as exogenous, whereas Alston & Venner (2002) developed a model in which the research effort was chosen by the biotech firm. See also Frisvold et al. (1999), Falck-Zepeda et al. (2000), Qaim (2003), and Lapan & Moschini (2004).

The basic model also assumes competition in the market for the commodity and the absence of any other market distortions. Models of research benefits have been extended to incorporate various types of market distortions, for example, (*a*) those resulting from the introduction of distortions associated with government policies such as farm commodity programs or trade barriers, including the failure to impose optimal trade taxes in the large-country case; (*b*) those resulting from the exercise of market power by middlemen (e.g., Huang & Sexton 1998); and (*c*) those resulting from environmental externalities (e.g., Antle & Pingali 1994). In this context, the main effect of a market distortion is to change the distribution of research benefits, with comparatively small effects on the total benefits. These changes in the distribution of benefits (and the total benefits) depend on the nature of the market distortion, along with the other market characteristics and the nature of the research-induced technological change, which together determine the potential research benefits in an undistorted setting.

Alston et al. (1988) identified and Alston & Martin (1995) subsequently proved a key aspect of the relationship between the distorted and undistorted research benefits. Specifically, research benefits in the presence of a distortion (ΔW^{ACT}) are equal to benefits in the absence of the distortion (ΔW^{MAX}) minus the effects of research on the deadweight losses from the distortion (ΔDWL, where we define $DWL = W^{ACT} - W^{MAX}$)—i.e., $\Delta W^{ACT} = \Delta W^{MAX} - \Delta DWL$. Thus, research benefits may be smaller or greater than in the absence of the distortion, depending on whether the research-induced technological change exacerbates or mitigates, respectively, the deadweight loss from the distortion—a result that depends, in turn, on the specific nature of a distortion and the other features of the market in which it applies. This simple but powerful result encompasses many ideas and is broadly applicable to any second-best analysis, not just this specific category. It helps to account for a variety of specific results in the literature on research benefits in a distorted market setting (e.g., Murphy et al. 1993, Chambers & Lopez 1993). For instance, immiserizing technological change requires that the effect of research be to worsen the consequences of an existing distortion sufficiently to more than outweigh the maximum potential benefits, which is a rather extreme outcome.

2.3. Political Economy Models

Models of agricultural research in a distorted market setting have been used to draw inferences about implications of market distortions for the rate of investment in agricultural research and thus the rate and direction of technological change (e.g., Hayami & Ruttan 1971, Schultz 1978, Mellor & Johnston 1984). Further wrinkles are added if we treat the distortions as endogenous, being determined jointly with the research investment and thus the technological change in a political economy or interest group model: Studies in this vein include, among others, Rausser (1982), Gardner (1988), de Gorter & Zilberman (1990), Rausser & Foster (1990), de Gorter et al. (1992), Alston & Pardey (1993), Foster & Rausser (1993), and de Gorter & Swinnen (1998, 2002). For instance, de Gorter & Zilberman (1990) used a model of industry technology with inelastic demand in which, consistent with the discussion in Section 2.1, farmers would lose from research in an undistorted setting but would benefit from research in the presence of a target price policy. Thus, they suggest we can account for and justify farm support policies as having been introduced to make possible socially beneficial research that otherwise would not have been politically acceptable to agricultural interests.

Political economy models that suppose agricultural research and farm program policies are chosen jointly to maximize a single criterion function typically involve two important abstractions from reality. First, the models assume a single government choosing combinations of policies to maximize a single criterion function. However, in countries such as the United States, the policies are chosen by different governments. Farm program policies are determined federally, whereas public agricultural research investments are predominantly the province of state government agencies, albeit using funds from a mixture of sources including state governments and various arms of the federal government.[10,11] Second, the models treat the consequences of today's R&D policies as though they are felt immediately along with the effects of today's farm commodity policies, but the impacts of today's research are realized only after long lags, measured in decades. The research policies that are interacting with and determining the impacts of today's commodity programs were implemented by the governments in power 20 years ago—the agricultural R&D policies established under George H.W. Bush, not George W. Bush, will determine the impact of farm program policies to be introduced by President Obama.[12]

The extent to which the results from the models are conditioned by these abstractions remains a matter for conjecture. To be sure, research policies chosen by any of the 50 state governments will be influenced by the present and prospective price policies to be implemented by the federal government, and the price policies introduced by the federal government in its periodic farm bills will have been influenced by the federal and state agricultural R&D programs over the previous decades. However, the relationships are many dimensional and multiperiod, with recursive rather than simultaneous causation, and thus are unlikely to be represented accurately by a simple static trade-off of welfare among producers, consumers, and taxpayers to maximize a single objective function.

3. RESEARCH THAT CREATES DATA ON RESEARCH INSTITUTIONS, INVESTMENTS, AND IMPACTS

A significant part of the economic literature includes studies that describe, document, and quantify the institutions that fund, regulate, and conduct agricultural research as well as the investments that they make. These "descriptive" studies are of value in their own right, but they also provide an institutional frame of reference and data for econometric and other modeling studies. Although documenting the institutional-descriptive studies alone would take much more time than we can spend in this review, we mention a few key

---

[10]Over the past several decades in particular, federal government departments and agencies other than agriculture, such as the National Science Foundation, National Institutes of Health, Department of Defense, and the Environmental Protection Agency, account for a larger, and now sizable, share of the federal funds directed to public agricultural R&D in the United States.

[11]de Gorter et al. (1992, p. 30) recognized the issue of multiple governments and asserted that "there is no reason to believe that disaggregating the decision process would refute [their] results." Gordon Rausser has advised us in a personal communication that Rausser et al. (2009) formally demonstrate that, even when agricultural research is the result of policies chosen by different governments, a criterion function can be derived that is based on a weighting of consumer, producer, and taxpayer interests.

[12]Given very long agricultural R&D lags, it does not seem reasonable to use a model that requires an implicit assumption that commodity program policies set in a given farm bill will be fixed for the period in which the R&D policies set in the same farm bill will have effect. For instance, consider the dramatic changes in farm program policies in 1985, 1996, and 2002 (e.g., see Alston & Sumner 2007).

studies that documented institutions in the context of making broader contributions to the literature on the economics of research. Notable contributions to the literature on U.S. agricultural research policy that provided institutional history, documented data on investments, or both include Ruttan (1982), Huffman & Evenson (1993, 2006), Kerr (1987), and Alston & Pardey (1996, 2006). Studies taking an international perspective include Hayami & Ruttan (1971), Evenson & Kislev (1975), Baum (1986), Pardey et al. (1991, 2006), Alston et al. (1999), and World Bank (2008).

Work has also been undertaken to develop concepts and measures related to agricultural science effort (in terms of public and private research investments, training and employment of research staff, and the like) and research output (in terms of new crop varieties and livestock breeds, patents, plant breeders rights, publications, and so on). In addition, substantial investments have been made in conceptual and empirical development of other measures (e.g., of prices and quantities of agricultural inputs and outputs) that are useful for measuring production relationships in agriculture, including research outcomes (e.g., the impacts on prices, production, consumption, and trade as well as the total benefit from research and its distribution).

Studies of the relationship between research and productivity rely on the painstaking and demanding work of the economist who makes the data on inputs and outputs used in studies of production more generally. As noted by Griliches in his Presidential Address to the American Economic Association:

> We ourselves do not put enough emphasis on the value of data and data collection in our training of graduate students and in the reward structure of our profession. It is the preparation skill of the econometric chef that catches the professional eye, not the quality of the raw materials in the meal, or the effort that went into procuring them (Griliches 1994, p. 14).

In his Waugh lecture to the American Agricultural Economics Association, Gardner discussed the importance of data creation and of having econometricians and other data users know how the data they use were created:

> Agricultural economists and other social scientists tend to take data as facts. . . The problem is the data are not facts. Facts are what is really there. Data are quantitative representation of facts, which statistical workers and economists concoct (Gardner 1992, p. 1074).

> I call the study of how primary statistical information is made into economic data "factology." The neglect of factology risks scientific ruin (Gardner 1992, p. 1067).

Gardner drew specific attention to the measurement of agricultural inputs (especially capital), outputs, and productivity as instances where a lot of effort and judgment goes into the creation of the "data," such that the data themselves are very much transformed from the raw material used to make them, and consequently areas where factology matters more than most. The same point applies perhaps even more forcefully to studies of the returns to agricultural R&D, when they involve significant further transformation of data on research investments and productivity that already had embodied in them a great deal of judgment, much of which may not be apparent to the user. Unfortunately, the lessons from Gardner's lecture have not been embraced by all practitioners, but some progress has been made with developing and documenting improved measures of agricultural inputs, outputs, and productivity as well as agricultural research investments, which are the raw materials for many studies of returns to agricultural R&D.

Andersen (2005) reviewed previous studies of U.S. agricultural productivity patterns and documented the evolution of approaches and results.[13] This literature shows an evolution from national fixed-weight indexes to state-level Divisia approximations using Fisher-ideal or Tornqvist-Theil indices, with increasing use of the appropriate index number theory (and other economic theory) combined with less aggregated data to reduce index number bias and other distortions in the measures.

Two separate long-term endeavors, one led by Eldon Ball at the U.S. Department of Agriculture (USDA)-Economic Research Service and the other by Philip Pardey at the University of Minnesota, have produced alternative state-level data sets that entail substantial differences in spite of essentially common purposes and similar basic information (for details and discussion, see Acquaye et al. 2000, 2003; Andersen 2005; Andersen et al. 2008; Alston et al. 2009). The data from Andersen et al. (2009) were developed specifically for measuring the economic consequences of U.S. public agricultural research, and the creation of these and the corresponding data on research investments has been by far the most demanding part of that long-standing project culminating in the book by Alston et al. (2009).

Compared with measures of productivity and its elements, measures of investment in research (and counterpart measures of stocks of scientific knowledge) have attracted much less effort and attention in the literature. This relative neglect could be comparatively pernicious. It takes a lot of work to develop measures of agricultural research investments. Appropriate measures of public agricultural research investments are not published in suitably long time series, in the relevant form, by any government agency. However, some data have been compiled by Huffman & Evenson (1993), the National Science Foundation (2008), Robbins & Moylan (2007), and Pardey & Andersen (2009). Guidelines for compiling such data include work by the Organization for Economic Cooperation and Development (2002, 2005). For international data, see Pardey et al. (2006) and the Agricultural Science and Technology Indicators (ASTI) Web site at http://www.asti.cgiar.org/.

To derive the relevant measures of public research spending requires delving through various government documents and sorting out those elements from particular spending lines that are truly research and truly applied to agriculture. It also requires going across places and backward through time, dealing with changing definitions, changing reporting procedures, and inevitable omissions. The long agricultural R&D lags mean

---

[13]Barton & Cooper (1948), Loomis & Barton (1961), and Baron & Durost (1960) were among the first researchers to compile national indexes of inputs, outputs, and productivity in U.S. agriculture. These authors calculated fixed-weight indexes, where the weights were equal to the average price of each subaggregate over a few selected years (see also Griliches 1960). The USDA published fixed-weight (Laspeyres) indexes of inputs, outputs, and productivity annually in *Changes in Farm Production and Efficiency* until the early 1990s. Griliches & Jorgenson (1966, 1967) were among the first to apply Divisia aggregation procedures to productivity measures of the general economy. According to Capalbo & Vo (1988, p. 101), Brown (1978) was the first researcher to compile Divisia indexes of inputs and outputs in U.S. agriculture. More recent studies of U.S. agricultural productivity include Ball (1985), Evenson et al. (1987), Capalbo & Vo (1988), Craig & Pardey (1990a,b; 2001), Jorgenson & Gollop (1992), Huffman & Evenson (1992, 1993), Ball (1994), Pardey et al. (1994), Ahearn et al. (1998), Ball et al. (1997), Ball & Nehring (1998), Ball et al. (1999), Acquaye et al. (2000, 2003), and Alston et al. (2009).

that time-series econometric studies require many years of data on both investments in R&D and productivity. Many studies have been constrained by the lack of suitably long time series, and researchers have resorted to estimation devices that almost surely have distorted the findings—such as imposing restrictions on the lag distribution length and shape or creating estimates of past data using crude extrapolations from the present, a data step that is not always apparent to the reader of the distilled research product. Data on private research investments have been particularly difficult to obtain, even in relatively short time series, because the information is proprietary—and even public companies are not obliged to publish the relevant information in their annual reports in a way that would be useful to economics researchers: For compilations of U.S. private sector agricultural R&D data, see Huffman & Evenson (1993), Klotz et al. (1995), Fuglie et al. (1996), Echeverría & Byerlee (2002), and Dehmer et al. (2009).

4. ATTRIBUTION PROBLEMS IN MODELS OF RESEARCH IMPACTS

In modeling the effects of research on agricultural productivity the two principal areas of difficulty are in identifying the research lag structure (the temporal attribution problem) and in the treatment of knowledge spillovers whether they are among different firms within an industry, different industries within a country or other geopolitical entity, or among countries (the spatial and institutional-cum-sectoral attribution problem).

4.1. Temporal Aspects of the R&D Attribution Problem

Research takes a long time to affect production, and then it affects production for a long time. Once formed, innovations and knowledge take time to be diffused and affect productivity, and so the overall lag between R&D spending and productivity growth reflects a confluence between the lags involved in knowledge creation and in its subsequent use. One element of the attribution problem, then, is in identifying the specifics of the dynamic structure linking research spending, knowledge stocks, and productivity.

A large number of previous studies have regressed a measure of agricultural production or productivity against variables representing agricultural research and extension, often with a view to estimating the rate of return to research. Alston et al. (2000) provided a comprehensive reporting and evaluation of this literature (see also Schuh & Tollini 1979, Norton & Davis 1981, Evenson 2001, Alston et al. 2009).

Only a few studies have presented much in the way of formal theoretical justification for the particular lag models they have employed in modeling returns to agricultural research. Alston et al. (1995) presented a conceptual framework based on a view that agricultural production uses service flows from a stock of knowledge (e.g., see Rausser 1974), which is augmented by research (e.g., see Griliches 1979).[14] The specification of the determinants of the lag relationship between research investments and

---

[14]The fact that science is a cumulative process, in which today's new ideas are derived from the accumulated stock of past ideas, influences the nature of the research-productivity relationship as well. This makes the creation of knowledge unlike other production processes.

production, which involves the dynamics of knowledge creation, depreciation, and utilization, is crucial. A finite lag distribution relates past investments in research to current increments to the stock of knowledge. However, even if knowledge depreciates in some fashion over time, under reasonable views of the nature, rate, and form of depreciation of knowledge, some effects of research will persist forever. As a practical matter, analysts end up representing these effects with a finite distributed lag that represents the confounded effects of the lags in the knowledge creation process and the dynamics of depreciation of the knowledge stock. In such a context, it is difficult to have precise views about the nature of the reduced-form empirical lag relationship between research investments and productivity, in terms of its overall length and shape, apart perhaps from a perception that there will be an initial "gestation" or "invention" lag (before research has any effects), an "adoption" lag during which the lag weights rise to a maximum, and, eventually, declining weights as the impact of past research investments on current productivity fades into unimportance.

Table 2 summarizes some key features of research lag distribution models applied in studies of agricultural productivity in Organization for Economic Cooperation and Development countries. This table represents a reworked version of table 5 in Alston et al. (2000). Until quite recently, it was common to restrict the lag length to be less than 20 years. In the earliest studies, available time series were short and lag lengths were very short, but the more recent studies have tended to use longer lags. Most studies have restricted the lag distribution to be represented by a small number of parameters, both because the time span of the data set is usually not much longer than the assumed maximum lag length and because the individual lag parameter estimates are unstable and imprecise given the high degree of collinearity between multiple series of lagged research expenditures.[15]

In their application using long-run, state-level data on U.S. agriculture, Alston et al. (2009) found in favor of a gamma lag distribution model with a much longer research lag than most previous studies had found—for both theoretical and empirical reasons.[16] Their empirical work supported a research lag of at least 35 years and up to 50 years for U.S. agricultural research, with a peak lag in year 24. Alston et al. (2008) also documented the adoption lags for particular agricultural technologies and their results are consistent with relatively long overall lags. This comparatively long lag has implications for both econometric estimates of the effects of research on productivity and the implied rate of return to research.

4.2. Spatial Aspects of the R&D Attribution Problem

Compared with the research lag structure, the issue of spatial attribution has received less attention in the literature on agricultural R&D and has been approached differently in the

---

[15]Common types of lag structures used to construct a research stock include the de Leeuw or inverted-V (e.g., Evenson 1967), polynomial (e.g., Davis 1980, Leiby & Adams 2002, Thirtle & Bottomley 1988), and trapezoidal (e.g., Huffman & Evenson 1989, 1992, 1993, 2006; Evenson 1996). A small number of studies have used free-form lags (e.g., Ravenscraft & Scherer 1982, Pardey & Craig 1989, Chavas & Cox 1992).

[16]The detailed arguments are laid out in Alston et al. (1995) and some earlier evidence is presented by Pardey & Craig (1989) and Alston et al. (1998) (see also Huffman & Evenson 1989). Alston et al. (1998) discussed the issue of knowledge depreciation drawing on the previous literature, and these arguments are restated and refined by Alston et al. (2008), and Alston et al. (2009).

Table 2 Research lag structures in studies of agricultural productivity[a]

Characteristic	Number of estimates Count	1958–1969	1970–1979	1980–1989	1990–1998	1958–1998
				Percentage		
Research lag length (benefits)						
0–10 years	253	9.7	6.2	17.9	12.7	13.4
11–20 years	537	41.9	22.0	38.8	22.8	28.5
21–30 years	376	0.0	20.7	12.0	25.9	19.9
31–40 years	178	0.0	4.3	5.6	14.3	9.4
40 up to ∞ years	141	0.0	9.5	6.6	7.6	7.5
∞ years	102	35.5	7.5	2.9	5.4	5.4
Unspecified[b]	109	12.9	13.1	3.2	4.9	5.8
Unclear[c]	190	0.0	16.7	12.7	6.3	10.1
Total	1,886	100.0	100.0	100.0	100.0	100.0

[a]Based on the full sample of 292 publications reporting 1886 observations. Adapted from Alston et al. (2000).
[b]Unspecified estimates are those for which the research lag length is not made explicit.
[c]Lag length is unclear.

literature on industrial R&D. In the more-recent literature, however, increasing attention has been paid to accounting for the fact that knowledge created within a particular geopolitical entity can have impacts on technology elsewhere, with implications that may matter to both the creators of the spillouts and the recipients of the spillins (for a review of this literature, see Alston 2002).

Some of the earliest work on these matters was done in applications to agriculture. The analysis by Griliches (1957) of the generation and dissemination of hybrid-corn technology throughout the United States was a seminal study in the economics of diffusion as well as the spatial spillover of an agricultural technology. This work inspired others on adoption of individual technologies, some of which entailed spatial spillovers. For example, Evenson & Kislev (1973) analyzed spillovers related to wheat and maize research, Araji et al. (1995) looked at spillovers regarding potato research, and Maredia et al. (1996) and Traxler & Byerlee (2001) investigated wheat spillovers. Pardey et al. (1996) analyzed the U.S. effects of rice and wheat varieties developed by international research centers in the Philippines and Mexico, and Pardey et al. (2006) assessed international and institutional crop varietal spillovers into Brazil.

Other studies have sought to assess the overall effects of agricultural research on productivity, including spillover impacts, with regression-based methods using more aggregate (region- or state-specific as well as national) measures of R&D. For example Huffman & Evenson (1993) found that a sizable share (upwards of 45%) of the benefits from research conducted in U.S. State Agricultural Experiment Stations was earned as interstate spillovers.

Whether they were concerned with spillovers or not, the past studies have imposed implicit or explicit assumptions about the spatial spillover effects of agricultural research based on geopolitical boundaries. For example, most past studies of the effects of U.S. agricultural research on productivity have implicitly assumed that agricultural research is totally fungible, such that U.S. national agricultural output depends on the national aggregate of U.S. spending on public agricultural R&D, regardless of where it was spent or by whom (e.g., Griliches 1964, Evenson 1967, White & Havlicek 1982, Chavas & Cox 1992, Alston et al. 1998). In contrast, some studies at the level of individual states proposed that research efforts by individual states have spillover effects only among states within the same (subnational) geopolitical region, whereas research outside a region does not affect its agricultural productivity (e.g., Khanna et al. 1994, Yee & Huffman 2001).[17] Several other studies, beginning with Huffman & Evenson (1989), incorporated geoclimatic information while retaining the restriction that technology spillovers occur only among neighboring states within contiguous geopolitical regions. Huffman & Evenson (1992, 1993, 2001, 2006), Huffman & Just (1994, 1999), and McCunn & Huffman (2000) subsequently used the same set of constructed spillover weights.

Many studies, however, simply ignored the effects of research in other states or by the federal government, and almost all of the regression-based studies of agricultural R&D have ignored the possibility of international spillovers, unless they were specifically emphasizing that possibility.[18] Looking more broadly at the literature, few studies of national systems, irrespective of the method used, have allowed for either spillins or spillouts—in their meta-analysis, Alston et al. (2000) identified less than 20% of studies allowing for any spillovers.

The modeling decisions—either to ignore spillovers or to represent them using measures based on physical proximity—have been at least to some extent driven by the limitations of available data and the requirements for parsimonious models. Even when we are conscious of the possibility of interstate or international spillover effects (and not totally hamstrung by data limitations), it is not clear what we ought to do about them. Clearly, however, restrictive assumptions are inevitable.

5. EVIDENCE ON THE ECONOMIC CONSEQUENCES OF AGRICULTURAL R&D

Alston et al. (2000) conducted a meta-analysis of 292 studies that reported estimates of returns to agricultural R&D, and they reported an overall mean internal rate of return for their sample of 1852 estimates of 81.3% with a mode of 40% and a median of 44.3% (see **Table 3**). After dropping some outliers and incomplete observations, they conducted regression analysis using a sample of 1128 estimates with a mean of 64.6%, a

---

[17]Citation patterns in the patent applications and in professional published literature indicate that spatial spillovers are much more pervasive.

[18]Bouchet et al. (1989) is an exception. In addition, studies of the effects of the CGIAR centers on agricultural productivity in adopting countries using other than regression methods have emphasized the spillins of technology (e.g., Brennan & Fox 1995, Pardey et al. 1996, Brennan et al. 1997, Brennan & Bantilan 1999, Brennan 2007). Alston (2002) reviewed these studies. Brennan (2007) reported a more-recent application to wheat spillovers from CIMMYT to Australia.

Table 3 Lag structures and rates of return to agricultural R&D[a]

	Estimates		Rate of return				
	Number	Share of total	Mean	Mode	Median	Minimum	Maximum
Characteristic	Count		Percentage				
Research lag length							
0–10	370	20.9	90.7	58.0	56.0	−56.6	1,219.0
11–20	490	27.7	58.5	49.0	43.7	−100.0	677.0
21–30	358	20.2	152.4	57.0	53.9	0.0	5,645.0
31–40	152	8.6	64.0	40.0	41.1	0.0	384.4
40 to ∞ years	113	6.4	29.3	20.0	19.0	0.3	301.0
∞ years	57	3.2	49.9	20.0	35.0	−14.9	260.0
Unspecified	205	11.6	48.7	25.0	34.5	1.1	337.0
Unclear	27	1.5	43.1	27 and 60	38.0	9.0	125.0
Research gestation lag							
Included	468	59.2	65.5	46.0	47.1	−14.9	526.0
Omitted	314	39.7	96.7	95.0	58.8	0.0	1,219.0
Unspecified or unclear	8	1.0	25.1		24.1	6.9	55.0
Total	790	100.0	77.5	46 and 58	50.2	−14.9	1,219.0
Spillovers							
Spillins	291	16.7	94.5	95.0	68.0	0.0	729.7
Spillouts	70	4.0	73.7	95.0	46.4	8.9	384.4
No spillovers	1,428	81.7	78.8	49 and 57	40.0	−100.0	5,645.0

[a]Based on a full sample of 292 publications reporting 1886 observations. For all characteristics, the sample excludes two extreme outliers and includes returns to research only and combines research and extension so that the maximum sample size is 1772. For the research gestation lag, the sample includes only observations with an explicit lag shape, resulting in a sample size of 790 observations. For spillovers, 25 observations were lost owing to incomplete information, resulting in a sample size of 1747 observations. Some estimates have spillover effects in both directions. Based on data reported in Alston et al. (2000).

mode of 28%, and a median of 42.0%. They found results that were generally consistent with expectations, but in many cases they could not distinguish statistically significant effects on the estimated rates of return associated with the nature of the research being evaluated, the industry to which it applied, or the evaluation methodology, because the signal-to-noise ratio was too low. Nevertheless, a predominant and persistent finding across the studies was that the rate of return was quite large. The main mass of the distribution of internal rates of return reported in the literature is between 20% and 80% per annum.

Alston et al. (2000) concluded that the evidence suggests that agricultural R&D has paid off handsomely for society, but they raised a number of concerns about the methods used in the studies that were likely to have led to upwards biases in the estimates. In particular, they suggested the studies may have suffered from bias associated with (a) using research lag distributions that were too short (the results showed that increasing the research lag length resulted in smaller rates of return, as theory would predict); (b) "cherry picking" bias in which only the most successful research investments were evaluated; (c) attribution biases associated with failing to account for the spillover roles of other private and public research agencies, in other states or other countries, in contributing to the measured benefits; or (d) other aspects of the methods used.

5.1. Recent Evidence on U.S. Agricultural R&D

More recently, Alston et al. (2009) modeled state-specific U.S. agricultural productivity for the period 1949–2002 as a function of public agricultural research and extension investments over 1890–2002. In this study, careful attention was paid to the types of methodological issues raised by Alston et al. (2000) and emphasized in this section, in particular to modeling the research lag distribution and the state-to-state spillovers of research impacts. Spillovers (or agroecological similarity or technological closeness) between states were represented using a measure based on output mix correlations—an adaptation of the approach of Jaffe (1986, 1989) who constructed a measure of technological distance between firms based on patent data. The research lag distribution was estimated using a flexible gamma distribution model. The results supported relatively long research lags (an overall lag length of 50 years with a peak impact at 24 years but with most of the impact exhausted within 40 years), with a very substantial share of a state's productivity growth attributable to research conducted by other states and the federal government. These results mean that the national benefits from a state's research investment substantially exceed the own-state benefits, adding to the sources of market failure in agricultural R&D because state governments may be expected to ignore or at least (heavily) discount the spillover benefits to other states.

Table 4 summarizes the results from the authors' preferred model, showing the distribution of own-state and national benefits from state-specific and federal investments in agricultural research and extension in the United States, expressed in terms of benefit-cost ratios and internal rates of return.[19] The results show that marginal increments in investments in agricultural research and extension (R&E) by the 48 contiguous U.S. states generated own-state benefits of between $2 and $58 per research dollar, averaging $21 across the states (the lower benefit-cost ratios were generally for the states with smaller and shrinking agricultural sectors, especially in New England). Allowing for the spillover benefits into other states, state-specific agricultural research investments generated national benefits of between $10 and $70 per research dollar, averaging

---

[19]There are compelling reasons to report benefit-cost ratios rather than internal rates of return in this instance, as discussed by Alston et al. (2009). Some internal rates of return are reported here to facilitate comparisons with other studies.

Table 4 Benefit-cost ratios and internal rates of return for U.S. agricultural R&D[a]

Returns to	Benefit-cost ratio (3% real discount rate)		Internal rate of return	
	Own-state	National	Own-state	National
State research and extension	Ratio		Percent per year	
48 states				
Average	21.0	32.1	18.9	22.7
Minimum	2.4	9.9	7.4	15.3
Maximum	57.8	69.2	27.6	29.1
Selected states				
California	33.3	43.4	24.1	26.1
Minnesota	40.6	55.4	24.7	27.3
Wyoming	12.7	23.6	16.8	20.9
Regions				
Pacific	21.8	32.9	20.2	23.5
Mountain	20.0	31.6	19.0	22.7
Northern Plains	42.4	54.5	24.9	27.0
Southern Plains	20.2	31.0	19.5	22.7
Central	33.7	46.8	23.1	25.9
Southeast	15.1	26.7	17.6	22.0
Northeast	9.4	18.4	14.0	19.0
USDA Research		17.5		18.7

[a]Source: Alston et al. (2009).

$32 across the states. The marginal benefit-cost ratio for USDA intramural research was comparable, at $18 per dollar invested in research.

The benefit-cost ratios in **Table 4** are generally large and might seem implausibly large to some readers. In fact, however, these ratios are consistent with internal rates of return at the smaller end of the range compared with the general results in the literature as reviewed by Alston et al. (2000) and summarized in **Table 3**, and as discussed by others (e.g., Evenson 2001, Fuglie & Heisey 2007). Specifically, the estimates of own-state "private" rates of return ranged from 7.4% to 27.6%, with an average of 18.9% per annum across the states, the estimates of national "social" rates of return ranged from 15.3% to 29.1%, with an average of 22.9% per annum across the states, and the rate of return to USDA intramural research was 18.7% per annum.

6. CONCLUSION

The literature on the economics of agricultural R&D is large. In this review, we have concentrated on some key areas where results may be fragile or distorted as a result of modeling choices made by economists. The creation of the "data" used in our analyses is a critical step. Because the interpretation of results often depends crucially on the data, it is incumbent on the data user to invest at least as far as knowing how the data were made, but there is no mechanism for enforcing this investment and it does not appear to have been a focus of effort. Like the work of creating data, factology is not well rewarded within the agricultural economics profession. Even so, the available data have significantly improved as a result of the efforts of a few individuals.

Along with the data, models used for measuring research benefits have improved over the years. Analysis has revealed some areas where findings are sensitive to modeling choices, including the representation of technological change in the model, the treatment of spillovers, and the R&D lag distribution. These are essentially empirical questions that are often difficult to resolve with the available data but must be settled, and they can have substantial impacts on the findings. The issue of how to go about specifying the research-induced technical change is largely unresolved. Better progress has been made with lags and spillovers. The trend has been to find larger spillover impacts and longer research lags in studies that test for these aspects. Models that inappropriately ignore spillovers or truncate the lag are likely to find higher rates of return to research as a result. Other specification choices—such as how to deal with market distortions from market power of firms, government policy, or environmental externalities—have relatively important effects on estimates of the distribution of benefits and relatively little effect on estimates of the total benefits.

Agricultural economists have invested extensively in quantifying the payoffs to agricultural R&D, but for the most part, these studies have referred to total benefits to the relevant society, rather than to particular groups in society. Partly, this may reflect the fact that findings regarding distributional impacts are comparatively sensitive to aspects of specification that often must be chosen arbitrarily; thus the results are fragile. An example is Cochrane's technology treadmill argument suggesting that, among farmers, only the early adopters of new technology benefit, and even they do so only temporarily (Cochrane 1958, Herdt & Cochrane 1966). As shown in this review, specific conditions must hold for this argument to be true (it requires a relatively inelastic demand and a multiplicative supply shift), and they probably do not hold in most applications.[20] But what we do not have is compelling, direct econometric evidence to show that farmers have in fact benefited from technological change. It says something about our models and measures that we have not yet been able to address this issue definitively.

As a profession, we have amassed a persuasive body of evidence demonstrating that the world as a whole and individual nations alone have benefited enormously from productivity growth in agriculture, a substantial amount of which has been enabled by technological

---

[20]Even considering agriculture in aggregate in the United States, the relevant demand is likely to be quite elastic (see Alston 2007), which is sufficient for farmers to benefit, even if research causes a multiplicative supply shift, for which there is no evidence. For any individual agricultural industry for any individual country, demand is likely to be highly elastic because of international trade. The relevant demand is likely to be highly inelastic in a case where the analysis applies to relative aggregated commodities in the world as a whole—e.g., global producer benefits from increases in the supply of wheat—or highly localized markets in a developing country where lack of adequate infrastructure circumscribes the market reach of agricultural producers.

change resulting from public and private investments in agricultural R&D. The evidence suggests that the benefits have been worth many times more than the costs. This is so, even if we discount the estimates heavily because we suspect they may have been upwardly biased, perhaps inadvertently through unfortunate choices of methods or limitations in the available data of the types discussed in this review. An implication is that the substantial government intervention notwithstanding, the world is continuing to underinvest in agricultural R&D.

SUMMARY POINTS

1. The total gross annual research benefits depend primarily on the size of the research-induced supply shift and the scale of the industry to which it applies.

2. The distribution of the benefits between producers and consumers depends on the relative elasticities of supply and demand, on the nature of the research-induced supply shift, and, less importantly, on the functional forms of supply and demand.

3. The very specification of technology defined at the industry level or the use of a representative firm model will condition distributional results. If simple models (such as the Cobb-Douglas model or the Constant Elasticity of Substitution model) are used to represent the production function, then factor-augmenting technological change—whether neutral across all factors or biased to augment just one factor—or the inclusion of research as a separate input will imply proportional (pivotal or otherwise divergent) supply curve shifts.

4. The possibility of losses to producers in aggregate as a consequence of research-induced technical change is often discounted, on the grounds either that demand is relatively elastic or that a parallel research-induced supply shift is relatively likely (or that the pivotal shift seems comparatively unlikely), but concrete empirical evidence on that issue has been elusive to date.

5. Models of research benefits have been extended to incorporate various types of market distortions, such as farm commodity programs or trade barriers, the exercise of market power by middlemen, and those resulting from environmental externalities. The main effect of a market distortion in this context is to change the distribution of research benefits, with comparatively small effects on the total benefits.

6. A significant part of the economic literature includes studies that describe, document, and quantify the institutions that fund, regulate, and conduct agricultural research as well as the investments that they make. These "descriptive" studies are of value in their own right but they also provide an institutional frame of reference and data for econometric and other modeling studies.

7. In modeling the effects of research on agricultural productivity, the two principal areas of difficulty are in identifying the research lag structure (the temporal attribution problem) and in the treatment of knowledge spillovers whether they are among different firms within an industry, among different industries within a

> country or other geopolitical entity, or among countries (the spatial and institutional-cum-sectoral attribution problem).
>
> 8. A predominant and persistent finding across the economic returns-to-research studies is that the measured rate of return is quite large. The main mass of the distribution of internal rates of return reported in the literature is between 20% and 80% per annum.

DISCLOSURE STATEMENT

The authors are not aware of any affiliations, memberships, funding, or financial holdings that might be perceived as affecting the objectivity of this review.

ACKNOWLEDGMENTS

The work for this project was supported in part by the University of California, the University of Minnesota, the USDA's Economic Research Service, Agricultural Research Service, CSREES National Research Initiative, the Giannini Foundation of Agricultural Economics, and the Bill and Melinda Gates Foundation. We thank Gordon Rausser for helpful comments and suggestions.

LITERATURE CITED

Acquaye AKA, Alston JM, Pardey PG. 2000. *A disaggregated perspective on post-war productivity growth in U.S. agriculture: Isn't that spatial?* Presented at NC-208 Conf. Agric. Product. Data Methods Meas. USDA-ERS, Washington D.C.

Acquaye AKA, Alston JM, Pardey PG. 2003. Post-war productivity patterns in U.S. agriculture: influences of aggregation procedures in a state-level analysis. *Am. J. Agric. Econ.* 85(1):59–80

Ahearn M, Yee J, Ball VE, Nehring R. 1998. Agricultural productivity in the United States. *Econ. Res. Serv. USDA Info. Bull. 740*

Akino M, Hayami Y. 1975. Efficiency and equity in public research: rice breeding in Japan's economic development. *Am. J. Agric. Econ.* 57(1):1–10

Alston JM. 2002. Spillovers. *Aust. J. Agric. Resour. Econ.* 46(3):315–46

Alston JM. 2007. Benefits and beneficiaries from U.S. farm subsidies. *AEI Policy Series: Agricultural Policy for 2007 Farm Bill and Beyond*. Washington DC: Am. Enterp. Inst. http://www.aei.org/research/farmbill/publications/pageID.1476,projectID.28/default.asp)

Alston JM, Andersen MA, James JS, Pardey PG. 2009. *Persistence Pays: U.S. Agricultural Productivity Growth and the Benefits from Public R&D Spending*. New York: Springer. In press

Alston JM, Craig BJ, Pardey PG. 1998. *Dynamics in the creation and depreciation of knowledge, and the returns to research*. Discuss. Pap. 35, EPTD, Int. Food Policy Res. Inst.

Alston JM, Edwards GW, Freebairn JW. 1988. Market distortions and the benefits from research. *Am. J. Agric. Econ.* 70(2):281–88

Alston JM, Marra MC, Pardey PG, Wyatt TJ. 2000. A meta analysis of rates of return to agricultural R&D: *ex pede herculem? Res. Rep. 113*, IFPRI, Washington, DC

Alston JM, Martin WJ. 1995. Reversal of fortune: immiserizing technological change in agriculture. *Am. J. Agric. Econ.* 77:251–59

Provides comprehensive documentation and meta-analysis of studies estimating returns to agricultural R&D.

Provides comprehensive coverage of concepts, models, and methods used by economists to measure research benefits and set priorities.

Alston JM, Norton GW, Pardey PG. 1995. *Science Under Scarcity: Principles and Practice for Agricultural Research Evaluation and Priority Setting.* Ithaca, NY: Cornell Univ. Press

Alston JM, Pardey PG. 1993. Market distortions and technological progress in agriculture. *Technol. Forecast. Soc. Change* 43(3/4):301–19

Alston JM, Pardey PG. 1996. *Making Science Pay: The Economics of Agricultural R&D Policy.* Washington, DC: Am. Enterp. Inst.

Alston JM, Pardey PG, Smith VH, eds. 1999. *Paying for Agricultural Productivity.* Baltimore, MD: Johns Hopkins Univ. Press

Alston JM, Pardey PG. 2001. Attribution and other problems in assessing the returns to agricultural R&D. *Agric. Econ.* 25(2-3):141–52

Alston JM, Pardey PG. 2006. Farm productivity and inputs. In *Historical Statistics of the United States—Millennial Edition*, ed. S Carter, S Gartner, M Haines, A Olmstead, R Sutch, G Wright. Cambridge, UK: Cambridge Univ. Press

Alston JM, Pardey PG, Taylor MJ, eds. 2001. *Agricultural Science Policy: Changing Global Agendas.* Baltimore, MD: Johns Hopkins Univ. Press

Alston JM, Pardey PG, Ruttan VW. 2008. *Research lags revisited: concepts and evidence from U.S. agriculture.* Presented at Econ. Hist. Assoc. Meet., New Haven, CT

Alston JM, Sumner DA. 2007. Perspectives on farm policy reform. *J. Agric. Resour. Econ.* 32(1):1–19

Alston JM, Venner R. 2002. The effects of the U.S. Plant Variety Protection Act on wheat genetic improvement. *Res. Policy* 31(4):527–42

Alston JM, Wohlgenant MK. 1989. Measuring research benefits using linear elasticity equilibrium displacement models. Appendix to "The returns to the Australian wool industry from investment in R&D," JD Mullen, JM Alston. *Rural Resour. Econ. Rep. 10*, Sydney: NSW Agric. Fish.

Andersen MA. *Pro-cyclical productivity patterns in U.S. agriculture.* PhD thesis. Univ. Calif., Davis

Andersen MA, Pardey PG, Craig BJ, Alston JM. 2009. *Measuring capital inputs using the physical inventory method: with application to U.S. agriculture.* Work. Pap., InSTePP, Univ. Minn. St. Paul. In prep.

Antle JM, Pingali PL. 1994. Pesticides, productivity, and farmer health: a Philippines case study. *Am. J. Agric. Econ.* 76:418–30

Araji AA, White FC, Guenthner JF. 1995. Spillovers and the returns to agricultural research for potatoes. *J. Agric. Resour. Econ.* 20(2):263–76

Ball VE. 1985. Output, input, and productivity measurement in U.S. agriculture. *Am. J. Econ.* 67(3):475–86

Ball VE. 1994. Measuring agricultural productivity in U.S. agriculture. In *Evaluating Research and Productivity in an Era of Resource Scarcity*, ed. WB Sundquist, ch. 7; Proc. NC-208 Symp., Orlando, Florida, March 1993; Staff Pap. P94-2, Dep. Agric. Appl. Econ., Univ. Minn.

Ball VE, Bureau JC, Nehring R, Somwaru A. 1997. Agricultural productivity revisited. *Am. J. Agric. Econ.* 79(4):1045–63

Ball VE, Gollop FM, Kelly-Hawke A, Swinand GP. 1999. Patterns of state productivity growth in the U.S. farm sector: linking state and aggregate models. *Am. J. Agric. Econ.* 81(1):164–79

Ball VE, Nehring R. 1998. *Patterns of state productivity growth in the U.S. farm sector.* Econ. Res. Serv. Staff Pap. 9804, US Dep. Agric.

Barton GT, Cooper MR. 1948. Relation of agricultural production to inputs. *Rev. Econ. Stat.* 2:117–26

Barton GT, Durost DD. 1960. The new USDA index of inputs. *J. Farm Econ.* 42(5):1398–410

Baum WC. 1986. *Partners Against Hunger: The Consultative Group for International Agricultural Research.* Washington, DC: World Bank

Bouchet F, Orden D, Norton GW. 1989. Sources of growth in French agriculture. *Am. J. Agric. Econ.* 71(2):280–93

Brennan JP, Bantilan MCS. 1999. Impact of ICRISAT research on Australian agriculture. *Aust. Cent. Int. Agric. Res. Rep. 1*, NSW Dep. Agric.

Brennan JP. 2007. Beyond semi-dwarf wheat yield increases: impacts on the Australian wheat industry of on-going spillovers from the International Maize and Wheat Improvement Center. *Aust. J. Agric. Resour. Econ.* 51(4):385–401

Brennan JP, Fox PN. Impact of CIMMYT wheats in Australia: evidence of international research spillovers. *Econ. Res. Rep. 1/95*, NSW Dep. Agric.

Brennan JP, Singh IP, Lewin LG. 1997. Identifying international rice research spillovers in New South Wales. *Agric. Econ.* 17(1):35–44

Brown R. 1978. *Productivity returns and the structure of production in U.S. agriculture, 1974-47*. PhD thesis. Univ. Wis., Madison

Capalbo SM, Vo TT. A review of the evidence on agricultural productivity and aggregate technology. In *Agricultural Productivity: Measurement and Explanation*, ed. SM Capalbo, JM Antle, ch. 3. Washington, DC: Resour. Future

Chambers RG, Lopez R. 1993. Public investment and real price supports. *J. Public Econ.* 52:73–82

Chavas J-P, Cox TL. 1992. A nonparametric analysis of the effects of research on agricultural productivity. *Am. J. Agric. Econ.* 74:583–91

Cochrane WW. 1958. *Farm Prices: Myth and Reality*. Minneapolis, MN: Univ. Minn. Press

Craig BJ, Pardey PG. 1990a. *Multidimensional output indices*. Staff Pap., Dep. Agric. Appl. Econ., Univ. Minn. St. Paul

Craig BJ, Pardey PG. 1990b. *Patterns of agricultural development in the United States*. Staff Pap., Dep. Agric. Appl. Econ., Univ. Minn. St. Paul

Craig BJ, Pardey PG. 2001. Input, output, and productivity developments in U.S. agriculture. See Alston et al. 2001, ch. 5

Davis JS. 1980. A note on the use of alternative lag structures for research expenditure in aggregate production function models. *Can. J. Agric. Econ.* 28:72–6

Davis GC, Espinoza MC. 1998. A unified approach to sensitivity analysis in equilibrium displacement models. *Am. J. Agric. Econ.* 80:868–79

de Gorter H, Nielson DJ, Rausser GC. 1992. Productive and predatory public policies: research expenditures and producer subsidies in agriculture. *Am. J. Agric. Econ.* 74:27–37

de Gorter H, Swinnen JJM. 1998. Endogenous commodity policies and the social benefits from public research expenditures. *Am. J. Agric. Econ.* 80:107–15

de Gorter H, Swinnen JJM. 2002. Political economy of agricultural policy. In *Handbook of Agricultural Economics, Volume 2*, ed. BL Gardner, GC Rausser, ch. 36. Amsterdam: Elsevier

de Gorter H, Zilberman D. 1990. On the political economy of public good inputs in agriculture. *Am. J. Agric. Econ.* 72:107–15

Dehmer S, Pardey PG, Alston JM. 2009. *The shifting structure of private food and agricultural R&D in the United States since the 1950s*. Work. Pap., InSTePP, Univ. Minn. St Paul. In prep.

Duncan RC. 1972. Evaluating returns to research in pasture improvement. *Aust. J. Agric. Econ.* 16(3):153–68

Duncan RC, Tisdell C. 1971. Research and technical progress: the returns to the producers. *Econ. Rec.* 47(117):124–9

Echeverría RG, Byerlee D, eds. 2002. *Agricultural Research Policy in an Era of Privatization*. Wallingford, UK: CAB Int.

Evenson RE. 1967. The contribution of agricultural research to production. *J. Farm Econ.* 49: 1415–25

Evenson RE. 1996. Two blades of grass: research for U.S. agriculture. In *The Economics of Agriculture Volume 2, Papers in Honor of D. Gale Johnson*, ed. JM Antle, DA Sumner, ch. 11, pp. 171–203. Chicago, IL: Univ. Chicago Press

Evenson RE. 2001. Economic impacts of agricultural research and extension. In *Handbook of Agricultural Economics, Volume 1A: Agricultural Production*, ed. BL Gardner, GC Rausser, ch. 11. New York: Elsevier

Evenson RE, Kislev Y. 1973. Research and productivity in wheat and maize. *J. Polit. Econ.* 81:1309–29

Description of the technology treadmill hypothesis stating that, among farmers, only the early adopters benefit from new technology, and then only temporarily.

Evenson RE, Kislev Y. 1975. *Agricultural Research and Productivity*. New Haven, CT: Yale Univ. Press

Evenson RE, Landau D, Ballou D. 1987. Agricultural productivity measures for US states 1950-82. In *Evaluating Agricultural Research and Productivity*, ed. WB Sundquist. St. Paul, MN: Univ. Minn.

Falck-Zepeda JB, Traxler G, Nelson RG. 2000. Surplus distribution from the introduction of a biotechnology innovation. *Am. J. Agric. Econ.* 82(2):360–69

Foster WE, Rausser GC. 1993. Price distorting compensation serving the consumer and taxpayer interest. *Public Choice* 77(2):275–91

Frisvold GB. 1997. Multimarket effects of agricultural research with technological spillovers. In *Global Trade Analysis*, ed. TW Hertel. New York: Cambridge Univ. Press

Frisvold G, Sullivan J, Raneses A. 1999. Who gains from genetic improvement in U.S. crops? *AgBioForum* 2(3–4):237–46

Freebairn JW. 1992. Evaluating the level and distribution of benefits from dairy industry research. *Aust. J. Agric. Econ.* 36(2):141–66

Fuglie KO, Heisey PW. 2007. *Economic returns to public agricultural research*. Econ. Brief 10, Econ. Res. Serv., USDA

Fuglie KO, Ballenger N, Day K, Klotz C, Ollinger M, et al. 1996. Agricultural research and development: public and private investments under alternative markets and institutions. *Agric. Econ. Rep. 735*, USDA, Washington, DC

Gardner BL. 1988. *Price supports and optimal spending on agricultural research*. Work. Pap. 88-1, Dep. Agric. Resour. Econ., Univ. Maryland

Gardner BL. 1992. How the data we make can unmake us: annals of factology. *Am. J. Agric. Econ.* 74(5):1066–75

Griliches Z. 1957. Hybrid corn: an exploration in the economics of technological change. *Econometrica* 25:501–22

Griliches Z. 1958. Research costs and social returns: hybrid corn and related innovations. *J. Polit. Econ.* 66(5):419–31

Griliches Z. 1960. Measuring inputs in agriculture: a critical survey. *J. Farm Econ.* 42(5):1411–27

Griliches Z. 1964. Research expenditures, education and the aggregate agricultural production function. *Am. Econ. Rev.* 54(6):961–74

Griliches Z. 1979. Issues in assessing the contribution of R&D to productivity growth. *Bell J. Econ.* 10(1):92–116

Griliches Z. 1994. Productivity, R&D, and the data constraint. *Am. Econ. Rev.* 84(1):1–23

Griliches Z. 2001. R&D and productivity: the unfinished business. See Alston et al. 2001, ch. 3

Griliches Z, Jorgenson DW. 1966. Sources of measured productivity change: capital input. *Am. Econ. Rev.* 56(1/2):50–61

Griliches Z, Jorgenson DW. 1967. The explanation of productivity change. *Rev. Econ. Stud.* 34(3):249–83

Harberger AC. 1971. Three basic postulates for applied welfare economics: an interpretive essay. *J. Econ. Lit.* 9(3):785–97

Hayami Y, Ruttan VW. 1971. *Agricultural Development: An International Perspective*. Baltimore, MD: Johns Hopkins Univ. Press

Herdt RW, Cochrane WW. 1966. Farm land prices and farm technological advance. *J. Farm Econ.* 48(2):243–63

Huang S-Y, Sexton RS. 1998. Measuring returns to an innovation in an imperfectly competitive market: application to mechanical harvesting of processing tomatoes in Taiwan. *Am. J. Agric. Econ.* 78:558–71

Huffman WE, Evenson RE. 1989. Supply and demand functions for multiproduct U.S. cash grain farms: biases caused by research and other policies. *Am. J. Agric. Econ.* 71:761–73

Huffman WE, Evenson RE. 1992. Contributions of public and private science and technology to U.S. agricultural productivity. *Am. J. Agric. Econ.* 74:752–56

Seminal economic study of the diffusion of agricultural technologies.

The first production function estimates with an added R&D variable.

Huffman WE, Evenson RE. 1993. *Science for Agriculture: A Long-Term Perspective*. Ames, IA: Iowa State Univ. Press

Huffman WE, Evenson RE. 2001. Structural and productivity change in US agriculture, 1950–1982. *Agric. Econ.* 24(2):127–47

Huffman WE, Evenson RE. 2006. *Science for Agriculture: A Long-Term Perspective*. Oxford, UK: Blackwell. 2nd ed.

Huffman WE, Just RE. 1994. Funding, structure, and management of public agricultural research in the United States. *Am. J. Agric. Econ.* 76:744–59

Huffman WE, Just RE. 1999. Agricultural research: benefits and beneficiaries of alternative funding mechanisms. *Rev. Agric. Econ.* 19:2–18

Jaffe AB. 1986. Technological opportunity and spillovers of R&D: evidence from firm's patents, profits, and market value. *Am. Econ. Rev.* 76(5):984–1001

Jaffe AB. 1989. Characterizing the 'technological position' of firms with application to quantifying technological opportunity and research spillovers. *Res. Policy* 18(2):87–97

Jorgenson DW, Gollop FM. 1992. Productivity growth in U.S. agriculture: a postwar perspective. *Am. J. Agric. Econ.* 74(3):745–50

Kerr NA. 1987. *The Legacy: A Centennial History of the State Agricultural Experiment Stations, 1887-1987*. Columbia, MO: Missouri Agric. Exp. Stn.

Khanna J, Huffman WE, Sandler T. 1994. Agricultural research expenditures in the United States: a public goods perspective. *Rev. Econ. Stat.* 76(2):267–77

Klotz C, Fuglie K, Pray C. *Private sector agricultural research expenditures in the United States: 1960-1992*. Staff Pap. 9525, Econ. Res. Serv. USDA

Lapan H, Moschini G. 2004. Innovation and trade with endogenous market failure: the case of genetically modified crops. *Am. J. Agric. Econ.* 86(3):634–38

Leiby JD, Adams GD. 2002. The returns to agricultural research in Maine: the case of a small Northeastern experiment station. *Northeast. J. Agric. Resour. Econ.* 20:1–14

Lindner RK, Jarrett FG. 1978. Supply shifts and the size of research benefits. *Am. J. Agric. Econ.* 60 (1):48–58

Lindner RK, Jarrett FG. 1980. Supply shifts and the size of research benefits: reply. *Am. J. Agric. Econ.* 62(4):841–44

Loomis RA, Barton GT. 1961. Productivity of agriculture: United States, 1870–1958. *USDA Tech. Bull. 1238*

Lynam JK, Jones PG. 1984. *Benefits of technical change as measured by supply shifts: an integration of theory and practice*. Mimeogr., Cent. Int. Agric. Trop.

Martin WJ, Alston JM. 1997. Producer surplus without apology? Evaluating investments in R&D. *Econ. Rec.* 73(221):146–58

Maredia MK, Ward R, Byerlee D. 1996. Econometric estimation of a global spillover matrix for wheat varietal technology. *Agric. Econ.* 14:159–73

McCunn A, Huffman WE. 2000. Convergence in productivity growth for agriculture: implications of interstate research spillovers for funding agricultural research. *Am. J. Agric. Econ.* 82(3):370–88

Mellor JW, Johnston BF. 1984. The world food equation: interrelations among development, employment and food consumption. *J. Econ. Lit.* 22:531–74

Moschini G, Lapan H. 1997. Intellectual property rights and the welfare effects of agricultural R&D. *Am. J. Agric. Econ.* 79:1229–42

Mullen JD, Alston JM, Wohlgenant MK. 1989. The impact of farm and processing research on the Australian wool industry. *Aust. J. Agric. Econ.* 33:32–47

Murphy JA, Furtan WH, Schmitz A. 1993. The gains from agricultural research under distorted trade. *J. Public Econ.* 51(2):161–72

Muth R. 1964. The derived demand curve for a productive factor and the industry supply curve. *Oxf. Econ. Pap.* 16:221–34

Natl. Sci. Found. 2008. *Science and Engineering Indicators 2008*, Vols. 1–2. Arlington, VA: NSF

Systematic assessment of the implications of parallel, pivotal, and divergent shifts in supply on the magnitude and distribution of the benefits from research.

Norton GW, Davis JS. 1981. Evaluating returns to agricultural research: a review. *Am. J. Agric. Econ.* 63(4):685–99

Oehmke JF, Crawford EW. 2002. The sensitivity of returns to research calculations to supply elasticity. *Am. J. Agric. Econ.* 84(2):366–69

Org. Econ. Coop. Dev. 2002. *Frascati Manual: Proposed Standard Practice for Surveys on Research and Development.* Paris: OECD

Org. Econ. Coop. Dev. 2005. *Oslo Manual: Guidelines for Collecting and Interpreting Innovation Data.* Paris: OECD. 3rd ed.

Pachico D, Lyman JK, Jones PG. 1987. The distribution of benefits from technical change among classes of consumers and producers: an ex *ante* analysis of beans in Brazil. *Res. Policy* 16:279–85

Pardey PG, Alston JM, Christian JE, Fan S. 1996. Hidden harvest: U.S. benefits from international research aid. *Food Policy Rep.*, IFPRI, Washington, DC

Pardey PG, Alston JM, Piggott RR, eds. 2006. *Agricultural R&D in the Developing World: Too Little, Too Late?* Washington, DC: Int. Food Policy Res. Inst.

Pardey PG, Andersen MA. 2009. *A long-run price index and the real cost of U.S. agricultural research.* Work. Pap., InSTePP, Univ. Minn. St. Paul. In prep.

Pardey PG, Beintema NM, Dehmer S, Wood S. 2006. Agricultural research: a growing global divide? *Food Policy Rep.* 17, IFPRI, Washington, DC

Pardey PG, Craig B. 1989. Causal relationships between public sector agricultural research expenditures and output. *Am. J. Agric. Econ.* 71:9–19

Pardey PG, Craig BJ, Deininger KW. 1994. A new look at state-level productivity growth in U.S. agriculture. In *Evaluating Research and Productivity in an Era of Resource Scarcity*, ed. WB Sundquist, ch. 6; Proc. NC-208 Symp. Orlando, Florida, March 1993; Staff Pap. P94-2, Dep. Agric. Appl. Econ., Univ. Minn.

Pardey PG, Roseboom J, Anderson JR. 1991. Topical perspectives on national agricultural research. In *Agricultural Research Policy: International Quantitative Perspectives*, ed. PG Pardey, J Roseboom, JR Andersen, ch. 8. Cambridge, UK: Cambridge Univ. Press

Petersen WL. 1967. Returns to investment in poultry research in the United States. *J. Farm Econ.* 49(3):656–70

Qaim M. 2003. Bt cotton in India: field trial results and economic projections. *World Dev.* 31(12):2115–27

Rausser GC. 1974. Technological change, production, and investment in natural resource industries. *Am. Econ. Rev.* 64(6):1049–59

Rausser GC. 1982. Political economic markets: PERTs and PESTs in food and agriculture. *Am. J. Agric. Econ.* 64(5):821–33

Rausser GC, Foster WE. 1990. Political preference functions and public policy reform. *Am. J. Agric. Econ.* 72(3):641–52

Rausser GC, Zussman P, Swinnen J. 2009. *Political Power and Endogenous Policy Formation.* Cambridge, UK: Cambridge Univ. Press. In press

Ravenscraft D, Scherer FM. 1982. The lag structure of returns to research and development. *Appl. Econ.* 14:603–20

Robbins CA, Moylan CE. 2007. *Research and Development Satellite Account Update: Estimates for 1959-2004.* Washington, DC: Bur. Econ. Anal.

Rose RN. 1980. Supply shifts and the size of research benefits: a comment. *Am. J. Agric. Econ.* 62(4):834–7

Ruttan VW. 1982. *Agricultural Research Policy.* Minneapolis, MN: Univ. Minn. Press

Schultz TW. 1953. *The Economic Organization of Agriculture.* New York: McGraw-Hill

Schultz TW. 1978. On economics and politics of agriculture. In *Distortions in Agricultural Incentives*, ed. TW Schultz, ch. 1. Bloomington, IN: Indiana Univ. Press

Foundational study of the economic benefits from agricultural R&D.

Schuh GE, Tollini H. 1979. *Costs and benefits of agricultural research: state of the arts*. Work. Pap. 360, World Bank

Scobie GM. 1976. Who benefits from agricultural research? *Rev. Mark. Agric. Econ.* 44(4):197–202

Smale M, Zambrano P, Falck-Zepeda J, Gruére G. 2006. *Parables: applied economics literature about the impact of genetically engineered crop varieties in developing economies*. EPT Discuss. Pap. 158, IFPRI

Thirtle CG, Bottomley P. 1988. Is publicly funded agricultural research excessive? *J. Agric. Econ.* 31:99–111

Tintner G. 1944. A note on the derivation of production functions from farm records. *Econometrica* 1:26–34

Traxler G, Byerlee D. 2001. Linking technical change to research effort: an examination of aggregation and spillovers effects. *Agric. Econ.* 24:235–46

Voon JP, Edwards GW. 1991. The calculation of research benefits with linear and nonlinear specifications of demand and supply functions. *Am. J. Agric. Econ.* 74(3):415–20

White FC, Havlicek J. 1982. Optimal expenditures for agricultural research and extension: implications of underfunding. *Am. J. Agric. Econ.* 64(1):47–55

Wise WS, Fell E. 1980. Supply shifts and the size of research benefits: a comment. *Am. J. Agric. Econ.* 62(4):838–40

Wohlgenant MK. 1997. The nature of the research-induced supply shift. *Aust. J. Agric. Resour. Econ.* 41(3):385–400

World Bank. 2008. *World Development Report 2008: Agriculture for Development*. Washington, DC: World Bank

Wright BD, Pardey PG. 2006. The evolving rights to intellectual property protection in the agricultural biosciences. *Int. J. Technol. Global.* 2(1/2):12–29

Wright BD, Pardey PG, Nottenburg C, Koo B. 2007. Agricultural innovation: economic incentives and institutions. In *Handbook of Agricultural Economics*: Volume 3, ed. RE Evenson, P Pingali, ch. 6. Amsterdam: Elsevier

Yee J, Huffman WE. 2001. *Rates of return to public agricultural research in the presence of research spillovers*. Presented at Annu. Meet. Am. Agric. Econ. Assoc., Chicago

Zhao X, Griffiths WE, Griffith GR, Mullen JD. 2000. Probability distributions for economic surplus changes: the case of technical change in the Australian wool industry. *Aust. J. Agric. Resour. Econ.* 44:83–106

Supply and Demand of Electricity in the Developing World

Madhu Khanna[1] and Narasimha D. Rao[2]

[1]Department of Agricultural and Consumer Economics, University of Illinois, Urbana-Champaign, Illinois 61801; email: khanna1@illinois.edu

[2]School of Earth Sciences, Stanford University, Stanford, California 94305; email: ndrao@stanford.edu

Annu. Rev. Resour. Econ. 2009. 1:567–95

First published online as a Review in Advance on June 26, 2009

The *Annual Review of Resource Economics* is online at resource.annualreviews.org

This article's doi:
10.1146/annurev.resource.050708.144230

1941-1340/09/1010-0567$20.00

Key Words

privatization, energy efficiency, elasticities, reforms

Abstract

This paper reviews the literature that has sought to quantify the determinants of electricity demand and supply efficiency in developing countries. We examine the causal relationship between electricity consumption and economic growth, price and income elasticities of demand, and the barriers to adoption of energy-efficient equipment. We also examine the performance outcomes of economic policies affecting the electricity sector, including institutional reforms such as privatization and regulation. We find that electricity demand is driven by GDP, prices, income, the level and characteristics of economic activity/urbanization, and seasonal factors. The magnitude of their effects differs across countries, time periods, and studies even for the same country. These demand studies suffer from a number of limitations, including data availability and price distortions that limit responsiveness of demand to price signals. The literature is inconclusive on whether reforms, particularly privatization, improved supply efficiency. Effective regulation, competitive markets, and appropriate sequencing of reforms are important factors that influence the outcomes of privatization. There is a need for more quantitative analysis of the social welfare and distributional impacts of privatization of the electricity sector in developing countries.

1. INTRODUCTION

World energy consumption is expected to grow by 55% between 2005 and 2030, with electricity use doubling and coal consumption increasing by 73%. Three-fourths of this increase in energy consumption is projected in developing countries, and nearly half from China and India. The International Energy Agency (2007) estimated that meeting electricity demand in developing countries would require an annual investment of at least $165 billion. In the face of this projected growth, financial resource constraints, and concern about the growing contribution of developing countries to climate change, it is important to understand the determinants of electricity demand and the factors that influence growth and efficiency of electricity supply in developing countries. These will influence the extent to which economic growth and price signals influence trends in electricity consumption, the potential to expand supply from existing capacity, the need for investment in new capacity, and the policy reforms needed to do so.

This paper reviews the existing literature that has sought to quantify the relationship among electricity consumption, economic growth, and other determinants of electricity demand in developing countries. Specifically, we examine the causal relationship between electricity consumption and economic growth in developing countries, which has implications for how changes in electricity consumption will affect economic growth and the investments needed in new generation capacity to meet future needs. Reverse causality from GDP to electricity consumption would imply that electricity conservation may be implemented with little adverse impact on GDP. We also examine the available empirical evidence on the responsiveness of electricity demand to changes in prices and the incentives and barriers to adoption of energy-efficient equipment. The determinants of electricity demand at the national, sectoral, and household levels and the drivers of changes in energy intensity are analyzed for specific developing countries.

On the supply side, the historically state-owned electricity sector in developing countries has been operating at a loss, is dependent on state subsidies for operating expenses, and has limited ability to generate resources for investment in modern equipment. Developing countries undertook sweeping reforms of their electric sectors in the 1990s. A key motivation for these reforms was to attract private investment to increase supply and provide universal access to electricity at affordable prices. These reforms included a shift to private ownership, corporatization, and unbundling of vertically integrated utilities; introduction of independent regulators; and, to a lesser extent, creation of markets for electricity generation. Efforts aimed at these reforms have had mixed success. Moreover, the institutional structure and regulatory framework of the sector and the pricing policies adopted have had implications for the efficiency of the electricity sector and the incentives to adopt new technologies. We examine the effects of reforms in ownership, regulations, and other economic policies in developing countries on the performance of their electricity sector.

Approximately 40% of the population in developing countries does not have access to electricity, with the proportions of rural populations served by electric power grids ranging from 98% in Thailand and 85% in Mexico to only 2%–5% in Sub-Saharan Africa (Martinot et al. 2002). Excluding China, the population without electricity has increased steadily since 1990 (International Energy Agency 2007). The high costs of delivering electricity from centralized energy systems require large investments in establishing transmission and distribution grids that can penetrate remote regions. This has led to interest in small-scale decentralized energy generation, based on renewable energy sources that may be either connected to the grid or a stand-alone system. We review the experience with rural electrification in developing countries.

In Section 2, we present the electricity demand model that provides a framework for examining the empirical determinants of electricity consumption. In Section 3, we review the econometric evidence on the determinants of electricity consumption at various levels of aggregation, including a review of the evidence on the direction of causality between electricity consumption and growth. Section 4 describes the conditions in the electric-supply sector and its efficiency. Section 5 reviews the evidence on the drivers of reform, the efficiency and economic outcomes of reforms, and rural electrification. This is followed by the conclusions in Section 6.

2. AN ELECTRICITY DEMAND MODEL

The demand for electricity is a derived demand by households for lighting, cooking, and heating and by firms to operate equipment to produce goods and services. Household production theory can be used to specify a model for residential demand for electricity in which households purchase "goods" on the market that are used as inputs to produce final commodities that provide utility. More specifically, a household combines electricity and capital equipment to produce a composite energy commodity. The household's utility function can be written as

$$U = U(E(R,K), X; T),   \tag{1}$$

where E is the electrical energy–based services produced using the household production function $E(R, K)$, K is capital stock consisting of appliances, R is rate of utilization of that capital stock, X is a composite numeraire good, and T is household tastes and preferences. By choosing R and K, the household automatically determines the desired level of consumption of electricity E^*, while taking prices of inputs E and K, good X, and income Y as given. We can similarly represent a firm's problem of choosing the amount of electricity and other inputs to consume to maximize profits associated with the production of a marketable output (say, Y for ease of representation below) taking prices of output and inputs and technology (T) as given.

One can view the optimization problem of the household/firm as a two-stage problem: In the first stage, the household/firm minimizes the cost of producing E, whereas in the second stage, it maximizes utility/profits. This maximization yields input demand functions for R and K:

$$R = R(P_E, Y; T), \text{ and}   \tag{2}$$

$$K = K(P_E, P_K, Y; T),   \tag{3}$$

where P_E is the price of electricity and P_K is the price of the electrical appliances. Equations 2 and 3 reflect the long-run equilibrium demand for R and K. This model is static; it assumes an instantaneous adjustment to new equilibrium values when prices or income/output change. Households/firms can respond to an increase in the price of electricity by lowering the rate with which they utilize the existing stock of appliances in the short run and by adjusting their capital stock in the long run to be more electricity efficient.

A structural model would simultaneously estimate the level of capital stock and the level of energy consumption. In the absence of equipment stock and utilization rate data, a reduced-form static model can be specified as follows:

$$E^* = E(P_E, P_K, Y; T). \tag{4}$$

A log-log regression equation of the following form is typically estimated, assuming that desired consumption, E_t^*, is the same as actual consumption of electricity, E_t:

$$\ln E_t^* = \alpha + \beta_P \ln P_E + \beta_Y \ln Y. \tag{5}$$

To the extent that it is reasonable to assume that cross-sectional differences in consumption of electricity represent not only variation in the utilization rate but also stock adjustment, estimates based on cross-sectional data can be interpreted as long-run elasticities, whereas those based on time-series data are measures of short-run adjustments.

To allow for dynamics in the determination of demand for electricity, one can distinguish between E_t and E_t^* at time t where the difference reflects constraints in instantaneously adjusting capital stock to desired levels warranted by changes in economic variables (see Bohi & Zimmerman 1984). A Koyck partial adjustment model is assumed as follows:

$$E_t - E_{t-1} = \Phi(E_t^* - E_{t-1}), \tag{6}$$

where $0 < \Phi < 1$ reflects the speed of adjustment that is instantaneous if $\Phi = 1$. Substituting Equation 5 in Equation 6 specified in logarithmic terms we obtain

$$\ln E_t = \Phi\alpha + \Phi\beta_P \ln P_E + \Phi\beta_Y \ln Y + (1 - \Phi)\ln E_{t-1}. \tag{7}$$

This reduced-form dynamic model can be used to obtain short-run elasticities and income elasticities as follows (see Houthaker & Taylor 1966):

$$\varepsilon_P^{SR} = \frac{\partial \ln E_t}{\partial \ln P_E} = \phi\beta_P; \quad \varepsilon_Y^{SR} = \frac{\partial \ln E_t}{\partial \ln Y} = \phi\beta_Y, \tag{8}$$

whereas the corresponding long-run elasticities (obtained when the capital stock-adjustment process is completed) are

$$\varepsilon_P^{LR} = \beta_P; \quad \varepsilon_Y^{LR} = \beta_Y. \tag{9}$$

Two alternative adjustment models, a cumulative adjustment model and a flexible distributed lag model, have been considered in the literature (Westley 1984). The former considers a fixed portion of the capital stock to be adjusted each year and the desired stock is attained in a finite time unlike a partial adjustment model where actual stock approaches but never reaches the desired level. The latter includes the same lag pattern for all explanatory variables and recognizes that it takes time to respond to changed economic conditions.

3. ECONOMETRIC ANALYSIS OF THE DEMAND FOR ELECTRICITY

The determinants of the demand for electricity have been studied econometrically both at a macroeconomic, economy-wide (or sectoral) level and at a microeconomic, household/firm level. We now discuss the types of determinants examined, the methods used, and the findings of these studies for developing countries.

3.1. Relationship Between Electricity Consumption and GDP

The framework presented above treats income Y_t as given at a household level at a point in time in analyzing the demand for electricity. At the macroeconomic level, this may not be reasonable. Instead, the relationship between E_t and Y_t (interpreted as GDP) could be bidirectional; the consumption of electricity can both constrain growth in GDP and be determined by it. A number of studies have focused on examining the relationship between E_t and Y_t and the direction of causality between the two. The standard Granger test (Granger 1969) can be used to examine the causal relation between E_t and Y_t if the variables are stationary. Unit root tests are first conducted to test if the data are stationary. If the variables are nonstationary but cointegrated, an error correction model can be used to infer the existence of a causal relationship. Short time spans of the data sets used for testing causality weaken the power of the unit root test and of the cointegration and causality tests. In a recent study of the causality between GDP and electricity consumption for ten developing countries, Chen et al. (2007) used panel unit root tests and panel cointegration tests that allow for heterogeneity among individual members of the panel.

Studies examining the direction of causality between economic growth and electricity consumption for a wide range of developing countries find mixed evidence across different countries, and sometimes even for the same country with different data sets, time periods, and methodologies (see reviews in Jumbe 2004, Chen et al. 2007). These reviews show a unidirectional relationship running from electricity to GDP in almost the same number of instances (16 cases) as the reverse relationship (11 cases). A bidirectional relationship or no causality is observed in only a few cases. Variances in country-specific conditions, such as the extent to which electricity is consumed for economic activities versus basic human activities and the efficiency with which it is used, can be used to explain some of the differences in causality. However, some of these differences may also be attributed to the use of traditional tests of statistical significance with small samples. Chen et al. (2007) used panel data methods and statistical tests with data for ten newly industrializing and developing countries in Asia for the period 1971–2001 and found a significant long-run bidirectional causality between real GDP and electricity consumption and a short-run causality from economic growth to electricity consumption. Their findings suggest that electricity conservation policies may be feasible in the short run without adversely impacting economic growth. They may also be indicative of inefficient and wasteful use of electricity in developing countries, and thus the level of consumption does not affect economic growth. The presence of a bidirectional relationship in the long run shows the importance of increasing investment in electricity infrastructure and reducing wastage of electricity to support and meet the needs of high economic growth rates.

3.2. Determinants of the Aggregate Demand for Electricity

Several studies have sought to quantify the responsiveness of aggregate electricity demand to income and to other determinants of electricity demand such as electricity price using national/sectoral data for electricity consumption, real GDP, real electricity price, and other relevant explanatory variables. The latter include measures of temperature, urbanization, stock/prices of appliances, prices of other energy forms, and a lagged measure of electricity consumption to determine the rate of adjustment in consumption to changes in economic variables.

A number of econometric issues underlie the estimation of the price responsiveness of electricity demand, making this more difficult than the typical estimation of demand curves (Taylor 1975). Unlike standard goods, consumers of electricity do not face a single price, but rather a price schedule, with decreasing or increasing block pricing. The marginal price is dependent on the amount of consumption and influences the level of consumption. The use of average price as the determinant of electricity consumption is based on the assumption that consumers respond to the price obtained from their electricity bills (Branch 1993). Both the *ex post* marginal and average prices are determined simultaneously with the level of consumption; thus, their inclusion as explanatory variables leads to correlation between price and the error term of the electricity demand equation. Taylor (1975) recommends including both the marginal price of the last block consumed and the average price as predictors in the demand function, but he recommends using actual values from the price schedules and not *ex post* values. Additionally, explanatory variables such as the lagged dependent variable, per capita income, prices of electricity, and stock of electric appliances are likely to be endogenous and lead to simultaneity bias in the reduced-form dynamic model of electricity demand. Many recent studies use cointegration techniques to avoid spurious regressions between variables that may be driven by time trends and to control for endogeneity of the explanatory variables (see Pesaran et al. 1998).

The estimation of elasticities poses additional challenges in developing countries because of their unique characteristics that influence the choice of model and data used. For example, in many countries [as discussed in the case of India (Bose & Shukla 1999) and Lebanon (Nasr et al. 2000)], electricity demand is supply constrained and not demand driven. This can limit the meaningful inclusion of price in the electricity demand equation in countries with severe rationing (e.g., Lebanon), where consumers rely on autogeneration devices or there is significant theft of electricity (e.g., India) (**http://news.bbc.co.uk/2/hi/business/4802248.stm**), and where electricity use is not metered and is charged for at a fixed rate. For example, in the agricultural sector in India and in Thailand, a single meter may serve several households owned by their landowner (Sathaye & Tyler 1991). Consumers in a number of developing countries regularly face electricity outages, and the amount of downtime should be considered in estimating demand for electricity from utilities (Westley 1984). The use of partial adjustment models is problematic in transition economies because of the overinvestment in industrial and social capital during the times of the Soviet Union. Thus, previous period's capital stock may not constrain electricity consumption in industrial and service sectors (Atakhanova & Howie 2007). Additionally, a distinction may be needed between access to electricity and demand for electricity because universal access to electricity is not a common reality, unlike in developed countries (Berndt & Samaniego 1984).

The studies reviewed here and listed in **Table 1** assume that supply of electricity and supply of capital equipment are perfectly elastic; none of these studies account for the interdependence between price and quantity [an exception is Diabi (2002), who included the price of appliances as an explanatory variable]. This is similar to the treatment of prices in most energy demand studies for developed countries

Table 1 Price and income elasticity of demand for electricity[a]

Study	Country and time period	Sector	Price elasticity		Income elasticity	
			Short run	Long run	Short run	Long run
Lundmark (2001)	Namibia 1980–1996	Aggregate	−0.51	−0.863		
De Vita et al. (2006)	Namibia 1980–2002	Aggregate		−0.298		0.589
Pouris (1987)	South Africa 1950–1983	Aggregate		−0.9		
Whittaker & Barr (1989)	South Africa 1950–1983	Aggregate		−1.02		
Lin (2003)	China 1952–2001	Aggregate		−0.04		0.86
Lin (2003)	China 1978–2001	Aggregate		−0.02		0.78
Ma et al. (2008)	China (1995–2004)	Aggregate	−0.68			
Bates (1993)	India	Residential	−0.05	−0.22		
Bates (1993)	India	Industrial	−0.18	−0.14		
Bates (1993)	India	Agriculture	−0.2	−0.2		
Bose & Shukla (1999)	India 1985–1994	Residential	−0.65		0.88	
Bose & Shukla (1999)	India 1985–1995	Commercial	−0.26		1.27	
Bose & Shukla (1999)	India 1985–1996	Agriculture	−1.35		0.82	
Bose & Shukla (1999)	India 1985–1997	Small industrial			0.49	
Bose & Shukla (1999)	India 1985–1998	Large industrial	−0.45		1.06	
Eltony & Hajeeh (1998)	Kuwait (1975–1995)	Commercial	−0.33	−0.98	0.33	0.81
Eltony & Al-Awadhi (2007b)	Kuwait (1975–2003)	Commercial	−0.33	−1.64	0.34	0.5
Eltony & Al-Awadhi (2007a)	Kuwait (1975–2005)	Residential	−0.22			
Bates (1993)	Pakistan	Industrial	−0.05			
Bates (1993)	Pakistan	Commercial	−0.07			
Mahmud (2000)	Pakistan (1972–1993)	Aggregate	−0.24 to −0.32	−0.24 to −0.32		
Bates (1993)	Philippines	Residential	−0.15			

(continued)

Table 1 (cont.)

Study	Country and time period	Sector	Price elasticity		Income elasticity	
			Short run	Long run	Short run	Long run
Bates (1993)	Philippines	Commercial	−0.18			
Bates (1993)	Philippines	Agriculture	−0.20			
Diabi (1998)	Saudi Arabia 1980–1992	Aggregate	−0.003 to −0.12	−0.004 to −0.14	0.095–0.326	0.11–0.49
Diabi (1998)	Saudi Arabia 1980–1993	Aggregate		−0.14		
Holtedahl & Joutz (2004)	Taiwan (1955–1995)	Residential	−0.15	−0.16	0.23	1.04
Bates (1993)	Thailand	Residential	−0.18			
Bates (1993)	Thailand	Commercial	−0.15			
Bates (1993)	Thailand	Agriculture	−0.20			
Buranakunaporn & Oczkowski (2007)	Thailand (1977–1979)	Manufacturing	−0.30	−0.82		
Halicioglu (2007)	Turkey (1968–2005)	Residential		−0.52		0.7
Atakhanova & Howie (2007)	Kazakhstan 1994–2003	Aggregate			0.36–0.72	
Atakhanova & Howie (2007)	Kazakhstan 1994–2004	Industrial			0.48–0.86	
Atakhanova & Howie (2007)	Kazakhstan 1994–2005	Service	−0.12		0.85–0.75	
Atakhanova & Howie (2007)	Kazakhstan 1994–2006	Residential	−0.22	−1.1	0.12	0.59
Nahata et al. (2007)	Russia 1992–2000	Urban residential	−0.165			
	Russia 1992–2001	Rural residential	−0.28			
	Russia 1992–2002	Industrial	−0.45			
	Russia 1992–2003	Others	−0.33			
	Russia 1992–2004	Agriculture	−0.13			
Bates (1993)	Argentina	Residential	−0.85	−0.07 to −0.19		
	Argentina	Industrial	−0.15	−0.42 to −0.56		

Table 1   (cont.)

Study	Country and time period	Sector	Price elasticity		Income elasticity	
			Short run	Long run	Short run	Long run
Balabanoff (1994)	Argentina 1970–1990	Aggregate				1.00
Bates (1993)	Brazil	Aggregate	−0.2	−0.83		
	Brazil	Residential	−0.02	−0.22		
	Brazil	Industrial	−0.22	−0.60		
	Brazil	Commercial	−0.03	−0.26		
Balabanoff (1994)	Brazil 1970–1990	Aggregate		−0.43		1.73
	Chile 1970–1990	Aggregate				1.65
Westley (1992)	Colombia 1958–1976	Industrial		−0.25		1.12
Balabanoff (1994)	Colombia 1970–1990	Aggregate		−0.18		1.88
Westley (1989)	Costa Rica 1970–1979	Commercial		−0.3 to −0.7		0.3–0.7
Westley (1992)	Costa Rica 1970–1979	Residential		−0.5		0.2
	Costa Rica 1970–1980	Commercial		−0.5		0.5
	Dominican Republic 1960–1980	Residential		−0.5		0.45
	Dominican Republic 1960–1980	Commercial		−0.45		0.55
	Dominican Republic 1960–1980	Industrial		−0.65		1.25
Balabanoff (1994)	Ecuador 1970–1990	Aggregate				1.95
Ramcharran (1990)	Jamaica 1970–1986	Aggregate			1.65	
	Jamaica 1970–1987	Residential			1.21	4.17
	Jamaica 1970–1988	Small industrial	−0.26	−0.43		
	Jamaica 1970–1989	Large industrial	−0.19	−0.52		

(continued)

Table 1 (cont.)

Study	Country and time period	Sector	Price elasticity		Income elasticity	
			Short run	Long run	Short run	Long run
Westley (1992)	Paraguay 1970–1977	Residential/commercial	−0.5		0.375	
Westley (1984)	Paraguay 1970–1977	Aggregate	−0.56		0.42	
Balabanoff (1994)	Peru 1970–1990	Aggregate				0.7
Bates (1993)	Mexico	Residential	−0.11	−0.23		
	Mexico	Industrial	−0.05	−0.38		
	Mexico	Commercial	−0.02	−0.13		
	Mexico	Agriculture	−0.01	−0.15		
Westley (1992)	Mexico 1962–1979, 1970–1978	Residential		−0.47		0.73
Berndt & Samaniego (1984)	Mexico 1962–1972	Residential	−0.35	−0.81	1.31	1.8
	Mexico 1970–1978	Residential	−0.04	−0.11	0.66	1.37

[a]Based on aggregate data.

(Bohi & Zimmerman 1984).[1] The studies reviewed here use an average price of electricity as the explanatory variable, with a few exceptions that include De Vita et al. (2006) and Westley (1989). None of these studies develop a method to incorporate multistep block pricing (Taylor 1975).

Studies using the reduced-form dynamic equation include Ramcharran (1990), De Vita et al. (2006), Atakhanova & Howie (2007), Berndt & Samaniego (1984), Diabi (2002), and Westley (1989). A few studies use the distributed lag model, which includes a series of lagged electricity prices to estimate long-run price elasticity (Pouris 1987, Whittaker & Barr 1989, Bose & Shukla 1999, De Vita et al. 2006). Others use cross-section data to estimate a sectoral cost function (Mahmud 2000, Buranakunaporn & Oczkowski 2007, Ma et al. 2008) or a linear expenditure system (Brenton 1997). These latter studies estimate not only own- and cross-price elasticities for electricity and other energy inputs in production, but also the elasticity of substitution between various energy forms.

Table 1 shows that the price elasticity of demand for electricity is rather low, ranging between -0.85 and -0.04 with an average value of -0.4 in the short run and between -1.02 and -0.11 with an average value of -0.6 in the long run. A 60-country analysis by Brenton (1997) shows that price elasticity of electricity increases with income. Despite low price elasticities of demand in individual countries, a cross-country study of electricity prices (corrected for purchasing power parity) and electricity consumption per unit GDP for 49 countries (27 OECD and 22 non-OECD countries) in 1996 showed a strong inverse relationship (International Energy Agency 1999). Demand for electricity is also income inelastic, more so in the short run. In general, demand for electricity in commercial and service sectors tends to be more income/output elastic than in the residential sector. Burney (1995) used cross-sectional data on per capita electricity consumption for 93 countries for 1990 to estimate income elasticity of electricity consumption and found that per capita electricity consumption increases not only with income but also with the rate at which income increases. Demand for electricity also increases with socioeconomic development (literacy rates, industrialization, and urbanization). The impact of these variables is greater for high-income countries, but there is no definite pattern across regions and income groups, implying that the responsiveness of electricity consumption to these variables depends on country-specific factors.

Other variables such as climatic factors and urbanization have been included as explanatory variables in several studies and found to be important. De Vita et al. (2006) found that low temperatures significantly raise electricity consumption in Namibia, whereas Berndt & Samaniego (1984) found that maximum temperatures are significantly positively associated with electricity demand but minimum temperatures have an insignificant effect in lowering demand in Mexico. Diabi (2002) found that variations in temperature across time but not regions affect demand for electricity in Saudi Arabia. Nasr et al. (2000) found that degree days have a significant positive effect on electricity consumption

---

[1] Electricity demand studies for the United States covering various time periods in the 1960s and 1970s show that the short-run own-price elasticity of electricity ranged between -0.1 and -0.35, with the majority of the studies finding an estimate less than -0.2. The own-price long-run elasticity ranged between -0.35 and -2.5, with the majority of studies finding it to be approximately -1.0. Income elasticity estimates ranged between 0 and 2; short-run income elasticities were typically considerably less than 1, whereas long-run income elasticities were closer to 1 (Bohi & Zimmerman 1984, Taylor 1975). Short-run price elasticities were not found to differ according to either average or marginal prices, but long-run elasticities varied considerably across studies depending on the measure of price used primarily because of differences in the estimated adjustment coefficients.

in Lebanon during the period that rationing becomes nonexistent and electricity consumption becomes more demand driven. Urbanization is expected to increase demand for electricity by providing greater access to the grid and by increasing use of electrical appliances as exposure to media and advertising in big cities increases. Several studies found electricity consumption in developing and developed countries significantly increased with urbanization (see reviews in Berndt & Samaniego 1984, Holtedahl & Joutz 2004, Halicioglu 2007).

Cross-price elasticities for electricity consumption are seldom estimated or found to be significant in the single-equation electricity demand equations reviewed above.[2] However, studies estimating translog cost functions for the manufacturing sector in Pakistan (Mahmud 2000), Thailand (Buranakunaporn & Oczkowski 2007), and China (Ma et al. 2008) do show significant substitution possibilities between electricity and natural gas, coal and electricity, and diesel and electricity. Furthermore, responsiveness of electricity consumption is also influenced by power shortages. Bose & Shukla (1999) estimated the elasticity of electricity consumption with respect to power shortages from electric utilities in India and found that a 1% increase in power shortages decreases electricity consumption by 0.21% in the residential sector and by 0.3% in the commercial sector, and has no impact on the agricultural and industrial sectors. This suggests that captive generation is being used to substitute for utility-based electricity in India.

Berndt & Samaniego (1984) extended the standard demand model described above by including demand for electricity hookups in Mexico. They included the share of population having access to electricity as an explanatory variable in Equation 7 and examined the factors that determine access to electricity instead of treating it as exogenous. They estimated a two-equation system and examined the partial income elasticity for electricity (for the population that already has access to electricity) and the total income elasticity for electricity that includes the effect of income on increasing the demand for access to electricity. They found that total income elasticities are 40% larger than partial income elasticities in both the short run and the long run.

Estimates of the rate of adjustment of demand vary considerably across countries and across sectors within a country. It is relatively slow in all sectors in Jamaica (Ramcharran 1990) and Kazakhstan (Atakhanova & Howie 2007), possibly because of the high cost of replacing electrical equipment, and very high in Saudi Arabia (Diabi 2002). Lagged prices are typically not found to be statistically significant determinants of future electricity consumption (De Vita et al. 2006, Bose & Shukla 1999).

3.3. Household Demand for Electricity

A number of studies have sought to explain the determinants of electricity demand at the household level using detailed microdata gathered from household surveys. In developing countries, much of the energy used by households has traditionally come from fuels such

---

[2]Because equipment is typically constrained to use a particular type of energy, prices of other energy forms are not relevant (unless the equipment has dual fuel-burning capacity or if there is autogeneration of electricity using diesel fuel or kerosene as in some developing countries). A few studies have examined cross-price elasticities for electricity consumption with respect to diesel (De Vita et al. 2006), kerosene prices (Bose & Shukla 1999), oil (Holtedahl & Joutz 2004), and appliance prices (Diabi 1998) and found them to be statistically insignificant (possibly owing to limited opportunities for switching between grid electricity and other fuels) or to have the wrong signs (e.g., Diabi 1998, Bose & Shukla 1999).

as biomass, kerosene, and candles. The energy ladder model has been used to conceptualize the phases in fuel switching from universal reliance on biomass to transition fuels such as kerosene or coal and finally to liquefied petroleum gas, natural gas, or electricity (Heltberg 2004). Sathaye & Tyler (1991) provide early survey-based evidence of the effects of rising income levels, availability of fuels, urbanization, government policies, and household activity patterns (such as extent of female employment) on the transition from solid fuels to liquefied petroleum gas for cooking and on the number of electric appliances owned per household. More recently, Pachauri & Jiang (2008) found that urban households in both India and China consume a larger share of electricity and fossil-based energy sources than rural households, with the transition to modern energy types in urban areas increasing with income and education.

Demand for electricity is, thus, expected to be driven by size, income, and education of the household; dwelling type and size; weather variables; prices of electricity and of alternative fuels (in recently electrified country studies these could include prices of paraffin or candles); as well as the cost and availability of suitable appliances (which could depend on access to credit). A number of recent studies have estimated this demand using average price of electricity as an explanatory variable and a logarithmic functional form.[3] Elasticity estimates obtained by the studies using household-level survey data are presented in **Table 2**. These estimates (with the exception of those for Nairobi) are consistent with those obtained from aggregate demand studies in showing that demand for electricity is price and income inelastic. Filippini & Pachauri (2004) found that price elasticity differs across seasons; it is more inelastic in summer than in other seasons, and Tiwari (2000) found that income elasticity increases as income increases. Although electricity demand is price and income inelastic in both developing and developed countries, estimates for developing countries are relatively higher. This indicates that, as income levels in these countries increase, electricity consumption will experience a relatively larger increase than it would in developed countries.[4] The low price elasticity implies that future increases in price of electricity are unlikely to lead to much reduction in demand; an exception is provided by Tiwari (2000), who found that the elasticity is −0.84 for the upper-income class in Mumbai. These studies show considerable heterogeneity in the demand for electricity across households with different sizes, demographic characteristics, and locations (with varying levels of urbanization). Some studies analyze the influence of differences in the composition of home appliances on electricity consumption by constructing an index that captures the average electricity requirement of each appliance rather than just the number of appliances (Tiwari 2000, Jung 1993) or a count of end uses of each type in each dwelling (Eiswerth et al. 1998). Such studies indicate these measures have statistically significant effects on electricity demand.

---

[3]No *a priori* functional form is suggested by theory, and Zarnikau (2003) found no conclusive evidence in favor of one type of parametric form as compared with others. A logarithmic is typically chosen for ease of interpreting the coefficients as elasticities and for reducing the effect of extreme electricity expenditures and incomes on parameter estimates.

[4]Branch's (1993) review of studies estimating demand for electricity using household data for the United States shows that the income elasticity ranges between 0.14 and 0.4, whereas the price elasticity ranges between −0.11 and −0.55. Differences among these studies arise as a result of variances in methods and data used, such as the measure of income (categorical versus continuous measures), price (average or marginal), the level of aggregation of the data, and treatment of appliance stocks. Despite the range in the estimates, these studies indicate that electricity consumption is price and income inelastic in the United States.

Table 2 Determinants of household demand for electricity[a]

Study	Country and time period	Price elasticity	Income elasticity	Other significant variables
Louw et al. (2008)	South Africa: 2002	—	0.23–0.53	Price of paraffin and candles, cooking appliance ownership
Filippini & Pachauri (2004)	India: 1993–1994	−0.29 to −0.51	0.6–0.64	Price of LPG, dwelling size, urbanization, household size, demographic characteristics
Tiwari (2000)	India: 1987–1988	−0.7	0.34	Type of dwelling, dwelling size, age of household, index of power requirement of appliances owned
	Lower income	−0.76	0.28	
	Middle income	−0.65	0.19	
	Upper-middle income	−0.61	0.28	
	Upper income	−0.84	0.40	
Hughes-Cromwick (1985)	Nairobi: 1981	−0.34	1.6	Household size, number of electric appliances

[a]Based on household survey data. Abbreviation: LPG, liquefied petroleum gas.

3.4. Intensity of Electricity Consumption

In addition to understanding the price and GDP responsiveness of demand for energy, considerable effort has been devoted to studying the mechanisms leading to a change in energy intensity in industry in developing countries, particularly as interest in the potential for energy efficiency improvements to reduce costs and greenhouse gas emissions has grown. Changes in energy efficiency over time could be autonomous or induced by various economic forces. Sanstad et al. (2006) investigated the rate of autonomous energy efficiency improvement in various energy-intensive industries in India, Korea, and the United States by estimating industry-specific translog cost functions with capital, labor, energy, and materials as inputs and using data for varying periods prior to 1996. They found evidence of declining energy efficiency in several industries in each of the three countries, implying that technological change in the past has been energy using rather than energy saving. Other studies have examined changes in the intensity of the relationship between energy consumption and GDP over time and sought to decompose the change in aggregate energy intensity into the impact due to a change in industrial activity composition (i.e., structural effect) and a change in sectoral energy efficiency (i.e., intensity or efficiency effect). Following Ang & Zhang (2000), we define the aggregate energy intensity, at time t, as a summation of sectoral data:

$$I_t = \sum_{i=1}^{n} S_{it} I_{it}, \tag{10}$$

where I_t represents aggregate energy intensity ($= e_t/y_t$), e_t is total energy consumption, y_t is total output, S_{it} is the production share of sector i ($= y_{it}/y_t$), and I_{it} is the energy intensity of sector i ($= e_{it}/y_{it}$). A change in I_t may be due to changes in the sectoral energy intensity or due to structural change in the output mix of the economy. The primary objective of an energy decomposition analysis is to quantify these two effects. Ang & Zhang (2000) reviewed the developments in the methods used for decomposition analysis and the studies that have applied it in industrial energy demand analysis, whereas Liu & Ang (2007) reviewed the evidence from applications of this technique to developed and developing countries. The latter study found that, in the past three decades or so, industrialized countries experienced a decline in aggregate energy intensity while developing countries observed periods of increases and decreases in their energy intensity (with the exception of China where energy use has been decreasing consistently). The energy-GDP ratio rises as per capita income increases in low-income countries, reaching a plateau in middle-income countries, and then declines in high-income countries. A key driver behind changes in the aggregate energy intensity for industry has been subsector energy intensity change; product-mix change has played a smaller role in changing energy intensity. In the case of China, in particular, they found that the bulk of evidence suggests that both intensity change and structural changes led to reductions in energy intensity, with the impact of intensity change being larger in absolute terms.

Only a few studies have applied this approach to decompose the causes of change in electrical energy intensity in developing countries. Applying this approach to decompose the trends in electricity consumption and industrial production in Singapore and Taiwan, Ang (1994) found similar results to those above in that changes in sectoral energy intensity explain much of the change in aggregate electricity intensity in both countries in the 1970s and 1980s. Chen & Wu (1994) used an input-output decomposition method to provide a more detailed breakdown of the causes of increase in electricity use in Taiwan between 1976 and 1986. They found that growth in final demand (particularly due to exports) was the dominant cause of increased electricity use followed by a trend toward substitution of electricity for oil, whereas technological change in capital, labor, energy, and materials had a negative effect on electricity use. Steenhof (2006) analyzed the change in electricity demand in the industrial sector in China from 1998 to 2002. China has experienced a significant decline in energy intensity per unit of GDP; in 2001, it was only 28% of what it had been in 1980. However, electricity consumption (and therefore coal consumption) grew at 8% per annum while coal consumption grew at 2.3% per annum between 1990 and 2002.

Steenhof (2006) explains that electricity consumption has been driven primarily by an increase in industrial activity and by shifts in the type of fuel used from oil and natural gas toward electricity as industrial processes have switched from heat energy to electrical energy. By 2002, the intensity of electricity use per unit of economic activity had also fallen to 83% of 1998 levels. Fisher-Vanden et al. (2004) used decomposition analysis to find that productivity change is a dominant factor explaining the decline in intensity of electricity use in the industrial sector in China over 1997–1999. Using regression analysis to determine the contribution of various factors to this increase in productivity, they found that increases in electricity prices and R&D expenditures as well as change in ownership from state-owned to foreign-invested firms contributed to an increase in the productivity of electricity use.

A few studies have also examined the potential for increasing end-use efficiency in the electricity sector and the barriers to realizing that potential. An early survey of industrial companies in India in 1992–1993 by Parikh et al. (1994) showed the electricity savings that could be achieved through investment in demand-side management through better housekeeping practices, more cogeneration, and more-efficient electric motors. This and other studies also point to the barriers to the adoption of energy-efficient technologies, such as lack of information about available technologies among consumers, high discount rates, subsidized energy prices, uncertainty about cost savings, high up-front costs, requirements for rapid payback, and high rate of return on investments (see review in Reddy & Shrestha 1998). Among these barriers, lack of awareness and initial cost were ranked as the foremost reasons for nonadoption of a variety of electricity-efficient technologies in a survey of consumers in the residential, industrial, and commercial sectors in India in 1996 (Reddy & Shrestha 1998). Pricing electricity at marginal cost could create economic incentives for increasing energy efficiency (Reddy 2003).

Efficiency improvements lower the effective cost of energy consumption, which can offset a part of the expected energy savings. Jin (2007) reviewed existing discussions in the literature on the existence and magnitude of the rebound effect that show that the effect is country and sector specific. Studies using U.S. data provide estimates of this effect ranging from 2%–13% to 60%–70% (Grepperud & Rasmussen 2004). Investigating the responsiveness of residential electricity consumption to reductions in real electricity price over the 1975–2002 period in South Korea, Jin (2007) found evidence of a short-term rebound effect of 38% and a long-term rebound effect of 30%. Roy (2000) found the potential for even larger rebound effects in the case of a nonelectrified village in India that switched from kerosene lamps to increasingly efficient solar lanterns for lighting. The existence of supply constraints on electricity that, in turn, lead to a considerable unmet demand for electricity and low income levels can be expected to result in a large rebound effect and an increase in demand for electricity even with an increase in energy efficiency.

We now turn to the literature that uses economic tools to analyze factors influencing the supply of electricity and the performance of the industry in developing countries. This includes studies that have examined the technical efficiency of the electricity-generating industry as well as studies examining the institutional structure of the electricity sector, the reforms that have been undertaken, and their influence on the performance of the sector.

4. ELECTRICITY SUPPLY SECTOR

The electricity supply sector in developing countries had been established and operated by the respective governments with the objective of catalyzing economic development and providing access to a larger share of the population. Electric utility companies were vertically integrated in their provision of electricity generation, transmission, and distribution in the belief that they provide economies of scale (Jamash et al. 2004). Williams & Ghanadan (2006) described the key features of this sector prior to reforms in the 1990s. Most utilities providers were unable to earn revenues sufficient to cover costs and were dependent on the government for operating expenses. Supply was unable to keep pace with demand, and the sector suffered from lack of investment in new equipment, high system losses, low efficiency, and poor quality of service. Electricity pricing was characterized by direct government subsidies, cross subsidization for agriculture and residential consumers by industrial consumers, limited use of meters, and an inability to prevent theft and to collect revenues.

4.1. Efficiency of Electricity-Generating Plants

A study of the long-term trends in efficiency of electricity generation in non-OECD countries for the period 1971–2005 shows that the gap between their efficiency of coal-based electricity generation and that of the OECD countries has widened

(Maruyama & Eckelman 2009). The authors found that global energy consumption could be reduced by 5% and global greenhouse gas emissions by 8% if all countries were brought up to the standards of the countries that lead the world in efficiency.

The performance of standard electricity-generating plants in a country relative to the best practice in that country and the causes of inefficiency among these plants has been examined by a large number of studies using parametric and nonparametric methods to construct efficiency scores. These studies typically use stochastic frontier analysis or data envelopment analysis (DEA). The former involves estimating a parametric cost or production function using a statistical method that allows for random unobserved heterogeneity among firms. It allows for the separation of inefficiency from a best-practice frontier and from statistical noise due to unobserved factors. DEA, a nonparametric approach, relies on linear programming to construct a transformation frontier made up of best-practice firms and computes efficiency of other firms relative to the frontier. DEA methodology does not make any allowances for shocks of statistical errors and thus is very data dependent (Pollitt 1993). A discussion of the advantages and disadvantages of using DEA over stochastic frontier methods can be found in Pombo & Taborda (2006).

Studies using DEA to quantify operational inefficiencies and to identify the causes of inefficiency in electricity plants in developing countries include those for India (Chitkara 1999), Nepal (Jha & Shrestha 2006), Singapore (Chang & Tay 2006), Hong Kong (Wang et al. 2007), Taiwan (Yang 2006), and Iran (Sadjadi & Omrani 2008). Some of these studies also estimate the changes in productivity over time using the Malmquist index. There is no consensus on which outcome variables best measure the performance of electricity-generating and -distributing plants. The efficiency of generating units is measured using multiple variables that include coal and oil consumption, auxiliary consumption, peaking capacity, and energy loss rate, whereas the efficiency of distributing units is measured by energy delivered, number of employees, number of customers, and size of service area. These studies show considerable inefficiencies among electricity-generating plants. They also show how efficiency could be improved by decreasing operational and maintenance expenditures, reducing overstaffing, increasing training of operating personnel, and operating at an optimal scale. DEA studies have been criticized because a small perturbation in the data could lead to big changes in ranking of firms based on efficiency (Sadjadi & Omrani 2008). Sadjadi & Omrani (2008) applied a recently developed optimization technique that allows for uncertainty in data and parameters with DEA and leads to a solution that is robust to possible realizations of uncertain parameters. Using data for electricity distribution units in Iran for 2004, they demonstrated the reliability of this approach by comparing their results with those obtained using the stochastic frontier approach. Recent developments in DEA include its application to estimate environmental efficiency of electricity plants. For example, in India, Murty et al. (2007) used the directional output distance function to estimate the potential for firms to increase good output and reduce pollution nonproportionally relative to the frontier. They found that the marginal cost of abatement increases with overall abatement but decreases with increase in plant capacity.

Relatively few studies have used the stochastic production frontier approach to estimate technical inefficiency among electricity-generating plants in developing countries (see review in Khanna et al. 1999). A recent study by Shanmugam & Kulshreshtha (2005) uses this approach to measure the technical efficiency of coal-based power plants in India over the period 1995–2002. They found that efficiency varies across plants and regions but is relatively constant over time and that newer plants are more efficient than older plants.

Empirical evidence on the effects of the limited private ownership that existed in the electricity sector in the prereform era shows that privately and publicly owned firms were virtually equally efficient. Pollitt (1995) was one of the first to analyze econometrically the impact of privatization on the electric-supply industry using an international sample of electricity-generating plants. His evidence indicates that private ownership leads to better investment planning and lower generation costs in the long run and that privately owned plants are slightly more efficient (2%–5%) than publicly owned plants. In the short term, when technology is fixed, no evidence of cost efficiency due to private ownership is found. Yunos & Hawdon (1997), who used DEA to compare the efficiency of electricity production in 27 developing countries in 1987, found that public-sector firms performed as well as private-sector firms.

The mixed effects of ownership are also found by Khanna & Zilberman (1999a), who econometrically examined the energy efficiency of 63 electricity-generating plants in India over the period 1988–1991. They distinguished between plants that are state owned and those that are owned by the central government and compared them with those that are privately owned. They found that privately owned plants were statistically significantly more energy efficient than state-owned plants but not more efficient than those owned by the central government, which had greater managerial autonomy than state-owned plants and were not guaranteed government subsidies.

In another study, Khanna et al. (1999) estimated a stochastic frontier cost function using panel data and parametric and semiparametric methods with alternative assumptions about the distribution of the error term for electricity-generating plants in India over the period 1988–1991. They investigated the extent and sources of inefficiency by incorporating the hypothesized sources directly in the cost function. They found significant inefficiency among these power plants; the distributional assumptions about the error term influence the value of average inefficiency. Publicly owned plants are more inefficient than privately owned plants, and low capacity utilization is a significant determinant of inefficiency. However, like Khanna & Zilberman (1999a), they also found that plants owned by the central government were less inefficient than those owned by the state government, indicating that even among publicly owned plants, managerial autonomy and appropriate incentives for cost minimization can reduce technical inefficiency. All these studies focused on the period before privatization was introduced.

5. REFORM OF THE ELECTRICITY SECTOR IN DEVELOPING COUNTRIES

Starting in the 1990s, many OECD countries and more than 70 developing and transition countries began to reform their electricity sectors. The motivations for reform and the institutional context in which it occurred were fundamentally different in developing countries from those in developed countries. In the latter case, electricity deregulation was motivated by the objectives of improving efficiency, increasing competition, enhancing customer choice, and lowering prices. In developing countries, the driving forces can be categorized into "push" and "pull" factors (Zhang et al. 2008). The push factors include disillusionment with public enterprises as a result of high costs and unreliable supply as well as the needs to expand the grid, improve the sector's financial health, increase revenue for the state, and raise the rate of investment in the sector. In many cases, electric-sector reform was a part of a broader economic liberalization agenda to introduce fiscal responsibility following the macroeconomic crises of the 1980s. The pull factors include the desire to achieve the benefits demonstrated by the pioneering experiences with reform in Chile and other Latin American countries and the advocacy for reform by the International Monetary Fund and the World Bank through their institutional reform programs.

A number of theoretical arguments can be made in favor of private ownership and market-oriented reforms leading to efficiency. Property rights theories suggest allocating property rights of assets to owners that have efficiency maximization as their objective, whereas bureaucracy theories recognize that civil servants and politicians who may be responsible for running publicly owned utilities are not primarily interested in the profitability of the enterprise or in minimizing its costs. Both suggest efficiency gains from private ownership. In contrast, theories of regulation suggest that the regulations that need to accompany privatization of utilities with asymmetric information about their private costs create incentives for overinvestment and not for cost minimization (see Pollitt 1997). Arguments can also be made for unbundling ownership among generators, transmitters, and distributors (see Pollitt 2008) and for enhancing competition and facilitating privatization, thereby increasing transparency in business operations and making efficient foreign and domestic takeovers more likely (but with the recognition that this unbundling will impose upfront costs for reorganization).

By the end of the 1990s, reform was still in its early stages in most developing countries and less than 20% of the countries in South Asia and Sub-Saharan Africa had taken key steps to reform the system (Jamash et al. 2004). A survey of 115 developing countries in 1998 found that corporatization and commercialization of the state utility had been undertaken by 40% of countries but only 20% had privatized utilities and 29% had laws to unbundle and/or privatize the sector. Later surveys confirmed that as of 2000 the extent of reform in this sector was limited and varied considerably across developing countries (more details of these surveys are in Bacon & Besant-Jones 2001).

Studying the economic causes of privatization by 83 developing countries by 1987, Ramamurti (1992) showed that privatization was more likely to be pursued by countries with high budget deficits, high foreign debt, greater dependence on the World Bank and the International Monetary Fund, as well as a relatively rapidly expanding private sector. The determinants of reform of the electricity sector, in particular, have been examined by several studies using econometric techniques and data from a cross section of countries (see review in Jamash et al. 2004). These studies show that less risky countries (i.e., those with better policy and institutional environments, with greater judicial independence, and with an economic ideology favoring competition and private ownership) were likely to have undertaken more steps toward reform. Countries in Latin America were likely to have undertaken more reform steps than those in the Middle East and Africa. These studies suffer from a number of shortcomings, due to the availability and quality of data, including a narrow specification of the dependent variable, endogeneity of some explanatory variables (such as political risk that was likely to have been reduced by privatization, implying reverse causality), omitted variables bias, and lack of a temporal dimension.

5.1. Implications for Performance of Privatizing the Electricity Sector

A number of studies have examined the effects of privatization on economic performance across industries and countries (see surveys by Megginson & Netter 2001,

Parker & Kirkpatrick 2005) and concluded that privately owned firms are more efficient and profitable and increase their capital investment spending than are comparable state-owned firms. However, these reviews also show that privatization alone may not be sufficient to generate economic gains; effective regulation and competition need to be present to realize the potential gains from privatization. Most of these studies focused on the telecommunication industry and included data for developing and developed countries, which may conceal differences among these countries.

Similar evidence of the need for effective regulation to support successful privatization is found for the electricity sector in developing countries (Zhang et al. 2008). Electricity markets have to be well designed and governed to ensure efficiency, and real-time balancing of demand and supply of electricity is needed. Credible regulatory institutions and a political will to restore prices to reflect long-run marginal costs and introduce competition need to accompany privatization to achieve its full benefits. After controlling for privatization and competition, Cubbin & Stern (2006) econometrically examined the relationship between the quality of regulatory governance and the level of generation capacity per capita for electricity-supply industries in 28 developing countries over the period 1980–2001. Even after controlling for autocorrelation and endogeneity, they found that having both a regulatory law and an autonomous regulator and using license fees to fund the regulatory agency had positive and statistically significant impacts on generation capacity per capita. Using crude indicators for competition and privatization, they found that, although introduction of competition did have a significant impact on generation capacity levels, the effects of privatization were weak and mixed. Additionally, the quality of overall country governance and the quality of the regulatory laws have a positive effect on generation capacity, and this effect increases over time with experience and regulatory reputation. In addition to regulation, well-defined and credible political institutions were positively and significantly correlated with generating capacity.

The need for a legal and regulatory framework to be in place before privatization of the power supplier is emphasized by Bacon & Besant-Jones (2001), who discuss the optimal sequencing of reform steps to ensure its long-term sustainability, the optimal timing of reform, and the difficulties in making power suppliers pass on productivity gains in the form of lower prices to consumers in noncompetitive retail markets for electricity. Pollitt (1997) highlighted the political and regulatory preconditions for successful reform. He also emphasized that the realization of efficiency gains depends on restructuring publicly owned assets and better government management as well as on improving competitiveness of labor, capital, and product markets.

Recent studies by Zhang et al. (2005, 2008) examine the roles of privatization, competition, and regulation and the effect of the sequence of these reforms on various measures of performance. The first study used panel data for 25 developing countries for the period 1985–2001 and found that having an independent regulator before privatizing is associated with higher electricity availability and more generating capacity, whereas introducing competition before privatization has favorable impacts on service penetration, capacity expansion, capacity utilization, and capital productivity. The second study examines the impact of reforms on electricity generated, labor productivity, generation capacity, and capacity utilization in 36 developing and transitional economies over the period 1985–2003. Using panel data methods to control for country-specific effects and including the reform variables separately as well as their interactions, Zhang et al. (2008) found that privatization improves performance only when it is coupled with the existence of an independent regulator. Regulation on its own seems to be ineffective, because regulation of state-owned enterprises by the government is likely to lack credibility. However, they did find strong support for the positive effects of competition by itself on all measures of performance, suggesting that guaranteeing exclusivity in power purchase to new generators and independent power producers may diminish incentives for efficiency and improved economic performance.

Jamash et al. (2004) reviewed studies analyzing the effects of reform in the electricity sector in developing and developed countries on productive efficiency. These studies show that privatization increases efficiency when accompanied by a competitive market. In contrast, Plane (1999) examined the benefit of reform in the presence of market power in Cote d'Ivoire where the electric utility shifted from public ownership to private operation as a monopoly. He estimated a stochastic frontier function using data for 1959–1995 with gross production of electricity as the dependent variable and found that productive efficiency improved significantly as a result of privatization in 1990. He attributed this increase in efficiency to organizational innovations that accompanied privatization, such as decentralization of management, in-house training of employees, and better information management. Gains in efficiency were associated with a reduction in costs and a decrease in the relative price of electricity, which benefited consumers.

A few other country-specific studies have analyzed the impact of reforms in the electricity sector on efficiency using DEA. Pombo & Ramirez (2005) and Pombo & Taborda (2006) analyzed the implications of the 1994 sector-wide reforms in Colombia that introduced competition and incentives for utility efficiency and established a new regulatory agency, a market system for wholesale electricity transactions, and a bidding system for its pool electricity market in the region. Pombo & Ramirez (2005) examined the impact of privatization on efficiency of thermal power plants over the prereform (1988–1994) and postreform (1995–2000) periods. They showed that new market entrants, use of newer technologies, and regulatory policy led to an increase in the productive efficiency of plants. Ownership did not have a significant effect on efficiency. Pombo & Taborda (2006) examined the efficiency and productivity of power distribution utilities in Colombia from 1985–2001. They found that, after the reform, plant efficiency and productivity increased mainly among the largest electric utilities and that the implementation of regulatory reform was a key determinant of these efficiency gains. Other studies of electricity distribution companies in Turkey (Bagdadioglu et al. 1996) and the Philippines (Pacudan & de Guzman 2002) using DEA show that these companies suffer from scale inefficiency. The former shows that privately owned companies were more efficient than those publicly owned, possibly owing to an absence of universal supply obligations for those companies and thus the potential for improved scale efficiency. The latter study indicates that demand-side management strategies have a potential for improving scale efficiency.

A number of case studies reviewing the electricity sector's experience with privatization provide a mixed picture of its success (see Besant-Jones 2006). These studies indicate that reforms in Latin America improved efficiency, labor productivity, capacity utilization, and supply quality while reducing frequency of blackouts and electricity losses and led to gains in social welfare. Reforms also improved the fiscal position of governments by approximately 1% of GDP (see Pombo & Taborda 2006, Besant-Jones 2006, Zhang et al. 2005). However, distributional effects of the reforms were mixed. Although lower income groups benefited as a result of improved access to electricity supply, most of the productivity gains with privatization were initially kept by generators and were passed on to purchasers of electricity only in the presence of competitive wholesale markets and regulatory price reviews. Birdsall & Nellis (2003) found that privatization worsened employment and raised electricity prices. In addition, although privatization reduced theft of electricity, it also increased payments by the poor for electricity. Case studies for other developing countries (see Parker & Kirkpatrick 2005) document the difficulties in maintaining competitiveness in the sector; the costly disputes between investors, regulators, and governments; and the drop in private-sector investment in the electricity sector since the late 1990s (for a discussion of the experience in India, see Bhattacharyya 2007).

5.2. Economic Policy Distortions Affecting the Electricity Sector

Government intervention in the electricity sector is not limited to ownership. It often involves setting the retail price of electricity and the price of key inputs for electricity generation that distort consumption decisions, choice of inputs, and incentives to adopt energy efficient technologies. These policies affect not only economic growth but also the environment because electricity generation relies heavily on fossil fuels, especially coal, which contributes to both air pollution and global warming.

An early review of economic policies in developing countries by Bates (1993) identified several policies that distorted energy consumption decisions. In particular, he found that, in 1990, 60% of the less developed countries had an electricity price that was below its long-run marginal cost (the weighted average ratio of retail price to cost is 62%). He also found that countries commonly gave cross subsidies from industrial to residential consumers, from industry to agriculture, and across regions. Despite reforms, the retail price of energy continued to be approximately 20% below its marginal cost even in 1999 (International Energy Agency 1999). The desire to promote universal access to electricity and to maintain its affordability as well as the political and social difficulties of raising electricity prices have led to a continuation of subsidies and, as in the case of India, to the reintroduction of free electricity for the agricultural sector in 2004 (Bhattacharyya 2007). These policies have raised demand and inefficient use of electricity and imposed a heavy fiscal burden on the government that has hampered investment in modernization and expansion of capacity in the sector. A number of countries (e.g., India) historically restricted imports of energy-efficient equipment and protected domestic suppliers of energy-inefficient equipment. Furthermore, input prices for the electricity sector are also distorted. For example, low coal prices, incorrect price differentials between different grades of coal, and an import tariff on high quality coal all led to a lack of incentives to produce and use efficiency-enhancing high-quality coal for electricity generation and discouraged investment in coal washeries in India (Bates 1993).

These economic policy distortions have implications not only for efficiency but also for emissions generated by the electricity sector. Khanna & Zilberman (1999b, 2001) applied the putty-clay framework to examine incentives for a power plant to adopt high-quality coal, which can raise its energy efficiency and increase production capacity even with the existing capital equipment. They showed that eliminating existing policy distortions in India, such as an import tariff on high-quality coal and imposing a carbon tax, could induce adoption of higher quality coal and reduce carbon emissions while increasing electricity generation and social welfare.

In addition to the need to reduce economic policy distortions to foster an electricity sector that functions efficiently, there is also a need for policies that correct market prices to reflect the environmental costs of electricity production. However, the design of such environmental policies needs to consider the other economic policy distortions existing in the electricity sector in order to be efficient. Khanna (2003) discussed the importance of identifying the policy distortions that influence carbon emissions from electricity generation and of tailoring policies to the underlying source of the problem. Standard policy prescriptions such as a carbon tax or emissions standards and a disregard for existing distortions result in high costs of carbon abatement. She found that the marginal costs of carbon abatement for the electricity sector in India are lowest with an emissions tax that accompanies domestic policy reforms and highest with an emissions tax in the absence of other policy reforms.

5.3. Decentralized Electricity Generation

International donors have promoted decentralized electricity generation in developing countries since the 1970s. However, the success of such an approach in providing rural electricity has been mixed, and there are very few examples of broader success in establishing viable and self-sustaining distributed generation models that expand beyond their initial, limited scope. A study of 120 World Bank projects for rural electrification since the 1980s shows that the objective of 75% of them was to improve energy supply; 60% of them had the objective of increasing rural incomes (including environmental benefits), and 7% had an explicit poverty-reduction objective (World Bank 2008).

There is a large literature analyzing the technical and economic factors that influence the feasibility of decentralized energy generation, using renewable energy technologies, and the choice between grid-connected and stand-alone power generation. Most of these studies are context and technology dependent and have limited geographical scope. They also tend to focus on technology assessment and not on the institutional factors that can affect widespread reliance on distributed power generation (see review in Kaundinaya et al. 2009). Local institutional weaknesses, lack of mechanisms for financing and cost recovery, and a policy that emphasizes incentives for capital and equipment over maintenance and performance have limited the sustainability of many programs (World Bank 2008). Meta-analyses that draw on details of individual projects could help determine broader, generalizable determinants of economic viability, sustainability, and commercial scalability of rural electrification projects. Research on the environmental benefits of distributed systems is also lacking, perhaps because environmental objectives have not driven projects in developing countries.

Zerriffi (2007) examined the experience with rural electrification in Brazil, Cambodia, and China, all of which have very different institutional, regulatory, and policy environments. He identified institutional factors important for the success of rural electrification and suggested the need to shift the emphasis from whether a given technology can provide electricity to how it will do so. Policies for promoting rural electrification need to be carefully designed. Subsidies can be used to ease the burden of high initial costs but should not be used to provide electricity at below cost because they are unsustainable in the long run and harm the creation of viable markets.

On the demand side, rural electrification is key to enabling households to move up the energy ladder and shift from low-efficiency and polluting biomass-based fuels to electricity. Studies show that electricity in rural areas is primarily used for lighting and for powering televisions and radios. Electricity is used for cooking in only a minority of homes.

Rural electrification confers a number of benefits, in the form of improved health benefits due to reduced indoor air pollution, improved health knowledge through increased access to television, and better nutrition from improved knowledge and storage facilities from refrigeration. Other benefits include increased leisure time, greater educational attainment among children in electrified households, and increased agricultural productivity. A monetized estimate of the willingness to pay for some of these benefits based on the avoided cost of alternative energy forms (such as candles, kerosene, and batteries), in select developing countries, is approximately $50 per household per month. Actual connection costs vary between $150 and $2000 per household, depending on the location and size of the community; thus, the household willingness to pay is expected to be well above the average supply cost (World Bank 2008).

Most of the benefits from rural electrification have historically been captured by the nonpoor because poor households are often unable to afford the connection once the grid is available and progressive tariff structures prove to be regressive. Similarly, off-grid systems are typically expensive, and information about available subsidies is poorly disseminated, resulting in the exclusion of poor consumers.

6. CONCLUSIONS

The review of electricity demand studies demonstrates that such demand is driven by GDP, prices, income, level and characteristics of economic activity/urbanization, and seasonal factors. The magnitude of the effects of these factors differs across countries and time periods, and even within studies of the same country. These demand studies suffer from a number of data limitations. Most of these studies use aggregate (national/sectoral level) time-series data and suffer from small sample sizes, use of explanatory variables such as price and real income that do not vary a great deal over this period, and multicollinearity among variables (Westley 1992). The accuracy of some of these data for some countries may also be questionable (for concerns about underreporting of energy consumption and overreporting of GDP by China's Statistical Authorities, see Fisher-Vanden et al. 2004). Survey data from households vary cross sectionally but may not provide much variation in electricity price unless it varies substantially across locations.

Furthermore, several characteristics of the electricity sector of developing countries pose problems for the estimation of elasticities. The prevalence of supply rationing, theft, subsidies, and captive generation reduce the influence of price. Rather than model the block tariff structure, most studies assume users respond to *ex post* average price. Most of the elasticity estimation studies reviewed here used a reduced-form dynamic equation to estimate price and income elasticities instead of structural models in which capital stock is endogenously determined.

On the supply side, the literature on efficiency estimation and the effects of reforms on efficiency has dominated other types of economic analyses. The literature is inconclusive on whether reforms, particularly privatization, improve supply efficiency. Evidence, based mostly on econometric studies, indicates other drivers, such as regulatory performance and competition, influenced efficiency. In terms of supply growth, reforms led to short-lived acceleration of electric generation from the private sector in the 1990s. The Asian crises and other factors led to a slowdown in this trend. Empirical evidence suggests that institutional capacity, sequencing of reforms, and complementary policies that promote competition and regulatory capacity are needed for privatization to be successful. These can also reduce the adverse distributional outcomes of privatization and lead to increased access and transfer of the efficiency gains to the poor. There is a need for more quantitative analysis of the broader impacts that privatization of rural electrification has in developing countries in terms of poverty reduction, access to electricity, employment, distribution of income, long-term economic growth, and social welfare.

DISCLOSURE STATEMENT

The authors are not aware of any affiliations, memberships, funding, or financial holdings that might be perceived as affecting the objectivity of this review.

ACKNOWLEDGMENT

We thank Alexander Kiyoshi Mino for his careful and extensive literature search and assistance with this paper.

LITERATURE CITED

Ang BW. 1994. Decomposition of industrial energy consumption: the energy intensity approach. *Energy Econ.* 16:163–74

Ang BW, Zhang FQ. 2000. A survey of index decomposition analysis in energy and environmental studies. *Energy* 25:1149–76

Atakhanova Z, Howie P. 2007. Electricity demand in Kazakhstan. *Energy Policy* 35:3729–43

Bacon RW, Besant-Jones J. 2001. Global electric power reform, privatization and liberalization of the electric power industry in developing countries. *Annu. Rev. Energy Environ.* 26:331–59

Bagdadioglu N, Waddams Price CM, Weyman-Jones TG. 1996. Efficiency and ownership in electricity distribution: a non-parametric model of the Turkish experience. *Energy Econ.* 18:1–23

Balabanoff S. 1994. The dynamics of energy demand in Latin America. *OPEC Energy Rev.* 18 (4):467–88

Bates RW. 1993. The impact of economic policy on energy and the environment in developing countries. *Annu. Rev. Energy Environ.* 18:479–506

Berndt ER, Samaniego R. 1984. Residential electricity demand in Mexico: a model distinguishing access from consumption. *Land Econ.* 60:268–76

Besant-Jones JE. 2006. *Reforming power markets in developing countries: What have we learned?* Discuss. Pap. 19, Energy Min. Sect. Board, World Bank

Bhattacharyya SC. 2007. Sustainability of power sector reform in India: What does recent experience suggest? *J. Clean. Prod.* 15:235–46

Birdsall N, Nellis J. 2003. Winners and losers: assessing the distributional impact of privatization. *World Dev.* 31:1617–33

Bohi DR, Zimmerman MB. 1984. An update on econometric studies of energy demand behavior. *Annu. Rev. Energy* 9:105–54

Bose RK, Shukla M. 1999. Elasticities of electricity demand in India. *Energy Policy* 27:137–46

Branch ER. 1993. Short-run income elasticity of demand for residential electricity using consumer expenditure. *Energy J.* 14:111–21

Brenton P. 1997. Estimates of the demand for energy using cross-country consumption data. *Appl. Econ.* 29:851–59

Buranakunaporn S, Oczkowski E. 2007. A dynamic econometric model of Thailand manufacturing energy demand. *Appl. Econ.* 39:2261–67

Burney NA. 1995. Socioeconomic development and electricity consumption. A cross-country analysis using the random coefficient method. *Energy Econ.* 17:185–95

Chang Y, Tay TH. 2006. Efficiency and deregulation of the electricity market in Singapore. *Energy Policy* 34:2498–508

Chen S, Kuo H, Chen C. 2007. The relationship between GDP and electricity consumption in 10 Asian countries. *Energy Policy* 35:2611–21

Chen CY, Wu RH. 1994. Sources of change in industrial electricity use in the Taiwan economy, 1976–1986. *Energy Econ.* 16:115–20

Chitkara P. 1999. A data envelopment analysis approach to evaluation of operational inefficiencies in power generating units: a case study of Indian power plants. *IEEE Trans. Power Syst.* 14:419–25

Cubbin J, Stern J. 2006. The impact of regulatory governance and privatization on electricity industry generation capacity in developing economies. *World Bank Econ. Rev.* 20:115–41

De Vita G, Endresen K, Hunt LC. 2006. An empirical analysis of energy demand in Namibia. *Energy Policy* 34:3447–63

Diabi A. 2002. The demand for electric energy in Saudi Arabia: an empirical investigation. *OPEC Energy Rev.* 22:13–29

Eiswerth ME, Abendroth KW, Ciliano RC, Ouerghi A, Ozog MT. 1998. Residential electricity use and the potential impacts of energy efficiency options in Pakistan. *Energy Policy* 26:307–15

Eltony MN, Al-Awadhi MA. 2007a. The commercial sector demand for energy in Kuwait. *OPEC Energy Rev.* 31:17–26

Eltony MN, Al-Awadhi MA. 2007b. Residential energy demand: a case study of Kuwait. *OPEC Energy Rev.* 31:159–68

Eltony MN, Hajeeh M. 1999. Electricity demand by the commercial sector in Kuwait: an econometric analysis. *OPEC Energy Rev.* 22:23–32

Filippini M, Pachauri S. 2004. Elasticities of electricity demand in urban Indian households. *Energy Policy* 32:429–36

Fisher-Vanden K, Jefferson GH, Liu H, Tao Q. 2004. What is driving China's decline in energy intensity? *Resour. Energy Econ.* 26:77–97

Granger CWJ. 1969. Investigating causal relations by econometric models and cross-spectral methods. *Econometrica* 37:424–38

Grepperud S, Rasmussen I. 2004. A general equilibrium assessment of rebound effects. *Energy Econ.* 26:261–82

Halicioglu F. 2007. Residential electricity demand dynamics in Turkey. *Energy Econ.* 29:199–210

Heltberg R. 2004. Fuel switching: evidence from eight developing countries. *Energy Econ.* 26:869–87

Holtedahl P, Joutz FL. 2004. Residential electricity demand in Taiwan. *Energy Econ.* 26:201–24

Houthaker HS, Taylor LD. 1966. *Consumer Demand in the United States*. Cambridge, MA: Harvard Univ. Press

Hughes-Cromwick EL. 1985. Nairobi households and their energy use: an economic analysis of consumption patterns. *Energy Econ.* 7:265–78

Int. Energy Agency. 1999. *World Energy Outlook: Looking at Energy Subsidies: Getting the Prices Right*. Paris: IEA

Int. Energy Agency. 2007. *World Energy Outlook: China and India Insights*. Paris: IEA

Jamash T, Newbery D, Pollitt MG, Mota R. 2004. *Electricity sector reform in developing countries: a survey of empirical evidence on determinants and performance*. Policy Res. Work. Pap., World Bank

Jha DK, Shrestha R. 2006. Measuring efficiency of hydropower plants in Nepal using data envelopment analysis. *IEEE Trans. Power Syst.* 21:1502–11

Jin SH. 2007. The effectiveness of energy efficiency improvement in a developing country: rebound effect of residential electricity use in South Korea. *Energy Policy* 35:5622–29

Jumbe CBL. 2004. Cointegration and causality between electricity consumption and GDP: empirical evidence from Malawi. *Energy Econ.* 26:61–68

Jung TY. 1993. Ordered logit model for residential electricity demand in Korea. *Energy Econ.* 15:205–9

Kaundinaya DP, Balachandra P, Ravindranath NH. 2009. Grid-connected versus stand-alone energy systems for decentralized power—a review of literature. *Renew. Sustain. Energy Rev.* In press. doi:10.1016/j.rser.2009.02.002

Khanna M. 2003. Policies for carbon abatement in the presence of regulatory distortions: the electricity sector in India. In *India and Global Climate Change: Perspectives on Economics and Policy from a Developing Economy*, ed. M Toman, U Chakravorty, S Gupta, pp. 131–65. Washington, DC: Resour. Future Press

Khanna M, Mundra K, Ullah A. 1999. Parametric and semi-parametric estimation of the effect of firm attributes on efficiency: the electricity generating industry in India. *J. Int. Trade Econ. Dev.* 8:419–30

Khanna M, Zilberman D. 1999a. Barriers to energy-efficiency in electricity generation in India. *Energy J.* 20:25–42

Khanna M, Zilberman D. 1999b. Freer markets and the abatement of carbon emissions: the electricity-generating sector in India. *Resour. Energy Econ.* 21:125–52

Khanna M, Zilberman D. 2001. Adoption of energy efficient technologies and carbon abatement: the electricity generating sector in India. *Energy Econ.* 23:637–58

Lin BQ. 2003. *Electricity demand in the People's Republic of China: investment requirement and environmental impact*. Work. Pap. 37, Asian Dev. Bank

Liu N, Ang BW. 2007. Factors shaping aggregate energy intensity trend for industry: energy intensity versus product mix. *Energy Econ.* 29:609–35

Louw K, Conradie B, Howells M, Dekenah M. 2008. Determinants of electricity demand for newly electrified low-income African households. *Energy Policy* 36:2814–20

Lundmark R. 2001. Changes in Namibia's energy market. *Scand. J. Dev. Altern. Area Stud.* 20:103–12

Ma H, Oxley L, Gibson J, Kim B. 2008. China's energy economy: technical change, factor demand and interfactor/interfuel substitution. *Energy Econ.* 30:2167–83

Mahmud SF. 2000. The energy demand in the manufacturing sector of Pakistan: some further results. *Energy Econ.* 22:641–48

Martinot E, Chaurey A, Lew D, Moreira JR, Wamukonya N. 2002. Renewable energy markets in developing countries. *Annu. Rev. Energy Environ.* 27:309–48

Maruyama N, Eckelman MJ. 2009. Long-term trends of electric efficiencies in electricity generation in developing countries. *Energy Policy* 37:1678–86

Megginson WL, Netter JM. 2001. From state to market: a survey of empirical studies on privatization. *J. Econ. Lit.* 39:321–89

Murty MN, Kumar S, Dhavala KK. 2007. Measuring environmental efficiency of industry: a case study of thermal power generation in India. *Environ. Resour. Econ.* 38:31–50

Nahata B, Izyumov A, Busygin A, Mishura A. 2007. Application of Ramsey model in transition economy: a Russian case study. *Energy Econ.* 29:105–25

Nasr GE, Badr EA, Dibeh G. 2000. Econometric modeling of electricity consumption in post-war Lebanon. *Energy Econ.* 22:627–40

Pachauri S, Jiang L. 2008. The household energy transition in India and China. *Energy Policy* 36:4022–35

Pacudan R, de Guzman E. 2002. Impact of energy efficiency policy on productive efficiency of electricity distribution industry in the Philippines. *Energy Econ.* 24:41–54

Parikh JP, Reddy BS, Banerjee R. 1994. *Planning for Demand-Side Management in the Electrical Sector*. New Delhi, India: Tata/McGraw-Hill

Parker D, Kirkpatrick C. 2005. Privatization in developing countries: a review of evidence and policy lessons. *J. Dev. Stud.* 41:513–41

Pesaran MH, Smith R, Akiyama T. 1998. *Energy Demand in Asian Economies*. Oxford: Oxford Univ. Press

Plane P. 1999. Privatization, technical efficiency and welfare consequences: the case of the Cote D'Ivoire electric company. *World Dev.* 27:343–60

Pollitt MG. 2008. The arguments for and against ownership unbundling of energy transmission networks. *Energy Policy* 36:704–13

Pollitt MG. 1993. *Technical efficiency in electric power plants.* Work. Pap., Dep. Appl. Econ., Univ. Cambridge

Pollitt MG. 1995. *Ownership and Performance in Electric Utilities.* Oxford: Oxford Univ. Press

Pollitt MG. 1997. The impact of liberalization on the performance of the electricity supply industry: an international survey. *J. Energy Lit.* 3:3–31

Pombo C, Ramirez M. 2005. *Privatization in Colombia: a plant performance analysis.* RES Work. Pap. 3151, Inter-Am. Dev. Bank

Pombo C, Taborda R. 2006. Performance and efficiency in Colombia's power distribution system: effects of the 1994 reform. *Energy Econ.* 28:339–69

Pouris A. 1987. The price elasticity of electricity demand in South Africa. *Appl. Econ.* 19:1269–77

Ramamurti R. 1992. Why are developing countries privatizing? *J. Int. Bus. Stud.* 23:225–49

Ramcharran H. 1990. Electricity consumption and economic growth in Jamaica. *Energy Econ.* 12:65–70

Reddy BS. 2003. Overcoming the energy efficiency gap in India's household sector. *Energy Policy* 31:1117–27

Reddy BS, Shrestha RM. 1998. Barriers to the adoption of efficient electricity technologies: a case study of India. *Int. J. Energy Res.* 22:257–70

Roy J. 2000. The rebound effect: some empirical evidence from India. *Energy Policy* 28:433–38

Sadjadi SJ, Omrani H. 2008. Data envelopment analysis with uncertain data: an application for Iranian electricity distribution companies. *Energy Policy* 36:4247–54

Sanstad AH, Roy J, Sathaye JA. 2006. Estimating energy-augmenting technological change in developing country industries. *Energy Econ.* 28:720–29

Sathaye J, Tyler S. 1991. Transitions in household energy use in urban China, India, the Philippines, Thailand, and Hong Kong. *Annu. Rev. Energy Environ.* 16:295–335

Shanmugam KR, Kulshreshtha P. 2005. Efficiency analysis of coal-based thermal power generation in India during post-reform era. *Int. J. Global Energy Issues* 23:15–28

Steenhof PA. 2006. Decomposition of electricity demand in China's industrial sector. *Energy Econ.* 28:370–84

Taylor LD. 1975. The demand for electricity: a survey. *Bell J. Econ.* 6:74–110

Tiwari P. 2000. Architectural, demographic and economic causes of electricity consumption in Bombay. *J. Policy Model.* 22:81–98

Wang JH, Ngan HW, Engriwan W, Lo KL. 2007. Performance-based regulation of the electricity supply industry in Hong Kong: an empirical efficiency analysis approach. *Energy Policy* 35:609–15

Westley GD. 1984. Electricity demand in developing countries. *Rev. Econ. Stat.* 66:459–67

Westley GD. 1992. *New Directions in Econometric Modeling of Energy Demand with Applications to Latin America.* Washington, DC: Inter-Am. Dev. Bank

Westley GD. 1989. Commercial electricity demand in a central American economy. *Appl. Econ.* 21:1–17

Whittaker J, Barr GD. 1989. The price elasticity of electricity demand in South Africa. *Appl. Econ.* 21:1153–57

Williams JH, Ghanadan R. 2006. Electricity reform in developing and transition countries: a reappraisal. *Energy* 31:815–44

World Bank. 2008. *The Welfare Impact of Rural Electrification: A Reassessment of the Costs and Benefits.* IEG. Washington, DC: World Bank

Yang C. 2006. Assessing the performance and finding the benchmarks of the electricity distribution districts of Taiwan power company. *IEEE Trans. Power Syst.* 21:853–61

Yunos JM, Hawdon D. 1997. The efficiency of the national electricity board in Malaysia: an inter-country comparison using DEA. *Energy Econ.* 19:255–69

Zarnikau J. 2003. Functional forms in energy demand modeling. *Energy Econ.* 25:603–13

Zerriffi H. 2007. *Making small work: business models for electrifying the world.* Work. Pap. 63, Program Energy Sustain. Dev., Stanford Univ.

Zhang YF, Parker D, Kirkpatrick C. 2005. Competition, regulation and privatisation of electricity generation in developing countries: Does the sequencing of the reforms matter? *Q. Rev. Econ. Financ.* 45:358–79

Zhang YF, Parker D, Kirkpatrick C. 2008. Electricity sector reform in developing countries: an econometric assessment of the effects of privatization, competition and regulation. *J. Regul. Econ.* 33:159–78

Energy Efficiency Economics and Policy

Kenneth Gillingham,[1] Richard G. Newell,[2,3,4,*] and Karen Palmer[3]

[1]Precourt Energy Efficiency Center, Stanford University, Stanford, California 94309; email: kgilling@stanford.edu

[2]Nicholas School of the Environment, Duke University, Durham, North Carolina 27708; email: richard.newell@duke.edu

[3]Resources for the Future, Washington, D.C. 20036; email: palmer@rff.org

[4]National Bureau of Economic Research, Cambridge, Massachusetts 02138

Annu. Rev. Resour. Econ. 2009. 1:597–619

First published online as a Review in Advance on June 26, 2009

The *Annual Review of Resource Economics* is online at resource.annualreviews.org

This article's doi: 10.1146/annurev.resource.102308.124234

1941-1340/09/1010-0597$20.00

*Corresponding author

Copyright © 2009 by Annual Reviews. All rights reserved

Key Words

appliance standards, market failures, behavioral failures

Abstract

Energy efficiency and conservation are considered key means for reducing greenhouse gas emissions and achieving other energy policy goals, but associated market behavior and policy responses have engendered debates in the economic literature. We review economic concepts underlying consumer decision making in energy efficiency and conservation and examine related empirical literature. In particular, we provide an economic perspective on the range of market barriers, market failures, and behavioral failures that have been cited in the energy efficiency context. We assess the extent to which these conditions provide a motivation for policy intervention in energy-using product markets, including an examination of the evidence on policy effectiveness and cost. Although theory and empirical evidence suggests there is potential for welfare-enhancing energy efficiency policies, many open questions remain, particularly relating to the extent of some key market and behavioral failures.

1. INTRODUCTION

Energy efficiency and conservation have long been critical elements in the energy policy dialogue, and they have taken on a renewed importance as concerns about global climate change and energy security have intensified. Many advocates and policy makers hold that reducing the demand for energy is essential to meeting these challenges, and analyses tend to find that demand reductions can be a cost-effective means of addressing these concerns. With such great policy interest, a significant literature has developed over the past 30 years, providing an economic framework for addressing energy efficiency and conservation, as well as empirical estimates of how consumers respond to policies to reduce the demand for energy.

We begin by defining a few terms to put the literature in context. First, it is important to conceptualize energy as an input into the production of desired energy services (e.g., heating, lighting, motion), rather than as an end in itself. In this framework, energy efficiency is typically defined as the energy services provided per unit of energy input. For example, the energy efficiency of an air conditioner is the amount of heat removed from air per kilowatt-hour (kWh) of electricity input. At the individual product level, energy efficiency can be thought of as one of a bundle of product characteristics, alongside product cost and other attributes (Newell et al. 1999). At a more aggregate level, the energy efficiency of a sector or of the economy as a whole can be measured as the level of gross domestic product per unit of energy consumed in its production (for analyses of the determinants of energy intensity at the state and national levels, see, for example, Metcalf 2008, Sue Wing 2008).

In contrast, energy conservation is typically defined as a reduction in the total amount of energy consumed. Thus, energy conservation may or may not be associated with an increase in energy efficiency, depending on how energy services change. That is, energy consumption may be reduced with or without an increase in energy efficiency, and energy consumption may increase alongside an increase in energy efficiency. These distinctions are important when considering issues such as the "rebound effect," whereby the demand for energy services may increase in response to energy efficiency–induced declines in the marginal cost of energy services. The distinction is also important in understanding the short- versus long-run price elasticity of energy demand, whereby short-run changes may depend principally on changes in consumption of energy services, whereas longer-run changes include greater alterations of the energy efficiency of the equipment stock.

One must also distinguish between energy efficiency and economic efficiency. Maximizing economic efficiency—typically operationalized as maximizing net benefits to society—is generally not going to imply maximizing energy efficiency, which is a physical concept and comes at a cost. An important issue arises, however, regarding whether private economic decisions about the level of energy efficiency chosen for products are economically efficient. This will depend on the economic efficiency of the market conditions the consumer faces (e.g., energy prices, information availability) as well as the economic behavior of the individual decision maker (e.g., cost-minimizing behavior).

Market conditions may depart from efficiency if there are market failures, such as environmental externalities or imperfect information. Aside from such market failures, most economic analysis of energy efficiency has taken cost-minimizing (or utility/profit-maximizing) behavior by households and firms as a point of departure in analysis. Some literature, however, has focused more closely on the decision-making behavior of economic actors, identifying potential "behavioral failures" that lead to deviations from cost minimization and motivated at least partly by results from the field of behavioral economics. Much of the economic literature on energy efficiency therefore seeks to conceptualize energy efficiency decision making, to identify the degree to which market or behavioral failures may present an opportunity for net-beneficial policy interventions, and to evaluate the realized effectiveness and cost of actual policies.

This line of research has important implications both for assessing the cost of correcting market failures—such as environmental externalities—and for clarifying the role of policies that are oriented toward the correction of behavioral failures. For example, if behavioral failures lead to underinvestment in energy efficiency, then some reductions in energy-related emissions could be available at low or even negative cost. At the same time, policies that provide an efficient means of correcting environmental externalities—such as an emissions price—may not be well suited to inducing these relatively low-cost energy and emission reductions. In principle, a set of policies addressing both market and behavioral failures could, therefore, potentially provide a more efficient overall response. In practice, the value of individual policy components depends on the extent of existing market problems and the ability of specific policies to correct these problems in a net beneficial manner.

This article views the literature through this perspective and begins by introducing the notion of energy efficiency as an investment in producing energy services. After presenting evidence of energy market influences on energy efficiency, we then turn to identifying and examining empirical evidence on a range of market and behavioral failures that have been discussed in the energy efficiency literature. We then address the implications of this evidence for policy interventions and briefly review the empirical evidence on the effectiveness and cost of policy, including price policies and information policies. Finally, we provide overall conclusions. We limit the scope of this study primarily to energy efficiency and conservation in buildings and appliances and do not address transportation in detail. Nonetheless, most of the same conceptual and empirical issues carry over to transportation as well.

2. ENERGY EFFICIENCY AS AN INVESTMENT IN PRODUCING ENERGY SERVICES

From an economic perspective, energy efficiency choices fundamentally involve investment decisions that trade off higher initial capital costs and uncertain lower future energy operating costs. In the simplest case, the initial cost is the difference between the purchase and installation cost of a relatively energy-efficient product and the cost of an otherwise equivalent product that provides the same energy services but uses more energy. The decision of whether to make the energy-efficient investment requires weighing this initial capital cost against the expected future savings. Assessing the future savings requires forming expectations of future energy prices, changes in other operating costs related to the energy use (e.g., pollution charges), intensity of use of the product, and equipment lifetime. Comparing these expected future cash flows against the initial cost requires discounting the future cash flows to present values. Holding consumption of energy services constant, a privately optimal decision would entail choosing the level of energy efficiency to minimize the present value of private costs, whereas economic efficiency at a societal level would entail minimizing social costs. This makes energy efficiency different in character from many other product attributes for which there may not be a well-defined notion of what constitutes optimal or "rational" behavior on the part of the individual.

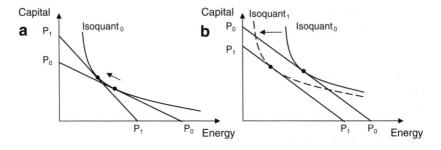

Figure 1

(*a*) Energy efficiency–improving substitution versus (*b*) energy-saving technological change.

This conceptualization of the problem maps directly into a production function framework, where capital and energy are viewed as inputs into the production of energy services. Along an isoquant describing a given level of energy services, the cost-minimizing level of energy use (and thus energy efficiency) is found at the point of tangency where the marginal increase in capital cost with respect to energy reduction is equal to their relative price (in present-value terms) (**Figure 1**). As described above, the relative price will depend on the capital cost of efficiency improvements, the discount rate, expected energy prices, equipment utilization, and decision-time horizon. This framework applies at the household level as well as at a broad sectoral or multisectoral level where energy and capital are used to produce energy services.[1]

Focusing on the household level as an example, greater energy efficiency can be driven by market forces in two ways within this production function framework. First, households may move along the energy-services isoquant by substituting capital for energy in response to a change in relative prices (**Figure 1a**, with relative prices changing from P_0 to P_1). Second, technological change that shifts the isoquant in a way favoring (i.e., biased toward) greater energy efficiency (**Figure 1b**, with isoquant$_0$ shifting to isoquant$_1$) could change the production possibilities available to households. In contrast, energy conservation not driven by energy efficiency improvements would be associated with a lower level of energy services (i.e., a lesser isoquant).

Market failures can be represented within this framework as a divergence of the relative prices used for private decisions from the economically efficient prices. For example, both unpriced environmental externalities and missing information on the energy intensity of product use would tend to lower the relative price of energy, leading to choices of inefficiently low energy efficiency (e.g., P_0 compared with P_1 in **Figure 1a**). Note that this framework presupposes optimizing behavior by the consumer, given available information—an assumption subject to debate within the behavioral economics literature, as discussed below.

The next section further explores the role of energy markets in governing energy efficiency decisions. Section 4 then identifies potential market and behavioral failures that may lead to suboptimal decisions.

---

[1]Understanding the economic forces governing the rate and direction of energy-related technological change at the product, sectoral, and aggregate levels has been an important area of research, particularly in the context of climate change modeling. For a review of literature devoted to this topic, which is beyond the scope of this paper, see Gillingham et al. (2008).

3. ENERGY MARKET INFLUENCES ON ENERGY EFFICIENCY

Energy markets and market prices influence consumer decisions regarding how much energy to consume and whether to invest in more energy-efficient products and equipment. An increase in energy prices will result in some energy conservation in the short run; however, short-run changes in energy efficiency tend to be limited owing to the long lifetimes and slow turnover of energy-using appliances and capital equipment. Nonetheless, if an energy price increase is persistent, it also is more likely to significantly affect energy efficiency adoption, as consumers replace older capital equipment and firms have time to develop new products and processes.

The extent of demand responsiveness to changes in price is captured in the price elasticity of energy demand. **Table 1** presents the ranges of energy own-price elasticity estimates in the literature. Long-run price elasticities are larger than short-run elasticities, corresponding to more energy efficiency improvements as capital turns over. On average, natural gas price elasticities are greater than electricity or fuel oil elasticities. Note that, because they are based on actual consumer behavior, these price elasticity estimates include any increase in consumption of energy services that might occur in response to a lower unit cost of energy services resulting from increased energy efficiency (i.e., the rebound effect).

Other studies have focused specifically on factors influencing technology adoption, finding that higher energy prices are associated with significantly greater adoption of

Table 1 Ranges of estimates of energy own-price elasticities[a]

	Short run		Long run	
	Range	References	Range	References
Residential				
Electricity	0.14–0.44	Dahl (1993)	0.32–1.89	Bernstein & Griffin (2005), Hsing (1994)
Natural gas	0.03–0.76	Bohi & Zimmerman (1984), Dahl (1993)	0.26–1.47[b]	Bohi & Zimmerman (1984), Dahl (1993)
Fuel oil	0.15–0.34	Wade (2003)	0.53–0.75	Dahl (1993), Wade (2003)
Commercial				
Electricity	0–0.46	Dahl (1993),	0.24–1.36	Wade (2003), Dahl (1993)
Natural gas	0.14–0.29	Dahl (1993), Wade (2003)	0.40–1.38	Wade (2003), Bohi & Zimmerman (1984)
Fuel oil	0.13–0.49	Dahl (1993), Wade (2003)	0.39–3.5	Wade (2003), Newell & Pizer (2008)
Industrial				
Electricity	0.11–0.28	Bohi & Zimmerman (1984), Dahl (1993)	0.22–3.26	Bohi & Zimmerman (1984), Dahl (1993)
Natural gas[b]	0.51–0.62	Bohi & Zimmerman (1984)	0.89–2.92	Dahl (1993), Bohi & Zimmerman (1984)
Fuel oil	0.11	Dahl (1993)	0.5–1.57[c]	Bohi & Zimmerman (1984)

[a]Absolute values shown; all values are negative.
[b]Estimates drawn largely from regional studies.
[c]Estimates for 19 states.

energy-efficient equipment (Anderson & Newell 2004, Hassett & Metcalf 1995, Jaffe et al. 1995). Further upstream in the technology development process, Newell et al. (1999) and Popp (2002) found energy-efficient innovation is also significantly determined by energy prices (for a review, see Popp et al. 2009). Empirical estimates, therefore, demonstrate a substantial degree of responsiveness of energy utilization as well as energy-efficient technology adoption and innovation to changes in energy price.

4. POTENTIAL MARKET AND BEHAVIORAL FAILURES

Much of the literature on energy efficiency focuses on elucidating the potential rationales for policy intervention and evaluating the effectiveness and cost of such interventions in practice. Within this literature, there is a long-standing debate surrounding the commonly cited "energy efficiency gap." There are several ways to view this gap. At its core, the gap refers to a significant difference between observed levels of energy efficiency and some notion of optimal energy use (Jaffe et al. 2004). That notion of optimal energy use has at times focused on maximizing physical energy efficiency, which will not generally coincide with maximal economic efficiency because energy efficiency comes at a cost. Within the investment framework described above, the energy efficiency gap takes the form of under-investment in energy efficiency relative to a description of the socially optimal level of energy efficiency. Such underinvestment is also sometimes described as an observed rate or probability of adoption of energy-efficient technologies that is "too slow."

Often, the efficiency gap is illustrated by a comparison of the market discount rate and relatively high "implicit discount rates" that are implied by consumer choices over appliances with different costs and energy efficiencies (Hausman 1979). The empirical evidence is relatively well established; in a number of studies published primarily in the late 1970s and early 1980s, analysts using a variety of methodologies found implicit discount rates ranging from 25% to over 100% (Sanstad et al. 2006, Train 1985).

Economists have posited a number of explanations to account for part or all of the apparent gap: hidden costs not accounted for by the analyst, including search costs as well as reductions in other product attributes (e.g., lighting quality) (Jaffe et al. 2004); lower energy savings than assumed by the analyst, owing in part to heterogeneity of consumers (Hausman & Joskow 1982); uncertain future energy savings implying rational consumers should put more weight on the initial cost (Sutherland 1991); the irreversibility of energy efficiency investments and the associated option value of waiting to invest (Hassett & Metcalf 1993, 1995; van Soest & Bulte 2000); and the possibility that consumers are appropriately forming expectations about future energy prices but energy analysts are using incorrect proxies for these expectations (Jaffe et al. 2004). For example, studies have found that actual savings from past utility-sponsored programs achieved 50%–80% of predicted savings (Hirst 1986, Sebold & Fox 1985), although a more recent study by Auffhammer et al. (2008) suggests that utilities have improved their abilities to predict savings. Similarly, Metcalf & Hassett (1999) found that, once all costs are accounted for, the realized return to attic insulation is much below the returns promised by engineers and manufacturers, and at 9.7%, it is consistent with the interest rate suggested by standard investment theory. Others have argued that the energy efficiency gap must not exist because rational optimizing consumers would not be willing to ignore large benefits—the proverbial $20 bill on the sidewalk (Sutherland 1996).

Conversely, other papers that examined these explanations for why there may not be a gap found some of them lacking. Metcalf (1994) found that the uncertainty of future energy savings described in Sutherland (1991) should actually lead a rational investor to require a rate of return that is lower than the market discount rate, because energy efficiency investments will tend to serve as a hedge against other risks. Sanstad et al. (1995) showed that the option value analysis of Hassett & Metcalf (1993, 1995) suggests an implicit discount rate much lower than observed implicit discount rates, even when taking irreversibility into account. Howarth & Sanstad (1995) discussed heterogeneity and hidden costs as possible concerns, but they suggested that analysts are cognizant of these issues and are careful to take them into account. For example, Koomey & Sanstad (1994) paid close attention to confounding factors such as heterogeneity and hidden costs and still found high implicit discount rates for efficient ballasts for commercial lighting and consumer purchases of refrigerators.

Other papers focus on distinguishing market barriers to the adoption of energy-efficient technologies from market failures. Market barriers can be defined as any disincentives to the adoption or use of a good (Jaffe et al. 2004). Market barriers may or may not be market failures in the traditional welfare economic sense. Potential market barriers described in the broader energy efficiency literature occasionally include such factors as low energy prices, fluctuating energy prices, or high technology costs, which are clearly not market failures on their own. Systematic biases in consumer decision making that lead to underinvestment in energy efficiency relative to the cost-minimizing level are also often included among market barriers. Following the review by Shogren & Taylor (2008) of behavioral economics, however, we classify these biases as "behavioral failures." In the present context, we consider behavioral failures to represent consumer behavior that is inconsistent with utility maximization or, in the current context, with energy-service cost minimization. In contrast, market failure analysis is distinct in presupposing individual rationality and instead focusing on the conditions surrounding interactions among economic agents and society.

There is an economic rationale for policies to correct market barriers if they represent market or behavioral failures (Shogren & Taylor 2008). **Table 2** provides a summary of potential market and behavioral failures relating to energy efficiency and conservation, along with policy responses that have been implemented, or could be implemented, to address these problems in cases where they are found to be significant. We focus on the most commonly raised market and behavioral failures but do not prejudge whether they are empirically significant problems for energy efficiency and conservation.[2] The remainder of this section discusses each of these potential concerns in turn. Then in Section 5, we review experience with policies that have been proposed and implemented, in part, as a response to these concerns.

4.1. Energy Market Failures

The common theme in energy market failures is that energy prices do not reflect the true marginal social cost of energy consumption, either through environmental externalities,

---

[2]In addition to the issues discussed below, Fischer (2005) developed the economic theory supporting a role of price discrimination in imperfectly competitive markets in diminishing producers' incentives to improve energy efficiency of low-end products. Ruderman et al. (1987) discussed the effects of inseparability of product features on markets for energy efficiency, although associated inefficiencies should be minimal in competitive markets.

Table 2 Commonly cited market and behavioral failures relevant to energy efficiency along with potential policy responses

Potential market failures	Potential policy options
Energy market failures	
Environmental externalities	Emissions pricing (tax, cap and trade)
Average-cost electricity pricing	Real-time pricing, market pricing
Energy security	Energy taxation, strategic reserves
Capital market failures	
Liquidity constraints	Financing/loan programs
Innovation market failures	
R&D spillovers[a]	R&D tax credits, public funding
Learning-by-doing spillovers	Incentives for early market adoption
Information problems	
Lack of information, asymmetric information	Information programs
Principal-agent problems	Information programs
Learning by using	Information programs
Potential behavioral failures	**Potential policy options**
Prospect theory	Education, information, product standards
Bounded rationality	Education, information, product standards
Heuristic decision making	Education, information, product standards

[a]R&D, research and development.

average-cost pricing, or national security. Environmental externalities associated with the production and consumption of many sources of energy lead to emissions of greenhouse gases and other air pollutants resulting in costs that are borne by others—that is, they are not internalized by the individual energy consumer. Absent policy, an environmental externality leads to an overuse of energy relative to the social optimum and, hence, underinvestment in energy efficiency and conservation. Although there is no debate over the existence of environmental externalities, the magnitude of such externalities and their degree of internalization are uncertain and hard to measure. Gillingham et al. (2006) reviewed the literature on environmental externalities from the production of electricity and found that past policies to reduce electricity use provided monetized benefits from the reduction in CO_2, nitrous oxides (NO_x), sulfur dioxide (SO_2), and fine particulate matter (PM_{10}) that were on the order of 10% of the direct value of the electricity savings. Environmental externalities, largely in the form of air emissions, also exist with other fossil fuels, such as home-heating oil or propane. To the extent that energy prices do not currently internalize these externalities (which varies by pollution type), the market will provide a level of energy efficiency that is too low from a societal point of view. The economically optimal policy response is to price emissions, which will indirectly stimulate greater energy efficiency.

Prices faced by consumers in electricity markets also may not reflect marginal social costs due to the common use of average-cost pricing under utility regulation. Average-cost pricing could lead to under- or overuse of electricity relative to the economic optimum. On one hand, to the extent that average costs are above marginal costs as a result of amortized fixed costs, consumers face a price above the economically optimal price, thus encouraging underuse of electricity. On the other hand, average-cost prices depend on the average cost of the mix of generators used to produce electricity. Market-based pricing produces daily or hourly wholesale prices that reflect the cost of the marginal generator and retail prices that typically reflect the average of these marginal costs over a period of months. Time-of-use (TOU) prices vary in a preset manner by time of day or season, whereas real-time pricing (RTP) directly conveys information about the current marginal cost of generation and transmission in the price, updated at an hourly or even more frequent basis. If consumers face prices that are at times too low (peak times) and at other times too high (off-peak), they will overuse electricity during the peak times and underuse it during the off-peak relative to the social optimum (Joskow & Tirole 2007).

RTP and, to a lesser degree, TOU pricing can partly alleviate this market failure (which could alternatively be described as a policy failure). Of course, the cost of implementing TOU pricing or RTP may exceed the benefits, and there may be other market failures related to the adoption of real-time meters (Brennan 2004). However, recent evidence from the Anaheim Critical Peak Pricing Experiment suggests that, with recent technology advances, a variation of RTP implemented during peak periods has significant potential to improve social welfare, with little effect on use in off-peak periods (Wolak 2006). Whether there would be conservation of total energy use with a comprehensive RTP scheme during all time periods is less clear. Similarly, the effect of TOU pricing or RTP on energy efficiency investments is unclear and would depend on the pricing that exists during the time those investments would be used.

Some authors have suggested that there are national security external costs from the United States' dependence on certain energy sources—particularly oil from unstable regions of the world—that consumers do not face in energy prices or therefore take into account in their energy-use decisions (Bohi & Toman 1996, Bohi & Zimmerman 1984). Although these concerns are associated primarily with transportation-related consumption of oil, they are relevant to building energy consumption through fuel oil consumption for heating and the association between natural gas and oil markets. Economic and other analyses of the national security risks of energy consumption are not entirely satisfying, in part because of the lumpiness of the problem. On the margin, reducing oil consumption would not likely change the associated security risks, nor the military and diplomatic expenditures undertaken in response. Nonetheless, a long-term larger reduction may reduce these risks, and to the extent that these risks are not fully reflected in the price of relevant energy resources, there will be a resulting underinvestment in energy efficiency.

4.2. Information Problems

Information problems are consistently raised in the energy efficiency literature and, along with behavioral failures, are often given as the primary explanation for the energy efficiency gap (Sanstad et al. 2006). Specific information problems cited include consumers' lack of information about the availability of and savings from energy-efficient products, asymmetric information, principal-agent or split-incentive problems, and externalities associated with learning by using. The following descriptions take the consumers' perspective, but several of these same information problems have been studied in the context of decision making by firms (DeCanio 1993, 1994a,b; DeCanio & Watkins 1998; Stein 2003). As discussed in Section 5, if such problems are significant and correctable, they may warrant labeling and other information programs.

Lack of information and asymmetric information are often given as reasons why consumers systematically underinvest in energy efficiency. The idea is that consumers often lack sufficient information about the difference in future operating costs between more-efficient and less-efficient goods necessary to make proper investment decisions (Howarth & Sanstad 1995). This argument can be consistent with cost-minimizing behavior, if we assume that under perfect information consumers would reach a privately optimal outcome. Alternatively, information problems may occur when there are behavioral failures, so that consumers are not appropriately taking into account future reductions in energy costs when making present investments in energy efficiency. We discuss information problems in the context of behavioral failures in Section 5.

Asymmetric information, where one party involved in a transaction has more information than another, may lead to adverse selection (Akerlof 1970). In the context of energy efficiency, adverse selection could imply that sellers of energy-efficient technologies that would provide clear *ex post* benefits to consumers are unable to perfectly transfer this information to buyers if the energy efficiency is unobserved (Howarth & Sanstad 1995). The sellers of every product would have an incentive to suggest that the energy efficiency of the product is high, but because the buyers cannot observe the energy efficiency, they may ignore it in their decision. The model by Howarth & Andersson (1993), which incorporates explicit transaction costs of transferring information, formally describes how this circumstance could lead to an underinvestment in energy efficiency. Whereas transaction costs in this context may be a source of market failure, transaction costs in general may be legitimate and not a reason for intervening in markets.

The principal-agent or split-incentive problem describes a situation where one party (the agent), such as a builder or landlord, decides the level of energy efficiency in a building, while a second party (the principal), such as the purchaser or tenant, pays the energy bills. When the principal has incomplete information about the energy efficiency of the building, the first party may not be able to recoup the costs of energy efficiency investments in the purchase price or rent charged for the building. The agent will then underinvest in energy efficiency relative to the social optimum, resulting in a market failure (Jaffe & Stavins 1994). Murtishaw & Sathaye (2006) attempted to quantify the magnitude of the principal-agent problem for four end uses: space heating, refrigerators, water heating, and lighting. They found that the principal-agent problem is potentially relevant to 25% of refrigerator energy use, 66% of water heating energy use, 48% of space heating energy use, and 2% of lighting energy use, although they did not quantify the degree to which energy efficiency decisions in these cases have actually been inefficient. Levinson & Niemann (2004) found that tenants whose electric bills are included in their rental contracts consume significantly greater energy than tenants who pay their own electric bills.

Positive externalities associated with learning by using can exist where the adopter of a new energy-efficient product creates knowledge about the product through its use, and others freely benefit from the information generated about the existence, characteristics, and performance of the product. This phenomenon is not unique to energy efficiency

(Jaffe et al. 2004). In the context of demand-side management programs, some studies have distinguished learning-by-using spillovers into "free drivers" and program spillovers (Blumstein & Harris 1993, Eto et al. 1996). Free drivers are nonparticipants who install energy-efficient products as a result of hearing about them from program participants. Program spillovers occur when the participating household installs additional energy-efficient products, without rebates, as a result of the information they learned through participation in the program.

4.3. Liquidity Constraints in Capital Markets

Blumstein et al. (1980) first described liquidity constraints that hinder access to financing for energy-efficient investments as a market barrier. Some purchasers of equipment may choose the less energy-efficient product owing to lack of access to credit, resulting in underinvestment in energy efficiency and reflected in an implicit discount rate that is above typical market levels. This effect is a variation of a market failure associated with a lack of access to capital that is widely discussed in the development economics literature, and it applies to any capital-intensive investment, not just energy-efficient products (Ray 1998). The extent to which liquidity constraints are an issue in energy efficiency has yet to be established empirically. Some evidence indicates that only a small percentage of home improvements are funded by loans, which could imply liquidity constraints are important for only a small fraction of energy efficiency investments or that liquidity constraints effectively force most energy efficiency investments to be self-financed (Berry 1984).

In industry and government, a common financing constraint is the institutional disconnect between capital and operating budgets, but energy-services performance contracts have developed to fill this niche. In some cases, such as for industrial customers, energy-service providers pay the capital cost and receive a share of the resulting savings. In other cases, such as for government and institutional customers, the customer can borrow at a lower interest rate than the energy-service provider, so it makes greater financial sense for the customer to make the investment. In such cases, the energy-service providers recommend energy efficiency improvements, guarantee the operating cost savings, and pay the difference if those savings are not realized—often allowing for the repayment of the capital cost to be treated as an operating expense (Zobler & Hatcher 2003). In addition, if liquidity constraints are an issue for energy efficiency investments, then they will also constrain other types of investments, and any potential solution would have to reach well beyond energy efficiency policy.

Golove & Eto (1996) described a case of asymmetric information where consumers are unable to transfer information to their lenders about the relative certainty of operating cost savings from an efficiency investment. Thus, the lender cannot determine the likelihood of repayment and is less likely to approve of the loan. Golove & Eto claimed the resulting credit constraints imply that consumers should be given a lower interest rate than lenders are willing to offer, and thus consumers faced with the higher interest rate may underinvest in energy efficiency. The extent of this potential problem has not been measured empirically to our knowledge, and this problem of information transfer may apply to other costs as well, possibly altering the result. Energy-efficient mortgages from some lenders address this problem by crediting a home's energy efficiency when determining the interest rate or the size of the mortgage. Warranties may also address this problem privately.

4.4. Innovation Market Failures

R&D spillovers may lead to underinvestment in energy-efficient technology innovation owing to the public good nature of knowledge, whereby individual firms are unable to capture the full benefits from their innovation efforts, which instead accrue partly to other firms and consumers. This is not particular to energy efficiency innovation; rather, it is a general feature of technological innovation, which manifests empirically as a social rate of return to R&D that is approximately two to four times higher than the private rate of return (Griliches 1995, Hall 1996, Nadiri 1993). If energy is underpriced relative to the social optimum, this innovation problem will be magnified in the context of energy-saving technologies (Goulder & Schneider 1999, Jaffe et al. 2005, Schneider & Goulder 1997).

Learning by doing (LBD) refers to the empirical observation that, as cumulative production of new technologies increases, the cost of production tends to decline as the firm learns from experience how to reduce its costs (Arrow 1962). LBD may be associated with a market failure if the learning creates knowledge that spills over to other firms in the industry, lowering the costs for others without compensation to the original investing firm (Fischer & Newell 2008, van Benthem et al. 2008). In the energy context, LBD processes have been empirically investigated and applied primarily to fledgling low-carbon electricity-generating technologies in the context of energy and climate policy modeling. The empirical evidence on learning in terms of energy-using equipment is very limited, and what does exist focuses generally on product cost reductions rather than learning specifically with respect to improving energy efficiency (see, e.g., Bass 1980). It is also difficult to empirically distinguish learning from other factors that affect product costs and prices. Further research is needed to examine learning in energy-efficient technologies and ascertain the degree to which the learning spills over to other firms. The potential for positive externalities from LBD is not unique to energy: It may occur with any new technology that displays nonappropriable learning characteristics.

4.5. Behavioral Failures

The behavioral economics literature has drawn attention to several systematic biases in consumer decision making that may be relevant to decisions regarding investment in energy efficiency. Similar insights can be gained from the literature on energy decision making in psychology and sociology (e.g., see Stern 1985; Lutzenhiser 1992, 1993). Frameworks incorporating such departures from perfect rationality have intuitive psychological appeal as well as an empirical basis from behavioral economic and psychological studies. The crucial question is whether these deviations from perfect rationality lead to significant *systematic* biases in energy efficiency decision making, and if so, whether these biases lead to under- or overinvestment in energy efficiency. Due to the limited economics literature in this area, in many cases we reference literature from other social sciences that bears directly on energy consumption–related behavior.

The behavioral economics literature draws upon cognitive psychology and other disciplines to inform experimental and theoretical analyses aimed at understanding how consumers make decisions. Behavioral economists tend to relax the classical microeconomic assumption of rational choice and replace it with bounded rationality or other heuristic decision-making methods (McFadden 1999). Behavioral economics has been motivated by evidence that consumers are not perfectly rational—even if they are given perfect information—and has developed a positive theory designed to understand how consumers make decisions in practice. In the energy efficiency context, the most relevant and common rationality assumption is that of behavior that minimizes present-value costs for a given level of energy-service provision.

The evidence that consumer decisions are not always perfectly rational is quite strong, beginning with the research by Tversky & Kahneman indicating that both sophisticated and naïve respondents will consistently violate axioms of rational choice in certain situations (e.g., see Tversky & Kahneman 1974, Kahneman & Tversky 1979). Since then, an entire literature has developed examining when and how people violate the axioms of rational choice. Surveys of this literature of behavioral decision theory include Camerer (1997), McFadden (1999), Machina (1989), Rabin (1997), and Thaler (1991). Shogren & Taylor (2008) provide a review specifically in the context of resource and environmental economics. Our review follows the primary theme of behavioral economics by focusing on consumer decisions. Firms may also face some of the same issues, although competitive forces serve to moderate the significance of behavioral failures for firms (Shogren & Taylor 2008).

The three primary themes that emerge from behavioral economics and have been applied in the context of energy efficiency are prospect theory, bounded rationality, and heuristic decision making. The prospect theory of decision making under uncertainty posits that the welfare change from gains and losses is evaluated with respect to a reference point, usually the status quo. In addition, consumers are risk averse with respect to gains and risk seeking with respect to losses, so that the welfare change is much greater from a loss than from an expected gain of the same magnitude (Kahneman & Tversky 1979). This can lead to loss aversion, anchoring, status quo bias, and other anomalous behavior (Shogren & Taylor 2008).

Bounded rationality suggests that consumers are rational but face cognitive constraints in processing information that lead to deviations from rationality in certain circumstances (Simon 1959, 1986). Heuristic decision making is related closely to bounded rationality and encompasses a variety of decision-making strategies that differ in some critical way from conventional utility maximization in order to reduce the cognitive burden of decision making. For example, Tversky (1972) developed the theory of elimination by aspects, wherein consumers use a sequential decision-making process where first they narrow their full choice set to a smaller set by eliminating products that do not have some desired feature or aspect (e.g., cost above a certain level), and then they optimize among the smaller choice set, possibly after eliminating further products.

Not much economic literature empirically tests these behavioral hypotheses to uncover whether there is a systematic bias, either negative or positive, in decision making related to energy consumption. Hartman et al. (1991) empirically examined whether the status quo effect posited in prospect theory holds in the consumer valuation of reliable electric service. Though reliable electric service is only somewhat related to energy efficiency, they found that the status quo effect is significant in this case, suggesting that consumers are irrationally reluctant to move from the status quo and accept more likely interruptions in electricity service.

Empirically testing bounded rationality is even more difficult, for there is no single consensus model of bounded rationality in energy decision making (Sanstad & Howarth 1994). Friedman & Hausker (1988) developed a theoretical model using a particular structure of bounded rationality in which consumers do not have the ability to optimize their energy consumption in response to a tiered-rate structure of electricity prices. The model indicates that consumers will overconsume energy if the rate structure is increasing and underconsume if it is decreasing. Friedman (2002) tested this theoretical model using electric-utility data and exploited the increasing block structure of electricity rates to find that the empirical specification consistent with bounded rationality (and leading consumers to overconsume electricity) has more predictive power than one based on utility maximization.

Heuristic decision making in energy is similarly difficult to test empirically, although several papers in psychology have done so. Kempton & Montgomery (1982) used a survey technique to find that consumers use simple heuristic techniques to determine their energy consumption, and these techniques systematically lead to underinvestment in energy efficiency. For example, Kempton & Montgomery found that, for decisions regarding energy-efficient investments, consumers tended to use a simple payback measure where the total investment cost is divided by the future savings calculated using the energy price today, rather than the price at the time of the savings—effectively ignoring future changes in real fuel prices. Kempton et al. (1992) used similar methods, finding that consumers systematically miscalculate payback for air conditioner investments, again leading to overconsumption of energy.

Yates & Aronson (1983) found that consumers attach disproportionate weight to the most psychologically vivid and observable factors, often called the salience effect. The salience effect may influence energy efficiency decisions, potentially contributing to an overemphasis on the initial cost of an energy-efficient purchase, leading to an underinvestment in energy efficiency (Wilson & Dowlatabadi 2007). This may be related to evidence suggesting that decision makers are more sensitive to up-front investment costs than energy operating costs, although this evidence may also be the result of inappropriate measures of expectations of future energy use and prices (Anderson & Newell 2004, Hassett & Metcalf 1995, Jaffe et al. 1995).

Loewenstein & Prelec (1992) developed a theoretical model of intertemporal choice that replaces the utility function with a value function that is more elastic for outcomes with large absolute magnitudes than for outcomes with small magnitudes, consistent with evidence in Thaler (1981) and Holcomb & Nelson (1992). Thus, in this value function framework, discounting depends on the magnitude of the outcome. Applying this to the case of energy efficiency investments, flows of electricity savings are typically smaller than the annual returns from other types of investments and thus would be subject to higher rates of discount. Loewenstein & Prelec posited that their model may capture a behavioral bias that implies a systematic underinvestment in energy efficiency relative to the consumers' cost-minimizing choice. To our knowledge, the model has not been empirically tested in the context of energy efficiency.

This review reveals that the empirical literature testing behavioral failures specifically in the context of energy decision making is very limited. The literature in psychology and sociology discusses these biases further and provides some additional evidence of such biases (e.g., for a review of the approaches in the different fields as applied to energy, see Wilson & Dowlatabadi 2007). The available evidence suggests that systematic biases may exist in consumer decision making that could lead to overconsumption of energy and underinvestment in energy efficiency. However, more fully understanding the magnitude of these biases, disentangling them from informational and other market failures, and measuring the ability of practicable policies to address these behavioral failures remain important areas for future research.

5. ENERGY EFFICIENCY POLICY

Although the literature has identified a number of potential market and behavioral failures that are relevant to energy efficiency, for policy responses to improve economic efficiency, they must successfully reduce these failures and the associated benefits must exceed the cost of implementing the policy. In Section 4, we identified a number of relevant market failures, several of which are not unique to energy efficiency and conservation. For example, R&D spillovers exist throughout the economy, and motivate general policies such as patent protection, R&D tax credits, and basic research funding. Policy decisions specific to energy efficiency R&D arise mainly in the context of determining the level and allocation of public-research spending among different purposes (for a related discussion, see Newell 2008). LBD spillovers are similar in that any emerging technology may exhibit nonappropriable gains from learning, raising questions over the appropriate bounds on policy.

The environmental externalities avoided by energy efficiency and conservation largely result from emissions associated with burning fossil fuels. Economic theory suggests that if consumers are optimizing and there are no other market imperfections, a first-best policy to address the environmental externalities would ensure that the external cost from emissions is added to the energy price, such as through a Pigouvian tax or cap-and-trade system. The resulting internalization of the externality would lead to reduced energy demand (more conservation) and more energy efficiency investment.

To assess the amount of energy savings from such an emissions price policy, one can examine the price elasticity of energy demand discussed earlier, which is typically done in the context of a computable general equilibrium model or other aggregate energy-economic model. In the context of climate policy, such modeling typically finds that a significant portion of cost-effective emissions reductions are achieved through energy efficiency and conservation, alongside renewable energy, nuclear power, and carbon capture and storage applied to coal (Clarke et al. 2006, Weyant et al. 2006). Policies to promote energy efficiency directly are second-best responses to environmental externalities, however, because they do not discriminate among the emissions intensities of different energy sources, do not provide an incentive for reducing consumption of energy services, and tend to apply only to a subset of sources. Instead, policies to promote energy efficiency may be the appropriate response to demonstrated behavioral failures, particularly in contexts where that behavior has broader societal implications (e.g., environmental externalities).

The remaining discussion focuses on the economic rationale, effectiveness, and cost of policies that are specifically targeted to energy efficiency grouped into three broad categories: information programs, incentives, and product standards. Before turning our attention to these issues, we briefly review some generic issues that arise in measuring the effectiveness and cost of energy efficiency policies. For a more detailed review of these issues, see Gillingham et al. (2006).

5.1. Issues in Measuring Energy Efficiency Policy Effectiveness and Cost

The literature on energy efficiency and conservation policy evaluation is extensive and has become more sophisticated with time. There are a few critical issues common to energy efficiency policies. First, *ex ante* studies dominate much of the energy efficiency policy literature, particularly for evaluating product standards. These studies form a valuable starting point for understanding future policy, but they do not demonstrate that policies have been effective or net beneficial in actual implementation. As more energy efficiency and conservation policies have been implemented, the literature is shifting to *ex post* studies that examine the historical effectiveness and cost of energy efficiency and conservation policies in order to improve future policy making.

One of the major criticisms of the energy efficiency and conservation policy evaluation literature is that "free riders" are not always properly accounted for. Free riders are consumers who would have invested in energy efficiency or conserved energy absent the policy, but who receive additional benefits from the policy (Joskow & Marron 1992). Benefits from free riders should not be counted in the benefits from the policy, but costs (that are not simply transfers) should be included in the costs of the policy. As discussed above, papers in the broader energy efficiency literature point to an offsetting effect of "free drivers," where nonparticipants in the program are induced to invest in energy efficiency or conserve energy as a result of having observed program participants (Blumstein & Harris 1993, Eto et al. 1996, Geller & Attali 2005).

Another common criticism of energy efficiency policy evaluations is that they either ignore or inappropriately account for the rebound effect, such that energy efficiency improvements decrease the marginal cost of energy services, thereby increasing demand and inducing less-than-proportional reductions in energy use. There is an extensive debate in the literature about the importance of the rebound effect in the context of energy efficiency standards (for a review, see Gillingham et al. 2006), but some empirical evidence suggests it may be numerically small in the case of energy efficiency standards (Dumagan & Mount 1993). For example, Davis (2008) examined the case of clothes washers and found a relatively small, but not insignificant, rebound effect of -6%. For recent evidence in the household transportation context, see Small & Van Dender (2007).

5.2. Information Programs

Information programs typically aim to induce energy efficiency investments by providing information about potential energy savings or examples of energy savings. Some programs attempt to promote energy conservation, particularly for electricity during times when the electricity grid is stressed. Historically, many information programs have been part of utility demand-side management (DSM) programs, and others have been federal programs such as Energy Star, appliance labels, and home energy ratings for new homes. Information programs also include programs that provide feedback to consumers about their energy consumption.

Information programs are motivated by the informational problems and behavioral failures noted above. The intention is that, by providing greater and more reliable information, issues of uncertain future returns and asymmetric information may be lessened. Additional information may also lower the cognitive cost of energy decision making or help guide consumers toward better decisions.

Information programs vary greatly, both in their method and implementation, and evidence of their effectiveness is mixed. Weil & McMahon (2003) offered anecdotal evidence that product labeling requirements can be successful in increasing energy-efficient investments, but Levine et al. (1995) found that the Energy Guide product labeling requirements were fairly ineffective. The Energy Guide label has been revised in a recent rule made to improve its effectiveness. According to some studies, voluntary

Energy Star labels appear to have achieved significant savings by inducing greater energy efficiency (Webber et al. 2000). For example, Howarth et al. (2000) presented evidence that the voluntary Environmental Protection Agency Green Lights program (now part of Energy Star) and Energy Star office products program have been effective in increasing energy efficiency investments by increasing access to information.

Anderson & Newell (2004) examined industrial energy audits and found that, although plants accept only approximately half of the recommended projects, most plants respond to the costs and benefits presented in the energy audits and, with the additional information, adopt investments that meet hurdle rates consistent with the standard investment criteria the audited firms say they use. Newell et al. (1999) found that the responsiveness of energy-efficient product innovation to energy prices increased substantially after product labeling was required. Stern (1985) suggested that many early energy conservation information programs (particularly DSM programs) were not very effective. Fischer (2008) examined the psychological literature on feedback programs (i.e., programs that provide consumers real-time information about their electricity consumption) and found feedback induces energy conservation with typical savings of 5%–12%. Reiss & White (2008) examined data from the 2000–2001 California electricity crisis and found that, in times of crisis, conservation appeals and information programs can produce sustained reductions in energy demand. Data indicating the cost effectiveness of these programs are not readily available.

5.3. Financial Incentives

Incentive programs provide financial motivation for energy efficiency investments through direct subsidies, tax credits, tax deductions, rebates, or loan subsides. Financial incentives have also been used to promote energy conservation in the electricity market during times of peak load. In addition, financial incentives have been used to encourage the development of new energy technologies, such as through prizes for highly energy-efficient products (Gillingham et al. 2006). Incentive programs have been primarily implemented as part of utility DSM programs. These programs are broadly motivated by the concerns mentioned above, in effect responding to the perceived underinvestment in energy efficiency by subsidizing such investment.

The findings from empirical evidence on the effectiveness of financial incentives are mixed. Stern (1985) suggested financial incentives are not very effective in inducing initial interest in energy efficiency improvement programs, but they may help induce energy efficiency investments by those already participating in the programs. Using a survey about the conservation tax credits of the early 1980s, Carpenter & Chester (1984) found that, although 86% of those surveyed were aware of the credit, only 35% used it, and of those who used it, 94% would have invested anyway. Several studies econometrically estimate the effect of state tax incentives on all conservation investments and find mixed results. Hassett & Metcalf (1995) attempted to correct previous methodological errors and estimated that a change of 10 percentage points in the tax price for energy investment increases the probability of making an energy efficiency investment by 24%. Williams & Poyer (1996) also found that despite the free-rider issue, tax credits increased the probability of an energy efficiency investment using data on the 1980s tax credit. These results suggest that financial incentives may be effective, but further research is needed to determine their cost effectiveness.

There is a fairly extensive literature examining the cost effectiveness of utility DSM programs, which typically contain financial incentives along with information programs. Common values in the literature of the "negawatt cost" or the full life-cycle cost (i.e., total expense of running the program and installing equipment) per kilowatt-hour saved as a result of a DSM program, range from below $0.01/kWh to above $0.20/kWh saved (in real 2002 dollars). For comparison, the U.S. average residential electricity price has been in the range of $0.08–0.09/kWh (in real 2002 dollars) over the past ten years (Energy Information Administration 2008). A debate in the literature continues regarding negawatt costs, with recent econometric evidence by Loughran & Kulick (2004) suggesting utilities are overestimating energy savings, thus leading to costs on the high end. However, an analysis on the same data by Auffhammer et al. (2008) points out that the savings summary statistic used by Loughran & Kulick (2004) was unweighted, and thus in this case, it underestimates the national average of electricity saved per dollar spent on DSM programs. Auffhammer et al. (2008) found a weighted average negawatt cost in the range of 0.05–0.13 $/kWh based on the model by Loughran and Kulick and failed to reject the null hypothesis that the utility-reported savings estimates are correct on average. These figures include only costs to the utilities, however, not to the energy end user; consumer costs may be in the range of 60–70% of utility costs (Nadel & Geller 1996). Taking utility estimates of costs and effectiveness as given, Gillingham et al. (2004) calculated a cost effectiveness for all DSM programs of $0.034/kWh (in 2002 dollars) saved in 2000 using only utility costs and utility self-reported savings.

5.4. Product Standards

Product standards set a minimum level of energy efficiency that all covered products on the market must meet. In some cases, standards may be differentiated by size and type of the product, such as refrigerator standards that may be different for mini fridges than they are for full-sized refrigerators. Energy efficiency standards are politically motivated by the full range of concerns noted above. From an economic perspective, other policy responses tend to be more direct, efficient responses to the market failures described. For example, if consumers are making rational decisions and there is heterogeneity in their preferences for energy efficiency, product standards could lead to a loss in economic efficiency by forcing behavior change on those who gain relatively little from energy efficiency (e.g., those who do not use the product often) (Hausman & Joskow 1982). On the other hand, verified behavioral failures could provide an economic rationale for product standards.

The literature on product standards focuses for the most part on appliance standards, for which there are primarily ex ante estimates of cost and effectiveness based on government regulatory analysis. Using engineering estimates of the energy savings and energy prices, Meyers et al. (2003) found a cumulative net benefit of $17.4 billion over 1987–2000 for the 1987–2000 appliance standards. With projections of future energy savings added, they found a cumulative net benefit of the current standards of $154 billion for 1987–2050 (both figures in 2003 dollars). Taking these estimates as given, Gillingham et al. (2004) calculated an implied cost effectiveness of $0.028/kWh saved in 2000.

These net-benefit estimates have, to our knowledge, not been subject to independent verification in the economic literature. Because these analyses do not include a valuation of environmental or security externalities, their net benefits arise solely from implicit modeling assumptions that are different from the way consumers behave in the absence of product standards (i.e., implicitly modeling behavioral failures). The implication is either that consumers are not minimizing costs, or that the model is making incorrect assumptions. Further empirical research evaluating the degree to which each of these cases is more correct would be valuable.

6. CONCLUSION

The literature on the economics of energy efficiency and conservation has embodied significant debate over the past few decades, yet many outstanding issues remain. The heart of the debate centers on the issues of identifying the economically efficient level of energy efficiency, of determining whether policy directed specifically toward energy efficiency is necessary to bring us to this level, and, if this is so, of determining its net benefits in practice. We identify potential market and behavioral failures that may help to explain this gap, although quantitative evidence on the magnitude of many of these potential failures is limited.

Many of the commonly cited market failures are not unique to energy efficiency, and addressing them calls for a much broader policy response, such as an economy-wide price on greenhouse gases to address climate change, comprehensive innovation policy to increase innovative effort, and electricity market reforms moving toward marginal cost pricing. Conversely, information and behavioral failures—to the extent that they are substantial—tend to motivate more specific energy efficiency policies, provided that the benefits of the policies exceed the costs. Further research in this vein is essential to clarify better the potential for energy efficiency policies to increase economic efficiency.

DISCLOSURE STATEMENT

K.P.'s research is funded in part by unrestricted gifts to the Resources for the Future (RFF) Electricity and Environment Program from the Simons Foundation, Allete Power, First Energy, Pennsylvania Power & Light, Constellation Energy, and the Edison Electric Institute. This research was funded in part by a special gift from Exelon Corporation for work on energy efficiency, by the RFF Electricity and Environment Program, and by the U.S. Environmental Protection Agency STAR Fellowship program.

ACKNOWLEDGMENTS

We appreciate the very helpful research assistance of Maura Allaire as well as useful comments from James Sweeney, Timothy Brennan, Maximilian Auffhammer, Richard Howarth, Danny Cullenward, and Sebastien Houde.

LITERATURE CITED

Akerlof G. 1970. The market for lemons: quality uncertainty and the market mechanism. *Q. J. Econ.* 84:488–500

Anderson S, Newell R. 2004. Information programs for technology adoption: the case of energy-efficiency audits. *Resour. Energy Econ.* 26:27–50

Arrow K. 1962. The economic implications of learning by doing. *Rev. Econ. Stud.* 29:155–73

Auffhammer M, Blumstein C, Fowlie M. 2008. Demand-side management and energy efficiency revisited. *Energy J.* 29:91–104

Bass F. 1980. The relationship between diffusion rates, experience curves, and demand elasticities for consumer durable technological innovations. *J. Bus.* 53:51–67

Bernstein M, Griffin J. 2005. *Regional Differences in the Price-Elasticity of Demand for Energy.* Santa Monica, CA: RAND Corp.

Berry L. 1984. The role of financial incentives in utility-sponsored residential conservation programs: a review of customer surveys. *Eval. Program Plann.* 7:131–41

Blumstein C, Harris J. 1993. The cost of energy efficiency. *Science* 261:970

Blumstein C, Kreig B, Schipper L, York C. 1980. Overcoming social and institutional barriers to energy efficiency. *Energy* 5:355–72

Bohi D, Toman M. 1996. *Economics of Energy Security.* Norwell, MA: Kluwer Acad.

Bohi D, Zimmerman M. 1984. An update on econometric studies of energy demand behavior. *Annu. Rev. Energy* 9:105–54

Brennan T. 2004. Market failures in real-time metering. *J. Regul. Econ.* 26:119–39

Camerer C. 1997. Progress in behavioral game theory. *J. Econ. Perspect.* 11:167–88

Carpenter EH, Chester TS. 1984. Are federal energy tax credits effective? A Western United States survey. *Energy J.* 5:139–49

Clarke L, Wise M, Placet M, Izaurralde C, Lurz J, et al. 2006. *Climate change mitigation: an analysis of advanced technology scenarios.* Work. Pap. 16078, Pac. Northwest Natl. Lab.

Dahl C. 1993. *A survey of energy demand elasticities in support of the development of the NEMS.* Work. Pap., Colorado Sch. Mines, US Dep. Energy

Davis L. 2008. Durable goods and residential demand for energy and water: evidence from a field trial. *Rand J. Econ.* 39:530–46

DeCanio SJ. 1993. Barriers within firms to energy-efficient investments. *Energy Policy* 21:906–14

DeCanio SJ. 1994a. Agency and control problems in U.S. corporations: the case of energy-efficient investment projects. *J. Econ. Bus.* 1:105–24

DeCanio SJ. 1994b. Why do profitable energy-saving investment projects languish? *J. Gen. Manag.* 20:62–71

DeCanio SJ, Watkins W. 1998. Investment in energy efficiency: Do the characteristics of firms matter? *Rev. Econ. Stat.* 80:95–107

Dumagan JC, Mount TD. 1993. Welfare effects of improving end-use efficiency: theory and application to residential electricity demand. *Resour. Energy Econ.* 15:175–201

Energy Information Administration. 2008. *Electric Power Monthly with Data for September 2008.* Washington, DC: US Dep. Energy/EIA

Eto J, Vine E, Shown L, Sonnenblick R, Payne C. 1996. The total cost and measured performance of utility sponsored energy-efficiency programs. *Energy J.* 17:31–52

Fischer C. 2005. On the importance of the supply side in demand-side management. *Energy Econ.* 27:165–80

Fischer C. 2008. Feedback on household electricity consumption: a tool for saving energy? *Energy Effic.* 1:79–104

Fischer C, Newell R. 2008. Environmental and technology policies for climate mitigation. *J. Environ. Econ. Manag.* 55:142–62

Friedman L. 2002. Bounded rationality versus standard utility-maximization: a test of energy price responsiveness. In *Judgements, Decisions, and Public Policy*, ed. R Rowda, J Fox, pp. 138–73. New York: Cambridge Univ. Press

Friedman L, Hausker K. 1988. Residential energy consumption: models of consumer behavior and their implictions for rate design. *J. Consum. Policy* 11:287–313

Geller H, Attali S. 2005. *The Experience with Energy Efficiency Policies and Programmes in IEA Countries: Learning from the Critics.* Paris: Int. Energy Agency

Gillingham K, Newell R, Palmer K. 2004. *Retrospective examination of demand-side energy efficiency policies.* Discuss. Pap. 04-19, Resour. Future

Gillingham K, Newell R, Palmer K. 2006. Energy efficiency policies: a retrospective examination. *Annu. Rev. Environ. Resour.* 31:161–92

Gillingham K, Newell R, Pizer W. 2008. Modeling endogenous technological change for climate policy analysis. *Energy Econ.* 30:2734–53

Golove W, Eto J. 1996. *Market barriers to energy efficiency: a critical reappraisal of the rationale for public policies to promote energy efficiency.* Work. Pap. LBL-38059:UC-1322, Lawrence Berkeley Natl. Lab.

Goulder L, Schneider S. 1999. Induced technological change and the attractiveness of CO_2 emissions abatement policies. *Resour. Energy Econ.* 21:211–53

Griliches Z. 1995. R&D and productivity: econometric results and measurement issues. In *Handbook of the Economics of Innovation and Technical Change*, ed. P Stoneman, pp. 52–71. Oxford: Blackwell

Hall B. 1996. The private and social returns to research and development. In *Technology, R&D, and the Economy*, ed. LR Smith, CE Barfield, pp. 140–83. Washington, DC: Brookings Inst. Am. Enterp. Inst.

Hartman R, Doane M, Woo C-K. 1991. Consumer rationality and the status quo. *Q. J. Econ.* 106:141–62

Hassett KA, Metcalf GE. 1993. Energy conservation investment: Do consumers discount the future correctly? *Energy Policy* 21:710–16

Hassett KA, Metcalf GE. 1995. Energy tax credits and residential conservation investment: evidence from panel data. *J. Public Econ.* 57:201–17

Hausman J. 1979. Individual discount rates and the purchase and utilization of energy-using durables. *Bell J. Econ.* 10:33–54

Hausman JA, Joskow PL. 1982. Evaluating the costs and benefits of appliance efficiency standards. *Am. Econ. Rev.* 72:220–25

Hirst E. 1986. Actual energy savings after retrofit: electrically heated homes in the Pacific Northwest. *Energy* 11:299–308

Holcomb J, Nelson P. 1992. Another experimental look at individual time preference. *Ration. Soc.* 4:199–220

Howarth R, Andersson B. 1993. Market barriers to energy efficiency. *Energy Econ.* 15:262–72

Howarth RB, Haddad BM, Paton B. 2000. The economics of energy efficiency: insights from voluntary participation programs. *Energy Policy* 28:477–86

Howarth RB, Sanstad AH. 1995. Discount rates and energy efficiency. *Contemp. Econ. Policy* 13:101–9

Hsing Y. 1994. Estimation of residential demand for electricity with the cross-sectionally correlated and time-wise autoregressive model. *Resour. Energy Econ.* 16:255–63

Jaffe A, Newell R, Stavins R. 2004. The economics of energy efficiency. In *Encyclopedia of Energy*, ed. C Cleveland, pp. 79–90. Amsterdam: Elsevier

Jaffe A, Newell R, Stavins R. 2005. A tale of two market failures: technology and environmental policy. *Ecol. Econ.* 54:164–74

Jaffe A, Stavins R. 1994. The energy efficiency gap: What does it mean? *Energy Policy* 22:804–10

Jaffe A, Stavins R, Newell R. 1995. Dynamic incentives of environmental regulations: the effects of alternative policy instruments on technology diffusion. *J. Environ. Econ. Manag.* 29:S43–63

Joskow P, Tirole J. 2007. Reliability and competitive electricity markets. *Rand J. Econ.* 38:60–84

Joskow PL, Marron DB. 1992. What does a negawatt really cost? Evidence from utility conservation programs. *Energy J.* 13:41–74

Kahneman D, Tversky A. 1979. Prospect theory: an analysis of decisions under risk. *Econometrica* 47:263–91

Kempton W, Feuermann D, McGarity A. 1992. I always turn it on "super": user decisions about when and how to operate room air conditioners. *Energy Build.* 18:177–91

Kempton W, Montgomery L. 1982. Folk quantification of energy. *Energy* 7:817–27

Koomey J, Sanstad A. 1994. Technical evidence for assessing the performance of markets affecting energy efficiency. *Energy Policy* 22:826–32

Levine M, Koomey J, McMahon J, Sanstad A, Hirst E. 1995. Energy efficiency policy and market failures. *Annu. Rev. Energy Environ.* 20:535–55

Levinson A, Niemann S. 2004. Energy use by apartment tenants when landlords pay for utilities. *Resour. Energy Econ.* 26:51–75

Loewenstein G, Prelec D. 1992. Anomalies in intertemporal choice: evidence and an interpretation. *Q. J. Econ.* 107:573–97

Loughran D, Kulick J. 2004. Demand-side management and energy efficiency in the United States. *Energy J.* 25:19–41

Lutzenhiser L. 1992. A cultural model of household energy consumption. *Energy* 17:47–60

Lutzenhiser L. 1993. Social and behavioral aspects of energy use. *Annu. Rev. Energy Environ.* 18:247–89

Machina M. 1989. Dynamic consistency and non-expected utility models of choice under uncertainty. *J. Econ. Lit.* 32:1622–68

McFadden D. 1999. Rationality for economists? *J. Risk Uncertain.* 19:73–105

Metcalf G. 2008. An empirical analysis of energy intensity and its determinants at the state level. *Energy J.* 29:1–26

Metcalf GE. 1994. Economics and rational conservation policy. *Energy Policy* 22:819–25

Metcalf GE, Hassett KA. 1999. Measuring the energy savings from home improvement investments: evidence from monthly billing data. *Rev. Econ. Stat.* 81:516–28

Meyers S, McMahon JE, McNeil M, Liu X. 2003. Impacts of U.S. federal energy efficiency standards for residential appliances. *Energy* 28:755–67

Murtishaw S, Sathaye J. 2006. *Quantifying the effect of the principal-agent problem on US residential use.* Work. Pap. LBNL-59773, Lawrence Berkeley Natl. Lab.

Nadel S, Geller H. 1996. Utility DSM: What have we learned? Where are we going? *Energy Policy* 24:289–302

Nadiri IM. 1993. *Innovations and technological spillovers.* Work. Pap. 4423, NBER

Newell R. 2008. *A U.S. innovation strategy for climate change mitigation.* Discuss. Pap. 2008-15, Brookings Inst. Hamilton Project

Newell R, Jaffe A, Stavins R. 1999. The induced innovation hypothesis and energy-saving technological change. *Q. J. Econ.* 114:941–75

Newell R, Pizer W. 2008. Carbon mitigation costs for the commerical building sector: discrete-continuous choice analysis of multifuel energy demand. *Resour. Energy Econ.* 30:527–39

Popp D. 2002. Induced innovation and energy prices. *Am. Econ. Rev.* 92:160–80

Popp D, Newell R, Jaffe A. 2009. Energy, the environment, and technological change. In *Handbook of Economics of Technical Change*, ed. B Hall, N Rosenberg. Oxford: North-Holland

Rabin M. 1997. Psychology and economics. *J. Econ. Lit.* 36:11–46

Ray D. 1998. *Development Economics.* Princeton, NJ: Princeton Univ. Press

Reiss P, White M. 2008. What changes energy consumption? Prices and public pressures. *Rand J. Econ.* 39:636–63

Ruderman H, Levine M, McMahon J. 1987. The behavior of the market for energy efficiency in residential appliances including heating and cooling equipment. *Energy J.* 8:101–24

Sanstad A, Blumstein C, Stoft S. 1995. How high are option values in energy efficiency investments. *Energy Policy* 23:739–43

Sanstad A, Hanemann M, Auffhammer M. 2006. *End-use Energy Efficiency in a "Post-Carbon" California Economy: Policy Issues and Research Frontiers.* Berkeley, CA: Calif. Clim. Chang. Cent.

Sanstad AH, Howarth RB. 1994. *Consumer rationality and energy efficiency.* Presented at Proc. Summer Study Energy Effic. Build., Berkeley, CA

Schneider S, Goulder L. 1997. Achieving carbon dioxide emissions reductions at low cost. *Nature* 389:13–14

Sebold FD, Fox EW. 1985. Realized savings from residential conservation activity. *Energy J.* 6:73–88

Shogren J, Taylor L. 2008. On behavioral-environmental economics. *Rev. Environ. Econ. Policy* 2:26–44

Simon H. 1959. Theories of decision-making in economics and behavioral science. *Am. Econ. Rev.* 49:253–83

Simon H. 1986. Rationality in psychology and economics. *J. Bus.* 59:209–24

Small K, Van Dender K. 2007. Fuel efficiency and motor vehicle travel: the declining rebound effect. *Energy J.* 28:25–51

Stein J. 2003. Agency, information, and corporate investment. In *Handbook of the Economics of Finance*, ed. G Constantinides, M Harris, R Stulz. Amsterdam: Elsevier

Stern P, ed. 1985. *Energy Efficiency in Buildings: Behavioral Issues*. Washington, DC: Natl. Acad. Press

Sue Wing I. 2008. Explaining the declining energy intensity of the U.S. economy. *Resour. Energy Econ.* 30:21–49

Sutherland RJ. 1991. Market barriers to energy efficiency investments. *Energy J.* 12:15–34

Sutherland RJ. 1996. The economics of energy conservation policy. *Energy Policy* 24:361–70

Thaler R. 1981. Some empirical evidence on dynamic inconsistency. *Econ. Lett.* 8:201–7

Thaler R. 1991. *Quasi-Rational Economics*. New York: Russell Sage Found.

Train K. 1985. Discount rates in consumers' energy-related decisions: a review of the literature. *Energy* 10:243–53

Tversky A. 1972. Elimination by aspects: a theory of choice. *Psychol. Rev.* 79:281–99

Tversky A, Kahneman D. 1974. Judgement under uncertainty: heuristics and biases. *Science* 185:1124–31

van Benthem A, Gillingham K, Sweeney J. 2008. Learning-by-doing and the optimal solar policy in California. *Energy J.* 29:131–51

van Soest DP, Bulte E. 2000. Does the energy-efficiency paradox exist? Technological progress and uncertainty. *Environ. Resour. Econ.* 18:101–12

Wade S. 2003. *Price Responsiveness in the AEO2003 NEMS Residential and Commercial Buildings Sector Models*. Washington, DC: US Dep. Energy/EIA

Webber CA, Brown RE, Koomey JG. 2000. Savings estimates for the ENERGY STAR voluntary labeling program. *Energy Policy* 28:1137–49

Weil S, McMahon J. 2003. Governments should implement energy-efficiency standards and labels— cautiously. *Energy Policy* 31:1403–15

Weyant JP, de la Chesnaye FC, Blanford GJ. 2006. Overview of EMF-21: multigas mitigation and climate policy. *Energy J.* Spec. Issue Multi-Greenh. Gas Mitig. Clim. Policy: 1–32

Williams M, Poyer D. 1996. The effect of energy conservation tax credits on minority household housing improvements. *Rev. Black Polit. Econ.* 24:122–34

Wilson C, Dowlatabadi H. 2007. Models of decision making and residential energy use. *Annu. Rev. Environ. Resour.* 32:169–203

Wolak F. 2006. *Residential customer response to real-time pricing: the Anaheim Critical-Peak Pricing Experiment*. Work. Pap. 151, Energy Inst. Cent. Study Energy Mark., Univ. Calif. Berkeley

Yates S, Aronson E. 1983. A social psychological perspective on energy conservation in residential buildings. *Am. Psychol.* 38:435–44

Zobler N, Hatcher K. 2003. Financing energy efficiency projects. *Gov. Financ. Rev.* Feb. 14–18

Recent Developments in Renewable Technologies: R&D Investment in Advanced Biofuels

Deepak Rajagopal,[1] Steve Sexton,[2]
Gal Hochman,[2] and David Zilberman[2*]

[1]Energy and Resources Group, University of California, Berkeley, California 94720;
email: deepak@berkeley.edu

[2]Department of Agricultural and Resource Economics, University of California,
Berkeley, California 94720; email: zilber@are.berkeley.edu

Annu. Rev. Resour. Econ. 2009. 1:621–44

First published online as a Review in Advance on
May 21, 2009

The *Annual Review of Resource Economics* is
online at resource.annualreviews.org

This article's doi:
10.1146/annurev.resource.050708.144259

1941-1340/09/1010-0621$20.00

*Corresponding author

Key Words

energy, transportation, innovation, adoption, policy

Abstract

Investment in renewable energy, both in research and development
and in commercial production, has risen significantly during the
current decade. Although a variety of different renewable sources
have been targeted for expansion, biomass technologies, especially
those for converting biomass to liquid biofuels for transportation,
have cornered a large share of the new investments. Cutting-edge
knowledge in genomics and biotechnology, process chemistry, and
engineering is being applied to produce new types of energy feedstock and process them into novel biofuels. If these investments
bear fruit, liquid biofuels have the potential to displace a substantial amount of oil over the next few decades, with limited negative
impact on food supply and the natural habitat. Energy-security and
food-security constraints and environmental considerations will
determine which technologies emerge as winners. The search for
new transportation fuels is also giving rise to the development of
new paradigms in innovation, commercialization, and regulation.

1. INTRODUCTION

Investment in renewable energy, both in research and development (R&D) and in production capacity, has grown as a sum of public and private investment during the current decade (International Energy Agency 2008b). The world has witnessed a similar rise in demand for renewable energy before, most notably in the aftermath of the 1973 OPEC oil embargo. As spectacular as the rise in investments was then, the following decade witnessed a steep fall in oil prices and a fall in demand for renewable energy. Consequently, R&D spending on renewable energy also declined (Margolis & Kammen 1999, Rausser & Papineau 2008). However, post-9/11 geopolitics of oil, economic growth in non-OECD countries, peak oil concerns, and consensus on mitigating climate change suggest that current interest is likely to be sustained (Himmel et al. 2007, *The Economist* 2008, Royal Society 2008).

Investments in R&D are risky because of technological uncertainty. Private investments tend to be less forthcoming because of innovation spillovers, the insufficiency of patent regimes for internalizing the benefits of R&D, and credit constraints (Arrow 1962, Alston & Pardey 1996, Jacobsson & Bergek 2004, Jaffe et al. 2005, Kobos et al. 2006). Investments in production capacity or consumption infrastructure are also susceptible to market uncertainties from, for example, fluctuations in energy prices. This creates a disincentive for irreversible capital expenditures and can cause a decline in production capacity as firms go bankrupt (Hochman et al. 2008). These problems are further magnified in the case of clean technologies because of incomplete markets for environmental goods or energy security.

Government policies have played an important role in stimulating demand and supply of alternative energy. Subsidies for production, consumption, and R&D have provided incentives for investment, whereas mandates for renewable fuels have guaranteed a market for those investments (Fischer & Newell 2008, Rajagopal & Zilberman 2008). The government stimulus in response to the economic crisis of 2008 is seen as an opportunity to increase spending on renewable energy projects, which can reduce dependence on imported oil and generate domestic jobs (*The Economist* 2008, Seib 2008). Global renewable energy initiatives can also draw inspiration from the Brazilian sugarcane ethanol program, PROALCOOL, which began in the 1970s and continues today. As a result of this program, domestic sugarcane ethanol composes 50% of current transportation fuel consumption in Brazil (Weidenmier et al. 2008).[1]

Several different renewable resources such as biomass, solar, wind, geothermal, and hydropower are currently in the R&D stage (Carr 2008). On the basis of the form of use, a majority of these can be grouped under either electric power generation or transportation.[2] A closer look reveals an increase in emphasis on technologies for transportation. One possible explanation is that, although both electric power generation and transportation are reliant on fossil fuels, transportation is much less diversified (approximately 99% dependent on crude oil) and depends on imports from regions that are unstable and hostile to the major oil-consuming nations. Several technologies are in the running as alternatives to oil. Biofuels, hybrids, plug-in electrics, compressed natural gas, or hydrogen-fueled

---

[1]During the same time, Brazil also reduced its share of imported oil from 70% to only 10%; this was achieved in part by increasing domestic oil production.

[2]Another form of use is heat (e.g., solar thermal and improved cook stoves), but investment in renewable technologies for heating is small compared with that of electricity and transportation.

vehicles can each become a significant player under the right economic and policy conditions. However, because of simplicity and cost advantages, liquid biofuels appear to have a head start in this race.

This paper is a review of recent trends in the liquid biofuel industry. The rest of the paper is organized as follows: Section 2 is an overview of the energy outlook and R&D investment in biofuels. Section 3 is a brief review of the technology spectrum for advanced biofuels. Section 4 is a review of the economics of biofuels from a private-sector perspective. Section 5 deals with issues of intellectual property arising from the public-private model of innovation and entrepreneurship. Section 6 deals with the market failure in renewable energy and reviews common mechanisms used to support renewable fuels, their effectiveness in achieving policy objectives, and their economic efficiency. Section 7 concludes this review.

2. OUTLOOK FOR OIL AND R&D IN BIOFUELS

In nearly every country with the exception of Brazil, oil accounts for more than 98% of energy used in transportation (International Energy Agency 2004). The International Energy Agency predicts that global demand for oil will reach 106 million barrels per day by the year 2030 (excluding biofuels) compared with 85 million barrels per day in 2008 (International Energy Agency 2007). The potential to increase production of conventional oil is predominantly in the OPEC regions (International Energy Agency 2007). Large investments are being made by OPEC and non-OPEC nations in costly and increasingly polluting sources of oil such as deep-sea drilling, enhanced oil recovery, oil sands, coal liquefaction, and gas liquefaction (Energy Information Administration 2008). According to New Energy Finance, approximately 98% of the overall energy R&D by private companies is for conventional fuels (**http://www.climatechangecorp.com/content.asp? ContentID=5209**). But given the environmental risk of increased reliance on fossil fuels, there is significant government support for clean nonfossil technologies to address the energy challenge. Nonfossil fuel resources include nuclear energy, energy efficiency, renewable energy, hydrogen and fuel cell technologies, and energy storage (International Energy Agency 2008b).

One of the many channels of government support is R&D funding. Total spending on energy R&D by International Energy Agency members has been increasing since 2000. Nuclear energy receives the lion's share of the total R&D budget, whereas fossil fuels have received the bulk of the increase in budget since 2000. As of 2006, funding for renewable energy R&D has also increased from $0.8 billion to $1.18 billion (all amounts noted are in U.S. dollars) (International Energy Agency 2008b).

In 2004, renewable energy accounted for 13.1% of the global primary energy supply. Biomass accounted for 79.4% of global renewable energy (International Energy Agency 2008a). More than 98% of the biomass was consumed for heat and electricity, whereas liquid biofuels (ethanol and biodiesel) accounted for just 1.4% of biomass energy. Furthermore, liquid biofuels currently supply less than 1% of energy used in transportation worldwide (Energy Information Administration 2008). However, liquid biofuels are considered to have the potential to displace a substantial amount of oil over the next few decades (International Energy Agency 2004). The U.S. Department of Energy believes it is possible to replace 30% of current U.S. gasoline consumption with biofuels by 2030 (Perlack et al. 2005, Energy Efficiency Renewal Energy Program 2007). Several other countries have also adopted ambitious targets and policies for liquid biofuels (International Energy Agency 2004, Renewable Energy Network 2008, Rajagopal & Zilberman 2008).

In the United States between 2002 and 2007, the combined budget of the U.S. Department of Energy and U.S. Department of Agriculture for biomass research increased from $97 million to $140 million (2002 dollars). During the same time, total spending on solar, wind, geothermal, and hydrogen technologies declined (Rausser & Papineau 2008). The U.S. federal biomass policy as outlined in the Energy Independence and Security Act of 2007 allocates several million dollars for R&D and demonstration projects for advanced biofuels, especially those that achieve the greatest reductions in greenhouse gases (GHG) (Energy Efficiency Renewal Energy Program 2007).

Increase in public sector support for bioenergy has been complemented by private sector investment in R&D, which also places a large emphasis on liquid biofuels. Several biotech companies have received funding to develop technologies that break down lignocellulose and help turn it into fuel (Schubert 2006). Between 2002 and 2007, venture-capital funding in the United States for biofuels increased from $2.5 million to $298 million (nominal dollars), second only to solar technologies (Rausser & Papineau 2008). Major oil companies have entered into partnerships worth hundreds of millions of dollars with universities and agribusiness companies to develop new biofuel technologies (Sheridan 2007). Cutting-edge developments in the fields of genetic engineering, biology, and chemistry are being applied to engineer new varieties of crops and aquatic biomass optimized for energy production as well as new types of microbes for degrading lignocellulose into sugars and for synthesizing novel biofuels and bio-based substitutes to petrochemicals (Ragauskas et al. 2006, *The Economist* 2007, Moose 2008, Schaffer 2008).

The emergence of biomass as a potentially major source of future energy is in some ways a return to the past. Prior to the industrial revolution, wood and charcoal supplied energy for heating and cooking in homes, while domesticated animals supplied energy for agriculture and transport. The replacement of animal power with machine power is claimed to have freed up 80 million acres of U.S. land—land that had been used to grow grass and other feed for the millions of animals used by humans (**http://bioenergy.ornl. gov/papers/misc/switgrs.html**). With the advent of coal and petroleum in the mid- and late-nineteenth century, respectively, the world began a rapid transition away from biomass to fossil fuels. Similarly, during the beginning of the twentieth century, many industrial materials such as dyes, solvents, and synthetic fibers were made from trees and agricultural crops, which were replaced by petrochemicals by the late 1960s (Ragauskas et al. 2006). This time, however, the biomass renaissance is relying on cutting-edge science.

3. TECHNOLOGY SPECTRUM

The energy supply chain comprises four main stages: (*a*) extraction or production of raw material, (*b*) processing into fuel or electricity, (*c*) distribution and retail, and (*d*) end use. In the case of energy from biomass, the first stage is cultivation and harvesting of feedstock (or, simply, the collection of wastes). After collection, the feedstock is transported to a biorefinery where it is processed to produce electricity, fuels for transportation, or other industrial chemicals and materials, which substitute petrochemicals (Perlack et al. 2005). We review some of the major technologies undergoing R&D.

3.1. Feedstock

Table 1 lists the major types of crops that can be used as feedstock for biofuels. Ethanol can be produced from any feedstock that is sugar, starch, or cellulose based. Approximately 90% of the global production of ethanol comes from Brazilian sugarcane and U.S. corn (Worldwatch Institute 2006). Biodiesel is produced from oils, which can be extracted from a variety of sources such as oil seeds, palm, algae, and waste oil. Currently, more than 90% of the global biodiesel production is from rapeseed and soy. Furthermore, between 2000 and 2005, global production of ethanol doubled while that of biodiesel quadrupled (Martinot 2005), with biodiesel composing approximately one tenth of total liquid biofuel.

Current biofuels are produced entirely by using parts of plants that provide food for humans. Therefore, appropriation of edible plant matter for biofuel production has an adverse impact on the food situation, which is facing major challenges even without biofuels (Runge & Senauer 2007, Sexton et al. 2009). This is somewhat mitigated if coproducts of biofuel can replace the displaced food. Furthermore, edible plant matter makes up a small portion of the total photosynthetic output, the bulk of which is nonedible cellulosic matter. More than half of all harvested dry matter is in cereal and legume straws; in tops, stalks, leaves, and shoots of tuber, oil, sugar, and vegetable crops; and in prunings and litter of fruit and nut trees that are not fit for human consumption (Smil 1999).

Calculations suggest that using first-generation biofuel technologies for the entire global harvest of sugarcane, maize, wheat, sorghum, sugar beet, and cassava can supply approximately 85% of global gasoline consumption. Cellulosic feedstock may be able to supply the same fuel using less than half the amount of land required by food crops (Rajagopal & Zilberman 2008). Other calculations suggest the United States, Canada, and the European Union would require between 30% and 70% of their respective current crop area if they replaced just 10% of their transport fuel consumption with biofuels (OECD 2006). The high productivity of lingocellulosic biomass explains the emphasis of current R&D.

Table 1 Biofuel feedstocks

Feedstock	Crops/waste	Example(s)
Sugar	Stalk	Sugarcane, sweet sorghum
	Root	Sugar beets
Starch	Cereals	Corn, wheat, barley, rye, sorghum
	Root crops	Potatoes, cassava
Lignocellulose	Energy crops	Switchgrass, Miscanthus, poplar, willows
	Forestry residue	Wood thinnings
	Agricultural waste	Rice straw, wheat straw, corn stover, sugarcane residue
	Solid waste	Municipal solid waste, paper waste, dung
Lipids	Oil seeds and nuts	Rapeseed, soybean, oil palm, coconut, sunflower, peanut, jatropha curcas
	Algae	Microalgae
	Waste oil	Used vegetable oil, animal fat

Cellulosic biomass under investigation includes a variety of materials: Examples are agricultural wastes, including those resulting from conventional ethanol production such as corn stover and sugarcane bagasse; forestry residues such as wood wastes, municipal solid wastes, and wastes from pulp/paper processing; dedicated crops such as fast-growing woody trees (poplars) and shrubs (willows); and grasses such as switchgrass and Miscanthus (Perlack et al. 2005, Somerville 2006). The cellulosic components of these materials range between 30% and 70%.

The goal of biofuel research is to optimize plants for producing biomass for biofuels. To increase biomass production from plants, many avenues are being explored: for example, manipulation of photosynthesis to increase the capture of light energy; manipulation of genes involved in nitrogen metabolism; delaying or prevention of flowering, which allows for the transfer of more photosynthetic energy to cellulose-rich parts of the plant; development of regulators for delaying the dormancy in winter; and ways to increase the growth phase (Ragauskas et al. 2006). Biofuel prospects will receive a major boost if the feedstock can be grown on marginal lands, as these are more abundant than fertile lands, are not used for food production, and tend to be low in biodiversity and carbon stocks. However, marginal lands have poor soil and high levels of biotic and abiotic stressors. Therefore, research is aimed at developing new crop varieties that can grow at elevated rates under conditions of drought, extreme temperature, high pest pressure, salinity, etc. (Vinocur & Altman 2005). Biofuel production from cellulosic feedstock requires pretreatment processes that disrupt the lignocellulose and remove the lignin, thereby allowing the access of microbial enzymes to break down cellulose into fermentable sugars. Both the pretreatments and the production of enzymes in microbial tanks are expensive. Therefore, plant genetic engineering is being applied to develop new crop varieties with less lignin, crops that self-produce enzymes for cellulose and lignin degradation, or plants that have increased cellulose or an overall biomass yield (McLaren 2005, Sticklen 2006, Moose 2008).

Plants optimized for cellulose production are likely to require significantly less nitrogen and other nutrients and thus reduce contribution to GHG (Khanna et al. 2009, Moose 2008). Harvesting crop residues for biofuel production can have a negative impact on soil fertility, which depends on regional yield, climatic conditions, and cultural practices. Developing a tool for optimizing removal rates that ensure sustained soil productivity is an agronomic challenge (Wilhelm et al. 2004, Khanna et al. 2008).

A handful of investors and researchers have their eye set on algae, an aquatic feedstock for biofuel production. Algae reproduce faster than any terrestrial plant, and it is claimed that they can yield up to 20,000 gallons per acre of fuel per year, which is 50 times as much fuel produced from an acre of corn. Depending on how they are processed, algae could yield biodiesel, ethanol, hydrogen, as well as other products (Schubert 2006).

3.2. Processing

For any given combination of feedstock and end fuel, there are several alternative conversion processes (see **Figure 1**). Technologies for processing of sugar, starch, or oil seeds are commercially mature today. Ethanol is produced using yeast-based fermentation of sugars and starch, whereas biodiesel is produced by transesterification of vegetable oil. For further details on these technologies, refer to Faaij et al. (1997), Demirbas (2001),

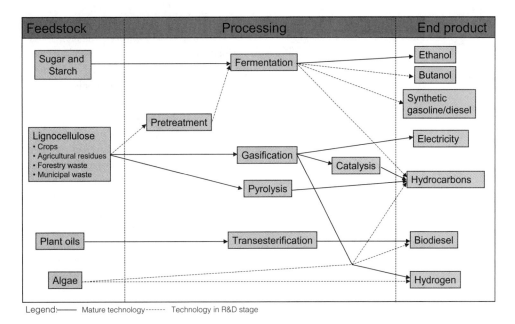

| Feedstock | Processing | End product |

Figure 1

Major biofuel pathways.

Tijmensen et al. (2002), Schubert (2006), Farrell & Gopal (2008), and Rajagopal & Zilberman (2008).

The success of cellulosic biofuels hinges on achieving breakthroughs in processing lignocellulose into simple sugars at low cost (Somerville 2006). Lignocellulose has a complex interlinked structure that is recalcitrant to simple processes that are used for depolymerizing (i.e., breaking down) sugar- and starch-based feedstock (Lynd 1996, McLaren 2005, Himmel et al. 2007, Wyman 2008, Sexton et al. 2009). Several biotech companies and government laboratories are being funded to engineer enzymes and microorganisms to optimize lignocellulose degradation and help turn lignocellulose into fuel (Schubert 2006). Lignocellulose first requires chemical pretreatment, which can open up the biomass to further action by microbial enzymes that break it down into simpler sugars and eventually into ethanol or butanol. Pretreatment can be done using different chemical catalysts, but these are currently uneconomical. Pretreatment designs have to balance cost of capital, chemicals, and the recovery of fuel and catalysts (Eggeman & Elander 2005). Subsequent to chemical pretreatment, the biomass is subjected to biological breakdown into simple sugars. The focus of R&D is in low-cost synthesis of enzymes that break down cellulose into sugars and of microbes that can ferment sugars into fuels (Ragauskas et al. 2006, Schubert 2006, Somerville 2006, *The Economist* 2007, Himmel et al. 2007, Stephanopoulos 2007). Consolidated bioprocessing, which features enzyme production, hydrolysis, and fermentation in one step, is another promising approach (Lynd et al. 2005). It exploits enzyme-microbe synergy to lower the cost and increase efficiency in conversion compared with sequential processes. If leap-forward technology advances are made in pretreatment, the biological conversion steps of enzyme production, enzymatic hydrolysis, and fermentation cost can be as low as approximately $0.60/gal (Wyman 2008).

Once broken down into simple sugars, the sugars can be fermented to produce ethanol or butanol or can be used as building blocks to produce bigger hydrocarbons such as diesel or other industrial chemicals. One line of research aims to exploit genetically engineered microorganisms (such as *Escherichia coli* infused with genes from other microbes) that can convert sugar into novel biofuels such as synthetic gasoline, diesel, and jet fuel (*The Economist* 2007, Sheridan 2007, Schaffer 2008). Employing the synthetic biologic approach, some biochemists and microbiologists are dissecting the gut of wood-chewing termites and the intestine of grass-chewing ruminants to gain a better understanding of the mechanism of cellulose breakdown in nature (Schubert 2006, Schaffer 2008). This approach aims to engineer/synthesize new complex, biologically based (or inspired) systems, which display functions that do not exist in nature. Another possibility is pure chemical conversion of carbohydrates into higher-chain hydrocarbons using new catalysts (Kunkes et al. 2008). The advantage of all these methods is they can utilize carbohydrates produced from a variety of sources including sugar, starch, and cellulose and deliver fuels that are similar to existing transportation fuels. The economic implication is that future biorefineries can respond to market conditions by switching between inputs or by adjusting the optimal mix of various outputs they produce.

As an alternative to the above chemical/biological processing, lignocellulose can be converted using thermochemical processes into a variety of liquids such as ethanol, methanol, methyl-tertiary butyl ether, gasoline, and diesel (Bain 2003). This relies on the same technologies that turn coal into liquid fuel from syngas (Department of Trade and Industry 2007, Rudloff 2007). In this case, biomass undergoes gasification to produce an intermediate product, "syngas," which is then converted to gasoline or diesel using chemical catalysis (termed the Fischer-Tropsch process). Although this process was used to convert coal into liquid fuels during World War II, its application to biomass presents additional technical challenges (Schubert 2006). Another thermochemical pathway is pyrolysis (i.e., the conversion of biomass in an oxygen-deficient environment). In this process, biomass is converted into bio-oils, which can be used as biofuels. Although several commercial pyrolysis technologies exist, bio-oils have significant drawbacks such as low volatility, high viscosity, coking, and corrosiveness. Furthermore, bio-oils are a mixture of different compounds and require costly processes to isolate useful biofuels (Farrell & Gopal 2008).

Cellulosic ethanol is slowly moving into production. A few pilot plants are in operation; the largest one is operated by Iogen, a biotech company based in Ottawa, Canada. This facility produces approximately 260,000 gallons of ethanol from wheat straw. The technology employed is pretreatment using high temperatures and acid hydrolysis, followed by enzymatic conversion to sugar, which is then followed by fermentation into ethanol using yeast (Schubert 2006).

Beyond biofuels, biomass conversion technologies are being developed to extract a wide range of materials—such as solvents, lubricants, and plastics, which are currently produced from petroleum—as well as high-value chemicals such as fragrances, flavoring agents, and other chemicals that can be used in food and health supplements. For instance, starch can be processed into either polylactide to make a biodegradable bioplastic or 1,3-propanediol to make an improved polyester-type product. The major impediment to the use of biomass is the development of methods to separate, refine, and transform it into chemicals and fuels (Ragauskas et al. 2006).

3.3. Distribution and End Use

Different biofuels impose varying requirements for distribution and end-use infrastructure. Although technical challenges also exist, these are less daunting compared with those at the feedstock production and processing stages. The challenges for distribution relate to building infrastructure (for example, new pipelines for transportation of biofuel) and to increasing the fleet of flexible-fuel vehicles, which are economic rather than technological in nature (see Section 4 for more detail).

3.4. Technology Summary

A variety of biofuel technologies exist at each stage of development, each of which is at a different level of technological maturity. In the case of first-generation biofuels based on sugar, starch, and oil-seed crops, the technologies for all four stages are mature. But despite the initial optimism about first-generation biofuels, the future of biofuels lies in the second generation (Khanna et al. 2009, Royal Society 2008, Woordburn 2008). This involves new feedstock (cellulosic energy crops, wastes, and algae) and new conversion technologies that use microbiological processes to convert feedstock directly into synthetic gasoline/diesel or into butanol, all of which are in the R&D stage. Compared with ethanol or biodiesel, the final products produced by these technologies are expected to be more easily compatible with existing infrastructure for distribution and end use (*The Economist* 2007). There is disagreement about when lignocellulosic conversion will begin to operate on an industrial scale—anywhere between 2015 and 2030 is projected. However, it is certain that bringing down the costs is key and this requires technological breakthroughs, which in turn require sustained investment and public support. The long-term outlook for oil and the emerging regulatory environment indicate the possibility of this outcome.

4. PROFITABILITY OF BIOFUEL INVESTMENTS

Energy producers are facing a market characterized by a widening gap between demand and supply of cheap oil. The price of oil is expected to average $100 per barrel between 2008 and 2015 (in real-year 2007 dollars) and rise to $120 by the year 2030 (International Energy Agency 2007). Ethanol and biodiesel are economical at this price range (given assumptions on feedstock cost), whereas technological breakthrough in conversion technologies can deliver cost reductions making second-generation biofuels profitable at these oil prices. Producers are also expecting a regulatory environment that in the future will be hostile to carbon-intensive fuels and also encourage domestic sources. But while environmental benefits are important, technologies that are low cost will be more profitable and hence more likely to succeed in the marketplace (Rausser & Papineau 2008).

4.1. Production Cost

The cost of production of biofuel depends on the cost of feedstock and cost of conversion. For first-generation technologies, the cost of feedstock composes the bulk of the final cost of producing biofuel, and this varies across feedstock and locations (International Energy Agency 2004, OECD 2006). Depending on the type used, feedstock accounts for 50%–80% of the final cost and has a huge effect on producer returns (Khanna et al. 2009).

For every dollar increase in price per bushel of corn, the cost of producing ethanol increases by $0.35 per gallon ($0.52 in energy equivalent terms) to a gallon of gasoline (Caesar et al. 2007, Tyner & Thaeripour 2007). Thus, a tripling of corn price from $2.00 per bushel to $6.00 per bushel requires a $2.00 increase in the price of ethanol for producers to retain their margins. Events in 2008 were trying for biofuel producers: The relative price of corn increased more than that of gasoline, and when corn prices declined, gasoline prices fell even more in relative terms (http://www.cattlenetwork.com/Content.asp?ContentID=272026). The net impact has been that several biofuel producers including VeraSun Energy (the largest publicly traded ethanol maker in the United States), Greater Ohio Ethanol, Gateway Ethanol, and Beatrice Biodiesel have all filed for bankruptcy protection, while Pacific Ethanol (the largest manufacturer on the West Coast) posted a $55-million loss during the third quarter of 2008 despite a 56% increase in sales over 2007 (**http://www.ethanolproducer.com/article.jsp?article_id=4925&q=bankrupt&category_id=41**). In the long term, by mandating more than doubling the current corn-ethanol consumption, the U.S. Energy Independence and Security Act of 2007 lowers crop prices. As a result, slower expansion of capacity may revive margins of more ethanol producers.

However, second-generation biofuels produced using wastes from agriculture, forestry, municipal sources, as well as purpose-grown grasses and woody crops have lower feedstock cost than do current biofuels (Wyman & Goodman 1993, Lynd 1996). In addition, researchers believe that the first cellulosic feedstock to be used will come from wastes rather than dedicated energy crops because of cost advantages. Estimates suggest that approximately 142.5 million tons of wastes can be procured at a cost ≤$45 per delivered dry ton and approximately 186.5 million tons of wastes at a cost ≤$56 per delivered dry ton (both amounts are in 1994 dollars) (Lynd 1996). At a technical conversion efficiency of 100 gallons per dry ton of waste, this implies production of approximately 15.3 and 20 billion gallons of ethanol, respectively. However, among waste-based feedstock, only municipal solid wastes have the advantage of being able to utilize an existing collection and transportation infrastructure from the source to the biorefinery (Perlack et al. 2005).

Although second-generation technologies are likely to impose lower feedstock cost, they are projected to impose a higher cost for conversion. Khanna et al. (2008) compare the projected cost of producing ethanol using corn and three other cellulosic feedstocks in the United States (see **Table 2**). The share of nonfeedstock costs is much higher for stover and switchgrass, whereas these costs are lower for Miscanthus because of considerably higher yield per hectare.

Although not yet commercial, algal biofuels are promising because they may yield 100 times more oil per acre than soybean and 50 times more fuel per acre than corn (Schubert 2006). Conservative economic estimates from a pilot facility put the final cost of producing synthetic gasoline or diesel in large volumes by using current microalgae technology at more than $8.00 per gallon. However, with coordinated R&D to improve our understanding of basic algal biology and to process algal biofuel, these costs are likely to decline (**http://www1.eere.energy.gov/biomass/pdfs/algalbiofuels.pdf**).

Butanol is a biofuel that unlike ethanol can be shipped in gasoline pipes and used in gasoline internal combustion engines without modification. Butanol currently costs more to produce than grain-based ethanol (approximately $4.00 per gallon), but it is also more energy dense, containing 30% more energy per gallon than ethanol. With technological breakthroughs, it may become cost competitive with cellulosic ethanol (Bullis 2008).

Table 2 Cost of production of biofuels from alternative feedstocks (in $/gallon)[a]

Feedstock	Feedstock cost[b]		Opportunity cost of land		Nonfeedstock cost	Coproduct credit	Total cost per gallon of ethanol		Feedstock cost at farm gate[c]	
	High cost	Low cost	High cost	Low cost			High cost	Low cost	High cost	Low cost
Corn	1.82	1.82	—	—	0.78	0.48	2.12	2.12	1.82	1.82
Corn stover	1.21	1.03	0.70	0.74	1.46	0.12	3.26	3.11	1.71	1.56
Switchgrass	1.18	0.89	1.44	1.52	1.46	0.12	3.96	3.71	2.41	2.20
Miscanthus	1.01	0.65	0.59	0.63	1.46	0.12	2.95	2.61	1.40	1.06

Source: Khanna et al. (2008).

[a]Owing to space limitations, costs of biofuel from corn stover in the high-yield scenario are not reported. These costs are as follows: feedstock cost, $0.55/gal; opportunity cost of land, $0.53/gal; total cost, $2.42/gal; and feedstock cost at farm gate, $0.87/gal.

[b]Includes transportation cost, but excludes opportunity cost of land.

[c]Excludes transportation cost, but includes opportunity cost of land.

4.2. Coproducts from Biorefining

In addition to feedstock and oil prices, coproduct revenues, conversion efficiency, and coal and natural gas prices can significantly affect net margins for biofuel plants (Tiffany & Eidman 2003). Revenues from coproducts such as distiller grains remaining from corn ethanol and oil cake from biodiesel production can be used as animal feed or as organic fertilizer. Likewise, bagasse from sugarcane or lignin from cellulose processing can be used to produce steam and electricity generation. Similar to a modern oil refinery, which handles multiple varieties of crude oil and produces different fuels such as gasoline, diesel, jet fuel, heating oil, and petrochemicals, biorefineries of the future would process a variety of feedstock and produce a range of products. In addition to biofuels, high-value chemicals such as pharmaceuticals and polymers will result as coproducts and thereby lead to higher competitiveness of biofuels (Hayes et al. 2005, Corma et al. 2007). Although synergies between the production of fuels and chemicals from biomass are high, one complicating factor is the size of markets for organic chemicals, which tends to be relatively small compared with that for liquid fuels. Thus, identifying chemical coproducts for biorefinery production so as not to exceed the market demand will be a challenge, as large quantities of liquid fuels are produced at these facilities (Worldwatch Institute 2006). Locating biorefineries near areas of high demand for both products and coproducts will also enhance profitability.

4.3. Distribution and End Use

A low cost of production is not sufficient to ensure adoption of a biofuel. The cost of delivered energy depends on the cost of distribution and end-use consumption. If the existing shipping infrastructure for feedstock is leveraged for biofuel and finished fuel, then the cost of biofuels is lowered. For example, a major advantage of corn or sugarcane ethanol is the fact that harvesting, storing, and shipping the crops and the final fuel require minimal new infrastructure. However, ethanol is not amenable to shipping in gasoline pipeline because of its hygroscopic properties; thus, it is transported through rail-, road-, and waterways. Demand for ethanol has not achieved a scale sufficient to justify investments in a dedicated pipeline infrastructure, which is the cheapest form of transportation. However, the first movement of ethanol via pipeline began to occur near the end of 2008 (Khanna et al. 2009).

From an end-use standpoint, ethanol or biodiesel can be used in existing automobile engines with no engine modifications at low levels of blending such as 5%–10%. However, higher blending levels require flexible-fuel vehicles, which are marginally costlier. Synthetic gasoline and diesel are compatible with the current fleet of automobiles, whereas butanol requires modifications to current internal combustion engines at levels higher than those required for ethanol (Bullis 2008). Compatibility with the existing distribution and end-use infrastructure is a significant roadblock faced by vehicles using alternative technologies that are competing with liquid biofuels, for example electric, compressed natural gas, and hydrogen vehicles. The lower incremental vehicle and refueling costs associated with biofuels provide them with a distinct advantage (International Energy Agency 2004).

4.4. Issues of Adoption

Although point estimates of average profitability provide some indication of which technologies may succeed, in reality there could be low levels of adoption. The rich literature on technology adoption describes several factors that influence the decision of a producer or consumer to invest in a technology. Whereas the earliest models explained adoption simply as a process of imitation, the newer models recognize heterogeneity among potential adopters and the role of risk and uncertainty in an integrated framework (Feder et al. 1985, Katz & Shapiro 1986, Besley & Case 1993, Sunding & Zilberman 2001, Hall & Khan 2003). But with biofuels, the reality is more complex because successful deployment requires coordinated adoption across several stages of production. For instance, a farmer's decision to adopt a new crop such as Miscanthus will depend on whether he has a contract with a cellulosic biorefinery, and a cellulosic biorefinery will be built if supply of feedstock from nearby farms is assured and a distribution infrastructure is in place. New distribution infrastructure, in turn, will be provided if there is sufficient retail demand for the product, and this demand depends on the availability of a fleet of flexible-fuel cars, which are costlier than regular cars. Yet, only with sufficient demand will automobile manufacturers supply costlier flexible-fuel cars (Sexton et al. 2009). This scenario provides an example of the familiar "chicken-egg" argument that can result in underinvestment.

Similar to the high-tech industry, the synthetic biology industry could emerge as one that depends on standardized parts to develop new products. Just as companies develop software programs that run on multiple operating systems or game consoles, synthetic biologists are developing a parts-based agenda in engineering new microbial organisms for commercial use (Henkel & Maurer 2007). At least one company claims dramatic progress in assembling several dozen parts inside yeast and bacteria to synthesize the antimalarial drug artemisinin and is betting on a similar approach for synthesizing novel bioproducts from sugars (Schaffer 2008). The need for compatibility between parts in this approach raises familiar issues such as network effects and the rise of dominant firms (e.g., Microsoft) within the biofuel industry (Henkel & Maurer 2007).

5. ISSUES OF INNOVATION AND ENTREPRENEURSHIP

The development of renewable energy technologies will be driven by a series of forces that have, in recent years, given rise to the "entrepreneurial university" and the establishment of an education-industrial complex. In the most dynamic sectors of the economy—biotechnology and nanotechnology—there is growing appreciation for the capacity of universities to create commercially valuable innovations. This recognition has led universities to seek to capitalize on their knowledge creation in ways they have not historically done.

5.1. University and Industry Roles in Innovation

An evaluation of the incentives and constraints facing researchers leads to the conclusion that universities have a comparative advantage in basic research, whereas industry is relatively efficient at applied research. Graff et al. (2002) assumed researchers are motivated by fame, fortune, and freedom, where freedom is defined as the ability to control one's research agenda. Universities provide faculty with freedom to satisfy their curiosity through research and opportunities for fame derived from successful research but a small probability of achieving fortune. In contrast, industry provides researchers with a greater likelihood of achieving fortune, but at the expense of freedom and (to some extent) fame (Graff et al. 2002). Industry researchers are directed to develop products and innovations that will enhance firm profitability.

Given these incentives, researchers self-select into either of these settings. This self-selection process equips the college campus with a creative faculty motivated by fame and endows industry with a people motivated by fortune. Hence, universities are considered to have a comparative advantage in basic research and industry in applied research (National Science Foundation 1953, 1954; Bush 1960; Rausser & Ameden 2004). The public-good attributes of basic research (Arrow 1962, Griliches 1992, Stiglitz & Wallsten 2000, Salter & Martin 2001) make it an appropriate fit for the university environment. Applied research, with its focus on solving particular problems, can be better motivated by a profit incentive, making it a better fit for industry. The division of research labor between industry and academia, therefore, allows both the university to pursue its traditional mission of providing an intellectual commons and the firm to pursue its profit motive.

The search for alternative fuels will rely on basic science much as technological breakthroughs in medicine, agriculture, and information technology have (Somerville 2006, Whitesides & Crabtree 2007, National Renewable Energy Laboratory 2008). Economical cellulosic technologies will be achieved only with improved knowledge of depolymerization (Somerville 2006, Stephanopoulos 2007). The conversion of sugars into novel biofuels with the help of synthetic microbes relies on synthetic biology, an emerging hot field that draws from classical genetic engineering (Ferber 2004, Himmel et al. 2007). Similarly, electric vehicles as well as wind and solar energy all stand to benefit immensely from breakthroughs in the chemistry behind energy storage technologies (Government Accountability Office 2006, Whitesides & Crabtree 2007). However, the private sector is likely to underinvest in basic research. In addition to the problems of an incomplete market for environmental goods and the inability to appropriate fully the benefits from R&D (discussed in Section 6), the long-term horizon of research in alternatives and uncertainty about future oil prices provide an inconsistent incentive for investment by private firms (Gallagher et al. 2006). Public investment in energy research, particularly basic research, is therefore needed to approach socially optimal levels of investment. Gallagher et al. (2006) suggest there is considerable capacity to capitalize on comparative advantages in research across sectors, including industry, academia, and national laboratories.

The complementarities between university and industry research have been fully appreciated only in recent decades (Peters & Fusfeld 1983, Fairweather 1988, Geisler & Rubenstein 1989, Rausser & Ameden 2004). In line with their mission of maintaining "intellectual commons," universities have historically placed innovations in the public domain (Hofstadter 1996). Administrators now recognize, however, that they can increase the benefit to society and enhance university prestige and revenue if they license knowledge to firms that, by virtue of having rights to technologies, will invest in their development and deployment (Etzkowitz et al. 2000). Firms have little incentive to commercialize a technology in the public domain because competing firms can freely capitalize on R&D investments by others (Graff et al. 2002).

5.2. Models of Intellectual Property Rights Management

Four principal models of intellectual property rights management by the university have emerged (Graff et al. 2002). The open-source model is the dominant paradigm, as publication of knowledge is deemed the objective of university research and necessary for ensuring the quality and progress of research (Merton 1973, Nelkin 1984). The collaboration model, which has been popular in parts of Europe, confers rights to the researcher, who is free to enter into contracts with industry to share knowledge. In the licensing model, the university claims property rights to innovations and negotiates the transfer of rights to interested industry partners through offices of technology transfer, which are a new development particularly prevalent in the United States as a consequence of the 1980 Bayh-Dole Act (Argyres & Liebeskind 1998, Mowery & Sampat 2005). In the venture-formation model, university professors provide expertise to start-ups or actively participate in business operations and derive the bulk of their research support outside the university. Although such arrangements can be complicated, they offer the university and its researchers opportunities for profits, encourage local economic growth, and foster an entrepreneurial spirit (Audretsch & Feldman 1996, Zucker et al. 1998, Zucker et al. 2000). For examples of alternative energy ventures, see Woordburn (2008).

The foregoing models assume a one-way relationship between basic research by public institutions and applied research by private firms. Industry in these models is a consumer of knowledge produced by the academe. In reality, however, collaboration has become a two-way relationship with industry seeking to influence research agendas and secure intellectual property rights ex ante (Rausser & Ameden 2004, Bercovitz & Feldman 2007). The rise of an interactive educational-industrial complex is a response to declining (at least in relative terms) public funding for research, growing importance of innovation in an increasingly knowledge-driven economy, and increasing numbers of innovations with applications to industry (i.e., biotechnology) (Etzkowitz et al. 1998, Henderson et al. 1998, Etzkowitz et al. 2000).

5.3. The Education-Industrial Complex

The drive to find sustainable energy has brought a renaissance in the education-industrial complex. A number of major research universities have received in excess of $10 million from companies—among them are University of California, Davis; University of California, Berkeley; University of Illinois; Georgia Institute of Technology; Texas A&M University; Iowa State University at Ames; and Stanford University for biofuel and renewable energy research (Sheridan 2007). By 2008, dozens of other firms researching technology for next-generation biofuels, including agricultural companies, enzyme and catalyst developers, and feedstock producers, had invested in in-house R&D and funded research at universities and national laboratories (Schubert 2006, Woordburn 2008).

Although collaborative partnerships between industry and public research institutions can offer considerable benefits (Department of Energy 1995, Stiglitz & Wallsten 2000), they also present risks to both parties. The incentives of industry and the academe are partly aligned, at best (Geisler & Rubenstein 1989, Slaughter & Leslie 1997). University administrators should be concerned about erosion of research autonomy, control over university's education mission, and the impact of intellectual property rights agreements on the "intellectual commons" (Argyres & Liebeskind 1998). The entrepreneurial university is viewed as a threat to the integrity of academic research (Krimsky et al. 1991, Pelikan 1992, Brooks 1993). Industry executives should be concerned that academic researchers do not share the firm's profit motives. Early industry-university collaborations were criticized for these reasons (Rausser & Ameden 2004, Rudy et al. 2007). The imbroglio over the University of California, Berkeley/Novartis agreement is a case in point (Rausser & Ameden 2004). By far the most ambitious collaboration to date, the $500-million, 10-year agreement of University of California, Berkeley, with British Petroleum and partner institutions Lawrence Berkeley National Laboratory and University of Illinois, Urbana-Champaign, to form the Energy Biosciences Institute has attracted similar criticism (Delvicchio 2007a,b). Though little empirical evidence exists to confirm the worries of those skeptical of university-industry partnerships, debate continues as to whether they threaten the intellectual commons, disinterestedness in research, academic freedom, and basic research (Kenney 1986; Slaughter 1988; Brooks 1993; Delvicchio 2007a,b).

To the extent that interactive university-industry collaboration alters the research agenda in favor of applied research over basic research, the benefits of existing technologies may not be fully realized, and future scientific progress may be hindered (Kenney 1986, Feller 1997, Herdt 1999, Rausser et al. 2008). Herdt (1999) suggested that, despite gains in biotechnology, plant biologists remain "functional illiterates" in need of additional knowledge to unlock the potential of biotechnology. He contends that such knowledge will not be acquired with the focus on applications of existing technologies. Profit-driven innovation may also ignore areas of research that may greatly improve the human condition yet provide little benefit to corporations, such as technologies to benefit poor populations with little purchasing power (Herdt 1999, Serageldin 1999, Pingali & Traxler 2002). A research alliance that leverages the complementarities and potential synergies between public research institutions and private companies can help developing countries in particular to narrow the gap between themselves and the developed world in cutting-edge research (Rausser et al. 2000).

5.4. Emerging Industrial Alliances

The energy industry will become increasingly science based with the shift away from traditional fossil fuels. Firms will face new organizational imperatives that may lead to vertical and horizontal integration. Their capacity to innovate will rely on access to basic science and critical technologies (Etzkowitz et al. 1998). In the new energy landscape, traditional methods of knowledge acquisition (such as licensing) are insufficient for firm innovation. Rather, firms will rely on access to basic science and key technologies to remain competitive in the transition to renewable energy sources (Etzkowitz et al. 1998).

The aggressive investment by large oil companies in renewable energy research and life sciences is consistent with the strategies of major chemical companies in the 1990s that sought to capitalize on biotechnology. Dow, DuPont, and Monsanto acquired the major seed companies in North America, as well as small biotechnology start-ups, in an unprecedented industry consolidation (Graff et al. 2003). In the field of biofuels, industry restructuring is already evident with agricultural commodities companies such as Cargill and Archer Daniel Midland constituting the largest producers of crop-based liquid fuels. R&D on genetic screening, modification, and creation of new germplasms for cellulosic crops and enzymes as well as engineering of microbes for depolymerization of lignocellulose are being undertaken by smaller biotech firms such as Mendel, LS9, Amyris, OPX Biotechnologies, Genencor, and Synthetic Genomics (Schubert 2006, Woordburn 2008). These start-up biotechnology firms may be acquired by large, horizontally integrated firms, much as their predecessors were a decade ago, or they may persist as did diffuse research enterprises in the pharmaceutical and semiconductor industries (Graff et al. 2003).

Because profitable biofuel production requires coordination among feedstock producers, livestock producers, and gasoline processors and retailers, as well as access to technology, we can expect the integration of big oil with big agribusiness. Partnerships such as British Petroleum with DuPont, ConocoPhillips with Archer Daniel Midland, Shell PLC with Iogen, and Chevron with Weyerhauser to produce biofuels are indicators of such a future. These partnerships and the focus in university research parallel developments in agriculture and the life sciences 10 years ago with the emergence of biotechnology. They foreshadow consolidation in renewable fuels and driven by oil producers.

6. POLICY

Clean-energy technologies are disadvantaged by various imperfections in energy markets. The lack of a price on pollution and on energy security, knowledge spillovers from investment in R&D, imperfect competition and information, poorly functioning capital markets, principal-agent problems, and investor myopia are some well-known sources of failure that afflict energy markets. Market uncertainty can also lead to underinvestment because of risk aversion and irreversibility. Energy producers are susceptible to periods of boom and bust as oil prices fluctuate. Long periods of low oil prices make renewable fuels uncompetitive. They create a disincentive for irreversible capital expenditures (Hochman et al. 2008). Yet another source of failure is the infant-industry argument, which states there is a need for special incentives given learning-by-doing effects (on the supply side) and learning-by-using effects (on the demand side) (Jaffe et al. 2005). Some technologies also need coordinated investment at multiple stages from production to end-use infrastructure. In such cases, coordination costs and network effects may discourage investment. Given these conditions, the supply of clean energy in a free market is likely to be less than socially optimal.

These obstacles, in conjunction with political-economic considerations, have led governments to pursue a range of policies to stimulate investment in clean energy. Approximately 60 countries had adopted renewable-fuel support programs by 2007, including 23 developing countries (Rajagopal & Zilberman 2008, Renewable Energy Network 2008). These policies are not equally efficient and are associated with varying magnitudes of excess burden (Fischer & Newell 2008). Roughly speaking, the various government policies affecting alternative energy technologies can be grouped under two categories: adoption-inducing policies and innovation policies.

6.1. Adoption-Inducing Policies

Adoption-inducing policies tend to stimulate demand and supply of new technologies that either are already technically mature or are likely to become mature in the near future. Mandates for biofuels, excise tax credits for blending ethanol with gasoline or biodiesel with diesel, tax credits on purchase of flexible-fuel vehicles, low-interest loans, and guarantees on construction of biorefineries are some of the ways by which governments have stimulated production and consumption of biofuels. However, adoption-inducing policies carry the risk of technological lock-in. A particular technology may become so entrenched in the marketplace that it stifles the development of other superior technologies (Jaffe et al. 2005). Thus investments in first-generation biofuels may hinder adoption of second-generation or investments in biofuels may hinder development of better alternatives to biofuels. In the absence of appropriate safeguards, policies such as mandates for biofuel can lead to deforestation and, hence, prove counterproductive (Royal Society 2008). de Gorter & Just (2007a,b) argued that, contrary to the belief that ethanol policies mitigate the harmful effects of farm subsidies, they increase the deadweight-loss cost of corn production subsidies. Hence, policymakers ought to exercise caution when pursuing policies that increase diffusion of certain technologies over others. We must highlight another common inefficiency of all policies that do not directly tax pollution but instead subsidize cleaner alternatives: They do not provide incentives to reduce the use of polluting technologies, to improve efficiency, or to conserve energy. Policies that mandate fuel efficiency standards could also, by reducing the cost of travel, lead to more travel and higher net emissions in the worst-case scenario (Austin & Dinan 2005).

6.2. Innovation Policies

Innovation policies target the issue of low investment levels in energy R&D. In addition to the knowledge externality argument, financial-market reasons may also lead to underinvestment in innovation. There is evidence that small and innovative firms experience higher cost of capital, which is mitigated only partially by the existence of venture-capital firms (Hall 2002). Patent incentives apart, the two major policies governments pursue are public provision of R&D through grants to both public and private institutions and the provision of tax incentives for investment in R&D by private firms. The aim of R&D policies is to increase expenditure on research and lower the future cost of renewables. R&D policies, however, do not provide incentives for demand-side improvements in the form of energy efficiency and energy conservation or for shifting from dirtier to cleaner fossil fuels (Fischer & Newell 2008).

Even though the public-good nature of R&D presents a clear rationale for intervention, it is ex ante unclear what the optimal level of R&D in energy ought to be. One interesting line of research comparing historical data on investments in public and private R&D to that suggested by theory showed that a several-fold increase in energy R&D investment is both warranted and feasible (Nemet & Kammen 2007). Given a budget for energy R&D, the optimal allocation of this budget across different competing technologies must be determined. Because the outcome of any scientific research project is uncertain, it is generally in society's interest to fund a diverse set of technological initiatives that target the problem at hand (Dasgupta & Maskin 1987). This is a problem of ex ante portfolio analysis under risk and uncertainty and is a topic that requires further research (Rausser & Papineau 2008). Other questions future research needs to address should include the following: Who should be funded to pursue this research? What mix of patents and open source incentives is most likely to deliver high innovation at least cost? How ought research personnel be compensated?

Both adoption and innovation policies are technology oriented. Environmental policies, in contrast, target a specific type of market failure, namely an environmental externality. Environmental policies that rely on mechanisms such as emission fees and tradable emission permits are technology neutral, whereas performance standards can be either technology neutral or technology specific—which technologies can be excluded or included depends on how the standard is set. Technology-neutral policies have the potential to induce both adoption and innovation without picking technology winners. Currently in the planning stage, one of the first policies to target reduction of GHG emissions from transportation is the state of California's Low Carbon Fuel Standard on transportation fuels (**http://www.energy.ca.gov/low_carbon_fuel_standard/index.html**; **http://gov.ca. gov/index.php?/fact-sheet/5155/**).[3] In sum, the motivation for biofuel policies extends beyond addressing environment externalities.

7. CONCLUSIONS

The stakes are enormous. Replacing a sizeable share of crude oil brings hundreds of billions of dollars into play. Liquid biofuels is just one in a portfolio of alternatives to oil. However, biofuels today attract a major share of investment in alternative technologies for transportation. This is not entirely without reason. In the near term, biofuels such as ethanol and biodiesel allow producers, consumers, and governments to take advantage of existing domestic infrastructure and respond quickly to oil shocks. In the long term, if technological breakthroughs are achieved, biofuels can supply a much larger share of energy for transportation with limited negative impact on food supply and natural habitat.

The R&D investments in biofuels are concentrated around applying cutting-edge knowledge in genomics and biotechnology, process chemistry, and engineering to convert new types of feedstock into novel biofuels and biomaterials. There is an ongoing race to determine the cheapest feedstock, the most efficient conversion technology for feedstock, and finally the most useful products. This race is not occurring in isolation. In addition to

---

[3]The European Union's Emission Trading Scheme, which launched in 2003, is a multisector cap-and-trade program covering emissions from 11 different types of industries, including oil refinery. In contrast, the Low Carbon Fuel Standard is aimed exclusively at transportation fuels.

technological factors, there are energy security considerations as well as environmental and food-supply constraints that will affect the success of these investments. The search for better biofuels is also leading to the development of new paradigms in innovation, production, and regulation. Some patterns that are arising include the reemergence of an educational-industrial complex as the model for development of new knowledge; the interlinking of food and energy supply; the integration of big oil and agribusiness; the use of standardized parts in biotechnology; and the amalgamation of environmental, agricultural, and energy policy goals. R&D focused on biofuels may have positive spillovers, with some new traits and technologies providing clues for increasing productivity of food crops or improving human health. Despite rapid technological advances, agricultural biotechnology remains confined to a handful of crops such as maize, soy, and cotton, as well as a few traits such as pest resistance and herbicide tolerance. The drive toward next-generation biofuels is set to change this trend.

That said, investment in exploration of new fossil fuels dwarfs investment in nonfossil alternative energy. Therefore, fossil fuel technologies may emerge the winners in the race for future energy. The risk from such a scenario is an increase in GHG emissions with its attendant implications for anthropogenic climate change. Policies that compensate for GHG benefits and for fuel security will improve the economics of biofuels. Improvements in production efficiency of biofuel and agriculture will reduce competition to land and other resources and improve the outlook for biofuels. Developments in other alternative technologies will also affect the expansion of biofuels. The biological revolution is in its infancy and the future is uncertain, but policies can play an important role in delivering a sustainable biofuel future. The economic principles we laid out will also be relevant in the future.

DISCLOSURE STATEMENT

The authors are not aware of any affiliations, memberships, funding, or financial holdings that might be perceived as affecting the objectivity of this review.

ACKNOWLEDGMENT

We thank the Energy Biosciences Institute for financial support. David Zilberman is a member of the Giannini Foundation of Agricultural Economics.

LITERATURE CITED

Alston J, Pardey P. 1996. *Making Science Pay: The Economics of Agricultural R&D Policy.* Washington, DC: Am. Enterp. Inst.

Argyres N, Liebeskind J. 1998. Privatizing the intellectual commons: universities and the commercialization of biotechnology. *J. Econ. Behav. Organ.* 35(4):427–54

Arrow K. 1962. *Economic Welfare and the Allocation of Resources for Invention.* Princeton, NJ: Princeton Univ. Press

Audretsch D, Feldman M. 1996. R&D spillovers and the geography of innovation and production. *Am. Econ. Rev.* 86(3):630–40

Austin D, Dinan T. 2005. Clearing the air: the costs and consequences of higher CAFE standards and increased gasoline taxes. *J. Environ. Econ. Manag.* 50(3):562–82

Bain R. 2003. *Biopower Technical Assessment: State of the Industry and Technology.* Golden, CO: Natl. Renew. Energy Lab. Oak Ridge Natl. Lab.

Bercovitz J, Feldman M. 2007. Fishing upstream: firm innovation strategy and university research alliances. *Res. Policy* 36(7):930–48

Besley T, Case A. 1993. Modeling technology adoption in developing countries. *Am. Econ. Rev.* 83:396–402

Brooks H. 1993. *Research Universities and the Social Contract for Science.* Cambridge, MA: MIT Press

Bullis K. 2008. Cheaper butanol from biomass: a startup has raised $25 million for inexpensively producing biofuel. *MIT Tech. Rev.* Oct. 27

Bush V. 1960. *Science, the Endless Frontier.* Washington, DC: US Natl. Sci. Found.

Caesar W, Riese J, Seitz T. 2007. Betting on biofuels. *McKinsey Q.* 2:53–63

Carr G. 2008. The power and the glory. *Economist*, June 19: Spec. Rep.

Corma A, Iborra S, Velty A. 2007. Chemical routes for the transformation of biomass into chemicals. *Chem. Rev.* 107(6):2411–502

Dasgupta P, Maskin E. 1987. The simple economics of research portfolios. *Econ. J.* 97(387):581–95

de Gorter H, Just D. 2007a. *The economics of a biofuel consumption mandate and excise-tax exemption: an empirical example of U.S. ethanol policy.* Work. Pap. 2007-20, Dep. Appl. Econ. Manag., Cornell Univ.

de Gorter H, Just D. 2007b. *The welfare economics of an excise-tax exemption for biofuels.* Work. Pap. 2007-13, Dep. Appl. Econ. Manag., Cornell Univ.

Delvicchio R. 2007a. Cal's biofuel deal challenged on campus. *San Franc. Chron.* Mar. 8:A1

Delvicchio R. 2007b. UC, faculty reach deal on biofuels institute. *San Franc. Chron.* April 20:B5

Demirbas A. 2001. Biomass resource facilities and biomass conversion processing for fuels and chemicals. *Energy Convers. Manag.* 42(11):1357–78

Dep. Energy. 1995. *Energy R&D: Shaping Our Nation's Future in a Competitive World. Final Report of the Task Force for Strategic Energy Resource Development.* Washington, DC: U.S. Dep. Energy

Dep. Trade Ind. 2007. *Meeting the energy challenge.* White Pap., UK Dep. Trade Industry

The Economist. 2007. Advanced biofuels: ethanol, schmethanol. *Economist*, Sept. 27: http://www.economist.com/science/displaystory.cfm?story_id=9861379

The Economist. 2008. Clean technology in the downturn: gathering clouds. *Economist*, Nov. 6: http://www.economist.com/business/displaystory.cfm?story_id=12562281

Eggeman T, Elander R. 2005. Process and economic analysis of pretreatment technologies. *Bioresour. Technol.* 96(18):2019–25

Energy Effic. Renew. Energy Program. 2007. *Federal Biomass Policy: Energy Independence and Security Act.* Washington, DC: US Dep. Energy

Energy Info. Admin. 2008. *Energy Information Administration Outlook.* Washington, DC: Energy Info. Admin.

Etzkowitz H, Webster A, Gebhardt C, Terra B. 2000. The future of the university and the university of the future: evolution of ivory tower to entrepreneurial paradigm. *Res. Policy* 29(2):313–30

Etzkowitz H, Webster A, Healey P. 1998. *Capitalizing Knowledge: New Intersections of Industry and Academia.* Albany, NY: SUNY Press

Faaij A, van Ree R, Waldheim L, Olsson E, Oudhuis A, et al. 1997. Gasification of biomass wastes and residues for electricity production. *Biomass Bioenergy* 12(6):387–407

Fairweather J. 1988. *Entrepreneurship and Higher Education: Lessons for Colleges, Universities, and Industry.* Las Vegas, NV: Assoc. Study Higher Educ.

Farrell A, Gopal A. 2008. Bioenergy research needs for heat, electricity, and liquid fuels. *Mater. Res. Soc. Bull.* 33(4):373–80

Feder G, Just R, Zilberman D. 1985. Adoption of agricultural innovations in developing countries: a survey. *Econ. Dev. Cult. Change* 33(2):255–98

Feller I. 1997. Technology transfer from universities. *Higher Educ. Handb. Theory Res.* 12:1–42

Ferber D. 2004. Synthetic biology: microbes made to order. *Science* 303:158–61

Fischer C, Newell R. 2008. Environmental and technology policies for climate mitigation. *J. Environ. Econ. Manag.* 55(2):142–62

Gallagher K, Holdren J, Sagar A. 2006. Energy-technology innovation. *Annu. Rev. Environ. Resour.* 31(1):193–237

Geisler E, Rubenstein A. 1989. *University-Industry Relations: A Review of Major Issues.* Dordrecht: Kluwer Acad.

Gov. Account. Off. 2006. Key challenges remain for developing and deploying advanced energy to meet future needs. *Rep. Congr. Req. 07-106,* Gov. Account. Off., Washington, DC

Graff G, Heiman A, Zilberman D. 2002. University research and offices of technology transfer. *Calif. Manag. Rev.* 45(1):88–115

Graff G, Rausser G, Small A. 2003. Agricultural biotechnology's complementary intellectual assets. *Rev. Econ. Stat.* 85(2):349–63

Griliches Z. 1992. The search for R&D spillovers. *Scand. J. Econ.* 94:29–42

Hall B. 2002. The financing of research and development. *Oxf. Rev. Econ. Policy* 18(1):35–51

Hall B, Khan B. 2003. *Adoption of new technology.* Work. Pap., NBER

Hayes DJ, Fitzpatrick S, Hayes MHB, Ross JRH. 2005. The biofine process, production of levulinic acid, furfural and formic acid from lignocellulosic feedstocks. In *Biorefineries—Industrial Processes and Products. Status Quo and Future Directions,* Vol. 1, ed. B Kamm, PR Gruber, M Kamm, ch. 7. Weinheim, Ger.: Wiley

Henderson R, Jaffe A, Trajtenberg M. 1998. Universities as a source of commercial technology: a detailed analysis of university patenting, 1965-1988. *Rev. Econ. Stat.* 80(1):119–27

Henkel J, Maurer S. 2007. The economics of synthetic biology. *Mol. Syst. Biol.* 3:117–20

Herdt R. 1999. *Enclosing the global plant genetic commons.* Presented at China Cent. Econ. Res., Peking

Himmel M, Ding S, Johnson D, Adney W, Nimlos M, et al. 2007. Biomass recalcitrance: engineering plants and enzymes for biofuels production. *Science* 315(5813):804–7

Hochman G, Sexton S, Zilberman D. 2008. The economics of biofuel policy and biotechnology. *J. Agric. Food Ind. Organ.* 6(2): artic. 8

Hofstadter R. 1996. *Academic Freedom in the Age of the College.* Piscataway, NJ: Transaction Publ.

Int. Energy Agency. 2004. *Biofuels for Transport: An International Perspective.* Paris: OECD/Int. Energy Agency

Int. Energy Agency. 2007. *Renewables in Global Supply: An IEA Factsheet.* Paris: OECD/Int. Energy Agency

Int. Energy Agency. 2008a. *World Energy Outlook.* Paris: Int. Energy Agency

Int. Energy Agency. 2008b. *International Energy Agency R&D statistics database.* http://www.iea.org/textbase/stats/rd.asp

Jacobsson S, Bergek A. 2004. Transforming the energy sector: the evolution of technological systems in renewable energy technology. *Ind. Corp. Change.* 13(5):815–49

Jaffe A, Newell R, Stavins R. 2005. A tale of two market failures: technology and environmental policy. *Ecol. Econ.* 54(2-3):164–74

Katz M, Shapiro C. 1986. Technology adoption in the presence of network externalities. *J. Polit. Econ.* 94(4):822–41

Kenney M. 1986. *Biotechnology: The University-Industrial Complex.* New Haven, CT: Yale Univ. Press

Khanna M, Hochman G, Rajagopal D, Sexton S, Zilberman D. 2009. Sustainability of food, energy and environment with biofuels. *CAB Rev. Perspect. Agric. Vet. Sci. Nutr. Nat. Resour.* In press

Khanna M, Önal H, Chen X, Huang H. 2008. *Meeting biofuel targets: implications for land use, greenhouse gas emissions and nitrogen use in Illinois.* Presented at Farm Found./USDA Conf. Transit. Bioecon. Environ. Rural Dev. Impacts, St. Louis, MO

Kobos P, Erickson J, Drennen T. 2006. Technological learning and renewable energy costs: implications for US renewable energy policy. *Energy Policy* 34(13):1645–58

Krimsky S, Ennis J, Weissman R. 1991. Academic-corporate ties in biotechnology: a quantitative study. *Sci. Technol. Human Values* 16(3):275–87

Kunkes E, Simonetti D, West R, Serrano-Ruiz J, Gartner C, Dumesic J. 2008. Catalytic conversion of biomass to monofunctional hydrocarbons and targeted liquid-fuel classes. *Science* 322 (5900):417–21

Lynd L. 1996. Overview and evaluation of fuel ethanol from cellulosic biomass: technology, economics, the environment, and policy. *Annu. Rev. Energy Environ.* 21(1):403–65

Lynd L, Zyl W, McBride J, Laser M. 2005. Consolidated bioprocessing of cellulosic biomass: an update. *Curr. Opin. Biotechnol.* 16(5):577–83

Margolis R, Kammen D. 1999. Underinvestment: the energy technology and R&D policy challenge. *Science* 285(5428):690–92

Martinot E. 2005. *Renewables 2005: Global Status Report*. Washington, DC: Worldwatch Inst.

McLaren J. 2005. Crop biotechnology provides an opportunity to develop a sustainable future. *Trends Biotechnol.* 23(7):339–42

Merton R. 1973. The normative structure of science. In *The Sociology Of Science: Theoretical and Empirical Investigations*. Chicago, IL: Univ. Chicago Press

Moose S. 2008. *Technology, research and development for the bioeconomy*. Presented at Farm Found. Conf. Transit. Bioecon. Environ. Rural Dev. Impacts, St. Louis, MO

Mowery D, Sampat B. 2005. Universities in national innovation systems. *The Oxford Handbook of Innovation*, ed. J Fagerberg, DC Mowery, RR Nelson, ch. 8, pp. 209–39. Cambridge, UK: Oxford Univ. Press

Nelkin D. 1984. *Science as Intellectual Property. Who Controls Research?* London: Macmillan

Nemet G, Kammen D. 2007. US energy research and development: declining investment, increasing need, and the feasibility of expansion. *Energy Policy* 35(1):746–55

Natl. Renew. Energy Lab. 2008. *Basic Research*. Boulder, CO: Natl. Renew. Energy Lab.

Natl. Sci. Found. 1953. *Federal Funds for Science: 1950-51 and 1951-52*. Washington, DC: NSF

Natl. Sci. Found. 1954. *Federal Funds for Science: Fiscal Years 1953, 1954 and 1955*. Washington, DC: NSF

Org. Econ. Coop. Dev. 2006. *Agricultural market impacts of future growth in the production of biofuels*. Work. Pap., OECD

Pelikan J. 1992. *The Idea of the University: A Reexamination*. New Haven, CT: Yale Univ. Press

Perlack R, Wright L, Turhollow A, Graham R, Stokes B, Erbach D. 2005. *Biomass as feedstock for a bioenergy and bioproducts industry: the technical feasibility of a billion-ton annual supply*. Tech. Rep. A357634, US Dep. Energy/ US Dep. Agric.

Peters L, Fusfeld H. 1983. *Current US University-Industry Research Relationships: Selected Studies*. Washington, DC: NSF

Pingali P, Traxler G. 2002. Changing locus of agricultural research: Will the poor benefit from biotechnology and privatization trends? *Food Policy* 27(3):223–38

Ragauskas A, Williams C, Davison B, Britovsek G, Cairney J, et al. 2006. The path forward for biofuels and biomaterials. *Science* 311(5760):484–89

Rajagopal D, Zilberman D. 2008. Environmental, economic and policy aspects of biofuels. *Found. Trends Microecon.* 4(5):353–468

Rausser G, Ameden H. 2004. Public-private partnerships needed in horticultural research and development. *Calif. Agric.* 58(2):116–19

Rausser G, Papineau M. 2008. *Managing R&D risk in renewable energy*. CUDARE Work. Pap., Dep. Agric. Resour. Econ., Univ. Calif. Berkeley

Rausser G, Simon L, Ameden H. 2000. Public–private alliances in biotechnology: Can they narrow the knowledge gaps between rich and poor? *Food Policy* 25(4):499–513

Rausser G, Simon L, Stevens R. 2008. Public vs. private good research at land-grant universities. *J. Agric. Food Ind. Organ.* 6(2): artic. 4

Renew. Energy Netw. 2008. *Renewables 2007: Global Status Report*. Paris: Renew. Energy Policy Netw.

Royal Soc. 2008. *Sustainable Biofuels: Prospects and Challenges. Policy Document 01/08*. London: Royal Soc.

Rudloff M. 2007. First commercial BTL production facility—the Choren beta plant Freiberg. *Proc. Eur. Energy Biomass Conf., 15th, Berlin*. Florence/Munich: ETA/WIP

Rudy A, Coppin D, Konefal J. 2007. *Universities in the Age of Corporate Science: The UC Berkeley-Novartis Controversy*. Philadelphia, PA: Temple Univ. Press

Runge C, Senauer B. 2007. How biofuels could starve the poor. *Foreign Aff.* 86(3):41–53

Salter A, Martin B. 2001. The economic benefits of publicly funded basic research: a critical review. *Res. Policy* 30(3):509–32

Schaffer A. 2008. Breeding the oil bug. *Pop. Sci.* 272:68–96

Schubert C. 2006. Can biofuels finally take center stage? *Nat. Biotechnol.* 24:777–84

Seib GF. 2008. In crisis, opportunity for Obama. *The Wall Street Journal*, Nov. 21:A2

Serageldin I. 1999. Biotechnology and food security in the 21st century. *Science* 285(5426):387

Sexton S, Rajagopal D, Hochman G, Zilberman D. 2009. Biofuels: the good, the bad, the ugly. *Calif. Agric. Spec. Collect. Biofuels*. In press

Sheridan C. 2007. Big oil's biomass play. *Nat. Biotechnol.* 25(11):1107–201

Slaughter S. 1988. Academic freedom and the state: reflections on the uses of knowledge. *J. Higher Educ.* 59(3):241–62

Slaughter S, Leslie L. 1997. *Academic Capitalism: Politics, Policies, and the Entrepreneurial University*. Baltimore, MD/London: Johns Hopkins Univ. Press

Smil V. 1999. Crop residues: agriculture's largest harvest? Crop residues incorporate more than half of the world's agricultural phytomass. *Bioscience* 49(4):299–308

Somerville C. 2006. The billion-ton biofuels vision. *Science* 312:1277

Stephanopoulos G. 2007. Challenges in engineering microbes for biofuels production. *Science* 315 (5813):801–4

Sticklen M. 2006. Plant genetic engineering to improve biomass characteristics for biofuels. *Curr. Opin. Biotechnol.* 17(3):315–19

Stiglitz J, Wallsten S. 2000. Public-private technology partnerships: promises and pitfalls. In *Public-Private Technology Partnerships*, ed. P Vaillancourt Rosenau, pp. 37–53. Cambridge, MA: MIT Press

Sunding D, Zilberman D. 2001. The agricultural innovation process: research and technology adoption in a changing agricultural sector. *Handb. Agric. Econ.* 18(1A):207–62

Tiffany D, Eidman V 2003. *Factors associated with success of fuel ethanol producers*. Staff Pap. P03-7, Dep. Appl. Econ., Coll. Agric. Food Environ. Sci., Univ. Minn. http://www.apec.umn.edu/staff/dtiffany/staffpaperp03-7.pdf

Tijmensen M, Faaij A, Hamelinck C, van Hardeveld M. 2002. Exploration of the possibilities for production of Fischer Tropsch liquids and power via biomass gasification. *Biomass Bioenergy.* 23 (2):129–52

Tyner WE, Thaeripour F. 2007. *Future biofuels policy alternatives*. Presented at Farm Found. Conf. Biofuels, Food, Feed Trade-offs, St. Louis, MO

Vinocur B, Altman A. 2005. Recent advances in engineering plant tolerance to abiotic stress: achievements and limitations. *Curr. Opin. Biotechnol.* 16(2):123–32

Weidenmier M, Davis J, Aliaga-Diaz R. 2008. *Is sugar sweeter at the pump? The macroeconomic impact of Brazil's alternative energy program*. Work. Pap., NBER

Whitesides G, Crabtree G. 2007. Don't forget long-term fundamental research in energy. *Science* 315 (5813):796–98

Wilhelm W, Johnson J, Hatfield J, Voorhees W, Linden D. 2004. Crop and soil productivity response to corn residue removal: a literature review. *Agron. J.* 96(1):1–17

Woordburn D. 2008. *Think GreenTech*. San Francisco, CA: Think Panmure LLC

Worldwatch Inst. 2006. Biofuels for transport: global potential and implications for energy and agriculture. *Worldwatch Inst. Rep. Ger. Minist. Food, Agric. Consum. Protect.*, Ger. Agency Tech. Coop./Ger. Agency Renew. Resour., London

Wyman C. 2008. Cellulosic ethanol: a unique sustainable liquid transportation fuel. *Mater. Res. Soc. Bull. Harnessing Mater. Energy* 33

Wyman C, Goodman B. 1993. Biotechnology for production of fuels, chemicals, and materials from biomass. *Appl. Biochem. Biotechnol.* 39(1):41–59

Zucker L, Darby M, Armstrong J. 2000. *University science, venture capital, and the performance of US biotechnology firms*. Mimeogr., Univ. Calif. Los Angeles

Zucker L, Darby M, Armstrong J. 1998. Geographically localized knowledge: spillovers or markets? *Econ. Inq.* 36(1):65–86

Fuel Versus Food

Ujjayant Chakravorty,[1,2] Marie-Hélène Hubert,[1,2] and Linda Nøstbakken[2]

[1]Department of Economics and [2]Department of Marketing, Business Economics, and Law, University of Alberta, Edmonton, Canada T6G 2R6; email: ujjayant@ualberta.ca, mhubert@ualberta.ca, linda.nostbakken@ualberta.ca

Annu. Rev. Resour. Econ. 2009. 1:645–63

First published online as a Review in Advance on July 9, 2009

The *Annual Review of Resource Economics* is online at resource.annualreviews.org

This article's doi: 10.1146/annurev.resource.050708.144200

Key Words

agricultural production, biofuel economics, climate policy, environmental regulation, land allocation

Abstract

Many countries have actively encouraged the production of biofuels as a low-carbon alternative to the use of fossil fuels in transportation. To what extent do these trends imply a reallocation of scarce land away from food to fuel production? This paper critically reviews the small but growing literature in this area. We find that an increase in biofuel production may have a significant effect on food prices and, in certain parts of the world, in speeding up deforestation through land conversion. However, more research needs to be done to examine the effect of newer generation biofuel technologies that are less land intensive as well as the effect of environmental regulation and trade policies on land-use patterns.

1. INTRODUCTION

In 2004, an estimated 14 million hectares (ha) worldwide were being used to produce biofuels and their by-products, representing approximately 1% of global cropland (IEA 2006). In recent years, many countries have adopted policies to encourage the supply of energy from land-based sources. Several factors are contributing to this trend, including the need for cleaner energy sources, a desire for less dependence on foreign countries for vital energy supplies, and the perceived benefits from boosting a domestic agriculture sector that has been dependent on subsidies for survival.

Bioethanol and biodiesel account for the majority of fuel from land. However, these liquid forms of bioenergy supply only a small share of the world energy market—approximately 1% of world renewable energy supply and 1.8% of the world's transportation fuels. Almost 90% of biofuels are ethanol, and the remaining 10% are biodiesel.[1] Rajagopal & Zilberman (2007) divided the land-based fuels into three main categories: U.S. ethanol from corn, Brazilian ethanol from sugarcane, and German biodiesel from rapeseed. In Brazil, ethanol provides approximately 22% of gasoline demand, whereas in the United States, this share is less than 3% (OECD 2008). The global biofuel market is dominated by two countries: Brazil and the United States, who together supply three-quarters of the commodity.

Land-based fuel production has received much policy attention in recent years. Nonetheless, its current share is relatively small in most countries, except for Brazil. However, in the future, government policies that encourage renewable energy sources may result in a larger share of transportation fuels coming from land that historically has been used for food production, forestry, and other critical uses. Probiofuel policies have led to a rapid increase in acreage under biofuels in the United States, the European Union, and developing countries such as China and India, albeit from a very small base. Policies that encourage land-based fuel production may lead to a reduction in acreage used for food production, with a corresponding reduction in food supply and increase in food prices. Furthermore, land that is not well suited for agriculture, but is currently used for forestry or grasslands, may be converted for fuel production. Large-scale land conversion may in turn lead to a leakage of sequestered carbon into the atmosphere, which could significantly reduce the potential environmental benefits from substitution of gasoline by biofuels.

On the demand side, 99% of energy services in the transportation sector are currently provided by petroleum. Consumption in this sector is expected to increase by approximately two-thirds by the year 2030 (IEA 2007, Rajagopal & Zilberman 2007). Several substitutes such as solar, wind, nuclear, and other renewables exist to replace polluting fossil fuels in the electricity sector. However, first-generation biofuels are the only viable substitutes currently available in transportation. Other substitutes, such as second-generation biofuels and fuel cells, hold considerable promise but are still at the research and development stage.[2]

---

[1] Typically, conventional or first-generation biofuels are classified into two broad categories: ethanol and biodiesel. Conventional ethanol in OECD countries is produced mainly from starchy crops such as corn, wheat, and barley, but it can also be made from potatoes and cassava, sugarcane, and sugar beet. In tropical countries like Brazil, ethanol is produced exclusively from sugarcane, whereas molasses is used in India. Biodiesel is produced from transestherfication of vegetable oils or animal fats. Biodiesel can also be produced from used vegetable oils (Rajagopal & Zilberman 2007).

[2] The biofuel sources discussed above such as land-based corn and sugarcane are typically referred to as first-generation biofuels. A second generation of biofuels is derived from agricultural or forest by-products and residues such as straw, woodchips, and grasses. Only the cellulosic parts of the plant are used. Second-generation biodiesel can be produced from biomass by gasification or Fischer-Tropsch synthesis (OECD 2008). Other substitutes such as methanol, hydrogen, and synthetic diesel are produced via gasification from lignocellulosic biomass (Hamelinck & Faaij 2006).

With the agricultural sector also becoming a provider of clean energy, land availability and food needs can limit the growth in plant-based fuels production. World food requirements are likely to maintain a significant level of growth in the coming decades (FAO 2007). A change in dietary habits toward meat and dairy products is also expected to accompany the rise in per capita income and food consumption in developing countries (Cranfield et al. 1998, Delgado et al. 1999). This shift in food consumption preferences increases the demand for land because meat and dairy are intensive users of agricultural land. In addition, there is relatively little unused, arable land left available for a major expansion of current agricultural production (Wiebe 2003, FAO 2007). However, the use of second-generation biofuels produced from crop residues and high-yielding herbaceous energy crops are being explored as possible options that can mitigate the competition for land between food and energy production. Herbaceous crops are plants with soft rather than woody tissues. This energy source includes corn cover and wood chips, which are classified as crop residues, as well as high-yielding energy crops such as miscanthus and switchgrass. Although the total production costs of second-generation biofuels exceed that of first-generation biofuels (IEA 2009), they have the advantage of being less land intensive and being able to grow on lands of lower qualities (Khanna 2008).

This article provides a review of some of the major issues and economic trade-offs between fuel production for transportation and the production of food from land. The remainder of the paper is organized as follows: In Section 2, we discuss the main economic models that have been developed and used to study biofuel production and its economic and policy implications. Section 3 discusses the allocation of land between food and fuel. The economics of biofuels are presented in Section 4. In Section 5, we provide a brief overview of government policies toward biofuel production, including trade and agricultural policies, and discuss their potential impacts on biofuel and food production. We then discuss some of the environmental impacts of biofuel production in Section 6. Section 7 concludes the paper.

2. ECONOMIC MODELS OF BIOFUELS

Several models have been developed to study the interaction between biofuels and food. The production of biofuels and the development of the biofuel industry are highly dependent on land availability and food demand as well as on the price of conventional transportation fuels, mainly petroleum. Accordingly, the models that have been developed to study fuel versus food can generally be divided into two main categories, based on whether they describe only the agricultural sector or both the agricultural and transportation sectors. Below, we give a brief overview of some of these modeling efforts focusing particular attention on the underlying structure of the models.

2.1. Models of the Agricultural Sector

The main modeling efforts at the global level focusing only on the agricultural sector are led by the Food and Agricultural Policy Research Institute (FAPRI 2007) and the International Food Policy Research Institute (IFPRI) (Msangi et al. 2007). Both studies develop

---

They require much less land relative to first-generation biofuels. Third-generation biofuels may be produced from algae and biotech feedstocks. When developed, second- and third-generation biofuels are expected to be less land intensive.

partial equilibrium models to explore the potential impact of biofuels production on food prices, agricultural production, food security, and international trade in the medium term (until 2016 or 2020). In these models all prices are endogenous, but the scarcity of land resources is not considered explicitly and petroleum prices are taken as given. The impact of the development of biofuels is explored by introducing an exogenous demand for transportation. The models are used to project demand and supply for agricultural products, as well as to predict trade patterns between different regions of the world.

Three scenarios are defined and studied by the IFPRI model. A first scenario focuses on the recent boom in biofuels production, but it leaves out second-generation biofuels. The second scenario introduces second-generation biofuels, and the third adds improvements in crop productivity. The results are compared with a benchmark model without biofuels production. An increase in food prices in this model also affects caloric availability and child nutrition in poor-income economies. The FAPRI (2007) model considers only one scenario and aims at analyzing the expected impact of biofuels production on agricultural markets until the year 2016.

Other models of the agricultural sector incorporate endogenous demand for land. Schneider & McCarl (2003) extended the FASOM (Forest and Agricultural Sector Optimization Model) of Adams et al. (1996), which is a partial equilibrium model of the U.S. agriculture and forest sectors, in order to examine the potential role of biofuels production within a portfolio of land-based carbon mitigation strategies. This is an optimization model, where the objective is to maximize the economic surplus net of the costs of inputs under land-allocation constraints. To account for imperfect substitutability between alternative uses of land, available land is divided into different land types, and the model tracks land competition among food, feed, energy, and forest uses. It allows for land allocation among several crops, pastures, and forestry.

Other spatial models have been developed at the global level. IIASA (International Institute for Applied Systems Analysis), in a joint effort with FAO (2009), has developed a model of the global food system where production, consumption, and world food trade dynamics are projected for the near future. Because land quality differs dramatically across geographical areas, they are divided into different agroecological zones. One of the key features of this model is that it takes into account the spatial climate change impacts on agricultural yields. Scenarios have been defined to quantify the impacts of first- and second-generation biofuels on agriculture, the world food system, and land use. The study analyzes a scenario in which biofuel targets are implemented in current OECD countries as well as in some major developing countries.

Other studies have dealt with the impact of biofuel policies in the public economics tradition. One strand of this literature develops partial equilibrium trade models to analyze the interaction between biofuel policies such as tax credits or mandates and agricultural policies such as deficiency payments or farm subsidies (Hochman et al. 2008, de Gorter & Just 2009a). Another literature focuses on the welfare effects of tax credits and mandates in the United States (de Gorter & Just 2009b).

2.2. Models of Agriculture and Transportation

We divide our presentation of models of agriculture and transportation into two parts on the basis of whether the models are partial or general equilibrium. Most of the models presented below are set up within a general equilibrium framework.

2.2.1. Partial equilibrium models. The nature of land-based fuel production implies that biofuels compete with food production for scarce land resources. Hence, the opportunity cost of land must be taken into account when considering the production costs of biofuels. This is done by Chakravorty et al. (2008), who developed a stylized model within a Ricardian-Hotelling framework. In this dynamic framework, land allocation decisions are based on the rent maximization principle. The model focuses on the supply of biofuels in the context of scarce energy resources in which available land is allocated between the food and energy industries. The demand for clean energy is modeled by introducing an exogenous cap on the carbon stock in the atmosphere. Biofuel serves as a perfect substitute for petroleum and is considered carbon neutral.

Whereas the previous model is set in a resource economics tradition, another set of models evaluates the welfare and greenhouse gas effects of biofuels policies. These studies focus on U.S. biofuels policies. Elobeid & Tokgoz (2008) developed a partial equilibrium model of the world ethanol market to study the impact of U.S. trade barriers on the U.S. ethanol market. This model distinguishes among six regions: the United States, Brazil, the European Union 15, China, Japan, and the rest of the world. The model is used to analyze the implications of a U.S. tariff on ethanol imports as well as a tax credit on U.S. and Brazilian ethanol. Ando et al. (2009) explored the welfare and greenhouse gas effects of the U.S. Renewable Fuel Standard (RFS) in the presence of biofuels subsidies. Their study is based on the assumption of a closed economy with homogenous consumers that benefit from vehicle miles traveled. Vehicle miles are produced by blending gasoline and biofuels, but consumers suffer from disutility caused by congestion and greenhouse gas emissions. Finally, Lasco & Khanna (2009) extended the previous framework to that of an open economy (the United States versus Brazil).

2.2.2. General equilibrium models. The GTAP (Global Trade Analysis Project) model (Hertel 1997) has been altered to take into account land scarcity and has been combined with the GTAP-E model (Burniaux & Truong 2002), which is a model of the energy sector (Banse et al. 2008; Hertel et al. 2009a, 2009b). This model takes into account the heterogeneity of land across geographical areas by dividing the global land area into different agroecological zones (Lee et al. 2005). Each zone is defined according to the length of the growing season, and they are in turn subdivided into three climatic zones (tropical, temperate, and boreal). Land-use changes within each zone are determined by changes in relative rents, and the magnitude of these changes is driven by a constant elasticity of transformation. In the model, first-generation biofuels are used in conventional vehicles that are compatible with blends up to 10% bioethanol, and flexi-fuel vehicles are typically designed for blends of 85% ethanol. To treat biofuels and petroleum as complementary inputs, the altered GTAP model incorporates a constant elasticity of substitution production function for the transportation sector (McDougall & Golub 2008). The model allows for substitution between petroleum products and three types of biofuels: ethanol, biodiesel produced from oil, and biodiesel from vegetable oil. To take into account the fact that bioethanol can be produced from different feedstocks, ethanol production is modeled using a constant elasticity of substitution production function. The value of the elasticity of substitution between different fossil fuels and biofuels reflects existing technological barriers. Second-generation biofuels and other technologies currently at the research and development stage are not considered in this model.

General equilibrium models have been used to explore the impact of different mandatory blending policies on world agricultural production. Whereas some models focus on the impacts of the European directive on the world agricultural markets (Banse et al. 2008), others explore the consequences of the implementation of both E.U. and U.S. biofuels policies (Birur et al. 2008, Hertel et al. 2009b).

Reilly & Paltsev (2009) developed a model of transportation and agriculture based on the Massachusetts Institute of Technology Emissions Predictions and Policy Analysis model, which is a recursive-dynamic multiregional equilibrium model of the world economy (Paltsev et al. 2005). This is a bottom-up model built on the GTAP data set, and it gives a detailed representation of energy markets while accounting for regional production, consumption, and bilateral trade flows. The model estimates the emissions of greenhouse gases, including CO_2, as well as other air pollutants. Production and consumption sectors are modeled with constant substitution elasticities. Two biomass technologies are considered: the production of electricity and a liquid fuel from biomass. The demand for land is incorporated in the model, but even though the model is set up at the world level, land is treated as a homogeneous input. The model considers different energy sectors, such as heat, electricity, and transportation and accounts for the price-induced substitution of energy between polluting fossil fuels and clean bioenergy.

In the studies presented above, growth in agricultural yields is treated as exogenous. Keeney & Hertel (2008) have adopted the GTAP model with endogenous yield growth. For example, the recent increase in food prices is likely to induce technological progress in the agricultural sector. Induced innovation studies, such as Hayami & Ruttan (1971), have estimated long-run supply responses of agricultural yields to food prices. Keeney & Hertel (2008) incorporated such supply response functions into the GTAP model to consider the effect of technological progress.

The results from the above studies are discussed in the rest of the paper. In **Table 1**, we summarize the different approaches taken by the above models. Most of them focus on the economics of biofuels supply and in particular address the issue of government policy and how that can affect biofuels production. A smaller sample of the models explicitly considers environmental impacts from biofuels production. A fewer number explicitly consider the role of fossil fuel scarcity and the effect rising prices of energy may have on the supply of biofuels.

Next, we consider some of the main factors that are behind the increased demand for biofuels and discuss current trends in land allocation between food and biofuels.

3. THE ALLOCATION OF LAND BETWEEN FOOD AND FUEL: CURRENT TRENDS

Between 2004 and 2007, when both ethanol and biodiesel production grew rapidly in the United States and other countries, there was a dramatic increase in food prices for several commodities such as corn, wheat, and vegetable oils. This is in sharp contrast to the long-run decline in world food prices of almost 75% over the period 1974–2005 (*The Economist* 2007). Short-run increases in food prices were generally caused by supply shortages arising from poor harvests. In a recent study, Martin (2008) suggested that approximately one-quarter to one-third of the price increase in recent years can be explained by the increased production of energy from land. Other factors explaining the recent rise in

Table 1 Modeling structure employed by different studies

Sector	Reference	Land use and land-use changes	Economics of biofuels	Government policy toward biofuels	Environmental impacts of biofuels
Agricultural	FAPRI (2007)	No[a]	Yes[b]	Yes	No
	IFPRI (2007)	No	Yes	No	No
	Schneider & McCarl (2003)	Yes	Yes	Yes	Yes
	IIASA (2009)	Yes	Yes	Yes	Yes
	Hochman et al. (2008)	No	Yes	Yes	No
	de Gorter & Just (2009a)	No	Yes	Yes	No
	de Gorter & Just (2009b)	No	Yes	Yes	No
Agricultural and transportation	Chakravorty et al. (2008)	Yes	No	Yes	Yes
	Elobeid & Tokgoz (2008)	No	Yes	Yes	No
	GTAP models[c]	Yes	Yes	Yes	No
	Reilly & Paltsev (2009)	Yes	Yes	Yes	Yes
	Ando et al. (2009)	No	Yes	Yes	Yes
	Lasco & Khanna (2009)	No	Yes	Yes	Yes

[a]Indicates that the model does not account for the given factor.
[b]Indicates that the model includes the given factor.
[c]Sources: Birur et al. (2008), Hertel et al. (2009b).

world food prices are droughts and increased demand for agricultural products from highly populated developing countries.

An increase in corn prices—a commodity that can be used to generate energy—also leads to an increase in the price of meat and dairy products because corn accounts for more than half the cost of animal feed in countries such as the United States (Yacobucci & Schnepf 2007). Thus, large-scale conversion of corn to ethanol will affect the supply of corn in the world market. The United States exports two-thirds of the world's corn, and developing countries with large populations such as China and Mexico are large importers. In 2004, 11% of the corn harvested by U.S. farmers was used for ethanol production. As a result, a shift toward biofuels in the United States will inevitably result in higher prices of corn in these countries. In fact, the spike in the price of tortillas in Mexico during January 2007 was widely attributed to this phenomenon.

Approximately 1% of total world cropland was used to produce biofuels and their by-products in 2004 (IEA 2006). Brazil has the highest share of acreage devoted to biofuels production; sugarcane is currently produced on 5.6 million ha in Brazil, which accounts for approximately 10% of the country's cropland. Elsewhere, even though the acreage used for land-based energy production is quite small, not much new land is available for energy production. Future growth in biofuels supply will thus have to come from new technologies or from substitution of current acreage away from food to fuel production.

Of the total land available in the world (approximately 13.5 billion ha) forests cover 4.2 billion ha while agriculture (croplands and pastures) accounts for 5 billion ha, of which 1.6 billion ha are cropland. The remaining land is mainly urban and ill-suited for agriculture. The Food and Agriculture Organization (FAO 2008) considers an additional 2 billion ha as potentially suitable for agriculture. This estimate should, however, be treated with caution. First, according to Wiebe (2003), these 2 billion ha exhibit low crop yields and are highly vulnerable to land degradation, which undermines their long-term production capacity. Nonetheless, some biofuel crops, such as cassava, castor, and sweet sorghum, can be grown under unfavorable environmental conditions, but the energy efficiency of these crops is low. Second, the world's forests and wetlands supply valuable environmental services such as biodiversity conservation, carbon sequestration, and water filtration. As a result, some of these areas are or will likely be zoned for protection and hence unavailable for agricultural production. As surplus land availability is limited, an increased focus on biofuels will undoubtedly come at the expense of land under food production.

This increasing focus on biofuels and its attendant demand for crops may be offset in part by taking advantage of the potential for increased yields that lies in currently available technologies. Even if crop yields grow at a lower rate than in the past, actual yields are still far below their potential in most regions (FAO 2008). For instance, in Malaysia and Indonesia, which are the world's largest producers of biodiesel after the European Union, current palm oil yields amount to 4 tons per hectare, but they could potentially be increased to 6 tons per hectare with available know-how. In China, the average sugarcane yield is only 60 tons per hectare and has the potential to rise to approximately 85 tons per hectare.

4. THE ECONOMICS OF BIOFUELS

There are two important dimensions that need to be taken into account when considering the economics of biofuels: energy yields and production costs. Both are highly dependent on the feedstock used, and local conditions determine which feedstock can be used in which region of the world. For instance, in the United States, ethanol is produced from corn, which is a far more demanding plant in terms of land quality than sugarcane, which is used in Brazil. There are also large differences in the availability and in the quality of land between different regions (Wiebe 2003). For instance, surplus land available in the United States and in European countries is small compared to countries like Brazil and Indonesia. Thus, to determine where the production of biofuels will occur, it is crucial to consider not only the amount of land available but also its quality.

The economic potential for biofuels can be better understood by comparing the costs and yields of the major producers: Brazil and the United States. Brazilian ethanol is based on sugarcane and is by far the most efficient, with average yields of 1665 gallons per hectare. In the United States, ethanol from corn yields approximately 800 gallons per hectare (Seauner 2008). The sugar in sugarcane can be converted directly into ethanol, but in corn-based ethanol production, the carbohydrate must first be converted into sugar. Moreover, the cane stalks from sugarcane harvesting (bagasse) are burned to fuel the plant, which further reduces the cost of production. The higher efficiency of the transformation process leads to cheaper ethanol from sugarcane relative to corn. Producing one gallon of ethanol in Brazil costs approximately $0.83, whereas the corresponding amount for U.S. corn-based ethanol is $1.09 (all amounts noted are in U.S. dollars) (Lasco & Khanna 2009). Although ethanol can also be produced from other crops such as cereals and beets, the cost of these crops is even higher (Ryan et al. 2006). In comparison, biodiesel production in Germany is more expensive with average costs that are approximately twice those of U.S. ethanol. With crude oil prices of $35 per barrel or more, Brazilian ethanol is already economically competitive (FAO 2008).

In their study of the conversion of marginal lands into agricultural land, Banse et al. (2008) showed that increasing food prices are less important compared with studies where the endogenous demand for land is explicitly incorporated into the model. Banse et al. (2008) reported that most food prices follow a decreasing trend. The exception is oilseed, which shows a small price increase of 1% in their model. In contrast, the IFPRI model (Msangi et al. 2007) predicts a significant increase in oilseed and sugar prices.

Several studies evaluate the possible implications of the E.U. biofuels targets. Banse et al. (2008) found that to reach these targets European imports from land-abundant countries such as South America will have to increase. This will increase the share of all energy crops that the European Union imports from 42% to 53%. We return to this issue below when we look at the implications of government policies toward biofuels production.

Second-generation biofuels feedstocks, such as switchgrass and miscanthus, can be grown on marginal lands that are not productive in traditional agricultural uses (Hochman et al. 2008). In temperate areas such as Illinois, the energy yield of miscanthus can reach 1400 gallons per hectare compared to only 800 gallons per hectare produced from corn (Khanna 2008). However, their production costs are still high compared with the costs of producing first-generation biofuels (Rajagopal & Zilberman 2007). It costs $2.74 per gallon to produce ethanol from miscanthus, but only $2.12 for ethanol produced from corn (Khanna 2008). Other substitutes, such as methanol, hydrogen and synthetic diesel, may be produced via gasification from lignocellulosic biomass (Hamelinck & Faaij 2006). To date, few economic studies have examined the role of second-generation biofuels in the future energy mix. A study by IIASA (2009) reveals that production of lignocellulosic plants on approximately 125 million ha, an area representing less than 10% of current world croplands, would be sufficient to achieve a biofuels target share of 10% in world transport fuels in 2030. Under this scenario, mandatory or voluntary blending targets are implemented in major OECD countries including the United States, the European Union, and developing countries such as China and India.

Many studies analyze the relationship between biofuels and food prices. The competition for limited land resources between fuel and food results in important consequences, such as malnutrition and food shortages, especially in poorer regions. Analysis using the IFPRI model shows that biofuel production has a substantial impact on world food prices. The largest increase in prices is observed for oil seeds and sugarcane. When only first-generation biofuels are modeled, corn and oil seeds prices rise by 76% and 66%, respectively. However, when second-generation biofuels and productivity improvements are taken into account, these numbers fall to 45% and 49%, respectively, and accounting for crop productivity improvements renders the price effect even smaller, although still significant.

The IFPRI model also looks at the effects on calorie availability and child nutrition in poor-income economies, particularly focusing on Sub-Saharan Africa. The results of the first-generation biofuels scenario when compared with the no-biofuels case show an 11% reduction in daily calorie availability (275 calories) and a significant increase in the number of children suffering from malnutrition. The effects are obviously smaller when technological progress is considered, in the form of second-generation biofuels and improvements in crop productivity.

There is a close link between the profitability of biofuels and the prices of food and oil. Low food prices mean a lower opportunity cost of land, an input in the production of first-generation biofuels. In contrast, a high oil price is equivalent to a high output price for biofuels. From 2004 to 2007, low food prices combined with high oil prices considerably improved the profitability of biofuels, which resulted in high levels of investment in the biofuels industry. As a result, the United States currently has approximately 134 ethanol plants, compared with 63 plants in 2003. High food prices since 2008 have reduced investment in the biofuels industry. Hochman et al. (2008) employed a partial equilibrium trade framework to examine this stylized fact. Specifically, their model looks at the impacts of biofuels production on food prices within a dynamic system that takes into account inventory considerations. That is, food inventories will deplete relatively fast to meet biofuels demands, which in turn will change expectations and contribute to rising food prices. On the one hand, higher demand for biofuels can increase income of crop producers. Therefore, it undermines the needs for policy intervention—price supports, output restrictions, or deficiency payments—in the agricultural sector. On the other hand, low food prices can improve the competitiveness of biofuels compared with petroleum. It fuels investment in the bioenergy industry—building of new plants and research and development in second-generation biofuels. However, high food prices may depress bio-fuels competitiveness and slow down investments. This can cause bankruptcies at the firm level, as were observed in the U.S. farm sector in 2008.

Chakravorty et al. (2008) showed that, as the exhaustible resource (petroleum) becomes scarcer, its price increases, thereby making land-based fuel production (biofuels) competitive. As a consequence, land shifts out from food production to energy production, which leads to an increase in the price of food. Ultimately, the scarce petroleum resource is exhausted and all energy is supplied by land. The question of whether petroleum or biofuels should be used has also been analyzed in the modified GTAP model. This model accounts for the price increase in crude oil relative to the increase in agricultural prices. Results indicate that the demand for energy resources—petroleum versus biofuels—depends critically on the relative price of fossil fuel and land-based energy.

5. GOVERNMENT POLICY TOWARD BIOFUELS PRODUCTION

A range of different regulatory policies have been proposed and implemented. These include mandatory blending, i.e., regulations requiring that a certain amount of ethanol be blended with gasoline in transportation fuels, subsidies to biofuel producers, as well as trade barriers aimed at biofuels imports. Other highly relevant policies for the development of biofuels include carbon taxes or quotas. Although such regulations are not necessarily specific for biofuels, they still affect energy choice and hence the supply of biofuels indirectly. Next, we discuss some of these policies and examine their implications.

5.1. Mandatory Blending

Governments such as those of the European Union and the United States have established biofuel mandates to be achieved by target dates. For instance, the European Union expects its member states to ensure that biofuels and other renewables provide at least 5.75% of transportation fuels by the year 2010 and 10% by 2020 (Bureau et al. 2009). With an average share of renewables in the EU25 countries of only 2% in 2007 (OECD 2008), these goals may seem unrealistic. In the United States, the first RFS was instituted by the Energy Policy Act in 2005 (FAO 2008). It required modest levels of renewables to be blended into U.S. motor fuel: 4 billion gallons in 2006, increasing to 7.5 billion gallons in 2012. By comparison, the current level of biofuel use in the United States is close to 9 billion gallons (FAO 2008). Former President George W. Bush declared that the biofuels production target should be 35 billion gallons in 2017. The Energy Information and Security Act passed in 2007 expanded the RFS program by requiring the use of 36 billion gallons of ethanol per year by 2022, of which 21 billion gallons must be produced from second-generation feedstocks (Yacobucci & Schnepf 2007). Countries such as China, Japan, and Australia also have in place policies encouraging the production of biofuels (Rajagopal & Zilberman 2007). However, the Chinese government recently decided to slow down its ethanol plant expansion program because of worries that the rapid expansion could threaten the country's food security (Kojima et al. 2007).

The implementation of a mandate leads to a switch toward biofuels and away from gasoline in the country introducing the mandate (Ando et al. 2009). The impact of the policy on the world biofuels market depends on the market power of the country introducing the policy. If the country has market power, the additional demand of ethanol may lead to a rise in ethanol prices, which induces a substitution toward petroleum and away from ethanol in other countries (Lasco & Khanna 2009).

In terms of actual impacts of mandatory blending, the FAPRI model shows that ethanol production in the United States will expand much more rapidly than mandated by the Energy Policy Act of 2005, surpassing 7.5 billion gallons by 2008 and 12 billion gallons by 2010. However, in the absence of any incentives, the European Union is not expected to achieve the goal of a 5.75% share of renewable fuels by 2010. Biodiesel production in the European Union is expected to grow more slowly because of the increasing price of vegetable oil in the model and the assumption of stagnant future crude oil prices. If oil prices do not rise, then biofuel producers do not have an adequate incentive to supply the energy market.

Several other studies explore the impact of mandatory blending on the world agricultural sector. Some of them are focused on the European directive (Banse et al. 2008), while others consider the implementation of both E.U. and U.S. policies (Birur et al. 2008, Hertel et al. 2009b). All of them predict a positive impact on food prices as a result of mandatory blending. The implementation of mandatory blending in the European Union is projected to slow down the decline in the price of certain feedstocks such as cereals and sugar (Banse et al. 2008). The effect on world prices is more significant when policies are implemented in both the European Union and the United States. Because not much surplus land is available in Europe, it is expected that half the crops used in biofuels production must be imported to meet the target (Banse et al. 2008). In contrast, in the United States, the additional ethanol needed to meet these mandated targets will, to a large degree, be produced domestically. These studies also show that the impact of mandatory blending on land use will be substantial. It will have a major effect on greenhouse gas emissions because any conversion of forest lands into agriculture will cause carbon leakage and may undo some of the greenhouse gas reduction objectives the biofuels program is designed to achieve.

5.2. Carbon Taxes and Carbon Cap

Most countries levy a tax on gasoline and diesel, and excise tax reductions are the most widely used instrument to bridge the gap between the price of conventional and that of land-based fuels. However, the level of taxation varies across countries. In the United States, there is a fixed tax credit of $0.45 per gallon of ethanol blended with gasoline and a $1.00 per gallon tax credit for biodiesel (Rajagopal & Zilberman 2007). The excise tax credit may be justified by the presence of environmental externalities that cannot properly be corrected in end-user prices (Kojima et al. 2007). Ryan et al. (2006) estimated that the price difference between conventional and biofuels in Europe is equal to approximately $229 per ton of CO_2 equivalent (2006 prices), which is much higher than the actual price in 2006 of $17 per ton of carbon. However, instead of recommending the use of an excise tax or subsidy, Lasco & Khanna (2009) suggested imposing a differential carbon tax on biofuels on the basis of the carbon intensity. Although a subsidy increases the use of ethanol, which emits less greenhouse gases than does gasoline, the benefits of reduced greenhouse gas emissions are not enough to offset the increase in the demand for driving from lower gas prices.

Energy security is another important driver of biofuels policy. Countries such as the United States have stressed the need to develop the domestic biofuels market so as to reduce their dependence on foreign oil (Taheripour & Tyner 2007). Currently, the United States imports 60% of its oil. The question is how much is the United States willing to pay for this added energy security in terms of higher gasoline prices. If energy security is highly valued, that will translate into a strong incentive program for biofuels production. Carbon taxes that may emerge under a cap and trade program being actively considered in the United States will also encourage the displacement of conventional fuels by land-based fuels. Carbon trading has already been introduced in the European Union, although prices are relatively low in this early phase of trading and setting sectoral targets.

Schneider & McCarl (2003) explored the potential role of biofuels production in a portfolio of climate mitigation options for the United States. The agricultural sector offers a wide range of strategies to mitigate climate change, including biological sequestration from conversion of agricultural land into forests, the adoption of new techniques for soil carbon sequestration, and the displacement of fossil fuels by biofuels. The authors used an optimization model, and for each level of carbon prices, they determined the least costly mitigation strategies. Their results show that biofuels are not viable below a carbon price of $40 per ton. However, for carbon prices above $70, biofuels dominate all other agricultural mitigation strategies.

Reilly & Paltsev (2009) examined the least costly strategy for reaching different carbon-concentration targets (450–750 parts per million). They found that the development of bioelectricity is expected to be insignificant owing to the availability of competitive carbon-free substitutes for electricity (nuclear and solar). However, because other substitutes for petroleum such as fuel cells and hydrogen are not mature enough at this stage, biofuels are the only viable substitute in terms of cost and emissions savings. To meet these carbon targets, biofuels production rises substantially in their model, leading to an increase in world food prices. From 2010 to 2020, world food prices are projected to increase by approximately 10%. When a mandatory blending target is imposed in the European Union and the United States, the increase in prices is expected to be approximately 9% for coarse grains in the United States, 10% for oilseeds in the European Union, and 11% for Brazilian sugarcane.

In a recent study using a Ricardian-Hotelling framework, Chakravorty et al. (2008) analyzed the impact of pollution regulation on the transition to biofuels and on food prices. The demand for a clean environment is expressed in terms of a cap on the carbon stock. The immediate implication of this cap is a rise in energy prices, which speeds up the adoption of biofuels and leads to a rise in food prices. The importance of these effects depends on the level of land scarcity, the demand for food, the level of the regulatory constraint, and the availability of fossil fuels.

5.3. Trade Barriers and Other Market Distortions

Government policies aimed at restricting trade are also of crucial importance to the biofuels industry. Such policies are motivated by a desire for increased energy security and the perceived benefits of supporting heavily subsidized domestic agricultural sectors. Trade policies will have a major impact on where biofuels are produced. For instance, the United States currently imposes a 54 cents per gallon import tariff on ethanol. In addition, the Food Conservation and Energy Act of 2008 provides various incentives to the domestic farm sector to produce first-generation biofuels and for using cellulosic feedstocks (Ando et al. 2009). This includes a differential subsidy for corn ethanol ($0.45 per gallon) and cellulosic ethanol ($1.01 per gallon). Brazil is the main exporter of ethanol into the U.S. market; consequently, lifting this tariff would have a major impact on both U.S. and Brazilian production. U.S. ethanol is economically viable only at crude oil prices exceeding $58 per barrel, whereas Brazilian ethanol is much cheaper. Hence, trade liberalization may result in an increase in exports of ethanol from Brazil to the United States.

The U.S. government protects domestic production by imposing trade barriers and introducing domestic market distortions such as a tax credit to refiners blending ethanol with gasoline. Several studies (Elobeid & Tokgoz 2008, de Gorter & Just 2008, Lasco & Khanna 2009) analyzed the impact of trade liberalization by removing U.S. trade barriers and tax credits in the ethanol market and studying the resulting spillover effects on other markets such as petroleum and agriculture. Removing import tariffs along with the subsidy induces a switch toward gasoline and away from ethanol in fuel composition. de Gorter & Just (2008) estimated that demand for ethanol will decrease by 90%, whereas Lasco & Khanna (2009) and Elobeid & Tokgoz (2008) found a more modest effect of approximately 6% and 2%, respectively. Lasco & Khanna (2009) explained the difference in magnitudes by the various assumptions regarding the elasticity of substitution and the supply elasticity of gasoline.[3] Because the United States has market power in the world ethanol market, an increase in the world ethanol price causes a reduction in Brazil's ethanol consumption.

International trade in food products is highly protected. An estimated 75% of total agricultural support to OECD countries is provided by market access barriers (Anderson et al. 2006). Liberalization of food markets will impact food and crop prices as well as the competitiveness of biofuels. The European Union and the United States have a range of policies that encourage overproduction of sugar, which in turn leads to a lower world market price of sugar. The sugar market is one of the most distorted agricultural markets, and world prices are estimated to be 40% below the price level that would prevail in a free market (Kojima et al. 2007). These policies have stimulated the production of ethanol in Europe and encouraged Brazil to divert its production of sugar from exports toward ethanol production. Hence, a liberalization of the highly protected European sugar market is likely to result in increased prices of sugar in Europe, which will reduce the competitiveness of European biodiesel.

6. ENVIRONMENTAL IMPACTS OF BIOFUELS PRODUCTION

Contrary to popular impression, biofuels are not carbon neutral. Life Cycle Assessment studies have estimated the amount of carbon emitted by the biofuels production process from "well to wheel" (Rajagopal & Zilberman 2007, Peña 2008). **Table 2** shows the direct emissions savings from using biofuels relative to gasoline measured in CO_2 equivalent. Savings from ethanol produced from sugarcane in Brazil are higher than the savings from corn in the United States. Furthermore, savings from second-generation biofuels tend to be larger than those of first-generation biofuels. Note that the stage at which most of the carbon emissions occur differs between gasoline and biofuels (Peña 2008). Most carbon emissions are released into the atmosphere during the combustion of gasoline, but for biofuels, emissions are generated during the various stages of fuel production. This is important when considering climate policy.

More recent studies have attempted to calculate the overall change in emissions by also accounting for the effects of land-use changes (Fargione et al. 2008, Searchinger et al. 2008). This work aims at recognizing the effects of additional acreage coming from deforested lands or from conversion of grasslands into cropland, which releases stored carbon into the atmosphere. Turning grasslands into croplands is estimated to release between 134 tons of carbon per hectare in the United States and 165 tons per hectare in Brazil (Fargione et al. 2008), whereas conversion of forest can release between 600 and 1000 tons of carbon per hectare (FAO 2008). In a recent study, Fargione et al. (2008) found that the carbon lost by converting rainforests, savannas, or grasslands into land for biofuels production outweighs the carbon savings from substitution of gasoline and diesel by biofuels. Such conversions release 17 to 420 times more carbon, depending on the crop and ecosystem, than the annual savings from replacing fossil fuels. Given such effects, corn-based ethanol, instead of resulting in a 20% reduction in carbon emissions, as previously thought, may double emissions over a 30-year period.

---

[3]In de Gorter & Just (2008), gasoline and ethanol are perfect substitutes, whereas in Elobeid & Tokgoz (2008), they are perfect complements. Lasco & Khanna (2009) took a middle approach and defined the two as imperfect substitutes.

Table 2 Overview of direct emission savings from biofuels compared with reference fossil-fuel vehicle[a]

Biofuel	Generation	Feedstock	Low	Best estimate	High
Bioethanol	1st	Sugar crops	0.7	1.2	2.2
		Starch crops	0	0.4	0.9
		Brazilian sugarcane	2.4	2.9	3.3
	2nd	Lignocellulosic crops	2.6	2.5	2.4
		Lignocellulosic residues	2.7	2.6	2.5
Biodiesel	1st	Oil seeds	0.5	1.3	1.8

[a]Measurements in tons of CO_2 equivalents per 1000 gallons.
Source: Ryan et al. (2006).

Deforestation is another negative environmental impact that results from the increased production of biofuels (Curran et al. 2004). It also has negative implications for carbon sequestration and the protection of biodiversity. The demand for biofuels has already been cited as a factor responsible for an increase in deforestation. One example is in Indonesia where increased deforestation resulted in a 70% rise in palm oil prices during 2007 (Yacobucci & Schnepf 2007).

Deforestation has negative implications for carbon sequestration and the protection of biodiversity (IIASA 2009). However, these problems may be avoided by using abandoned agricultural lands. Khanna et al. (2009) suggested that land shortages in the United States may be alleviated by bringing into cultivation areas currently protected by the Conservation Reserve Program (35 million acres). A recent study has estimated the potential for bioenergy production at the global scale from using such lands (Campbell 2008). Taking into account the potential for bioenergy, which includes both bioelectricity and biofuels, these results show that approximately 8% of current primary energy demand may be produced on the 400 million ha of abandoned lands.

Several studies have examined the greenhouse gas effects of biofuels policies (Ando et al. 2009, Lasco & Khanna 2009). Lasco & Khanna (2009) compared U.S. carbon emissions under different policy scenarios. If the current U.S. mandate is imposed, the level of carbon emissions is systematically higher than under optimal policy intervention (which internalizes the external effects induced by greenhouse gas emissions). These papers focus on the implications of biofuels policies on the energy markets, abstracting from interactions with other markets, such as agricultural or land markets. Biofuels policies may have implications on land allocation and indirect carbon emissions in land-abundant countries such as Brazil, Indonesia, and Malaysia (IIASA 2009). These studies also neglect the effects of such policies on carbon emissions from the rest of the world. If biofuels mandates are introduced in a country that has market power in the biofuels market (as the United States and the European Union have for ethanol and biodiesel), world biofuels prices may increase. This, in turn, may result in biofuels exports from other countries and increased petroleum consumption in their domestic sectors (carbon leakage). Thompson et al. (2009) found that assumptions about land-use responses in Brazil will have a significant effect on U.S.-Brazil trade in ethanol and ethanol prices in the

United States. That is, these market effects as well as their environmental impacts in terms of deforestation and carbon emissions are highly sensitive to assumptions regarding model parameters.

The production of biomass relies on water resources, which are becoming increasingly scarce in many regions. With more acreage under biofuels, irrigated land areas may expand. This may increase the demand for water and make it more expensive. Increased competition for water may cause a decline in agricultural yields and slow down the growth of food production (Rajagopal & Zilberman 2007). The issue of water availability is all the more important in countries such as India and China that already suffer from water shortages (Berndes 2002, de Fraiture et al. 2008).

7. CONCLUDING REMARKS

The future of the biofuels industry will be an increasingly important issue in the decades to come. The demand for transportation is projected to double by 2030 (IEA 2007). Nuclear power, solar energy, and wind energy can substitute for petroleum and coal to meet demand for electricity and heating. These resources have some advantages: They are largely inexhaustible and carbon neutral. However, the only viable substitute for transportation energy in the near future is first-generation biofuels. The production of this resource is limited by the availability of land, which is also used for food production. Serious concerns have been raised regarding the carbon benefits of biofuels production and use. It is well-known that carbon is released into the atmosphere during the production of biofuel. However, policies that encourage biofuels production may also lead to encroachment into forest lands, thereby speeding up the rate of deforestation, which results in the release of more carbon into the atmosphere. These trends, if significant, may offset the reductions in carbon emissions that the large-scale adoption of biofuels was intended to achieve in the first place.

Even in the absence of regulation to encourage the production of biofuels, the supply of biofuels is expected to lead to rising food prices. Models show that corn and oil seed prices may increase by 65–75% by the year 2020. However, when more advanced second-generation biofuels that use less land are introduced, these figures decline to 45–50%.

Many policies have been introduced with the aim of increasing the production and use of biofuels. Mandatory blending requirements have been implemented in the United States and various E.U. countries. These policies are projected to induce substantial increases in world biofuels production in the near future. They are also expected to adversely impact agricultural production in the rest of the world because these domestic biofuels targets can be met only through large-scale imports from land-abundant countries such as Brazil that enjoy a comparative advantage in producing low-cost biofuels from sugarcane. Trade in biofuels may induce significant land-use changes and deforestation in the developing countries. However, protectionist policies in the developed economies will likely reduce these adverse environmental impacts. More economic studies need to be done to take into account the increase in the carbon footprint of biofuels because of land-use changes, which may, according to some estimates, release much larger amounts of carbon into the atmosphere than the carbon savings from the displacement of petroleum by biofuels.

Relative to other climate mitigation options for the agricultural sector, the substitution of fossil fuels by biofuels is still expensive. Modeling studies suggest that displacing fossil fuels by biofuels can be a competitive climate mitigation strategy if the price of the carbon is above $70 per ton. Next-generation biofuels may be superior in terms of their land-use requirements, but they may also be more costly to produce.

From the point of view of economic research, the issue of fuel versus food is a promising one. The allocation of land away from food to the production of biofuels will depend on an array of factors, some of which exhibit a significant degree of uncertainty. First, although current biofuel technologies are land intensive, newer generation biofuels may use land more efficiently. Therefore, the impact of biofuel supply on food production may be limited. Second, protectionist policies that limit imports of clean energy based on trade and national security considerations may have a positive environmental effect by limiting land conversion and deforestation in developing countries that have a cost advantage in the supply of biofuels. Third, the price of nonrenewable resources such as crude oil will determine how quickly consumers switch to the cleaner alternative. This shift will also be determined by government cap and trade programs and investment decisions such as those providing subsidies and tax credits to fueling stations that cater to flexible-fuel vehicles. Understanding the effects of these policies will require economic models that build on the limited number of important existing studies and that integrate approaches from agriculture and resource economics as well as industrial organization.

DISCLOSURE STATEMENT

The authors are not aware of any affiliations, memberships, funding, or financial holdings that might be perceived as affecting the objectivity of this review.

ACKNOWLEDGMENTS

The authors thank the Canada Research Chair program, the Social Science and Humanities Research Council (SSHRC) of Canada, and the Center for Applied Business Research in Energy and the Environment (CABREE) at the University of Alberta for generous financial support. They also thank David Zilberman for valuable comments and suggestions, which improved the paper significantly.

LITERATURE CITED

Adams DM, Alig RJ, Callaway JM, McCarl BA, Winnett SM. 1996. *The forest and agricultural sector optimization model (FASOM): model structure and policy applications*. Res. Pap. PNW-RP-495, US Dep. Agric., For. Serv., Pac. Northwest Res. Stn.

Anderson K, Martin W, Valenzuela E. 2006. The relative importance of agricultural subsidies and market access. *World Trade Rev.* 5(3):357–76

Ando AW, Khanna M, Taheripour F. 2009. *Market and social welfare effects of the renewable fuels standard*. See Khanna et al. 2009. In press

Banse M, van Meijl H, Tabeau A, Woltjer G. 2008. *Impact of EU biofuel policies on world agriculture and food markets*. Eur. J. Agric. Econ. Pap. 6476, 107th Semin., Sevilla, Spain

Berndes G. 2002. Bioenergy and water—the implications of large-scale bioenergy production for water use and supply. *Glob. Environ. Change* 12:253–71

Birur DK, Hertel TW, Tyner WE. 2008. *Impact of biofuel production on world agricultural markets: a computable general equilibrium analysis*. GTAP Work. Pap. 53, Purdue Univ.

Bureau JC, Guyomard H, Jacquet F, Tréguer D. 2009. *European biofuel policy: How far will public support go?* See Khanna et al. 2009. In press

Burniaux J, Truong T. 2002. *GTAP-E: an energy-environmental version of the GTAP model.* GTAP Tech. Pap. 16., Cent. Glob. Trade Anal., Purdue Univ.

Campbell JE, Lobell DB, Genova RC, Field CB. 2008. The global potential of bioenergy on abandoned agriculture lands. *Environ. Sci. Technol.* 42:5791–94

Chakravorty U, Magné B, Moreaux M. 2008. A dynamic model of food and clean energy. *J. Econ. Dyn. Control* 32:1181–203

Cranfield JAL, Hertel TW, Eales JS, Oreckel PV. 1998. Changes in the structure of global food demand. *Am. J. Agric. Econ.* 80(5):1042–50

Curran L, Trigg N, McDonald AK, Astiani D, Hardiono YM, et al. 2004. Lowland forest loss in protected areas of Indonesian Borneo. *Science* 313(5660):1000–3

de Fraiture C, Giordano M, Liao Y. 2008. Biofuels and implications for water use: blue impact of green energy. *Water Policy* 10(Suppl. 1):67–81

de Gorter H, Just DR. 2008. The economics of the US ethanol import tariff with a blend mandate and tax credit. *J. Agric. Food Organ.* 6(6):1–21

de Gorter H, Just DR. 2009a. The welfare economics of a biofuel tax credit and the interaction effects with price contingent farm subsidies. *Am. J. Agric. Econ.* 91(2):477–88

de Gorter H, Just DR. 2009b. The welfare economics of biofuel tax credits and mandates. See Khanna et al. 2009. In press

Delgado C, Rosegrant M, Steinfeld H, Henui S, Courbois C. 1999. *Livestock to 2020. The next food revolution.* Discuss. Pap. 28, Int. Food Policy Res. Inst., Food Organ. Agric. Int. Livest. Res. Inst.

Elobeid A, Tokgoz S. 2008. Removing distortions in the U.S ethanol market: What does it imply for the United States and Brazil? *Am. J. Agric. Econ.* 90(4):918–33

FAO. 2007. *The State of Food and Agriculture: Paying Farmers for Environmental Services.* Rome: Food Agric. Organ.

FAO. 2008. *The State of Food and Agriculture: Prospects and Perspectives. Biofuels: Risks.* Rome: Food Agric. Organ.

FAPRI. 2007. *US and World Agricultural Outlook.* Ames, IA: Food Agric. Policy Res. Inst., Iowa State Univ./Univ. Mo.-Columbia

Fargione J, Hill J, Tilman D, Polasky S, Hawthorne P. 2008. Land clearing and the biofuel carbon debt. *Science* 319:1235–38

Hayami Y, Ruttan VW. 1971. Induced innovation and agricultural development. Staff Pap. Ser. 71, Dep. Agric. Appl. Econ., Univ. Minn., St-Paul

Hamelinck CN, Faaij A. 2006. Outlook for advanced biofuels. *Energy Policy* 34(17): 3268–83

Hertel TW. 1997. *Global Trade Analysis: Modeling and Applications.* Cambridge, UK: Cambridge Univ. Press

Hertel TW, Rose S, Tol RSJ, eds. 2009a. *Economic Analysis of Land Use in Global Change Policy.* New York: Routledge

Hertel TW, Tyner WE, Birur D. 2009b. Biofuels for all? Understanding the global impacts of multinational mandates. In *Economic Analysis of Land-Use in Global Climate Change Policy*, ed. TW Hertel, S Rose, RSJ Tol. New York: Routledge

Hochman G, Sexton SE, Zilberman D. 2008. The economics of biofuel policy and biotechnology. *J. Agric. Food Ind. Organ.* 6(8):1–22

IIASA. 2009. *Biofuels and Food Security: Implications of an Accelerated Biofuels Production.* Vienna: Int. Inst. Appl. Syst. Anal.

IEA. 2006. *World Outlook 2006.* Paris: Int. Energy Agency

IEA. 2007. *World Outlook 2007.* Paris: Int. Energy Agency

IEA. 2009. *From 1st to 2nd Generation Technologies.* Paris: Int. Energy Agency

Keeney R, Hertel TW. 2008. *The indirect land-use impacts of U.S. biofuels policies: the importance of acreage, yield and bilateral trade response.* GTAP Work. Pap. 52, Purdue Univ.

Khanna M. 2008. Cellulosic biofuels: Are they economically viable and environmentally sustainable? *Choices* 23(3):16–21

Khanna M. 2009. *Transition to a bioeconomy: environmental and rural development impacts.* Proc. Farm Found./USDA Conf., St. Louis, Mo. http://www.farmfoundation.org

Khanna M, Hochman G, Rajgopal D, Sexton SE, Zilberman D. 2009. Sustainability of food, energy and environment with biofuels. *CAB Rev. Perspect. Agric. Vet. Sci. Nutr. Nat. Resour.* 4(28): In press

Khanna M, Scheffran J, Zilberman D, eds. 2009. *Handbook of Biofuels Economics and Policy.* New York: Springer. In press

Kojima M, Mitchell D, Ward W. 2007. *Considering Trade Policy for Liquid Biofuels.* Washington, DC: World Bank Energy Syst. Manag. Assist. Program

Lasco C, Khanna M. 2009. US-Brazil trade in biofuels: determinants, constraints and implications for trade policy. See Khanna et al. 2009. In press

Lee H-L, Hertel TW, Sohngen B, Ramankutty N. 2005. *Towards an integrated land-use database for assessing the potential for greenhouse gas mitigation.* GTAP Tech. Pap. 25, Cent. Glob. Trade Anal., Purdue Univ.

Martin A. 2008. Fuel choices, food prices and finger-pointing. *New York Times*, Mar. 15, pp. B1, B6

McDougall RM, Golub A. 2008. *A revised energy-environmental version of the GTAP model.* GTAP Tech. Pap., Cent. Glob. Trade Anal., Purdue Univ.

Msangi S, Sulser T, Rosegrant M, Valmonte-Santos R, Ringler C. 2007. *Global Scenarios for Biofuels: Impacts and Implications.* Washington, DC: Int. Food Policy Res. Inst.

OECD. 2008. Economic assessment of support biofuels policies. *Organ. Econ. Coop. Dev. Draft Rep.*, Paris

Paltsev S, Reilly J, Jacoby H, Eckaus R, McFarland J, et al. 2005, The MIT Emissions Predictions and Policy Analysis (EPPA) model: Version 4. *MIT Rep. 125*, Joint Program Sci. Policy Glob. Change, Cambridge, MA. http://web.mit.edu/globalchange/www/MITJPSPGC_Rpt125.pdf

Peña N. 2008. *Biofuels for transportation: a climate perspective.* Solut. White Pap., Pew Cent. Clim. Change

Rajagopal D, Zilberman D. 2007. *Review of environmental, economic, and policy aspects of biofuels.* Policy Res. Work. Pap. 4341, World Bank

Reilly J, Paltsev S. 2009. Biomass energy and competition for land. See Hertel et al. 2009a, ch. 8

Ryan L, Convery F, Ferreira S. 2006. Stimulating the use of biofuels in the European Union: implications for climate change policy. *Energy Policy* 34:3184–94

Schneider UA, McCarl B. 2003. Economic potential of biomass based fuels for greenhouse gas emission mitigation. *Environ. Resour. Econ.* 24:291–312

Searchinger T, Heimlich R, Houghton RA, Dong F, Elobeid J, et al. 2008. Use of U.S. croplands for biofuels increases greenhouse gas through emissions from land-use change. *Science* 319:1238–40

Seauner B. 2008. Food market effects of a global resource shift toward bioenergy. *Am. J. Agric. Econ.* 90(5):1226–32

Taheripour F, Tyner W. 2007. *Ethanol subsidies: Who gets the benefits?* Work. Pap., Purdue Univ.

The Economist. 2007. Food prices: cheap no more. *Economist*, Dec. 6, http://www.economist.com/printedition/displayStory.cfm?Story_ID=10250420

Thompson W, Meyer S, Westhoff P. 2009. *Potential for uncertainty about indirect effects of ethanol on land-use in the case of Brazil.* Work. Pap., Univ. Mo., Columbia

Wiebe K, ed. 2003. *Land Quality, Agricultural Productivity, and Food Security.* Cheltenham, UK/Northampton, MA: Edward Elgar

Yacobucci BD, Schnepf R. 2007. Ethanol and biofuels: agriculture, infrastructure, and market constraints related to expanded production. *CRS Rep. RL33928*, Natl. Counc. Sci. Environ., Washington, DC

The Economics of Genetically Modified Crops

Matin Qaim

Department of Agricultural Economics and Rural Development,
Georg-August-University of Goettingen, 37073 Goettingen, Germany;
email: mqaim@uni-goettingen.de

Annu. Rev. Resour. Econ. 2009. 1:665–93

First published online as a Review in Advance on
June 26, 2009

The *Annual Review of Resource Economics* is
online at resource.annualreviews.org

This article's doi:
10.1146/annurev.resource.050708.144203

Key Words

agricultural biotechnology, consumer acceptance, impacts,
regulation, technology adoption

Abstract

Genetically modified (GM) crops have been used commercially for
more than 10 years. Available impact studies of insect-resistant and
herbicide-tolerant crops show that these technologies are beneficial
to farmers and consumers, producing large aggregate welfare gains
as well as positive effects for the environment and human health.
The advantages of future applications could even be much bigger.
Given a conducive institutional framework, GM crops can contribute significantly to global food security and poverty reduction.
Nonetheless, widespread public reservations have led to a complex
system of regulations. Overregulation has become a real threat for
the further development and use of GM crops. The costs in terms
of foregone benefits may be large, especially for developing
countries. Economics research has an important role to play in
designing efficient regulatory mechanisms and agricultural innovation systems.

1. INTRODUCTION

A genetically modified (GM) crop is a plant used for agricultural purposes into which one or several genes coding for desirable traits have been inserted through the process of genetic engineering. These genes may stem not only from the same or other plant species, but also from organisms totally unrelated to the recipient crop. The basic techniques of plant genetic engineering were developed in the early 1980s, and the first GM crops became commercially available in the mid-1990s. Since then, GM crop adoption has increased rapidly. In 2008, GM crops were being grown on 9% of the global arable land (James 2008).

The crop traits targeted through genetic engineering are not completely different from those pursued by conventional breeding. However, because genetic engineering allows for the direct gene transfer across species boundaries, some traits that were previously difficult or impossible to breed can now be developed with relative ease. Three categories of GM traits can be distinguished: First-generation GM crops involve improvements in agronomic traits, such as better resistance to pests and diseases. Second-generation GM crops involve enhanced quality traits, such as higher nutrient contents of food products. Third-generation crops are plants designed to produce special substances for pharmaceutical or industrial purposes.

The potentials of GM crops are manifold. Against the background of a dwindling natural resource base, productivity increases in global agriculture are important to ensure sufficient availability of food and other raw materials for a growing population (von Braun 2007). GM crops can also bring about environmental benefits. Furthermore, new seed technologies have, in the past, played an important role for rural income growth and poverty alleviation in developing countries (e.g., Hazell & Ramasamy 1991, Fan et al. 2005). These effects are also expected for GM crops (FAO 2004). Finally, nutritionally enhanced crops could help improve the health status of consumers (e.g., Bouis 2007, Unnevehr et al. 2007).

In spite of these potentials, the development and use of GM crops have aroused significant opposition. Public reservations are particularly strong in Europe, but they have also spilled over to other countries and regions through trade regulations, public media, and outreach efforts of antibiotech lobbying groups (e.g., Pinstrup-Andersen & Schioler 2001, Miller & Conko 2004, Herring 2007, Paarlberg 2008). The major concerns are related to potential environmental and health risks, but there are also fears about adverse social implications (e.g., Altieri 2001, Friends of the Earth 2008). For instance, some believe that GM technology could undermine traditional knowledge systems in developing countries. Given the increasing privatization of crop improvement research and proliferation of intellectual property rights (IPRs), there are also concerns about the potential monopolization of seed markets and exploitation of smallholder farmers (e.g., Sharma 2004).

Because GM crops are associated with new potentials and issues, their emergence has also triggered substantial research dealing with economic and policy aspects. This article reviews the available research on the economics of GM crops. Section 2 gives a brief overview of the status of commercialized GM crops and expected trends for the future. Then, work related to the analysis of impacts at the micro and macro level is discussed. Whereas Sections 3 and 4 address impacts of first-generation GM applications, Section 5 refers to second-generation crops from an ex ante perspective. Sections 6 and 7 focus on consumer acceptance and the economics of regulation, including aspects of biosafety as well as food labeling and IPRs. In the concluding section, policy and research implications are discussed.

2. STATUS OF GM CROPS

2.1. Commercialized GM Crops

The commercial application of GM crops began in the mid-1990s. Since then, the technology has spread rapidly around the world, both in industrialized and developing countries (**Figure 1**). In 2008, GM crops were being grown on 125 million ha in 25 countries. The countries with the biggest share of the GM crop area were the United States (50%), Argentina (17%), Brazil (13%), India (6%), Canada (6%), and China (3%) (James 2008). Strikingly, among the countries of the European Union (EU), only Spain grows GM crops on a significant scale. Although a few other EU countries have approved individual GM technologies, the commercial area is still negligible, because of public-acceptance problems and unfavorable regulatory frameworks.

In spite of the widespread international use of GM crops, the portfolio of available crop-trait combinations is still very limited. At present, only a few first-generation technologies have been commercialized. The dominant technology is herbicide tolerance (HT) in soybeans, which made up 53% of the global GM crop area in 2008. HT soybeans are currently grown mostly in the United States, Argentina, Brazil, and other South American countries. This technology accounts for 70% of worldwide soybean production.

GM maize is the second-most dominant crop and covered 30% of the global GM area and 24% of total maize production in 2008 (James 2008). GM maize involves HT and insect resistance, partly as separate and partly also as stacked technologies. Insect resistance is based on different genes from the soil bacterium *Bacillus thuringiensis* (Bt). These Bt genes control the European corn borer, the corn rootworm, and different stemborers (Romeis et al. 2008). Bt maize is grown mostly in North and South America, but it is also planted to a significant extent in South Africa and the Philippines.

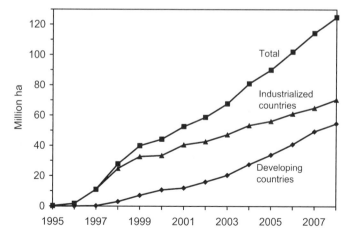

Figure 1

Development of the global area using genetically modified crops (1995–2008).
Source: James (2008).

GM crops with significant area shares also include cotton and canola. Bt cotton with resistance to bollworms and budworms is particularly relevant in developing countries. In 2008, India had the largest Bt cotton area with 7.6 million ha, followed by China with 3.8 million ha. South Africa, Argentina, Mexico, and a few other countries use this technology as well. In the United States, Bt and HT cotton are employed, partly with stacked genes. Until now, HT canola was grown mostly in Canada and the United States. A few other GM crops, including HT alfalfa and sugarbeet as well as virus-resistant papaya and squash, have been approved in individual countries, so far covering only relatively small areas.

2.2. GM Crops in the Pipeline

A couple of GM technologies previously developed for food crops either were never commercialized or were withdrawn from the market because of consumer-acceptance and marketing problems. Examples include Bt and virus-resistant potato as well as HT wheat. Yet, such technologies may be reintroduced, should public acceptance improve. A number of other GM crop technologies that provide insect resistance or HT are ready to be commercialized. For instance, Bt rice has been field tested extensively in China and other countries (Huang et al. 2005, Cohen et al. 2008). Different Bt vegetables—including eggplant, cauliflower, and cabbage—are likely to be commercialized soon in India and other countries in Asia and Africa (Krishna & Qaim 2007, Shelton et al. 2008). HT rice is also in a relatively advanced phase within the research and development (R&D) pipeline (Hareau et al. 2006).

Other first-generation GM technologies that are being developed include fungal, bacterial, and virus resistance in major cereal as well as root and tuber crops (Halford 2006). Their market introduction can be expected in the short to medium run. Plant tolerance to abiotic stress—such as drought, heat, and salt—is also being worked on intensively. Yet, because the underlying genetic mechanisms are complex, the work is at a more basic level, so significant commercial releases can be expected only in the medium run (Herdt 2006, Ramasamy et al. 2007).

Second-generation GM technologies in the pipeline include product quality improvements for nutrition and industrial purposes. Examples are oilseeds with improved fatty acid profiles; high-amylose maize; staple foods with enhanced contents of essential amino acids, minerals, and vitamins; and GM functional foods with diverse health benefits (Jefferson-Moore & Traxler 2005, Pew Initiative on Food and Biotechnology 2007).

Enhancing food crops with higher nutrient contents through conventional or GM breeding is also called biofortification. A well-known example of a GM biofortified crop is Golden Rice, which contains significant amounts of provitamin A. Golden Rice could become commercially available in some Asian countries by 2012 (Stein et al. 2006, Potrykus 2008). Other biofortification projects include the development of GM sorghum, cassava, banana, and rice enhanced with multiple nutrients (Qaim et al. 2007). Such crops may become commercially available over the next 5–10 years.

Third-generation GM crops involve molecular farming where the crop is used to produce either pharmaceuticals such as monoclonal antibodies and vaccines or industrial products such as enzymes and biodegradable plastics (Moschini 2006, Halford 2006). Although concepts have been proven for a number of these technologies, product development and regulatory aspects are even more complex than they are for first- and second-generation crops. Substances produced in the plants must be guaranteed not to enter the regular food chain with a zero-tolerance threshold. Therefore, plants that are not used for food and feed purposes will likely be chosen for product development, or approvals for third-generation GM crops will be given for use under contained conditions only. In either case, this brief overview reveals that the GM crops available so far represent only a very small fraction of the large future potentials of plant genetic engineering.

3. MICROLEVEL IMPACTS OF FIRST-GENERATION GM CROPS

Because HT and insect-resistant Bt crops have already been used for a number of years, numerous microlevel impact studies have been carried out in different countries. Many such studies are based on random sample surveys, comparing the performance of adopters and nonadopters of GM crops (Kalaitzandonakes 2003, Naseem & Pray 2004, Qaim 2005, Gandhi & Namboodiri 2006). However, such with-without comparisons can be associated with a selectivity bias. On the one hand, if adopting farmers are more skillful than their nonadopting counterparts, the net technological impacts may be overestimated, because the group of adopters may show better performance even without GM technology. On the other hand, if the technology is adopted only by farmers under specific conditions, net impacts may be underestimated. For instance, Bt technology is expected to be particularly beneficial in high pest pressure environments. Therefore, simply comparing the productivity of adopters in high pest pressure environments with that of nonadopters in low pest pressure environments would lead to a downward bias in impact assessment.

Different approaches have been used to reduce a potential selectivity bias. For instance, some authors have observed developments over time, involving several rounds of data collection (e.g., Pray et al. 2002, Sadashivappa & Qaim 2009). Others have combined survey data of GM farmers with calculations of what would have been without technology adoption (e.g., Gianessi et al. 2002, Brookes & Barfoot 2008). In addition, within-farm comparisons have been made in situations where adopting farmers continued to use conventional crops on part of their land (e.g., Qaim & de Janvry 2005). Econometric approaches to deal with selectivity issues are explained below.

3.1. Farm-Level Impacts of HT Crops

HT crops are tolerant to certain broad-spectrum herbicides such as glyphosate and glufosinate, which are more effective, less toxic, and usually cheaper than selective herbicides. Accordingly, farmers who adopt HT technology benefit in terms of lower herbicide expenditures. Total herbicide quantities applied were reduced in some situations, but not in others. In Argentina, herbicide quantities were increased significantly (Qaim & Traxler 2005), in large part owing to the fact that herbicide sprays were substituted for tillage. In Argentina, the share of soybean farmers using no-till doubled to almost 90% since the introduction of HT technology (Trigo & Cap 2006), whereas in the United States and Canada, no-till practices expanded through HT adoption (Kalaitzandonakes 2003, Fernandez-Cornejo & Caswell 2006). In terms of the yields achieved, no significant difference between HT and conventional crops is seen in most cases. Only in a few examples when certain weeds were difficult to control with selective herbicides did the adoption of HT and the switch to broad-spectrum herbicides result in better weed control and higher crop yields. These include HT soybeans in Romania and HT maize in Argentina (Brookes & Barfoot 2008).

Overall, HT technology reduces the cost of production through lower expenditures for herbicides, labor, machinery, and fuel. Yet, because HT crops were developed and commercialized by private companies, a technology fee is charged on seeds, which varies among crops as well as countries. Several early studies for HT soybeans in the United States showed that the fee was of a similar magnitude or sometimes higher than the average cost reduction, so that gross margin effects were small or partly negative (e.g., Duffy 2001, Fernandez-Cornejo et al. 2002). Comparable results were also obtained for HT cotton and HT canola in the United States and Canada (Fulton & Keyowski 1999, Marra et al. 2002, Phillips 2003, Naseem & Pray 2004). The main reasons for farmers in such situations to continue using HT technologies were easier weed control and savings in terms of management time. Fernandez-Cornejo et al. (2005) showed that the saved management time for U.S. soybean farmers translated in part into higher off-farm incomes. Moreover, farmers are heterogeneous, such that many adopters have benefited in spite of zero or negative mean gross margin effects. The average farm-level profits seem to increase over time, partly as a result of seed-price adjustments and farmer-learning effects.

In South American countries, the average gross margin effects of HT crops, especially HT soybeans, are larger than in North America (Trigo & Cap 2006). While the agronomic advantages are similar, the fee charged on seeds is lower, as HT technology is not patented there. Many soybean farmers in South America use farm-saved GM seeds. Qaim & Traxler (2005) showed that the average gross margin gains through HT soybean adoption are in a magnitude of more than $20 per ha for Argentina.

3.2. Farm-Level Impacts of Bt Crops

Insect-resistant Bt crops have different effects than do HT crops. Bt crops produce proteins that are toxic to larvae of some lepidopteran and coleopteran insect species. Therefore, Bt is a pest-control agent that can be used as a substitute for chemical insecticides. Following Lichtenberg & Zilberman (1986) and Zilberman et al. (2004), this can be expressed in a damage-control framework:

$$Y = F(x)[1 - D(z, Bt; N)],$$

where Y is the effective crop yield, and $F(\cdot)$ is potential yield without insect damage, which depends on variable inputs, x. $D(\cdot)$ is the damage function determining the fraction of potential output being lost to insect pests; it can take values in the 0–1 interval. Crop losses depend on exogenous pest pressure, N, and they can be reduced through the application of chemical insecticides, z, and/or the use of Bt technology. If pest pressure is high and farmers use a lot of chemical insecticides in the conventional crop, Bt adoption should lead to substantial insecticide reductions.[1] However, Bt technology can also impact effective crop yields. Even though the Bt gene does not affect potential yield, $F(\cdot)$, it can lead to a reduction in crop losses, $D(\cdot)$, when there is previously uncontrolled pest damage, thus leading to a higher Y.

---

[1]Pemsl et al. (2008) pointed out that natural pest-control agents such as beneficial insects could also reduce crop losses but that these are often suppressed through chemical insecticides. Therefore, even without Bt, a reduction in chemical insecticides may be possible in specific situations. However, compared with chemical insecticides, Bt is much less harmful to beneficial insects (Shelton et al. 2009).

Insecticide reduction and yield effects are closely related: Farmers who use small amounts of insecticides in their conventional crop in spite of high pest pressure will realize a sizeable yield effect through Bt adoption, whereas the insecticide reduction effect will dominate in situations when farmers initially use higher amounts of chemical inputs. The same principles also hold for other pest-resistant GM crops. In general, yield effects will be more pronounced in developing rather than in developed countries, because pest pressure is often higher in the tropics and subtropics and resource-poor farmers face more severe constraints in chemical pest control (Qaim & Zilberman 2003).

3.2.1. Empirical evidence. The Bt-insecticide-yield linkages are diagrammed in **Figure 2** using field trial data with Bt cotton in India. As shown, Bt does not completely eliminate the need for insecticide sprays because some crop damage still occurs when the technology is used. The reason is that Bt toxins are very specific to certain pest species, whereas other insect pests, especially sucking pests, remain unaffected.

What do the agronomic impacts look like under practical farmer conditions? **Table 1** confirms that both insecticide-reducing and yield-increasing effects can be observed internationally. Yield effects of Bt cotton are highest in Argentina and India. For Argentina, the explanation is simple: Conventional cotton farmers underutilize chemical insecticides, so that insect pests are not effectively controlled (Qaim & de Janvry 2005). In India, however, insecticide use in conventional cotton is much higher (Qaim et al. 2006). This suggests that factors other than insecticide quantity influence damage control in conventional cotton and, thus, the yield effects of Bt technology. These factors include insecticide quality, insecticide resistance, and the correct choice of products and timing of sprays.

For Bt maize, similar effects are observable, albeit generally at a lower magnitude (**Table 1**). Except for Spain, where the percentage reduction in insecticide use is large, the more important result of the use of Bt maize is an increase in effective yields. In the United States, for instance, Bt maize is used mainly against the European corn borer, which is not

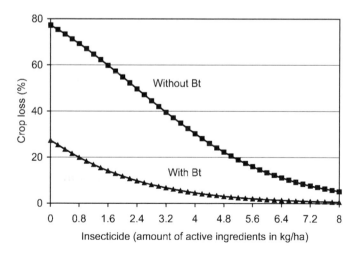

Figure 2

Relationship between insecticide use and cotton crop losses with and without Bt in India.
Source: Qaim & Zilberman (2003).

Table 1 Average farm-level agronomic and economic effects of Bt crops

Country	Insecticide reduction (%)	Increase in effective yield (%)	Increase in gross margin (US$/ha)	Reference(s)
Bt cotton				
Argentina	47	33	23	Qaim & de Janvry 2003, 2005
Australia	48	0	66	Fitt 2003
China	65	24	470	Pray et al. 2002
India	41	37	135	Qaim et al. 2006, Sadashivappa & Qaim 2009
Mexico	77	9	295	Traxler et al. 2003
South Africa	33	22	91	Thirtle et al. 2003, Gouse et al. 2004
United States	36	10	58	Falck-Zepeda et al. 2000b, Carpenter et al. 2002
Bt maize				
Argentina	0	9	20	Brookes & Barfoot 2005
Philippines	5	34	53	Brookes & Barfoot 2005, Yorobe & Quicoy 2006
South Africa	10	11	42	Brookes & Barfoot 2005, Gouse et al. 2006
Spain	63	6	70	Gómez-Barbero et al. 2008
United States	8	5	12	Naseem & Pray 2004, Fernandez-Cornejo & Li 2005

often controlled by chemical means (Carpenter et al. 2002).[2] In Argentina and South Africa, mean yield effects are higher because pest pressure is more severe than it is in temperate climates. The average yield gain of 11% shown in **Table 1** for South Africa refers to large commercial farms. These farms have been growing yellow Bt maize hybrids for several years. Gouse et al. (2006) analyzed on-farm trials that were carried out with smallholder farmers and white Bt maize hybrids in South Africa. They found average yield gains of 32% on Bt plots. In the Philippines, average yield advantages are 34%.

Preliminary evidence based on field-trial observations also exists for other Bt crops. Huang et al. (2005) observed high insecticide reductions but relatively small yield effects for Bt rice in China, whereas Krishna & Qaim (2008b) reported significant insecticide and yield effects for Bt eggplant in India.

---

[2]More recently, a different Bt maize technology has been commercialized in the United States to control the corn rootworm complex, against which significant amounts of chemical insecticides are used in conventional agriculture. However, representative studies on the impacts of this new Bt maize technology under farmer conditions are not available.

3.2.2. Econometric estimates. Econometric analyses with different model specifications confirm the net insecticide-reducing and yield-increasing effects of Bt technology. For Bt maize, Fernandez-Cornejo & Li (2005) provided estimates for the United States, and Yorobe & Quicoy (2006) did so for the Philippines. More studies are available for Bt cotton: Huang et al. (2002a) employed an insecticide-use model and a production function with a damage-control specification to estimate the effects in China. A similar analysis was done by Qaim & de Janvry (2005) in Argentina. Bennett et al. (2006) estimated Cobb-Douglas-type production functions for a sample of farmers in India.

Qaim et al. (2006) also estimated productivity effects of Bt cotton in India, differentiating between Bt gene and germplasm effects. They showed that part of the impact variability observed in India during the first years of adoption was due to the incorporation of the Bt gene in only a few cotton varieties that were not suitable for all locations. In such situations, a yield drift can be observed; that is, the positive Bt gene effect is counteracted by a negative germplasm effect. This underlines the finding that the benefits of GM can be fully realized only when the technology is inserted into a number of locally adapted varieties.

Thirtle et al. (2003) used a stochastic frontier approach with data from farmers in South Africa to show that Bt adoption helps to increase the technical efficiency of cotton production in the small-farm sector. Kambhampati et al. (2006) did a similar analysis for India. Many of these econometric analyses used instrumental variable approaches to avoid or reduce selectivity issues and problems of endogeneity. One study by Crost et al. (2007) also used panel data techniques for the estimation of Bt productivity effects.

3.2.3. Gross margin effects. The gross margin effects of Bt technologies are also shown in **Table 1**. In all countries noted, Bt-adopting farmers benefit; that is, the economic advantages associated with insecticide savings and higher effective yields more than outweigh the technology fee charged on GM seeds. The absolute gains differ remarkably among countries and crops. On average, the gross margin gains are higher for Bt cotton than for Bt maize, and they are also higher in developing as opposed to developed countries. In addition to agroecological and socioeconomic differences, the GM seed costs are often lower in developing countries, owing to weaker IPRs, seed reproduction by farmers, subsidies, or other types of government price interventions (Basu & Qaim 2007, Sadashivappa & Qaim 2009).

Agricultural policies are also partly responsible for the different gross margin effects. For instance, in the United States, China, and Mexico, the cotton sector is subsidized, which encourages intensive production schemes and high overall yields. The situation is similar for maize in Spain. By contrast, Argentinean farmers are not subsidized; instead, they face world-market prices. Especially for cotton, world-market prices have been declining over the past 10 years, thus eroding the economic benefits resulting from technological yield gains. Furthermore, within countries, farmer conditions are heterogeneous so that the effects are variable (Qaim et al. 2006, Pemsl & Waibel 2007).

3.3. Poverty and Distribution Effects

Seventy-five percent of all poor people in the world are smallholder farmers or rural laborers. Therefore, GM crops may also have important implications for poverty and income distribution in developing countries. If only rich farmers were to benefit, inequality would increase. Yet, if resource-poor farmers could access GM crops suitable for their situations, the poverty and equity effects may be positive. Apart from technological characteristics, this also depends on the institutional setting at national and local levels (Qaim et al. 2000, Evenson et al. 2002). For instance, strong IPRs and high seed prices as well as information, credit, and infrastructure constraints can hinder poor farmers' proper access to GM seeds, even if the underlying technology is suitable for smallholder agriculture (e.g., Qaim & de Janvry 2003, Thirtle et al. 2003, Qaim 2005, Edmeades & Smale 2006).

So far, HT crops have not been widely adopted in the small-farm sector. Smallholders often weed manually, so that HT crops are inappropriate, unless labor shortages or weeds that are difficult to control justify conversion to chemical practices. The situation is very different for Bt crops. Especially in China, India, and South Africa, Bt cotton is often grown by farms with less than 3 ha of land (Huang et al. 2002a,b; Qaim et al. 2008). In South Africa, many smallholders grow Bt white maize as their staple food (Gouse et al. 2006). Several studies show that Bt technology advantages for small-scale farmers are of a similar magnitude as those of larger-scale producers. In some cases, the advantages can be even greater (Pray et al. 2001, Morse et al. 2004, Qaim et al. 2008).[3]

However, few studies exist that have analyzed wider socioeconomic outcomes, including effects on rural employment and household incomes. This dearth of broader microlevel research may be the reason for the ongoing controversy surrounding the poverty and rural development implications of GM crops. Subramanian & Qaim (2009a,b) provide the first comprehensive work in this direction. Building on a village social accounting matrix and multiplier model, they examined direct and indirect effects of Bt cotton adoption in India. Their results show that the technology is employment generating, especially for hired female agricultural laborers, which is due to significantly higher yields in need of harvesting. The technology also generates employment in other sectors linked to cotton production, e.g., trade and services.

Simulated impacts on household incomes are shown in **Figure 3**. Each additional hectare of Bt cotton produces 82% higher aggregate incomes than are obtained from conventional cotton, implying a remarkable gain in overall economic welfare through technology adoption in India. For landless households, the positive income effects are relatively small. More female employment for cotton harvesting is counteracted by less male employment for spraying operations. However, all types of farm households—including those below the poverty line—benefit considerably more from Bt than from conventional cotton. These findings demonstrate that GM crops can contribute significantly to poverty reduction and rural development, when they are suited to the small-farm sector and embedded in a conducive institutional environment.

3.4. Environmental and Health Effects

In addition to the economic and social impacts of GM crops, there are also environmental and health implications. In the public debate, potential environmental risks, such as undesirable gene flow or impacts on nontarget organisms, are often in the fore. Food safety concerns are also raised. Shelton et al. (2009), Weaver & Morris (2005), and

---

[3]Especially for India, biotech critics still report that Bt cotton ruins smallholder farmers. However, such reports do not build on representative data (Qaim et al. 2006, 2008). Gruère et al. (2008) showed that the occasional claim of a link between Bt cotton adoption and farmer suicides cannot be substantiated.

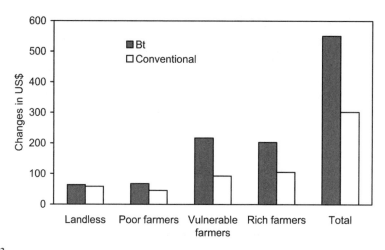

Figure 3

Household income effects of Bt cotton compared with conventional cotton in India. The results are based on simulations with a social accounting matrix and multiplier model for a typical cotton-growing village in the Indian state of Maharashtra. Two simulations were run, both considering an expansion in the village cotton area by 1 ha. The first scenario assumes that the additional hectare is cultivated with Bt cotton, whereas the second assumes that it is cultivated with conventional cotton. Accordingly, differences between the two scenarios can be interpreted as net impacts of Bt technology adoption. Adapted from Subramanian & Qaim (2009a).

Bradford et al. (2005) have reviewed such risks, concluding that most are not specific to the technique of genetic modification but would be present for any conventionally produced crops with the same heritable traits. Although potential risks need to be further analyzed and managed, GM crops can also induce substantial environmental and health benefits.

3.4.1. Environmental benefits. Adoption of HT crops does not lead to reductions in herbicide quantities in most cases, but selective herbicides, which are often relatively toxic to the environment, are substituted by much less toxic broad-spectrum herbicides. Moreover, tillage operations are cut and no-till practices expanded, helping to reduce soil erosion, fuel use, and greenhouse gas emissions (Qaim & Traxler 2005, Brookes & Barfoot 2008).

For Bt crops, the main environmental benefits are related to reductions in chemical insecticide applications. Reductions in pesticide use have been particularly significant in cotton, the most pesticide-consuming crop worldwide. Brookes & Barfoot (2008) estimated that between 1996 and 2006 Bt cotton was responsible for global savings of 128 million kg of pesticide active ingredients, reducing the environmental impact of total cotton pesticides by 25%. **Figure 4** shows that Bt adoption leads to overproportional reductions in the most toxic insecticides.

In the first years of Bt crop deployment, it was predicted that insect populations would soon develop Bt resistance, which would undermine the technology's effectiveness and lead to declining insecticide reductions over time. However, until now, Bt resistance has not been observed under field conditions, which may be due to successful resistance management strategies, such as the planting of non-Bt refuges (Hurley et al. 2001, Bates et al. 2005). In countries where no such strategies are implemented, Bt resistance has also not been reported. However, other factors can lead to changes in Bt effects over time.

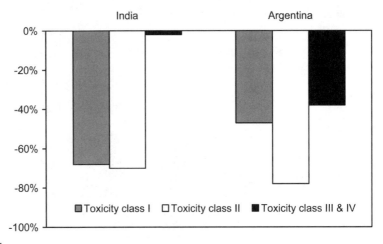

Figure 4

Insecticide reductions through Bt cotton by toxicity class. Results are based on within-farm comparisons obtained from surveys in different cotton-growing regions of India and Argentina. Following the
international classification of pesticides, toxicity class I comprises the most toxic products, whereas
toxicity class IV comprises the least toxic products. Based on data from Qaim & Zilberman (2003),
Qaim et al. (2006), and Qaim & de Janvry (2005).

In China, for instance, insecticide applications increased again after several years of Bt
cotton use, in spite of the absence of Bt resistance. Wang et al. (2006) attributed this to
secondary pests, which may have become more important through the Bt-induced reduction in broad-spectrum insecticides. Their analysis, however, was based on only one year
of observations with increased insecticide applications, making conclusive statements premature (Hu et al. 2006). Using data collected over a period of five years, Sadashivappa &
Qaim (2009) did not find any evidence of secondary-pest outbreaks in India.

GM crops may also help preserve agrobiodiversity. Conventional breeding leads to new
crop varieties. If a particular new variety produces a large productivity gain, it may spread
widely, potentially replacing a large number of older varieties and landraces. This occurred to some extent during the Green Revolution in Asia (Cooper et al. 2005). Developing additional conventional varieties with similar characteristics can be a long and costly
process. In contrast, the development of GM traits through genetic engineering can be
backcrossed at moderate costs into numerous varieties.[4] Therefore, instead of replacing
local varieties, GM versions of these varieties can be made available. Indeed, in most
countries where GM technologies have been commercialized, a large number of varieties
carrying specific GM traits can be observed (e.g., Qaim 2005, Trigo & Cap 2006, Qaim
et al. 2008). More than a technical question, the impact of GM technologies on varietal
diversity depends on the design of IPR and biosafety policies, breeding capacities, and
other institutional conditions (Zilberman et al. 2007).

3.4.2. Health benefits. GM crops, especially Bt crops, are also associated with health
benefits. Direct health advantages for farmers are a result of less insecticide exposure

---

[4]This is also one reason why genetic engineering is a complementary tool and not a substitute for conventional
breeding. GM traits will always have to be incorporated into locally adjusted germplasm.

during spraying operations. Often, the health hazards for farmers applying pesticides are greater in developing as opposed to developed countries because environmental and health regulations are more lax, most pesticides are applied manually, and farmers are less educated and less informed about negative side effects. Pray et al. (2001) and Huang et al. (2003) showed that the frequency of pesticide poisonings was significantly lower among Bt cotton adopters than among nonadopters in China. Hossain et al. (2004) used econometric models to establish that this observation is causally related to Bt technology. Bennett et al. (2003) made the same observation for Bt cotton in South Africa, and there is first evidence that similar effects can also be expected for other Bt crops in smallholder agriculture, such as Bt rice in China (Huang et al. 2005, 2008). Using econometric estimates and a cost-of-illness approach, Krishna & Qaim (2008b) projected that Bt eggplant in India may produce farmer health benefits worth approximately $4 million per year.

For consumers, Bt crops can yield health benefits through lower pesticide residues in food and water. Furthermore, in a variety of field studies, Bt maize was shown to contain significantly lower levels of certain mycotoxins, which can cause cancer and other diseases in humans (Wu 2006). Especially in maize, insect damage contributes significantly to mycotoxin contamination. In the United States and other developed countries, maize is carefully inspected, so lower mycotoxin levels may be most responsible for reducing the costs of testing and grading. But in many developing countries, strict mycotoxin inspections are uncommon. In such situations, Bt technology could contribute to lowering the total health burden (Wu 2006, Qaim et al. 2008).

4. MACROLEVEL IMPACTS OF FIRST-GENERATION GM CROPS

Numerous studies using macrolevel economic surplus models have analyzed the broader welfare effects of GM crops. When the market of only one single crop is considered, partial equilibrium models are used, whereas general equilibrium models are employed when indirect effects and spillovers to other markets and sectors are also of interest.

4.1. Partial Equilibrium Approaches

Whenever new crop technologies are adopted on a large scale, the productivity increase will cause the crop's supply curve to shift downward, leading to a change in producer and consumer surplus (Alston et al. 1995). Because most GM technologies currently available have been commercialized by the private sector, technology rents accrued by innovating companies need to be considered (Moschini & Lapan 1997).

Price et al. (2003) estimated that in the late 1990s Bt cotton generated a total annual economic surplus gain of approximately $164 million in the United States, of which 37% was captured by farmers, 18% by consumers, and 45% by the innovating companies. Falck-Zepeda et al. (2000b) also reported similar results. Because Bt cotton adoption in the United States has increased since then, absolute surplus gains are higher today, but relative surplus distribution remains approximately the same (Fernandez-Cornejo & Caswell 2006).

For Bt cotton in China, Pray et al. (2001) estimated economic surplus gains of approximately $140 million in 1999, with only 1.5% going to the innovating companies and the rest captured by farmers. IPR protection in China is weak, and use of farm-saved Bt cottonseeds is widespread. Under these conditions, it is difficult for companies to capture innovation rents. Cotton consumers did not benefit in 1999 because the government controlled output markets, thus preventing a price decrease. Recently, markets have been liberalized, so Chinese consumers now benefit from Bt cotton technology. In India, Bt cotton surplus gains were projected at $315 million for 2005 (Qaim 2003). Because cotton prices there are not fully liberalized, consumer benefits were not considered. Farmers capture two thirds of the overall surplus gains; the rest accrues to biotech and seed companies. Bt cotton in India is commercialized in hybrids, so use of farm-saved seeds is low. Thus, the private sector innovation rent is higher than in China.

For Bt maize in the United States, Wu (2002) estimated a total surplus gain of $334 million in 2001. Approximately half of the gain accrued to producers, followed by industry profits (31%). The consumer share was relatively small. For Bt maize in Spain, Demont & Tollens (2004) calculated welfare gains of approximately $2 million in 2003, of which 60% went to farmers and 40% to seed companies. The relatively low absolute gain is due to the fact that Bt maize in 2003 covered only an area of approximately 25,000 ha. Similar effects were shown during the early years of Bt maize adoption in the Philippines (Yorobe & Quicoy 2006).

A number of studies have examined the partial equilibrium effects of HT soybeans (e.g., Moschini et al. 2000, Falck-Zepeda et al. 2000a, Qaim & Traxler 2005). Most of these studies use multiregion models. Worldwide welfare gains of HT soybeans were on the order of US$1 billion in the late 1990s. Gains have grown since then as a result of increased adoption. At the global level, downstream sectors and consumers are the main beneficiaries, capturing more than 50% of surplus gains. The effects vary strongly by country, however. Within the United States, farmers capture approximately 20% of the national welfare gains versus almost 60% accruing to Monsanto as the innovating company. By contrast, in Argentina, the farmer surplus share is 90%. These differences are largely due to different levels of IPR protection (Qaim & Traxler 2005).

In addition to such ex post studies, ex ante studies for GM crops have also been carried out in different countries. Examples include analyses for Bt maize and different HT crops in the EU (Demont et al. 2004, 2008), HT rice in Uruguay (Hareau et al. 2006), Bt eggplant in India (Krishna & Qaim 2008b), drought-tolerant rice in India and Bangladesh (Ramasamy et al. 2007), and virus- and insect-resistant sweet potato in Kenya (Qaim 2001). These ex ante studies confirm that GM crops can bring about sizeable welfare gains, with distributional effects dependent on IPRs and other institutional conditions.

4.2. General Equilibrium Approaches

Many of the available general equilibrium studies use the multiregion computable general equilibrium (CGE) model and associated database of the Global Trade Analysis Project (Hertel 1997). This model captures the vertical and horizontal linkages between markets within regions and between regions via bilateral trade flows. The results of several global impact studies are summarized in **Table 2**.

Bt cotton adoption entails global welfare gains in the range of $0.7–1.8 billion per year. The differences across studies partly reflect the use of different versions of the basic model. More importantly, however, the assumed technology adoption rates in different regions matter. Because Bt adoption continues to increase, the aggregate welfare gains are increasing too. Most CGE studies for Bt cotton to date found the biggest regional welfare effects occurred in China (e.g., Huang et al. 2004, Frisvold & Reeves 2007), but India, where the technology was commercialized later, has been catching up rapidly. Anderson et al. (2008)

Table 2 Projected global welfare gains from GM crops (CGE model results)[a]

Reference	Crop	Year of study	Annual welfare gain (US$)
Frisvold & Reeves (2007)	Bt cotton	2005	1.4 billion
Elbehri & MacDonald (2004)	Bt cotton	2001	1.8 billion
Anderson & Yao (2003)	Bt cotton	2005	1.4 billion
Anderson et al. (2008)	Bt cotton	2001	0.7 billion
Nielsen & Anderson (2001)	GM oilseeds and maize	—	9.9 million
Anderson & Yao (2003)	GM soybean and maize	—	7.0 billion
Hareau et al. (2005)	Bt rice	—	2.2 billion
Hareau et al. (2005)	Drought-tolerant rice	—	2.5 billion
Hareau et al. (2005)	HT rice	—	2.1 billion
Anderson & Yao (2003)	GM rice	—	2.0 billion

[a]Abbreviations: CGE, computable general equilibrium; GM, genetically modified; HT, herbicide tolerant.

estimate that widespread adoption of Bt cotton in India and other countries of South Asia will result in additional regional welfare gains on the order of $1 billion per year.

Larger international markets result in bigger effects for GM oilseeds and maize. With widespread international adoption of HT and insect resistance in these crops, annual welfare gains could be approximately $10 billion (Nielsen & Anderson 2001). A ban on production and imports by the EU, however, could reduce these global gains by two thirds, because of foregone benefits for domestic consumers and the far-reaching influence of EU policies on international trade flows and production decisions in exporting regions (Tothova & Oehmke 2005).

For GM rice, large global welfare gains are projected as well. For other rice technologies, such as Bt, HT, and drought tolerance, and assuming moderate adoption levels in rice-producing regions, Hareau et al. (2005) estimated global welfare gains of $2.1–2.5 billion per year, with India and China gaining the most. Huang et al. (2004) projected that the welfare gains in China alone could reach over $4 billion when different first-generation GM rice technologies are widely adopted. The studies available to date provide lower bound estimates of the global welfare effects of GM crops, because positive environmental and health externalities have not been properly quantified.

5. POTENTIAL IMPACTS OF SECOND-GENERATION GM CROPS

First-generation GM crops involve direct productivity and income effects, which can be evaluated at the micro level and then integrated into macrolevel modeling approaches. Second-generation crops, which involve enhanced quality attributes, must be evaluated differently. Quality improvements generally lead to a marginal utility increase and a higher willingness to pay (WTP) among consumers. In a market model, this can be represented as an upward shift in the crop's demand function. There are no ex post impact studies available for second-generation GM crops, because such crops have not been widely adopted. However, several authors have carried out conceptual analyses and ex ante simulations of the welfare effects under different conditions in developed countries (e.g., Jefferson-Moore & Traxler 2005, Giannakas & Yiannaka 2008).

In developing countries, the situation is different, especially when looking at technologies that are targeted to the poor, such as biofortified GM crops. Widespread production and consumption of biofortified staple crops could reduce micronutrient deficiencies, improve health outcomes, and provide economic benefits (Bouis 2007). Yet, it is uncertain if they would command higher market prices, because the poor are often not aware of their micronutrient deficiencies and may not be willing or able to pay a quality premium. Therefore, biofortified crops in developing countries may not lead to an upward shift in demand, so social welfare effects must be evaluated differently (Qaim et al. 2007).

Dawe et al. (2002) looked at the potential nutritional effects of Golden Rice by analyzing likely improvements in vitamin A intakes in the Philippines. This approach implicitly builds on a measure of program success that has been used for other micronutrient interventions, namely the achieved reduction in the number of people with micronutrient intakes below a defined threshold. However, since micronutrient intake is not an end in itself but only a means to ensure healthy body functions, it is more appropriate to go further and quantify health outcomes directly. Zimmermann & Qaim (2004) and Stein et al. (2006) suggested an alternative approach in their analyses of the potential health benefits of Golden Rice. They defined the benefit of the technology as the difference in health costs related to vitamin A deficiency with and without Golden Rice.

In their ex ante analysis, Stein et al. (2008) used representative household data from India to show that Golden Rice could reduce the health costs of vitamin A deficiency by up to 60%. They also calculated a high cost-effectiveness of Golden Rice, which compares favorably with other nutrition and health interventions, and a high social rate of return, which compares favorably with other agricultural R&D investments (Qaim et al. 2007). Anderson et al. (2005) used a macro CGE model to simulate the benefits of Golden Rice at the global level. Modeling consumer health effects among the poor as an increase in the productivity of unskilled laborers, they estimated worldwide welfare gains of over $15 billion per year, with most of the benefits accruing in Asia. In China, for instance, Golden Rice was projected to entail a 2% growth in national income (Anderson et al. 2005).

Significant economic and health benefits can also be expected for other biofortified crops, such as iron- and zinc-dense staple foods or crops containing higher amounts of essential amino acids (Qaim et al. 2007). The potentially high cost-effectiveness of biofortification in developing countries is due to the fact that the approach is self-targeting to the poor, with biofortified seeds spreading through existing formal and informal distribution channels. However, possible issues of consumer acceptance must be considered. Especially when no price premium is paid in the output market, suitable strategies to convince farmers to adopt such crops are needed. A combination of quality traits with interesting agronomic traits may be a practicable avenue.

6. CONSUMER ACCEPTANCE OF GM CROPS

In spite of the great potential of GM crops and the benefits that have already materialized, public attitudes toward the technology are often negative, and consumer acceptance remains an issue.[5] Consumer perceptions are often dominated by health, environmental,

---

[5]This is in contrast to pharmaceutical applications of GM technologies, which are widely accepted by the public.

social, and ethical concerns, which are not always based on the best information but which have emerged as important driving forces of biotechnology policies (Miller & Conko 2004, Paarlberg 2008). One reason for the partial acceptance may be that most GM crops now available involve agronomic traits with limited direct benefits to consumers. Consumer acceptance may increase when second-generation, quality-enhanced GM foods or crops with combined agronomic and quality traits are introduced.

Aspects of GM crop acceptance have been widely analyzed in the literature; most studies determine consumers' WTP for GM-free foods or the willingness to accept a discount for GM foods. These findings help us understand the values consumers attach to the GM attribute especially in the absence of observable market data. There are two approaches used for estimating WTP. The first approach involves choice modeling or contingent valuation surveys to obtain stated-preference data from consumers. Most of the available studies for GM crops build on this approach, both in developed (e.g., Lusk 2003, McCluskey et al. 2003, Moon & Balasubramanian 2004) and developing countries (e.g., Kimenju & De Groote 2008, Krishna & Qaim 2008a). The advantage of stated-preference surveys is that representative data can be obtained. The disadvantage, however, is the potential hypothetical bias, as consumers state their preferences without any direct financial implications. The second approach avoids this bias through experimental auctions, although samples are usually smaller and not representative of the total population. The experiments are often designed such that participants bid with real money or are presented with opportunities to exchange a given GM product for a corresponding GM-free product or vice versa. Such experimental auctions have been used for analyzing consumer acceptance in the United States and the EU (e.g., Huffman et al. 2003, Lusk et al. 2006).

Lusk et al. (2005) provide a meta analysis, regressing the WTP results from individual studies on a set of explanatory variables. Across all studies in the analysis, the weighted mean WTP for GM-free products is a premium of 23% more than that for GM products. However, remarkable differences arise. The WTP is significantly higher in Europe than in the United States, and it is significantly lower for processed than for fresh GM foods. Studies using experimental auctions result in a lower WTP for GM-free foods on average. Individual analyses also show a significant influence of consumer characteristics such as age, education, income, or gender, but the direction of the influence is not uniform.

A difference in WTP for GM and GM-free products indicates that many consumers do not consider these options as perfect substitutes. In that case, introducing GM technology would be associated with a negative externality, which would need to be accounted for in welfare economics studies (Giannakas & Fulton 2002, Lapan & Moschini 2004). However, past experience shows that both stated-preference and experimental data do not always correctly predict actual consumer behavior. Moreover, consumer responses are strongly dependent on the type of information available at a certain point (Huffman et al. 2003), so GM acceptance may potentially change rapidly. The public media play an important role. Especially in Europe, media reports about GM crops have been predominantly negative.

In general, available studies suggest that second-generation GM foods will be more acceptable to consumers than first-generation products (Lusk et al. 2005). This supports the hypothesis that GM acceptance levels will rise when quality-enhanced crops with more direct consumer benefits become available. There are also indications that consumers in developing countries have more positive attitudes toward GM food than their counterparts in developed countries (e.g., Kimenju & De Groote 2008, Krishna & Qaim 2008a).

One possible explanation is that they are generally poorer and sometimes food insecure; thus they may be more open to productivity-increasing technologies.

7. ECONOMICS OF GM CROP REGULATION

Because GM crops are associated with several potential market failures, the technology is heavily regulated. For instance, GM crops may be associated with environmental and health externalities, so biosafety and food safety regulations have been put in place. For consumers, the GM characteristic of food products is a credence attribute, indicating that labeling regulations can help to reduce transaction costs and problems of asymmetric information. The development of GM technologies leads to public goods that can easily be reproduced, so IPR protection is needed as an incentive for private sector R&D investments. However, because every regulation is associated with trade-offs, the optimal level should be determined on the basis of solid economics research (Just et al. 2006).

7.1. Biosafety and Food Safety

Governments have an important role in ensuring that novel foods are safe for human consumption and that novel agricultural inputs do not cause major negative impacts on the environment and long-term agricultural production possibilities. Most countries, with the notable exception of the United States, consider GM crops to be novel foods, regardless of the characteristics of their final product. Hence, new laws and institutions to regulate potential biosafety and food safety issues have been established, requiring that GM products be approved before they may be grown in, consumed in, or imported into a country (Herdt 2006). Because approval processes are not internationally harmonized, they have become a major barrier to the spread of GM crops and technologies around the world. For instance, the EU has not yet approved some of the GM maize technologies that are used in the United States and Argentina, which obstructs trade not only in technologies but also in commodity and food markets. In the EU, this is related to public-acceptance problems. In other parts of the world, however, the lack of GM crop approvals is often due to human and financial capital constraints. Smaller developing countries, in particular, have been unable to legislate and operate a biosafety regulatory system to date. This has shut them off from some of the international markets (Pray et al. 2006).

In countries where a biosafety system is in place, most of regulators' efforts are put into preventing the commercialization of products that may harm people or the environment (i.e., type I errors). Often, regulators are extremely cautious, requiring many regulatory trials over a long period of time. However, lengthy biosafety and food safety testing procedures come at a cost. Kalaitzandonakes et al. (2007) estimated the private compliance costs for regulatory approval of a new Bt or HT maize technology in one country at $6–15 million. Commercializing the same technology in other countries will entail additional costs. Beyond these direct regulatory costs, there are indirect costs in terms of foregone benefits (preventing the use of safe products is referred to as type II errors). Pray et al. (2005) estimated that a two-year delay in the approval of Bt cotton in India led to aggregated losses to farmers of more than $100 million.

Such high regulatory costs slow down overall innovation rates. They also impede the commercialization of GM technologies in minor crops and small countries, as markets in such situations are not large enough to justify the fixed-cost investments. Expensive regulations are also difficult to handle by small firms and public sector organizations, thereby contributing to the further concentration of the agricultural biotech industry. Were such lengthy and complex procedures necessary to regulate high-risk products, then the costs involved would be justified. But this does not seem to be the case. Because the use of genetic engineering does not entail unique risks, it is illogical to subject GM crops to a much higher degree of scrutiny than conventionally bred crops (Bradford et al. 2005). The regulatory complexity observed today appears to be the outcome of the politicized public debate and the lobbying success of antibiotech interest groups (Miller & Conko 2004).

Some reform of the GM regulatory framework will be necessary, and economists have an important role in this respect in terms of quantifying costs and benefits. Lichtenberg & Zilberman (1988) suggested a safety rule approach for more efficient pesticide legislation under uncertainty. The same approach could also be useful in the context of GM crops. It combines a probabilistic risk assessment model with a safety rule decision mechanisms that is equivalent to the use of significance levels for statistical decision making (Sexton et al. 2007). The safety rule approach can be employed for cost-benefit or risk-benefit analyses. Hence, transparent criteria and maximization techniques are used to bring science and objectivity to decision-making processes that are often influenced by political economy considerations and a precautionary approach.

7.2. Labeling and Coexistence

Several countries have introduced or considered introducing a food-labeling system. In general, mandatory or voluntary labeling is possible. Mandatory labeling is often used to warn consumers of specific health risks (e.g., cigarettes), whereas voluntary labeling is more common to differentiate products with desirable characteristics for marketing purposes (e.g., organic). Both systems can convey the same information to consumers. Given that only GM products that are considered to be safe are approved for market release, no warning of risks is required on labels. Therefore, the issue is mainly one of heterogeneous consumer preferences, which—from an economics perspective—would be best addressed through voluntary labeling of GM-free products (Golan et al. 2001). The EU, however, has established a mandatory system, which is more costly and can reinforce the notion that GM products are inherently unsafe. The motivation underlying the EU approach is that consumers have a right to know, which is different from the need to know approach in the context of risk communication. Moschini (2008) argued that the right to know approach is too open ended and potentially unbounded, because it can be invoked for virtually anything.

Labeling involves market segregation and a system of identity preservation, which can be quite costly. The cost is negatively correlated with the threshold levels allowed for the adventitious presence of GM material. Again, these thresholds are not related to risks but are a political decision; very low thresholds can lead to prohibitive segregation costs. Giannakas & Fulton (2002) and Lence & Hayes (2005) showed that labeling in general and segregation costs in particular can influence the welfare effects of GM crops significantly. Dissimilar approaches across countries can also lead to serious problems in international trade.

Labeling and segregation are also related to coexistence. The EU, in particular, has established rules to ensure the coexistence of GM crops with conventional and GM farming, which involve a number of technical and legal specifications, from minimum distance requirements for cultivation to liability and insurance measures (Beckmann et al. 2006). The high degrees of complexity, uncertainty, and direct costs associated with these coexistence rules represent clear disincentives for EU farmers to adopt GM crops (Demont & Devos 2008, Breustedt et al. 2008).

7.3. Intellectual Property Rights and Public-Private Partnerships

In the United States and most other developed countries, living organisms and parts thereof have been patentable since the 1980s. This has spurred a tremendous amount of private sector biotechnology research. Nowadays, more than 75% of all patents in agricultural biotechnology are held by the private sector, mostly by a few large multinational corporations (Graff et al. 2003). Although strong patents and other forms of IPRs provide an incentive for private sector R&D, they are associated with higher prices and the usual static welfare losses in monopoly situations. As noted above, the degree of IPR protection in a country has an influence on GM crop adoption and benefit distribution. When GM seed prices are too high, resource-poor farmers face access problems (Qaim & de Janvry 2003). Therefore, the optimal level of IPR protection and enforcement is situation specific (Giannakas 2002).

The proliferation of IPRs on genes, processes, and technologies has led to access and freedom-to-operate problems within the biotechnology industry. Because the development of a single GM crop may require the use of dozens of patented intermediate technologies, licenses have to be negotiated with multiple parties, involving high transaction costs (Santaniello et al. 2000). In that sense, the freedom-to-operate problem may contribute to further industry concentration. Public sector research organizations, in particular, are at a disadvantage because they often have relatively little to offer in return for licenses from private companies. Even the largest public sector patent holders, such as the University of California and the United States Department of Agriculture, own less than 2% of total agricultural biotechnology patents versus the more than 10% owned by individual multinational companies such as Monsanto and DuPont (Graff et al. 2003).

However, public sector organizations combined hold 24% of the patents, and in some areas they could develop GM crops without relying on patents from the private sector. Graff & Zilberman (2001) suggested an IPR clearinghouse mechanism to reduce transaction costs for such public sector collaborations and joint ventures. A working example is the Public Intellectual Property Resource for Agriculture (PIPRA), bringing together intellectual property from more than 40 universities and public agencies and helping make their technologies available to innovators around the world (http://www.pipra.org).

Such public sector initiatives are important, as certain research and technology areas will not be addressed by private companies because of the limited size of the potential markets or other constraints. Examples include technologies designed especially for poor farmers and consumers in developing countries (Qaim et al. 2000, Lipton 2001). In such areas, more public research is needed. Moreover, more public-private partnerships should be sought to harness the comparative strengths of both sectors (Rausser et al. 2000, Byerlee & Fischer 2002). Usually, universities are better suited to carry out basic research, whereas private companies have advantages in more applied research and development

(Rajagopal et al. 2009). There are numerous examples of public-private research cooperation in agricultural biotechnology, but none of these projects has yet led to a commercialized GM crop. Ex ante studies show that well-designed partnerships can be advantageous for all parties involved (Krishna & Qaim 2007, 2008b). Nonetheless, more research is needed to develop best practices for the transfer of technologies and know-how as well as the development and commercialization of GM crops.

8. CONCLUSION

GM crops have been used commercially for more than 10 years. To date, most of the GM crops employed have been HT and insect resistant. Available impact studies show that these crops are beneficial to farmers and consumers and produce large aggregate welfare gains. Moreover, GM crops bring about environmental and health benefits. GM crops may also be well suited for small-scale farmers, because such seed technologies are scale neutral. The empirical evidence shows that Bt crops in particular can have significant income-increasing and poverty-reducing effects. Farmers in developing countries sometimes benefit more than farmers in developed countries, which is partly a result of weaker IPR protection and, thus, lower seed prices. Yet, income distribution effects also depend on the wider institutional setting, including farmers' access to suitable seed varieties, credit, information, and other input and output markets. More public and institutional support will be needed to realize the benefits for the poor on a larger scale.

GM technologies currently in the research pipeline include crops that are tolerant to abiotic stresses and crops that contain higher amounts of nutrients than traditional crops. The benefits of such applications could be much greater than the ones already observed. Against the background of a dwindling natural resource base and growing demand for agricultural products, GM crops could contribute significantly to food security and sustainable development at the global level. New technologies are crucial for the necessary production increases.

In spite of these potentials, public opinion regarding GM crops remains divided, especially in Europe. Concerns about new risks and lobbying efforts of antibiotech groups have led to complex and costly biosafety, food safety, and labeling regulations, which slow down innovation rates and lead to a bias against small countries, minor crops, small firms, and public research organizations. Overregulation has become a real threat for the further development and use of GM crops. The costs of regulation in terms of foregone benefits may be large, especially for developing countries. This is not to say that zero regulation would be desirable, but the trade-offs associated with regulation should be considered. In the public arena, the risks of GM crops seem to be overrated, while the benefits are underrated.

Economics research has an important role to play in finding ways to maximize the net social benefits. More work is needed to quantify possible indirect effects of GM crops, including socioeconomic outcomes as well as environmental and health impacts. Furthermore, economists need to contribute to the design of efficient regulations and innovation systems in light of changing framework conditions. Although the gradual move from public to private crop improvement research is a positive sign of better-functioning markets, certain institutional factors seem to contribute to increasing industry concentration. This could lead to adverse outcomes in terms of technology development and access. Such issues need further analysis.

SUMMARY POINTS

1. GM crops have been used commercially for more than 10 years in developed and developing countries. So far, herbicide-tolerant and insect-resistant Bt crops have been the primary ones employed.

2. Impact studies show that these crops are beneficial to farmers and consumers and produce large aggregate welfare gains. In many cases, farmers in developing countries benefit more than farmers in developed countries.

3. Moreover, GM crops bring about environmental and health benefits. Bt crops in particular allow significant reductions in chemical pesticides.

4. Bt crops can also be suitable for small-scale farmers. Evidence from India and other developing countries shows that they contribute to higher household incomes and poverty reduction, when embedded in a conducive institutional environment.

5. Future GM crop applications, involving tolerance to abiotic stress and higher nutrient contents, may lead to much larger benefits.

6. Against the background of a dwindling natural resource base and growing demand for agricultural products, GM crops can contribute significantly to food security and sustainable development at the global level.

7. In spite of these potentials, public opinion still regards the use of GM crops as controversial. Concerns about new risks have led to complex and costly biosafety, food safety, and labeling regulations.

FUTURE ISSUES

1. Overregulation has become a real threat for the further development and use of GM crops. The costs in terms of foregone benefits may be large, especially for developing countries.

2. Economics research has an important role to play in finding ways to maximize the net social benefits. More work is needed to quantify possible indirect effects of GM crops, including socioeconomic outcomes as well as environmental and health impacts.

3. Furthermore, economists need to contribute to designing efficient regulatory mechanisms and innovation systems.

4. Although the gradual move from public to private crop-improvement research is a positive sign of better-functioning markets, certain institutional factors seem to contribute to increasing industry concentration.

5. Especially with a view to small-scale farmers, more public research and institutional support are needed to complement private sector efforts.

DISCLOSURE STATEMENT

The author is not aware of any affiliations, memberships, funding, or financial holdings that might be perceived as affecting the objectivity of this review.

ACKNOWLEDGMENTS

Constructive comments from David Zilberman and Steve Sexton are gratefully acknowledged. Most of my research related to the economics of GM crops was supported financially by the German Research Foundation (DFG).

LITERATURE CITED

Alston JM, Norton GW, Pardey PG. 1995. *Science Under Scarcity: Principles and Practices of Agricultural Research Evaluation and Priority Setting.* Ithaca, NY: Cornell Univ. Press

Altieri MA. 2001. *Genetic Engineering in Agriculture: The Myths, Environmental Risks and Alternatives.* Oakland, CA: Food First

Anderson K, Valenzuela E, Jackson LA. 2008. Recent and prospective adoption of genetically modified cotton: a global computable general equilibrium analysis of economic impacts. *Econ. Dev. Cult. Change* 56:265–96

Anderson K, Jackson LA, Nielsen CP. 2005. Genetically modified rice adoption: implications for welfare and poverty alleviation. *J. Econ. Integr.* 20:771–88

Anderson K, Yao S. 2003. China, GMOs and world trade in agricultural and textile products. *Pac. Econ. Rev.* 8:157–69

Basu AK, Qaim M. 2007. On the adoption of genetically modified seeds in developing countries and the optimal types of government intervention. *Am. J. Agric. Econ.* 89:784–804

Bates SL, Zhao JZ, Roush RT, Shelton AM. 2005. Insect resistance management in GM crops: past, present and future. *Nat. Biotechnol.* 23:57–62

Beckmann V, Soregaroli C, Wesseler J. 2006. Coexistence rules and regulations in the European Union. *Am. J. Agric. Econ.* 88:1193–99

Bennett R, Morse S, Ismael Y. 2003. Bt cotton, pesticides, labour and health: a case study of smallholder farmers in the Makhathini Flats, Republic of South Africa. *Outlook Agric.* 32:123–28

Bennett R, Kambhampati U, Morse S, Ismael Y. 2006. Farm-level economic performance of genetically modified cotton in Maharashtra, India. *Rev. Agric. Econ.* 28:59–71

Bouis H. 2007. The potential of genetically modified food crops to improve human nutrition in developing countries. *J. Dev. Stud.* 43:79–96

Bradford KJ, Van Deynze A, Gutterson N, Parrott W, Strauss SH. 2005. Regulating transgenic crops sensibly: lessons from plant breeding, biotechnology and genomics. *Nat. Biotechnol.* 23:439–44

Breustedt G, Müller-Scheeßel J, Latacz-Lohmann U. 2008. Forecasting the adoption of GM oilseed rape: evidence from a discrete choice experiment in Germany. *J. Agric. Econ.* 59:237–56

Brookes G, Barfoot P. 2005. *GM Crops: The Global Socioeconomic and Environmental Impact—The First Nine Years.* Dorchester: PG Econ.

Brookes G, Barfoot P. 2008. *GM Crops: Global Socioeconomic and Environmental Impacts 1996–2008.* Dorchester: PG Econ.

Byerlee D, Fischer K. 2002. Accessing modern science: policy and institutional options for agricultural biotechnology in developing countries. *World Dev.* 30:931–48

Carpenter J, Felsot A, Goode T, Hammig M, Onstad D, Sankula S. 2002. *Comparative Environmental Impacts of Biotechnology-Derived and Traditional Soybean, Corn, and Cotton Crops.* Ames, IA: Counc. Agric. Sci. Technol.

Cohen MB, Chen M, Bentur JS, Heong KL, Ye G. 2008. Bt rice in Asia: potential benefits, impact, and sustainability. See Romeis et al. 2008, 8:223–48

Cooper J, Lipper LM, Zilberman D, eds. 2005. *Agricultural Biodiversity and Biotechnology in Economic Development*. New York: Springer

Crost B, Shankar B, Bennett R, Morse S. 2007. Bias from farmer self-selection in genetically modified crop productivity estimates: evidence from Indian data. *J. Agric. Econ.* 58:24–36

Dawe D, Robertson R, Unnevehr L. 2002. Golden Rice: What role could it play in alleviation of vitamin A deficiency? *Food Policy* 27:541–60

Demont M, Cerovska M, Daems W, Dillen K, Fogarasi J, Mathijs E, et al. 2008. Ex ante impact assessment under imperfect information: biotechnology in new member states of the EU. *J. Agric. Econ.* 59:463–86

Demont M, Devos Y. 2008. Regulating coexistence of GM and non-GM crops without jeopardizing economic incentives. *Trends Biotechnol.* 26:353–58

Demont M, Tollens E. 2004. First impact of biotechnology in the EU: Bt maize adoption in Spain. *Ann. Appl. Biol.* 145:197–207

Demont M, Wesseler J, Tollens E. 2004. Biodiversity versus transgenic sugarbeet: the one euro question. *Eur. Rev. Agric. Econ.* 31:1–18

Duffy M. 2001. *Who benefits from biotechnology?* Presented at Am. Seed Trade Assoc. Meet., 5-7 December, Chicago, Ill.

Edmeades S, Smale M. 2006. A trait-based model of the potential demand for a genetically engineered food crop in a developing economy. *Agric. Econ.* 35:351–61

Elbehri A, MacDonald S. 2004. Estimating the impact of transgenic Bt cotton on west and central Africa: a general equilibrium approach. *World Dev.* 22:2049–64

Evenson RE, Santaniello V, Zilberman D, eds. 2002. *Economic and Social Issues in Agricultural Biotechnology*. Oxfordshire, UK: CABI Publ.

Falck-Zepeda JB, Traxler G, Nelson RG. 2000a. Rent creation and distribution from biotechnology innovations: the case of Bt cotton and herbicide-tolerant soybeans in 1997. *Agribusiness* 16: 21–32

Falck-Zepeda JB, Traxler G, Nelson RG. 2000b. Surplus distribution from the introduction of a biotechnology innovation. *Am. J. Agric. Econ.* 82:360–69

Fan S, Chan-Kang C, Qian K, Krishnaiah K. 2005. National and international agricultural research and rural poverty: the case of rice research in India and China. *Agric. Econ.* 33:369–79

FAO. 2004. *The State of Food and Agriculture 2003-04; Agricultural Biotechnology: Meeting the Needs of the Poor?* Rome: FAO

Fernandez-Cornejo J, Caswell M. 2006. *The First Decade of Genetically Engineered Crops in the United States. Economic Information Bulletin 11*. Washington, DC: US Dep. Agric.

Fernandez-Cornejo J, Hendricks C, Mishra A. 2005. Technology adoption and off-farm household income: the case of herbicide-tolerant soybeans. *J. Agric. Appl. Econ.* 37:549–63

Fernandez-Cornejo J, Klotz-Ingram C, Jans S. 2002. Farm-level effects of adopting herbicide tolerant soybeans in the USA. *J. Agric. Appl. Econ.* 34:149–63

Fernandez-Cornejo J, Li J. 2005. *The impacts of adopting genetically engineered crops in the USA: the case of Bt corn*. Presented at Am. Agric. Econ. Assoc. Annu. Meet., 24–27 July, Providence, RI

Fitt G. 2003. Implementation and impacts of transgenic Bt cottons in Australia. *ICAC Rec.* December:14–19

Friends of the Earth. 2008. *Who Benefits from GM crops? The Rise in Pesticide Use. Agriculture and Food Issue 112*. Amsterdam: Friends Earth Int.

Frisvold G, Reeves J. 2007. *Economy-wide impacts of Bt cotton*. Presented at Annu. Beltwide Cotton Conf., Natl. Cotton Counc. Am., New Orleans

Fulton M, Keyowski L. 1999. The producer benefits of herbicide-resistant canola. *AgBioForum* 2:85–93

Gandhi VP, Namboodiri NV. 2006. *The adoption and economics of Bt cotton in India: preliminary results from a study*. Work. Pap. 2006-09-04, Indian Inst. Manag.

Gianessi LP, Silvers CS, Sankula S, Carpenter JE. 2002. *Plant Biotechnology: Current and Potential Impact for Improving Pest Management in US Agriculture: An Analysis of 40 Case Studies.* Washington, DC: Natl. Center Food Agric. Policy

Giannakas K. 2002. Infringement of intellectual property rights: causes and consequences. *Am. J. Agric. Econ.* 84:482–94

Giannakas K, Yiannaka A. 2008. Market and welfare effects of second-generation, consumer-oriented GM products. *Am. J. Agric. Econ.* 90:152–71

Giannakas K, Fulton M. 2002. Consumption effects of genetic modification: What if consumers are right? *Agric. Econ.* 27:97–109

Golan E, Kuchler F, Mitchell L. 2001. Economics of food labeling. *J. Consum. Policy* 24:117–84

Gómez-Barbero M, Berbel J, Rodriguez-Cerezo E. 2008. Bt corn in Spain—the performance of the EU's first GM crop. *Nat. Biotechnol.* 26:384–86

Gouse M, Pray C, Schimmelpfennig D, Kirsten J. 2006. Three seasons of subsistence insect-resistant maize in South Africa: Have smallholders benefited? *AgBioForum* 9:15–22

Gouse M, Pray C, Schimmelpfennig D. 2004. The distribution of benefits from Bt cotton adoption in South Africa. *AgBioForum* 7:187–94

Graff GD, Cullen SE, Bradford KJ, Zilberman D, Bennett AB. 2003. The public-private structure of intellectual property ownership in agricultural biotechnology. *Nat. Biotechnol.* 21:989–95

Graff G, Zilberman D. 2001. An intellectual property clearinghouse for agricultural biotechnology. *Nat. Biotechnol.* 19:1179–80

Gruère GP, Mehta-Bhatt P, Sengupta D. 2008. *Bt cotton and farmer suicides in India: reviewing the evidence.* Discuss. Pap. 00808, Int. Food Policy Res. Inst.

Halford NG, ed. 2006. *Plant Biotechnology: Current and Future Uses of Genetically Modified Crops.* Chichester, UK: John Wiley & Sons

Hareau GG, Mills BF, Norton GW. 2006. The potential benefits of herbicide-resistant transgenic rice in Uruguay: lessons for small developing countries. *Food Policy* 31:162–79

Hareau G, Norton GE, Mills BF, Peterson E. 2005. Potential benefits of transgenic rice in Asia: a general equilibrium analysis. *Q. J. Int. Agric.* 44:229–46

Hazell P, Ramasamy C. 1991. *The Green Revolution Reconsidered: The Impact of High-Yielding Rice Varieties in South India.* Baltimore, MD: Johns Hopkins Univ. Press

Herdt RW. 2006. Biotechnology in agriculture. *Annu. Rev. Environ. Resour.* 31:265–95

Herring RJ. 2007. The genomics revolution and development studies: science, poverty and politics. *J. Dev. Stud.* 43:1–30

Hertel T. 1997. *Global Trade Analysis: Modeling and Applications.* New York: Cambridge Univ. Press

Hossain F, Pray CE, Lu Y, Huang J, Hu R. 2004. Genetically modified cotton and farmers' health in China. *Int. J. Occup. Environ. Health* 10:296–303

Hu R, Huang J, Lin H, Rozelle S. 2006. *Bt cotton in China: Are secondary insect infestations offsetting the benefits in farmer fields?* Presented at Int. Consort. Agric. Biotechnol. Res. Conf., 10th, Ravello, Italy

Huang J, Hu R, Pray C, Qiao F, Rozelle S. 2003. Biotechnology as an alterative to chemical pesticides: a case study of Bt cotton in China. *Agric. Econ.* 29:55–68

Huang J, Hu R, Rozelle S, Pray C. 2005. Insect-resistant GM rice in farmers' fields: assessing productivity and health effects in China. *Science* 308:688–90

Huang J, Hu R, Rozelle S, Pray C. 2008. Genetically modified rice, yields and pesticides: assessing farm-level productivity effects in China. *Econ. Dev. Cult. Change* 56:241–63

Huang J, Hu R, Rozelle S, Qiao F, Pray CE. 2002a. Transgenic varieties and productivity of smallholder cotton farmers in China. *Aust. J. Agric. Resour. Econ.* 46:367–87

Huang J, Hu R, van Meijl H, van Tongeren F. 2004. Biotechnology boosts to crop productivity in China: trade and welfare implications. *J. Dev. Econ.* 75:27–54

Huang J, Rozelle S, Pray C, Wang Q. 2002b. Plant biotechnology in China. *Science* 295:674–77

Huffman WE, Shogren JF, Rousu M, Tegene A. 2003. Consumer willingness to pay for genetically modified food labels in a market with diverse information: evidence from experimental auctions. *J. Agric. Resour. Econ.* 28: 481–502

Hurley TM, Babcock BA, Hellmich RL. 2001. Bt corn and insect resistance: an economic assessment of refuges. *J. Agric. Resour. Econ.* 26:176–94

James C. 2008. *Global status of commercialized biotech/GM crops: 2008. ISAAA Briefs 39*. Ithaca, NY: Int. Serv. Acquis. Agri-Biotech Appl.

Jefferson-Moore KY, Traxler G. 2005. Second-generation GMOs: Where to from here? *AgBioForum* 8:143–50

Just RE, Alston JM, Zilberman D, eds. 2006. *Regulating Agricultural Biotechnology: Economics and Policy*. New York: Springer

Kalaitzandonakes N, ed. 2003. *The Economic and Environmental Impacts of Agbiotech*. New York: Kluwer

Kalaitzandonakes N, Alston JM, Bradford KJ. 2007. Compliance costs for regulatory approval of new biotech crops. *Nat. Biotechnol.* 25:509–11

Kambhampati U, Morse S, Bennett R, Ismael Y. 2006. Farm-level performance of genetically modified cotton—a frontier analysis of cotton production in Maharashtra. *Outlook Agric.* 35:291–97

Kimenju SC, De Groote H. 2008. Consumer willingness to pay for genetically modified food in Kenya. *Agric. Econ.* 38:35–46

Krishna VV, Qaim M. 2007. Estimating the adoption of Bt eggplant in India: Who benefits from public-private partnership? *Food Policy* 32:523–43

Krishna VV, Qaim M. 2008a. Consumer attitudes toward GM food and pesticide residues in India. *Rev. Agric. Econ.* 30:233–51

Krishna VV, Qaim M. 2008b. Potential impacts of Bt eggplant on economic surplus and farmers' health in India. *Agric. Econ.* 38:167–80

Lapan HE, Moschini G. 2004. Innovation and trade with endogenous market failure: the case of genetically modified products. *Am. J. Agric. Econ.* 86:634–48

Lence SH, Hayes DJ. 2005. Genetically modified crops: their market and welfare impacts. *Am. J. Agric. Econ.* 87:931–50

Lichtenberg E, Zilberman D. 1986. The economics of damage control: why specification matters. *Am. J. Agric. Econ.* 68:261–73

Lichtenberg E, Zilberman D. 1988. Efficient regulation of environmental health risks. *Q. J. Econ.* 103:167–78

Lipton M. 2001. Reviving global poverty reduction: what role for genetically modified plants? *J. Int. Dev.* 13:823–46

Lusk JL. 2003. Effect of cheap talk on consumer willingness to pay for Golden Rice. *Am. J. Agric. Econ.* 85:840–56

Lusk JL, Jamal M, Kurlander L, Roucan M, Taulman L. 2005. A meta analysis of genetically modified food valuation studies. *J. Agric. Resour. Econ.* 30:28–44

Lusk JL, Traill WB, House LO, Valli C, Jaeger SR, et al. 2006. Comparative advantage in demand: experimental evidence of preferences for genetically modified food in the United States and European Union. *J. Agric. Econ.* 57:1–21

Marra MC, Pardey PG, Alston JM. 2002. *The payoffs to agricultural biotechnology: an assessment of the evidence*. EPTD Discuss. Pap. 87, Int. Food Policy Res. Inst.

McCluskey JJ, Ouchi H, Grimsrud KM, Wahl TI. 2003. Consumer response to genetically modified food products in Japan. *Agric. Resour. Econ. Rev.* 32:222–31

Miller HI, Conko G. 2004. *The Frankenfood Myth—How Protest and Politics Threaten the Biotech Revolution*. Westport, CT: Praeger

Moon W, Balasubramanian SK. 2004. Public attitudes towards agro-biotechnology: the mediating role of risk perceptions on the impact of trust, awareness and outrage. *Rev. Agric. Econ.* 26:186–208

Morse S, Bennett R, Ismael Y. 2004. Why Bt cotton pays for small-scale producers in South Africa. *Nat. Biotechnol.* 22:379–80

Moschini G. 2008. Biotechnology and the development of food markets: retrospect and prospects. *Eur. Rev. Agric. Econ.* 35:331–55

Moschini G. 2006. Pharmaceutical and industrial traits in genetically modified crops: coexistence with conventional agriculture. *Am. J. Agric. Econ.* 88:1184–92

Moschini G, Lapan H. 1997. Intellectual property rights and the welfare effects of agricultural R&D. *Am. J. Agric. Econ.* 79:1229–42

Moschini G, Lapan H, Sobolevsky A. 2000. Roundup Ready soybeans and welfare effects in the soybean complex. *Agribusiness* 16:33–55

Naseem A, Pray C. 2004. Economic impact analysis of genetically modified crops. In *Handbook of Plant Biotechnology*, ed. P Christou, H Klee. 51: 959-91. Chichester, UK: John Wiley & Sons

Nielsen CP, Anderson K. 2001. Global market effects of alternative market responses to genetically modified organisms. *Weltwirtsch. Arch.* 137:320–46

Paarlberg RL. 2008. *Starved for Science: How Biotechnology is Being Kept Out of Africa.* Cambridge, MA: Harvard Univ. Press

Pemsl DE, Gutierrez AP, Waibel H. 2008. The economics of biotechnology under ecosystem disruption. *Ecol. Econ.* 66:177–83

Pemsl D, Waibel H. 2007. Assessing the profitability of different crop protection strategies in cotton: case study results from Shandong Province, China. *Agric. Syst.* 95:28–36

Pew Initiative on Food and Biotechnology. 2007. *Applications of Biotechnology for Functional Foods.* Washington, DC: Pew Initiat. Food Biotechnol.

Phillips PWB. 2003. The economic impact of herbicide tolerant canola in Canada. See Kalaitzandonakes 2003, 7:119–40

Pinstrup-Andersen P, Schioler E. 2001. *Seeds of Contention: World Hunger and the Global Controversy over GM Crops.* Baltimore, MD: Johns Hopkins Univ. Press

Potrykus I. 2008. Golden Rice—from idea to reality. Bertebos Prize lecture. *Presented at Bertebos Conf., 7–9 September, Falkenberg, Sweden*

Pray CE, Bengali P, Ramaswami B. 2005. The cost of biosafety regulations: the Indian experience. *Q. J. Int. Agric.* 44:267–89

Pray CE, Huang J, Hu R, Rozelle S. 2002. Five years of Bt cotton in China—the benefits continue. *Plant J.* 31:423–30

Pray CE, Ma D, Huang J, Qiao F. 2001. Impact of Bt cotton in China. *World Dev.* 29:813–25

Pray CE, Ramaswami B, Huang J, Bengali P, Hu R, Zhang H. 2006. Costs and enforcement of biosafety regulation in India and China. *Int. J. Technol. Glob.* 2:137–57

Price GK, Lin W, Falck-Zepeda JB, Fernandez-Cornejo J. 2003. The size and distribution of market benefits from adopting agricultural biotechnology. *Tech. Bull.* 1906, US Dep. Agric., Washington, DC

Qaim M. 2001. A prospective evaluation of biotechnology in semi-subsistence agriculture. *Agric. Econ.* 25:165–75

Qaim M. 2003. Bt cotton in India: field trial results and economic projections. *World Dev.* 31: 2115–27

Qaim M. 2005. Agricultural biotechnology adoption in developing countries. *Am. J. Agric. Econ.* 87:1317–24

Qaim M, de Janvry A. 2005. Bt cotton and pesticide use in Argentina: economic and environmental effects. *Environ. Dev. Econ.* 10:179–200

Qaim M, de Janvry A. 2003. Genetically modified crops, corporate pricing strategies, and farmers' adoption: the case of Bt cotton in Argentina. *Am. J. Agric. Econ.* 85:814–28

Qaim M, Krattiger AF, von Braun J, eds. 2000. *Agricultural Biotechnology in Developing Countries: Towards Optimizing the Benefits for the Poor.* New York: Kluwer

Qaim M, Pray CE, Zilberman D. 2008. Economic and social considerations in the adoption of Bt crops. See Romeis et al., 12:329–56

Qaim M, Stein AJ, Meenakshi JV. 2007. Economics of biofortification. *Agric. Econ.* 37(Suppl. 1): 119–33

Qaim M, Subramanian A, Naik G, Zilberman D. 2006. Adoption of Bt cotton and impact variability: insights from India. *Rev. Agric. Econ.* 28:48–58

Qaim M, Traxler G. 2005. Roundup Ready soybeans in Argentina: farm level and aggregate welfare effects. *Agric. Econ.* 32:73–86

Qaim M, Zilberman D. 2003. Yield effects of genetically modified crops in developing countries. *Science* 299:900–2

Rajagopal D, Sexton S, Hochman G, Zilberman D. 2009. Recent developments in renewable technologies: R&D investment in advanced biofuels. *Annu. Rev. Resour. Econ.* 1:621–44

Ramasamy C, Selvaraj KN, Norton GW, Vijayaraghavan K, eds. 2007. *Economic and Environmental Benefits and Costs of Transgenic Crops: Ex-Ante Assessment*. Coimbatore: Tamil Nadu Agric. Univ.

Rausser G, Simon L, Ameden H. 2000. Public-private alliances in biotechnology: Can they narrow the knowledge gaps between rich and poor? *Food Policy* 25:499–513

Romeis J, Shelton AS, Kennedy GG, eds. 2008. *Integration of Insect-Resistant Genetically Modified Crops within IPM Programs*. New York: Springer

Sadashivappa P, Qaim M. 2009. *Effects of Bt cotton in India during the first five years of adoption.* Presented at Int. Assoc. Agric. Econ. Triennial Conf., Beijing, China

Santaniello V, Evenson RE, Zilberman D, Carlson GA, eds. 2000. *Agriculture and Intellectual Property Rights: Economic, Institutional and Implementation Issues in Biotechnology*. Oxfordshire, UK: CABI Publ.

Sexton SE, Lei Z, Zilberman D. 2007. The economics of pesticides and pest control. *Int. Rev. Environ. Resour. Econ.* 1:271–26

Sharma D. 2004. *GM Food and Hunger: A View from the South*. New Delhi: Forum Biotechnol. Food Secur.

Shelton AM, Fuchs M, Shotoski FA. 2008. Transgenic vegetables and fruits for control of insects and insect-vectored pathogens. See Romeis et al., 9:249–71

Shelton AM, Naranjo SE, Romeis J, Hellmich RL, Wolt JD, et al. 2009. Setting the record straight: a rebuttal to an erroneous analysis on transgenic insecticidal crops and natural enemies. *Transgenic Res.* In press. doi: 10.1007/s11248-009-9260-5

Stein AJ, Sachdev HPS, Qaim M. 2006. Potential impact and cost-effectiveness of Golden Rice. *Nat. Biotechnol.* 24:1200–1

Stein AJ, Sachdev HPS, Qaim M. 2008. Genetic engineering for the poor: Golden Rice and public health in India. *World Dev.* 36:144–58

Subramanian A, Qaim M. 2009a. The impact of Bt cotton on poor households in rural India. *J. Dev. Stud.* In press

Subramanian A, Qaim M. 2009b. Village-wide effects of agricultural biotechnology: the case of Bt cotton in India. *World Dev.* 37:256–67

Thirtle C, Beyers L, Ismael Y, Piesse J. 2003. Can GM-technologies help the poor? The impact of Bt cotton in Makhathini Flats, KwaZulu-Natal. *World Dev.* 31:717–32

Tothova M, Oehmke JF. 2005. Whom to join? The small-country dilemma in adopting GM crops in a fragmented trade environment. *Q. J. Int. Agric.* 44:291–310

Traxler G, Godoy-Avila S, Falck-Zepeda J, Espinoza-Arellano J. 2003. Transgenic cotton in Mexico: a case study of the Comarca Lagunera. See Kalaitzandonakes 2003, 10:183–202

Trigo EJ, Cap EJ. 2006. *Ten Years of Genetically Modified Crops in Argentine Agriculture*. Buenos Aires: Argent. Counc. Inf. Dev. Biotechnol.

Unnevehr L, Pray C, Paarlberg R. 2007. Addressing micronutrient deficiencies: alternative interventions and technologies. *AgBioForum* 10:124–34 von Braun J. 2007. The world food situation: new driving forces and required actions. *Food Policy Rep. 18*, Int. Food Policy Res. Inst., Washington, DC

Wang S, Just D, Pinstrup-Andersen P. 2006. *Tarnishing silver bullets: Bt technology adoption, bounded rationality and the outbreak of secondary pest infestations in China.* Presented at Am. Agric. Econ. Assoc. Annu. Meet., Long Beach, Calif.

Weaver S, Morris M. 2005. Risks associated with genetic modification: an annotated bibliography of peer-reviewed natural science publications. *J. Agric. Environ. Ethics* 18:157–89

Wu F. 2002. *Bt or not Bt? Tools for regulatory decisions concerning genetically modified corn.* PhD thesis. Eng. Public Policy, Carnegie Mellon Univ.

Wu F. 2006. Bt corn's reduction of mycotoxins: regulatory decisions and public opinion. See Just et al. 2006, 9:179–200

Yorobe JM Jr, Quicoy CB. 2006. Economic impact of Bt corn in the Philippines. *Philipp. Agric. Sci.* 89:258–67

Zilberman D, Ameden H, Graff G, Qaim M. 2004. Agricultural biotechnology: productivity, biodiversity, and intellectual property rights. *J. Agric. Food. Ind. Organ.* 2(2): artic. 3

Zilberman D, Ameden H, Qaim M. 2007. The impact of agricultural biotechnology on yields, risks, and biodiversity in low-income countries. *J. Dev. Stud.* 43:63–78

Zimmermann R, Qaim M. 2004. Potential health benefits of Golden Rice: a Philippine case study. *Food Policy* 29:147–68

ANNUAL REVIEWS
A Nonprofit Scientific Publisher

Annual Reviews – Your Starting Point for Research Online
http://arjournals.annualreviews.org

- Over 1280 Annual Reviews volumes—more than 28,800 critical, authoritative review articles in 37 disciplines spanning the Biomedical, Life, Physical, and Social sciences—available online, including all Annual Reviews back volumes, dating to 1932

- Personal subscriptions include permanent online data rights to the volume regardless of future subscription status. Online data rights include access to full-text articles, PDFs, Reviews in Advance (as much as 6 months ahead of print publication), bibliographies, and other supplementary material

- All articles are fully supplemented, searchable, and downloadable—see http://resource.annualreviews.org

- Access links to the reviewed references (when available online)

- Site features include customized alerting services, citation tracking, and saved searches

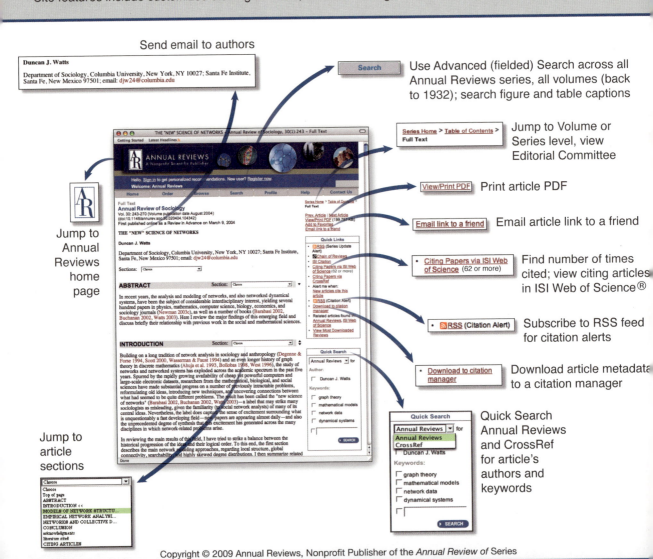

Send email to authors

Use Advanced (fielded) Search across all Annual Reviews series, all volumes (back to 1932); search figure and table captions

Jump to Volume or Series level, view Editorial Committee

Print article PDF

Email article link to a friend

Find number of times cited; view citing articles in ISI Web of Science®

Subscribe to RSS feed for citation alerts

Download article metadata to a citation manager

Quick Search Annual Reviews and CrossRef for article's authors and keywords

Jump to Annual Reviews home page

Jump to article sections